W9-BKT-287

Encyclopedia of Human Behavior

Volume 4 R - Z INDEX

Editorial Advisory Board

ENCYCLOPEDIA OF HUMAN BEHAVIOR

EDITOR-IN-CHIEF

V. S. Ramachandran

University of California, San Diego
La Jolla, California

VOLUME 4 R-Z INDEX

ACADEMIC PRESS

San Diego New York Boston London Sydney Tokyo Toronto

This book is printed on acid-free paper. ♾

Academic Press, Inc.
A Division of Harcourt Brace & Company
525 B Street, Suite 1900, San Diego, California 92101-4495

United Kingdom Edition published by
Academic Press Limited
24–28 Oval Road, London NW1 7DX

Library of Congress Cataloging-in-Publication Data

Encyclopedia of human behavior / edited by V. S. Ramachandran.
p. cm.
Includes index.
ISBN 0-12-226920-9 (set). -- ISBN 0-12-226921-7 (v. 1)
ISBN 0-12-226922-5 (v. 2) -- ISBN 0-12-226923-3 (v. 3)
ISBN 0-12-226924-1 (v. 4).
1. Psychology--Encyclopedias. I. Ramachandran, V. S.
BF31.E5 1994
150'.3--dc20 93-34371
CIP

PRINTED IN THE UNITED STATES OF AMERICA
95 96 97 QW 9 8 7 6 5 4 3 2

Contents

R

S

READING

Charles A. Weaver III
Baylor University

Glossary

Dyslexia A specific reading problem, in a person with near-normal (or higher) intelligence, proper instruction, and adequate motivation.

Orthography The written symbols of a language.

Perceptual span The amount of material that can be detected by the eye in a single glance; in reading, the perceptual span has been estimated to be no more than about 20 characters, and is asymmetrical, extending about 15 characters to the right of the fixation and about 4 characters to the left (for English readers; the pattern is reversed in Hebrew readers, who read from right to left).

Phonological recoding The process of converting the written symbols of a language into their sound-based counterparts. Usually, this sound-based counterpart involves internal (rather than external) speech.

Phonology The spoken part of a language, consisting of phonemes.

Saccade Literally, "jumps." The rapid, ballistic movements of the eyes during reading; saccades occur no often than four or five times per second in reading.

READING is the process by which individuals decode a written language. Readers must translate from a written language (called an "orthography") to its underlying sound-based components (called the "phonology"). Learning this process involves knowledge of the phonetic structure of language, and requires literally hundreds of hours of practice. Though early readers rely on sounding out the components of words, skilled readers are able to access the words automatically, without phonological mediation. Several causes of dyslexia (learning difficulties specific to reading) will be discussed, including perceptual difficulties, faulty eye movements, and genetic factors. Finally, the relationship between reading and literacy will be addressed.

I. INTRODUCTION

The most important thing that humans do—and no other species *can* do—is develop and use a spoken language. Furthermore, we seem to acquire that language easily and innately, much as we master a skill like walking.

Unlike spoken language skills, which develop without too much cognitive awareness, learning to read requires much practice, instruction, and effort. That process often begins with picture books where one comes to understand that those symbols mean something. Eventually, one learns to identify letters, and then groups of letters to sound out words.

Language use is the single most impressive cognitive skill humans possess. Yet, a child of 5 years has mastered most of the subtleties (if not yet the vocabulary) of language use. Language is fundamentally important to human culture; it has been around for as long as our species has been around. Every human—given normal neural development and a normal environment—will develop spoken language. Across a variety of different cultures, children seem to go through the same developmental sequences, at approximately the same age in developing language skills.

While the development and use of *spoken language* in humans is innate, written language is a skill which is not innate, nor is it a skill that all humans can or will acquire. Reading clearly hinges on the spoken language, but reading is not something we are innately predisposed to do.

II. HISTORICAL REVIEW

A. The History of Written Language

Though true writing systems did not develop until about 5000 years ago, some types of written communication were used long before then. The earliest kinds of written communication are termed "logographs." In logographs, each symbol represents an object, and the picture is drawn to resemble that object. For example, a person trying to communicate a "tree" would draw a picture of a tree. On the surface, this may seem like a good basis for language, however some words may be difficult—if not impossible—to draw. How would one draw a symbol for "honesty," or "anger?" Nouns are more easily drawn, but verbs, adverbs, and adjectives are considerably more difficult. Also, the absolute number of symbols needed in a logographic language would be overwhelming. In fact, Chinese is the only popular language today that uses logography.

Logographs such as the Chinese use are a fundamentally different type of language than English. English is what is known as an "alphabetic" language. In alphabetic languages each symbol stands for a sound, and reading is accomplished by decoding the letters into their sounds. Languages vary with respect to how "good" this mapping is. Italian, for example, has a very good symbol-to-sound map, English somewhat less so. Alphabetic languages all derive from Phoenician, which was developed a little more than 3000 years ago. The earliest Phoenician languages contained only consonants. While this may seem confusing, n xmpl wll shw hw ths knd f wrtng cn b ndrstd wth lttl trbl (that is, "an example will show how this kind of writing can be understood with little trouble"). Later, the Greeks added the vowels; in fact, all European written languages derive from the Greek alphabet, which is relatively unchanged in the past 2000 years. (The other alphabetic systems, widely used in the Near and Middle East—Hebrew, Arabic, the languages of India—derive from the Aramaic alphabet.)

B. Early Reading Research

Research in the reading process has a history almost as old as psychology itself. Workers in Wundt's laboratory, set up in Leipzig over 100 years ago, were keenly interested in many aspects of the reading process. They studied concepts like perceptual span—how much information can you take in from the periphery when your eyes are not moved—inner speech, rate, and the nature of eye movements, etc. This work culminated in the publication of Huey's book, *The Psychology and Pedagogy of Reading* in 1908. Huey's book, even today, remains highly readable, and current research has served to substantiate Huey's basic findings.

With the rise of behaviorism in American psychology, work on the reading process came to a standstill. To the extent research was done, it was in promoting one approach to reading or another, and the work was much more applied in nature. Beginning in the late 1950s, and especially in the 1960s, researchers' interest in reading was rekindled. Since about 1970, research has flourished. A number of specialized scientific journals specifically devoted to reading research were developed. In 1984, *The Handbook of Reading Research* was published, followed 6 years later by a second volume of the same name.

III. PERCEPTUAL PROCESSES IN READING

The reading process is constrained by the limitations of the human information processing system. For example, readers can only move their eyes so quickly, and can only see so much in the periphery of their vision. Images that hit the retina last for only a fraction of a second before fading. Also, readers have a limited capacity short-term memory store that can easily get overloaded. Each of these stages brings a "bottleneck" into the reading process, limiting how fast the process can operate.

A. Eye Movements

The seminal work on eye movements was conducted in the late 1800s, but recent techniques have allowed a more thorough investigation into exactly how readers move their eyes. Everyone has the impression, as they are reading, that the eyes are moving smoothly across the page. In fact, the eyes are moving in a very jerky, abrupt manner. These eye movements are called "saccades," French for "jumps." You can easily demonstrate this to yourself. Sit across the table from a friend, and have that friend read while you are looking over the book. Notice that your friend's eyes jump, maybe 3 or 4 times a second. Ask your friend what they thought they experienced; inevitably, they thought their eyes were moving smoothly across the page. [*See* EYE MOVEMENTS.]

Saccades impose the first limitation on reading. Each eye movement in reading has two components: a stage where the eyes move to the next word (during which almost no information can be extracted) and a time when the eyes focus on the word, called "fixations." During reading, most research estimates that the movement stage takes about 25 msec, while the fixations last considerably longer, from 200 to 250 msec (about one-fifth to one-fourth of a second). We are limited to a maximum of five saccades per second.

B. Perceptual Span

The second major determinant in reading rate is what is called the "perceptual span." Visual acuity is best for information at the center of the retina, called the "fovea." The fovea is lined with cells (called "cones") that perceive sharp detail. Farther into the periphery of the retina, acuity fades. Again, you can demonstrate this for yourself. Hold a book a foot or so in front of you, and focus on one word on the page. *Without moving your eyes,* try to recognize words on either side of where you are focusing (you'll probably have difficulty not moving your eyes). You can recognize some letters, probably, but you'll also see how rapidly the information becomes unusable. [*See* VISUAL PERCEPTION.]

George McConkie and Keith Rayner have developed a powerful technique for measuring perceptual span in reading, called the "moving window." Most eye movement recorders in current research operate by shining a harmless laser beam on the eye. The eye reflects some of that light back to a computer, and as the eye movements change, the computer records these changes. McConkie and Rayner made use of this technique, but went a bit further. Imagine a computer screen with a text written on it, and then imagine that the text was covered up by a series of X's. The display looked something like what is shown in Figure 1. By recording the eye movements, McConkie and Rayner were able to determine where the readers were looking. Then, they gradually removed the X's that were covering up the text, revealing what was underneath. Each time the readers moved their eyes, the "window" moved along with them. When this window was small, readers had to move their eyes many times to uncover even a single word. But as the window got bigger and bigger, subjects could make larger eye movements, thus speeding up their reading. At some point, though, increasing the size of the window no longer resulted in an increase in reading speed. The point at which the reading rate levels off indicates the limits of the perceptual span. Adding more information outside that span has no effect, because it cannot be perceived. Using this technique, McConkie, Rayner, and their colleagues found that readers' maximum perceptual spans were about 20 characters, extending about 15 characters to the right of the fixation, and about 4 to the left. (This assymetry is reversed in readers of Hebrew, who read from right to left.) Research on eye movements and perceptual span is important when considering speed reading, a topic which will be covered later.

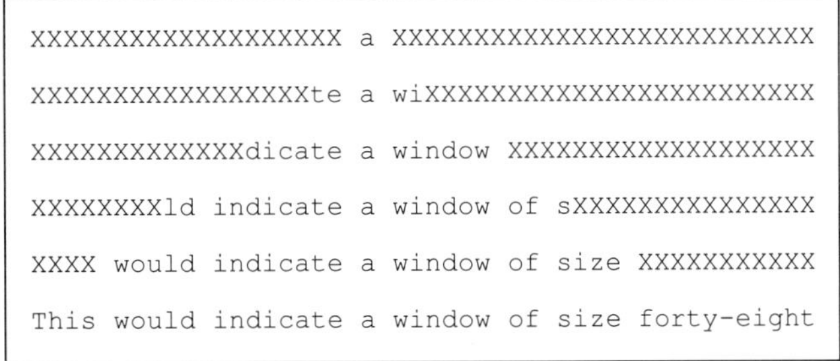

FIGURE 1 An example of the moving window procedure. Each line indicates a larger window.

The numbers listed above report maximum rates. What goes on in more typical reading situations? About 10–15% of the time, our saccades are actually *backwards*. Furthermore, saccades of 20 characters are highly uncommon. Usually, saccades average about 8 characters, or about one word. Though there is some evidence that readers do not focus on every word (readers sometimes skip short, frequently occurring words like "the" and "of"), researchers now believe that readers do focus on the great majority of words in a passage. Therefore, typical reading rates for normal college readers average about 250 words per minute.

IV. THE ROLE OF PHONOLOGY IN READING

After the perceptual limitations described above, the next bottleneck in the reading process lies with our limited capacity short-term memory (STM) spans. STM can hold only a few items (about 7, by most estimates), and without constant rehearsal, lasts no more than 12–15 sec. Thus, efficient use of STM is critical for good reading. [*See* MEMORY.]

A. A Model of Working Memory

A current model of STM was derived by Alan Baddeley, though he prefers the term "working memory" (WM). Critical to the understanding of WM is recognizing the importance of phonology, or "sound." Most of the work in WM is done using a phonological code. Furthermore, speech is of particular importance. Since our reading is done by means of recoding visual information into inner speech (even skilled readers rely on inner speech), the WM model deserves a brief discussion.

The WM model has three main components, as outlined in Figure 2. There is a "central executive" component, which works as a controller, more or less. It corresponds roughly to the concept of "attention." There is also a component which handles visual information, which is termed the "visual–spatial sketchpad." This component handles spatially oriented information. Obviously, this module will be important in the reading process.

The final component—and in many ways the most important one—is the phonological loop. The loop itself is composed of two smaller components, the "phonological store" and the "articulatory control process." The phonological store consists of a limited duration (about 2 sec) trace of what was just heard. This is the brief "echo" you can sometimes hear in your head following a loud noise. Next time you listen to a favorite piece of music, try to notice how long the auditory image lingers after the piece is finished. You should be able to tell that it lasts about 1–2 sec, and then is gone. You can still call up your memory of that piece, but it is not the same as the lingering trace.

All auditory information can gain access to the phonological store, but speech *automatically* gains access to it. Have you noticed how disruptive speech can be when you are trying to read, yet how easy you might be able to read in an airplane, where the

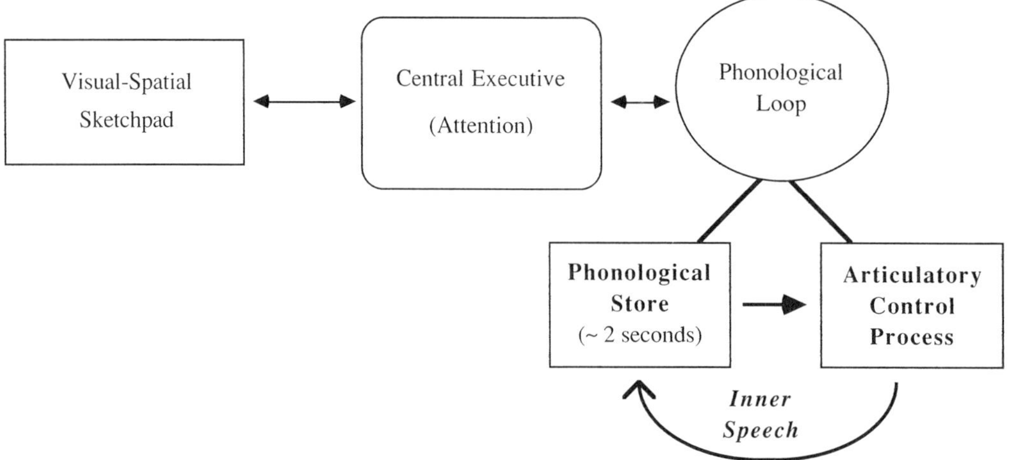

FIGURE 2 Baddeley's model of working memory. [Adapted from Alan Baddeley (1990), "Human Memory: Theory and Practice." Copyright © 1990 Allyn and Bacon. Reprinted with permission.]

noise is much louder? That is because the speech that you are hearing automatically gains access to this part of your working memory, whereas the plane noise does not. You may remember this phenomenon from college—many college students claim to be able to study while listening to music, yet most report that they find it easier to study when listening to (instrumental) classical music. Why? The classical music contains no words.

WM spans last longer than the 1–2 sec indicated by the phonological store by means of the articulatory control process. One function of the articulatory control process is to "refresh" the information in the phonological store, making it last longer. The process of refreshing the loop results in what we call "inner speech," the voice we all hear in our head when thinking and reading. (Note that this is *not* to be confused with the "voices in the head" heard by schizophrenics.)

The translation from written to phonological information is the second major function of the articulatory control process. This is done through a process known as "phonological recoding." Readers take the visual input and convert it into its corresponding sound. This is obvious when watching a child learn to read (as they sound out letters and words), but adults do it too (as shall be seen shortly).

B. How Phonology Influences Reading

The progression of reading by children usually goes from oral reading, to reading while moving lips, to moving while subvocalizing, to "silent" reading. However, recent studies indicate that even highly skilled readers read by means of recoding information—so much so that small movements of the vocal tract can be detected as these people read. Again, a demonstration will help make things clearer. Which sentence do you find it takes you longer to read "silently?"

(a) Miss Jones' lobster sauce shop rarely sells halibut.
(b) Miss Smith's fish sauce shop seldom sells shellfish.

The two are roughly comparable in length, but most people find the second much more difficult to read. If we were not recoding, we would not have this trouble.

It is worth noting that "inner speech" and "subvocalization" are not necessarily the same thing. Some studies have shown that if subvocalization is eliminated (by having readers recite "la la la" while reading, for example), but inner speech is not disrupted, reading progresses fairly normally (especially if the material is not difficult). But if inner speech is prevented, reading is seriously impaired. [*See* Inner Speech, Composing, and the Reading–Writing Connection.]

The importance of inner speech and reading can be seen clearly when examining congenitally deaf individuals. Only one-fourth of congenitally deaf individuals will learn to read at a level we would consider literate. This almost certainly has to do with the lack of external phonological input for these readers. The 5-year-old hearing child learns to read by pairing symbols, that are (at first) unknown, with sounds that are quite familiar. The deaf child does not have this set of sounds on which to draw.

Further evidence of the importance of phonology in reading can be taken from those deaf readers who do learn to read. Interestingly, readers—despite never having "heard" these words pronounced—make phonetic judgments similar to those of hearing readers. For example, they respond differently to rhyming words ("save" and "wave") than the nonrhyming, but orthographically similar words ("have" and "cave"). They can also name the real-world equivalents for nonwords which would be pronounced similar to real words in English ("cruise" for "krews," and "broom" for "brume"). They show similar effects of reading tongue-twisters, as well. In short, though they have never heard external sounds, the inner speech of congenitally deaf readers seems to parallel that of hearing readers.

V. DEVELOPMENTAL ASPECTS OF READING

Since reading is such a complex skill, it is not surprising that it takes many hundreds of hours to hone that skill. Prereaders must first acquire a set of skills basic to the reading process, and many children gain these skills outside of the school setting.

A. Fluent Letter Identification

The first skill that must be mastered by children is being able to identify letters quickly and accurately. Many early studies showed that this ability was the best predictor of early reading success; prereaders who were fluent with the alphabet learned to read more easily. Unfortunately, the process is not quite as simple as having the children learn to recite the alphabet. Instead, the child needs to develop a certain fluency with the alphabet, so that letters are named "automatically." If the child can immediately name the letters, the limited cognitive resources can be devoted to "higher" reading processes, such as word recognition. Alphabetic fluency, especially in English, also plays the facilitating role of associating symbols with sounds—most letter names "say" what sound they make. The better "B," for example, maps to the sound [bee]. Since this matching of symbols to sounds underlies reading, learning the letters fluently will give the child an extra edge.

B. Phonetic Awareness

A second skill is required in reading process, what psychologists call "phonetic awareness." Earlier, reading was defined as the process of matching symbol to *sound*. A more accurate characterization would be to say that reading is a process of matching symbols to *phonemes*. A phoneme is more accurately defined as a category of sounds. An analysis of different speakers all trying to make the same sound, say "[bee]," there are some subtle differences across different speakers. Yet those sounds are heard as being the same, because the categories important to speech have been learned. Across all different languages, there are close to 100 different phonemes. English, however, uses only about 45 of them. [*See* PHONETICS.]

The process of learning which phonemes are important in the language your culture speaks is an excellent illustration of the innateness of language to humans. A 9-month-old Japanese infant will respond to a change from [ra] to [la], which is a phoneme distinction that the Japanese language does not make. (It is partly this lack of a distinction that gives natives of Japan their characteristic accent when speaking English.) Just a few months later, the same child, raised in a Japanese-speaking environment, will no longer differentiate those two sounds. Therefore, the very young children seem to be biologically prepared to identify important categories of speech, those relevant to their native language.

Though speakers innately develop the categories necessary for phoneme detection, they are not innately *aware* of them. Prereaders who develop an awareness of these phonemes will be at a great advantage in reading, which hinges upon putting the symbols with the appropriate phonemes. Early instruction clearly helps. An example of this instruction would be asking a child, "Take the word 'mop,' and replace the [m] with a [t]. What new word do you get?" As children develop an awareness of how phonemes can be manipulated, they begin to appreciate things like alliteration or rhyme. Dr. Seuss, either by design or clever intuition, uses rhyme and alliteration very effectively, which can communicate this phonemic awareness to children.

"Sesame Street" is another example of how these two tasks can be combined in ways that children find interesting. "Sesame Street" will often display a letter, say "S," and then do several things. First, they will repeat the letter name ("ess") while showing the child the symbol. Next they often use that letter in ways which exploit the phonemic similarities. For example, the "S" will be a snake, while the narrator might say, "Simon, the slippery snake, slides slowly." Such lessons combine symbol–phoneme match, segmenting of phonemes in real words, and give the child a concrete image (the picture of the snake, which looks like the letter) to aid learning.

C. Enhancing Children's Reading Readiness

What can parents do to enhance their child's reading potential? One leading authority states, without hesitation, that the single most important thing parents can do to enhance their child's reading ability is reading aloud to them. This serves several critical functions. It gives them practice with comprehension skills, especially if the parent asks the occasional questions while reading, such as, "what else do you think the bunny could do to get away?" It gives them practice matching letters to sounds, as they watch the letters on the page. It gives them exposure to written words, which will be much more important once letter skills are mastered. Equally important, though, it shows the child that reading and literacy are to be valued, and reading is something that the parent does. Not all cultures share this set of values—in some cultures, the children that wish to go off by themselves and read a book under a tree are seen as "odd," or even "antisocial."

Some estimates indicate that children whose parents read to them each night enter school with some 1500 hours of practice with print. In addition, children may spend nearly that much time watching

Sesame Street. Other children, though, have virtually no print exposure before schooling. It is impossible for schooling to make up for so many lost hours of informal instruction. Furthermore, those children who come to school with so much practice are also likely to read at home. The less-practiced readers are not. A child in the 90th percentile of reading ability (meaning, one who reads better than 90% of his or her peers) reads *two hundred times* more text than does the child in the 10th percentile. It is unrealistic to believe that formal education can make up for such differences.

D. Phonetics or Whole-Word?

During the middle part of this century, debate raged among teachers of reading, centering around a single question: should reading be taught using a "whole-word" method, which focused on reading entire words without sounding them out? Or, should beginning reading stress a phonetic approach, teaching reading through phonics? For the earliest reading, the question is now virtually settled: phonetic, code-based instruction is vital to learning to read any alphabetic language. "Whole-word" or "whole-language" approaches, which abandon the teaching of symbol–phoneme matches are misguided. Most "whole-language" approaches rest on the assumption that since spoken language was learned by attending to whole words in context (itself a dubious assumption), reading should follow a similar progression. As has been pointed out throughout this chapter, though, reading is not simply a natural extension of spoken language.

As reading skills develop, the educational emphasis shifts to so-called "higher" reading skills, like comprehension. No one denies that the final reading process involves recognizing whole words in context. But learning to read solely through reading whole words in context would be like trying to teach someone to ski by placing them at the top of a steep mountain. A skilled skier could navigate that mountain, because that skier learned some basic skills and practiced for many hours. But that does not mean a beginning skier should learn to ski that way.

The last 25 years of research provides clear evidence that phonics instruction is necessary. Despite this, the popularity of whole-language instruction remains: to quote one authority, "staggering." It is likely, though, that as this research becomes more widely known, the emphasis will (appropriately) shift toward "phonics first."

The beginning reader, then, reads by matching symbol to phoneme, and then stringing the phonemes together to recognize words. This is a tedious process. As a result, the beginning reader will run into the problems associated with the limited-capacity working memory buffer. Readers may well forget the first sounds of a word by the time they get to the end of the word. (Adult readers often have similar problems with words when sentences are too long. Everyone is familiar with the experience of forgetting the beginning of a sentence by the time we get to the end of it.) Eventually, then, reading progresses beyond this "sounding-out" stage.

As the reading process develops, middle-school readers begin to recognize similarities among words. They use these regularities to allow them to recognize familiar words, rather than having to sound every word out. With much practice they begin to recognize words directly. This additional way of accessing words has been incorporated into what has been called a "dual-route" theory of reading. One of the routes, as we have already seen, involved phonological mediation—the words are accessed by their sounds. Skilled readers, though, begin to bypass the mediated route (at least, most of the time). Skilled readers begin to access words directly.

That is not to say that the role of "inner speech" becomes any less important. As has been stressed throughout, inner speech is crucial to reading. What happens as reading becomes more skilled, though, is that words themselves become directly accessible. Rather than having to match each symbol to each phoneme, and then combining the phonemes to recognize the word, we can now recognize words directly. When words are retrieved from the lexicon, it can be done without the help of the individual letter-to-phoneme mappings.

There is an important lesson with respect to reading here. Skilled reading requires direct, automatic access to words. As with any skill, the way reading becomes automatic is through practice, and much of it. Grade-school children vary dramatically in the level of print exposure they have, but it is not unreasonable to expect the average sixth-grade reader to read one million words a year. Even so, even more practice allows the child additional opportunities to develop fluent automatic access to words. Therefore, children should be encouraged to read *anything*. Parents may shake their heads in disbelief when the child picks out another book about baseball, or another Nancy Drew mystery. The temptation is to direct the child away from reading these "popular" books, and into something that will be "good for them." However, developing these basic reading skills *is* good for them. A child is much better off, in terms of developing reading skills, reading 10,000 pages of Nancy Drew than 2500 pages of the "classics." Children should be encouraged to read everything—magazines, newspaper, comic books, even cereal boxes! All of these serve as important practice, and hasten the development of skilled reading.

E. Speed Reading

Advertisements for "speed reading" courses are everywhere. Sometimes the claims are fairly modest—some claim that these programs can double your reading rates, for example. Sometimes, though, the claims are extraordinary—"increase your reading rates to 10,000 word per minute, *with no loss of comprehension!*" Such claims are impressive, and if they could work, would be a great benefit. The question, of course, is do they work?

The answer is twofold, in some respects. First, it is impossible to increase true *reading* to 10,000 words per minute, for reasons which will be explained later. However, some of these readers may be developing a related, and also highly useful skill—skimming. During skimming, readers are aware that they are not reading every word, but when they finish, they can often tell the "gist" of the passage. Under the best possible circumstances, skimming rates might be several thousand words per minute. Skimming an article can be useful, as readers might be able to learn much of what was in the article in a shorter period of time.

That having been said, that is not the same as true reading. The limitations on reading are physiological and perceptual, not purely cognitive. The two main determinants in the true upper limits of reading rates have been discussed earlier: the rate of the saccades and the perceptual span. As was mentioned before, readers are limited, by the limitations of our neurons, to a maximum of about five saccades per second. Perceptual spans are limited by the resolution power of the retina outside of the fovea. The only way to increase saccades rate would be to increase the rate of firing of our neurons. The only way to increase the resolution power of the retina would be to add additional cones in the parafoveal regions. Neither, obviously, can be done.

F. Maximum Reading Rates

How fast can readers read, then? By using very generous estimates, we can make an educated guess. Assume that a reader makes five saccades per second, and makes no backward saccades at all (a very generous estimate). Next, assume the reader can see three words with each saccade (also very generous). Thus, the reader can see 15 words per second, and, since there are 60 sec in a minute, can read 900 words per minute. It is unlikely that few, if any, readers approach that figure. Few typically read half that fast. Theoretically, though, the maximum rate on true reading would be something less than 900 words per minute.

VI. DYSLEXIA

Dyslexia is a specific reading problem. We might define dyslexia as a specific reading (not language) problem in individuals who

1. have roughly normal intelligence
2. have been provided adequate instruction
3. have been raised in a culturally appropriate environment
4. have a desire to read
5. show no sign of neurological deficits

Such a definition excludes many people—individuals who were never schooled, those with inadequate levels of intelligence to read, those with brain damage, etc. Those reading-impaired individuals should not be confused with true dyslexics. The term "dyslexia" has traditionally been reserved for those readers who, despite otherwise normal educational achievement, fail to read. Often, readers will be diagnosed as dyslexic if they read two grade levels below where they should be reading, or if they are 2 standard deviations below the mean reading ability for their peers (roughly, the bottom 3% of the distribution).

One caveat: the term "dyslexia" is a catch-all term, embodying a number of different reading problems. It is extremely unlikely that all readers diagnosed with dyslexia suffer the same cause. To say someone has dyslexia is in some ways no more informative that a physician telling someone they have a virus.

When discussing dyslexia, researchers ask, are dyslexics *qualitatively* different than normal readers? Or are they simply readers at one of the distribution? Half the people in any given grade read below average (that is what the "average" means!). In addition, 2.5% of readers will read 2 standard deviations below their grade level. That is true because reading ability, like every other trait, is normally distributed. If dyslexics are simply those readers at the bottom end of the distribution, doing things like normal readers, but just not as well, then they need not be separated from other readers. If, however, they are entirely different, doing things normal readers do not, then something special may be going on. [*See* DYSLEXIA.]

A. Developmental and Acquired Dyslexia

Dyslexia researchers make several classifications of dyslexia. First, they distinguish between *acquired dyslexia* and *developmental dyslexia*. Acquired dyslexia is defined as some type of dyslexia which can be attributed to known brain damage. Developmental dyslexia, on the other hand, is dyslexia for which there is no identifiable brain damage. For present purposes, developmental dyslexia is of greater interest. Developmental dyslexics account for the majority of the individual diagnosed, and are the most frustrating for parents, teachers, and researchers. Often, these are bright, motivated students, doing well in other subjects, who simply cannot read.

When researching developmental dyslexia, it is instructive to compare them with a group of readers known as "backward readers." Backward readers may also read two grade levels below their age-appropriate peers, but backward readers also have a level of intelligence 2 years below their peers. That is, they may be 10 years old, reading at an 8-year-old level, but have an IQ of 80 (which is a way of saying they have the level of intelligence of an average 8-year-old). Several differences are striking. While backward readers are almost equally divided between males and females, about three-fourth of all dyslexics are male. In addition to the obvious IQ difference, backward readers show other signs of neurological impairment, such as movement problems. Perhaps most striking, and most surprising, is the prognosis for the two. The prognosis for dyslexics is poor; currently, educators have a fairly low success rate with dyslexics. In contrast, the prognosis for backward readers is comparatively good. The backward-reading child may always read at a level below their age, but they will continue to make progress. Ironically, then, if two 10 year olds—one a bright but dyslexic child, the other a less-intelligence backward reader—are in the same remedial reading class, chances are very good that in 5 years, the less-intelligent child will be reading better.

B. What Acquired Dyslexia Says about Developmental Dyslexia

Before examining possible causes of developmental dyslexia, two kinds of acquired dyslexia, surface dyslexia and deep dyslexia, deserve mention. Both are cause by brain damage, but the resulting outcomes are quite different. Surface dyslexics appear to read only by using the phonological route. Not all words are equally accessible through the phonological route. English has a number of irregular words, where the symbols do not correspond directly to the phonemes. Examples would be words like "island," "colonel," and "stomach." A surface dyslexic will read those words as "iz-land," "kol-o-nell," and "stow-match." The surface dyslexic, then, seems to have lost the direct-access route of reading.

By contrast, deep dyslexics read only using the direct-access route. They have lost the ability to sound out words using their phonological route. Thus, they make errors of a different sort. They may be shown the word "dresser," and they'll say "bureau." Or, when given the word "car," they might say "automobile." Notice that the errors will often serve to preserve meaning, though the reader changes the exact wording used.

These two dyslexia types are perhaps the strongest evidence we have for a dual-route model of reading. As is so often the case in psychology, researchers learn about normal functioning by looking at what is lost in abnormal cases.

C. Potential Causes of Developmental Dyslexia

The underlying cause of acquired dyslexia is clear: brain damage. Neurologists can usually pinpoint the areas of damage through sophisticated tests (though the treatment is much less successful). However, the cause (or more correctly, the causes) of developmental dyslexia remains a puzzle. Since dyslexia is a term which lumps together a variety of disabilities, it is not surprising to find out that there is no single underlying "cause."

About 10 years ago, dyslexia was commonly thought of as a disorder where readers saw letters reversed and/or out of order. Now, researchers believe that kind of perceptual problem to be relatively rare, and uncharacteristic of most dyslexics. When compared to normal children on perceptual/spatial tasks (which did not involve verbal materials), dyslexics typically perform as well as normal readers. Despite anecdotal evidence to the contrary, dyslexics do not consistently reverse letters or numbers.

Researchers have long known that the eye movements of dyslexics were abnormal. Dyslexics take longer to make saccades. When they make a saccade, they typically move their eyes ahead fewer letters than do normal readers. They make longer regressive saccades than do normal readers, and their regressive saccades are more frequent. In short, they move their eyes much less efficiently. However, the fact that dyslexics have faulty eye movements begs the question, are the faulty eye movement the *cause* of the dyslexia, or are they are *result* of poor reading behavior? After all, if an unfamiliar language were presented to readers of English (especially a language that was written from right to left), their eye movements would be considerably less efficient than skilled readers of that language. If faulty eye movements are the cause of the reading problems, though, then eye movement training potentially could be a useful treatment.

Recent evidence indicates that the faulty eye movements are the result of faulty reading, not the cause of it. If normal readers are given very difficult texts to read, their eye movements become similar to those of dyslexics. If dyslexics are given easy material to read, their eye movements become much more like those of normal readers. Therefore, it seems unlikely that dyslexia is caused by faulty eye movements.

Recently, Richard Olson and his colleagues at the University of Colorado undertook an enormous project designed to analyze the word recognition skills of dyslexic twins. Olson was able to find monozygotic twins (which share 100% of their genetic material) and dizygotic twins (which share only 50% of their genetic material). Through the use of sophisticated analyses, not only were they able to determine the concordance rates among the twins (that is, the likelihood that one twin would be dyslexic given that the other was also dyslexic), but also the cause of the dyslexia (whether it was caused by genetic factors or external factors, such as teaching).

Olson's group made several remarkable findings. First, he found that the concordance rate among identical (monozygotic) twins was very high, with genetic factors accounting for roughly 40% of the dyslexia. More interesting, though were the results separating phonological and orthographic (letter-based) factors. The influence of genetics on phonological skill was over 90%—the very nature of the phonological store (to use Baddeley's term) was alomost entirely genetically determined. By contrast, their was no influence of genetics on the orthographic skills (identifying letters, etc.). Those skills were determined exclusively by external factors, such as schooling and reading practice.

These results reinforce an important point made throughout this chapter: the role of phonology in reading is paramount. Individuals who suffer from phonological deficits (resulting in shorter working memory spans) are at risk for reading problems. Working memory space is an extremely valuable resource, and those who use it more efficiently will be better readers.

Finally, one other potential cause of dyslexia must be mentioned. Some proportion of the individuals who suffer from dyslexia, in truth, probably never learned the basic phonological mapping skills. The task is daunting, especially to the typical first grader. Though things seem to be changing in recent years, historically reading remediation with dyslexics has not been successful. Educators are becoming aware now that the phonetic principle *must* be acquired for reading to proceed. Skipping a child who is having trouble with those skills to a more advanced reading level is certain to fail. Until children grasp the phonemic, alphabetic principle, remedial education should be directed there.

That brings with it a whole host of additional problems, though. As every parent knows, children can be rather cruel toward their classmates who are in remedial education. The fifth-graders, then, who are taken out of the classroom so that they can be in the first- or second-grade reading class are likely to be derided. They will see themselves as stupid, or as lazy, or both. Reading will become a source of discomfort to them. They will dread lessons in school (and their motivation and attention will suffer). They will hate reading outside of school (which is so important in the development of skilled reading). They will also see reading as a form of punishment, and will not see it as a source of pleasure. Their problems will likely compound, but more as a result of social factors than as a result of educational factors.

VII. LITERACY

Finally, any discussion of reading would not be complete without at least a brief mention of the role of reading in literacy. In recent years, a number of scholars have forcefully argued that American educators are creating a "culturally illiterate" society. Though our children are learning to read, they do not read what society in the past has deemed culturally important.

Reading researchers typically have several reactions to the push toward cultural literacy. First of all, they all are sympathetic to the loss of what seemed to be culturally shared knowledge. References to Shakespeare have been replaced by references to "Wayne's World." Works of literature that have inspired readers for so many generations are certainly worth reading. Parents wish our 15 years olds could read "Romeo and Juliet" as they did, and see the wonderful, terrible lessons. Professors wish college freshmen would come to their first class with some knowledge of who Poe was, and what a reference to a "golden calf" meant. At one level, reading researchers join the outcry.

At a second level, though, they disagree. Literacy is built upon a reading public, and despite the advances we have made in terms of studying the reading process, illiteracy rates in America are still astonishingly high (some report high school illiteracy rates of 25%). If the children are not taught to read in the first few years of their schooling, any chance of a "culturally literate" society is lost. Therefore, the focus on teaching skills before content seems to be a more than reasonable trade-off, especially early in the educational process.

VIII. SUMMARY

As has been stated through this article, reading is more than a logical extension of spoken language. Though its ties to speech are clear, reading involves very different skills, and vast amounts of practice. Early reading which stresses phonics has proven to be the most successful approach, and prereaders who have the basic building-blocks of reading—letter detection skills and phonemic awareness—are at a great advantage. As reading becomes more skilled, the reliance on phonological mediation lessens. Words become directly accessible, and the reading process becomes more efficient.

Skilled reading is the result of several factors. Readers must possess a nonintuitive grasp of their spoken language (phonemes). They must learn the symbols-to-phonemes match inherent in our alphabetic language. They must gradually learn to recognize patterns of letters (and eventually, words). All of these factors require many hundreds of hours of practice.

Bibliography

Adams, M. J. (1990). "Beginning to Read." MIT Press, Cambridge, MA.

Barr, R., Kamil, M. L., Mosenthal, P., and Pearson, P. D. (1991). "The Handbook of Reading Research," Vol. II. Longman, New York.

Crowder, R. G., and Wagner, R. K. (1992). "The Psychology of Reading," 2nd ed. Oxford University Press, New York.

Flesch, R. (1985). "Why Johnny Can't Read," 2nd ed. Harper and Row, New York.

Pearson, P. D., Barr, R., Kamil, and Mosenthal, M. L. (1984). "The Handbook of Reading Research," Vol. I. Longman, New York.

Perfetti, C. A. (1985). "Reading Ability." Oxford University Press, New York.

Rayner, K., and Pollatsek, A. (1989). "The Psychology of Reading." Prentice–Hall, Englewood Cliffs, NJ.

Vellutino, F. R. (1979). "Dyslexia: Theory and Practice." MIT Press, Cambridge, MA.

REASONING

Willis F. Overton
Temple University

Glossary

Cognition Set of psychological processes that involve the construction, acquisition, maintenance, and utilization of knowledge.

Competence Abstract, universal idealization of a system of thought or reasoning. Also termed mental structures.

Deductive inference Inference process that moves from the universal to the particular, and premises provide absolute certainty for the conclusion.

Embodiment A theory of mind claiming that mind emerges from the biocultural field as a self-organizing activity system.

Implication A relation holding between propositions of the form "If *p* then *q*," where it could not possibly be the case that the antecedent clause or premise *(p)* is true, and the consequent clause or conclusion *(q)* is false, and where there is a relevance relation between the antecedent and conclusion. Also called "logical truth," "entailment," and "validity."

Inductive inference Inference process that moves from the particular to the general, and premises provide probable or contingent evidence for the conclusion.

Logical necessity A relation holding among propositions where a conclusion follows with absolute certainty from the premises.

Procedure Actual or real-time strategy employed during thinking or reasoning. Provides access to and implementation of competence.

Reasoning The form of thinking that involves inference. Inference can be either inductive or deductive; hence, there is inductive reasoning and deductive reasoning.

Thinking Psychological process involving the construction and manipulation of symbols.

REASONING must be understood as one set of psychological processes that form part of a more general set of processes known as cognition. Cognitive processes are all those that involve the construction, acquisition, maintenance, and utilization of knowledge. Thus, cognitive processes include, at least, perception, thinking, language, memory, and problem solving. Of these cognitive processes, thinking—defined as the construction and manipulation of symbols—is most central to our interest because reasoning is a particular type of thinking. Reasoning is thinking that involves inference which is the process where one proposition (i.e., a set of symbols) is arrived at and accepted on the basis of other propositions that were originally accepted. The originally accepted propositions are called premises and these provide the evidence from which inferences are made to the proposition called a conclusion. Reasoning then, is distinguished from other types of thinking such as associative thinking, fantasy thinking, productive thinking, and creative thinking that do not directly involve the inference process.

Reasoning is a specific type of thinking, but there are also several types of reasoning. Usually these are divided into inductive reasoning processes and deductive reasoning processes. Deductive reasoning is unique because it is the only type of reasoning in which the inference process leads from general propositions to particular propositions, and the premises provide absolutely conclusive ("necessary") evidence for the truth of the conclusions. Other types of reasoning, including for example, pragmatic reasoning (based on knowledge of context), statistical reasoning (based on probability), and modal reasoning (based on both possibilities and necessities), involve inductive inferences. In this case the inference process leads from the particular to the general. In inductive reasoning, premises provide probable, not necessary, evidence for conclusions.

While the general focus of this article is on reasoning, the specific focus involves the nature, origin, and development of deductive or formal reasoning. This is a domain that is central to scientific reasoning and hypothesis testing, and it is the domain that is central to the production of coherent arguments which can guide a good deal of day to day life. Even if, as some critics claim, everyday reasoning involves more pragmatic and probabilistic inductive thought than deductive thought, an understanding of that nature of deductive reasoning forms a necessary foundation for considerations of when and under what conditions this type of reasoning is displaced by pragmatic reasoning and other types of thought.

I. REASONING AND LOGIC

In order to clarify the specific nature of deductive reasoning and to clearly differentiate it from both inductive reasoning and logic consider the following examples:

1. All trains from Philadelphia to Washington stop in Baltimore.
   The train on Track 6 goes from Philadelphia to Washington.
   Therefore, the train on Track 6 stops in Baltimore.
2. All the trains I have ever seen that go from Philadelphia to Washington
   have stopped in Baltimore.
   Therefore, all trains from Philadelphia to Washington stop in Baltimore.

Example 1 involves deductive inference, and example 2 involves an inductive inference. Here it is important to be clear that logic and deductive reasoning are not identical. Logic is a discipline of study that is not, in itself, interested in the reasoning processes (i.e., inductive reasoning and deductive reasoning) that produce these examples. The reasoning processes are the domain of cognitive and cognitive–developmental psychology. Logicians are interested in the products of the reasoning processes which they term *arguments*. From the perspective of psychology, examples 1 and 2 involve types of inferences—a deductive reasoning inference and an inductive reasoning inference, respectively—but from the perspective of logic, example 1 is a deductive argument, and example 2 is an inductive argument. Logic identifies and analyzes arguments that are accepted as correct or incorrect. Logical reasoning concerns mental processes that are related to logical arguments. [*See* LOGIC.]

For the logician, an argument is a sequence of sentences or propositions of which one (the conclusion) is said to follow from the others (premises), and the premises are said to provide evidence for the truth of the conclusion. Deductive arguments have the characteristic of being *valid* (correct) or *invalid* (incorrect). To say that a deductive argument is valid is to say that it is absolutely impossible to find situations in which the argument has true premises and a false conclusion. Thus, the conclusion necessarily or logically follows from the premises in a valid deductive argument. Inductive arguments cannot be valid/invalid because the premises provide only probable evidence for the truth of the conclusion. Regardless of how many trains to Washington that one sees stop in Baltimore, there may be some trains that go straight through.

The sentences that compose deductive arguments are true or false, but the argument itself is valid or invalid. Further, a valid argument may have true premises and a true conclusion (e.g., all parents have children; all fathers are parents; therefore, all fathers have children); false premises and a false conclusion (e.g., all children have siblings; all fathers are children; therefore, all fathers have siblings); or false premises and a true conclusion (e.g., all children have siblings; all brothers are fathers; therefore, all brothers have siblings). The validity of a deductive argument is relatively independent of the truth of its premises and conclusion. The only relation precluded by a valid deductive argument is true premises and a false conclusion.

The *truth* of a sentence or a propositions in a deductive argument is best understood through the concept *possible worlds*. Roughly, a possible world is any situation that is conceivable or imaginable and can be described by a consistent story. This means there are many possible worlds (e.g., the worlds of novels, films, myths, etc.). The common sense familiar world—called the *actual world*—is one of these possible worlds. A sentence is true in a given possible world when the sentence correctly describes that possible world. Furthermore, a sentence is logically or necessarily true when it is true in all possible worlds.

The distinction between validity and truth leads to another important distinction that is often not kept clear when people investigate deductive reasoning. This is the relationship between the validity and the *soundness* of a deductive argument. For an argument to be sound it must be valid, but it must also be the case that each of the premises are true in the actual world. Thus, some arguments will be valid but not sound, but all sound arguments will also be valid.

Logic then is concerned with identifying valid and invalid arguments. More generally, it is concerned with identifying the forms or patterns of valid arguments regardless of their specific content. Logicians begin this task from simple sentences and the *sentential connectives* that join them together (i.e., "not" called *negation;* "and" called *conjunction;* "or" called *disjunction;* "if . . . then" called the *conditional;* "if and only if" called the *biconditional*) and demonstrate valid and invalid arguments related to these connectives. The elementary arguments that are established as valid are building blocks for elementary *argument forms* or *rules of inference* that are used to analyze more complex arguments. The simplest of these argument forms are Modus Ponens, Modus Tollens, and the Hypothetical Syllogism:

1. Modus Ponens
   If p then q
   $\underline{p}$
   Therefore, q.
2. Modus Tollens
   If p then q
   Not $\underline{q}$
   Therefore, not p.
3. Hypothetical Syllogism
   If p then q
   If q then r
   Therefore, if p then r.

In these and other valid argument forms any content can be substituted for p, q, r and the argument remains valid (i.e., the argument remains valid in all possible worlds).

The general deductive system that incorporates the connectives and inference rules is called a *propositional* or *sentential* logic. A more powerful system that includes the propositional logic, but goes beyond it, is variously called *quantificational, predicate,* or *first-order* logic. This system has features concerned with the internal structure of propositions and the quantification of propositions (i.e., all, some, none) along with the features described by the propositional logic. The simplest kind of quantified arguments are the *syllogisms*. For example:

All B are A
Some C are B
Therefore, some C are A

Deductive propositional and predicate logics ultimately are formalizations of the commonsense correct deductive arguments that people engage in on a day to day basis. The logics are attempts to establish rules according to which such arguments proceed. A logic is a theory of the nature of arguments. By establishing the rules of valid deductive arguments, a logic also pinpoints the nature of error or incorrect arguments. When logic is seen in this fashion, it again helps to illustrate the distinction between logic and logical reasoning. If logic is composed of the rules of arguments, then logical reasoning concerns psychological processes that somehow reflect these rules. The major question then for psychology concerns the way in which the psychological processes of reasoning come to reflect these rules.

Although it was a major controversy in the past, a strong consensus has recently developed indicating that virtually all normal adults demonstrate the *capacity* to reason successfully on complex deductive reasoning tasks. This is not to say that deductive reasoning cannot be undercut by pragmatic factors. There is, in fact, a body of data which suggests that the individual can indeed be diverted from reasoning deductively by factors such as the plausibility of premises and various kinds of real world knowledge. However, these findings simply reinforce the distinction between what people do in many everyday settings and what they are capable of doing. Given that there is strong evidence that normal adults demonstrate a capacity to reason deductively, the question of significance is how they come to develop this capacity. Of secondary interest is the question of what factors produce suboptimal reasoning when the capacity for optimal reasoning is available to the individual. [*See* DEDUCTIVE REASONING.]

II. REASONING AS COMPETENCE VERSUS REASONING AS PROCEDURAL

Historically, there have been two alternative proposals, each designed to present a sufficient theoretical account of deductive reasoning. One of these has been called a competence or mental logic approach, the other has been called a procedural approach. The competence alternative claims that the rules of logical arguments can be understood as relatively adequate models of normative, idealized, abstract operations of mind in this domain. Thus, the claim is made that the individual in some sense acquires and has access to the operations characterized by these rules. However, it is emphatically denied that these operations need be conscious. The rules, thus described, constitute a competence, and the competence is held to be a significant feature of the explanation for adequate performance on deductive reasoning tasks. It is important to note, however, that the competence is not to be thought of as mental representations used in actual reasoning. Competence is an idealization of the system of thought that the normal adult has access to. It constitutes an epistemic (i.e., universal) model. The actual individual mental representations used in accessing and implementing this competence constitutes a procedural model.

Within the group of investigators who agree that competence is a necessary feature for understanding logical reasoning a primary issue of disagreement concerns the manner in which competence is acquired. Some claim that competence is primarily innate; others claim that competence is partially innate and the rest directly learned; others that language structures provide the basic forms out of which logical deductive competence is abstracted; and others claim that competence emerges out of the general cognitive activity of the organism interacting with its world.

The procedural group has a strong commitment to the use of information processing and computational models as explanatory devices. Furthermore, and most importantly, in contrast to the epistemic models developed by the competence group, the models of the procedural group are pragmatic and instrumental in nature. These models are characterized by being attempts to imitate real or actual actions in real time rather than being abstract idealizations of logical rule systems. There have been a range of specific models employed by this group to attempt to account for performance on deductive reasoning tasks. Some simple information processing models claim that direct real world experiences stored in memory as counterexamples are sufficient to explain reasoning with conditional or other propositions. For example, presented with the conditional proposition "If a student strikes a teacher, then the student is suspended," the individual begins with a memory search. If a counterexample or a generalization of a counterexample is retrieved from memory (i.e., a student who has struck a teacher and not been suspended), the individual asserts that the rule is false, otherwise he asserts it as true. Other procedural theorists also claim that direct real world experiences are sufficient. However, experiences are represented as inductions from pragmatic activities such as permissions, obligations, and causations. The inductions form generalized knowledge structures called "pragmatic reasoning schemas." When similarly structured material is presented at a later time the schema is elicited and this provides a richer source of examples from which to draw inferences than if the schema is not elicited. Johnson-Laird's work on mental models represents the most systematically developed procedural computational model of deductive reasoning. Johnson-Laird's mental models are presumed actual procedures and representations derived from the real world that the individual employs when processing specific reasoning tasks in real time.

In examining theories of the nature of deductive reasoning we thus find that this domain is currently being explained by two broad classes of seemingly incompatible theories—*competence* theories and *procedural* theories. Competence theories describe normative abstract idealizations taken to represent operations of mind that are relatively enduring, universal, and applicable to a broad range of phenomena. The competence—also called mental structures—thus described, has been formulated in terms of the rules of deductive logic when the domain of explanation is deductive reasoning. Competence is primarily formal or syntactic in nature. Procedural or process theories describe specific representations and procedures as these are applied in real time to local problems. Procedural theories suggest that the solution to deductive problems occurs through inductively derived strategies. Procedures involve specific contents and are primarily semantic in nature.

III. CRITIQUES OF COMPETENCE AND PROCEDURES

It is important to note—but not surprising—that critiques presented against each class of theory have been argued from the strength of the critic's theory to the weakness of the theory under review. Critiques of competence theories focus on the failure of deductive competence to account for concrete events such as situational effects, content effects, and pragmatic factors that occur in actual chronological time (real time) Johnson-Laird's objections are typical. He argues that, according to competence theories, people should not make mistakes, and semantic content should not influence task solutions. "The most glaring problem is that people make mistakes. They draw invalid conclusions, which should not occur if deduction is guided by mental logic" (1983, p. 25). "The underlying assumption of any formal logic . . . is that deductions are valid in virtue of their form, not their content. . . . If . . . a rule of inference is laid down in the mind, it should apply whatever the content of the proposition" (pp. 29–30).

Johnson-Laird's and similar objections hold only if competence theories are understood as being procedural in nature. That is, they hold only if the claim is made that competence operates as an effective procedure in real time which should, therefore, inevitably produce the correct answer regardless of content or other situational factors. The significant fact here, of course, is that competence theories need not and do not make such a claim. Competence theories make the epistemic claim that when deductive competence is properly accessed and implemented it will lead to valid solutions. Proper access and implementation are procedural issues. Competence theorists may be criticized for failing to develop a procedural component as part of a general theory of reasoning. But, this is a very different thing than expecting a competence theory to be a procedural theory.

Critiques of procedural theories have focused on the inadequacy of procedures to account for the specifically logical (i.e., necessary and universal) features of deductive reasoning. Recent empirical work suggests that the direct memory and pragmatic positions are not sufficient to account for logical features that go beyond the effects of local content. Further, Braine argues that the principal value of the pragmatic approach has been in demonstrating the facilitative effect of local content, rather than as a general account of deductive reasoning. Evans raises the methodological question of whether memory and pragmatic investigations can, in principle, yield general explanations of *deductive reasoning* since their designs are based on features that go beyond the information given.

Russell has reviewed the concept of mental models and concludes that a mental model is not an account of "comprehension or logical understanding itself, but rather, a way of conceptualizing the real-time mental life of a rule-follower." Others in turn, argue that logic enters mental models in implicit and unanalyzed ways through the theory of reference and through the effective procedures Johnson-Laird describes. And Braine maintains that mental models can, at best, account for only a small subset of reasoning problems.

IV. TOWARD AN INTEGRATED COMPETENCE–PROCEDURAL THEORY

The apparent incompatibility between competence and procedural theories can be maintained only to the degree that one type of theory is understood as a substitute for the other. To the extent that they are seen as individuated but interrelated components of a general theory of reasoning the incompatibility vanishes. The rejection of any position that maintains that competence and procedural theories can substitute for each other forms the foundation for the construction of a general competence–procedural theory of deductive reasoning. This idea is both the thesis of, and the point of development for, the rest of this chapter.

From the integrative competence–procedural position, competence theory is designed to explain the comprehension or understanding of logic. Competence describes general performance specifications but it is neutral on how the system is to be accessed or implemented. Procedural theory is designed to explain the real-time processing that provides access to, and the implementation of, competence.

Before exploring, in some detail, a specific competence–procedural theory of reasoning, a preliminary metatheoretical issue needs to be presented. In general, the type of cognitive theory that gets generated to explain any domain depends to a great degree on the kind of theory of mind that operates as the foundation for understanding cognitive processes. If one accepts a blank slate theory of mind, then all knowledge acquisitions, including the reasoning process, will tend to be understood as the result of direct learning or direct environmental instruction. If one holds to a computational theory of mind, then the tendency is to see the basic processes as prewired into the system and specific content as a direct acquisition from the environment. Procedural theories and some competence theories (e.g., Braine) have historically been formulated within the context of these two understandings of the nature of mind.

Recently, a theory of mind, called embodiment theory, has been gaining support as a coherent alternative to either of these earlier perspectives. Embodiment theory of mind rests on an understanding of mind as a self-organizing system. Mind is understood according to the same categories that are fundamental to other self-organizing systems, chief among these being the categories of differentiation, integration, and emergent levels of organization. Mind is considered to be a web of beliefs, intentions, and desires that emerge from the organism's activity as it operates in a biocultural field. From this perspective mind is neither a disengaged subjective concept derived from an isolated and reified biology nor a set of equally disengaged cultural and linguistic norms. Mind is an emergent organization that through activity differentiates from the biocultural field and further transforms itself into novel forms of organization that are characterized by terms such as thinking and reasoning. It is within this understanding of mind that the following competence–procedural theory of reasoning is proposed.

V. A COMPETENCE–PROCEDURAL THEORY OF REASONING

To a significant extent this embodied theory of reasoning grows out of the later writing of Jean Piaget. It is most unfortunate that these later writings have thus far not been adequately examined by investigators in the field of reasoning because they offer a coherent integrative approach that moves far beyond Piaget's early work in the field of reasoning. In his early work, Piaget focused on the mental structures that serve the function of deductive reasoning in the adult. He described the organization of these structures as a propositional calculus and characterized this variously as the "INRC group," the structure of formal thought, second order operational structures. Whatever its detailed characterization, the organization has always been understood as the competence of the normal adult with respect to mathematical–logical or deductive reasoning. Further, the theory is designed to describe and explain the transformations in cognition that lead to this adult level of competence. To achieve this developmental task Piaget described several forms of mental organization that emerge during ontogenesis and represent weaker, less flexible, less mobile approaches to reasoning. For infancy he described the development of an organization of action that, lacking symbols, does not constitute reasoning but represents a kind of logic of action (sensorimotor schemes and the *structures d'ensemble*) that serves as a weak prototype for later reasoning. For toddler-hood and childhood he described the transformation of the logic of action into a symbolic competence and then a representational reasoning characterized by a class logic of hierarchies, relations, and quantifiers (concrete operational thought, concrete operational structures, groupings). This form of reasoning constitutes logical reasoning but is limited by not being interpropositional in nature. The interpropositional deductive reasoning or formal reasoning is the final form of reasoning competence. It emerges and becomes available for logical problem solving during adolescence.

In the latter part of his career Piaget, moved to expand his theory of logical reasoning by focusing increased attention on the nature of strategies or procedures that develop to access and implement the developing competence as that competence becomes available. The increased focus on procedures in no way devalued the competence analysis; it simply increased the scope of the general theory. In the most contemporary extension of the theory, Piaget describes the individual as developing two types of cognitive systems, competence systems and procedural systems. Competence systems function to understand the world. They are composed of the relatively stable, relatively enduring, and universal structures just described. This is the epistemic subject, and the organization of structures is considered to be complete, as in the highest level of formal reasoning competence, or incomplete, as in concrete operational logic, or the logic of sensorimotor action.

Procedural systems function to assure success on problems. They are composed of individuated real-time action systems that may be sequentially ordered but are not enduring in the way that the competence systems endures. A procedure is an action means to an end or goal. It is context dependent, and context includes both the available competence and information inputs (e.g., success at baking a cake requires stirring, mixing, and beating, but a recipe and ingredients form the necessary context for these procedures). A procedural system constitutes the psychological subject, and procedures are considered to be sufficient or insufficient, rather than complete or incomplete.

Because the kinds of procedures that can be used to account for the actual processing of deductive problems are limited only by functional criteria—real-time processing and sensitivity to inputs, outputs, and internal states—the number of candidates for designation as procedures is large. For example, it could be the case that people process deductive problems by actually thinking in terms of truth tables, by actually thinking in terms of Venn diagrams, by actually thinking in terms of natural deductive procedures, by mental models, by pragmatic methods, or by various methods employing direct experience. Further, procedures may reflect individual differences or individual strategies. As a consequence, different people may—at different times and under different circumstances—use different procedures as they attempt to access and implement available competence in efforts directed at solving deductive reasoning problems.

The variety of potential specific procedural models has noteworthy implications for the relationship between competence and procedures. A significant—but frequently misunderstood—point is that empirical research designed to examine the viability of particular procedural models is not directly relevant to the adequacy of the notation system used in the formalization of competence models. Thus, for example, Braine suggests that empirical work has generally shown that people do not actually use truth tables in solving deductive problems. This research is valuable in ruling out truth tables as a procedural model. However, the research is irrelevant to the question of whether truth functional rules should be used as the notation for a model of competence. The observation that people seldomly think in terms of truth tables would be relevant to the adequacy of the competence model only under the assumption that there is or must be an identity between competence and procedures. However, identity implies that the one could be a substitute for the other. This position has already been rejected as an impediment to an adequate account of the broad range of empirical findings that are currently available concerning reasoning.

A. Developmental Origins of Competence and Procedures

The integration of a competence perspective and a procedural perspective into a competence–procedural theory of reasoning requires a specification of how these systems arise out of the embodied activity of the organism and how these systems develop and become transformed from infancy through adulthood. At birth the organism is fundamentally a self-organizing activity matrix that is undifferentiated with respect to psychological processes. The initial organization present at birth is primarily biological in nature. This system is differentiated into systems and subsystems arranged as an integrated set of hierarchies at the biological level, but it is neutral (undifferentiated) with respect to psychological processes and systems. Psychological organization and processes differentiate out of this neutral matrix through both sensory and motoric activity. Thus, the acquisition of both competence and procedural systems initially emerges from the embodied experiences of the organism. Following sufficient development at this sensorimotor level, further differentiations and integrations lead to the emergence of new systems that are characterized as "representational" or "conceptual," and this is identified as the preoperational level. The process continues and ultimately leads to a level at which the acquired system can be characterized as a relatively complete logic system and the procedures that access and implement this competence. This level is identified as the level of reflective or formal deductive reasoning.

The process that accounts for the development within levels of cognitive organization and accounts for the reorganization from level to level is the embodied activity which Piaget defined as assimilation/accommodation. Assimilation and accommodation are two sides of the same general activity—adaptation—and each is present in every cognitive act. Assimilation is the component of any cognitive act that transforms the surrounding to conform to the current organization of the organism. Thus, it is the activity component that interprets (even at a bodily level of interpretation) the actual world resistance that it comes up against. Assimilation is an act of *integration* in that the resistance the activity meets is transformed into the organization of the system. Assimilation, therefore, is the activity that gives meaning to the world. When the infant sucks—what a third-person adult observer would call the mother's breast—a suckable is created by the infant. This suckable is a part of the infant's organized activity and the meaning of the object is just that activity.

Accommodation is secondary to assimilation. It is embodied activity that is dependent on the resistances which assimilation meets. Accommodation is the act of differentiation. While assimilation imposes necessity by projecting outward the current organization, accommodation opens possibilities through the partial failures of these projections as they are reflected inward. Accommodation reflects the fact that every activity leads to a change in the organization of the system. It is the progressive component of the assimilation/accommodation dialectic. Just as affirmations naturally lead to negations in a dialectic model, accommodations are the natural result of assimilations. Accommodation are *differentiations* that occur in the system. Just as a suckable is created when the infant sucks the mother's breast, this suckable is now a novel feature and hence a differentiation of the suckable system.

1. The Origin of Procedures

Beginning from initial biological organization and activity, early *psychological differentiations* yield classes of motor schemes designed to *interpret* the resistances of the actual world, and *implement* actions that succeed in that world. These schemes become *interpretative/implementation procedures* (Piaget's presentation and procedural schemes) and they further differentiate, at representational and reasoning levels, into classes of procedures described earlier (e.g., mental models, Venn diagrams).

An important developmental consequences follows from this account of the origin of the procedural system. The initial psychological cognitive system is procedural in nature. However, this system develops in the context of a biological competence. Thus, the root competence that forms the foundational context for interpretation/implementation psychological procedures is neither psychological nor representational in nature. This root competence is organized sensory and motor activity itself. This means that any strictly nativist account for the later acquisition of logical competence is rejected at the start. While biology (organized activity) is essential, it is essential in the constraints and opportunities it introduces and not through providing an unlearned set of specific logical rules or elements.

2. The Origin of Competence and Necessity

It is beyond the scope of this paper to present a detailed description of the manner in which sensorimotor procedures lead to the mental structures that constitute a sensorimotor competence characterized by a logic of action and the way that, in turn, this competence acts as context for the procedures developed at the level of representations. It is also beyond the scope of this paper to follow in detail this recursive and directional process through the incomplete reasoning competence system of the late representational level, and the relatively complete competence system of the formal reasoning level. However, a sketch of this process needs to be presented because it involves the development of the understanding of "necessity"; a concept that is central to all deductive reasoning.

In essence, the position being described here makes the claim that logical necessity is not a concept that is inductively derived from the observed world. Rather, logical necessity is the expression of a systemic feature of a logical model. This is analogous to the way that water is a systemic expression of a model of H_2O. Water has characteristics that are not elements of the system H_2O and logical necessity is a characteristic that is not a specific element of the system of logic. The logical model that yields logical necessity is the relatively complete deductive competence system of the adolescent or young adult.

Competence derives from a synthesis of procedural necessities (i.e., assimilations) and possibilities (i.e., accommodations), developed first at the sensorimotor level. The infant's early understanding of "the real" (that which is), "the necessary" (that which must be), and "the possible" (that which might be) are constructions (deriving from organized action and the resistance it meets) that differentiate out of the initially psychologically neutral activity matrix. Necessity is the expression of integrations realized through the activity of assimilation. Possibility is the expression of differentiations realized through the activity of accommodation. To illustrate this, consider further the example of sucking. Newborn sucking (biological assimilation) yields a result. It is when sucking meets a resistance (in the sense of failing to yield a result) that a compensation (accommodation) occurs. This variation of the original assimilation creates a new potential possibility that—when actualized—becomes a new assimilation (sensorimotor). Here then we have the first sensorimotor differentiation into necessity (assimilation), possibility (potential variations or accommodations), and reality (continued resistances). This is not, however, logical necessity. Psychologically it is still the necessity of a feeling of "must."

This sensorimotor procedural origin of necessity and possibility establishes the procedural base for progressive (higher level representational and reasoned levels) coordinations of possibilities—with their flexibility—and necessities—with their self-regulating system character—into increasingly complete competence systems. This means that the understanding of logical necessity that becomes evident first in childhood and adolescence is never the direct product of innate biological hardware as nativists often suggest, nor is it the product of inductive generalization drawn from direct observations of the world. Logical necessity is characteristic of a logical model—from the point of view of logic—or the deductive competence system—from the point of view of psychology. The developmental question is not how either the brain or the world generates feelings of "must." The developmental question is how an action understanding of "must" becomes transformed into a propositional understanding of "logical necessity."

Having *seen* a thousand trains going to Washington and stopping at Baltimore may yield a *contingent* (i.e., based on empirical knowledge) truth, and a very strong feeling that this train *must* stop at Baltimore; it does not, however, yield logical necessity. Possessing a competence system of understanding that generates integrations such as "All *A*'s are *B;* this is an *A;* therefore, this is a *B*" does yield logical necessity, and this is independent of any particular set of empirical observations concerning *A*'s or *B*'s. If all trains to Washington stop at Baltimore, and this is a train to Washington, then this train will stop in Baltimore. This statement is a logical necessity, and this has nothing to do with empirical observations of trains. The logical necessity comes from the formal or syntactical organization among the parts of the sentence, or more generally, among sets of propositions. It is this organization, beginning in biology as an initial pattern of action, becoming transformed through actions in the world into the sensorimotor "must," and undergoing transformations onto the planes of representations and logics, that comes to constitute the relatively complete deductive competence system of the adult.

In summary, the relatively complete deductive reasoning competence system takes the form of a logical deductive model, and the system differentiates out of sensorimotor procedures. As both the competence system and the procedural system advance, become transformed, and become projected onto higher levels of knowing (i.e., the representational or conceptual, followed by class logical reasoning and leading to interpropositional logical reasoning), reasoning competence increasingly comes to more adequately serve the function of logical comprehension or logical understanding. Interpretative/implementation procedures increasingly serve the function of providing access to, and implementation of, the available competence.

B. The Specific Nature of Competence: Meaning, Implication, and Relevance

In describing deductive competence as a system of understanding that takes the form of a logical deductive model, it becomes clear that it is important to consider the specific character of the logical model chosen to describe the system. The issue here is that the model chosen has implications for the theory of the development of the system as well as for the specific nature of the system itself.

Historically, logic was viewed as a kind of Platonic ideal. That is, logic was considered to be a set of absolute truths, and this set was independent of the experiences and understandings of humans. Given this view, it is not surprising that the logical models that were developed were primarily "extensional" in nature, and dealt with truth as a relationship of correspondence between sentences and the actual or real world. These truth-functional models (e.g., the propositional calculus) were, in fact, used by Piaget as a notational device to describe the deductive competences of the reasoning levels. However, because Piaget's general theory takes a rationalist or constructivist position, and asserts that all knowledge—including logical knowledge—is ultimately a product of human actions, the use of the realist truth-functional models has been seen recently as something of an embarrassment for the theory. In other words, it seemed somewhat odd for a system that is so radically intensional or constructivist at its root, to be so radically extensional or realist in its description of logical competence. Toward the end of his career, Piaget began to deal with this seeming inconsistency in two ways. On the one hand, he initiated some suggestions that might ultimately lead to changes in the notation of the competence model; moving from a propositional calculus toward a natural deductive system. On the other hand, he devoted more attention to describing how the competence system could be better understood as an intensional system that subsumed an extensional system. That is, he developed the groundwork to demonstrate that a seemingly extensional system, can in fact, emerge out of the embodied constructions of the individual.

The possible revision of Piaget's theory to a new notation system for the formal reasoning competence model was tentative and highly technical and will not be elaborated here. The effort to make the whole logical competence model more coherent by explicitly subsuming the extensional to the intensional, however, requires comment because it provides a foundation for further elaborations of an embodied theory of the development of reasoning.

Piaget made several strategic moves in his modification of the competence model: (a) There was a reaffirmation that the competence system is a system of meanings, and these arise out of the embodied experiences of the organism. Thus, whatever the specific character of the deductive competence system, it must arise out of the meaning system that the organism constructs through its actions. (b) The concept of *implication* was made central to the nature of the competence system. Implication has always had an important place in the system, but now it became the root concept. (c) It was suggested that an embodied form of implication represents an early sensorimotor acquisition, and provides the base for later developmentally transformed and elaborated forms of implication, which only give the appearance of being extensional. (d) The logical concept of *relevance* was introduced as an important bridge between meaning and implication.

The reaffirmation that all meaning, and, hence, all knowledge, arises out the sensory actions and the motoric actions of the individual requires little comment. This has always represented the core of Piaget's constructivism and it is codified in the concept assimilation which is understood as the primary cognitive process. As stated earlier, the organism gives meaning to the world through its actions; in particular, the actions defined by assimilation. Thus, logical knowledge must be rooted in, and derived from, early meanings, and not imposed by some independent set of external truths.

Implication is a relation that holds between premises and conclusion, or between antecedent and consequence, as in the proposition "If *p*, then *q*." When the relation of implication holds we can then say that *p implies q*. In fact, when *p* implies *q*, the argument is defined as a deductive argument. The issue then, is to specify exactly what defines this relation between antecedent and consequence (premises and conclusion). The answer is that the relation is defined as implication if and only if, it *could not possibly* be the case that the antecedent (premise) is true, and the consequent (conclusion) false. Thus, the implication relation is defined by being a logical necessity (*could not be the case in any possible world*). This relation is also referred to as *logical truth, entailment,* and *validity*.

Implication then, is a necessary relationship that leads from one state of affairs to another. But we have already seen that from an embodiment position "necessity" is rooted in organized actions of the individual beginning at the sensorimotor level. Thus, implication at a interpropositional formal reasoning level as, for example, in the Modus Ponens argument ("If *p*, then *q; p;* therefore *q*"), finds its primitive and incomplete origins in the preconceptual sensorimotor level (e.g., If I pull on the blanket, then I will bring the toy on top of the blanket closer). At the sensorimotor level, implication is clearly a relation between actions and not between symbols. As a consequence, an intensional, intuitive, but nonsymbolic, sense of "must" becomes available to the infant. At the representational level the intensional "must" appears in verbal form. At the formal reasoning level, the *matrix* of meanings that have been intensionally generated produce an understanding of logical necessity that has the appearance of being purely extensional in nature.

Implication was made central to the competence model, in part, to clarify how a *seemingly* external state of affairs like logical truth and validity can emerge out of the organized embodied activities of the individual. In the earlier system, implication played a critical role in formal reasoning, but implication had no clear direct roots in the early system of meanings. Instead, implication was understood to be an operation that was built up from the primitive operations "and," "or," and "not" that were acquired at the concrete operational level of reasoning. Implication then, in the original system, represented an integration of these atomic elements, and this integration emerged at the level of formal reasoning. In the modified system it is still predicted that a full deductive understanding of implication, including its various equivalent transformations (i.e., "not *p* or *q*"; "not the case that, *p* and not *q*"), will not be available until adolescence. However, primitive analogues of implication, including action implication as already described, and causal sequences that mimic implication, and are incorporated in language, will be available at earlier levels.

Although this discussion of implication demonstrates the critical role of meaning (i.e., precursors of logical necessity is are assimilations, and hence, meanings), it does not capture the full importance of meaning in the system. The introduction of the logical concept of *relevance* both forms an important bridge between meaning and implication, and expands on the definition of implication itself. For any conditional proposition ("If *p,* then *q*") there may be some identifiable meaningful relationship, linkage, or connection between the antecedent *(p)* and consequent *(q)* clauses, or there may be none. For example, for the conditional proposition, "If he is a bachelor, then he is unmarried," there is an identifiable relationship that is *definitional* in nature. For the conditional, "If you use your computer on the job, then it is tax deductible," there is an identifiable relationship and it is *conventional* in nature. However, for the conditional, "If the moon is made of blue cheese, then oceans are full of water," there is no identifiable meaningful connection between antecedent and consequence. The presence of a meaning relationship between antecedent and consequence is termed *relevance* in logic.

Relevance is a condition that is used in logic to distinguish genuine implication, or simply implication, from a weaker form of implication termed "material implication." Thus, the concepts *implication logical truth, entailment,* and *validity* require not only a necessary relationship between antecedent and consequence as discussed earlier, but also a relevance relationship.

Piaget uses the relevance relationship, which he calls "meaning implication" or "signifying implication," to further establish the central role of implication in the new competence system. This, in turn, further demonstrates both that the apparent extensional system develops out of the meaning system and that primitive forms of implication precede the relatively complete form evident in formal deductive reasoning. Piaget accomplishes these purposes by arguing that a relevance connection—defined as assimilation—is basic to any action sequence that involves knowing, from the sensorimotor to the formal deductive level.

At the sensorimotor level, the relevance connection occurs between actual actions (e.g., the sensorimotor, not verbal sense of "If I pull on the blanket, then I will bring the toy on top of the blanket closer"). If toy–blanket is not assimilated (given a meaning linkage) to pulling the blanket, then the *action implication* vanishes. At the representational level, the action meanings become incorporated in language (e.g., "If it rains, then the bicycle will get wet"). Here, the *causal implication* occurs only if a relevance relationship is formed such that "wet bicycle" is given a meaning linkage to "rain." Finally, at the formal reasoning level, the relevances and logical necessities join to form the deductive competence system that operates as a structured whole. This system, representing a developmental transformation of the earlier systems, permits the kind of logical understandings that involve *genuine implication,* (entailment, logical truth, and validity) that are evident in traditional deductive reasoning problems.

In conclusion, Piaget's most recent writings offer at least an outline of a general theory of the nature, origin, and development of reasoning. The theory begins from an embodiment assumption, and pictures the development of reasoning, and cognition generally, as a series of differentiations and integrations of knowledge structures. These begin with actual actions and at each new major level of integration the resulting novel structures become transformed into representational and logical systems. With respect to offering a comprehensive theory of reasoning, a key feature of Piaget's approach is that—consistent with the thesis of the present work—it recognizes the necessity of both competence and procedural systems. It is also consistent with a large body of research data and with the recent movement in the field of cognition toward a more embodied perspective concerning the nature and development of all forms of knowing.

Bibliography

Caverni, J., Fabre, J., and Gonzalez (Eds.) (1990). "Cognitive Biases." North Holland, Amsterdam.

Cheng, P. W., and Holyoak, K. J. (1985). Pragmatic reasoning schemas. *Cog. Psychol.* **17,** 391–416.

Evans, J. St. B. T. (Ed.) (1983). "Thinking and Reasoning." Routledge & Kegan Paul, London.

Inhelder, B., and Piaget, J. (1958). "The Growth of Logical Thinking from Childhood to Adolescence." Wiley, New York.

Johnson-Laird, P. N. (1983). "Mental Models." Harvard University Press, Cambridge, MA.

Macnamara, J. (1986). "A Border Dispute: The Place of Logic in Psychology." The MIT Press, Cambridge, MA.

Overton, W. F. (Ed.) (1990). "Reasoning, Necessity, and Logic: Developmental Perspectives." Erlbaum, Hillsdale, NJ.

Overton, W. F. (1991). Competence, procedures and hardware: conceptual and empirical considerations. In "Criteria for Competence: Controversies in the Assessment of Children's Abilities," (M. Chandler and M. Chapman, Eds.) pp. 19–42. Erlbaum, Hillsdale, NJ.

Overton, W. F. (1994). Contexts of meaning: The computational and the embodied mind. In "The Nature and Ontogenesis of Meaning" (W. F. Overton and D. S. Palermo, Eds.) Erlbaum, Hillsdale, NJ.

Piaget, J. (1987). "Possibility and Necessity," Vols. 1 and 2. University of Minnesota Press, Minneapolis.

Piaget, J., and Garcia, R. (1991). "Toward a Logic of Meaning." Erlbaum, Hillsdale, NJ.

Russell, J. (1987). Rule-following, mental models, and the developmental view. In "Meaning and the Growth of Understanding" (M. Chapman and R. A. Dixon, Eds.) pp. 23–48. Springer-Verlag, New York.

RELAXATION

Jonathan C. Smith
Roosevelt University

Glossary

Autogenic training A complex and highly structured European approach to relaxation and treatment that incorporates a wide range of techniques, including imagery and self-suggestion.

Casual relaxation Everyday relaxing activities generally not taught as part of a formal relaxation program. Examples: jogging, music, reading, sports. Not considered in this article.

Cognitive–behavioral relaxation theory A perspective that defines relaxation in terms of reduced physical arousal; cognitive (mental) relaxation skills; and assumptions, attitudes, and philosophies conducive to relaxation.

Cognitive–behavioral relaxation training A comprehensive approach to relaxation based on the idea that different approaches have different effects and work for different people. Students are taught a variety of techniques and then develop a relaxation program or script that meets their needs

Cue-controlled relaxation An abbreviated approach to relaxation in which a word (for example, "calm") is first paired with a relaxation exercise and eventually presented in place of the exercise.

Meditation An approach to relaxation in which one calmly attends to a simple stimulus and calmly returns attention after every distraction.

Progressive relaxation A physical approach to relaxation that involves tensing up and letting go of muscles while attending to and differentiating sensations of tension and relaxation.

Relaxation response A perspective that defines relaxation in terms of reduced physiological arousal. Also, Herbert Benson's breathing meditation.

Yoga A set of Oriental approaches to philosophy and religion that incorporates a wide variety of stretching, breathing, imagery, and meditation exercises as well as numerous restrictions on diet, sexual behavior, and exercise. Western yoga focuses mostly on Hatha yoga stretching exercises.

RELAXATION is reduced tension. Physical relaxation is a wholesale reduction of physical stress arousal across a wide range of body organs and systems; mental relaxation involves passively and receptively focusing on a restricted stimulus and acquiring assumptions, attitudes, and personal philosophies conducive to relaxation. Strategies for evoking both physical and mental relaxation are as old as civilization itself and have evolved from religion, magic, and science. Today, relaxation is used widely in psychotherapy, stress management, and medicine, as well as for performance enhancement, self-exploration, and personal growth. This article considers formal approaches to relaxation often taught by health professionals.

I. MODELS OF RELAXATION

In everyday life, people define relaxation in a variety of often contradictory ways. To some, relaxation is feeling "sleepy and drowsy," and to others, "restful and alert." It is "an absence of muscle tension" or being "refreshed and energized for action." And relaxation can be "quiet absorbtion in a task" or "distant detachment from tasks," and so on. Relaxation exercises are equally diverse and range from actively tensing up or stretching muscle groups to passively meditating on a simple stimulus. Formal theories of relaxation attempt to identify what underlies such diverse experiences and practices, provide criteria for determining the degree of relaxation one may have reached in relaxation training, and explain differences among relaxation strategies.

Encyclopedia of Human Behavior, Volume 4

A. The Relaxation Response Model

Historically, relaxation has been defined in physical terms. The relaxation response, popularized by cardiologist Herbert Benson, is the opposite of the emergency fight-or-flight stress arousal response. Under stress, the brain's hypothalamus automatically triggers a constellation of physiological changes mediated by the sympathetic nervous system and various endocrine glands. For example, heart rate, blood pressure, breathing, muscle tension, and brain activity increase to awaken and energize one for vigorous emergency activity (such as running from a wild dog or to the goalpost in football). In the relaxation response, the hypothalamus triggers decreased sympathetic nervous system activity, often accompanied by increased parasympathetic nervous system activity. This automatically evokes a reduction in physical tension or arousal. A key feature of the relaxation response model is that various relaxation strategies are interchangeable because they have the same effect, reduced arousal. Research supports the notion that many approaches to relaxation reduce arousal. [*See* STRESS.]

Many variations of the relaxation response model have emerged over the years, including the specific effects model. This perspective identifies two types of arousal, somatic (physical) and cognitive (stressful mental activity or worry). Physical relaxation approaches, such as massage and yoga stretching, should work better for somatic tension, whereas cognitive techniques such as imagery and meditation should work for cognitive arousal. Research support for the specific effects model is weak.

B. Cognitive–Behavioral Relaxation Theory

The most comprehensive approach to understanding relaxation considers both physical and mental factors. Cognitive–behavioral relaxation theory, developed by psychologist Jonathan C. Smith, identifies three components of relaxation; (1) reduced arousal, or the relaxation response; (2) deployment of cognitive relaxation skills of focusing, passivity, and receptivity; and (3) acquisition of relaxation cognitive structures, that is, assumptions, attitudes, and personal philosophies conducive to deepened relaxation. The relaxation skill, focusing, involves attending to a restricted stimulus for an extended period of time; passivity is ceasing unnecessary goal-directed and analytic activity; and receptivity is the ability to tolerate and accept new experiences. When one casually relaxes, say, by reading a novel, one focuses on the book (and not distracting worries), passively ceases possibly competing activities (the urge to study, mow the lawn, and so on), and receptively accepts whatever new and unexpected experiences the novel may bring. These same skills are involved in all forms of relaxation, whether it be passively and receptively focusing on a yoga stretch, a fantasy image, a simple prayer, or a meditation.

Cognitive–behavioral relaxation theory emphasizes the importance of relaxation cognitive structures. A relaxer must relinquish assumptions, attitudes, and philosophies that create tension, for example, "I must be perfect at everything," "I must always be in control," and "I am a worthless person." These must be replaced by cognitive structures more conducive to relaxation, for example, "Live one day at a time," "I accept myself for who I am," and "God's will be done." Finally, cognitive–behavioral relaxation theory states that the many approaches to relaxation that have evolved over the centuries have different effects and work for different people. This is most apparent not in

TABLE I
Relaxation Word List Reflecting Subjective Experiences Reported in Relaxation

Absorbed	Carefree	Drowsy	Happy	Laid back	Passive	Reverent	Strengthened
Accepted	Childlike	Energized	Harmonious	Light	Patient	Selfless	Thankful
Accepting	Clear	Fascinated	Healing	Limp	Peaceful	Sensuous	Timeless
Asleep	Complete	Floating	Heavy	Liquid	Playful	Silent	Tingling
Assured	Confident	Focused	Hopeful	Loose	Pleased	Simple	Trusting
At ease	Contented	Forgetting	Indifferent	Loved	Prayerful	Sinking	Unafraid
Awake	Creative	Free	Infinite	Loving	Refreshed	Soothed	Untroubled
Aware	Delighted	Fun	Inspired	Mysterious	Relaxed	Speechless	Warm
Beautiful	Detached	Glorious	Joyful	Mystical	Rested	Spiritual	Whole
Blessed	Dissolving	Glowing	Knowing	Optimistic	Restored	Spontaneous	Wonderful
Calm	Distant						

lowered physiological arousal, but in the rich array of subjective experiences people report when relaxing (see Table I), as well as the changes in cognitive structures they report.

II. APPROACHES TO RELAXATION

A. Progressive Relaxation

Progressive relaxation is perhaps the approach to relaxation most used by health professionals. Physician and psychologist Edmund Jacobson introduced progressive relaxation in the 1920s. He trained subjects to detect and recognize increasingly subtle levels of muscle tension. The strategy, sometimes called "Jacobsonian Relaxation," involved generating and letting go of the smallest amount of tension possible. Subjects focused on two or three muscle groups a session, eventually covering over 50 muscle groups in a training period that could last up to a year.

Jacobson's method was cumbersome, although his gentle and minimal strategy of letting go of tension is still used. Today, mental health professionals are likely to use abbreviated versions of progressive relaxation that involve attempting to create a considerable level of relaxation in the first session by effortfully generating and releasing tension (see Table II). Often up to 16 muscle groups are targeted in a single session. As training progresses, muscle groups are combined (for example, the hands and arms are tensed up together rather than as separate exercises) until one can essentially do what Jacobson taught: simply detect and let go of tension without first overtly creating tension. In the most abbreviated form of progressive relaxation, called conditioned or cue-controlled relaxation, a person thinks a relaxing cue word, such as "calm," while practicing progressive relaxation. Eventually, the cue itself is enough to evoke relaxation.

TABLE II

Popular Approaches to Relaxation Ranked (1 = high, 9 = low) According to Focusing, Passivity, Receptivity, and Conduciveness to Relaxation Structure Formation

1. Zen / mindfulness / vipassana ("attend to the flow of all stimuli")
2. Concentrative meditation (transcendental meditation, mantra meditation, Benson's "relaxation response" method, counting breaths)
3. "Contemplative" exercises that involve passively waiting for associations to arise concerning a selected topic or stimulus (autogenic "unconscious answers")
4. Imagery / visualization exercises (nature/outdoor, travel, water, indoor, wise person/healing forces imagery themes)
5. Autogenic exercises that focus on internal organs and structures (abdomen, heart, spine)
6. Autogenic exercises that focus on surface (skin, skeletal muscles) sensations ("warmth/heaviness/tingling")
7. Breathing exercises
8. Yoga stretching (Hatha yoga)
9. Progressive relaxation

Most explanations of progressive relaxation focus on the role of directing attention and creating a relaxation "rebound effect." Throughout training, one attends to and differentiates subtle sources of tension. The goal is to eventually learn to detect tension that might ordinarily go unnoticed and to recognize when relaxation is occurring. Another goal, especially of the more contemporary, abbreviated approaches, is first to create considerable muscle tension by tightening up and then letting go. This permits a relaxation rebound in which the release of tension creates a greater level of relaxation than could be achieved by simply willing muscles to relax.

B. Yoga Stretching

The word yoga comes from a Sanskrit word that can mean to bind, join, attach, or yoke. It can also mean to direct and concentrate attention, to use and apply, or to unite or commune with God. These meanings reflect the many goals of traditional yoga, a set of oriental approaches to philosophy and religion that incorporate a wide variety of stretching, breathing, imagery, and meditation exercises as well as numerous restrictions on diet, sexual behavior, and exercise.

Contemporary Western teachers of yoga have largely avoided that part of yoga that is religious, philosophical, and pseudoscientific and focused on Hatha yoga stretching exercises (see Table III). This can be relaxing for many reasons: stretching releases muscle tension, increases the flow of blood to the muscles cleansing the by-products of tension, stimulates the joints, diverts attention from stressful worry, and so on.

C. Breathing Exercises

Breathing exercises can be found in just about every relaxation discipline. However, they are emphasized in Prana yoga and a Western form of natural

TABLE III
Sample Abbreviated Progressive Relaxation Exercises

Hand squeeze

While keeping the rest of your body relaxed, squeeze the fingers together by making a fist.

Do this *now*.

Squeeze the fingers together, making them tighter and tighter. Let the tension build completely.

Notice the tension . . . and *let go*.

PAUSE

Let yourself relax.

Let the tension go. You might want to think of a tight ball of string slowly unwinding.

Focus on your hand as it begins to relax more and more.

Attend to the good feelings as the momentum of relaxation begins to carry the tension away.

Right arm squeeze

While keeping the rest of your body relaxed, squeeze your lower and upper right arm together, bending at the elbow. You might want to imagine you are trying to touch your shoulder with your hand.

Do this *now*.

Let the tension build until the squeeze feels most satisfying and complete.

Squeeze them together more and more.

And *let go*.

Let your arms go limp like a floppy rag doll.

Enjoy the feelings of relaxation you create as your muscles smooth out.

Compare how your right arm feels with your left arm.

Just notice what it feels like as the muscles start to become more and more deeply relaxed.

Shoulder squeeze

This time move your attention to your shoulders. Keep the rest of your body relaxed.

Squeeze them in whatever way feels best . . . by shrugging them up . . . by pulling them behind you . . . or by making a slow circling motion.

Squeeze them *now*.

Feel the good tension as it grows to a point where it is most satisfying and complete.

Squeeze every muscle fiber.

Notice how you can generate a complete squeeze.

And *let go*.

Let the momentum of relaxation begin to melt away tension.

Let your muscles go and think about the pleasant feelings of relaxation in your shoulders.

Give your shoulder muscles time to relax.

Let relaxation flow into every muscle.

Back of neck squeeze

This time mover your attention up to your neck and gently tilt your head back. While keeping the rest of your body relaxed, gently press the back of your head against your neck *now*.

Let the tension grow, this time not too tightly.

Create a good, complete squeeze.

And *let go*.

PAUSE

Let the muscles of your neck relax like a floppy rag doll.

Let the tension unwind.

Enjoy the feelings of relaxation.

Let the momentum of relaxation carry the tension away.

Source: Adapted, with permission, from Smith, J. C. (1989). "Relaxation Dynamics: A Cognitive–Behavioral Approach to Relaxation," pp. 69–75. Research Press, Champaign, IL.

childbirth called Lamaze. Most breathing exercises have among their goals an emphasis on diaphragmatic (or "stomach") breathing, and increased control over breathing pace, volume, pauses, and rhythm. Specifically, the exercises usually require one to breathe more slowly, taking in more air with each inhalation, increasing the pauses between each breath, and breathing in an even, rather than jerky, manner (see Table IV).

D. Autogenic Training

Autogenic training is a popular European approach to relaxation with historical links to hypnosis. Developed in the 1930s by dermatologist Johannes Schultz and elaborated in the 1960s by Wolfgang Luthe, the contemporary system is a sequence of exercises based on the idea that passively thinking suggestive phrases and images can bring about relaxation and changes in health. Autogenic training begins with six standard exercises that involve mentally repeating verbal formulas designed to suggest heaviness, warmth in the extremities, an easily beating heart, relaxed breathing, abdominal warmth, and a cool forehead. Emphasis is placed on the process of passive volition, that is, repeating suggestive phrases while maintaining complete indifference about their consequences.

In the United States, autogenic training usually stops with the six standard exercises. However, tra-

TABLE IV
Sample Abbreviated Yoga Stretching Exercise

Arm and side stretch

Let both your arms fall limply to your sides.

PAUSE

Slowly, smoothly, and gently circle your right arm and hand up and away from you.

PAUSE

Let your arm extend straight, and circle higher and higher.

PAUSE

Let it circle to the sky.

PAUSE

And then circle your arm over your head so your hand points to the other side . . . stretch and arch your body as you reach and point farther and farther.

PAUSE

Now gently and easily

PAUSE

Circle your arm back over your head . . . to your side

PAUSE

Finally to the resting position.

PAUSE

And let your arm hang.

Back stretch

Now, focus your attention on your back, below your shoulders.

Slowly, smoothly, and gently relax and bow over.

PAUSE

Let your arms hang limply.

PAUSE

Let your head fall forward, as you bow forward farther and farther in your chair.

PAUSE

Do not force yourself to bow over . . . let gravity pull your body toward your knees . . . farther and farther. It's OK to take a short breath if you need to.

PAUSE

Feel the stretch along the back.

PAUSE

Let gravity pull your body forward, as far as it will go.

PAUSE

Then gently and easily sit up.

PAUSE

Take your time.

PAUSE

Inch by inch, straighten up your body.

PAUSE

Until you are seated comfortably in an upright position.

Back of neck stretch

Now, while sitting erect, let your head tilt easily toward your chest.

PAUSE

Try not to force it down.

PAUSE

Simply let gravity pull your head down.

PAUSE

Farther and farther.

PAUSE

Feel the stretch in the back of your neck

PAUSE

As the force of gravity easily and slowly pulls your head down

PAUSE

And when you are ready

PAUSE

Gently and easily lift your head.

Source: Adapted, with permission, from Smith, J. C. (1989). "Relaxation Dynamics: A Cognitive–Behavioral Approach to Relaxation," pp. 94–99, 100–101. Research Press, Champaign, IL.

ditional training continues with a variety of special exercises. Organ-specific formulas tailor the standard suggestions to patient needs. For example, back sufferers may think, "My back is warm." In addition, intentional formulas are targeted to behavioral changes ("I will study more and drink less.")

Finally, a series of seven "meditative," or imagery, exercises are presented. Patients begin by focusing on the color sensations that spontaneously occur with eyes closed in relaxation. Then, the colors that appear most frequently are attended to, until they can be produced and modulated on demand. Patients proceed to visualize simple concrete objects, abstract constructs (such as truth, justice, and friendship), emotional states, and other people. Eventually, exercises are directed toward seeking "answers from the unconscious," that is, asking a question ("What is the source of my rage?") and passively waiting for a spontaneous answer.

E. Imagery

Imagery is widely used in psychotherapy and stress management, both as a relaxation strategy, and for other purposes. Images often form an important part of hypnotic induction, and the production of hallucinated images is frequently a suggested hypnotic response. Advanced autogenic training also involves a graduated series of both simple and complex images. Some forms of meditation incorporate a variety of simple images. Used alone for relaxation, imagery is often called thematic imagery, guided imagery, creative visualization, self-hypnosis, fantasy, and guided daydreaming.

Imagery can be classified according to the modality of its content: visual, verbal, auditory, olfactory, tactile, gustatory, or kinesthetic. Typically, the content is visual, with other sense modalities introduced as elaborations. Common imagery themes include: outdoor nature imagery (forests, plains, mountains), water imagery (beaches, brooks, lakes, oceans, rain), travel imagery (riding a plane, boat, or car; floating), indoor imagery (a cabin, cathedral, childhood home), and the wise person (Buddha, Mother Theresa) or healing forces (soothing sunlight, healthy immune system).

F. Meditation

Meditation, like yoga, is one of the oldest approaches to relaxation and is often associated with religion and spirituality, most notibly Transcendental Meditation (TM), Yoga, and Zen Buddhism. However, in the West, meditation is usually secularized and reduced to these simple instructions:

Calmly attend to a simple stimulus
After every distraction
calmly return your attention
. . . again and again and again

Concentrative meditation techniques, such as TM and beginning forms of Zen, involve attending to a preselected stimulus, such a meaningless sound or syllable called a mantra, the flow of breath, simple counting, a mental image, or an external image. More advanced forms of meditation, variously called Zen openness, *shikan-taza* (Japanese for "just sitting"), mindfulness or vipassana, involve attending to the flow of all stimuli.

G. Hypnosis and Biofeedback

Hypnosis and biofeedback are considered elsewhere in this encyclopedia; however, both are used in relaxation. Generally, hypnosis begins with an induction procedure that incorporates suggestions of drowsiness and relaxation while restricting a client's attention. Eventually, a series of suggestions are presented to enhance the ability to respond to a series of hypnotic tasks ("Your eyelids are so heavy they cannot be opened. . . . Your arms and legs are so heavy they cannot be lifted"). At the end of induction, relaxation can be offered as a suggestion on its own. [*See* HYPNOSIS.]

Biofeedback uses complex electronic and mechanical equipment to detect physiological activity usually outside of awareness, for example, heart rate, blood pressure, muscle tension, stomach contractions, electrical activity of the cerebral cortex, and emotional perspiration. Signals reflecting level of activity are then converted to an audible or visible signal. Just as a thermometer enables one to "see" one's body temperature, biofeedback equipment enables a client to see or hear a variety of subtle internal processes. When used in relaxation training, biofeedback is a useful way of training a client to detect tension and quickly determine when a relaxation technique is working. [*See* BIOFEEDBACK.]

H. Combination Approaches and Cognitive–Behavioral Relaxation Training

Many approaches to relaxation, including traditional yoga and autogenic training, combine strategies. Typically, physical approaches, such as progressive relaxation and yoga stretching, are presented first, followed by breathing or imagery, and ending with meditation. Cognitive–behavioral relaxation training, based on cognitive–behavioral relaxation theory, is a contemporary combination approach based on the premise that traditional sequences of techniques are not an accident, but reflect a relaxation hierarchy in which techniques can be ranked according to focusing, passivity, receptivity, and conduciveness to relaxation structure formation. (see Table V).

In cognitive–behavioral relaxation training, a client is first taught a variety of techniques, rather than one or two. Typically, approaches low on the hierarchy (progressive relaxation, yoga, breathing) are presented first followed by higher-level approaches (imagery, meditation). To help clients discover the unique effects of each approach, care is taken to teach relatively "pure" forms; that is, stretching not mixed with breathing and imagery, imagery not mixed with stetching and breathing, and so on. Then a relaxation program or tape is con-

TABLE V
Sample Abbreviated Breathing Exercises

Bowing and stretching breathing

As you inhale, reach and stretch. Arch your back and gently circle both arms up toward the sky, like the hands of a clock or the wings of a great bird. When you are ready to exhale, slowly circle your arms down so they are hanging heavily, and gently bow over, as before, squeezing out all the air. Let gravity pull your body down farther and farther. There is nothing for you to do.

Continue breathing this way for a while.

Inhaling through nose

Breathe in through your nose as smoothly and gently as possible. Take a full breath.

PAUSE

And relax, letting yourself breathe out naturally, without effort.

PAUSE 5 SECONDS

Continue breathing this way, breathing in and out quietly and evenly at your own pace.

Exhaling through lips

Take a slow deep breath and pause.

And breathe out slowly through your lips, letting the flow of air be as smooth and gentle as possible. Continue breathing out, emptying all the air from your stomach and chest.

PAUSE

Then breathe in through your nose.

PAUSE

Continue breathing this way, making the stream of air that passes through your lips as you exhale as smooth and gentle as possible.

PAUSE 5 SECONDS

Let the tension flow out with every breath.

Source: Adapted, with permission, from Smith, J. C. (1989). "Relaxation Dynamics: A Cognitive–Behavioral Approach to Relaxation," pp. 123, 126–127. Research Press, Champaign, IL.

structed incorporating those exercises most appropriate for client needs. Finally, special suggestions, affirmations, and words (Table I) are incorporated to deepen and link relaxation to client assumptions, attitudes, and personal philosophies supportive of relaxation. To see the difference between traditional and cognitive–behavioral approaches to yoga stretching, compare Tables IV and VI.

III. USES OF RELAXATION

Relaxation has been described as the widely applied "aspirin" of psychotherapy. Various relaxation strategies have had modest value for treating:

> alcohol abuse, anxiety, arthritis, asthma, bruxism, bulimia, cancer, cigarette smoking, dental fear, depression, diabetes, drug abuse, dysmenorrhea, eczema, esophageal spasm, hair pulling, hemophilia, herpes, hyperactivity, hypercholesterolemia, hypertension, hyperventilation, infertility, insomnia, irritable colon, menopausal hot flashes, headaches, motion sickness, nail biting, obesity, pain, panic disorder, phantom limb, phobias, Raynaud's disease, seizures, sexual dysfunctions, test anxiety, tics, tinnitus, and ulcers.

The diversity of this list probably reflects the ease with which relaxation is taught and the large number of disorders potentially impacted by stress arousal.

For minor problems, relaxation may have value when used alone. However, in most clinical contexts, relaxation is presented as part of other treatments. Relaxation can be used at the onset of psychotherapy, to build rapport and reduce client inhibitions and defensiveness. It is a formal part of many approaches of behavior therapy, including desensitization and stress inoculation training. In both these approaches the client and therapist construct a list of problem situations ranked from least to most stressful. For example, if a client's problem is "shyness in meeting others" the list might include "talking to acquaintances over the phone" (least stressful) and "meeting a total stranger in a cafeteria (most stressful). Then the client visualizes each situation, starting with the most easy. At the slightest sign of tension, the client ceases visualizing and starts practicing a previously taught relaxation exercise. When relaxed, the client continues until he or she can visualize an entire situation without anxiety. Once a situation has been mastered, the next most stressful one is tackeled.

Behavioral medicine and health psychology treatments have found considerable use for relaxation. In pain management, relaxation can be a useful tool for diverting attention or reducing tension that can

TABLE VI
Sample Abbreviated Cognitive–Behavioral Relaxation Training Script Emphasizing Yoga Stretching (Compare with Table IV)

Imagine you are a palm tree standing by the ocean beach. As the wind blows, big waves crash against the shore. Each wave releases its tension as the water runs up and dissolves into the sand. The warm sun shines overhead, a source of life and energy for all the world.

PAUSE

A long, slow gust of wind sighs through the leaves.

PAUSE

Slowly, smoothly, and gently bow over and stretch completely. There is no need to force yourself; let gravity pull.

PAUSE 10 SECONDS

Feel the stretch completely, all along your arms and torso.

COMPLETE STRETCH

As the gust subsides, gently unstretch and release your tension. Take a deep refreshing breath and exhale, letting out your tension.

PAUSE

A wave crashes against the shore, releasing its energy into the sand.

PAUSE

The sun overhead bathes you in an ocean of peaceful clear light.

PAUSE

The wind begins to grow more gentle.

PAUSE

Even more easily than before, slowly reach up and stretch. Stretch all the way, barely moving a leaf.

PAUSE

Gently return to your upright position, as a wave quietly releases its tension against the shore. Take a full breath and relax.

At the end of the stretch, let yourself settle into stillness in the warm sun.

COMPLETE STRETCH. REPEAT FOR NECK, FACE, AND LEGS

Let yourself enjoy this relaxation. You have the capacity within for creating peace and calm. Let your mind attend to the good sensations you have created.

PAUSE

The waves have settled into quiet ripples lapping against the shore.

PAUSE

As you let yourself sink deeper into a pleasant state of inner calm, very slowly and easily rock back and forth to the easy rhythm of the waves.

PAUSE 10 SECONDS

Let your movements be so gentle that they barely stir the air. Let your breathing be slow and easy.

PAUSE 10 SECONDS

You have few cares or concerns as you attend only to this soothing rocking motion.

PAUSE

Quietly overhead, the sun continues to touch all with its delicate and gentle rays.

PAUSE

The wind becomes completely quiet and the ocean is still.

PAUSE

Let your body become completely motionless as you settle into a deeply peaceful calm.

PAUSE

It is good to let your mind center on the warm sun against your skin. This is your meditation focus. It reminds you that you can trust your innermost thoughts and feelings. It is okay to put past worries aside and live in the present moment.

PAUSE

Whenever your mind wanders, that's okay.

PAUSE

Gently return to the sun as it bathes you in peaceful life-giving light.

PAUSE 5 MINUTES

aggravate pain. It is often used to prepare for and recover from surgery or uncomfortable medical procedures. Relaxation is often incorporated in programs designed to enhance physical health, prevent illness, and facilitate recovery from illness. Finally, relaxation is a useful component of programs designed to treat various risk behaviors, including overeating, smoking, alcohol abuse, and substance abuse. Here, relaxation techniques can reduce craving, divert attention from potential temptations, and provide a satisfying substitute activity.

Relaxation is frequently part of programs claimed to enhance performance and personal growth. Goals include reducing interfering tension before sports, enhancing the diversity of associations in creative brainstorming activities, and enriching the appreciation of art and literature. Finally, virtually every religion, both traditional and new, has an important role for relaxation. Various rituals, prayers, and centering activities are essentially variations and combinations of the nine major types of relaxation outlined earlier (Table I). When used in a religious or spiritual context, relaxation exercises are presented to reduce active attempts at analysis and control in order to appreciate potentially hidden resources or "powers."

Bibliography

Bernstein, D., and Borkovec, T. (1973). "Progressive Relaxation Training: A Manual for the Helping Professions." Research Press, Champaign, IL.

Lichstein, K. L. (1988). "Clinical Relaxation Strategies." Wiley, New York.

Smith, J. C. (1990). "Cognitive–Behavioral Relaxation Training: A New System of Strategies for Treatment and Assessment. Springer, New York.

Smith, J. C. (1989). "Relaxation Dynamics: A Cognitive–Behavioral Approach to Relaxation." Research Press, Champaign, IL.

Smith, J. C. (1993). "Understanding Stress and Coping." Macmillan, New York.

Risk-Compensating Behavior

Mark Thayer
San Diego State University

Nasser Daneshvary
University of Nevada at Las Vegas

Glossary

Exogenous Outside the control of the individual decision-maker.

Expected utility Satisfaction that one can reasonably expect to obtain in an uncertain situation; measured as the sum of the possible outcomes times their respective probabilities.

Probability Likelihood that an event will occur.

Risk Probability that an event with negative consequences will occur; the opposite of safety.

Utility Satisfaction one derives from an activity (e.g., consumption).

RISK-COMPENSATING BEHAVIOR occurs when individuals, in response to an exogenous improvement in safety, voluntarily accept greater risk. The impact is to partially or fully offset the exogenous safety improvement, reducing its overall effectiveness. This behavior is consistent with a utility maximization decision process in which individuals respond optimally to exogenous stimuli. Risk compensation has been extensively researched and found to exist in a variety of situations. The decision process that yields risk compensation and the associated empirical evidence are discussed here.

I. BACKGROUND

The justification for legislation requiring safety belt use in automobiles is the reduced risk of death and/or injury, given the occurrence of an accident. Likewise, other attempts to reduce risk in the home (e.g., tamper-proof packages), while recreating (e.g., sunscreens), and/or in the work place (e.g., OSHA regulations) are designed to create a safer local environment.

However, the expected results from these risk-reducing activities can be partially or fully offset if individuals behave in a risk-compensating manner. Risk compensation occurs when individuals, in response to an exogenous improvement on safety, voluntarily accept greater risk by reducing individual safety activities. The net effect is a reduction in the effectiveness of the safety-enhancing program.

There exist numerous examples of risk-compensating behavior in home, recreation, and work place situations. Tamper-proof packages for household cleansers and prescription drugs were designed to reduce accidental household poisonings. However, the increased safety was offset by risk compensation as these items were made more accessible to children through inadequate storage practices and caused a documented increase in household poisonings after the adoption of tamper-proof packages. Likewise, individuals have apparently decided to spend more time in the sun in response to the availability and use of sunscreen products. Thus, increased sunscreen use has had little impact on the number of cases of melanoma and non-melanoma (basal and squamous cell) skin cancer. The Occupational Safety and Health Administration (OSHA) has been regulating health and safety conditions in the work place for two decades. However, the policies of OSHA are generally viewed as ineffective as workers compensate for safety regulation by behaving in a riskier manner; that is, workers reduce individual safety due to the perception that they are protected by government policy. Thus, while work-related death rates have been reduced over the past 20 years (from 18 to 9 deaths per 100,000 workers), 10,500 workers lost their lives in 1990 and the incidence of lost workdays has steadily increased. A

Encyclopedia of Human Behavior, Volume 4

specific example of work place risk compensation occurred in major league baseball. The number of hit batsman in major league baseball increased markedly from the 20-year period before compared to the 20-year period immediately after the introduction of batting helmets. Thus, player behavior responded to safer batting.

Risk-compensating behavior is often described as an optimal response to a change in the existing situation. The individual decision-maker is confronted with new information and adjusts in an effort to increase utility or satisfaction producing activities. For instance, an increase in exogenous safety allows activities that were formerly avoided because of their inherent danger. Thus, the birth control pill, by reducing the probability of unwanted pregnancy, allows increased sexual activity. Improved automobile safety allows greater speed and driving under what were formerly hazardous road conditions. Modern word processors allow greater typing speed than conventional typewriters since the penalty of an error is significantly reduced. [*See* DECISION MAKING, INDIVIDUALS.]

Risk compensation is also applicable in converse conditions. An increase in exogenous risk often causes individuals to behave in a safer manner. Thus, as weather causes a deterioration in road conditions, drivers generally compensate by driving slower.

In the next section we describe in detail the decision process that underlies risk-compensating behavior. This is followed by a discussion of the empirical results concerning driving behavior, the most studied example of risk compensation.

II. THEORETICAL CONSTRUCT

Risk compensation is derived from an economic model of behavior. In general, individuals possessed with full knowledge are assumed to behave in an optimal manner and maximize utility or satisfaction, subject to an income constraint. In this context safety or risk is only one argument in the utility function. Note that the objective is to maximize overall utility not minimize risk. The primary outcome of this model is that individuals will choose activity levels to the point where the incremental or marginal benefits equal the incremental or marginal costs of any specific action. As with other utility producing goods, an optimal level of safety will be chosen by the utility maximizing individual.

In the real world there exists considerable uncertainty concerning the effects (benefits and/or costs) of possible decisions. Thus, the standard utility maximizing model is not applicable to situations characterized by uncertainty. In these uncertain situations individuals are assumed to maximize *expected* utility, which is the algebraic sum of outcomes multipled by their respective probabilities. The optimal conditions for this model specify that individuals will undertake action until the incremental expected benefits equal the incremental expected costs. This decision process can be seen in the following model, where subscripts refer to partial derivatives. Let

s = individual safety measures.

e = exogenous safety measures beyond control of the individual, such as required seat belt use laws.

P = $P_{(s,e)}$, probability that an individual is involved in an accident where probability is influenced by individual actions ($P_s < 0$, $P_{ss} > 0$) and exogenous factors ($P_e < 0$, $P_{ee} > 0$); that is, as individual and exogenous safety measures increase, the probability of an accident declines with a declining rate due to diminishing returns.

L = $L_{(s,e)}$, loss associated with an accident where loss is influenced by individual actions ($L_s < 0$, $L_{ss} > 0$) and exogenous safety measures ($L_e < 0$, $L_{ee} > 0$).

D = $D_{(e,g)}$, disutility associated with practicing individual safety ($D_s > 0$, $D_{ss} > 0$) and from exogenous safety measures ($D_e > 0$, $D_{ee} > 0$). Disutility may also result from the interaction of individual and exogenous actions ($D_{se} > 0$).

Also note that no assumption is made concerning the relationship between s and e in either the probability function P or the loss function L. If P_{se} and L_{se} are nonnegative then individual and exogenous actions are substitutes in production. However, if these values are negative then individuals perceive s and e as complementary goods; that is, goods that make each other more valuable.

The individual is assumed to maximize expected utility (U), constrained by income (I). In the simplest case there are only two states of the world; the accident occurs with probability P and the accident does not occur with probability $1 - P$. This simple optimization problem is written as: maximize

$$U = P_{(s,e)}[I - D_{(s,e)} - L_{(s,e)}] + [1 - P_{(s,e)}][(I - D_{(s,e)}],$$

or

$$U = I - D_{(s,e)} - P_{(s,e)}L_{(s,e)}. \quad (1)$$

The individual will take safety measures until the benefits of additional action (benefits of reduction in expected loss) are just offset by the additional disutility. Thus, optimal individual safety effort, determined by maximizing Eq. (1) with respect to s, will conform to

$$-D_s = P_sL + PL_s, \quad (2)$$

where the right-hand side is the extra benefits (change in probability times the loss function plus change in the loss times the probability) and the left-hand side is the additional disutility.

The relationship between individual and exogenous safety measures can be determined by treating Eq. (2) as an implicit function and using the implicit function rule to solve for ds/de.

$$ds/de = (D_{se} + P_{se}L + P_sL_s + P_eL_s + PL_{se})/(-D_{ss} - P_{ss}L - 2P_sL_s - PL_{ss}). \quad (3)$$

The theoretical construct can be used to make a number of predictions concerning risk-compensating behavior. First, $ds/de < 0$ if individual and exogenous actions are assumed to be substitutes (see description above) in the probability and loss functions. This is the formula for compensating behavior. That is, increases in exogenous safety measures relax the constraint and allow the individual to substitute exogenous safety for individual safety. The individual reallocates scarce resources, purchasing less individual safety and more of other utility producing goods.

However, it should noted that the sign of ds/de is indeterminate if s and e are assumed to be complementary in reducing risk and loss. In this case risk-compensating behavior does not always occur and will depend on the extent that complementarity produces additional safety that offsets the extra disutility of any exogenous safety measure. The manner in which individuals treat individual and exogenous safety measures is an empirical question. *A priori* one might expect that relatively risk averse individuals would demonstrate the least amount of compensating behavior. That is, exogenous safety measures might not be offset by reductions in individual actions. Likewise, risk preferers or risk lovers may be relatively strong candidates for compensating behavior. In the next section we present the relevant data concerning this hypothesis.

The second prediction of the model is that risk compensation will be heightened in situations in which there exist individual activities that substitute directly for the exogenous safety measures. If none exist then there is no opportunity for risk-compensating behavior.

Third, risk compensation (ds/de) will be large when the probability change (P_e) corresponding to the change in exogenous risk is large. Thus, one can expect that policies that have a large (small) effect on perceived risk will (not) produce compensating behavior, *ceteris paribus*.

Fourth, the benefits of risk taking must be relatively large to induce risk-compensating behavior. If there is little to be gained in terms of utility from risk taking then the individual will lack the necessary incentive to alter behavior.

Finally, risk compensation will be larger for exogenous safety measures that affect the accident probability than those measures that affect the severity of damage from the accident. For example, illegal immigration from Mexico is largely unaffected by a change in apprehension rates since illegal immigrants just make more attempts to enter the United States. Thus, risk compensation offsets any increase in apprehension rates. In this case a change in the severity of punishment would likely have a greater impact due to the occurrence of less risk compensation.

III. EMPIRICAL RESULTS: DRIVING BEHAVIOR

Individuals drive automobiles to achieve transportation (and other) objectives. During any specific driving session the individual is protected by a combination of individual and exogenous safety measures. The individual can drive in a defensive manner, wear a safety belt, refrain from drinking and driving, and choose relatively safe routes (e.g., minimal cross traffic). In addition, government agencies can mandate safe equipment (e.g., enclosed gasoline tanks and air bags) and alter behavior through legislation (e.g., safety belt laws). Thus, driving provides ideal conditions for studying risk-compensating behavior.

The existence and magnitude of risk compensation in driving have been studied extensively. Most of the previous work has focused on the effectiveness of mandatory safety belt laws. Safety belt use has increased dramatically since the introduction of legislation requiring safety belt use. A 1992 survey of 3000 United States citizens indicated that 64% always buckle up. This is a 236% increase from the 19% usage rate of 1984, before the enactment of safety belt laws. In addition, only 8% hardly ever use a safety belt, down from 40% in 1984. Anecdotal evidence suggests that properly worn seat belts can reduce the risk of death by 75% and serious injuries by 66%.

However, the existing scientific studies (those that control for confounding variables) are not uniform in their assessment of the effectiveness of seat belts. For example, recent empirical results for Australia and New Zealand suggest that seat belt use is negatively correlated with the number of traffic fatalities. The same pattern was found to exist between a variety of injury rates and seat belt use in California. In addition, it has been estimated that fatalities in the 25 United States jurisdictions with seat belt laws were 6.6% lower than that forecast for the no seat belt law scenario for these states. This improvement amounts to approximately 1300 lives saved. Finally, it has been estimated that 100% usage of seat belts could reduce fatalities by 40%.

On the other hand, a number of studies have pointed out that, contrary to conventional wisdom, seat belt laws may not reduce the number of total fatalities. For safety belt use, the basic inference is that utilizing the safety belt provides the driver with an additional sense of security which translates into relatively more reckless driving. There is a potential for offsetting or compensating behavior for the driver of the automobile.

Several studies tested the impact of automobile safety regulation on both occupant and nonoccupant death and injury rates. Two primary results emerge: (1) occupant's lives are saved at the expense of motorcyclists, bicyclists, and pedestrians; and (2) the severity of accidents is reduced but the frequency of accidents increases. The earliest studies, conducted in the mid-1970s, using aggregate time series and cross-section data indicated that occupants' lives were saved at the expense of pedestrian deaths and a larger number of nonfatal accidents. These results were recently verified utilizing aggregate time series data for New Zealand. The findings were that a mandatory seat belt law, enacted in 1972, was negatively correlated with the deaths of automobile occupants and positively associated with deaths of motorcyclists, bicyclists, and pedestrians. In fact, this study indicated complete offsetting in that *total* deaths showed no relationship to seat belt use (savings in occupant deaths were just offset by the increase in nonoccupant deaths). Other recent work provides further evidence of offsetting behavior, demonstrating that both nonoccupants and rear seat passengers are more at risk when seat belt laws are in effect. As an aside, it seems that other automobile safety equipment (e.g., air bags) also reduces fatalities, but the number of accidents and other associated injuries have increased.

The studies discussed above generally indicate a risk-compensation effect, although the magnitude of the effect is subject to interpretation. However, these studies provide no information concerning the individual decision process that generates risk compensation. Each of the studies is inherently limited since it employs aggregate time series or cross-section data.

In a recent study researchers attempted to develop a more detailed understanding of risk compensation by using individual-specific observations obtained from a regional survey. The also accounted for individual preferences toward relative risks and controlled for other individual-specific variables (besides seat belt use) which might affect driving performance. These confounding factors included the number of years individuals have worn seat belts, age, miles driven to work, education level, sex, and annual income. Finally, they used a more sensitive indicator of risk-compensating behavior. As discussed above, the aggregate studies have analyzed the impact of safety belts or safety belt laws on the number of fatalities and/or the number of accidents. However, these are rare events and much risk compensation may occur without the occurrence of an accident or a fatality. Thus, these researchers analyzed the impact of an individual's seat belt usage on the number of moving violations or tickets. The premise was that if seat belt using drivers are practicing risk compensation by taking additional risks then such behavior would result in a larger number of moving violations, *ceteris paribus*.

Econometric models based on individual-specific survey data were estimated to investigate the relationship between seat belt usage and the number of citations for moving violations. The analysis incorporated the risk preferences of individuals as revealed by the degree of precaution exhibited against everyday risks. The results indicated that risk-compensating behavior was undertaken only by those individuals who were not strongly risk averse. Conversely, seat belt use was associated with relatively fewer moving violations for the individuals who exhibited risk aversion. Thus, individuals who had a relatively low regard for various risks practiced greater risk compensation. On the other hand, risk averse individuals did not compensate (for the additional safety provided by a seat belt) by driving more recklessly. Clearly, tastes for risk were an important dimension of risk-compensating behavior. Taken together, the results imply that individual risk preferences are an important dimension which should be considered when testing for risk-compensating behavior.

IV. CONCLUDING REMARKS

A commonly used approach for assessing the effectiveness of an exogenous change in safety is to examine the technological aspects of the change. For example, if occupant movement can be restrained with a safety belt during the occurrence of an automobile accident then one can make a prediction concerning the number of injuries and lives saved given safety belt usage. However, this technological approach ignores any behavioral change that may accompany the technological change. To the extent that behavioral change occurs then the estimate of injuries and lives saved will be in error. In general, individuals tend to compensate for exogenous safety changes and behave in a riskier manner, reducing the effectiveness of the exogenous change. Thus, a technological approach is incomplete and a more general model of behavior must be used to accurately assess exogenous safety changes. This is objective of the economic model of behavior discussed above.

Risk compensation has several important implications for the design of social policies that promote safety in the home, work place, and while recreating. First, programs should be designed to achieve the largest direct impact on safety since risk compensation (an indirect effect) will reduce their effectiveness. For example, seat belt laws that are enforced as primary laws (one can be stopped for not wearing a seat belt) will provide greater overall risk reductions than those enforced as secondary laws (one must be stopped for another violation before the seat belt law can be enforced). Risk compensation will occur in both situations but primary laws will provide greater direct risk reductions, which translates into greater overall risk reductions. Second, policies should be designed to reduce the expected loss from the event rather than the probability of the event. Policies that affect the probability of the event (e.g., better tires, shorter stopping distances and turning radii, wider traffic lanes) provide direct feedback to the individual and heighten the potential for risk compensation. However, policies that reduce the loss given occurrence of the event (e.g., high penetration resistant windshields, breakaway sign posts, seat belts) provide less direct feedback and reduce risk compensation.

There exist many policies that can be adopted to enhance safety and not be subject to offset associated with risk compensation. However, the anticipation of risk-compensating behavior should be an inherent part of policy design.

Bibliography

Asch, P., Levy, D. T., Shea, D., and Bodenhorn, H. (1991). Risk compensation and the effectiveness of safety belt use laws: A case study of New Jersey. *Policy Sci.* **24,** 181–197.

Blomquist, G. (1986). A utility maximization model of driver traffic safety behavior. *Accident Anal. Prev.* **18**(5), 371–375.

Blomquist, G. (1991). Motorist use of safety equipment: Expected benefits or risk incompetence? *J. Risk Uncertainty* **4,** 135–152.

Campbell, B., Campbell, F. (1988). Injury reduction and belt use associated with occupant restraint laws. In "Preventing Automobile Injury: New Findings from Evaluation Research (J. Graham, Ed.). Auburn House, Dover, MA.

Evans, W. N., and Graham, J. D. (1991). Risk reduction or risk compensation? The case of mandatory safety-belt use laws. *J. Risk Uncertainty* **4**(1), 61–73.

Garbacz, C. (1990). Estimating seat belt effectiveness with seat belt usage data from the Centers for Disease Control. *Econ. Lett.* **34**(1), 83–88.

Garbacz, C. (1991). Impact of New Zealand seat belt law. *Econ. Inq.* **29**(2) 310–316.

Garbacz, C. (1992). Do front seat belt laws put rear seat passengers at risk? *Popul. Res. Policy Rev.* **11,** 157–168.

Hemenway, D. (1988). "Prices and Choices: Microeconomic Vignettes." Ballinger, Cambridge, MA.

Lave, L., and Weber, W. (1970). A benefit–cost analysis of auto safety features. *Appl. Econ.* **4**(1), 265–275.

Loeb, P. D. (1993). The effectiveness of seat belt legislation in reducing various driver-involved injury rates in California. *Accident Anal. Prev.* **25**(2), 189–197.

McCarthy, P. (1986). Seat belt usage rates: A test of Peltzman's hypothesis. *Accident Anal. Prev.* **18**(5), 425–438.

Singh, H., and Thayer, M. A. (1992). Seat belt use and driving behavior. *Econ. Inq.* **30**(4), 640–658.

Todaro, M. P., and Maruszko, L. (1987). Illegal migration and U.S. Immigration reform: A conceptual framework. *Pop. Dev. Rev.* **13**(1), 101–114.

SCHIZOPHRENIA

Mark F. Lenzenweger
Cornell University

Irving I. Gottesman
University of Virginia

Glossary

Affective illness Mental illness characterized by a prominent and persistent disturbance in mood such that persons are depressed, sad, gloomy, and, often, suicidal (major or unipolar depression); a mood disorder can also result in excitement, euphoria, and manic behaviors (manic-depression or bipolar illness).

Delusion A firmly held false belief that is completely inconsistent with external reality and resistant to evidence to the contrary (e.g., believing that alien forces from Mars are controlling one's thoughts and actions).

Diathesis-stressor model A theoretical model that holds psychopathology is the interactive result of a diathesis (predisposition) for illness that is triggered by environmental stressors. In the case of schizophrenia, the diathesis is largely genetically determined.

Epidemiology The study of the frequency, rate, and distribution of illness in a population as well as those factors increasing risk for an illness in a population.

Hallucination A perceptual experience in any sensory modality in the absence of actual relevant and sufficient stimuli (e.g., "hearing" an external voice comment on one's actions in the absence of any other person).

Schizophrenia Severe psychotic mental illness characterized by massive disruption in thought, behavior, and emotion. Persons with schizophrenia frequently suffer from hallucinations, delusions, and thought disorder. They frequently withdraw from social relations and have great difficulty in occupational functioning.

Thought disorder Disruption in the form, or organization, of thought as reflected in a person's speech (e.g., incoherence; neologism, an invented word that has no meaning to listeners).

SCHIZOPHRENIA is the most severe and devastating form of mental illness known to humankind occurring around the world and affecting approximately 1% of its population. It is a life-long disease that results in the disorganization of thought, feelings, and behaviors, frequently beginning early in life before the age of 25. The illness is determined largely by genetic factors, although environmental factors play an important as yet unspecified role in the development of schizophrenia. At this time there is no cure for the condition; however, psychopharmacological medications do help to control the most disabling of schizophrenic symptoms. Research remains to be done to specify the nature of the genetic determinants of schizophrenia and how they bring about the emergence and unfolding of the condition.

I. INTRODUCTION

Everyday encounters with the misuse of the terms "schizophrenia" or "schizophrenic" to refer to the foreign policy of the United States, the stock market, or any other disconfirmation of one's expectations does an injustice to the enormity of the public health problems and profound suffering associated with this most puzzling disorder of the human mind. Current surveys of the general U.S. population done in door-to-door fashion lead to the projection that 1.85 million Americans above the age of 16 have or have had an episode of schizophrenia. By the year 2000, a scant decade from now, that number will grow to 2.06 million victims. World-wide projections can be shown to be quite close to these rates, whether they come from rural India or industrialized England, Japan, or Denmark, according to recent reports from the World Health Organization.

Schizophrenia is the most severe form of mental illness known to humankind. It is characterized by massive psychological and behavioral disorganization indicating a loss of contact with reality. The suffering individual frequently experiences frightening hallucinations, delusions, and thought disorder. Schizophrenia is still diagnosed today as it was at the turn of the century: by its psychopathology—that is, by its abnormal patterns of thought and perception as inferred from language and behavior. We wish we had a definitive neuropathology to pinpoint a valid diagnosis of schizophrenia, but that goal still eludes the field. Three ingredients go into an accurate diagnosis: (1) a careful interview with the patient to determine symptoms currently present and absent, (2) a mental and physical health history of the patient, and (3) a mental health history of the patient's biological relatives.

Clinicians are aided in their diagnostic work by knowledge of the family history, even though 89% of all schizophrenics do not have a schizophrenic parent, and fully 81% do not have a schizophrenic parent, sister, or brother. From its earliest descriptions, schizophrenia was said to "run in families." That tendency could implicate either genes or environment, or a combination of both. Within the past 75 years, reliable studies of schizophrenics and their relatives have established that this familial tendency is largely due to some aspect of genetic inheritance. We believe that genes in and of themselves do not result in schizophrenia, but that they establish a predisposition or substrate—an inherited diathesis or vulnerability—that, when combined with the consequences of environmental stress, tip the scale into illness.

It is essential to note that schizophrenia is a mental illness, a psychosis, a form of insanity, and not simply, as Ronald Laing, Thomas Szasz, or Herbert Marcuse and others have argued, the manifestation of a deviant or alternative lifestyle or evidence that society itself is sick. Moreover, no environmental factor, by itself, has ever been proved to cause schizophrenia. In more than 100 years of study, no one has found a single case of schizophrenia caused solely by the conditions of the patient's upbringing. The alleged causal environmental conditions—such abnormal rearing causes as early death of parents, odd marriages by odd parents, weird parent–child relations, and such adverse life events as war, poverty, disastrous interpersonal relations, and brain insults—occur very widely, but people experiencing any of those conditions rarely become schizophrenic although they may feel distressed or experience "nervous breakdowns." During the same 100-year period, although the pattern of inheritance was not yet clear, the necessary role of genetics was established with circumstantial and indirect evidence, at least on scientific grounds. Uncertainty on the diagnostic front, however, perpetuates uncertainty in regard to definitive causes.

There is not yet a blood test, urine or cerebrospinal fluid analysis, or CT (computerized tomography), rCBF (regional cerebral blood flow), PET (positron emission tomography), or MRI (magnetic resonance imaging) brain imaging scan that can establish an unchallenged diagnosis of schizophrenia. New enhancements so that information from the electrical and magnetic fields of the brain can be used to specify the possible structural or functional abnormalities in schizophrenics are imminent. Eventually, there will be some highly specific physical method for detecting schizophrenia as well as the predisposition to it. We know that something goes wrong chemically and/or physically in the brain of a schizophrenic, but we do not yet know what. The antipsychotic medications used to treat (i.e., control the symptoms of, but not cure) schizophrenia since 1953 give clues about excesses or deficiencies of various neurotransmitter substances or receptor sites in the brain, but these are only clues. Study continues on all fronts, but no approach has yielded *the* answer.

Schizophrenic symptoms can be slightly, moderately, severely, or absolutely disabling. The first onset can appear from puberty and adolescence to well into a person's 50s and 60s, though relatively few cases begin after age 55. The first episode can, when untreated, last a few weeks or many years. Recovery runs the gamut from what is euphemistically called "complete social recovery"—recovery to a level tolerable in society, but probably not to the highest level of predisease functioning—to chronic incapacitation. And the life history of a schizophrenic can include only one or two episodes of decompensation (mild, moderate, or severe) or more episodes, progressively more severe and occurring at ever-shorter intervals.

Although some scientists and clinicians have spoken of a group of schizophrenias, we believe that schizophrenia is, at its core, *essentially* one entity, one clearly definable mental disorder that must be studied in unity along the whole continuum of its manifestations. Opinions to the contrary are easily found. The generic name of the disease is schizophrenia—on that mental health workers agree.

II. CLINICAL DESCRIPTION AND DIAGNOSIS

As noted above, the diagnosis of schizophrenia is made after a careful examination of the patient's mental and physical health history. According to the *Diganostic and Statistical Manual of Mental Disorders—Revised* (DMS-III-R), the standard nomenclature for making psychiatric diagnoses in the United States, the diagnosis of schizophrenia is *guided* by these criteria:

A. Presence of Characteristic psychotic symptoms in the active phase: either (1), (2), or (3) for at least one week:
   (1) two of the following:
      (a) delusions
      (b) hallucinations throughout the day for several days or several times a week for several weeks, each hallucinatory experience not being limited to a few brief moments
      (c) incoherence or marked loosening of associations
      (d) catatonic behavior
      (e) flat or grossly inappropriate affect (emotional tone)
   (2) bizarre delusions (i.e., involving a phenomenon that in the person's culture would be regarded as totally implausible, e.g., thought broadcasting, being controlled by a dead person)
   (3) prominent hallucinations [as defined in (1b) above] of a voice with content having no apparent relation to concomitant depression or elation, or a voice keeping up a running commentary on the person's behavior or thoughts, or two or more voices conversing with each other

B. During the course of the disturbance, functioning in such areas as work, social relations, and self-care is markedly below the highest level achieved before onset of the disturbance.

C. Schizoaffective disorder (a combination of schizophrenic and mood symptoms) and mood disorder (depression or mania) with psychotic features have been ruled out.

D. Continuous signs of the disturbance for at least 6 months.

E. It cannot be established that an organic factor (e.g., brain tumor or trauma, drug intoxication, etc.) initiated and maintained the disturbance.

F. If there is a history of autistic disorder (a childhood onset psychosis), the additional diagnosis of schizophrenia is made only if prominent delusions or hallucinations are also present.

For a diagnosis of schizophrenia, criteria A through F must all be met. A former arbitrary criterion, that age of onset must be 45 years or younger, has been dropped from DSM-III-R for good reason. About 10% of schizophrenics have their first hospital admission after age 45.

Both the DSM-III-R and the World Health Organization International Classification of Mental Disorders (ICD, the standard outside the United States) are helpful in drawing a diagnostic picture. According to the DSM-III-R, schizophrenia represents a group of disorders characterized by the presence of a thought disorder. The DSM directs attention to the patients' misinterpretations of reality; delusions and hallucinations; inappropriate emotional and social response; and withdrawn, regressive, or bizarre behavior. The ICD dwells more on a fundamental disturbance of personality and a frequent sense of being controlled by outside forces, as well as on the DSM's delusions and bizarre perceptions and inappropriate emotional and social behavior. It has always omitted the arbitrary DSM-III age cut-off of 45. Both classification systems assume that organic brain disease of various origins has first been excluded as a diagnostic possibility.

Schizophrenia diagnosis requires delineating some length of time during which the patient has suffered symptoms. The DSM-III-R requires 6 months' duration in order to avoid false diagnoses of schizophrenia for short-lived reactions to drugs or disasters (earthquakes, combat, plane crashes) that mimic many of the symptoms in genuine schizophrenia. The duration period is arbitrary and can lead to an underdiagnosis of genuine schizophrenia. The duration criterion gives rise to the use of another term, *schizophreniform* psychosis, used for cases that resemble schizophrenia and which have lasted more than 2 weeks but less than 6 months. Europeans use the term schizophreniform psychosis more literally for cases in which the investigator does not want to exclude the possibility of true schizophrenia. In either instance, the term allows the diagnostician to red flag an interim decision for later reconsideration. Everyone has a breaking point in the face of either acute or cumulative stress that may result in some kind of "psychogenic psychosis"; it is usually not schizophrenia and disappears after the stressors (or toxins) are removed.

Schizophrenia is easily confused, particularly at first onset, with the other large category of severe "functional" mental illness, major affective disorders (depressive psychosis, mania, or manic-depressive illness), especially when bizarre delusions are present. The two illnesses appear at times so similar that misdiagnosis in both directions may contaminate some of the treatment and research literature. Mental health workers believe they are separate illnesses because they respond, by and large, to distinctive treatment, have different natural histories and outcomes, and have different family illness patterns. But until we can confirm a diagnosis chemically or by some genetic test, we cannot be absolutely sure of the purity of our research data or treatment recommendations.

In this context, it is important to identify the primary characteristics of what is termed "schizophrenia spectrum" or schizotypic psychopathology. Schizotypic individuals, although *not* schizophrenic *per se,* display symptoms and behaviors that many researchers believe are attenuated forms of schizophrenic symptoms that endure in a trait-like way over the lifespan of schizotypic persons. For example, for most of his or her adult life a schizotypic person may have no close relationships or friends as well as display markedly odd speech and thought processes, intense anxiety when around other people, peculiar behavior and emotional expressions, and increased suspiciousness of others. A relation between schizotypic psychopathology and schizophrenia was suspected after it was found that schizotypic people are found in increased numbers among the biological relatives of persons with schizophrenia. Moreover, schizotypic individuals have been found to display patterns of performance on laboratory and psychological tests that are strikingly similar to those found among people who actually suffer from schizophrenia. So, although not schizophrenia by definition, schizotypic psychopathology is a form of mental illness related to schizophrenia and one that may help us understand the causes of schizophrenia proper.

A. What Schizophrenia Is Not

Because the reading public is as often misled by popular accounts in films, biographies, and novels, it is important to recognize false examples of schizophrenia. For example, people with multiple personalities, such as the heroine in *The Three Faces of Eve,* are not schizophrenics; they suffer from a rare form of hysterical neurosis (i.e., schizophrenia and multiple personality disorder are not synonymous). Mark Vonnegut (son of Kurt Vonnegut) in *The Eden Express* describes himself as having some symptoms occurring in schizophrenia, such as alterations of the senses and somatic, grandiose, religious, and persecutory delusions and hallucinations, but the clear descriptions of manic and depressive episodes come closer to meeting criteria for bipolar affective disorder (formerly termed manic-depressive psychosis). Debora Blau, the fictional adolescent of *I Never Promised You a Rose Garden,* has some symptoms that overlap with those seen in schizophrenia (almost delusional concerns about her body and health, grandiose delusions, paranoid traits, suicide attempts) but comes closest to meeting the criteria for somatization disorder (also known as Briquet's syndrome) with her dramatic spells of blindness, deafness, paralysis, and hallucinations.

III. HISTORY OF THE CONCEPT: EARLY OBSERVATIONS AND LATER INSIGHTS

The general historical observations with respect to schizophrenia go something like this: Though somewhat arguable, there is no compelling ancient description of schizophrenia, although early healers, including the father of medicine, Hippocrates (460–377 B.C.), carefully described other forms of madness such as the "sacred disease" (epilepsy), mania, and melancholia (depression). At least Hippocrates attributed madness to the brain—as opposed to possession by the gods, the conventional classical explanation for bizarre behavior—but thought it was the result of "abnormal moisture" of the brain. Once adequately described clincially in 1809, however, schizophrenia seems to have bounded into the 19th century view all over the Western world and to have increased rapidly for a hundred years. If valid, such an observation demands an explanation.

One theory for such a rapid increase holds that a tendency toward this kind of mental breakdown may have always been present in humans, but emerged as an incapacitating illness only under the stress of losing personal space in increasingly urbanized and industrialized societies. Although no one has ever ruled out stress as a contributing factor, it now seems clear that it does not "cause" schizophrenia by itself. Closely allied, but slightly different, is a second theory: that the social changes caused by the breakdown of traditional family and cultural patterns—patterns that had remained much the same from ancient times up to the industrial revolution in the 18th century—created more insanity of all types, and thus more schizophrenia. As larger and larger numbers of asylums, or madhouses, were built in Western Europe over the course of the 19th century to accommodate the insane, these concentrated gatherings enabled observers to differentiate carefully, for the first time, among various forms of madness. Only with the coming of these asylums were physicians able to define different mental illnesses by describing the differences in symptoms, in course, and in outcome, because only then could they observe large enough numbers of insane persons for long enough periods of time.

Much more simple, but also more radical, is the third theory: that schizophrenia is a disease that acutally did not exist prior to the 17th or 18th century. That's why no one had described it any earlier and why 19th century observers saw such an increase in insanity. It came and it spread, perhaps transmitted by an infectious viral agent, parallelling the AIDS story. Perhaps schizophrenia was spread like the psychoses caused by syphilitic invasion of the central nervous system: that condition, called general paralysis of the insane (G.P.I.), general paresis, or dementia paralytica, may have resulted from a mutated bacterium that appeared in France soon after the Napoleonic wars and spread throughout the West.

Each of these three theories appears to account for the sudden appearance of large numbers of sufferers from schizophrenia, however, each must accommodate the fact that, since about 1900, there has been no notable increase in the incidence of schizophrenia anywhere in the world. Industrialization has spread, family breakdowns have, if anything, increased, and no antischizophrenic viral agent has been invented.

Few, if any, early historical documents, including the Old and New Testaments, provide support for the existance of schizophrenia. Later documents provide little more solid evidence for the illness. Descriptions of patients at St. Bartholomew's Hospital in London (the "mother hospital" of the English-speaking world) translated from Latin manuscripts in the 12th century reveal only four possible persons with schizophrenia, having both auditory and visual hallucinations, delusions, and recovery among 57 "chronicles of miracles." No unambiguously schizophrenic character appears in Shakespearean drama despite the Bard's skill in a word-painter of other kinds of behavioral deviances; he did use such words as *lunatic, mad, insane,* and *fool* to refer to severe mental illness. Careful notes and symptom checklists compiled by the 17th century English physician–astrologer Richard Napier (1559–1634) on more than 2000 mental patients do not reveal any clear cases of schizophrenia. The term *neurosis* was not introduced until 1783, when it referred generically to a disordered nervous system in the absence of fever; *psychosis* did not appear as a term until the middle of the 19th century. Still, we cannot find unmistakable reports of schizophrenia under these or other names in early medical accounts.

The first clinically adequate descriptions of schizophrenia appeared independently in England and France in the same year—1809. In *Observations on Madness,* John Haslam (1764–1844), Superintendent of the Bethlem Hospital in London, described what we recognize today as unmistakable schizophrenia. Also in 1809, Philippe Pinel (1745–1826), a French physician, clearly characterized cases of typical schizophrenia; cases Benedict Morel (1809–1873) would subsequently term *demence prococe* (in Latin, *dementia praecox* or the early/premature loss of mind). Later, Emil Kraepelin (1856–1926), the famous German clinical psychiatrist, became the definitive categorizer and organizer of the abnormal language and behavior that comprise the substance of contemporary psychopathology, anticipating its development as a branch of the neurosciences. (Karl Jaspers, a younger contemporary of Kraepelin complemented the unfolding understanding of schizophrenia from a phenomenological–descriptive angle by specifying the pathology of mental processes.) His clinical analyses of schizophrenics stand, for the most part, as the descriptive terms used today. He unified the formerly distinct categories above and gave this comprehensive malady the name *dementia praecox*. Kraepelin believed that an adolescent who developed hallucinations and delusions, behaved bizarrely, and remained ill in this way for an extended period of time suffered from the illness Morel had described under this rubric, but he also included patients suffering from catatonia and hebephrenia. Kraepelin defined the disease as a series of clinical pictures with a common feature: termination in "mental weakness." He also admitted that the deterioration did not always occur, that the patients did not all remain chronically ill, and that dementia sometimes began after adolescence.

After long and careful observation, Kraepelin classified his dementia praecox patients according to two criteria: their symptoms and the course of their illness. By 1896, often using terms borrowed from others, he divided his patients into three types: *hebephrenic, catatonic,* and *paranoid.* In 1913 he added dementia *simplex* (those patients with only subtle, "negative" symptoms) to his classificatory scheme. These descriptions not only characterized the patients' symptoms, but indicated severity of the psychoses, moving from simple and paranoid, the least severe, to hebephrenic, the most. By measuring the severity of the patient's illness, Kraepelin also was predicting some correlation between how ill the patient was and the degree of recovery to be expected, a so-called prognosis.

The second leading figure in establishing the clinical picture of schizophrenia as well as naming the disorder was Eugen Bleuler. Bleuler was a teacher and colleague of Carl Jung's and an early member of Sigmund Freud's Psychoanalytic Society and he contributed much more than a name to the study of schizophrenia. Interestingly, however, Bleuler's important contributions in this area came more in spite of his Freudian associations than because of them. Although Bleuler was not in basic disagreement with Kraepelin, his 1911 publication on this illness stretched Kraepelin's findings in some ways. Bleuler believed Kraepelin's descriptions were based on secondary, rather than primary, symptoms and that the primary problem was the disordered thought process. He argued that the primary symptoms were a loosening of associations (connecting unrelated ideas, for instance), autism (complete self-centeredness), affective disturbance (inappropriate emotions and actions), and ambivalence (not being able to make up one's mind). Delusions, hallucinations, and catatonia, Bleuler believed, resulted from these more fundamental disturbances. Bleuler's 1911 text, not available in English until 1950, also showed that he was eager to take into account the psychodynamic ideas of Freud and Jung.

IV. EPIDEMIOLOGICAL CONSIDERATIONS

A. Morbid Risk, Prevalence, and Incidence

Epidemiology is the branch of science that studies the rates and frequencies with which illnesses occur in a population. There are several important concepts used by epidemiologists that will help our understanding of the amount of schizophrenia in the world today. The first concept is known as the *lifetime morbid risk* (MR)—the likelihood that someone will suffer an episode of schizophrenia between birth and death. In addition to lifetime MR, there are two other counts that are important in the study of schizophrenia: *incidence* and *prevalence*. The *incidence* of schizophrenia is the number of new cases that occur within a period, usually one year, expressed as a rate per 1000 or 10,000 of the general population. For schizophrenia, incidence is currently put at 4 *new* cases per year per 10,000 adults.

The *prevalance* of schizophrenia is based on the total number of patients alive at any specific time; this number would include those who have been ill in the past but who are not obviously psychotic and under "official" care at the time of study. Prevalence is expressed as a rate per 1000 either for the total population or for only the people over the age at which the risk for developing the disorder begins, usually fixed at age 15 for schizophrenia. Current estimates of the lifetime prevalence of schizophrenia are around 1.6%, or 16 cases per 1000 individuals in the adult population.

The value most often accepted as representing the lifetime morbid risk of schizophrenia in the general population is 1.0%. That is, one out of every 100 people born today and surviving to at least age 55 will develop into a diagnosable case of schizophrenia. The earliest census studies (1928) coming out of Germany had established the risk at 0.85% based on a very small sample and that figure is used in the older literature. The currently accepted value is not, after all, so far from the "lucky" guess.

It is important to clarify what the lifetime risk of developing schizophrenia means and what it does not mean. It means that, for the purposes of research into the causes of schizophrenia, a "normal" rate of schizophrenia is considered to be 1% and any higher occurrence in any studied group must be due to some increase in risk factors—perhaps an inherited component, an extremely stressful environment, injuries, or illnesses. Moreover, a 1% lifetime risk for schizophrenia does not mean that every single individual has that risk. To arrive at that average we counted individuals from families who in five generations have never had a case of schizophrenia occur as well as individuals born to two schizophrenic parents. The individual who has had no schizophrenic relative for generations has an even lower than 1% risk whereas the individual who has two schizophrenic parents has a lifetime risk for developing schizophrenia themselves of between 36 and 55%.

B. Age at Onset of Schizophrenia

Systematic observations since the time of Kraepelin reveal that schizophrenia has a variable age of onset: Almost no cases appear before the age of puberty; the number of new cases sharply increases between the ages of 15 and 35 and then slowly drops off; very few new cases appear after age 55. Half of all male schizophrenics experience the onset of their illness by age 28; for females the age is 33. It should be noted that representative average ages of onset for DSM-III diagnosed schizophrenics are lower: 21 years for males and 27 for females.

The sex difference in age of onset shows up around the world and represents an enigma. The total lifetime morbid risk does not differ significantly by sex. Can the sex difference at onset be attributed to differences in the rate of brain maturation timing, to the greater vulnerability of males burdened with testosterone, to the protective effects of estrogen in females, to greater societal demands on males to "grow up" before they are as socially and physically mature as their female age-mates, or what? We don't know, but efforts to find the answers to such questions will certainly add to the knowledge necessary for solving the puzzle of schizophrenia.

C. Distribution of Schizophrenia by Social Classes

Ever since a 1939 study showed that the first-admission rates for schizophrenia were 102 per 100,000 among those living in the slums of central Chicago and diminished in a gradient to less than 25 per 100,000 in affluent neighborhoods on the periphery of the city, researchers have used the information to support opposite conclusions about the nature and direction of the possible causal factors involved. Similar variations have been demonstrated in 16 subsequent studies in other cities and countries, and that social or occupational class rather than local ecological conditions has been pinpointed as the determining variable for these gradients. Social class is less powerful in rural areas as a predictor of increased rates of schizophrenia.

Two principal explanations for the higher rates of schizophrenia among the "underclass" have been proposed. The "breeder" hypothesis, or stress-as-cause, suggests that the cumulative stress induced by proverty, social disorganization in the form of crime and broken homes, and child abuse/neglect in the lower classes are responsible for breeding more schizophrenia. The "drift" hypothesis suggests that a downward social class migration of mentally impaired (that is, mentally inefficient, not mentally retarded) workers on their way to becoming overt schizophrenics overloads the lower class with schizophrenics. These about-to-become schizophrenics are, in effect, immigrants who carry their predisposition with them and "ruin" the reputation of their new neighborhood, namely, that of the inner-city, blue-collar working class. A complementary hypothesis, supported by data, is that social selection traps some preschizophrenics in the lower class from which they originated, whereas their normal siblings and peers are more likely to improve their status as a result of secular improvements in educational and economic opportunities (compared to their parents' generation). Careful research conducted in the United Kingdon, United States, and Israel has provided clear evidence that lower SES levels do not cause schizophrenia, but rather individuals with schizophrenia tend to "drift downward" in the SES distribution once the disease process has "turned on."

Support for the downward drift hypothesis, however, does not disprove a role for stressors, although it may well mean that stress triggers the development of schizophrenia rather than causes the disease itself. After all, the vast majority of those born into the lower class do not become schizophrenics. Conversely, we asume that some persons predisposed to schizophrenia and born poor might have escaped the illness had they been able to avoid poverty's insults to development and psychological integration; for example low birth weight is associated with poverty and with central nervous system damage. If not born with low birth weight, a person otherwise predisposed to developing schizophrenia might well avoid such an outcome. Almost all research confirms that the stressors which may trigger schizophrenia—interpersonal stress, brain trauma and disease, drug intoxication, and the like—are not unique to poverty. At present, the alleged stressors all lack a proven one-to-one relationship to schizophrenia and appear to be too widespread in the population to explain the causes of schizophrenia. [*See* STRESS.]

D. Schizophrenia around the World

The universality of schizophrenia across time (the past 200 years) and space (from the pastoral villages of Botswana in Africa to industrialized societies) has been challenged repeatedly, often with little high-quality empirical data. In 1988 the World Health Organization reported the completion of yet another major study which should set many of the speculations to rest. Schizophrenia *is* universal, and the variation across cultures as different as rural Chandigarh, India, and Nottingham, England, is demonstrably modest. It seems safe to conclude that the incidence of schizophrenia in most human populations around the world today is rather similar; even if a rate two or three times as high as the values here are found, it represents a small real difference—8 or 12 cases instead of 4 cases per 10,000 adults. Still, unexplained pockets of very low rates, such as those reported in the Southwest Pacific (Papua, New Guinea), and very high rates, such as those reported in Western Ireland and a region in Croatia (one of the republics of the former Yugoslavia), if confirmed, demand explanations.

In summary, today we find human beings afflicted with schizophrenia in all societies and in all socioeconomic strata within these societies. Differences in frequency over time and space (cultures, subcultures) have sometimes been observed, but they are difficult to interpret easily. However, many of the reported variations cannot be other than artifacts of inaccurate reporting (untrained observers, small samples, idiosyncratic conventions about diagnoses) and perhaps simpler explanations relating to changes in life-expectancy and to social mobility will suffice.

V. GENETICS OF SCHIZOPHRENIA

A. The Diathesis–Stressor Framework and Polygenic Model

Is schizophrenia genetically influenced? Such a simplistic question cannot do justice to the accumulation of knowledge from research into the complex multifactorial causes and contributors to the phenomenon of schizophrenia. Passionate partisan debate has raged for decades on both extremes of the Nature to Nurture or heredity to environment continuum of explanatory causes, with one side asserting that heredity and biology were irrelevant and the other, that environment and psychosocial factors were irrelevant. The heredity–environment controversy with respect to the causes of schizophrenia is a remnant from a broader, sociopolitical and ideological battle of longstanding known as the Nature *versus* Nurture Controversy. [*See* BEHAVIORAL GENETICS.]

Current research strongly indicates that genetic factors are essential as a *diathesis* (predisposition) but that they are not sufficient, by themselves, for the development of schizophrenia. Within a broad framework known as "diathesis–stressor" theory, the vast array of facts gathered by both those scientist–clinicians typecast as hereditarians and those typecast as environmentalists can be reconciled without "appeasement" on either side. Demonstration of a significant role for genetic factors in the etiology of schizophrenia conveys *no* implications of therapeutic nihilism, either psychotherapeutic or pharmocotherapeutic.

The development of all human characteristics requires contribution from both genes and environments; in this sense, all characteristics are "acquired" rather than simply inherited or written on a blank slate. For schizophrenia, the unresolved problems are to identify the specific genes, together with their importance as causal factors in the disease, their chemical products, and their mechanisms for modulating behaviors, and to identify the specific environments (physical and psychosocial) together with their contributions to the disease, and their mechanisms for modulating behaviors.

The basic evidence for the importance of genetic factors in the etiology of schizophrenia comes from the simultaneous considerations of the results of family, twin, and adoption studies conducted from 1916 to 1992. The overall pattern of scientific data clearly supports the familiality of schizophrenia—

the tendency of schizophrenia to run in families—and it can be interpreted as largely due to the sharing of genes rather than due to the sharing of environments and experiences. In a sense, schizophrenia is the kind of common genetic disorder studied by scientists who follow coronary heart disease, mental retardation, or diabetes, and thus not like such rare genetic diseases as Huntington disease (HD) or phenylketonuria (PKU, a form of mental retardation), each with clear, simple Mendelian inheritance patterns associated with dominant (HD) or recessive (PKU) modes of inheritance from parents to children.

Much more complex patterns of familial aggregation of pathology have been observed for diabetes, moderate mental retardation, Alzheimer disease, coronary heart disease, manic-depression (bipolar and unipolar affective disorder), epilepsy, and cleft lip and palate, to name a few. The patterns observed for schizophrenia strike the observer as being in the same ball park as the conditions just mentioned: for none of these do we find large numbers of families in which the risks to first-degree relatives appear to be close to the expected 50% rates for Mendelian dominant disorders or 25% for recessive diseases. Furthermore, a patient with such a *multifactorial–polygenic* condition requiring an accumulation of more than two relevant genes as well as relevant environmental contributors most often comes from a family in which neither parent manifests it and, usually, none of the siblings or children do either. Paradoxically, these are some of the very reasons to suspect polygenic inheritance as a root cause of such "atypically" familial disorders.

The vast majority of gene-influenced human variation—both normal and abnormal—arises from polygenic effects which, when plotted on paper, take the shape of a bell-shaped, or "normal," curve. Height, IQ test scores, and blood pressure values are nice textbook examples. The numerous polygenes associated with a particular disease co-act with each other and other factors to produce pathology, although they themselves are not yet individually detectable. They are not differnt in kind from the major genes that cause Mendelian conditions, but each has only a "small" effect on trait variation as compared to the total variation for that trait. Therefore, the expression of the trait depends much less on which polygenes in the specific system a person has (e.g., height, blood pressure, IQ) than on the total number pulling him or her toward an extreme. A feature of special interest in the study of schizophrenia and other major mental disorders is the allowance such polygenic systems have to store and conceal genetic contributors to *the liability to developing* the disorder, somewhat analogous to carrier status for recessive diseases.

For polygenic characteristics, what is inherited is a *predisposition* toward developing the disorder—a loading of nature's dice that increases the risk of, in this instance, developing schizophrenia. We believe that a relative of a schizophrenic inherits a combined genetic part of the liability for schizophrenia that is much greater (for a son or daughter) or a little greater (for a first cousin) than that for a member of the general population who is genetically unrelated to a schizophrenic. With the increases in liability go increases in risk that exceed the ordinary population risk of about 1%.

The strength of a diathesis–stressor framework that incorporates a polygenic basis for the diathesis is that it fits the results of many careful studies of schizophrenia. However, a single-major-locus genetic hypothesis or a "mixed-model" genetic hypothesis (competing genetic models) may be correct for a few of the cases (or some small fraction) of schizophrenia; a certain amount of etiological heterogeneity is to be expected with multifactorial disorders. Regardless of the specific genetic model that guides specific investigations into schizophrenia, a plurality of data-informed scientists researching schizophrenia accept the diathesis–stressor formulation or something close to it.

To be certain, *no* purely environmental theory has been borne out by any study. No one has ever proved that environmental factors alone can be a sufficient cause of true schizophrenia in any person not related to a schizophrenic. Schizophrenia has been diagnosed after, for instance, a head injury or the flu, but these trauma-induced schizophrenia-like psychoses are no longer accepted as true schizophrenia; the majority are now seen as parts of the broader category of organic brain syndromes associated with physical disorders.

Family, twin, and adoption studies of schizophrenia provide the grist for our mill. Each contributes to the genetic argument, complementing the others. No one method alone yields conclusive proof or disproof. For schizophrenia, devoting too many resources to a similar kind of random, long-shot search for genetic markers, absent some candidate genetic marker that is logically related to the neurochemical and pathophysiological facts established by research, would be like investing in penny stocks on the Denver Stock Exchange. However, once in awhile someone makes a fortune by just such speculation.

B. Family Studies of Schizophrenia

If transmissible genetic factors contribute to developing schizophrenia, the disorder should cluster in affected families at a higher rate than the 1% affected in the general population. That a disease is familial, however, does not necessarily mean that it is genetic. As we have already cautioned, it may be transmitted through families not by genes but through some cultural practice, some infectious source, or some kind of learning by imitation. When we look at family studies to decide whether the variable is something genetic, we want to ask if the pattern of risks rises and falls as a function of the genetic overlap rather than as a consequence of shared experience. Do closer relatives, who have more genes in common, have a higher risk, and does that risk diminish as family relatedness diminishes? Furthermore, if the relatives are not overtly affected with schizophrenia, do they have something specifically odd or different about them that might provide clues to their having inherited a "diluted" form of schizophrenia, that is, schizophrenia spectrum disorder?

Table I summarizes the lifetime risks of being affected with schizophrenia for the various kinds of relatives of a schizophrenic. The table shows the degree of genetic relationship for different groupings of relatives from which the percentage of genes various family members share in common with a schizophrenic proband can be compared. The data come from pooling information from about 40 reliable studies conducted in Western Europe from 1920 to 1987. There is some danger in pooling such information, because the study designs are not exactly alike, but pooling after the judicious removal of the poorest data gives a clear and stable summary pattern not obtainable from any one or two studies.

TABLE I
Risks of Schizophrenia (Definite and Probable) for Relatives of Schizophrenics

Relationship	Morbid risk (%)
General population	1
Spouses of patients	2
Third-degree relatives	
First cousins	2
Second-degree relatives	
Uncles/aunts	2
Nephews/nieces	4
Grandchildren	5
Half-siblings	6
First-degree relatives	
Parents	6
Siblings	9
Children	13
Siblings with one schizophrenic parent	17
DZ twins	17
MZ twins	48
Children of two schizophrenics	46

Source: Gottesman (1991). Reproduced with permission.

Table I presents the risks of developing schizophrenia for first-degree (parents, sibs, children), second-degree (uncles, nephews, grandchildren, half-sibs), and third-degree (first cousins) relatives of schizophrenics. Additionally, it gives the risks for fraternal twins, who are also first-degree relatives and for identical twins who could be called zero-degree relatives because they are really genetic clones of one another. Risks for spouses, who are highly unlikely to be related genetically, are presented to allow testing the idea of being able to induce schizophrenia in someone simply by sharing an intimate physical and psychological relationship. Table I also includes the risks of schizophrenia for the children of two schizophrenics, showing them to be nowhere near the 100 or 75% risks required to support simple Mendelian-style recessive and dominant genetic disorders (as well as simple environmental models of familial transmission). The pooled studies represent large enough samples to be quite reliable and an enormous amount of information is summarized in Table I that bears careful study.

Overall, the pattern of risk figures in the relatives of schizophrenics strongly supports the conclusion that the magnitude of the increased risk varies with the amount of gene sharing and not with the amount of experience sharing. Identical twins and offspring of dual matings are higher than first-degree relatives, who are higher than second-degree relatives, who are higher than third-degree relatives, who are higher than spouses and the basic risk of 1% in the general population.

We would like to note that among schizophrenics who do become parents, the ratio of mothers to fathers is two to one. This striking fact, coupled with the high risk for schizophrenia among the children of schizophrenics, has led some partisans to proclaim that it confirms the notion that pathogenic mothering causes schizophrenia. The term "schizophrenogenic mother'' was coined by the psychoanalyst Frieda Fromm-Reichmann in 1948 during the heyday of explanations favoring child-rearing attitudes as the central cause of schizophrenia, with no reference whatsoever to ''genes.'' The more neutral and, we believe, valid explanation is that age of onset is earlier in males, thus reducing the likelihood of their finding a mate, and that marriage and procreation occur earlier in females, thus allowing the future female schizophrenic increased opportunity to marry and start a family before she becomes ill. The net effect of such social forces of selection results in twice as many children being born to schizophrenic mothers as to schizophrenic fathers, thus feeding the myth of schizophrenogenic mothering. In the three studies that provide data on the matter, the *risk* of developing schizophrenia in the offspring of schizophrenic mothers is the same as that observed in the offspring of schizophrenic fathers. The phrase ''schizophrenogenic mother'' can now be expunged from the scientific literature.

C. Twin Studies of Schizophrenia

Although the family studies reviewed in the last article show that the relatives of schizophrenics are more likely to be schizophrenic than the general population, these only *implicate* genes as the source of this familial illness. It could still be argued that the excess risk is caused by shared family environment/experience, or psychological contagion. The classical studies of identical (monozygotic, MZ, or one-egg) and fraternal (dizygotic, DZ, or two-egg) twins reared together test the idea that genes are the cause of the familiality. The strategy derives from the fact that identical twins share 100% of these genes and their environment, whereas fraternal twins share, on average, 50% of their genes and also 100% of their environment. In most studies same-sex fraternal twins are used to eliminate possible variations due to sex differences within a pair. If shared family environment is of primary importance in causing schizophrenia, then all co-twins, regardless of zygosity, would be similar. Identical pairs would be no more alike (no more concordant for schizophrenia) than fraternal pairs. If genes are more important, then identical twins should be considerably more concordant for schizophrenia than fraternal twins.

The separation of twins into MZ and same-sex DZ pairs can be accomplished routinely by a combination of blood typing and observations of general similarity in appearance (eye and hair color and texture, height, weight), sometimes including fingerprint analyses. It is sufficient here simply to appreciate the conceptual simplicity of the method:

Identical twin similarity for schizophrenia (is due to) = 100% of genetic variance + 100% of environmental variance.
Fraternal twin similarity for schizophrenia (is due to) = 50% of genetic variance + 100% of environmental variance.
Therefore, identicals − fraternals similarity = 50% of the genetic variance in the liability to developing schizophrenia.

Altogether the world research literature on schizophrenia contains only a dozen systematic studies, each labor intensive and each precious for the leverage it gives in understanding the complexities of the contributors to the causes this psychosis. Six early twin studies (conducted prior to 1953) showed remarkably similar concordance rates without the dubious corrections for age; they were dubious because they assumed no correlation in the age of onset for pairs of relatives but, the correlation in the age of onset for twin pairs is considerable. Despite the stability of the twin findings with respect to schizophrenia and their implications for the importance of genetic factors in causing schizophrenia, standard texts in psychopathology have ignored or belittled them.

The six modern twin studies that have been reported since 1963—four from Scandinavia, one from the United States, one from the United Kingdom—generally report lower identical twin concordance rates than earlier studies but similar fraternal rates. On the surface their MZ findings range more widely, actually from zero to 50%, but the zero from the preliminary reports of the Finnish study is a fluke. Since virtually all of these studies include twins who are still alive and discordant, their results are not yet final. For instance, the Finnish study first reported no concordance among rather young identical twins, but follow-up some years later resulted in a 36% concordance. Each time researchers recheck on their original subjects, new rates may result, but changes will be minor after 5 to 10 years following diagnosis in the first twin of identical pairs.

Table II presents a survey of these newer studies. It gives a technically more correct and more genetically informative measurement called a *probandwise*

TABLE II
Concordance Rates for Schizophrenia in Newer Twin Studies

	MZ pairs (total probandwise)		DZ pairs (total probandwise)	
	Pairs	Rate(%)	Pairs	Rate(%)
Finland, 1963/1971	17	35	20	13
Norway, 1967	55	45	90	15
Denmark, 1973	21	56	41	27
United Kingdom, 1968/1987	22	58	33	15
Norway, 1991	31	48	28	4
United States, 1969/1983	164	31	268	6
Pooled concordance (excluding U.S.)				
Median	146	48	212	15
Weighted mean		48		16
Pooled concordance (all studies)				
Median	310	46	480	14
Weighted mean		39		10

Source: Gottesman (1991). Reproduced with permission.

concordance. For a pairwise concordance, a pair, both of whom are schizophrenic, is counted as one pair in the numerator and in the denominator. For a probandwise concordance, concordant twins are counted as two pairs both in the numerator and in the denominator but only when those pairs contain schizophrenics both of whom are identified *independently* from the "official" register of cases. Probandwise rates are unbiased ones in regard to "sampling" and the only ones that are directly comparable to population risks. If we were able to report probandwise rates for the earlier studies we would have done so, but the necessary information was not available.

The twin study we lean most heavily upon for our insights reports on the British data collected by the second author of this article (I.I.G.) and his co-investigator, the late James Shields of the United Kingdom. In 1948 Eliot Slater, whose own twin study is among the classical ones above, initiated a new twin register designed to avoid sampling biases that is maintained at the Genetics Unit of the Maudsley-Bethlem Hospital and Institute of Psychiatry in London. Sixteen years later Gottesman and Shields collected follow-up information from fieldwork and hospital interviews to select 62 schizophrenic subjects from 57 pairs of twins from a total register of 479 disordered twins—the total yield from about 45,000 consecutive psychiatric admissions. Unlike most schizophrenic samples, this one had a higher representation of cases with a good prognosis because subjects were selected from consecutive outpatient admissions as well as from consecutive inpatient admissions. As it turned out, however, by 1965 all the outpatient schizophrenic twins had been hospitalized, even if only for a few weeks. The Maudsley-Bethlem study was designed so as to answer most of the dissatisfactions with the earlier twin studies in regard to genetic biases, sampling biases, and diagnostic uncertainty.

This sample was refined by using the blindfold diagnoses of a panel of six judges rather than chart diagnoses or the investigators' own evaluations. That removed two pairs of identical twins from the study. The concordance rates resulting from the six-judge consensus were 58% for MZ and 12% for DZ at the level of schizophrenia-like "functional" psychoses. These rates are not age-corrected because the discordant twins were followed initially for 3 to 27 years (age-corrections are typically statistically applied to risk and concordance figures to take into account the variations in risk for the illness that are linked to age). Age-correcting would have raised the rates artificially because the healthy co-twins had, in effect, already "used up" their risk for a future schizophrenia. Even though a number of these original subjects were still within the risk period for developing schizophrenia, a further check of national health insurance records after 20 more years (1985) found only one new schizophrenic in the total sample, and she was a co-twin from a DZ pair, raising the rate 3% to that reported in Table II.

Overall, we believe the pooled probandwise concordances for schizophrenia in Table II give the most accurate picture of risk among identical and fraternal twins for industrialized societies in the last half of the 20th century. Given the perspective above about design differences between the classical and the new studies, we see the entire array of twin findings as fulfilling a basic requirement of "hard science"—replication. Undeniably, when twins are reared together, the identical twin of a schizophrenic is much more likely to be schizophrenic than the fraternal twin of a schizophrenic. No one or two concordance rates provide the last word from twin studies, but the findings are consistent and very orderly. Excluding the V.A. chart-based study (designated United States 1969/1983 in Table II), the pooled data in Table II results in an identical twin concordance rate of 48% and a fraternal rate of 16%. These results indicate that shared genes certainly have something to do with the source of schizophrenia. However, the fact that only half of the identical twin pairs are concordant for recognizable schizophrenia tells us that something important beyond genetic factors is required to complete the solution to the puzzle of causation.

There is reasonably good agreement among the recent twin studies of schizophrenia. The similar picture is partly a consequence of using the probandwise method of calculation and partly the result of thorough sample investigation and longer follow-up. But it is similar also because modern investigators are agreeing more on diagnostic criteria and taking the middle of the road more often. We favor a standard that accepts as concordant, co-twins who are schizophrenic or probably shizophrenic, virtually all of whom have been hospitalized for a functional (i.e., not obviously organic) psychosis, one that is not likely to be an affective psychosis. For the second phase of data analysis we would add the co-twins with genetically relevant schizophrenia spectrum disorders (known as schizotypic conditions), but currently there is disagreement over the definition and assessment of such conditions. Developments in brain imaging, in cognitive neuroscience, and in molecular genetics should soon remove many of the ambiguities of clinical diagnoses that rely only on behavior.

The kinds of environmental experiences examined in identical twins discordant for schizophrenia seem insufficient to account for discordance. Not many low birthweight babies, or children tied to the apronstrings of constricting and inconsistent mothers, or submissive twins who have difficulties in fending for themselves because of their close relationship actually develop schizophrenia. Such factors may, however, be important in determining illness and health among identical twins who have a predisposition to schizophrenia. For some scientific problems, the occurrence of identical twins reared apart from birth seems to give us an ideal "natural experiment" to resolve some of the conflicts over the relative importance of nature and nurture. For schizophrenia, however, these cases are very rare and the circumstances that create them are unusual, to say the least.

Fourteen pairs of identical twins reared apart, in which at least one member has been diagnosed as schizophrenic, have been described in the scientific literature, but the sample is too small for generalization. Of these, however, 64% are concordant, a value somewhat higher than the concordance rate of 48% for identical twins reared together. These data, however, are clearly consistent with genetic influences operating to bring about schizophrenia.

Studying the adult offspring born to concordant and discordant MZ and DZ twins produces unique evidence for testing the idea that the genotype for schizophrenia can be completely invisible or unexpressed in a "carrier" and yet be transmitted to the next generation. If the risk of schizophrenia to the offspring of schizophrenic MZ twins is like that of the offspring of ordinary schizophrenics, about 13%, and if the risk to the offspring of the clinically healthy MZ co-twins is close to the population rate of 1%, it would provide very powerful evidence *for* the role of the environment (the rearing factors associated with a schizophrenic parent) in causing schizophrenia. Alternatively, it would raise further questions about nongenetic phenocopies of schizophrenia in the ill MZ twin. If, on the other hand, the risk to the children of the healthy MZ co-twin matches that in the children of the sick MZ twin, it *undermines* the significant causal role for shared rearing factors such as social class and for *the unshared factor of a schizophrenic parent.*

In a Danish study of the offspring of concordant and discordant twin pairs, the risks of developing schizophrenia for the offspring of the two groups of MZ twins are quite high and indistinguishable from each other. However, the risk for the offspring of schizophrenic DZ twins is virtually the same as for the two groups of MZ twins. The risk for the children of healthy DZ co-twins, actually the nieces and nephews of schizophrenics, is close to that reported in Table I for such relatives in the literature, only 2.1%.

The data from this unusually well-followed-up sample of Danish schizophrenic twins and their offspring support a strong role for genetic factors in the etiology of schizophrenia. No support is found for the suggestion that rearing by a schizophrenic parent is necessary or sufficient to produce schizophrenia in offspring. Our data do not support the hypothesis that nongenetic factors such as putative viruses or cerebral injuries or toxins frequently lead to monozygotic discordance because the offspring of the phenotypically normal MZ co-twins of schizophrenics had the same risk of developing schizophrenia as if they were the children of schizophrenics. It would appear that the genotype for schizophrenia can remain completely unexpressed and silent to clinical detection, be transmitted, and then be expressed in the next generation when the sons and daughters encounter a different constellation of relevant stressors.

By way of an interim summary, the facts about the risks for schizophrenia obtained from family studies of schizophrenics—their parents, siblings, children, and more distant relatives—all suggested that schizophrenia was familial, that is, it was much more common among relatives than among members of the general population. As one line of evidence that the familiality was not merely the result of sharing experiences, rather than genes, the classical genetic strategy involving the comparison of concordance rates in identical and fraternal twins of schizophrenics was detailed. The observed rates in twins and other relatives suggest that genetic factors are important but that they are not adequate for explaining all the observations. Still unclear is the role played by possible shared experiences within the family for which the study of children adopted away from their schizophrenic parents is required.

D. Adoption Studies

Both the critics and the skeptics could complain that the masses of family and twin data presented, which strongly implicate genetic factors of one kind or another in the etiology of schizophrenia, can be explained away by some kind of environmental contagion. The "vector," or agent, of that contagion could be some kind of within-family psychological phenomenon, such as the presence of a so-called schizophrenogenic mother or the "affective style" (expressed attitudes) or "communication deviance" between patently normal parents and between such parents and *some* of their children. The vector would have to work like a time bomb, not unlike the delayed action of "slow viruses" implicated in some physical diseases such as the neurological disease kuru which even had a familial pattern of affection; recall that the age of onset of schizophrenia ranges over the interval from puberty to the middle 50s. Virus theories about the etiology of schizophrenia have a following among some serious scientists. However, recent reviews of this literature note that it is very important to separate viruses as causes of mental disorder, from impaired immunological functioning as a consequence of the stress of being mentally ill; neither psychiatric nurses nor the spouses of schizophrenics have elevated rates of schizophrenia.

When the parents who provide the genes to their children are not the same as the rearing parents, an opportunity is provided for disentangling the genetic and the experiential factors that predispose an individual to the development of schizophrenia later in life. The traditional family studies of schizophrenia have already shown that the children of patients do indeed have a very high risk for developing the same disorder at a rate some 13 times the general population rate. In adoption studies of schizophrenia, the adoptee of interest receives his or her genes (and prenatal environment) from "birth parents," one of whom is schizophrenic, and his or her rearing environment and experiences from adoptive parents who have been carefully screened through interviews and hospital record-checks for psychological health and economic security. On the face of it such an arrangement disentangles heredity from environment and permits a clearer examination of both classes of contributing forces. Ideally, well-designed adoption studies could support the genetic interpretation of the observed familiality of schizophrenia, or they could embarrass such interpretations and point to psychological (or even infectious) contagion.

Four variations of the adoption research strategies exist. The first and most used looks at the grown-up, adopted-away offspring of birth parents (mothers and sometimes fathers) who are known to be or have been diagnosed as schizophrenic. The second design starts with grown-up adoptees who have been diagnosed as having schizophrenia and then proceeds to evaluate the current and retrospective psychiatric statuses of their biological *and* their adoptive families. The third variation, termed cross-fostering, also very difficult to conduct, starts with the children of normal, or at least psychiatric-recordless, parents who have been adopted into homes where an adoptive parent, apparently within normal limits psychologically at the time of adoption, later came to be diagnosed as a schizophrenic. The final design, with no completed examples yet in hand, examines the adopted-away children of schizophrenics and their adoptive parents prospectively and longitudinally, as well as the physical and emotional environments to which they are exposed in their adoptive homes; once the yield of schizophrenic adoptees is sufficient, their families and experiences can be contrasted with those of the still-healthy adoptees so as to specify the contributory and triggering events for schizophrenia as well as the protective ones.

Implicit in these strategies is the question of whether the presence of a schizophrenic parent is a relevant *environmental* factor in the development of their offspring's schizophrenia when it does occur. Does the simple presence of such a "pathogen" lead to the kinds of stresses, double binds, negatively expressed emotions, marital skews and schisms, communication deviances, and so on, that purportedly lead to the development of schizophrenia in those so exposed? If so, we would expect that removing children from such homes via the adoption process would result in a lower risk than the average of 13% usually observed among the offspring of schizophrenics reared at home. We know that about 87% of persons with a schizophrenic parent do not develop clinically overt cases of schizophrenia. From this observation alone it is clear that the presence of a sick parent is not sufficient as an environmental cause of schizophrenia; and, because only about 10% of schizophrenics have a psychotic mother or father, such a parent is not necessary as a genetic cause of schizophrenia either.

The only "experimentally" controlled environmental factor in adoption research strategies is the postnatal presence or absence of a schizophrenic parent who rears the child. Because we do not yet understand *which* aspects of such rearing experiences may be causal or contributory in the chain of events leading to schizophrenia, we cannot compare these aspects directly in the two kinds of household involved. The bottom line from this discussion is that the adoption results cannot be used to assess *general* environmental contributors to liability for developing schizophrenia and cannot be used to dismiss or belittle the importance of psychosocial or ecological factors, other than the one controlled factor, in a first episode of schizophrenia or in subsequent episodes. Overall, synthesizing the results of the several adoption investigations, the broad genes-plus-environment hypothesis for explaining the cause of schizophrenia is strengthened by the adoption studies. As listed in Table III they show that sharing an environment with a schizophrenic parent or another schizophrenic generally does *not* account for the familiality of cases. The adoption studies clearly demonstrated that an individual's genetic endowment was more closely linked to the expression of schizophrenia in them or their family members than was any facet of his or her rearing environment. One of the favorite notions before 1966 was that genes inherited from a schizophrenic did predispose a person to schizophrenia, but that the transmitter of the genes who also raised the person transmitted a schizophrenogenic environment as well. Both the necessity and the sufficiency of the specific kinds of schizophrenogenic environments provided by schizophrenic parents have been weakened by the adoption results. Recall that 90% of schizophrenics do not have schizophrenic parents.

VI. SCHIZOPHRENIA, SOCIETY, AND SOCIAL POLICY

A more comprehensive appreciation and understanding of the syndrome of schizophrenia, with all of the ramifications for the impact of society on it and for the impact of schizophrenia on society, can be derived from a consideration of the facts about patterns of mortality (death) and morbidity (disease susceptibility), crime and violence, and aspects of reproduction (sexuality, fertility or "fitness," marriage, and divorce). All of these facts fall under the umbrella of the definition of "social biology"—knowledge about the biological and sociocultural factors that influence the structure of human populations—and have direct implications for implementing social policy.

Current research reveals that even today the mortality rate among schizophrenics is twice that of the general population. Suicides, accidents, and cardiovascular disease are sources of excess mortality among schizophrenia sufferers. Suicide is *the* most frequent and alarming cause of excess mortality among schizophrenics, far surpassing any other cause. Although received wisdom would correctly implicate suicide as a major cause of death among sufferers from the major affective disorders (depression and manic-depression), it comes as a surprise to learn that schizophrenics kill themselves almost as frequently. In the World Health Organization 10-country follow-up study of psychiatric patients, it was found that schizophrenics constituted 80% of the fatalities in the first 5 years. Of the 19 suicides, 14 had a diagnosis of schizophrenia, indicating that the risk of suicide is as great or greater than among patients with affective disorders. [*See* SUICIDE.]

A recurring observation made by clinicians working with schizophrenics is that the symptoms of depression and anhedonia (absence of pleasureable feelings) often co-occur at such a high rate that their presence is not a useful clue to the prediction of

TABLE III
Five Adoption Studies of Schizophrenia Summarized

Study	Index case	Group in which prevalence was measured (*N*)	% Sc (95% CI)	Controls	Group in which prevalence was measured (*N*)	% Sc (95% CI)
Heston *et al.*	Sc mothers	Their adopted away offspring (47)	10(2–18)	Mothers not Sc	Their adopted away offspring (50)	0
Rosenthal *et al.*	Sc mothers and fathers	Their adopted away offspring (69)	19(10–30)	Parents not mentally ill	Their adopted away offspring (79)	10(5–19)
Kety *et al.*	Sc who were adopted as children	Biological parents (66)	12(6–23)	Adoptees with no psychiatric history	Biological parents (65)	6(2–15)
		Biological half-siblings (104)	19(12–28)		All siblings of adoptees (143)	6(3–12)
		Adoptive parents (63)	2(0–9)		Adoptive parents (68)	4(1–12)
Wender *et al.*	—	Children of Sc parents raised by normals (69)	19(10–30)	—	Children of normals raised by Sc (28)	11(2–28)
Tienari	Sc mothers	Their adopted away offspring (117)	11(6–18)	Parents not psychotic	Their adopted away offspring (148)	1.4(0.2–5)

Source: Hanson, D. R., and Gottesman, I. I. (1992). Schizophrenia. In "The Genetic Basis of Common Diseases" (R. A. King, J. I. Rotter, and A. G. Motulsky, Eds.) New York: Oxford. Reproduced with permission.

Note: Sc, schizophrenic; CI, confidence interval (the range within which the true value will be found 95% of the time such studies are replicated). For the Tienari study, the diagnoses presented are preliminary and include all psychoses in addition to schizophrenia; only for offspring over the age of 20.

suicide attempts. However, once the "facets" of depression are differentiated so that a particular feature—pervasive hopelessness—can be discerned, that may well be a clinical clue worth attending to as a harbinger of suicidal behavior. [*See* DEPRESSION.]

Obtaining a balanced perspective about the relationship between violence and schizophrenia is extremely difficult. The thirst of the media leads inexorably to an exaggeration of any genuine relationships that may exist, but dispassionate sources of information are available to help us attain a more accurate perspective. Knowing that a person has some kind of mental disorder does *not* permit an accurate prediction about her or his "dangerousness," however. In fact, it has been concluded that of every three mentally disordered persons predicted to be violent by an expert psychologist or psychiatrist, only one will go on to commit a violent act. In short, psychiatric diagnoses are the poorest predictors of violence. The best include the same demographic factors found useful in predicting violence in the general population of the United States—age, sex, social class, and a prior history of violence.

The seriously mentally ill make a trivial contribution to violent acts in society; you are safer visiting a patient in a mental hospital than you are on the streets of any major American city after dark. From this vantage point, the life-threatening behavior of some schizophrenics can be seen as isolated episodes.

Clinical impressions about the sexual behavior of schizophrenic men and women are usually so idiosyncratically anecdotal that they provide no guarantees about their usefulness in understanding other cases. In general, it is clear that there is something very special about the process of schizophrenia that leads to a low probability of successful marriage.

The fertility of the mentally ill has attracted the attention of "do-gooders" and "do-badders" for more than a century. Marital fertility is somewhat lower for schizophrenics compared to the general population. However, both the marriage rate and the relative rate of reproduction (a product of fertility rate times marriage rate) are much lower, especially for male schizophrenics. Therefore, the major "mechanism" of lower fertility rates is via lower rates of marriage.

VII. CONCLUSION AND FUTURE DIRECTIONS

What has not been accomplished, obviously, is the parallel mission to complete the big picture for understanding the origins of schizophrenia. The preceding material reflects an effort to describe the facts, certain and uncertain, that inform a view of (1) the nature of predisposing factors to schizophrenia and how they may be transmitted within families and (2) how diathesis (predisposition) or vulnerability interacts *epigenetically* with stressors to produce episodes of dysfunction frequently followed by degrees of improvement.

Readers of this article will likely have to conclude that, based on the cumulative credible evidence, a large, rather specific, and important genetic factor(s), in conjunction with putative, unspecified nongenetic factors for most cases, leads to the development, over varying lengths of time, of varying severities of schizophrenia(s). Resistance to such a balanced conclusion, when it appears, must be based on ideological reasons.

Given the existence of an important genetic predisposition to the liability for developing schizophrenia, it becomes important to build theories or models for how that predisposition becomes actualized into episodes of overt schizophrenic behaviors and to build other models for how that predisposition may be transmitted across generations. Such models can serve as maps for both the specialist researcher and the informed layperson to the continent of schizophrenia, telling us where we are, where we need to go, and where there are uncharted territories or inconsistent data requiring further exploration. If the models are to do their job of making sense out of the data, they must be dynamic, that is, they must take account of the changes in phenotype over time from normal to disordered to social recovery and, too often, back to disordered. Schizophrenia is almost always an episodic mental disorder. Recoveries from such episodes were known even before the era of active neuroleptic treatments and then, as now, about 20% of the persons diagnosed as suffering from schizophrenia could be expected to resume useful lives outside the hospital.

At the present stage of our knowledge it is more accurate to call schizophrenia a heavily genetically influenced disorder rather than a genetically determined disorder so as to avoid any hereditarian implication of "inevitability." Some human malfunctions, whether medical or behavioral, are better than others for providing useful clues to the kinds of research strategies into causes and treatments for schizophrenia. Coronary heart disease, diabetes, mental retardation, and epilepsy—all complex, multifactorially influenced syndromes with demonstrable genetic components—would be at the top of a recommended list.

Unlike a genetic disease like galactosemia or an environmental disease like measles, schizophrenia fits somewhere in between along with diabetes and coronary heart disease. For the latter two conditions the unspecified genetic predisposition must share the spotlight with an array of environmental contributors (diet, exercise, smoking, lifestyle, pregnancy, etc.) some of which lead to some people with the vulnerability developing the disorder. With such middle-of-the continuum conditions, the facts suggest that the environmental factors may be interaction effects only—that is, only those unlucky persons with "sensitive genotypes" feel the effects.

What relevance do the new advances in the neurosciences have for schizophrenia? Only the "flavor" of these exciting advances relevant to schizophrenia can be provided in summarizing statements, but the interested reader can pursue in-depth treatments via the bibliography for this article. "How does the brain really work?" is no longer a rhetorical question. The accumulation of partial answers to how it works, as well as how it malfunctions, feed directly into questions about the causes and treatments for schizophrenia (and other forms of psychopathology). An adult brain contains some 100 billion neurons and the typical neuron has about 1500 synapses, or connections, to other neurons; the total number of synapses across which electrical/chemical signals are transmitted or blocked is mind-boggling. At each synapse there may be one million receptor molecules that mediate the communication with other neurons, families of chemicals known collectively as neurotransmitters and neuromodulators. [*See* SYNAPTIC TRANSMITTERS AND NEUROMODULATORS.]

The king of putative neurotransmitter dysregulation in schizophrenia is dopamine, but there are other contenders for the throne that cannot yet be ruled out such as serotonin, acetylcholine, and GABA. Driving the dopamine hypothesis about the "intermediate cause" of schizophrenia is the idea of *overactivity* of neurons containing or using dopamine in mesolimbic, basal ganglia-nigrostriatal, and mesocortical regions of the brain. Because the most effective drugs used to treat schizophrenia block dopamine receptors (hence transmission of signals), and because agents that make schizophrenia worse, such as PCP and amphetamines, increase dopamine levels, the hypothesis has made sense and has had remarkable survival in a rapidly changing bioscience environment.

Such indirect evidence about the role of dopamine is now being replaced by still controversial direct evidence obtained from the use of PET, positron emission tomography, to visualize the density of D2 (one specific kind of dopamine receptor) receptors in the caudate-putamen regions of the brains of living schizophrenics. However, PET research with psychiatric patients is still a "rare bird" and much more remains to be learned.

By careful examination of schizophrenics *before* they become dysfunctional (i.e., as children), it should become possible to distinguish between those facets of disturbance that are indicators of the genetic predisposition to developing schizophrenia versus those that are signs of incipient schizophrenia or those that may be accommodations to the disorder itself. Deficits in sustained attention and subtle eye movement dysfunctions represent aspects of psychobiological functioning that high-risk researchers are focusing on in their work. Valid predictors of adult schizophrenia may indeed be forthcoming from high-risk studies of the young offspring of schizophrenic mothers and fathers, but three possibilities must be considered before such predictors are equated with biological or possibly even genetic markers for schizophrenia: (1) the deviance may merely reflect maladaptive reactions to being reared by and with a parent with major mental illness (hence the importance of complementary prospective adoption study designs), (2) the deviance may reflect nonspecific liability to developing schizophrenia, that is potentiators or correlates of potentiators for the specific liability itself (hence the importance of *psychiatric* as well as *normal* control groups), and (3) childhood predictors might represent the earliest signals of already-started schizophrenia (hence not useful for identifying contributors to the liability but very important as an early-warning signal for the initiation of intervention). A fourth possibility is that the group of "outliers" having deviance in childhood arose by chance and small-sample fluctuations. The proof of the pudding in high-risk research designs will only come from thorough follow-ups of the children until the expected yield of bona fide schizophrenics emerge, unless valid genetic markers are, in the meantime, discovered. Additional clues in the discovery of valid predictors of adult schizophrenia may come from careful examination of schizotypic individuals (persons who carry a liability for schizophrenia but who have not expressed the illness in full-blown form), especially since many of these individuals have never been exposed to the effects of anti-psychotic medication, institutionalization, and the stigma attached to the diagnosis of schizophrenia.

The current breathtaking pace of discovery of genes affecting health is so phenomenal that it can be followed on the front pages of *The New York Times, The Wall Street Journal,* and the evening television news without even reading such scientific journals as *Nature,* published only weekly. Such breakthroughs have virtually all been relevant to major gene disorders, that is, the rare mendelian forms of disease with their prototypical 50 and 25% recurrence risks among siblings. It is only a question of time and informed initiative before the revolution of human genetics reaches the more complex phenotypes of the major mental disorders such as schizophrenia. However, unfortunately, the search for genetic linkage to schizophrenia with the available genetic markers and a simple single major locus model has not resulted yet in replicated positive linkage findings.

So ends our exploration of schizophrenia. Space constraints have limited us to a fairly cursory treatment of the vast and rich research literature on this most puzzling disorder. We make no claim that our review has been exhaustive. The interested reader is strongly encouraged to consult the resources list in the bibliography below for more detailed expositions, particularly *Schizophrenia Genesis* by I. I. Gottesman.

Bibliography

Dohrenwend, B. P., Levav, I., Shrout, P. E., Schwartz, S., Naveh, G., Link, B. G., Skodal, A. E., and Stueve, A. (1992). Socioeconomic status and psychiatric disorders: The causation–selection issue. *Science* **255,** 946–952.

Erlenmeyer-Kimling, L. (1987). Biological markers for the liability to schizophrenia. In "Biological Perspectives of Schizophrenia" (H. Helmchen and F. A. Henn, Eds.). Wiley, New York.

Gottesman, I. I. (1991). "Schizophrenia Genesis: The Origins of Madness." Freeman, New York.

Hafner, H., Gattaz, W. F., and Janzarik, W. (Eds.) (1987). "Search for the Causes of Schizophrenia." Springer-Verlag, Berlin.

Lenzenweger, M. F. (1993). Explorations in schizotypy and the psychometric high-risk paradigm. In "Progress in Experimental Personality and Psychopathology Research" (L. J. Chapman, J. P. Chapman, and D. Fowles, Eds.), Vol. 16, pp. 66–116. Springer, New York.

Lenzenweger, M. F., and Korfine, L. (1992). Confirming the latent structure and base-rate of schizotypy: A taxometric analysis. *J. Abnormal Psychol.* **101,** 567–571.

McGue, M., and Gottesman, I. I. (1989). Genetic linkage in schizophrenia; Perspectives from genetic epidemiology. *Schizophrenia Bull.* **15,** 281–292.

Meehl, P. E. (1990). Toward an integrated theory of schizotaxia, schizotypy, and schizophrenia. *J. Pers. Disorders* **4,** 1–99.

Moldin, S. O., and Erlenmeyer-Kimling, L. (in press). Special Issue: Update on Risk Indicators in Schizophrenia. *Schizophrenia Bull.*

Watt, N. F., Anthony, E. J., Wynne, L. C., and Rolf, J. E. (Eds.) (1984). "Children at Risk for Schizophrenia: A Longitudinal Perspective." Cambridge University Press, New York.

Self-Defeating Behaviors

Rebecca Curtis
Adelphi University

Glossary

Fear of success Irrational avoidance of success, possibly unconscious.

Learned helplessness Failure to act in situations in which action would be rewarding as a consequence of experiencing uncontrollable events in the past.

Masochism Hurting oneself physically, possibly in conjunctions with sexual activities, or in work or relationships.

Self-fulfilling prophecy When an expectation of an experience makes it more likely for an experience to occur, or appears to have led to the experience's occurrence, a self-fulfilling prophecy is said to exist.

Self-handicapping Choosing to engage in an activity in advance which will hurt one's performance.

Self-injurious behavior Action causing physical harm, such as self-mutilation.

SELF-DEFEATING BEHAVIORS are actions leading to a lower reward–cost ratio than is available through an alternative course of action. These behaviors might be called simply "maladaptive," but, in many cases, they involve a person's basic sense of identity. Negligence of health maintenance, underachievement, self-handicapping, helplessness, self-defeating excuse-making, anxiety about success, and avoidance of accurate information about one's abilities are types of self-defeating behaviors distinct from the other psychological problems frequently referred to as personality and psychiatric disorders. The term "self-defeating behaviors" is usually associated with behaviors which occur among normal people, and not the full range of psychiatric symptoms. People may be aware that a behavior is self-defeating, but not know how to refrain from engaging in it, unaware of an alternative behavior, or unaware of the lack of rewards or great costs involved in the maladaptive behavior. The behavior itself must be intentional, even if the consequences of the behavior are not. Self-defeating behaviors have been categorized as (1) "trade-offs" when they offer short-term benefits at harmful long-term costs; and (2) "counterproductive strategies" when a person chooses an approach that does not lead to the consciously desired outcome. Behaviors involving self-mutilation are not usually included among self-defeating behaviors, but are called self-injurious or sometimes self-destructive behaviors.

I. HISTORICAL BACKGROUND

The idea that people engage in defensive behavior was first introduced by Sigmund Freud in his 1894 work entitled *The Defence of Neuro-Psychoses*. Freud regarded neurotic behaviors as defending the ego against threatening sexual and aggressive impulses. Although Anna Freud acknowledged that ego defenses might protect against external as well as instinctual threats, it was Alfred Adler who insisted first that symptoms were unconsciously created to guard the self against esteem losses from external threats. Adler believed that people constructed obstacles to safeguard the self and ideal self, and, when victorious in the face of these obstacles, enhance their prestige in the estimation of others.

The understanding of this "obstacle-constructing" or self-defeating behavior was central to Adlerian therapy.

Karen Horney also saw neurotic symptoms as ways to maintain self-esteem. She believed neuroses provided an alibi for the lack of accomplishment. Aggression, withdrawal, and dependence upon others were primary styles of self-defeating behaviors she described as ways of protecting the self against humiliation and abandonment. [*See* SELF-ESTEEM.]

II. THE DEVELOPMENT AND CHANGE OF SELF-DEFEATING BEHAVIORS

Self-defeating behaviors occur when people have experienced an insufficient number of rewards based upon their actions for self-actualizing behaviors. When maladaptive beliefs about oneself, others, and social causality are developed, further self-defeating behaviors occur, consistent with the maladaptive beliefs. To the extent a person anticipates unpleasant outcomes or an inability to cope effectively with potentially unpleasant events, the person will be unlikely to engage in self-enhancing behaviors or the behaviors necessary to appropriately regulate the maladaptive views of the self and of the world. The person need not be aware of what is being avoided. When people are unsuccessful in attaining progress toward goal-attainment through increased effort, they must consider giving up the goal for which they are striving, or changing their beliefs about themselves. People may hold goals such as believing they are capable of performing a task, winning the love of someone to whom they are attracted, or attaining their parents' love, for example. If they give up such a goal, they must change their beliefs and tolerate any painful feelings of anger or sadness associated with failure to attain the goal. If people are unwilling to change their beliefs about goal attainment and experience any unpleasant affect associated with failure, they explain their failure with maladaptive attributions (excuses) and continue to engage in behaviors attempting to confirm an erroneous expectancy. Changing a belief frequently requires engaging in expectancy-disconfirming or risk-taking behaviors. New expectations and theories about oneself, others, or social causality are then formed. Some of the specific techniques about psychotherapy for self-defeating behaviors are described later in the section on treatment.

III. EXPECTANCY CONFIRMATION AND SELF-FULFILLING PROPHECIES

A. Interpersonal Situations

People choose to be with others who confirm their self-views. College students are more likely to choose as roommates students who verify their self-views, even negative ones. When people receive particularly unpleasant information about themselves from others, spouses and close friends help bring individuals back to their usual self-views. But when people receive unusually positive information, their intimate associates also discredit the new information and bring individuals back to their former views of themselves. Acquaintances are less likely to discredit the new information.

When people erroneously believe that others will reject them, they engage in behaviors that make their beliefs come true, such as avoiding initiating interactions with other people or disagreeing more with them. People who are not confident others will like them are also more likely to talk too much or too little, be too controlling or not controlling enough, or reveal too much or too little of an intimate nature. These behaviors are all examples of self-fulfilling prophecies. [*See* SELF-FULFILLING PROPHECIES.]

B. Work Situations

When people have failed at a series of problems, they have lower expectations of success and persist less on future problems than people who have been successful. High achievers not only have a high motivation to succeed, but also high expectations of success, and low anxiety about failure. A low anxiety about failure allows people to choose tasks that are challenging. Thus, they achieve at greater levels. People low in motivation to achieve choose tasks that are inappropriately difficult or inappropriately easy. If they fail on a very difficult task, they can attribute their failure to the difficulty of the task. If they succeed on an easy task, they attribute their success to the ease of the task, not to their ability. High achievers choose tasks which give them more information about their ability—moderately difficult tasks.

Expectations are learned from the environment, as well as from personal experience. When told that women perform better than men on a task, women, for example, actually perform better than when told that men perform better. Hearing that people with one's own particular personality style perform better leads people to be more successful than hearing that another personality style performs better. Such phenomena are referred to as "self-fulfilling prophecies." In some situations the expectations of other people influence one's performance. For example, teachers were led to believe that some students in their class would "bloom" in intelligence during the year. The students chosen to be "bloomers" had been selected randomly. These students, in fact, showed significant increases on intelligence test scores at the end of the year. Follow-up studies designed to determine what the teachers did differently with these students showed that they required more work and were less likely to accept answers that were only partially correct, but did not spend more time with these students or praise them more.

Although low expectations lead to poor performance, unrealistically high expectations can lead people to persist at tasks when their efforts are no longer profitable and can lead to catastrophic losses. In business matters, this behavior is known as "throwing good money after bad." The individual has "too much invested to quit" then becomes all the more determined to persist in the face of failure. People may feel it is humiliating to admit that their judgment was wrong or that other people were right. Knowing when to quit can be as important as not giving up too soon. People with high expectations can be immunized against the pathology of high expectations by being told they have been given some insoluble problems.

Parents of children with low expectations of success are more likely to provide their children with answers to problems than parents of children with high expectations of success. Giving a child an answer, rather than providing hints about how to arrive at an answer, conveys to a child that she or he cannot solve the problem on her or his own.

People sometimes fail in order to escape the high expectations of others in the future. Such failure is not self-defeating if a person must fail to avoid greater demands.

IV. SPECIFIC TYPES OF SELF-DEFEATING BEHAVIORS

A. Self-Handicapping

What happens when people have favorable, but uncertain expectations regarding the future? If failure has painful implications for one's identity, people may engage in strategies called "self-handicapping" behaviors in order to protect their favorable, but fragile, self-views. The term was originally defined by researchers Steven Berglas and Edward Jones as "any action or choice of performance setting that enhances the opportunity to externalize (or excuse) failure and to internalize (reasonably accept credit for) success." Only the first definition constitutes self-defeating behavior. The second definition is a strategy frequently used by athletes to enhance the competitiveness of a game. Self-handicapping is based upon two attributional principles. These are the *discounting principle,* whereby failure under extenuating circumstances is not taken as evidence of incompetence, and the *augmentation principle,* whereby success under hardship is seen as proof of particularly high ability.

Men who were told that they were successful on tasks regardless of their actual performance later chose to take a drug described as "debilitating" as opposed to a drug described as "facilitating" before performing similar tasks again. Men who were told they were successful only when they were *actually* successful chose the facilitating drug. The experimenters reasoned that the men chose the debilitating drug so that if they performed poorly, they could attribute their poor performance to the drug and not to their lack of ability. Self-handicapping is one type of behavior that occurs after people have experienced successes seemingly independent of their actions.

Genetic predisposition renders some people more prone to alcohol abuse. Many studies, however, have examined the use of alcohol and other substances as self-handicaps. Self-handicappers drink more than nonhandicappers, but do not report drinking any more unless they are in a situation in which the alcohol can serve as a handicap. Apparently, the impressions of others outweigh their desire to deceive themselves. In a study in which men were told that their social skills were going to be evaluated and were given an opportunity to drink as much as they wanted, heavy drinkers who were told that alcohol would hurt their performance drank more than heavy drinkers who were told it would help their performance. The light drinkers who were told that alcohol would hurt their performance were the participants who drank the least in the study. The use of alcohol as an excuse works for men in some situations. Men accused of wife abuse were rated as being less responsible for their actions if they were intoxicated. Interestingly, women who were abused were rated as being more responsible if they were intoxicated. Recovering alcoholics, it must be pointed out, attributed more blame to a drinking husband. On a hopeful note, participants in one study did not use alcohol to self-handicap when given access to a familiar performance-enchancing strategy—i.e., study materials.

In our culture, there is apparently less social stigma attached to using a performance-inhibiting substance than there is to exhibiting personal weaknesses. Referring to oneself as an alcohol abuser can be preferable to the implications of being a hit-and-run driver or a child molester. In these situations, people are willing to trade up from one very derogatory personality attribution to another less deprecating one.

Low effort, test anxiety, shyness, hypochondriasis, disruptive moods, and substance abuse are excuses people can create in advance of situations. For example, athletes identified as low self-handicappers increased their practice before important meets, whereas those identified as high self-handicappers engaged in less practice. Their low effort provides in advance an excuse for failure.

People only report test anxiety as affecting their performance when their self-esteem is threatened and when it has not been ruled out as a plausible excuse for a poor performance. When told that anxiety does not affect performance on a particular, but important, test, high test anxious participants report they have expended less effort than others. This suggests that their tendency to self-handicap extends beyond their use of test anxiety. Similarly, women who are high in hypochondriasis only report that their physical symptoms have hurt their performance when told that physical symptoms can have such an effect or no mention is made of them, but not when told that such physical conditions do not have negative effects on performance.

One common form of self-handicapping is procrastination. Procrastinators report low self-esteem and self-confidence, high social anxiety, depression, neurosis, lack of energy, noncompetitiveness, self-consciousness, and disorganization. Procrastination allows people to protect their self-esteem by attributing a failure to lack of time rather than to a lack of ability. But procrastination is not always self-defeating. It can also occur when people have conflicting goals.

Researchers have found self-handicapping to be more common among men than among women. Men are more likely to attribute success to their ability than are women, even when the successes are independent of their actions. Women, then have no reason to try to protect a belief about an ability they do not think they possess. When women do self-handicap, it is by reporting test anxiety, low effort, and traumatic experiences, rather than by creating an impediment to performance. Test anxiety probably reflects a chronic uncertainty about ability level, not a particular situation in which people were made to feel uncertain by nonveridical feedback. Differences between men and women also exist in the ways shyness has been displayed. Men tend to avoid social situations, whereas shy women tend to act passively pleasing.

A scale for measuring the tendency to engage in self-handicapping behaviors was developed by Edward Jones and Frederick Rhodewalt. This scale has two major factors. The first factor involves a proclivity for excuse-making and blaming external circumstances. The second factor reflects concern for effort and motivation. When threats to self-esteem occur, those who score high on the scale are more likely to claim a handicap than those who score low on the scale. The high scorers are more likely to call themselves underachievers. High self-handicappers are low in self-esteem and high in the extent to which they monitor somatic functioning, consistent with the idea that they are likely to attend to their bodily functions for self-handicapping purposes. High self-handicapping is not related to conscious measures of the need for achievement.

Although related to self-esteem, self-handicapping is a different construct. For example, when self-esteem is controlled, high self-handicappers anticipating a difficult test indicate they will exert less effort than low self-handicappers and both high and low self-handicappers expecting an easy test. Controlling for level of self-esteem, self-handicappers still consider extenuating circumstances to have a greater effect on their performance.

The favorable, but fragile self-esteem of many self-handicappers seems similar to that of persons believed to be narcissistic in personality style. In psychoanalytic theory, narcissism develops when a parent is more concerned with a child's image than with the child himself or herself. The child is used to fulfill the parents' needs. For example, Alice Miller has described how parents may develop the child's intellectual capacities to bolster their own sense of self-worth. The child seeks insatiably for admiration, but admiration is not the same as love. The child is forced to derive a feeling of love from the attributes the parents value. Otto Kernberg has argued that a parent is cold and rejecting and that the child must rely on herself or himself for love instead of the parent. Heinz Kohut has maintained that narcissistic children do not find a way to overcome their disappointments and seek out idealized parental surrogates throughout adulthood to compensate for their low self-esteem. Social-learning theorists hypothesize that narcissistic disorders are induced by praising children too much for attributes the parents use for fulfillment of their own needs. The sense of entitlement, intolerance of criticism, and fantasies of unlimited power, success, and brilliance of narcissists represent a "proactive" attempt to comfort themselves when they fail to meet the unrealistic expectations developed from unwarranted parental praise. [*See* NARCISSISTIC PERSONALITY DISORDER.]

B. Pessimism and Helplessness

Both animals and people frequently become helpless when unpleasant events or, in some cases, pleasant ones, happen regardless of what they do. If people feel as if they have no control over events, they likely become pessimistic and depressed regarding the future. When people explain uncontrollable events by believing that there is something global, enduring, and stable about their personality which is the cause, they are most at risk for depression. For example, if someone performs poorly at work or in school, attributing the failure to a lack of ability is attributing the failure to a stable, enduring, global, and internal characteristic.

Attributing a social rejection to being unlikable is a similar type of attribution. College students who have such an explanatory style usually have poor grades. Those who obtain higher grades attribute their failures to a lack of effort (an "unstable" quality) or to the difficulty of the material (an "external" cause). Women are more likely than men to explain events in the self-defeating, pessimistic, fashion. When combined with aptitude test scores, an optimistic explanatory style reliably predicts performance in college. An optimistic explanatory style also predicts performance in work situations, such as success in the sales of life insurance. The politicians who are elected to office are also those with the more optimistic styles.

Any uncontrollable event, including success, can lead to depression when a person believes she or he is not deserving of the reward. This occurs, for example, when people believe that they have been rewarded in some way not for what they have achieved, but because of being the spouse or child of a famous person, or because of something they did in the past, independent of their current activities. This type of depression is called a "success depression."

Researchers have investigated the type of parenting style that leads to pessimism and depression. Loss is believed to be the major predictor of depression, including loss of control over rewarding experiences. The loss of a close relationship, job, status, or esteem can precipitate a depression, but parenting styles such as physical and verbal abuse, including criticism (uncontrollable punishments) or praise regardless of behavior (uncontrollable rewards) also predisposed children to depression. Women are roughly twice as likely as men to become depressed. Certainly, lower rewards may account for this phenomenon. Researchers who have investigated the evaluations given to girls and boys by teachers and parents have found that failures of girls were attributed to their inadequacy, whereas boys are less likely to receive such comments. The feedback given to boys referred to their behavior. Attributing failure to internal, global, stable factors, such as lack of ability, is the attributional style correlated with depression. Girls are more frequently taught this style by parents and teachers. When feedback is changed in experimental settings, the attributional style of women changes. When women have been instructed to attribute their failures to a lack of effort, their self-defeating, self-perpetuating style of low expectations in the presence of men, poor performance, low self-reward, and debilitating attribution of successes to luck and failures to lack of ability is changed. [*See* ATTRIBUTION; LEARNED HELPLESSNESS.]

C. Choosing to Suffer and Masochism

Research investigating the conditions leading people to choose to suffer has found that if people are expecting an unpleasant event to happen, they are more likely to make something else unpleasant happen in the waiting period. This is a variation of the self-fulfilling prophecy phenomenon. A self-fulfilling prophecy is when a person makes something more likely to happen which she or he is expecting to happen. In the case of "choosing to suffer," a person makes something else unpleasant happen. Research investigating the choice to suffer has found that people are especially likely to choose to engage in an unpleasant activity, such as self-administering shocks, if they are probably going to be required to engage in another unpleasant activity, such as tasting caterpillars and grasshoppers, than if they are certainly going to have to engage in the other unpleasant action. People are more likely to choose to suffer if they are expecting the unpleasant event for a long time than for a short time. They are also more likely to choose to suffer if they change their conceptions of themselves during the waiting period than if they change their conceptions of the situation. Examples of changing one's self-conception during the waiting period are thinking that either one is brave, a positive quality, or thinking one deserves to suffer, a negative quality. An example of changing one's concept of the situation is the thought that maybe the unpleasant event is not so bad after all. People given an opportunity to hurt themselves have been shown to expect better outcomes in the future than those not given such a choice. This behavior may represent superstitious thinking or a portrayal of the work ethic that suffering will be rewarded. Studies on masochistic-like behavior in animals and humans has shown that such behaviors occur when both animals and people are trying to escape or avoid situations they expect to be even more anxiety-provoking than the one they "choose." People learn behaviors that are ultimately harmful to themselves to avoid worse situations. The learned behaviors continue in situations in which the anxiety-provoking event or stimulus is no longer present, but its absence is not clearly discernible.

For many years, many psychoanalysts described a cluster of behaviors that were called masochistic. Freud thought that masochistic behaviors arose from the child's fantasies of being beaten and guilt over sexual feelings. Wilhelm Reich described the masochistic character as displaying chronic feelings of suffering, with annoying complaints and demands, provocation, awkward social behavior, and intense passion for tormenting others. He believed that masochism could be explained on the basis of an actual or fantasied nonfulfillment of an inordinate demand for love. Like narcissistic behaviors, masochistic behaviors are ways children learn to take care of their parents in order to help the parents take care of them.

D. Fear of Success

Although the notion of a "fear of success" dates back to Freud and was more recently postulated to account for the poor performance of women in the presence of men, both men and women who score high in fear of success are more likely to procrastinate, less likely to engage in special assignments required to obtain an A in a course, have greater indecisiveness and conflict, find it more difficult to choose a major, are more dissatisfied with their majors, change their majors more frequently, and are more likely to take leaves of absence from school. Although women speak less in class than men, are less likely to tell others when they make high grades, and more likely to tell others when they make poor grades, they are not more likely than men to score high on recent measures of fear of success. They are apparently, frequently realistically, more likely to fear being rejected for being more successful than men.

People who fear success are more likely to miss meetings in alcohol detoxification programs and weight-reduction workshops. Whereas people who do not fear success usually perform better after success and worse after failure, the reverse is true for high success-fearers. People who do not fear success perform better on a subsequent task after reading self-affirming statements, but success-fearers perform better after reading self-derogating statements.

Does the fear of failure explain the behavior of these people as well as the fear of success? Although those who score high in the fear of success also score high in the fear of failure, their strategy appears to be one of neither achieving too much nor failing too much. Their strategy allows them to do well, but not so well that they offend or hurt others. They are less likely to sabotage success in cooperative than competitive situations. "Clutch players" on athletic teams have been found to be high in the fear of success. In a "clutch," their ability to help out their team and their fear of failure outweigh their concerns about out-starring their teammates.

Parents of children who are high in the fear of success give more hints and instructions on experimental tasks, criticize their children more, and make more comments about their child to the experimenter. Parents of success-fearers preempt their child's independence, apparently made anxious about the child's failure. On a word-construction test, they moved their child's letters, gave the child words, and sometimes pushed the youngster away and made the words themselves.

The fear of success has been hypothesized to come both from problems of being more successful than parents, siblings, or a spouse, and parents' anxiety over children's separations and independence. If a parent becomes anxious when the child (or adult child) is more successful, the child will also become anxious about the consequence of the success for the parent. This phenomenon seems to occur among women concerned about the parent of either gender, but is more likely among men who are worried about their fathers. Parents sometimes become anxious when their children become independent. This occurs especially when children leave the home for nursery or elementary school and leave their parents' residence as young adults. The school phobias of children are usually a consequence of a parent's anxiety, frequently how the mother will find meaning in her life without a child at home all day in need of her care. Sometimes parents are content to let their children move out of the house, but are unwilling to let adult children develop values, such as religious beliefs different from their own. When adult children feel conflicted about the consequences of their independence for their parents, they sabotage their successes so that they require the assistance they know their parents wish to give them. People are not usually fully aware of their concerns about their parents which lead to sabotaging their success.

E. Health Negligence

Compliance with physicians' instruction ranges form 20 to 82%. Compliance with medical regimens ranges from 60 to 78%. Some people may not realize that symptom-alleviation and cure are not the same and discontinue treatment when the symptoms disappear. Others are making choices favoring short-term goals over long-term ones. Avoidance of check-ups, examinations, and mammographies and failures to exercise, to use dental floss, and to use condoms are in this category. In still other cases, there are benefits of illness which outweigh the costs, such as escaping obligations of work, family, and friends, providing excuses for poor performance, and attracting attention and support in a manner likely perceived as more legitimate than from psychological distress. Therefore, people sometimes engage in activities that make illness more likely, or fail to engage in preventive behaviors. Particular styles of avoiding unpleasant emotions are also being found by health psychologists to relate to an increased incidence of physical illness. These patterns are described in the following section.

Eating disorders, such as binge eating and anorexia, have received increasing attention in recent years. Both binge eaters and anorexics suffer from high standards and expectations, particularly those of others. These disorders frequently occur among high-achieving women, or women from high-achieving families. Anorexia can be a way of staying in control, particularly with an over-controlling parent, or a way of avoiding the feminine role implications of menstruation and pregnancy. Because of the life-threatening nature of these disorders, hospitilization may be required.

Dieters with low self-esteem are more likely to engage in binge eating than are dieters with high self-esteem. Binge eating has been viewed as a way of avoiding feelings of emotional emptiness and painful recognition of the self's shortcomings. Focusing attention on the simple, here-and-now, bodily processes of biting, tasting, chewing, and swallowing food may be a way of restricting awareness to simple sensations and away from broad questions about the meaning of one's life. Bulimics (who make themselves regurgitate after eating) score very low on scales that measure meaningful, existential thinking. Overeating and obesity can be a way of providing an excuse for social rejection that is less painful to accept that rejection for other aspects of one's personality or feelings of sexual anxiety.

Unprotected sexual behavior, leading to the possibilities of pregnancy and Acquired Immune Deficiency Disease, is linked to a conflict over goals. Men who think it makes sense to use condoms, but for whom it is especially important to be seen as "good at sex" and to enjoy themselves, are less likely to use condoms than men with less conflict about their goals. More pervasive personality patterns such as "thinking, but not doing" and "doing without thinking" are also involved.

F. Self-Deception

1. Selective Recall

Self-deception is a motivated distortion of self-knowledge. Although it remains unclear if people selectively attend to information consistent with their prior views and attitudes, it is clear that people are more likely to consciously recall information which is consistent with their views of self and others, especially when they are anxious. The effects of having been exposed to inconsistent information are often revealed, however, when people are not questioned directly, indicating that selective recall may take place at the conscious, but not the unconscious, level.

2. Avoidance of Accurate Diagnostic Information

When people have received success feedback that is independent of their actual performance, they are likely to avoid situations that give them accurate information about their abilities. This is a way of maintaining an illusion of success when one is actually uncertain about one's abilities. The accurate assessment of one's abilities requires risk-taking and tolerating the failures which occur. The inability or unwillingness to tolerate failure creates a defensive, self-defeating posture.

C. Avoidance and Destructive Expression of Emotions

Three styles of coping with stress are related to physiological dysfunction and ill-health. These are as follows: (1) the rational–anti-emotional style, (2) the helpless, hopeless, lacking-in-autonomy style, and (3) the angry, aggressive style. People who report that they are *not* bothered by stressful stimuli, when physiological measures indicate that they *are* distressed, have medically significantly higher blood pressure than people who report their psychological distress. They also report more illnesses and more visits to their physicians' offices. From a psychoanalytic viewpoint, this first style, characterized by the avoidance of the conscious experiencing of unpleasant emotions, has been called repression and dissociation. Regarding the second style, people may consciously feel helpless or accommodating to others, but avoid the feeling of fearing abandonment if they are not accommodating. Although disputed by physicians, this style has been linked to death from cancer. The third style has been linked to coronary illness. A person may be aware of feeling angry or controlling, but unaware of a wish to hurt others or a fear of being harmed by others. Although the studies upon which these conclusions are drawn must be replicated, the avoidance of anxiety and depression clearly occurs at considerable physiological cost. Relaxation, disclosure to others, and large social support networks are known, on the other hand, to result in improved immune functioning. [*See* COPING.]

V. PSYCHIATRIC SYNDROMES AND PERSONALITY DISPOSITIONS

A. The Relations between Self-Defeating Behaviors and Psychiatric Syndromes

People with poor expectations regarding the future in many areas of their lives or one very important area are frequently depressed. Severe anxiety about failure leads to poor performance and a choice of tasks inappropriate to one's ability level. Persons who are depressed frequently use alcohol or other drugs to escape their painful feelings. Therefore, people with self-defeating styles of behavior are likely to hold diagnoses of depression, anxiety, or substance abuse. To the extent that people are aware of choosing to hurt themselves, however, the sense of being in control of their destiny, even an unpleasant one, may enable them to feel less depressed and anxious than a lack of control would make them feel.

Self-criticism, guilt, disinterest in caring partners, failure to complete tasks, and chronic pessimism are all characteristics of people suffering from depression. Therefore, some clinicians have considered self-defeating personality disorder as a mild variant of chronic depression. Some patients treated with antidepressant medications and lithium (used from bipolar affective disorder) have shown improvement. It remains unclear, however, if the depressogenic cognitive style is the cause or result of the somatic aspects of depression. Therapy that focuses upon the cognitive restructuring of the pessimistic cognitive style is often more effective than psychopharmological interventions. It is generally thought that antidepressant medication is not effective unless a person is exhibiting biological signs of depression, such as changes in sleeping and eating patterns and psychomotor inertia. [*See* DEPRESSION.]

People with mood disorders such as depression and mania obviously engage in many self-defeating behaviors. Depressed people reveal too many of their personal feelings to others, becoming too intimate, too soon. Depressed men are angry to others around them. Depressed people are less likely to initiate positive social interactions. These behaviors all lead to social rejection, causing more depression.

B. The Relation between Self-Defeating Behaviors and Personality Disorders

Personality disorders are self-defeating patterns of behaving. Therefore, it is possible to specify the self-defeating behaviors characteristic of obsessive, passive–aggressive, antisocial, paranoid, etc., styles. [*See* Personality Disorders.]

A particular cluster of behaviors not listed previously as a personality disorder, called "self-defeating personality disorder," has been proposed to account for the following behaviors; (1) choosing people and situations that lead to mistreatment or rejection when alternatives are available; (2) sacrificing oneself for the benefit of others; (3) depression after positive events; (4) lack of interest in others who are kind; (5) provoking others and then feeling hurt; (6) rejecting opportunities for pleasure; (7) rejecting others' offers to help; and (8) failing to accomplish tasks crucial to one's personal goals. This proposal for a personality disorder classification was controversial with many mental health professionals for fear that abused women would be labeled as having a personality disorder and blamed for their abuse. Current proposals for this personality disorder classification specify that persons who have been abused may not be given this classification so that the victim is not blamed for the violence of another.

Critics of the self-defeating personality disorder (SDPD) classification have been skeptical about its value because the behaviors described are similar to those of dependent and passive–aggressive personality styles. Tolerance of an abusive spouse was included at one time as a criterion for dependent personality disorder. Masochists have been described an annoying, provocative, complaining, and indirectly hostile—characteristics of the passive–aggressive style. Similarities with some theorists' views of the narcissistic personality style have already been discussed. It is estimated that at least 70% of the people who meet the criteria for SDPD also meet the criteria for dependent personality disorder and that at least 50% of those diagnosed as SDPD meet the criteria for borderline and avoidant personality disorders. There is considerable overlap among many of the personality disorders, however, not just the self-defeating style. If the implications for treatment differ from those of other styles, the self-defeating personality cluster will likely be listed as a separate disorder in the *Diagnostic and Statistical Manual of Mental Disorders* of the American Psychiatric Association. The fact that sacrificing oneself too greatly for the needs of others is considered self-defeating is, of course, a point of view reflective of the dominant, contemporary Western culture. In many cultures, such behavior would be considered exemplary of good mental health.

VI. TREATMENT OF SELF-DEFEATING BEHAVIORS

When behaviors are not crucial to a person's identity, information alone may lead to change. For example, upon learning that smoking is a serious health hazard, many people stop smoking. Many times people can get the insights they need into what is going wrong from asking friends and family members. The risk of asking is almost all that is required. When self-views that are central to one's identity are involved, however, change may not be so simple. Once a person has an identity as someone who suffers or as a victim, changing one's identity may require going through a period with no identity or self-definition at all. This is a frightening experience which many people will undergo only in the safe atmosphere of therapy with a professional.

Treatment for depression has been described in the section above on self-defeating personality style. Although all types of therapy can be regarded as treating self-defeating behaviors, some specifics about treating self-handicapping and self-defeating behaviors from different theoretical orientations are provided.

A. Empathic Therapies—Client-Centered or Experiential Approaches

Empathic techniques are believed to be very helpful in treating self-handicapping and narcissistic behaviors. In client-centered or experiential therapy the clinician responds to the client with an attitude of unconditional positive regard in the hope that the client will internalize a sense of self-acceptance. It is hoped that from this experience, self-handicappers will feel valued and respected for who they are as people, not for what they *do*.

B. Cognitive–Behavioral Therapies

Behavioral clinicians might suggest some sort of skills acquisition, such as assertiveness training for symptoms of shyness, or relaxation-training for symptoms of anxiety. Some clinicians have found, however, that self-handicappers perceive the obligation to perform as reminiscent of the demands made by their parents, resulting in nonproductive struggles with the clinician resulting in noncompliance or resistance. A treatment which asks no questions and makes no recommendations about performance may be more successful. [*See* COGNITIVE BEHAVIOR THERAPY.]

Clinicians may explore the thoughts and feelings about situations self-handicappers are avoiding prior to giving permission to approach the situations. Then self-handicappers can be taught to substitute positive self-statements for negative ones and to endure unpleasant feelings rather than seek symptomatic relief. Self-handicappers can also be helped to determine internal standards of success rather than accept externally imposed standards. Family therapy is useful in altering dysfunctional standards generated by parents.

C. Psychoanalytic Therapies

Psychoanalysts have described the difficulties treating people formerly described as masochistic who would be called self-defeating today. Any successes patients experience may make them so anxious that they will hurt themselves to reduce the anxiety that something more frightening will happen if they do not inflict suffering upon themselves. For example, a man may have learned to criticize himself to keep his father from criticizing him even more severely. If he is helped to refrain from self-criticism, he may become very anxious, expecting a cruel blow from fate. Some clinicians suggest encouraging these patients to let themselves suffer in a small way after a success so that they will not become overwhelmingly anxious.

Psychoanalysts have made progress in treating narcissistic personality disorders. In the psychoanalytic self-psychology approach, the analyst makes no comments that could be interpreted as critical, letting the patient idealize the analyst and internalizing the self of the other they wish to be. Of primary importance is the analysts' attunements to the patient's emotional experience, making up for the deficits of the parents in this regard. These patients frequently need the sense that they are admired to stay in therapy.

D. Group Therapies and Personal Growth Groups

Groups therapies are very useful for discovering and changing self-defeating interpersonal styles. If information about the consequences of behaviors and exploration of the feelings occurring when those behaviors are exhibited is not sufficient for change, then individual treatment may be recommended.

E. Substance Abuse Programs

Abuse disorders are extremely difficult to treat successfully in outpatient therapy. The most successful treatments for substance abuse disorders are residential programs of at least 2 months duration and Alcoholics Anonymous and similar "anonymous" groups. Unless abusers are helped to establish a new support network, return to the environment in which the abuse occurred usually results in recidivism. [*See* SUBSTANCE ABUSE.]

VII. CONCLUSIONS

Although people have long oberved self-defeating behaviors in themselves and others, it is only recently through scientific study in the laboratory that mental health professionals have gained knowledge of the conditions leading to these behaviors or making them more likely in normal individuals without any biological predisposition. Such knowledge is now making possible more effective means of treating them, and it is hoped, the dissemination of knowledge which can help prevent them.

Bibliography

Baumeister, R. F. (1989). "Masochism and the Self." Lawrence Erlbaum, Hillsdale, NJ.

Baumeister, R. F., and Scher, S. J. (1988). Self-defeating patterns among normal individuals; Review and analysis of common self-destructive tendencies. *Psychol. Bull.* **101,** 343–362.

Curtis, R. (Ed.) (1989). Self-defeating behaviors: Experimental research, clinical impressions, and practical implications. Plenum, New York.

Higgins, R. L., Snyder, C. R., and Berglas, S. (1990). "Self-Handicapping: The Paradox that Isn't." Plenum, New York.

Seligman, M. E. P. (1991). "Learned Optimism." Knopf, New York.

SELF-EFFICACY

Albert Bandura
Stanford University

Glossary

Affective processes Processes regulating emotional states and elicitation of emotional reactions.

Cognitive processes Thinking processes involved in the acquisition, organization, and use of information.

Motivation Activation to action. Level of motivation is reflected in choice of courses of action, and in the intensity and persistence of effort.

Perceived self-efficacy People's beliefs about their capabilities to produce effects.

Self-regulation Exercise of influence over one's own motivation, thought processes, emotional states, and patterns of behavior.

PERCEIVED SELF-EFFICACY is defined as people's beliefs about their capabilities to produce designated levels of performance that exercise influence over events that affect their lives. Self-efficacy beliefs determine how people feel, think, motivate themselves, and behave. Such beliefs produce these diverse effects through four major processes. They include cognitive, motivational, affective, and selection processes.

A strong sense of efficacy enhances human accomplishment and personal well-being in many ways. People with high assurance in their capabilities approach difficult tasks as challenges to be mastered rather than as threats to be avoided. Such an efficacious outlook fosters intrinsic interest and deep engrossment in activities. They set themselves challenging goals and maintain strong commitment to them. They heighten and sustain their efforts in the face of failure. They quickly recover their sense of efficacy after failures or setbacks. They attribute failure to insufficient effort or deficient knowledge and skills which are acquirable. They approach threatening situations with assurance that they can exercise control over them. Such an efficacious outlook produces personal accomplishments, reduces stress, and lowers vulnerability to depression.

In contrast, people who doubt their capabilities shy away from difficult tasks which they view as personal threats. They have low aspirations and weak commitment to the goals they choose to pursue. When faced with difficult tasks, they dwell on their personal deficiencies, on the obstacles they will encounter, and all kinds of adverse outcomes rather than concentrate on how to perform successfully. They slacken their efforts and give up quickly in the face of difficulties. They are slow to recover their sense of efficacy following failure or setbacks. Because they view insufficient performance as deficient aptitude it does not require much failure for them to lose faith in their capabilities. They fall easy victim to stress and depression. [*See* SELF-DEFEATING BEHAVIORS.]

I. SOURCES OF SELF-EFFICACY BELIEFS

People's beliefs about their efficacy can be developed by four main sources of influence. The most effective way of creating a strong sense of efficacy is through *mastery experiences*. Successes build a robust belief in one's personal efficacy. Failures undermine it, especially if failures occur before a sense of efficacy is firmly established.

If people experience only easy successes they come to expect quick results and are easily discouraged by failure. A resilient sense of efficacy requires experience in overcoming obstacles through persev-

Encyclopedia of Human Behavior, Volume 4

erant effort. Some setbacks and difficulties in human pursuits serve a useful purpose in teaching that success usually requires sustained effort. After people become convinced they have what it takes to succeed, they persevere in the face of adversity and quickly rebound from setbacks. By sticking it out through tough times, they emerge stronger from adversity.

The second way of creating and strengthening self-beliefs of efficacy is through the *vicarious experiences* provided by social models. Seeing people similar to oneself success by sustained effort raises observers' beliefs that they too possess the capabilities to master comparable activities to succeed. By the same token, observing others fail despite high effort lowers observers' judgments of their own efficacy and undermines their efforts. The impact of modeling on perceived self-efficacy is strongly influenced by perceived similarity to the models. The greater the assumed similarity the more persuasive are the model's successes and failures. If people see the models as very different from themselves their perceived self-efficacy is not much influenced by the models' behavior and the results they produce.

Modeling influences do more than provide a social standard against which to judge one's own capabilities. People seek proficient models who possess the competencies to which they aspire. Through their behavior and expressed ways of thinking, competent models transmit knowledge and teach observers effective skills and strategies for managing environmental demands. Acquisition of better means raises perceived self-efficacy.

Social persuasion is a third way of strengthening people's beliefs that they have what it takes to succeed. People who are persuaded verbally that they possess the capabilities to master given activities are likely to mobilize greater effort and sustain it than if they harbor self-doubts and dwell on personal deficiencies when problems arise. To the extent that persuasive boosts in perceived self-efficacy lead people to try hard enough to succeed, they promote development of skills and a sense of personal efficacy.

It is more difficult to instill high beliefs of personal efficacy by social persuasion alone than to undermine it. Unrealistic boosts in efficacy are quickly disconfirmed by disappointing results of one's efforts. But people who have been persuaded that they lack capabilities tend to avoid challenging activities that cultivate potentialities and give up quickly in the face of difficulties. By constricting activities and undermining motivation, disbelief in one's capabilities creates its own behavioral validation.

Successful efficacy builders do more than convey positive appraisals. In addition to raising people's beliefs in their capabilities, they structure situations for them in ways that bring success and avoid placing people in situations prematurely where they are likely to fail often. They measure success in terms of self-improvement rather than by triumphs over others.

People also rely partly on their *somatic and emotional states* in judging their capabilities. They interpret their stress reactions and tension as signs of vulnerability to poor performance. In activities involving strength and stamina, people judge their fatigue, aches, and pains as signs of physical debility. Mood also affects people's judgments of their personal efficacy. Positive mood enhances perceived self-efficacy, and despondent mood diminishes it. The fourth way of modifying self-beliefs of efficacy is to reduce people's stress reactions and alter their negative emotional proclivities and misinterpretations of their physical states.

It is not the sheer intensity of emotional and physical reactions that is important but rather how they are perceived and interpreted. People who have a high sense of efficacy are likely to view their state of affective arousal as an energizing facilitator of performance, whereas those who are beset by self-doubts regard their arousal as a debilitator. Physiological indicators of efficacy play an especially influential role in health functioning and in athletic and other physical activities.

II. EFFICACY-ACTIVATED PROCESSES

Much research has been conducted on the four major psychological processes through which self-beliefs of efficacy affect human functioning.

A. Cognitive Processes

The effects of self-efficacy beliefs on cognitive processes take a variety of forms. Much human behavior, being purposive, is regulated by forethought embodying valued goals. Personal goal setting is influenced by self-appraisal of capabilities. The stronger the perceived self-efficacy, the higher the goal challenges people set for themselves and the firmer is their commitment to them.

Most courses of action are initially organized in thought. People's beliefs in their efficacy shape the types of anticipatory scenarios they construct and rehearse. Those who have a high sense of efficacy, visualize success scenarios that provide positive guides and supports for performance. Those who doubt their efficacy, visualize failure scenarios and dwell on the many things that can go wrong. It is difficult to achieve much while fighting self-doubt.

A major function of thought is to enable people to predict events and to develop ways to control those that affect their lives. Such skills require effective cognitive processing of information that contains many ambiguities and uncertainties. In learning predictive and regulative rules people must draw on their knowledge to construct options, to weight and integrate predictive factors, to test and revise their judgments against the immediate and distal results of their actions, and to remember which factors they had tested and how well they had worked.

It requires a strong sense of efficacy to remain task oriented in the face of pressing situational demands, failures, and setbacks that have significant repercussions. Indeed, when people are faced with the tasks of managing difficult environmental demands under taxing circumstances, those who are beset by self-doubts about their efficacy become more and more erratic in their analytic thinking, they lower their aspirations, and the quality of their performance deteriorates. In contrast, those who maintain a resilient sense of efficacy set themselves challenging goals and use good analytic thinking which pays off in performance accomplishments.

B. Motivational Processes

Self-beliefs of efficacy play a key role in the self-regulation of motivation. Most human motivation is cognitively generated. People motivate themselves and guide their actions anticipatorily by the exercise of forethought. They form beliefs about what they can do. They anticipate likely outcomes of prospective actions. They set goals for themselves and plan courses of action designed to realize valued futures.

There are three different forms of cognitive motivators around which different theories have been built. They include *causal attributions, outcome expectancies,* and *cognized goals*. The corresponding theories are attribution theory, expectancy-value theory, and goal theory, respectively. Self-efficacy beliefs operate in each of these types of cognitive motivation. Self-efficacy beliefs influence causal attributions. People who regard themselves as highly efficacious attribute their failures to insufficient effort, those who regard themselves as inefficacious attribute their failures to low ability. Causal attributions affect motivation, performance, and affective reactions mainly through beliefs of self-efficacy. [*See* ATTRIBUTION.]

In expectancy-value theory, motivation is regulated by the expectation that a given course of behavior will produce certain outcomes and the value of those outcomes. But people act on their beliefs about what they can do, as well as on their beliefs about the likely outcomes of performance. The motivating influence of outcome expectancies is thus partly governed by self-beliefs of efficacy. There are countless attractive options people do not pursue because they judge they lack the capabilities for them. The predictiveness of expectancy-value theory is enhanced by including the influence of perceived self-efficacy.

The capacity to exercise self-influence by goal challenges and evaluative reaction to one's own attainments provides a major cognitive mechanism of motivation. A large body of evidence shows that explicit, challenging goals enhance and sustain motivation. Goals operate largely through self-influence processes rather than regulate motivation and action directly. Motivation based on goal setting involves a cognitive comparison process. By making self-satisfaction conditional on matching adopted goals, people give direction to their behavior and create incentives to persist in their efforts until they fulfill their goals. They seek self-satisfaction from fulfilling valued goals and are prompted to intensify their efforts by discontent with substandard performances.

Motivation based on goals or personal standards is governed by three types of self-influences. They include self-satisfying and self-dissatisfying reactions to one's performance, perceived self-efficacy for goal attainment, and readjustment of personal goals based on one's progress. Self-efficacy beliefs contribute to motivation in several ways: They determine the goals people set for themselves; how much effort they expend; how long they persevere in the face of difficulties; and their resilience to failures. When faced with obstacles and failures people who harbor self-doubts about their capabilities slacken their efforts or give up quickly. Those who have a strong belief in their capabilities exert greater effort when they fail to master the challenge. Strong perseverance contributes to performance accomplishments.

C. Affective Processes

People's beliefs in their coping capabilities affect how much stress and depression they experience in threatening or difficult situations, as well as their level of motivation. Perceived self-efficacy to exercise control over stressors plays a central role in anxiety arousal. People who believe they can exercise control over threats do not conjure up disturbing thought patterns. But those who believe they cannot manage threats experience high anxiety arousal. They dwell on their coping deficiencies. They view many aspects of their environment as fraught with danger. They magnify the severity of possible threats and worry about things that rarely happen. Through such inefficacious thinking they distress themselves and impair their level of functioning. Perceived coping self-efficacy regulates avoidance behavior as well as anxiety arousal. The stronger the sense of self-efficacy the bolder people are in taking on taxing and threatening activities. [*See* MOTIVATION, EMOTIONAL BASIS.]

Anxiety arousal is affected not only by perceived coping efficacy but also by perceived efficacy to control disturbing throughts. The exercise of control over one's own consciousness is summed up well in the proverb: "You cannot prevent the birds of worry and care from flying over your head. But you can stop them from building a nest in your head." Perceived self-efficacy to control thought processes is a key factor in regulating thought produced stress and depression. It is not the sheer frequency of disturbing thoughts but the perceived inability to turn them off that is the major source of distress. Both perceived coping self-efficacy and thought control efficacy operate jointly to reduce anxiety and avoidant behavior.

Social cognitive theory prescribes mastery experiences as the principal means of personality change. Guided mastery is a powerful vehicle for instilling a robust sense of coping efficacy in people whose functioning is seriously impaired by intense apprehension and phobic self-protective reactions. Mastery experiences are structured in ways to build coping skills and instill beliefs that one can exercise control over potential threats. Intractable phobics, of course, are not about to do what they dread. One must, therefore, create an environment so that incapacitated phobics can perform successfully despite themselves. This is achieved by enlisting a variety of performance mastery aids.

Feared activities are first modeled to show people how to cope with threats and to disconfirm their worst fears. Coping tasks are broken down into subtasks of easily mastered steps. Performing feared activities together with the therapist further enables phobics to do things they would resist doing by themselves. Another way of overcoming resistance is to use graduated time. Phobics will refuse threatening tasks if they will have to endure stress for a long time. But they will risk them for a short period. As their coping efficacy increases the time they perform the activity is extended. Protective aids and dosing the severity of threats also help to restore and develop a sense of coping efficacy.

After functioning is fully restored, the mastery aids are withdrawn to verify that coping successes stem from personal efficacy rather than from mastery aids. Self-directed mastery experiences, designed to provide confirmatory tests of coping capabilities, are then arranged to strengthen and generalize the sense of coping efficacy. Once people develop a resilient sense of efficacy they can withstand difficulties and adversities without adverse effects.

Guided mastery treatment achieves widespread psychological changes in a relatively short time. It eliminates phobic behavior and anxiety and biological stress reactions, creates positive attitudes, and eradicates phobic ruminations and nightmares. Evidence that achievement of coping efficacy profoundly affects dream activity is a particularly striking generalized impact.

A low sense of efficacy to exercise control produces depression as well as anxiety. It does so in several different ways. One route to depression is through unfulfilled aspiration. People who impose on themselves standards of self-worth that they judge they cannot attain drive themselves to bouts of depression. A second efficacy route to depression is through a low sense of social efficacy. People who judge themselves to be socially efficacious seek out and cultivate social relationships that provide models on how to manage difficult situations, cushion the adverse effects of chronic stressors, and bring satisfaction to people's lives. Perceived social inefficacy to develop satisfying and supportive relationships increases vulnerability to depression through social isolation. Much human depression is cognitively generated by dejecting ruminative thought. A low sense of efficacy to exercise control over ruminative thought also contributes to the occurrence, duration, and recurrence of depressive episodes. [*See* DEPRESSION.]

Other efficacy-activated processes in the affective domain concern the impact of perceived coping self-efficacy on biolgical systems that affect health functioning. Stress has been implicated as an important contributing factor to many physical dysfunctions. Controllability appears to be a key organizing principle regarding the nature of these stress effects. It is not stressful life conditions *per se,* but the perceived inability to manage them that is debilitating. Thus, exposure to stressors with ability to control them has no adverse biological effects. But exposure to the same stressors without the ability to control them impairs the immune system. The impairment of immune function increases susceptibility to infection, contributes to the development of physical disorders, and accelerates the progression of disease. [*See* STRESS AND ILLNESS.]

Biological systems are highly interdependent. A weak sense of efficacy to exercise control over stressors activates autonomic reactions, catecholamine secretion, and release of endogenous opioids. These biological systems are involved in the regulation of the immune system. Stress activated in the process of acquiring coping capabilities may have different effects than stress experienced in aversive situations with no prospect in sight of ever gaining any self-protective efficacy. There are substantial evolutionary benefits to experiencing enhanced immune function during development of coping capabilities vital for effective adaptation. It would not be evolutionarily advantageous if acute stressors invariably impaired immune function, because of their pervalence in everyday life. If this were the case, people would experience high vulnerability to infective agents that would quickly do them in. There is some evidence that providing people with effective means for managing stressors may have a positive effect on immune function. Moreover, stress aroused while gaining coping mastery over stressors can enhance different components of the immune system.

There are other ways in which perceived self-efficacy serves to promote health. Lifestyle habits can enhance or impair health. This enables people to exert behavioral influence over their vitality and quality of health. Perceived self-efficacy affects every phase of personal change—whether people even consider changing their health habits; whether they enlist the motivation and perseverance needed to succeed should they choose to do so; and how well they maintain the habit changes they have achieved. The stronger the perceived self-regulatory efficacy the more successful people are in reducing health-impairing habits and adopting and integrating health-promoting habits into their regular lifestyle. Comprehensive community programs designed to prevent cardiovascular disease by altering risk-related habits reduce the rate of morbidity and mortality.

D. Selection Processes

The discussion so far has centered on efficacy-activated processes that enable people to create beneficial environments and to exercise some control over those they encounter day in and day out. People are partly the product of their environment. Therefore, beliefs of personal efficacy can shape the course lives take by influencing the types of activities and environments people choose. People avoid activities and situations they believe exceed their coping capabilities. But they readily undertake challenging activities and select situations they judge themselves capable of handling. By the choices they make, people cultivate different competencies, interests, and social networks that determine life courses. Any factor that influences choice behavior can profoundly affect the direction of personal development. This is because the social influences operating in selected environments continue to promote certain competencies, values, and interests long after the efficacy decisional determinant has rendered its inaugurating effect.

Career choice and development are but one example of the power of self-efficacy beliefs to affect the course of life paths through choice-related processes. The higher the level of people's perceived self-efficacy the wider the range of career options they seriously consider, the greater their interest in them, the better they prepare themselves educationally for the occupational pursuits they choose, and the greater is their success. Occupations structure a good part of people's lives and provide them with a major source of personal identity.

III. ADAPTIVE BENEFITS OF OPTIMISTIC SELF-BELIEFS OF EFFICACY

There is a growing body of evidence that human accomplishments and positive well-being require an optimistic sense of personal efficacy. This is because ordinary social realities are strewn with difficulties. They are full of impediments, adversities, setbacks, frustrations, and inequities. People must have a robust sense of personal efficacy to sustain the perseverant effort needed to succeed. In pursuits strewn with obstacles, realists either foresake them, abort their efforts prematurely when difficulties arise, or become cynical about the prospects of effecting significant changes.

It is widely believed that misjudgment breeds personal problems. Certainly, gross miscalculation can get one into trouble. However, the functional value of accurate self-appraisal depends on the nature of the activity. Activities in which mistakes can produce costly or injurious consequences call for accurate self-appraisal of capabilities. It is a different matter where difficult accomplishments can produce substantial personal and social benefits and the costs involve one's time, effort, and expendable resources. People with a high sense of efficacy have the staying power to endure the obstacles and setbacks that characterize difficult undertakings.

When people err in their self-appraisal they tend to overestimate their capabilities. This is a benefit rather than a cognitive failing to be eradicated. If efficacy beliefs always reflected only what people can do routinely they would rarely fail but they would not set aspirations beyond their immediate reach or mount the extra effort needed to surpass their ordinary performances.

People who experience much distress have been compared in their skills and beliefs in their capabilities with those who do not suffer from such problems. The findings show that it is often the normal people who are distorters of reality. But they display self-enhancing biases and distort in the positive direction. People who are socially anxious or prone to depression are often just as socially skilled as those who do not suffer from such problems. But the normal ones believe they are much more adept than they really are. The nondepressed people also have a stronger belief that they exercise some control over situations.

Social reformers strongly believe that they can mobilize the collective effort needed to bring social change. Although their beliefs are rarely fully realized they sustain reform efforts that achieve important gains. Were social reformers to be entirely realistic about the prospects of transforming social systems they would either forego the endeavor or fall easy victim to discouragement. Realists may adapt well to existing realities. But those with a tenacious self-efficacy are likely to change those realities.

Innovative achievements also require a resilient sense of efficacy. Innovations demand heavy investment of effort over a long period with uncertain results. Moreover, innovations that clash with existing preferences and practices meet with negative social reactions. It is, therefore, not surprising that one rarely finds realists in the ranks of innovators and great achievers.

In his delightful book titled *Rejection,* John White provides vivid testimony that the striking characteristics of people who have achieved eminence in their fields is an inextinguishable sense of personal efficacy and a firm belief in the worth of what they are doing. This resilient self-belief system enabled them to override repeated early rejections of their work.

Many of our literary classics brought their authors countless rejections. James Joyce's *Dubliners* was rejected by 22 publishers. Gertrude Stein continued to submit poems to editors for 20 years before one was finally accepted. Over a dozen publishers rejected a manuscript by e. e. cummings. When he finally got it published, by his mother, the dedication read, in uppercase: "With no thanks to. . ." followed by the list of 16 publishers who had rejected his manuscript.

Early rejection is the rule, rather than the exception, in other creative endeavors. The Impressionists had to arrange their own exhibitions because their works were routinely rejected by the Paris Salon. Van Gogh sold only one painting during his lifetime. Rodin was rejected three times for admission to the Ecole des Beaux-Arts.

The musical works of most renowned composers were initially greeted with derision. Stravinsky was run out of town by enraged Parisiens and critics when he first served them the *Rite of Spring*. Entertainers in the contemporary pop culture have not fared any better. Decca records rejected a recording contract with the Beatles with the nonprophetic evaluation, "We don't like their sound. Groups of guitars are on the way out." Columbia records was next to turn them down.

Theories and technologies that are ahead of their time usually suffer repeated rejections. The rocket pioneer Robert Goddard was bitterly rejected by his scientific peers on the grounds that rocket propulsion would not work in the rarefied atmosphere of outer space. Because of the cold reception given to innovations, the time between conception and technical realization is discouragingly long.

The moral of the *Book of Rejections* is that rejections should not be accepted too readily as indicants of personal failings. To do so is self-limiting.

In sum, the successful, the venturesome, the sociable, the nonanxious, the nondepressed, the social reformers, and the innovators take an optimistic view of their personal capabilities to exercise influence over events that affect their lives. If not unrealistically exaggerated, such self-beliefs foster positive well-being and human accomplishments.

Many of the challenges of life are group problems requiring collective effort to produce significant change. The strength of groups, organizatons, and even nations lies partly in people's sense of collective efficacy that they can solve the problems they face and improve their lives through unified effort. People's beliefs in their collective efficacy influence what they choose to do as a group, how much effort they put into it, their endurance when collective efforts fail to produce quick results, and their likelihood of success.

IV. DEVELOPMENT AND EXERCISE OF SELF-EFFICACY OVER THE LIFESPAN

Different periods of life present certain types of competency demands for successful functioning. These normative changes in required competencies with age do not represent lock-step stages through which everyone must inevitably pass. There are many pathways through life and, at any given period, people vary substantially in how efficaciously they manage their lives. The sections that follow provide a brief analysis of the characteristic developmental changes in the nature and scope of perceived self-efficacy over the course of the lifespan.

A. Origins of a Sense of Personal Agency

The newborn comes without any sense of self. Infants' exploratory experiences in which they see themselves produce effects by their actions provide the initial basis for developing a sense of efficacy. Shaking a rattle produces predictable sounds, energetic kicks shake their cribs, and screams bring adults. By repeatedly observing that environmental events occur with action, but not in its absence, infants learn that actions produce effects. Infants who experience success in controlling environmental events become more attentive to their own behavior and more competent in learning new efficacious responses than do infants for whom the same environmental events occur regardless of how they behave.

Development of a sense of personal efficacy requires more than simply producing effects by actions. Those actions must be perceived as part of oneself. The self becomes differentiated from others through dissimilar experience. If feeding oneself brings comfort, whereas seeing others feed themselves has no similar effect, one's own activity becomes distinct from all other persons. As infants begin to mature, those around them refer to them and treat them as distinct persons. Based on growing personal and social experiences they eventually form a symbolic representation of themselves as a distinct self.

B. Familial Sources of Self-Efficacy

Young children must gain self-knowledge of their capabilities in broadening areas of functioning. They have to develop, appraise, and test their physical capabilities, their social competencies, their linguistic skills, and their cognitive skills for comprehending and managing the many situations they encounter daily. Development of sensorimotor capabilities greatly expands the infants' exploratory environment and the means for acting upon it. These early exploratory and play activities, which occupy much of children's waking hours, provide opportunities for enlarging their repertoire of basic skills and sense of efficacy.

Successful experiences in the exercise of personal control are central to the early development of social and cognitive competence. Parents who are responsive to their infants' behavior, and who create opportunities for efficacious actions by providing an enriched physical environment and permitting freedom of movement for exploration, have infants who are accelerated in their social and cognitive development. Parental responsiveness increases cognitive competence, and infants' expanded capabilities elicit greater parental responsiveness in a two-way influence. Development of language provides children with the symbolic means to reflect on their experiences and what others tell them about their capabilities and, thus, to expand their self-knowledge of what they can and cannot do.

The initial efficacy experiences are centered in the family. But as the growing child's social world rapidly expands, peers become increasingly important in children's developing self-knowledge of their capabilities. It is in the context of peer relations that social comparison comes strongly into play. At first, the closest comparative age-mates are siblings. Families differ in number of siblings, how far apart in age they are, and in their sex distribution. Different family structures, as reflected in family size, birth order, and sibling constellation patterns, create different social comparisons for judging one's personal efficacy. Younger siblings find themselves in the unfavorable position of judging their capabilities in relation to older siblings who may be several years advanced in their development.

C. Broadening of Self-Efficacy through Peer Influences

Children's efficacy-testing experiences change substantially as they move increasingly into the larger community. It is in peer relationships that they broaden self-knowledge of their capabilities. Peers serve several important efficacy functions. Those who are most experienced and competent provide models of efficacious styles of thinking and behavior. A vast amount of social learning occurs among peers. In addition, age-mates provide highly informative comparisons for judging and verifying one's self-efficacy. Children are, therefore, especially sensitive to their relative standing among the peers in activities that determine prestige and popularity.

Peers are neither homogeneous nor selected indiscriminately. Children tend to choose peers who share similar interests and values. Selective peer association will promote self-efficacy in directions of mutual interest, leaving other potentialities underdeveloped. Because peers serve as a major influence in the development and validation of self-efficacy, disrupted or impoverished peer relationships can adversely affect the growth of personal efficacy. A low sense of social efficacy can, in turn, create internal obstacles to favorable peer relationships. Thus, children who regard themselves as socially inefficacious withdraw socially, perceive low acceptance by their peers, and have a low sense of self-worth. There are some forms of behavior where a high sense of efficacy may be socially alienating rather than socially affiliating. For example, children who readily resort to aggression perceive themselves as highly efficacious in getting things they want by aggressive means. [*See* PEER RELATIONSHIPS AND INFLUENCES IN CHILDHOOD.]

D. School as an Agency for Cultivating Cognitive Self-Efficacy

During the crucial formative period of children's lives, the school functions as the primary setting for the cultivation and social validation of cognitive competencies. School is the place where children develop the cognitive competencies and acquire the knowledge and problem-solving skills essential for participating effectively in the larger society. Here their knowledge and thinking skills are continually tested, evaluated, and socially compared. [*See* COGNITIVE DEVELOPMENT.]

As children master cognitive skills, they develop a growing sense of their intellectual efficacy. Many social factors, apart from the formal instruction, such as peer modeling of cognitive skills, social comparison with the performances of other students, motivational enhancement through goals and positive incentives, and teachers interpretations of children's successes and failures in ways that reflect favorably or unfavorably on their ability also affect children's judgments of their intellectual efficacy.

The task of creating learning environments conducive to development of cognitive skills rests heavily on the talents and self-efficacy of teachers. Those who are have a high sense of efficacy about their teaching capabilities can motivate their students and enhance their cognitive development. Teachers who have a low sense of instructional efficacy favor a custodial orientation that relies heavily on negative sanctions to get students to study.

Teachers operate collectively within an interactive social system rather than as isolates. The belief systems of staffs create school cultures that can have vitalizing or demoralizing effects on how well schools function as a social system. Schools in which the staff collectively judge themselves as powerless to get students to achieve academic success convey a group sense of academic futility that can pervade the entire life of the school. Schools in which staff members collectively judge themselves capable of promoting academic success imbue their schools with a positive atmosphere for development that promotes academic attainments regardless of whether they serve predominantly advantaged or disadvantaged students.

Students' belief in their capabilities to master academic activities affects their aspirations, their level of interest in academic activities, and their academic accomplishments. There are a number of school practices that, for the less talented or ill prepared, tend to convert instructional experiences into education in inefficacy. These include lock-step sequences of instruction, which lose many children along the way; ability groupings which further diminish the perceived self-efficacy of those cast in the lower ranks; and competitive practices where many are doomed to failure for the success of a relative few.

Classroom structures affect the development of intellectural self-efficacy, in large part, by the relative emphasis they place on social comparison versus self-comparison appraisal. Self-appraisals of less able students suffer most when the whole group studies the same material and teachers make frequent comparative evaluations. Under such a monolithic structure students rank themselves according to capability with high consensus. Once established, reputations are not easily changed. In a personalized classroom structure, individualized instruction tailored to students' knowledge and skills enables all of them to expand their competencies and provides less basis for demoralizing social comparison. As a result, students are more likely to compare their rate of progress to their personal standards than to the performance of others. Self-comparison of improvement in a personalized classroom structure raises perceived capability. Cooperative learning structures, in which students work together and help one another also tend to promote more positive self-evaluations of capability and higher academic attainments than do individualistic or competitive ones.

E. Growth of Self-Efficacy through Transitional Experiences of Adolescence

Each period of development brings with it new challenges for coping efficacy. As adolescents approach the demands of adulthood, they must learn to assume full responsibility for themselves in almost every dimension of life. This requires mastering many new skills and the ways of adult society. Learning how to deal with pubertal changes, emotionally invested partnerships, and sexuality becomes a matter of considerable importance. The task of choosing what lifework to pursue also looms large during this period. These are but a few of the areas in which new competencies and self-beliefs of efficacy have to be developed.

With growing independence during adolescence some experimentation with risky behavior is not all that uncommon. Adolescents expand and strengthen their sense of efficacy by learning how to deal successfully with potentially troublesome matters in which they are unpracticed as well as with advantageous life events. Insulation from problematic situations leaves one ill-prepared to cope with potential difficulties. Whether adolescents foresake risky activities or become chronically enmeshed in them is determined by the interplay of personal competencies, self-management efficacy, and the prevailing influences in their lives. Improverished hazardous environments present especially harsh realities with minimal resources and social supports for culturally valued pursuits, but extensive modeling, incentives, and social supports for transgressive styles of behavior. Such environments severely tax the coping efficacy of youth enmeshed in them to make it through adolescence in ways that do not irreversibly foreclose many beneficial life paths.

Adolescence has often been characterized as a period of psychosocial turmoil. While no period of life is ever free of problems, contrary to the stereotype of "storm and stress," most adolescents negotiate the important transitions of this period without undue disturbance or discord. However, youngsters who enter adolescence beset by a disabling sense of inefficacy transport their vulnerability to distress and debility to the new environmental demands. The ease with which the transition from childhood to the demands of adulthood is made similarly depends on the strength of personal efficacy built up through prior mastery experiences. [*See* ADOLESCENCE.]

F. Self-Efficacy Concerns of Adulthood

Young adulthood is a period when people have to learn to cope with many new demands arising from lasting partnerships, marital relationships, parenthood, and occupational careers. As in earlier mastery tasks, a firm sense of self-efficacy is an important contributor to the attainment of further competencies and success. Those who enter adulthood poorly equipped with skills and plagued by self-doubts find many aspects of their adult life stressful and depressing.

Beginning a productive vocational career poses a major transitional challenge in early adulthood. There are a number of ways in which self-efficacy beliefs contribute to career development and success in vocational pursuits. In preparatory phases, people's perceived self-efficacy partly determines how well they develop the basic cognitive, self-management, and interpersonal skills on which occupational careers are founded. As noted earlier, beliefs concerning one's capabilities are influential determinants of the vocational life paths that are chosen.

It is one thing to get started in an occupational pursuit, it is another thing to do well and advance in it. Psychosocial skills contribute more heavily to career success than do occupational technical skills. Development of coping capabilities and skills in managing one's motivation, emotional states, and thought processes increases perceived self-regulatory efficacy. The higher the sense of self-regulatory efficacy the better the occupational functioning. Rapid technological changes in the modern workplace are placing an increasing premium on higher problem-solving skills and resilient self-efficacy to cope effectively with job displacements and restructuring of vocational activities. [*See* COPING.]

The transition to parenthood suddenly thrusts young adults into the expanded role of both parent and spouse. They now not only have to deal with the ever-changing challenges of raising children but to manage interdependent relationships within a family system and social links to many extrafamilial social systems including educational, recreational, medical, and caregiving facilities. Parents who are secure in their parenting efficacy shepherd their children adequately through the various phases of development without serious problems or severe strain on the marital relationship. But it can be a trying period for those who lack a sense of efficacy to manage the expanded familial demands. They are highly vulnerable to stress and depression. [*See* PARENTING.]

Increasing numbers of mothers are joining the work force either by economic necessity or by personal preference. Combining family and career has now become the normative pattern. This requires management of the demands of both familial and occupational roles. Because of the cultural lag between societal practices and the changing status of women, they continue to bear the major share of the homemaking responsibility. Women who have a strong sense of efficacy to manage the multiple demands of family and work and to enlist their husbands' aid with childcare experience a positive sense of well-being. But those who are beset by self-doubts in their ability to combine the dual roles suffer physical and emotional strain.

By the middle years, people settle into established routines that stabilize their sense of personal efficacy in the major areas of functioning. However, the stability is a shaky one because life does not remain static. Rapid technological and social changes constantly require adaptations calling for self-reappraisals of capabilities. In their occupations, the middle-aged find themselves pressured by younger challengers. Situations in which people must compete for promotions, status, and even work itself, force constant self-appraisals of capabilities by means of social comparison with younger competitors.

G. Reappraisals of Self-Efficacy with Advancing Age

The self-efficacy issues of the elderly center on reappraisals and misappraisals of their capabilities. Biological conceptions of aging focus extensively on declining abilities. Many physical capacities do decrease as people grow older, thus requiring reappraisals of self-efficacy for activities in which the biological functions have been significantly affected. However, gains in knowledge, skills, and expertise compensate some loss in physical reserve capacity. When the elderly are taught to use their intellectual capabilities, their improvement in cognitive functioning more than offsets the average decrement in performance over two decades. Because people rarely exploit their full potential, elderly persons who invest the necessary effort can function at the higher levels of younger adults. By affecting level of involvement in activities, perceived self-efficacy can contribute to the maintenance of social, physical, and intellectual functioning over the adult lifespan. [*See* AGING, PERSONALITY, AND ADAPTATION.]

Older people tend to judge changes in their intellectual capabilities largely in terms of their memory performance. Lapses and difficulties in memory that young adults dismiss are inclined to be interpreted by older adults as indicators of declining cognitive capabilities. Those who regard memory as a biologically shrinking capacity with aging have low faith in their memory capabilities and enlist little effort to remember things. Older adults who have a stronger sense of memory efficacy exert greater cognitive effort to aid their recall and, as a result, achieve better memory. [*See* MEMORY.]

Much variability exists across behavioral domains and educational and socioeconomic levels, and there is no uniform decline in beliefs in personal efficacy in old age. The persons against whom the elderly compare themselves contribute much to the variability in perceived self-efficacy. Those who measure their capabilities against people their age are less likely to view themselves as declining in capabilities than if younger cohorts are used in comparative self-appraisal. Perceived cognitive inefficacy is accompanied by lowered intellectural performances. A declining sense of self-efficacy, which often may stem more from disuse and negative cultural expectations than from biological aging, can thus set in motion self-perpetuating processes that result in declining cognitive and behavioral functioning. People who are beset with uncertainties about their personal efficacy not only curtail the range of their activities but undermine their efforts in those they undertake. The result is a progressive loss of interest and skill.

Major life changes in later years are brought about by retirement, relocation, and loss of friends or spouses. Such changes place demands on interpersonal skills to cultivate new social relationships that can contribute to positive functioning and personal well-being. Perceived social inefficacy increases older person's vulnerability to stress and depression both directly and indirectly by impeding development of social supports which serve as a buffer against life stressors.

The roles into which older adults are cast impose sociocultural constraints on the cultivation and maintenance of perceived self-efficacy. As people move to older-age phases most suffer losses of resources, productive roles, access to opportunities, and challenging activities. Monotonous environments that require little thought or independent judgment diminish the quality of functioning, whereas intellectually challenging ones enhance it. Some of the declines in functioning with age result from sociocultural dispossession of the environmental support for it. It requires a strong sense of personal efficacy to reshape and maintain a productive life in cultures that cast their elderly in powerless roles devoid of purpose. In societies that emphasize the potential for self-development throughout the lifespan, rather than psychophysical decline with aging, the elderly tend to lead productive and purposeful lives.

V. SUMMARY

Perceived self-efficacy is concerned with people's beliefs in their capabilities to exercise control over their own functioning and over events that affect their lives. Beliefs in personal efficacy affect life choices, level of motivation, quality of functioning, resilience to adversity, and vulnerability to stress and depression. People's beliefs in their efficacy are developed by four main sources of influence. They include mastery experiences, seeing people similar to oneself manage task demands successfully, social persuasion that one has the capabilities to succeed in given activities, and inferences from somatic and emotional states indicative of personal strengths and vulnerabilities. Ordinary realities are strewn with impediments, adversities, setbacks, frustrations, and inequities. People must, therefore, have a robust sense of efficacy to sustain the perseverant effort needed to succeed. Succeeding periods of life present new types of competency demands requiring further development of personal efficacy for successful functioning. The nature and scope of perceived self-efficacy undergo changes throughout the course of the lifespan.

Bibliography

Bandura, A. (1986). "Social Foundations of Thought and Action: A Social Cognitive Theory." Prentice-Hall, Englewood Cliffs, NJ.

Bandura, A. (1991). Self-efficacy mechanism in physiological activation and health-promoting behavior. In "Neurobiology of Learning, Emotion and Affect" (J. Madden, IV, Ed.), pp. 229–270. Raven Press, New York.

Bandura, A. (1991). Self-regulation of motivation through anticipatory and self-regulatory mechanisms. In "Perspectives on Motivation: Nebraska Symposium on Motivation" (R. A. Dienstbier, Ed.), Vol. 38, pp. 69–164. University of Nebraska Press, Lincoln.

Lent, R. W., and Hackett, G. (1987). Career self-efficacy: Empirical status and future directions. *J. Vocational Behav.* **30,** 347–382.

Maddux, J. E., and Stanley, M. A. (Eds.) (1986). Special issue on self-efficacy theory. *J. Soc. Clin. Psychol.* **4**(3).

Schunk, D. H. (1989). Self-efficacy and cognitive skill learning. In "Research on Motivation in Education." (C. Ames and R. Ames, Eds.), Vol. 3, pp. 13–44. Academic Press, San Diego.

Schwarzer, R. (Ed.) (1992). "Self-Efficacy: Thought Control of Action." Hemisphere, Washington, DC.

White, J. (1982). "Rejection." Addison-Wesley, Reading, MA.

Wood, R. E., and Bandura, A. (1989). Social cognitive theory of organizational management. *Acad. Management Rev.* **14,** 361–384.

Self-Esteem

Roy F. Baumeister
Case Western Reserve University

Glossary

Defensive self-esteem A pattern in which people falsely pretend to have high self-esteem. Self-doubts and insecurities are masked by portraying oneself in a highly favorable manner.

Downward comparison When appraising oneself in relation to other people, one chooses people who are faring badly, so that one gains by comparison.

Efficacy The successful exercise of control over the environment, often resulting in a positive sense of self as capable.

Individual differences Sources of variation among people. Specifically, some people have higher self-esteem than others.

Reflected appraisal Receiving evaluative messages from other people. Self-esteem is based partly on how the individual perceives that he or she is regarded by others.

Self-handicapping Creating a barrier or obstacle to one's own performance, so that future, anticipated failure can be attributed to the obstacle rather than to lack of ability.

SELF-ESTEEM is the evaluative dimension of self-knowledge, referring to how a person appraises himself or herself. High self-esteem refers to a favorable evaluation of self, similar to the meaning of words *confident, proud, self-respecting, conceited.* Low self-esteem indicates a less positive or negative evaluation of the self, as indicated in words such as *insecure, self-doubting, lacking in confidence, self-critical.* Self-esteem may be used to refer to a person's appraisal of himself or herself as a whole (global self-esteem) or can be discussed with respect to evaluation of self in some particular dimension or sphere (domain-specific self-esteem).

I. IMPORTANCE OF SELF-ESTEEM

Interest in self-esteem has been high among both professional researchers and the general public. The public's interest arises in part from the hope that self-esteem may provide the key to solving social problems. The California Task Force to Promote Self-Esteem and Personal and Social Responsibility concluded that a lack of self-esteem was central to most social problems facing California and the United States today, and it expressed faith that a dose of high self-esteem would operate as a social vaccine against drug abuse, school failure, crime, delinquency, teenage pregnancy, and other problems. Reliable evidence to justify such faith is largely absent at present. Even when certain social problems have indeed been linked to low self-esteem, the correlations are inadequate to prove causality; thus, low self-esteem may be a result rather than a cause of delinquency or educational failure. Still, the available evidence, although ambiguous and incomplete, can be taken as consistent with the faith in self-esteem as a social vaccine.

Research interest in self-esteem is part of a broader research focus in self and identity. Self-esteem has been shown to be an important and central feature of self-knowledge, and it has been linked to a broad range of thoughts, feelings, and actions.

Research interest in self-esteem can be sorted into two broad categories. The first is the basic assumption that people want and perhaps need a modicum of self-esteem. This motivation to think well of oneself has been assumed to be universal and to underlie many patterns of human response such as efforts to succeed, a quest for social approval, pleasure at developing skills, ambition, competitiveness, group loyalty, and derogation of rival groups. The second interest is concerned with individual differences in self-esteem. That is, some people have higher self-esteem than others, and many studies have sought to examine the correlates and consequences of high versus low self-esteem.

II. THE DESIRE FOR SELF-ESTEEM

Most social scientists accept the assumption that people desire to think well of themselves, although theorists differ as to the strength and scope of that wish. The need for self-esteem is treated as an axiom or explanatory principle rather than a testable theory; that is, it is used to interpret why people do things rather than being subjected to experiments designed to investigate whether people do actually seek to think well of themselves.

Despite the impossibility of objective proof, considerable evidence fits the theory that people are guided by a strong, fundamental desire for self-esteem. People claim credit for successes but deny blame for failures. They exaggerate and overestimate their abilities. They overestimate how many people agree with their opinions and underestimate how many people can match their abilities. They systematically choose to compare themselves with others who are less gifted or worse off than themselves. They deny or conceal their shortcomings and advertise their virtues and positive traits. They identify themselves with successful groups and distance themselves from failing or stigmatized groups.

The universality of a need for self-esteem is also suggested by the fact that people who fail to satisfy that need show signs of stress and deprivation. In particular, self-esteem has a significant impact on happiness, such that people who think well of themselves are happier than people with low self-esteem. Low self-esteem, in contrast, has been repeatedly and strongly linked to depression.

Emphasis on individual self-esteem may be particularly strong in modern, Western societies. In other cultures and historical periods, self-esteem was based on group ties and position in society, such as one's family lineage and class honor. In such societies, self-esteem was largely a fixed and unchangeable quality. It is plausible that as personal attributes are regarded as more changeable and more individual, self-esteem has become more vulnerable and hence more of a pressing concern in modern Western societies than it was in past eras. Nonetheless, it is apparent that people who ranked at the bottom of traditionally structured societies (e.g., slaves, who were consensually regarded as having minimal worth as persons) struggled to find some basis for positive self-esteem despite the culture's treatment of them as worthless.

Self-esteem is built up through two main routes. The first is based on experiences of efficacy—that is, the direct and successful personal exercise of control over the environment. The second is reflected appraisal, which means receiving evaluations from other people: Self-esteem is based partly on how the individual perceives that he or she is regarded by others. Someone who has had many experiences of success and direct control, and who is also clearly loved, admired, and respected by significant other people, will almost certainly have high self-esteem. [*See* SELF-EFFICACY.]

III. ASSESSMENT OF SELF-ESTEEM

Because of the widespread interest in studying self-esteem, many measures have been developed. Nearly all of them are based on asking the person to rate himself or herself in response to a series of questions covering various aspects or dimensions of the self-concept. Each answer receives a certain number of points depending on how favorable it is, and points are summed across questions to furnish a total self-esteem score. Some measures have multiple subscales, which may for example furnish different scores for social self-esteem, physical abilities self-esteem, intellectual or work self-esteem, and beliefs about one's physical attractiveness.

The measurement of self-esteem is plagued by several problems. One is the problem of defensive self-esteem; that is, someone who is actually insecure may rate himself or herself in a very favorable fashion on the questionnaire, as a means of denying personal problems and inadequacies, or as a way of making a good impression on the researchers. Measures of socially desirable responding (which seek to assess the person's tendency to exaggerate his or her good qualities in order to project a highly positive image) are sometimes used in connection with self-esteem scales in order to sort defensive self-esteem from genuine self-esteem.

A second problem is the frequent use of unreliable or unvalidated measures. Because self-esteem seems intuitively obvious, many researchers devise their own scales and measures rather than using established ones. These practices raise problems of interpretation and foster inconsistencies among findings.

Some researchers think that self-esteem is a changing state rather than a stable trait. That is, someone may have high self-esteem in the morning but have low self-esteem in the afternoon (after receiving a major rejection or failure, for example). Efforts to measure state self-esteem have been hampered by the repeated finding that self-esteem measures are remarkably stable across time, however, supporting the trait view. [*See* TRAITS.]

Still, it does appear that each person's self-esteem does fluctuate around a baseline (trait) level. Major success and failure experiences and significant episodes of reflected appraisal can raise or lower the state self-esteem from that baseline level, although after a period of time has elapsed people tend to return to their initial level of self-esteem. Also, some people fluctuate more than others, and instability of self-esteem has been linked to several patterns. For example, people with unstable high self-esteem show unusually strong tendencies toward anger and hostility, presumably because they feel vulnerable and sensitive to threats from others. Thus, aggressors and bullies are most likely to be people with favorable but fluctuating views of themselves, who seek to attack and dominate others in order to support their vulnerable egotism. In contrast, people with secure and stable high self-esteem tend not to be aggressive. [*See* AGGRESSION.]

Despite these problems, several reliable and valid measures of self-esteem exist. The most commonly used one is the Rosenberg Self-Esteem Scale, a brief and straightforward measure. Its brevity makes it convenient to administer, but some consider it too short, too obvious, and unrealistically unitary, and some researchers complain that it fails to predict behavior effectively, possible because of those shortcomings. A Feelings of Inadequacy Scale was developed by Janis and Field to measure self-esteem and this scale has been revised several times by other researchers. It has been popular among researchers because it often yields significant findings and (in some revised versions) offers ample supplementary information through multiple subscales. It has been criticized for focusing excessively on social confidence and for phrasing most questions in terms of negative self-appraisals, but revised versions have sought to correct these problems. A third measure, the Texas Social Behavior Inventory, also focuses heavily on social self-esteem and has been gaining in popularity among researchers. In addition to these, there are numerous other scales, including various specialized scales for use with children, clinical samples, and other special populations.

IV. UNDERSTANDING INDIVIDUAL DIFFERENCES IN SELF-ESTEEM

Systematic comparisons of people with high self-esteem against people with low self-esteem have revealed multiple differences and broad patterns. In general, people with high self-esteem are easy to understand: They expect to succeed at things in general and they anticipate that others will like them. People with low self-esteem have been more difficult to understand, however, and researchers have gone through many theories depicting them as irrational, self-hating, insecure, conflicted, self-destructive, and the like.

A first problem is deciding whom to classify as having low self-esteem. The standard practice is to administer a self-esteem measure to a large sample of people and then divide the scores in half, defining anyone who scores below the median as having low self-esteem. Unfortunately, median self-esteem scores tend to be high, raising some ambiguity as to whether people who score below it are truly low in self-esteem or only relatively low. Thus, people who score high in self-esteem are quite genuinely high, but most people who score low may be regarded as having intermediate or moderate self-esteem in an absolute sense. Efforts to select people with extremely low self-esteem scores find relatively few available, and these may suffer from mental illness or other disturbances, thereby confounding efforts to study low self-esteem. This encyclopedia entry will follow the standard practice of considering anyone who scores below the median in self-esteem as being low in self-esteem.

Recent work has furnished an increasingly clear picture of people with low self-esteem. In the first place, they appear to suffer from a lack or incoherence of self-knowledge. Their discussions of themselves tend to be inconsistent, contradictory, hesitant, uncertain, and confused, in contrast to the self-knowledge of people with high self-esteem.

Second, it appears that they share the desire to think well of themselves, just like people with high self-esteem. This contradicts some theories which asserted that people with low self-esteem desire failure or rejection or derive satisfaction from proving themselves to be worthless. People with low self-esteem desire to succeed and receive approval from others, and they feel happy in response to such positive events, even though they tend not to expect frequent successes and may respond to praise or social approval with some element of skepticism. Low self-esteem is created by a failure to satisfy the need for self-esteem, not by a lack or inversion of that need. Put another way, low self-esteem is marked more by the absence of positive things rather than the presence of negative things to say about oneself.

Third, people with low self-esteem tend to have some aspects of themselves about which they are proud and confident. In other words, very few people have appraisals of themselves that are unfavorable in all respects and spheres. People with low self-esteem tend to guard these isolated positive qualities jealously.

Fourth, low self-esteem can be understood as a lack of coping resources, leaving the person vulnerable to stressful and threatening events. People with high self-esteem can withstand some failures and setbacks because they can fall back on all their other positive attributes to give them confidence and make themselves feel good. The same failure or setback may be much more devastating to someone with low self-esteem, however, because he or she does not see as many other positive traits on which to fall back. [*See* COPING.]

Fifth, people with low self-esteem seem guided by a broad motivation to protect themselves and their fragile self-esteem. They seek to minimize risks and avoid situations containing any possibility of losing self-esteem. In contrast, people with high self-esteem seem much less worried about the possibility of losing esteem and are guided by persistent motivations to enhance the self through gaining additional approval or achieving new and better successes. People with high self-esteem will accept risks because they are confident they can succeed, whereas those same risks will be avoided by people with low self-esteem because they anticipate possible failure.

Sixth, the ambitions of people with low self-esteem may have a focus or goal different from that of people with high self-esteem. People with high self-esteem consider themselves to be already doing reasonably well, and so they focus their efforts on improving further so as to be exceptional and outstanding. Such a goal requires identifying one's strengths and potentialities and cultivating these. In contrast, people with low self-esteem tend to be more concerned with problems, deficiencies, and inadequacies, and so to them the most pressing need is to remedy these deficiencies rather than to build their strengths. Their immediate goal is to be passable rather than to be exceptional.

Lastly, people with low self-esteem suffer from some degree of inner, motivational conflict. They want to do well and succeed, but they are also insecure about subjecting themselves to pressures and high expectations. There is some evidence that large, unexpected successes make people with low self-esteem uncomfortable, create stress, and cause health problems for them. Although conceptions of "fear of success" or "rejection of success" have now largely been discredited and discarded, there is still some evidence that people with low self-esteem respond to success with mixed feelings, particularly if they may have to repeat or sustain that success in further performances.

V. MAINTAINING SELF-ESTEEM

People use a variety of strategies to protect their self-esteem against loss or damage. The multiplicity of strategies attests to the importance of maintaining one's self-esteem.

A common strategy is to interpret events in a biased, self-serving fashion. Events that reflect badly on the self are often attributed to external causes or surrounded with mitigating circumstances, so that implications regarding one's worth as a person are denied. Moral transgressions are interpreted in ways that downplay their harmful consequences or emphasize extenuating circumstances, thereby diminishing blame. Poor performances are labeled as transitory lapses or blamed on bad luck, lack of effort, unfairness, and other causes that shift the onus away from a lack of capability.

Attributing one's apparent failures to external causes may be a central reason for the surprisingly high levels of self-esteem maintained among stigmatized or disadvantaged minority groups. Although it was long believed that blacks, women, and other stigmatized groups would suffer from low self-esteem, research continued to find that these groups had average self-esteem levels that were equal to or higher than the average self-esteem levels among culturally dominant groups (such as white males). One reason, apparently, is that these disadvantaged individuals find it relatively easy to attribute failures and setbacks to prejudice, discrimination, and unfairness on the part of the system or the dominant group, and so these setbacks do not endanger the individual's self-esteem.

People sometimes set up situations so as to ensure that they will have excuses when things go wrong. In self-handicapping, for example, people create barriers to their own performance (such as by drinking too much alcohol, not getting enough sleep, or not preparing adequately) so that future, anticipated failure can be blamed on the handicap rather than seen as proof of low ability. Potential threats to self-esteem are thus deflected and defused in advance.

Another strategy is to minimize exposure to criticism or negative feedback. Some people simply refuse to pay attention to critical feedback, and as a result it is forgotten with relative ease. People distract themselves from threatening news or unpleasant facts, and so potential threats to self-esteem are deflected without even having to exert effort at rationalization.

When threats cannot be denied or deflected, people defend self-esteem by bracketing the threat off in time, thereby denying implications for the present and future. In bygone eras involving oppressively high standards of virtue and piety, it was common for adolescent males to behave in ways they themselves regarded as sinful—but then at the end of adolescence to put all these events behind them by means of a religious conversion experience, after which the "born again" individual could begin with a clean, virtuous slate.

Compensation is an important strategy for dealing with threats to self-esteem. If events call one's virtue or ability into question in one sphere, one can turn attention instead to another sphere where one's virtue or ability seems more secure. Sometimes people will respond to a loss of esteem in one area by raising or exaggerating their self-appraisal on other, unrelated dimensions, with the result that there is not net or total loss of self-esteem.

Yet another mechanism invokes downward comparison, that is, comparing oneself to others who have done worse or are in a poorer position. This is another strategy that can be employed by stigmatized or disadvantaged minority group members to maintain high self-esteem; they may compare themselves exclusively with members of their own group, thereby avoiding any risk to self-esteem that might arise from comparing oneself against the better-off majority. It is also a strategy used following trauma or other unexpected setbacks that can jeopardize self-esteem. By comparing oneself against other victims who have it worse, one can conclude that one is actually doing quite well under the circumstances.

Using these techniques (and it is likely that further research will identify yet more) enables people to protect themselves against losing self-esteem. There are individual differences in preferences among the various techniques and in overall use of them. Initially it was believed that people with low self-esteem simply failed to use defensive techniques, but research has found that they use them pervasively and systematically, in contrast to people with high self-esteem who resort to them only occasionally (such as after a major, unexpected failure). At present, the emerging consensus is that people with low self-esteem are more defensive in general, but people with high self-esteem show the more dramatic and extreme forms of defensive reactions, on an occasional basis.

Bibliography

Baumeister, R. F. (Ed.) (1993). "Self-Esteem: The Puzzle of Low Self-Regard." Plenum, New York.

Baumeister, R. F., Tice, D. M., and Hutton, D. G. (1989). Self-presentational motivations and personality differences in self-esteem. *J. Pers.* **57,** 547–579.

Campbell, J. D. (1990). Self-esteem and clarity of the self-concept. *J. Pers. Soc. Psychol.* **59,** 538–549.

Coopersmith, S. (1967). "The Antecedents of Self-Esteem." Freeman, San Francisco.

Fleming, J. S., and Courtney, B. E. (1984). The dimensionality of self-esteem: II. Hierarchical facet model for revised measurement scales. *J. Pers. Soc. Psychol.* **46,** 404–421.

McFarlin, D. B., and Blascovich, J. (1981). Effects of self-esteem and performance feedback on future affective preferences and cognitive expectations. *J. Pers. Soc. Psychol.* **40,** 521–531.

Rosenberg, M. (1979). "Conceiving the Self." Basic Books, New York.

Shrauger, J. S. (1975). Responses to evaluation as a function of initial self-perceptions. *Psychol. Bull.* **82,** 581–596.

Taylor, S. E., and Brown, J. D. (1988). Illusion and well-being: A social psychological perspective on mental health. *Psychol. Bull.* **103,** 193–210.

Wylie, R. C. (1979). "The Self-Concept," Vol. 2. University of Nebraska Press, Lincoln, NE.

SELF-FULFILLING PROPHECIES

John H. Fleming and Debra J. Manning
University of Minnesota

Glossary

Behavioral confirmation Confirmation of an expectancy based on direct behavioral evidence provided by a target.

Confirmatory bias The tendency for perceivers to search for evidence that fits their prior expectations and to ignore or discount disconfirming information.

Expectancy A belief, often erroneous, that is (usually tentatively) held about a person on the basis of his or her group or category membership (category-based expectancy), or on the basis of some second-hand or other information about the specific person (target-based expectancy).

Perceiver In the expectancy confirmation process, the person who holds an expectancy about another person and acts on it to bring about a self-fulfilling prophecy.

Perceptual confirmation Confirmation of an expectancy as a result of interpreting ambiguous information or behavior (rather than direct behavior) in line with an expectancy.

Self-fulfilling prophecy A belief, often erroneous, that when acted on by the believer brings about the conditions that make it come true.

Stereotype In the expectancy confirmation process, an expectancy based on a person's group or category membership.

Target In the expectancy confirmation process, the person about whom an expectancy is held by a perceiver.

SELF-FULFILLING PROPHECIES are beliefs, often erroneous beliefs, that when acted on by the believer come true. Self-fulfilling prophecies have been described under a variety of names—the Pygmalion and Galatea effects, experimenter expectancy effects, and behavioral and perceptual expectancy confirmation effects, to name a few. Whatever their name, self-fulfilling prophecies are a pervasive and intriguing aspect of social life that have important implications for social and interpersonal relations. Self-fulfilling prophecies are also relevant to the study of stereotyping and prejudice, academic performance, interpersonal relationships, and impression formation.

I. HISTORY AND OVERVIEW OF THE PHENOMENON

A. The "Pygmalion" Myth

Long before psychologists and sociologists had identified, labeled, and examined the self-fulfilling prophecy effect, the phenomenon had already been described in literature and demonstrated by traveling circus magicians. The concept of the self-fulfilling prophecy has its origins in Greek mythology and the story of Pygmalion. According to the myth, Pygmalion was a sculptor who created a statue of a woman so beautiful that he fell desperately and unrequitedly in love with it. Seeing Pygmalion's anguish, Aphrodite, the goddess of love, took pity on him and brought the statue—named Galatea—to life. The theme of the Pygmalion myth—that wanting something to be true can actually make it come true—has since appeared repeatedly in literature, most notably in George Bernard Shaw's *Pygmalion,* in which

Eliza Doolittle, a young woman of little social grace or status, is transformed into a woman of refined character and delicate manner by her teacher, Professor Henry Higgins. With her outward appearance altered to accommodate her new role, Miss Doolittle publicly presents her new self with such confidence that even those at a "high-society ball" find her performance convincing. Thus, Miss Doolittle's and Professor Higgins's beliefs created a version of reality that was further validated by the behavior of others around them.

B. The "Clever Hans" Phenomenon

The powerful effect of expectations was also demonstrated by two members of a traveling magic show, a horse known as "Clever Hans" and his trainer, Wilhelm von Osten. Clever Hans was billed as an extraordinary animal who could correctly answer factual questions, do arithmetic with a high degree of accuracy, and answer questions about musical harmony. Many were in awe of the animal's hoof-tapping performances and proclaimed the ability a result of superior intelligence. However, a great deal of skepticism also arose and alternative explanations were sought for the phenomenon. How else could the horse actually know the answers to the questions posed? After repeated observations of both horse and trainer, skeptics concluded that Clever Hans was simply responding to a behavioral cue provided by his master. When Hans had tapped the correct number of times, his trainer, who believed in the horse's ability and expected correct responses, inadvertently leaned forward slightly. After pairing this movement with the food given for a correct response, Hans learned to tap until the cue, giving the illusion of implicit knowledge actually possessed by the trainer.

The self-fulfilling nature of beliefs is not limited to fiction or to the barnyard. Self-fulfilling prophecies manifest themselves in all aspects of life, from the kicker who "chokes" and misses the crucial field-goal attempt after his coach expresses his uncertainty about the kicker's ability, to students who excel simply because their teachers expect them to do well. They show themselves in runs on banks that are believed to be in financial difficulty (and that ultimately lead to the bank's decline) and in presidential campaign momentum in which one candidate's lead increases simply because he or she is perceived to be the front-runner. It seems to be an undeniable fact of life that beliefs can create reality. Over the past 40 years, however, psychologists have sought to understand how.

II. EARLY CONCEPTUALIZATIONS OF THE SELF-FULFILLING PROPHECY IN PSYCHOLOGY AND SOCIOLOGY

A. Thomas Merton and the Self-Fulfilling Prophecy

Following World War II, the United States became home to a large number of displaced Europeans. It was at this time that social science research turned to the issue of racial and ethnic stereotyping and the consequences that such beliefs were having on our increasingly diverse society. In 1948 sociologist Robert Merton published his classic treatise on racial stereotyping and offered an operational definition of the self-fulfilling prophecy. He described this phenomenon as an initially false definition of a situation that evokes a new behavior that makes the originally false conception come true. Merton asserted that the stereotyped beliefs we hold about members of certain ethnic or racial groups may lead us to act in ways that come to elicit behavior from others that supports those beliefs. For example, Merton notes that during the early part of the 20th century, African-American workers were frequently excluded from union membership because of a pervasive belief on the part of union leadership that they "were incorrigibly at odds with the principles of unionism." This belief was presumably supported by the observation that when unions called strikes, many of the strike-breakers (pejoratively referred to as "scabs") were African-Americans. However, Merton also notes that being excluded from union membership and being victimized by pervasive discrimination meant that the doors of economic opportunity were largely closed to most African-American workers. Consequently, when good-paying jobs became available during periods of union unrest, it was not surprising that African-Americans were lined up to take advantage of the opportunity to work as replacements for strikers. This, in turn, fueled unionists' assertions that African-American workers were anti-union. Without some kind of intervention, this self-fulfilling cycle can, and often does, continue unabated. Beyond its description of the mechanisms of social ills, however, Merton's formal conceptualization of the self-fulfilling prophecy has provided a theoretical framework for an entire generation of research on expectancy effects. [*See* PREJUDICE AND STEREOTYPES.]

B. Early Self-Fulfilling Prophecy Research

In an elaboration of one of Merton's other examples, researchers have investigated the effects of expectancy confirmation in negotiation settings. Merton had suggested that the expectation of war may lead one nation to behave toward another in ways that actually give rise to conflict. For example, fearing an attack from a neighbor, a country may begin to mass its forces on the border to fend off the anticipated attack. Seeing these troop movements and fearing their implications, the neighboring country may respond by moving its forces to the border, which could trigger a preemptive strike. This action–reaction spiral of escalation may actually precipitate conflict, creating a reality of the initial expectation. In these studies participants were assigned the task of negotiating with others who were expected to be either competitive or cooperative in nature. This research demonstrated that the participants had evoked responses that were consistent with their initial expectations. That is, partners believed to be competitive came to behave competitively, whereas partners believed to be cooperative behaved cooperatively. Similarly, Strickland's research on surveillance and trust in the workplace showed that increased monitoring of workers' behavior leads to less trust and subsequent untrustworthy behavior. In effect, supervisors may actually bring about that which they fear by treating their subordinates as untrustworthy.

C. Experimenter Expectancy Effects

Further evidence for the self-fulfilling nature of social expectations has been provided by Robert Rosenthal and his colleagues. They were concerned with the ways in which researchers may influence the outcomes of their own research. The effect of experimenters' expectations on the actual outcomes of their research was demonstrated in a clever study in which students conducting a maze learning experiment were told that they were responsible for either "maze bright" or "maze dull" rats. Although these animals had been randomly labeled and actually came from the same group of rats, those rats that students believed to be bright actually performed better than those rats that students believed to be dull. Perhaps not unlike Clever Hans, the animals responded in ways that confirmed the students' expectations. That experimenters' expectations can actually influence the results of their studies presents a significant dilemma for researchers of both human and animal behavior. Demonstrations of experimenter expectancy effects such as these have led to precautions and procedures now considered a standard part of psychological research. But what about the world outside the laboratory? How do our expectancies of others' performances or personalities influence their behavior? Moreover, how do those expectancies influence our future perceptions of others?

III. EARLY PSYCHOLOGICAL RESEARCH ON SELF-FULFILLING PROPHECIES (EXPECTANCY EFFECTS)

A. The Expectancy Confirmation Sequence

To simplify our discussion of self-fulfilling prophecies and of the processes through which they come about, we must first define some terminology. As we do so, we will also describe a prototype of the self-fulfilling prophecy or expectancy confirmation sequence originally presented by John Darley and Russell Fazio. The sequences begins with a belief, or an *expectancy,* that is held (presumably tentatively) by a person that we will call the *perceiver*. Because the social-psychological study of self-fulfilling prophecies has traditionally involved social interaction and expectations about people, the sequence also requires a second person, about whom the belief is held, called the *target* of the expectancy. Expectancies can be beliefs based on a person's membership in any one of a variety of social categories (sometimes called *stereotypes* or *category-based expectancies*), or they can be beliefs based on second- or third-hand information about a specific target person (sometimes called *target-based expectancies*). The next step in the sequence is for the perceiver to act on the basis of the expectancy. For example, if you expect someone with whom you are to interact to be warm and friendly, you may act in a warm and friendly manner yourself. Next, the target interprets the behavior of the perceiver (i.e., "She acted warm and friendly") and responds in a manner consistent with that behavior (i.e., "I think I'll act warm and friendly in return"). The perceiver observes the target's response, interpreting it in line with his or her prior expectation, and infers that the behavior accurately reflects the target's personality (i.e., "I was right. She is friendly and warm!"). This outcome is referred to as *expectancy confirmation* or *behavioral confirmation*. If, in addition, the target then *internalizes* the expectancy (i.e., comes to see himself or herself as warm and friendly as a result of the interaction), a self-fulfilling prophecy has been born. There are numerous permutations of this basic sequence, and not all researchers agree that an expectancy must be internalized before it can become a self-fulfilling prophecy. Nonetheless, this sequence will serve as a basic template for our discussion of the research and theory related to expectancy confirmation processes and self-fulfilling prophecies. [*See* EXPECTATION.]

B. Self-Fulfilling Prophecies in the Classroom

The results of Rosenthal's early research into experimenter expectancy effects led to interesting questions about the potential effects that teachers' expectations may have on students' performances. In a highly controversial study by Rosenthal and school principal Lenore Jacobson, teachers in an elementary school were led to believe that certain children in their classrooms could be expected to "bloom" intellectually during the school year. This prediction was ostensibly based on a new (and, in reality, bogus) intelligence test administered at the time other actual IQ tests were given in the fall. Whether the children were labeled bloomers or not (i.e., given no label) was determined randomly (i.e., there was no reason to expect that bloomers were any different from their peers at the start of the school year). However, IQ tests given at the end of the academic year showed some dramatic differences between those children who were expected to get smarter and those who were not: On average, the IQs of bloomers were 4 points higher than those of children who were not expected to show increases in academic performance, a statistically significant difference. In some cases, the increase was as high as 30 points. In short, teachers' beliefs became reality by virtue of the ways in which they treated the school children. Rosenthal and Jacobson concluded that the teachers provided quantitatively as well as qualitatively different instruction and feedback to the children for whom they had high expectations. Subsequent research aimed at replicating these effects has yielded mixed results. However, reviews of this literature have generally lent credence to the notion that a teacher's expectations about a student's performance can have a profound effect on that student's actual performance. By giving them more time to respond to questions, more opportunities to demonstrate competency, and by providing greater reinforcement for success, teachers can inadvertently facilitate the success of those students they believe to have the greatest potential. However, by giving students they believe to have the least potential less time to respond to questions, fewer opportunities to demonstrate competency, and by providing little reinforcement for success, teachers can also inadvertently undermine the success of those students.

C. The Self-Fulfilling Nature of Perceiver Expectancies: Behavioral Confirmation

Social psychologists have also been interested in determining the effects of expectancies in more casual social interactions. Many of our expectations about others are based on visible or overt characteristics, such as one's age, race, or gender. The stereotyped beliefs associated with these kinds of categories undoubtedly influence our behavior toward people belonging to these groups. In one investigation, Mark Snyder and his colleagues used a getting acquainted situation to demonstrate the self-fulfilling nature of the physical attractiveness stereotype, which is based on the belief that "what is beautiful is good." The researchers led male research participants to believe that their female partners (targets) were either physically very attractive or very unattractive via a photograph. After receiving this attractiveness information, the men engaged in brief telephone conversations with their partners, who remained unaware of the expectancy. These conversations were recorded and later analyzed. Results confirmed that those women erroneously believed to be attractive actually came to behave in a more friendly, outgoing, flirtatious, and socially attractive manner than those thought by their partners to be unattractive.

The pernicious self-fulfilling effects of interracial stereotypes were demonstrated in a provocative study by Carl Word and his colleagues. In that research, white participants served as interviewers for a fictitious job. These subjects interviewed both white and black applicants. Word and his colleagues were particularly interested in the white–black dyads. They found that the white interviewers in these dyads conducted more distant interviews, engaging in less conversation, spending less time, and acting in a less friendly fashion than did interviewers in white–white dyads. Not surprisingly, the white–black interviews were less successful than their white–white counterparts. In a second portion of the research, interviewers were trained to treat applicants like the original interviewers had treated the black applicants. White applicants interviewed by these interviewers also did poorly and felt bad about their interviews. Clearly, the nonverbal behavior of the interviewers was responsible for the black applicants' poor interview performance and created an interracial self-fulfilling prophecy.

D. The Self-Fulfilling Nature of Target Expectancies

In a related study, Amerigo Farina and his colleagues used a slightly different configuration to illustrate how expectations produce their effects. Instead of providing perceivers with an expectancy about the characteristics of their targets, the perceivers were told that the targets had an expectancy of friendliness about *them*. Perceivers were led to believe that their targets thought that they were a former mental patient, a homosexual, or a "normal" person. The target actually received no such information. The participants were then asked to complete a specific task and to limit their subsequent conversation to task-relevant topics. Recordings of the interactions were later analyzed. The results showed that perceivers who thought their target to have a negative expectancy of them actually came to elicit behavior from the target that was less friendly and more aloof than did those perceivers who thought they were viewed as "normal." In other research, participants were led to believe that their partners either liked or disliked them on the basis of an interests questionnaire. In reality, the partners held no such beliefs. After interacting with the partners, the behaviors of the "liked" participants were judged to be more friendly and they were judged to be more likable by their partners, whereas the "unliked" participants were actually judged to be less likable.

That people can be induced to be more or less friendly or socially warm has been sufficiently demonstrated. Another interpersonal characteristic that has reliably been shown to produce the self-fulfilling prophecy effect is competitiveness. As alluded to by Merton, people's beliefs about others' competitive or cooperative nature may contribute greatly to the relations that are developed with those others and the eventual outcomes of the relations. In a study by Harold Kelly and Anthony Stahelski, participants were asked to engage in a prisoner's dilemma game with another person and to choose either a cooperative or competitive game-playing strategy. The researchers then arranged for participants who had chosen opposite strategies to play the game. Competitors, believing the appropriate game-playing strategy to be one of competitiveness, actually came to elicit competitive behavior from their cooperative partners. The initially cooperative participants soon came to apply a tit-for-tat strategy and reciprocated their partners competitive initiatives. These competitive responses then served as evidence for competitors' assumptions about the appropriateness of their chosen strategy and about the preferred strategy of their partners. For competitors, the world was as it was expected to be. [*See* COMPETITION; SOCIAL VALUES.]

E. Perceptual Confirmation of Perceiver Expectancies

Thus far, our discussion of the self-fulfilling prophecy has focused on *behavioral confirmation,* that is, situations in which a person who holds an erroneous belief (the perceiver) about another person (the target) behaves toward the target as if the initial belief were correct, thereby eliciting behavior from the target that confirms the initial expectation. Expectancy effects can also occur at the level of *perceptual confirmation*. Specifically, even if targets do not provide any actual behavioral evidence to support perceivers' beliefs, perceivers may *perceive* that such evidence was provided, thus perpetuating their erroneous beliefs.

One of our main tasks as social perceivers is to understand and explain other people's behavior. However, much of our behavior is open to multiple interpretations; often our intentions and motives are ambiguous. Because human behavior is often ambiguous, people can "read" things into behavior that may or may not be there. That is, they can see what they want to see in other people's behavior. How people interpret the ambiguous behavior of a target-person may be related to their expectancies about that particular target (i.e., how would we expect that "type" of person to behave?). Research has shown that we often operate with a "confirmation bias," seeking information that is consistent with what we already believe to be true and ignoring inconsistent information. John Darley and Paget Gross attempted to demonstrate this perceptual process in a seductively simple study. All of their participants viewed two videotape clips of "Hannah," a 10-year-old girl. For half of the participants, the first clip portrayed Hannah in very pleasant surroundings, on a playground with new, upscale equipment and clean sidewalks. For the other participants, the first clip featured Hannah in much less pleasant surroundings—the playground in which she played was unmistakably in a poor neighborhood, with old tires for swings and littered grounds. The second video segment was exactly the same for both groups. In this tape Hannah was shown taking some tests of mental ability in which her performance is scored as she goes along, answering some items correctly and others incorrectly. After viewing both tape segments participants were asked to provide their impressions of Hannah and her academic potential. As predicted, the expectancy provided by the first tape (i.e., Hannah's likely socioeconomic status), significantly influenced participants' perceptions of her subsequent performance. If Hannah had been seen in an impoverished rather than an enriched environment, she was thought to have less academic potential and to be less likely to succeed as an adult, even though her actual test-taking performance was identical for all subjects! For the perceivers in this study (and perhaps for many of us social perceivers) "seeing is believing."

F. The Self-Fulfilling Effects of Labeling

Perceptual confirmation can occur in a wide variety of contexts and thus can have far reaching consequences particularly for those who are continually the targets of stereotyped beliefs or are likely to be stigmatized, such as members of minority groups, mobility-impaired and physically challenged individuals, or individuals with disfigurements, scars, or mental disabilities. These beliefs often serve as labels and, once applied, may operate as a perceptual filter through which perceivers then process all subsequent information. A demonstration of just such a process was provided in a controversial field study by David Rosenhan and 9 of his colleagues. All 10 men sought and received admission to 10 different mental hospitals; the information they provided was factual (with the exception of their professions as psychologists) and they all complained of voices in their heads that said "bump" and "thud." Upon admission, most received a diagnosis of undifferentiated schizophrenia. Once inside the hospital the new patients acted as they normally would, sometimes taking notes on their observations. None were detected as fakes by the hospital staff and all were released on their own initiative after no less than 2 weeks. When some of the staff were questioned about their wards, they reported seeing evidence of schizophrenia among these pseudo-patients—notes taken to document their stay were interpreted as paranoid tendencies or delusional behavior. In fact, the only people who seemed at all skeptical of Rosenhan and his colleagues were the other patients in the mental hospital, the people who were actually mentally ill!

The self-fulfilling effects of social labels have also been demonstrated in contexts other than mental hospitals. In an elegant study conducted by Robert Kraut, experimenters posing as survey researchers canvassed neighborhoods with a fictitious questionnaire that assessed the likelihood that people would give to charity. Half of those polled were randomly labeled as likely to give to charity and half were labeled as unlikely to contribute. Approximately 2 weeks later, other experimenters went through the same neighborhoods collecting charitable donations. When the donations were analyzed, the researchers discovered that those who had been labeled as charitable givers had in fact donated significantly more than had those who had been labeled as unlikely to contribute, even though the labels had been assigned at random! In effect, being given a label was sufficient to produce the expected behavior in those so labeled.

IV. CURRENT THEORETICAL AND EMPIRICAL WORK ON SELF-FULFILLING PROPHECIES

The research we have described is but a small sample of the considerable work that has been devoted to understanding the workings of self-fulfilling prophecies. As we have argued, self-fulfilling prophecies emerge in all aspects of people's daily lives and affect a broad spectrum of human social behavior. Because of their importance, self-fulfilling prophecies continue to be a rich area of psychological investigation and a great deal of attention has been focused on them.

A first generation of research and theory had as its goal to describe and document the existence of the self-fulfilling prophecy (or the so-called "expectancy confirmation process" or "Pygmalion effect"). Although useful, early explanations for the expectancy confirmation process generally eschewed accounts of those circumstances under which expectancy confirmation does not occur in favor of documenting those under which it does occur. These early explanations also did not adequately incorporate the various needs and goals of perceivers that might make the effect more or less likely to emerge. A number of more recent approaches to understanding how self-fulfilling prophecies produce their effects have been offered and a second generation of research is now under way to more clearly delineate the antecedents and dynamics of the process. This work, in turn, may generate answers to a number of related questions and intriguing observations of both theoretical and practical import. Some approaches, such as those offered by Lee Jussim and by Steven Neuberg and Susan Fiske, focus on the social–cognitive factors, such as attentional, memorial, and information processing limitations and biases, that determine whether a belief will become reality. Others, such as those offered by Mark Snyder and his colleagues and by John Darley, James Hilton, and their colleagues, approach self-fulfilling prophecies from a motivational perspective, examining the ways in which people's motives and goals determine whether an expectancy will come true or be abandoned instead.

A. Perceiver-Induced Constraint

Edward E. Jones has suggested that the crucial mechanism for the emergence of self-fulfilling prophecies is a pervasive phenomenon known in social psychology as *correspondence bias* or the *fundamental attribution error*. Briefly, correspondence bias is the tendency for observers to infer that another person's behavior was caused by internal (or what are called *dispositional*) factors, such as the person's true beliefs or personality, rather than by situational factors, such as coercion or constraint, even when observers are told that the person had no choice but to engage in the behavior. In the classic experimental demonstration of the effect, research participants prepared essays supporting or opposing Fidel Castro. Observers then read the essays and rated the essay-writers' true attitudes toward Castro. Some were told that the position advocated in the essay (pro- or anti-Castro) had been freely chosen, whereas others were told that the essay position was determined by chance. Clearly, observers reading the randomly assigned (or constrained) essays should have had little information on which to base a judgment about the writers' true attitudes; after all, the essays had been assigned randomly. Despite this, however, these observers rated the writers' attitudes toward Castro to be consistent with their essay presentations. In other words, even constrained behavior is used to form judgments of other people's opinions and personalities. [*See* ACTOR–OBSERVER DIFFERENCES IN ATTRIBUTION.]

The correspondence bias effect has been demonstrated numerous times and in a variety of contexts. It is one of the most robust effects in the social-psychological literature and continues to be the object of intensive theoretical and empirical scrutiny. In addition, it has been implicated as one of the social phenomena essential to the creation of self-fulfilling prophecies. In a demonstration of the role that correspondence bias can play in the self-fulfilling prophecy sequence, Daniel Gilbert and Edward Jones had research participants take part in an opinion study in which one participant (the inducer) posed biased political questions to another participant (the responder). Inducers posed questions following a prescribed sequence, and were instructed to request the responder to provide a predetermined liberal or conservative response. One schedule contained a high proportion of liberal responses and the other contained a high proportion of conservative responses. Inducers asked each question and then requested a response by signaling for either the conservative or the liberal response with one of two lights. Responders then simply read the requested response from a sheet of prepared answers. Thus, responders' behavior was completely constrained and under the direct control of the inducers. Even under these highly constrained conditions, inducers judged predominantly liberal responders to be significantly more liberal than the predominantly conservative responders. Inducers used responders completely constrained responses as the basis for their opinion ratings! In the context of the self-fulfilling prophecy, this *perceiver-induced constraint* effect suggests that perceivers who hold expectancies about others can induce those others to behave in ways that are consistent with their original expectations, and then use that induced behavior to make judgments about those persons' personalities.

B. Other Perspectives on the Expectancy Confirmation Process: Interaction Goals

Other perspectives have also been offered. Using expectancy confirmation processes as a means to examine person perception in general, the interaction goals perspective suggested by John Darley and his colleagues focuses on the effects of individuals' goals and expectations on the course and outcome of social interaction. At the heart of their approach is an emphasis on the goal-driven nature of human interaction and a recognition of the important role that interaction goals play in shaping human interaction. The main insight offered by the interaction goals framework is that a perceiver's general motives, interaction goals, and information about the nature of his or her fellow interactants all combine to generate the perceiver's specific interaction tactics.

These researchers have provided evidence that the goals of perceivers with negative expectancies affect the preinteraction information-seeking strategies that perceivers use during an interaction with a target. For example, if perceivers hold a negative expectancy about another person (e.g., that he or she may crumble under pressure) and know that they may have to rely on that person for a future stress-related task, perceivers will actively seek information about the expectancy, even though it may incur a cost in terms of social awkwardness. These perceivers, however, may actually discover that the initial expectancy was false. In contrast, if perceivers hold the same negative expectancy but have as a goal to simply conduct a casual conversation with the target, perceivers may avoid seeking information about the expectancy to ensure that the interaction proceeds smoothly. This kind of avoidance strategy obviously circumscribes the information base upon which perceivers can later draw to form impressions of the target, and this, in turn, results in different final impressions of the target. These perceivers are unlikely to uncover any evidence disconfirming the initial belief and a self-fulfilling prophecy emerges. For example, imagine that you are having lunch with someone you have heard may become angry when academic grades are discussed. To ensure that your interaction proceeds smoothly, it is unlikely that you will raise the topic of grades with this person unless some important outcome is dependent on raising the issue. Unfortunately, this kind of "walking on eggshells" precludes your discovery that the person does not get angry when talking about grades—on the contrary, he likes the topic. Because you avoided the topic of grades in the service of your interaction goals, you will never discover that your original belief was false. Moreover, it is possible that the effort involved in avoiding the topic may also contribute to your belief that your original expectancy must have been true! Building on this work, Darley and his colleagues have proposed a general theoretical framework for studying self-fulfilling prophecies and interpersonal expectancy effects based on a consideration of interaction goals. Clearly, individuals' interaction goals and the interaction tactics they engender can have profound effects on their encounters with others. For this reason, applying an interaction-goals approach to interpersonal interaction promises to be both useful and fruitful.

C. A Functional Approach

Attention to motivational goals in the behavioral confirmation process is also important in Snyder and his colleagues' recent work applying the functional approach. The functional theory of attitudes and behavior proposes that these phenomena are held and carried out in the service of specific motivational goals (i.e., the theory is concerned with the plans and goals, the needs and purposes that are served by attitudes and behavior). Moreover, the theory holds that the same attitude or behavior may serve different functions for different people. Snyder and his colleagues believe that self-fulfilling prophecies occur because people's behaviors are guided by specific motivations and that by changing a person's motivational goals, the behavioral confirmation process can be redirected in such a way that perceivers and targets will *not* enact a negative self-fulfilling prophecy. For example, in one study male perceivers were given motivational instructions that requested that they either "get to know" or "get along with" their partners in an upcoming getting acquainted telephone conversation. Prior to these instructions, they were given a picture of either an obese or normal weight woman (the target) and told that the picture was of their partner. The women were unaware of both the picture and the motivational instructions. The conversations were recorded and analyzed. Results showed that only when the perceivers were instructed to "get to know" their partners did the targets confirm the expectancy (i.e., women believed to be obese were less friendly, less socially skilled, and less flirtatious than those believed to be normal weight). Perceivers instructed to "get along with" their partners did not, however, elicit behavioral confirmation of the negative expectancy. Snyder explains that in order for a self-fulfilling prophecy to occur, certain motivational components are necessary and that we can predict when expectancy confirmation will occur and when expectancy disconfirmation will occur if we know the motivations underlying the behavior of perceivers and targets.

D. Self-Verification Processes

Based on the research and theory presented here, expectancy confirmation would appear to be the inevitable outcome of most social interactions. Fortunately, however, it is not. Most of the more recent approaches to expectancy confirmation processes recognize the need to identify not only those conditions under which expectancies will be confirmed, but importantly, also those under which they are disconfirmed. Darley and his colleagues' interaction goals approach and Snyder's functional approach both address this issue in some detail. In addition to these perspectives, however, William Swann and his colleagues' work has focused on self-verification—the process through which a person's identity is upheld in the face of countervailing expectancies. That research has generally demonstrated that when an issue or dimension is personally relevant and important, targets can be successful as short-circuiting the normal expectancy confirmation cycle, defeating rather than fulfilling an erroneous prophecy.

E. Conclusion

In the story of Pygmalion, a man's desired state of reality was bestowed upon him by a goddess from above. Since then, we have discovered that human beliefs and desires can create a reality of their own without the aid of superhuman beings. The testimony of the power of beliefs to create social reality has been borne out in psychological research over the past several decades and continues to be the focus of research examining the most complex of psychological phenomena, motivations and goals. In the realm of human behavior, the self-fulfilling prophecy appears to be one of the most pervasive and intriguing phenomena of all. But self-fulfilling prophecies are double-edged swords. The very same process that can stimulate school children to rise to their highest potentials can kindle and perpetuate a cycle of conflict and destruction among nations. The process that can reinvigorate struggling corporations can also perpetuate racism and sexism. Therein lies the fascination and the paradox of the self-fulfilling prophecy. The challenge is to understand how to harness its positive powers, and to neutralize its sometimes pernicious consequences.

Bibliography

Darley, J. M., and Fazio, R. H. (1980). Expectancy confirmation processes arising in the social interaction sequence. *Am. Psychol.* **35,** 867.

Hilton, J. L., and Darley, J. M. (1991). The effects of interaction goals on person perception. In "Advances in Experimental Social Psychology" (M. Zanna, Ed.), Vol. 24, pp. 235–267. Academic Press, San Diego.

Hilton, J. L., Darley, J. M., and Fleming, J. H. (1990). Self-fulfilling prophecies and self-defeating behavior. In "Self-defeating Behaviors: Experimental Research, Clinical Impressions, and Practical Implications" (R. Curtis, Ed.), Chapt. 3, pp. 41–65. Plenum, New York.

Jones, E. E. (1990). "Interpersonal Perception." Freeman, New York.

Jones, R. A. (1977). "Self-Fulfilling Prophecies." Erlbaum, Hillsdale, NJ.

Rosenthal, R., and Jacobson, L. (1968). "Pygmalion in the Classroom." Holt, Rinehart & Winston, New York.

Snyder, M. (1984). When belief creates reality. In "Advances in Experimental Social Psychology" (L. Berkowitz, Ed.), Vol. 18, pp. 247–305. Academic Press, New York.

Snyder, M. (1992). Motivational foundations of behavioral confirmation. In "Advances in Experimental Social Psychology" (M. Zanna, Ed.), Vol. 25. Academic Press, San Diego.

SEMANTIC MEMORY

Christine Chiarello
Syracuse University

Glossary

Episodic memory An autobiographical memory of a particular experience.

Exemplar A member of a semantic category.

Prototype The most representative, or average, member of a category.

Retrieval The process of accessing information from memory.

Semantic priming The facilitation in response time that occurs when an item to be recognized is preceded by an item of related meaning.

SEMANTIC MEMORY refers to the long-term store of general information we have about the world. Semantic memories are not tied to specific events which were experienced at a particular time, in a particular place. Rather, they represent our knowledge base of concepts and their relationships. Semantic memories are necessary to understand language, to think, and to interpret the meaning of all types of information that we receive.

I. THE NATURE OF SEMANTIC MEMORY

Memories are often thought of as echoes of our past, reflecting (perhaps imperfectly) the inflections and nuances of specific events as we have experienced them. But, in addition to such episodic memories, long-term memory also contains a wealth of information representing our general knowledge base. For example, we "know" the meanings of words in our vocabulary, everyday facts (e.g., forks and spoons are utensils for eating, rather than writing), and even very abstract ideas (e.g., everyone loses in a war). Although we constantly access this type of information, retrieval of such semantic memories is not experienced as "remembering," perhaps because it seems to be effortless and is not accompanied by a sense of reminiscence. In general, semantic memories are more resistant to forgetting than episodic memories. They also support our ability to draw inferences, which allows us to "know" something that we have not explicitly learned. For example, we can infer that power lawn mowers are combustible based on the separate notions that such mowers use gasoline, and gasoline is combustible. Such general, conceptual information constitutes an essential part of our long-term memory store. Without it we would be unable to recognize objects, to comprehend language, and to behave intelligently. [*See* MEMORY.]

II. CONCEPTS AND CATEGORIZATION

Concepts are mental representations of objects, entities, and events that enable us to categorize our experiences as instances of more general classes. In this way we can recognize commonalities across unique experiences and respond appropriately despite minor differences in appearance. But how are categories defined? What do all members of a category have in common? Research into human categorization suggests that most, if not all, categories comprise loose coalitions of members with partially overlapping relations to each other, and fuzzy boundaries between categories. This contrasts with the more classical view of categories as defined by a set of necessary and sufficient properties which are shared equally by all members of the category, with clearly demarcated borders between categories. The philosopher Wittgenstein pointed out the inadequacies of the latter view in his analysis of the concept of *games*. While we would all agree that

Encyclopedia of Human Behavior, Volume 4

chess, baseball, tic-tac-toe, and children playing "house" each represents an example of *games,* it is impossible to identify a set of defining properties that they all share. For example, while many games involve competition and winners and losers, some children's games do not. Even with careful philosophical analysis, no single attribute was found to be shared by all examples of *games*. Equally careful consideration of more common object categories, such as *birds* or *furniture,* yields similar results. Rather than requiring the extraction of a set of defining features, human categorization is better captured by two structural properties: (1) family resemblances among members of the category, and (2) graded membership within and between categories. We will first consider how these properties characterize the use of common, concrete categories. Then we will expand our view to consider other types of categories, and how categories are constructed and combined.

A. Family Resemblances, Typicality, and Basic Level Concepts

Although there may be no defining set of criteria for category membership, many features are shared among members of a category. For example, some features of *fruit* are: has seeds, is sweet, grows on trees, has a peel, is edible. Some fruits (apples, oranges) have all these properties, while others have differing subsets of properties. Lemons grow on trees, have seeds and a peel, and are edible, but are not sweet, while grapes are sweet, have seeds and a peel, are edible but do not grow on trees. (Note that having seeds cannot be a *defining* property of *fruit,* since some nonfruits such as sunflowers also have seeds.) Many other partially overlapping sets of features are evident when considering the entire class of fruits. Members of a category such as *fruit* seem to resemble each other in the same way that members of a family do: there may be no single feature (hair color, height, nose size and shape, freckles) that characterizes every family member, yet each has some features in common with some other members, hence the family resemblance. Thus, it appears that categories are structured via probabilistic family resemblances. Knowing a category means knowing the constellation of features that characterize the category, and the extent to which various exemplars instantiate these features.

This view of category structure implies that there may be no clearly defined boundary between one category and another, and that not all members of the category are equally representative of it. There is not threshold number of fruit-features an instance must have to be classed as a *fruit*. Rather, the fewer features it shares with other fruits, the less "fruity" it is. Thus, while apples and oranges are clearly "fruity" fruits, watermelons are less so, and avocados are very atypical fruits. In other words, there is graded membership within categories. Indeed, those instances that share relatively few features with other members of the category frequently give rise to border disputes (Is a tomato a fruit or vegetable? Is a porpoise a fish or a mammal?). Such disagreements characterize human categorization, and imply that the boundaries between many categories are ill-defined.

While category boundaries may be difficult to determine, there is generally high agreement among people in how good an example of the category a given instance is: nearly everyone agrees that an apple is a very typical fruit, and that an avocado is not. These typicality ratings can predict many categorization phenomena. Typical category members are generally learned first during childhood, and are the first instances mentioned when people are asked to list members of a category. When one is given an instance, and asked to categorize it, response speed varies with typicality. Most importantly, instances rated most typical of a category are those which also have: (1) the highest degree of family resemblance with other members of the category, and (2) the least resemblance to members of other, contrasting categories. For example, apples share numerous features with many other fruits, but relatively few features with vegetables and flowers. Because of its strong family resemblance, the most typical category member may best represent the category as a whole. Thus, categorization may involve comparison of a given instance to a *prototype* that best represents the category. The prototype may be the most typical example of the category, or it may represent the "ideal" of the category derived from a composite of the most typical members. In either case, due to its high degree of family resemblance, the prototype both best represents the category as a whole and is most distinctive from instances of other contrasting categories. [*See* CATEGORIZATION.]

Thus far, we have considered some aspects of the internal structure of categories. An equally important part of our conceptual knowledge consists of the relationship between categories. Many everyday categories are hierarchically organized with respect to more and less inclusive categories. For example, the category *apple* subsumes a set of less inclusive, subordinate categories (macintosh apple, granny smith apple, etc.). Likewise, the category *apple* is itself subsumed by a more inclusive, superordinate category, *fruit,* which also is subsumed by a yet more inclusive category, *food.* This hierarchy provides us with the flexibility to make fewer or greater conceptual distinctions among entities, in response to the task at hand: e.g., the distinction between varieties of apples is not relevant to determining nutritional value, but may be important in deciding how to make the best applesauce. However, there is evidence that one level of the hierarchy, the basic level, is the most useful for most common cognitive activities.

Basic level categories are those such as *apples, cars,* and *desks* which seem to capture the level at which we usually interact with our environment. It has been determined that basic level concepts represent the most inclusive level of categorization which has the following properties. (1) Basic level categories have the largest number of attributes common to members of the class (e.g., examples of *desks* share many more properties than examples of *furniture*). (2) Common movement patterns are used when interacting with basic level, but not superordinate, objects (e.g., similar movements are used with all kinds of chairs, but not all types of furniture). (3) Basic level objects are similar in shape (e.g., the class of cars can be recognized by an outline drawing of their shape, while the class of vehicles cannot). (4) A mental image can be generated to represent the basic level class as a whole. (5) Objects are generally named at the basic level (e.g., a photo of a particular automobile will be named as a car more frequently than as a vehicle or a sedan). Thus, this level of categorization may be the most fundamental. Indeed, basic level categories, and their labels, tend to be learned earliest by children.

Thus far we have seen that concrete object categories are hierarchically organized with a particular level of abstraction being most basic, and that category membership is graded and organized around family resemblances. But semantic memory includes many other kinds of conceptual structures such as abstract ideas, events, and even new categories constructed "on the fly." It is important to understand the ways in which these semantic memories are similar to, and differ from, common object categories.

B. Abstract Concepts and Scripts

Abstract concepts, such as *patriotism* or *subtraction,* do not have concrete referents in the world. When persons are given a word and asked to think of a context or circumstance in which it might appear, there is much greater difficulty doing this for abstract than for concrete terms. This suggests that abstract concepts are not as strongly connected to other elements of our knowledge base as are concrete concepts (see Section III.A below). Despite this, at least some abstract categories (such as *crimes*) have graded membership. There is good agreement that some criminal activities (murder, theft) are more typical of the category than others (treason, animal abuse). In addition, the more typical members are those that share the greatest number of features with other members of the category. However, other abstract categories (such as *rules*) do not show such typicality effects. One property that appears to distinguish abstract and concrete concepts is the range of potential category members. While it is possible to exhaustively catalog concrete category membership (there are a finite number of *fruits*), this may be impossible for many abstract categories (new *rules* are constantly being generated). Finally, while there has been little research into whether there are basic levels for abstract categories many of these do appear to be hierarchically organized (shoplifting and burglary are types of *thefts,* and theft is subsumed into the more inclusive category of *crimes*). In at least one domain, computer programming, one level of the conceptual hierarchy does appear to be treated as basic. Expert programmers prefer to classify programming instructions as "sorts" and "searches," rather than at the more superordinate (algorithms) or subordinate (binary searches) levels. It may be that a basic level exists for those abstract categories about which we possess a great deal of detailed knowledge.

A different type of conceptual structure may underlie our knowledge of events and situations (e.g., grocery shopping, going to a restaurant). We are here concerned with generic knowledge of these activities, and not with any specific episode that may have been experienced. This type of knowledge structure, which consists of a complex sequence of stereotyped activities organized around a goal, has been termed a script. The grocery shopping script would consist of roles (shopper, cashier), props (grocery cart, price scanner), and a standardized sequence of events or scenes (enter store, get cart, select items, wait in line, pay cashier, leave store) that are needed to achieve the goal (buy food). Scripts have two major functions. When attempting to achieve a routine goal, the relevant script can be retrieved from memory and used to organize our behavior in attaining the goal. In addition, scripts serve as frameworks for comprehension. When interpreting a story or conversation, the relevant scripts are used to fill in the "gaps" in the narrative that may not be explicitly stated. Thus, they are used to generate inferences and can produce "misrememberings" when an unmentioned, but typical, action is recalled as part of a specific instance in which it did not occur.

There is good agreement across individuals on the elements of various scripts, their order, and organization (such as scene boundaries). This event knowledge has a family resemblance structure. No one element of a script defines whether a given instance will be considered an example of the script. Although "paying for food" is an important component of the grocery shopping script, a particular instance might not include any purchases, and "paying for food" is also a part of other scripts (eating in a restaurant). Scripts are both hierarchically and temporally organized. Some script actions are in a subordinate relation to other script actions (paying includes subactions of removing one's wallet, extracting money, etc.), in addition to having a standard order of occurrence. Thus, although scripts represent a more complex memory structure, they share some organizational properties with simple object categories, as well as having characteristics unique to the representation of events.

C. Category Construction

Concepts can be constructed either by combining two or more simple concepts or by creating an entirely novel category when there is no concept available to suit our current needs. As we will see, category construction reveals the intricate web of semantic knowledge that is brought to bear in the categorization process.

1. How Are Concepts Combined?

The logic of sets would lead one to predict that combined concepts represent either the union or the intersection of the simple concepts being combined. However, neither is characteristic of the manner in which humans form combined concepts. For example, *gray clouds* are not the union of all gray things and all clouds. But the meaning of gray clouds is also not captured by intersection of the properties of gray things and the properties of clouds. A salient feature of gray clouds is that they are threatening, but this is not a general property of either gray things or clouds. Investigation of combined concepts reveals a number of characteristics suggesting that a complex interaction between the properties of simple concepts takes place when they are combined to form a new composite category.

First, membership in combined categories is frequently overextended: although blackboards are not considered to be *furniture,* they are considered to be *school furniture*. Thus, the *furniture* category is overextended to include blackboards, when it is combined with the category of *school things*. Overextension is most likely to occur when an item (blackboard) is a very good example of one of the original categories (school things), and, at best, a very marginal member of the other category (furniture).

Second, the typicality of an item within a combined category may differ from the typicality of the same item within each of the constituent simple categories. For example, a guppy is a very good example of a *pet fish,* but is neither a typical *fish,* nor a typical *pet*. Thus, typicality for exemplars of combined categories cannot always be predicted from the typicality structure of the original categories.

Third, the combined concept no longer has all the properties of each simple concept, nor only those attributes which are found in both simple concepts. Each constituent concept contributes some attributes to the combination, while other attributes are lost. Note that an attribute of one of the simple concepts must be lost when it is inconsistent with an attribute of the other category: while fish are frequently eaten, pets are not; thus, the "often eaten" property of fish is lost from the combination *pet fish*. The combined category may also have attributes (emergent properties) that neither simple concept possesses (threatening in the *gray clouds* example).

Finally, in some cases, one of the constituent concepts appears to dominate in the meaning of the combined concept, in that it contributes more attributes than the other simple concept. For example, *pet birds* have more attributes charateristic of *birds* than of *pets*.

In light of the characteristics listed above, it may be best to think of combined concepts as hybrids, rather than as the result of the addition or intersection of two simpler concepts. The hybrid concept may have its own prototype that is used to determine degree of membership in the new composite category. This hybrid prototype will "inherit" some properties from each "parent" concept, according to certain principles of transmission. For example, if an attribute is necessary for one of the parents (a fish must have gills), then it will tend to be transmitted (*pet fish* have gills). If the parents have inconsistent attributes, only one of these can be inherited (*pet fish* have scales, rather than fur). The fact that some parental traits dominate in transmission to offspring also appears to have its counterpart in the construction of hybrid concepts.

To the extent that conceptual inheritance is analogous to genetic inheritance, we would expect a wide variety of meaning structures in combined concepts, even given rather similar "parent" concepts. Note that while typical *pet birds* (canaries) are also fairly typical *birds*, typical *pet fish* (guppies) are not typical *fish*. Can all characteristics of combined concepts be accounted for in terms of inheritance? Emergent properties are those that are present in the hybrid concept, but absent in both parents, and thus not inheritable. Many emergent properties appear to depend upon aspects of world knowledge that are not represented in either constituent concept: gray clouds are threatening based on our knowledge that they may signal an impending storm. Thus, a rather broad array of knowledge may contribute to the interpretation of combined concepts. This need not invalidate the inheritance view. The expression of any inherited trait is subject to modification by the environment. If our knowledge of the world is considered to be the environment within which conceptual combination takes place, then both the meanings of constituent concepts and other world knowledge should contribute to the interpretation of hybrid concepts.

2. Ad Hoc Categories

There are situations in which it is necessary to classify objects or events in a truly novel way. Ad hoc categories are those constructed "on the fly," when retrieval of previously stored concepts, or their combinations, is inadequate to meet a current cognitive need. For example, one can readily list "*things to take out of one's home during a fire*" even though the various items were not previously categorized in this manner. Like common object categories, ad hoc categories have an internal structure, characterized by graded membership. Thus, for example, there is strong agreement across persons that children and other family members are more typical of things to take out during a fire than are stereos and blankets. But unlike common object categories, typicality is not determined by similarity to a prototype based on family resemblance. Indeed, the members of ad hoc categories are frequently quite dissimilar from each other on most perceptual dimensions (consider the lack of attributes shared among children, cats, money, family photos, important documents). Rather, ad hoc categories are structured by the goals the category serves: e.g., the most typical things to remove in a fire are those that best serve the goal "preserving what is precious or irreplaceable." Thus, membership decisions are based on only those properties that are relevant to achieving the goal. Many ad hoc categories appear to be organized around an ideal that the goal is aiming toward. For example, the ideal of the category "*things to eat on a diet*" may be "possesses zero calories," since such items will best achieve the goal of losing weight. Foods that are considered the best examples of the category are those that most closely approximate the ideal of zero calories. Thus, membership is graded according to similarity to an ideal, rather than via degree of resemblance to an instance that best represents the category as a whole.

Because ad hoc categories are not well-established in memory, our ability to construct and use them reveals the interface between semantic memory retrieval and higher level reasoning skills. At least some aspects of creativity and problem solving depend on the ability to form novel classifications, and to envision how seemingly disparate objects or ideas can be recruited toward the achievement of a complex goal. These more dynamic aspects of category construction and classification illustrate the importance of semantic memory in mental activities involving insight and creativity.

D. Summary

The previous discussion demonstrates some of the variety of conceptual structures that make up semantic memory. We have seen that concepts comprise a category of rather diverse members (common objects, abstract ideas, events, etc.), each of which shares a partially overlapping set of properties with other exemplars of this category. While most, but not all, concepts have a graded membership structure, this may or may not co-occur with a prototype based on family resemblance. Some concepts (scripts, ad hoc categories) are goal oriented, while others (object categories) are not. Thus, there may be no set of defining properties that characterizes every type of conceptual structure. To some extent, common objects may represent the "prototypical" variety of concept, since object concepts share many properties with other types of concepts. It is important to acknowledge that our notion of *concepts* is itself a concept, having an internal structure not unlike that of other semantic memory constructs.

III. ACCESSING SEMANTIC MEMORY

The preceding discussion has focused on the content of semantic memory. We will now consider how semantic memory is accessed. In order to actually make use of this rich knowledge base for various cognitive activities, information must be retrieved with great speed and accuracy. At any given moment in processing, most conceptual information is not in active use, remaining in a quiescent background state. However, when we think of a concept, hear or read its name, or see the object it represents, its meaning is activated, and brought to the forefront of our cognitive processing. Activated concepts can be retrieved into working memory to participate in whatever conscious mental processes we are currently engaged in. In order to understand how this memory activation operates, we must consider how concepts are interrelated in semantic memory.

A. Semantic Networks and Spreading Activation

Semantic memories are organized by similarity of meaning. To a large extent concepts are defined in terms of other concepts. To understand a given concept, we must make reference to other closely related concepts (e.g., a *cat* is a *small animal* and a common *pet*, etc.). Semantic networks are frequently used to graphically represent the interrelations among concepts. Figure 1 shows a portion of a semantic network. The ellipses, referred to as nodes, represent concepts. Nodes for closely related concepts are connected via links, which can vary in strength: the *tiger–lion* link is stronger (closer in the network) than the *tiger–circus* link. Typical instances of a category (cat) will have stronger connections to other category members and to the superordinate (animal), than will atypical instances (zebra). Abstract concepts (such as *fierce*) will have fewer connections with other concepts in the network as

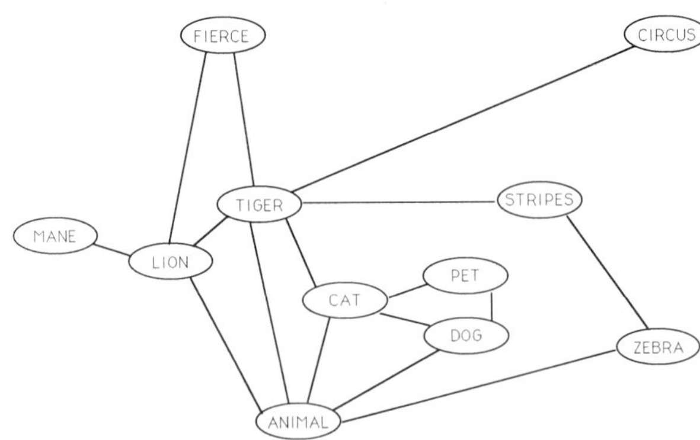

FIGURE 1 Illustration of a portion of a semantic network. The ellipses represent concept nodes, and the lines links between semantically related concepts.

compared to concrete concepts, which may contribute to why they are more difficult to comprehend.

Thinking about a concept, or encountering a word or object that it represents, will entail activating the memory node that represents the concept. Once a concept node has become activated, activation will propagate through the network via the links between related nodes. Each node encountered will receive some of this activation, producing a cognitive "chain reaction." In other words, an activated concept will tend to trigger other related concepts by briefly raising their activation levels. This spread of activation through the semantic network represents a kind of memory search. This can be seen in a free association task, where persons are given a word, and are asked to respond with "the first word(s) that comes to mind." The word *tiger* will tend to produce free association responses such as *lion, cat,* and *fierce,* presumably because activaton from *tiger* has spread to strongly related concepts (*lion, fierce*), causing the latter to more easily come to mind.

There are several characteristics of the activation process that constrain the extent to which activation will spread through the network. First, unless we continue to attend to a given concept, its activation level will decrease over time (decay rate). An activated node will only temporarily be more accessible for processing, usually for less than a second. Second, the amount of activation that spreads between an activated node and its neighbors will depend on the strength of the link (e.g., *tiger* will activate *lion* to a greater extent than *circus*). Third, activation decreases as it traverses successive nodes (semantic distance). Thus, little activation will reach concepts that are only very indirectly related to each other (*zebra—mane*). The decay rate, varying connection strengths, and semantic distance together ensure that most semantic memory activations will be fleeting, and that only a portion of the total semantic network will be activated at any moment in time. The activated portion of the network will represent those ideas that are potentially relevant to information we are currently processing.

The accessibility of concept nodes within semantic memory will vary with the degree of activation they have received. As a consequence of spreading activation, when a given concept is accessed, other concepts related in meaning will also temporarily be more available for processing. Semantic priming research indicates that this results in faster retrieval of related concepts. When asked to recognize a target word such as CAT, persons will make faster responses when they have just previously seen a related prime word such as DOG, as compared to an unrelated word (PEN). Investigations of this semantic priming effect have revealed some important properties of retrieval from semantic memory. Spreading activation has a very rapid onset: priming can occur when the interval between the presentation of prime and target words is less than 1/20th of a second. Priming occurs between words which are directly associated (LION–TIGER), and between words that are not directly associated (LION–STRIPES), but are linked via an intervening association (e.g., TIGER)—see Figure 1. Less priming occurs between words that are only weakly associated (TIGER–CIRCUS), than between words that are more strongly associated (TIGER–LION). In general, then, ease of retrieval is at least partly determined by the organization of information within semantic memory (i.e., interconnectedness within the semantic network).

B. Retrieval Failures

It is arguable whether we ever truly forget a semantic memory. Rather, the inability to recall a fact or a name may be better thought of as a temporary retrieval failure. When asked to answer questions such as "What rock group sang 'Color My World'?" or "What stringed instrument is played horizontally using the fingers?" people frequently are unable to immediately recall the answer, but may report that they "know that they know it." This puzzling phenomenon, termed feeling of knowing, represents a partial retrieval failure. On the one hand, we are able to judge, with some accuracy, whether some information is represented within our semantic memory, but, on the other hand, we are unable to access this information directly. Feeling of knowing experiences may play an important role in directing semantic memory searches. If the sought-after information is stored in memory, then a more extensive search could result in a successful retrieval. But if the information is not available in memory, then a continued search would be unproductive.

Feeling of knowing states can be experimentally induced by posing difficult general information questions, and asking persons to rate their confidence that they do possess the knowledge, in those cases where they could not recall the information requested. Accuracy of the feeling of knowing rating can then be assessed by comparing it to performance in a subsequent recognition test in which the correct answer must be chosen from several possibilities. If accurate, a confident feeling of knowing rating would be associated with a correct recognition response. In general, strong feelings of knowing are more accurate than not, although they do not provide a completely reliable index of semantic memory contents.

What causes feelings of knowing? Two different mechanisms could produce such experiences. The information provided in the memory query would be expected to initiate a spreading activation process in long-term memory. If the relevant concept receives some activation, but not enough to permit retrieval into working memory, then the residual activation could provide an indication that the information is indeed available in one's memory. Partial memory activation would be expected to be available only for a brief time after the initial recall attempt (due to the decay rate), but it could contribute to some spontaneous feeling of knowing experiences. People could also rely on general knowledge of their own semantic memory contents (metamemory) when giving feeling of knowing judgments. For example, someone with considerable musical knowledge could provide high feeling of knowing estimates for the above questions, regardless of the activation level of the sought-after concept (e.g., "Since I'm pretty familiar with musical instruments I probably know it, even though I can't recall it just now"). Familiarity does influence performance in a wide variety of judgment tasks. In particular, it has been shown that fairly accurate feeling of knowing estimates can be based on topic familiarity under conditions (1-week test intervals) in which residual memory activation could not be present.

The most important point to emphasize is that knowledge of one's own semantic memory states (current activation levels) and/or contents (metamemory) can be used to guide memory search, under conditions in which more automatic retrieval processes have not succeeded.

IV. ALTERATIONS IN SEMANTIC MEMORY FUNCTION

Because we continue to accumulate knowledge throughout the lifespan, the content, and perhaps the organization, of semantic memory should change over a lifetime. Many individuals will have acquired a high degree of expertise in one or more areas of knowledge (e.g., car repair, nuclear physics, cooking). One component of this expertise is a richly developed, domain-specific, body of semantic knowledge. Attempts to develop computer systems to simulate such expertise ("expert systems") have revealed that it is the possession of a highly organized, domain-specific knowledge base, rather than specialized memory retrieval or inferencing processes, that is the key to expert performance. Thus, there can be an enhancement of semantic memory throughout one's life, at least in those areas in which one can be regarded as an expert. But what about disruptions of semantic memory? We will now consider the extent to which normal aging, and brain injury/disease, alters semantic memory function.

A. Effects of Normal Aging on Semantic Memory

The elderly are often characterized as being forgetful, and "losing their memories." Like most caricatures, these difficulties are exaggerated, but contain a grain of truth with respect of episodic memory. In contrast, semantic memory is extremely resiliant to loss with normal aging. The healthy elderly perform as well as younger adults on a variety of measures of semantic memory function. Indices of categorization, word association, and script knowledge do not vary with advancing age. Feeling of knowing is as accurate in old, as in younger, adults. Language comprehension does not decline with age, and, in at least one respect, it may improve. Older adults typically have more extensive vocabularies than the young. Although the elderly will respond more slowly in most experimental tasks, semantic priming research indicates no age differences in the rate at which activation spreads within the semantic network. This implies that the speed of semantic memory retrieval is not slowed as a consequence of normal aging.

There is one phenomenon related to semantic memory retrieval which is more likely to be disrupted among the elderly. Older individuals more frequently experience "tip of the tongue" states, in which the name of an object or person is temporarily inaccessible. However, this does not appear to be due to failure to activate the appropriate concept in semantic memory. Semantic information is available in such states, but cannot be used to access the appropriate name code. Thus, it is the interface between semantic memory and output processes which may be impaired in the elderly, rather than any disruption within semantic memory itself.

In general, then, there is little evidence that semantic memory diminishes with age, nor that semantic memories cease to be stored beyond a certain age. Thus, the slowed responses and sensory losses that accompany normal aging do not signal any deterioration within conceptual memory.

B. Breakdowns in Semantic Memory after Brain Injury

Although the brain changes that accompany normal aging do not appear to disturb semantic memory function, frank injuries to the brain, whether due to disease or accidents, can profoundly disrupt the use of semantic memory. Two particularly dramatic examples are provided by patients with Alzheimer's disease and by brain-injured persons who appear to have category-specific knowledge deficits.

1. Semantic Memory in Alzheimer's Disease

The dementia that accompanies Alzheimer's disease (AD) affects a wide range of cognitive functions including language, memory, attention, and reasoning. In particular, mild to moderately impaired AD patients exhibit a constellation of deficits involving semantic memory. For example, their ability to generate members of even very familiar semantic categories is markedly diminished in both quantity and quality. On average, they will list only half as many category members as nondemented persons, and they will also generate many items that are not part of the category. AD patients have difficulty naming objects (often making errors semantically related to the item—SWEEP for BROOM), and providing a name when given a definition. Their word association responses are also abnormal, and become increasingly idiosyncratic as the disease progresses.

Many types of semantic judgments are impaired. For example, AD patients have difficulty answering yes/no questions about a presented object (e.g., a saw) such as "is it used for cutting?" despite adequate visual perceptual abilities. In light of the above symptoms, it is not surprising that spontaneous speech in AD is characteristically vague and semantically impoverished. Thus, while their statements are grammatically well-formed, little content is conveyed to the listener. Finally, AD patients do poorly on tests of general world knowledge, and in describing everyday activities (script knowledge).

These deficits appear to indicate a wide-spread loss of information from semantic memory. However, other findings indicate that a great deal of conceptual knowledge is intact. AD patients, for example, show normal or near-normal semantic priming which suggests that the semantic network (concept nodes and their interconnections) is grossly intact. It is also the case that many of the semantic deficits described above can be ameliorated by seemingly minor changes in the task. For example, while AD patients are very poor at generating category members when given the name of the category (FURNITURE), they can provide the appropriate category label when given a exemplar (i.e., CHAIR). This implies that they have difficulty searching a category to retrieve specific exemplars, yet can use an exemplar to access the appropriate superordinate. Along the same lines, AD patients have difficulty determining whether a given concept (*fish*) has a specific attribute (*fins*), yet can correctly judge that the concept and attribute are related in meaning. While the latter only requires one to determine that there is a connection between *fins* and *fish* in semantic memory, the former depends on an evaluation of this information (fish *have* fins, but do not *eat* fins). Apparently, the connections between concepts and their attributes are intact, but the ability to make more specific judgments about the nature of these attributes is compromised.

To summarize, when the task requires a directed search of semantic memory, or when an evaluation of semantic memory contents is needed, AD patients perform poorly. However, indirect probes of the integrity of semantic memory (as in semantic priming) do not suggest any major deterioration. Such findings make it unlikely that knowledge of concepts and semantic categories is lost in AD. Instead, it appears that it is the ability to make intentional use of this information that is impaired by this dementing illness. [*See* ALZHEIMER'S DISEASE.]

2. Category-Specific Knowledge Deficits

While semantic memory dysfunction in AD is not restricted to any particular class of concepts, other brain injuries (caused by encephalitis, head injury, or stroke) can result in deficits specific to a small set of semantic categories. For example, a patient might have great difficulty naming fruits and vegetables, yet have no difficulty naming other objects, including other types of food. A more frequently reported dissociation is between the ability to access information about living vs nonliving things. Such patients are impaired at naming, defining, and describing the attributes of various animals and plants, but not inanimate objects such as types of vehicles or furniture (the converse can also occur, but is much less frequent). Does this mean that various categories are represented in different "regions" of semantic memory such that brain damage can "cleave" semantic memory along category boundaries? This would be a remarkable conclusion, if supported.

Further analysis of cases of living/nonliving knowledge deficits suggests that a more fundamental distinction among kinds of knowledge is involved. Concrete concepts are characterized by both sensory and functional properties. In general, living things are distinguished more by sensory attributes than by function (e.g., visual, tactile, and taste attributes distinguish *apples* and *bananas* more so than differences in their functions). In contrast, inanimate objects are distinguished more by their use than by their appearance or sensory quality (consider the differences between *cups* and *bowls*). Therefore, if sensory and functional knowledge could be selectively distrupted, this would likely affect some categories more than others. Thus, impaired access to sensory knowledge should be more detrimental to living than to nonliving things, while impaired access to functional information should affect nonliving more than living things. There is some reason to prefer this interpretation. Although some patients are generally more impaired accessing living vs nonliving concepts, there are some categories that violate this animacy distinction. For example, individuals who show good performance for most inanimate objects, but poor performance on living things, may also have great difficulty with selected inanimate categories such as *musical instruments* in which sensory properties may be more important than function.

The existence of category-specific deficits implies some segregation within semantic memory of various types of knowledge. However, this need not indicate that there is a brain "center" for each individual category. Rather, different components of meaning (such as appearance and function) may be stored separately, and then activated and combined when concepts are retrieved. Brain injury, then, could selectively disrupt access to some meaning components, which would affect some categories to a greater extent than others.

C. Summary

Semantic memory is not static. Its contents and organization will evolve as new knowledge is acquired and assimilated. Semantic memory can be enhanced over a lifetime, particularly in areas in which one has developed particular expertise. Conceptual memory does not deteriorate as a consequence of normal aging, but it can be impared by brain injury or disease. In the latter cases, semantic memory function can be altered either globally, as in Alzheimer's disease, or within a more restricted domain (category-specific deficits).

V. CONCLUSION

Nearly all cognitive activities will, to some extent, require the use of semantic memory. It is the foundation upon which many cognitive processes are built. Recognition, comprehension, thinking, and reasoning all depend on rapid and accurate access to this highly organized knowledge base. Categories of diverse types enable us to flexibly classify objects, events, and abstractions in response to changing environmental demands. Thus, in a very real cognitive sense, "knowledge is power."

The study of semantic memory has applications that extend beyond the confines of the psychology laboratory. Formal education is structured to enrich the content and improve the accessibility of semantic memory. A better understanding of how semantic memories are formed, organized, and accessed can lead to the development of improved learning techniques and educational practices. Further study of semantic memory impairments is likely to yield insights into how the human brain stores and accesses information. In addition, continued advances in our understanding of the human knowledge system can assist in the development of more sophisticated artificial intelligence systems.

Bibliography

Damasio, A. R. (1990). Category-related recognition defects as a clue to the neural substrates of knowledge. *Trends Neurosci.* **13,** 95–98.

Light, L. L., and Burke, D. M. (1988). "Language, Memory, and Aging." Cambridge University Press, New York.

Nebes, R. D. (1989). Semantic memory in Alzheimer's Disease. *Psychol. Bull.* **106,** 377–394.

Neely, J. H. (1991). Semantic priming effects in visual word recognition: A selective review of current findings and theories. In "Basic Processes in Reading: Visual Word Recognition" (D. Besner and G. Humphreys, Eds.), Erlbaum, Hillsdale, NJ.

Schwanenflugel, P. (Ed.) (1991). "The Psychology of Word Meanings." Erlbaum, Hillsdale, NJ.

SEMANTICS

Cliff Goddard
University of New England, Australia

Glossary

Argument An expression about which something is being said (predicated); either a referring expression (a noun phrase) or a proposition.

Compositionality The fact that the meaning of a complex expression, such as a sentence, is composed from the meanings of its constituents, such as words.

Meaning relations A cover term for semantic relations such as synonymy (same meaning), antonymy (opposite meaning), hyponymy (semantic inclusion).

Metalanguage Any system of representation used to describe another such system; a semantic metalanguage is any system of terms and rules used to describe meanings in ordinary language.

Polysemy A situation in which a single lexical item has several distinct, yet related, meanings; as for example, the verb *cry* or the noun *chip*.

Semantic field A set of words sharing some components of meaning, such as kinship terms, cooking verbs, colors, parts of the body.

Semantic primitive A fundamental term in a semantic metalanguage, i.e., a term regarded as impervious to further semantic analysis.

SEMANTICS is the study of how meanings are expressed in human languages. Since this is the basic function of language, semantics is crucial to understanding the nature of human language abilities. Another concern of semantics is the relationship between language, culture, and cognition. It is possible to study vocabulary, grammar, intonation patterns, and even usage conventions from a semantic point of view, but the greatest amount of research to date has concerned word meanings. The prime theoretical problem in semantics is to decide on the optimal metalanguage for semantic representation, that is, the best system for describing meanings.

I. ISSUES IN MEANING DESCRIPTION

To state the meaning of a linguistic expression is to give an equivalent expression in some metalanguage of semantic representation. This may consist of technical constructs (such as semantic features or markers) or logical symbols, or it may be a standardized subset of ordinary language. An ideal semantic metalanguage would be (a) universal, i.e., equally applicable to all languages, (b) maximally intelligible and explicit, and (c) comprehensive, i.e., capable of analyzing natural language in its entirety.

The idea of meaning analysis seems logically to imply the existence of a set of indefinable terms or semantic primitives. Modern linguists differ on whether it is possible to identify semantic primitives, whether they would be the same for all languages, and whether they would be expressible through ordinary words. Among those who endorse their existence, from otherwise different perspectives, are Jerrold Katz, Ray Jackendoff, Igor Mel'čuk, and Anna Wierzbicka. These scholars assume that the terms of semantic description are discrete elements, each clearly separate from the other, analogous to words in this respect. Others, such as George Lakoff and Ronald Langacker, reject this assumption and advocate systems incorporating scalar values and diagrammatic representations.

Linguistic semanticists agree that their goal is to account for the semantic competence of speakers, that is, the knowledge and skills which enable speakers to express and interpret meanings in context. Minimally, this involves accounting for meaning relations and for the compositionality of meaning. Semantics has been influenced by many adjacent fields, including philosophy and logic, psychology, anthropology, and artificial intelligence studies. Within generative linguistics, semantics occupies an oddly marginal place due to the Chomskyan view that the most interesting properties of the language faculty are syntactic, not semantic.

Semantics is often treated as a predominantly theoretical pursuit, with many introductory texts devoting their attention to theories about the nature of meaning in the abstract, such as reference-based theories, the use theory, the stimulus–response theory, conceptualist theories, Platonism, structuralism and semiotic approaches. The emphasis of this article, however, is on methodologies for empirical investigation.

II. CLASSICAL PRINCIPLES

The classical principles for definition were established by Aristotle. First, a good definition must be framed in words which are simpler and more easily understood than the word being defined. Second, no word can be used in a definition whose own definition depends on the word being defined. Violating these principles results in the faults of obscurity and circularity. Third, a good definition must correctly predict the range of use of the word defined, being neither too broad nor too narrow. Definitions which do no meet this criterion lack descriptive adequacy.

Conforming to these principles is no easy matter, and conventional dictionaries abound with violations. The Macquarie Dictionary, for instance, defines *demand* as *claim as a right* or *ask for with authority,* though *claim, right,* and *authority* are no less obscure than *demand.* On investigating further in the same dictionary, circularity quickly comes to light: *claim* is itself defined in terms of *demand.* Defining (or, pseudo-defining) words in circular or obscure terms accomplishes nothing, since it fails to make meaning explicit and intelligible.

A simple example of a descriptive inadequacy is *bachelor: unmarried man,* because this definition predicts a range of application which is too broad (priests and widowers are not bachelors). Definitions can also be too narrow. For instance, neither of the Macquarie Dictionary's definitions for *demand* predicts that a mugger saying *Give me all your cash or you're dead* qualifies as a *demand.*

III. COMPONENTIAL ANALYSIS

Though the work summarized in this section makes use of similar techniques and methods of representation, a fuller treatment would distinguish at least three trends: a European school beginning with Louis Hjemslev and running through to Algirdas Greimas, Bernard Pottier, and Eugenio Coseriu, an anthropological tradition begun by Floyd Lounsbury and Harold Conklin, and a syntactically oriented trend found in American generativism, notably with Jerrold Katz and Ray Jackendoff, and in the early work of George Lakoff and James McCawley.

A. Principles and Basic Approach

Underpinning componential analysis (henceforth, CA) is the structuralist principle that things do not exist in themselves but in relation to one another, as parts of an overall system. For a structuralist, the meaning of a word is the totality of its possible relations with other words.

CA begins by comparing and contrasting words within a semantic field. A notation of semantic features or components is devised to summarize the similarities and contrasts. Such analyses are not intended to be exhaustive. Only that part of the meaning is captured which is necessary to account for the meaning relations within the semantic field at hand. (Some analysts admit the existence of additional supplementary or distinguishing features, but these are regarded as secondary in importance.) The examples in (1) are from the semantic fields of human stage-of-life terms and items of furniture for sitting on.

(1a)	*man*	[+ADULT, +MALE]
	woman	[+ADULT, −MALE]
	boy	[−ADULT, +MALE]
	girl	[−ADULT, −MALE]
(1b)	*chair*	[+BACK, +SINGLE PERSON]
	stool	[−BACK, +SINGLE PERSON]
	bench	[±BACK, −SINGLE PERSON]

Relations between semantic fields can be accommodated by means of additional features. For instance, the similarities and differences between *man, woman, boy, girl,* on the one hand, and *stallion, mare, colt, filly,* on the other, could be captured by adding the features HUMAN or EQUINE, respectively, to the analyses in (1a).

In (1), the features constitute an unordered "bundle," but for many other cases it is necessary to specify what individual features apply to. An analysis like *father* = [+PARENT, +MALE] would not bring out that fatherhood is a one-way relationship between two individuals. For this purpose, CA uses variables, bracketing and logical symbols such as "&" (conjunction) and "=" (identity), some borrowed from the predicate calculus, a system of formal logic. These provide a kind of syntax for componential representation. Some simplified examples follow.

(2)		
	X is *father of* Y:	X[+MALE, PARENT OF (Y)].
	X is *mother of* Y:	X[−MALE, PARENT OF (Y)].
	X is *brother of* Y:	X[+MALE] & PARENT OF(X) = PARENT OF (Y)
	X is *sister of* Y:	X[−MALE] & PARENT OF (X) = PARENT OF (Y)
	X is *grandfather of* Y:	X[+MALE] & X[PARENT OF(PARENT OF (Y)]
	X is *grandmother of* Y:	X[−MALE] & X[PARENT OF (PARENT OF (Y)]

Propositions may function as arguments. In *Max caused the cat to die,* both *Max* and *the cat to die* are arguments of the predicate *cause,* even though *the cat to die* is itself a proposition with its own internal structure. In CA terms, *kill* is often described as the same in meaning as *cause to die.* As shown in (3), this portrays *kill* and *die* as standing in the same semantic relationship that obtains between pairs like *melt* (transitive) and *melt* (intransitive), and *break* (transitive) and *break* (intransitive), an analysis with some intuitive appeal.

(3)		
	X *kills* Y:	X[CAUSE([(Y)DIE])]
	X *melts* Y:	X[CAUSE([(Y)MELT])]
	X *breaks* Y:	X[CAUSE([(Y)BREAK])]

The breakdown in (3) can be carried further. Arguably, *die, melt,* and *break* all share the component [BECOME]; *die* also contains [−ALIVE], *melt* also contains [LIQUID], and so on. Example (4) shows, in simplified form, how the relationship between converse antonyms like *give* and *take* can be analyzed.

(4)		
	X *gives* Y to Z	X[CAUSE([(Z)HAVE(Y)])]
	X *takes* Y from Z	X[CAUSE([(Z)NOT HAVE(Y)])]

Sophisticated CA can become quite complex, as shown by the examples below, which are current in the literature. (5) is for the transitive verb *climb,* (6) for the verb *chase.* Notice that these employ labeled bracketing and nodes, devices intended to make it possible to effect a mapping between semantic and syntactic (phrase) structure. (In (5), the predicate GO is written preceding its arguments, following the ordering convention of predicate calculus.)

(5) *climb:* $[_{\text{Event}}\ \text{GO}(\ [_{\text{Thing}}]_i,\ [_{\text{Path}}\ \text{TO}\ (\ [_{\text{Place}}\ \text{TOP-OF}\ [_{\text{Thing}}]_j]\ )]\ )\ ]$

(6) *chase:*

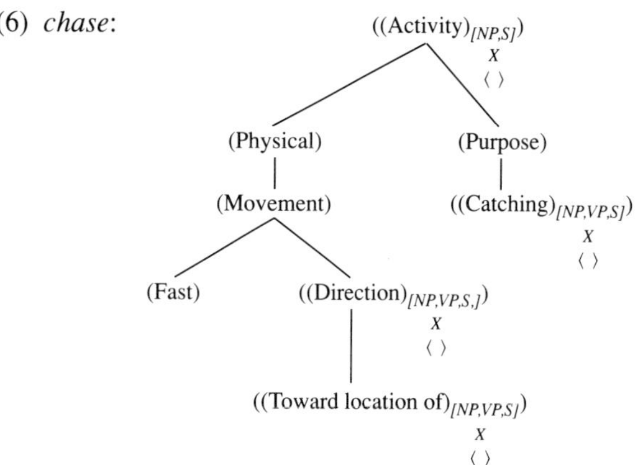

CA enables an explicit account of meaning relations. For instance, that *give* and *take* are converses, that *stallion* and *mare* are hyponyms of *horse,* that *kill, melt,* and *break* are felt intuitively to belong to the same "natural class" (causative verbs). Furthermore, assuming a procedure for combining the meanings of individual words, CA will be able to account for the contradictory nature of *my mother is a man,* for the entailment relationship between *I killed him* and *he died,* and so on.

CA can illuminate differences in meaning structure between languages. The Yankunytjatjara language of Central Australia has a classificatory kin system, in which the word *mama* applies not only to one's father, but also to his brothers, male cousins, wife's sisters' husbands, and so on. Similarly, *ngunytju* takes in not only one's mother, but her sisters, female cousins, husband's brother's wives, and so on. Clearly, there is a logical principle at work, which is arguably captured in (7).

(7)		
	X is Y's *mama:*	X[KIN, +MALE, +SENIOR] & X[LINEAL(Y)] & X[GENERATION: +1(Y)]
	X is Y's *ngunytju:*	X[KIN, −MALE, +SENIOR] & X[LINEAL(Y)] & X[GENERATION: +1(Y)]

Here the feature LINEAL contrasts with COLLATERAL; GENERATION is a multi-valued feature showing how the generation level of the individual stands in relation to oneself. In this way unitary meanings can be attributed to the Yankunytjatjara words and the structural dimensions of the system clearly laid bare.

B. Problems with Componential Analysis

The most serious critique of CA concerns its metalanguage. Componential symbols like [HUMAN],

[MALE], [ADULT], [CAUSE], [NOT], and [PARENT] must be identical in meaning to the corresponding English words, for two reasons. First, the representations can only be understood on the basis of the English words; second, the analyses can only be tested and supported by reference to judgments about what is and is not acceptable in ordinary language. (If [MALE] did not mean the same as English *male,* the anomaly of *male woman* could not be explained from the analysis of *woman* as: [-MALE, ADULT].) The technical metalanguage of CA is therefore a disguised subset of ordinary language.

This situation leaves CA open to charges of obscurity and circularity. The concept of *parents,* for instance, is more complex than either *father* or *mother,* and presumably demands explication in terms of them, e.g., *X's parents = X's father and mother*. This means the analyses in (1a) are circular. Similarly, it is impossible to explicate the complex and obscure notions of *lineal descent* and *generation* without drawing on the concepts of *father* and *mother*. This undermines the attractiveness of (7), which was intended to free our interpretation of the Yankunytjatjara concepts from reliance on these English terms.

A second metalanguage objection is that CA makes no attempt to standardize the inventory of semantic features or to constrain its size. Notwithstanding, it is questionable whether the componential technique could ever provide a comprehensive analysis of the entire vocabulary of a language, because it proves impossible to apportion all lexical meanings into clearly delimited semantic fields.

A third criticism is that the descriptive corpus of CA remains extremely limited, despite the approach having been extant for over 50 years, and much of it is of low descriptive adequacy. (An analysis equating bachelor with *unmarried man* is a standard example in the CA literature. Finally, CA can be criticised on account of its overly cut-and-dried nature. Since a given feature must either be present or absent, there is no obvious way to accommodate the apparent "fuzziness" or vagueness of many words.

IV. COGNITIVE SEMANTICS

Under this heading are treated theorists who seek psychologically realistic models of meaning, often based on perception and denying any sharp break between knowledge of language and knowledge about the world. The leading theorists are George Lakoff and Ronald Langacker.

A. Prototypes, Basic-Level Concepts and Metaphor

In seminal work, psychologist Eleanor Rosch established the existence of prototype effects, the phenomenon whereby some members of a category are more central and more salient than others. Rosch asked people to rate items on how well they exemplified categories such as *furniture, fruit, vehicle, bird, toy,* and *clothing*. People rate *robin* and *chair* as very good examples of *bird* and *furniture,* for instance, whereas *penguin* and *telephone* rate as poor examples. Asked to list members of a category, people list higher-rated items earlier than lower-rated ones. They make more rapid judgments on category membership about higher-rating items than lower-rated ones. It is tempting to conclude from such effects, which have also been found in relation to concrete objects, speech acts, colors, and many other areas, that categorization is inherently fuzzy and that meanings cannot be faithfully portrayed in clear or absolute terms. [*See* CATEGORIZATION.]

Cognitive semantics (henceforth, CS) rejects the basic premise of componential analysis, i.e., that meanings can be characterized in a set of necessary and sufficient conditions. Insofar as attributes of meaning can be identified at all, CS is inclined to see them either as continuous variables or as factors in a network of "family resemblance"; meanings, in the CS view, have no clear boundaries.

CS also diverges from its predecessors on the nature of the relationship between words in a semantic field and the superordinate or generic term which covers them all; for instance, the relationship between *apple, orange,* and *banana,* on the one hand, and *fruit* on the other. CA assumes that it is the specific terms which are more complex; that each individual fruit contains the general component FRUIT plus individual components differentiating one fruit from another. CS rejects this, arguing that *apple, orange,* and *banana* are "basic level concepts," closer to concrete experience, acquired earlier by children, and conceptually simpler than more abstract generic concepts. A good deal of psychological research appears to support this conclusion.

The role of metaphor in language and cognition is another powerful theme in CS. Ordinary speech abounds in conventionalized metaphors, such as the following (from the semantic domain of anger): *to blow one's top, get hot under the collar, get steamed up, explode*. It has been argued that expressions like these follow from implicit "conceptual metaphors," such as ANGER IS THE HEAT OF LIQUID IN A CONTAINER.

The role of metaphor goes far beyond this, however. Many proponents of CS see metaphor as a fundamental faculty of the mind, enabling the creation of abstract concepts, through imaginative projection, from basic-level ones. It is argued that the relatively abstract semantic domains of time and cognition are modeled on the concrete experiences of movement and perception. In apparent support of this, studies of semantic change show that future tense morphemes often originate as movement verbs, and that words for thinking often start out as perception verbs. As well, there is systematic polysemy between the relevant domains in many languages. In English, for instance, one can speak of the future and the past as *ahead* and *behind*, and use the verb *see* in a cognitive sense, as in *I see what you mean*.

B. Scenarios, Fuzzy Sets, and Image-Schemata

There are numerous descriptive and analytical concepts under development in this rapidly changing field. Almost universally accepted in one form or another is the notion that some meanings incorporate elaborate "scenarios" or "scripts," with a narrative-like structure and a cast of dramatis personae. George Lakoff and Zoltán Kövecses' influential analysis of English *anger* is a five-stage scenario involving the Self and a Wrongdoer. The scenario also makes use of "scales of intensity" and makes reference to physiological reactions. The first two stages are shown in (8). Subsequent stages portray an attempt to control the anger, a loss of control leading to an outbreak of angry behavior, and a final stage of retribution such that the intensity of the retribution balances that of the offense, and the angry disappears.

(8) *Stage 1—Offending Event:* Wrongdoer offends S. Wrongdoer is a fault. The offending event displeases S. The intensity of the offense outweighs the intensity of the retribution (which equals zero at this point), thus creating an imbalance. The offense causes anger to come into existence.
Stage 2—Anger: Anger exists. S experiences physiological effects (heat, pressure, agitation). Anger exerts force on the Self to attempt an act of retribution.

Cognitive scenarios do not break completely with CA insofar as they are still composed of discrete (word-like) elements. Other modes of representation, however, resort to scalar values in an attempt to model variability in word use. A much-cited study by Linda Coleman and Paul Kay suggested that the cognitive schema underlying *lie* has the three components shown in (9). Although each of these is dichotomous, they are logically independent, so that overall membership in the category *lie* is a gradient phenomenon. For instance, standard social lines like *How nice to see you!,* which satisfy conditions (a) and (b) but not (c), are on this view literally "partial lies." Partial category membership can be formalized within a mathematical system known as "fuzzy set theory."

(9) Components of *lie:*
  (a) The proposition being asserted is false.
  (b) The speaker believes it to be false.
  (c) In uttering the proposition, the speaker intends to deceive the addressee.

A study by William Labov proposed gradient membership not only in the overall category, but also in the constitutive properties. Labov investigated use of *cup, mug, bowl,* and *vase,* in reference to drawings of a range of differently shaped containers, and taking into account the influence of functional settings. He proposed the representation in (10) as a definition of *cup*. Note that the ratio of width to height is a continuous variable (though having an optimal value), and that even the discrete features contribute in a scalar fashion to an overall probability rating.

(10) The term *cup* is used to denote round containers with a ratio of width to depth of $1 \pm r$, where $r \leq r_b$, and $r_b = \alpha_1 + \alpha_2 + \ldots \alpha_v$ and α_i is a positive quality when the feature i is present and 0 otherwise.

Feature 1 = with one handle
2 = made of opaque vitreous material
3 = used for consumption of food
4 = used for the consumption of liquid food
5 = used for consumption of hot liquid food
6 = with a saucer
7 = tapering
8 = circular in cross-section

Cup is used variably to denote such containers with ratios width to depth $1 \pm r$, where $r_b \leq r \leq r_t$ with a probability of

$r_t - r/r_t - r_b$. The quantity $1 \pm r_b$ expresses the distance from the modal value of width to height.

An even greater departure from conventional definition dispenses with propositional representation entirely. Philosopher Mark Johnson, who has worked closely with George Lakoff, believes that meanings derive from the preconceptual structuring of bodily experience into "kinesthetic image-schemata," which are impossible to represent in propositional terms. The concepts *in* and *out,* for instance, are said to have their origin in our kinesthetic apperception of the body as a CONTAINER as we ingest, excrete, inhale, and exhale. This embodied understanding is imaginatively projected into conceptual terms, giving rise to the myriad uses of *in* and *out,* many of which are of an abstract nature, as in particle-verb constructions like *figure out* and *carry out.*

Ronald Langacker is another theorist who uses diagrams to depict meaning structure. He maintains that semantic (including grammatical) structure has its basis in psychological processes such as perceptual scanning, figure–ground organization, and focusing. The examples in (11) are adapted from the work of Langacker's colleague Susan Lindner, who identified these three basic image schemata for the English verb-particle *out.* The label "TR" designates a "trajector" which moves or is oriented with respect to a "landmark" (LR), concepts said to be generalizations of the notions of figure and ground.

(11a) Image schema for *out*$_1$
e.g., *John went out of the room, Pick out the best theory, Drown out the music.*

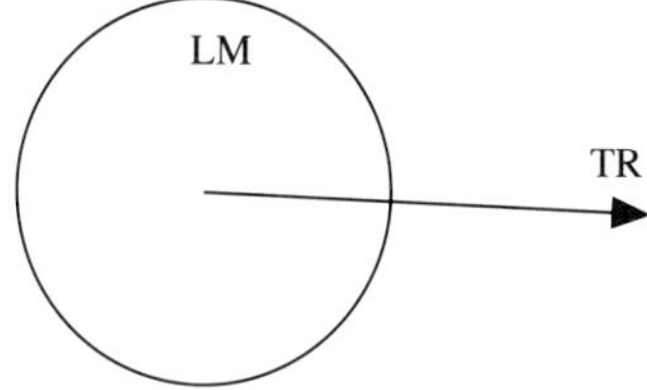

(11b) Image schema for *out*$_2$
e.g., *Pour out the beans, Send out the troops, Write out your ideas.*

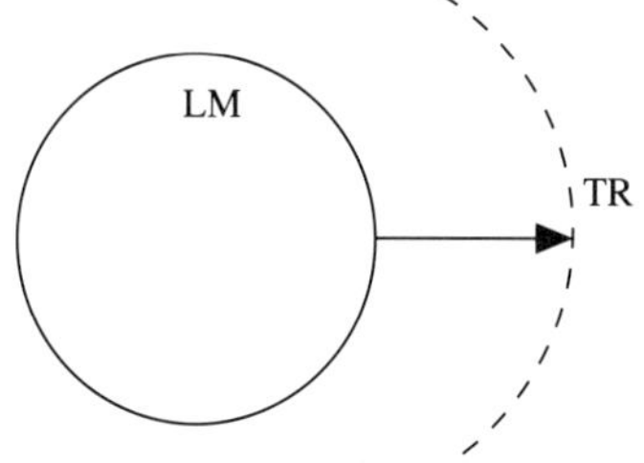

(11c) Image schema for *out*$_3$
e.g., *The train started out for Chicago.*

C. Difficulties and Objections

One difficulty with CS is the proliferation of representational devices and explanatory mechanisms, which are often described in a rather hazy fashion. There is also a dearth of discussion on how they are supposed to interact with one another. It is particularly unclear how diagrams and kinesthetic image-schemata can be made to interface with the propositional aspects of meaning. CS can also be criticized for a tendency to make sweeping assertions about psychological processing on the strength of linguistic evidence alone, without independent empirical support.

Though most cognitive semanticists employ propositional representation to some extent, they seldom consider theoretical and methodological questions of metalanguage and therefore fall easy prey to obscurity and circularity. For instance, the scenario for *anger* cited in (8) employs the terms *offending* and *retribution,* which are as semantically complex as *anger* itself (if not more so), and stand in as much need of explication. Reliance on a complex and obscure metalanguage hampers the articulation of subtle semantic relations. For instance, the complex notion of *offense* obscures the cognitive, judgmental element in *anger.*

The treatment of prototype effects leaves much to be desired. Despite the rhetoric about conceptual structures, the formulations offered in CS studies are often simply statistical models of the experimental data. Moreover, the results of many prototype studies are almost certainly artifacts of the experimental design, the much-used questionnaire on category inclusion being a case in point. If people are asked to rank robins, eagles, chickens, pelicans, and bats on a seven-point scale of birdiness, naturally a scale of birdiness emerges. Nonetheless, speakers have clear intuitions that a bat is definitely not a bird, whereas a pelican definitely is, albeit of a rather atypical kind. Despite the prototype effect, it is arguable that there are certain necessary semantic components to the concept *bird,* including having feathers and a beak, and laying eggs.

It is faulty logic to jump from the existence of a prototype effect to the conclusion that a concept lacks clear conceptual boundaries. Telling evidence of this was a study which asked people to rate numbers for their degree in membership in the categories ODD NUMBER and EVEN NUMBER. The subjects did so willingly, producing graded responses for what are undeniably clear-cut categories.

V. NATURAL SEMANTIC METALANGUAGE

The tradition behind this approach may be called Leibnizian. Many 17th century rationalists believed in "simple ideas," but it was Leibniz who inaugurated empirical investigation of the lexicon as a method for identifying indefinable notions. In the 20th century, this program was revived by Andrzej Bogusławski and Jurij Apresjan. Its main theoretical figure today is Anna Wierzbicka.

A. Principles and Methodology

The natural semantic metalanguage (henceforth, NSM) approach is based on reductive paraphrase, i.e., explication by way of a semantically equivalent expression couched in simpler terms in natural language. The approach rejects logical symbols, technical neologisms, binary features, and the like on the grounds that any such formalism must ultimately be explained and understood through natural language. As practiced by Wierzbicka, the approach is committed to exhaustive analysis in discrete terms. It posits a set of indefinable semantic–conceptual primitives, held to exist as word meanings in natural language. The semantically primitive words and their rules of combination make up a mini-language, known as "natural semantic metalanguage," with the same expressive power as the full natural language. It is hypothesized that the NSMs derived from various languages are semantically equivalent—essentially, that the semantic cores of all human languages coincide.

Since 1972 Wierzbicka has worked against the background of a hypothesized complete inventory of semantic primitives. The current inventory, whose primary English exponents are listed in (12), numbers about three dozen.

(12) Proposed NSM lexico-semantic primitives

SUBSTANTIVES:
I, you, someone, something, people
DETERMINERS AND QUANTIFIERS:
this, the same, other, one, two, many, all
MENTAL PREDICATES:
think, say, know, feel, want
PARTONOMY AND TAXONOMY:
have parts, kind of
META-PREDICATES:
no, if, can, because, like, very
TIME AND PLACE:
when, where, before, after, under, above
ACTIONS AND EVENTS:
do, happen
EVALUATORS AND DESCRIPTORS:
good, bad, big, small

Two main criteria govern the admissibility of a meaning as a semantic primitive: (a) it must resist all attempts at decomposition; (b) it must have a lexical (or morphemic) exponent in every language. It is expected that semantically primitive meanings will be versatile, that is, be found as building blocks in the meanings of many other words. The combined inventory listed above has enormous generative capacity.

Resistance to decomposition can readily be illustrated with the elements *I* and *this*. A putative paraphrase for *I* along the lines of "the person who says this" cannot be valid because the sentence *The person who says this must be a fool* does not mean the same as *I must be a fool*. Attempts to explain the meaning of *this* in terms of "spatial deixis" only obscure it. "Deixis" is hardly a simpler and clearer concept than *this*, and in any case *this* is not an inherently spatial concept at all; one can talk of *this time, this song, this word* just as well as of physical objects.

When checking for lexical exponents of primitives, care is needed to take account of the confounding effects of polysemy and of nonsemantic factors. Common words are often polysemous, so it is to be expected that exponents of semantic primitives will frequently be so. For example: English *feel* is polysemous between its semantically primitive sense (as in *I feel good/bad*), its action sense (*I felt her pulse*), and its cognitive sense (*I feel it's wrong*).

Semantic equivalents may have differing ranges of use in different languages. If in a particular language the exponent of *want* can also mean "love," "like," and "need," then obviously it will be more frequent than its monosemic equivalent in another language. A more subtle factor is how the lexical element figures in the expressive dynamics of the language as a whole. For example, in Yankunytjatjara the exact equivalent of *because* (one sense of the ablative case-marker-*nguṟu*) is not particularly common in ordinary discourse because the language has grammaticized this meaning into a pair of common purposive constructions. Social and cultural factors can also cause range of use differences. For example, Thai *chán* "I" has an extremely narrow range of use because in Thai society references to oneself are generally expected to be accompanied by expressions of humility or inferiority.

Detailed cross-linguistic testing of the proposed natural semantic metalanguage is at a relatively early stage. Nonetheless, studies indicate that the primitive inventory set out above can be isolated in languages as diverse as Japanese, Yankunytjatjara, Ewe (West Africa), French, and Thai, as well as English. Practical semantic work has also been carried out with in the NSM framework in Polish, Russian, Arrernte (Australia), Chinese, and Mbula (PNG), aside from the other languages already mentioned.

B. Reductive Paraphrase Explications

A striking feature of the NSM descriptive corpus is its size and diversity, taking in lexical, grammatical, and illocutionary studies. Much of this work does not stick solely to the minimal metalanguage, however. It is often feasible in the investigation of a particular semantic area to employ terms which, while not absolutely simple, are clearly relatively simpler than the words being defined; for instance, in explicating colors to use the verb *see*. Further, it is often necessary to allow for contextual variation in the form by which a semantically primitive meaning is expressed. For instance, combinations of *someone* with determiner-like elements such as *this* and *the same* sound strange in English and may confuse; in this context the word *person* functions as a semantic equivalent (an "allolex") of *someone*, i.e., the phrases *this person* and *the same person* can be regarded as identical in meaning to the unusual-sounding expressions just mentioned. Similarly, *me* functions as an allolexic variant of *I*, *not* as a variant of *no*, and so on.

Wierzbicka's work in lexical semantics includes speech act verbs, ethnopsychological terms, the names of simple and complex artifacts, colors, mass nouns, kin terms, body parts, natural kinds, functional categories, ideological and value terms, among others. Some examples follow.

(13) presents NSM explications for two negative English emotion words, *angry* and *sad*. In line with what psychologists know as a cognitive view of emotion, they make reference to the experience of interconnected thoughts and wants of certain kinds. They also incorporate aspects of scenario representation, evoking a prototypical situation. The presence of *like* in the framing structures (e.g., *X thinks something like this, X feels like this*) accommodates a degree of indeterminacy in use. Comparing (13a) and (13b) will make the point that NSM explications can capture subtle nuances of meaning, while being directly accessible to the semantic intuitions of native speakers.

According to (13a), anger is prototypically triggered by a negative judgment about something that someone has done. This judgment is coupled with a volitional response: a refusal to accept what has happened and a desire to act. Thus, the attitude of an angry person is active. There is no actual specific action implicated, but the experiencer is aware of a potential impulse to do "something bad" to the culprit. According to (13b), sadness is prototypically triggered by the perception that a bad event has taken place and the wish that things were otherwise. The emotional tone is further established by a wilingness to take action, coupled with the realization that none is possible, which evokes a feeling akin to helplessness and resignation.

13a. X feels angry =
X feels something
sometimes a person thinks something like this:
  this person did something bad
  I don't want this
  I want to do something
  I would want to do something bad to this person
because of all this, this person feels something bad
X feels like this

13b. X feels sad =
X feels something
sometimes a person thinks something like this:
  something bad happened
  I would want: this didn't happen
  if I could, I would do something
  I can't do anything
because of all this, this person feels something bad
X feels like this

An example from the domain of kinship is given in (14), for the English concept *mother*. Interestingly, this combines components of both biology (birth-giver) and social expectation (caregiver). It has been argued in the CS literature that the concept of motherhood does not require a biological component, because of the existence of adoptive mothers and so-called "donormothers," who provide eggs for *in vitro* fertilization. This overlooks the fact that without modifiers the unmarked sense of *mother* is clearly that of birth-giver, and that the expression *the real mother* is confined to birth-giver. It is true that the words *real mother,* and even *mother* itself, can occur in reference to caregiver only, as in *she gave birth to me, but she was never a (real) mother to me,* but there are subtle syntactic and semantic factors to be taken into account; for instance, the difference between *a (real) mother to me* (caregiver) and *my real mother* (birth-giver). Combining both biological and social expectation components paves the way for an explanation of these subtleties. The expected caregiver role also helps account for the use of *mother* in similes (*she was like a mother to me*), and even to explain its secondary meaning in relation to nuns.

(14) X is Y's mother =
before Y was a person
Y was inside X and was like a part of X
because of this people would think:
X wants to do good things for Y
X doesn't want bad things to happen to Y

Perhaps the most challenging and controversial finding of NSM studies is that the semantics of "life-forms" (e.g., *animal, bird, fish*), natural kinds (e.g., *dog, horse, mouse*), and manufactured objects (e.g., *cup, bottle, bicycle*) are astonishingly complex, far more so than the meanings of abstract and relational concepts. Wierzbicka's explications for *cup* and *cat,* for instance, run to over 60 lines each, despite containing many semantically complex terms—verbs like *drink, hold, spill, scratch,* and *jump,* and nouns like *liquid, mouth, hair,* and *hands.* If each such complex term were explicated to the level of primitives, the semantic content of apparently simple words like *cat* and *cup* would appear simply astronomical.

Part of the reason for their Byzantine intricacy is that the proposed explications contain a great deal of knowledge that other theorists would regard as encyclopedic. For example, that *cats* lick themselves to keep clean, that they play with the creatures they catch, that they meow and purr. Wierzbicka's definition of *cup* includes a detailed description of the action-sequence for which a cup is made and even of the prototypical situation of use (by some people sitting around a table sharing tea from a pot). Wierzbicka maintains that all this detail is part of the tacit knowledge contained within the meaning of such words and (unlike many cognitive semanticists) insists that, in principle, there is a boundary between linguistic and encyclopedic knowledge, albeit not positioned where traditional wisdom would have it.

A noteworthy finding of NSM work on manufactured objects is the relative importance of intended function, as opposed to outward physical characteristics. The purpose of a manufactured object unifies what would otherwise be a collection of arbitrary physical properties. The smallish size of a cup , its tapering shape and delicate handle all make sense for a thing designed to be drunk from in sips, set down on a saucer in-between times, and able to refilled when necessary. The larger size of a mug, its cylindrical shape and sturdy base make sense for a thing designed to hold sufficient liquid not to need refilling and to be suitable for use anywhere, so to speak, including being held in the hand for long periods. Elaborate specifications like this have some affinity with the conviction of cognitive semanticists that ordinary words are embedded within complex cultural scenarios.

As mentioned, other NSM semantic work has addressed morphosyntactic phenomena (e.g., expressive derivation, passives, causatives, complementation) and illocutionary phenomena (e.g., discourse particles, interjections, indirect speech acts, conversational routines). Lately the method has been extended to take in genre structure, speech styles and culture-specific communicative styles.

C. Problems and Difficulties

Though the gargantuan size and complexity of reductive paraphrase explications strikes some as literally impossible to believe, such reactions carry little force in themselves. Similar responses no doubt came from many who peered through the newly invented telescope or microscope.

Legitimate doubts center on the viability of a universal semantic metalanguage. It is far from certain that all the proposed semantically primitive meanings can be expressed by lexical means in all languages. Though decisive counterexamples are not known at this point, it is known that lexical exponents underlying the part–whole relationship and taxonomy are difficult to locate in some languages. Contrary to the predictions of the NSM hypothesis, it is sometimes claimed that there are languages in which it is impossible to express a purely hypothetical meaning or to distinguish clearly between temporal and causal notions (i.e., to distinguish between *if* and *when,* or between *after* and *because*). Such reports are usually anecdotal and based on scanty data, however.

As with the proposed NSM lexicon, so too with its syntax. The criticism has frequently been made of Wierzbicka's work that she has failed to identify the elementary combinatorial patterns envisaged for the lexical primitives, and that her definitions often take advantage of English-specific syntax. These criticisms are well-founded. The truth is that NSM work on syntactic patterns is only now beginning in real earnest.

VI. MEANING–TEXT MODEL

The meaning-text model (henceforth, MTM) is the formal framework of the Russian linguists Jurij Apresjan, Igor Mel'čuk, and Alexander Zholkovsky (known as the Moscow School, though the latter two are now based in North America). The MTM aims to provide an integrated description not only of the meanings of all the words and fixed phrases in a language, but of their syntactic and collocational properties as well. The goal is to enable "automatic paraphrasing," whereby given any sentence all its synonymous and near-synonymous equivalents could be produced. This would pave the way for automatic translation between languages.

A. Semantic Approach of the MTM

The Moscow School pursues propositional-style representation and recognizes the need for a standardized, non-arbitrary metalanguage. Though their early work in the late sixties sought to identify semantic primitives, they have since become less interested in the fine details of semantic metalanguage. Instead, they have concentrated on describing large sections of the lexicon, a trend pioneered by Apresjan's work on Russian and continued in the "Explanatory-Combinatorial Dictionaries" (ECDs) of Russian and French being produced by Mel'čuk and colleagues.

In the MTM, the meaning of a lexical unit is conceived of as a "semantic network," in which a set of simpler meanings are combined using a logical syntax based on the predicate calculus. Such networks also can be stated in a simplified fashion, resembling lexicographic definitions as in (15) (note that each of these applies to only one of several senses of the word defined). Notice that the lexical unit being defined is presented in a specified syntactic frame.

(15) a. X reveals Y to Z = X immediately causes that Y becomes known to Z
b. X improves = The value of the quality of X becomes higher
c. X escapes from Y through Z = X, being trapped in Y, moves out of Y via Z.

A key MTM principle is that a lexical unit and its decomposition should be mutually substitutable without any change of meaning, according to the judgment of native speakers (though stylistic differences are unavoidable). Thus, the decompositions above should be substitutable for all ordinary uses of *reveal, improve,* and *escape* in the relevant senses.

Though controlled and standardized, the metalanguage of the ECDs is not supposed to consist primarily of primitives. The use of intermediate constituents in a gradual process of semantic decomposition is considered desirable both for greater manageability and to make the semantic links between lexical items explicit. Examples (16a) and (16b) illustrate further decompositions of *becomes* and *known.* These should be substitutable into higher-level definitions, so that (16c), for example, should be synonymous with (15a).

(16) a. Y becomes W = Y begins to be W
b. Y is known to Z = information "Y" is in Z's psyche
c. X reveals Y to Z = X immediately causes that the information "Y" begins to be in Z's psyche.

B. Difficulties and Objections

In the quest for automatic paraphrasing, the MTM aims not at exact synonymy, but at an approximate "quasi-synonymy," whereby a single sentence could have hundreds or even thousands of semantic "equivalents." Since speakers can differentiate much subtler meaning differences than this, it can be argued that the MTM linguists have set their sights too low to faithfully model ordinary semantic competence. Compromising on semantic accuracy also undermines substitutability as a validity test for semantic decompositions.

The claim that the semantic metalanguage used in the ECDs is free of circularity and obscurity is open to question; (16) b, for instance, embodies the dubious claim that *information* and *psyche* are semantically simpler than *known*. As they themselves recognize, the MTM linguists will ultimately have to settle on a set of semantic primitives and show how their putative intermediate units can be constructed from the primitives. Even so, their work is remarkable for its thoroughness, its consistency, and its scope.

VII. SEMANTICS, COGNITION, AND BEHAVIOR

It is important to recognize that expressing meanings through language is itself human behavior (indeed, pre-eminently so) and therefore deserving of study in its own right in the panoply of the human sciences. It is wrong to look at language, and cultural phenomena generally, solely from the point of view of the possible explanatory value in relation to other behavior. This is not to deny that insights from semantics may be of value and interest to adjacent disciplines, particularly cultural anthropology and psychology. Two questions of great significance for the human sciences generally are: What do languages have in common semantically and conceptually? And how do they differ?

It is customary in linguistics to distinguish between substantive and formal universals, which concern the identities of individual elements and the nature of their combinatorial relationships, respectively.

As for substantive semantic universals, while Charles Fillmore, James McCawley, Jerrold Katz, Alexander Zholkovsky, and Ray Jackendoff (among others) have all hazarded probable examples at one time or another, their suggestions have been sketchy and remain untested cross-linguistically. The set of conceptual primitives proposed by Anna Wierzbicka is by far the most detailed and testable hypothesis in the literature, but it is too early to anticipate to what extent it will hold up to rigorous cross-linguistic scrutiny.

Taking account of findings from the study of grammatical typology, it does seem likely however that the semantic systems of all languages will be found to share a reasonable number of concepts and distinctions, such as first and second person pronouns, a distinction between persons and things, deixis, quantification, the concepts of identity ("sameness") and of similarity, ways of expressing volition ("wanting"), cognitive notions, negation, concepts akin to those of agency ("doing") and event ("happening"), notions of time and place ("when" and "where"), systems of taxonomic and part–whole classification, and terms of evaluation and dimension. To this list could be added, for the majority of languages at least, some concepts of causation, the hypothetical and the potential.

Little is known about formal semantic universals, except at a very general level, for instance, that compositionality is found in all languages and that it is possible to form referring expressions (i.e., the equivalents of noun-phrases, in meaning, if not in structure) in all languages. The X-bar theory of phrase-structure may be seen as a hypothesis about the syntactic compositionality of meaning. Two lexical fields where valuable cross-linguistic work has been done, however, are those of color terminology (Brent Berlin, Paul Kay, and colleagues) and ethnobiology (Cecil Brown and colleagues).

The question of semantic differences between languages bears directly on the Sapir–Whorf hypothesis, viz., that languages influence thinking and perception. Presumably, language-specific concepts and distinctions must mediate a speaker's experience of the physical and social world, and play a role in cognition to some extent. But to what extent? In what domains? What is the relative contribution of lexical, grammatical, illocutionary, and discourse semantics? How do linguistic and cultural knowledge interrelate, if indeed it is possible to disentangle them at all? With recent improvements in semantic methodology it is reasonable to believe real progress can be made in the empirical investigation of such questions. Awareness of semantic differences between languages can also help minimize ethnocentrism, particularly anglocentrism, in cross-cultural studies. In this respect, there is a valuable interchange opening up between semantics and the emerging discipline of "cultural psychology," as seen in the recent works of Jerome Bruner and Richard Schweder. All in all, perhaps the most exciting aspect of the study of semantics is its potential to contribute to progress on problems of common concern across the human sciences.

Bibliography

Allan, K. (1986). "Linguistic Meaning," 2 vols. Routledge & Kegan Paul, London/New York.

Apresjan, J. D. (1992). "Lexical Semantics: User's Guide to Contemporary Russian Vocabulary." [English translation of "Leksičeskaja Semantika—Sinonimečeskie sredstva jazyka." Nauka, Moscow. 1974.] Karoma, Ann Arbor, MI.

Eco, U., Santambrogio, M., and Violi, P. (1988). "Meaning and Mental Representations." Indiana University Press, Bloomington.

Goddard, C., and Wierzbicka, A. (Eds) (1994). "Semantic and Lexical Universals—Theory and Empirical Findings." John Benjamins, Amsterdam.

Jackendoff, R. (1990). "Semantic Structures." MIT Press, Cambridge.

Lakoff, G. (1987). "Women, Fire and Dangerous Things." Chicago University Press, Chicago.

Langacker, R. W. (1987). "Foundations of Cognitive Grammar," Vol. 1. Stanford University Press, Stanford, CA.

Mel'čuk, I. A. (with a lexicographic team). (1988). "Dictionnaire Explicatif et Combinatoire du Français Contemporain. Recherches Lexico-Sémantiques." Vol II. Presses de l'Universite de Montreal, Montreal.

Taylor, J. R. (1989). "Linguistic Categorization. Prototypes in Linguistic Theory." Clarendon, Oxford.

Wierzbicka, A. (1992). "Semantics, Culture, and Cognition." Oxford University Press, Oxford.

Sensation Seeking

Jim H. Patton
Baylor University

Glossary

Bordom susceptibility An aversion to repetitive experience, routine work, or predictable people with a reaction of restless discontent when unavoidably exposed to such experience.

Disinhibition The need to seek release in uninhibited social activities with or without the aid of alcohol.

Experience seeking Seeking of novel experiences through travel, music, art, and a spontaneous, nonconforming life style with similarly inclined persons.

Sensation seeking The motivation or need for a variety of sensations and the willingness to take physical and social risks in order to experience this range of sensations.

Thrill and adventure seeking A desire to engage in physical activities involving elements of speed, danger, novelty, and defiance of gravity (e.g., parachuting, scuba diving).

THE TRAIT OF sensation seeking (SS) takes its definition from almost 30 years of research conducted by Marvin Zuckerman in the area of optimal arousal or stimulation level. Sensation seeking, as originally conceptualized by Dr. Zuckerman, described only the "sheer quantity and intensity" of external stimulation sought by an individual. Subsequent factor analytical work revealed that a more precise definition of sensation seeking would include the need for varied, novel, and complex stimulation. Therefore, a more contemporary definition of sensation seeking would be the motivation or need for a variety of sensations and the willingness to take physical and social risks in order to experience this range of sensations. According to Zuckerman, sensations from such activities as skydiving, scuba diving, motorcycle riding, and other activities involving speed and risk, provide sensations that are primary reinforcers for people who score high on Zuckerman's Sensation Seeking Scale.

I. THEORETICAL AND HISTORICAL BACKGROUND FOR SENSATION SEEKING

A. Evolutionary Underpinnings of Sensation Seeking

Zuckerman draws heavily on evolutionary theory and comparative psychology to reach the conclusion that there is considerable variation in animals' levels of exploration, approaching novel stimuli, and levels of risky play. Zuckerman believes that the tendency to engage in these activities is, to a large extent, biologically determined for any one individual. There is mounting evidence that Zuckerman may indeed be correct. Ultimately Zuckerman believes that SS is related to reproductive success. He reasons that in order for animals to survive they must command enough territory to sustain themselves and engage in mating behavior. When resources become scarce in one area animals must have a willingness to explore new territories in search of new sources of sustenance. Indeed, the animal who may have explored novel territory before resources become scarce would have the advantage since time would be saved in time of stress. The same logic applies to mating; those animals most willing to explore the possibilities of new mates would be more likely to meet with success. However, those animals who endured too many risks in search of resources or mates run a greater risk of meeting with misfortune and would likely pass fewer copies of their genes into future generations. So, there is always a trade off between sensation seeking in the service of reproductive success and danger to the individual organism which might remove him or her from the gene pool. In Zuckerman's view, therefore, sensation seeking is an instinctive drive in the service of reproductive success.

B. Instincts, Needs, and Drives

This notion of instinct influencing human as well as animal behavior is not a new one. It was popularized in the 1920s. Some objected to the notion of instinct and Woodworth first offered the construct of "drive" as a substitute. Since that time various categorizations and hierarchies of drives have been postulated by various theorists. These various drives are usually seen as the result of some physiological deficit (e.g., hunger, thirst) and impel behavior until they are reduced usually by some consumatory act. For instance, you become hungry (drive) because your blood sugar is low (physiological deficit). When you eat (consummatory act) your blood sugar goes up and you feel less hungry (deficit and drive reduced). Some theorists saw problems with the use of drive as a theoretical construction because of its necessary dependence on a physiological deficit for activation. The notion of need, as elaborated by Henry Murray, is very close to the notion of drive but avoids some of the theoretical objections. Needs tend to do more than energize behaviors, as drives do, needs also direct behaviors toward certain particular goals. In addition, needs may include a cognitive/mental component that allows an organism to express a need driven behavior even when the physiological deficit relating to drive is absent. For example, John may choose to eat, because he likes the taste of chocolate, and is in the presence of chocolate, even if he is not hungry. In other words, John is not hungry, that is, driven to eat the chocolate by a physiological deficit. Rather, the chocolate is available and John especially likes it. So, he eats. Robert, on the other hand, might just as well avoid eating the chocolate under the same circumstances if perhaps he was on a diet. Robert might like the chocolate as well as John yet pass it by because his "need" to be thin takes precedence over his affinity for the chocholate. As you can see, the concept of need allows for a more active decision making role on the part of the organism.

For our purposes it is important to note that one grouping of Murray's needs includes those that are directed toward the enjoyment of sensations. Like other researchers, Zuckerman has drawn upon Murray's theoretical underpinning to explore an area of personality of interest to him and to develop a test to measure a latent trait, sensation seeking, of importance to understanding human behavior.

C. Inhibition and Arousal

Zuckerman's theory also depends heavily upon Pavlov's work. Pavlov claimed that organisms differ in terms of the type of nervous system they possess. He conceived of two nervous system types, one a weak, shy nervous system, prone to nervousness and shyness, while the other was a strong, gregarious type. In a sense, to seek environmental stimulation is to overcome inhibitions to the contrary. Seeking out stimulation in the face of physical or social danger often requires disinhibition of protective tendencies. Some organisms seem to find it very difficult to overcome the anxiety barriers generated by social or physical danger. Other organisms seem to "tread where angels fear to go." Cattell and Eysenck have termed the tendency toward being disinhibited in social situations extroversion, one pole of the continuum of an introversion–extroversion personality dimension. Introverts are individuals who shy away from environmental interaction while extroverts do exactly the opposite. Eysenck has recently noted the relatedness of his theory of extroversion to theories of arousal and the physiological underpinnings thereof. Sensation seeking is most probably an important component or corollary of extroversion. [*See* EXTRAVERSION–INTROVERSION.]

Another corollary of sensation seeking relates to levels of arousal. Since the end of the last century investigators and theoriests have been interested in what constitutes an optimal level of stimulation. Each from our own experience can recall situations where a stimulus at a certain level may be pleasurable yet, when experienced at a different, often more intense, level the stimulus becomes a painful one. Think of music. When your favorite music is experienced through stereo headphones at 50–60 dB it can be stimulating or soothing depending on the character of the music. Additionally, one's attention to the music may drift. One can either focus on the music or let it drift into the background. However, when volume is increased to around 80 dB the music is most difficult to ignore and begins to resemble noise as well as provoke attention. At 120 dB the music is painful and aversive. Organisms exposed to high levels of noise may appear very aroused as they attempt to avoid the aversive stimulus. Freud observed that stimulus intensity can drive internal "intracerebral excitement" or arousal.

Citing the work of Wundt, Freud, Yerkes-Dodson, Hebb, and Duffy as background, Zuckerman reaches the conclusion that there is an optimal range of stimulus contact, intensity, and novelty that is most pleasurable or most conducive to better learning or performance for each individual. In this view individuals may seek stimulation to maintain an optimum level of arousal so as to maximize their pleasure. It is also clear that different levels of arousal may affect performance such as learning efficiency. Interestingly, the level of arousal necessary for optimal learning may vary as a function of the difficulty of the task to be learned. As task difficulty increases less intense stimulation is necessary for optimal learning. For the easiest tasks higher levels of stimulation are necessary. As task difficulty increases the necessary level of stimulation drops off to an optimal intermediate level for the most difficult tasks. When levels of stimulation are too low in relation to task difficulty performance suffers as it does when stimulation levels are too high. Elizabeth Duffy studied several indices of physiological arousal, including EEG, as measures of mental effort. She observed that individuals vary in arousal due to either genetic or environmental factors and that these differences affect their personality or temperament.

Since the late 1940s Hans J. Eysenck has defined personality along three dimensions: introversion vs extroversion, neuroticism or emotional instability vs stability, and psychoticism or tough-minded asocial tendencies vs socialized humaneness. To date the first two dimensions have been much better researched than the third. In the 1960s Eysenck proposed that extroverts have a higher optimal level of stimulation than do introverts. Capitalizing on an increased understanding of how cortical arousal is achieved Eysenck linked his theorizing to differential levels of sensitivity of the brainstem ascending reticular activating system (RAS). The RAS is responsible for modulating the level of cortical arousal, among other things, through a feedback loop system. Stimulation can impact the system from the senses or from the "emotional brain" or limbic system. According to this schema, the introvert would have a very sensitive activating system predisposed to producing a high level of cortical arousal with minimal sensory input. Conversely, the extrovert would need much higher levels of stimulation to gain comparable levels of activation.

In the late 1960s Eysenck began to increasingly emphasize the role of genetics in personality theory. Taking the animal literature as a point of departure Eysenck observed that selective breeding could produce animals of different temperaments. He reasoned that personality traits such as extroversion, and perhaps more narrow traits such as impulsivity or sensation seeking, might have a common or correlated genetic basis. Eysenck realizes that genes code for proteins (e.g., enzymes and receptors), not behavior. However, he maintains that the glands and neurons that use these proteins to produce neuromodulators and hormones, as well as their receptors, may heavily influence behavioral tendencies. Eysenck also realizes the necessary influence of environment. In fact, extreme environmental conditions may outweigh genetic influences. But for most of us, in Eysenck's view, genetics makes a considerable contribution to personality. This is a view shared by many psychologists today—that both genetics and environmental influence are significant, at least equal, contributors to behavioral tendency.

Subsequent research in a number of laboratories has led investigators to believe that people differ in their genetic predisposition to need external stimulation in order to stay aroused. Those who need little stimulation to be optimally aroused (reading might suffice) would be at one end of the continuum. Others who require a constant barrage of varied, novel, and high-intensity external stimulation, say rock climbers, would be at the other end. It may also be the case that the level of stimulation needed to produce optimal learning may in some way be related to psychopathology. For instance, attention-deficit disorder may be the result of under arousal in the context of a classroom learning situation. When arousal is augmented with a stimulant, say Ritalin, learning improves. Level of arousal has also been linked to personality traits such as introversion–extroversion, impulsivity, and sensation seeking by researchers such as Eysenck, Zuckerman, Barratt, Revelle, and their colleagues. Finally, sensation seeking and related personality constructs such as those listed above have been placed in central positions in more global multivariate schemes of personality such as the currently popular "Big Five" structure championed by Goldberg.

II. MEASUREMENT OF SENSATION SEEKING

A. The Sensation Seeking Scale

Zuckerman's theory postulates that there are individuals in our midst who vary in terms of the stimulation they need to negotiate the environment. In order to categorize individuals Zuckerman has composed the Sensation Seeking Scale (SSS). Form V, the lastest version of the SSS, is a 40-item paper-and-pencil forced-choice questionnaire. Items on the SSS separate into four factors:

1. *Thrill and adventure seeking* (*TAS*). Items reflecting a desire to engage in physical activities involving elements of speed, danger, novelty, and defiance of gravity (e.g., parachuting, scuba diving).
2. *Experience seeking* (*ES*). Items reflecting seeking of novel experiences through travel, music, art, and a spontaneous, nonconforming lifestyle with similarly inclined persons.
3. *Disinhibition* (*Dis*). Items describing the need to seek release in uninhibited social activities with or without the aid of alcohol.
4. *Boredom susceptibility* (*BS*). Items reflecting an aversion to repetitive experience, routine work, or predictable people with a reaction of restless discontent when unavoidably exposed to such experience.

The SSS provides an overall score and subscores for each of the factors. Factor, internal, and retest reliability data indicate that the SSS is psychometrically sound and it continues to be refined. The scales are moderately intercorrelated suggesting that they all tap different aspects of a more global factor.

B. Characteristics of Sensation Seekers

Using data from self-report inventories of drug use along with SSS scores researchers have found significant relationships between high scores on the SSS and extent of drug use, particularly marijuana, hashish, amphetamines, and psychedelic drugs. Drug experience typically correlates with all four scales not just the ES scale. In comparative studies with other personality tests it is clear that the SSS most clearly measures the trait most closely correlated with drug use. But cigarette use and alcohol consumption have been related to SS. These relationships are not as clear as those from the drug use data. The alcohol consumption data show that while ethanol consumption is related to high scores on all four scales it is most clearly related to the disinhibition subscale. [*See* SUBSTANCE ABUSE.]

Sensation seekers are different in terms of their sexual experience, thrill seeking, and preference for complexity. Sexual experience in college students and sexual responsiveness, arousability, and frequency in young married women are related to the broad SS trait as measured by the SSS. Sensation seekers participate in a greater variety of heterosexual activities, with more partners. Driving is a readily recognized outlet for thrill seeking in many members of the population. There is a very strong linear relationship between the speeds at which survey respondents reportedly drive on highways having 55 MPH speed limits and all of the SS scales. Sensation seekers have strong preferences for particular types of stimulation. High SS prefer complex as opposed to simple graphic designs when asked to rate designs. High SS persons also prefer complex music such as classical or jazz to more bland popular music. Sensation seekers prefer spicy or sour foods and even prefer novel smiles versus mundane ones.

High sensation seekers are more prone to volunteer for various types of unusual experiments and activities including experiments in sensory deprivation, hypnosis, drug effects, encounter groups, and gambling instruction. Sensation seekers seem to prefer novel activities. Interestingly, in experiments that are boring or monotonous (e.g., sensory deprivation, meditation) sensation seekers are more likely to drop out early or seek additional stimulation. However, in experiments involving social interaction sensation seekers seem to enjoy themselves while low sensation seekers seem to show anxiety, often withdraw, and report not liking the experience. Sensation seekers who volunteer for gambling experiments tend to bet more and at higher odds. Finally, sensation seekers who take scuba lessons tend to stay under longer and dive deeper on their first free dive than others. Groups such as volunteer salvage divers and volunteer firefighters have even higher SS scores. The TAS subscale was predictive of how far female subjects would go in looking over an exposed parapet 16 stories high and has also predicted fear reactions in other phobic situations such as exposure to snakes.

Zuckerman has used the behavior and physiological reactions of high and low sensation seekers to develop a model for risk-taking. High sensation seekers generally appraise the risk in a situation as less than low sensation seekers. Given equal levels of risk appraisal high SS anticipate more positive arousal whereas low SS anticipate feelings of fear or anxiety. Zuckerman theorizes that the relative balance between the states of fear vs sensation seeking, as risk increases, determines for any one individual whether that individual will engage in the activity at hand.

Scores on the SSS have been correlated with other personality tests. Those who score high on the SSS also tend to score high on Eysenck's extroversion scale. In fact high SSS scores are more reflective of the "impulsive" component of extroversion than the "sociable" component. Sensation seekers tend to be nonconformists and risk takers guided more by their selfish interests than by societal convention or the needs or opinions of others. In persons with low sensation seeking scores, as activities get more risky anxiety increases. However, in high SS individuals, as risk increases anxiety or fearfulness decreases. Sensation seeking increases as a function of age until adolescence, then declines from the 20s on. Older persons tend to score lower on Thrill and Adventure Seeking and Disinhibition. Males generally score higher than females especially on the Disinhibition scale but also on the Thrill and Adventure Seeking scales while scores on Experience Seeking are equivalent.

Sensation seeking has been correlated with a number of biological variables, lending credence to Zuckerman's claim of heritability. In a series of experiments Zuckerman and two biologically oriented researchers, Monte S. Buchsbaum and Dennis L. Murphy, articulated the biological phenomena associated with SS. This research showed a strong convergence of both animal and human research between SS and low monoamine oxidase (MAO) levels, augmenting of the average evoked sensory potential, and levels of gonadal hormones. According to Zuckerman and his colleagues, the behavioral correlates of these variables are: hypersexuality, social dominance, sociability, aggression, exploration of novel situations, play, and general activity. In humans, manic-depressive tendencies and psychopathy are associated with both SS and its biological correlates. These results are strongly supportive of Zuckerman's claim that SS is a genetically influenced trait or temperament.

C. The Place of Sensation Seeking in a Global Personality Theory

Personality researchers have provided evidence that the "Big Five" personality constructs represent an adequate structure for describing the most basic major dimensions of personality. The Big Five are (I) Extroversion or Surgency, (II) Agreeableness, (III) Conscientiousness, (IV) Emotional Stability, and (V) Culture or Intellect or Openness to Experience. Researchers such as Tupes, Christal, Digman, Costa, McCrae, Goldberg, and Hough have been major contributors in this area. Researchers have found that the Big Five model has held up across language domains, using both adjectival and questionnaire-type assessments, and across methods of analysis. However, as Hough observes, while the Big Five may represent the superstructure of personality, it does not have enough fine grain detail to adequately predict such behaviors as job success. Some personality researchers have criticized the Big Five noting that the trait domain underlying the Big Five superfactors is complex and is not easily fit by a consistent set of superfactors. In any case, the first three Big Five factors seem the most stable. Sensation seeking fits into Factor I: Extroversion or Surgency. Some facets of Factor I include: talkative, extroverted, assertive, forward, daring, flamboyant, sociable, zestful, dominant, active, persistent, mischievous, confident, bold, uninhibited, flirtatious, explosive, adventurous, spontaneous, opportunistic, and exhibitionistic. These are easily recognizable correlates of sensation seeking.

However, because some aspects of personality overlap and there are several schemes one might use to divide up the personality trait domain, one could find components of sensation seeking loading on other factors. The important thing to realize is that sensation seeking attributes load heavily on Factor I and that this factor is one of the major descriptors of human personality. This is consistent with Zuckerman's assertion that sensation seeking is an important biologically relevant and determined personality trait. While sensation seeking and Extroversion or Surgency are not identical, sensation seeking is a major component of Factor I and therefore important in any dimensional theory of personality, no matter what the name a particular researcher assigns this factor. This factor is also stable across a number of investigational domains mentioned above. If this were not so, there would be considerable reason to doubt claims made for the biological relevance and determinism of this Extroversion or Surgency factor. [*See* TRAITS.]

III. BIOLOGICAL CORRELATES OF SENSATION SEEKING

A. Orienting Responses

An orienting response (OR) is a physiological and behavioral reaction to a stimulus of moderate intensity. Pavlov was the first to use the term in his animal research and believed that the OR was an analog of human curiosity. The OR can also be considered a measure of focused attention that is at maximal strength at levels of intermediate arousal. If a stimulus which initially elicits an OR is repeated several times the intensity of the OR diminishes, a phenomenon called habituation. A defensive reaction (DR) occurs when an aversive stimulus is presented and the subject wishes to avoid that stimulus. The assumption is that sensation seekers have a higher curiosity or willingness to investigate moderately intense novel or complex stimuli. Therefore, sensation seekers should have stronger orienting responses to these stimuli. This is in fact what Zuckerman and others have found when they compared subjects with various scores on the SSS for strength of orienting response. High sensation seekers had larger galvanic skin responses in response to novel visual and auditory stimuli. Both high and low sensation seekers habituated at the same rate to repeated stimuli, however. In fact when several levels of sensory intensity are included in an experiment, the high SS subjects respond with a stronger OR to the moderately intense stimuli and with a DR to very intense stimuli. Low SS subjects form DRs to both the moderate and the intense stimuli. Further confirmation that OR is reflective of SS is the fact that young subjects have stronger ORs than older subjects. It is interesting to note that persons experiencing a high state of anxiety and arousal tend to be distractible and give weak ORs.

Orienting response strength can be related to psychopathology. People with anxiety disorders and schizophrenics who are behaviorally inactive tend to demonstrate weak ORs. Stimuli in their environments do not seem to interest them. These same schizophrenics tend to score low on the SSS, as one would predict. Schizophrenics who are more active, as well as psychopaths, tend to display strong ORs. Additionally, extreme psychopaths have a tendency to give strong ORs to stimuli such as needle punctures and strong shocks. These same stimuli would elicit a DR in most humans. Display of a strong OR to an intense stimulus is also a characteristic of high sensation seekers. Some researchers, Hare for instance, believe there might be a strong genetic or biological component to extreme psychopathy. This hypothesis would make sense if psychopathy is some how related to sensation seeking. [*See* ANXIETY DISORDERS; SCHIZOPHRENIA.]

B. Average Evoked Responses

An evoked response is an EEG signal recorded from the brain in response to an external stimulus. Because of the sometimes random state of the brain which might exist when each particular stimulus is presented, the EEG signals are averaged over many trials. This "averaged evoked response" is a model of what the electrical activity in the brain is in response to certain stimulus inputs. The time-locked half-second-averaged EEG yields a characteristic complex wave form dependent on the nature of the stimulus delivered and the recording site. These average evoked response (AER) wave forms are fairly consistent within an individual. [*See* EEG, COGNITION, AND DEMENTIA.]

There are many ways to quantify AERs but one simple way developed by Buchsbaum is to measure the amplitude of a certain component of the wave form and plot it as a function of the stimulus intensity that produced it. If increasing levels of stimulus intensity produce increasing amplitude of AER in an individual, that person is called an "augmentor." Conversely, if increasing levels of stimulus intensity produce a reduction in AER amplitude then the person is called a "reducer." These differences are often most apparent at more intense stimulus magnitudes. Augmentors are thought to be involved in stimulus intake and reducers stimulus rejection. There is a close parallel between augmenting and reducing and the orienting response vs defensive reaction continuum.

Buchsbaum and a number of colleagues, including Zuckerman, have tried to relate SS to the AER. In general these studies have found that normal people who are augmentors tend to be high scorers on the SSS, that augmenting decreases with age, and that augmentors have low endorphin levels. Psychiatric patients who are augmentors tend to be manics (and their well relatives), delinquents, heroin users, psychopaths, alcoholics, process schizophrenics, and to have low levels of the enzyme monoamine oxidase (MAO). Normal people who display a tendency to be reducers score low on the SSS, and have high endorphins. Psychiatric patients who are reducers tend to be stimulant users, hospitalized reactive schozphrenics, insomniacs, and have high MAO levels. These results agree substantially with other work describing sensation seekers. Of special note is the fact that manic patients are most often augmentors. Lithium, a standard treatment for bipolar affective disorder, prevents mania in many patients and may also reduce the number and severity of depressive swings in the disorder. Lithium also has a tendency to change the augmenting pattern to a reducing pattern and seems most effective in bipolars who are the most significant augmentors. Augmenting of the cortical evoked response seems to involve another postulated aspect of the biological makeup of sensation seekers: the capacity to react to stimuli of high intensity without displaying a defensive reaction.

C. Monoamine Oxidase and Neurotransmitters

MAO is a mitochondrial-bound oxidizing enzyme found in many body tissues but especially liver and nervous tissue. In nervous tissue MAO acts to remove used or excess aminergic neurotransmitters from systems where they are used. The aminergic neurotransmitters include: dopamine, norepinephrine, and serotonin. In general terms, MAO is one important component in the regulatory system that governs how and how well certain classes of our neurons transmit information. The involved neurotransmitter systems are present in all mammalian species and, as will be discussed in a subsequent section, are important in orchestrating survival behaviors. It is also important to note that two of these amine neurotransmitters, dopamine and norepinephrine, also known as catecholamines, operate within very narrowly defined functional boundaries. Their amounts are closely regulated by neuronal machinery, presumably because their particular levels are so important in regulating survival behaviors. [*See* Synaptic Transmitters and Neuromodulators.]

Normal subjects who are high on the SSS tend to have low levels of MAO. The converse is true of low SSS score subjects who have high levels of MAO. Other characteristics of subjects with low MAO are that they are usually younger and are male. Psychiatric patients with low levels of MAO are most likely diagnosed as manics (their well-relatives also tend to have low MAO), alcoholics, chronic paranoid schizophrenics. These same patients tend to be augmenters. Patients with high MAO levels may be many things, but in common they are reducers. People who are not yet diagnosable but are at risk also show differences in MAO levels. Those at risk with low MAO levels are most typically socially active, criminal, and drug users while those with high MAO activity are typically not very socially active.

What is of significance, regarding these chemical and behavioral findings, is that the inverse relationship between SS and MAO level is a possible indicator of correlations between behavioral traits and levels of catecholamines in the brain. MAO, as an enzyme, is subject to variability as a result of genetic makeup. Within limits variable amounts of MAO might bias behavior one way or another. For instance, a moderately low level of MAO might occur in a person who is a sensation seeker, gregarious, an augmentor, and social drinker who likes to party. However, this individual may live a relatively normal life. Yet a person with an even lower level of MAO might fall into a high-risk category, perhaps drinking to excess, using other drugs, and having a driving while intoxicated conviction (criminality) along with a court ordered psychiatric referral. Still lower levels of MAO might predispose one to be an outright alcoholic, have bipolar disorder, or a schizophrenic episode. As MAO decreases, behaviors related to sensation seeking increase in frequency. Sensation seeking seems to be very closely related to neurochemical variables that are heavily influenced by genetics.

IV. A BIOSOCIAL MODEL OF SENSATION SEEKING

A. Catecholamines and Mammalian Behavior

In the past 20 years we have learned numerous and striking facts about the anatomical and chemical milieu of the mammalian nervous system. These advances are due largely to technological advances in various types of chemical assay techniques. Even 10 years ago it was possible for the most sophisticated laboratories to analyze neurotransmitter concentrations from a single neural vesicle, not a neuron but a vesicle, using a technique called GC-MS (gas chromatograph–mass spectrometer). GC-MS is now financially and technologically within reach of almost any serious neurochemistry lab. Additionally, there are other new methods that allow analysis of very small amounts of neurochemical at sites within the brains of living behaving animals as an ongoing process. The result of these technological advances is twofold. One, we know that the brain is much more complex than we envisioned even 10 years ago. There are more neurotransmitters or neuromodulators and receptor types than we dreamed. The possible interactional processes between these neurotransmitter systems and their receptor subtypes are mind boggling, yet tremendously exciting. Two, we know that the traditional amine neurotransmitters, those that we discovered early in our quest, are tremendously important for regulating fundamental survival behaviors.

Even with limited knowledge one must reach the conclusion that dopamine (DA), norepinephrine (NE), and serotonin (5-HT) are important. For instance, the major drug classes that alleviate some of the complex symptomology of schizophrenia all act on a type of DA receptor. While a defect in the DA system itself may or may not be at the root of a predisposition to schizophrenia, there is little doubt the DA system is involved directly in modulating the behaviors central to the disorder. Similar claims could be made for the drugs useful in treating affective disorder. These drugs mostly have their impact on the NE and 5-HT systems. Stimulants, useful in attention deficit disorder, a disorder often accompanied by impulsive sensation seeking behavior, have effects on NE and DA systems. The point here is clear: the synthesis and uptake enzymes, transport mechanisms, release mechanisms, receptors, and end product enzymes for these neurotransmitter systems are key points in their regulation. And, because these neurotransmitter systems must stay within relatively narrow limits for normal behavior to occur, these same key points represent important opportunities for genetic and environmental manipulation of the qualitative and quantitative output of these neurotransmitter systems. This is the mechanism of genetic control of some very important survival behaviors. Of importance to the current topic is the fact that sensation seeking is an important personality variable and has been shown to be related to levels of an important enzyme in these monoamine pathways, MAO.

Neurotransmitter systems are expensive mechanisms for nature to evolve. As a consequence a single neurotransmitter is typically used in a variety of locations and perhaps for several purposes. It is the receptor and its activity on the target neuron that ultimately determines the particular function of a particular neurotransmitter at that location. So, for instance, DA occurs in several important pathways in the nervous system. Two of the major applications of DA involve motor systems and hormonal regulation. These two systems are critical since both function as components in larger systems serving important adaptive behaviors: being able to move and regulating metabolism. Another important system utilizing DA modulates motivation and reinforcement. This system is more germane to the present topic.

DA in the medial forebrain bundle activates several structures in the area of the hypothalamus. There is ample evidence of both DA and NE in pathways mediating self-stimulation though evidence is conflicting on which is of more relative importance. The self-stimulation paradigm is one where an animal presses a bar or performs some other operant in order to receive small electrical currents delivered to a site in its brain. Brain sites that evoke high rates of pressing, and therefore high rates of stimulation, are said to be reinforcing sites. Conversely, sites where animals will not press for stimulation or where they press to avoid stimulation are not reinforcement sites. The self-stimulation paradigm is thought to be our best animal demonstration of the neural basis of reinforcement. And reinforcement, of course, is what causes animals to repeat activities that produce or occur in contiguity with it. Evidence suggests that DA is the more important catecholamine and drug studies suggest that when DA action is blocked or decreased by some mechanism, then self-simulation behavior decreases. Cocaine, which largely operates through its influence on DA systems, is highly addictive and reinforcing. In fact animals will bar press in order to self-administer cocaine in much the same way they will bar press for electric current. Experiments using paradigms such as self-stimulation, self-administration, and other techniques coupled with administration of various drugs have resulted in a behavioral taxonomy for monoaminergic neurotransmitters.

Norepinephrine seems instrumental in mechanisms of reward, reinforcement in learning, and satiety mechanisms. Dopamine is important for the control of motor behavior, circling behavior, postural behavior, stereotyped behavior, hyperactivity syndrome, general motor activation, the reception and analysis of sensory information, incentive and motivation systems, and emotional states. Serotonin levels and activity in the brain have proven to be important for inhibition of motor, social, and sexual behavior. Though these systems seem at times to overlap and even to be in conflict, the overall function of these neurochemicals is to modulate incentive, environmental search, reinforcement, and perhaps facilitate learning by strengthening consolidation via influence on attention or activation. General categories of adaptive behavior such as incentive, motor activation, and inhibition of motor, social, and sexual behavior, as well as environmental search and reinforcement, are obviously linked to sensation seeking.

It seems obvious that the research conducted by Zuckerman and his colleagues relating sensation seeking to MAO levels directly relates to the chemical neurobiology data base representing our understanding of the fundamental behavioral correlates of these neurotransmitters. The results of the two lines of research are in agreement. This should not come as any great surprise since, if Zuckerman is right in assuming sensation seeking is an important genetically determined and biologically relevant personality variable, there ought to be some underlying physiological mechanism mediating sensation seeking. That seems exactly the case.

B. Genetics and Variability in Monoamine Systems

In view of the highly complicated and controlled nature of the feedforward and feedback systems that regulate production and release of neurotransmitters it is not surprising that malfunctions of these systems will occur. These malfunctions may lead to subtle differences in behavior still within the normal range or more serious distortions of neural performance and therefore to neurological or psychiatric disorders. Huntington's disease is an example of a neurological disease where a defect is genetically transmitted as an autosomal dominant trait with full penetrance—half of the children of parents with the disease will become afflicted themselves. The prevailing neurochemical hypothesis of Huntington's is that it is a *hyper*dopaminergic–*hypo*cholinergic–*hypo*GABAergic imbalance in brain dopamine, acetylcholine (cholinergic), and γ-amino butyric acid (GABA) neurotransmitter systems.

Biogenic aminergic neurotransmitters are also thought to have a special role in a number of genetically influenced mental disorders. Schizophrenia and manic-depressive disorder are genetically influenced psychiatric disorders, shaped by heredity and marked by biochemical changes in the brain related to catecholamine systems. There is little reason to doubt that natural genetic variability within normal ranges exists in these same systems. MAO, as one component of the monoaminergic systems, is but one point of genetic input in this complicated system. Since Zuckerman has convincing evidence that sensation seeking varies as a function of MAO activity and there are firm theoretical links between monoaminergic system activity and behaviors related to sensation seeking, there is a very good chance that sensation seeking's genetic component is due to variability in monoaminergic system activity. We all know, however, that genetics is only one piece of the puzzle.

C. Social Influences on the Expression of Sensation Seeking

We are all sensation seekers to some degree. However, most of us tend to express our sensation seeking tendencies through socially acceptable avenues. Many of the behaviors indicative of sensation seeking canvassed on Zuckerman's SSS such as the TAS and the ES are reflective of the kinds of risk taking common to middle- and upperclass American people. These two scales, the TAS and ES, also show the greatest differences between British and American samples, indicating a cultural influence. Cultural influences obviously have a heavy impact on the types of behaviors individuals choose to express the trait of SS.

As this piece is being written we are in the midst of a cultural trend called bungee jumping. Bunjee jumping is an activity where an individual has a bundle of large rubber band-type cords attached to his or her ankles and also to a platform 80 or more feet high. The activity takes its name from the name of the rubberized cords, bunjee cords. Of course, the bunjee cords are much shorter than the height of the platform. When the person jumps from the platform the cords tip the person upside down and begin to stretch, bringing the individual to a brief stop in mid-air. Then the cords retract and a short period of bouncing occurs followed by the jumper being lowered to the ground. All types of people, mostly young, mostly male, pay $50 on up to "jump" into space. There are jumping platforms located on cliffs over rivers, some jump from helicopters, and a recent fad is for cranes to show up on vacant lots adjacent to university campuses. The screams and squeals of jumpers are amazing as are their postjump accounts. This exercise clearly is a socially acceptable form of sensation seeking, perhaps extreme sensation seeking. Zuckerman feels that the more deviate the form of sensation seeking activity, vis a vis cultural norms, the more likely the behavior is biologically, genetically, driven. That is to say, bunjee jumping is likely a culturally acceptable expression of sensation seeking that requires a person above average in sensation seeking as a participant. However, peer pressure or some other mechanism might be sufficient to get some people who might not be such active sensation seekers to give it a try. After all, its safe and "everybody is doing it." However, the more uncommon the form of sensation seeking is within a culture, the more it violates cultural taboos, the more likely the participants are examples of people who are driven by the basic genetically determined trait. An example of such behavior might be poly-drug use, especially IV drug users sharing needles with other users. This behavior is not only socially disapproved but highly dangerous from any of a number of public health perspectives. It is hard to talk an average person into sharing a needle and much more likely that those who do share needles tend to engage in other sensation seeking activities. These people most likely represent the genetic extreme of high sensation seeking.

Another important question is whether a person might be susceptible to having their phenotypic expression of sensation seeking raised or lowered by the environment they find themselves exposed to as they grow up. A great deal of evidence exists that would support the hypothesis that developmental environment might influence trait expression. For instance, birth order may be a variable that influences level of sensation seeking. First-born children and only children of both sexes tend to score higher on the SSS than children born later in the birth order. Zuckerman reasons that the quality and quantity of time parents spend with first born (until a second born arrives) and only children sets a higher optimal level of stimulation for these children. Zuckerman further notes that many parents who believe, mistakenly he thinks, that extraordinary early stimulation is necessary for optimal intellectual development may be creating sensation seekers rather than intellectually gifted offspring. [*See* BIRTH ORDER, EFFECT ON PERSONALITY AND BEHAVIOR.]

In the final analysis there is still much work to be done on the social influences impacting the expression of sensation seeking. Important questions that need to be addressed include those such as: Is there a critical period? However, even if the details of social influence on sensation seeking are not well understood there is little doubt that environment helps determine both the avenues of expression of sensation seeking, especially those socially acceptable avenues, as well as helping to influence the level of the trait expressed in any individual.

D. A Biosocial Model of Sensation Seeking

Zuckerman and his colleagues have done a convincing job of outlining the trait of sensation seeking. As with many traits, the extremes would represent maladaptive behavior and some middle, optimal range would confer an evolutionary advantage. Also, the extremes would likely be rather resistant to environmental modification, being more firmly fixed by genetics. Those individuals in the middle range of sensation seeking tendency would also be most susceptible to environmental influence both in terms of the amount of sensation seeking they display and the avenues they choose to display it. The malleability of the trait to the influence of the environment only serves to make the trait more adaptive by allowing some modification to suit the individual curcumstance of each individual. A trait that leaves an individual hard-wired at birth would offer little flexibility and likely provide for little adaptiveness beyond a very narrow niche.

Zuckerman and his colleagues, then, have compiled a remarkable literature outlining the nature of sensation seeking and its expression across a number of species. They have also made considerable progress in identifying physiological correlates and biochemical markers for the trait. What remains to be done is a more complete and accurate placement of this very important trait within the general schema of the trait structure necessary to globally describe human behavior. Also awaiting accomplishment is a more thorough description of what environmental circumstances and time courses are most influential in their impact on the level and expression of the sensation seeking trait. There is no doubt that researchers will continue to search for answers to these questions since sensation seeking is so closely linked to important questions of the human condition: reproduction, violence, criminality, excitement, productivity, and exploration, among others.

Bibliography

Barratt, E. S., and Patton, J. H. (1983). Impulsivity: Cognitive, behavioral, and psychophysiological correlates. In "Biological Bases of Sensation Seeking, Impulsivity, and Anxiety (M. Zuckerman, Ed.). Lawrence Earlbaum, Hillsdale, NJ.

Buss, D. M. (1991). Evolutionary personality psychology. *Annu. Rev. Psychol.* **42,** 459.

Digman, J. M. (1990). Personality structure: Emergence of the five-factor model. *Annu. Rev. Psychol.* **41,** 417.

Eysenck, H. J. (1983). A biometrical-genetical analysis of impulsive and sensation seeking behavior. In "Biological Bases of Sensation Seeking, Impulsivity, and Anxiety (M. Zuckerman, Ed.). Lawrence Earlbaum, Hillsdale, NJ.

Zuckerman, M. (1979). "Sensation Seeking: Beyond the Optimal Level of Arousal." Lawrence Earlbaum, Hillsdale, NJ.

Zuckerman, M. (1983). A biological theory of sensation seeking. In "Biological Bases of Sensation Seeking, Impulsivity, and Anxiety (M. Zuckerman, Ed.). Lawrence Earlbaum, Hillsdale, NJ.

Zuckerman, M. (1990). The psychophysiology of sensation seeking. *J. Personality* **58,** 313.

Zuckerman, M. (1991). "Psychobiology of Personality." Cambridge University Press, New York.

Zuckerman, M., Buchsbaum, M. S., and Murphy, D. L. (1980). Sensation seeking and its biological correlates. *Psychol. Bull.* **88,** 187.

SENSE OF SMELL

Steve Van Toller
University of Warwick, United Kingdom

Glossary

Anosmia Total loss of the ability to detect smells.

Aromacology A number of related disciplines involving the use of fragrances or essential oils to produce relaxation or cures for medical illnesses.

Cognition The processes of thought and information processing in the brain.

Emotion Often held to be the opposite of cognition, emotion is a feeling state.

Neuropsychology The study of the brain processes, anatomical, physiological, and biochemical, and how they relate to behavior.

Sensory evaluation The use of scientific techniques applied to measurements and analysis of assessments, made by consumers or sensory panelists, of odor or flavor characteristics.

Specific anosmia An inability to detect certain odors or types of odors in a person with otherwise normal olfactory ability.

THE SENSE OF SMELL is largely a neglected human sense; Helen Keller called it the fallen angel of the senses. Smell, like taste, is a particulate sense and detection of an odor requires the olfactory receptors to be stimulated by volatile molecules. With certain odors the number of molecules required for detection may be as low as 40. On average a person breathes in about 8 liters (23×10^6 molecules) of air per minute containing a variable number of odorous molecules. In order to be odorous a molecule must have a molecular weight between 15 and 300. For example, alcohol (C_2H_5OH) with a molecular weight of 46 is odorous, whereas sugar ($C_{12}H_{22}O_{11}$) having a molecular weight of 342 is not.

Compared to animals humans are relatively insensitive in terms of their ability to detect smells. An average human is able to detect 1 g (7×10^{21} molecules) of butyric acid (an unpleasant, sweaty-foot odor) dispersed uniformly throughout a 10-storey building. A good German shepherd dog would be able to detect the same amount of material distributed over the area of a small city like Dublin at a uniform level of between 200 and 300 feet. In addition to volatility, an odorous molecule must also be soluble in water and fats. Within the animal kingdom, fish are among the most sensitive creatures in terms of ability to detect odors. Salmon swim back to their hatching stream to spawn from areas in the oceans where they mature, such as the Sargossa sea, by using their sense of smell. The distances involved can be as much as 12,000 miles. However, in olfactory comparisons made between dogs and humans who were wheeled around with their noses close to the ground, humans performed at levels that were not markedly inferior to the performance of the tested dogs. Of course this type of testing permitted the use of cognitive abilities which would favor the humans. The sense of smell was an important early sense in terms of evolution. In fact, Le Gros Clark said that Descartes statement *cogito ergo sum* should be changed to *olfacio ergo sum*. This reformulation indicates that it was the developing sense of smell that allowed prediction and anticipation and, as such, the sense of

Encyclopedia of Human Behavior, Volume 4

smell might be argued to be the forebearer of cognition.

I. THE NOSE

The nose is often spoken of as being the organ of the sense of smell but its primary function is to adjust the temperature and humidify the breathed-in air that is taken down to the delicate cells of the lungs. To produce these changes, the incoming breathed air is passed over and between three layers of nasal turbinates which are richly lined with blood vessels. The nose is pyramidal in shape and at its apex there is a small chamber which contains the olfactory tissues. In humans this sensory tissue covers a total area of about 625 mm^2, half being in the left-hand side of the nose and half in the right-hand side of the nose. The nose is divided into two sides by a nasal septum. Olfactory cells are thought to have a life cycle of about 28 plus or minus 7 days. In addition to the nonfunctional developing and degenerating olfactory receptors, there are other types of cells—support cells, mucus secretory cells, and cells that aid required metabolic processes. The total number of olfactory cells in a human has been estimated to be comparable with the number of visual receptor cells (5×10^6).

II. THE OLFACTORY SYSTEM

Unlike our understanding of the mechanisms of the visual and the auditory senses, we still do not understand the processes of how incoming odors are coded and classified by the brain. It has recently been suggested that the mechanism is similar to that of the bodily immune system with families of protein receptor types for each type of odor. A molecular genetic study proposed that there are families of transmembrane receptor proteins which, in a fashion similar to the recognition of the toxic material by the immunological system of the body, come to identify odors. Such a process could be very flexible and would allow for learning processes to occur. However, the biochemical mechanisms have still to be worked out in detail. The electrical information generated in the tiny olfactory nerves (fila olfactorium, 1st cranial nerve) passes into the brain via small "pepperpot-like" holes in the cribriform plate on the underside of the skull and enters the two olfactory bulbs which lie on the undersurface of the brain. On entering the bulbs, the nerves interact with external granule cells, tufted cells, and mitral cells before passing from the olfactory bulbs into complex circuits of the mid-brain areas called the limbic system. The reduction in cell numbers in the olfactory bulb from input to output is in the order of 1000 to 1, indicating that an important function of the olfactory system is to detect small amounts of odor.

A. The Trigeminal Nerve and Vomeronasal Systems

In addition, nerves of the trigeminal system (5th cranial nerve), which also have a powerful influence upon the sense of smell are found both lining the nasal passageways and intermixed with olfactory receptor cells. Unlike the olfactory nerve, the trigeminal nerve is a touch sense and stimulation of this system causes the characteristic reflex withdrawal movements seen when ammonia, smelling salts, or other trigeminal stimulants are smelled. The 5th cranial nerve also has extensive innervation to the facial and mouth regions. For example, it is the trigeminal nerve which causes lacrimation when onions are peeled. Some animals possess, in addition to the olfactory and the trigeminal nerves, a vomeronasal chemoreception (Jacobson's organ). This important chemoreceptive sense consists of a pit-like structure in the roof of the mouth. Its action can be observed in mammals when they make a yawning-type (Flehman) response. This response serves to draw air into the vomeronasal pit. The classical action of this system is observed in snakes who sample air by extruding their forked tongues, which they then withdraw and place into their vomeronasal pits to sample the molecules they have gathered. Humans have a functional vomeronasal system during the embryonic stages of human development in the womb but the system appears to become vestigial following birth.

B. Olfactory Pathways in the Brain

The electrochemical information initiated by odorous molecules is passed into the brain via the olfactory bulbs. Here the olfactory recepter cells encounter arrays of nerve cells which are designed to maximize detection of olfactory stimuli. The olfactory nerves leave the olfactory bulb and enter a complex circuit in the brain collectively called the limbic system. The limbic system is related to motivational, emotion, and feeling states and behaviors. It is a complex circular system involving overall 122 regions and associated tracts having a vital role in the orchestration of the various systems of central nervous systems; these also include the autonomic nervous systems and the hormonal systems. Interestingly, the original name for the limbic system was the rhinencephalon or nose-brain. From its intimate input and connections with the limbic system it can be readily appreciated how the associations of smells with emotion and motivation occur. [*See* LIMBIC SYSTEM.]

III. ANOSMIA

The olfactory nerves, being very small, are extremely vulnerable, and anosmia or loss of the ability to sense smells is more common than generally supposed. Although there are a number of causes for loss of the sense of smell, a large number of cases arise either from viral infections that destroy the tiny olfactory nerves or from a blow to the head that causes shearing and rupturing of the olfactory nerves as they pass through the cribriform plate. Anosmias arising from physical obstruction, brain neuropathology and hormonal dysfunctions are fewer in numbers. Additionally, there are some anosmia cases arising from hereditary factors. In general, hereditary factors are hard to prove because the possibility of an early head trauma is difficult to rule out.

A. Specific Anosmia

Individuals have different sensitivities to smells; in addition, each person will have an individual portfolio of odors that either they are not be able to smell or to which they have very high thresholds. Thus, individuals have a different olfactory portfolio of specific anosmias. People's specific anosmias have a marked bearing on how their behavior is influenced by the sense of smell. Specific anosmia may lead to some self-selection for certain work or professions in which smell plays an important part.

IV. SENSORY EVALUATION

Almost all commercial products are given an odor by their manufacturer, which is designed to invoke favorable attributes in the customers' perception of the product. For example, many supermarkets now bake bread on their premises and part of the purpose is to fill the food shopping areas with the very pleasant pyrazine smells from the baking and roasting processes. In order to evaluate smells given to products, commercial industries have developed a number of sensory evaluation techniques. By using such techniques it is possible to measure the absolute detection thresholds of an odor, which occurs at the point where a smell can be reliably detected. At higher concentrations the naming threshold occurs when a smell can be reliably named. In addition, difference measures can be used to establish such things as odor similarities and dissimilarities. Various psychometric scales can be used to evaluate smells in terms of their strength, pleasantness, familiarity, and other attributes. Basically, there are three main headings under which an odor can be categorized: first, a sensory aspect which is stable over time, such as the onioness of an onion or the fishiness of a fish; second, a hedonic dimension which refers to the pleasantness or unpleasantness of an odor, normally conceived as a unidimensional scale of opposites; third, there is a set of attributes that have been learned either by personal associations or via social and cultural factors. The particular psychometric method used will depend on the purpose of the study being undertaken. As sensory testing involves complex variables and their interactions, special descriptive statistical techniques, such as multidimensional scaling and principle components analysis, have been developed to allow easy overviews of the complex data. Manufactures using odor in their product need to balance two basic customer needs, familiarity and odor novelty. This is often done over time by moving or drifting the odor along an identified critical dimension. In addition to the more obvious characteristics of an odor outlined above, panelists and ultimately the customer bring to the sampling situation a number of psychological factors that can have a strong influence on testing and purchasing decisions. Recently, sensory evaluation attempts have centered on individual psychological reactions.

V. ELECTRONIC NOSES

Another area of developing interest is sensor technology using "electronic noses" in which various gas-sensing devices such as inorganic semiconductors or conducting polymers can be "tuned" to individual odor notes and used to detect a particular odor. Arrays of polymers each tuned to different odor notes allow for more complex odors to be monitored routinely. The initial application for such devices lies in commerce where in many production processes it is of value to be able to detect and monitor certain odors, particularly off-odor notes and taints. Such devices in the future could have immense value in allowing anosmics to detect dangerous or off-flavors. Also, it is possible that in the future such devices may become sufficiently sensitive to allow the early detection of illness by examining bodily odor notes produced by the underlying biochemical metabolic processes. Thus, it would be possible to detect faulty or abnormal metabolic processes relatively cheaply. At the present time electronic noses or similar analogue-sensing devices fall far below human performance in terms of threshold detection levels and in the range of their olfactory ability. An area related to studies of electronic noses is that of increased understanding of how neural networks interconnect and are able to learn. The characteristics of the olfactory system make it particularly well suited for neural network studies and it has been used in a number of such studies.

VI. KEY IMPACT ODORANTS

A typical food odorant can be composed of many thousands of constituent smells which can be identified by using physical techniques such as gas chromatography and mass spectometry. It has been shown that critical odorants called key impact odors and occurring at very low levels may play a role out of proportion to their physical presence in a particular food smell. An example are the furans in coffee which at levels of 10^{12} impart the pleasant coffee aroma; at increased levels of 10^{9} the aroma becomes distinctly unpleasant and smells of stale overpercolated coffee. Another example are the delicious roasting notes of the pyrazines which again are found at very low concentrations and although chemically identified in the late 1800s were ignored for many years because they were present at physically low levels. It is likely that animal notes used in perfumes act as key impact odorants. It is also possible that key impact odorants acting as semiochemical signals may be eventually identified in body odors.

VII. AGE EFFECTS

A. Babies and Infants

Within hours of birth a baby comes to recognize its mother by her odor. Similarly, mothers have been shown to identify their own babies by odor after postpartum contact periods as short as 10 min. This suggests that odor plays an important role in the vital bonding behavior between the baby and its carer. It is now felt that reaction to the maternal smell either is an innate response or has properties that result in it being learned very rapidly. Experiments carried out on bottle-fed babies have demonstrated that the breast odor of a lactating mother is very attractive to babies despite the fact that their primary nutrient reinforcement is derived from bottled milk. It is unlikely that the olfactory bonding in the postpartum period involves complex cognitive functions (metaphoric) and must relate to conditioning or associative learning (metonymic) between a particular odor and reinforcing event such as comfort or feeding. Olfactory processes are functional during the later fetal developmental stages and, while in the womb, the fetus will be able to detect aromatic substances released by the mother's circulation into the amniotic fluid surrounding the developing fetus. This suggests that the sense of smell may operate at an early proto-cognitive stage allowing vital and salient semiochemical information to be passed to the baby before the main cognitive processes are functional.

B. Developmental Factors

There has been a long and vigorous debate about whether young children have the same hedonic reactions to smells as do adults. The basis of this debate was whether reactions to smells were innate (brain hardware) or learned (brain software). Early research studies suggested that young children's smell "likes and dislikes" were very different from those of adults and that the adultlike response did not develop until about the age of 5–6 years when young children begin to assimilate social values and ideas. The earlier studies were complicated by the fact that they required a verbal response from young children. This made the task difficult for children because a complex verbal response (metaphor) was required. Additionally, young children often, compliantly, give the response they feel is required by the experimenter. Recently studies have been carried out which allow the child to respond without using verbal labels. In these studies children gave the smells to either a well-established pleasant character or a well-established unpleasant character taken from a young children's television program. This type of study allows the children to make a metonymic response and does not require complex metaphoric verbal responses. Such studies have shown that the likes and dislikes of young children and adults are similar. It has been pointed out that children often have personal comforters in which odor plays an important and vital role in invoking security and safety.

C. Aging

Between the ages of 20 and 80 years of age the average decline in olfactory ability is about 20%. Unlike the other sensory systems of vision and hearing, there is no sensory compensation, such as that provided by spectacles or hearing aids. Diminution of the ability to smell, which is usually overlooked or ignored, can lead to a severe loss in the quality of life. This type of natural olfactory loss has been identified by the name presbyosmia in the hope that such a name will result in the problem being more widely recognized and action taken to alleviate it. The reasons for this aging loss are not fully understood but it might result from cellular or metabolic malfunction or calcification of the cribiform plate reducing the number of functional olfactory nerves. It is interesting to note that when the elderly eat they tend to prefer more highly flavored foods such as port and other fortified wines and strong gamey meats. As a consequence of the olfactory losses, the elderly often have less interest in eating. The quality of life for the elderly can be improved by using herbs and cooking techniques that serve to enhance flavor.

VIII. BODY ODOR

Although diet and the environment have an influence on personal body odor, genetic factors have a strong influence and each person has a distinctive smell. Human body smells are derived mainly from the apocrine sweat glands located on the scalp, cheeks, and underarm axillary and breast regions, and the genital areas of the body. As well as their average larger body size, males also have larger apocrine glands and tend to support more body bacteria. Both of these factors serve to produce a strong male body odor. It has been suggested by ethologists that the action of raising one's arms is a dominance response serving to increase body size and release the body odor of a person. There have been a number of studies devoted to the characterization of body odors and the commerical development of agents to suppress such odors. Dogs have been used to detect body odors taken from clothing and instruments used by criminals, and such evidence has been used to secure convictions in Holland. A number of behavioral studies have shown that humans can distinguish other individuals by body smell. Furthermore, humans can distinguish body odors taken from different parts of the body.

Cross-cultural studies have shown that the odor of strangers are remembered as unpleasant while those of friends are more likely to be recalled as being pleasant. In one experimental study, unseen T-shirts of partners were rated as more pleasant than unseen T-shirts of strangers. Thus, group bonding, in part, appears to be related to smell. In a study carried out using German and Japanese subjects, odors from family members were often rated pleasant whereas odors of strangers were rated unpleasant. It has also been suggested that the elderly more easily adapt to residential facilities when they are first exposed to the different cultural and social smells they will encounter. This indicates that it may be important to integrate a person into the smell of a group to achieve a satisfactory and smooth integration.

It is a well-established finding from a number of replicated experiments that females living together or leading close lives tend to show menstrual synchrony. This is often not apparent to the participants of the groups. It is not understood how this synchrony occurs but body odor may be a factor. The phenomenon of menstrual synchrony illustrates the possible influence of body odors at low levels of awareness.

A. Semiochemistry

Semiotics is the science of signals and clearly, as mentioned above, smells of all types carry valuable information. The sense of smell is the dominant sense throughout the animal kingdom, serving to carry salient information. Many species of insects are specifically controlled by species-relevant odors called pheromones. For example, termite colonies are regulated by levels of the various odors within the colony. After a conflict with a neighboring colony, decrease in the odor level relevant to soldier or fighter termites will cause the young in the colony to develop as replacement fighter termites. This process continues until the odor rises to an appropriate level for the adequate protection of the colony. The vast majority of species in the animal kingdom mate with members of their species that have a certain smell. The value of odor carrying sexual information is that it acts as a parsimonious biological system. Animals only need to react in a certain way to others who have a specific smell; all other smells are ignored. Homo sapiens developed as cognitive creatures and needed to break away from such an efficient but nevertheless restrictive process which produces stereotypical behavior patterns and limits diversity. For various cultural and social factors, the sense of smell has incorrectly been relegated to a position of an inferior if not an insignificant sense. Humans tend to consider their visual and auditory sensory systems to be more important than their sense of smell. However, recent research is beginning to show that the sense of smell may have more important effects than has been previously supposed. Certainly, in common with other animals, Homo sapiens are well endowed with glands that excrete bodily odors. Indeed, it has been claimed the Homo sapien's initial survival, considering that they are relatively puny members of the animal kingdom, was due to their unpalatable smell. A recent book has referred to humans as scented apes. Thus, humans have the means for biological semiochemical communication. In all known human cultures, fragrances and/or perfumes are applied to parts of the body and there has recently been an increase in the anthropological knowledge related to this area. As mentioned earlier it has also been shown that humans can detect and gain information from the bodily smells of other humans. In certain sufferers, genetic biochemical abnormalities result in an unpleasant body smell. An example is called the fish-odor syndrome (trimethylaminuria) where unfortunate sufferers' breath and sweat smell strongly of fish. The defect is due to faulty oxidation metabolism and the sufferers are unable to convert the smelly amine into its odorless form. Not surprisingly such sufferers tend to lead isolated and withdrawn lives. In China and Japan people tend to have low levels of natural body odors, and body odors are seen as abnormal. It has been claimed that the Japanese developed room deodorizing systems in order to remove the smell of people from Western cultures from Japanese hotel rooms.

IX. MEMORY

Memory has been described as the main attribute of olfaction; this is because it is often linked with strong episodic events from the past. Most people feel that there is a distinct and special relationship between the sense of smell and memory and tend to believe that the sense has special links with memories often invoking Proust's remembrance of things past which was based on the flavor of petites madeleines dipped into his tea. This overlooks the fact that the other senses could also have invoked such memories; however, in any event, the smell caused Proust to begin, by his account, a somewhat painful process of reintegration in which, as an adult, he reconstructed and reinterpreted the past. However, compared to the visual and auditory systems, odors are less likely to be interfered with by conflicting and similar stimuli and, as a consequence, are likely to lay down purer traces of information. Thus, when revived, perhaps many years later, they evoke a purer recall. In addition, an olfactory memory is more likely to be involved in a traumatic or an emotional episode and this will result in the trace having additional "power" in terms of brain processing. A recent study has claimed to support the view that smells can recall earlier memories if the subject is primed to respond to a smell in a subjective way. This study also found that females were better in terms of recall than males. In general, empirical research studies that have been carried out on smell memory have demonstrated that it is different in degree rather than different in kind to memories evoked by the other sensory systems. [*See* MEMORY.]

X. EMOTION

Belief about a special relationship between the sense of smell and emotion is very widespread. Emotion permeates all areas related to the sense of smell—no other aspect of behavior is more closely related to smell, by the general public. However, very little theoretical or experimental knowledge is available about this particular relationship. It is true that one of the main dimensions of the sense appears to be hedonic, meaning pleasant sensation, and people can easily react to a smell in terms of whether they like it. However, experimentally testing the relationship between smell and hedonism is not simple. As pointed out earlier, the olfactory brain pathways are closely involved with the limbic system which is intimately bound up with moods, feelings, and emotions. Various reports have been made about the effects of pleasant and unpleasant odors on feeling and mood states and, in general, it has been shown that a pleasant odor will have a positive effect on judgments. Curiously, unpleasant odors are rated as more unpleasant when presented to the right nostril.

Smell and emotion are two very old brain systems. Both are neglected in terms of education and this, in no small part, adds to the confusion and difficulty that people have when trying to express themselves beyond the level of a mere hedonic "like" or "dislike" reaction. Both systems were too important to be left at the level of mere hind-brain reflexes despite the common assumption that both are systems which humans might be better without. However, the truth is far from this and both systems can be argued to be important defining characteristics of the human races. At each evolutionary stage in the development of the human brain both of these systems were integrated into the newer developing brain areas in profound and subtle ways. Thus, emotion and the sense of smell have permeated all the brain areas and are involved in most reactions. For example, all animals eat. Humans eat but are also able to raise eating to the levels of aesthetic dining in which smell and taste come together into the synthesis of flavor. Both smell and emotion appear to have few primary or innate biological actions and most of their reactions are learned or secondary. This creates considerable individual variation and makes for difficulties in interpretations. A recent suggestion is that smells produce changes in the chemical endorphine transmitter substances of the brain, thus creating positive and negative mood states. However, although this is a credible suggestion, it is too soon to confirm such ideas.

XI. SMELL AND NEUROPHYSIOLOGY

Psychophysiology is the recording and use of physiological measurements, such as heart rate, skin conductance, electroencephalography, which occur at very low levels of subjective awareness, as indices of psychological events and information processing by subjects.

The main value of these techniques is that the measurements can be taken with the subject being unaware that they are being tested. One well-known method is electroencephalography (EEG) which refers to the recording of AC electrical signals from the outer cortical layers of the brain. Records are made by attaching electrodes to a person's scalp. The earliest attempts to understand how EEG relates to olfactory stimulation was made in the 1950s but the techniques then available made interpretation of the waxing and waning squiggly analogue ink traces difficult. Over the last decade methods of recording EEG and a number of related EEG techniques have been improved and new attempts have been made to understand how the brain processes olfactory information at the cortical level. By using fast Fourier transformation techniques EEG activity can be represented by colored typographical maps which relate to the level of electrical activity on the brain's surface. Olfactory studies recording EEG from both adults and infants have shown a number of interesting effects; such findings may help us to understand how the brain processes olfactory information. [*See* BRAIN ELECTRIC ACTIVITY.]

Another measurement of brain electrical activity is the contingent negative voltage (CNV) signal, which is a DC signal. In the CNV situation subjects are presented with an initial signal and told that when a second signal occurs they are to react, usually by pressing a switch, as fast as they can. Prior to the first signal the subject is primed by breathing odorized air. It has been claimed that certain odors produce positive changes while others produce negative changes in DC voltage. This method requires that a large number of trials be averaged to obtain a reliable signal. Another EEG related measurement, also involving averaging over trials, is evoked potentials (EPs). EPs are the summated activity from large numbers of actively firing neurons following presentation of a stimulus. The EP records the underlying electrical activity during several hundred milliseconds following presentation. The various positive and negative electrical peaks plus their latencies are held to be a function of underlying processing of information by the brain. The very small signal of an EP (12 μV), relative to the background random electrical noise (60 μV) in the brain, requires repetitions to improve signal strength. It has been shown that olfactory evoked potentials (OEPs) are different from chemosomatosensory evoked potentials (CSEPs) elicited mainly by the trigeminal system. The ability to separate the trigeminal and olfactory components by using evoked potentials has allowed a procedure to be devised which allows for accurate diagnosis of anosmics. One of the findings obtained by this technique is that when using a pure odorant (i.e., without trigeminal components) it is not possible for subjects to say whether the odor is being presented to the left or the right nostril. This indicates that unlike the other sensory systems, localization is not possible for the sense of smell.

At the present time the EEG and related techniques have shown a number of interesting and provocative findings but we still lack understanding of many of the subtleties related to the sense of smell and brain function. Recent introduction of nonlinear techniques of analysis called Chaos theory now allows analysis of brain EEG using nonlinear methods. The value of Chaos theory is that, despite the name, it allows for a complete overview rather than looking at the various elements that make up the whole.

In addition to attempts to understand the underlying electrical activity of the brain there are a number of progressive neurodegenerative diseases in which the sense of smell shows parallel impairment. Patients suffering from these illnesses, usually related to aging complaints, are found to have an impaired ability to recognize and remember odors at an early stage of the illness. The best example of this class of disease is Alzheimer's disease which produces presenile dementia in sufferers. In autopsied brain material taken from former Alzheimer sufferers it has been shown that the central neuropathology and neurochemical changes are also found in the olfactory tissues. Such findings have led to the suggestion that testing olfactory ability may serve as a diagnositc test for Alzheimer's disease. The main caution for this approach relates to the fact that although it is true that the main brain areas affected by the neurodegenerative changes in Alzheimer's disease are concerned with olfactory processing, these brain areas are also concerned with cognitive aspects such as memory and information processing plus emotion and moods.

XII. PERFUMES AND FRAGRANCES

The word perfume comes from the Latin word *per fumar,* which means "from smoke." The name illustrates Homo sapien's early activity in burning aromatic woods and herbs for the aromas they released, initially in religious ceremonies where aromatic woods, resins, and herbs were burned as offerings and also to influence the worshipers. Frankincense and myrrh are quoted as important aromatic substances in a number of religious beliefs. Later perfumes and fragrances were used by royalty and the very rich. From the earliest known human history perfumes and fragrances have been used to anoint and fragrance the body and all known human races make use of herbs. For example, the Trobrianders of the Pacific wear sweet smelling plants on their upper arms. Today we have arrived at an egalitarian state concerning fragrances worn on the body and a large percentage of the population wash off their natural body smells and replace them with perfumes or aftershave fragrances. This human activity is, in part, due to advertisements and encouragement of a large perfume and fragrance industry, but it is practiced in all societies and appears to be a fundamental human activity.

Perfumes are arranged into genealogies and all perfumes and fragrances can be fitted into one or other of the genealogical families. The perfume types used for females generally are green notes, floral notes, aldehydic notes, chypre notes, oriental notes, leather notes, fougere notes. The perfume types used for males generally are green notes, citrus notes, lavender notes, spicy notes, floral notes, chypre notes, fougere notes, woody notes, leather notes, musky notes. A perfume consists of a complex mixture of fragrances called odor accords. It will contain top notes which will evaporate immediately after application of the perfume, middle notes which will evaporate over a longer period and finally bottom notes which may last for a considerable time. The latter bottom notes consist of fragrances with heavy molecular weights, often including animalic odors, giving "body" or "roundness" to a perfume.

XIII. AROMATHERAPY

Aromatherapy is the use of aromatic substances, usually essential oils, to influence moods and behaviors. It is very popular at the present time and, in no small part, this is due to the fact that journalists have given publicity to its practices. Aromatherapy can be divided into a number of different areas: aesthetic, medical–clinical, psychoaromatherapy, holistic aromatherapy. In practice these range from aromatherapy used for pleasure to a belief in the efficacy of certain odors to effect specific medical cures. It is a most popular method of treatment and at times it can be very effective, but the question is how much of the effect is due to the particular odor being used? Aromatherapy involves a number of factors, such as touch, dialogue, and rapport, that are also efficacious in helping patients. There is also the question of placebo effects which can show very powerful effects. Thus, the actual odors used in any treatment may not be very important in terms of the overall treatment. Aromatherapists tend to generalize from particular cases and rarely use adequate and necessary controls to check for any placebo effects. Thus, although aromatherapists tend to use scientific terms and ideas to boost their credibility, very few studies have been reported in a way that would allow them to be scientifically evaluated. Practitioners tend to range from strict vitalists, who believe that the only a natural essential odor will effect a cure, to those who adopt a more lasseiz faire attitude. As an alternative therapy it clearly has an important role but, at the present time, it lacks scientific credibility.

XIV. ENVIRONMENTAL SMELLS

The salubrious parts of urban areas tend to be upwind of the prevailing wind conditions. This ensures that the affluent get the least polluted air. For example, the prevailing winds of the UK are from the west; therefore, the poorest areas of UK cities are generally located on the east sides. Recently, there have been a number of attempts to use odors to improve the environment. A company in Japan has produced an industrial computerized air conditioning system which circulates odors throughout the building and the odors are changed during the day. During the initial periods of the morning and after the lunch break, workers are refreshed by citrus smells, such as orange and lemon. In the midmorning periods, floral odors are circulated throughout the building complex "to help improve concentration." Woodlands scents are circulated "to relax the workers" during the lunch break period and toward the end of the working day. Production is said to have improved as a result of odorizing the environment. In addition, in certain parts of Tokyo odors are released into certain streets to odorize the surrounding areas. A series of experiments related to human vigilance has shown that odors can be used to improve performance, with the smell of peppermint being particularly effective. Other research experiments have shown that odors can be used to aid relaxation and reduce stress. These latter studies tie in with the claims of the aromatherapists. The findings of these studies support the idea that changes of sensory state produce stimulation that can improve performance of many types of behavior. The effects are complex as shown by a recent experiment which demonstrated a positive improvement in performance of subjects who had been led to believe that they were working in the presence of an odor design to improve concentration. In fact, odorless water had been sprayed into the testing area. This clearly relates to placebo effects which are well-known interfering variables found in many human experiments.

XV. CONCLUSIONS

In comparison with the senses of vision and hearing, relatively little research has been carried out on the sense of smell but in the last decade the number of studies devoted to this neglected area has increased considerably and this is reflected in a number of edited books that have appeared in the last few years. Odor has been shown to play an important but, as yet, poorly understood role in human social behavior and interaction. An important current development involves increased understanding of body odor and individual body odor mapping. We still need to understand how odors affect moods, emotions, and cognitive states. As yet, the olfactory mechanisms mediating relaxation are not understood but, again, appear to be effective. An important part of the ongoing olfactory studies is to understand the neuroanatomical and neurochemical underpinnings of this sensory system. At the present time we find a situation where there is a plethora of information and facts concerning olfaction but very little in the way of theories to tie the facts together. It is to be hoped that the theoretical stage will come about during the next decade. It has been suggested that the collective name for research into the various areas of olfation should be called Aromacology. A name for this collective area might serve to focus research and identify an important but previously neglected area of human behavior.

Bibliography

Davis, J. L., and Eichenbaum, H. (Eds.) (1991). "Olfaction: A Model System for Computational Neuroscience." MIT Press, Cambridge, MA.

Getchell, T. V., Doty, R. L., Bartoshuk, L. M., and Snow, J. B. (Eds.) (1991). "Smell and Taste in Health and Disease." Raven Press, New York.

Laing, D. G., Doty, R. L., and Breipohl, W. (Eds.) (1991). "The Human Sense of Smell." Springer-Verlag, New York.

Muller, P. M., and Lamparksy, D. (Eds.) (1991). "Perfumes: Art, Science and Technology." Elsevier Applied Science, London.

Serby, M. J., and Chobor, K. L. (Eds.) (1992). "Science of Olfaction." Springer-Verlag, New York.

Stoddart, D. M. (1990). "The Scented Ape: The Biology and Culture of Human Odour." Cambridge University Press, Cambridge.

Van Toller, S., and Dodd, G. H. (Eds.) (1988). "Perfumery: The Psychology and Biology of Fragrance." Chapman & Hall, London.

Van Toller, S., and Dodd, G. H. (Eds.) (1992). "Fragrance: The Psychology and Biology of Perfume." Elsevier Applied Science, London.

SENTENCE PROCESSING

Brian MacWhinney
Carnegie Mellon University

Glossary

Articulatory planning The mental activity of ordering words and sounds into a sequence for the control of movements of the larynx, lips, and jaws.

Competition The form of mental processing that treats mental traces in terms of their relative strengths or activations and which selects out the strongest as the winners.

Cue reliability Grammatical cues that are high in reliability are ones that point to the correct grammatical interpretation whenever one relies on them.

Garden-pathing The type of processing that occurs when one follows out a particular interpretation of a sentence that turns out in the end to be wrong and which then needs to be retraced to derive the correct interpretation.

Lexicon The mental representation of the words and grammatical markings in our language.

Modularity The theory of mental processing that attempts to minimize or restrict the competitive interaction between processes.

Proposition A relation between words in which one word functions as the predicate and the other words function as arguments, taking assigned roles determined by the logical form of the predicate.

SENTENCE PROCESSING is the mental activity in which we engage when we produce and comprehend sentences. This activity includes many component processes. When we listen to or read sentences, we must link words together into phrases; we must determine the parts of speech of ambiguous words; we must assign words and phrases to grammatical roles; and finally we must derive a deeper conceptual interpretation of the underlying meaning of the sentence. When we produce sentences, we must select a starting point that includes a sentence topic and a main verb; we must decide which material should be foregrounded into the main clause and which material backgrounded into subordinate clauses and adverbial phrases. We must then take our plans for the words to be included in an utterance and reduce them to a set of articulatory gestures. Both comprehension and production involve a finely tuned interleaving of these various complex processes that typically occurs against a backdrop of noise, interruptions from other speakers, and competing cognitive tasks. Despite its great complexity, sentence processing is a skill that is smoothly executed for many hours every day of the year by billions of human beings in hundreds of languages all around the world.

I. SENTENCE COMPREHENSION

In order to understand sentences, we first need to pick out the words of which they are composed. The process of identifying the words in a sentence is known as "lexical access." This type of access is a necessary preliminary to all other aspects of sentence comprehension. In reality, lexical access involves very different operations depending on whether we are reading sentences or listening to them. When we are reading English text, words are neatly segmented by spaces. Using the rather inconsistent spelling rules of English, we can associate the written forms of words with their auditory forms. Together, the written and auditory forms are used to activate the underlying meanings of the word. In

Encyclopedia of Human Behavior, Volume 4

aural comprehension, the process is not guided by the clear markings of the written form. In fact, there are no strong and fully reliable cues to word segmentation in English. For example, it is easy to misperceive a word like "nitrate" as being "night rate." Despite the absence of clear segmentation cues, we are able to use our rich lexical knowledge to directly pick out the auditory forms of words from the speech stream. Although frequent words are detected more quickly, even relatively rare words are recognized smoothly and with hesitation. [*See* PHONOLOGICAL PROCESSING AND READING.]

A. Incremental Processing

There are at least four major levels of processing that occur during comprehension of a sentence. First, *auditory processing* uses input sound patterns to extract a set of phonological cues. Second, *lexical processing* uses phonological cues to activate particular lexical items or words. Third, *grammatical processing* matches up lexical items into relational structures. Fourth, *conceptual processing* extracts meaning from these relational structures. It is important to realize that sentence processing involves the simultaneous interaction of each of these four levels. We do not wait until we have completed all auditory processing before attempting lexical processing. Nor do we complete all grammatical processing before attempting any conceptual processing. Take as an example the sentence "The boy chased the baboon into the bedroom." As soon as we hear the first two words "the" and "boy," we immediately begin to relate them to each other and then to the following verb "chased." Moments after hearing "chased," we begin to construct an interpretation of the activity in which there is a boy doing some chasing. We do not need to wait until we have heard all the words in the sentence to begin to extract these meanings. In this sense, sentence processing is both interactive and incremental—we tend to make decisions about material as soon as it comes in, hoping that the decisions that we make will not be reversed.

B. Garden-Pathing

However, sometimes these decisions must indeed be reversed. There are times when the initial decisions that we have made take us down the "garden path." A classic example of garden-path processing occurs with sentences such as "The communist farmers hated died." It often takes the listener awhile to realize that it was the communist that died and it was the farmers who hated the communist. Inclusion of a relativizer to produce the form "The communist that farmers hated died" might have helped the listener sort this out. A somewhat different example is the sentence "The horse raced past the barn fell." Here, we need to understand "raced past the barn" as a reduced relative clause with the meaning "The horse who was raced past the barn." If we do this, the appearance of the final verb "fell" no longer comes as a surprise.

Garden paths arise when a word has two meanings, one of which is very common and one of which is comparatively rare. In a sentence like "The horse raced past the barn fell" the use of the verb "raced" as a standard transitive verb is much more common than its use as the past participle in a reduced passive. In such cases, the strong meaning quickly dominates over the weak meaning. By the time we realize our mistake, the weak meaning is fully suppressed by the strong meaning and we have to try to comprehend the sentence from scratch. A classic garden-path example from Karl Lashley is the sentence "Rapid righting with his uninjured left hand saved from destruction the contents of the capsized canoe." If this sentence is read aloud, listeners find it extremely difficult to understand the second word as "righting" rather than "writing."

C. Ambiguity

Standing in contrast to garden-path sentences, are sentences with ambiguous grammatical structures. For example, there are two readings of the sentence "Flying planes can be dangerous." The planes can be either dangerous to their pilots and passengers or dangerous to onlookers down on the tarmac. Both interpretations of the participle "flying" are fairly strong. Because the two readings are of similar strength, they can compete with each other and no garden-pathing arises. Another example of this type is "He bought her pancakes" in which "her" can be either the possessor of the pancakes or the recipient of the pancakes. Both meanings are strong and can compete with each other during sentence processing, yielding a clear ambiguity.

D. Modularity

The four types of processing mentioned earlier (auditory, lexical, grammatical, and conceptual) are fully intermixed in real time. We do not wait until the end of the sentence to complete a lower level before moving on the to the next level. However, it is not yet clear whether the interaction between these levels is completely immediate. For example, it appears that during the first 300 msec after hearing a word, we attend primarily to its auditory shape, rather than the degree to which it fits into some grammatical context. Take as an example the sentence "The sailors took the port at night." Here the word "port" could refer to either the wine or the harbor. We can ask subjects to listen to sentences like this while watching a computer screen. Directly after subjects hear the word "port," we can present one of these three words on the computer screen: "wine," "harbor," and some control word such as "shirt." If we do this, we will find that the recognition of both "wine" and "harbor" is facilitated in comparison to the control word "shirt." If we change the sentence to something like "The sailors drank the port at night," we would expect perhaps that the context would bias the subject to respond more quickly to "wine" than to harbor, because one is not likely to drink a harbor. However, in some studies there is evidence that both "wine" and "harbor" are facilitated in comparison to the control word "shirt," even when the context tends to bias the "wine" reading of "port." This facilitation is fairly short-lived and the preference for the contextually appropriate reading soon comes to dominate.

This type of result indicates that, in the first fraction of a second after hearing a word, we rely most strongly on auditory cues to guide our processing. This is not to say that context is not present or not being used as a cue. However, during the first fraction of a second, we need to focus on the actual auditory form in order to avoid any "hallucinatory" effects of paying too much attention to context too soon in processing.

E. Shadowing

Children often try to tease one another by immediately repeating the other person's words even as they are being produced. Some skilled shadowers can repeat words with only a 300-msec delay. However, most of us can shadow at around an 800-msec delay. If a distortion is added to the end of a word, shadowers will usually correct this distortion immediately. For example, if the word "cigarette" is distorted to "cigaresh," the shadower will immediately and unconsciously correct it to "cigarette." This indicates that the shadower takes in enough of the word to derive a unique lexical item and then simply predicts the shape of the rest of the word, essentially ignoring the additional auditory information. The speed with which this is done provides yet another indicator of the "on-line" and immediate nature of sentence processing.

F. Reconstruction

The type of reconstruction that occurs during shadowing can also occur directly during comprehension. For example, we may tend to think that we hear a final "s" on the word "cat" if it occurs in a sentence like "The cat sit under the table." It is difficult for listeners to believe that the sentence was not actually "The cats sit under the table." In general, we often use syntactic patterns to correct for problems in the sentences we hear, thereby patching up the various errors made by other speakers, even before they really come to our attention.

II. SENTENCE PRODUCTION

There are many similarities between sentence comprehension and sentence production. In both activities, we rely heavily on the words in our lexicon to control syntactic structures. Both activities make use of the same patterns for determining grammatical structures. The most important difference between sentence comprehension and sentence production is based on the fact that, when producing utterances, we are in full control of the meanings we wish to express. In comprehension, on the other hand, we are necessarily followers—we need to piece together the meanings composed by others.

The processing of sentences in production also involves at least four structural levels. The first level governs the formulation of what we want to say or *message construction*. The second involves the reduction of our ideas to a set of words through *lexical access*. The third structures these words into utterances through *positional patterning*. The fourth activates a series of verbal gestures through *articulatory planning*. As in the case of comprehension, these four stages are conducted not in serial order, but in parallel. Even before we have finished the complete construction of the message underlying a sentence, we begin the process of articulating the utterance. Sometimes we find out in the middle of an utterance that we have either forgotten what we want to say or do not know how to say it. It is this interleaved quality of speech production that gives rise to the various speech errors, pauses, and disfluencies that we often detect in our own speech and that of others.

Speech errors come in many different forms. Some involve simple slurring of a sound or retracing of a group of words. Others provide more dramatic evidence of the nature of the language planning process. Some of the most entertaining types of speech errors are *spoonerisms,* which owe their name to an English clergyman by the name of William Spooner. Instead of "dear old queen," Spooner produced "queer old dean." Instead of "ye noble sons of toil," he produced "ye noble tons of soil." Instead of "I saw you light a fire in the back quad, in fact you wasted the whole term," he said "I saw you fight a liar in the back quad, in fact you tasted the whole worm." These errors typically involve the transpositions of letters between words. Crucially, the resulting sound forms are themselves real words, such as "liar" "queer," and "worm." The tendency of these errors to produce real words is known as the "lexical bias" and indicates the extent to which the lexicon itself acts as a filter or checker on the articulatory process.

Another illuminating group of errors are named after a character named Mrs. Malaprop in the play "The Rivals" by Sheridan. Some examples of *malapropisms* include "Judas Asparagus" for "Judas Iscariot," "epitaphs" for "epithets," or even "croutons" for "coupons." Some malapropisms can be attributed to pretentious use of vocabulary by uneducated speakers, but many of these errors are true slips of the tongue. In a malapropism, the two words have a similar sound, but a very different meaning. The fact that speakers end up producing words with quite the wrong meaning suggests that, at a certain point during speech planning, the processor handles words more in terms of their phonological form than the meaning they express. It is at this point that malapropisms can occur.

When two words end up directly competing for a single slot in the output articulatory plan, the result is a lexical *blend*. For example, a speaker may want to describe both the flavor and the taste of some food and end up talking about its "flaste." Or we might want to talk about someone's spatial performance and end up talking about their "perfacial performance." These errors show the extent to which words are competing for placement into particular slots. When two words are targeting the same slot, one will usually win, but if there is no clear winner there can be a blend.

Another remarkable property of speech errors is the way in which grammatical markers seem to operate independently of the nouns and verbs to which they attach. Consider an "exchange" error such as "the floods were roaded" for "the roads were flooded." In this error, the plural marker "s" and the past tense marker "ed" go to their correct positions in the output, but it is the noun and the verb that are transposed. This independent behavior of stems and their suffixes indicates that words are being composed from their grammatical pieces during sentence production and that grammatical markers contain clear specifications for their syntactic positions.

Some of the earliest thinking on the subject of speech errors was done by Sigmund Freud at the beginning of the century. He believed that slips of the tongue could provide evidence for underlying anxieties, hostilities, and worries. From this theory, arose the notion of a "Freudian slip." We now know that the majority of speech errors are not of this type, but it still appears that at least some could be viewed in this way. For example, if a speaker is discussing some activities involving a local barber, he might say "He made hairlines" instead of "He made headlines." These errors indicate contextual influences from competing plans. However, even examples of this type of contextual influence do not necessarily reveal underlying hostilities or neuroses.

III. MESSAGE CONSTRUCTION

The basic goal of both sentence comprehension and sentence production is the linking of formal linguistic expression to underlying conceptual meanings. A common way of thinking about these underlying meanings is in terms of a *conceptual dependency* graph. As an example, take the set of propositions underlying the first sentence of Lincoln's Gettysburg Address.

1. Forefathers set forth a nation.
2. Nation was new.
3. Nation was on this continent.
4. Setting forth occurred four score and seven years ago.
5. Nation was conceived in liberty.

6. Nation was dedicated to a proposition.
7. Proposition is: all men are created equal.

Lincoln brought together these varying underlying propositions into a single grammatical whole by foregrounding some material into the main clause ("forefathers set forth a nation") and backgrounding other material into relative clauses and modifiers.

In the classical rhetorical theory of the Greeks and Romans, the art of combining ideas into sentences was called "arrangement." In our everyday speech, we continually engage in simple forms of arrangement. For example, if we want to point out that there is a dent in the side of the refrigerator, we can say "Someone knocked a dent in the refrigerator" or we can say "The refrigerator got a dent knocked into it." In the first case we avoid the pseudo-passive construction, but are forced to point a finger at a specific perpetrator of the deed. In the second case, we background or deemphasize the doer of the activity, focusing instead on the result. These choices between what to foreground and what to background are being made in every sentence we produce.

Another choice we make is between alternative perspectives on a single action. For example, we could describe a picture by saying "The girl gave a flower to the boy." If that is the form we select, we are taking the viewpoint or perspective of the girl and describing the activity of giving from her vantage point. Alternatively, we could say "The boy got a flower from the girl." In this alternative form, we view the action from the perspective of the recipient. Depending on whether we choose to view the action from the viewpoint of the giver or the receiver, we will use either the verb "give" or the verb "get." Language is full of choices of this type, and sentence production can be viewed as involving a continual *competition* between choices for perspectives and foregrounding. The various points of view we could take and the various ideas that we want to express are continually in competition with one another for expression. At a given point in time, only one set of ideas can be expressed. In the end, we can never express all available information or all possible perspectives and we must make hard choices to pick some winners and leave some ideas unexpressed.

In comprehension, we also face a vigorous competition in our match of ideas to linguistic form. The first phrase in a sentence plays a crucial role as a starting point for the construction of the meaning underlying the sentence. In English, this first word is often the subject of the sentence, but it can also be some other adverbial phrase or a preposed topic, as in sentences such as "Ice cream and bananas, Bill really likes 'em swimming in chocolate sauce." Once we have established this initial starting point, the verb and additional nouns and phrases attached to the verb are all related propositionally to the starting point. If we are lucky, the process of attaching material to this starting point goes smoothly, but if there are ambiguities or garden-pathings, we may be forced to undo some of our initial propositional connections.

The construction of relations between words depends strongly on a set of grammatical cues for *cohesion* relations. These cues include pronouns and articles that mark which of several preceding objects is being pointed to in a current sentence. For example, in a slight variation on the nursery rhyme, we can say, "Jack and Jill went up the hill to fetch a pail of water. He fell down and broke his crown and she came tumbling after." In this sequence, we know that "he" refers to Jack and that "she" refers to "Jill." This co-reference between the pronoun and its antecedent is part of much more extensive system of cohesion markings that we use to construct stories and larger discourses. Underlying this system is the notion of givenness and newness. When something has already been mentioned, it is "old" material, and we can refer to it with an article like "the." When it is "new" material, we can refer to it using an article like "a." Across groups of sentences, the sentence processing mechanism depends heavily on these cues for the linking of propositions.

The construction of propositional meanings is guided by our default assumptions about language and the world. For example, if we hear a sentence describing "Indians and cowboys," we may tend to recall it as having been about "cowboys and Indians." In general, the exact surface form of sentences often fades within seconds after we hear them. This is particularly true of the commonplace, predictable material that is used in textbooks or in experiments on sentence processing. However, if one examines memory for more lively, charged, interpersonal communications, a very different picture emerges. For this type of discourse, memory for the specific working of jokes, compliments, insults, and threats can be extremely accurate, extending even over several days. Often we are careful to note the exact phrasing of language spoken by our close associates, since we assume that this phasing contains important clues regarding aspects of our interpersonal relations. For material that contains no such interpersonal content, we focus only on underlying meaning, quickly discarding surface phrasings.

IV. THE ROLE OF SYNTACTIC THEORY

Sentence comprehension depends on at least some use of grammatical knowledge. We have to use the order in which words occur to distinguish the meaning of "The dog is chasing the bear" from that of "The bear is chasing the dog." We often cannot derive the correct interpretation of even the simplest of sentences without paying attention to word order and other grammatical markings. But how and when do we impose our ideas about grammatical structures on the incoming stream of words? Some researchers believe that the impact of grammar is full and immediate particularly during the first 500 msec after hearing a word. Consider these example sentences:

The spy shot the cop with a revolver.
The spy saw the cop with a revolver.

In the first sentence, we can say that the prepositional phase, "with a revolver" modifies or attaches to the noun "cop." In the second sentence, the prepositional phrase "with a revolver" modifies or attaches to the verb "shot." These assignments seem immediate and direct, occurring during the processing of the prepositional phrase itself. Some studies have suggested that a universal property of the basic human sentence processing mechanism known as "minimal attachment" biases the listener toward the correct interpretation in the first sentence and forces a mild garden path in the second. However, other studies have questioned these claims, demonstrating that these biases can easily be shifted around with other materials. Evidence for the direct action of complex syntactic structures on sentence processing is currently minimal.

On the other hand, there is a great deal of evidence for effects that depend directly on the association between individual words. In the examples given above, a direct lexical effect from the verb "shot" tends to bias the listener to thinking of the revolver as an instrument more than in the case of the verb "saw." Sometimes lexically based expectations can be fairly complex. Consider these sentences:

John criticized Mary, because she hadn't delivered the paper on time.
John apologized to Mary, because he hadn't delivered the paper on time.
?John criticized Mary, because he hadn't delivered the paper on time.
?John apologized to Mary, because she hadn't delivered the paper on time.

Processing of the first two sentences is quick and easy, because the gender of the pronoun matches that of the expected agent. However, the processing of the second pair is more problematic because the gender of the pronoun forces the selection of an unexpected causor of the criticism or the apology.

Another lexical effect centered around the verb involves the degree to which a verb anticipates a direct object or complement. For some listeners, this sentence leads to a garden path: "Since Jay always jogs a mile seems like a short distance to him." The natural tendency here is to assume that "a mile" is the complement of the verb "jog." It appears that even verbs that are sometimes intransitive and do not require direct objects tend to be processed as taking objects or complements, if there is a noun immediately following the verb. It is expectations of this type, centered in individual words and operating through our general understanding of relations in the world, that most strongly determine the time course local syntactic effects in sentence processing.

V. CROSS-LINGUISTIC COMPARISONS

What stands out most clearly when one compares sentence processing across languages is the fairly tight relation between the time course and ultimate results of sentence processing and the reliability of specific grammatical cues in the language. Consider a comparison of these sentences from English and Spanish:

The lion kisses the cow.
El león besa la vaca. (The lion kisses the cow.)

A major difference between the two languages revolves around the use of variable word orders. In Spanish, it is possible to invert the word order and produce "la vaca besa el león" while still meaning that the lion is kissing the cow. This inversion is even clearer if the particle "a" is added to marker the direct object as in these variant orderings in which the two nouns are moved into different places around the verb "besa."

El león besa a la vaca.
A la vaca la besa el león.
La besa el león a la vaca.
La besa a la vaca el león.

These differences between English and Spanish can be traced to the relative cue validities of word order and object marking in the two languages. In English, it is virtually always the case that the noun that appears before the verb is the subject of the sentence. If the verb is an active verb, the preverbal noun is almost always the actor. This means that the cue of preverbal positioning is an extremely reliable guide in English to assignment of the actor role. In Spanish, no such simple rule attains. Instead, the best cue to assignment of the actor role is the presence of the object marker particle "a." If one of the nouns in a two-noun sentence is marked by "a," then we know that the other noun is the agent or subject.

Other languages have still other configurations of the basic cues to sentence interpretation. For example, Hungarian makes reliable use of a single case marking suffix on the direct object. German uses the definite article to mark case and number. The Australian language Warlpiri marks the subject with a variety of complex case markings. Navajo places nouns in front of the verb in terms of their relative animacy in the Navajo "Great Chain of Being" and then uses verbal prefixes to pick out the subject. These languages and others also often rely on number agreement between the verb and the noun as a cue to the subject. English also requires subject–verb agreement, but this cue is often missing or neutralized. In languages like Italian or Arabic, subject–verb agreement marking is extremely clear and reliable.

When one looks at the ways in which languages deal with complex structures such as relative clauses, a parellel picture of processing based on relative cue reliability also emerges. For example, in Japanese the basic order of sentences is noun–noun–verb, rather than the noun–verb–noun order found in English. In addition, Japanese places relative clauses before the head noun, rather than after the head noun. Japanese marks subject and object with case particles or postpositions. All of these differences lead to great contrasts between the processing of conceptually similar relative clause structures in English and Japanese. However, what appears to be constant in all languages is the fact that relative clause structures that involve any extreme "stacking up" of nouns or verbs are comparatively difficult to process. In English, this occurs in center-embedded clauses such as "The dog the rat the cat chased bit barked." In Japanese, this concept would be rendered as "cat-by chased rat-by bit dog barked." The Japanese form of the utterance is relatively easy to process, but a pattern such as "dog cat-by chased rat-by bit barked" is difficult in Japanese, since it involves a greater stacking up of nouns and verbs, although not quite as extreme as in the English version.

These cross-linguistic comparisons point out the extent to which all processing requires the linking of nouns to verbs in a smooth and conceptually driven fashion. Any stacking up of unattached, unrelated nouns puts a burden on short-term memory that then impedes further processing. Effects such as this can be treated in terms of the general concept of *cue cost*.

When monolingual speakers come to learning a second language, they need to fundamentally retune their sentence processing mechanism. First, they need to acquire a new set of grammatical devices and markings. Second, they need to associate these new devices with the correct cue validities. Third, they need to reorganize their expectations for particular sequences of cues and forms. Initially, the learner simply transfers the cues, cue validities, and habits from the first language to processing of the second language. Over time, the cue validities change smoothly, until they eventually match that of the native monolingual.

VI. THE DEVELOPMENT OF PROCESSING

When children come to the task of language learning, they have no idea which language they are being asked to learn, so they must be equally well prepared to pick up virtually any possible human language. What they learn first in a given language is primarily influenced by the clarity of its marking or its *dectability*, as well as its cue reliability. English-speaking children quickly learn to rely on the preverbal positioning cue, whereas Spanish-speaking children soon learn to rely on the use of the particle "a" to make the direct object. Although cue reliability is the primary determinant of the order of acquisition of grammatical markings, there are some deviations from this general rule. In particular, children are slow to pick up difficult patterns such as subject–verb agreement marking. It appears that what makes this type of marking particularly difficult for the child is the fact that markings on one grammatical phrase must be carried over to and matched by properties on another grammatical phrase. This type of processing across a distance is a cue cost factor that limits full acquisition of this type of structure until age 5 or 6.

In general terms, young children have not yet organized their processing systems in a way that provides maximally quick and efficient processing. In reaction time experiments measuring sentence comprehension, children are markedly slower than adults. In tasks requiring picture descriptions, young children often fail to organize a variety of concepts into a single well-structured sentential package. Increases in expressive skills continue well into the adolescent years. Although all of the basic syntactic structures of the language are usually mastered by age 3, it takes many more years to coordinate the use of these various devices in actual sentences, particularly in sentence production.

VII. DISORDERS IN SENTENCE PROCESSING

Although all of us learn the basic structure of our language, we vary greatly in our abilities to control language smoothly and to use language to delight and persuade others. Even in the first years of life, there are often vast differences between the ways in which children come to grips with language learning. Some children are able to produce their first two-word sentences even by the time of their first birthday, whereas other children remain speechless as late as 3 or even 4 years of age. Classic examples of children with language delay include Albert Einstein and Lord Macauley. In some cases, these children speak secretly with their peers or siblings long before engaging in conversations with adults. A short period of language delay is also found in children suffering from chronic ear infections or disorders of the trachea. When these disorders are corrected, these children quickly pick up the missed stages of development and soon come to talk like their age-matched peers.

There are other children who have various forms of organic disorders or brain injuries that lead to long-term and sometimes permanent disabilities in language processing. The general term for children with normal cognitive abilities, but with specific disorders in language processing is *specific language impairment* or SLI. Children with SLI fall into two further groups—those with impairments specific to language production and those with impairments to both production and comprehension. The root cause of disorders in production often involves problems with the timing of articulation or sentence formulation. The causes of a general language impairment can include problems with auditory processing, central timing problems, or problems in lexical access.

Adults who have suffered from strokes or other injuries to the brain can develop somewhat different language problems. Patients whose only problem lies in the smooth and rhythmic articulation or words are said to suffer from *dysarthria*. Patients whose only problem is the finding of the correct word for objects and activities are said to suffer fron *anomia*. Patients with more central language disorders are said to suffer from *aphasia*. If the patient tends to speak in a telegraphic fashion, omitting grammatical markings and other small words, the standard classification is for *expressive aphasia*, which is also known as agrammatism, nonfluent aphasia, or Broca's aphasia. If the disorder leads to too great a use of verbal material, the classification is for *fluent aphasia*, which is also called Wernicke's aphasia. When the ability to imitate is specifically impaired, the diagnosis of *conduction aphasia* is often used. The localization of these various forms of aphasia in particular areas of the brain is difficult to achieve, although both anterior and posterior areas around the Sylvian fissure are typically involved in all of the aphasias. [*See* APHASIA.]

Aphasia has a standard pattern of effects on language loss in different languages. This pattern is determined by the relative cue reliability of grammatical markers in each language. As we noted earlier, the strongest cue for sentence processing in English is the preverbal positioning of the subject. This particular cue remains well-preserved in English-speaking aphasics, whereas the weaker cue of subject–verb agreement is virtually totally destroyed. On the other hand, Italian-speaking aphasics show the opposite pattern, with a strong preservation of subject–verb agreement and a fairly minimal use of word order cues. In terms of sentence production, aphasics also show a strong sensitivity to the relative importance of grammatical markings in their language. English-speaking aphasics retain the subject–verb–object word order of the English and Turkish-speaking aphasics retain the subject–object–verb order of their language. German-speaking aphasics retain the definite article, since it is a crucial marker of case and number, whereas Hungarian-speaking aphasics drop the article, since it is not a crucial marker in their language.

The various characteristics found in aphasics' comprehension of language can be mimicked in normal subjects by exposing them to a high level of noise or additional concurrent tasks while listening to complex sentences. Noise and cognitive load can also have strong effects on sentence processing in the weaker language of bilinguals. For example, a German–English bilingual with relatively weaker English abilities will start to resemble an English aphasic when subjected to a slight amount of noise. These results suggest that the language processing system relies on a core set of computational resources for many different purposes. Various forms of damage or temporary impairment to this core set of resources tends to affect those aspects of language processing that require particular care or attention.

VIII. OVERVIEW

Together these many facts gathered from different languages and different types of speakers point toward a view of sentence processing as highly interactive and competitive. During comprehension, there is a struggle between words for recognition in the input speech stream. Grammatical roles activated by verbs compete for nominal arguments and nominals compete for roles. Phrases compete for alternative attachments and pronouns compete for alternative referents. In production, ideas compete for expression, words compete for slots, and everything competes for final articulation. Given this massive struggle between forms and functions, it is remarkable how effortless language processing often seems and how easy it is for us to pour our ideas into words.

Bibliography

Altmann, G. (Ed.) (1989). "Parsing and Interpretation." Erlbaum, Hillsdale, NJ.

Bates, E., Wulfeck, B., and MacWhinney, B. (1991). Crosslinguistic research in aphasia: An overview. *Brain Language* 1–15.

Carlson, G., and Tanenhaus, M. (Eds.) (1989). "Linguistic Structure in Language Processing." Kluwer, Dordrecht.

Clark, H., and Clark, E. (1977). "Psychology and Language: An Introduction to Psycholinguistics. Harcourt, Brace, Jovanovich, New York.

Just, M., and Carpenter, P. (1992). A capacity theory of comprehension: Individual differences in working memory. *Psychol. Rev.* 122–149

MacWhinney, B., Osman-Sági, J., and Slobin, D. (1991). Sentence comprehension in aphasia in two clear case-marking language. *Brain Language* 41, 234–249.

MacWhinney, B. (1992). Transfer and competition in second language learning. In "Cognitive Processing in Bilinguals." (R. Harris, Ed.), Elsevier, Amsterdam.

MacWhinney, B., and Bates, E. (Eds.) (1989). "The crosslinguistic Study of Sentence Processing." Cambridge University Press, New York.

Miller, J. (Ed.) (1991). "Research on Child Language Disorders: A Decade of Progress." Pro-Ed, Austin, TX.

SEX ROLES

Jan D. Sinnott
Towson State University

Glossary

Femininity Behavior and qualities shown by women.

Masculinity Behavior and qualities shown by men.

Roles Organized patterns of interpersonal behaviors congruent with a culture.

Role stereotypes Rigid ideas about appropriate role behaviors.

SEX ROLES can be defined as role-related behavior ascribed by society to women because they are women and to men because they are men. The designation of an individual as a woman or a man may be done by the individual, by the society, or by both. Factors used as designation criteria are not consistent. The field of sex roles is one in which definitions have had more than usual importance. The questions in this field are emotionally loaded ones which are tied to social expectations, history, taboos and strong biological urges. Definitions determine what is studied, and what is seen as unchangeable or "given" by nature over the life span. Sex roles, roles once seen as simple and unchanging, are now seen by psychologists as more complex, more context-determined, and more malleable.

I. FURTHER DEFINITIONS AND MODELS

Several definitions and further distinctions need to be made to avoid confusion. The first distinction can be made between *sex* and *gender*. In 1979, Unger attempted to clarify the distinction between sex and gender for the discipline of Psychology. She argued that sex should be limited to the biological bases of producing the two primary genders: the presence of XX or XY chromosomes, hormonal output from the gonads, internal and external reproductive anatomy, and secondary sex characteristics. Gender on the other hand is what culture does with the evidence of biological sex. Ultimately the culture creates expected behavior patterns or styles which are deemed gender specific. A second distinction can be made between *sex roles* and *sex role stereotypes*. The former include the actual behaviors of males and females which have considerable variability. The latter are oversimplified socially shared perceptions of idealized "male" or "female" actions, perceptions which usually allow little variability. Third, *sexuality* differs from *sex roles*. The roles are overt behaviors of many kinds, including sexuality, linked to "maleness" and "femaleness." Sexuality is the behavior directly associated with having sex or being sexually involved. Fourth, *gender identity,* one's sense of oneself as essentially "male" or "female," may or may not be reflected in one's *roles* or one's *sexuality*. Fifth, *gender schemes* are the cognitive constructs used to conceptualize "male" or "female" roles or identity, and, although held very deeply by the person, may not be congruent with his or her behavior.

Gender differences, defined as distinctions that can be made between maleness and femaleness or between males and females themselves, are a problematic category. Psychologists often find it hard to decide how *much* difference is a true difference. We often confuse differences in perceptions or constructs of sex roles with differences in actual behavior of males and females. Yet decisions about "differences" often lead to broad public policy decisions.

Defining and measuring sex roles in polarized terms (i.e., "male" vs "female") may be erroneous. According to Rabin, the idea that there are only two biological sexes needs reexamination. There are numerous examples from biology that indicate more possibilities than just two complementary sexes. We find hermaphroditic species which contain both reproductive capacities within one body, and even one all-female species of whiptail lizard which reproduces parthenogenetically. There are large numbers of coral reef fishes and tropical sand fishes which change sex. The popular polarization of the enormous range of human variability into two boxes at opposing ends of the human spectrum may be the consequence of normative thinking in the social sciences added to our penchant for creating dualities by ignoring the overlapping frequency distribution curves for male and female performance. Even when a statistically significant sex difference in performance in math skill or verbal skills can be demonstrated, this larger overlap between distributions means that the individuals whose performance falls within the overlap area cannot be distinguished on the basis of gender. Many females excel in math. Many males do poorly in math but excel in verbal skills. Differences that emerge are far more likely to be individual differences than actual gender differences separating all women from all men. So the most useful approach may be to think of and to measure maleness and femaleness on a continuum.

Confusion among these terms and models leads to negative results for science and for individuals. Conceptualizations of sex roles have been a function of philosophy, history, economics, and politics. Awareness that sex roles exist, and are influential, and that this occurs at all times in life, has also been a function of those four forces. These influences quietly shape the choice of problems to investigate and research projects to pursue. Most scientists in a given field accept some view of the world that dominates their field and choose problems accordingly. Driven by a need for cognitive consistency, individuals adopt the new view as "natural." In a world at war, for example, the role of a man is seen as that of a warrior, "naturally," and the role of a woman "naturally" becomes that of a worker/mother; after a return to peace, the woman may be "naturally" redefined as mother (only) while the now suddenly "nonwarlike" male is redefined as worker. Theories of adjustment, development, and mental health are quick to conform to the demands of the belief system and historical situation. Social psychology has made it clear that even radical shifts in ideas and behavior are accepted to maintain thinking consistency, provided motivation is high enough. Researchers in human development are not immune to these general laws. We study what seems important at the time.

II. GENDER ROLE DEVELOPMENT ACROSS THE LIFE SPAN

A. Childhood Developmental Theories

Early views of sex role development considered masculine and feminine roles as biologically based and, once established in childhood, consistent throughout the life span. The testing movement provided the impetus to quantify and validate such views. Masculinity and femininity were conceptualized as marking the two extreme endpoints of a continuum. Individuals were assumed to be optimally adjusted if their biological sex and their sex role identity were the same. An individual who deviated from a prescribed sex role was seen as one whose psychosexual development was inadequate, rather than as possibly a person who was flexible in meeting changing environmental demands. This view reflected the Freudian approach which depicted sex role identification in terms of resolution of the Oedipal conflict. Such a resolution involved the identification of a boy with his father and the girl, in a somewhat more circuitous way, with her mother. The possible learned nature of sex roles came to the forefront with the advent of social learning theory, cognitive developmental theory, biologically oriented inquiries, anthropological investigation, and the life span approach.

B. Social Learning Theory

Whereas Freud and other functionalists implied that sex roles merely unfold out of an innate potential, the social learning theorists such as Bandura posited that such roles were learned via imitation and observation of parents and other adult models. Reinforcement then led to the establishment of behavioral patterns. Although changes in reinforcement contingencies allowed the possibility for sex role change, it was assumed that the sex typed roles did not change significantly during one's life span. Modeling the behaviors of the same sex was thought to begin at a very early age and to be reinforced into adulthood. However, research that has focused on modeling of adult behavior or global personality traits shared by parent and child has *not* found that children closely follow the behavior or personality of the same-sex adult.

C. Cognitive Developmental Theory

A cognitive developmental approach such as Kohlberg's, held that the child's perception of sex role identification precedes sex appropriate behavior. The child discovered that two sexes existed, thought about himself or herself as being a boy or a girl, considered differences between the sexes, and came to some fairly stable notions as to what "boy/man" versus "girl/woman" connoted. Some of the same behavioral factors that the social learning theorists proposed were also expected, except that cognitive identification with a same-sex parent *preceded* the modeling of behaviors in terms of observation and imitation. The cognitive developmentalists also assumed that both children and adults maintained a relatively consistent concept of themselves as male or female, and that the search for congruence between beliefs and behavior led to the maintenance of appropriate roles. This view may be contrasted with the social learning view in which reward is the key to the persistence of sex appropriate behavior. Both theoretical viewpoints, however, emphasize the establishment of such an identity early in life with consistency in adulthood.

The learning perspective on sex roles has also received a valuable contribution from the biological perspective of Money and Ehrhardt. These researchers have studied children who genetically, and on the basis of prenatal hormones, would have been expected to develop the gender identity of one sex but because of mishap (for example, structural damage or deformity of the genitals) were assigned to the opposite sex. Interview data collected from the families of such children indicated that seeming acceptance of the assigned sex and gender role identity development proceeded commensurate with the child's acceptance of assigned gender identity. While these studies are by no means conclusive, they do point out the overwhelming impact of socialization.

D. Anthropological Investigations

Anthropological study has supported the learned nature of sex roles and has led to questioning the notion of consistent, appropriate behaviors for each gender. The large impact of culture on any given society's notion of what is appropriate male and female behavior has been exemplified by Mead's comparison of three primitive societies. Both the men and women of the Arapesh tribe were described as being passive, nurturant, cooperative, and sensitive, traits perceived as feminine in American culture. The Mundugamore men and women were characterized as aggressive, suspicious, and uncaring, traits perceived as masculine in American culture. The Tchambuli men behaved in ways our society typically defines as feminine while the women exhibited what we might define as stereotypically masculine traits. The importance of culture-specific specialization has been expounded in numerous articles and books with respect to more modern societies as well.

The anthropological perspective has been used by researchers such as Gutmann to explore the function of sex roles in terms of survival of the species. Cultural universals are presumed to reflect basic human propensities; their consistency is assumed to be of some importance in terms of survival. Proponents of the learning approach, which emphasizes socialization, view exceptions to cultural universals as evidence for the greater impact of environment on heredity. Opponents point out that a few exceptions do not make a case against biological mechanisms but rather show evolutionary change within some special environmental conditions.

E. Adult Developmental Theories

The life span approach to sex role development has been a relatively recent phenomenon. Neugarten, Gutmann, and Block explored changes in male and female role expectations during adulthood that were based upon social expectation and major developmental tasks. Block and Riegel viewed the manifestation of cultural sex roles as a function not only of biological demands and past learning experiences but of the nature of economic systems, the historical moment, and the philosophical system within which they are defined. Thus, sex roles in this perspective imply dynamic change based upon the individual change and the social and cultural climate.

Loevinger's milestones of ego development and their extrapolations to sex role development form the basis of Block's approach. In the earliest period, the main development concerns of the child are genderless, and identity constitutes a mere naming of gender: "I am a boy/girl." Later, conformity to learned patterns becomes the main task; this is reflected in the development of sex role stereotypes and sex role bifurcation. This conformist stage is followed by one of self-criticism based on comparison with an abstract ideal, thereby moderating the stereotypical role. With the advent of autonomy, individualization results as conflicts, aroused during the conformity and conscientious stages, are resolved. At this point, differentiation of sex role is said to occur. The highest, most integrated level of functioning finds the individual evolving a complex identity which combines aspiration, experience, and previously polarized traits. In sex role terms, this period is one of androgyny.

Hefner, Rebecca, and Oleshansky have proposed a life span approach to the development of sex role identity. Their hierarchical stages include: (1) global, undifferentiated sex roles; (2) polarized, or traditional masculine/feminine roles, and (3) transcendent roles which combine both masculinity and femininity. While the young child most likely has not defined a sex role and the adolescent most likely has overdefined it, the adult synthesizes roles into more complex wholes. For individuals who have "transcended" masculinity and feminity, psychological adjustment is no longer tied to these dichotomous sets of traits, or even the blend of androgyny. Unfortunately, the measurement of "transcendence" as distinct from androgyny has not yet been fully operationalized.

Garnets and Pleck have presented a concept called sex role strain analysis. Their viewpoint combines social learning and life span development. They feel that the ultimate harm of traditional sex roles is the devaluation an individual may experience if he or she does not conform to traditional standards set by sex role norms. Thus, strain results from discrepancy between the individual's self-perception and his or her perceptions of social expectations. Garnets and Pleck also measure the degree of salience of sex role characteristics for the individual.

Sinnott described a postformal theory of adult sex role development. A number of investigators have recently addressed the topic of "postformal" operations, i.e., those structures of thought which are a stage more complex in organization than Piaget's formal operations. More work on postformal, mature adult thought is being done, possibly since the idea of cognitive development beyond adolescence is an appealing one. The question of interest here is: How might formal and postformal operations be related to a life span model of sex role development? To address this question it is necessary to examine some aspects of postformal operations and the argument itself more closely. The argument is a postmodern one.

What kind of case is being made for a relation between cognitive development, especially formal and postformal operations, and sex roles? To oversimplify, it is the same type of case that Kohlberg makes about cognitive development and early sex role development and about cognitive and moral development. Social relations, of which sex roles and moral development are examples, may be seen as based upon cognitive skills. As cognitive skills develop, the social relations can be understood and can become more complex, too. At those times, when the world can be known in a manner more complex than an abstract, formal one, roles also might be known in a way that is more complex. Having thought of the role in a complex way, one could then live it in a complex way. [*See* COGNITIVE DEVELOPMENT; MORAL DEVELOPMENT.]

How would roles be known in postformal terms? To answer this question, one must look at theories of postformal operations. According to Kramer, authors of these theories all state that postformal thought is: (1) a distinct stage, (2) which subsumes formal operations, and (3) which incorporates a relativistic view of truth. Generally, then, a postformal cognitive stage could underlie a view of sex roles in which roles are not absolute but are created relative to the actor. Some given formal structure of roles would be consciously chosen based on some belief system that is a subjective view of "truth" from among a number of formal role structures. Further, what constitutes a given role would be known to be somewhat arbitrary and based partly on the perceiver's own experiences and resultant ideas of the role. The postformal concept of sex roles, then, includes a necessary subjectivity. It operates by laws like those of the new physics as described by Sinnott.

The role taken, or the role which one perceives that another takes, becomes what is agreed on by the persons in the interaction. The reality of the role is therefore determined by a system of beliefs held by the persons in the interaction. The individual is not in a roleless, undefined state, nor in possession of an absolute unchanging role, which is a permanent descriptor of one's identity. Rather he or she is constantly, perhaps even consciously, creating a flexible role definition in relation to individuals and circumstances in context. In the framework of Kelly's theory of personality, persons are always constructing a new social meaning for the self in the context of evolving social structures within a given society's institutions.

Role behaviors also may be seen as attempts to solve everyday life problems. Individuals learn to act in a way which helps them meet their goals. In the context of problem solving, which is a cognitive function, postformal thought-based roles might permit greater creativity in using strategies to solve problems where the problem goal is unclear. Most everyday problems fall into this category.

F. Systems Theory and Adult Sex Roles

Systems theory is a theory of interacting processes and the way they influence each other over time to permit the continuity of some larger whole. Systems act so as to continue. Systems change because their own balances are not optimal or because they are influenced by other systems. Some authors who provide excellent descriptions of these general ideas are van Bertalanffy and Miller. Miller's discussion of *living* systems is especially useful to consider for a discussion of sex roles. Individuals, societies, and cells all appear to use similar processes to create boundaries, to take in stimulation, to process information, to act, and to change. For example, for cells, information may be chemical and may be filtered by cell walls; for persons, information may be conceptual and may be filtered by perceptions; for societies information may be news and be filtered by censors. Cells, persons, and societies all exist in relation to each other which further complicates matters. Within systems theory, roles are structures of the social system which are equivalent to organs in the physical/person system; they are organized ways of ensuring that some vital function is performed.

As living systems—be they cell, person, or society—develop and age, they appear to proceed through a regular set of stages. They begin in disorder, that is, with a few parts concrete and defined. They become more orderly, defined, and bounded over time. They become rigid before they disintegrate and die as systems. System changes may be further described in chaos theory and complexity theory.

How does this relate to sex role development over the life span? Consider the person and society as living systems, each seeking continuity and meeting survival needs. These needs include control of information and energy flow. Sex roles are ways person and social systems can regulate the flow of information and energy (effort) while taking care of survival needs. The early stages of these systems are disordered in regard to roles, i.e., no roles are apparent. For example, the newborn is sex roleless, and a group of strangers is roleless as a group. Later stages are associated with more concretized roles; in the person and in the group, masculinity and femininity may emerge. Final stages find the roles rigid and inflexible, so they would fail to respond to the pull of new needs. This failure of response leads to disorder and a search for new, more complex order. Systems theory suggests that this may be the kind of transition we are seeing in societies now, and in the individual after the reproductive period and parental imperative (Gutmann). The person having rigid roles (sex roles or other roles), faced with new demands, might adapt with new complex integrations of role related behaviors, or might keep a *dys*functional system.

III. MAJOR CONFLICTS IN THE FIELD OF SEX ROLE RESEARCH

Six major conflicts have emerged in the field. Future research is likely to focus on these, as well as moving along to others. First, are roles fixed or flexible? Early theorists saw roles as fixed, at an early age, for life. More recent theorists see roles established, then evolving, based on age, societal demands, etc. Second, how central are roles to personality? In more traditional societies sex roles seem to be a core organizing principle of personal functioning; in less traditional cultures, they seem to be adopted and cast off with less impact on the person's sense of self. Third, how closely do roles relate to identity? This is a subdivision of the second question. Fourth, should roles be measured taking into account context and self-perception *vs* actual behavior? If roles need not be fixed, *context* might be extremely important to self-description since success as a parent (for example) often requires different traits than success as an employee. In another example, the single female parent may best use a combined role the earlier theorists labeled "masculine" as well as "feminine." Also, one's consistent self-concept, as perceived by the self, may be very different from what witnesses see the person actually doing, since the person may be verbally expressing what he or she has been told *should* be said. Fifth, are stereotypes, sexism, and power politics inherent in sex roles? Some theorists maintain that since roles have always been connected to power, domination, discrimination, and stereotypes, that this is a part of their dynamics. Other theorists maintain that roles could be conceived of (and studied) as value free and power neutral. Sixth, should we study *change* over time in roles? Developmental studies have demonstrated that changes seem to occur, based on age and history. How important are they for day to day applications of sex role knowledge?

Consideration of these conflicts, and the issues on which theorists agree, leads to several recommendations for future research and theory (Sinnott, 1987). Several conclusions can be drawn from the early and the recent literature on life span sex role development.

1. We must not jump to conclusions that responses on a scale will be predictive of behavior. Individuals may say that they are "masculine" by their scale responses, but may mean they are masculine in regard to stereotyping concepts. They may rate themselves differently in other situations, may act other than their ratings, and their behavior may vary from situation to situation. They may do what is most rewarding and that may happen to be masculine. They may score themselves masculine due to development of an identity labeled masculine. They may do so since masculine behavior is socially desirable. They may change in self-definition due to life stage demands, or when their own concept of masculinity is no longer like their behavior, even if to everyone else they are still "masculine," by some other definition. And they may label themselves or act as they perceive society expects them to do. Since all these factors may underlie their responses to the scale, it is hard to predict behavior based on scale responses.

2. Responses to sex role instruments do mean something. What is meant may be tempered by each person's perception of unspoken situational constraints and other factors mentioned above. If individuals respond appropriately they are matching themselves to global standards designed to reflect the clearest opposition between gender-assigned roles.

3. Masculinity, feminity, and androgyny have been shown to be adaptive. Depending upon the situational demands, subject to the constraints above, any of the roles might be adaptive. The real question is, what is the most useful role in a certain setting: masculine, feminine, both, or neither? Useful may mean "liable to be rewarded" or "consistent," or "workable by some external criterion." Androgyny may be the most adaptive response in terms of the last criterion; masculinity may be the most adaptive in terms of the first.

4. Sex roles are meaningful in terms of social expectations. The concept of global, oppositional, gender-linked roles is present for all members of society, and society imposes these role expectations on individuals so long as the real characteristics of those individuals are not known. So whatever complex designation of role and behavior one adopts, the general "other" is still seen as conforming to the global stereotypes. Individuals also perceive role expectations projected by others, and, to the degree they are conformists, attempt to conform to them.

5. Sex roles are meaningful ways to order one's sense of self as socially efficacious, to create a sense of personal conformity, and to order self-concept. The creation of the self concept is partially accomplished by acting, and noticing that the self is the center of effective acts. Roles permit structured action likely to work in a society. They also are labels that live on beyond the individual and can be generalized to many situations. Knowing a sex role without knowing the meaning of that role to the person is to take only half a step toward knowledge.

6. The meaning of sex roles depends on age and developmental stage. Meanings are related to modes of cognition and social demands at each period. They are also related to the previous history and experience of the person and the historical period in which the society finds itself. Infants can know roles in direct physical forms, but cannot know them abstractly. The concrete operational person can know roles in the abstract, and the formal operational person can build logical systems of roles. The postformal person can see roles relativistically, as co-created by persons in them.

7. Models of sex role changes over time can be of many types. Change can be more complex than increase or decrease in global qualities. Change might occur on one dimension but not on another, or in global role traits but not in behavior, or visa versa. Change might be triggered by specific events or might represent an accretion over time. It may be reversible. Change might result from diffusion of a self-concept until

its meaning is so muddy that it can become something new. Change might depend on past rates of change. It is useful for investigators to be clear about their underlying model of change as they discuss sex role development.

8. Sex role complexity and adult sex role development may be linked to cognitive abilities like postformal thought or problem-solving skills. Roles have been linked to cognitive processes such as concept formation. As cognitive operations become more complex, their associated roles might be seen as multifaceted rather than undimensional.

9. Sex role development related questions (e.g., "Am I being feminine?" "What is the masculine thing to do at any age?") may be conceptualized in decision theory or problem solving theory as ill-structured problems. This means among other things that they have an unclear goal. Decisions must be made about the nature of the goal as a part of solving the problem. Problem-solving literature can be a guide to dimensions we need to test to understand the process of solving sex role behavior/self-concept problems. This application of cognitive theory has not yet been attempted.

10. Sex role developmental theories suggest new physics concepts and might make use of them. A multivariate approach needs to be taken in sex role studies, in that adjacent centers of causality—other persons, the social order—cause changes in an individual's sex roles. The person, in turn, causes changes in the social order by his or her perception of roles and by action on that perception. It is clear that one's vantage point in measuring sex roles is very important in drawing conclusions about the results. These models have companion models in the physical sciences that could be used in studies of change, both change in a person and change among systems.

11. Sex role development theory can make use of ideas in systems theory. Personal and social systems are connected by many roles, among them sex roles. Theories of living systems give us an outline of the processes within and between those two systems. The flow of information can be studied within and between systems and roles are part of that information flow. A study of system boundaries can be conceptualized as a study of rigid or flexible roles and the capability of society or person to perceive or enact them. Future studies can take this model of living systems into account. Models of complexity and chaos may also be useful.

12. Emerging ideas suggest that in the future roles will be orchestrated consciously by the person, rather than being imposed consciously or unconsciously by society, or being left to the mercy of unexamined forces. Each child may grow up aware that she or he has a wide spectrum of role possibilities that can be acted out.

Future work should address the following questions and issues:

1. Role stereotypes (positive and negative), role related behavior, and gender-linked expectations all must be considered as potentially different phenomena in sex role research. The nature of test questions themselves is important. The scope, nature, variability, and contextual factors in each must be explored.

2. Roles must not be assumed to be linked to actual behavior or to be predictive of behavior, without evidence.

3. Role strength must be considered; one can be considered masculine, feminine, or androgynous only relative to some standard.

4. Perceptions, intentions, belief systems, and meanings are important neglected variables in sex role research.

5. Sex role life span research should be integrated with Piagetian approaches, cognitive work in general, problem-solving research.

6. Sex role development research should use models of change over time from new physics, chaos theory, complexity theory and systems theory to broaden the repertoire of multivariate approaches at its disposal and better reflect the reality of these complex multisystem changes.

7. The impact of roles on society and the species and the utility of roles of society and species need to be considered.

8. Learning and developmental effects need to be considered jointly in future research.

9. What is adaptive depends on situation, developmental stage, reward and punishment contingencies, past history, and the energy available state of the person–system at that time.

10. People have different styles of achieving the same goal or enacting the same intention, or reporting the same attitude.

11. Self-concept personal continuity, and personal effectiveness are seldom examined but enter into the picture of sex role development.

12. Methodological issues need to be clarified, especially including longitudinal research on factor changes. But current approaches still give useful information with careful interpretation.

Bibliography

Carter, D. B. (Ed.) (1987). "Current Conceptions of Sex Roles and Sex Typing; Theory and Research." Praeger, New York.

Devor, H. (1989). "Gender Blending; Confronting the Limits of Quality." Indiana University Press, Bloomington, IN.

Lips, H. M. (1991). "Women, Men, and Power." Mayfield, Mountain View, CA.

Sinnott, J. D. (1986). "Sex Roles and Aging; Theory and Research from a Systems Perspective." S. Karger, NY.

Sexual Behavior

John D. Baldwin and Janice I. Baldwin
University of California at Santa Barbara

Glossary

Erotophiles People who like and have positive attitudes about sex.

Erotophobes People who have a fear or phobia about sexuality and sexual cues.

Kinsey scale A continuum of different levels of heterosexual to homosexual orientation, with 0 being pure heterosexual and 6 being pure homosexual.

Psychogenic Excitation that has its origins in mental activity.

Scripts Patterns of talk and action that people learn from other people, books, movies, and other media. There are sexual scripts for dealing with every stage of relationships, from meeting a potential partner to making love.

Sexual orientation The degree to which a person is sexually attracted to the other sex, the same sex, both sexes, or neither sex.

HUMAN SEXUAL BEHAVIOR is influenced by countless biological, psychological, and social factors. From an evolutionary perspective, sexual behavior functions primarily to assure reproduction; and throughout most of human evolution, sexual activity was closely related to pregnancy and childbearing. Sexual behavior is usually pleasurable and may at times seem like an end in itself, but before the development of reliable birth control techniques, the link between sex and reproduction was much closer. The pleasures of sex also help create social bonds between two people, but these bonds are often not strong enough by themselves to guarantee monogamy. Most cultures have surrounded sexuality with symbolic qualities, ritual meaning, or moralistic implications that often function to increase monogamy and family orientation. This social overlay makes human sexuality far more complex than the relatively basic reproductive activities seen in other primates. Some societies have discovered special ways in which sexual pleasures can be heightened and enjoyed for themselves, without always being linked with pregnancy. The development of increasingly effective birth control and abortion techniques in the past three decades has allowed considerable separation of sexual activity from reproduction and the subsequent sexual revolution.

I. A MULTI-FACTOR MODEL OF SEXUALITY

As late as the early 1900s, it was common to "explain" human sexual behavior in terms of instincts. For example Freud postulated a sexual instinct and "explained" people's sex drive in terms of an instinctual energy he called libido. Gradually instinct theories have been recognized as weak hypothetical constructs and replaced by more detailed models of the biological, psychological, and social causes of motivation and behavior. Current theories of sexuality recognize that sexual behavior involves multiple components that interact complexly. The most basic elements of this multifactor model of sexual behavior are the reflex mechanisms that cause vaginal lubrication, penile erection, other genital responses, and orgasm. These reflexes influence and are influenced by both instrumental learning and classical conditioning, which in turn are affected by the type of home, community, and culture in which a person lives. Finally, as children develop more cognitive capacities, they can increasingly plan unique and creative ways of directing their sexual experiences.

A. Reflexes

The sexual responses of the genitals are mediated by several reflex centers located in the lower spinal cord. The most basic way to activate the sexual reflexes is by touch to the genitals. Nerves connecting the gentials to the spinal reflex centers respond to touch as the *unconditioned stimulus* that activates them—without the need for any prior conditioning. The reflex mechanisms then activate all the genital changes associated with sexual arousal, such as vaginal lubrication, penile erection, and—after enough stimulation—orgasm. They also send signals to and respond to signals from the brain. The connections with the brain allow sexual responses to influence and be influenced by learning, memory, and thought.

The sex reflexes operate from birth, but the hormonal changes of puberty lead to increasing sexual sensitivity and spontaneous responses in the genitals. The reflexive and inborn facets of sexual behavior are not, by themselves, adequate for assuring intercourse or successful reproduction. Considerable learning is needed for an individual to become sexually active. Since learning is influenced significantly by individual, social, and cultural variables—and each person has a unique history of learning experiences—there is considerable variability in human sexual activities both within and between societies.

B. Perception and Instrumental Learning

The neural pathways that connect the reflex centers in the lower spine to the brain connect with the sensory centers in the cerebral cortex, allowing people to perceive many types of sensations from the genitals. Some of these perceptions enter into long-term memory and influence later thoughts and actions.

In addition, some of the neural inputs from the genitals innervate the pleasure and pain centers in the brain, such that certain types of genital stimulation are experienced as pleasant, while other types are painful. Through instrumental learning (also known as operant conditioning), people usually learn to repeat those activities that are followed by pleasurable, rewarding experiences and avoid those followed by aversive sensations. We learn to do things that are instrumental in attaining pleasure (such as those things leading to orgasm) and avoiding pain (or reinforcement) and punishment help assure that most people learn sexual practices that are instrumental in attaining sexual pleasure—which, before the advent of birth control, often served the biological function of promoting pregnancy and the reproduction of the species. [*See* Operant Learning.]

The more rewarding—and less aversive—a person's experiences with sex, the more positive associations and memories the person tends to have about sex; and this usually translates to greater sexual motivation—or "sex drive"—if there are no biological problems that detrimentally affect the sexual response systems.

C. Classical Conditioning

The sexual reflex is among the reflexes that are capable of being conditioned via classical conditioning (also known as Pavlovian conditioning). Namely, when a neutral stimulus is paired repeatedly with the unconditioned stimulus of appropriate touch to the genitals, that neutral stimulus gradually becomes a *conditioned stimulus* capable of eliciting the sexual reflex. In common parlance, these conditioned stimuli are called "erotic stimuli" or "sexual turn-ons." Usually, the more frequently that an erotic stimulus or turn-on has been paired with the unconditioned stimulus to touch to the genitals, the more capable that conditioned stimulus is of eliciting sexual responses—unless a person has so many negative associations with or biological problems affecting sex that they suppress the sexual response. [*See* Classical Conditioning.]

Through classical conditioning, almost any stimulus that is frequently paired with and is predictive of the sexual arousal can become an erotic stimulus or sexual turn-on. The specific stimuli that people respond to as sexually exciting differ from person to person, depending on each individual's prior sexual experiences. Many people learn to respond to pictures or fantasies of nude bodies as erotic stimuli, if these have been paired with masturbation or sexual interactions in the past. Some come to find "talking dirty" to be sexually arousing, if such talk has been a common part of their exciting sexual experiences. Although many people would be offended by vulgar language and do not understand how anyone could find it sexually exciting, the principles of classical conditioning allow us to understand that almost *any* stimulus can become an erotic stimulus or sexual turn-on, for those individuals who have experienced it in conjunction with sexual excitement.

When people learn to imagine their erotic stimuli (in the absence of any external stimuli), they gain the ability to fantasize about their turn-ons. Since having sexual fantasies is often pleasurable, many people learn this cognitive activity—unless guilt or other bad feelings punish such fantasies. Some people cultivate elaborate sexual fantasies because of the pleasure and sexual arousal that they bring.

Nerves that connect the cortex to the sexual reflex mechanisms in the lower spinal cord allow cortical activity—such as seeing or fantasizing about sexual turn-ons—to activate the sexual reflexes. This is called *psychogenic* stimulation of the sexual reflexes, since the excitation is psychological in origin. For some people, psychogenic stimulation only produces a mild sexual response, such as slight vaginal lubrication or partial penile erection; but in other people, the response can be quite strong, sometimes leading to orgasm. There is a great deal of variation among people in the strength of these psychogenic responses, these differences being due to the number and intensity of positive and negative learning experiences that any given individual has had with sexuality.

During sexual intercourse, fantasies and psychogenic sexual stimulation can add to the total excitement that enhances the sexual response. Fantasies also serve to distract people from some of the stimuli that can inhibit the sexual response—e.g., guilt about sexual activities, fears of not being attractive enough to one's partner, or fears about the adequacy of one's sexual performance.

The sexual reflexes can be inhibited by aversive conditoning. Any of a variety of sex-related stimuli can become associated with fear, worry, or anxiety—depending on each individual's unique history of classical conditioning. For one person, fears of becoming pregnant can interfere with the sexual response, whereas another person may have no fears of pregnancy. Fear of not pleasing one's partner, not being able to have orgasms, or anything else can inhibit the sex reflex. Given the pervasive social attention to physical attractiveness—especially for females—some people feel anxious that their partner will not think that their body is attractive enough. [*See* ANXIETY AND FEAR.]

D. Nonsocial and Social Learning

Some learning is clearly social, as when we watch other people's actions—perhaps via movies or videos—and learn from them. However, sexual learning may occur alone, as when a child explores touching his or her body, discovers masturbation, and pairs certain fantasies with sexual activities. But even these relatively nonsocial activities, done in private, are usually not devoid of social influence. For example, the child's frequency of masturbation is influenced by the degree to which the parents accept or punish masturbation. Each individual's choice of fantasy images used during masturbation is often affected by prior social experiences.

Social learning theory emphasizes that we learn a great deal from observing the actions and listening to the words of others, who are called *models*. Although sexual intercourse is usually not done publicly in our society, people learn about sex in private from observing and listening to their sexual partners. People also learn the sexual activities of *symbolic models* presented in magazines, books, movies, TV, and videos. In addition, there are many sex-related activities—such as meeting, becoming intimate, and suggesting sexual activities—that are modeled more often in public than is sexual behavior per se. Once information is acquired by observing others, people may later attempt similar actions. The degree to which they fully adopt the behavior depends on how instrumental it is in bringing them rewarding effects. Did a sexual position modeled in a video bring pleasure or complaints from one's partner?

Not only do people learn the physical activities of sex by observing and listening to others, they learn how others talk about sex and play out sexual roles. Patterns of talk and action are often called "scripts," and sexual scripts are involved at every stage from meeting a potential partner to making love. For example, there are countless opening lines a person can use to meet another, and research indicates that women are more discerning among them than are men. Men like almost all types of opening lines that women use to strike up a conversation; but women tend to like direct and innocuous lines and be turned off by cute-flippant lines from men. There are the countless scripts for dealing with sex, and they vary from society to society—from subculture to subculture. This can create confusion when people move from one social sphere to another or try to become intimate with someone from a different subculture.

E. Cognitive and Social Psychology

Cognitive psychology adds another level of complexity to the multifactor model of sexuality. Our perceptual experience enters inputs from all sense modalities into thought and memory. Our thoughts are composed mostly of visual imagery, sounds, and the inner words we "hear" in our minds as we think to ourselves. Whereas sexy pictures can influence our visual sexual fantasies, the sexual scripts we learn tend to influence the inner words we use to think about sex. When teens see TV shows or movies in which certain lines or scripts lead to sexually exciting outcomes, they may find themselves rehearing those words in their minds and then using parts of combinations of those scripts with others.

Social psychology stresses how much each individual is influenced by his or her position in society. Two people living in the same country—but exposed to different subsets of the multiple cultures possible within a society have access to different models, media, books, videos—which provide them with different ideas about sexual conduct. Some obtain vast amounts of information about sex, birth control, and relationships, while others obtain little. From each person's unique perspective on life, each develops personal views and opinions. As a result, two people can interpret the same event very differently: Two people can see the same erotic movie, and one calls it interesting while the other calls it repulsive pornography.

Cognitive and social psychology emphasize the importance of people's cognitive processes in interpreting their situations, creating unique and personal plans of action and making novel contributions to their social interactions. People are not passive receptacles, only being shaped by society. They are active, creative makers of their own social lives. They modify and creatively reconstruct the scripts and action patterns learned from society, producing their own unique contributions and social constructions. Creativity stems from many sources, two of which, for example, are fantasy and problem solving. People often invent creative fantasies, involving images and scripts, that can lead to plans for doing sexual activities they have never done before. People may consciously attempt to create a special sexual experience that is uniquely their own. Through the creative recombination of different scripts, fantasies, and novel ideas, people can construct sexual plans and actions that differ from anything they have ever seen used by others. Though perhaps not radically different from their culture, their actions are creative variations. Problems often cause people to search for creative solutions. When people face a problem, such as increasing boredom with sex after 10 years of marriage, the problem may stimulate creative efforts to devise novel and interesting sexual experiences.

As millions of creative people invent novel ideas and share them with others, the total contributions have their impact in changing the sexual practices of the larger society. Many new ideas are lost after being tried a few times, but others (usually the most rewarding ones) spread and become widely popular. Magazines and books may help popularize a sexual position or fantasy. People also change their society by voting, for example using the ballot to express their values about abortion, nude beaches, pornography, and other sex-related topics. By showing how people's values and creative thoughts affect their society, cognitive and social psychology empower people to take a stronger role in changing social conditions related to sexuality, gender, and reproductive rights.

F. Sex Drive

Psychology used to conceive of behavior is a function of drives and people today still talk about sex drive and libido. But with the development of multifactor models of behavior, the concept of drive is now seen as simplistic. People's desires and motivations for sex result from the multiple causes, some biological and others social–psychological in origin.

Testosterone heightens sexual motivation in males—and probably in females. (Normally women have small amounts of testosterone in their bodies that are adequate for promoting sexual interest.) Good health tends to facilitate sexual desire and pleasure; whereas illness, depression, drug abuse, and other biomedical factors tend to reduce sexual motivation. Also, the more prior rewards and less prior punishment a person has experienced with sex, the stronger the person's sexual interest and motivation tends to be. Punishment related to sex leads to inhibition that can reduce a person's sexual motivation. The more sexual turn-ons and fantasies a person developed (via classical conditioning), the more likely his or her sexual interest will be piqued by numerous events of everyday life that might not be perceived as sexual by another [who has not eroticized those stimuli]. Also, the more sexual scripts a person has learned, the more the person tends to think and act in sexual ways.

There is no single "normal" level of sexual desire. Two people with high sexual desire may be very happy with their sexual life having sexual interactions every day; and two people with low sexual desire may have an equally satisfactory sex life, engaging in intercourse twice a month. Sexual desire is most likely to be a problem in a couple's relationship when the two have discrepant sexual desire—one wanting sex much more than the other.

II. SEXUAL ORIENTATION

Although many people think that there are only two types of sexual orientation—heterosexual and homosexual—the issue is much more complex. There is a continuum of positions between these two extremes with bisexuality lying in the middle. The definitions of these three terms set the stage for understanding the whole continuum. "Heterosexuals" are people whose primary erotic, psychological, emotional, and social interest is in members of the other sex—even though that interest may not be overtly expressed. "Homosexuals" are people whose primary erotic, psychological, emotional, and social interest is in members of the same sex—even though that interest may not be overtly expressed. "Bisexuals" have both of these capacities. [*See* SEXUAL ORIENTATION.]

Alfred Kinsey was the first sex researcher to provide a method of describing sexual orientation on a continuum, with 0 being pure heterosexual, 3 being bisexual, and 6 being pure homosexual. People who are at position one are mostly heterosexual, but have some homosexual orientation. Each higher number represents greater homosexual orientation. Kinsey and his coresearchers actually devised two separate scales. One measured *overt sexual experience,* and the other *psychosexual reactions,* such as erotic feelings, emotions, and fantasies. In most cases a person's position on one scale is the same as on the other scale. However, there are cases in which people's overt sexual behavior does not completely parallel his or her psychosexual reactions. For example, some homosexuals can respond sexually to the other sex, even though they find that their emotional and psychological attachment is to the same sex. Also, a person can be a homosexual and never engage in sexual relations with a member of the same sex.

III. DEVELOPMENTAL PATTERNS OF SEXUAL BEHAVIOR

Developmental models of human conduct are useful in showing how the numerous elements of a multifactor model interact across the lifespan. They help avoid debates about nature and nurture by clarifying how both biological and environmental factors influence behavior at each phase of life.

A. Childhood

The sexual reflexes function from the first days of life: Soon after birth, many boys have penile erections; and some girls, vaginal lubrication and clitoral tumescence. Even before birth, ultrasound studies suggest that erections may occur in male fetuses.

In the first year of life, many babies show the simplest forms of masturbation. Early in infancy, babies explore their environments and their own bodies, touching and looking at many parts of the anatomy with as much interest as they show for the world around them. Out of simple curiosity, they touch their arms, legs, and other parts, and discover their genitals in this process. Touch to the genitals elicits the sexual response, along with pleasurable feelings that reward genital self-stimulation. There are documented cases of babies learning to masturbate to orgasm before 1 year of age (though boys do not ejaculate any fluid before puberty). There is, however, considerable variation among children in early sexual self-stimulation, depending largely on their parents' response to the activity. Some parents punish and suppress early sexual behavior; whereas others are more accepting. Children who are punished for genital exploration may not learn to touch their genitals. Punishment may in fact condition inhibitions and fears about self-touching.

Sometimes children are inquisitive to learn what other children's bodies look like. Since children's play is not always monitored closely by adults, sexual exploration can lead in many possible directions. Often it leads to nothing more than one child's simply looking at and briefly touching the other child's body, but other outcomes are possible. A 9-year-old brother and his younger sister may innocently engage in mutual sexual exploration and discover that sexual play is pleasurable. In rare cases, after weeks of repeated sex play, they may discover intercourse, without knowing that adults would disapprove. Only later may the children discover that these activities are called "incest" and deemed unacceptable in the larger society.

In cultures where people sleep together in a common room or hut, children may see their parents making love and later imitate coital activities during play with other children. There is a great deal of variability among cultures in childhood sexuality; and in societies where parents do not inhibit their children, sexual exploration and play continue throughout childhood: There is no biologically determined "latency period" for sexuality.

In homes where early childhood sexual exploration is punished and little sexual information is given to the child, children can grow up with little knowledge and considerable guilt about touching their sexual organs or masturbating. Small degrees of such inhibition may not have long-lasting effects on the person's sexuality; but high levels of guilt and sexual ignorance can make it difficult for a person to develop a happy, uninhibited sexual life in subsequent years. Children who have negative socialization about sex often develop erotophobia, which is a fear of phobia of sexuality and sexual cues, leading to negative attitudes about sex. In contrast, a positive sexual socialization tends to lead to erotophilia, positive attitudes about sexuality and sexual cues.

In most societies, including ours, there is a double standard that imposes more sexual inhibitions, guilt, and erotophobia on girls than on boys. Parents are more likely to disapprove of masturbation for girls than boys. Girls are given fewer names for their genitals and are less likely to know the correct names than are boys, and few girls are told they have a clitoris. As a result, girls are less likely to masturbate or talk about their genitals than are boys.

B. Early Adolescence

Puberty usually begins between ages 9 and 13 in girls and 10 and 14 in boys. Most girls begin to menstruate between 11 and 14. Boys usually begin to be able to ejaculate at 11 or 12. The hormonal changes of puberty make the genitals more sensitive and more responsive. Adolescents—especially males—begin to experience spontaneous sexual arousal during the daytime and at night—in the form of nocturnal sexual arousal, erections, and orgasms. As a result teenagers typically become increasingly interested in sexuality—unless they have been made to feel very guilty or inhibited about sex.

Boys typically develop sexual interests earlier and more intensely than girls. This is due to both biological and social factors. For biological reasons, boys usually begin to notice sexual arousal—such as spontaneous penile erections—2 or 3 years earlier than girls notice their first sexual arousal. Boys have more penile erections and orgasms—both while awake and sleeping—than girls have noticeable sexual arousal and orgasms. Boys are more likely than girls to be aware of their spontaneous sexual arousal and find it intense. Nocturnal erections occur during dream sleep and boys often wake in the morning with erections, which can help them discover the heightened level of pleasure that comes from masturbation after the onset of puberty. Also, boys have more nocturnal orgasms—or wet dreams—than do girls, and these are often coupled with sexual imagery that promote the development of sexual fantasies. As a result, the sexologist John Money calls wet dreams "nature's own pornography show"—just one more reason why boys tend to develop more erotic turn-ons and sexual fantasies than girls do.

There are exceptions to these generalizations. Erotophobic boys may deny their emerging sexuality, and erotophilic girls may actively explore their sexuality, even though they experience fewer biological impulses to aid them than boys do. However, most boys feel sexual arousal and interest much more often each day than most girls do.

Boys are much more likely than girls to learn to masturbate to orgasm during the adolescent years. This is due, in part, to the more frequent occurrences of spontaneous sexual arousal and orgasm in boys and the double standard that imposes less punishment and social inhibitions on boys than girls. In our culture, many boys also experience peer pressure to experiment with sexuality, gain sexual knowledge, and become "sexperts." Talk in the male peer group often turns to sex, and many boys feel pressure from their peers to lose their virginity and prove their manhood. Success is greeted with social approval, which rewards even more interest in sex.

Girls, in contrast, tend to experience a more cautious socialization about sex. Yes, there is talk about sex in their peer groups, what it feels like and who is doing it. There is a great deal of variation among girls' peer groups, but these groups are more likely to pass on messages of caution about sex than are boys' peer groups. Girls learn that their more sexually active peers are called "sluts," or worse, and fear of social disparagement can make many girls reluctant to earn that label. Girls' peers may share frightening stories about girls who were taken advantage of by boys, stories of unwanted pregnancies and the subsequent problems, stories showing that STDs create many more complications for females than for males. In addition, girls may contiue to hear words of caution from their parents.

Boys tend to want sex more than girls and to push more for it, while girls are more likely to play the gate-keeper role, wanting to know if he really cares about her before proceeding all the way to sexual intercourse. Hence, many girls and boys go through a period of petting or "fooling around" before engaging in sexual relations. Because physical touch to the skin, lips, and other body parts are all pleasurable, it is not surprising that couples enjoy the sensations of touching, fondling, kissing, and hugging. In such close interactions, pressure and touch to the genital areas are quite likely, which can heighten sexual arousal.

Erotic petting may be inhibited in societies that make young people feel guilty about premarital sex; or it can be facilitated in societies that inundate their youth with movies, videos, and stories of people doing sexual activities. Societal messages also influence the next step of sexual exploration: Societies with clear messages that premarital sex will be strongly punished may suppress further sexual exploration until marriage (or at least engagement); but such prohibitions are not very strong in most Western societies.

C. Premarital Sex

Many cultures have strict rules against premarital sex. Since most people throughout history have not had effective means of birth control, premarital sexual activity often led to pregnancy; and young unmarried mothers usually could not find marriage partners. Males often did not want to marry a pregnant woman or a woman with a child—unless it was theirs—because they did not want to devote their child-rearing efforts to raising someone else's children. In such cultures, virginity is very important; and a man may give a woman back to her family if she is found (or suspected) not to be a virgin at marriage. Naturally, there is much variation among cultures, and some societies allow a certain amount of premarital sex, perhaps with a fiance just before marriage.

Since the advent of the sexual revoluton, many modern Western nations have experienced significant increases in premarital sexuality, this being due to the development of increasingly effective forms of birth control, the decreasing influence of rigid religious codes, and increased secular culture showing sexy images in videos, TV, and movies. In the United States, increasing premarital sex has led to an increasing amount of teenage pregnancy and teenage abortion, in part because many parents and teachers have been reluctant to provide good birth control information to teenagers. Even though a majority of American parents want sex eduation in the schools, a vociferous minority tends to block it in many schools. In Western Europe and Canada, where rates of teenage premarital sexual activity are similar to those in the United States, the teen pregnancy and abortion rates are considerably lower. For example, the pregnancy rate among 15 to 19 year olds is 96 per 1000 in the United States, compared to 35 per 1000 in Sweden and 14 per 1000 in the Netherlands. In modern Western European countries, teenagers are given better sexual education and better access to birth control services than in the United States. Also traditional religious influence is less powerful/influential in Europe.

While the prevalence of premarital sexual intercourse has gradually increased, the age of onset has gradually declined. For example, Alfred Kinsey, a pioneer sex researcher, found that half of the women he interviewed some 40 years ago had intercourse before marriage; but Morton Hunt found that 81% of 18- to 24-year-old married women had done so in the early 1970s. In 1971, only 46% of unmarried 19-year-old women had engaged in intercourse; but this percentage increased to 55% in 1976 and 69% in 1979. This trend for increasing early sexuality is believed to have leveled off in the 1980s. In 1990, 54% of high school students grades 9 to 12 have had sexual intercourse.

Most parents do not tell their children or adolescents many details about the scripts for sexual intercourse, and many signal a reluctance or unwillingness to talk about premarital sex. As a result, many teens turn to their peers and the media for this information. These multiple and different sources often provide confusing or inaccurate information, with jumbled and often contradictory messages about the events surrounding first sex. Because it can be difficult to tell which of the countless different scripts presented by the media and peers is the best, adolescents often experiment with numerous lines and scripts, combining elements from various ones, not knowing which ones will work best for them until they have tried many. The less accurate information they have, the more likely they are to make mistakes. Because many of the scripts used on TV and in movies do not work well in everyday life, adolescence can involve much frustrating experimentation and embarrassment. (The more accurate information that teens receive from parents, sex educators, and books, the more likely they are to be well prepared for adolescent sexual exploration and first intercouse.)

In a study of girls' experiences around the time they have their first sex, Sharon Thompson found that many girls worried about a boy's putting a "big thing in small hole." Many did not know the ways that boys are likely to approach them for first sex and are surprised by the rapidity with which first sex occurred. Some were taken advantage of because they did not have realistic expectations and scripts for dealing with the boys. Those girls who were least likely to be abused or taken advantage of during their early sexual activities had mothers who talked honestly with them about the sexual scripts needed for good experiences with sex. First intercourse is usually less problematic for boys than girls. Typically, boys have orgasm and like losing their virginity. Girls are less likely to orgasm and less happy about their loss of virginity. However, after a year or two of sexual experience, many females and males begin to learn which scripts work best, how to have better sex, and how to avoid some of the problems related to sex—such as pregnancy, sexually transmitted disesase (STDs),and abusive partners.

Although some parents may believe that a guilt-inducing sex socialization will keep their child from experimenting with premarital sex, the erotophobia they condition in their children can create serious problems. Erotophobic teens often feel so guilty about sex that they avoid sex education information and do not learn effective means of birth control. This can leave them vulnerable to sexual accidents if their erotophobia is overcome by curiosity about sex or pressure from another person to experiment with sex. Although students with high sex guilt may begin sex as early as students with low sex guilt, they wait about a year longer than those with low sex guilt before using contraception. Erotophobic people can become pregnant and contract sexually transmitted diseases as easily as other people; and their lack of knowledge about sex puts them at a greater risk of such mishaps, since they have not planned ahead for sex and have limited knowledge about ways to avoid the problems.

Since AIDS has become a serious health problem, considerable effort has been directed at teaching adolescents safer sexual practices—such as the use of condoms and avoiding anal sex. Although some teens are following this advice, many teens are not using condoms for safer sex. In 1991, 46% of high school students reported using condoms during their last sexual intercourse. Since one-fifth of all people with AIDS contracted the virus as teens, there is room for improvement in education and honest communication with teens about sex. [*See* AIDS AND SEXUAL BEHAVIOR.]

D. Cohabitation

Although cohabitation is less common in the United States than in France or Sweden, increasing numbers of people are living with a partner without being married. In the United States, approximately 4% of unmarried adults are cohabiting, in contrast to 1% in 1960.

In the early 1950s, the typical age of marriage was about 20 years in women and 22.5 in men. Today it is about 24 in women and 26 in men. Since teens are also beginning sex at earlier ages than in the 1950s, it is clear that many young people are spending more years of their lives as sexually active but unmarried than was true before the sexual revolution. Some individuals have 2 to 5 years before they enter a relationship that will lead to marriage; for others it may be 10 years or more. Those who postpone marriage are more likely to cohabit than those who do not.

People who cohabit tend to be more liberal, and less religious, and more critical of marriage as an institution than people who do not cohabit. Although cohabitation is becoming increasingly routine before marriage, there is no evidence that it helps people make better choices of marital partners. Most cohabiting unions do not lead to marriage, dissolving relatively quickly. Also, cohabitors are more likley to divorce than people who do not cohabit, perhaps because they are more critical of marraige both before and after the wedding.

E. Marriage

In their 20s and 30s, married couples typically engage in coitus two or three times a week. Erotophiles often seek out ways to expand their sexual lives, add new activities and keep their erotic love strong. Many erotophobes expected that sex would be good once it was legitimated by marriage; but even after marriage, many erotophobes continue to feel that sex is "dirty," "sinful," or "base"; and these feelings can interfere with the enjoyment of intimate sexual relations for years or all through life. [*See* MARRIAGE.]

The frequency of intercourse usually declines as people age. Many married people report that sexual relations are most fulfilling in the first year after marriage and that the quality of their sexual experience declines thereafter. People also report a decline in communication, listening, respect, and romantic love after marriage. These changes are not biologically determined or inevitable; but they do indicate that many people do not devote much attention to making their marriages successful. They also suggest that many people do not have the time, effort, or skill to solve their marital and sexual problems and/or that the multiple other demands of adult life—jobs, careers, children, socializing—are so demanding or rewarding that their marriages become neglected.

Heterosexual couples commonly engage in noncoital sex play before penile–vaginal intercourse. Foreplay typically lasts some 5 to 15 minutes, though the time varies from couple to couple and from time to time for any given couple. Various stimulative techniques are used in foreplay, including touching, caressing, and kissing of the genitals, breasts, lips, and other body parts. Couples use a variety of positions for engaging in intercourse, which usually lasts approximately 10 minutes. While the male-on-top, face-to-face position is very common, couples are increasingly using the female-on-top position. Side-by-side positions and combinations of female superior and side-by-side positions are also used. Rear-entry positions are less commonly explored.

Many couples engage in oral–genital stimulation. Hunt's research found that 90% of people married less than 25 years had engaged in oral sex during the preceding year. Anal intercourse is not a common practice for most couples. Hunt's data indicate that for married people between 18 and 35, approximately 50% of men and 25% of women had engaged in anal intercourse on at least one occasion. A 1991 study of men ages 20–39 found that 20% had engaged in anal intercouse, 75% had performed oral sex, and 79% had received it.

Gay and lesbian couples use manual and oral stimulation of the genitals, breasts, and anus, along with caressing, kissing, and body rubbing for sexual arousal. Since the advent of AIDS, many gay males have reduced their use of anal sex, since it is one of the activities most likely to transmit HIV (the virus that causes AIDS).

Although females tend to be less interested in sex than males in the teens and 20s, female sexual interest tends to increase in the 20s, 30s, and 40s. Many of the inhibitions that girls learned while young are gradually overcome. As women learn how to avoid irresponsible partners, unwanted pregnancies, and STDs, they learn how to avoid some of the problems that had caused them to worry about sex earlier. Also, many learn how to have orgasms more easily, making sex more exciting and fulfilling. Many overcome guilt and other inhibitions as supportive sexual partners, the legitimacy of marriage, and access to more reliable information about sex counteract earlier fears and myths (ignorance). These factors have led many to the generalization that male sex drive peaks at 20 while females peak in their 30s or 40s. This generalization is somewhat misleading, since (1) many males have very strong sexual interests all through young and middle adulthood, and some even longer, and (2) increasing numbers of young women have fewer sexual inhibitions or are overcoming their sexual inhibitions at an earlier age than their mothers did. Modern books, courses, and workshops on sexuality help them do this.

People in their teens and 20s often explore novel sexual positions and activities, but married couples often settle into a few favorite positions after they have explored a range of possibilities and discovered the ones they like the best. This can eventually lead to boredom with sex. If married couples report that they are losing interest in sex because it has become too routine, sexual therapists and marriage counselors sometimes give couples books that show multiple sexual positions and encourage them to try novel ones. There are several good books—such as *Sexual Awareness* by Barry McCarthy and Emily McCarthy, *How to Make Love to the Same Person for the Rest of Your Life, and Still Love It* by Dagmar O'Connor, and *The New Joy of Sex* by Alex Comfort—that contain pictures of multiple sexual positions, describing the pros and cons of each for males and females.

F. Extramarital Sex

Although marriage vows require faithfulness, studies reveal that a considerable number of people break the traditional marital contract. Hunt's survey in the 1970s found that 50% of married men and 20% of married women had at least one extramarital relationship by the age of 45. However, the rates for younger women were similar of those of men. Other more recent surveys of magazine readers indicate higher rates of extramarital sex. For example, a *Cosmopolitan* survey found that 60% of the women and 75% of men had extramarital sexual experience. There is historical and cross-cultural evidence that extramarital sex has been common at other times and in other societies. Although most individuals attempt to keep their extramarital affairs secret, they do not always succeed; and the discovery that there has been extramarital sex can be very damaging to the quality of a marriage, undermining trust and sometimes leading to divorce.

Some people, most notably Nena and George O'Neil in the book *Open Marriage,* recognize that secret affairs are common yet potentially deleterious to marriage and advocate "open marriage" as an alternative. Built on the assumption that most people want both a committed relationship and freedom, open marriage is designed to allow a couple to see other people and decide if this should include sexual relations or not. There are too few studies on open marriage to know how common it is. One study found that in 15% of marriages, both partners had agreed that extramarital sex was acceptable under certain circumstances.

G. Divorce

About 50% of marriages end in divorce in the United States, though there has been a gradual decline in divorce since its peak in 1981. For many couples, marital happiness is the highest in the first year of marriage. As incompatibilities and fights begin to detract from the feelings of love, many couples cease to feel the passion and commitment needed to keep a relationship together. The peak in divorce occurs at 1.5 years after marriage. Many married people stop trying as hard at making their relationship work, and many experience a decline in marital happiness, sexual pleasure, and love. This need not occur if people continue to value their relationship and put time and effort into it. Unfortunately, the numerous obligations of adulthood—job, parenthood, maintaining a home—can take so many hours a week that many adults simply do not have the time to devote to their relationship. Thus, one study found that "difficulty in communication" was the most common reason given for divorce. Other reasons were unhappiness and incompatibility. Also, the birth of the first child is one of the greatest stresses on a relationship, and the sooner the child comes after marriage, the greater the chances of divorce. Waiting a couple of years before beginning a family allows a couple to solve many of their interpersonal problems and establish a stable relationship before adding the complexities of childrearing. Counselors, marriage workshops, and books can help, too. [*See* DIVORCE.]

Bibliography

Crooks, R., and Baur, K. (1993). "Our Sexuality," 5th ed. Benjamin/Cummings, Redwood City, CA.

Heiman, J., and LoPiccolo, J. (1988). "Becoming Orgasmic: A Sexual Growth Program for Women." Prentice-Hall, New York.

Kaplan, H. S. (1987). "The Illustrated Manual of Sex Therapy," 2nd ed. Brunner-Mazel, New York.

Masters, W. H., Johnson, V. E., and Kolodny, R. (1992). "Human Sexuality," 4th ed. Harper Collins, New York.

Reinisch, J. M. (1990). "The Kinsey Institute New Report on Sex." St. Martin's Press, New York.

Silverstein, J. (1986). "Sexual Enhancement for Men." Vantage Press, New York.

Thompson, S. (1990). Putting a big thing into a little hole: Teenage girls' accounts of sexual initiation. *J. Sex Res.* **27,** 341–361.

Zilbergeld, B. (1992). "The New Male Sexuality." Bantam Books, New York.

Sexual Disorders

Ronald M. Doctor and Bryan Neff
California State University at Northridge

Glossary

Biological sex Refers to one's status as male or female in terms of basic physiological characteristics, e.g., chromosomes, hormones, genitalia, etc.

Exhibitionism A paraphilic condition in which sexual gratification is obtained by inducing surprise, fear, or disgust in an unsuspecting person by the "flashing" of one's genitalia.

Fetishism A paraphilia that involves sexual gratification through rubbing, fondling, or usage of body parts or nonhuman objects such as underwear, garders, shoes, silk, etc.

Gender identity Refers to a person's psychological identification with culturally defined traits and behaviors that constitute being a man (masculine) or woman (feminine).

Gender identity disorders Sexual disorders in which a person experiences a psychological confusion or mismatch between their biological sexual characteristics and their culturally assigned gender identity.

Paraphilias Sexual disorders that are characterized by an intense focus upon (1) nonhuman objects, (2) the suffering or humiliation of oneself or a partner, or (3) children or other nonconsenting persons; and result in great personal distress or disturbance.

Sexual orientation One's emotional and physical attraction toward the same sex (homosexual), opposite sex (heterosexual), or both (bisexual).

Transsexualism An extreme form of gender identity disorder in which a person exhibits a life-long sense of gender incongruence (e.g., feeling trapped in the body of the opposite sex) and an overriding desire to undergo sex reassignment surgery.

Transvestism A paraphilia that is marked by a compulsion to cross-dress in clothing of the opposite sex. The amount of cross-dressing can be partial or regular. Most transvestites are heterosexual.

Voyeurism A paraphilic condition characterized by a recurrent, intense, and sexually oriented act that involves the observation of unsuspecting people who are naked, disrobing, or engaged in sexual activity.

SEXUAL DISORDERS encompass the full range of human sexual thoughts, feelings, and actions that are generally regarded as abnormal, dysfunctional, or disordered. With three exceptions (homosexuality, sexual addictions, and rape), the disorders discussed here are listed in the *Diagnostic and Statistical Manual Version III-R* (DSM-III-R) used in psychiatry and psychology as a means of listing the various diagnostic categories treated with psychotherapy or medications. Since the DSM-III-R represents our current cultural values regarding human sexuality, it will serve as the basis for identifying various "disorders" that we feel are unacceptable in mainstream society. The disorders discussed are listed under "sexual disorders" in the DSM-III-R with the exception of the gender identity disorders, which are represented in the DMS-III-R under Disorders Usually First Evident in Infancy, Childhood, or Adolescence. From our frame of reference, however, the gender identity disorders, while they begin in childhood, have a profound effect on adult behavior and the ways in which adults cope with this disorder. Homosexuality has been excluded from the DSM-III-R but remains a topic in the sexual disorders literature and cannot be excluded as a form

Encyclopedia of Human Behavior, Volume 4

of sexual variation that has significant socio-cultural history. The sexual addictions were excluded from the diagnostic system but are included in this discussion for information purposes since the terminology has been used extensively in the public literature and media. Finally, rape, which is not represented in the DSM-III-R, is discussed in this article, although we emphasize its aggressive and violent nature rather than sexual nature. Rape, as with such crimes as murder, are usually considered symptoms of other underlying problems, not a disturbance in itself.

I. INTRODUCTION

Few topics regarding human behavior hold as much interest and as much pathos as that of deviations and dysfunctions in human sexuality. What constitutes deviations and dysfunctions, however, are heavily dependent on contemporary cultural attitudes and values and these are often blind to the past history of sexuality in the culture.

We know, for example, that sexuality was represented in the rock art of the earliest human cultures. Paleolithic (30,000 to 10,000 B.C.) rock art, for example, is replete with both human and animal fertility symbols that were thought to endow the represented forms with abundant offspring. The Egyptians (3000 B.C.) are thought to have added power to the concept of fertility as represented in their symbols. In Western culture, our sexual values came mostly from the Judeao–Christian traditions. The Judaic tradition emphasized reproductive sexual behavior without guilt. The core concern was to protect the integrity of marriage with all other considerations of secondary value. Strict laws of adultry were applied to women but the husband was instructed only to "not covet your neighbor's wife. . . ," otherwise sex outside the marriage was tolerated. While the Jews were nomadic and their values emphasized family and procreation, sexual values for the Greeks emanated from their more settled agricultural lifestyle. Here family was still central but the Greeks allowed far more freedom of sexual expression in varied forms. For example, bisexuality was common among Greek males. Since beauty was the primary value or attraction, sexual behavior and arousal could arise in response to both boys and young or mature women of beauty. With the rise of Christianity more ascetic beliefs began to emerge. In general, sex had a procreative function, not the pleasure role noted with the Greeks and Hebrews. By the 18th century, religious views of life shifted from emphasis on eternal life in heaven to attaining happiness on earth and romantic love was valued. Sexual "deviations" started to become cultural issues with particular emphasis on homosexuality and masturbation. As venereal diseases became widespread, cultural values shifted to the physician as the arbiter of sexual morality, and to the repression of sexual behavior, particularly that of males. In the 20th century sexual notions are clearly shifting towards a continuum of behaviors. Modern sexologists not only have described the physiological, emotional, and psychological aspects of sexual behavior but have also highlighted the various forms of sexual behavior that exist whether in overt or covert forms.

This article deals with the full range of human sexual thoughts, feelings, and actions that are generally regarded as abnormal, deviant, or disordered. Our focus will be on these extremes but it should be noted that "deviant" and "disordered" are concepts that rest upon the assumption of a medical, disease, or psychiatric model of behavior that dichotomizes human actions into two qualitatively seperate categories of "normal" and "abnormal." Some sexologists, on the other hand, view these sexual behavior variations not as diseases to be cured but as atypical expressions representing quantitative rather than qualitative differences. To them, sexual behavior falls on a broad continuum with the extremes being vunerable to labels like "disordered" and "abnormal." Here we are dealing with differences in intensity and narrowness of behavior rather than qualitatively different behaviors. We can see this, for example, in the husband who might be aroused by his wife wearing lingerie versus the fetish individual who can only become sexually aroused by lingerie. Furthermore, the demarcation between abnormal and normal categories is not fixed or absolute. Rather, it consists of an ever changeable subjective value judgment derived from psychiatric, cultural, and political forces. For example, masturbation, once considered a sin then a disease, is now acceptable and understood. Likewise, homosexuality was actually removed from the psychiatric nomenclature due to political pressures and changes in culture norms. These are examples of the changeable nature of categorization and labeling and the subjective social value judgments they represent.

Our discussion will follow closely the psychiatric nomenclature and diagnostic categories since these represent our current values regarding human sexuality and the types of behaviors that are considered unacceptable in mainstream society. We will use the terms or labels often used in psychiatry and law to denote these patterns. Although it is not a psychiatric disorder, we will discuss homosexuality since it is a form of sexual behavior that has socio-cultural historical relevance and is still a controversial topic among some peoples. We will also discuss rape, gender identity disorders, and sexual addictions which are listed in the psychiatric diagnostic system but not under sexual disorders.

The behavioral area of sexual dysfunctions is not discussed since it usually represents inhibitions in sexual drive or performance and is not as comprehensive a manifestation of one's being as are the problems and stresses characteristic of sexual disorders. Finally, we will briefly discuss the topic of rape, emphasizing its aggressive and violent nature rather than sexual nature.

Our starting place in discussing sexual disorders is to focus on the notion of "sexual identity." A person's sexual identity can be seen as an interrelationship among the three basic elements of human sexual behavior, namely, biological sexual characteristics, gender identity, and sexual orientation. In the diagram below you can see that sexual identity is formed from the interaction between biological sex characteristics (such as male and female sex organs, hormones, etc.), gender identity (or one's identification with or feeling of feminity or masculinity), and sexual orientation (homo-, bi-, heterosexual, or other objects of stimulation as found, for example, in the paraphilas). In examining the gender identity disorders we will be discussing biological sex and gender identity. On the other hand, when we discuss the paraphilias, we will be focusing in part upon sexual orientation. [*See* SEX ROLES.]

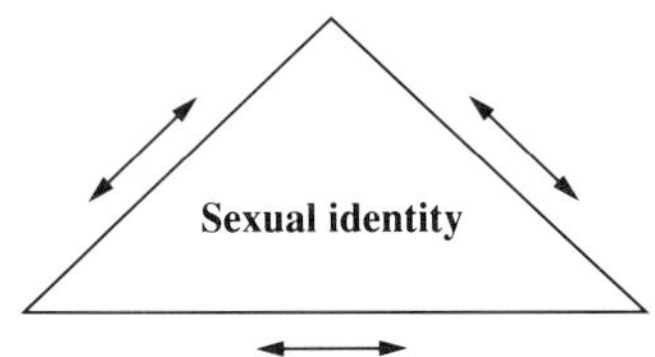

II. GENDER IDENTITY DISORDERS

A person with gender identity disorder (GID) experiences a confusion or mismatch between biological sexual characteristics and their culturally assigned gender identity. The identity problem is psychological in nature rather than a biological ambiguity. Biologically, they are dimorphic (male vs female) in terms of chromosomal, gonadal, gential development, and hormonal levels. The ambiguity exists in terms of the individual's identification with culturally defined traits that constitute being a woman or man, i.e., the degree of femininity or masculinity the person exhibits through thoughts, feelings, and their actions. Not all people are comfortable with what they feel is their true sense of being a woman or man and their biological sex. The amount of disturbance can range from a mild sense of inappropriateness, to feeling like a woman trapped in a male's body, and vice versa.

GID should not be confused with transvestitism, homosexuality, and hermaphroditism. Transvestites, as we will see later in more detail, cross-dress for fetishistic pleasure, and, with few exceptions, rarely find an incongruity between their sex and gender. A person who is emotionally and sexually attracted to a member of their same sex is, likewise, not inherently disturbed in regards to their gender identity. Finally, the hermaphrodite has to some degree the sexual organs for both sexes. Since this confusion stems from being biologically intersexed, the hermaphrodite's dilemma is not considered a psychological disorder. Once again, those with GID are unambiguously biologically formed in one sex, and their confusion is at the emotional and psychological levels.

GIDs are conceptually divided into three categories: GID of childhood, GID of adolescence and adulthood (not transsexual), and transsexualism. Let us look at each of these three categories.

A. Gender Identity Disorder of Childhood

GID of childhood is reserved for prepubescent children and is relatively uncommon. The sex ratio for the population in general is unknown, yet through clinical work it appears that there are many more boys than girls diagnosed with this condition. Generally, the age of onset for both sexes is age 4; however, in some cases it may appear as early as age 2. The majority of children will return to their expected gender roles by puberty, while the remaining minority will continue experiencing what is called "gender dysphoria" or role confusion. Reliable predictions of adult pathology, based upon nontypical childhood behavior have proved elusive. The primary symptoms needed to make a diagnosis are: (1) a persistent and severe discomfort regarding her or his own biological sex, and (2) a belief that they are, or desire to be, of the opposite sex. Such feelings and behaviors are chronic and problematic, thereby transcending any normal variation of stereotypical gender roles, such as being a "tomboy" or a "sissy."

A female with this disorder exhibits intense feelings of frustration at being a girl with a corresponding desire to become a boy, or, in some cases, they may even believe that they are of the opposite gender already. They often seek male peers and are repulsed by traditional feminine toys, games, etc., preferring instead the masculine equivalents. Lastly, there is an intense disgust toward and rejection of their anatomy, often illustrated by beliefs that they will grow a penis or not go through normal female pubescent body changes. The overall pattern with males is identical to the female description except that the specifics are reverse. For example, GID boys typically show severe distress at being a boy, they engage in cross-dressing, and prefer female toys, peers, and so on. They are repulsed by their genitalia, often wishing that it would disappear or that they would grow up and become a woman.

A major difference between the two sexes is found in the fact that many more boys than girls are treated for this condition. It is thought that differential socialization patterns may account for the discrepancy in prevalence rates. For example, boys are more often subjected to rigid parental expectations and therefore any nontypical gender behavior is often more apparent. Boys also tend to display more signs of secondary pathology, e.g., depression, anxiety, and withdrawal, perhaps due to harsher social consequences from peers for their feminine-like behavior. On the other hand, females who cross the gender lines ("tomboys") tend to be more readily accepted than "sissies," or boys who violate gender expectations.

B. Gender Identity Disorder of Adolescence or Adulthood (Nontranssexual)

A person with this condition must have reached puberty, exhibit reoccurring discomfort with their biological sex, and habitually cross-dress. Motivation for wearing the apparel of the opposite sex is for emulation purposes, not for fetishistic pleasure. They are psychologically identified with the opposite sex and exhibit intermittent to constant cross-dressing. Despite the person's sense of discomfort, they usually have no preoccupations with changing their sex to match their gender identity.

Some researchers theorize that GIDs should be conceptualized on a continuum rather than as separate diagnostic categories. Accordingly, they might prefer the term *transgenderism,* which can be seen as an intermediate stage between the two extremes of GID of childhood and secondary transsexualism, i.e., someone who after a period of time decides to make a sex change. The transgenderist is someone who is living permanently in the role of the opposite sex *but* does not have the desire for a complete sex change. Essentially, their change is in gender, not in sexual biological characteristics.

C. Transsexualism

The transsexual condition can be distinguished from other GIDs essentially because of a life-long sense of gender incongruence or inappropriateness and a persistent preoccupation or obsessive quest for sex realignment or "reassignment" surgery. This preoccupation for sex change surgery must be present for a least 2 years to be diagnosed transsexualism. As you can see, we are now at the more extreme end of the GID continuum.

Some theorists have attempted to distinguish between primary and secondary transsexualism, with the former evidencing a history of gender dysphoria since childhood while the latter may be long-term cross-dressers or transgenderists but they seek reassignment surgery later in life usually after experiencing a traumatic stressor.

Secondary pathology for transsexuals is common and most often includes anxiety and depression. For those who are driven to change their sex, the difficulty in getting the funds to pay for surgery can result in self-mutilation and even suicide. In a culture that defines their dilemma as pathological and abnormal, transsexuals have many stories to relate about the pain and suffering they experience. This brief glimpse into the recollection of a girl "trapped" in a male body should partially convey their struggle for recognition as legitimate human beings:

> . . . I wanted above all to walk down the hall at school and be looked at and respected as were the normal girls. Yes, normal girls; for I was a girl with all my heart, but I was not a normal girl. I was a freak of a girl, one who

> had to look like a boy. . . . (Benjamin, 1966, p. 199)

It is generally believed that transsexualism is present in about 1 out of 30,000 males and 1 out of every 100,000 females. More males seek out treatment than females, with ratios as high as 8 to 1. In the United States alone, it is estimated that there are between six and ten thousand postoperative transsexuals, i.e., people who have had sex change operations.

D. Etiology of Gender Identity Disorders

As the current body of knowledge now stands, the causal roots of GID remain undiscovered. The various approaches that attempt to explain this particular disorder can be broken down into the biological/medical, psychodynamic, and developmental/learning models. The first approach purposes genetic, hormonal, neurological, and chromosomal abnormalities as a causal factor. Despite a few leads, such as the effects of prenatal hormones on gender behavior, there is meager amount of data to support the notion of biology as a sole or even major influence. The psychodynamic model emphasizes early childhood and personality development. Causal roles are attributed to difficulty with mother–child relations and the failure to psychologically identify with the parent of the opposite sex. Again, this is not a universal or even major phenomenon. Furthermore, it is very difficult to tease out what is the chicken and what is the egg. In other words, do parents shape children's behavior or does the child's behavior shape the parents' difficulty with the relationship? Finally, the importance of socialization processes and the acquisition of atypical childhood behaviors via modeling or conditioning represents the learning and developmental point of view. Unfortunately, contrary to both the psychodynamic and learning models, there is very little indication that the family environment has any serious effect in the development of gender identity disorders for substantial numbers of cases. For example, in a study by R. Green (*American Journal of Psychiatry*, 1978), of 16 children who were raised by transsexuals all were found to have heterosexual orientation with no disturbance in their gender identity.

E. Treatment Approaches to Gender Identity Disorders

The general consensus is that many or all behavioral and psychodynamic treatments for GID are ineffective. Behavioral therapies have produced a few "successes" in strongly motivated clients, but even then some of the behavioral modification techniques used have raised disturbing moral questions. For example, reports of behavior therapies describe asking children to overemphasize the gender identity differences so as to produce aversive social reactions which, persumably, would diminish these opposite-sex behaviors and attitudes. In contrast, psychodynamic treatments aim at resolving childhood conflicts in the hope of producing acceptance of one's sex and the corresponding gender identity. After many case histories and grueling therapeutic hours, personality reorganization approaches have almost always ended in total failure. Both approaches subject children to personal pain in addition to the feelings of failure they must experience in therapies that are ineffective.

For transsexuals, sex reassignment treatment (sex change surgery) has proven in a majority of cases to be successful in bringing happiness and relief. After a careful screening process, a qualified individual must undergo intensive counseling and instruction on matters of grooming, vocation, legal rights, voice training, and the proper use of stereotypical gender role mannerisms. Then they may begin hormonal therapy in order to produce the desired secondary sex characteristics, e.g., breasts in males, facial/body hair modification, changes in body fat distribution, and some voice alteration. After living and working in one's new gender role for 1 to 2 years, only then can the candidate undergo genital reconstruction. The artificially constructed vagina is much more realistic in appearance and function than its male counterpart. While female genitalia is capable of lubrication and orgasm, the penis is less sensitive and lacks natural erectile capacities. Though limited in number and with sometimes inconclusive findings, some follow-up studies have indicated an 80 to 85% satisfaction rate for transsexual operations, with male-to-female transsexuals usually faring better than their counterparts. Dissatisfaction is usually the result of poor surgical techniques and personal and social instability that preceded surgery.

III. THE PARAPHILIAS

The term *paraphilia* is derived from the notion of a deviation or separation (para-) from what most people are attracted to (-philia). Originally, these were called "perversions," but modern terminology generally describes then as "deviations" or, more recently, as "variations." The DSM-III-R describes these deviations as ". . . recurrent sexual urges and sexually arousing fantasies generally involving either (1) nonhuman objects, (2) the suffering or humiliation of oneself or one's partner (not merely simulated), or (3) children or nonconsenting persons." The diagnosis, however, is made only if the person has acted on there urges or is greatly disturbed or distressed about them. Paraphilic fantasy (such as sex with animals, arousal from undergarments, sado-masochistic thoughts, cross-dressing, or sex with children, etc.) as such is not sufficient to warrant clinical diagnosis. These preoccupations must be intense and recurrent, or undesired and disturbing to the individual, the preferred or exclusive forms of sexual gratification, or acted out overtly to be considered pathological. The paraphilias are usually multiple in nature rather than singular. They are almost exclusively confined to men with the exception of masochism, in which we see a significant number of females.

Current views of paraphilias have been heavily influenced by Freudian theory and analysis of sexual behavior. Within the psychodynamic model, a healthy or natural sexual relationship consists of opposite sexed partners whose object is coitus (sexual gratification through intercourse). These deviation in sexual orientation involve the use of an object other than the opposite sex partner, such as one of the same sex (homosexual), children (pedophilia), close relative (incest), animals (zoophilia), inanimate objects (fetish), or even dead people (necrophilia), as sexual objects. Likewise, instead of seeking coitus, departures include watching others (voyeurism), exposing genitals (exhibitionism), infliction of pain (sadism), or suffering pain (masochism) as deviant aims. In the paraphilias, the erotic object has a role or characteristic that is more important than their personality and personal characteristics of the object and the aim is to enact the paraphilic fantasy.

Mainstream diagnostic systems have been strongly influenced by these two major departures from object and aim. Alternatively, others have argued that perhaps the impact on others should be used as the diagnostic criterion. Here, fetishes and transvestism, and perhaps gender identity disorders, would be excluded in that they usually have little or no direct negative impact on others. All this is brought to your attention to highlight the subjective and consequently changing nature of diagnosis and categorization. Basically, as with most other mental illness categories, we are dealing with social value judgments rather than specific "diseases" and as such cultural and political values and attitudes influence the diagnostic process.

A. Pedophilias

The pedophile (derived from the Greek for "child lover") sexually prefers children of either sex for erotic gratification. It is usually thought that perpetuators must be at least 10 years older than their victims, but this age difference may differ considerably depending on circumstances. Pedophilia is also called "child sexual abuse" and "child molestation." Child molestation is most often perpetrated by males and usually involves such actions as manipulation of the child's genitalia, stroking of the body, forcing the child to manipulate the adult's genitalia, and, to a lesser degree, intromission. Pedophilia is the most common form of paraphilias and involves the most vulnerable victims—children.

Heterosexual men are responsible for most sex abuse against girls. Two out of three sexually abused children, however, are girls. *Conservative* estimates are that 10% of females and 2% of males were sexually abused as children. There is no well-delineated personality for the pedophilic. However, the concept of the "dirty old man" as perpetuator is misguided in that most pedophiles are in their late 30s with only about 5% being aged men. If we had to generalize, we could say that pedophiles are generally immature developmentally even though they may have married and have children of their own. Second, we often see the behavior under stress, i.e., during stressful life periods often accompanied by marital and sexual problems. Alcohol is consistently involved in pedophilic encounters. The majority of victims are relatives, neighbors, or acquaintances; and encounters, while usually brief, occur in series of extended contacts. Generally the younger the child, the more immature the perpetuator. Actual penetration and coitus occur in only 4% of cases. Interestingly, the vast majority (80%) of perpetuators have themselves been abused as children.

B. Incest

Incest is treated here as a subcategory of pedophilia. However, since pedophiles differ in age from their victim, incest may not necessarily meet the criteria. For example, the majority of incest cases seem to involve cousins and siblings who might be similar in age. Incest (from the Latin "impure") is a form of pedophilia involving close relatives, most commonly between cousins but parent–child or sibling–sibling incest is the most repugnant and most often the focus of treatment or criminal proceedings. Taboos against incest are present in all cultures, particularly against mother–son incest. Surveys among adults indicate that 14% of males reported having had sexual contact with a relative before adulthood (95% of which were heterosexual in nature) and 9% of females have had such contact. Most of these experiences were with cousins and essentially involved some form of "petting." Among a university sample, however, 10% of females reported incestuous relationships with their fathers (including stepfathers). Almost 90% of cases brought to court for incest involve father–daughter while only 5% are father–son incidents. Transgenerational incest seems to occur in about 10% of incest cases but probably has different dynamics than immediate parents and children or children and children.

The studies of incest have concluded that these events occur within seriously disturbed or dysfunctional families and that a code of silence develops in which these events are not spoken about and often repressed by the victims. Furthermore, the parents in this unhappy marriage typically consist of a domineering, authoritative, and impulsive husband and a dependent and emotionally distant wife. The husbands often also abuse the wives as well as the children.

Incest is a criminal as well as psychological disorder. The experience of incest is traumatic and psychologically damaging to the children involved (and even to those who know about it). Criminal prosecution does not erase the trauma of incest. These deep psychological scars must eventually be addressed in order for the victim to heal and live a fully mature life.

C. Voyeurism

Voyeurs are also called "peepers" or "Peeping Toms." The psychiatric diagnostic system describes this condition as a recurrent, intense, and sexually oriented "act of observing unsuspecting people, usually strangers, who are either naked, in the process of disrobing, or engaging in sexual activity. . . ." Looking (or "peeping") provides sexual arousal but no actual sexual contact with the observed person is sought. Orgasm, usually produced by masturbation, may occur during the voyeuristic activity, or later in response to the memory of what the person has witnessed. Often these people enjoy the fantasy of having a sexual experience with the observed person, but in reality this does not occur. In its severe form, peeping constitutes the exclusive form of sexual activity.

Lady Godiva's ride through the streets of Coventry to remit an oppressive tax was watched by no one from the town—out of respect and gratitude for her actions—with the exception of Tom the tailor, who peeped through the curtains and for this act went blind. The "Peeping Tom" of today does not go blind literally but they are almost always men. To be considered a paraphilia, there must be a recurrent and intense preoccupation with looking from hiding or secret places. Just looking at live nudes or pictures of nudes is not a paraphilia.

Voyeurs tend to be younger men (convicted age is 23.8 years), unmarried and with little or no alcohol, drug, or other mental illness problems. While they tend to be a heterogeneous as a group, they do commonly have deficiencies in heterosexual relationships. As a matter of fact, it has been conjectured that the voyeuristic practices are a safe and protected way of avoiding a possible relationship with a woman.

D. Exhibitionism

The legal term for exhibitionism is "indecent exposure" because of the shock or offensive value of the act to others. Again, this is mainly a male disorder. Like other paraphilias, it involves repetition, intensity, and sexual urges or arousing fantasies of at least 6 months duration. For the exhibitionist or "flasher" gratification seems to come from the disgust, shock, fear, and surprise of the unsuspecting usually female victims. There is usually a compulsive, driven quality to this behavior (as with most paraphilias) but they are also prone to be caught as they return to the same situation or place repeatedly. There is some evidence that at some level they may wish to be caught and that this consequence is deliberate and desired. The exhibitionists' behavior has a distinctive hostile air to it and this, coupled with the fact that they often have serious sexual problems might suggest intense, perhaps unconscious, hostility exists toward women. As a group they tend to be younger (30s) with about 30% married, 30% divorced or separated, and 40% never married. They are often above average in intelligence and do not have more serious forms of mental illness.

Anxiety, which forms a part in all the paraphilias, is also apparent in exhibitionists both in terms of the excitement or anxiety associated with the act itself and with the desire for anxiety relief that results from the act. There is also evidence that exhibitionists are sexually aroused by stimuli that usually have little or no arousal potential for most people (such as seeing fully clothed women in normal activities) and thus may misread the motives and intentions of others (perhaps seeing them as sex crazed as they are). A fairly large percentage of women (between 45 and 50%) report having seen or had direct contact with a "flasher."

E. Fetishism

Fetishism involves sexual arousal from some inanimate or nonliving object. Exposure to the object or preference for the object is usually necessary to maintain erectile states. Common objects include shoes, sheer stockings, gloves, toilet articles, undergarments particularly underpants, and many tactilely stimulating substances (soft fetishes) such as fur, velvet, and silk garments, and smooth solid objects (hard fetishes) that can be rubbed and fondled such as shoes, leather objects, and so on.

In ancient cultures, fetishes were objects that had magical powers. For the fetishist the object itself is endowed with sexual power and the owner is of little or no interest. Panties, stockings, and garders may be alluring and channel excitment to the wearer but to the fetishist, the object itself is the allure and goal, not the user.

Almost any object can acquire fetish properties. One mechanism for acquisition is classical conditioning in which a neutral object comes to acquire arousal properties by association with sexual arousal and stimulation (i.e., masturbating with the object present). By this process, any stimulus, even body parts, can become a fetish object.

Orgasm may occur with the fetish alone or the fetish object may need to be present during intercourse in order to maintain stimulation toward orgasm. Again, poorly developed heterosexual relationships are found in fetishes as in other paraphilias. Here, however, there is usually a strong mother–son bond with the fetish individual. Fetishes usually develop during adolescence. They are seldom distraught enough by the behavior to seek out psychotherapy and they are usually not overt or foolish enough to be arrested or detected.

F. Transvestism

The Latin *trans* meaning "across" and *vestia* meaning "dress" for the term for "cross-dressing" or "transvestism." As pointed out earlier, transsexuals often manifest cross-dressing as a first expression of opposite sex feelings. This behavior, along with men who dress in "drag" to attract other men for sexual purposes, is not usually considered manifestations of transvestism. Likewise, female impersonators and actors who play female parts are not included under this diagnosis. To qualify as transvestism, there must be a compulsive desire to cross-dress and an intense frustration when the practice is interfered with. The transvestite is usually heterosexual in orientation, married, and otherwise masculine in appearance, demeanor, and sexual preference. The cross-dressing, while compulsive, is done in secret and does not lead to homosexuality or gender identity problems—although transvestites report feeling like a woman during the cross-dress episodes. Often wives will be overt or covert conspirators in the cross-dressing activities. Cross-dressers will often seek each other out for social occasions while made up as women.

The compulsion to cross-dress begins by adolescence, although most children who cross-dress will "grow out of it" by adulthood. Some male transvestites recall their parents forcing them to wear girls clothing as a form of humiliation and punishment. As an adult, however, the wearing of women's clothing usually has more significance than just sexual arousal or punishment. If affords the transvestite male an opportunity to escape from pressures and responsibilities. Some males only *partially* cross-dress, usually by covertly wearing female undergarments under their male clothing. Others are *complete* cross-dressers, who overtly carry out this practice either occasionally or, for some, all the time.

G. Sadomasochism (S-M)

The term *sadomasochism* is derived from the family names of two historical characters. The first is the French nobleman Marquis de Sade (Donatien Alphonse Francois was his "first" name, 1740–1814), whose writing consisted of vivid accounts of pain inflicted on one partner in sexual encounters of various kinds. *Sexual sadism* is defined as the inflection of physical pain and/or personal humiliation and degradation on a sexual partner. While de Sade portrayed infliction of excruciating pain on individuals, most sadism involves mild to moderate pain. It is estimated that about 5% of men and 2% of women have obtained sexual pleasure by inflicting pain on a regular basis.

While sadists inflict pain on willing or nonconsenting partners, sexual masochists (from Leopold von Sacher-Masoch, a German novelist who described this behavior in the late 19th century) enjoy suffering for erotic excitement as a preferred form of sexual activity. While sadists overwhelmingly tend to be men, masochists are more often females. The study of sadomasochism has only just begun. What little is known about these practices comes mainly from case studies, i.e., examination of S-M activities at centers for such activities or through paid dominance and submission sexual surrogates hired for these purposes.

Sadomasochistic activities center on use of dominance–aggression and submission in sexual activities. Terms that denote these activities abound such as bondage and domination (B-D), master–mistress, dominatrix, humiliation, restraints, whipping, leather/rubber, slave, bottom or submissive, and so on. Activities often involve elaborate interactions, sometimes with predetermined code words that will lead to the immediate release of a victim if desired and often use fetishistic trappings such as leather/rubber garments, chains, whips, shackles, harnesses, and other props. Rarely do sadomasochistic practices lead to physical injury, mutilation, or death. Victims, however, may be nonconsenting or willing and, not infrequently, paid sexual partners. The most frequent S-M activities are spanking, master–slave bondage, humiliation situations, oral–anal S-M contexts, whipping, and to a lesser degree, verbal abuse, enemas, torture, "golden showers" (urinating on someone), and use of toilet articles.

There is a well-defined S-M subculture that includes paraphernalia sex shops, stages for bondage scenes, magazines, prostitutes trained in S-M skills, and videos. Participants are predominantly heterosexual males with a greater concentration of bisexual female participants. Sadomasochistic activities are defined as paraphilias if they are recurrent and intense. To just tie up a sexual partner occasionally is not S-M activity.

H. Miscellaneous Paraphilias

Sexual arousal can become conditioned to a wide variety of eliciting stimuli. In this section, we will describe some relatively uncommon paraphilias that involve usual and sometimes noxious objects of sexual arousal. The miscellaneous paraphilias described below not only occur rarely but are often not detected due to their secretive nature and the fact that persons who engage in these acts are rarely motivated to seek treatment for their behavior.

A number of paraphilias are difficult to clarify. Some seem closely linked to fetishism but instead of body parts, body discharges take on erotic significance. Coprophilia, for example, involves erotic fascination with feces; klismaphilia with enemas; urophilia with urine; and mysophilia with filth. These stimuli may excite or be used for orgasm. Soiling others—by urinating or defecating on them—can also serve sadomasochistic purposes and is sometimes seen in assaults and rape situations.

Some paraphilias may have a sexual goal that is not immediately obvious. For example, pyromania (fire setting) and kleptomania (stealing for excitement) are thought to sometimes represent sexualized activities and thereby qualify as paraphilias.

Frotteurism (or toucherism) is a paraphilia that involves sexual gratification or arousal by rubbing against or fondling an unsuspecting, nonconsenting person. The frotteur acts on urges to touch, rub, or fondle usually in crowed places, often accompanied by fantasies of having sex with the singled-out person. Contact is brief to avoid detection.

Finally, the 20th century has brought a host of telephone scatologia, or efforts to seek sexual gratification by making obscene telephone calls. Anonymity and escape from detection are enhanced in use of this media for contact.

IV. CAUSAL MODELS AND TREATMENTS

Several key observations and assumptions should be noted before addressing the etiology and treatment of sexual disorders. First, contemporary sexologists have had little success in identifying specific causal factors and in designing and implementing successful treatment modalities. Such a state is due, in part, to limited theoretical models and problematic methodology. Criticism of existing causal models have been in terms of their myopic and/or reductionistic focus. In other words, most theories have focused solely on cognitive/emotional, behavioral, or environmental elements rather than on how all three elements interact and affect an individual's sexual identity. Another factor may be methodological problems, e.g., the difficulty in forming operational definitions for, and measuring such abstract concepts as, gender identity or sexual orientation. A more important and subtle point however, is the view that by separating the range of sexual behaviors into specific categories and calling these "abnormal," we are, by this process alone, not asking the critical questions about *how* sexual identity and orientation develop as a phenonomen. Instead, we are caught up in treating our categorizations as if they are real and true medical diseases or abnormalities. In fact, it appears that sexual expression can vary greatly and lies on a continuum. Even though experience and socialization can affect the location of one's position on the continuum, we know very little about how individuals get to a particular place on the continuum in the first place.

Biologial theories have predominated as causes of sexual disorders. The specific biological determinant or process would have to be in the male and not female structures. No absolute causative biological mechanisms have been identified. Most behavioral scientists see very little value in the psychoanalytic or psychodynamic theories. Both deficient psychosexual development and Oedipal fixations have been used to account for sexual disorders. Repressed hostility is thought to be at the roots of most paraphilias and the disorder allows a symbolic acting out of these repressed urges.

Learning theory models emphasize classical conditioning or associative learning linking sexual arousal with previously neutral objects or situations, masturbation becoming a key activity for this linking to occur. Learning theory seems to account for some paraphilias and for some portion of the sexual disorders but it lacks sufficient empirical power and predictability.

As mentioned previously, treatments for the paraphilias and other sexual disorders are very ineffective and positive effects seem to be confined to highly motivated clients with milder forms of the disorders. Biological treatments essentially attempt to dull or reduce sexual drive. The behavior therapies utilize counter-conditioning and desensitization methods. Various forms of group therapies (structured in a self-help manner) seem to be effective with the motivated client.

V. SEXUAL ADDICTION

How far do normal sexual activity levels extend? Where do we draw the line for pathological levels of sexual activity? Again, changes in social values have defined different patterns and points on the sexual activity continuum as pathological at different times. As a matter of fact, lack of precision in defining this category and the subjective nature of judgments resulted in the elimination of sexual addiction from the paraphilias in the DSM-III-R edition.

The terms "sexual addiction" and "sexual compulsion" began to appear in the scientific and clinical literature in the 1970s. They soon became popular terms to describe individuals who seemed obsessed with sexual behavior, i.e., nymphomaniacs, etc. Usually, sexual activity had to reach a level where it interfered with their job, relationships, career, or even their health. The behavior was often described as uncontrolled sexual behavior but functional analysis showed that it tended to lower anxiety states and probably helped enhance self-esteem and the sense of power and control.

Critics of the use of these concepts or diagnostic categories argued that they lacked precision and behavioral clarity, that they were often unreliable, and full of subjective judgments. Critics pointed out that the concepts did not fit our knowledge of the addictions nor of the compulsive processes. Furthermore, they were often applied to gay men with many partners and thus seemed discriminatory.

Supporters of this category argued that frequency was not the issue, rather one had to look at the purpose and meaning to the individual as critical components. Here, seeking out transient relationships in an indiscriminate manner certainly had the ring of self-defeating and self-destructive patterns of behavior that qualified as paraphilias. At this point, however, sexual addiction is an historical term.

VI. RAPE

Rape (Latin, "to seize") or the actual act of seizing a person by physical force or threat is an extreme form of sexual aggression and coercion. Rape is technically a legal term but it can be viewed from a psychological perspective. Current definitions of rape have extended the violation to deliberate intrusion into the emotional, physical, or rational integrity of the individual and even debasement through voyeurism ("visual rape"). Legally, rape is divided into statutory (seduction of a minor) and forcible seizure of an unwilling partner over age 18. Recent attention has been focused on "date rape" or the use of coercion by dates, acquaintances or even boyfriends. The victims are almost always women. No woman is entirely safe from rape. Almost 100,000 rapes are reported each year but estimates are the majority of rapes go unreported. Most occur outside or in the victim's home. National studies have found that the incidence of rape has increased more rapidly than any other type of violent crime.

There are many factors and levels of causation to rape. Certainly, cultural and subcultural attitudes toward women and about men contribute to the setting for rape. Psychological studies of rapists have identified some broad typologies of rapists. These types were derived from a psychological examination of rape cases. In none of these cases was it found that rape was motivated by sexual satisfaction. All the cases were characterized by a predominance of power motive or anger. This lead to the classification of rapists as (1) power assertive types (intimidation and control), (2) power reassurance types (to compensate for an underlying sense of weakness and inadequacy), (3) anger–retaliation type (rage, hatred, and violence predominate), and anger–excitation rape (the pathological sadist).

Prediction of rape from psychological profiles is not possible even though a proportion of rapists are obviously disturbed. The literature in this area is replete with instances of rape, in which, prior to the attack, the rapist had given no hint whatsoever of being a dangerous person. Conviction rates for rape are low and treatment or therapeutic interventions have generally been ineffective and disappointing. In addition to the need to develop adequate predictive and therapeutic measures for rapists, there is a tremendous need to improve treatments for the traumatized victims of these violent crimes.

VII. HOMOSEXUALITY

Sexual orientation, as it relates to homosexuality, is one's erotic attraction toward the same sex. Sexual orientation is a part of one's sexual identity, which, in turn, is primarily related to physical and emotional disposition, and is simultaneously interconnected yet distinct from biological and gender identity.

In Western culture, the most prominent means of conceptualizing sexual orientation is in terms of hetero- versus homosexuality. Traditionally, such distinctions are oversimplified and create oppositional positions. For these reasons, some theorists would rather conceive of orientation as being on a continuum, with heterosexuality and homosexuality at either end and in between a vast gradation of overlap reflecting bisexuality. Dichotomous thinking, coupled with rigid cultural values biased in favor of the heterosexual majority have led to a lengthy history of intolerance towards and oppression of homosexual and bisexual individuals.

Two forces helped shape negative and oppressive attitudes toward homosexuality. The first was Judeo-Christian values and beliefs that held that nonprocreative sexual acts were regarded as "sins against nature" and consequently frowned on in the culture. The second force was the rise of medicine and psychology as powerful authorities and arbiters of social morality by defining and controlling "deviant" and "diseased" behaviors. This control led to the condemnation of many fringe or nontraditional sexual practices with homosexuality in the forefront. Psychiatry, for example, included homosexuality in their diagnostic manual thus sanctioning intervention and treatment. Sin was now replaced by pathology. Being identified as mentally ill meant that homosexuals could be stripped of their civil and human rights while the heterosexual population looked on.

Under fire from within and outside their ranks, on December 15, 1973, the American Psychiatric Association board of trustees voted to remove homosexuality from the categories of mental illness. After much struggle and debate, homosexuality was replaced with a new category, ego-dystonic homosexuality, denoting those homosexual individuals who were distressed by their orientation and wanted to become heterosexual. This compromise category did not last for long, as many professionals and lay persons could see that it was just another more subtle means of perpetuating prejudice and oppression. Finally, all reference to homosexuality was removed from the official nomenclature and the following excerpt was inserted in the DSM-III-R:

> This category [ego-dystonic] has been eliminated for several reasons. It suggested to some that homosexuality itself was considered a disorder. In the United States almost all people who are homosexual first go through a phase in which their homosexuality is ego-dystonic. Furthermore, the diagnosis of ego-dystonic homosexuality has rarely been used clinically and there have been only a few articles in the scientific literature that use the concept.

A. Prevalence

The problem in measuring the prevalance of homosexuality is that it must be operationally defined.

Renowned sex reseacher Alfred Kinsey chose to operationally define sexual orientation on a continuum in terms of behavior frequency of homo-, hetero-, and degree of combined sexual behaviors. The following scale was developed:

0. Exclusive heterosexual with no homosexual
1. Predominately heterosexual, only incidental homosexual
2. Predominately heterosexual, but more than incidental homosexual
3. Equally heterosexual and homosexual
4. Predominately homosexual, but more than incidental heterosexual
5. Predominately homosexual, but incidental heterosexual
6. Exclusively homosexual

What resulted from his pioneering assessment of the sexual practices of the American public was surprising. Kinsey found that 37% of males surveyed had had physical contact to the point of orgasm, at least once, with another man. In addition, another 4–6% were either primarily or exclusively homosexual. It was found that of the females questioned, 13% had at least one such encounter with another female.

To conceive of homosexuality in strict behavioral terms challenged the more prevalent practice of using the terms to represent a personality deficit. The latter approach, of course, leads to social stigmatization. Kinsey also avoided applying sexual orientation labels in an either/or manner, by conceiving of sexuality as a range of behaviors on a continuum. Despite his popularity, his results were criticized on methodological and theoretical grounds. Specifically, grave doubts were raised about the generalizability of his data from the limited sampling he used. Other researchers conducting surveys with better sampling methods found similar to much lesser rates of incidence; usually between 4 and 16% homosexual behavior of some kinds. Theoretically, Kinsey was criticized for being too reductionistic by trying to conceptualize the homosexual experience in terms of the frequency of same sex behaviors. Regardless of the precise percentages and how one exactly conceives of it, homosexuality is and has been a pervasive part of our culture and population.

Since the early 1970s, there appears to have been a radical rethinking of how we treate those of homo- or bisexual orientations. Still, some lay persons and professionals find these orientations pathological and must seek causes and roots for these disorders. Katchadourian responds to these efforts in the following manner:

> Those who accept homosexuality as an illness seek its causes. Those who do not, object to this approach. "Causes" implies that there is something wrong; why not seek the "causes" of heterosexuality? The search for the origins of sexual orientation—homosexual or heterosexual—is a more legitimate quest.

The causal agents responsible for producing any sexual orientation are basically unknown. If we hope to gain insight by relying on a single explanation, then we will surely miss the dynamic and interactive nature of sexual identity. Whether the theoretical model is based upon genetic inheritance, developmental influences, or psychodynamic conflict, the nature of sexual orientation, regardless of sexual preference, seems better understood as having multiple roots.

B. Treatments

Contemporary thought rejects the outdated notion of homosexuality and bisexuality as diseases to be treated and cured. Attempts by professionals to change or convert homosexuals into heterosexuals have almost always been exercises in futility. Despite long and intensive therapeutic hours, psychoanalysis has had no success. With their aversive counter-conditioning techniques, the behavioral therapies have only faired marginally better. Irrespective of the theoretical model, when a person (homosexual or not) is forced into the therapy room, not only is change highly unlikely but the chances for negative psychological consequences are greatly increased.

An apparent exception to this lack of success was the Masters and Johnson sex therapy study, which reported to have "helped" two-thirds of those who volunteered for a 2-week treatment program. Criticisms of their work include the fact that the male and female participants were carefully screened to ensure that they exhibited high levels of desire to change and were the beneficiaries of very supportive partners. In addition to such biases in sampling, further analysis of the follow-up data revealed that the claimed failure rate of only 28% was probably too low. Perhaps a rate of about 45% would be more accurate.

C. Differences in Health and Personality

As pointed out earlier, psychiatrists have conceptualized the homosexual as inherently pathological and heterosexual as "normal." Numerous scientific studies have compared homosexuals who sought treatment against normal heterosexuals who were *not* in treatment. Differences were found between these groups on health and personality variables. More recent studies, with improved methodology, have shown that very few differences in pathology actually exist between equivalent heterosexual and homosexual samples. Differences in depression and suicide rates previously attributed to pathology or flaws in the individuals are now seen from a broader socio-psychological level of causation, i.e., environmental pressures to live up to one's societal status as deviant.

Another area in which scientific bias has played a mystifying role is in the realm of personality differences between homo- and heterosexuals. Specifically, there have been studies showing gay men were more feminine than straight men and that lesbians were more masculine than their heterosexual counterparts. Once again, such findings have been shown to be based on methodologically flawed clinical/nonclinical designs. Once corrected for biased sampling, such studies show that the differences in gender identity are minimal. Yes, "butch" lesbians and effeminate gays exist, but as a stereotype they are not representative of the homosexual and bisexual population as a whole.

Bibliography

American Psychiatric Association. (1987). "Diagnostic and Statistical Manual," 3rd ed., revised. Washington, DC.

Bancroft, J. (1983). "Human Sexuality and Its Problems." Churchill Livingston, London.

Bayer, R. (1987). "Homosexuality and American Psychiatry: The Politics of Diagnosis." Princeton University Press, NJ.

Benjamin, H. (1966). "The Transsexual Phenomenon." Julian Press, New York.

Bullough, V. L., and Brundage, J. (1982). "Sexual Practices in the Medieval Church." Prometheus, Buffalo, NY.

Carnes, P. J. (1983). "The Sexual Addiction." CompCase, Minneapolis.

Docter, R. F. (1988). "Transvestites and Transsexuals: Toward a Theory of Cross-Gender Behavior." Plenum, New York.

Freeman, E. B. (1988). "Intimate Matters: A History of Sexuality in America." Harper and Row, New York.

Finkelhor, D. (1984). "Child Sexual Abuse." Free Press, New York.

Gonsiorek, J. C., and Weinrich, J. D. (Eds.) (1991). "Homosexuality: Research Implications for Public Policy." Sage, Newburry Park.

Katchadourian, H. A. (1989). "Fundamentals of Human Sexuality," 5th ed. Holt-Rinehart and Winston, San Francsico.

Sexual Orientation

Kathryn Kelley and Lori Dawson
University at Albany, State University of New York

Glossary

Bisexuality Referring to a sexual orientation in which sexual behavior, affection, and fantasies are directed toward members of both genders.

Gay A man with a homosexual orientation.

Heterosexuality Referring to a sexual orientation in which sexual behavior, affection, and fantasies are directed toward members of the opposite gender.

Homophobia The irrational fear or intolerance of those who engage in homosexual acts.

Homosexual bias Religious and moral objections to homosexuality, the belief that such behavior is deviant, and the acceptance of various myths about homosexuals.

Homosexuality Referring to a sexual orientation in which sexual behavior, affection, and fantasies are directed toward members of the same gender as oneself.

Lesbian A woman with a homosexual orientation.

Sexual orientation The combination of physical sexual activity, interpersonal affection, and erotic fantasies that are directed at the members of the opposite sex, the same sex, or both.

WITHIN THE FIELD of study devoted to human sexuality, few topics evoke as much discussion and controversy as does the area of sexual orientation. Predominantly negative societal views about nonheterosexual orientations affect the study of sexual orientation. The literature on homosexuality has been politicized, and sensitivity to the effects of this bias is useful. The etiology of homosexuality occupies a prominent position in this subfield, despite the fact that little is known about the precursors of the typical orientation, heterosexuality. In the initial section, the defining characteristics of sexual orientation and the relative distribution of its categories are discussed. Second, historical and contemporary findings about sexual orientation are brought to bear upon theories used to examine it. Developmental issues relating to homosexuality across the lifespan are also included. The close relationships of homosexuals and bisexuals are characterized, and issues about parenting receive attention. Social and legal phenomena are described, particularly in relation to stereotypes, homophobia, sexual activity, and participation in military service.

I. NUMERICAL DISTRIBUTION OF THE SEXUAL ORIENTATIONS

Controversy surrounds the deceptively simple question regarding the percentage of people occupying each category of sexual orientation. The characteristics of the sample and questions used to identify orientation affect the obtained distribution. The operational definition of sexual orientation includes criteria related to behavior, fantasy, attraction, self-identification, and combinations of these variables. The use of behavioral criteria can imply confounding factors, because it may lead to the inclusion of people as homosexual who are engaging in same-sex activity for reasons independent of sexual arousal, i.e., domination in prison settings. A similar situation exists with respect to fantasy; some married men may fantasize and be attracted to other men, but engage in sexual activity only with their wives. Self-reports may misclassify people who are sexually active with both genders but identify themselves as either heterosexual or homosexual rather than bisexual. An example of this is men who consider themselves heterosexual, but engage in sexual acts, often secretly, with other men. The tearoom trade—involving impersonal, anonymous sex acts in public places such as restrooms—is a site for this type of activity.

The incidence of gay married men is difficult to obtain through conventional research, but it is estimated that 2 to 4% of married men engage in homosexual activity, and that 10 to 20% of homosexual men have been married. Conversely, some people who consider themselves homosexual nonetheless apply the public label of heterosexuality or bisexuality to avoid ridicule and stigmatization.

Recently, multidimensional criteria have begun to receive the most agreement as appropriate to define sexual orientation. Fritz Klein's definition focuses on seven related and perhaps impermanent criteria: sexual attraction, sexual behavior, sexual fantasies, emotional preference, social preference, self-identification, and lifestyle. These variables are assessed with respect to the three time frames of past, present, and the ideal future. Few studies have used this multifactorial approach, although a strong, positive correlation has been observed between self-identified sexual orientation and an index of behavioral and attraction criteria.

More commonly, estimates of homosexuality have utilized only behavioral criteria. In 1948 and 1953 Alfred Kinsey and colleagues provided the statistics most widely quoted in subsequent years. A seven-point continuum of sexual orientation ranged from zero representing exclusively heterosexual to six, representing exclusively homosexual. The figures for United States adults indicated that 37% of men and 19% of women had at least one homosexual experience in adulthood. Ten percent of men and 3% of women identified themselves as primarily or exclusively homosexual. Reanalysis of the Kinsey data by one of his coauthors, for example, led to revised estimates of primarily or exclusively homosexual adults to 4% of men and 1.5% of women. More recent data have indicated similar findings, with approximately 5% of men and 2% of women identified as homosexual. Hesitancy to report homosexual tendencies in face-to-face interviews can bias such estimates, and the percentages may be regarded as lower boundaries of the true estimate of homosexuality. Homosexual groups maintain that the percentage of population represented by their orientation is closer to 10%. Few studies have included females in these estimates; existing data indicate the incidence of female homosexuality to be approximately half that of male homosexuality. An additional limitation to these data stems from the practice of combining bisexuals and homosexuals instead of distinguishing these orientations.

II. THEORIES OF HOMOSEXUALITY

Theories of the origin of homosexuality concentrate on two basic comparisons, that between biological determinism and socialization and the nature vs nurture controversy. Socialization theories have not conclusively explained sexual orientation to date, and biological theories are receiving renewed attention. A combination of nature and nurture explanations is the more likely explanation than either factor in isolation.

A. Biological Theories of Homosexuality

The three most commonly studied biological bases of behavior are genetic hereditability, hormonal differences, and divergent brain structure and function.

1. Genetic Hereditability

An approach useful to assessing genetic hereditability is the study of monozygotic (MZ) and dyzygotic (DZ) twins. MZ twins, sharing identical genetic material, typically show a higher concordance rate for a heritable trait than DZ twins with less similar genetic material. Frank Kallmann's early twin studies reported a nearly perfect concordance rate for orientation among MZ male twins. Later studies on male twins have indicated substantial genetic influence on the basis of predicted differences in concordance. Less concordance for sexual orientation has been observed among female twins. Correspondence in sexual orientation among non-twin family members of the same gender has also been observed.

Criticisms of this research included methodological shortcomings and lack of replicability. Careful screening of subjects with respect to verifiable information has been recommended in such studies. Ascertainment bias, in which similar relatives are more likely to be found and assessed than dissimilar ones, results in a higher probability of observing a pair with the same orientation. Thus, this source of bias should also receive attention in this type of research. The confounding and artifactual aspects of the studies on hereditability of sexual orientation interfere with the definitive interpretation of their results.

2. Hormonal Influences on Homosexual Orientation

Two distinct categories of hormonal influences on sexual orientation exist: prenatal hormonal effects and differential reactions to hormones in adults. Subjects in these studies are either human or animal, and the applicability of findings about hormone-induced sexual behaviors among animals to human sexuality is questionable.

During gestation, gonadal sex hormones affect fetal feminization and masculinization and also have an organizing effect on certain parts of the brain, particularly the hypothalamus. The mammalian pattern is for genital development and brain differentiation to be female unless masculinized with androgens. Because purposeful administration of excess hormones during gestation is unethical in human studies, certain prenatal syndromes can provide information about atypical variations in hormone levels.

Two of these prenatal syndromes involve variation in androgen. In congenital adrenal hyperplasia (CAH), also known as androgenital syndrome, an excess of androgen produces masculinized genitals in genetic females. Childhood play in girls with CAH resembles stereotypically boylike behavior, called tomboyism; the source of this difference compared to non-CAH sisters could be prenatal hormone exposure, or having ambiguous genitalia and receiving differential treatment from parents regarding gender role encouragement. Other differences include a higher incidence of female homosexuality in both self-identification and history of sexual relationships, especially among the variant of CAH associated with a salt-losing metabolism. Interestingly, males with CAH indicate a decreased incidence of homosexuality.

Androgen-insensitivity syndrome (AIS) affects genetic males by reducing the utilization of testosterone. The gonadal male has testes in addition to female genitalia, but no uterus or oviducts. AIS individuals and genetic females do not differ from each other in sexual arousal or orientation. Psychiatrist John Money interprets the syndrome as an indication that neither chromosomal sex, gonadal sex, nor hormonal cyclicity determines heterosexual orientation in women. Research on AIS also cannot differentiate the determinants of female sexual orientation as androgen-produced organization of the brain from female socialization.

A syndrome affecting some men who otherwise have the typical chromosomal and gonadal composition is 5-α reductase deficiency, also known as dihydrotestosterone (DHT)-deficiency syndrome. Without the enzyme needed to convert testosterone into DHT, external genitalia are ambiguous at birth. Often raised as girls, they experience puberty with the development of masculine secondary sex characteristics. A switch in gender identity can subsequently occur. Cultural valuation of the male role appears as feasible an explanation for this shift as biological determinism, in which pubertal testosterone masculinized the brain and stimulated attraction toward women.

Maternal stress stimulates the production of adrenaline and corticosterone that can interfere with fetal production of testosterone. Animal studies have shown severe maternal stress to increase homosexual-like behavior. However, contradictory results exist among studies on human males, implying little support for the maternal stress theory.

Direct assessment of hormone levels and hormonal reactions has implicated a hormonal feedback mechanism in sexual orientation. Some studies have illustrated that estrogen administration to homosexual males resulted in less decrease in the production of luteinizing hormone (LH) than in heterosexual males. However, when individual and lifestyle factors that affect testicular hormone production were controlled—age, alcohol use, etc.—the difference disappeared. In controlled studies of the hormone levels of lesbians and heterosexual women, no significant differences typically result. Thus, evidence about the contribution of hormonal levels to sexual orientation is conflicting, and lifestyle and individual characteristics also affect observed differences. [*See* HORMONES AND BEHAVIOR.]

3. Brain Structure

Differences between male and female animals occur in brain structure, and are known as sexual dimorphisms. The preoptic area of the hypothalamus, related to LH feedback and other effects, has been the site of a search for sexual dimorphisms in humans. To date, a reliable difference has not been related to sexual orientation, although one portion of the preoptic area was observed to be smaller in homosexual than heterosexual men. Criticism of this study on methodological grounds has included the notation that the cause of death (acquired immune deficiency syndrome) among the homosexuals could have confounded the results. However, a dimorphism based on sexual orientation in men has been demonstrated in the suprachiasmatic nucleus, although this difference has been interpreted as more an effect of orientation and its associated characteristics than a cause. In general, brain dimorphism in relation to sexual orientation remains to be demonstrated reliably and validly. [*See* HYPOTHALAMUS.]

B. Socialization Theories

The four major accounts of sexual orientation that focus on socialization are: family patterns, childhood gender nonconformity, early sexual experiences, and cross-cultural studies.

1. Family Patterns

The original research on family patterns as the source of homosexuality grew out of psychoanalytic tradition. Sigmund Freud himself, however, did little theorizing about homosexuality. In Freudian terms, individuals are born polymorphous perverse, with an essentially bisexual nature having the capability of enjoying sexual gratification from any source independently of gender. Through cultural proscriptions, heterosexuality is reinforced as the socially appropriate form of sexual expression. Therefore, all humans, theoretically, have latent homosexual desires. An improper resolution to the psychosexual Oedipal complex results in homosexuality, which Freud viewed as benign although some later psychoanalysts developed a decidedly more negative stance.

Empirical studies initially supported some of the elements of a dysfunctional family pattern in the etiology of homosexuality. These elements have included maternal dominance and one or both parent's psychological distance from and rejection of offspring. However, lack of replicability, contradictory results, cross-cultural inconsistencies, and methodological problems such as the use of clinical samples have placed this support in doubt. The use of retrospection for assessment purposes is known to create bias in subjects' memory. For example, homosexual adults who may have strained relationships with parents could be reporting unsatisfactory aspects of childhood on the basis of greater recall of more accessible information.

2. Childhood Gender-Role Nonconformity

When retrospecting about their childhood, homosexuals of both genders have recalled having rejected the stereotypic gender role. Examples of differences in early and middle childhood behavior have included: cross-gender toy play and activities like athletics, typically some cross-dressing, sissy or tomboy behaviors, and gender of friends. The absence of masculine behaviors in boyhood has predicted the development of bisexual or homosexual identity in adulthood. Socialization in societies with strong gender-role stereotypes heightens the likelihood of this relationship. Gender-role nonconformity has been shown to be less predictive of later homosexual or bisexual orientation in women than men. Controversy exists about the significance of this nonconformity, whether it represents a cause or indicator of atypical sexual orientation.

3. Early Sexual Experiences

A model of the effects of early sexual experiences on homosexual orientation has been proposed by psychologist Michael Storms. According to this model, the rate of sexual maturation affects later orientation by limiting sexual experimentation to the homosociality phase when boys' most likely sexual contacts would be boys instead of girls. Some support exists for this account, in the role that affective responses to early sexual experiences have in predicting adult sexual orientation. However, the few months of difference in the onset of sexual exploration between homosexuals and heterosexuals casts doubt on the importance of pubertal timing. The theory also does not provide a clear model for lesbianism, given that the incidence of early negative experiences with males but not positive ones with females differs between heterosexual and homosexual women. Precisely how they differ has been disputed. Thus, early sexual activity may positively reinforce homosexual tendencies in some young men, but it does not appear to affect significantly sexual orientation in general.

4. The Cross-Cultural Perspective

Observations of sexual behavior across cultures provide a wider perspective about the influence of socialization on sexual orientation. In a classic report by Clellan Ford and Frank Beach on 76 cultures, most societies accepted and tolerated homosexuality, and several practiced ritualized forms of homosexuality as rites of passage. Far more anthropological research has been conducted on male, than on female, homosexuality. Cross-cultural variation in its form, ritualization, and occurrence indicates the malleability of variables that affect sexual orientation. It also argues against biological and genetic factors as the primary determinants of orientation.

C. The Interactionist Model

Interactionist models rely on the confluence of biological/genetic and socialization/experiential factors as determinants of sexual orientation. The relative contributions of these factors vary among these models, but sexual behavior and orientation are likened to other forms of human behavior in their multifactorial etiology. Examples are Milton Diamond's Biased Interaction model and John Money's theory of sexual identity development. Diamond, a biologist, described how social experiences affect gender identity and sexuality, and proposed that genetic and hormonal influences greatly affect them. This position contrasts with Money's basic stance that the two factors interact, but that environmental factors play the greater role. The social expression of sexuality's biological base is at the heart of these models. Eventually scientific research may indicate that both biological and experiential factors jointly determine sexual orientation. For heterosexuals and some homosexuals, one set of factors may be found to predominate.

III. DEVELOPMENTAL ISSUES RELATING TO HOMOSEXUALITY

Specific developmental issues have been applied to homosexuality. This section discusses identity formation and the coming out process, adolescence, and aging.

A. Identity Formation and the Coming Out Process

The definition of coming out varies, and the narrowest concept involves telling others about one's homosexual orientation. A broader conceptualization describes the lengthy developmental process of recognizing one's own sexual preferences and arriving at an integration of orientation into everyday life. Thus, identity formation implies a broad context, while coming out can be viewed as one aspect of the identity process.

Identity formation begins in adolescence, and models of this process postulate common elements while differing in others such as applicability to one or both genders. In 1990 Vivienne C. Cass based a model for both genders on clinical experience. In the first of the six stages, identity confusion, individuals develop a sense that homosexuality has become relevant in their lives, and confusion and inconsistency about sexuality occur. Other themes of this stage include the occurrence of homosexual fantasy, perhaps avoidance of overt homosexual behavior, and feelings of isolation and alienation. The second stage, identity comparison, clarifies the implications of the atypical orientation and may increase alienation from former support systems due to the abandoning of heterosexual expectations (e.g., marriage and family) and privilege (familial and societal acceptance). Faking a heterosexual lifestyle, called passing, may avoid negative consequences. Temporary adherence to bisexuality, exaggerated public heterosexual displays, and demonstrations of homophobic attitudes have been traced to this stage's personal identity confusion.

The last four stages signal a resolution to the turmoil. Identity tolerance, stage three, extends to one's own orientation in contact with similar others. The lack of social skills can interfere with progress. Next, identity acceptance can occur by developing positive identification and increased contact with other homosexuals. A homosexual support system helps to dissipate alienation as the person begins to integrate into the homosexual subculture. In stage five, identity pride, identification with the gay and lesbian community leads to increased pride and awareness. Anger and community activism occur, along with a tendency to dichotimize one's existence between gay and heterosexual orientations. Communication about being homosexual takes place in this stage, typically to friends expected to be tolerant and later to relatives. The final stage, identity synthesis, leads to a reduction of divisiveness and anger. Orientation becomes integrated as one aspect of the individual's personal identity.

B. Special Issues in the Lives of Homosexual Adolescents

According to theories of social and personality development, the primary tasks of adolescence and young adulthood revolve around formation of identity and intimate relationships. Adolescents who are acquiring a homosexual identity experience additional stress which limits their ability to accomplish the basic developmental tasks. [*See* ADOLESCENCE.]

The homosexual adolescent begins to realize that sexual orientation implies membership in a stigmatized minority group. Typically this occurs without familial and cultural support systems available to members of racial, ethnic, and religious minority groups. In a survey of homosexual adolescents, they reported relatively high incidence of assault, verbal abuse by peers, problems in school, and problems with substance abuse and mental health. They are five times more likely to attempt suicide than heterosexual adolescents, in more serious ways. The U.S. National Center for Health Statistics has estimated that approximately 30% of the 5000 annual suicides are precipitated by issues related to sexual orientation and sexual identity. Awareness and proactive solutions to this problem appear to be insufficient to date in the professional community. Although support from the homosexual community could aid the acquisition of a positive identity, access is limited. Reluctance among homosexual teachers and other potential resources stems from fear of accusations that they are attempting to recruit young people. The legal ramifications of dealing with minors about sexual orientation also prevent intervention.

Instead of forming meaningful intimate relationships, homosexual adolescents become experts at camouflaging their orientation, known as hiding. This practice results in invention of heterosexual dates, distancing from family and former friends, and loss of self-esteem. Sexual encounters are used as a technique for learning about and moving toward the homosexual culture. Safer sex practices, particularly relevant to gay adolescents, are inhibited by the reluctance to label themselves homosexual and plan for the possibility of engaging in sexual activity. Dropping out of school interferes with learning about the risks of sexually transmissable diseases (STDs) including acquired immune deficiency syndrome (AIDS), caused by the HIV virus. Given that 21% of HIV-infected persons are 20 to 29 years old and the long latency of HIV, infection probably occurred during adolescence. Thus, the male adolescent has been described as being in grave danger of contracting STDs including AIDS.

Descriptions of parents' relationships with homosexual children typically include negative reactions to their child's disclosure of orientation. Initial shock, guilt, and denial evolve into strained relationships which tend toward more dysfunction in parent–daughter than parent–son pairs. The most positive type of parent–child relationship is characterized by continued contact with denial, in which parents know little about the child's personal life except perhaps having met the child's same-sex partner. Almost half of these parent–child relationships consist of varying degrees of negativity, with about 1 in 10 characterized by positive interactions among parents, offspring, and the offspring's partner.

C. Differences in Personality

Although differences are assumed to exist between heterosexuals and homosexuals with respect to various personality dimensions, empirical research on this point is conflicting. Except for sex roles, few studies show consistent and significant individual differences based on sexual orientation. Homosexual adults have been shown to express atypical sex roles more commonly than heterosexuals. Thus, homosexual men may be found to admit greater femininity, and lesbians more masculinity, than their heterosexual counterparts. However, B. R. Simon Rosser has found this association to depend on the rigidity of gender roles in a particular society.

Variations in psychological adjustment have also been investigated. The results have ranged from no difference to a difference that depends on the individual's adaptation to the homosexual orientation and on involvement in the gay community. Worse adjustment has been found among maladapted, uninvolved homosexuals, and the societal stigma associated with their orientation has been offered as an explanation of this relationship.

D. Homosexuality and Aging

While many of the problems related to aging in Western societies are universal, special issues apply to aging among homosexuals. The cohort of homosexuals over age 60 grew up in a period of less social tolerance, before the gay civil rights movement of the 1970s. Secretiveness about one's homosexual orientation was more common. Yet older homosexuals express high levels of life satisfaction and acceptance of aging, especially for those active in the homosexual community. Raymond Berger catalogued the experiences of older male homosexuals, and concluded that these individuals do not fit negative cultural stereotypes by presenting more psychological maladjustment than heterosexual males their age. Like many surveys of homosexuals, this work overrepresented white, educated men active in some form of homosexual community and so may be biased. Similar studies of lesbians yielded comparable results, except that women reported less frequent sexual activity, sometimes due to the unavailability of a suitable partner for a long-term relationship.

The social and psychological mid-life crisis common to heterosexuals applies less widely to homosexuals. Explanations for this difference center on the latter's more general flexibility in sex roles and androgyny. Homosexuals reevaluated their role in society during the course of homosexual identity formation as young adults, perhaps making the mid-life examination less likely. For lesbians who may have rejected the male-centered norm for physical attractiveness, bodily changes associated with aging may be viewed as less important.

Particular legal and social complications do affect aging homosexuals more than heterosexuals. When a partner falls ill, homosexuals have no legal visitation rights in hospitals or nursing homes. In case of death, less social support is available for the surviving homosexual partner. Blood relatives can make claims against the property of a deceased family member who was homosexual, ignoring the needs of the survivor who was unable to derive the benefits of a legal marriage.

IV. GAY, LESBIAN, AND BISEXUAL RELATIONSHIPS

The commonalities and differences in the relationships of lesbians and gay men will be addressed in this section. A large-scale study on homosexual relationships was conducted by Alan Bell and Martin Weinberg in 1978. Based on their sample of nearly 1000 homosexuals of both genders, five distinct types of relationships emerged: close-coupled, open-coupled, functional, dysfunctional, and asexual. Close-coupled relationships are fairly permanent and are marked by sexual exclusivity and strong emotional commitment. Open-coupled relationships had some emotional commitment but were not monogamous. Functional individuals had a high frequency of sexual activity, but not commitment. Dysfunctional individuals also had a high number of sexual partners but experienced sexual difficulty and regrets about their orientation. Finally, asexual individuals showed little or no sexual interest or activity, had many sexual problems, and had regrets about their orientation.

A. Lesbian Relationships

Lesbian relationships perhaps resemble close heterosexual couplings more than they do gay male relationships. Lesbians have been described as regarding their own relationships in the same way. The facts that both partners are women and that lesbian pairings are considered deviant undoubtedly affects the course of their relationships. Common themes affecting relationship stability are dominance, dependence, and similarity. High levels of sexual satisfaction in conjunction with commitment and closeness are also found in lesbian relationships. Stereotypic role-playing, anonymous or impersonal sexual activity, and unequal division of labor are less commonly found in lesbian than in gay male or heterosexual relationships.

Dissolution of lesbian relationships, typically after a monogamous status of long duration, may not result in total estrangement of former partners. The reason for this may originate from the close-knit nature of lesbian communities and friendship networks. Characteristically, lesbian communities are founded on interacting social networks based on sexual orientation, with a strong sense of feminist values. The communities serve as an institutional base of organizations and settings which provide places and structures for lesbian interaction. The activities are centered around women's music, art, and political activism, and involvement affects self-acceptance, self-esteem, and having a positive lesbian identity.

B. Gay Male Relationships

Characteristics of gay male relationships were described in detail by David McWhirter and Andrew Mattison in 1984. Gay male couples with a mean longevity of 8.9 years were interviewed. The researchers devised a theory of six stages describing the phases of gay male relationships. During the first year of the relationship, blending occurs; romantic love, income sharing, and division of labor occupy the couple. The next 2 years involve nesting and such practical matters as homemaking and finding compatibility. In the third stage, maintaining takes place for 2 years through establishing traditions, taking risks, and resolving conflict. The rest of the first decade deals with the building stage, in which relationship stability provides support for the individual to develop productive, independent interests. The fifth stage (releasing) occupies the second decade, described as a period of trust, merging finances, and taking each other for granted. Renewing takes place in the final stage, characterized by reliance on security and memories, shifting perspectives, and restoring the partnership.

Differences consistently occur between lesbians and gay males in the frequency of impersonal sexual activity and the number of sexual partners. Fully half of gay men have been described as having had more than 50 sexual partners in their lifetime. Lesbians, in contrast, typically have had fewer than 10 partners. The incidence of impersonal sex has varied with the impact of AIDS, at least temporarily.

C. Bisexual Relationships

In Kensey's findings over four decades ago, 46% of men reported having sexual experiences with partners of both genders. Relatively little information exists about bisexuality, and many samples in research on homosexuality have included bisexuals. Collapsing across categories of sexual orientation is common in works on homosexuality. Reasons for this practice include facilitating statistical analysis, increasing the size of the homosexual sample, and conforming to theoretical bias. Interpretation of the data supports conclusions about homosexuals, while not thoroughly examining a sizable bisexual component. A portion of samples labeled homosexual has thus reported engaging in marital and homosexual sex contemporaneously, for example. In 1978 Bell and Weinberg presented a breakdown of their sample, comparing behavior and feelings. They reported that 26% of white, homosexual males had some bisexual contact and that 42% expressed bisexual attraction. Similarly, 32% of white lesbians had engaged in bisexual behavior and half expressed bisexual attraction. The interpretation of the data supports conclusions about homosexuals, while negating the existence of a sizable bisexual component.

How to define bisexuality within the concept of sexual orientation has challenged some theorists. William Masters and Virginia Johnson used the term ambisexual in 1979 to denote those individuals who have no preference about the gender of their partner. These authors give the term additional meaning, however, by indicating that an ambisexual is one who as a sexually mature individual has "never evidenced interest in a continuing relationship" (p. 146). Other researchers have defined bisexuality more broadly and less negatively, such as designating as bisexual several of the middle categories on the Kinsey scale. The defining characteristic focuses on engaging in sexual activity with both genders, either consistently or variably after reaching sexual maturity.

The multifactorial approach to defining sexual orientation extends to bisexuality. Sexual behavior may be expressed as bisexual, but the affection, fantasy, desire, and self-definition may all vary. In her 1976 study of female sexuality, Shere Hite noted that a significant number of women, who were heterosexual by self-definition, spontaneously expressed a desire to try a sexual relationship with another woman. Some women identify themselves as bisexual even though they have never had sexual experiences with women. In other studies sizable proportions of men have also expressed bisexual desire and/or attraction, without engaging in the corresponding behavior. Additionally, heterosexuals commonly report having had homosexual fantasies, with or without the desire to act on them.

Negative attitudes toward bisexuals have been reported in studies assessing samples of the other two orientations. Only recently have bisexuals become more visibly organized. One claim by bisexual activits is that theirs is the true orientation. Objections to the notion that bisexuals are sexually promiscuous are also found in activism. However, comparatively little is known about bisexual patterns, so that evidence has not been available to support the objections.

D. Parenting

An estimated 6 to 14 million children in the United States have gay, lesbian, or bisexual parents. Some of these children were conceived in a heterosexual union, while others are among the growing number of children conceived through artificial insemination of lesbians. The latter technique uses sperm from an anonymous donor, avoiding the custody issues faced by parents of children from former heterosexual relationships. In some states, homosexual orientation is sufficient grounds to prohibit child custody, or a major obstacle to it. The homosexual or bisexual parent may spend considerable amounts to support a custody claim, with only a small chance of success.

Lesbian mothers confront discrimination and social stigmatization, in addition to the custody battles described above. In lesbian couples, the woman who is artificially inseminated becomes the biological mother with legal custody. Few states allow a nonbiological mother to adopt a child when the biological mother has custody, particularly when lesbianism is involved. However, a small number of states are beginning to allow homosexual couples to adopt children.

Similarities have been demonstrated between heterosexual and lesbian mothers' maternal attitudes and parenting effectiveness. Differences in parenting style tend to be neutral or not harmful for children, in areas such as gender-role expectations. Relationships between lesbian mothers and their children's father, in the case of former marriage, tend to be more congenial and to encourage more contact between fathers and children. Similar patterns have been reported among gay fathers. However, gay fathers may experience more difficulties within the homosexual community than do lesbians. Less tolerance of children, as a sign of heterosexual activity, exists in the gay male community.

The impact of having a homosexual parent on children indicates this method of rearing children to have some drawbacks, but that the overall result resembles the typical outcome of childrearing. In comparisons of children with lesbian vs heterosexual mothers, both gender-related and other developmental characteristics do not differ between the two groups. Children with lesbian mothers attempt to avoid embarrassment and teasing by hiding their situation from friends and by disclosing it to few. Less information about gay fathers' effect on children exists, especially in comparison to children of heterosexual parents. In general, research so far has not demonstrated that children of homosexual parents differ on major psychological or developmental factors.

V. STEREOTYPES AND PERCEPTIONS OF HOMOSEXUALS

Stereotypes of homosexuals involve attitudes that they are abnormal, deviant, and maladjusted. A majority of American adults have in surveys expressed the opinion that homosexuality is always or almost always wrong. Negative stereotypes about male homosexuals also include the belief that many are child molesters, although empirical studies have found that the vast majority of child molesters are heterosexual males. Evidence of negative stereotypes has also been documented in media portrayals of homosexuals as victims or villains. [*See* Prejudice and Stereotypes.]

A. Homophobia

The term homophobia denotes irrational fear, revulsion, and condemnation of homosexuals. Demographic factors such as gender, age, and religious conservatism affect its extremity. Homosexuals have reported in surveys that they have been victimized by anti-gay jokes, verbal threats or harassment, and physical assault, some of which has occurred in the workplace. The incidence of hate crimes, known as gay bashing, has increased in recent years. A less extreme form of negative stereotyping is termed homosexual bias, often based on moral or religious objections.

B. Legal Restrictions

Legal issues pertaining to homosexuality include restrictive legislation against sexual acts. Sodomy (oral–genital or anal sexual activity) laws are one example of this legal restriction. Currently just under half the states have sodomy laws. Enforcement typically occurs only against homosexuals, including in states where heterosexual sodomy (oral–genital or anal sexual activity) is also illegal. In the case of Bowers vs Hardwick, the U.S. Supreme Court refused to extend the constitutional right of privacy to homosexual sodomy, while avoiding a ruling on heterosexual sodomy also covered by the Georgia law in question.

A second example of restriction of homosexuals involves U.S. immigration law. Since 1917, homosexuals have been prohibited from coming into the country, on grounds that they were regarded as possessing a basic psychopathic personality. The U.S. Immigration and Naturalization Service removed the ban on homosexuals in 1979, followed by a congressional reenactment of the ban. Enforcement varies, and a similar restriction applies to anyone who is HIV positive.

C. Civil Rights Issues

In regard to civil rights, constitutional law has various classifications which are subject to different levels of court scrutiny. A class of people being discriminated against may possess certain features that term it as suspect. Enhanced constitutional protection applies to suspect classes, which must have been subjected to a long history of persecution due to irrational stereotypes. The suspect class has also been unable to obtain protection from the government's legislative branch, and has experienced discrimination because of a trait that is immutable. Homosexuals meet the first two criteria, but immutability is controversial. If homosexuality can be changed, then it is not immutable; the search for genetic and biological causes of sexual orientation thus has become significant for claims of the justifiability of civil rights protection.

D. Legalized Discrimination

Currently no federal protections in the United States bar discrimination based on sexual orientation. A minority of states and local governments have established this protection providing legal recourse in cases of discrimination regarding employment, housing, or education. Some companies have established nondiscrimination programs and diversity training, and have extended benefits coverage to the partners of homosexuals.

Homosexuals are excluded from the military and other classified government service. The U.S. Defense Department's Uniform Code of Military Justice prohibits anal and oral intercourse, and this rule is typically enforced only among homosexuals. Enforcers known as courtesy patrols follow suspected homosexuals to monitor their behavior. The U.S. military has recently discharged approximately 1500 people per year because of homosexuality, and most of the expulsions involve lesbians. Statistics have revealed that homosexual soldiers less often abuse drugs (including alcohol) and have fewer disciplinary problems than heterosexual soldiers.

The practice of denying homosexuals security clearance on the basis of possible blackmail has been questioned. Gregory Herek studied this policy and in 1990 concluded that government created the problem by refusing to allow openness about homosexual orientation. Homosexuals were found to be at no greater risk to be blackmailed than heterosexuals.

Policies of other governments suggest that banning open homosexual orientation is not highly problematic. Of the NATO allies, only Britain and the United States exclude homosexuals from military service. The other countries vary in restrictions about living quarters and jobs assigned to homosexuals.

Bibliography

Barret, R., and Robinson, B. (1990). "Gay Fathers." D.C. Heath, Lexington, MA.

Blackwood, E. (Ed.) (1986). "The Many Faces of Homosexuality: Anthropological Approaches to Homosexual Behavior." Harrington Park Press, New York.

Burch, B. (1993). "On Intimate Terms: The Psychology of Difference in Lesbian Relationships." University of Illinois Press, Urbana, IL.

Curry, H., and Clifford, D. (1989). "A Legal Guide for Lesbian and Gay Couples," 5th ed. Nolo Press, Berkeley, CA.

Geller, T. (Ed.) (1990). "Bisexuality: A Reader and Sourcebook." Times Change Press, Ojai, CA.

Kelley, K., and Byrne, D. (1992). "Exploring Human Sexuality." Prentice-Hall, Englewood Cliffs, NJ.

Masters, W., and Johnson, V. (1979). "Homosexuality in Perspective. Little, Brown & Co., Boston.

McWhirter, D., Sanders, S., and Reinisch, J. (Eds.) "Homosexuality/Heterosexuality: Concepts of Sexual Orientation." Oxford University Press, New York.

Puterbaugh, G. (Ed.) (1990). "Twins and Homosexuality: A Casebook." Garland, New York.

Rosser, B. R. (1991). "Male Homosexual Behavior and the Effect of AIDS Education: A Study of Behavior and Safer Sex Practices in New Zealand and South Australia." Praeger, New York.

SIGN LANGUAGE

Karen Emmorey
The Salk Institute for Biological Studies

Glossary

Iconic An expression or symbol such as a word or sign is iconic if it resembles the concept or object that it denotes.

Modality Language modality refers to the medium in which it is perceived and/or produced (visual–manual vs aural–oral for signed and spoken languages, respectively).

Morphology The system of word/sign formation and the rules governing the internal structure of words/signs.

Phonology The system of rules and constraints that operate on the sounds of spoken language or on the manual and nonmanual units of sign language.

Syntax The system of rules and principles for constructing the gramatical sentences of a language.

SIGN LANGUAGES are used primarily by deaf people throughout the world. They are languages that have evolved in a completely different medium, using the hands and face rather than the vocal tract and perceived by eye rather than by ear. They have arisen as autonomous languages not derived from spoken language and are passed down from one generation of deaf people to the next. Deaf children with deaf parents acquire sign language in the same way that hearing children learn spoken language. Sign languages are rich and complex linguistic systems which conform to the universal properties found in all human languages. As with spoken language, the left hemisphere of the brain is critically involved in processing sign language, indicating that the general brain basis for language is modality independent. American Sign Language (ASL) is the language used by deaf people in the United States and parts of Canada.

I. MYTHS ABOUT SIGN LANGUAGE

Myth 1: *Sign language is universal.* Sign language is *not* a universal language shared by deaf peoples of the world. There are many different sign languages that have evolved independently of each other. Just as spoken languages differ in grammatical structure, in the types of rules that they contain, and in historical relationships, signed languages also differ along these parameters. For example, despite the fact that American Sign Language (ASL) and British Sign Language are surrounded by the same spoken language, they are mutually unintelligible. Sign languages are generally named for the country or area in which they are used (e.g., Austrian Sign Language, German Sign Language, Hong Kong Sign Language). The exact number of sign languages in the world is not known.

Myth 2: *Sign language is made up of pictorial gestures and is similar to mime.* An important property of human language is that the form of words is generally *arbitrary*. For example, there is no relation between the English word "frog" or the French word 'grenouille" and an actual frog. In contrast, many signs have a discernible relation to the concepts that they denote. For example, the sign for "tree" in American Sign Language is made with the forearm held upright with the fingers spread wide. One could say that the forearm represents the trunk and the fingers represent the branches of the tree. In Danish Sign Language the sign for "tree" differs from the ASL sign, but it also bears a perceptible relation to a tree: the two hands outline the shape of a tree starting with a round top and ending with the trunk. Although both of these signs are iconic and resemble mime, they have been conventionalized in different ways by the two sign languages.

Encyclopedia of Human Behavior, Volume 4

Although some signs have iconic properties, most signs do not bear a clear resemblance to what they denote. For example, the ASL sign for "apple" is made with the knuckle of the index finger touching the cheek (see Fig. 1a) and bears no resemblance to an apple or to eating an apple. For most signs, the relationship between the form and the meaning is not transparent. In addition, the iconicity of signs is generally irrelevant to the way the language is organized and processed.

Furthermore, pantomime differs from a linguistic system of signs in important and systematic ways. The space in which signs are articulated is much more restricted than that available for pantomime. For example, pantomime can involve movement of the entire body as well as any part of the body. In contrast, signing is constrained to a space extending from just below the waist to the top of the head, and the entire body is never involved. In addition, sign languages have an intricate compositional structure in which smaller units (such as words) are combined to create higher level structures (such as sentences), and this compositional structure is found at all linguistic levels (phonology, morphology, syntax, and discourse). This complex and hierarchical compositional structure is not present in pantomime.

Myth 3: *Sign language is a pidgin form of spoken language using the hands and has no grammar of its own.* American Sign Language has been mistakenly thought to be "English on the hands." However, ASL has an independent grammar that is quite different from the grammar of English. For example, ASL allows much freer word order compared to English. English contains tense markers (e.g., *-ed* to express past tense), but ASL (like many languages) does not have tense markers that are part of the morphology of a word; rather tense is expressed lexically (e.g., by adverbs such as "yesterday"). There are no indigenous signed languages that are simply a transformation of a spoken language to the hands.

One might ask "If sign languages are not based on spoken languages, then where did they come from?" However, this question is as difficult to answer as the question "Where did language come from?" We know very little about the very first spoken or signed languages of the world, but research is beginning to uncover the historical relationships between sign languages, as has been done for spoken languages. For example, part of the origin of American Sign Language can be traced to the establishment of a large community of deaf people in France in 1761. These people attended the first public school for the deaf, and the sign language that arose within this community is still used today in France. In 1817, Laurent Clerc, a deaf teacher from this French school, established the first deaf public school in the United States and brought with him French Sign Language. The gestural systems of the American children attending this school mixed with French Sign Language to create a new form that was no longer recognizable as French Sign Language. ASL still contains a historical resemblance to French Sign Language, but both languages are mutually unintelligible.

Myth 4: *Sign language cannot convey the same subtleties and complex meanings that spoken languages can.* On the contrary, sign languages are equipped with the same expressive power that is inherent in spoken languages. Sign languages can express complicated and intricate concepts with the same degree of explicitness and eloquence as spoken languages. The linguistic structuring which permits such expressive power is described in the next section.

II. LINGUISTIC STRUCTURE OF AMERICAN SIGN LANGUAGE

American Sign Language is one of the most widely studied sign languages. A brief description of ASL structure is provided here—a complete description would require a large volume (the full characterization of any grammar is lengthy). The description is designed to illustrate that signed languages exhibit the same properties and follow the same universal principles as spoken languages and that signed languages provide unique insight into the nature of language itself.

A. Phonology

Phonology is the study of the sound patterns found in human languages; it is also the term used to refer to the system of knowledge that speakers have about the sound patterns of their particular language. But do sign languages have a phonology? Is it possible to have a phonological system that is not based on sound? In spoken languages, words are constructed out of sounds which in and of themselves have no meaning. The words "cat" and "pat" differ only in the initial sounds which have no inherent meanings of their own. Sounds may be combined in different ways to created different words: "bad" differs from

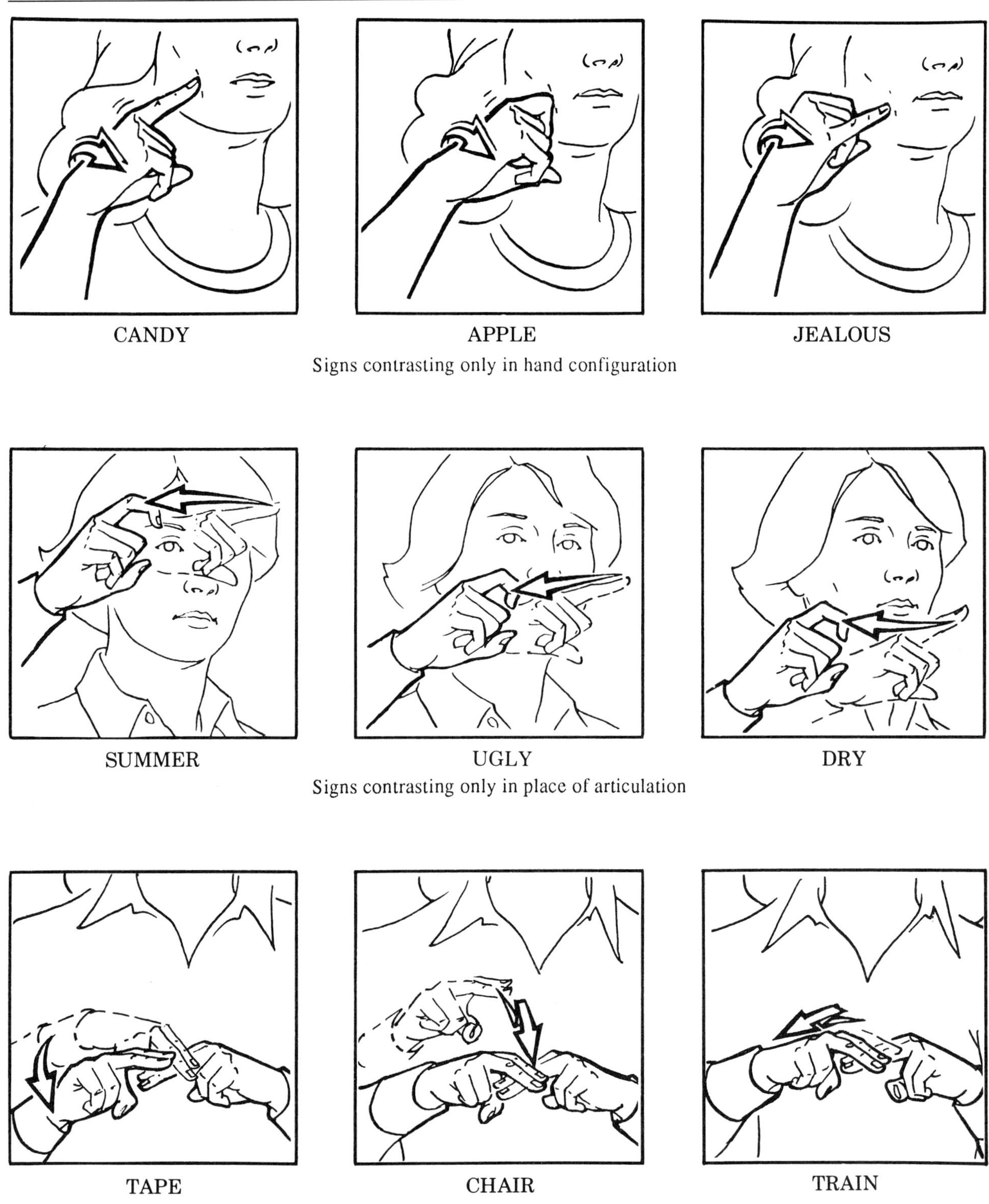

FIGURE 1 Illustration of part of the phonological system of American Sign Language. These signs contrast the different phonological parameters of ASL, which are themselves meaningless but can be combined to create lexically meaningful signs.

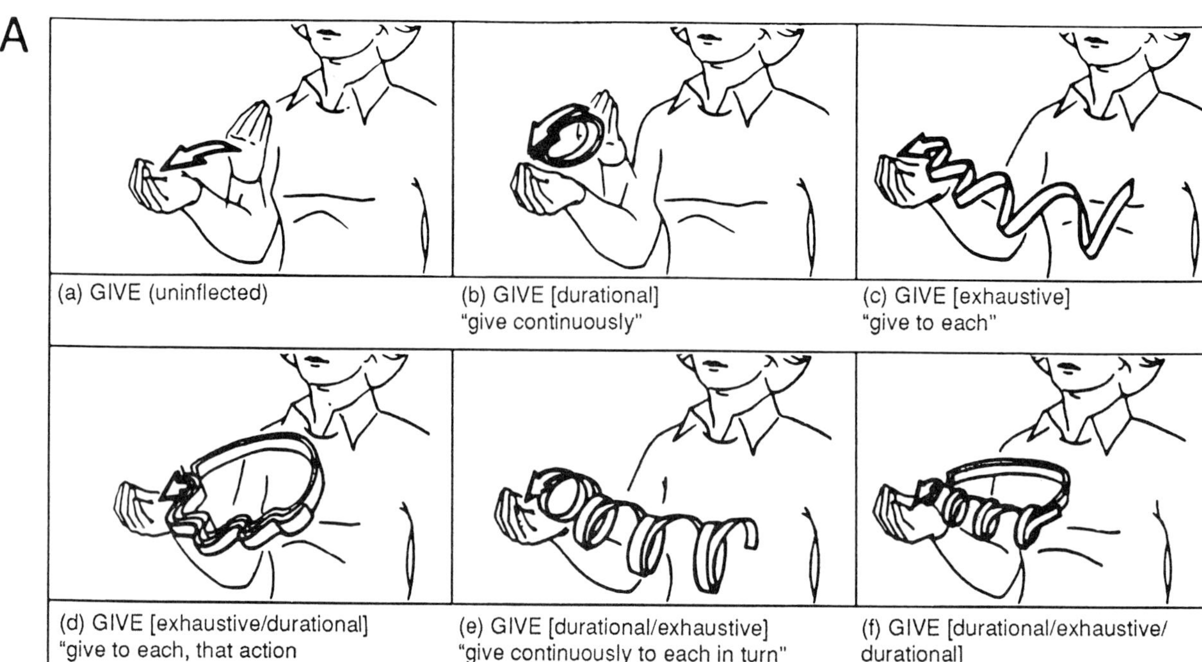
A
(a) GIVE (uninflected)
(b) GIVE [durational]
"give continuously"
(c) GIVE [exhaustive]
"give to each"
(d) GIVE [exhaustive/durational]
"give to each, that action recurring over time"
(e) GIVE [durational/exhaustive]
"give continuously to each in turn"
(f) GIVE [durational/exhaustive/durational]
"give continuously to each in turn, that action recurring over time"

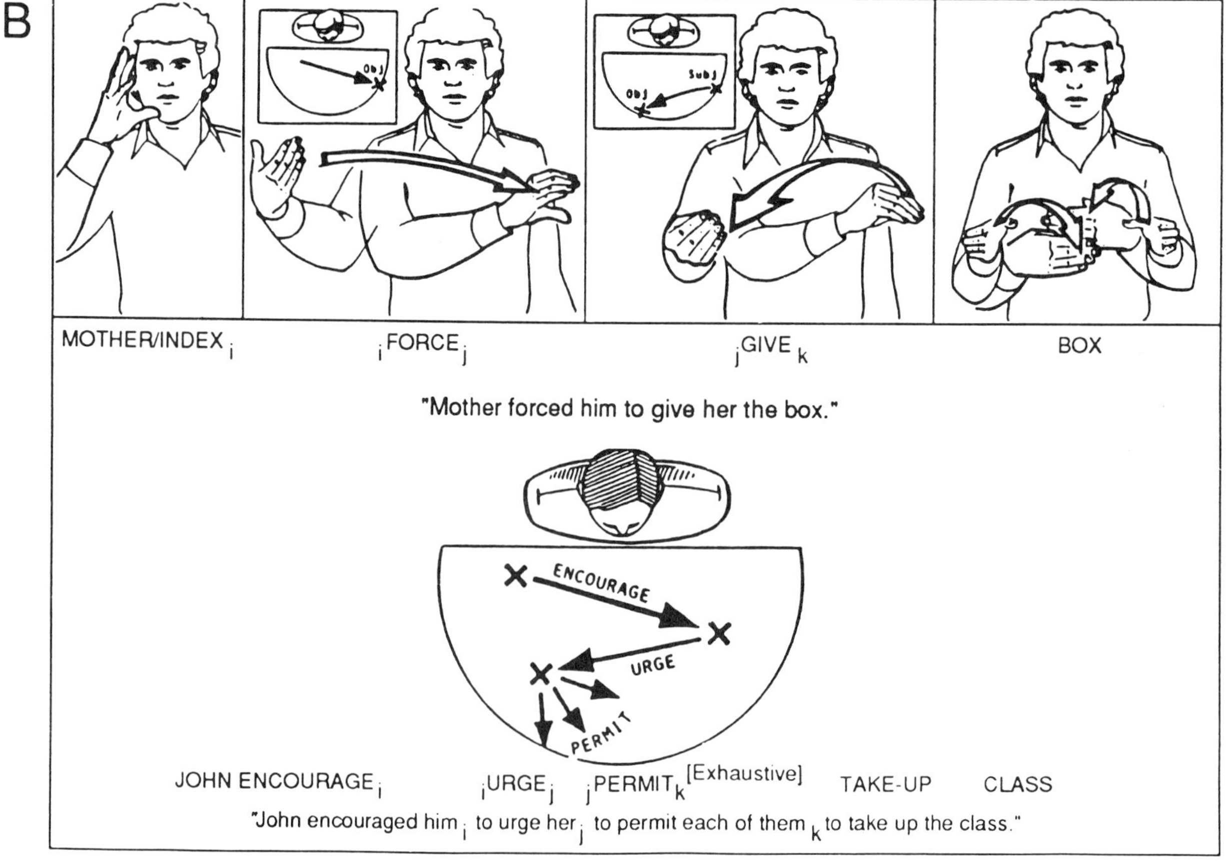
B
Obj
Subj
Obj
MOTHER/INDEX$_i$
$_i$FORCE$_j$
$_j$GIVE$_k$
BOX
"Mother forced him to give her the box."
ENCOURAGE
URGE
PERMIT
JOHN ENCOURAGE$_i$
$_i$URGE$_j$
$_j$PERMIT$_k$[Exhaustive]
TAKE-UP
CLASS
"John encouraged him$_i$ to urge her$_j$ to permit each of them$_k$ to take up the class."

"dab" only in how the sounds are sequenced. Similarly, signs are constructed out of components that are themselves meaningless and are combined to create words.

Signs are composed of four basic phonological parameters: handshape, location, movement, and palm orientation. American Sign Language contrasts about 36 different handshapes, but not all sign languages share the same handshape inventory. For example, the "t" handshape in ASL (the thumb is inserted between the index and middle fingers of a fist) is not used by Danish Sign Language; Swedish Sign Language contains a handshape formed with an open hand with all fingers extended except for the ring finger which is bent—this hand configuration is not used in ASL. Figure 1a illustrates three ASL signs that differ only in handshape. Signs also differ according to where they are made on the body or face. Figure 1b shows three signs that differ only in location. Movement is another contrasting phonological parameter that distinguishes minimally between signs as shown in Figure 1c. Several different path movement types occur in ASL, e.g., circling, arc, straight, and signs can contain "internal" movement such as wiggling of the fingers or changes in handshape. Finally, signs can differ solely in the orientation of the palm; for example, the sign WANT (signs are notated as English glosses in uppercase) is produced with a spread hand with the palm up, and FREEZE is produced with the same handshape and movement (bending of the fingers and movement toward the body), but the palm is facing downward. These meaningless phonological elements are combined and sequenced to create lexical signs.

ASL exhibits other phonological properties that were once thought to be only found in speech. For example, ASL contains phonological rules similar to those found in spoken languages. ASL contains deletion rules in which an element (such as a movement or a handshape) is deleted from a sign and assimilation rules in which one element is made more similar to a neighboring element. ASL signs also have a level of syllabic structure which is governed by rules similar to those that apply to syllables in spoken languages. The fact that signed languages exhibit phonological properties despite the completely different set of articulators (e.g., the hands vs the tongue) attests to the universality and abstractness of sublexical structure in human languages. [*See* PHONOLOGICAL PROCESSING AND READING.]

B. Morphology

ASL contains the same basic form classes as spoken languages, nouns, verbs, adjectives, pronouns, and adverbs, but it has a very different system of word formation. In English and in most spoken languages, morphologically complex words are most often formed by adding prefixes or suffixes to a word stem. In ASL, these forms are created by nesting a sign stem within dynamic movement contours and planes in space. Figure 2a illustrates the base form GIVE along with several inflected forms which can be embedded within one another and which convey slightly different meanings. ASL has many verbal inflections which convey temporal information about the action, e.g., whether the action was habitual, iterative, or continual. These inflections do not occur in English, but they are found in other languages of the world.

Another set of inflections applies to a subset of ASL verbs and indicates the subject and/or object of the verb (see Fig. 2b). In ASL, noun phrases are associated with points in a plane of signing space, and verbs can move between these spatial points to indicate the subject or object. For example, if MOTHER has been associated with a point on the signers right and BOY with a point on the signers left, then if the verb FORCE moves from right to left, it would mean "She forces him" (see Fig. 2b). If the verb were to move left to right, it would mean "He forces her." The first spatial endpoint of the verb agrees with the subject, and the final endpoint agrees with the object; thus, these verbs are called "agreeing" verbs. Other inflections can also be added to indicate plural objects or reciprocal ("each other").

FIGURE 2 Morphology and syntax in American Sign Language. (A) The uninflected sign GIVE is illustrated in (a), and GIVE with single inflections are shown in (b) and (c). The figure shows different embedded combinations of infections which have distinct meanings (d, e, and f). Note that these inflections are produced simultaneously rather than as prefixes or suffixes. (B) Syntactic spatial mechanisms in ASL. The figure illustrates the association of nouns with loci in space (indicated by subscripts), and movements of verbs between these loci (indicated by arrows). The spatial endpoints of these verbs agree with the spatial loci established for the subject and object of the sentence.

Like English, ASL has rules that govern how compound nouns and verbs are formed. An example of an English compound is the word "blackboard" which does not mean a board that is black (blackboards can even be white) and which has a different stress pattern than the phrase "black board." ASL compounds also have different meanings and stress patterns compared to noun phrases. For example, the ASL compound BLACK-NAME which means "bad reputation" is formed by combining the sign BLACK with the sign NAME. In isolation the sign NAME contains two beats, but within the compound it contains only one beat. Compounding is a common morphological process in ASL, as it is in many languages.

Finally, ASL does not have many prepositions, and instead encodes spatial relations through morphological devices. ASL uses a system of *classifiers* which are pronominal forms that classify an object according to its semantic and/or visual–geometric properties. Many of the world's languages have classifier systems (especially Bantu languages) in which a different pronoun is used for humans, for animals, for inanimate objects, etc. ASL classifiers are embedded in verbs of motion and location which describe the movement and position of objects and/or people in space. For example, to express "the bicycle is beside the fence" a vehicle classifier is used for bicycle and is positioned in space next to a visual–geometric classifier for fence ("long-sectioned-rectangular object"). The ASL expression tends to be much more explicit compared to the English preposition "beside" because the ASL classifier verbs of location also indicate the orientation and precise location of the fence and bicycle with respect to each other (e.g., whether the bicycle is close to the fence, facing the fence, etc.). Again, although this system appears mimetic, it is not. ASL expressions of location and motion have an internal structure comprised of a limited set of movements, locations, and manners of movement which are constrained by linguistic rules.

C. Syntax

The basic canonical word order for ASL is subject–verb–object; however, ASL word order is much more flexible compared to English. ASL morphology can mark the relationship between words, and ASL does not need to rely on word order to convey grammatical relations such as subject or object. For example, the object of the verb can appear as the first word of the sentence, if it is morphologically marked as a topic, e.g., CAT(topic), DOG CHASE, "As for the cat, the dog chased it." Topics are distinguished by a specific facial expression (see below). Similar to Italian and unlike English, ASL allows "subjectless" sentences. For example, it is possible to sign the following: TODAY SUNDAY. MUST VISIT MY MOTHER. In English these two sentences would require subjects (subjects are bolded): "Today, **it**'s Sunday. **I** must visit my mother." The constraint on overt subjects is just one of the ways in which the syntax of ASL differs from English (but is similar to other languages).

Personal pronouns in ASL are expressed with either a flat handshape (fingers together) to indicate possessive case ("my," "your") or with a closed fist and extended index finger (pointing) to indicate nominative ("I," "you"). For referents that are physically present, the pronominal sign is directed at the physical referent; thus, first person reference is made by the signer pointing to his or her own chest, and second-person pronominal reference is made by pointing to the addressee's chest. Similarly, when referents are actually present, third-person pronouns are produced by pointing to the appropriate persons. Although these pronoun signs appear to be simple pointing gestures, they are not. The ASL system of pronouns has the same grammatical properties found in spoken languages. For example, the pronominal signs are compositional unlike pointing gestures, and the component parts convey different grammatical distinctions. Hand orientation indicates grammatical person (e.g., first vs second person), handshape contrasts grammatical case (e.g., possessive vs nominative), and movement (an arc vs pointing) indicates grammatical number (plural vs singular).

Many of the syntactic functions that are fulfilled in spoken languages by word order or case marking are expressed in ASL by spatial mechanisms. For example, when noun phrases are introduced into ASL discourse, they may be assigned an arbitrary locus in the plane of signing space. Once a referent has been associated with a locus, the signer may then refer to that referent by using a pronominal sign directed at the locus. In addition, verbs can move with respect to these loci to indicate subject and object relations (see Morphology above). Generally, these loci remain fixed in space, but under certain discourse conditions, the loci can *shift* such that they are associated with different referents. In addition, spatial loci can be embedded within different subspaces of the reference plane, and there is evidence for more than one signing plane (e.g., nonspecific reference and counterfactuals may use diagonal and/or higher planes of space). Overall, the syntactic system of ASL is used to express the same linguistic *functions* found in the world's languages, but the *form* these functions take is explicitly spatial. The use of space for syntactic functions is a unique resource afforded by the visual modality of sign language. [*See* SYNTAX.]

D. Linguistic and Emotional Facial Expression

The face carries both linguistic and emotional information for ASL signers. Both hearing and deaf people use their face in the same way to convey emotional information—these expressions (e.g., happy, sad, angry) are universal. However, ASL signers also use facial expressions to convey linguistic contrasts. Linguistic and emotional facial expressions differ in their scope and timing and in the face muscles that are used. Grammatical facial expressions have a clear onset and offset, and they are coordinated with specific parts of the signed sentence. Emotional expressions have more global and inconsistent onset and offset patterns, and they are not timed to co-occur with specific signs or parts of a signed sentence. Examples of linguistic facial expression include marking for adverbials, topics, questions, conditionals, and relative clauses.

Grammatical facial expressions are critical to the syntax of ASL because they distinguish several different syntactic structures. For example, consider the following two ASL clauses: TODAY SNOW, TRIP CANCEL ("It's snowing today; the trip is canceled"). These are two co-ordinate main clauses. However, if the first clause is produced with a conditional facial expression (the eyebrows are raised, the head is tilted slightly to the side, and the shoulders move slightly forward), the syntactic structure is altered. The first clause becomes a conditional subordinate clause, and the meaning changes to "If it snows today, the trip will be canceled." The only difference between the two structures is the facial marking that co-occurs with the first clause. Facial behaviors also represent adverbs which appear in predicates and carry different specific meanings. For example, two ASL sentences may have exactly the same signs and differ only in the facial adverbials which co-occur with the signs. The facial expression "mm" (lips pressed together and protruded) indicates an action done effortlessly; whereas the facial expression "th" (tongue protrudes between the teeth) means "awkwardly" or "carelessly". These two facial expressions accompanying the same verb (e.g., DRIVE) convey quite different meanings ("drive effortlessly" or "drive carelessly").

Researchers are studying facial expressions in ASL for insight into the interface between biology and behavior. Emotional expressions are produced consistently and universally by children by 1 year of age. Emotional facial expressions also appear to be associated with specific neural substrates that are distinct from those involved in language. How does the linguistic system underlying the use of grammatical facial expressions interact with the biologically programmed use of emotional facial expressions? Current research suggests that different neural systems may subserve linguistic and emotional facial expressions—the left hemisphere appears to be involved in producing linguistic facial expressions, whereas the right hemisphere is important for producing emotional facial expressions. In addition, although deaf children produce emotional facial expressions very early (as do hearing children), they acquire linguistic facial expressions later and with a quite different pattern of development which reflects their (unconscious) analysis of these facial signals as part of a linguistic system. [*See* FACIAL EXPRESSIONS OF EMOTION.]

E. Finger Spelling and the Manual Alphabet

The manual alphabet used in ASL consists of 26 different handshapes which correspond to the 26 letters of the English alphabet. Other signed languages have different fingerspelling systems; for example, British fingerspelling uses a two-handed system. Fingerspelling is often used when there is no existing ASL sign (e.g., for place names) and is somewhat separate from the grammar of ASL—grammatical rules do not apply to *novel* fingerspelled words.

However, fingerspelled words can become "lexicalized" or enter the sign vocabulary if they are used repeatedly in one or several contexts. These fingerspelled signs are quite distinct from fingerspelled English words because they have undergone significant phonological reshaping and have become incorporated into the ASL grammar over time. For example, N-O was a fingerspelled word meaning "no" which has been incorporated into the ASL lexicon. The sign #NO (the # indicates a lexicalized fingerspelled sign) has a different movement than the fingerspelled word (N-O moves to the right slightly whereas #NO moves forward slightly), and #NO contains modified alphabet handshapes such that neither the N nor the O handshapes appear as they do in the original fingerspelled word. Further evidence that the sign #NO is part of the ASL lexicon is that it can undergo a morphological rule which creates a verb which can be inflected. The verb SAY-NO-TO is derived from #NO and can inflect for subject and object as an agreeing verb (see Morphology above).

F. Dialects, Accents, and Language Use

Very often speakers in different geographic regions or from different social groups show systematic differences in language use, and these groups are said to speak different dialects of the same language. The same phenomenon occurs for signed languages. For example, ASL signers from the Northeast and Southern regions of the United States often use different signs for the same object (compare British and American dialectal differences in word use: gas/petrol, diaper/nappy, elevator/lift). Southern signers also produce the two-handed form of signs more often than non-Southerners (some signs have both one-handed and two-handed forms that do not differ in meaning). The deaf black community in the United States also has its own dialect of ASL. Certain signs (e.g., FLIRT, SCHOOL) have black forms which originate from the time when schools for the deaf were racially segregated. These signs are used most often when black deaf individuals interact with each other and form part of the culture of the black deaf community. Both regional and black signing dialects also differ phonologically, but these systematic differences in pronunciation have been less well studied. In some regional dialects, the thumb may be extended while producing certain signs without changing meaning (e.g., FUNNY, BUTTER); this difference in pronunciation may be perceived as an accent. Similarly, when signers of Chinese Sign Language learn ASL, they may have an accent derived from small phonetic differences between CSL and ASL. For example, the closed fist handshape is slightly different for ASL and CSL. In ASL, the hand is relaxed and only the very tip of the thumb protrudes above the first, but in CSL the fist is more rigid, and the entire top joint of the thumb protrudes. When CSL signers produce ASL signs, they may maintain the handshape from CSL, and this phonological difference may be perceived as a foreign accent.

In addition to regional and social dialects, different "situational dialects" or language styles can be found for users of ASL. The signing style used for formal lectures differs from that used for informal conversations or narratives. Formal ASL is slower paced, uses a larger signing space, tends to use two-handed variants of signs, and shows less coarticulation. In contrast, for causal or informal signing, signs that are made near the face may be produced lower down, one-handed signs predominate, and signs are often articulated such that they "overlap." For example, the sign THINK is made with a "1" handshape touching the forehead, and the sign PLAY is made with a "Y" handshape (thumb and pinky extended, other fingers closed). When THINK occurs before PLAY in casual signing, the signer may "anticipate" the handshape for PLAY and produce THINK with a "Y" handshape and extended index finger. This kind of anticipation or coarticulation does not occur as frequently in formal signing. These phonological and lexical changes are not unlike those found for formal and informal speech.

G. Sign Poetry and Song

Poetry and song are forms of artistic expression that make use of linguistic patternings of sound, rhythm, and grammar. How are poems and songs expressed in a language without sound? ASL poetry exhibits some internal structuring that is parallel to that found in oral languages, but it also contains poetic structure that is intrinsic to its visual–spatial modality. Like spoken poetry and song, ASL can rhyme by manipulating the phonological structure of words (see Phonology above). Signs can rhyme if they share the same handshape or the same movement, and a poem may contain signs that all share a single handshape or group of handshapes that are formationally similar. Rhythmic structure within a sign poem can be created by manipulating the flow of movement between signs and by rhythmically balancing the two hands. The use of space is a poetic device that is intrinsic to the visual modality. Signs move through space and are clustered and separated within space to produce an additional dimension of structure within a poem. Sign poetry also takes advantage of the visual modality by using "cinematic" techniques such as zooms, close-ups, and visual panning.

The poetic and literary tradition for English is hundreds of years old. For ASL, this tradition is developing within our generation through organizations such as the National Theater of the Deaf. The nature of ASL literature is similar to the "oral" literature of storytelling and potery that exists in communities which do not have a writing system. Songs and stories are passed down from generation to generation which reflect the culture of the society. Similarly, deaf culture is strongly reflected in the themes of ASL stories and poems. For example, poems and stories often express the value of sign language to the deaf community—a common language is a major determinant of any culture. Other themes include the origins of the deaf community, the relationship between hearing and deaf people, and shared cultural experiences such as growing up in a residential school for the deaf.

III. SIGN LANGUAGE ACQUISITION

A child acquiring a sign language appears to be faced with a quite different task than a child acquiring a spoken language. A completely different set of articulators is involved, and the language is perceived with a different sensory system. Do the properties of sign languages affect the course and timing of language acquisition? For example, do the iconic properties of sign languages aid in their acquisition? Do the spatial properties of sign language present special challenges for the acquisition process? Recent research has addressed these questions, and the results are briefly described here. This research is based on deaf children acquiring ASL as a native language from their deaf parents. The general finding is that deaf children acquire sign language in the same way as hearing children acquire a spoken language: both groups pass through the same linguistic milestones at the same time. These findings suggest that the capacities which underlie language acquisition are maturationally controlled and that the psychological, linguistic, and neural mechanisms involved in language acquisition are not speech specific.

A. Babbling and First Signs

Just as hearing babies babble prior to producing their first word, deaf babies babble with their hands prior to producing their first sign. Babbling occurs between about 7 and 10 months of age, and is characterized by a rhythmic syllabic organization for both speech and sign. Just like vocal babbling in hearing infants, manual babbling is produced with a subset of manual phonetic units found in sign languages of the world and is produced without meaning or reference. The fact that babbling occurs in babies exposed to sign language suggests that babbling in general is not simply a result of the maturation of the motor system governing vocal articulation, but rather babbling may be the product of the maturation of a modality-neutral linguistic capacity.

Children acquiring both spoken and signed languages go through a stage in which isolated single words are produced. There is some evidence that first signs in ASL emerge earlier than first words in English. First signs have been reported as early as 6 months, whereas first words tend to appear between 11 and 13 months. The apparent early appearance of first signs is not tied to iconicity since the majority of first signs are not particularly iconic. For example, MILK which is a frequent first sign (and first word) is made with movements similar to milking a cow. While this sign may be iconic for adults, it is not iconic for children. The ostensible early appearance of first signs may be due to the early motor development of the hands compared to the vocal tract. However, some recent research has questioned the early appearance of first signs and has suggested that first words and signs may appear at about the same time.

Similar to spoken languages, early lexical signs tend to be uninflected, i.e., just the stem or base form of the word is produced. In addition, children often make phonological substitutions and alterations within their first signs. Thus, just as hearing children acquiring English might say "baba" for "bottle", deaf children simplify and alter adult signs; e.g., the "baby" sign for MOMMY is often produced with a "1" handshape (loose fist with index finger extended) rather than the correct spread hand (fingers not touching) and contact to the chin is with the index finger rather than the thumb. The phonological alterations in both sign and speech tend to reflect articulatory ease, with more difficult sounds and handshapes acquired later.

The semantic relations that are expressed in children's early word combinations are also the same for speech and sign. Children sign and talk about the existence and nonexistence of objects, actions on objects, possession of objects, and locations of objects. The expression of semantic relations occurs in the same order for both signed and spoken languages: existence relations appear first, followed by action and state relations, then locative relations. The last semantic expressions to emerge for both types of languages are datives, instruments, causatives, and manners of action.

B. Acquisition of Morphology and Syntax

All children make "mistakes" when learning language, and deaf children learning ASL make the same kinds of errors that hearing children make when acquiring English. For example, English-speaking children go through a stage in which they overgeneralize the past tense marker *-ed,* producing forms such as *comed, goed,* and *broked.* Similarly, children acquiring ASL overgeneralize verb morphology. For example, once children have learned to inflect verbs for subject and object (see above), they may overextend this marking to verbs which do not permit this inflection. These "mistakes" provide a view into the child's developing grammar and indicate that children do not simply imitate adult utterances but instead have an internal system of rules that may or may not match the adult grammar.

Children learning English (and other spoken languages) make errors with personal pronouns, substituting "you" for "me" and vice versa. Pronoun reversals are not that surprising in child speech, given the shifts that occur between speakers and listeners using "I" and "you." Children often construe "you" as a name for themselves. For ASL, one might predict a different course of acquisition for these pronouns because of their iconic properties, i.e., "you" is indicated by pointing to the addressee and "me" is indicated by pointing to oneself. Both hearing and deaf children use pointing gestures prelinguistically. This raises the question of how deaf children move from prelinguistic gestural communication to linguistic–symbolic communication when the form (pointing) is virtually identical. Is the acquisition of pronouns early and error-free for children acquiring ASL—do they capitalize on the iconic nature of ASL pronouns? The surprising answer is no; despite the transparency of pointing gestures, deaf children do not use ASL pronouns earlier than children acquiring English, and they make pronoun reversals in early signing. Children acquiring ASL seem to go through three stages: (1) the use of gestural (nonlinguistic) pointing, (2) the use and misuse of pronouns as lexical signs (i.e., "you" as a name), and (3) the correct use of pronouns within a grammatical system.

Children acquiring ASL must master the syntactic use of space which is quite intricate and complex (see Syntax above). At age 3, children do not use spatially indexed pronouns to refer to people or objects that are not physically present. By age 4, children begin to associate noun phrases with abstract loci in space, but they make errors. For example, children may fail to correctly maintain the unique association between a locus and a noun phrase producing sentences in which it is not clear who is doing what to whom. Similarly, children acquiring English produce sentences with unidentified "he's" and "she's." By age 5, ASL learning children provide an abstract locus for noun phrases when one is required, and generally maintain this association appropriately. Verb agreement between these loci is also produced correctly. The complete spatial reference system (including shifting space) is not acquired until age 7 or 8—the same age at which English-speaking children master the reference system of English.

Understanding the nature of language acquisition for a signed language has provided important and profound insight into the nature of human language and the human capacity for language. The maturational mechanisms underlying language are not tied specifically to speech but appear to be linked to a more abstract linguistic capacity such that the acquisition of visual–manual and aural–oral languages are acquired according to the same maturational time table. Furthermore, linguistic symbolic systems are essentially and fundamentally arbitrary, and children acquiring ASL ignore its potential iconicity and construct linguistic rules according to grammatical principles which are not grounded in form-meaning similarities.

C. Acquisition of Sign Language Late in Childhood: Evidence for a Critical Period for Language Acquisition

The majority (90%) of deaf children are first exposed to sign language later in life—only deaf children who have deaf signing parents are exposed to sign language from birth. Children who have hearing parents who do not sign may have no effective language exposure in infancy and early childhood. These children typically acquire sign language when they enter a residential school for the deaf and become immersed in the language, using it to converse with other deaf children and adults. Some children may not enter a residential school until high school. Unfortunately, deaf children rarely acquire competence in English and often have no primary language until they acquire a sign language. This population of deaf signers provides a unique opportunity to investigate the "critical period" hypothesis for language acquisition. Essentially, this hypothesis posits that a child must be exposed to language within a particular critical or sensitive period in development in order to acquire language normally and completely. Exposure to language past this critical period will result in imperfect and abnormal language acquisition. Because most individuals are exposed to their native language from birth, this hypothesis has been difficult to test.

Recent research with deaf adults who were not exposed to sign language until late in childhood or adulthood supports the critical period hypothesis for language acquisition. There is a nearly linear relationship between the age at which a deaf person was first exposed to ASL and their performance on tests of ASL grammar and processing—the later the exposure to language, the worse their grammatical knowledge and performance. Crucially, these differences are not due to the number of years of signing experience—the native signers and the "late" signers in these studies were equated for the number of years of practice with ASL, and most had been signing for 20 or 30 years. The production and comprehension of ASL morphology are strongly affected by age of acquisition, with those exposed to the language early in life outperforming those exposed at later ages. Late learners of ASL are not entirely incompetent in their use of ASL morphology, but they lack the grammatical analysis and highly consistent use of linguistic structures that is displayed by native signers. Similar critical period effects have also been found with spoken languages for second language learning. Researchers hypothesize that these effects are due to the maturational state of the child at the time of language exposure. A precise account of the mechanisms underlying the maturational change involved in the critical period for language acquisition remains a goal for future research.

IV. BRAIN ORGANIZATION FOR SIGN LANGUAGE

Sign language exhibits properties for which each of the cerebral hemispheres of hearing people shows different predominant functioning. The left hemisphere has been shown to subserve linguistic functions, whereas the right hemisphere subserves visual–spatial functions. Given that ASL expresses linguistic functions by manipulating spatial relations, what is the brain organization for sign language? Is sign language controlled by the right hemisphere along with other visual–spatial functions or does the left hemisphere subserve sign language as it does spoken language? Or is sign language represented equally in both hemispheres of the brain? Recent research has shown that the brain honors the distinction between language and nonlanguage visual–spatial functions. Thus, despite the modality, signed languages are represented primarily in the left hemisphere of deaf signers, whereas the right hemisphere is specialized for nonlinguistic visual–spatial processing in these signers.

Damage to the left hemisphere of the brain in deaf signers leads to sign aphasias similar to those observed with spoken language. Aphasias are disruptions of language that follow certain types of brain injury. For example, adult signers with left hemisphere damage may produce "agrammatic" signing which is characterized by a lack of morphological and syntactic markings and is often accompanied by halting effortful signing. For example, an agrammatic signer will produce single sign utterances which lack the grammatically required inflectional movements and use of space. Similarly, "agrammatic" aphasia in spoken language is characterized by effortful speech and a lack of grammatical markers, such as the past tense *-ed* or plural *-s* in English. Lesions to a different area of the left hemisphere produce a different kind of aphasia characterized by fluent signing or speaking, but with errors in the selection of grammatical markers and syntactic errors. A signer with this type of lesion may sign fluently but will not correctly utilize syntactic spatial loci and will produce incorrectly inflected signs. Differential damage within the left hemisphere produces differential linguistic impairments, and these impairments reflect linguistically relevant components for both sign and speech. [*See* APHASIA.]

In contrast, right hemisphere damage produces impairments of many visual–spatial abilities, but does *not* produce sign language aphasias. When given tests of sign language comprehension and production, signers with right hemisphere damage perform normally, but these same signers show marked impairment on nonlinguistic tests of visual–spatial functions. For example, when given a set of colored blocks and asked to assemble them to match a model, right hemisphere damaged signers have great difficulty and are unable to capture the overall configuration of the block design. Similar impairments on this task are found with hearing, speaking subjects with right hemisphere damage. In contrast, left hemisphere damage does not impair performance on most visual–spatial tasks for either signers or speakers. The poor performance of right hemisphere damaged signers on nonlinguistic visual–spatial tasks, such as perceiving spatial orientation or understanding spatial relations between objects, stands in marked contrast to their unimpaired visual–spatial linguistic abilities. The brain exhibits a principled distinction between linguistic and nonlinguistic visual–spatial functions.

The brain organization for sign language indicates that left hemispheric specialization for language is not based on hearing and speech. The underlying basis for left hemisphere specialization is the fundamental nature of linguistic functions rather than the sensory modality which conveys the language. Investigations of the neural underpinnings of signed and spoken languages are currently making use of *in vivo* techniques which can probe linguistic and visual–spatial processing in the intact brain. By contrasting signed and spoken languages, these studies can illuminate in greater detail the determinants of brain substrate for language and visual–spatial cognition.

Bibliography

Klima, E. S., and Bellugi, U. (1988). "Signs of Language." Harvard University Press, Cambridge MA.

Newport, E., and Meier, R. (1985). The acquisition of American Sign Language. In "The Crosslinguistic Study of Language Acquisition" (D. Slobin, Ed.), Vol. 1. Erlbaum, Hillsdale, NJ.

Padden, C. (1988). Grammatical theory and signed languages. In "Linguistics: The Cambridge Survey" (F. Newmeyer Ed.), Vol. 2. Cambridge University Press, New York.

Poizner, H., Klima, E. S., and Bellugi, U. (1987). "What the Hands Reveal about the Brain." MIT Press, MA.

Reilly, J., McIntire, M., and Bellugi, U. (1991). Faces: The relationship between language and affect. In "From Gesture to Language in Hearing and Deaf Children" (V. Volterra and C. Erting, Eds). Springer-Verlag, New York.

SLEEP: BIOLOGICAL RHYTHMS AND HUMAN PERFORMANCE

Roseanne Armitage
University of Texas Southwestern Medical Center at Dallas

Glossary

Biological rhythm Predictably recurrent change in physiology or behavior with a fixed period length.

Desynchronous EEG Low-voltage, fast-frequency brain activity.

Sleep architecture Pattern of changes in sleep stages during sleep.

Synchronous EEG High-voltage, slow-wave brain activity.

SLEEP is a distinct behavioral state that is defined on the basis of postural changes, reduction in response to external stimuli, and the presence of characteristic changes in brain wave activity, changes in temperature, and a variety of hormonal and neuroendocrine changes. Interest in sleep goes well beyond scientific inquiry. Poets, philosophers, and artists have contemplated the mysteries of sleep for centuries. Further, sleep is one of the few areas of scientific discovery to which all people can relate. Most everyone has experienced first-hand, the effects of both good and poor sleep. The following article will review our current knowledge of sleep physiology, biological rhythms, and the impact of sleep on daytime performance.

I. SLEEP EEG MEASUREMENT

Research on sleep electroencephalography (EEG) dates back to the mid-1930s, although the majority of scientific discoveries have taken place since 1951, when Aserinksy and Kleitman first identified rapid eye movement (REM) sleep in infants. Sleep EEG is recorded from electrodes affixed to the scalp that detect underlying bioelectrical potentials from the brain. Electrodes placed at the outer ridges of the eyes and under the chin monitor changes in eye movement (electroculograms or EOG) and muscle activity (electromyograms or EMG), respectively. These signals are then amplified by a factor of 10,000–50,000 and the resulting voltage values are displayed on paper. Recent advances in microcomputer technology have permitted the development of "paperless" polygraph systems where EEG data are displayed on a computer monitor and stored on large-volume disks or tape. [*See* BRAIN ELECTRIC ACTIVITY; EEG, COGNITION, AND DEMENTIA.]

II. REM AND NREM SLEEP ARCHITECTURE

Five distinct stages of sleep have been identified based on the appearance of certain EEG characteristics that recur throughout the night. REM sleep, the stage most often associated with good dream recall, is characterized by a pattern of low-voltage, mixed-frequency, desynchronous EEG activity. Binocularly symmetrical rapid eye movements (REMs) and inhibition of motor activity (atonia or paralysis of antigravity muscles) are also associated with REM sleep. Only the diaphragm and extraocular muscles are active in this sleep stage. REM has been called paradoxical or active sleep because the pattern of EEG activity closely resembles that of wakefulness. It is somewhat akin to being awake in a body that is asleep.

Four stages of nonrapid eye movement (NREM) sleep have also been identified in humans. Stage 1 sleep is characterized by relatively low-voltage, fast-frequency EEG in the absence of REMs. Stage 1 sleep occurs at the beginning of the night and during the transition between other sleep stages. Stage 2 sleep is associated with sinusoidal spindle activity (12–14 cps) and biphasic, single delta waves (0.5–2 cps), called K-complexes. Background EEG activity in Stage 2 is generally higher voltage and slower frequency than Stage 1 or REM sleep. Stages 3 and 4 sleep are considered slow-wave or deep sleep, based on the predominance of delta waves. A sleep record with 20–50% delta is classified as Stage 3 and more than 50% delta identifies Stage 4 sleep.

In a healthy adult, the first episodes of Stage 1 identify sleep onset followed by the emergence of Stage 2, approximately 10 min later. Delta activity gradually appears, with a descent to slow-wave usually within the first hour of sleep. The first episode of REM occurs during the second hour of sleep and subsequent REM periods occur approximately 90 min after the previous one. Each REM period lengthens progressively, with three of four REM periods in a given night. An illustration of typical sleep architecture is shown in Figure 1.

NREM sleep comprises 70% of total sleep time, and approximately 50% of the night is spent in stage 2 sleep. REM constitutes 20–25% of total sleep time whereas 10–15% of the night is devoted to slow-wave sleep. Stage 1 and intermittent wakefulness generally make up less than 10% of the night.

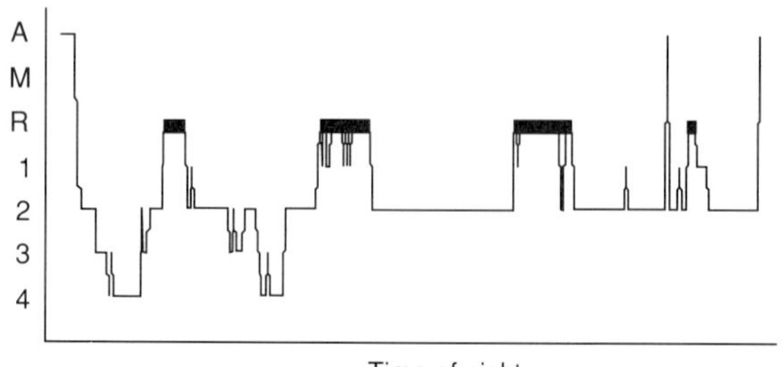

FIGURE 1 Typical sleep architecture in a normal healthy adult. A-awake, M-movement, R-REM sleep, 1-Stage 1 sleep, 2-Stage 2 sleep, 3-Stage 3 sleep, 4-Stage 4 sleep.

III. AGE EFFECTS ON SLEEP

Human infants spend about 16 hr a day sleeping with 50% of total time in REM sleep, whereas premature infants have over 75% REM-sleep time. By age 2, REM sleep drops to less than 35% of total sleep. The percentage of REM further decreases to adult levels (20%) by age 5 or 6. The REM/NREM sleep cycle is approximately 50 min in length in neonates, lengthening to 90–100 min by early adolescence, and remains relatively constant throughout adulthood.

In general, the latency to the first REM period shortens to less than 70 min in the elderly, coupled with a decline in the amount of slow-wave sleep. There is some evidence to suggest that body temperature, usually at its lowest point in slow-wave sleep, is altered in the elderly, perhaps accounting for the decline in Stages 3 and 4 sleep. Overall, total sleep time is reduced in older adults, often accompanied by early morning awakenings. The ontogenetic changes in sleep architecture have been used as evidence for the functional significance of REM sleep.

IV. CONTROL MECHANISMS AND FUNCTIONS OF SLEEP

The mechanisms controlling sleep and wakefulness have been identified through animal research using electrode implants. As such, our knowledge is limited to the sleep stages that are similar in humans and animals, namely REM and slow-wave sleep. Little is known, for example, about the control mechanisms or functions of other NREM sleep stages, as they are identifiable in humans, but not usually in animals. Notable exception is recent work exploring computer-quantified EEG frequencies in low-amplitude NREM sleep in rats. As the precise frequency characteristics that underlie each sleep stage become known, exploration of animal models of EEG regulation may identify the mechanisms involved in initiating and maintaining low-voltage NREM sleep.

Slow-wave sleep is presumed to be controlled by limbic forebrain structures including the basal forebrain, anterior hypothalamus, preoptic area, and thalamus. Electrical stimulation of these areas will result in drowsiness followed by sleep. The thalamus has been implicated in the generation of spindle activity, but is not necessary for the generation of cortical slow waves, which persist even after ablation of this region. There are also regions of the medulla, that when stimulated, produce cortical synchronization in an awake animal. Stimulation of this region during sleep will, however, produce wakefulness. Thus, a complex interaction of various areas in the brain regulates sleep and wakefulness. Catecholamine and adrenergic neurotransmitters have been implicated in the control of this sleep stage. The depletion of monoamines and dopamine, for example, results in the initiation of sleep. [*See* HYPOTHALAMUS; LIMBIC SYSTEM; SYNAPTIC TRANSMITTERS AND NEUROMODULATORS.]

Slow-wave sleep is associated with a reduction in cerebral metabolic rate, decreased temperature, and increased energy conservation. This sleep phase has been implicated in body and cell repair, leading to the view that slow-wave sleep serves a restorative–metabolic function and is required for homeostasis.

REM sleep is associated with acetylcholine, a neurotransmitter that is antagonistic toward catecholamines. Levels of acetylcholine are presumed to be highest in REM sleep, intermediate in wakefulness, and lowest in slow-wave sleep. These two major classes of neurotransmitters are presumed to have reciprocal interactive effects on the regulation of sleep stages. In dwelling electrode studies in animals have shown an increase in synchronous theta (4–8 cps) activity in the hippocampus during REM. REM sleep is largely controlled by the brainstem, not the cortex. The pons also generates distinct ponto-geniculo-occipital (PGO) waves during REM, that are not observable in scalp-recorded EEG. Phasic REMs, and middle-ear muscle potentials, presumed to controlled by similar mechanisms, have been taken as evidence for PGO activity in humans.

Increased cerebral metabolism and activation of the visual cortex are found in REM sleep. This sleep stage is considered vital in facilitating structural differentiation and maturation of the central nervous system in neonates. REM deprivation in animals results in poor neural growth and development, interferes with the acquisition of new skills, and eventually leads to death. The prevalence of REM sleep in infant mammals argues strongly in favor of its role in neural developement.

There is no one sleep center, but several areas in the forebrain and brainstem connected through ascending and descending projections to the cortex seem to initiate sleep.

V. BIOLOGICAL RHYTHMS

During approximately the same time period as the discovery of REM sleep, a vigorous growth of biological-rhythm research occurred. Of primary interest were rhythms in physiology and behavior with a period of approximately 24 hr, termed circadian (from the latin *circa dies:* about a day). Circadian rhythm research has formed the basis for theories on jet-lag effects, shift work, and biological clocks that control rhythms. The term ultradian (*ultra dies*), used to identify shorter duration rhythms such as the 80- to 120-min REM/NREM sleep cycle, was introduced a few decades later. Infradian rhythms, with a periodicity longer than 24 hr, have also been identified, of which lunar and menstrual cycles are examples.

Biological rhythms are presumed to be controlled by an internal clock or pacemaker that responds to a variety of exogenous (external) and endogenous (internal) influences. Light and temperature can be strong exogenous entrainers of biological rhythms, altering the periodicity and the strength or amplitude of rhythms, depending on time of exposure. Internal entrainment mechanisms can include neuroendocrine function, hormones, and neurotransmitter release, among others. Further, the need for energy conservation and homeostasis may be the driving force behind rest and activity cycles.

Circadian rhythms are presumed to be controlled by the suprachiasmatic nucleus (SCN) located in the anterior hypothalamus, also implicated in the regulation of temperature and slow-wave sleep. Ablation of the SCN will result in arrhythmic activity cycles that can be restored to a 24-hr period by transplantation of SCN cells from another animal. Light is the primary stimulator for the SCN, relayed through specialized photoreceptors. Very recent work has shown that the timing of exposure to light can be manipulated to disrupt sleep schedules, or alternatively, to improve sleep in shift workers. Bright light exposure has also been used to diminish the effects of jet-lag and as a treatment for seasonal depression.

Given that most functions within the brain are subsumed by several regions, is unlikely that a single pacemaker system controls all circadian and ultradian rhythms. It seems more plausible to assume that multiple pacemakers control the timing of physiology and behavior. Considerable debate remains over whether circadian and ultradian rhythms are, in fact, independent processes, or whether they are likely to be controlled by the same oscillatory mechanisms. Further research is necessary to resolve these issues.

Humans may be somewhat unique in that they are able to override sleepiness and to ignore cues of light and darkness. Occupational accidents are, however, examples of the impact of pushing the biological clock too far. Nuclear power-plant accidents such as Three-Mile Island and Chernoble, the Exxon Valdez oil spill, and increased air and auto accidents at night have all been attributed to trying to maintain alertness when the body is biologically prepared for sleep. Stated differently, these accidents result from unsuccessful attempts to override the biological clock that controls sleep and wakefulness. Trying to stay awake between 3 and 5 A.M. is the most difficult, as any shift-worker, diligent student, or sleep researcher can attest.

VI. THE BRAC HYPOTHESIS

In the mid-1960s, Kleitman theorized that variations in task performance, attention spans, and fatigue in wakefulness were related to the sleep cycle. This ground-breaking theory, the so-called basic rest–activity cycle (BRAC), suggested that similar mechanisms controlled rhythms in physiology and behavior throughout the 24-hr period. He further proposed that the 80- to 120-min REM/NREM sleep cycle had a waking analog. A variety of circadian and ultradian rhythms related to the sleep cycle have since been identified.

VII. RHYTHMS IN SLEEP PHYSIOLOGY

Growth hormone, body temperature, testosterone, melatonin, a variety of pituitary hormones, metabolic function, and blood constituents all show circadian rhythms related to the sleep/wake cycle. Melatonin, luteinizing hormone, prolactin, and growth hormone, for example, show peak concentrations during the night, particularly in slow-wave sleep. Urine flow and electrolytic concentrations show ultradian rhythms during sleep and are coupled with phase of the REM/NREM cycle.

VIII. RHYTHMS IN COGNITIVE ACTIVITY

A. Dreaming

In addition to the physiological changes associated with the sleep cycle, Kleitman and colleagues suggested that REM sleep was associated with dreaming. Early work indicated that detailed dream recall could only be obtained following REM awakenings, and led to the assumption that the appearance of REMs signified dreaming. More recent work has shown that dream recall rates are generally higher following awakenings from REM sleep (70–100%), lowest following slow-wave sleep (0–25%), and intermediate from Stage 2 awakenings (25–60%). It is clear from this research that REM sleep cannot be equated with dreaming. However, dream *recall* is facilitated in REM sleep, largely due to the presumed activation of memory and linguistic capabilities in this sleep stage. [*See* DREAMING.]

Individual differences also contribute to dream recall. In surveys of university students, about 10% remember dreams every morning upon awakening. Approximately 10% of students rarely recall a dream, whereas the majority of students recall dreams one to four times a week. In addition, cognitive style seems to play a role in recall. Individuals with more flexible and fluid cognitive styles tend to be remember more dreams, in support of the proposed relationship between creative thinking and dreaming. [*See* CREATIVE AND IMAGINATIVE THINKING.]

At the height of interest in hemispheric asymmetries and laterality, several theorists proposed that dreaming was correlated with greater activation of the right hemisphere. Although EEG and dream studies conducted since 1980 clearly indicate that neither good dream recall or manifest content is correlated with EEG asymmetries, the purported link between the right hemisphere and REM sleep remains a strong influence on current views.

B. Hemispheric Asymmetries in Sleep EEG

Early work suggested that EEG amplitude was lower in the left hemisphere during NREM stages and lower in the right hemisphere during REM sleep. Decreased EEG amplitude is generally interpreted to reflect a higher degree of cortical activation, suggesting that REM was associated with greater activation of the right hemisphere and that the left hemisphere was involved with NREM sleep. Several studies attempted to replicate this finding without success. More recent research tends to support the view that REM sleep is associated with small interhemispheric differences, not greater activation of the right hemisphere. Nevertheless, the notion that the two sides of the brain are differentially activated during REM and NREM sleep initiated a number of task-performance studies following awakenings from sleep.

C. Cognitive Task Performance and Hemispheric Asymmetries during Sleep

Most cognitive tasks are presumed to be lateralized; mathematical and logical tasks are associated with the left hemisphere of the brain, whereas visuospatial tasks are presumed to be mediated by the right hemisphere, in most right-handed individuals. The mode of presentation and the complexity of tasks is, however, critical. It is important to note that only stimuli presented to the right visual hemifield project directly to the left hemisphere. Similarly, stimuli presented to the left hemifield have a direct pathway to the right hemisphere. The presentation of stimuli outside the hemifields will project to both hemispheres and cannot be used to assess functional lateralization. These technical issues are important to bear in mind when interpreting task-performance data and their relationship to sleep stages.

D. Perceptual After-Effects

Lavie and colleagues have conducted a number of studies on perceptual after-effects following REM and NREM awakenings. The idea behind their work has been that if REM sleep was associated with increased cortical arousal of the right hemisphere, the duration of perceptual after-effects should be greater following awakenings from REM compared to Stage 4 sleep. In several studies they obtained longer-duration after-effects following REM awakenings, although these differences were not always significant. Their results support the view that cognitive processing is enhanced in REM sleep.

E. Mathematical and Spatial Tasks

Lavie and colleagues have also investigated performance on digit-span and word-fluency tasks, presumed to involve left hemisphere processing, and dot localization, pattern recognition, and spatial tasks, mediated by the right hemisphere. Better performance on left-hemisphere tasks was obtained following NREM awakenings. Performance on dot-localization tasks was most accurate following REM awakenings and significantly worse following NREM sleep. Other tasks did not, however, show significant differences between REM and NREM awakenings. Further research has also suggested that tactile tasks show a left-hand superiority following awakenings from REM sleep.

Taken together, these data suggest that a shift in cognitive-task performance is likely to occur in REM sleep. It is debatable, however, whether this shift is associated with unique characteristics and functions of the right hemisphere. As EEG studies suggest small asymmetries in REM sleep, it seems more reasonable to postulate that information processing in general is facilitated in REM. The cognitive and electrophysiological profile may be less disrupted in the transition from REM to wakefulness than from NREM to wakefulness. Performance data alone, however, suggest at least some lateralized tasks are enhanced following REM awakening.

IX. ULTRADIAN RHYTHMS IN WAKEFULNESS

One strategy for testing the BRAC hypothesis is to monitor ultradian rhythms in task performance in wakefulness. In addition to their work in sleep, Lavie and colleagues have investigated rhythms in perceptual phenomena in wakefulness and have shown 80- to 120-min rhythms in the duration of after-effects. Performance on spatial and mathematical tasks may also show an ultradian rhythm, but not always at 80–120 min. Further, manipulation of the demand characteristics of studies will alter the periodicity of performance. Offering monetary incentives for peak performance will suppress rhythmicity, further evidence of our ability to override the biological clock that controls sleep and wakefulness.

These data are suggestive of a BRAC but are not conclusive. Because two rhythms have the same periodicity does not indicate they are controlled by the same mechanism(s). A more accurate test of the BRAC hypothesis requires 24-hr monitoring of performance and associated physiological variables such as EEG. If rhythms in EEG activity are continuous throughout sleep and wakefulness, no phase shift will occur in the transition from sleep to wakefulness or *vice versa*. Such an endeavor is, however, very labor intensive and, to date, has not been published.

A. Gender Differences

Several studies have shown that 80- to 120-minute rhythms in task performance are more pronounced among females. Hemispheric asymmetries in EEG activity, collected during the task performance episode, may also differentiate males from females. Males show larger interhemispheric differences during both mathematical and spatial tasks. Females, on the other hand, show small EEG differences associated with accurate performance on both types of tasks. While females may show stronger rhythms in wakefulness, the opposite effect has been observed during sleep. Ultradian rhythms in sleep EEG may be considerably stronger among males and generally of a shorter periodicity. This finding suggests that the mechanism or clock that controls rhythms in females may be stronger during the daytime. Perhaps females are more influenced by time and environmental cues that entrain or drive the biological clock. Most biological rhythm and sleep research, however, is conducted on male subjects. In studies where both male and female subjects were included, less than 30% analyzed potential gender effects. Even fewer take phase of the menstrual cycle into account, despite the known thermogenic influences of progesterone and other gonadal hormones that are likely to alter sleep architecture. Thus, there is insufficient work identifying gender differences and what factors may contribute to differential biological-rhythm control in males and females. What work has been completed suggests the timing of biological rhythms in sleep and wakefulness do show gender effects.

X. SLEEP DEPRIVATION EFFECTS ON PERFORMANCE

There is ample anecdotal information on the effect of sleepiness on performance in wakefulness, independent of the BRAC hypothesis. There are natural fluctuations in alertness during the waking hours such as a dip in performance in the afternoon, usually following lunch. Some researchers have taken this as evidence for pressure to nap, like the afternoon siesta observed in some Latin and European cultures. Others have suggested this "postlunch dip" is the result of insufficient nocturnal sleep. Kleitman, among others, has suggested that performance fluctuations reflect the endogenous, circadian pacemaker at work, though the nature of the tasks themselves may influence performance. There is strong evidence to suggest that daytime alertness is under the control of both the sleep cycle and an endogenous circadian rhythm, independent of sleep. These two processes are likely to function interactively to control sleep and performance.

The impact of sleep on performance has been evaluated in numerous studies on sleep deprivation and shift work. Shift work is associated with increased daytime sleepiness, decreased performance on rote tasks, and increased accidents, as reported above. Shift work also has an impact on the quality of sleep obtained during the daytime, reducing total sleep time and increasing the amount of wakefulness after sleep onset.

Performance also shows a monotonic decline as a function of sleep deprivation. Reaction time is slower following total sleep deprivation and accuracy on memory tasks is generally reduced. Sleep deprivation also results in decreased concentration and an increase in distractive thoughts during task performance.

The precise effects of REM sleep deprivation on performance have been harder to identify. Some early work suggested that reaction time may actually improve with REM deprivation, and only a few studies have identified associated performance decrements. More recent work in animals suggests that REM deprivation interferes with learning an avoidance task. Appetitive tasks performance does not appear to be influenced by REM deprivation. Humans show decreased performance on logic tasks for several days following REM deprivation. College students are still able to recite the rules of tasks, but are unable to apply them.

Additionally, REM deprivation has an impact on sleep physiology during recovery periods. A REM-rebound phenomenon has been observed where the amount of REM on subsequent recovery nights is increased, and the latency to the first REM period is shortened. Further, as the length of REM deprivation increases, attempts to enter REM sleep become more frequent. In essence, it becomes harder to stop the emergence of REM sleep as the deprivation period increases. However, follow-up studies indicated strong individual differences in the amount of REM rebound.

Both REM and total sleep deprivation have an impact on mood, resulting in irritability and increased negative affect that may also contribute to poor performance. Research in the mid-1960s suggested that five nights of REM deprivation resulted in profound psychological disturbances. Subsequent studies, however, did not find dramatic personality changes following a week of REM deprivation. A few studies suggest that sleep deprivation and, in particular, REM deprivation, may alleviate depression. The mood alleviation effects are, however, short-lived.

Slow-wave sleep deprivation also results in a rebound on recovery nights. In general, it is harder to stop individuals from entering slow-wave than it is to deprive them of REM sleep, suggesting that the "pressure" for slow-wave sleep may be greater and may reflect an increased biological need for deep sleep. On the other hand, slow-wave sleep deprivation does not produce a larger performance decrement than REM deprivation nor is slow-wave rebound and recovery stronger. Total sleep deprivation is likely to have more deleterious effects on mood and performance than does selective deprivation of REM or slow-wave sleep. It should be noted, however, individual differences may have a strong impact on sleep deprivation effects. A case study of a young man who was sleep deprived for 264 hr revealed few mood or performance difficulties. Further, recovery sleep lasted a mere 14 hr and subsequent sleep was its usual 8-hr duration.

This resilience to the effects of sleep deprivation reflects our ability to override the biological clock that regulates sleep and wakefulness and to compensate for sleepiness. It is only when the pressure for sleep becomes overwhelming that serious performance and alertness decrements occur. Further, the effects of sleep deprivation may be cummulative, building up over many days before performance deterioration is noticeable. As the more recent REM-deprivation studies have shown, although performance decrements may be subtle, they may have serious consequences. Occupational accidents may result from subtle alterations in decisional processes that may result from too many nights of sleep restriction or total deprivation.

The impact of sleep disruption can also be seen in psychiatric disorders such as depression, obsessive–compulsive disorders, and anxiety disorders, where difficulty in sleeping is used as one of the diagnostic criteria. Most notably, REM sleep abnormalities such as shortened REM latency and increased total REM time have been offered as biological markers of depression. Further, depression has been linked to abnormalities of the hypothalamic-pituitary-adrenal axis, implicated in the control of sleep/wake cycles, and several sleep-related biological rhythm disturbances have been reported in this group. Thus, the effects of sleep loss and disturbance in biological rhythms have an impact that extends across several scientific disciplines.

Our understanding of the regulation of sleep and wakefulness has improved tremendously over the past three decades. New fields of research and medicine have emerged as a result of the discovery of REM sleep and interest in sleep/wake cycles. Sleep-disorders medicine, the study and diagnosis of insomnia, narcolepsy, sleep apnea, and REM behavioral disorders, among others, has emerged as separate discipline within sleep research. Chronobiology, the study of biological rhythms, owes its origins in part to sleep research. Courses in sleep and dreams now appear in college curricula and several graduate programs now offer specializations in sleep research.

Bibliography

Antrobus, J., and Bertini, M. (Eds.) (1992). "The Neuropsychology of Dreaming Sleep." Erlbaum, NJ.

Kryger, M., Roth, T., and Dement, W. (Eds.) (1989). "Principles and Practice of Sleep Medicine." Saunders, Philadelphia.

Moffitt, A., Kramer, M., and Hoffmann, R. (Eds.) (1993). "The Functions of Dreaming." State University of New York Press, Albany.

Niedermeyer, E., and Lope da Silva, F. (Eds.) (1982). "Electroencephalography." Urban and Schwarzenberg, Baltimore.

Spring, S., and Deutsch, G. (Eds.) (1981). "Right Brain–Left Brain." Freeman, San Francisco.

Touitou, Y., and Haus, E. (Eds.) (1992). "Biologic Rhythms in Clinical and Laboratory Medicine." Springer-Verlag, Berlin.

Wauquier, A., Dugovic, C., and Radulovacki, M. (Eds.) (1989) "Slow Wave Sleep: Physiological, Pathophysiological, and Functional Aspects." Raven Press, New York.

Webb, W. (Ed.) (1982). "Biological Rhythms, Sleep and Performance." Wiley, Chichester.

SOCIAL COGNITION

Howard Lavine, Eugene Borgida, and Laurie A. Rudman
University of Minnesota

Glossary

Category accessibility The readiness or ease with which a stored category is activated from memory and used to encode stimulus information.

Cognitive heuristics Mental rules of thumb used for reducing complex judgmental tasks to simpler procedures.

Cognitive process The mental operations that are used to make a judgment or engage in behavior.

Concept activation The process of bringing an element of knowledge from long-term memory into preconscious or conscious awareness.

Schemas Abstract knowledge structures containing the attributes of a stimulus, along with the rules specifying the interrelationships among the stimulus attributes.

Social stereotypes Knowledge structures that contain beliefs and expectations about the attributes of people belonging to specific social groups.

SOCIAL COGNITION represents a scientific approach to the study of human social behavior that has provided insights into a diversity of topic areas within the field of social psychology. As such, social cognition is not associated with any one theory or tied to any specific area of research. From a social cognition perspective, the manner in which social information is encoded, stored, and retrieved from memory is critical to an understanding of how we perceive other people and the social world. Below, we sketch the framework of social cognition, discuss its relation to traditional social psychology and cognitive psychology, and consider its origins and intellectual history. Finally, we illustrate how social cognitive approaches have contributed to an understanding of social behavior by presenting a selective overview of theory and research in several substantive domains.

I. TRADITIONAL SOCIAL PSYCHOLOGY AND SOCIAL COGNITION

Cognitive processes have long been accorded a central role in social psychological theories. However, because cognitive processes are not directly observable, they cannot be measured easily. What distinguishes social cognition from traditional social psychology is the relatively more formal way in which such unobservable processes are treated. Traditional social psychological research has generally inferred the existence of cognitive processes on the basis of overt behavioral data. By using outcome data to explore questions of process, traditional social psychology has, in effect, employed S-R methodologies to test S-O-R (stimulus–organism–response) models of social behavior. In contrast, the major thrust of social cognition research is to provide conceptual models of, and consequently more detailed evidence for, the mediating role of cognitive processes.

To illustrate how traditional social psychology and social cognition differ in emphasis, consider research on the relationship between attitudes and behavior. In one line of research, social psychologists have traditionally manipulated the amount of experience an individual has with an attitude object, and then measured both attitudes and behavior. This research indicates that attitudes formed on the basis of direct experience are more strongly related to behavior than are attitudes formed in the absence of such behavioral experience. Within this approach, however, only the beginning and end of the presumed causal sequence are actually studied; the cognitive mechanisms responsible for translating experience-based attitudes into behavior are not directly assessed. In subsequent social cognitive research focusing on the cognitive mechanisms underlying this phenomenon, it has been shown that attitudes based on direct behavioral experience are more cognitively accessible—that is, more easily retrievable from memory—than attitudes formed on an indirect basis. Moreover, this research has shown that people who can quickly retrieve their attitudes from memory demonstrate higher attitude–behavior correspondence than those whose attitude retrieval is slower. Therefore, one reason why attitudes based on direct experience are more predictive of behavior is that they are more accessible in memory than attitudes formed via indirect means.

This research illustrates how social cognition research, compared to traditional social psychological research, brings the processes that mediate social behavior into clearer focus by attempting to measure them directly rather than inferring them from behavior. Moreover, by directly incorporating cognitive processes into theoretical models of social behavior, considerable explanatory power is gained; we move beyond the realm of merely predicting behavior, and enter into the realm of explaining behavior.

II. COGNITIVE PSYCHOLOGY AND SOCIAL COGNITION

If the purview of cognitive psychology is the study of cognitive structure and process, is social cognition merely the application of cognitive psychology's theories and methods to a social context? Although there have been varied responses to this question, the answer is probably a little yes and largely no. To be sure, the two are similar in important respects. Broadly speaking, cognitive psychology and social cognition share the common dual concerns of representation (structure) and process. Moreover, the methodological tools employed by researchers in the two fields are similar. However, despite these surface similarities, fundamental underlying differences between social and nonsocial cognition also exist. As social psychologists Leonard Martin and Leslie Clark recently observed, "we do not think about people in the same way that we think about other things." Perhaps most importantly, in social—as opposed to nonsocial—cognition we are simultaneously perceivers and the targets of perception. This fact has important implications for social perception and behavior. For example, research has documented that the manner in which we categorize others strongly influences the way in which we think about them and interpret their behavior. Our impressions of others also directly influence our behavior toward them, which has in turn been shown to influence their actual behavior. In this way, whether we categorize an African-American dentist as an African-American or as a dentist is likely to determine how we perceive that person, how we treat her, and consequently how she comes to perceive and behave toward us.

Social cognition also differs from non-social cognition in that the former is more highly intertwined with emotion; in the social domain, more than in others, our feelings influence our thoughts and vice versa. For example, research shows that people are often better able to recall information to the extent that it is affectively congruent with their current mood state. In a somewhat different vein, research shows that our attributions about the causes of other people's behavior affects the emotions we experience toward them. If we believe that Laszlo failed his chemistry test because he neglected to study, we may feel anger or disgust toward him. In contrast, if we attribute the failure to illness, we may pity Laszlo. [*See* ATTRIBUTION.]

As we have tried to illustrate, social cognition has much in common with both traditional social psychology (e.g., its emphasis on social stimuli) and cognitive psychology (e.g., its emphasis on cognitive structure and process). However, social cognition is synonymous with neither. It is a perspective within social psychology that highlights the ways in which the organization and processing of social information guide social perception and behavior. To better appreciate the work of contemporary social cognition, we turn now to a brief discussion of the historical background and intellectual origins from which social cognition has arisen.

III. HISTORICAL BACKGROUND AND INTELLECTUAL ORIGINS

Social psychologists have always stressed that people are thinking organisms. At the turn of the century, a cognating, evaluating self was already at the center of social psychological inquiry in the writings of Cooley, James, McDougall, and Mead. Even when the rest of psychology suffered from a dearth of mentalism during the reign of behaviorism, social psychologists continued to accord cognitive constructs a central place in their theorizing. By World War II, an influx of gestalt scientists escaping fascism found an intellectual home in American social psychology, with its emphasis on unobservable processes. For example, Kurt Lewin and Fritz Heider concentrated in unique ways on how the organization and representation of perceptual and cognitive elements affect the inferences people make about the social world.

Moreover, the war itself dominated the attention of many seminal thinkers in the field. German and American psychologists alike wondered how a highly evolved nation like Germany could undergo such a massive and rapid "attitude change" as to blind the German people to the overthrow of humanitarian values and the genocide of millions. Focusing on the powerful Nazi propaganda machine, some social psychologists investigated the factors that influence attitude indoctrination and persuasion, while others focused on persuasion as a form of authoritarian compliance. But the Holocaust also brought to the forefront the problems of stereotyping, prejudice, and discrimination that continue to occupy the field today. Thus, the war was instrumental in terms of introducing both cognitively oriented scientists and phenomena into the newly developing area of social psychology. [*See* PERSUASION.]

Nonetheless, it was not until the early 1970s that social cognition began to emerge as a subfield of social psychology in its own right. Researchers working in the area of social perception began to apply models of human cognition and memory that were being developed in experimental psychology as a consequence of the cognitive revolution. Conferences, journals, texts, and graduate seminars devoted to the cross-fertilization of cognitive and social psychology soon developed. Developments within social cognition were informing and influencing social psychologists' understanding of social behavior—from attribution to stereotyping, and from impression formation to persuasion.

Although the subfield of social cognition is relatively young, it has been argued that its influence can be traced to two philosophical orientations: The first, which has been referred to as the elemental perspective, focuses on how different pieces of information are combined to form organized cognitive structures; the second, which has been termed the holistic perspective, focuses on the subjective nature of perception, and on the organizational principles that guide higher-order cognitive and perceptual processing.

Within the elemental school, associative network models have probably had the greatest influence on social cognition. Developed within cognitive psychology in the 1960s and 1970s, these models were concerned with two fundamental problems of cognition: First, how is information in the external world represented and organized within the person? That is, how is information cognitively structured? Second, what are the psychological mechanisms that operate on cognitive structures? That is, how is perceived and stored information processed? In answer to the first question, associative network models suggest that cognitive structures arise through the pairing or association of cognitive elements in memory based on their similarity, their temporal or spatial contiguity, and their frequency and recency of association. In a similar fashion, more complex cognitive structures are built up through these basic principles of association. Structurally, these models posit that concepts are represented as verbal propositions or nodes in long-term memory, and that relations among them are represented by links among the nodes. Associative network models also incorporate assumptions about the processes that operate on memory structures. The most important of these is the metaphor of concept activation. When a concept is encountered in the environment (e.g., when I see a dog), its corresponding memory node is activated, resulting in conscious awareness of that concept. This activation then emanates outward, spreading along the associative pathways to other concepts with which the activated concept is linked in memory. This process of "spreading activation" brings into conscious awareness those concepts with which the originally activated concept (dog) is linked (e.g., the concept of "attack" may be brought into conscious awareness). The degree to which a given concept activates other linked concepts is governed by the strength of association between them.

Associative network theories thus rely on the premise that complex cognitive structures are built up from and composed of relatively independent cognitive elements, a process referred to as "bottom-up" processing. In contrast, adherents of holistic or "top-down" notions of cognition emphasize that the entire configuration of information represented within a given cognitive structure is a unitary structure within itself, which operates as an indivisible cognitive unit. The cardinal axiom of this school is that the whole is more than the sum of its parts.

An early exemplar of this orientation is provided by the influential psychologist Sir Frederick Bartlett, who emphasized the constructivist nature of social perception. Bartlett demonstrated that stimuli are perceived and remembered as higher-order units rather than as collections of independent elements strung together. Bartlett's work also foreshadowed important developments in social cognition with the notion that information in the environment is processed within the interpretive framework provided by a given cognitive structure. In fact, a major theme of Bartlett's research was that social perception is often distorted in the direction of cultural expectations and previous experience. Indeed, as will become evident below, subsequent research has shown that cognitive structures can have wide ranging effects on perception; they influence the aspects of the stimulus environment to which people attend, the manner in which such information is interpreted and encoded, and the information that is most likely to be available for later retrieval. In essence, this approach highlights the inherently subjective nature of perception, thought, and memory.

In the remainder of this essay, we first discuss generally how the organizational structure of social knowledge influences social perception and behavior. To this end, we consider evidence concerning the contents of social knowledge and the rules that govern its organization, focusing on three particular content areas: stereotyping, the self, and close relationships. Next, we review evidence regarding the manner in which various cognitive processes give rise to social perception and behavior. It should be noted, however, that we have chosen to discuss the effects of structure and process separately for the purpose of clarity of exposition; in reality, they are interdependent facets of social cognition.

IV. THE CONTENT AND STRUCTURE OF SOCIAL KNOWLEDGE

Although social cognition researchers have described various types of cognitive structures, we focus on the structural concept that has been employed in most social cognition research: schemas. Schemas consist of abstract generic knowledge about the attributes of a stimulus, and about the interrelationships among the stimulus attributes. The stimulus may be any of a wide variety of entities, including objects, persons, social categories, events, or situations. For example, a schema about the social group "scientists" may contain descriptive information in the form of beliefs, expectations, and knowledge about scientists (e.g., scientists are "ingenious," "unsociable," "eccentric," and "no fun at parties"). The schema would also provide information about the way in which the attribute information is related (e.g., "scientists are eccentric because they are very intelligent").

As we illustrate below, schemas have been most widely investigated by social cognition researchers with respect to their facilitation in the construction of social reality. Social situations are often ambiguous, and consequently open to many interpretations. An important function of schemas is that they serve as frameworks or a lens for interpreting ambiguous information. Schemas about the attributes of social groups, or social stereotypes, can serve as behavioral expectancies for individual members of those groups. Such behavioral expectations are often based on visually prominent characteristics such as gender, race, and age. For example, research by S. A. Sagar and Janet Schofield on racial stereotyping has shown that when a black and a white child engage in identical ambiguously aggressive behaviors, such behaviors are viewed as being more aggressive when performed by the black child.

Not only are social situations often ambiguous, they are often exceedingly complex; they contain overwhelming amounts of information, more than we can possibly process or store. Thus, another function of schemas is that they allow us to simplify and organize otherwise unmanageably complex stimulus environments. This often occurs by categorizing people as members of groups (e.g., based on sex, race, age), and subsequently perceiving them in stereotypic terms rather than as complex individuals with idiosyncratic attributes. Much social cognition research has shown that people selectively encode and better remember stimulus information that is consistent with their operative schema than information that is schema irrelevant. In one study, David Hamilton and Terrence Rose presented participants with descriptions of people of different occupational groups—accountants, salesman, and doctors—using an identical set of trait adjectives. Some of these trait adjectives were associated with the stereotypic schema of each occupation (e.g., wealthy–doctors, talkative–salesman, timid–accountants), while others were not part of the stereotypic occupational schemas. Following the presentation of the trait information, participants were asked to recall how frequently each trait had described a member of each occupational group. Although each trait had been used to describe each group with equal frequency, participants' frequency estimates were biased in the direction of their schemas: doctors were recalled as being described as thoughtful and wealthy, accountants as perfectionistic and timid, and salesman as enthusiastic and talkative. In addition, when information was presented in such a way that there was a correlation between the behavioral information and occupational status, participants were more likely to detect the correlation when it was stereotype consistent than stereotype irrelevant. This research shows that what is encoded and remembered is in part dependent on the existing cognitive structures that people bring to their social situations. [*See* PREJUDICE AND STEREOTYPES.]

In addition to contending with often ambiguous and complex social environments, we are often called on to make judgments and inferences based on incomplete information. Schemas often serve us well in this endeavor by allowing us to "go beyond the information given," enabling judgments and inferences based on limited information. Implicit personality schemas, or schemas about which personality traits go together, are especially likely to affect inferences based on limited stimulus information. For example, if we observe someone being friendly, we may spontaneously ascribe to them the traits of extroversion and kindness.

Finally, several programs of research have examined the antecedents and consequences of schema activation for understanding the dynamics of social interaction. This research finds that schemas influence not only what stimulus features we attend to and encode, but also how we behave toward others. Perhaps most important, research on behavioral confirmation suggests that schema activation results in self-fulfilling prophesies. Studies have shown that when our beliefs and schemas lead us to perceive others in stereotypic terms (e.g., as an African–American) rather than as a unique individual, our behavior (e.g., unfriendly) elicits from them confirmatory behavior (e.g., hostility), thus bolstering our pre-existing schemas. This dynamic provides an important insight into the reasons why social stereotypes are so difficult to change. [*See* SELF-FULFILLING PROPHECIES.]

In summary, we have shown that schemas about others influence each stage of social information processing, from the initial interpretation and encoding of information, to retrieval, judgment, and behavior. We have attempted to illustrate that social perception consists of an intricate interplay between objective stimulus qualities and organized prior knowledge that we bring to and impose upon the situation. We now briefly turn to an examination of research on self-schemas.

Social cognition research on the representation of the self has focused on the organization of self-attributes (e.g., personality traits, social roles, activity preferences, behavioral experiences) within different social situations. Thus, we may hold different sets of beliefs about the self within the work context (e.g., diligent, ambitious), the family context (e.g., flexible, nurturing), and informal social contexts (e.g., reserved, anxious). Research has shown that self-schemas influence how we perceive both others and ourselves. With regard to the former, Hazel Markus and her colleagues have found that we tend to perceive others in terms that are relevant to our self-schemas. Patricia Linville has suggested that various aspects of the self and their associated attributes comprise an overall associative network of the self. Linville has shown that structural variations in self-representations have important implications for people's emotional and physical well-being. The central structural concept in Linville's model is self-complexity. Self-complexity refers to the number of self-aspects a person possesses and the extent to which different self-aspects are interrelated in the network. Self-aspects include social roles, types of activities, relationships, self-defining traits, and future aspirations. High self-complexity is defined by having many self-aspects that are structurally independent (i.e., self-aspects with few common attributes). For instance, a woman who is competitive at her job but nurturing with friends is more complex than a woman who is competitive both at work and with friends.

Linville has provided evidence that self-complexity acts as a buffer against depression and stress-related illness. This is because when a negative event threatens a self-attribute (e.g., the women are overlooked for a promotion, threatening the self-attribute "competitive"), the negative thoughts and feelings associated with the event are likely to affect all of the self-aspects to which the threatened self-attribute is associated. Thus, the woman who is competitive at work and with friends is likely to experience more negative emotion than the woman who is competitive at work but nurturing with friends.

A relatively recent extension of self-schemas concerns relationship schemas, which involve mental representations of "self-with-other." That is, in addition to having conceptions of self and others, people in relationships share a relational schema containing the traits, attitudes, and feelings that characterize their identities when they are together. In addition, these relationship schemas may also contain interpersonal scripts that regulate their communication and behavior toward one another. These scripts may be a product of cultural norms or societal roles (e.g., a doctor-and-patient script, or a teacher-and-student script). On the other hand, people in consensual relationships often forge their own idiosyncratic scripts that dictate who they are with one another. For example, a man may be harsh and demanding at work but weak and dependent with his wife at home. Similarly, a woman may be generally assertive except in the presence of her domineering father. Relationship schemas are acquired conjointly through a process of trial-and-error learning. The outcome resembles a series of if–then statements (e.g., "If I'm assertive, he'll shout at me; if I appear helpless, he'll give in") that often become routinized so that neither participant is aware of the covert rules governing their behavior. Because a person has many relationships and each may have its own interactional pattern, relationship schemas are a way of conceptualizing William James' observation that "a man has as many social selves as there are individuals who recognize him."

V. THE PROCESSING OF SOCIAL INFORMATION

Thus far we have described generally how the cognitive representation and organization of social information influences social perception and behavior. We now turn our attention to the processes that operate on these cognitive structures, which together produce social cognition. We should note, however, that social cognition researchers have generated a variety of process models to explain a diverse range of social behaviors and our review of them is necessarily selective.

In early social cognition research beginning in the late 1960s, theorists developed models of social judgment and behavior in which the social thinker was regarded as a highly logical and quasi-scientific information processor. When people's reasoning did not consistently conform to the tenets of these rational models, such departures were viewed as being caused by the intrusion of emotional (e.g., defensive) factors.

Research in the 1970s on social inference began to suggest quite a different view of the social thinker. Research at this time suggested that people often look for cognitively less effortful strategies, or short cuts, for perceiving the social world. This view of the social thinker has given rise to what Shelly Taylor has termed the "cognitive miser." We process complex cause–effect relationships, form impressions of people, respond to persuasive messages, and reason about all sorts of matters by adopting simplified strategies that emphasize efficiency rather than accuracy. As will be seen below, these problem-solving strategies often produce reasonably adequate solutions. When cognitive biases and errors did occur, they were viewed not as the result of intrusive defensive or emotional processes, but due to inherent limitations in the cognitive system.

Although social cognition research has generated ample evidence that people often behave as cognitive misers, more recent research conducted in the 1980s and 1990s finds that there are circumstances in which people will adopt more deliberative, complex cognitive strategies that more closely approximate prescriptive models of social cognition. The recognition that people vary their processing efforts on the basis of both situational constraints and motivational factors such as needs and goals has given rise to a view of the social thinker as a pragmatic information processor, or what Susan Fiske and Shelly Taylor have termed the "motivated tactician." This more sophisticated view of the social thinker recognizes the intricate interplay between motivational and cognitive factors in producing social perception and behavior. A major goal of social cognition research has been to determine the conditions under which people will choose various cognitive strategies, and to understand their consequences. While social thinking is often the product of the simplified cognitive strategies employed by the cognitive miser, under certain circumstances social thinking is more complex and systematic, driven by a range of needs and goals. Below, we illustrate how these different types of information processing have been central to the development of social cognition theory within several topic domains in social psychology.

A. Attribution Theory

The central question posed by attribution theory is how people use information to make causal judgments. Early attribution approaches delineated complex sets of decision rules that, if followed, allowed the social perceiver to accurately determine whether an actor's behavior is caused by his or her enduring personality traits (a dispositional attribution) or some feature(s) of the external situation (a situational attribution). A great deal of subsequent attribution research has found that social perceivers often deviate in their causal reasoning from the tenets of these early prescriptive models. The most persistent departure from these models centers on people's apparent insensitivity to the situational factors that shape social behavior. Dozens of studies have found that people attribute others' behavior to dispositional factors, even when such behavior is clearly constrained by situational forces. This tendency to overattribute causality to the actor's dispositions and to neglect constraining situational information has been termed the "fundamental attribution error." [*See* ACTOR–OBSERVER DIFFERENCES IN ATTRIBUTION.]

More recent social cognition research within the attribution area has been directed to the development of models that are more descriptive of the actual mental events that govern people's attributional reasoning. Several recent models have suggested that causal attributions result from two successively activated processes. The first process involves the spontaneous encoding of the actor's behavior in terms of relevant dispositional qualities. This process is believed to occur relatively automatically, requiring only a modicum of effort and cognitive capacity. In a second, more effortful and deliberative process, perceivers are believed to adjust their dispositional inferences on the basis of whatever constraining factors may be present in the situation. Several studies have shown that this second process is relatively easy to disrupt (e.g., when perceivers' cognitive capacities are overloaded) while the first process is impervious to the presence of other ongoing cognitive activities. This research, which contrasts the dispositional inference process as automatic and the situational "correction" process as deliberate, provides a cognitive process explanation for the fundamental attribution error.

B. Cognitive Heuristics

Various approaches have been taken to understanding social judgment and decision-making processes. Early approaches emphasized well-developed routines involving formal rules of information integration (e.g., Bayes Theorem) for arriving at judgments and decisions. As in the attribution area, however, a considerable amount of research has shown that human judgment and decision making deviates from the cognitive calculus of these formal models.

Beginning with the seminal work of Daniel Kahneman and Amos Tversky in the mid 1970s, social cognition researchers have attempted to discern the basic processes through which various judgmental errors and biases occur. This effort has uncovered several simplifying rules of thumb, or cognitive heuristics, that people use for solving complex problems. In this section, we briefly review the nature of two well-researched heuristic principles.

1. Representativeness

The representativeness heuristic is used for making judgments about probability, such as the probability that outcome A was generated from process B, or the probability that instance A is a member of class B. For example, in judging the probability that a person is a member of a specific social category, this heuristic involves a consideration of the extent to which the person shares the attributes stereotypically associated with the social category. In general, this is a reasonable problem-solving strategy: representative members of a category are more probable than less representative members. However, when other relevant information is ignored, such as the frequency of that social category in the population, use of the representativeness heuristic can lead to judgmental errors. For example, imagine a small-framed person who smokes a pipe, wears wire-rimmed glasses, and likes to read. Following such a description, suppose you were asked whether the person was more likely to be a truck driver or a poetry professor at an Ivy League university. Although truck drivers are far more numerous in the population than Ivy League poetry professors, research has found that a majority of people asked this question rated the person as more likely to be a poetry professor. This and many other examples of the representativeness heuristic show that people tend to overrely on individuating information at the expense of base rate information when making judgments about probability.

2. Availability

The availability heuristic involves judging the probability or frequency of an event on the basis of the ease with which instances of the event can be brought to mind. Consider the question: Which is more common, death by shooting or death by emphysema? One way to answer this question would be to consult the proper epidemiological records on causes of death. Given limited time and resources, however, we are more likely to think about this problem by generating instances of each cause of death from memory. We then make a relative probability judgment based on the sample of evidence that we have generated. To the extent that we generated representative samples of the population, the availability heuristic provides an efficient means of answering this type of question. However, our samples are often biased. For example, the media are more likely to report deaths from gun violence than from emphysema. This may cause instances of the former to be easier to generate from memory, and thus seem more prevalent in the population than is actually the case.

C. Impression Formation

As we discussed above, social behavior is often inherently ambiguous; its meaning is importantly determined by the interpretive concepts applied by the perceiver. A fundamental process through which impressions are formed is to construe behavioral information in terms of previously stored categories, such as personality traits. However, if a given behavior can have multiple meanings, how does the perceiver go about deciding which trait category best fits that behavior? For example, does complimenting a co-worker on his or her physical appearance exemplify ingratiation, innocent flirting, or sexism? A great deal of research indicates that people will interpret and evaluate the behavior of others on the basis of whatever category information comes to mind most easily when the judgment is made. The readiness or ease with which a stored category is activated from memory and used to encode stimulus information is referred to as category accessibility. [*See* Categorization.]

If impression formation hinges on the activation of accessible categories, what factors influence accessibility? One set of determinants is the frequency and recency with which a given category has been activated in the past. Tory Higgins and his colleagues have demonstrated that ambiguous behavioral information will be assimilated to a trait concept that has been made temporarily accessible in a prior experimental context. Their procedure involved a priming task in which participants were exposed to concepts associated with either the trait "reckless" or the trait "adventurous" in an initial word perception task. Then, in an ostensibly unrelated study on reading comprehension, participants read about a person who had engaged in several behaviors that could either be construed as reckless or adventurous (e.g., skydiving). The results indicated that participants were more likely to categorize the stimulus person's behavior in terms of the trait category activated in the priming task than the other equally applicable but less accessible trait category. Moreover, participants' evaluations of the target person were more favorable when categorized as adventurous than reckless. Finally, participants' recollections of the target person's behaviors were distorted in the direction of their initial trait categorizations; originally ambiguous behaviors were recalled as unambiguously reckless or adventurous at a follow-up session one week later.

In addition to temporary increases in accessibility brought about by external contextual information, accessibility may also be influenced by individual differences in the particular types of categories that people habitually use to make sense of the social world. Higgins, his colleagues, and others have shown that these "chronically" accessible concepts are more likely to be used when interpreting a person's behaviors than equally relevant but relatively inaccessible concepts.

More recent models of impression formation have emphasized the interaction of prior knowledge structures (e.g., stereotypes) and external stimulus information in the impression formation process. At the crux of these process models is the notion that people rely on a variety of strategies in forming impressions of other people. These processes can be differentiated on the basis of the perceiver's degree of attention to the target person's individuating attributes. At the "category-based" end of the continuum, people rely on social stereotypes to form impressions. Thus, category-based impression formation involves perceiving people in terms of their stereotypic attributes (e.g., perceiving all women as nurturing and dependent) regardless of their individual qualities. At the other end of the continuum, perceivers form impressions by encoding and integrating the target person's individuating attributes while disregarding category membership.

According to these models, the perceiver attempts to confirm the initial, immediate, and automatic categorization of the target person. If the attributes are judged to be adequately consistent with the chosen category label, the category will be confirmed. Once confirmed, any further thoughts, feelings, and behaviors toward the target person will be based on the perceiver's stereotypic category label. If, however, the perceiver is highly self-involved with the target person (e.g., she's the new boss), he or she may form an impression based on the target's attributes to the exclusion of category-based information.

What happens, however, when the attribute information is inconsistent with the initial category label? When initial categorization fails, perceivers attempt to retrieve a new category capable of organizing the attribute information. This recategorization process may involve employing a subcategory that retains some of the features of the original category, but includes some inconsistent features as well. For example, an independent and assertive woman may be categorized as a "career woman." Recategorization employs both category-based processes and the use of individuating attribute information, and thus lies somewhere in the middle of the continuum of impression formation processes. As with category confirmation, if the recategorization process is successful, the perceiver's thoughts, feelings, and behaviors toward the target will reflect those associated with the new category. If, on the other hand, the perceiver fails to access a new category to subsume the attribute information and, in addition, has the cognitive resources and motivation, she will form an impression by integrating (e.g., averaging) the individuating information on an attribute-by-attribute basis.

Impression formation models suggest some important properties of social perception. First, consistent with stereotyping research and the "cognitive miser" perspective, these models posit that category-based (i.e., top-down) processes generally have priority over individuated processing. Thus, much of the time we tend to perceive people in terms of their visible group memberships rather than as unique individuals. More interestingly, the extent to which we form impressions based on our stereotypes versus individuating information is determined both by our goals in the situation and the extent to which the target person's attributes fit an activated category. For example, if our outcomes in the situation depend on another person, we may be more likely to devote cognitive effort to processing that person's individual attributes than if our outcomes are unrelated to the behavior of that person. [*See* IMPRESSION FORMATION.]

D. Attitude–Behavior Relations

The social cognition approach has also strongly influenced the ways in which social psychologists have researched social attitudes and their relationship to various forms of social behavior. For example, our understanding of the conditions under which attitudes guide and predict behavior has been substantively enriched by research on the underlying cognitive processes by which attitudes influence behavior. Russell Fazio and his colleagues, in particular, have argued that attitudes influence behavior through either a deliberative or a spontaneous process. The deliberative process can be viewed as relatively "data-driven." It involves a person's effortful consideration of the specific attributes (or "data") associated with an attitude object and of the potential consequences of engaging in a particular behavior. Whether your attitude toward buying a new home predicts purchase behavior, for example, may depend in part on your reasoned assessment of the various pros and cons associated with the new house.

By contrast, a more spontaneous or "theory-driven" process approach assumes that behavior sometimes flows more effortlessly from the activation of a person's attitude (hence, "theory") from memory. This model assumes that once attitudes are spontaneously activated, they serve as a perceptual framework through which the attitude object and the situation are selectively perceived. For example, positive attitudes facilitate attention to and encoding of positive characteristics of the attitude object to the relative exclusion of the attitude object's negative qualities. If, for example, we are asked to sign a petition to increase parking at the university, our attitude toward this issue may be automatically activated. If the attitude is positive, we are likely to think about the positive benefits of this policy (e.g., ease of parking) while neglecting to consider the negative qualities (e.g., increased congestion). Our definition of the immediate situation is thus defined by our positive attitude toward the issue. In this case, our attitude should serve as a strong behavioral cue, and lead to attitudinally consistent behavior. However, if when approached by the petitioner our attitude on the issue is not activated, we may base our behavior on other cues, such as whether we are late for an appointment. In this case, our attitudes are less likely to guide and thus be consistent with our behavior. In sum, by examining the various conditions that facilitate or inhibit the processes associated with these models of the attitude–behavior relationship, social psychologists have gained valuable insights into how social attitudes influence and predict behavior.

E. Attitude Change

The influence of theory and research from social cognition also may be found in the way social psychologists have been studying persuasion processes. A general theme of persuasion research involves the role of self-generated cognitions in processing persuasive communications. When a person receives or anticipates a persuasive message, for example, an attempt is made to relate the information and arguments contained in the message to the preexisting knowledge and attitude that the person has about the issue. In so doing, the person will generate a number of issue-relevant cognitions that may support the advocated position (pro-arguments) or may oppose the position (counterarguments). If these self-generated cognitions are primarily favorable, then persuasion will be the likely result; but if the cognitions are primarily unfavorable, then resistance to persuasion will be more likely. Therefore, how various features of a persuasion situation influence the amount of pro or counterargumentation has been the goal of considerable research to date.

Persuasion researchers in this tradition have hypothesized that two different modes of information processing may mediate attitude change. Richard Petty and John Cacioppo, for example, have proposed an elaboration likelihood model (ELM) of persuasion that distinguishes between central and peripheral modes of processing. Central processing occurs when people are both motivated and able to engage in message-relevant elaboration or processing of a persuasive communication. By contrast, peripheral processing refers to those factors in a persuasion setting that produce attitude change, but with minimal message-relevant elaboration of the content of the persuasive communication. For example, research has shown that peripheral persuasion cues like communicator attractiveness or likability or message length often mediate persuasion when either the motivation or ability for message-relevant thinking is low. These cues usually have less impact on attitudes when motivation and ability are high and the persuasive implications of such cues are attenuated by message recipients' central processing.

A second influential dual process model of persuasion has been proposed by Shelly Chaiken and her colleagues. The heuristic–systematic model (HSM), like ELM, assumes that people are generally motivated to form and hold valid, accurate attitudes. In addition, the HSM is based on the "principle of sufficiency"—that people cannot know with certainty that their attitudes are accurate and so they strive for a sufficient level of confidence in their attitudes. The HSM hypothesizes that people generate these sufficiency judgments either through an effortful and analytic approach to message processing (the "systematic" mode) or through a less effortful approach to message processing (the "heuristic" mode). In heuristic processing, for example, the persuasive communication activates simple rules of thumb which people consciously or unconsciously rely on to make sufficiency judgments (e.g., "longer messages are stronger messages"; "consensus implies correctness"; or "experts know best"). These simple heuristics mediate persuasion, yet they involve much less effort and cognitive capacity than persuasion produced through more systematic processing of the message.

While different in several respects, both models of persuasion have yielded interesting and important insights into the psychological factors that influence how people respond to persuasive communications. And, consistent with the social cognition approach, ELM and HSM underscore the extent to which attitudinal reactions to a persuasive communication will depend more on people's cognitive appraisals of message content than on their learning of the arguments themselves. [*See* ATTITUDE CHANGE.]

In conclusion, the social cognition perspective views people as active participants in the construction of their social worlds. While maintaining a strong commitment to cognitive models, social cognition has evolved to incorporate motivational influences and the role of emotion in social information processing. Social cognition has also begun to influence theory and research in other disciplines such as political science, sociology, law, and marketing. The challenge for social cognition as it evolves is to link these processes of social construal to a deeper understanding of social interaction and behavior in complex, real-world settings.

Bibliography

Fiske, S. T. (1993). Social cognition and social perception. *Annu. Rev. Psychol.* **44,** 155–194.

Fiske, S. T., and Taylor, S. E. (1991). "Social Cognition," 2nd ed. McGraw-Hill, New York.

Landman, J., and Manis, M. (1983). Social cognition: Some historical and theoretical perspectives. In "Advances in Experimental Social Psychology" (L. Berkowitz, Ed.), Vol. 16, pp. 49–123. New York, Academic Press.

Markus, H., and Zajonc, R. B. (1985). The cognitive perspective in social psychology. In "The Handbook of Social Psychology" (G. Lindzey and E. Aronson, Eds.), Vol II, 3rd ed. Random House, New York.

Martin, L. L., and Clark, L. F. (1990). Social cognition: Exploring the mental processes involved in human social interaction. In "Cognitive Psychology: An International Review" (M. W. Eyesenck, Ed.). Wiley, Sussex, England.

Sherman, S. J., Judd, C. M., and Park, B. (1989). Social cognition. *Annu. Rev. Psychol.* **40,** 281–326.

Uleman, J. S., and Bargh, J. A. (Eds.) (1989). "Unintended Thought." Guilford, New York.

Wyer, R. S., Jr., and Srull, T. K. (Eds.) (1984). "Handbook of Social Cognition" Vols. 1–3. Erlbaum, Hillsdale, NJ.

SOCIAL COMPARISON

Kirsten M. Poehlmann and Robert M. Arkin
The Ohio State University

Glossary

Comparison other A person to whom one compares one's abilities, opinions, or emotions.

Downward social comparison Comparing oneself to an inferior other; when stressed or threatened, people tend to select worse off others for social comparison.

Related attribute An attribute different from, but linked to, an attribute being assessed, as in the case of practice obscuring the impact of talent on performance.

Self-enhancement A process by which one improves one's self-esteem or self-concept.

Self-evaluation A process by which one obtains an accurate assessment of some dimension of the self.

Self-improvement A process by which one seeks to improve some dimension of the self.

Self-serving bias A tendency to view oneself favorably.

Similarity hypothesis A central tenet of the original social comparison theory. States that, to achieve an accurate appraisal, people select comparison others who are like themselves.

Social comparison A subjective evaluation of one's own characteristics achieved by comparing oneself to others.

Unidirectional drive upward A need or motivation that causes people to strive to improve their ability and performance levels.

A SOCIAL COMPARISON is a subjective evaluation of one's own characteristics (such as an ability, opinion, or performance) in relation to the perceived characteristics of others. Social comparison theory states that when no objective, physical standard is available, people seek to evaluate themselves by comparison to others. Social comparison theory and research attempt to identify when, why, and to whom people compare themselves, as well as to examine the consequences of these comparisons.

I. ESSENTIAL PROPOSITION

A. Outline of Social Comparison Theory

Social comparison theory rests on the premise that people have a drive to evaluate their abilities and opinions. People want these self-evaluations to be accurate, according to Leon Festinger, who proposed the theory in 1954. This desire for accurate self-evaluation reflects the negative consequences that can result from holding incorrect opinions and/or inaccurate appraisals of ability. Though ideal for accurate assessment, objective, nonsocial standards are rare. In the absence of these standards, Festinger reasoned, people evaluate their abilities and opinions by comparison with those of others. Festinger hypothesized that a lack of comparison, by reference to a subjective standard or an objective standard, causes uncertain and unstable self-evaluations.

Though less preferred, then, the subjective standard afforded by engaging in social comparison can reduce uncertainty and instability in self-evaluations. In sum, social comparison as conceptualized by Festinger serves the important function of providing useful information about the self, thereby reducing uncertainty, and preparing the individual for effective future action.

Although not explicit in Festinger's depiction of social comparison, the roots of the theory can also be seen in philosophical and sociological writings on social context and self-concept. For instance, in 1902 Charles Horton Cooley coined the term "looking-glass self'' to describe how others serve as a mirror in which to see oneself. George Herbert Mead similarly noted in 1934 that people often come to know themselves by imagining the interpersonal evaluations of significant others and then incorporating these perceptions into self-concept.

B. Importance of Social Comparison Theory

The development of social comparison theory marks a pivotal point in social psychology. It crystallized one major focus in social psychology on information gathering and processing, in particular information relevant to one's identity, and spawned a multitude of theories that stem from this theme. Its advent turned many researchers from examining group processes toward cognitive processes. In the case of social comparison, the social information is gathered and processed by an individual with the purpose of development, maintenance, and change in self-concept and self-evaluation. Later theoretical advances expanded on this important refocusing on information gathering and processing.

For instance, the need for affiliation is one of the many themes in social psychology linked to the need to reduce uncertainty, as outlined in social comparison theory. Excusing the sexist language, one of the most profound observations about human behavior is that ''man is by nature a social animal'' (Aristotle, *Politics,* ca. 328 B.C.). You may be alone as you read this chapter, but if you think for a moment about your daily activities, you surely have a remarkable array of experiences that include the company of others. Gregariousness and the many needs that are met through affiliation with others (e.g., approval, support, comfort, friendship, prestige) were the logical first explanations for ''man . . .'' the social animal. But social comparison theory adds that people have a drive to evaluate themselves and, when physical standards are not available, satisfy this need by comparing themselves to others. It therefore stands to reason that people have a ''cognitive'' need to associate with others in addition to the more ''pragmatic,'' interpersonal needs met by affiliation. According to this view, then, affiliation results in part from the desire of people to feel as though they have a handle on reality, that they have an essentially correct view of the world, and in particular an accurate appraisal of themselves. Contemporary research supports this idea.

Attribution theory is another important development in social psychology that owes a debt to the advent of social comparison ideas. An attribution is an explanation or inference that a person makes about why he or she, or another person, behaved in a certain way. The theory deals with the rules of thumb the average individual uses in attempting to discern the causes of some behavior. In law, for instance, judges and juries are asked to draw the distinction between murder and manslaughter; the distinction rests on the attribution of intent to the perpetrator. Attribution theory would thus consider the thought processes judges and juries use to gather and use information to make that attribution and decide the appropriate penalty. [*See* ATTRIBUTION.]

Social comparison and attribution theory share common ground in terms of the factors thought to motivate an individual to obtain relevant information. In the case of social comparison, uncertainty and the need for self-evaluation stimulate information gathering and use. Comparison of oneself to others provides information useful in drawing an inference about one's own characteristics. In the case of attribution theory, the more general of the two theories, uncertainty also plays an important role in inspiring information gathering and use. While social comparison theory is centered on matters of self-evaluation, however, attribution theory extends the process to drawing inferences about oneself *and* others. For both theories, the search for information can be a highly logical and dispassionate matter or one driven by self-interest and bias.

One major attribution approach divides information into three categories: consistency, distinctiveness, and consensus. Consistency refers to whether the same behavior occurs at other times or places, as well as in the current situation. Distinctiveness concerns whether an object is causing a reaction that is unique, or if other objects or entities would cause the same reaction. Finally, consensus is in effect an application of social comparison principles. Consensus information is used to determine how a given person's reaction compares to the reactions of most other people.

Thus, both social comparison theory and attribution theory draw on information about consensus as people strive to make inferences about behavior. The cause of an action is determined by considering others' reactions to the same stimulus in the same situation: if everyone has an identical response, it is most likely the stimulus or situation that produced it. If, on the other hand, few people react the same way as the person in question, then something about that person is likely to be seen as the cause of the response. For instance, if Francis is the only person in class to answer every one of 50 test questions correctly, then it is probably something about Francis, rather than the test or the class, that produced this result. The relationship between social comparison and attribution theory will be addressed again in a later section of this article.

Attribution and affiliation are not the only topics that have evolved from social comparison theory. A diverse range of social psychological processes, including cognitive dissonance, group polarization, social facilitation, relative deprivation, and equity theory, all owe an intellectual debt to social comparison theory, and all of these topics draw on principles and findings in the social comparison literature. [*See* COGNITIVE DISSONANCE; EQUITY.]

C. Significant Theoretical and Research Questions

Research on social comparison is plentiful and diverse. However, most of the research deals with several basic questions, which will be addressed now. These themes include (a) the specific motives or goals underlying social comparisons, (b) features of comparison dimensions and attributes of comparison others in the social comparison process, and (c) the consequences of social comparisons.

II. PURPOSES OF SOCIAL COMPARISON

Why people seek to compare themselves to others is a central question in the social comparison literature. As already indicated, Festinger's answer was that people wish to reduce uncertainty and, in the absence of any objective, physical standard one can use to obtain accurate self-evaluations, social standards have to suffice. This section begins with an examination of this goal of accurate self-appraisal. However, extensions of the original theory of social comparison processes have added the additional goals of self-enhancement and self-improvement to Festinger's original formulation. The balance of this section describes briefly each of these major functions served by social comparison, along with some of the implications of each.

A. Self-Evaluation

Early work on social comparison addressed the goal of reducing uncertainty by obtaining accurate self-evaluations. A major theme in social psychology, then and now, is that people want to be accurate in their views of the world. Festinger's idea that people compare themselves to others to obtain accurate self-evaluations is consistent with this theme. Empirical research supports the notion that people strive to have accurate perceptions of the world. For instance, research has shown that people often choose to receive as much accurate information as possible about their performance on a laboratory task, even if that information will reflect badly on them. Similarly, when looking for challenging and similarly skilled tennis partners, a person desires an accurate idea of his or her own ability in order to match it to that of potential partners.

Despite the emphasis on accuracy present in much social psychological research, other motives for social comparison have also received attention and empirical support. In some instances, the goal of social comparison can be self-enhancement or self-improvement.

B. Self-Enhancement

Self-enhancement is another crucial motive sometimes served by social comparison. People routinely exhibit a self-serving bias, which is a tendency to view oneself favorably. There is widespread agreement regarding the existence, prevalence, and potency of a general self-serving tendency in self-evaluation. Time and again the research shows that people readily accept credit when told they have succeeded, yet are willing to attribute failure to any handy excuse. This self-serving bias is revealed in many situations in which people have unreasonably optimistic self-evaluations. For instance, students receiving an examination grade will accept personal credit by judging the exam a valid measure of their competence if they learn they have done well; those who do poorly are likely to criticize the exam as a poor indicator of their ability. A group of five co-workers who succeed on a project will each claim some 40% of the credit for the collective success; a group of five co-workers who fail on the project each assume personally only about 10% of the responsibility for the poor outcome. Only 12% of Americans feel old for their age, 22% feel their age, but a whopping 66% think that they are relatively young for their age. These biases reflect an attempt to see oneself in the best possible light.

A self-enhancement motive, directed at improving or protecting self-esteem, can also be seen in social comparison. The prototype is that most people see themselves as better than average. Most business people see themselves as more ethical than the average business person. Most drivers believe themselves to be safer and more skilled behind the wheel than the average driver. Myers reports that 70% of college students rate themselves as above the average of their peers in leadership ability. Only 2% indicate that they are below average. On a college entrance exam survey students rated their "ability to get along with one another"—a trait dimension that is both subjective (lacking an objective, physical standard) and socially desirable—and not one of the 829,000 students who responded rated himself or herself below average. Indeed, 60% rated themselves in the top 10%; 25% saw themselves in the top 1%. This is a stunning conclusion. By definition, only half of any population is actually better than average; however, if one concludes, even erroneously, that one is better than at least half of the population, self-enhancement is achieved.

Social comparison can serve this end if the gathering of information is biased in self-serving ways. The research shows that it is. For instance, a person may make him- or herself feel better after performing poorly on a test by imagining those who performed worse still. This comparison to those who are inferior or worse off is termed downward social comparison, and it frequently serves the function of self-enhancement. For example, women who have been diagnosed with breast cancer often comment on the fact that their situation is not too terrible because there are others who have a more advanced case of cancer, or who do not have as much social support, or who are much younger and have not yet had the chance to lead a full life. Thus, these women make themselves feel better by comparing themselves with those who seem to be in a situation that is worse. Downward social comparison will be discussed in greater detail in a subsequent section.

In addition to one's choice of comparison others, self-serving tendencies can affect the dimensions used to assess one's personal qualities. Individuals may choose to shade social comparisons in a way that enhances feelings of self-worth. In preparing for a job interview, an individual might emphasize to her- or himself the importance of enthusiasm, willingness to learn, and diligence, where she or he seems to excel over others, rather than focusing on the specific job criteria that are lacking. Not getting the job may come as a surprise. In considering one's relationship skills, good friends, good times, and numbers of acquaintances may spring to mind; one's three divorces, although well above the statistical average, are all written off as aberrant exceptions to an otherwise outstanding record. Recent research shows a correlation between possession of perceived talents and attributes and their rated importance. In one study, subjects were asked to rank their own intelligence, social competence, artistic or musical ability, athletic ability, and physical attractiveness; these rankings were strongly correlated with subjects' ratings of the importance of these dimensions. Thus, subjects indicated that the attributes that they felt the best about were highly important traits to possess.

C. Self-Improvement

Social comparison sometimes serves the goal of discovering ways to improve oneself. Festinger hypothesized a "unidirectional drive upward" for abilities which creates pressure to strive to improve. This goal of self-improvement reflects Western culture's emphasis on achievement or performance. The desire to improve oneself is apparent in numerous social psychological theories, principally achievement motivation.

There is relatively little research on social comparison and self-improvement, but some evidence indicates that comparisons are used for learning, self-improvement, and attaining high levels of social adjustment. Research on modeling, or imitation, suggests that merely by being in the presence of and watching (and thus comparing to) others, people learn how to perform specific tasks incidentally. Every parent knows that children learn a great deal from their playmates. But new research pushes back the earliest age at which children appear to learn skills from each other, to a point even before they acquire language. One implication is that day care can provide an enriching experience, merely because of the effects of modeling and children's tendency to expand the range of their everyday skills through their natural tendencies toward imitation, or mimicry. The evidence shows that children in good early day care have advantages in the long run. Those who enter day care before their first birthday are later rated by their third-grade teachers as more persistent, independent, verbally facile, confident, and socially adjusted than their peers without the day care experience. These findings and others show that children and adults are attuned closely to the behavior of others, compare their own performance, and then progress toward greater achievement.

D. Conflict among Social Comparison Objectives

The three motives of self-evaluation, self-enhancement, and self-improvement discussed above are all important functions of social comparison. Not surprisingly, fulfilling all three functions simultaneously is rare. One line of research has examined conditions under which people seek to realize a particular objective, rather than others.

Findings conflict about people's preference for one motive over another. In some cases, self-evaluation has been chosen over self-enhancement motives. Other research suggests, however, that people prefer self-enhancement to self-evaluation under some conditions. For instance, when there is a specific threat to self-esteem, self-enhancement motivation seems to win out over self-evaluation. Thus, social comparison can serve as a means of coping with threat, for example the prospect of disapproval. Other research shows that people tend to choose self-evaluation of their feelings only when self-enhancement is not possible.

The preference for self-enhancement over self-evaluation fits well with the finding that people are uncomfortable when they compare themselves with others who are superior. Upward comparisons, or comparisons to someone who is perceived to be superior, typically do not produce self-enhancement. It is surprising, then, that the majority of social comparison studies where upward comparison is possible indicate a preference for it. It is important to realize, however, that many of these studies present subjects with social comparison opportunities on dimensions that are not personally relevant, and thus the desire for self-enhancement may not be strong enough to outweigh the desire for self-evaluation.

The functions of self-enhancement and self-improvement are also often in conflict. Upward comparisons, with superior others, provide the information and/or models necessary for self-improvement, but these comparisons can also be damaging to self-esteem. People often sacrifice self-improvement benefits in favor of preserving self-esteem by avoiding upward comparisons. Two conditions have been shown to promote this. The desire to protect self-esteem is especially strong when self-esteem is already threatened, such as by hints of failure or disapproval, and when people believe their inferiority may be made public.

III. IMPORTANT FEATURES OF THE SOCIAL COMPARISON

Social comparisons can vary in a number of respects. Specific values on these dimensions are determined by the goal of the comparison, and they can have a significant effect on the consequences of the comparison.

A. Similarity Level of the Comparison Other

"Comparison other" is the term used to describe someone selected for social comparison purposes. Relative to an individual gathering social comparison information, the comparison other may be similar, the comparison other may be superior, and the comparison other can of course be inferior. Comparisons with a superior comparison other are referred to as upward comparisons; those with a comparison other who is inferior or worse off are termed downward comparisons.

1. Similar Comparison Others

The similarity hypothesis was a central proposition of Festinger's original conceptualization of social comparison processes. It states that people prefer to compare themselves to others who are similar to themselves. Festinger reasoned that the more discrepant another's opinions or abilities from one's own, the more difficult it is to obtain an *accurate* evaluation of one's own opinions or abilities. Thus, because the goal of the social comparison was conceptualized as an accurate self-evaluation, a person should be likely to choose similar over dissimilar comparison others whenever possible.

Comparing oneself to someone whose opinion or ability level is extremely divergent from one's own offers only very weak and ambiguous evaluative information. For instance, the chess novice does not gain much useful information by learning through comparison that the chess master is clearly better. Rather, the beginner is well-advised to assess ability by reference to another novice. A liberal college student is unlikely to calibrate the correctness of her or his opinion about a specific environmental issue by reading conservative columnists or attending meetings of the Young Republicans. Such activities might be useful in generating counterarguments, or refining one's perspective, but not in calibrating its accuracy. Instead, one's liberal friend, who is a member of "Friends of the Earth," is the better choice. From a range of comparison others, then, someone close to one's own opinion or ability is ordinarily selected; the goal of an accurate evaluation of one's abilities or opinions is best served by comparison to similar others.

A major development in social comparison research is an interpretation of the similarity hypothesis referred to as the related-attributes similarity hypothesis. This hypothesis asserts that to obtain a useful evaluation of an opinion or inference about ability one should compare oneself to people who are similar in attributes related to the opinion or ability in as many ways as possible. Taking social comparison of ability as the example, the ideal social comparison other should be similar in as many dimensions that could affect performance as possible. Goethals and Darley's attribution-based approach emphasized the fact that ability is not the only factor that influences performance, but performance is the only observable cue one has to infer ability. Numerous other factors—termed related attributes—also contribute to performance. Because of the related attributes, such as practice, which also contribute to performance level, accurate attributions about ability are terribly difficult unless one selects a comparison other comparable to oneself on these related attributes. Similarity on related attributes contributes to the goal of accurate self-evaluation by reducing the ambiguity that can otherwise obscure a clear inference about ability. For instance, a casual, weekend golfer can be certain that he or she cannot perform on the course as well as a former collegiate competitor. However, the casual golfer cannot be certain whether this difference in performance stems more or less from a difference in innate ability, a difference in training, or their current discrepancy in tee-times and practice.

Only truly related dimensions, ones that affect performance, should make equivocal one's evaluation of ability. Interestingly, people nevertheless often choose to compare themselves to others who are similar on dimensions that are unrelated to the one being evaluated. One intriguing example is that men and women both prefer to compare their intelligence to that of someone of their same sex, rather than a member of the opposite sex or the entire population, even though sex is an unrelated attribute in assessing intelligence.

Although similarity is important in obtaining an accurate evaluation of one's own abilities, the overall preference for comparison to similar others is qualified when the comparison dimension is unfamiliar to people and/or they do not know the range of possible scores. When the dimension is novel, people often prefer to learn the scores of those who seem to be most *dissimilar* to themselves. In particular, knowing the extreme scores, and thus the range from high to low, can help an individual understand an unfamiliar attribute by serving as a clear instance of the attribute and a clear example of its absence. To gauge the concept of generosity, for instance, one might imagine a particularly charitable friend and then imagine a particularly selfish acquaintance. By having a sense of the range of scores an individual has a better sense of the meaning of his or her own score. For instance, a boy who scores "18" on a newly developed test of verbal ability cannot know how to interpret this score without some context. However, if he knows the lowest score was a 1 and the highest score 19, on a test that can produce scores from 0 to 20, he has a much better sense of the meaning of his own score. Thus, comparison to dissimilar others can also serve the goal of accurate self-evaluation by providing important contextual information. The research shows that the absence of context does switch preference from similar to dissimilar others.

2. Superior Others (Upward Comparisons)

Upward comparison, to someone clearly superior, can serve both self-improvement and self-evaluative functions. Because one can look to a superior other as a model to be imitated, valuable information about one's status can be gained, and this information can inspire self-improvement. Overall, research shows that people prefer superior others to inferior others in assessing their abilities.

However, the tendency toward upward social comparison is qualified by feelings of hope versus despair. When people feel they are in control of a situation and can influence their outcomes, a superior other can serve as a model and lead to striving for self-improvement. However, when people feel out of control, and sense little prospect for improved performance, upward comparison can only serve to frustrate and inspire other negative emotions such as depression, dejection, and further hopelessness. The research shows that the tendency toward upward social comparison is qualified by such judgments about its utility.

Upward comparison seems antithetical to the powerful self-enhancement tendencies reviewed earlier. However, the apparent conflict can be reconciled. There are some situations in which upward comparison can lead to self-enhancement. For instance, one might compare oneself to another who is superior on the dimension being evaluated but more nearly similar on surrounding, related attributes. The overall similarity encourages one to draw inferences about one's potential and thus, can be self-enhancing. By contrast, comparison to someone who is superior on a given attribute, but dissimilar on relevant related dimensions, suggests that the related dimensions may be responsible for the other's superiority. Here, overall dissimilarity makes one's specific shortcoming seem irrelevant. Discovering, for instance, that one's pick-up basketball skills pale by contrast to those of a competitor, but that the competitor is a former collegiate athlete—in any sport—can relieve the sting of failure.

3. Inferior Others (Downward Comparisons)

The basic principle of downward comparison theory, as suggested by Thomas Wills in 1981, is that people can increase their feelings of subjective well-being through comparison with a less fortunate other. A corollary to this premise is that downward comparison is brought about by a decrease in subjective well-being.

Downward comparisons are most often viewed as a method of self-enhancement. This focus on self-enhancement is seen even in the basic principle of downward comparison cited above; people make their own situation seem better by using worse circumstances as a point of comparison.

An interesting line of research has focused on social comparisons made under threatening circumstances. In a study reported by Hakmiller in 1966, subjects who were given threatening feedback about the level of their hostility toward their parents chose to compare themselves to others who were supposedly even more hostile. The results of this and other studies have demonstrated that under conditions of threat people attempt self-enhancement through downward comparison.

4. Resolution of Seemingly Conflicting Literature

Upward and downward comparison have each received extensive attention in social comparison research, and many of the findings would seem to be in conflict. The fact that people prefer downward comparisons under some circumstances and upward comparisons in others has led to a tremendous amount of research aimed at discovering the antecedents (and consequences) of each type of comparison. One reconciliation focuses on the difference in the functions typically served by upward and downward comparisons; a second hypothesis emphasizes one's focus and various aspects of the information gained rather than the direction of the comparison; a third hypothesis deals with how people's emotional lives can influence their sampling of social comparison others.

a. Differences in Functions of Upward and Downward Social Comparisons

Downward and upward comparisons typically serve fundamentally different functions. Downward comparison rests on the premise that comparing oneself to less fortunate others is self-enhancing. Upward comparison, on the other hand, tends to serve a self-improvement and self-evaluation function. Further, the very nature of interaction with those less fortunate and those more fortunate seems to differ. People prefer to *compare* with those less fortunate (downward comparison) but to seek *information* from and *interact* with those more fortunate (upward contact). In sum, one major distinction is between the self-regulation of one's emotional life (downward comparison) and the self-regulation of goals, aspirations, and outcomes (upward comparison).

Shelley Taylor and others have reported extensive research exemplifying this distinction in an important domain of health psychology. Specifically, cancer patients prefer to make explicit comparisons to those who are worse off. However, they prefer to interact with and gain information from those who are better off and who are coping well, perhaps in an attempt to sustain an optimistic outlook and to learn how to cope better themselves. The preference for downward comparisons and upward contacts can coexist, then, since they serve different functions and are not mutually exclusive.

b. Focus of the Comparison

Upward and downward comparisons each provide two pieces of information. For instance, downward comparison indicates that one is better off than others, which should produce self-enhancement. However, a downward comparison can also imply that it is possible for one's situation to worsen, which could produce negative affect. Whether one concentrates on the positive information (one is better off than others) or the negative information (things could get worse) should produce very different results. Thus, the emotional response to an upward or downward comparison seems to depend not entirely on the direction of the comparison, but instead on one's focus on the positive or negative aspects of the information gained. Some research supports this distinction.

c. Focus on the Comparison Other

Ladd Wheeler and his colleagues have proposed another model which predicts that low subjective well-being will lead to upward rather than downward comparison. Doubtful subjective well-being, negative thoughts about the self, and a general sense of inferiority should cause one to notice others who are superior and then oversample them as comparison others. Wheeler and his colleagues provide evidence that negative mood can bias the comparison process in just this way. This finding is certainly consistent with the cyclical way in which depressive affect is known to stimulate depressive thinking, which in turn produces further depressive affect. People who can avoid this sort of catastrophising, and engage in a more self-serving cognitive bias, are best equipped to resist depression or emerge from the grips of this cyclical, negative spiral. Downward social comparison has even been used therapeutically to combat this phenomenon.

B. Attributes of the Comparison Dimension

The dimension being assessed is an important aspect of a social comparison. Just as there are subtle factors operating in the selection of comparison others, so too are there subtle and important variables associated with the comparison dimension.

1. Relevance and Importance

Personal relevance of a dimension plays an important role in the effects of social comparison on self-enhancement. For a dimension of little significance, learning that one's ability is low, compared to others, is not especially detrimental to self-worth. However, if the dimension is of considerable importance, a comparison indicating low ability can produce negative feelings. Fascinating research by Tesser and his colleagues draws a crucial distinction between dimensions personally and not personally relevant.

We have all had the experience of meeting someone for the first time and having to endure learning about their cousin who is first violin for the Cleveland Symphony, or their family tree, tracing their ancestry (through some circuitous path) to the estimable Grover Cleveland. People can attempt to feel good about themselves by basking in the reflected glory of another. To do this, people seek to establish relationships with high performing others or do what they can to enhance the appearance of the performance of persons to whom they are connected somehow.

There is a risk in doing this, though. The juxtaposition of oneself to a high performing, similar other can make oneself pale by contrast. The reflection process and the comparison process are, it seems, antagonistic. The former suggests the good performance of someone close to us enhances self-esteem; the latter suggests the good performance of someone close to us threatens self-esteem.

Tesser's reconciliation is that the reflection process and the comparison process are not always equally important. One's preexisting definition of self plays a crucial role in which of these two processes is invoked. Specifically, one's self-worth, or identity, rests for the most part on dimensions that are personally relevant. When another's performance is relevant to our own self-definition, which occurs with dimensions of personal importance, the comparison process swamps the reflection process and high performing, similar others constitute a threat. When another's performance is *not* relevant to our own self-definition, which occurs when an individual does not aspire toward excellence in that domain, the reflection process is the more important.

For instance, it is much easier to be happy for the academic success of a close friend, and even bask in her glory, if academic pursuits are not particularly important to one's own self-concept than if academics are crucial to one's own self-regard.

A most interesting extension is that people may actually adjust their self-concept in order to maintain their self-evaluation. Tesser assumes that people want to feel good about themselves, to evaluate themselves positively. Clearly, how people feel about themselves is at least partially determined by the social context in which they find themselves; he argues that an immensely important part of that context is the quality of the performance of important (including close) others. Therefore, two siblings, for example, inextricably linked (particularly if they are rather close in age) by their relationship, may seek to emphasize different domains of expertise in their lives: one artistic, one athletic, so as to simultaneously bask in the glory of the other while not disturbing the integrity or uniqueness of one another's own identity. Tesser's research documents the power of this self-evaluation maintenance process.

2. Desirability

Choice of a comparison other is affected by the desirability of the attribute in question. In comparison of their undesirable qualities, people tend to select similar others. While the dimension is no less undesirable, comparison with a similar other at least makes it possible to see the shortcoming as common. The false consensus effect is a robust tendency of people to overestimate the commonality of their opinions and their undesirable or unsuccessful behaviors. On matters of opinion, people find support for their positions by systematically overestimating the extent to which others concur. Similarly, when people behave undesirably or fail some task, they seek to reassure themselves by estimating that such behaviors or outcomes are commonplace.

In contrast, if the quality at issue is desirable, people tend to compare with dissimilar others, particularly those who may be inferior on the given quality. On matters of ability and when people behave desirably or successfully, one is more likely to observe a false uniqueness effect. That is, people tend to underestimate the commonality of their strengths, seeing their talents and admirable qualities and outcomes as relatively unusual. In this way, the overall merit of a positive trait or outcome is enhanced in value.

In sum, a similar or dissimilar comparison other can best serve the objective of self-enhancement under rather different circumstances. One's failings can be seen as normal if similar others are sought for purposes of social comparison; one's virtues seem rare and all the more virtuous if dissimilar, and inferior, others are sought for purposes of social comparison. The research supports the idea that choice of comparison other is determined in part by the desirability of the dimension. For instance, persons who drink heavily but use their seat belts would tend to overselect fellow heavy drinkers, but underrepresent seat-belt users in their social comparison of health and safety related behavior. Research by Jerry Suls and his colleagues supports this idea.

IV. CONSEQUENCES OF SOCIAL COMPARISON

Throughout this article we have touched on both the underlying motives for social comparison and, not surprisingly, the extent to which these objectives are realized. The theme is that how people feel and think about themselves is very much determined by social context. Social context is partly accidental (one can choose one's friends, but not one's family, the saying goes). But social context is importantly also the result of active choices among others for purposes of mere contact, significant companionship, and intimate relationships. The purpose of this section is to note that the social comparisons that result from both passive and active determinations of comparison others and comparison dimensions have a powerful impact on personal and social identity and self-evaluation. Social comparison research is sometimes criticized for giving less attention to the consequences of comparison than to its causes. But there is ample evidence that the consequences are huge.

One fun illustration is a classic study by Morse and Gergen, often referred to as the "Mr. Clean/Mr. Dirty" study. College students were actual applicants for a real job, and settled into a waiting room to complete some forms. Their self-esteem soared when they found themselves seated next to Mr. Dirty, who was unkempt and disorganized and who, finally, acted out and ensured he was not getting the offer. However, their self-esteem crashed in the other condition, when they were seated next to Mr. Clean, the applicant who was dressed in Sunday Best, held a well-stocked briefcase, and was poised and self-confident in demeanor. [*See* SELF-ESTEEM.]

Other research has shown that children surrounded in a primary school by others with relatively high ability suffer lower self-esteem than students in a context where the others are lower in ability. Two students attending colleges that differ dramatically in difficulty level, and which cause students to have to work more or less, can end up with different career aspirations. Ironically, the equally qualified student at the more competitive college has lower aspirations. This result could reflect the process of pluralistic ignorance, in which someone fails to share information with others and comes to an erroneous conclusion. Students at the competitive college could conclude that grades come easily to their peers, knowing only that they themselves are working very hard but assuming that their peers may not be. Of course, people are often wont to downplay in public their expenditure of effort, putting hard working people at a disadvantage in judging their ability. Students at the noncompetitive college know they do not work very hard, but still do well; the self-serving conclusion is that they are clearly quite capable people. In short, the optimism of the students at the less competitive college is borne of ignorance, too, but the research shows many clear benefits of optimistic thinking nevertheless.

In other research in an educational setting context mainstreamed mentally retarded children's perceptions of their competence were equal to those of normal children, but mainstreamed learning-disabled children's judgments of their competence were lower than their non-learning-disabled peers. The key difference was that retarded children compared themselves to their retarded peers; learning-disabled children compared themselves to the average students.

Research on relative deprivation shows that satisfaction with one's outcomes in life are more often determined by one's relative standing than any absolute level of one's outcomes. The research on relative deprivation offers many examples of the downtrodden, poor, or unfortunate who are not all that dissatisfied with their outcomes, while seemingly fortunate, well-heeled individuals feel unhappy or deprived. One ironic finding is that, just as an individual's or group's outcomes begin to rise, dissatisfaction is likely to set in. The research shows that one's level of aspiration rises even faster than one's outcomes, that this is true of social groups or classes, and the result is feelings of relative deprivation and dissatisfaction.

Affiliation is one major result of social comparison needs, and there are many consequences of affiliation itself; surprisingly, most are negative! Social ills, such as conformity, groupthink, group polarization, social loafing, deindividuation, pathological behavior, competition, and contagion seem to emerge naturally in the presence of large, and often even small, numbers of people. Psychologists are beginning to investigate how these social ills can be circumvented so that the rewards of affiliation (creativity, collaboration, collective effort, social comparison) are not a mixed blessing.

Emotional contagion is but one example of social contact run amok. Ordinarily, contact with others permits comparison of one's emotional life and, overall, reduction of uncertainty. Social contagion is the spread of heightened arousal throughout some population. It is a sort of collective excitement, one in which people seem to "catch" the mood of others around them. In particular, expressive people tend to attract attention, and to provide information once attended to; in ambiguous or uncertain circumstances, such individuals can have extreme reactions (e.g., fainting, high emotionality) and the spread of the mood and behavior can lead to disasters such as stampedes. Hysterical contagion refers to the quick spread of a disorder through a group when there is no medical explanation—other than the contagion of emotions. The quick spread of fainting spells in schools and the spread of insect bite disorders are but two documented cases.

Social comparison would not be necessary and would not occur if all of self-evaluation, the ways people think and feel about themselves, were always stable, confident, certain, optimistic, positive, etc. It is not, so we compare.

V. CONCLUSION

Four decades of theory development and research on social comparison processes since 1954 underscores the lasting power and usefulness of this important social psychological topic. One observer of social comparison theory described it as "everyone's second favorite theory," outstripped in rankings only by a given social psychologist's own personal specialty topic of interest. The point of this humorous observation was that nearly all social psychologists are drawn to the elegance, centrality, richness, and usefulness of the theory.

The development of social comparison theory and research was a turning point in the history of social psychology. The focus of research in the 1930s and 1940s was group processes, prejudice and aggression, and social perception. For the past 40 years social psychology has turned inward, to examine individuals' information gathering and processing tendencies, in particular concerning information relevant to one's identity.

Social comparison is also central to interpersonal processes, of course, as the motivations for social comparison are played out on the interpersonal stage. To a great extent, affiliation—the most basic of steps in social relations—is driven by the need for social comparison. However, as described—all too briefly in this chapter—important human affairs such as friendship, social support, group polarization, equity, and others, all stem from and depend on social comparison processes for their initiation and maintenance.

Most central, though, are the ways in which social comparison processes influence identity. Accurate self-evaluation is clearly important to one's welfare in everyday decision making. But self-enhancement appears to be a powerful and fundamental human need; social comparison seems as often driven by the need to feel good about oneself, to evaluate oneself positively. Finally, growth in the form of self-improvement depends to a great degree on purposeful and incidental learning that results from being in the presence of others. While often in conflict, these motives can co-occur, and people can oscillate among these objectives and others in the selection of comparison others and comparison dimensions.

In sum, how people feel and think about themselves is very much determined by social context; social context is partly accidental and partly the result of active choices among others for contact and companionship, and the results for social identity and self-evaluation are powerful indeed.

Bibliography

Festinger, L. (1954). A theory of social comparison processes. *Hum. Relat.* **7,** 117–140.

Latane, B. (Ed.) (1966). Studies in social comparison [Special issue]. *J. Exp. Soc. Psychol.* **2** (*Suppl.* 1).

Myers, D. (1990). "Social Psychology," 3rd ed. McGraw-Hill, New York.

Schachter, S. (1959). "The Psychology of Affiliation." Stanford University Press, Stanford, CA.

Social Comparison Theory. (1986). [Special issue]. *Pers. Soc. Psychol. Bull.* **12,** 261–299.

Suls, J. M., and Miller, R. L. (Eds.) (1977). "Social Comparison Processes: Theoretical and Empirical Perspectives." Hemisphere, Washington, DC.

Suls, J. M., and Wills, T. A. (Eds.) (1991). "Social Comparison: Contemporary Theory and Research." Erlbaum, Hillsdale, NJ.

Taylor, S. E., and Lobel, M. (1989). Social comparison activity under threat: Downward evaluation and upward contacts. *Psychol. Rev.* **96**(4), 569–575.

Wheeler, L., and Miyake, K. (1992). Social comparison in everyday life. *J. Pers. Soc. Psychol.* **62**(5), 760–773.

Wills, T. A. (1981). Downward comparison principles in social psychology. *Psychol. Bull.* **90**(2), 245–271.

Wood, J. V. (1989). Theory and research concerning social comparisons of personal attributes. *Psychol. Bull.* **106**(2), 231–248.

SOCIAL LOAFING

Steven J. Karau
Clemson University

Glossary

Coactive task A task in which individuals work in the real or imagined presence of others, but their inputs are not combined with the inputs of others.

Collective task A task in which individuals work in the real or imagined presence of others with whom they combine their inputs to form a single group product.

Coordination loss Decreased performance in groups due to an inability to synchronize individual efforts in the most efficient manner.

Social compensation A motivation gain effect in which an individual works harder collectively than coactively in order to compensate for the others in his or her group.

Social dilemma A situation in which individual interests are at odds with group interests such that behaviors that are beneficial or reinforcing to the individual are detrimental to the group.

Social facilitation The tendency for individuals to expend more effort when working coactively than when working alone.

Social inhibition A situation in which the presence of others serves to inhibit individuals from behaving as they would if they were alone.

SOCIAL LOAFING is the tendency for individuals to expend less effort when working collectively than when working individually or coactively. When working collectively, individuals work in the real or imagined presence of others with whom they combine their inputs to form a single group product. When working coactively, individuals work in the real or imagined presence of others, but their inputs are not combined with the inputs of others. Most tasks, at one point or another, require the efforts of groups working collectively to achieve success. Government committees, sports teams, organizational task forces, and symphony orchestras provide but a few examples of groups that combine individual efforts to form a single product. Because collective work settings are so common, it is important to determine the conditions under which individuals are likely to reduce their efforts when working collectively.

I. THE HISTORY OF SOCIAL LOAFING RESEARCH

The first experiment to suggest a possible decrement in individual motivation as a result of working in a group was conducted somewhere between 1882 and 1887 by Ringelmann. Male volunteers were asked to pull on a rope, tug-of-war fashion, as hard as they could in groups of varying sizes. The rope was connected to a strain gauge that measured the group's total effort. The results showed that as group size increased, group performance was increasingly lower than would be expected from the simple addition of individual performances. However, there were two possible causes for this performance decrement: (1) motivation loss or (2) coordination loss. Specifically, the reduced performance in groups could have occurred either because individuals socially loafed and reduced their efforts or because individuals were unable to synchronize their efforts in the most efficient manner, possibly pulling on the rope while others were pausing.

Motivation loss was separated from coordination loss in a classic 1979 experiment by Latané *et al.* Participants shouted and clapped as loudly as they could both individually and with others. While blindfolded and wearing headphones that masked the noise, college males shouted both in actual groups, and in pseudo-groups in which they shouted alone but believed they were shouting with others. Participants still reduced their efforts on the pseudo-group trials, even though they only thought they were working with others. Thus, Latané and colleagues demonstrated that a substantial portion of the decreased performance of groups was attributable to reduced individual effort, as distinct from coordination loss. They also coined the term "social loafing" for the demotivating effects of working in groups.

Since the late 1970s, nearly 80 studies on social loafing have been conducted in which individuals' coactive efforts were compared with individuals' collective efforts. Both laboratory experiments and field studies have been conducted using a wide variety of tasks and examining a range of subject populations varying in age, gender, and culture.

II. MAGNITUDE AND ROBUSTNESS

The bulk of the available research suggests that social loafing is moderate to strong in magnitude and consistently found across studies. Results of a recent meta-analysis (or quantitative integration of the literature) demonstrate that the magnitude of social loafing is comparable in size to that of a number of prominent social psychological effects. Social loafing has been found for a wide variety of tasks. These include evaluative tasks such as quality ratings of poems, editorials, and clinical therapists; cognitive tasks such as maze performance and vigilance tasks on a computer screen; creative tasks such as song-writing, finding items in a picture, and thought-listing; physical tasks such as rope pulling and swimming; and work-related tasks such as typing and job selection. Furthermore, although differences are occasionally found across samples, a number of studies have found significant social loafing regardless of participants' gender, nationality, or age. Thus, social loafing is robust and generalizable across tasks and subject populations.

III. EXPLANATIONS OF SOCIAL LOAFING

A number of explanations of social loafing have been proposed. No single unifying theory is currently viewed as entirely adequate for specifying why loafing occurs or the conditions under which the effect is more or less likely to emerge. However, taken as a whole, the theories that have been proposed provide potent insights into the determinants of motivation losses in groups. First, an overview of viewpoints that have received at least moderate consideration or research attention is presented, and then the empirical support for these views is discussed in terms of mediators and moderators of social loafing.

A. Social Impact Theory

According to Latané's social impact theory, people can be viewed as either sources or targets of social impact. The amount of social impact experienced in a situation is thought to be a function of the strength, immediacy, and number of sources and targets present. When individuals work collectively in a typical social loafing experiment, the experimenter serves as a single source of social impact, whereas other group members usually serve as multiple targets of social impact. Social impact theory suggests that the experimenter's request to try as hard as possible on the task should be divided across targets, resulting in reduced effort as group size increases. The division of impact is predicted to follow an inverse power function, with marginally decreasing impact as group size increases. When individuals work coactively, however, inputs are not combined, and each person feels the full impact of the experimenter's request and works hard. The strength of social impact theory appears to be its relative precision for specifying group size effects. The strength and immediacy factors, however, have been neglected by researchers and the theory has been criticized for not specifying the underlying psychological processes that it describes.

B. Arousal Reduction

Jackson and Williams have proposed a drive explanation to accompany a social impact approach to social loafing. They argue that the presence of other co-workers is drive-reducing because these others serve as co-targets of an outside source of social impact. Citing studies in which people faced with a fearful situation tended to prefer being in the company of others, they reasoned that the presence of others is not necessarily drive-inducing. Instead, the presence of others should only be drive-inducing when those others serve as sources of impact, but should be drive-reducing when they serve as co-targets. Presumably, working collectively leads to reduced drive and effort, resulting in decreased performance on simple tasks (where the dominant response is likely to be correct) and increased performance on novel, difficult tasks (where the dominant response is likely to be in error).

C. Evaluation Approaches

Many interpretations of social loafing invoke the concept of evaluation. These viewpoints suggest that social loafing occurs because, in most studies, individuals' inputs can only be evaluated in the coactive condition. In the collective condition, of course, individual inputs are combined into one group product. When working on collective tasks, individuals can "hide in the crowd" and avoid taking the blame for a poor group performance. Collective tasks may also lead individuals to feel "lost in the crowd" such that they cannot receive their fair share of the credit for a good group performance. The role of evaluation in social loafing is well documented (see Evaluation Potential, below). However, social loafing has also been found in studies in which individual inputs were identifiable in the collective condition. Therefore, although evaluation plays an important role, there are clearly other causes of social loafing.

D. Dispensability of Effort

Kerr and colleagues have suggested another possible cause of social loafing: Individuals may exert less effort when working collectively because they feel that their inputs are not essential to a high-quality group product. Moreover, this reduction in individual effort might occur even when each group member's contribution is completely identifiable. Thus, on some tasks, individuals may be unwilling to exert effort if they feel their input will have little impact on the resulting group product.

E. Equity in Effort

Another viewpoint proposes that people tend to match their co-worker's efforts when working collectively. According to this position, social loafing occurs because individuals expect others to slack off in groups and, therefore, reduce their own efforts in order to maintain equity. Support for this position was found in an initial study. However, the assumption that people expect others to loaf collectively is not supported in most studies that have assessed participants' expectations, and several recent studies have not supported this viewpoint. [*See* EQUITY.]

F. Expectancy-Value Approaches

Recently, several researchers have proposed that social loafing can be understood in terms of the expected utility of individual effort. Expectancy-value models of effort propose that individuals will be willing to exert effort on a task only to the degree that they expect their effort to be instrumental in obtaining valued outcomes. Relevant outcomes include such things as pay, self-evaluation, and feelings of purpose or belonging in one's group. According to this viewpoint, individuals engage in social loafing because they are more likely to perceive a strong contingency between their efforts and valued outcomes when working individually, rather than collectively. When working collectively, factors other than the individual's effort (such as the effort of others or the nature of the group task) frequently determine performance, and valued outcomes are often divided among all of the group members. Although this viewpoint is relatively new, it has received initial empirical support and shows promise as a potential organizing theory.

G. Self-Attention

Another perspective suggests that self-attention underlies social loafing. According to this viewpoint, working on a collective task leads to a decrease in the individual's self-awareness, leading them to disregard salient performance standards and to engage in less self-regulation. Thus, collective performance is lower than coactive performance because participants are more attentive to task demands and performance standards when working alone. Although this hypothesis is provocative, it is strongly in need of empirical support. There is some support for the notion that self-attention has an impact on different kinds of social behavior, but there is currently no evidence that self-attention mediates social loafing.

H. Summary

A number of theories have been advanced to explain social loafing, with some overlap in the underlying assumptions of several of the viewpoints. The current research evidence does not provide potent empirical support for any single unifying theory. This may be due to a tendency for researchers to focus on specifying the conditions under which social loafing can be reduced or overcome, rather than devising crucial tests of competing theories of underlying process. A number of experiments have found support for particular causes of social loafing or have isolated particular moderating factors. This may suggest that social loafing includes a class of phenomena with psychologically distinct mechanisms and that motivation loss in groups may be caused by a number of factors. For example, there is compelling evidence that reduced evaluation potential, dispensability of individual inputs, redundancy of inputs, and decreases in expected utility might all cause social loafing in some situations. However, little attempt has been made to integrate all of these moderators and causes into one unifying framework. Nevertheless, the tendency of researchers to focus on limiting conditions has provided a rich understanding of a number of factors that may reduce or eliminate social loafing. The research on limiting conditions also sheds some light on the adequacy of current theoretical approaches.

IV. MEDIATORS AND MODERATORS OF SOCIAL LOAFING

A. Evaluation Potential

As alluded to above, a number of studies have found that social loafing can be reduced or eliminated when evaluation potential is held constant across the coactive and collective conditions. In a prototypical study, individuals performed a shouting task coactively and collectively. Evaluation potential was manipulated such that individual inputs were always identifiable, never identifiable, or identifiable only in the coactive condition. Individuals only loafed when their inputs were identifiable in the coactive condition, but not in the collective condition. Recent studies have clarified the essential aspects of identifiability. One study demonstrated that participants only worked hard collectively when their inputs were both identifiable and comparable with those of others. When inputs were not comparable, there was no basis for evaluation, and identifiability had no impact. An additional question is identifiable to whom? In some of the previous research, identifiable participants were led to believe that only the experimenter would know their performance. In other research, they were led to believe that not only would the experimenter know, but so would they and their partners. In order to determine whose evaluation was important in eliminating loafing, a number of recent studies have varied who was given access to performance information. These studies have found that participants did not loaf on an additive task when they were the only ones to know their own score, and also did not loaf when given a standard by which to evaluate either their own performance or the performance of their group. This research suggests that evaluation by anyone (including oneself) may often be enough to eliminate social loafing. This research also demonstrates that in order for evaluation by any source (the experimenter, one's co-workers, or oneself) to be possible (a) the participant's inputs must be known or identifiable, and (b) there must be a standard (personal, social, or objective) present with which these inputs can be compared.

B. Dispensability of Inputs

It is notable in light of the research on evaluation potential that several studies using a different task and a slightly different paradigm have found effort reduction even in cases where individuals were identifiable. In these studies, individual effort was compared with group effort on disjunctive, threshold tasks in which the group was considered to have succeeded if any single group member reached a certain performance criterion. Furthermore, each individual's inputs were made identifiable to themselves, their co-workers, and the experimenter, whether they were working individually or in a group. The findings that individuals still reduced their efforts when working collectively suggest that some tasks and situations may lead individuals to perceive that their own contributions to the group product are dispensable, such that the goal can be reached even if they do not contribute much to the group effort. Thus, consistent with the dispensability viewpoint advocated by Kerr and others, social loafing might be caused in some situations by the perception that one's inputs to the collective task are unnecessary or irrelevant to group performance. These findings are also consistent with expectancy-value approaches to social loafing.

A related issue concerns the relatively uniqueness of one's individual inputs to the collective product. In most of the tasks used in social loafing research (for example, shouting and clapping, pumping air), individuals' inputs to the group product overlap or are redundant with those of their co-workers. This redundancy in inputs may lead individuals to feel that their inputs are unneeded or that their inputs will have little impact on the group performance. However, when individuals are generating unique products (for example, generating unusual uses for a unique object that other group members are not given), they are less likely to view their inputs as overlapping with those of their co-workers. Indeed, several studies have shown that individuals are less likely to engage in social loafing when their inputs to the collective product are made unique.

C. Expectations of Co-worker Performance

Expectations that group members have for how well their co-workers will perform may also influence motivation in collective settings. These expectations could be developed on the basis of co-workers' abilities or efforts, on interpersonal trust levels, or on other inferences made about group members. For many tasks, when an individual expects their co-workers to perform very well, then the final group outcome is not as dependent on their individual performance as when they expect their co-workers to perform poorly.

Consistent with this logic, several recent studies have found that individuals may actually increase their collective effort when they expect their co-workers to perform poorly on a meaningful task, an effect referred to as social compensation. These recent findings are in contrast to an initial study that reported a matching effect, such that individuals tended to work only as hard as they expected their partner to work. However, this initial study confounded the confederate co-worker's statement of her intended effort with her evaluation of the task. When task meaningfulness is held constant and high, participants tend to socially loaf when working with a co-worker who is expected to perform well and tend to socially compensate when working with a co-worker who is expected to perform poorly. A number of factors may interact with expectations of co-worker performance to determine when social loafing or social compensation will occur. For example, expectancy-value logic would suggest that social compensation is more likely to occur when individuals are working on meaningful tasks, when group size is small, and when the individual must continue as a member of the group. Research addressing these issues is currently in progress. [*See* EXPECTATION.]

D. Task Meaningfulness and Task Importance

Recently, a number of social loafing researchers have examined the impact that factors such as task attractiveness, task uniqueness, task meaningfulness, and personal involvement may have on individual effort in groups. These studies compare individual effort across coactive and collective settings on tasks that are designed to be viewed as relatively more or less meaningful or important. For example, one study manipulated personal involvement by having participants list their thoughts in response to a proposal to institute comprehensive exams at either the student's university (high personal involvement) or another, distant university (low personal involvement). Social loafing was only found in the low personal involvement condition. Another recent study found that social loafing was eliminated when participants were provided with incentives to work hard on the task. The findings of these studies suggest that the degree to which an individual is willing to exert effort may depend on the relative importance they attach to the task or the degree to which they view performing the task as pleasant or aversive. Consistent with expectancy-value theories, participants are less likely to loaf when they are doing something that they think is meaningful or important.

E. Group Cohesiveness and Group Identity

Another factor that might influence the likelihood of loafing is the importance of the group to the individual. It seems reasonable that when working with friends, teammates, or highly respected co-workers, individuals are more likely to be concerned with the outcome of the group performance and are less likely to loaf. Several theoretical viewpoints support such reasoning. For example, social identity theory suggests that people may obtain a positive social identity through the accomplishments of groups to which they belong, and group-level versions of social comparison theory suggest that individuals not only compare themselves with other individuals in order to obtain self-validation, but they also compare the groups to which they belong to other groups for the same reason. These perspectives all suggest that working in cohesive groups enhances individuals' concern for the evaluation of their group's performance. In expectancy-value terminology, working in cohesive groups increases the valence of rewards associated with favorable group outcomes. Although only a few studies have directly examined group cohesiveness, there is initial evidence that individuals are less likely to loaf in cohesive groups. In addition, the overall magnitude of social loafing is typically smaller in studies using participants that know each other than in studies using strangers as participants.

F. Group Level Comparisons

In a similar manner, providing individuals with a standard with which to compare their group's performance might also reduce or eliminate social loafing. When a group-level standard is provided, a superordinate group identity may be activated. An individual's concern for their group's performance might be enhanced even in noncohesive groups when a group-level standard is provided, because the group comparison has implications for the individual's self-evaluation. Consistent with this reasoning, several studies have shown that social loafing can be eliminated when a clear group-level comparison standard is provided. [*See* SOCIAL COMPARISON.]

G. Group Size

On most tasks, as group size increases, group performance becomes less dependent on the performance of any one individual. Therefore, performing in increasingly larger groups might lead individuals to feel that their outcomes are becoming increasingly less dependent on their efforts, thereby leading to increased social loafing. Indeed, most of the theories of social loafing would predict that individuals would be more likely to loaf in larger, rather than smaller groups, albeit for potentially different reasons. When group size is examined within individual studies, only weak support is found for a group size effect. In particular, two studies have found increased social loafing with increased group size, whereas seven additional studies have not found significant differences. However, recent meta-analytic results suggest that group size may indeed have a consistent effect. When the magnitude of social loafing was examined across all studies and group size was used as a predictor, a clear pattern emerged such that the overall amount of social loafing was larger as group size increased.

H. Gender

Recent gender research seems to suggest that women tend to be more group- or collectively oriented than men. For example, research on gender stereotypes has demonstrated that men are expected to possess high levels of agentic qualities (such as being independent and assertive), whereas women are expected to possess high levels of communal qualities (such as being friendly, unselfish, and concerned with others). Similarly, research conducted in small group settings has repeatedly shown that men tend to specialize in activity oriented toward task completion, whereas women tend to specialize in activity oriented toward meeting interpersonal demands within the group. Taken together, these findings suggest that men appear to be oriented toward individualistic and competitive concerns, whereas women appear to be oriented toward interpersonal and cooperative concerns. Extending this logic to social loafing suggests that women are more likely to view performing on collective tasks as important. Thus, while both sexes are likely to engage in social loafing, women might tend to loaf less than men. The empirical literature generally supports these conclusions. A number of studies have found significant levels of social loafing by both male and female participants. However, the magnitude of social loafing is often lower for women than for men, a pattern that becomes especially clear when comparing across all studies meta-analytically.

I. Culture

In a similar manner, the degree to which the dominant culture from which subject populations were selected emphasizes individualistic versus collectivistic concerns appears to moderate social loafing. Eastern or Oriental culture is often depicted as group- or socially oriented, whereas Western or American culture is often depicted as individualistically oriented. Therefore, individuals from Eastern cultures are more likely to view performing well on collective tasks as important than are individuals from Western cultures. A number of studies have examined social loafing cross-culturally, comparing effort levels in American participants to effort levels of participants in Japan, China, Taiwan, and other nations. Although there are exceptions in single studies, this research generally finds that individuals in Eastern cultures also engage in social loafing, but to a lesser degree than do individuals in Western cultures.

V. RELATIONSHIPS BETWEEN SOCIAL LOAFING AND OTHER PHENOMENA

A. Social Facilitation

Social facilitation refers to enhanced performance when working in the presence of others. Various theories associated with social facilitation suggest that the presence of others increases drive, arousal, or distraction, leading to improved performance on simple or well-learned tasks but leading to decreased performance on difficult or novel tasks. Both social loafing and social facilitation are concerned with the effects of the presence of others on performance and yet social loafing suggests that this presence decreases performance whereas social facilitation suggests that this presence increases performance for some tasks but decreases performance for other tasks.

The key to resolving this discrepancy appears to be in specifying whether the other people present are coactors (others who work on the same task but do not combine their outputs with the individual's) or co-workers (others who are working on the same task and combining their outputs with the individual's). Coactors serve as additional sources of social impact, whereas co-workers serve as co-targets of social impact. Therefore, in the social facilitation paradigm the number of individuals present across alone and coaction conditions is varied, whereas the number present across coactive and collective conditions in social loafing is held constant. As a result of this difference, explanations of social facilitation that rely on mere presence and distraction cannot explain social loafing, because the number of subjects present across conditions (and therefore the amount of drive, arousal, or distraction) remains constant. As previously mentioned, however, evaluation potential explanations may be able to account for both social loafing and social facilitation effects. As suggested by the arousal reduction viewpoint, the presence of others may serve to reduce the arousal associated with evaluation potential when these others are viewed as co-targets of an outside influence agent. Therefore, although it is perfectly reasonable to discuss social loafing and social facilitation as distinct phenomena due to their differing treatments of the presence of others, these two viewpoints are closely related. Future research might seek to specify the degree to which these two phenomena can be viewed as opposite effects with regard to evaluation potential.

B. Social Dilemmas

A social dilemma refers to a situation in which individual interests are at odds with group interests such that behaviors that are beneficial or reinforcing to the individual are detrimental to the group. Although the problems of social loafing and social dilemmas are typically treated separately and tend to use somewhat different research paradigms, there exists considerable conceptual overlap between these two areas. Recently, a handful of researchers have suggested possible relationships between social loafing and social dilemmas. At a general level, a social dilemma can be viewed as a reduction in individual effort to manage pooled resources and to consider long-term outcomes. Similarly, social loafing can be viewed as a social dilemma in which reducing one's effort at a task is a form of defecting from the group. Thus, both social loafing and social dilemma researchers are concerned with factors influencing the likelihood that individual behavior of one form or another will be detrimental to the group over time. Several methodological differences make it difficult to directly integrate social loafing and social dilemma research findings. As just one example, social dilemma studies typically do not include coactive control conditions with which to compare individual efforts within the group context. However, research in each area does produce novel insights for the other area.

C. Social Inhibition

A variety of situations have been found in which the presence of others serves to inhibit people from behaving as they would if they were alone. For example, members of groups are less likely than are individuals to help a victim in need, answer an intercom for a missing person, or take a free hamburger coupon in an elevator. One possible way to view these findings is as a reduction in individual effort in collectives highly similar to social loafing. However, a careful analysis suggests that the two phenomena differ in several respects and that they cannot be explained by the same underlying causes despite their superficial similarity. Specifically, (1) the groups in social inhibition studies are not true collectives in that individual outputs are not pooled into one group product, (2) social inhibition involves exercising restraint from doing what one would ordinarily do, whereas social loafing involves indulging in a socially undesirable behavior, and (3) whereas social loafing settings make individual actions less noticeable, social inhibition settings make individual actions more noticeable.

VI. CONCLUSIONS AND FUTURE DIRECTIONS

Individuals tend to engage in social loafing when working collectively. Social loafing appears to be moderate in magnitude and generalizable across tasks and subject populations. The tendency to engage in social loafing is moderated by a large number of variables, highlighting a number of conditions under which social loafing should be more or less likely to occur. For example, individuals are more likely to engage in social loafing when their individual outputs cannot be evaluated collectively, when working on tasks that are perceived as low in meaningfulness or personal involvement, when a group-level comparison standard is not available, when working with strangers, when they expect their co-workers to perform well, and when their inputs to the collective outcome are redundant with those of other group members. In addition, social loafing is robust across gender, culture, and tasks, although the magnitude of the effect is lower for women and for subjects from Eastern cultures.

Despite these potential mechanisms for reducing or eliminating the effect, social loafing is still likely to have serious consequences for a variety of everyday collective settings. First, social loafing is robust across both maximizing and optimizing tasks and across tasks that demand different kinds of effort. Second, although the magnitude of the effect is reduced among women and among individuals in Eastern cultures, significant levels of social loafing are still found for these subgroups. Thus, the effect is not restricted to laboratory studies of American males. Third, although social loafing is frequently eliminated when participants' scores cannot be evaluated collectively and when highly meaningful tasks are used, it is important to recognize that, in many real world contexts, individual inputs cannot be reliably identified or evaluated and people are frequently asked to work on mundane or uninspiring tasks. Even within occupations that appear to have a great deal of intrinsic value, at least some important aspects of the work are likely to be repetitive or dull. Finally, although several studies suggest that social loafing might be eliminated in highly cohesive groups, mere acquaintance with one's co-workers may not be sufficient to eliminate the effect. In many work settings, individuals do not know their co-workers very well or do not interact with them frequently enough to develop high levels of cohesiveness. Thus, social loafing is a problem that is likely to manifest itself in a number of everyday contexts.

The tendency of research to focus on limiting conditions for social loafing, rather than on underlying process, may have led inevitably to an erroneous view that social loafing is inconsequential. Nevertheless, this tendency to focus on moderating variables does have the positive consequence of suggesting a number of ways in which social loafing might be reduced or overcome in natural settings: Providing individuals with feedback about their own performance or the performance of their work group, monitoring individual performance or making such performance identifiable, assigning meaningful tasks, making tasks unique such that individuals feel more responsibility for their work, enhancing the cohesiveness of work groups, and making individuals feel that their contributions to the task are necessary and not irrelevant might all serve, under some conditions, to reduce or eliminate social loafing.

Future research could profitably proceed at a number of levels. An especially pressing need is to further substantiate social loafing outside of the laboratory in real-world settings such as industry, committees, juries, partnerships, and interpersonal relationships. Once the effect has been documented in such settings, attempts could be made to determine whether the moderating variables isolated in laboratory studies apply to other contexts as well. Additional research could further address the generalizability of social loafing, in terms of both dispositional and situational factors. Among the questions that might be more directly addressed are the following: What are the long-term effects of working collectively? Do people (in general, or particular subclasses) prefer tasks on which they can loaf? Is social loafing adaptive in some cases or does it allow individuals to devote their energies more fully to aspects of tasks that are within their particular domains of mastery and expertise? How might social loafing manifest itself within interacting groups such as decision making teams or juries, and how might individual efforts be measured in these contexts? Is it necessarily the case that the quality of the work suffers when people loaf? Can certain reward structures or goal-setting procedures reduce or eliminate social loafing? How aware are people of their social loafing in different settings? Does knowledge that one loafs in collectives affect the likelihood of loafing? These are just a few of the questions that future research can attempt to answer. Some of these questions form the basis of current, ongoing research on social loafing. The research reviewed in this summary supplies a consistent and highly diverse body of work from which to continue future investigations.

Bibliography

Harkins, S. G. (1987). Social loafing and social facilitation. *J. Exp. Soc. Psychol.* **23,** 1–18.

Harkins, S. G., and Szymanski, K. (1989). Social loafing and group evaluation. *J. Pers. Soc. Psychol.* **56,** 934–941.

Jackson, J. M., and Williams, K. D. (1985). Social loafing on difficult tasks: Working collectively can improve performance. *J. Pers. Soc. Psychol.* **49,** 937–942.

Karau, S. J., and Williams, K. D. (1993). Social loafing: A meta-analytic review and theoretical integration. *J. Pers. Soc. Psychol.* **65,** 681–706.

Kravitz, D. A., and Martin, B. (1986). Ringelmann rediscovered: The original article. *J. Pers. Soc. Psychol.* **50,** 936–941.

Latané, B., Williams, K., and Harkins, S. (1979). Many hands make light the work: The causes and consequences of social loafing. *J. Pers. Soc. Psychol.* **37,** 822–832.

Shepperd, J. A. (1993). Productivity loss in performance groups: A motivation analysis. *Psychol. Bull.* **113,** 67–81.

Williams, K. D., and Karau, S. J. (1991). Social loafing and social compensation: The effects of expectations of co-worker performance. *J. Pers. Soc. Psychol.* **61,** 570–581.

Social Support

Stephen J. Lepore
Carnegie Mellon University

Glossary

Buffering hypothesis Theory that social support is only beneficial to people who are under stress.

Invisible support Social support that is provided to a person without his or her awareness.

Social network The people with whom one has some form of regular social contact.

Social support Resources from the social environment that can be beneficial to psychological and physical health.

Support functions The quality of social relations a person has, as indicated by the material, emotional, and informational resources those social relations provide.

Support structures Quantitative indicators of the form, or nature, of a social network, such as its size or the frequency of contact with different members.

SOCIAL SUPPORT is the actual or perceived availability of resources in one's social environment that can be used for comfort or aid, particularly in times of distress. Social support is provided by one's social network, which is all of the people with whom one has some form of regular social contact. Most social networks include family, friends, and co-workers. Not all social networks are supportive, but those that are supportive tend to bolster the health and well-being of the recipients of the support. Social support appears to enhance individuals' physical and psychological health directly and indirectly by reducing the negative effects of stressors on health.

I. TYPES OF SOCIAL SUPPORT

Social networks have different dimensions that may influence the availability of social support or the effectiveness of social support in maintaining individuals' health and well-being. Two dimensions of primary importance are the *structural* and *functional* characteristics of social networks. Structural characteristics are quantitative indicators of the form, or nature, of a social network. Structural measures of support assess the degree to which individuals are socially integrated or isolated in their family and community. Structural aspects of social networks include its size, the amount of contact a person has with social network members, or how many people in a network know one another. Functional characteristics are quantitative indicators of the provisions, or resources, available from a social network. In other words, functional aspects of social networks are the things that people do for one another, such as provide emotional and material aid.

Social support depends on both the availability of a social network and the provision of particular resources through that network. Obviously, with a network size of zero one cannot receive any social support. Indeed, differences in social support availability might explain the different health prospects for socially isolated versus socially integrated people: as a group, social isolates have more health problems than do people who are integrated in a social network. Aside from such extreme situations, social network functions usually are more critical to an individuals' health than are structural factors, such as size or type of relations between social network members.

Social networks appear to be supportive, or helpful, in four primary ways: (a) they provide emotional comfort and enhance self-esteem; (b) they provide financial or other material aid; (c) they provide information or advice; and (d) they provide assistance or instrumental help. People often benefit from social support if it is tailored to a particular problem. For

Encyclopedia of Human Behavior, Volume 4

example, a person who needs help making a mortgage payment will probably get more benefit from a friend with money to loan than from one with advice to give. However, emotional support, or confirmation that one is loved and esteemed by others, appears to be beneficial to many individuals and under a number of diverse situations. People who cannot get financial support from friends can benefit psychologically by confiding in friends about their financial problems and worries. It is often comforting to have someone to talk to about one's problems, even if that person cannot solve the problems.

Finally, it should be noted that social support is not always directly provided by the social network. Sometimes people benefit from having supportive social relations without having any direct exchange of support. The mere perception that support is available is often enough to boost a person's morale or to reduce the negative impact of a stressful situation. Support also can protect individuals' mental and physical health when they are unaware that support has been provided. "Invisible support," or support that occurs without the recipients' knowledge, may protect people by preventing exposure to stressors. For instance, one could protect loved ones, or provide invisible support, by keeping bad news from them. Thus, the supportive functions of social networks are not always tangible to the recipient, but are nevertheless effective in maintaining the well-being of that person.

II. RELATION OF SOCIAL SUPPORT TO PHYSICAL AND PSYCHOLOGICAL HEALTH

Social support has been linked to lower levels of mortality, morbidity, and psychological symptomatology. Nearly a century ago, sociologist Emile Durkheim observed that more socially isolated people had a higher risk of committing suicide than people who were more socially integrated, or who had a number of regular social contacts. This was one of the earliest clues that interpersonal relationships might have a role in fostering and maintaining physical and psychological health. Since Durkheim's study, there has been ever-growing evidence that people who are more socially isolated, or less socially integrated, have more physical and psychological health problems, as well as higher rates of mortality. Moreover, the differential mortality rates cannot be explained by differences in major health-risk factors, such as blood pressure, cigarette smoking, or cholesterol levels in isolated versus integrated people.

It is possible that more socially integrated people have lower mortality risk than isolated people because there are health benefits associated with being socially integrated. There is some evidence that people who have more social ties to family or their community have low rates of psychiatric disorders, accidents, pregnancy complications, and tuberculosis. People who are more socially integrated also appear to be at lower risk for heart disease and death from heart disease than are their isolated counterparts. For example, women who are less socially integrated appear to be at greater risk for ischemic heart disease; men who are less socially integrated are likely to live longer after surviving a heart attack; Japanese-American men who are socially integrated appear to be less susceptible to coronary heart disease; and patients with myocardial infarctions are more likely to be isolated than are nonpatients.

The associations between social integration and health outcomes that range from psychiatric disorders to mortality suggest that there are health benefits derived from having social ties. Whether the health benefits of social integration are due to the supportive functions provided by social networks is not entirely clear. It may be that some other factor that is associated with social integration or social isolation is responsible for the different health outcomes of integrated versus isolated individuals. For example, isolated people may be economically disadvantaged relative to more integrated people. If isolated people are also indigent, their health problems may be explained by a lack of affordable or adequate health care. To determine whether social support actually has a role in maintaining or promoting health, it is important to look directly at the relation between the quality of social support that people receive and their health status. Knowing that a person has regular contact with their social network, or that they have a social network, only indicates that a person can potentially receive social support. Many people who have frequent contact with their social networks may perceive their network as unsupportive or, worse yet, view their social ties as a source of stress.

There is emerging evidence that social support per se, and not some other factor related to social integration or isolation, can influence physical health. However, scientific investigations of the relation between social support and health do not always present consistent or clear results. For example, one researcher has found that people who believe that they have adequate social support are at lower risk of mortality than people who believe they have inadequate social support. In contrast, other researchers have found that people who are satisfied with their marriage and social interactions with others do not have a lower risk of mortality than do their counterparts who are dissatisfied with their social relations. There are several reasons why studies present an inconsistent picture of the effects of social support on health. A primary reason is that social support is conceptualized and measured differently across studies. The remaining discussion will present additional evidence on the relation between support and health, but with particular attention given to the type of support and the mechanisms through which support is expected to influence health outcomes.

III. EXPLAINING THE POSITIVE EFFECTS OF SOCIAL SUPPORT

A. Social Support as Protection from Stressors

A central theory on the role of social support in health is that support functions by protecting, or "buffering," people from the inimical effects of life stressors. According to the stress-buffering theory, social support will have positive effects on the mental and physical health of people under high levels of stress, but have no effects on people with less or no stress. The rationale behind this theory is that social support somehow helps people to cope with the stress of life, thereby reducing the health toll of stress. People who have social support available to them but have no particular need for it would not be expected to gain any immediate health benefits from that support. [*See* STRESS.]

The buffering theory has been tested mainly with psychological rather than physical health outcomes. One of the reasons that so little is known about the role of social support in physical disease outcomes is that many of the major diseases, such as cancer and heart disease, develop over many years and are difficult to track. Thus, researchers are seldom able to identify and assess the social support networks of people before they develop a particular disease. Mental illnesses, on the other hand, have a relatively short onset and progression. Therefore, it is easier to test how social support influences mental illnesses than physical illnesses.

The stress-buffering effects of social support have been tested using both structural and functional measures of social support. Studies using structural measures, such as marital status and number of close friends, have consistently shown buffering effects on psychological health. People who are married or have a close friendship tend to experience less depression under stress than do people who lack significant social ties. People who have frequent contact with close friends during personal crises, such as health problems, divorce, and unemployment, also are happier and more satisfied with life than people who have relatively little contact with close friends. Although having close interpersonal relationships appears to protect people from the adverse psychological effects of stressors, having casual social connections does not seem to buffer stress. Casual social ties may develop through church membership, interaction with neighbors, or participation in clubs and organizations. People who have greater access to such ties tend to have less psychological distress and greater morale than people with relatively little access to such ties, but this is true regardless of the amount of stress in their lives. Thus, it appears that close social ties may be beneficial to mental health because they provide supports that help people to cope with stress, whereas more casual social ties may be beneficial to psychological well-being because they serve other functions, such as providing companionship.

There is only limited evidence that social support protects people from stress-related physical illnesses. For example, a study of male factory workers showed that workers with high levels of job-related stress had fewer health complaints if they perceived their spouse and supervisor to be supportive rather than unsupportive. A Swedish study has shown that greater levels of social involvement with co-workers appears to reduce the negative effects of work stress on coronary heart disease prevalence in men and women. Finally, an Israeli study has shown that highly anxious men who perceive their wives to be supportive have a lower incidence of angina pectoris than men who do not perceive their wives to be supportive. Again, it appears that close, or significant, social ties are most beneficial. There is no strong evidence that casual social ties, or simply the number of social ties one has, can reduce the negative effects of stress on health complaints. [*See* STRESS AND ILLNESS.]

B. Social Support and Health Behaviors

Social support networks may influence health by regulating individuals' health-related behaviors. For example, in contrast to relatively isolated people, people who are more socially integrated tend to smoke less, drink less alcohol, avoid between-meal snacks, eat breakfast, maintain a healthy weight, get adequate sleep, and engage in regular physical activity. Among the elderly, degree of social integration and contact, as well as perceived amount of social support available, is associated with better self-care. Among people trying to quit smoking, those who feel that they have others with whom they can discuss their problems are able to abstain from smoking for a longer period than those who do not feel that they have such confidant relations.

Social networks also may promote health by encouraging individuals to seek needed medical attention or to comply with medical treatments. For instance, the degree to which pregnant women consult with friends about health care issues has been shown to influence the degree to which they seek prenatal care. More generally, people who have relatively frequent interactions with friends tend to obtain preventive health care and seek help quickly when they are ill. Finally, compared to people who believe they have relatively little support from their spouse, friends, and health care providers, those who believe that they have high levels of support are more motivated to adhere to their medical regimen and are more acutely aware of the negative consequences of noncompliance. In turn, the heightened adherence motivation and awareness of the costs of noncompliance are associated with greater compliance. One way that support may protect people from stress is by increasing their medical adherence. For example, in a study of hypertension patients, those facing many life stressors were more likely to miss appointments with their physician than were those who had little stress. However, stressed patients who believed they had much support from significant others were less likely to miss appointments than stressed patients who felt they had little support.

C. Social Support and Physiological Functioning

If social support reduces stress-related health problems, it is possible that it does so by influencing physiological responses to stressors. A number of bodily changes tend to occur in people confronted by stressors. For instance, stress tends to activate the sympathetic nervous system, which causes increases in heart rate, blood pressure, and generalized arousal. The physiological responses to stressors are part of the body's coping mechanism. By increasing blood flow away from the organs and to the muscles, individuals are prepared to "fight" or "flee" in response to a stressor. Increased arousal also allows people to be more vigilant or attentive to their environment or threatening stimuli.

The most common biological markers of stress are increased heart rate and blood pressure, and elevated levels of hormones known as cortisol and catecholamines. Catecholamines are basically responsible for increasing bodily arousal, whereas cortisol is primarily useful in reducing swelling in tissue that might be damaged during fight or flight. Although increased arousal and production of catecholamines and cortisol are adaptive responses to stressors, they also can have harmful effects on health. For example, extreme levels of stress-induced arousal might lead to heart attacks and chronically high levels of stress-induced hormone production might contribute to heart disease. If social support can dampen the body's reaction to stressors, it might prevent stress-related illnesses and disease processes. Several laboratory studies have shown that people who are challenged by acute stressors, such as giving a speech or being socially harassed, experience smaller blood pressure and heart rate increases if they are in the presence of a supportive person than if they are alone or in the presence of a nonsupportive person. However, there is no evidence to date that social support in naturalistic settings, where people can experience very severe and repeated stressors, acts to reduce stress responding in the same way that it does in laboratory settings, with relatively mild stressors. [*See* CATECHOLAMINES AND BEHAVIOR.]

Social support also might be beneficial to health by enhancing immune system functioning. The immune system protects people from harmful viruses and antigens, which are noxious or toxic materials that enter the body. The most familiar defense mechanism of the immune system is the production of white blood cells that can circulate throughout the body to fight infections. When people are under stress, the immune system becomes compromised, producing fewer and less effective immune cells than normal. Findings from several studies suggest that social support may enhance immune functioning. For example, lonely people have poorer immune functioning than nonlonely people. In addition, higher social support appears to be related to enhanced immune functioning among the elderly and spouses of cancer patients.

IV. CONCLUSIONS

People who are socially integrated appear to be at lower risk for a variety of psychological and physical health problems, as well as mortality, than people who are relatively isolated. The psychological and health benefits of social integration are partly attributable to the supportive functions provided by social networks. People who receive social support from their social network, particularly if it is from significant others, such as spouses and family members, tend to have fewer psychological problems than people who do not receive support. To date, there is more evidence linking social support to psychological well-being than to physical health. However, several studies suggest that social support does play a role in physical health.

Several theoretical models have been posited to explain how social support can influence physical and psychological health. Social support appears to be particularly beneficial to individuals under stress. Therefore, support may operate by helping people to cope with stressors, which can be detrimental to physical and psychological health. Support also might function by promoting healthy behaviors, discouraging risk-taking and other unhealthy behaviors, and encouraging people to seek needed medical care or to adhere to medical regimens. Finally, social support appears to reduce stress-related arousal, dampen the production of catecholamines and cortisol, and to enhance immune functioning. These latter physiological effects of social support may prove to have health benefits.

Bibliography

Cohen, S., and Wills, T. A. (1985). Stress, social support, and the buffering hypothesis. *Psychol. Bull.* **98,** 310–357.

House, J. S., Landis, K. R., and Umberson, D. (1988). Social relationships and health. *Science* **241,** 540–545.

Vaux, A. (1988). "Social Support: Theory, Research, and Intervention." Praeger, New York.

Social Values

James K. Beggan
University of Louisville

Scott T. Allison
University of Richmond

Glossary

Competitors Individuals who tend to approach interdependence situations with the preference to maximize relative gain.

Cooperators Individuals who tend to approach interdependence situations with the preference to maximize joint gain.

Decomposed game An instrument used to assess social values that eliminates most social and strategic influences on responding.

Individualists Individuals who tend to approach interdependence situations with the preference to maximize own gain, regardless of the outcomes that are received by others.

Interdependence A situation in which an actor's outcomes depend on his or her own behavior and the behavior of one or more others; similarly, the others' outcomes depend on their own behavior and the behavior of the first actor.

Might vs morality hypothesis An interpretation of social values based on the assumption that people with different social values apply different meanings to the cooperation–competition dimension.

Prisoner's dilemma A choice situation where the rational pursuit of one's own interests can lead to outcomes that are suboptimal for the self and for others.

Social dilemma A choice situation that involves more than two people with a structure similar to that of a prisoner's dilemma.

Tit-for-tat A strategy where an actor who is interdependent with another selects the choice that the other person selected previously.

Triangle hypothesis An explanation for choices made in a prisoner's dilemma based on the assumption that people with different social values have different expectations regarding the behavior of others.

SOCIAL VALUES are stable preferences for certain patterns of outcome distributions to oneself and others. An example is the preference to gain as much as possible for oneself, regardless of what happens to others. In contrast, an individual may prefer a situation where the collective welfare of multiple parties is maximized, even at some personal cost. As will be described in greater detail below, there are a number of other types of social values. Social values have been shown to have a significant impact on choice behavior and decision-making in social situations.

I. ASSUMPTIONS UNDERLYING SOCIAL VALUES RESEARCH

To understand the operation of social values, it is necessary to make three assumptions about human behavior. These assumptions appear justified, as they are consistent with a large body of existing research, as well as human intuition. The first assumption is that when people evaluate outcomes, they operate according to the principle of hedonism. People generally prefer more of a good thing than less. For example, a large salary is superior to a small one. By the same principle, people prefer to minimize negative outcomes. A small pay cut is better than a large one.

The second assumption in social values research is that social relationships influence how outcomes are evaluated. This is a crucial assumption of the social values literature because it highlights the interpersonal nature of values. Further, this assumption differentiates the social values perspectives from other analyses of values that do not emphasize these social aspects. An individual may assess his or her outcomes in terms of both what he or she personally receives (i.e., in terms of the principle of hedonism) and what another person receives. Consider, for example, the husband who sees his wife's raise as an opportunity for both of them to have the roof of their house reshingled. In this example, the husband sees his wife's good fortune as a gain for himself. In contrast, the wife's sister may become jealous and view her sibling's good luck as a loss.

The third assumption in social values research is that individuals will behave in ways that allow them to obtain their preferred pattern of outcome distributions to the self and others. Thus, a husband who desires to make his wife happy will pick a restaurant he knows she likes. However, he will most likely make sure that it is a restaurant he likes as well.

II. TYPES OF SOCIAL VALUES

Researchers have identified a number of social values. These social values can be conceptualized as differing in terms of what one person receives relative to what another person receives. As a stylistic note, although social values can be considered for interdependence structures that involve two or more people, most work on the topic has focused on the dyad, or two-person group. This convention is adopted in the present discussion of social values. However, it is important to keep in mind that the present analysis could be extended to the interactions of three or more persons.

The three most common social values are cooperation, competition, and individualism. In cooperation, an individual is most satisfied with outcomes that maximize joint gain, measured as the sum of the individual gains. In competition, an individual is most satisfied with maximization of relative gain, defined as an outcome that provides as much more as possible to the self relative to others. Finally, in individualism, a person is happiest with an outcome that maximizes own gain, regardless of what is received by others.

Two additional social values of interest are altruism and aggression. In altruism, the actor prefers outcomes that maximize the outcomes of others, with no regard for his or her own outcomes. Aggression is the inverse of altruism. In aggression, the individual prefers outcomes that minimize the outcomes of the others, with no regard for his or her own outcomes. [*See* AGGRESSION; ALTRUISM AND HELPING BEHAVIOR.]

Three other social values have been defined at a theoretical level but do not appear frequently in the general population. Martyrdom refers to a preference for an outcome that maximizes the relative gain of others in comparison to the self. Masochism defines a preference to minimize one's own outcomes, regardless of the outcomes afforded to others. Finally, sado-masochism is the preference for outcomes that maximize the joint loss between an individual and other persons.

Researchers have also focused on other kinds of outcome distributions to the self and others. Examples of these include values such as equality (minimizing the difference between an actor's outcomes and the outcomes of others) and equity (making the ratio of an actor's costs and rewards proportional to the ratio of costs and rewards for others). Because the theoretical conceptualization of social values presented in the present paper has not considered these types of values to any great extent, they will not be examined in detail.

III. SOCIAL VALUES AND INTERDEPENDENCE

The preferences people have for certain patterns of outcome distributions (i.e., their social values) influence their behavior in situations of social interdependence. Social interdependence exists when the outcomes two (or more) people receive are determined by the behaviors of both of them. More specifically, in a two-person case, the outcomes actor A receives depends on both A's behavior and B's behavior. Similarly, the outcomes actor B receives are a function of both B's behavior and A's behavior. A large number of social situations are marked by this quality of social interdependence. The relationships between siblings, husbands and wives, the faculty in a psychology department, and the nations of the earth are all interdependent to a greater or lesser degree. People's social values influence the kinds of outcome distributions they find most attractive. Because people are assumed to behave in such a way that they will obtain their most attractive outcomes, social values can therefore be assumed to affect behavior in interdependent situations.

To illustrate how social values can influence behavior in situations of social interdependence, it is necessary to create an appropriate interdependence structure. A convenient way to accomplish this goal is to utilize a two-person, two-choice matrix game, such as the one presented in Table I. The "actor" can make either choice X or Y. The "other" can make either choice A or B. The outcome afforded to each player is a joint function of their simultaneous choices. The actor's points appear to the left of the comma for each cell in the matrix; the other's points are to the right of the comma. Thus, if the actor makes choice X and the other makes choice B, the actor will receive 1 point and the other will receive 4 points. Assuming the points represent positively valenced items, this outcome is very rewarding to the other but not very appealing to the actor. If the actor makes choice Y and the other makes choice A, the above outcomes for the players are reversed. On the other hand, if the actor makes choice X and the other makes choice A, then each player receives 3 points. Finally, if the players make the B–Y choice, they each receive 2 points.

Although the matrix situation presented in Table I seems rather straightforward, it actually represents a very complex social relationship that has received extensive study by economists, political scientists, and psychologists. Literally thousands of experiments on social interaction have been conducted using matrix games (such as the one in Table I) as idealized representations of human interaction. One reason for their popularity is the belief that the matrix game distills a basic quality of human social interaction, namely, its interdependent nature. A second reason is that the point values that create the interdependence structure can be manipulated very easily. By adjusting the point values in certain ways, scientists can create interdependence structures with a variety of properties. A third reason for the popularity of the matrix format is that it is simple to administer. It is quite easy to bring a person or group of people into a laboratory and ask them to make choices.

TABLE I
A Two-Person, Two-Choice Interdependence Game

	Other's choices	
Actor's choices	Choice A	Choice B
Choice X	3,3	1,4
Choice Y	4,1	2,2

Probably the most important reason the matrix game has received so much attention is that in games with certain interdependence structures, it is unclear which choice is rational. This creates a significant choice dilemma for players. The name given to such a matrix is the prisoner's dilemma. (Note: the matrix is called a prisoner's dilemma because it was originally presented in terms of choices faced by two prisoners.) The matrix presented in Table I has the structure of a prisoner's dilemma.

To understand how this matrix creates a problem in defining rationality, consider the perspective of the actor presented in Table I. The actor faces the problem of whether to choose X or Y. The choice of X will afford the actor either 3 points (if the other picks A) or 1 point (if the other picks B). Compare these outcomes with what will occur if the actor chooses Y. In this case, the actor will receive 4 points (if the other chooses A) or 2 points (if the other chooses B). From the standpoint of a rational actor, it seems as if it is more logical to choose Y and receive either 4 or 2 points rather than 3 or 1. However, because the matrix is symmetrical, the other will go through a similar thought process. If both players follow this logic, the mutual outcome is that the two players will end up in the Y–B cell, with 2 points each rather than the more profitable X–A cell. The dilemma of the prisoner's dilemma, then, is that a rational individual decision produces a suboptimal joint outcome.

Because of the potential for gain at the expense of the other, the Y and B choices are often termed the competitive or defecting choices. Because of the potential for maximum joint outcomes, the A and X choices are termed the cooperative or prosocial choices. Research on the relationship between social values and behavior in prisoner's dilemmas has shown that cooperators tend to pick the A or X (i.e., the cooperative or prosocial) option. This decision puts them at risk of being exploited but promises to afford greater joint benefit, assuming the other party also cooperates. In contrast, competitors tend to make the B or Y (i.e., competitive or defecting) choice. This decision will afford them maximum relative gain, if they can exploit the other. At the very least, it prevents them from receiving less than the other.

To understand why cooperators tend to behave as they do in the prisoner's dilemma (as well as other situations), consider how someone with a cooperative orientation would view the points displayed in the matrix. Because a cooperator attempts to maximize joint gain, he or she would add the values that accrue to each person. From the point of view of a cooperator, the X–A choice provides 6 points worth of joint benefit. The X–B and Y–A choices provide 5 points. The Y–B choice provides 4 points. Thus, for a cooperator the most attractive pair of choices is the X–A pair.

Contrast this perspective with a competitor's point of view. Someone attempting to satisfy a competitive social value would note the difference between what he or she gets and the other gets. For the X–A choice, the difference between the outcomes for the two players is 0. Likewise, the difference is 0 for the Y–B pair of choices. For a competitor, then, the only way to obtain a desired pattern of results is to make the B or Y choice (and hope that the other player makes an X or A choice, respectively).

An interesting fact is revealed when the preferred behavior of individualists is considered. Although individualists are motivated to maximize own gain (and are indifferent to the outcomes of others), in the matrix presented in Table I, the desire to maximize own gain will produce a choice identical to the one preferred by competitors: either the B or Y choice (again, with the hope that the other player makes an A or X choice, respectively). The fact that the preferred choice to satisfy competitive and individualistic goals are identical highlights an important problem faced and successfully resolved by researchers investigating social values. The problem was how to differentiate one type of value from another, given that these values must be inferred from some type of choice. This point is discussed below in greater detail.

IV. MEASURING SOCIAL VALUES

Thus far, social values have been described as preferences for a particular pattern of outcome distributions between oneself and another. Further, the definition notes that these preferences are stable across time. Therefore, it should be possible to measure a person's preferences. A number of methods have been developed to assess social values.

One method of measuring social values is to make inferences about values based on observed behavior. For example, if an individual is observed making a competitive choice, or better yet, a series of competitive choices, it might be concluded that this person's dominant social value is competitive. Although early work on social values often classified people in this fashion, this method of classification has a number of serious limitations. One important limitation is that it is often difficult to make inferences about values from observed behavior. As noted above, in the matrix game presented in Table I, the choice that maximizes own gain is confounded with the choice that maximizes relative gain.

A second limitation is based on the distinction between strategic and goal-oriented behavior. A goal-oriented behavior is an action that directly reflects an underlying social value. A strategic behavior refers to an action taken to influence another person to behave in a given manner. Making a competitive choice on a matrix game could reflect a genuine desire to gain a relative advantage over another. On the other hand, a competitive choice could also serve as retaliation to discourage future competitive behavior from another and reinforce cooperative actions. Punishing children for their transgressions is an instance of a hostile or aggressive action performed for socially beneficial reasons. Thus, a certain behavior might reflect more than one possible social value, and to the extent that it does, measurement becomes more difficult.

A third limitation in making inferences about social values from observed behavior is that researchers often use social values as the basis to predict behavior in a situation of social interdependence. It is circular to argue that an individual's social value (inferred from choice behavior on a social interdependence task) can be used to predict behavior in a social interdependence situation. To borrow from the language of the statistical tool regression analysis, the outcome variable becomes identical to the predictor variable.

To correct the limitations of the behavioral choice method, a number of researchers have developed alternative procedures to assess social values that eliminate or at least reduce the problem of distinguishing strategic and goal-oriented behavior. In addition, these procedures allow one to distinguish between different values which may be satisfied by an identical behavioral choice.

Probably the most widely used instrument to assess social values is the decomposed game (see Table II). In a decomposed game, subjects are presented with several (usually three) sets of options that provide outcomes to the self and a hypothetical

TABLE II
An Example of a Decomposed Game

	Choice		
	A	B	C
You get	55	30	60
Other gets	55	0	40

other. The subject is instructed to indicate which of the options they most prefer. This procedure is repeated over a series of trials with sets of options that differ in their point values. An individual is classified as having a particular social value if the majority of their selected options are consistent with a specific social value. To illustrate, in Table II, the left side of the table identifies who will receive a given outcome, either the self or the hypothetical other. The top of the table identifies three possible options the chooser can pick. If an individual picks choice B, this indicates a preference for 30 points for the self and 0 points for the other. Given the other available options, an individual who prefers B displays a competitive social value (a relative gain of 30 points, instead of 0 or 20). An individual trying to satisfy a cooperative motivation would prefer choice A (a joint gain of 110 points, compared to 30 or 100), whereas someone attempting to satisfy an individualistic motivation would prefer choice C (an own gain of 60 points, relative to own gain of 55 or 30).

The decomposed game technique has several advantages. First, by judicious choice of values for the trials, it is possible to distinguish a variety of subtle social values. For example, a problem with the decomposed game given in Table II is that cooperation (i.e., maximizing joint gain) is confounded with equality (i.e., both parties receive equal amounts). By using decomposed games that explicitly pit cooperative choices against equality choices, it would be possible to distinguish whether an individual had a cooperative social value or was revealing a preference for equality. Table III displays a second set of decomposed games that will accomplish this. An actor who prefers choice A, the desire to obtain 50 points for the self and 50 points for the other, rather than B, the desire to obtain 70 points for the self and 60 points for the other, reveals a preference for equality over joint gain, relative gain, or own gain maximization.

TABLE III
An Example of a Decomposed Game That Can Distinguish between Joint Gain Maximization and Equality Maximization

	Choice		
	A	B	C
You get	50	70	60
Other gets	50	60	40

A second advantage of the decomposed game format is that subjects do not actually interact with another person. As a result, the strategic aspect of the choice situation is removed. A third advantage of the decomposed game format is that it is easy to administer and score. A series of decomposed games can be completed in 10 to 15 min. With minor modifications (e.g., substituting tangible rewards for abstract points), the decomposed game measure has been used successfully with children as young as 4 years old.

The decomposed game measure also has some limitations. One important weakness is that a significant proportion of subjects do not display a clear preference for one social value and are therefore unclassifiable by the decomposed game method. A second limitation is that the decomposed game format does not accommodate the fact that people may demonstrate a variety of social values in a hierarchical fashion. For example, one person could make cooperative choices but switch to competitive ones if provided with the right opportunity. Another person might shift from making cooperative choices to individualistic ones, if presented with the right circumstances. Thus, the above two persons differ fundamentally in the structure of their cooperative social values; however, this difference would be undetected by a decomposed game measure. A third problem with the decomposed game format is similar to the one raised against classification based on actual choice behavior: the measurement technique is again very similar to the behavior that is being predicted by the measurement technique.

A second alternative method of assessing social values is based on a judgment procedure that requires subjects to evaluate the desirability of a variety of own–other outcome distributions. These ratings are used as the basis to construct a linear model that uses the values of outcomes to the self and to the other as the predictors of the desirability scores.

Because different social values will be associated with different weights assigned to the outcomes to the self and to the other, it is possible to use this judgment procedure to make very fine distinctions between different social values. This measure shares a number of advantages with the decomposed game method (e.g., because subjects evaluate own–other outcome distributions, strategic concerns are eliminated). In addition, the judgment procedure is quite different from the act of making choices in a setting of social interdependence. This reduces the validity of criticisms that the social values construct and the behavioral decisions that follow are two ways of measuring the identical construct. A disadvantage of the desirability judgment method is that it requires sophisticated techniques of statistical analysis such as regression and conjoint analysis.

V. WHEN SOCIAL VALUES AFFECT BEHAVIOR

Research on social values has focused on using the individual differences in outcome preferences to understand the sometimes wide variability in choice styles of people playing matrix games. Thus, it is not surprising that a great majority of research on social values has been conducted in the tradition of matrix games, especially the prisoner's dilemma. A general finding is that reliable differences in game play will be found among individuals with different social values. It is important to note, however, that although social values will influence behavior in interdependence settings, other factors may influence the choice persons make. In the matrix game presented in Table I, consider what might happen if the X–A cell had values of a million points each, and the points could be converted to dollars at a 1 to 1 ratio. With such high stakes, it is unlikely that even the most single-minded competitor would make such a great sacrifice to maximize relative gain.

Another situational factor that will influence game play is the behavior of the co-player. A co-player may cooperate, compete, or display some kind of mixed strategy. One mixed strategy that has received a great deal of attention is the tit-for-tat strategy. The tit-for-tat strategy is a simple rule that says, "Respond to another player the way that the other player responded to you the last time." Thus, if a co-player makes a cooperative choice, the tit-for-tat strategy dictates a cooperative choice. If an opponent behaves competitively, the tit-for-tat strategy dictates responding in kind. At the beginning of a series of choice trials, a tit-for-tat strategy cannot be used because an actor does not have information about a co-player's previous behavior. In this case, the tit-for-tat strategy opens with a cooperative choice, and then reflects an opponent's choices.

Despite its apparent simplicity, the tit-for-tat strategy affects the behavior of choice makers with different social values in different ways. More specifically, the choices of people with competitive social values are relatively unaffected by the behavior of an opponent. Given a cooperative opponent, they will make an exploitative choice to maximize relative gain. When paired with a competitive opponent, they will also make a defecting choice, to avoid falling behind. Because of their insensitivity to the behavior of opponents, competitors will also seek to exploit someone using a tit-for-tat strategy. Because a tit-for-tat strategy dictates responding in kind, the attempt to exploit will fail, and the competitor and the individual using the tit-for-tat strategy will end up deadlocked in mutual competition.

Individualists are very sensitive to the behavior of the other player. An individualist will exploit the cooperative choices of an opponent to reach the cell that provides maximum payoff to the self. If an opponent makes frequent competitive choices, the individualist will respond similarly to obtain a payoff of 2 rather than 1. However, individualists will show a high percentage of cooperative responses when paired against someone using a tit-for-tat strategy.

Even cooperators will modify their behavior if an opponent attempts to exploit them. If paired with a person using a tit-for-tat strategy or making cooperative choices, cooperators will display a high percentage of cooperative choices. However, if paired with a competitive other, cooperators shift to competitive responses.

The tendency of cooperators to behave competitively when matched against a competitor is significant from a theoretical viewpoint. This significance is based on the fact that by switching as they do, cooperators give up their most preferred outcome distribution, i.e., the maximization of joint gain. Examination of the values in Table I shows that when playing against an opponent who competes, a cooperator who cooperates will obtain a greater joint gain than a cooperator who competes (1 for self and 4 for the other, for a total of 5 vs 2 for self and 2 for the other, for a total of 4). It is likely the loss of their most preferred outcome distribution is more than made up for by being able to avoid making a "sucker" choice repeatedly.

Other research on social values has looked at how people behave in what are known as multiple-person prisoner's dilemmas or social dilemmas. These dilemmas are characterized by the same incentive structure as the prisoner's dilemma. Thus, there is a pressure to make a selfish choice that provides greater benefit to the self but runs the risk of producing inferior joint outcomes if other players behave in the same manner. In social dilemmas, however, the number of players can range from 3 to infinity. A large number of social problems have the structure of a social dilemma, such as deciding how much of a limited natural resource to use. As an example, consider the water shortage faced by much of California. The amount of water used by any one person is trivial in comparison to the total amount of water available. Thus, it is in any one person's best interests to take as much water as they desire. However, if everyone operates according to this principle, the collective outcome can be disastrous.

Although the role of social values in influencing behavior in social dilemmas has not received as much research attention relative to the prisoner's dilemma, available evidence paints a picture consistent with the results of research on the prisoner's dilemma. Empirical evidence suggests that in a social dilemma task, relative to competitors, cooperators are more likely to restrain self-interested behavior for the sake of collective interest. Competitors and individualists tend to respond to a shortage of resources by taking more. In the context of a water shortage, this means that competitors and individualists would be less likely to conserve water than cooperators. A possible motive to explain why individuals are willing to overuse a depleting resource is that they attempt to get what they can from the resource before it is exhausted, even though they recognize the potential negative long-term consequences of this decision.

Recently, researchers have extended the social values construct to other domains of social behavior. In a field study, researchers found that cooperators were more likely to donate hours of their time to a scientific investigation than either individualists or competitors. The results of this field study are wholly consistent with research on the prisoner's dilemma and social dilemmas. Further, the work contributes to demonstrating the external validity of the social values construct by suggesting that the results of laboratory investigations generalize to more realistic settings.

VI. WHY SOCIAL VALUES AFFECT BEHAVIOR

The question of what makes some people cooperative, others competitive, and still others individualistic is an important one. Although the literature on social values does not contain a definitive answer, a number of possible explanations have been suggested. One influential interpretation is known as the triangle hypothesis. According to this position, competitors believe that other people are likely to share their preference for relative gain maximization, whereas cooperators, and individualists to a lesser extent, believe there is wider variability in the possible responses of others. This assertion is known as the triangle hypothesis because the wide variability in the expectations of cooperators and individualists can be conceptualized as a base of a triangle, and the limited expectations of competitors serves as the narrow vertex of the triangle. A competitor's expectations that an opponent will compete serves also to justify a competitive stance. In contrast, because cooperators and individualists recognize that a co-player may adopt a variety of strategies, they realize that it is in their best interest to test a co-player before adopting one strategy over another.

Although a number of researchers have found support for the triangle hypothesis, other investigators have shown that to at least some extent even cooperators and individualists will also overestimate the number of people who have choice preferences like their own. However, the tendency of competitors to expect competition from others nicely explains the competitor's preference for competitive choices in terms of a self-fulfilling prophecy. A self-fulfilling prophecy refers to a situation where a person who expects a certain outcome actually brings it about through his or her own actions or failures to act. In the present context, an individual's expectancies about how others will behave in a prisoner's dilemma or social dilemma may affect his or her own willingness to make a cooperative choice. [*See* SELF-FULFILLING PROPHECIES.]

Consider an individual willing to make a cooperative choice on a prisoner's dilemma. What will happen if this person believes the opponent is likely to make a competitive choice? Most likely, the person will adopt a self-defensive pose and make a competitive choice. Regardless of whether the opponent intended to compete, it is likely that upon repeated trials of a prisoner's dilemma, the opponent will begin to make competitive choices, if only to avoid becoming a "sucker." In a paradoxical but understandable fashion, the person's defensive competitiveness creates in the opponent the exact type of behavior the person expected. Thus, the person comes to believe his or her competitive posture was warranted, based on actual events.

In contrast, consider an individual who believes that others may or may not cooperate. For this person, it is worth the effort to do a little exploration, i.e., begin with a cooperative position to determine whether the other will exploit it. This tactic allows an individual to discover whether an opponent is willing to cooperate. If so, both individuals can create a chain of mutual choices that maximize joint gain. In fact, if cooperators overestimate the number of people who will behave cooperatively, as some researchers have suggested, this could make a cooperative cycle even more likely.

The findings of empirical research are consistent with this line of reasoning. Over repeated trials, competitors develop a pattern of competitive interaction, regardless of the interaction preferences of opponents. Cooperators tend to show cooperative behavior, except when playing opposite an opponent who consistently shows competitive behavior. Individualists will exploit a consistently cooperative other; however, they will cooperate with a player who uses a flexible strategy of cooperating against cooperation but competing against competition.

Although the triangle hypothesis explains behavior in terms of expectancies about a co-player, little work has been done in formulating the origin of these expectancies. An additional point that deserves research attention concerns the causal direction among expectancies, choice, and the behavior of others. Do competitors expect competition in others because they initially adopt a competitive stance with others, and as a result encounter little but competitive social interactions? Or are the expectations of competitors created as a result of initial encounters with competition?

A second explanation for why some people cooperate, whereas others compete, is semantic in nature. According to the might vs morality hypothesis, cooperators and competitors conceptualize cooperation and competition in different ways. Cooperators tend to interpret the cooperation–competition dimension in terms of morality. From this perspective, cooperation is moral and good, whereas competition is immoral and bad. In contrast, competitors favor an interpretation of cooperation and competition in terms of power or potency. From this vantage point, cooperation is weak and competition is strong. Thus, the connotations applied to the two words supply shades of meaning that have important consequences for behavior. Cooperators choose to cooperate because they tend to believe that doing so is morally good, and not doing so is morally bad. In contrast, because competitors tend to view competition as a sign of strength, they are willing to engage in competitive actions.

The interpretation applied to cooperation and competition by individualists is not clear. Some research on the might vs morality hypothesis indicates that individualists interpret cooperation in a manner similar to competitors. Other research suggests that individualists are intermediate in their estimates of the perceived strength or morality of cooperative and competitive actions.

Although a number of studies have found support for the differential perceptions of cooperators and competitors regarding the competition–cooperation dimension, little attention has been devoted to understanding how people with different social values learn to interpret cooperation and competition in terms of goodness or strength. As with the expectancies about others' behavior that serve as the basis for the triangle hypothesis, the topic of how people learn to assign moral and power connotations to cooperation and competition should be a focus for future research.

VII. THE ORIGIN OF SOCIAL VALUES: A DEVELOPMENTAL PERSPECTIVE

Two influential interpretations of why social values affect behavior involve differential expectancies regarding the behavior of a co-player (the triangle hypothesis) and beliefs about the meaning and implications of cooperation and competition (the might vs morality hypothesis). Both these interpretations are limited in that they do not specify how these different expectations or beliefs develop. To shed light on this issue, it is useful to consider social values research conducted on children.

Much of the research conducted on children has focused on determining at what ages different social values manifest themselves in choice behavior. Research suggests that very young children attempt to satisfy individualistic social values. Between the ages of 4 and 5, competitive social values begin to manifest themselves. Finally, between the ages of 6 and 7 years, cooperative social values begin to appear.

Explanations for the development of social values in children have focused on two distinct processes. One explanation focuses on cognitive development, whereas the second focuses on the socialization process. The basis for the cognitive development interpretation rests on the simple fact that the tasks of maximizing own, joint, and relative gain differ in their computational difficulty. It is easiest to maximize own gain, as this merely requires that the individual compare the various outcomes that accrue to the self and choose the one that is largest. In contrast, maximizing joint or relative gain requires that an individual perform the required addition or subtraction before comparing the outcomes associated with possible choices. Given that the cognitive capacities of children develop over time, it is not surprising that they would use a less sophisticated decision strategy before more complex ones.

An alternative explanation for the development of social values is based on the socialization process. It is likely that as children grow older, they are exposed to both the benefits and disadvantages of cooperation and competition. No doubt, the value of cooperation is stressed within the family. In addition, in an educational environment, teachers are likely to encourage cooperation. On the other hand, many aspects of childhood—like the real world—encourage competition. At home, siblings are likely to compete for scarce resources, such as the use of particularly attractive toys, parental attention, and candy. At school, children come to realize that they can often attain the approval of the teacher by performing at a higher level than their peers. Evidence in support of the socialization hypothesis has been obtained in cross-cultural research on the development of social values. For example, a number of studies have shown that Mexican-American children tend to display more prosocial behavior than their Anglo-American counterparts. Given the likely assumption that people of different nationalities do not differ in their rate of cognitive development, it is probable that differences in the displayed rate of cooperative and competitive behavior result from differences in the socialization process.

Although children display a distinct maturation pattern in their tendency to perform cooperative or competitive actions, the body of evidence collected on adults suggests that over time one pattern or another becomes dominant in an individual's responses. Clearly, sufficient cognitive capacity is required for individuals to carry out cooperative and competitive transformations of outcomes to self and other. However, because this skill develops relatively early in the individual's life, the cognitive capacity argument cannot explain the variability in dominant social values among adults.

Both the triangle hypothesis and the might vs morality hypothesis implicitly favor an etiology based on the socialization process. Children may or may not come to expect competition from others based on their own observations, the stories they are told, and the actions of significant authority figures such as parents, teachers, and older siblings. Further, as these expectancies develop, they become tinged with associations that provide instruction regarding the potency or morality of cooperative and competitive behavior. Thus, it seems likely that a full understanding of the origin of social values will focus heavily on the learning process that occurs in the home, in educational settings, and elsewhere.

VIII. CONCLUSIONS

Much of the early interest in social values, as defined in the present article, focused on attempting to explain choice behavior in mixed-motive games such as the prisoner's dilemma. The assumption of this research was that individual difference variables, especially preferences for stable outcomes to oneself and another, could be used to reduce the amount of unexplained error variance that existed in matrix game research. Generally, research on social values has been successful in accomplishing this goal.

Other work on social values has been directed toward better understanding the origin of social values, and why they have their effect on behavior. Thus, research on social values has been conducted on children of a variety of nationalities and economic backgrounds. In addition, social values have also been examined in adults from different cultures. An important aspect of social values that has been examined concerns the manner in which people process information relevant to cooperative and competitive choice behavior in mixed-motive games. Evidence indicates that people with different social values conceptualize cooperation and competition in different ways (e.g., as indicators of morality or potency); moreover, these conceptualizations can have important effects on cooperative and competitive behavior.

Because of the complexity inherent in human behavior, a full understanding of social interdependence requires consideration of a great many factors. As the present review illustrates, the social values conceptualization appears to be a useful tool for coming to grips with this complexity. As such, it provides a useful framework for understanding a wide range of social behaviors: those that involve cooperation, competition, and conflict.

Bibliography

Knight, G. P., and Bohlmeyer, E. M. (1990). Cooperative learning and achievement: Methods for assessing causal mechanisms. In "Cooperative Learning: Theory and Research" (S. Sharan, Ed.). Praeger, New York.

Kuhlman, D. M., Camac, C. R., and Cunha, D. A. (1986). Individual differences in social orientation. In "Experimental Social Dilemmas" (H. A. M. Wilke, D. M. Messick, and C. G. G. Rutte, Eds.). Lang, New York.

Liebrand, W. B. G. (1986). The ubiquity of social values in social dilemmas. In "Experimental Social Dilemmas" (H. A. M. Wilke, D. M. Messick, and C. G. G. Rutte, Eds.). Lang, New York.

Luce, R. D., and Raiffa, H. (1957). "Games and Decisions." Wiley, New York.

Poundstone, W. (1992). "Prisoner's Dilemma." Doubleday, New York.

van Lange, P. A. M., and Kuhlman, D. M. (1990). Expected cooperation in social dilemmas: The influence of own social value orientation and other's personality characteristics. In "European Perspectives in Psychology" (P. J. D. Drength, J. A. Sergeant, and R. J. Takens, Eds.), Vol. 3. Wiley, Chichester, England.

SOCIOBIOLOGY

Harmon R. Holcomb III
University of Kentucky

Glossary

Adaptation A heritable trait that enhanced its bearer's fitness and evolved by natural selection.

Adaptive strategy A strategy for behaving in ways that enhance, or enhanced, its bearer's fitness.

Adaptive trait A trait that currently enhances its bearer's fitness.

Evolution A generational change in gene frequencies.

Fitness An organism's probability of or propensity for success at reproducing due to its heritable traits, e.g., running more swiftly than other deer helps a deer avoid being eaten by bears, increasing its relative chance of surviving and, hence, of reproducing.

Gene A replicator; a single segregating unit of DNA.

Natural selection Evolution in which differential reproduction is caused by variant heritable traits that differ in their design for reproductive success.

SOCIOBIOLOGY is the branch of evolutionary biology that studies social behavior in the social species. Human sociobiology studies human social behavior using the same basic evolutionary principles formerly applied to nonhuman species. The term "sociobiology" is associated especially with the controversial work of Edward O. Wilson and various popular, speculative works. Wishing to distance themselves from the sociobiology controversy, many researchers prefer other labels for the evolutionary biological study of human behavior: biosocial science, biosociology, biocultural science, evolutionary biological anthropology, evolutionary ecology, evolutionary ethology, evolutionary psychology, evolution and human behavior studies, human behavioral ethology, or socioecology.

I. RATIONALE

Human sociobiology emerged as a discipline or theoretical approach relatively recently. The important theoretical developments that form its basis include R. A. Fisher's and W. D. Hamilton's work on altruism and kinship, G. C. Williams' critique of group selection, Konrad Lorenz's and Nino Tinbergen's ethology, Robert Trivers' work on reciprocal altruism and parental manipulation, and John Maynard Smith's work on game theory. E. O. Wilson made the field visible by systematizing the preexisting body of knowledge, speculating about human nature, and theorizing about how genetic evolution is connected to mental and cultural processes and phenomena.

The evolutionary study of human adaptation can, of course, be traced back to Darwin. Ever since Darwin, evolutionists have been fascinated with identifying and explaining the similarities and differences human beings share with other species. Evolutionists describe and explain human behavior in ways designed to highlight variations both within our species and between our species and other species. They seek to comprehend the diversity of life in terms of ancestral conditions and general natural processes.

Humans are organisms, too. Humans are part of nature. Humans behave in ways that enable us to survive and reproduce. The same basic principles that apply to evolutionary change in general therefore must apply to our species, *Homo sapiens*. Natural selection has been the key to the evolution of all species studied so far. So it is reasonable to presume that understanding the evolution of our species will throw light upon human behavior. Given this historical, programmatic rationale for doing human sociobiology, evolutionists seek to explain why we do what we do in terms of the ways in which human behavior reflects our species' history of evolution by natural selection.

Evolutionists are well aware that many people vigorously deny the proposition that human social behavior is biologically, evolutionarily based. It has been thought that, although our bodies can be studied biologically, our social behavior cannot; that is what the social sciences are for. Thus, "sociobiology" is often regarded as a contradiction in terms, an extension of biology to areas where it has no business being. Common preconceptions lead us to think that if some behavior is "cultural" then it is not "biological," that if it is "social" then it is not "natural," that if it is "learned" then it is not "genetic," and so on. Whereas critics use such preconceptions to argue against sociobiology, sociobiologists challenge these preconceptions themselves. Whereas critics assume that genetic, evolved constraints are not relevant to anything specific about human social behavior or to contemporary social problems, advocates assume that evolution is relevant to many or all aspects of human sociality.

Thus, sociobiology is unlike normal science (in Kuhn's sense) in that the very idea of sociobiology is controversial. To report on human sociobiology as a collection of scientific facts or theories would be misleading. Whether it satisfies the norms of "science" or has uncovered "facts" or contains "applicable theories" is hotly contested, given the opposing assumption that evolution is irrelevant to human behavioral variation and has given us only a generalized capacity for culture and set of drives.

In the face of such resistance, evolutionists have argued in various ways that evolution is indeed relevant to human social behavior. The historical, programmatic rationale for sociobiology stated above can be developed to warrant extending the domain of evolutionary biology from behavior to social behavior to social institutions. Logically, these *relevance arguments* view human social phenomena as special cases of types of phenomena routinely described and explained in evolutionary terms generally. Even when successful, these arguments do not entail that the explanatory factors invoked in particular explanations are relevant to the phenomena explained or that the particular explanations are true. The following arguments govern the logic of theoretical extension in general.

Organisms develop their characteristics (their phenotype) as a result of a dynamic interplay between their set of inherited genes (genotype) and their environment. A phenotype includes morphology, physiology, and behavior. Human behavior is one aspect of the human phenotype (although human behavioral variation seems irreducible to biology). So, individual human behaviors and/or the psychological states that produce them have evolutionary explanations.

All populations of organisms are constituted by their individual members and reflect the phenotypes of their members. In particular, human societies are constituted by individual human organisms and reflect their individual forms of behavior. So, human social institutions have evolutionary explanations.

All evolutionary change is governed by a small set of evolutionary forces which guide population change in one direction rather than another by affecting changes in gene frequencies. The variation within a population from one generation to the next changes or not according to the interaction of these forces, e.g., genetic drift (random genetic change), mutation, natural selection, migration, immigration. In all species studied so far, natural selection has been the dominant, direction-giving force of evolutionary change. So, individual human behaviors and social institutions have explanations in terms of evolution by selection, via evolved psychological mechanisms.

How does natural selection work? Following Darwin, all evolution by natural selection involves three factors: variation, heredity, and fitness. Organisms in a local population vary. Some leave more offspring than others. Traits inherited from parents more successful at surviving and reproducing than others in the local population tend to increase in frequency in the next generation. These facts follow from basic statistics about who lives, who dies, and who reproduces.

Why do some organisms survive better than others? Why do some organisms reproduce better than others? These questions ask us to identify what constitutes fitness in nature. The basic evolutionary problem is not simply success at surviving and reproducing, but *design* for success at surviving and reproducing. The mechanism Darwin introduced into evolutionary thinking involves the way basic statistics are affected by fitness-related biases. Variant forms—whether morphological, physiological, or behavioral—can yield different aptitudes for success at surviving and reproducing (different fitnesses). When variant forms that confer differential fitnesses upon their bearers are inherited down the generations, the population evolves to a higher average fitness. In the simplest case, the individuals with the most fit variants will increase in the population from one generation to the next, resulting in cumulative evolutionary directional change as those variants increase in frequency in the population with each generation.

In sum, heritable variation in fitness results in evolution by natural selection. In all such cases, we can explain the evolution of the traits involved by identifying the selective advantages of evolved traits. The implication for human sociality is obvious: we can explain types of human individual behaviors and types of human social institutions by identifying the selective advantages that the behaviors and institutions give to the people who engage in those behaviors and participate in those institutions.

The preceding sorts of argument for the relevance of evolution to human social behavior are central to sociobiology's rationale and accepted by those who prefer a different label for their studies. The evolutionary perspective demands the evolutionary study of animal sociality (hence, animal sociobiology) and humans in particular (hence, human sociobiology). Without animal and human sociobiology, the overall picture of evolution in any species would be incomplete. One may "reject sociobiology" in the sense of rejecting a particular evolutionary approach, a particular application of evolutionary theory, an individual evolutionary study, and so forth. But to "reject sociobiology" in the sense of asserting in principle that evolution is irrelevant to human social behavior is to hold an incomplete picture of evolution.

In addition to these general, principled reasons for pursuing sociobiology, there are particular reasons involving levels of organization, natural selection, and altruism. Altruism is a source of theoretical incompleteness; it is a phenomenon which could not yet be incorporated into the big evolutionary picture without developing new concepts, theory, data, and methods. Historically, concern over how to explain altruism in nonhumans preceded the advent of human sociobiology as such. Speculations about humans began in earnest only after evolutionists removed altruism as a source of incompleteness in explaining the social behavior of nonhumans. As a result of being inspired by continuing successes in animal sociobiology, they began to address our incomplete understanding of human evolution. They tried to overcome preconceptions that make human social phenomena either irrelevant to or inconsistent with evolutionary theory, so that the evolution of human sociality could also be included in our picture of the social evolution of life. [*See* Altruism and Helping Behavior.]

II. ALTRUISM AND SELECTION PROCESSES

Both human and nonhuman organisms sometimes behave in many ways that give aid to others at their own expense. However, Darwinian individual selection favors traits that benefit their own possessor, not other population members or the group as a whole. Cooperation contains many opportunities for altruism, and so is a central defining feature of social behavior. A society may be defined as a local population of individuals of the same species organized in a cooperative manner. So, explaining altruism is a precondition for explaining social behavior. Indeed, E. O. Wilson, in his *Sociobiology: The New Synthesis* (1975), identified altruism as the central problem of sociobiology.

Behavioral ecologists often explained various human or nonhuman behaviors as "being good for the group." Given that overpopulation could destroy habitat and food resources, thereby leading to group extinction, Wynne-Edwards interpreted a host of phenomena in animals and birds as being due to group selection instead: flocking, territoriality, dominance hierarchies, altruism, and reproductive restraint are or appear to be the result of selection favoring the survival and reproduction of the group over that of its individual members.

Similarly, in the 1960s neofunctionalist ecological anthropologists, such as Roy Rappaport, Marvin Harris, and Andrew Vayda, explained a variety of individual human social behaviors and social institutions in terms of their functions for the group as a whole. But whereas Wynne-Edwards made explicit the need for "good of the group" explanations to be based on a process of group selection, neofunctionalist explanations of human behavior often left "good of the group" explanations unfounded. Anthropologists such as Alexander Alland, Lionel Tiger, and Robin Fox realized that the discussion over the relative efficacy of group selection and individual selection in evolutionary biology had important implications for neofunctionalist explanations in the social sciences.

In his *Adaptation and Natural Selection* (1966), George Williams subjected group selectionist explanations of nonhuman organisms to a devastating critique. Theoretically speaking, group selection can overcome the effects of individual selection only in a narrow set of conditions, conditions that make group selection the exception and individual selection the norm in fashioning adaptive behaviors. Therefore, he advanced a methodological principle of parsimony: one should not invoke group selectionist explanations if the phenomena can be explained by appeal to individual selection alone.

For instance, in *Animal Dispersion in Relation to Social Behavior* (1962), Wynne-Edwards interpreted the fact that some birds lay fewer eggs than physiologically possible as a reproductive restraint favoring the group, a population regulation mechanism. But David Lack provided empirical evidence showing that egg mortality increases with clutch size and that the actual number of eggs laid maximizes the individual bird's reproductive output in these conditions.

Similarly, anthropologists had interpreted the wide interbirth interval of 4 years among the !Kung San as a hunter–gatherer homeostatic mechanism for population regulation. Later work by Nicholas Burton Jones showed that shorter interbirth intervals increase mortality rate and that the optimal rate for individual reproductive success under their conditions is near the average. In both humans and nonhumans, females are maximizing individual reproductive success, not curtailing reproduction to control overpopulation.

Such empirical work underscores the fact that apparently altruistic behavior may be actually selfish, in the sense of being genetically adaptive at the level of the individual. So objections to adaptive evolutionary explanations, "such-and-such human behavior is not biologically adaptive," could be countered as based on ignorance of the constraints, of the complete set of costs and benefits at various levels of organization, or of the full array of selection processes.

Evolutionists expanded the array of selection processes to handle forms of altruism not covered by traditional models of individual selection. To do so, the genetic basis of selection has been reconceptualized. Since the only way for an individual to contribute to the next generation is to transmit genes via reproduction, an individual's behavior is adaptive to the extent that it perpetuates copies of genes qualitatively identical to those possessed by that individual.

The idea of the "selfish gene," popularized by Richard Dawkins in his *The Selfish Gene* (1976), is not a psychological concept. We have no drive to perpetuate our genes. We are not trying to behave adaptively. The concept of selfishness here is not one of intentions or unconscious urges. Rather, it is a conception of how selection processes fit together, i.e., it is an evolutionary concept about intrapopulation change from one generation to another.

We are motivated to behave in ways that lead to various results, and these results tend to be selected for or against insofar as they affect the relative number of copies of our genes that we contribute to later generations. Altruism toward offspring is favored if it perpetuates copies of the parent's genes better than available alternatives ("Darwinian individual selection"). Altruism toward kin is favored if it perpetuates copies of one's genes better than available alternatives ("kin selection").

W. D. Hamilton developed a precise mathematics for calculating when altruism to kin should evolve by selection. Altruism to kin is selected for as a function of (1) the benefit of the aid given by the altruist to the potential recipient, (2) the probability of risk to the donor of the aid, (3) the probability that the recipient of the aid bears a copy of the gene for altruism possessed by the donor ("coefficient of relatedness").

The phrase "gene for altruism" does not imply that there is a single gene that codes for altruism. It is shorthand for whatever genetic basis there is for acting altruistically, i.e., for whatever set of genes increases the probability of acting altruistically, given the current context of the physical constitution of the individual, the local environment, and the social environment. The "gene for behavior X" idea requires a genetic background for a behavior, but implies no particular view about individual development. The "gene for behavior X" idea used in evolutionary explanations incorporates a reference to the development of individual organisms without implying any tight sort of genetic control.

To make this point sharper, it is useful to distinguish *genetic determination* from *genetic determinism*. Genetic determination (or genetic causation) is relative to a context, and so does not imply genetic determinism, which ignores the way causation is context-bound. Genetic determinism envisages genes causing the same effect no matter what the environment or population or developmental pathway. Genetic determinism (which does not exist) implies that we cannot change a genetically caused behavior (e.g., John Doe's giving a job to his brother), behavioral predisposition (e.g., John Doe's nepotistic tendency), or behavioral strategy (e.g., John Doe's way of enhancing his fitness via altruism to his relatives).

Thus, the genetical theory of evolution does not prescribe any specific genetic limits on social change. Developmental genetics does not assert that genes determine organisms, although some might like to think that we could compute an organism from its genetic code. In order to know whether a behavior, behavioral predisposition, or behavioral strategy can be changed and how much it can be changed, we would have to try to change it by various means and wait and see what happens. This is how *norms of reaction* are devised, graphs that relate changes in phenotypes to changes in environments, changes in developmental pathways, and changes in genes.

At present, the known facts do not support the conclusion that biology (i.e., genes) imposes biological limits on human nature beyond obvious facts (e.g., men do not bear children), limits that make social changes proposed to solve social problems impossible or difficult by ordinary social means. Sociobiology lacks the requisite informational base in evolutionary and developmental genetics for prescribing social policies about how to change our society to bring about various effects. We know little about the modifiability of evolved behavioral strategies and psychological mechanisms. It is ideology, not the science in sociobiology, which says that genes "determine" and "fix" human social behavioral characters, making them inevitable results of the human genome. Evolution both constrains and enables human behavior. The issue over narrow biological limits and the absence of biological limits turns on the fact that evolutionary theory is predictive because genes in a given environment tend to produce a given behavior.

Critics often charge sociobiology with being a form of genetic determinism, a charge better levied at persons than at the field. Sociobiology as a discipline is committed to the idea of genetic determination on the basis of the application of evolutionary principles that make reference to genetic determination or genetic causation. Sociobiology as a discipline is not committed to the ideology of genetic determinism, even if some advocates of sociobiology express the ideology of genetic determinism despite facts about genes and the form of explanation proper to evolutionary studies.

Having clarified the meaning and implications of the phrase "gene for behavior X," we can better understand Hamilton's theorem. It states that genes for altruism will tend to increase in frequency in the population when K is greater than $1/r$, where K is the ratio of recipient's gain to altruist's cost and r is the fraction of genes identical by descent in the altruist and recipient. We have evolved to be altruistic toward our kin, and, as a consequence, many human behaviors can be explained using kin selection. Our clarification shows that these explanations do not imply an ideology of genetic determinism or a cynical view of human psychology.

Hamilton expanded the concept of fitness to include not only the individual's own reproductive output, but also the reproductive output of those who share one's genes due to common descent ("inclusive fitness"). We are selected to maximize our inclusive fitness, not our personal fitness. However, human society is full of cooperation with nonrelatives in addition to cooperation based on various family units. Robert Trivers showed how altruism toward nonrelatives could evolve if the beneficiary is likely to return the favor ("reciprocal altruism").

Basic human goals, often conceived of as needs in traditional social science, arise from evolutionary processes. Our goal of maintaining our bodies is established by mortality selection. Our goal of finding mates and preferring some mates to others is established by mate selection. Our goal of parenting is given by fertility selection. Our goal of helping our families is established by kin selection. Our goal of maintaining a reputation for fairness and morality is linked to reciprocal altruism.

Reciprocity is a basic relation that holds society together. A society requires cooperation among its members for its continued existence. We can trace the basis for social cohesion back to various sorts of reciprocity, identifying the ways in which social institutions make demands on the society's members that involve fitness-affecting behaviors.

Suppose you had a choice about whom to help, and behaved as if you had done your fitness calculations in situations where we keep the ratio of benefits to costs the same no matter who the recipient is. In this situation, selection favors the following preferences: aid to self over aid to another (since you share 100% of your genes with yourself), aid to more closely related relatives over aid to more distantly related relatives (since the closer the relative the greater number of shared genes arising from common descent), aid to relatives over friends (since you share more genes with relatives than with friends), aid to friends over strangers (since friends are more likely to reciprocate than strangers).

Of course, these preferences may change if the benefit/cost ratios vary among potential recipients. The theorem explains why humans are nepotistic, but also explains apparent exceptions. It will be more adaptive for me to give aid to a stranger rather than to a relative if I benefit reproductively more from the stranger's reciprocation than from nepotism.

The mathematical models employed in sociobiology provide sources for constructing and testing predictive hypotheses in a rigorous, quantitative, scientific manner. If we can calculate all the benefits and costs and degrees of relatedness involved in a given situation, then we can derive a mathematically precise, testable prediction about which of two alternative behaviors is more adaptive and determine the optimally adaptive behavior.

On the basis of such mathematical models, the diversity of nonhuman and human behavior can be unified and comprehended in a single evolutionary system of theories. Thus, altruistic phenomena as diverse as a human or nonhuman mother's altruism to offspring, sterile casts in the social insects, homosexuality in humans, warning cries of sentinel crows, nepotism, friendship, and so forth can be seen as the results of evolution by natural selection.

Perhaps the crucial new concept is that both phenotypically selfish and phenotypically altruistic behaviors evolve for the same reason: they are genetically selfish. Many people readily accept that animals behave in ways that are genetically selfish, but resist the thought that it is human nature for us to behave in genetically selfish ways. In response, sociobiologists developed explicit hypotheses and theories to deal with a basic source of resistance: the presumption that we transcend the nature of our primate ancestors through our minds and cultures.

III. EVOLUTION AND CULTURE

Humans do not passively receive our cultures as given, but actively manipulate them in ways that fit the preferences that enhance our fitnesses. Cultures are adaptive; if they were not minimally adaptive their members would cease to survive and reproduce. Our minds and cultures evolved as ways of altering our behavior to enhance our fitness over short time periods, tracking changes in our natural and social environment pertinent to our inclusive fitnesses. A culture is a way of life. Every species has a way of life. What is unique about human culture? A culture consists of shared, organized, socially transmitted information. We use our cultures (information transmitted socially, not genetically) to enhance our fitnesses and resist cultural changes that detract from our fitnesses.

Mortality selection concerns differential survival. Fertility selection concerns differential reproduction. These two modes of selection lead us to conceptualize the lifetime of an organism as involving two kinds of effort. *Somatic effort* consists of an organism's investment of matter/energy and information into its own bodily survival, via behaviors directed toward its own growth, development, and maintenance. *Reproductive effort* consists of its investment into reproduction, whether its own or that of others, via behaviors directed toward mating and parenting.

Human organisms have adapted minds, which enable us to receive, process, and act on cultural information and the material technology of the our cultures. Our minds are not arbitrary learning devices, but are tools fashioned according the basic selection criterion: to expend our somatic and reproductive effort in whatever ways maximize our genetic contribution to our evolving populations given the current constraints induced by our natural and social environments. Since other humans are at least as powerful a selective force as food, weather, climate, parasites, and so forth, we are adapted to group-living and to each other.

Animal sociobiology has developed a family of related mathematical models designed to help us compare actual expenditures of somatic effort devoted to getting food to various ideal *optimal foraging strategies*. These models treat decisions organisms make about what to eat ("diet breadth," "prey choice"), where to look for food ("patch choice"), where to live ("habitat choice"), with whom to forage ("group size"), and how long to forage ("time/energy budgets").

Human sociobiology has applied these optimal foraging models to a number of hunter–gatherer cultures: the Cree, Alyawara, Ache, Siona-Secoya, Ye'kwana, Yanomamo, Bari, Cuiva, and Yora, Inujjamuit, Efe, and Bushmen. By finding ways in which actual foraging deviates from the optimum strategy defined by simple models, we learn how various aspects of the culture are relevant to what counts as the optimum in the particular conditions experienced by that culture. An optimal strategy is, by definition, the strategy that maximizes fitness, given the constraints of the situation and the array of alternative strategies.

For instance, finding that various South American foragers favor plant over meat foods that have higher caloric returns, it is hypothesized that the local optimum defined in terms of calories alone must be made more complex and treat an optimal balance of both caloric and nutritional needs. Field studies oriented by the questions "What are they optimizing?" and "What are the constraints imposed by physiology, morphology, natural environment, and social environment that determine how the people should behave?" lead to richer, more complex theoretical models and to a more detailed understanding of particular people's ways of life as conditioned by the consequences of their behaviors for survival and reproduction.

In applying optimal foraging theory to the Ache of Paraguay, Hawkes and Hill attempted to account for the sexual division of labor, i.e., why in so many cultures men hunt and women gather. Traditional anthropological theories explain the fact that women do not forage for more than a few hours a day by postulating that they have limited needs and stop foraging when these needs are filled. As is often the case, evolutionists try to explain what other nonevolutionary accounts merely postulate, and so Hawkes and Hill pointed to the lack of reason for why fixed food requirements are set at one level or another and how or why they vary from culture to culture. Instead, an evolutionary hypothesis is that there is a direct, positive relation between foraging time and fitness, but that cultural constraints impose a threshold at which greater foraging activity does not lead to greater fitness.

This illustrates a basic orientation toward the problem of obtaining an evolutionary viewpoint on culture. In a nonoptimization approach, resource use varies as a function of different ways to achieve fixed culturally induced goals unrelated to biological fitness. In an optimization approach, resource use varies as a function of different ways to achieve culturally induced goals that in turn vary as different ways of achieving the ultimate goal of maximum fitness.

This orientation was first made into an explicit hypothesis by William Irons. He conjectured that in most human societies cultural success consists in accomplishing those things which make biological success probable. This hypothesis has been tested extensively in cross-cultural studies of reproductive effort. They bear out Iron's finding about the Yomut Turkmen, namely, that within a given culture, the wealthier, culturally more successful men have more surviving offspring than others. Cultural success is usually determined by a function of a variety of things in a given culture (e.g., wealth, hunting success, skill in warfare, position in a religious hierarchy), where this function varies from culture to culture independently of gene effects as far as we know. Within a culture, those who are more successful by the standards of that culture have, on average, higher biological fitness within that culture than the rest.

Studies of reproductive effort in animal sociobiology propose hypotheses based on a theory of sex-specific strategies for mating and parenting. In most (but not all) species, females, not males, bear children. Thus, a female contributes genes to the next generation through her own body and a male contributes genes through the bodies of one or more females. Males have virtually unlimited sperm, whereas females have a limited supply of eggs. Such physiological differences set up a behavioral difference. "The more mates, the more potential offspring" holds for males, not females.

The sex investing more potential reproductive output in an offspring should be more careful in choosing mates since it risks more. Not only does the bearing of offspring by females make their investment heavier, but females put much more reproductive potential at risk with each copulation or fertilization than males. To the extent that these conditions alone constrain optimal mate-choice strategies, selection favors males mating with as many females as possible and females mating with as few males as possible.

Laura Betzig, Monique Borgerhoff Mulder, and Paul Turke have collected together a number of field studies in their anthology, *Human Reproductive Behaviour* (1988). Among other things, they tested evolutionary predictions about male/female differences in mating strategies designed. These predictions hold under some (not all!) circumstances, and can be simplified as follows; the theory and data are quite a bit more complex.

Males are selected to compete with other males for as many female mates as possible, to compete with other males to exclude others from resources used to raise the children of other males and to acquire resources used to raise their own children, and to choose female mates according to signs of their potential success at bearing and raising children. Females are selected to compete with other females for as few male mates as possible, to compete with other females to exclude other females from potential male mates and to keep potential male mates for themselves, and to choose male mates according to signs of their relative potential for providing high quality genes, access to resources, or behaviors that enhance success at child bearing and child caring.

The field studies collected range from preindustrial cultures, such as the Yanomamo, Ache, Ifaluk, New Guinea Highlanders, to modern cultures, such as 19th century Utah Mormons and 20th century Kenyan Kipsigis. Despite wide variation in historical, social, cultural, and ecological contexts, the following supporting generalizations were found.

With respect to competition between males: (1) Men with fewer resources may be more likely to undertake risk, in order to increase their access to resources, or, more directly, to women. (2) Measures of success in male–male competition, including dominance, status, and wealth, positively correlate with measures of reproductive success, including fertility to date, age-specific or completed fertility, and mechanisms promoting fertility. (3) Dominance, status, and wealth positively correlate with a variety of mechanisms promoting men's reproductive success, including number of serial or simultaneous conjugal unions, number of reported extramarital liaisons, age at first marriage or reproduction, spouse's age at first reproduction, interbirth intervals, longevity, offspring survival, and probability of cuckoldry.

With respect to female and male choice of mates: (1) Women appear to choose men for the resources they offer and for their behavioral tendencies that signal potential child-caring success. (2) Dominant men successfully mate with the youngest, healthiest, most attractive women, since they are likely to have high reproductive potential. (3) Men choose faithful mates, since faithfulness enhances paternity confidence. (4) Men who are good providers choose wives for such indices of reproductive potential as youth and lack of children by another man.

Evolutionists evaluate the ongoing development of this body of empirical cross-cultural fieldwork in relation to studies of similar somatic and reproductive strategies in nonhuman organisms. The same evolutionary theory applies to humans and nonhumans alike. These applications take into account the facts particular to the species under study, including facts about psychological mechanisms and cultural variation not predictable on evolutionary grounds alone.

Such results testify to the ability of evolutionary biology to become relevant to and consistent with animal and human sociality not only as a matter of general principle, but also for specific cases, thereby removing obstacles to obtaining a complete picture of the evolution of life on earth.

IV. HUMAN NATURE, BIOLOGY, AND IDEOLOGY

The publication of E. O. Wilson's *Sociobiology: The New Synthesis* in 1975 triggered vigorous, heated debate over sociobiology among evolutionists, practitioners of the social and behavioral sciences, and the academic community in general. "The sociobiology controversy" became well known. Many people working at applying evolutionary perspectives to human behavior reject the label "sociobiology" in order to escape commitment to the doctrines and attitudes people associate with it.

On one hand, advocates brush aside complaints focusing on the sensationalized edicts of popularized sociobiology. They point to the rigorous work, as rigorous as can be expected for a relatively new field tackling very difficult problems. This work is found in diverse journals: *Ethology and Sociobiology, Journal of Social and Biological Structures, Human Nature, Behavioral Ecology and Sociobiology, Human Ecology, American Anthropologist,* and *Current Anthropology*.

On the other hand, critics view such work as only more subtly falling into the traps so obvious in popularized accounts of human nature. They point to the marketing of sociobiology in our society in the popular media, where all the worst interpretations and misapplications of evolutionary biology feed into naive preconceptions that rationalize the status quo with disastrously flawed science. Steven Jay Gould, Richard Lewontin, Leo Kamin, and Steven Rose have been the most vociferous critics of sociobiology who make people beware of the political dangers inherent in the alleged "science" of sociobiology. Sociobiology is taken to be an abuse of science that reflects and perpetuates politically dangerous ideologies.

From the point of view of this scientific and social critique, sociobiology views all human events as biologically, genetically determined through evolution ("biological determinism"). In its alleged "New Synthesis" of biological and social science, it takes social science to be reducible to biology on the grounds that humans are evolved organisms, one species among many. In its misapplication of hypotheses about fitness, natural selection, and genes to particular human populations, it too often operates from the assumption that all behaviors are optimally adaptive, a false assumption that draws attention away from the historical constraints. Historically speaking, it marks the emergence of 19th century Social Darwinism in our own time, e.g., the double standard between the sexes—that it's OK and to be expected that men cheat on their sexual partners more than women—is explained as an evolved genetic adaptation, therefore inevitable, and so a justifiable behavior.

For example, Philip Kitcher's *Vaulting Ambition: Sociobiology and the Quest for Human Nature* (1985) attacks the following sort of work ("pop sociobiology"). First, it offers a quick fix and final judgments, as opposed to pursuing difficulties so as to open up future lines of research. Second, it fails to include the biological and mathematical rigor needed to ensure the logic of its argument, but instead relies on a deeply flawed methodology of explanation and evidence as well as dubious or false assumptions. It thereby fails to achieve well-articulated and well-tested explanations worthy of the name of science. Third, it tries to climb a ladder from nature up to human nature through its hypotheses about adaptation, natural selection, and genes. It thereby provides a social weapon for those attracted to excusing social inequalities as part of our biological nature or otherwise providing alleged scientific support for the status quo.

Sociobiologists were quick to note that Kitcher did not examine some of the best evidence at the time, e.g., as cited in Patrick Gray's *Primate Sociobiology* (1985). They stress the improvement in method and evidence as the field develops, e.g., *Homicide* (1988), by M. Daly and M. Wilson. And they maintain that they are not engaged in the enterprise attributed to them by Kitcher and other critics. There is still little consensus on sociobiology's scientific and ideological status (e.g., on issues pursued in Fetzer's (1985) anthology *Sociobiology and Epistemology*).

The basic outstanding issue is whether the sociobiological extension of evolutionary ideas from animals to humans is legitimate, normal biology or whether it generates bad science or pseudoscience plagued by a host of flaws. As a result, people disagree about whether sociobiology illuminates or obscures human nature, whether sociobiology is radically new and should revolutionize the social and behavioral sciences, or whether it merely continues a tradition of crude biologism or reductionism.

If the facts do not support sociobiology, then we would like to explain why sociobiologists say what they say when the facts are not there. At issue is whether sociobiology is intrinsically sexist and racist and provides an excuse for the status quo or whether it merely gets misused that way. Our comments on altruism raise the question of whether the sociobiology of altruism provides a biological explanation of morality or whether it denies true altruism by saying that we are genetically selfish creatures.

Our discussion of adaptive explanation and optimality models raises the question of whether the adaptationist approach of sociobiology makes it unfalsifiable and thereby in violation of scientific method or whether its adaptive explanations are sufficiently testable to count as scientific.

To clarify the way the accusations arise, reconsider the mate selection theory previously reviewed. Disregarding the complexity of the theory, the charges focus on oversimplified generalizations, e.g., males are selected to choose as many mates as possible, whereas females are selected to choose as few mates as possible. This is readily interpreted to mean that humans are just like animals (an illegitimate extension of biology), with culture relegated to a means toward biological ends. It is a short step to read it as saying that males are selected to be promiscuous and females faithful (an abuse of language trading on anthropomorphism) since the theory makes these extreme differences the optimal strategies.

These interpretations sound like a crude biologism (making everything about humans out to be biologically based), since no nonbiological aspects of human social behavior are explicit in the theory and since the biological fact of being female or male is not differentiated from culturally constructed conceptions of masculinity and femininity.

Mate selection theory seems to fall into the trap of crude reductionism (reducing features of societies as wholes to the behavioral predispositions of their members), since the social institution of polygyny is a direct effect of men seeking many mates and females seeking one mate. It appears to be the conscious or unconscious expression of sexism (devaluing women due to spurious views about differences between men and women), since it lends itself to men rationalizing cheating on their female sexual partners by saying that "I can't help it; it's my biology making me do it."

Sociobiology in general seems to deliver a cynical view of human nature (one deeply distrustful of our higher spiritual aspects of compassion, love, and willingness to treat others as ends in themselves), since it views all of our behaviors as directed toward perpetuating copies of our genes and views all members of a population as engaged in a war of conflicting genetic interests.

Despite disclaimers, sociobiology's explanations are all too often constructed as unfalsifiable (they are built so that the facts always seem consistent with them even if the facts refute them), since the theory is so loose that an imaginative evolutionist can always think of some way of modifying the theory to make it fit the facts.

Whereas sociobiology's advocates treat it as good science free from ideological commitment, these accusations lead critics to treat it as bad science or pseudoscience in service of bad ideology. Sociobiology became politicized from the start, when it was reported to the public as a scientific theory of human nature, establishing narrow biological limits to social change (confusing biological determination with biological determinism). Explanations of behaviors implicated in the whole gamut of contemporary social issues were proposed, with speculations being treated as true and scientifically validated. To explain something, such as male promiscuity, was to show how it was rooted in our evolved genes, thereby making it beyond our control through the usual means of social change.

Sociobiologists deny that their work has these implications, ascribing misinterpretations to their skeptical critics. For example, sociobiology is a theory of human nature in the sense that it can transform our understanding of human behavior. But this does not mean that the behaviors and social institutions particular to our culture are part of the essence of being human or are fixed in our genes. Evolutionary imperatives yield variations in behavioral output given variations in the conditions of life.

Our current behaviors are not part of the essence of being human, since a general adaptive strategy is tailored to the particular psychological, cultural, historical, and individual context in which human organisms find themselves. Human behavior is not derivable from "biology alone," since these seeming "nonbiological" facts are necessary for the application of fitness-maximization principles. This cross-disciplinary facet of sociobiology's explanatory method permits its use in many diverse fields.

The theory (evolutionary theory) is not loose. The appearance of looseness is due to the difficulty of understanding the contextual constraints that form the antecedent conditions used in the application of general evolutionary principles (recall Hempel's covering-law model of explanation). Predictions are deduced from generalization plus antecedent conditions and antecedent conditions are induced from knowledge of the particular conditions of life of the organisms. This is the usual circle of deduction and induction in science. As we learn about the constraining conditions, the predictions are more and more refined.

Our current behaviors need not be fixed in our genes, except in the sense of the truism that all traits are fixed in genes and environments. Some sociobiologists study whether a given behavior has specific genetic antecedents. Few hold the extreme thesis that behaviors typically exhibit variations which correlate with genetic variations. Most hold the moderate thesis that variations in behavior are expressions of a similar human genotype for most human populations. It gives us physical abilities, psychological predispositions, and mental capacities that have tended to be adaptive in the evolutionary past. Connections of genes to behaviors are mediated by our brains (or minds). Sociobiologists are developing a complex psychology that treats adaptation at the psychological level ("evolved psychological mechanisms"), where specific behavioral outcomes are not supposed to be genetically determined, direct targets of natural selection.

Rather than genes determining our behaviors ("genetic determinism"), the most general genetic thesis is the standard view of causation. There are genetic, developmental, psychological, historical, and cultural conditions causally relevant to a given behavior in a given situation. Change any one causally relevant condition and, potentially, the behavior is changed. Change the genes and the behavior may be changed. Change the culture and the behavior may be changed. The extent that a behavior can be changed by one means or another is an empirical question, something to be investigated, rather than a dogma inherent in sociobiology. To explain some human behavior with the aid of sociobiology does not make it natural and good in the sense of being inevitable and desirable; it adds an evolutionary perspective to what we already know about the behavior, one that locates it within an evolutionary timescale for understanding the human species in relation to other species.

This viewpoint illustrates just one way in which sociobiologists vigorously defend their discipline against the sorts of accusations that so readily come to mind. No one, at least so far, has had the last word, and the proper interpretation of sociobiology with respect to its status as a science and as an ideology is a difficult problem that demands sophisticated understanding of evolutionary biology, human social behavior, scientific method, and the ideological dimensions of science. The controversy will continue and will itself be transformed in ways that will increase our understanding of sociobiology, science, and ideology.

At present there are three distinct uses to which sociobiology is put. First and foremost, it serves a scientific purpose within evolutionary biology, namely, attaining a more complete overall picture of the evolution of life, expanding it to include biological and social aspects in a single scheme. Second, it serves an extra-scientific purpose, namely, informing our overall picture of human nature. Third, it serves a cross-disciplinary scientific purpose, namely, adding an evolutionary dimension to the problems and proposed solutions in diverse disciplines: psychiatry, law, management theory, history, political science, ethical philosophy cognitive psychology, epistemology, religion, conflict studies, Marxist thought, aesthetics, sociology, linguistics, psychology, and anthropology.

Bibliography

Barkow, J. H. (1989). "Darwin, Sex, and Status." University of Toronto Press, Toronto.

Barkow, J. H., Cosmides, L., and Tooby, J. (Eds.) (1991). "The Adapted Mind." Oxford University Press, Oxford.

Betzig, L. L., Borgerhoff Mulder, M., and Turke, P. W. (Eds.) (1988). "Human Reproductive Behaviour." Cambridge University Press, Cambridge.

Cronk, L. (1991). Human Behavioral Ecology. *Annu. Rev. Anthropol.* **20,** 25–53.

Daly, M., and Wilson, M. (1988). "Homicide." Aldine, Hawthorne.

Holcomb, H. (1993). "Sociobiology, Sex, and Science." State University of New York Press, Albany.

Krebs, J. R., and Davies, N. B. (Eds.) (1991). "Behavioural Ecology," 3rd ed. Blackwell Scientific, Oxford.

Maxwell, M. (1993). "The Sociobiological Imagination." State University of New York Press, Albany.

Smith, E. A., and Winterhalder, B. (Eds.) (1992). "Ecology, Evolution, and Human Behavior." Aldine, Hawthorne.

Socioemotional Development

Ross A. Thompson and A. K. Ganzel
University of Nebraska

Glossary

Attachment The affectional tie that unites two or more people across time and place; applied especially to the emotional bonds formed between infants and their caregivers.

Emotional regulation The processes by which individuals are capable of monitoring, evaluating, and modifying their emotional reactions.

Functional emotions theory Theories that argue that the nature of emotion is fundamentally defined by the organism's ongoing transactions with the environment, especially goal attainment.

Insecure attachment Infants who do not maintain confidence in the caregiver's helpfulness, and instead show marked anxiety, avoidance, or disorganization when stressed in the company of that adult.

Internal working model An individual's representations of attachment, including conceptions of self and others who are attachment figures.

Secure attachment Infants whose confidence and trust in the caregiver enables them to explore and play comfortably, while confidently retreating to the caregiver as a "secure base" when threatened or alarmed.

Socioemotional development The intersection of social and emotional growth, reflecting the integration of complex developmental and environmental influences.

Strange Situation A widely used laboratory procedure for evaluating whether infants are securely attached or insecurely attached to their caregivers.

Structural emotions theory Theories that portray emotions as discrete, coherent constellations of physiological, subjective, and expressively activity that are organized on a neurophysiological level.

SOCIOEMOTIONAL DEVELOPMENT concerns the intersection of social and emotional growth. It addresses issues such as how emotion is expressed in social contexts, the social elicitors of emotional expressions, the social construction of emotional experience and emotional understanding, the social ramifications of emotional reactions, and the effects of emotion on social behavior. In a sense, socioemotional development is a conceptual rubric for both old and new research questions in developmental psychology. It includes, for example, the study of separation and stranger reactions in infancy, the development of attachments between infants and their caregivers, children's empathy and emotional understanding, their appreciation of emotional display rules, the psychosocial consequences of temperamental individuality, the growth of guilt, shame, and other moral emotions, and a range of other longstanding issues in the study of human development. Socioemotional development also includes newer studies of the growth of emotional regulation, children's representations of significant relationships, children's "emotion schemas" for how to act when aroused, and the emotional dimensions of disorders of developmental psychopathology like child maltreatment or depression.

This is clearly a very broad range of topics, and it is worthwhile inquiring what is gained by encompassing them within a general concept like "socioemotional development." The answer is that research on socioemotional development reflects a growing appreciation for the importance of emotion in organized behavioral functioning from early in life, especially in social contexts. By contrast with some traditional personality theories within psychology that emphasize the disorganizing, stressful character of emotional arousal, or its irrelevance to adaptive, strategic behavior, current views underscore how emotion can contribute to competent and constructive capacities from birth, whether emotion is enlisted to signal needs, motivate human attachments, organize social responses, heighten understanding of others, or aid in learning from the environment. To be sure, emotional arousal always retains its capacity to disorganize or undermine effective functioning, but the recognition that emotion need not always do so, and that from infancy it underlies many psychologically constructive behaviors, has contributed to a renewed appreciation of the important role of emotion in social life—hence, the term "socioemotional development."

I. SOCIOEMOTIONAL DEVELOPMENT AS AN INTEGRATIVE FIELD

Another characteristic of the study of socioemotional development is the integration of processes and influences from diverse developmental domains. By contrast with the general tendency of developmental scientists to study age-related accomplishments in one area of growth independently of others (e.g., cognitive development, or perceptual growth, or physical maturation, etc.), the field of socioemotional development requires its students to denote interrelationships between many different developmental and environmental processes that influence social and emotional growth. Consequently, this area fosters the reintegration of the developing person, in all its complexity.

A. Socioemotional Development and Other Developmental Domains

Socioemotional development depends on cognitive growth, for example, as emergent intellectual capacities become enlisted to appraise emotionally arousing events, reflect upon one's own emotional experiences, and understand the emotional expressions of others. As children grow cognitively, for example, they can better interpret the social meaning of subtle emotional cues (such as in facial expressions), and they can better appreciate that situations may evoke multiple (sometimes conflicting) simultaneous emotions in themselves and others. Socioemotional development also depends on the growth of self-understanding as children acquire a better appreciation of the situations that instigate their emotional arousal, the outcomes of their emotional expressions to others, and the strategies by which their emotion can be better managed or regulated for strategic purposes. One child may realize that watching scary movies is exciting and enjoyable for them while another appreciates that the same movies provoke uncomfortable fear (but which can be strategically managed by thinking of other things). Socioemotional development also draws on the growth of language and other communicative skills as they influence the expression of emotion and how it is socialized by others. Neurophysiological growth affects socioemotional functioning as brain centers relevant to the regulation and control of subcortical emotive processes gradually mature in the early years of life. Genetic and hereditary processes assume a significant role in the emergence of individual differences in many aspects of socioemotional reactivity, whether they concern tendencies toward sociability, shyness or other characteristics. In these and many other ways, a sophisticated understanding of socioemotional development requires integrating developmental processes across many different areas of growth.

It is important to recognize, however, that socioemotional growth is not just an outcome of these allied developmental processes but may also be, at times, a catalyst for their growth. A developing capacity for emotional regulation, for example, not only assists in the management of arousal but may also foster the child's intellectual and problem-solving skills in situations involving frustration, challenge, trial-and-error efforts, or delayed rewards. Language development aids in expressing emotion, but the growth of emotional understanding in childhood alters many of the pragmatics of language use. In these ways, therefore, socioemotional development has bidirectional associations with other developmental accomplishments: It grows as the result of allied achievements in other domains, but it also helps to advance these allied areas of growth.

B. Socioemotional Development in Bioevolutionary Context

One reason for viewing emotion as a contributor to organized, constructive psychological processes is that emotion is deeply rooted in the evolution of our species. Emotive processes are organized within neurophysiologically primitive subcortical structures in the human brain, and the universal recognition of facial expressions of basic emotions further suggests that emotion is an intrinsic feature of human functioning. Consequently, emotional arousal is associated with many biologically adaptive motivational tendencies: the impulse to flee potentially threatening events (fear), the capacity for self-defense (anger), quickly gathering information concerning unexpected events (surprise), and so forth. Furthermore, emotional expressions are potent social signals: they convey to others our arousal and action tendencies, and responses to these signals can often alter those action tendencies (such as when an attacker withdraws after perceiving the victim's anger).

These bioevolutionary influences suggest that socioemotional behavior should be regarded, in part, in terms of the adaptational demands encountered by our species during its long evolutionary history. Socioemotional functioning assumes added meaning, in other words, when integrated with its bioevolutionary context. Contemporary attachment theory argues, for example, that an infant's crying, following, contact-seeking, and other behaviors toward familiar adults reflects not just a baby's immediate learning history, but also an evolutionarily based predisposition to seek proximity to caregivers. They argue that such a predisposition, evolved over countless generations of human forebears, would have helped to ensure the survival of vulnerable young infants in settings where predation, natural dangers, desertion, and other risks posed formidable challenges to individual and species survival. Consequently, a young child who clings to a caregiver's leg—especially when threatened or uncertain—may not be unduly dependent or anxious, but instead reflecting bioevolutionary influences on his or her socioemotional behavior: the predisposition to seek protective contact with a nurturant adult.

C. The Intersection of Social and Emotional Behavior

A final indication of the integrative quality of contemporary research on socioemotional development is the synthesis of social and emotional behavior that this term suggests. Indeed, developmental researchers currently seldom study social behavior outside of its emotional context or, conversely, emotional reactions in nonsocial settings. In a sense, much of the meaning of social behavior derives from its emotional quality, whether researchers are studying an infant's friendliness or fearfulness in the presence of a stranger, a toddler's aggressive or sociable reactions toward peers, a grade-school child's emotional reactions to a parent's disciplinary practices, or an adolescent's sympathy with a friend whose feelings have been hurt. In similar fashion, most of the interesting questions guiding current research on emotional development concern its social functions, such as how children use the emotional expressions of others as cues for their own behavior (called "social referencing"), or how they manipulate their own expressions to accomplish social goals. Thus, the term "socioemotional development" reflects the recognition that, in research as in everyday life, the emotional and social dimensions of behavior are highly integrated.

As these introductory comments suggest, contemporary study of socioemotional development is extraordinarily broad and multifaceted—and consequently impossible to encompass within a short encyclopedic article. Our approach will instead focus on two topics that are currently generating considerable attention from developmental researchers: new ideas about the nature of emotional development, and new research about infant–parent attachment and its developmental significance. We have chosen these topics not only because they reflect current scientific interest, but also because they encompass some of the most important broader issues guiding inquiry into other areas of socioemotional development. We then conclude this short chapter with an outline of emerging future directions for this field.

II. NEW PERSPECTIVES ON EMOTIONAL DEVELOPMENT

For many years, developmental study of emotions was a subsidiary concern to researchers either because of traditional assumptions that emotional arousal was disorganizing and stressful (and thus undermined competent functioning) or because emotional development was regarded as a derivative of more important maturational or cognitive accomplishments. For example, infants' emerging wariness of strangers during the second half of the first year was long regarded as either a maturational phase (what one researcher called the "8-month anxiety") or as a by-product of cognitive achievements, such as the growth of a concept of object (and person) permanence. In either case, the emotions themselves were less interesting than their underlying constituents.

More recently, however, study of emotional development has flourished as researchers have realized that emotional growth is based on much more complex developmental processes, and that emotional reactions reveal the complex, organized quality of individual growth. Developmentalists now realize, for example, that an 8 month old's reaction to an unfamiliar adult is affected not only by cognitive and maturational prerequisites, but also by subtle aspects of the stranger's behavior, features of the setting, the presence of attachment figures, emotional cues from those figures, the child's temperament, the behavior of the stranger, the child's range of response options, and many other factors that are integrated in a surprisingly coherent and sophisticated fashion in the baby's emotional response, which may indicate not just fear or friendliness but gradations of shyness or wariness. Later developmental changes in stranger reactions occur as infants acquire more diverse social capacities for interacting with adults and as their own psychological independence from caregivers matures. Individual differences in stranger wariness or sociability are related both to the infant's range of social experiences and to the quality of the mother–infant relationship, and have important implications for the subsequent growth of social skills. In sum, emotional development provides a revealing look at the organization of developmental processes as they unfold over time. As a consequence, emotional development has now become a more primary interest in developmental psychology.

Accompanying this change in emphasis has been a change in perspective on emotion itself: developmental researchers are exploring whether structural or functional theories best account for the nature of emotion and for processes of emotional development. Their exploration has deepened our understanding of the role of emotion on social functioning throughout life.

A. The Influence of Structural Accounts of Emotional Development

Like the field of psychology more generally, developmental study of emotions in infants and children has been guided by structural theories of emotion. These theories portray emotions as discrete, coherent constellations of physiological, subjective, and expressive activity that are organized on a neurophysiological level, and are thus structured consistently across culture and history. In this view, humans possess a repertoire of basic emotions—including anger, fear, joy, sadness or distress, surprise, and disgust in most theories—that are differentiated by unique patterns of physiological activation, subjective experience, and expression (in particular, facial expression). The emotion of anger, for example, entails a distinct subjective experience, the physiological concomitants of that feeling (which accounts for the energized, aroused experience), and a unique constellation of facial expression and other behaviors. [*See* ANGER; ANXIETY AND FEAR; DISGUST; SURPRISE.]

The underlying biological organization of these discrete emotions does not mean that each appears at birth, however. Theories of emotional development from a structural orientation emphasize that certain basic emotions (like distress) are present in newborns, but that many emotions develop during the early months of life as the infant's cognitive skills and response capacities unfold. In subsequent years, of course, this repertoire of basic emotions is supplemented by an array of secondary emotions—like pride, gratitude, embarrassment, and guilt—that are not as strongly organized by biology and are thus more culturally variable.

Structural accounts of emotion have also had important implications for the measurement of emotion in children and adults. Researchers have used increasingly detailed systems for measuring facial expressions of emotion because of the belief that these expressions reliably index underlying subjective state, especially in young children prior to the socialization of cultural display rules for expressing emotion. In addition, developmental researchers have tended to study emotional growth by clearly distinguishing between different emotional states (especially primary emotions) and identifying how each develops in complexity during the early years of life. By assuming that the neurophysiological structure of emotional arousal is organized around discrete emotional states, in other words, developmental researchers have sought to understand the unique expressive patterns, cognitive correlates, and behavioral consequences of each type of emotion. [*See* FACIAL EXPRESSIONS OF EMOTION.]

Recently, however, structural accounts of emotional development have been challenged in several ways. Some emotions theorists have questioned whether emotional experience, expression, and arousal patterns cohere as consistently as structural accounts suggest. Some developmental researchers have noted, for example, that the facial expressions of young infants are often incongruous with their circumstances (for example, a baby who shows an expression of disgust while stretching, or surprise while staring at the soft light of a ceiling lamp), suggesting that the associations between emotional experience, expression, and arousal may not be neurophysiologically structured, but instead developmentally assembled. Furthermore, many students of emotion suggest that typical emotional experience consists not of the succession of a variety of discrete emotions, but rather subtly nuanced blends of a broad variety of emotional states that range in their intensity and temporal dynamics, and that these features of emotion are not well encompassed within structural accounts.

B. The Emergence of Functional Views

An alternative portrayal of emotional development that addresses some of these criticisms has recently been offered by functional theorists, who argue that the nature of emotion is defined not by biologically based constellations of expression, experience, and arousal, but rather by the organism's ongoing transactions with the environment. Emotions are fundamentally linked to an organism's goals and their attainment, and emotions not only reflect success or failure in goal-achievement but are also related to maintaining or changing relations between the organism and the environment (both internal and external) in ways relevant to these goals. The emotion of anger, for example, is central to the experience of goal-attainment being blocked by another, and the action tendencies associated with anger are directed toward removing these obstacles in ways that make the achievement of goals more probable. In this manner, functional emotions theorists emphasize the motivational qualities of emotional arousal, the importance of emotional expressions as social signals, the association between an individual's assessment of environmental events and emotional arousal, and the social construction of emotional experience. And although functional theorists refer to discrete emotions, their emotion taxonomy is broader and they also commonly speak of emotion "families" that are united by common patterns of organism–environment relations and action tendencies.

Functional views also affect how researchers study emotional development, since it cannot be assumed that facial expressions and other indices of primary emotions reliably reflect the emotional dimensions of organism–environment interactions. Instead, functionally oriented researchers tend to study broader constellations of emotional expression in terms of the specific situations in which they occur: for one child, for example, an angry expression and menacing posture may deter a peer's aggression, while for another child a tense shout of warning and calls to friends may accomplish the same functional goal. In each case, emotion figures prominently in altering transactions with the (social) environment in ways relevant to an individual's meaningful goals, but in ways that are revealed in much different behavioral constellations.

Emergent functional views of emotional development significantly broaden the scope of emotion research by linking emotion to goal states, individual appraisals of goal attainment, and broader motivational processes (indeed, one might worry that the study of emotion becomes unduly broadened as a consequence). They have also provoked interest in several current topics of research activity in the study of emotional development.

C. Current Topics in Emotional Development

1. Emotional Regulation

If emotion is centrally related to the transactions between the individual and the environment, then strategies for emotional regulation are essential for enlisting emotion optimally to support goal attainment. Consequently, developmental researchers have become interested in the processes by which individuals are capable of monitoring, evaluating, and modifying their emotional reactions—especially the intensive and temporal features of emotional behavior, which are often most relevant to competent functioning. Although infants and very young children rely primarily on others to manage their emotional arousal, emergent capacities for emotional self-regulation appear early in life. Whereas the newborn infant may cry uncontrollably, the toddler can seek assistance from others, the preschooler can reflect upon and talk about her feelings, the school-age child can redirect attention and use other deliberate strategies to reduce distress or anxiety, the adolescent can evoke personal strategies (like listening to favorite music) that manage emotion, and the adult can employ regulatory approaches that are emotion-specific (that is, strategies for managing anger may be different from those used to manage anxiety). Understanding the developmental constituents of these unfolding capacities for emotional regulation has thus become a new and important feature of the study of emotional development.

Research on emotional regulation is important not only for an understanding of normative processes of emotional development, but also for an appreciation of the origins of individual differences in emotion and emotional self-regulation and their psychosocial consequences. Developmental researchers who study children with behavioral problems—such as those who are unduly aggressive toward peers, or who are behaviorally inhibited in social interactions—have revealed that emotional self-management often assumes a significant role in their problems. Similarly, studies of children who are emotionally challenged—such as those who have been maltreated by parents, who are depressed, or who are raised by parents with an affective disorder—also reveal the importance of emotional self-regulatory strategies to an understanding of their condition. Thus, the study of emotional regulation is important not only as a normative feature of emotional development, but also for efforts to understand and assist children with socioemotional difficulties.

It is likely that many complex influences contribute to the emergence of developmental changes and individual differences in emotional self-regulatory capacities. Children must acquire a basic awareness of the situations requiring emotional self-control. They must develop a repertoire of strategies for managing their emotional arousal in necessary ways. As they do so, their knowledge of the social benefits of well-regulated emotion and the social rules governing emotional expression must increase also. Furthermore, growing maturity in emotional management probably also includes an ability to flexibly tailor one's regulatory skills to different situations and contexts, and the capacity to substitute a new strategy for an ineffective one. This requires the ability to sensitively evaluate the success of one's efforts to manage emotion. These are complex skills, and they suggest that the growth of emotional regulation is not a single unitary capacity, but a set of interrelated developmental processes. Individual differences in emotional management may derive from limitations in any one or a variety of these processes. Clearly, the emerging study of emotional regulation is an important but surprisingly complex topic in the developmental study of emotion.

2. Socialization of Emotional Expression and Experience

With its emphasis on the links between emotion and environmental transactions, functional accounts emphasize far more than structural accounts how emotion is socialized by the culture. Consequently, developmental researchers are examining these socialization influences in detailed social-interactional analyses and also in cross-cultural studies. Early findings are indicating that a child's emotional expressions are shaped through selective reinforcement and modeling beginning early in infancy, and that emotional expressions are further socialized as children acquire an understanding of cultural rules for emotional displays during the preschool and grade-school years. Equally important, a child's understanding of emotion is also socialized, beginning with the earliest verbal exchanges about emotions shared by parents and their toddlers, and continuing with active instruction and coaching about emotional experience and its expression by parents, peers, teachers, and other social agents. As a consequence, children acquire greater "emotional competence" in their culture as they learn to interpret, express, and manage their emotional experience in culture-specific ways. Elucidating how this competence is developmentally achieved is one of the more important research topics in the field of emotional development.

3. Individual Differences in Emotion

Finally, a third emerging research topic spurred by functional views of emotion is a renewed emphasis on individual differences in emotional experience and expression and their developmental origins. Variability in emotionality derives not just from individual differences in the self-regulatory capacities discussed earlier, but also from other diverse sources: biogenetic individuality that predisposes some children to be emotionally inhibited while others are more outgoing; "emotional biases" derived from early patterns of infant–mother interaction and the socialization of emotional experience in these contexts; and aspects of self-understanding that cause children to react emotionally to perceived incentives and challenges. Growing research attention to the origins of individual differences in emotional experience and expression reflects a recognition that emotional life quickly becomes individualized, reflecting a rich tapestry of influences that cause one's personal experience of emotion to be, at times, much different from that of others. [*See* INDIVIDUAL DIFFERENCES IN TEMPERAMENT.]

Taken together, current study of emotional development has focused attention on a number of basic issues in developmental study: To what extent are we products of our culture or of our biological organization? How does individual experience alter species-typical developmental processes? To what extent do developing persons learn to alter their own life experience by regulating arousal and its expression? Efforts to address these questions from the perspective of emotional development promise to advance long-standing debates on these and related questions.

III. ATTACHMENT AND THE ORGANIZATION OF RELATIONSHIPS

A second topic that continues to captivate students of socioemotional development concerns the origins and consequences of individual differences in parent–infant attachment. Contemporary attachment theory builds on a long legacy in developmental psychology: questions concerning the significance of the early mother–infant relationship for later adjustment, the relational origins of a growing sense of trust or security in the world at large, and the extent to which individuals approach new relationships biased by their early relationship history have been long articulated by developmental theorists, many of them from a psychoanalytic or neo-analytic orientation. In the 1970s and 1980s, however, renewed attention to these questions was generated by a provocative theory of attachment relationships proposed by John Bowlby, and the development by Mary Ainsworth of an insightful methodology for examining these attachments in young infants called the Strange Situation. These catalysts continue to guide contemporary attachment theory and research, but in some interesting new directions.

A. Attachment and the Organization of Development

The ethological attachment theory proposed by Bowlby integrated contemporary insights on early social and cognitive growth with emerging bioevolutionary perspectives on socioemotional development. In brief, he proposed that infants are motivated to remain close to familiar, trusted caregivers not only because of their reinforcement value, but also owing to the legacy of species evolution that made it advantageous for infants to remain close to protective, nurturant adults. The development of emotional ties, or attachments, to familiar caregivers is a natural consequence of this evolutionary legacy, built upon the infant's growing capacities to identify familiar persons and use behavioral strategies to stay close to them. Bowlby and Ainsworth argued further that while it is normative for infants to become attached, they vary in the extent of the security or confidence they obtain from these attachments. Most infants become securely attached, which means that they derive sufficient security from the caregiver's presence that they can explore and play comfortably, while confidently retreating to the caregiver as a "secure base" when threatened or alarmed. By contrast, the minority of infants who become insecurely attached seem not to maintain such confidence in the caregiver's helpfulness, and instead show greater anxiety, avoidance, or disorganization when stressed in the company of that adult.

Accompanying these theoretical proposals was the development of a research strategy for measuring these differences called the Strange Situation. This laboratory procedure consists of seven 3-minute episodes in which the infant (typically around 12 months of age) is observed with the mother, a stranger, and sometimes all alone. By observing closely the infant's behavior with each partner, but especially during reunions with the mother after having been separated from her, researchers have been able to distinguish the characteristics of securely attached and insecurely attached infants and to reliably classify infants into each group. More importantly, hundreds of studies employing the Strange Situation have helped to confirm the validity of these classifications, and have yielded a theoretically provocative account of the origins, stability, and cultural variability of attachment behavior in infants that will be reviewed below.

As a consequence, contemporary attachment theory has begun to explore the broader place of attachment in the organization of development. The importance of secure or insecure attachments to later social relationships, including how an individual conceptualizes the meaning of relationships (even parenting relationships as an adult) has received enhanced attention, and newer topics such as the effects of day care on attachment and clinical "disorders of attachment" have also emerged. Moreover, new methods for measuring individual differences in attachment in older children and adults have also recently been devised and are beginning to be validated. The reason attachment theory and research continues to dominate the study of socioemotional development is that it permits developmental scientists to explore these theoretical questions of longstanding interest with more incisive methods and research designs than were previously possible—yielding answers both expected and surprising.

B. Classic Issues in Attachment Research

In studies using the Strange Situation, researchers have begun to answer the questions that theorists had long posed concerning infant–mother bonding: why do some infants develop secure or insecure attachments, how stable do these attachments remain in the early years, and what are their long-term implications? In addition, cross-cultural studies have examined whether various cultural practices result in different kinds of attachment relationships than those commonly observed in the United States.

1. Origins of Individual Differences in Attachment

Consistent with theoretical expectations, researchers have found that infants are more likely to become securely attached if their caregivers are more sensitive, positive, and responsive to them in the early months of life. Maternal sensitivity is, in short, a primary determinant of the security of infant–mother attachment. Beyond this, however, other influences are also important. The father's involvement in care, the harmony of the marital relationship, socioeconomic stresses on the family, and the baby's temperamental qualities have all been found to influence the development of secure or insecure attachments. In a sense, these findings suggest that the "emotional climate" of the home that theorists have long implicated in the development of security and trust in infancy is multidetermined, involving contributions from other family members as well as mother, the family's broader living circumstances, and infants themselves.

2. Stability of Attachment and Prediction of Later Behavior

Once developed, how stable do these attachments remain in the early years of life? Do securely attached infants, for example, tend to remain that way? Although this important question has not been explored as systematically as it should, current evidence indicates that when caregiving conditions remain consistent, attachment relationships tend to remain stable over time. Infants who have developed secure attachments tend to maintain their security, for example, barring important changes in how they are cared for. On the other hand, when conditions of care change significantly—such as when the family experiences economic or legal stress, or the mother returns to work and the baby begins out-of-home care, or parents separate—attachment relationships often change, with some infants shifting from securely attached to insecure, and other babies changing in the opposite direction. As a result, researchers studying different samples of infants and mothers whose life circumstances vary significantly tend to report widely varying estimates of the proportion of infants who maintain the same quality of attachment over time.

This conclusion has important implications for the prediction of later behavior from whether an infant is securely attached or insecure. It suggests that the stability of the baby's conditions of care may be an important mediating factor. In general, researchers have found impressive associations between infant attachment and the child's sociability with peers, cooperation with parents, competence in exploration, and other markers of psychosocial growth in later years. But this has been found most often when there was consistency over time in the child's caregiving conditions, so that (for example) the nurturance and sensitivity of caregivers that initially fostered the baby's secure attachment continued to contribute to more optimal socioemotional functioning in the child at later ages. By contrast, in samples with significant changes in family circumstances or conditions of care, it has been more difficult to predict later behavior from the baby's attachment status—perhaps because the attachment relationship itself changed over time, or perhaps because caregiving influences changed to foster different behavior in offspring.

Taken together, these findings confirm theoretical expectations that the quality or security of early infant–mother attachment is an important cornerstone for later socioemotional growth. But many researchers have concluded that attachment is not alone important: the caregiving influences that initially fostered the baby's security must continue over time to ensure healthy later growth. In a sense, a secure or insecure attachment in infancy provides a provisional—rather than enduring—basis for later development. That foundation must be maintained to support later optimal socioemotional functioning.

3. Cross-Cultural Studies of Attachment

Given the bioevolutionary incentives for the growth of attachment relationships, developmental researchers have naturally been interested in whether patterns of attachment vary significantly cross-culturally. Do we find, for example, considerable consistency in the relative proportions of securely attached and insecurely attached infants in different cultural settings, or do these attachment patterns vary meaningfully owing to different normative practices of infant care? Questions like these address the extent to which attachment processes are affected by species-wide or culture-specific influences.

The answer is that both appear to be true. On one hand, there is cross-cultural variability in patterns of attachment, but on the whole this is not significantly greater than the variability in attachment patterns observed within cultures. In other words, the relative proportions of infants who are securely attached and insecurely attached are generally consistent across different cultural settings. On the other hand, there is evidence from several studies that culture-specific practices of infant care can significantly affect the formation of attachment relationships. In Japan, for example, where close and intimate contact between mother and baby is emphasized, infants often behave insecurely in the Strange Situation because they have had little prior experience with the separations from mother that this procedure requires. Similarly, infants reared on traditional Israeli kibbutzim—who are cared for in out-of-home settings from an early age—also show higher proportions of insecure attachments owing to their unique experiences of communal care.

Thus, although there is striking consistency in the patterns of attachment observed in different cultures, cultural practices concerning infant care are sometimes very important determinants of the security of attachment. This conclusion has alerted researchers to the need for cultural insight in understanding influences on attachment, and in devising alternative procedures for measuring attachment that are consistent with the normative early experiences of infants from different cultures.

C. Emerging Topics of Interest

These findings portray infant–mother attachment as a more multifaceted, dynamic process than traditional theories had suggested, while confirming that individual differences in attachment are significant determinants of later socioemotional development. Based on these findings, contemporary attachment researchers are currently broadening their theoretical and research work in new directions: exploring how children and adolescents represent the nature of attachment relationships conceptually, and examining how attachment relationships themselves change throughout life.

1. Internal Representations of Attachment Relationships

One of the most important advances in attachment theory has been the portrayal of attachment not only as a system of behavioral processes in infancy but also as a representational system of later years. That is, developmental scientists have begun to explore the nature of the concepts (or "internal working models") of oneself and of others that are believed to have their genesis in secure or insecure attachment relationships in infancy. In this view, for example, infants with secure attachments begin to develop representations of the self as loveable and worthy of affection, and concepts of others as trustworthy and supportive. This is believed to bias positively their subsequent social relationships because of the more confident expectations and self-referent beliefs they underlie. On the other hand, infants who are insecurely attached are likely to regard themselves and other people less positively, and this is likely to have a negative biasing effect on subsequent sociability. At its extreme, Bowlby believed that this could lead to later psychological disorders that derive from a legacy of insecure attachment relationships in the form of enduring negative internal "working models" of self and attachment figures.

This theoretical formulation has inspired a number of efforts to assess the nature of these "working models" as they develop. In recent years, attachment theorists have used doll-play procedures to explore the attachment-related beliefs of preschoolers, interviews to examine the attachment conceptions of 6 year olds, and retrospective self-reports and secondary-source methods to elucidate the attachment representations of adolescents and adults. Researchers have not yet examined whether these representations have a predictable relation to whether an individual was securely or insecurely attached as an infant, and for various reasons they may *not* be related: our representations of ourselves and others are based on many developmental catalysts besides attachment experiences in infancy, such that the internal "working models" of an adolescent or adult are likely derived not only from reconstructions of childhood experiences, but also from relationships experienced during the adolescent and adult years, including those with close friends, marital partner(s), and children. Consequently, a better understanding of the developmental origins of differences in the attachment-related representations of individuals after infancy, and their consequences for other aspects of socioemotional functioning, remains one of the most important research topics for future study of attachment processes.

2. Developmental Changes in Attachment Relationships

Of course, there are developmental changes not only in one's representations of attachment, but also in attachment relationships themselves throughout life. Although feelings of security, confidence, and trust in the parent are doubtlessly of paramount importance to the attachments of infants, parents quickly assume multidimensional roles in relation to children as offspring mature. They are not only sources of security but also salient play partners, teachers, and consultants; they are catalysts for the introduction of new experiences, interests, and competencies; they are reliable sources of love, affirmation, and support; they are mentors; they manage the distribution of resources that are valuable to the child; they mediate the child's relationships with kin, peers, and other adults; and, in their use of discipline and maturity demands, parents are sometimes frustrators of the child's wishes and desires as well as mediators and arbitrators of sibling relationships. In short, parent–child and parent–adolescent relationships are far more complex—behaviorally and psychologically—than are parent–infant relationships, and this must alter attachments with development.

The important challenge for attachment researchers, therefore, is to elucidate the changing quality of parent–offspring attachments over time, especially in relation to perceptions of security and trust that are foundational in infancy. Although security probably remains important to attachment throughout life, its preeminence may wane as children mature, become psychologically more independent, and have needs that extend far beyond the baby's need for protective nurturance. Attachment researchers are just beginning to examine developmental changes in children's experiences and understanding of the family system and their place in it, and exploring these developmental changes in attachment relationships remains a foundational concern for future work in attachment theory. In addition, understanding the interrelationships between multiple attachment relationships that a child experiences—not only with parents but also with siblings, extended kin, step-parents, out-of-home caregivers, and even teachers and peers—will contribute to a more multifaceted portrayal of attachment processes as they affect socioemotional growth throughout life.

Taken together, it is clear that attachment theory and research have moved far beyond the initial concern about the bioevolutionary origins of infant proximity-seeking that motivated the earliest theoretical and empirical efforts, and developmental scientists are now poised to extend their formulations to the construction of a truly lifespan view of attachment processes. Doing so, however, will require tackling formidably complex conceptual issues: what kinds of influences, for example, does one maintain from infancy through adulthood? How are self-referent belief systems constructed and perpetuated from the early years of life? How does one's experience of relationships affect other relationships? Readers will recognize that these questions have a long legacy in developmental psychology that will be maintained by future attachment studies.

IV. NEW ISSUES IN THE STUDY OF SOCIOEMOTIONAL DEVELOPMENT

Careful readers have realized that although the study of socioemotional development is potentially of lifespan importance, developmental theorists have focused largely on infancy and early childhood. Much less is known about socioemotional functioning during later childhood, and the research literature is virtually silent about adolescence and adulthood. There are many reasons for this: research on infancy and early childhood crystallizes long-standing issues of continuity and change in behavior that research on socioemotional development often addresses, and many of these processes can be more easily studied in young children. Moreover, as earlier noted, studies of attachment are extending to later ages in the effort to understanding the long-term significance of early attachment relationships. Nevertheless, the neglect of socioemotional processes at later ages is important because of the variety of important concerns meriting deeper exploration. A brief catalogue of such issues includes how socioemotional processes affect the prosocial and antisocial behavior of children and adolescents, how temperament relates to later personality individuality in the adult years, how "self-conscious" emotions like guilt, shame, pride, and embarrassment develop and affect behavior (and the sense of self), how sociocultural influences affect moral understanding and moral behavior, and how socioemotional processes relate to later disorders of developmental psychopathology.

Studying socioemotional processes at later years is quite a research challenge. Children and adolescents (not to mention adults) live in an ever-expanding variety of contexts (e.g., peer groups, schools, workplace settings, neighborhoods, social groups, etc.), and socioemotional processes salient in one setting likely relate in complicated ways to processes relevant to other settings. For example, the emotional quality of parent–child relationships likely affects peer interaction, but in complex and (at present) little-understood ways. Furthermore, by contrast with infants and young children, adolescents and adults are oriented not only toward present and past events but toward the future as well: their goals and expectations for their personal futures can significantly affect present socioemotional functioning in diverse ways.

Despite these challenges (or perhaps because of them), there is no shortage of important and interesting issues meriting further exploration in the study of socioemotional development. Rather than attempting a broader catalogue, we consider two issues in particular—socioemotional influences on peer relationships in middle childhood, and adolescent identity formation—to illustrate the potential insights offered by the study of socioemotional development extended to later ages.

A. Peer Relationships in Middle Childhood

Developmentalists have long recognized that peer relationships become increasingly important during middle childhood and adolescence, but they have only recently begun to elucidate how socioemotional processes both influence and derive from the quality of peer relationships. One promising approach concerns the study of differences in peer social status. Based on sociometric ratings by children themselves, researchers have distinguished children who are "popular" (i.e., well-liked), "controversial" (liked by some, disliked by others), "neglected" (ignored by most), and "rejected" (disliked by most). Not surprisingly, the rejected children have elicited the greatest concern and attention from developmental researchers. [*See* PEER RELATIONSHIPS AND INFLUENCES IN CHILDHOOD.]

Several studies indicate that children who are rejected by peers—often because of their aggressive behavior—are deficient interpreters of social cues. In particular, when they feel threatened, rejected children often interpret ambiguous social cues as hostile in nature, and thus overreact to benign peer encounters. In a sense, their deficient social information-processing leads to deficient socioemotional functioning that can have long-term consequences: even when they are not hostile, peers continue to reject these children because of their reputations.

However, it is likely that far more complex socioemotional processes contribute to peer rejection. For example, aggressive children may have limited skills at emotional regulation that affect their interpretation of social cues: when feeling threatened, for instance, their heightened arousal may bias their interpretation of social cues, constrain their consideration of response alternatives, and result in impulsive responses. There is also emerging evidence that these children are affected by parental power-assertion at home that causes them to generalize the frustration they experience in discipline encounters to peer relationships. Taken together, therefore, there is considerably more we have to learn about the origins of individual differences in peer relationships during middle childhood, especially when differences in socioemotional processes are manifested in problematic peer relationships.

B. Adolescent Identity Formation

"Adolescence" is connotatively synonymous with "transition," yet researchers have devoted surprisingly little attention to how the diverse changes of adolescence affect socioemotional processes or, conversely, how socioemotional functioning affects the success with which adolescents negotiate the changes they experience. [*See* ADOLESCENCE.]

The construction and elaboration of personal identity provides a good example of these complex, bidirectional influences. The question "who am I?" clearly reflects emergent cognitive capacities related to self-reflection and abstract thinking. Yet these cognitive capacities also conspire to produce an emotional response: teenagers become increasingly bothered by inconsistencies in their own behavior which may further motivate the search for identity. Identity formation is also linked to socioemotional aspects of friendship processes. The "self-conscious" emotions—particularly embarrassment—are highly salient to adolescents, and peer relationships provide a forum for exploring but protecting images of the self. The intimacy and trust provided by close friendships during adolescence provides an arena within which one can explore the question of who one is and (equally important) what one will become in the future.

Studying these processes is challenging because covert developmental processes like identity formation are revealed only globally when researchers rely on self-report measures, and such measures often fail to reveal the complex socioemotional influences that are often most informative. We hope that future studies of adolescent identity will increasingly employ the kinds of naturalistic observational strategies—supplemented by discourse analysis in the context of peer relationships—that have proven so informative in other areas of socioemotional study.

Taken together, it is clear that the study of socioemotional development builds on long-standing interests of developmental psychology concerning the role of emotion in social behavior, but also advances a number of new formulations concerning emotion as a behavioral organizer. This brief review suggests that there is considerable reason for optimism that exciting advances will continue to characterize future research in this area.

Bibliography

Ainsworth, M. D. S., Blehar, M. C., Waters, E., and Wall, S. (1978). "Patterns of Attachment." Erlbaum, Hillsdale, NJ.

Barrett, K. C., and Campos, J. J. (1987). Perspectives on emotional development. II. A functionalist approach to emotion. In "Handbook of Infant Development" (J. D. Osofsky, Ed.), 2nd ed. New York, Wiley.

Bowlby, J. (1969). "Attachment and Loss," Vol. 1. "Attachment." Basic Books, New York.

Garber, J., and Dodge, K. A. (Eds.) (1991). "The Development of Emotional Regulation and Dysregulation." Cambridge University Press, Cambridge.

Greenberg, M. T., Cicchetti, D., and Cummings, E. M. (1990). "Attachment in the Preschool Years." University of Chicago Press, Chicago.

Harris, P. L. (1989). "Children and Emotion." Basil Blackwell, Oxford.

Izard, C. E., and Malatesta, C. Z. (1987). Perspectives on emotional development. I. Differential emotions theory of early emotional development. In "Handbook of Infant Development" (J. D. Osofsky, Ed.), 2nd ed. Wiley, New York.

Lamb, M. E., Thompson, R. A., Gardner, W. P., and Charnov, E. L. (1985). "Infant–Mother Attachment." Erlbaum, Hillsdale, NJ.

Thompson, R. A. (Ed.) (1990). "Socioemotional Development." Nebraska Symposium on Motivation, Vol. 36. University of Nebraska Press, Lincoln.

SPATIAL ORIENTATION

John J. Rieser and Anne E. Garing
Vanderbilt University

Glossary

Beacon A single landmark or gradient.

Body axes The left–right or "x-axis," the front–back or "z-axis," and the head–toe or "y-axis." By convention the body axes are used to specify both the object locations relative to an observer and the degrees of freedom for actions used to change orientation.

Cognitive mapping Processes by which people come to know the straight line distances and directions relating objects and features of their surroundings that are mutually occluded from view and experienced along circuitous walks.

Dead reckoning Measuring the distance and direction of each leg of a trip and integrating to compute distance and direction from the starting point; typically refers to shipboard procedures.

Degrees of freedom for actions used to control orientation Facing direction can be controlled along each of the three body axes; rotating around the y-axis is called turn, around the z-axis roll, and around the x-axis pitch. Location can be translated along the same three axes; moving along the y-axis results in change in elevation relative to an object, along the x-axis in radial direction, and along the z-axis in distance (range).

Frame of reference Environmental information that is used to specify facing direction and location; logically it must consist of at least three points, or two points and a reference direction.

Navigating Locomoting to reach a particular destination, guided by reference either to a beacon or to an environmental framework, or by path integration.

Object-to-object relations Spatial layout, the network of straight line distances and directions among objects or places. Individual relations are sometimes called exocentric relations, and the network is called invariant spatial structure, denoting that the network remains the same when an observer moves.

Path integration Processes that account for the dead reckoning of humans.

Perceptual–motor coordination The degree to which the forces and directions of actions coincide with the distances and directions of the environmental goals of the actions.

Self-to-object relations The array of distances and directions relating an observer to objects and places, which changes whenever an observer moves. The individual spatial relations are sometimes called egocentric relations; the array is called perspective structure.

Visual–vestibular interaction Sensory processing in discrepant cue situations where vestibular information for posture or self-movement conflicts with visual information, sometimes resulting in disorientation or nausea. Especially relevant to space travel and to disorders of the inner ear.

SPATIAL ORIENTATION refers to the alignment or position of a body (or body part) relative to some reference system. Emphasis is on the whole body, typically: body tilt relative to gravity; facing direction or heading relative to magnetic poles, an object, or a place; and location (azimuth, altitude, and distance) relative to an object or place. Traditionally, emphasis has been on space perception and static cases of spatial orientation from a fixed position.

Recently, emphasis has shifted to dynamic cases of self-movement—how is it that people keep up to date on their changing spatial orientation while locomoting in different circumstances? Spatial orientation is essential for perceptual–motor coordination, since the force and direction of actions need to fit the distances and directions of the objects toward which the actions are directed. "To orient" refers to producing motoric actions serving to control spatial orientation. The four basic issues of spatial orientation are about (a) information (what reference information is used to guide action), (b) perception (what sensory systems are used to detect the actor–environment relation), (c) motoric action (how does the actor move in order to change position, and (d) perceptual–motor coordination (how does the actor know how much force to use to accomplish a given distance of movement). Much of the continuing research about spatial orientation relates to three practical problems: (a) Falling and controlling balance; (b) becoming lost and wayfinding; and (c) disorientation and nausea in conflicting cue situations, especially those involved in aeronautics and space travel.

I. GENERAL MATTERS: FUNCTIONS, HISTORY, PRINCIPLES, APPROACHES, AND APPLICATIONS

"Spatial orientation" and "orienting" can be broadly defined as all states and actions that are actively ordered in space. Typically, one thinks of the "states" as mental states involved in perceiving one's distance or direction relative to some destination object or position. But the states can also result from more primitive processes (not involving consciousness) or from higher processes (where spatial orientation is deduced from remembered facts). Typically, one thinks of the broad goals of spatial orientation as placing the body into a particular posture, stabilizing the body in a particular posture, moving part of the body with respect to a particular goal location, and locomoting to move the entire body with respect to a particular goal location. Examples abound across plant and animal species. They include plant tropisms (growth and movements to line up the roots, stems, and leaves with the direction of gravity and light); foraging and wayfinding on the return trip of honey bees and ants; and long distance migration without electronic aids by species as diverse as the monarch butterfly, arctic tern, and gray whale.

A. Functions

This article is focused on two of the major functions of human spatial orientation—postural orientation relative to gravity and navigating in order to find one's way from place to place. The two functions involve partly overlapping types of information, processes, and issues of investigation. Nevertheless, they relate to different contexts and practical applications, and are investigated by groups of researchers that overlap very little.

B. History

The rise of modern philosophy in the 17th century, with its emphasis on epistemology and the origins of the mind, marked a surge in interest in the perception of space and spatial orientation. Early thinkers focused on stationary observers and static objects, and worked to describe the visual cues that specified spatial relations. Nativists like Descartes and Kant assumed that minds are organized to understand the spatial meaning of cues without the benefit of experience. Empiricists like Hume and Berkeley, on the other hand, assumed that experiences associated with physical actions gave meaning to the visual cues.

Empiricists and nativists alike focused on static situations, an emphasis that was maintained through much of the 20th century. Although psychologists and others understood that people were typically in motion, they assumed that an understanding of perceiving in static situations would generalize to perceiving in dynamic situations where observer and/or objects are in motion. In the last 10 years, fueled largely by the insights and experiments of James Gibson and of Gunnar Johannson, emphasis has shifted toward dynamic situations in which observers and/or objects are moving. It seems clear that perceiving in dynamic situations is not the same as perceiving in static situations; indeed, motion of observer and object alike generates additional information that makes spatial orientation more precise.

C. Principles

The emphasis of this article is on two general principles that cross both the major functions of postural orientation and navigation. One principle is that spatial orientation is specified by multiple, independent, partially redundant sources of information. These, in turn, are often picked up by more than one sensory system, often including vision, audition, the somatosensory system, and the vestibular system. Given this, an understanding of intersensory integration is important. In some situations the multiple sources are redundant and specify the same orientation, whereas in other situations the multiple sources specify conflicting orientations.

How is it that these multiple sources of information are combined, typically resulting in a single perception of spatial orientation? One theoretical model that may account for orientation in some situations is a dominance model, where one source of information determines perception, dominating the other sources. Some observations of spatial orientation fit a dominance model. As an example of this consider the illusion of self-movement that occurs when one is actually stationary and a large region of the visual field moves. This situation is fairly common when driving an automobile and stopping beside a bus; if the bus moves forward while the automobile remains at rest, then the automobile's passengers feel as if they are moving backward. In situations like this, where one sensory modality specifies self-movement but the others specify stationarity, the information specifying self-movement typically dominates the information specifying stationarity; self-movement, not stationarity, is perceived. For example, illusions of self-turning occur in optokinetic drums (where truly stationary observers are surrounded by a visibly rotating cylinder); illusions of self-turning occur when a blindfolded, truly stationary observers step to compensate for movement of a platform turning under their feet; and illusions of to-and-fro motion occur in swaying rooms (where a truly stationary observer is surrounded by a visibly swaying room).

But simple dominance models do not generally fit discrepant cue situations where different sources of information specify different rates and/or directions of self-movement. The results in such situations are complex. Sometimes they seem to fit best with a switching model, where perception is determined first by one source of information and then it switches to another source. Other times they seem to fit best with a weighted combination model, where alternative sources of information are differentially weighted and combine to determine perception. Which model fits best also varies according to whether the dependent variable is perceived self-movement, eye movements, or nausea.

A second general principle is that both for postural control and for wayfinding, spatial orientation is achieved with two types of mutually supportive strategy. One is based on the spatio-temporal integration of information specifying self-movement, and the other is based on external frames of reference. Major issues of continuing investigation are how people acquire each strategy and its variants, how they combine the strategies when they are mutually supportive, and how they pick and choose among strategies when the strategies lead to mutually incompatible actions.

D. Approaches

Human spatial orientation is studied from a very wide array of approaches, notably cognitive sciences, neurosciences, computational sciences, and anthropology. Cognitive science approaches to the study of perception and control of postural orientation emphasize psychophysical methods to identify threshold levels of sensitivity, combined with linear and nonlinear models of intersensory integration. In addition cognitive science approaches to wayfinding and navigation depend on reaction time methods to infer the strategies used. Neurologists have long investigated the deficits in spatial orientation associated with broad areas of brain damage; and recently brain imagining techniques are being used to narrow the regions of damage associated with disorientation. Computer scientists specify spatial representations and computational processes that could be used for spatial orientation, and investigate how well their models simulate human behavior. Finally, cultural anthropologists have provided detailed descriptions of traditional methods of long distance navigation without instruments, for example those used to travel thousands of miles among the islands in the Southwestern Pacific Ocean.

E. Applications

Much continuing research about spatial orientation relates to practical problems. One problem is falling, especially falls associated in old age with decreases in visual contrast sensitivity, decreases in visual field size, decreases in vestibular sensitivity, and decreases in motor reaction time. A second problem is disorientation and nausea associated with discrepant cue situations, especially those where vestibular and biomechanical information specify one rate of acceleration and vision specifies a different rate. And a third problem is becoming lost and difficulties of wayfinding. These have been particularly well defined for persons who are blind or visually impaired, motorists, young children, and robotic explorers.

II. THE STRUCTURE OF SPACE, GEOMETRY OF SELF-MOVEMENT, CONTROL OF ORIENTATION, AND PERCEPTUAL–MOTOR COORDINATION

"Spatial structure" refers to the network of distances and directions relating objects and other features of the surroundings to each other. "Perspective structure" refers to a subset of those spatial relations, namely the distances and directions relating the actor to the surroundings.

A. Geometry of Self-Movement

It is useful to think about rotations in perspective (that is, changes in heading with no change in position) and translations in perspective (that is, changes in position with no change in heading). Rotations result in geometrically simpler changes in perspective than translations. During a rotation, one's self-to-object distances remain the same and the self-to-object directions all change by the same constant. During translations, one's self-to-object distances and directions both change, and the amounts of change depend on the amount of translation, but also on the particular self-to-object distance and direction of movement.

B. Control of Orientation

In open spaces people are free to translate in order to change their position along three dimensions, the z-axis (forward or backward), x-axis (left or right), and y-axis (up or down). People are fairly free, limited by walls and passages, to move throughout the x–z plane in most situations and typically restricted in movements along the y-axis (except when climbing, swimming, or flying). People can also rotate to change their facing direction along the same three axes; rotation around the z-axis is typically called roll (leaning sideways), around the x-axis pitch (tilting face up or face down), and around the y-axis yaw (turning). This amounts to six degrees of freedom of movement. The study of human postural control has emphasized the loss of control that results in falling forward, backward, and sideways. Study of human locomotion and navigation has emphasized keeping up to date on facing direction and movements within the x–z plane.

The same three orthogonal axes are often used to represent the spatial structure (spatial layout) of objects in a place using the rectangular coordinates of a Cartesian coordinate system (distances along the x, y, and z-axes), polar coordinates (distance from the origin and direction from a reference direction). In addition they can be used to represent the structure of the perspective available at a given point in a place; in this case, the origin of the coordinate system is typically centered at the person's body and the z-axis is aligned with the person's facing direction.

C. Spatial Orientation, Space Perception, and Perceptual–Motor Coordination

The topics included under spatial orientation are a subset of those included under space perception. Space perception typically subsumes object localization (processes through which one knows the locations of objects relative to one's own perspective or relative to other objects) and spatial orientation (processes through which one knows one's own position relative to objects or other external frameworks). Perceptual–motor coordination goes hand in hand with spatial orientation. Coordination means that the forces and directions of actions are tuned to the self-to-object distances and directions of the objects that are relevant to the actions. [*See* SPATIAL PERCEPTION.]

III. STATIC POSTURE AND SWAY RELATIVE TO GRAVITY

Two of the practical difficulties that motivate research to understand perception and control of posture involve the falls and physical injury associated with aging and the disorientation and nausea associated with motion or space sickness. Static posture and changes in posture are each picked-up by the visual, vestibular, and somatosensory systems. Psychophysical thresholds for each system are known, both for static postures and for body sway. But not known is how the multiple modalities of information are integrated to result in a single perception, especially in situations where they are discrepant.

A. Static Posture

Maintaining balance while standing still and while locomoting depends on keeping one's center of gravity over one's base of support. A person's center of gravity is typically changing, for example whenever the limbs move or when carrying a load, and actions need to compensate for such changes to avoid falling. The actions almost always involve moving the trunk, but often include moving the head or limbs as well.

The processes through which the center of gravity is controlled are not well understood, although they undoubtedly take into account the static masses of different limbs and torques generated during motion. But the ways human sensory systems detect gravity, and acceleration in general, are well understood. There are multiple sources of information. The different sources are constrained in different ways in different situations, and have different strengths and weaknesses.

In many ways vision provides the broadest amount of information, specifying the orientation of the eyes relative to gravity, as well as the eyes relative to the head, the head relative to the trunk, and the trunk relative to the different limbs. The direction of gravity is visible in many situations, specified for example by the up–down of carpentered environments, the direction things fall, the directions things grow, and the horizon. Whenever one or more of these are available, the tilt of the eyes' left–right axis and forward–backward axis relative to gravity can be seen to within about one degree. In addition, eye position relative to the head can be seen (specified by the shape of the visual field, as bounded by the eye sockets and nose), as can head position relative to the trunk (by view of the shoulders), and trunk position relative to limbs. [*See* VISUAL PERCEPTION.]

The otolith organs of the vestibular system are sensitive to static head tilt relative to gravity, and more generally specify linear accelerations of the head. The three semicircular canals are roughly lined up with the x-, y-, and z-axes of the body and, respectively, specify turning movements and other angular accelerations around each. The vestibular system operates without light; since it is sensitive to acceleration, illusions about the direction of gravity commonly occur during accelerations while in flight. Biomechanical information picked up by mechanoreceptors of the somatosensory system also specifies body tilt relative to gravity. For example, leaning on one's right side is specified by deep pressure on the left side and not the right side; leaning forward while standing still is specified by a pressure gradient on the soles of the feet, together with the muscular activity needed to keep from falling.

The different sources of information are typically highly correlated, that is, they specify the same orientation. In situations where one or more source of information is simply missing, for example vision does not occur in darkness, then the other sources completely determine perceived orientation. But in other situations the different sources each specify different orientations. For example, when standing still aboard a ship or place that begins to turn, the visual information from the immediate surroundings would specify standing still, whereas the vestibular and somatosensory input would specify the vehicle's turn. In such discrepant cue situations, the perception of orientation is not well understood. In some situations perception is based predominantly on one cue, whereas in others it is based on other cues or on a weighted mean of multiple cues. There is widespread study of visual–vestibular interactions in discrepant cue situations, motivated in part by the nausea and disorientation that arise in space flight.

B. Body Sway

Body sway is particularly relevant to falling and to difficulties maintaining balance. Body sway is periodic and typically quantified in terms of the amplitude and temporal frequency of the periods. Three major sensory systems are each sensitive to sway, and overlap in the ranges of sway to which they are most sensitive. For vision, optical flow specifies body sway; for example forward–backward sway of the head is specified by the looming and zooming of the frontal field; sideways sway is specified by left–right flow; vision is most sensitive to moderate frequency sways. Since sway typically combines linear and angular accelerations both the semicircular canals and the otoliths are sensitive to it, and are particularly sensitive to low frequency sways. Finally, the somatosensory system is responsive to sway, particularly flexion at the ankle joints, which are tuned to relatively high frequencies of sway.

IV. STATIC POSITION AND SELF-MOVEMENT

Traditionally, study has focused on the perception of stationary observers. In recent years the emphasis has changed to perception of moving observers.

A. Perceiving Static Self-to-Object Distances and Directions

Egocentric object localization and static spatial orientation refer to the same thing, namely perceiving self-to-object distances and directions. Depending on the situation, self-to-object distances and directions can be detected by looking and listening, as well as feeling by hand, feeling wind, feeling changes in temperature, or sniffing odorants. When looking, position along all three body axes is specified with precision; research has been focused on how different visual cues (for example those provided by binocular parallax, relative size and position, visual angle combined with familiar size) are integrated and result in a single perception. When listening, radial direction is detected with precision, whereas sensitivity to elevation is poor, and sensitivity to static distance is poor as well, depending largely on being familiar with the characteristic intensity of a sound; the same is true for using heat, wind, and odor for object localization.

B. Perceiving Self-Movement

The visual, auditory, vestibular, and somatosensory systems are also sensitive to self-movement. People perceive their self-movement in part because their self-movements result in afferent feedback, changes in self-to-object relations that are specified by looking, listening, smelling, and feeling wind or temperature. The sensory input directly specifies the changes in self-to-object distances and direction; and attention has been focused on quantitative models of the information. In addition, in cases of self-propelled movement, efferent and afferent information specify the biomechanical activities of self-movement. Attention is focused on how the somatosensory system integrates information specifying biomechanical activity with object locations remembered in the surroundings.

The geometry of self-movement is a key to understanding how it is perceived. During rotation, self-to-object distances remain constant whereas self-to-object directions all change at the same rate, equal to the rate of rotation. During translation along any straight line, self-to-object distances and directions both change. The rates of change are variable for different objects; the rates are a function of the object's distance from the observer and the object's direction relative to the observer's direction of movement. For example, when walking directly toward an object the self-to-object direction remains constant, whereas the angle toward an object that begins directly to the left changes rapidly. Similarly, for an object located directly to the side, the self-to-object distance and direction alike change slowly for objects that are far away compared to objects that are nearby.

The "flow" of these changing self-to-object distances and directions is picked up primarily by vision and audition (and is supplemented by sensitivity to wind, temperature, and odor). Mathematicians have shown that the flow rate and direction of change in self-to-object distances and directions on the different receptor surfaces provide a sufficient basis from which to compute rate and direction of self-movement. And psychophysical studies have shown that humans are sensitive to the flow rates.

V. NAVIGATING AND WAYFINDING

Navigating and wayfinding are essential skills for explorers. Research in this area relates to practical problems, for example difficulties with wayfinding by persons who are blind, search and rescue of children and others who become lost, the need for "smarter" artificial intelligence systems to explore and map other planets, and curiosity to understand ancient strategies used for long distance ocean travel without instruments.

One's distances and directions relative to features of the surroundings change during locomotion. Human navigation and wayfinding, keeping up to date on these changes, are accomplished through use of three mutually supportive procedures, namely heading toward a beacon, navigating by an external frame of reference, and path integration. Issues of continuing investigation are how people acquire each of these strategies, how broadly they adapt them for use in different situations, and how they pick or choose them or combine them in situations where a use of a single strategy will not suffice.

A. Piloting by Beacons

In some situations it is possible to detect the destination itself. This is readily done when it is possible to look at the destination, in which case its distance and direction are visible, and the underlying processes involve visual space perception. But even in these situations, it is important to consider how people know how to control their action to reach the destination. One method depends on use of feedback consisting of the visible consequences of walking. For example, when walking directly toward an object, its retinal image expands at a rate that is predictable, given the object's distance from the observer and the observer's rate of locomotion. People can adjust their walking in conjunction with visual feedback. However, it is clear that people can walk without vision, in order to reach destinations without feedback about the destination.

Beacons need not be visible. For example, sounds can serve as beacons. Radial localization of sound depends on cues available to stationary observers (including time, intensity, and phase differences at the two ears) and cues available to a walking observer (including the rate of change in intensity for a walking observer). In some situations, odors (in the case of a bakery) and temperatures (in the case of moving from the cool of deep shade to the heat of noon sun) can also serve.

B. Piloting by Frames of Reference

In many situations the destination itself is not perceptible, but other features of the surroundings are perceptible. When these other features are perceptible, they can serve as a frame of reference. For example, consider hiking in the woods and heading for a cabin that you know is sheltered in the valley that separates two mountain ridges that are visible. Although the valley is occluded from view, its location is visible as the intersecting point of the two ridges. If hikers know the cabin lies at the intersection of the two ridges, then the cabin's location can be "seen," specified by the ridges which serve as a frame of reference.

C. Piloting by Path Integration

Path integration and dead reckoning can be used without landmarks or external frames of reference. When used to navigate a ship, dead reckoning consists of measuring the distance and direction of each leg of a trip and using trigonometry to integrate the segments of the trip to compute current distance and direction from the starting point. Pedestrians, like sailors, are capable of path integration. To show this, people have been equipped with blindfolds to occlude their vision and sound systems to occlude their hearing, guided along a walk and asked to judge the distance and direction straight back to their starting place. The accuracy of their judgments decreases as a fairly linear function of the distances walked and the number of turns in the route walked.

Individuals differ widely in how accurately they accomplish dead reckoning. Children as young as 2 years of age can integrate across relatively short paths with only one or two turns, although they fail with longer or more complex routes. Adults differ widely from each other. For example, whereas some individuals walk complex 20-m paths and consistently judge the direction of their starting point within about 10 degrees error, others walk the same paths and completely lose track of their starting point.

D. Integrating Paths with Remembered Surroundings

People integrate paths walked with knowledge of their surroundings gained at an earlier time by looking or exploring. Ongoing paths can be integrated with the remembered layout of the surroundings via a path integration strategy and/or via an environmental frame of reference strategy. The two strategies depend on different types of information; they can operate alone or together in a mutually supportive fashion.

For the environmental frame of reference strategy, consider an example of hikers viewing a valley from a mountainside and then acting on the remembered view when exploring the valley's nooks and crannies later on foot. For the path integration strategy consider the example of a person who views a place from one observation point and then navigates without vision through the remembered place. To do this observers must keep up to date on changes in perspective associated with walking. Although path integration processes would account for how observers keep up to date on their starting point, the strategy could not account for how they integrate their path, in turn, with the remembered surroundings to keep up to date on the changing network of self-to-object distances and directions. Observers need perceptual–motor coordination. That is, they need to know the calibration of the scale of distances walked and turned relative to the scale of the remembered environmental distances and angles visually perceived at an earlier time. Perceptual learning seems to account for this calibration. While walking with vision, the flow of self-to-object distances and directions is visible, correlated with the biomechanical activity that causes the flow. One theory is that people learn this correlation, and then act on it to maintain their orientation when walking without vision.

VI. COGNITIVE MAPPING

Cognitive mapping refers to processes involved in coming to know the spatial layout of a place by spatially integrating objects and/or scenes perceived along circuitous walks. The problem is of particular interest because of difficulties experienced by some persons who are blind. It is clear that some strategies of cognitive mapping depend on path integration and other strategies depend on using environmental frames of reference. But the processes are not yet well understood, and three different metaphors are useful in helping to distinguish the alternatives.

One metaphor is map-making, which involves materials, episodic knowledge, and procedural knowledge to draw a map. The materials include paper, pencil, ruler to measure distances, and protractor to measure angles. The episodic knowledge includes information specifying the particular spatial relations that will be represented on the map—features of the path walked, the frame of reference, and the objects. The procedural knowledge involves knowing how to construct the map on paper and how to look at the map in order to read new distances of directions from it. It is clear that people come to know the spatial layout of places they have never viewed as a whole, and it is reasonable to name this knowledge a "cognitive map." But some have reified the idea of a map, assuming that a map-like representation resides in the mind and, given this, they take for granted that the processes are like those used to draw physical maps.

A second metaphor involves the representations and computations of analytic geometry, which provide a way to model knowledge of the changes in perspective. Within a geometrical model, observers' movements to new observation points correspond to rotations and translations of the origin and axes of a coordinate system through a field of objects whose locations are constant but whose coordinates change relative to the moving coordinate system. The model can be expressed in rectangular coordinates, polar coordinates, or any other coordinate system, and involves access to episodic and procedural knowledge. The episodic knowledge would be the self-to-object distances and directions specified relative to the initial observation point, together with the information about the path and/or frame. The procedural knowledge would include knowing how to assign coordinates to object locations, trigonometric equations to compute the new coordinates relative to the rotated/translated axes, equations to compute the new self-to-object distances and directions, and trigonometric tables to solve the equations.

Finally, a third metaphor involves perceptual learning, that people are sensitive to the correlated streams of environmental flow (picked up by vision and audition) and biomechanical information (picked up by the somatosensory system and the vestibular system) while walking. Knowing this correlation means they can anticipate the visible consequences of self-movement, even when walking in darkness or in situations where the to-be-anticipated features are occluded from view. Features of the model are perceptual sensitivities (to optical flow, biomechanical activity, and their correlation), memory representation of the surroundings, and representation of the learned correlation.

Bibliography

Cutting, J. E. (1986). "Perception with an Eye for Motion." MIT Press, Cambridge, MA.

Gibson, J. J. (1966). "The Senses Considered as Perceptual Systems." Houghton Mifflin, Boston, MA.

Henn, V., Cohen, B., and Young, L. (1985). Visual–vestibular interaction in motion perception and the generation of nystagmus. *Neurosci. Res. Prog. Bull.* **18,** 459–651.

Howard, I. P., and Templeton, W. B. (1966). "Human Spatial Orientation." Wiley, New York.

Lackner, J. R. (1985). Human sensory-motor adaptation to the terrestrial force environment. In "Brain Mechanisms and Spatial Vision" (D. Ingle, M. Jeannerod, and D. Lee, Eds.), pp. 175–209. MIT Press, Cambridge, MA.

Lee, D. N. (1980). The optic flow field: the foundation of vision. *Philos. Trans. R. Soc. London B* **290,** 169–179.

Rieser, J. J. (1991). Development and perceptual-motor control while walking without vision: The calibration of perception and action. In "Sensory-Motor Organizations and Development in Infancy and Early Childhood" (H. Bloch and B. Bertenthal, Eds.), pp. 379–408. Kluwer, Boston.

Rieser, J. J., Hill, E. W., Talor, C. R., and Bradfield, A. (1992). Visual experience, visual field size, and the development of nonvisualsensitivity to the spatial structure of outdoor neighborhoods explored by walking. *J. Exp. Psychol. Gen.* **121,** 210–221.

Schone, H. (1984). "Spatial Orientation: The Spatial Control of Behavior in Animals and Man." Princeton University Press, Princeton, NJ.

Warren, R., and Wertheim, A. H. (1990). "Perception and control of Self-Motion." Erlbaum, Hillsdale, NJ.

Waterman, T. H. (1989). "Animal Navigation." Freeman and Scientific American Library, New York.

Spatial Perception

H. R. Schiffman
Rutgers, The State University

Suzanne Greist-Bousquet
Kean College of New Jersey

Glossary

Accommodation The variable refractive capacity of the lens that brings an image into sharp focus on the retinal surface.

Albedo A property of surfaces that refers to the proportion of incident light that is reflected.

Binocular disparity The difference in the two retinal images that provides a strong impression of depth and three-dimensionality of space.

Convergence The tendency of the eyes to turn toward each other in a coordinated action to fixate on targets located nearby.

Horoptor The location of all points in space whose images fall on corresponding retinal points.

Invariants Constant characteristics of the pattern of light that are picked up by an observer in the perception of space.

Motion parallax The relative apparent motion of objects in the visual field as the viewer moves the head.

Stereopsis A perceptual experience of depth occurring as a consequence of the disparity of the images projected on each eye.

A PRIMARY ROLE of vision is to perceive space—to register the spatial arrangement of objects and surfaces in the environment. Indeed, objects are generally seen as solid forms lying at some distance in the terrain. The perception of space presents a most challenging problem: how is it possible that visual space is normally experienced as three-dimensional, yet the light-sensitive surface at the back of the eye (called the retina) is two-dimensional? The pattern of light which reaches the retina (called the retinal image) is also flat and two-dimensional. Part of the answer to this puzzle lies in the nature of the stimulation that arrives at the retina. For example, one sees differences in the brightnesses of different surfaces; objects are seen with varying degrees of clarity; some objects appear to partially cover other objects. Clearly, the pattern of stimulation contained in the visual image conveys information or "cues" that enable the perception of a three-dimensional space.

I. MONOCULAR CUES FOR SPATIAL PERCEPTION

A number of spatial cues require only a single eye for their reception and are labeled monocular cues.

A. Interposition

Interposition refers to the appearance of one object partially concealing or overlapping another (Fig. 1a). If one object is partially covered by another, the fully exposed one is perceived as nearer. When the images are of familiar objects, the effectiveness of interposition for showing relative distance is increased. However, interposition can provide only relative depth information—whether one object is nearer or farther than another from the observer—not precise depth or distance information.

B. Aerial Perspective

When viewing the terrain outdoors, objects in the far distance are generally seen less clearly than objects located close by. This effect is called aerial perspective and is due to the effect on light of very small particles in the atmosphere. Light rays traveling through suspended particles of dust, water vapor, and other atmospheric chemicals are scattered

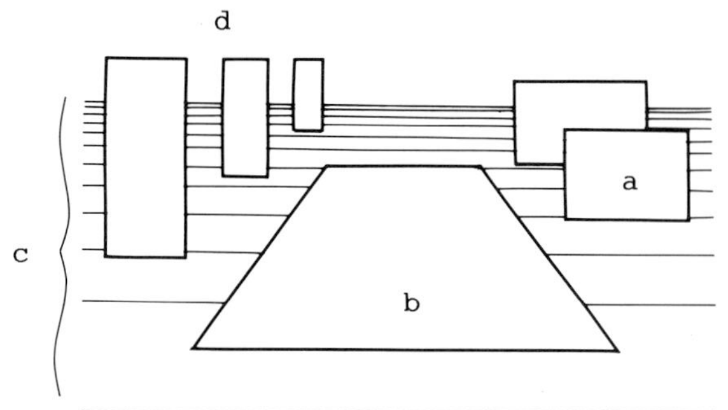

FIGURE 1 Select monocular spatial cues: interposition (a), linear perspective (b), texture gradient (c), and relative size (d).

somewhat, decreasing the clarity of the details and the overall lightness of the images of the objects reflected to the eye. Since light reflected from distant objects passes through more of the atmosphere than the light rays from nearby objects, the more distant objects appear hazy, dim, and even blurry. Thus, relatively large structures, such as buildings, appear closer when viewed on a clear day than on a hazy one. Aerial perspective may play a role in viewing over extensive distances.

C. Shading and Lighting

Generally, the surface of an object nearest the light source is the brightest. As the surface recedes from the light, it appears less bright and more darkly shadowed. This pattern of lighting and shading contributes to the perception of space. Lighting and shading can indicate the orientation of the surface relative to the light source.

D. Elevation

The horizon is higher in the vertical dimension of the visual field than is the foreground. Accordingly, objects appearing higher in the visual field are generally perceived as being located at a greater distance from the viewer than are objects that appear lower in the visual field. Elevation may play a role in the perception of both relative and absolute distance.

E. Linear Perspective

The perception of depth on a flat surface can be aided by the use of the geometric system of linear perspective. This involves systematically decreasing the size of more distant elements and the space separating them (Fig. 1b). The image of a three-dimensional object undergoes such a transformation as it is projected onto the retina. A typical example is railroad tracks. The parallel tracks appear to converge at a point in the distance called the "vanishing point."

F. Texture Gradients

A form of microstructure, generally seen as a grain or texture, is characteristic of most surfaces. This is obvious in many surfaces such as fields of grass, roads, and floors. The texture of these surfaces possesses a density change or texture gradient that structures the retinal image in a way that is consistent with the arrangement of objects and surfaces in the environment. When we look at any textured surface, the elements comprising the texture become denser as distance increases. As in linear perspective, the size of the elements and the distance separating elements decrease with distance (Fig. 1c). The gradient of texture provides the observer with information that he or she is viewing a receding distance. Information about the orientation of surfaces can also be provided by texture gradients.

G. Relative Size

The spatial cue called relative size applies when two similar or identical shapes of different sizes are viewed simultaneously or in close succession; in such cases the larger shape will appear closer to the viewer than the smaller (Fig. 1d).

H. Motion Parallax

When the observer or the objects in the visual scene move, a source of monocular information concerning depth and distance is produced. As the observer moves, objects located at different distances in the visual field appear to move at different velocities relative to each other. The relative apparent motion of objects as the observer moves the head is called motion parallax. Generally, when the head moves, elements of the visual field that lie close to the viewer appear to move faster than do distantly located elements; additionally, the apparent direction of movement differs for near and far objects. Both the relative velocities and the direction of the apparent movement depend on the location of the point at which the observer is gazing in the visual field (called the fixation point). The way in which motion paral-

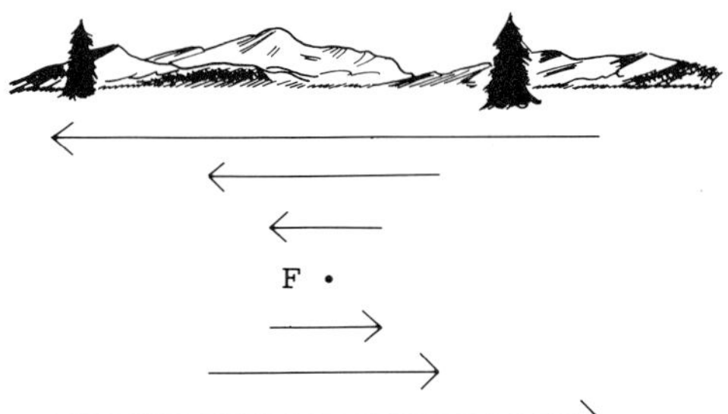

FIGURE 2 Schematic diagram of motion parallax. If an object located at F is fixated while the observer moves to the left, the images of the nearer objects appear to move to the right, whereas farther objects seem to move to the left. The length of the arrows indicates that the apparent velocity of objects in the field of view increases in direct relation to their distance from the fixation point.

lax occurs in one set of conditions is illustrated in Figure 2.

I. Accommodation

Accommodation is a physiological mechanism for focusing the lens in the eye to form a sharp retinal image. In humans, accommodation involves a change in the curvature of the lens—flattening the lens for focusing on distant targets and thickening it when focusing on nearby ones. This change in lens shape is accomplished by relaxing or contracting the set of muscles which are connected to the lens. It is possible that the signals which occur when adjusting these muscles furnish information to the brain about a target's spatial location. However, accommodation is probably limited as an effective source of spatial information. For humans, it would be of use only for distances up to about 2 m. For targets located beyond 2 m, accommodation is ineffective in furnishing accurate spatial information since the lens is limited in the extent to which it can be flattened.

J. A Direct Approach to the Perception of Space

J. J. Gibson has developed a theory which takes an adaptive, "ecological" approach to perception. This theory takes as its starting point the view that the information for perception is contained fully within the spatial and temporal patterns in the visual image. That is, light that is reflected from surfaces and objects in the environment possesses a structure that specifies the spatial characteristics of the visual world. According to this view, sufficient information is carried by this reflected light to account fully for the perception of the visual world.

Despite a moving observer, a changing environment and a changing retinal image, certain information remains constant. Such information is labeled invariants. Texture gradients offer invariant information (see Fig. 1c); that is, texture elements always appear finer or denser as distance increases, and they appear coarser with decreasing distance. A similar case exists with the information from motion parallax. The apparent velocity differences of different regions of the visual field resulting from movement of the observer directly reveal relative distance information.

Gibson's theory is one of direct perception which holds that invariant information about the spatial layout of the environment is picked up directly, rather than being the result of the processing and analysis of spatial cues. According to Gibson, there is no need for judgment or mediation by cognitive processes or thought. The information is "picked up" rather than "processed."

K. A Computational Approach to the Perception of Space

Another approach to the perception of space is found in a computational approach to perception. Like Gibson's approach, this approach assumes that the stimulus input contains the information necessary for perception. However, the computational approach suggests that the interpretation of the stimulus requires computations and further analysis. According to this view, spatial perception is the result of an overall process in which there is an analysis of the information in the retinal image. General physical knowledge and experience play a role in this analysis.

II. BINOCULAR CUES FOR SPATIAL PERCEPTION

Monocular cues furnish a good deal of spatial information. However, there are highly informative sources of spatial information which require the joint activity of both eyes; these are binocular cues for spatial perception.

A. Convergence

Convergence refers to the tendency of the eyes to turn toward each other in a coordinated action to fixate on targets located nearby. Targets located at some distance from the viewer, on the other hand, are fixated with the lines of sight essentially parallel to each other. Because the degree of convergence is controlled by muscles attached to the eyeballs, it is possible that different states of muscular tension for viewing near and far objects may furnish a cue to depth or distance. However, like accommodation, convergent eye movements as a source of spatial information would be useful only for nearby objects. [*See* EYE MOVEMENTS.]

B. Binocular Disparity

In humans, the two frontally directed eyes receive two slightly different or disparate images of the same three-dimensional scene. In the human, this is due to the fact that the eyes are set about 2 to 3 inches (5 to 7.6 cm) apart. The visual image seen by one eye is somewhat different than the visual image seen by the other eye. This difference in the two retinal images is called binocular disparity (or sometimes called binocular parallax).

The ability of the visual system to utilize binocular disparity information to detect the difference in depth between two objects is impressive. A depth difference between two objects which corresponds to 1 μm (0.001 mm) in retinal disparity can be detected. [*See* DEPTH PERCEPTION.]

C. Corresponding Retinal Points and the Horoptor

When a small target is fixated, it forms images on each retina. The fixated target will appear single, since the eyes are converged to project the target image on corresponding retinal points. That is, if the left retina and its image were superimposed on the right retina and its image, the images would correspond. A small target imaged on corresponding retinal points is fused by the visual system and so appears as a single target. In fact, for a given degree of ocular convergence (which depends on fixation distance), there exists a set of spatial locations that project onto corresponding retinal points. A small target at any one of these locations is seen as a single target. As shown in Figure 3, the location of all points in space that project onto corresponding retinal points and yield single images for a given degree of convergence produces an imaginary curved plane or zone called the horoptor.

Targets not lying on the horoptor of the fixated target—located either nearer or farther from the ob-

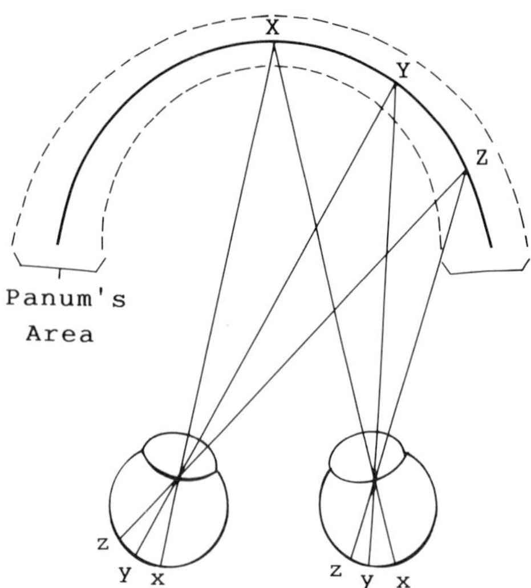

FIGURE 3 A depiction of the horoptor. The actual shape of the horoptor varies with fixation distance and ocular convergence. Images of the points X, Y, and Z will fall on corresponding retinal points and will be seen as single points. Points not lying on the horoptor or in the narrow area surrounding it (called Panum's fusion area) appear as double images.

server—will produce double images because they stimulate noncorresponding retinal points. Thus, targets located nearer or farther than a fixated target form images in different positions on each retina, giving rise to disparity. Ordinarily, the double images of nonfixated objects are not noticed.

D. Stereopsis

The unique appearance of depth with solidity, called stereopsis, arises from disparity information. An example of stereopsis is the entertaining depth effect experienced when viewing through a common stereo-viewer. The stereo-viewer presents two different pictures of the same scene taken with a stereo camera (a camera that has a double lens with each lens separated by about the same distance as the separation of the two eyes). Thus, two pictures are taken simultaneously. When the pictures are processed, mounted, and each presented by means of a stereo-viewer to the appropriate eye, the images fuse and the striking effect of stereopsis occurs. In general, two lawfully related images can be presented to each retina independently and stereopsis results—a vivid and compelling experience of a single three-dimensional scene.

III. THE VISUAL CLIFF

An important experimental analysis of the cues used for space perception in a number of animal species

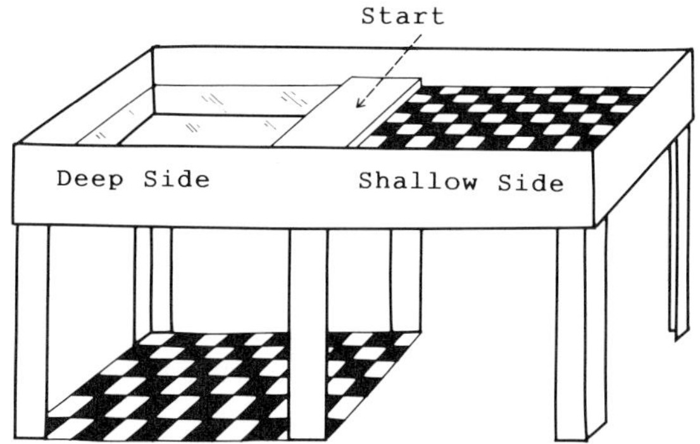

FIGURE 4 A diagram of the visual cliff.

has been made using an apparatus called the visual cliff (Fig. 4). A centrally located start platform divides the floor of the apparatus into two sides, each side furnishing different kinds of stimulation. The "shallow" side lies directly over a patterned surface; on the "deep" side the same patterned surface is placed some distance below. Actually, a sheet of glass extends over both the deep and shallow sides for safety and to equate sources of thermal, olfactory, and acoustic stimulation for both sides. Thus, with lighting equated for both sides, only intentional visual information is allowed. In the usual situation, an animal is placed on the start platform separating the shallow and deep surfaces. From this position the animal can see the shallow or "safe" side and the deep or "dangerous" side, an edge with a drop-off beyond it that is similar to what it would see if looking over the side of a cliff. A basic assumption of the visual cliff technique, of course, is that a tendency exists for animals to avoid a fall. As an adaptive mechanism preserving the species, it is reasonable to expect that most animals should be capable of depth perception; furthermore, this ability should be effective by the time the organism can locomote independently. The existence of this capacity is demonstrated by a preference for the shallow side. Indeed, based on research with a variety of animal species including primates and human infants, there is a strong tendency to avoid the deep side. The critical cue for perception on the visual cliff appears to be motion parallax.

IV. CONSTANCY IN THE PERCEPTION OF SPACE

As an observer changes positions in space and as an object moves in space, the retinal image of the object constantly changes. However, despite these changes in stimulation, the stable and enduring qualities of an object are perceived. This stability of perception in the presence of variation in physical stimulation is termed perceptual constancy.

A. Lightness Constancy

Lightness constancy refers to the fact that the lightness (and usually the color) of an object tends to remain relatively constant or stable despite changes in the amount of light striking it. Thus, for example, we perceive a patch of snow in dark shadow as white and a chunk of coal in sunlight as black, yet the physical intensity of the light reflected from the surface of the coal may be greater than that from the snow. In some manner we are taking into account information about the general conditions of lighting.

The surface property called albedo or reflectance is important to an understanding of lightness constancy. The albedo is the proportion of incident light that is reflected (i.e., the ratio of reflected/incident light) from an object or surface. It is independent of the degree of illumination. A sheet of paper may have an albedo of .80, for example; this means it reflects approximately 80% of the light it receives. If under ordinary conditions, a part of the paper is placed under dim illumination so that the sheet is not homogeneously illuminated, one still perceives the entire sheet as more or less uniformly light. The stability of the perception of the paper's lightness occurs because the entire surface of the sheet reflects a constant portion of the light received, even though the amount of incident light may differ for different parts of the paper's surface.

To utilize albedo, there must be indications of the general conditions of lighting. In fact, lightness constancy is poor when the sources of the incident lighting and the background illumination are obscured or lacking. If illumination is restricted to the object alone then the perceived lightness of the object will depend entirely on its illumination, and constancy is absent.

B. Size Constancy

The size of an object's image on the retina may undergo considerable changes as the object's distance from the viewer varies, but the size changes go relatively unnoticed under conditions of normal viewing. A man standing 7 m away looks about as tall as when he stands at 14 m away although the first image projected on the retina is twice the size of the second. Under normal viewing conditions, the perceived size of an object does not depend upon the retinal size of the object. Indeed, over a considerable range of distances, perceived size is somewhat independent of retinal size; this is termed size constancy. However, when cues to space are restricted or absent, size constancy is reduced.

C. Shape Constancy

An object typically appears to possess the same shape even when the angle from which it is viewed changes radically. This is called shape constancy. A typical window frame or a door appears to be more or less rectangular no matter at what angle it is viewed. Yet geometrically, it casts a rectangular image only when it is viewed from a certain position directly in front of a viewer.

Shape constancy operates to maintain the integrity of an object's shape. Shape constancy is impaired or eliminated when visual information as to an object's position relative to the viewer is lacking.

V. ERRORS IN THE PERCEPTION OF SPACE

The relative absence of a spatial context disturbs or reduces perceptual constancy. Similarly, when cues to space are lacking, are distorted, or are placed in apparent conflict with each other, distortions in the perception of the physical environment (called illusions) may result.

A. Transactionalism and the Ames Illusions

Transactionalism is an approach with particular relevance to constancy and the cues to space. The theoretical approach and related set of illusions (called Ames illusions) were devised by Adelbert Ames. Objects and surfaces such as floors, walls, and so on appear to be rectilinear despite the fact that the retinal images rarely include rectangles. The seeming contradiction between the perception and the optical stimulation led to the theoretical notion that experience with specific objects and surfaces plays a very important role in normal perception. Transactionalism is an empirical theory—it proposes that the perceptual world, in large measure, is constructed from experiences in dealing with the visual environment.

B. The Moon Illusion

The moon illusion refers to the phenomenon that the moon appears larger (as much as 1.5 times) when it is viewed at the horizon than at the zenith, although the projected images in both cases are identical.

There are diverse explanations of the moon illusion; all attempt to account for the striking difference in the apparent size of the moon when seen at the horizon and zenith. One such explanation proposes that the apparent size of the moon is affected by the angle of the eyes relative to the head. According to this account, the moon illusion is produced by changes in the position of the eyes in the head accompanying changes in the angle of elevation of the moon.

Another explanation of the moon illusion suggests that the horizon moon appears larger because it is viewed through filled space, such as trees, buildings, etc. In contrast, the zenith moon is viewed through empty space. The projected images of the moon in both cases are of identical size, but the horizon moon appears farther away. That it also appears larger follows from the linear relationship between apparent size and apparent distance. Thus, if two objects project the same retinal image but appear at different distances from the viewer, the object that appears farther from the viewer will be perceived as the larger. Applied here, the moon appears farther away at the horizon and, hence, appears larger.

C. Visual Geometric Illusions

There are hundreds of visual geometric illusions in which the length, size, shape, or direction of components of simple line figures are distorted. The illusion shown in Figure 5a, known as the Müller-Lyer illusion, is one of the most familiar geometric illusions. The apparent length of a line is distorted when arrowheads are added to the ends.

An example of the Ponzo illusion is shown in Figure 5b. Although the two horizontal lines are identical in length, the line located closer to the point of convergence of the two bounding lines appears to be longer. The Poggendorff illusion (Fig. 5c) involves a different sort of distortion: the two oblique line segments are actually aligned or collinear, yet to most observers an imaginary extension of the left line segment appears to be misaligned with the right line segment. Thus, in the Poggendorff illusion, the diagonal lines appear to be offset when intercepted.

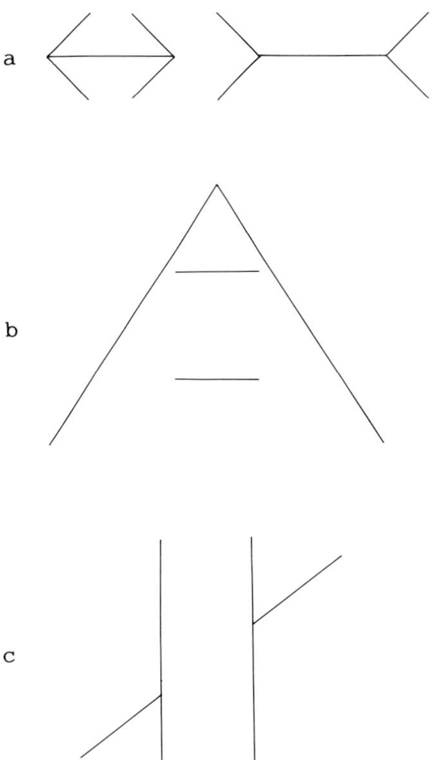

FIGURE 5 Three visual geometric illusions. The Müller-Lyer illusion (a), the Ponzo illusion (b), and the Poggendorff illusion (c).

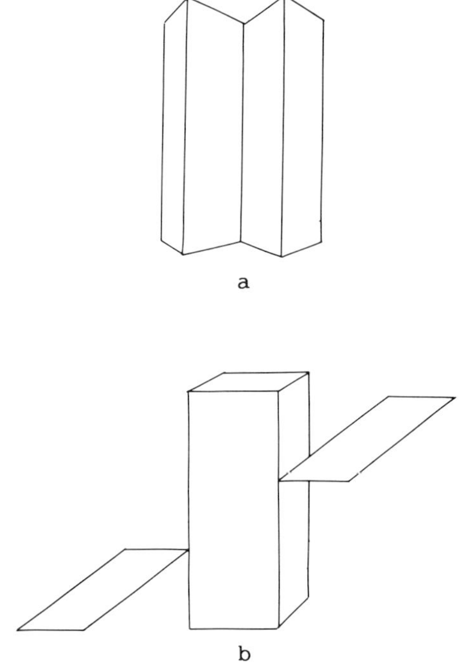

FIGURE 6 Elaborations of the Müller-Lyer and Poggendorff figures which illustrate the perspective constancy explanation for each illusion. (a) Perspective cues in the figure cause an apparent enlargement of the vertical projection of the farther corner to compensate for its apparently greater distance from the observer; perspective also produces an apparent shrinkage of the vertical projection of the nearer corner to compensate for its apparently shorter distance from the observer. When viewing such a building the vertical extents are seen as about the same height; thus, there is a compensation for apparent distance. When this compensation for apparent distance occurs in the Müller-Lyer figure, the line segments appear unequal. (b) The diagonal lines of the Poggendorff figure are processed as belonging to different horizontal planes rather than as a single continuous line. Such processing would disrupt the apparent collinearity of the diagonal lines.

D. Theoretical Explanations

There are a variety of theories to account for the distortions in the geometric illusions. One such theory is the perspective constancy theory which holds that certain stimulus features are indicators of apparent distance. In the case of the Müller-Lyer illusion, the perspective features furnished by the arrowheads or wings of the figure provide false distance cues. As a result, size constancy is inappropriately induced to compensate for the apparent distance of the line segments. The result is a consistent error in the perceived length of the lines. Figure 6a illustrates this effect.

The Ponzo illusion is closely linked to a perspective constancy explanation. The perspective feature, as applied here, is produced by the bounding converging lines that are ordinarily associated with distance. Accordingly, the perspective cue falsely suggests depth—the line that appears farther away is perceived as larger—thereby producing a size illusion.

The perspective constancy theory as applied to the Poggendorff illusion suggests that the diagonal lines are perceived as outlines of apparently receding horizontal planes that lie on different planes (Fig. 6b). The rectangle is perceived as lying on the frontoparallel plane (where all edges of the rectangle are perceived as equally distant from the observer). It is clear that such perspective processing disrupts the apparent collinearity of the obliques in the Poggendorff figure.

However appealing the perspective constancy theory is as an explanation for these (and other) visual geometric illusions, it is incomplete. The distortions in these illusions still occur when the figures are altered so as to change the depth features (for example, Fig. 7).

An alternative viewpoint suggests that the visual geometric illusions are caused by a number of fac-

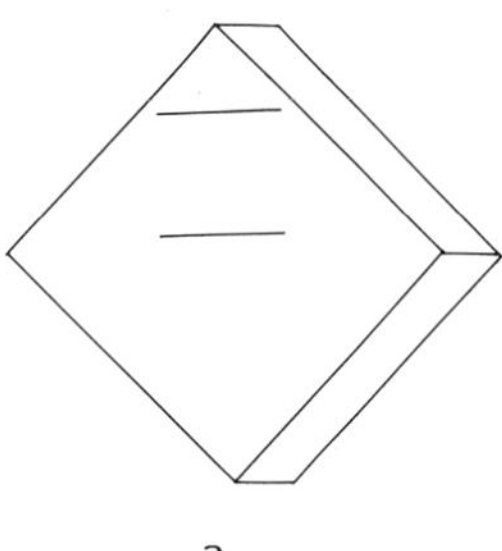

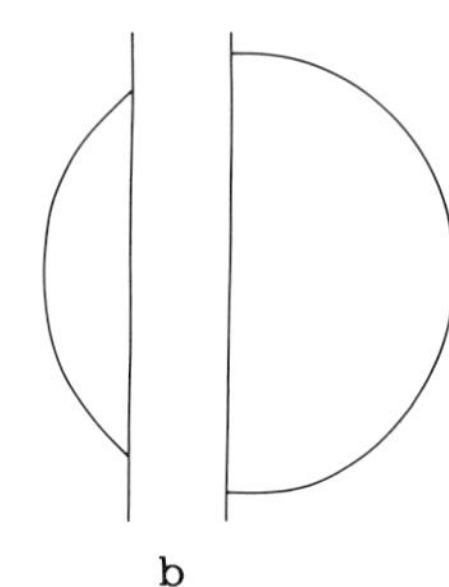

FIGURE 7 Variations of the Ponzo figure (a) and the Poggendorff figure (b) in which the perspective features are altered. (a) The diagonal lines cannot be interpreted as lines receding into the distance, yet the Ponzo illusion still occurs. (b) The diagonal lines are replaced by a circle which cannot be interpreted as line segments of different planes, yet Poggendorff-like misalignment still occurs.

tors. According to this theory, the illusions are produced by several different sources, such as the structure of the eye, neural interactions, and cognitive factors.

E. Ambiguous, Reversible, and Multistable Figures

There are a number of figures with inherent depth characteristics that may be ambiguously perceived with respect to their principle spatial orientation. After a brief period of inspection of Figure 8a, there is a spontaneous reversal in its spatial orientation. With continued inspection the reversal may occur periodically. This class of figures characterized by ambiguous and equivocal depth information is called ambiguous, reversible, or multistable figures.

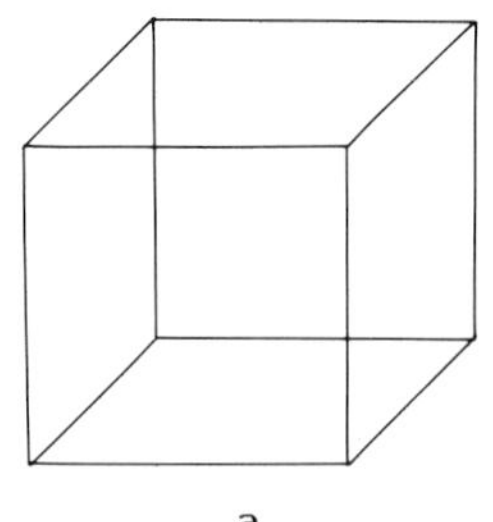

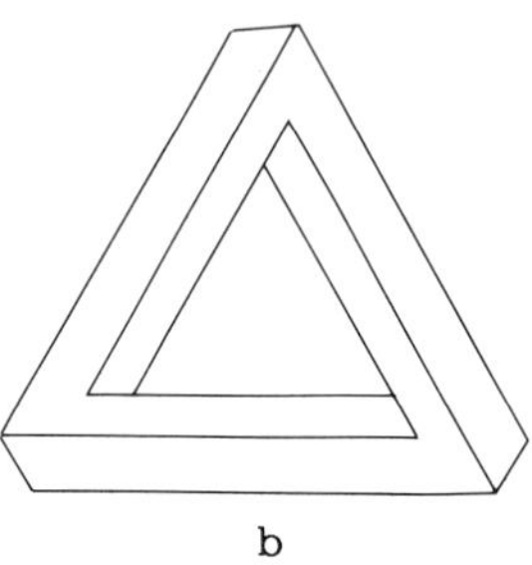

FIGURE 8 An ambiguous and impossible figure. After a brief inspection of (a), the cube spontaneously reverses in depth. An "impossible" triangle is presented in (b).

F. Impossible Figures

Impossible figures, as exemplified in Figure 8b, are displays which contain inconsistent and contradictory sets of depth information. When the components of these figures are viewed as a collection of individual line segments and angles, they appear as reasonable depictions of parts of a simple three-dimensional object in depth. However, when the entire figure is viewed as a unitary object, the depth characteristics of the individual features appear to be in conflict with each other and the figures appear spatially impossible.

Bibliography

Atkinson, R. C., Herrnstein, R. J., Lindzey, G., and Luce, R. D. (Eds.) (1988). "Stevens' Handbook of Experimental Psychology," 2nd ed., Vol. I. Wiley, New York.

Bruce, V., and Green, P. R. (1990). "Visual Perception: Physiology, Psychology and Ecology," 2nd ed. Erlbaum, Hillsdale, NJ.

Rock, I. (Ed.) (1990). "The Perceptual World." Freeman, New York.

Schiffman, H. R. (1990). "Sensation and Perception: An Integrated Approach," 3rd ed. Wiley, New York.

SPORT PSYCHOLOGY

Steven R. Heyman
University of Wyoming

Glossary

Clinical sport psychology The application of clinical psychological approaches for individuals in sport or athletic situations where an understanding of the particular nature of the sport or athletic environment is important to an understanding of the clinical issues.

Cognitive behavioral interventions Interventions and approaches to changing behaviors or feelings by changing what are assumed to be the causal cognitive processes.

Educational sport psychology The application of a variety of approaches to enhance athletic performance or to facilitate individual or team functioning.

Performance enhancement The application of psychological approaches to improve sport or athletic performance.

Research sport psychology The use of the scientific research method to study any of the many facets of sport, exercise, or athletic functioning.

Social facilitation The study of the effects of an audience on a performer's efforts.

SPORT is one of the most enduring of all human activities. Virtually from the beginning of any written human records, in civilizations across the world, accounts of sports and sport-related activities are found. For less than the last century has sport been studied scientifically, and sport psychology is an important part of that scientific study. It is an international field, holding the promise of becoming important not only to the understanding of competitive athletic abilities, but to areas of behavior that relate to many domains of human health and activity.

I. HISTORICAL BACKGROUND

Although the Greek Olympics (776 B.C. to A.D. 394) are recognized as enduring tributes to sport, it is a mistake to assume these were the first or oldest records of sport. Archeological artifacts indicate that such sports as boxing and wrestling were part of the Sumerian culture (3000 B.C.). Similarly, games and sports similar to some we would recognize today were recorded by the ancient Egyptians as well. In the ancient East, Chinese and Japanese records suggest that archery and charioteering were important activities. Although India is the birthplace of yoga, such sports as archery, wrestling, boxing, and javelin throwing were part of ancient India (2000–1000 B.C.). The well-preserved ruins of the Aztec and Mayan civilizations similarly record what seem to have been ball games and other sporting activities not unlike those that are played today.

The better, though still incomplete records from Greece and Rome indicate the central importance of sport to these cultures. Clearly for wealthy Greek citizens, part of the Homeric sense of "excellence" was skills in sport and physical activity. The ability of the Greek city-states to suspend wars so that the Olympics could take place attests to their valuing of sport. Victories enhanced the prestige not only of city-states, but also of the athletes. With the rise of Rome, the sports became increasingly professionalized and more violent. Gladiatorial games schools were established to train combatants. It would seem that training for sport in ancient Greece and Rome would have had to involve more than attention only to the physical components. They must have had an understanding of motivation and anxiety as they would relate to performance. One would wonder if in gladiatorial training there was not attention to the psychological components of understanding and competing with one's opponents. Unfortunately, so far as can be determined, records of the psychological components of training have not survived. With the end of the Olympic games and the rise of monastic Christianity, sport, and certainly its study, received little attention in Western history. As knighthood flourished, and jousting competitions spread, there were schools to train knights and soldiers, but, again, no records can be located that focus on what we would understand as the psychological components of such training. With the Renaissance, sport and games again became a part of leisure, and the rediscovery of Greek writings find the concepts of "sound mind, sound body" advocated by some. From the Restoration, through Colonial times, to the Civil War period, games and sport became increasingly popular in the United States, with the early forms of many of our ball games developing, and boxing and wrestling again becoming popular, as did many games of skill and of chance. By the end of the 19th century intercollegiate sports become entrenched in the United States, and the modern Olympics were instituted by Baron de Courbertin. As we know, the prevalence and popularity of sport and athletic activity have grown in the 20th century, and have become in many ways universal across cultures and within social classes in the West.

II. DEVELOPMENT OF SPORT PSYCHOLOGY IN THE LATE 19th AND EARLY 20th CENTURIES

A. Physical Activity as Part of a Well-Rounded Education

As the 19th century progressed, physical education for men and for women became incorporated into school curricula. Not only was this seen as an important part of a well-rounded and healthy life, but Victorian morality also assumed that "healthy" physical activity would channel the "urges" of young people into "productive" activity. As settlement houses were founded in the developing urban ghettoes of early 20th-century America, physical activity was included as a way of providing activities for young people, again with the assumption that such activities would drain off impulses that were seen as threatening to society.

B. The First Scientific Study

As scientific psychology developed in the mid- to late 19th century, many things were studied, but sport was not. Paradoxically, the study cited as the first experimental research in sport psychology was done by Triplett in 1898, and was cited by Gordon Allport as the first experiment in social psychology. In essence, Triplett studied the effects of the presence of others on an individual's performance. Of note here, his studies involved bicycle racers. Later in the 20th century, this research became the foundation for the study of social facilitation by social psychologists. The differential effects of the varying presence of observers are also of interest to contemporary sport psychology.

C. The Pioneering Role of Coleman Griffith

Dr. Coleman Griffith, a research psychologist, was brought to the University of Illinois in 1925 to study the behaviors of athletes and coaches, in part to help coaches improve the performance of the athletes. Based on his work, he wrote two texts that can be considered pioneering works in sport psychology. *The Psychology of Coaching* appeared in 1926, and in 1928 he published *The Psychology of Athletics*. He continued his work at the University of Illinois until 1932, when the funding for his laboratory was withdrawn, due to declining revenues at the University. He had an interesting exchange of letters about coaching with Knute Rockne, and apparently was hired by the Chicago Cubs in 1938 to study each of the baseball players.

D. Sport Psychology in the 1940s and 1950s

A small number of psychological studies of sport and athletic behavior appeared in the 1940s and 1950s, examining aggression, performance, coaching, and other behaviors, but there was no systemic focus to the study, nor were there organizations concerned primarily with the psychological bases of sport and physical activity. For most individuals, research or writing in the area of sport psychology was secondary to other interests or professional activities.

III. CONTEMPORARY SPORT PSYCHOLOGY

As a result of growing interest in sport psychology around the world, perhaps in part due to the growing importance of the Olympics during the Cold War, several hundred individuals took part in the First International Congress of Sport Psychology in Rome in 1965. These meetings have continued to occur on a regular basis. In 1967 the North American Society for the Psychology of Sport and Physical Activity (NASPSPA) took place in conjunction with the annual meeting of the American Association for Health, Physical Education, and Recreation. NASPSPA continues to meet on an annual basis.

Although research began to be conducted in a number of areas relating to sport and physical activity, much of the research of the 1950s and 1960s could be characterized as studying personality variables. Very often, any of a number of personality instruments would be given to athletes, to compare those who were more or less successful on a number of dimensions, or to compare athletes and nonathletes. While these research projects were important to the development of sport psychology, in retrospect they contained many flaws. There was no clear or consistent definition of "athlete" and "nonathlete." Most often team membership was the defining variable, but so many different types of teams, at so many different levels, were used that findings were inconsistent. Similarly, team membership often reflects a combination of skill level, motivation, and availability, but many "athletes" may not be on teams. Often the personality measures used, such as the Minnesota Multiphasic Personality Inventory (MMPI), were inappropriate to the populations and variables of interest. As studies were generally neither longitudinal nor cross-sectional, cause and effect were not understood and were confused. Thus, individuals experiencing success in sport might have personality variables such as confidence or low anxiety developed by their success, not causative of their success.

In the 1970s, and continuing to the present, as more and better trained researchers became involved with sport psychology, research moved away from basic personality scales to more complex research looking at person–team–environment interactions, as well as behaviors involved in physical activity. Personality instruments were developed that were more specific to sport, and some were developed to study specific sports or forms of physical activity. Rather than focusing on isolated variables, multivariate approaches to sport-related questions are being studied at present.

A. Development of Applied Sport Psychology

Bruce Ogilvie and Thomas Tutko published *Problem Athletes and How to Handle Them* in 1966. Although the title, in retrospect, is somewhat unfortunate, it was the first contemporary book to present a psychological approach to understanding and working with the problems that athletes might present. As more people became involved with sport psychology, interest in working with athletes also grew. As is not uncommon in many disciplines, a division began to develop between those who were more interested in research and those who were more interested in applied work, that is the application of psychological principles to work with athletes and sport participants. By the late 1970s a distinct area developed within sport psychology that has become known as applied sport psychology. Although this is only one area of sport psychology, it often is the area receiving the most attention, due to the high profile of certain Olympic teams or professional athletes who have worked with applied sport psychologists. Most of the books written for the lay person involving techniques or approaches to improve sport performance involve these approaches. This particular area of applied sport psychology is known as "performance enhancement."

1. Performance Enhancement

Performance enhancement involves the use of psychological approaches toward the improvement of athletic performance. Within sport psychology, the most commonly used approaches, and those that have received the most attention in research attempting to document their effectiveness, involve cognitive–behavioral approaches. These approaches are drawn from an area of psychotherapy known as cognitive–behavioral therapy. The key assumption behind these approaches is that our feelings and behaviors follow our thoughts, appraisal, or perceptions of events. If we can enhance or positively alter our cognitive processes, our behaviors will improve. [*See* COGNITIVE BEHAVIOR THERAPY.]

Two approaches are most common. Often used together, a person learns to relax physically and yet be cognitively alert, and in this state visually image (or perhaps experientially in some other sensory mode) the sport or physical activity. This preparation for physical activity, either to visualize a desired performance or to correct errors, has, in some research, been shown to be effective either without physical performance or in conjunction with physical practice.

Other approaches may involve a technique known as "thought stoppage." A person who perhaps begins a downward spiral of creating anxiety, or focusing increasingly on problem patterns, will learn to recognize this pattern early on, and will develop approaches to stopping these undesirable thoughts.

Perhaps one area of great mystery, inflated claims, and little research is hypnosis. Although studies of the effects of hypnosis on physical performance have occurred throughout this century, much of the earlier work was methodologically flawed. Given that people vary in their responsiveness to hypnosis, and perhaps only 10% of the population is highly responsive, it does not seem that hypnosis would accomplish more for most than relaxation and visualization. Although a few systematic studies of individuals have appeared relative to the effectiveness of hypnosis, there is no evidence to suggest as a widely used technique it would be particularly helpful to most individuals. It is an area, however, in which much more systematic research needs to be done. [*See* Hypnosis.]

IV. FUTURE OF THE FIELD

A. Current Definition of Areas

As currently defined by most individuals and organizations, there are three areas in sport psychology: clinical/counseling, education, and research. Clinical/counseling sport psychology involves working in a more traditional psychotherapeutic manner with athletes who are having personal problems, whether or not these problems are related to their sport. Some debate has taken place in the literature as to whether athletes have unique problems or experiences, but there is general agreement that performance demands, time commitments, publicity, and identity issues do have particular relevance to the experience of athletes and committed sport participants.

Educational sport psychology generally embraces the performance enhancement approaches, as well as activities including team cohesion development, and working with the parents and coaches of sport participants. It is not always possible to differentiate the activities and issues in this area from clinical/counseling sport psychology.

Research sport psychology encompasses most of the activities in the field, using the scientific method to study human behavior as it applies to sport, exercise, and physical activity. Some of the areas that would seem more obvious have been discussed previously in this section. There are many exciting frontiers: for example, the effects of exercise on mood are seen as an important area. This has taken on increased importance due to the AIDS pandemic. Research is examining whether individuals diagnosed as HIV+, or who have AIDS, can benefit both physically and psychologically from participation in various types of exercise and physical activity. It is particularly important for individuals advocating interventions to improve performance to document that these approaches will, in fact, work when rigorously tested.

B. Career Possibilities

The Division of Exercise and Sport Psychology of the American Psychological Association publishes a brochure entitled "Exercise and Sport Psychology: Graduate Training and Career Possibilities." Copies can be obtained by writing to the Division Services Office of the APA at 750 First Street N.E., Washington, DC 20002-4242. It discusses the possible job opportunities, and the education and training required, roughly paralleling the three tracks described above.

A great deal of debate has occurred in the sport psychology literature in the 1980s about the nature, role, and training requirements for sport psychology. Most of the graduate training programs in sport psychology currently are housed in departments of physical education (more often called kinesiology or sport science to reflect the scientific and research interests within these departments). Graduates of these programs, however, are generally not licensable or certifiable as psychologists under the laws of most states in the United States or Canadian provinces. While these programs can prepare individuals for work in educational and research sport psychology, given that the title "psychologist" is protected by law, it typically cannot be used by such individuals.

Only a few psychology departments offer graduate training including a sport psychology emphasis. Most often, graduates of these programs are trained as clinical or counseling psychologists, and can function both in more traditional roles and within one or more of the three domains in sport psychology.

It is to be hoped that over the next decade, graduate training programs will become more interdisciplinary, so that individuals interested in sport psychology will have a broader exposure both to traditional psychology courses, and supervised practicum experiences, as well as to coursework in the sport sciences, with appropriately supervised practice in sport psychology.

Unfortunately, for many individuals the allure of applied sport psychology or educational sport psychology, defined in terms of working with elite or professional athletes, is very attractive. There is a glamour connected to this, and the possibility of financial reward. The reality is, for the present and the foreseeable future, far less bright. As of 1992, only a handful, defined as less than 10 individuals, earn most or all of their income by direct work with athletes or teams. Although some professional teams hire consultants, this is usually on a part-time basis. College athletic programs and counseling centers have hired individuals to work with athletes, but often these are part-time positions.

Given the number of individuals interested in this particular area of sport psychology, even if more opportunities became available, the positions would still be highly competitive. Helping athletes with performance enhancement approaches should also be a time-limited role: presumably the person should develop the appropriate skills so as to make continued consultation unnecessary. Sport psychologists who have worked with individual athletes, and in particular with teams, have also discovered that they are treated in some ways like coaches: while the individual or team is winning, they are given a great deal of credit for the success. If losses should occur, however, the athlete or the team may well look for someone else, with the hope that they will provide greater success.

Research sport psychology includes incredibly diverse possibilities. Not only is there research on factors affecting athletic performance, and on the applied approaches attempting to enhance performance, but also many other areas within personality theory, social psychology, and clinic questions are also studied. There is also a clear overlap with health psychology, in that exercise and sport play roles other than recreational ones in our lives, although certainly the study of recreational sport pursuits is important. For example, much remains to be studied about why some individuals elect to participate in high risk sports, and why some individuals are highly successful while others are at personal risk. Similarly, youth sport is an important area of study, encompassing team dynamics, coach–athlete interaction, the role of parents and peers, and the effects of such participation on youngsters.

Sport psychology, although having roots going back over 100 years, is still a very new and developing field. In 1992 the APA received 25,000 slips indicating interest by graduate students in the 49 Divisions. Of these, 500 were for Division 47. It is to be expected that interest in this area will grow and develop. As additional professionals emerge, and graduate training expands, many more dimensions of human physical activity, exercise, sport, and athletics will utilize the knowledge and experience of psychologists. It is also to be expected that as the numbers of those training in sport psychology expand, the horizons of the field will expand greatly.

Bibliography

Cox, R. H. (1990). "Sport Psychology: Concepts and Applications," 2nd. ed. William C. Brown, Dubuque, IA.

Iso-Ahola, S. E., and Hatfield, B. (1986). "Psychology of sports: A Social Psychological Approach." William C. Brown, Dubuque, IA.

LeUnes, A. D., and Nation, J. R. (1989). "Sport Psychology: An Introduction." Nelson-Hall, Chicago, IL.

May, J. R., and Asken, M. J. (Eds.) (1987). "Sport Psychology: The Psychological Health of the Athlete." PMA, New York.

Straub, W. F., and Williams, J. M. (Eds.) (1984). "Cognitive Sport Psychology." Sport Science, Lansing, New York.

Williams, J. M. (Ed.) (1993). "Applied Sport Psychology: Personal Growth to Peak Performance," 2nd. ed. Mayfield, Mountain View, CA.

STRESS

Ronald M. Doctor
California State University at Northridge

Jason N. Doctor
University of California at San Diego and San Diego State University

Glossary

Appraisal A term used by Richard Lazarus to describe cognitive mediational processes that are linked with and produce stress responses.

Direct neurological enervation The "fight or flight" response involves neurological pathways of sympathetic nervous system enervation that produce rapid and intense physiological and psychological activation.

General adaptation syndrome A sequential three-stage physiological stress response pattern discovered by Hans Selye.

Hot reactors A term coined by Robert Eliot to denote cardiovascular reactors to everyday stress or challenges with elevated blood pressure and/or constricted vascular flow. This population often goes undetected and is susceptible to unexpected heart attacks and sudden death syndrome.

Rational emotive therapy (RET) This is a cognitive therapy developed by Albert Ellis to modify irrational thoughts that lead to disruptive emotions and behavior.

Relaxation response A term used by Herbert Benson to denote conscious activation of the parasympathetic or relaxation system through persistent training.

Social Readjustment Rating Scale (SRRS) Also called the Holmes-Rahe Scale or the Life Change Scale, it assesses various life stressors on a weighted basis. Total scores are predictive of health risk.

Stimulus specificity A term used to describe the fact that the particular physiological stress response depends, in part, on the stimulus the person receives or reproduces

Stress innoculation training (SIT) A therapy developed by Donald Meichenbaum as a multidimensional treatment package for stress prevention.

Sympathetic nervous system This is part of the autonomic or "automatic" nervous system that is involved in bodily activation or arousal.

THE TERM "stress" was introduced into the health psychology language by Hans Selye in 1926. Although the term "stress" is a household word, Selye actually preferred use of the descriptive term "strain" to denote his concept since it suggested structural changes whereas stress emphasized external factors. To him "stress" consisted of the "sum of all nonspecific changes (within an organism) caused by function or damage" or, more simply, "The rate of wear and tear in the body." More recently, he defined stress as "the nonspecific response of the body to any demand." He insisted that the stress response was nonspecific in that it produced a general but consistent set of reactions within the body and could be caused by a number of environmental "stressors." The nonspecific nature lies in the fact that any number of stressors can produce the same general, nonindividualized body response as a defense. Because Selye used animals for research and he focused exclusively on physiological reactions, his results are limited to these domains.

Other researchers have proposed that the stress response is mediated by covert or overt cognitive appraisal of events impinging on the individual that interprets these events as either threatening or not, and concomitantly assesses the individual's ability to handle the stressor. We will see later that person-

Encyclopedia of Human Behavior, Volume 4

ality traits have been isolated that affect this interpretative process. Finally, other definitions of stress emphasize the stimulus side of proposing that stress is really a stimulus or trigger for physiological, disease, and emotional responses.

So, we have moved from a simple physiological definition (wear and tear on the body) to emphasis on interpretative processes (threat and coping ability) and finally to views of stress as the stimulus or starting point for deviant physical, emotional, and mental activities.

I. INTRODUCTION

In the past two centuries, the greatest threat to human existence, aside from a nuclear holocaust, has been microbial disease. Vast numbers of humans have died from diseases, plagues, and epidemics. The Black Plague, for example, killed more than a third of the world population within just a few years. In this century, huge numbers have died from influenza epidemics. Even today, almost half of the world's population of children under the age of 5 years will die from some disease compounded with problems in malnutrition, inadequate sanitation, poor health services, or absence of vaccination programs. The actual technology for prevention of most diseases is available. Noting this fact, Jonas Salk concluded that we have advanced to the point where mankind can survive on this planet without a doubt at the physical level. But as microbial threats have come under control, a new and equally potent threat to lifespan has emerged in the form of habits in living, "lifestyle," or stress. Here, the overall manner in which we live our lives in such areas as occupation, hobbies, diet, exercise, attitudes and beliefs, emotional status, and world view can affect our health and longevity. Table I describes the leading causes of death before the age of 75 years. It can be seen that lifestyle stressors contribute greatly, more than environmental, biological and other factors, to premature death.

In the context of this article, lifestyle can be seen as primarily having to do with "stress." The study of stress has become the new frontier of research for the next century just as the study of disease has occupied our efforts in this century.

Today there is mounting evidence for the influence of psychological processes over organic processes. Psychological and medical researchers are beginning to work together to study the connection between "mind" and "body." There is a growing realization that the construct of mind (e.g., attitudes, beliefs, internalized statements, thought, and images) affects bodily processes which, in turn, influence our perceptions, thoughts, and attitudes. In the 1960s, researchers found that physiological functions such as blood pressure and heart rate, which were once considered completely involuntary (i.e., the province of the body), could be controlled voluntarily (i.e., by the mind). Moreover, if the mind could

TABLE I
Leading Causes of Death before the Age of 75

	Contribution percentage			
Cause of death	Lifestyle	Environmental	Biological	Other
Heart disease	54	9	25	12
Cancer	37	24	29	10
Motor vehicle accidents	69	18	1	12
Other accidents	51	31	4	14
Stroke	50	22	21	7
Homocides	63	35	2	0
Suicides	60	35	2	3
Cirrhorsis	70	9	18	3
Influenze/pneumonia	23	20	39	18
Diabetes	34	0	60	6
All factors combined	51	20	20	9

Source: The Center for Disease Control Publication (1984).

affect the beating of the heart or the constriction and dilation of blood vessels, it is possible that the mind could also affect such processes as the growth of cancer cells and the progress of an infection. We are now confident that the mind can influence the body. There is considerable evidence that we cannot treat mind and body as separate constructs, they are parts of the whole that have been artificially divided for separate study through history. How these parts and the whole express themselves will be explored in this article as we discuss the fascinating area of stress.

II. STRESS AS A PHYSIOLOGICAL RESPONSE

A. Selye's Triphasic Model

To Selye, the stress response followed a triphasic sequence that he called the general adaptation syndrome (GAS). This syndrome was divided into three consecutive stages that occurred with prolonged or chronic stressors. The first stage he called the alarm reaction stage. Here the body mobilized against the stressor in a defensive and protective manner in the form of an immediate activation of the sympathetic nervous division of the autonomic nervous system. Epinephrine is released, and heart rate, respiration, and blood pressure increase. Skeletal muscles tense and their blood supply enlarges. Sweat glands activate and the gastrointestinal system closes down its activities. In some cases, parasympathetic activation also accompanies sympathetic arousal. Presumably, as the stressor continues the organism moves into a more enduring phase called the resistance stage. In this phase, chronic hormonal and neurological changes emerge in an effort to adapt to the ongoing stressor and a dramatic reduction of most of the alarm reaction stage processes results. Of course, if the stressor is removed, the organism presumably returns to a more or less normal level of physiological activity. The first two stages could be repeated many times in the life of a person. However, eventually the "adaptive energy" becomes depleted and the body enters into the third stage of exhaustion in which organ damage and even death can occur. Table II lists the bodily reactions associated with each of these triphasic stages.

TABLE II
Physiological Reactions within Each Stage of the General Adaptation Syndrome (GAS)

Alarm stage
General sympathetic nervous system arousal
Skeletal muscular tension
Adrenal gland stimulation
ACTH and cortisol released
Growth hormone and prolactin secreted
Increased thyroid activity
Gonadotropin activity increased
Anxiety/panic symptoms may be experienced
Resistance stage
Reduction in adrenal cortical activity
Reduction in sympathetic nervous system activity
Homeostatic mechanisms engaged
Exhaustion stage
Enlargement of lymphatic structures
Target organ disease/dysfunction
Diathesis or increased vulnerability to disease
Psychological exhaustion: e.g., depression, avoidance, withdrawal
Physiological exhaustion: disease or death

B. Biologic Pathways for the Stress Response

The physiologic basis for the stress response seems to reside in the relationship of several layers of biological and neurological activity. The hypothalamus and the limbic systems in the brain are intimately involved in the stress response. The hypothalamus influences the autonomic nervous system and the endocrine system and therefore is a critical link to stress reactions. The limbic system is more complex and more advanced than the hypothalamus. It regulates emotional expression such as anxiety, grief, and depression. In turn, these emotions, as we will see later, are associated with eventual stress-related diseases. [*See* HYPOTHALAMUS; LIMBIC SYSTEM.]

Much is now known about the physiology of the stress response. There are three major biologic pathways for stress. The first is via *direct neurological enervation* of the sympathetic or "fight–flight" mechanism. This pathway tends to be responsive to acute stressors. Also, it, like the other two types of sympathetic nervous system (SNS) enervation, is almost always preceded by *cognitive* interpretations or appraisal of a perceived or imagined event which, in turn, determines the valence of the affective reaction in either positive or negative directions. Once a cognitive interpretation has been made (which could be subconsciously) as threatening, neural enervation of target organs may occur. Undoubtedly, this response follows descending pathways from the posterior hypothalamus (sympathetic activation) to thoracic and lumbar regions of the spinal cord and therein to end organ targets. No wonder so many people have back problems! This direct process accounts for immediate reactions but not for reactions that are more prolonged or chronic. A car moving in front of you on the road would activate this pathway. Likewise, "ego" assaults such as perceived failure or embarassment will trigger it.

A second physiologic reaction follows the *neuroendocrine pathways* studied initially by Selye. Here neuroendocrine activation tends to be triggered by intermittant or chronic stressors rather than the acute and sudden stressors more associated with direct neurologic pathway enervation. Likewise, psychological or cognitive factors are more likely to be involved in the neuroendocrine enervation. The key organ in this response system is the adrenal medulla which secretes catecholamine (norepinephrine or noradrenalin and epinephrine or adrenalin) that enervate somatic activity with much the same effects that direct neural enervation have on the person. Catecholamines, however, have a long-acting effect and thus prolong the adrenergic sympathetic response. [*See* CATECHOLAMINES AND BEHAVIOR.]

Endocrine responses, the third biological pathway for stress, produce even more sustained and disruptive reactions. Four well-established endocrine pathways for stress have been identified: adrenal cortical axis (e.g., ACTH), somatotropic axis (e.g., growth hormone), thyroid (e.g., thyrotropic releasing factor), and the posterior pituitary (e.g., vasopressin or antidiuretic hormone). Recently, it has also been found that the pituitary hormone testosterone plays a key role in the Type A coronary prone behavior pattern. There is a great deal of scientific interest in the endocrine pathways particularly because of their prolonged nature. [*See* HORMONES AND BEHAVIOR.]

C. Cognitive/Interpretative Models of Stress

Cognitive models of stress emphasize the role of cognitive factors as mediators of the stress response and of coping methods. It is generally accepted that cognitive factors precede physiological arousal, or, in some cases, are concommitant with it. Cognitive contributions involve primary appraisal (in which potential threat or jeopardy is assigned) and secondary appraisal (in which the person's capacity for dealing with the stressor is assigned). These appraisals may occur simultaneously or in sequence and are usually subconscious. Secondary appraisal depends on past experience, generalized beliefs about one's coping ability and available support. A third stage consists of coping responses. Coping responses are on a continuum and can be adaptive in the sense that the person works with their emotional reaction to the stimulus and/or develops a problem-solving attitude. Coping can also be maladaptive in which case the person reacts to emotions by adopting maladaptive, regressive, and self-destructive actions in the situation. There are five adaptive coping strategies for confronting a stressor. These include: seeking information, direct action toward the situation, inhibition of inappropriate emotional or behavioral reactions, intrapsychic efforts to deal with feelings and negative beliefs, and turning to others to work with feelings, gain support, and so on. [*See* COPING.]

III. TARGET ORGAN REACTIONS TO STRESS

Potential target-organ systems affected by the stress response include the cardiovascular and gastrointestinal systems, the skin, immune system, the brain, metabolic activity, and mental activity just to mention the more common. Which target organ is affected by stress induction seems to be a function of previous experience, conditioning, type and relative degree of activation, genetics, trauma, and so on. "Stimulus specificity" is a term used to describe the fact that the particular physiological stress response depends, in part, on the stimulus the person receives or reproduces. Pioneering work in this area came from a study reported by Wolf in 1947 of a patient who had a plastic window installed in his stomach so investigators could observe gastric activity in relation to various stimuli. The investigators found that gastric secretions were stimulus specific. For example, they decreased with anxiety stimuli but increased with anger-inducing stimuli. Subsequently, the differential effects of fear- and anger-eliciting stimuli have been studied on blood pressure, heart rate, muscle tension, respiration, and numerous other physiological and biochemical functions. These are examples of stimulus specificity.

IV. EMOTIONAL REACTIONS TO STRESS

Physiological, emotional, and mental response depends not only on the nature of the stressor but also on individualized response characteristics. Individualized response specificity has been noted in many studies. For example, Robert Eliot reports on the extensive research on cardiovascular reactions to stressors—particularly those that show "hot" or significant reactions in the form of elevated blood pressure and chemical changes when people are meaningfully challenged. Hot reactors may not show signs of high blood pressure when relaxed (in the doctor's office, for example) but will evidence significant reactions when challenged by competitive situations, potential failure situations, or extreme physical stress. Individualized reactions may take the form of increased output of blood ("output hot reactors") or increased blood pressure ("vasoconstrictive hot reactors") or some combination of the two types of reaction. The authors point out that since these are specific to stressor events and not chronic reactions, assessment is possible only under challenge conditions—which usually are not those present in typical blood pressure assessment conditions. These authors make a telling argument for the fact that hot reactors may be very susceptible to "sudden death syndrome" in which the person dies from an unpredictable and unexpected heart attack even when blood pressure studies seem normal.

Another area of individualized response specificity is that of particularized muscular reactions to stressors such as back spasms, headaches, and so on. Aside from specific reactions within systems of the body, there is also evidence of individualized response specificity in terms of *degrees* of response to stressors. So, "gastric reactors" may show extreme increases or decreases in secretions to stressors. Likewise, hot reactors show not only constrictive and output patterns but also individual degrees within these reaction patterns.

The specific but individualistic nature of the stress response runs counter to Selye's original hypothesis of a nonspecific physiologic response. Mason has pointed out, however, that Selye's experimental methods consistently produced a strong emotional response in the animals he studied. He hypothesized that it was the strength of this emotional reaction that created the illusion of a generalized nonspecific response to stressors. He also proposed that stress, whether it be a stimulus, response, or the interaction of these, be viewed as analogous to disease pathogens such as viruses and bacteria. Here, there are great *individual differences* in response to disease-producing pathogens as there are individual differences in response to stressors. Organismic factors make it difficult to predict group responses but do allow for individual predictions. The problem for future research will be to identify the various factors associated with the stress response and the differential weights of these factors for individuals. This will provide better prediction than is currently possible and permit the introduction of tailored preventative and treatment intervention strategies.

We have talked about physiological indices of stress. Below are listed a variety of emotional, behavioral, and physical signs of stress. Most of these signs are well known, some are less obvious. Most often the stress responses involve several or many of these "symptoms" or signs. You can see that once we move to nonphysiological measures of stress, the signs become complex, individualized, and more subtle.

Emotional signs

- Apathy—the "blahs," sadness, lack of pleasure in usually desired activities.
- Anxiety—apprehensiveness, tension, shakiness, arousal, off balance, fuzzy.
- Irritability—snappy, defensive attitude, standoffish, argumentative, angry, and reactive.
- Mental fatigue—difficulty concentrating, distractable, preoccupied, unable to focus or be creative.
- Overcompensation or denial—work as distraction, denial of problems or self, push others away, symptoms, suspicious, unwilling to slow down.

Behavioral signs

- Avoiding things—neglecting responsibilities and work, avoiding relationships and expression of personal feelings, unwilling to share, seclusion.
- Doing things to extremes—addictions, chemicals to modulate feelings, manic, poor judgment, and self-destructive behaviors.
- Personal neglect—accident proneness, poor personal habits, eating the wrong foods, lack of rest or recreation, poor work habits.
- Judgment problems—debts, petty crimes, anger and violent behavior, affairs, superficial relationships.

Physical signs

- Excessive worry about, or denial of, illness.
- Frequent illness.
- Physical exhaustion.
- Reliance on self-medication, including overuse of drugstore remedies (like aspirin).
- Ailments—headache, insomnia, appetite changes, weight gain or loss, indigestion,

nausea, nervous diarrhea, constipation, sexual problems.

V. ASSESSMENT TECHNIQUES

How do we go about assessing stress levels of people from nonphysiological indicators? Let's start with stress assessment techniques currently in use.

A. Questionnaire Assessments

The pioneering scale for measurement of stress was the Social Readjustment Rating Scale (SRRS) developed by Thomas Holmes and Richard Rahe (1967) and often called the "Holmes-Rahe Scale" or the "Life Change Scale." This scale does not actually measure stress itself but attempts to assess various life stressors in the person's recent experience. Forty-three possible life events or changes (of varying weights) are checked by respondents as to whether they have occurred within the past 12 months. The items and their weighted score values are presented in Table III. You might want to take this survey for yourself.

Total scores represent the predicted relative health risk to the person of becoming ill within the next 2 years. Cumulative weighted life change unit scores of 300 or more have been found to be predictive of major illness within 2 years for approximately 80% of high scorers. Risk of illness declines with total score values in a linear manner. Notice that stress is defined here as illness. The previous list of emotional, behavioral, and physical "signs" identified many stress responses that were less intense or acute than illness.

In an attempt to improve the SRRS predictability, Irving Sarason and his colleagues modified it by assessing not only life change events but also their desirability or valence in the person's life. The product created was called the Life Experiences Survey (LES). In a similar attempt to improve predictability, Lazarus and his colleagues developed the Hassles Scale of minor daily hassles or sources of minor adjustments that must be made much more frequently than major life events and often are the outcome of the life change event. For example, someone getting divorced may have to support two households, have increased responsibilities for cleaning, food preparation, laundry bills, and so on. Within the scale, negative hassles are offset by positives or uplifts in the final score.

The most commonly checked negative hassles are those related to weight, health of family members, and prices of goods. The most common positive uplifts are those related to good relationships and task completions. From extensive statistical analysis, Lazarus and Folkman concluded that daily "hassles are far superior to life events in predicting psychological and somatic symptoms. Hassles accounted for almost all the outcome variance attributable to life events, whereas life events had little or no impact on health outcomes independent of daily hassles."

The SRRS is the most widely used assessment of stressors in clinical and research work. However, as Monroe has pointed out, "The magnitude of the association reported (between score totals on stressor scales and stress reactions or illness) typically has been low. . . ." Other variables, both individual and environmental factors, intervene to affect outcome of life change events.

Several stress scales focus on the fact that the stress response is triggered by cognitive interpretation of "stressor" events. The Everly Stress and Symptom Inventory (ESSI) is a self-report inventory of 20 cognitive and affective states known to be highly correlated with activation of the physiological stress response. The ESSI also assesses coping strategies (10 positive and 10 maladaptive) and a 38-item symptom frequency scale of symptoms highly correlated with excessive stress arousal. This scale seems to have good predictive validity.

B. Physiological Measures of Stress Response

As we have seen, three biological systems are involved in stress response activation: neurological, neuroendocrine, and endocrine. Measures that have been developed that are primarily neurological in emphasis include electrodermal techniques such as GSR measures (useful to determine overall somatic arousal or arousal associated with a particular stressor), electromylographic measures (of muscle potential) and cardiovascular measures. Since stress responses involve the enervation of striated skeletal muscles, several of these physiological measures are sensitive to changes in muscle potential or byproducts of these changes. For example, research, has shown that muscle potential or overall electrical activity originating from relaxed muscles is a useful index of arousal. Once contraction occurs, however, the utility of this index significantly declines. Relaxed potential, on the other hand, provides an im-

TABLE III

The Social Readjustment Rating Scale[a]

Life event	Weighted score
1. Death of spouse	100
2. Divorce	73
3. Marital separation from mate	65
4. Detention in jail or other institution	63
5. Death of a close family member	63
6. Major personal injury or illness	53
7. Marriage	50
8. Being fired at work	47
9. Marital reconcillation with mate	45
10. Retirement from work	45
11. Major change in health or behavior of a family member	44
12. Pregnancy	40
13. Sexual difficulties	39
14. Gaining new family members (through birth, adoption, oldster moving in, etc.)	39
15. Major business readjustment (merger, reorganization, bankruptcy, etc.)	39
16. Major change in financial state (a lot worse or better off than usual)	38
17. Death of a close friend	37
18. Changing to a different line of work	36
19. Major change in the number of arguments with spouse (more or fewer, about child rearing, personal habits, etc.)	35
20. Taking out a mortage or loan for a major purchase (home, business, etc.)	31
21. Foreclosure on a mortage or loan	30
22. Major change in responsibilities at work (promotion/demotion, lateral transfer)	29
23. Son or daughter leaving home (for marriage, to attend college, etc.)	29
24. Trouble with in-laws	29
25. Outstanding personal achievement	28
26. Wife beginning or ceasing work outside the home	26
27. Beginning or ceasing formal schooling	26
28. Major change in life conditions (building a new home, remodeling, deterioration of home/neighborhood)	25
29. Revision of personal habits (dress, manners, associations, etc.)	24
30. Trouble with boss	23
31. Major change in working hours or conditions	20
32. Change in residence	20
33. Changing to a new school	20
34. Major change in usual type and/or amount of recreation	19
35. Major change in church activities (a lot more of fewer than usual)	19
36. Major change in social activities (clubs, dancing, movies, visits, etc.)	18
37. Taking out a mortgage or loan for a lesser purchase (for a car, TV, freezer, etc.)	17
38. Major change in sleeping habits (a lot more or less sleep, or a change in part of day when sleep occurs)	16
39. Major change in number of family get-togethers (more/fewer than usual)	15
40. Major change in eating habits (a lot more or less food intake, or very different meal hours or surroundings)	13
41. Vacation	13
42. Christmas	12
43. Minor violation of the law (traffic tickets, jaywalking, disturbing the peace, etc.)	11

Source: Holmes and Rahe (1967). *J. Psychosom. Res.* **J227,** 217–218. Reprinted with permission from Pergamon Press, Oxford, England.

[a] Instructions: This scale is useful for determining the clustering and cumulative effect of life events in your life. To use the scale, record the values to the events you have experienced during the past year. These weighted score values represent the average stressfulness of each life event on a scale of 0–100. Thus, if you experienced one personal injury or illness, record 53; if two injuries or illnesses record 53 twice.

portant baseline index of chronic states of stress arousal.

One particular location for electromylographic assessment has been noted as responsive to emotional arousal and that is the frontalis muscles of the forehead. These muscles not only respond to emotional stressors but there is evidence that they are also capable of eliciting stress responses by voluntary or "dual" enervation. Tensing the frontalis to mimic various emotional states can produce changes in GSR and heart rate. Experimentation is currently under way to determine the utility of other muscle groups in predicting and measuring stress responses.

Cardiovascular activity represents another major physiological response system for stress. Neural enervation directly affects heart rate and performance. Likewise, neuroendocrine enervation due primarily to the effects of epinephrine and norepinephrine has a direct and intense effect on ventricular speed and force of contraction.

Furthermore, although there are individual differences, vasoconstriction at peripheral sites such as fingers, toes, forearms, and calves can result from sympathetic activity. Reduced blood flow can be measured indirectly via reductions in skin temperature. Plethysmography (a measure of blood volume) is a more direct and more reliable measure of differential blood flow changes. For some individuals skin temperature can be determined by self-report, skin temperature devices, or just touching the individual's hands or feet to see if they are colder than other parts of the body.

Blood pressure is another physiological response that is particularly sensitive to acute stress and acute emotional arousal. Clinicians and scientists call this type of response "state-dependent" since it occurs when the eliciting stimulus is present in contrast to "trait-dependent" reactions that represent more chronic organismic changes due to stressor exposure (perhaps over a period of time).

Neuroendocrine responses are usually assessed by measurement of adrenal medullary catecholamine secretions: epinephrine (adrenelin) and norepinephrine (noradrenalin). These measures can be made directly by sampling urine, blood, or saliva or indirectly by looking at metabolites found usually in the urine.

Physical diagnosis of target organ effects is a form of assessment of the stress response after physiological damage has begun to occur. While there are some self-report scales of merit, such as the Seriousness of Illness Rating Scale and the Stress Audit Questionnaire, the main assessment tool is the physical examination usually conducted by a physician.

C. Personality Mediators of Stress

There is now general agreement in the psychological literature that personality design can contribute to the development of stress responses. Three examples from the recent psychological literature will help illustrate this relationship. The first is from the study of anxiety—particularly agoraphobia and panic disorders. Panic disorders involve a sudden, unpredictable, unexpected acute and intense anxiety reaction in which the individual experiences symptoms of excessive sympathetic system arousal. Agoraphobia often develops from panic attacks because agoraphobic individuals usually have social concerns and are more prone to utilize avoidance as a defense. Subsequent to a panic attack, the agoraphobic person usually dreads social situations (such as crowds, restaurants, theaters, and even driving) and either wishes to escape when in them or avoids the situation altogether. Edmond Bourne points out that research results have isolated "a deep seated sense of insecurity" coupled with excessive worry about safety or reactions of others, high standards, and expectations and "suppression of self-assertiveness" as personality characteristics associated with agoraphobia and often panic persons. These characteristics, in and of themselves, lead to the development of stress responses because so much of life contains potential social or personal stressors to these persons. [*See* AGORAPHOBIA; PANIC DISORDER.]

Likewise, Hans Eysenck reports on a series of grand longitudinal studies in which there is a significant association between stress prone personality "types" and chronic diseases associated with each type. He describes this study by saying that "In 1972, two sets of persons underwent detailed investigation . . . amounting to 2449 persons in all. . . . All were assigned one of four personality types [from their self-report test scores]. . . ." Persons were assigned randomly to behavior therapy or not (control). At a 7-year follow-up, 47.4% of the control group with cancer prone personalities had in fact developed cancer and died from it at that assessment time. Of the coronary prone personalities 15.4% had developed and died from CHD. In the behavior therapy condition, however, only 7.5% of the cancer prone personalities died from cancer and 4.2% of the CHD personalities had died from this disease. These studies not only demonstrate the strong association between personality, stress, and disease but also show that stress removal (by way of focused behavior therapy procedures) essentially eliminates the person's susceptibility to disease. These are very encouraging data since they clearly indicates that stress effects are reversible.

Finally, there is the pioneering work with cardiovascular disease and the Type A personality design identified and explored by "action–emotion complex" engaged in a chronic struggle to "obtain an unlimited number of poorly defined things from their environment in the shortest period of time." This compulsive, workaholic, aggressive, competitive style was best identified through face to face structured interviews and was consistently predisposed to premature coronary heart and artery disease. In contrast to the Type A behavior, a Type B was identified who was less aggressive, more relaxed, and set fewer deadlines. As studies have become more refined, the critical personologic factor to emerge as the central predictive variable for Type A vulnerability has been chronic states of hostility and cynicism. Issues of control and insecurity are also present but hostility and cynicism seem to carry the greater weight in the formation of coronary heart disease at an early age. [*See* TYPE A–TYPE B PERSONALITIES.]

Many psychological tests (generally of a self-report nature) have been developed to measure the "psychological" effects of stress. Without going into unnecessary detail, these tests include: the Minnesota Multiphasic Personality Inventory (MMPI), The Sixteen Personality Factor (16 P-F), Millon Clinical Multiaxial Inventory (MCMI), Taylor Manifest Anxiety Scale (TAS), State-Trait Anxiety Inventory (STAI), Affect Adjective Checklist (AACL), Subjective Stress Scale (SSS), and the Profile of Mood Scales (POMS). The format and purpose each of these instruments are quite different. Some measure personality on empirically determined factors and generate "profile" descriptions. Others are more singular and have only a few factors that relate to a specific trait or quality while others are scored in a more subjective fashion. All, however, can provide some measure of stress in the person's life. [*See* PERSONALITY ASSESSMENT.]

VI. STRESS AS A STIMULUS: DISEASE REACTIONS

Having talked about stress and personality in the previous section, we now turn to the effects of stress on particular diseases or target organs. Up until now we have been looking at stress as a response (to stressors). Now we are going to look at stress as a stimulus leading to particular health consequences. The systems of the body most stress susceptible are the cardiovascular system, gastrointestinal system, the skin, immune system, metabolic disease, and mental status. [*See* STRESS AND ILLNESS.]

Stress effects on the cardiovascular system are fairly well known and have been discussed in preceding sections. The Type A personality work as well as that of the "hot" reactors has been discussed elsewhere. The cardiovascular system seems particularly vulnerable to stress effects and damage. Cumulative stress, coupled with certain personality and behavioral factors, is strongly associated with the development of cardiovascular disorders.

Gastrointestinal disorders include peptic ulcers, ulcerative colitis, irritable bowel syndrome, and esophageal reflux as the most commonly studied GI disorders. Peptic ulcers can affect stomach or duodenal areas. The previously mentioned study in which stomach secretions were examined through a surgically installed window clearly demonstrated that anger and rage lead to increased secretions of acid and pepsin by the stomach. Feelings of depression, on the other hand, tended to decrease these secretions. While specific mechanisms have not been fully isolated, current thought is that peptic ulcers (both stomach and duodenal) have both genetic elements (e.g., secretion reactivity) and a learned element (perhaps suppressed rage or other feelings) and are thus multiply determined. Ulcerative colitis, or inflammation and ulceration of the inner colon tissue, also shows evidence of anger reactivity but usually within a compulsive, immature personality structure. It is thought that psychologic–emotional factors account for up to 74% of these disorders in adult and perhaps as high as 95% in children. Recent medical research indicates that a chronic bacterial infection (heliobater pylori) may be the underlying physical mechanism that is activated by lifestyle factors. Irritable bowel syndrome has clear physiological abnormalities associated with it but also shows clusters of personality traits such as compulsiveness, overresponsibility, sensitivity, and nonassertiveness. Esophageal reflux is a condition marked by substernal burning sensations with occasional radiation to arm or jaw and thus appears to mimic pain associated with coronary artery disease. It is often called "heartburn." Although the primary cause is physiological weakness in the lower esophageal soincter, psychological factors can trigger episodes. Again, emotional arousal combined with a compulsive mentalistic approach which does not allow resolution or expression of emotions is common here as with most GI disorders.

Respiratory disorders such as allergy, asthma, and hyperventilation can be triggered by acute and chronic stress conditioning often combined with or triggered by emotional reactions. Many muscular disorders have a stress-related component since the muscle system is often the end organ for stress arousal. Here pain, headaches, ringing in the ear, jaw tension, teeth grinding, awkwardness, stiffness, hyperventilation, dizziness, and so on can be tied to muscle tension as a response to stressors. Likewise, many skin disorders are related to stress including psoriasis, acne, hair loss (alopecia areata), and eczema. The immune system is particularly sensitive to excessive stress and shows an immunosuppression that can lead to the development of infectious and degenerative diseases. Two diseases of current concern—cancer and AIDS—are related to inhibition of immunocompetence. Studies are under way to try to isolate a cancer prone personality (Type C) that leads to cancer development. Such studies provide predictive power to identify people at risk much before actual disease or illness develops. As our predictive power increases, prevention takes on a greater focus and disease treatment—which occupies the vast majority of our health resources—becomes much less important.

These are just a few of the stress-related manifestation in the body. Mental and emotional activities and disorders can be stress related. As a matter of fact, current theories of psychopathology emphasize the *diathesis–stress* model in which the diathesis (the person's genetic, biological, and/or psychological vulnerability or preparatory condition) reacts to current social or interpersonal stressors to produce abnormal or maladjustive behaviors. The diathesis–stress model is used to account for and study most all forms of psychopathology and maladjustment including schizophrenia, depression, conversion disorders, obsessive–compulsive disorders, post-traumatic stress disorders, alcoholism, panic, and agoraphobia and many other disruptive and often debilitating conditions.

A. Models That Link Stress to Disease

Everly and Benson have proposed a "disorders of arousal" stress model for pathogenesis. According to these researchers, with prolonged stress arousal (or perhaps through genetic disposition) the limbic circuitry becomes hypersensitive for excitation. This neurologic hypersensitivity in the subcortical limbic system leads to a high propensity for hyperarousal on a chronic basis. This chronic excess arousal is evidenced by hyperstartle reactions and autonomic lability. More importantly, however, limbic hyperarousal and sensitivity eventually begin to affect low tolerance systems and physical as well as psychological disorders develop. Effective treatment for the disorder must include efforts to reduce chronic states of arousal. Furthermore, prevention is possible by focusing on lowering arousal and developing new coping skills. These methods are described more fully in the treatment section that follows.

VII. PSYCHOLOGICAL TREATMENT OF STRESS

There are many different models for the treatment of stress. Here we will discuss current approaches that seem to show promise as effective stress treatments. Models for the treatment of stress include: (1) behavioral treatments, which focus on operating on the stressful environment and reducing the stress response; (2) cognitive treatments, which focus on irrational thoughts and beliefs associated with the appraisal of stressful events; and (3) meditation which reduces stress through relaxation and attention focusing. While these models originate from markedly different theoretical standpoints they show surprising similarity in technique.

A. Behavioral Treatment

Behavior therapies for the treatment of stress are based on principles of learning investigated in the laboratory by operant and respondent psychologists. Researchers and their clinical counterparts, who have applied these principles to human populations, embrace the notion that psychology should be the study of observable events. In the area of stress, this means treatment should focus on identifying the stressful stimulus and reducing its salience or eliciting strength. With this stance that treatment should involve only the analysis and manipulation of natural events, behavior therapists have developed a set of very effective stress treatments.

1. Progressive Muscle Relaxation (PMR)

Is a technique that was originally developed by Edmund Jacobson (1938) a practicing physician. Jacobson proposed that stressful states were manifested and maintained by striate muscle tension. In his view, if people could learn to relax their muscles they could reduce their level of stress and the concomittant effects. Numerous studies have been conducted on PMR indicating that it is an effective stress treatment. The PMR strategy is as follows:

1. The participant is taken through the different muscle groups that will be used in the relaxation procedure and learns how to tense and relax these muscles.
2. The participant is then guided through a relaxation procedure where they tense and relax various muscle groups and learn to identify the feelings of relaxation and to release any excess tension.
3. With daily practice, the participant develops a less and less stressful and less anxious disposition. Muscle tension associated with daily activities is gradually replaced by a more relaxed muscle and emotional state.

Many people find the idea of tensing and releasing muscle counterintuitive. But, by tensing and letting go of a muscle what is achieved is an effect analogous to pulling back a pendulum and releasing it (i.e., extreme muscle tension swinging toward complete relaxation). With a properly trained clinician and a person suffering from severe levels of stress, PMR can be an enormous benefit. Integration of PMR into one's life also makes sense in terms of the Bensen–Everly "disorders of arousal" model described above in that such practice undoubtedly lowers chronic arousal or excitation levels in the limbic system and therefore lowers vulnerability to target organ effects. [*See* RELAXATION.]

2. Physical Exercise

There is much evidence supporting the notion that physical exercise reduces the stress response. The most accepted theory of why exercise is important in reducing stress is that it may represent a healthy release of the human stress response. Researchers posit various physiological mechanisms which explain the effect of exercise on stress. These include: (1) biochemical changes in bodily levels of various hormones and fatty acids; (2) postexercise muscle fatigue and subjective feelings of relaxation; (3) overall improvements in heart, respiratory, and metabolic functions.

Many behavior therapists in the area of behavioral medicine prescribe regular exercise to their clients who suffer from severe levels of stress. However, in order for physical exercise to be effective it should (1) be aerobic (at least a 20-minute period of increased oxygen demand) and rhythmic in nature: (2) not involve competition as this may increase stress.

3. Biofeedback

Biofeedback comprises several different procedures that systematically and continually measure and feedback to the individual a particular aspect of their physiological functioning. With this information the individual is able to modify their physiological functioning through cognitive and voluntary controls. The most common biofeedback measures are heart rate, electrical resistance of the skin (GSR) associated with sympathetic arousal, muscle tension, and temperature differentials. [*See* BIOFEEDBACK.]

Through biofeedback practice patients are able to enhance or invoke a generalized relaxation response and/or change the activity of a particular physiologic system which is in dysregulation due to stress. The reason biofeedback is considered a behavior therapy is that the type of feedback (e.g., unpleasant noise vs pleasant noise, green light vs red light, or alarm vs no noise) is contingent upon the physiological response. Thus, the person is able to learn how to regulate his or her physiology through operant learning techniques (i.e., by reinforcement and punishment contingencies between physiologic response and direction and intensity of feedback). By changing physiology basic changes occur in the nature of their stress response. Regular practice can produce a relatively permanent change.

Biofeedback has been applied to the following physiologic systems as a means of reducing the stress response:

1. Alpha brain wave activity (EEG)
2. Heart rate (EKG)
3. Galvanic skin resistance (e.g., palmer sweating; GSR)
4. Skin temperature
5. Muscle tension as assessed by electomyography (EMG) of the frontalis (forehead) muscles, trapezius (shoulder) muscles, and other specific muscle groups

B. Cognitive Treatments

Theories of mind and the notion that our bodies interact with forces outside of our space–time continuum have been posited by numerous philosophers since the time of Renee Descartes (who argued for a separation of mind and body). While some psychologists view the mind as collateral by-products of our genetics and learning history, many psychologists uphold the notion that the (unobservable) mind (both conscious and unconscious) has a significant influence over both our physiology and our behavior.

In the past 30 years, there have been several psychologists who have developed intervention strategies for treating stress that are aimed at restructuring cognitions (i.e., thinking) in order to reduce or alleviate stress. These therapies are known as cognitive and cognitive–behavioral therapies. Cognitive and cognitive–behavioral therapies for stress reduction are based on the assumption that what produces stress is the cognitive appraisal of the stressful stimulus. Thus, modifying or changing our interpretation of stressful stimuli may in fact remediate or reduce the stress response. [*See* COGNITIVE BEHAVIOR THERAPY.]

1. Rational Emotive Therapy

One of the first cognitive therapies, rational emotive therapy (RET), was developed by Albert Ellis. According to Ellis, all psychological disorders, including the stress response, arise from irrational thinking patterns. These patterns of thinking fit into an "A-B-C-D-E" paradigm. "A," the activating event, is a real external event which the individual experiences (as stressful). "B", belief, symbolizes the series of irrational self-verbalizations the person goes through after experiencing A (e.g., "I can't handle the situation" or "This is horrible and awful"). "C," the consequence, refers to the emotions and the behavior which result from B (e.g., the stress response). According to RET theory, the ABC sequence is the mechanism by which psychological disorders develop. Through RET, the therapist teaches the client to "D," dispute, the irrational cognitions they are having in response to A. By disputing such irrational cognitions and replacing them with rational cognitions, "E" will be experienced, i.e., the positive emotional effect of appropriately confronting one's irrational beliefs. Ellis' paradigm can be applied to a wide variety of psychological disorders as well as normal stressful reactions but is a particularly important intervention tool in the area of stress. Rational emotive therapy provides systematic coping mechanisms that a client can apply to a wide variety of stressful situations.

2. Beck's Cognitive Therapy

Aaron Beck's therapy like that of Ellis' is grounded in this idea of rationalism; however, Beck emphasizes that our thoughts need to be tested against available empirical data. In Beck's view, irrational thoughts and ideas regarding environmental stimuli lead to dysfunctional responses. Thus, changing a person's responses to their environment is best accomplished by changing thoughts. According to Beck rational thinking results from objective data-based interpretations of situations (i.e., hypothesis testing). Beck suggests that people should use three questions to test the validity of their thinking. They are as follows:

1. "What is the evidence for or against my belief?"
2. "Is there another way of looking at the situation?"
3. "What will be the outcome of the situation if my current thought is correct?"

Applied to stress, these three questions regarding the evidence for a belief, alternative explanations of a situation, and implications of the situation if the belief is in fact true, provide the person with a rational way of appraising a situation. Again, the cognitivists hold that by modifying or changing our appraisal of a situation the stress response is reduced. Beck's therapy represents another means to this end.

3. Stress Inoculation Training

In an effort to combine some of the approaches used by behavior therapists with those used by cognitive therapists like Beck and Ellis, Donald Meichenbaum has put together a multidimensional treatment package which addresses the environment, the stress response, and cognitive appraisal. This therapy is known as stress inoculation training (SIT).

Stress inoculation includes three phases of treatment. These phases are as follows:

Phase 1: Education In this phase people are told that their stress response has a modifiable cognitive component. Specifically, they are told that their appraisal of "stressful" situations leads to a stress response. In order to prevent the stress response people are instructed that they need to change their irrational self-statements to rational self-statements.

Phase 2: Acquisition In this phase people are given training in coping skills such as relaxation training and coping self-verbalizations. Through relaxation training they are able to control to some degree the intensity of the stress response.

Coping self-verbalizations provide verbal prompts which can be used to elicit appropriate behavior (e.g., "Relax. Take a slow deep breath" or "When the anxiety comes on, just pause and relax").

Phase 3: Application In this phase people apply the skills they have learned in phases one and two to stressful situations. This can be done covertly via visualization (e.g., "Imagine your boss just told you that you need to write a 20 page report by Friday") or *in vivo* as stressful situations arise in the person's everyday life.

SIT represents a multidimensional treatment aimed at improving coping strategies through changes in thinking and behavior. Moreover, SIT is a flexible treatment framework which can be applied to a wide array of stressful situations. Ultimately, the person should become an expert at SIT and be able to effectively cope with stress throughout their lifetime.

4. Meditation

Meditation has its origins almost 3500 years ago in ancient India. Since that time meditation has been disseminated very successfully throughout the eastern world. Over the centuries, different types of meditation have developed. However, only in the past 30 years has meditation achieved popularity in the United States.

Meditation has been defined as the act of focusing and calming. There are several different types of meditation which facilitate focusing and calming.

1. Problem contemplation—this involves trying to solve a paradoxical problem from a detached position.
2. Visual concentration—this involves focusing on a visual image (e.g., a flower, flame, tree, etc.) with a calm mind.
3. Mental repetition—involves the repetition of a phrase or "mantra" silently to one's self. There are mantra chants in the Hindu religion.
4. Physical repetition—focusing on one's breathing or rythmic movement during prayer can facilitate focusing and increase one's meditative state. The Zen use breath concentration as a form of mantra.

According to Benson, one of these four procedures combined with a quiet environment, a passive but alert attitude, and a comfortable position are necessary components for a successful meditative experience. The goal of meditation is to achieve complete focus. With complete focus comes a reduction of an individual's stress response.

VIII. CONCLUSIONS

The study of stress has led us back to the study of the whole person. Mind and body—concepts that were separated by Descarte into different areas of study—are now reforming as a single area of study but one with many interactive components. We are now sure that mind and body act as a singular unit, each influencing the other. There is some question as to whether we need to artificially separate them or design a science that studies them as a unit of data. We also know that through mental processes we can achieve access to and change the body reactions. This will undoubtedly in the future help prevent disease and give people opportunity to intervene in their own lives to enhance their health and happiness. The study of stress, which began at essentially the physiological level, is transforming into a new paradigm that represents the leading edge for a reintegration of our knowledge of the human being. It is an exciting area of study and one that will carry us into the next generation of knowledge about the human condition.

Bibliography

Benson, H. (1975). "The Relaxation Response." Morrow, New York.

Bourne, E. J. (1990). "The Anxiety and Phobia Workbook." New Harbinger, Oakland, CA.

Eliot, R. S., and Breo, D. (1989). "Is It Worth Dying For?" Bantam Books, New York.

Everly, G. S. (1989). "A Clinical Guide to the Treatment of the Human Stress Response." Plenum, New York.

Friedman, M., and Rosenman, R. (1974). "Type A Behavior and Your Heart." Knopf, New York.

Selye, H. (1956). "The Stress of Life." McGraw-Hill, New York.

Williams, R. (1989). "The Trusting Heart." Times Books, New York.

STRESS AND ILLNESS

Tracy B. Herbert and Sheldon Cohen
Carnegie Mellon University

Glossary

Adherence The degree to which patients follow the medical recommendations of practitioners.

Health behavior Activity undertaken by people who believe they are healthy in order to prevent future health problems.

Illness behavior Activity of people who feel ill with the purpose of determining the state of their health or finding a remedy.

Immune system The organs and structures that protect the body against harmful substances such as bacteria and viruses.

Neuroendocrine system An array of glands controlled by the nervous system that secrete hormones into the bloodstream.

Stress The condition that results when person/environment transactions lead the individual to perceive a discrepancy between the demands of a situation and the person's resources.

Sympathetic nervous system A division of the autonomic nervous system that enables the body to mobilize and expend energy during physical and emotional arousal.

THE RELATIONSHIP between stress and illness is the focus of a good deal of research performed in the field of health psychology. Health psychology is devoted to understanding the psychological factors associated with health and illness. One specific area of interest is determining the psychological factors related to the etiology of disease. Stress is one of the factors often studied that many people believe is related to health and disease. In fact, substantial evidence exists for associations between increased stress and reports of symptoms of disease as well as use of health services. Provocative evidence also exists for associations between increased stress and verified organic illness. In this chapter then, we will discuss stress, and specifically, focus on the mechanisms through which it might be possible for stress to influence health and illness.

I. DEFINING STRESS AND ILLNESS

A. What Is Stress?

Almost everyone has experienced the surge of adrenaline that comes with something sudden and unexpected, like when a speeding car almost hits us. One often hears people say they feel "stressed" because they are overworked, or they have "too much stress" in their lives. What is stress? Is it the adrenaline surge? The overwork? The way we feel emotionally? According to Lazarus and Folkman, two psychologists who have been important in developing a psychological theory of stress, stress is defined neither by an environmental event nor by a person's physiologic response to it. Rather, stress is defined by the person's *perception* of the environmental event. This perception involves the appraisal of potential harms, threats, and challenges posed by the event, as well as the individual's perceived ability to deal (or cope) with the harms, threats, and challenges. Thus, stress arises when a person appraises a situation as threatening or otherwise demanding, perceives that it is important to respond, and does not have an appropriate coping response immediately available. When individuals experience stress, or make a stress appraisal, they also characteristically experience negative emotions (e.g., anxiety, depression), changes in physiology, and changes in behavior patterns that increase risk for disease and mortality. [*See* STRESS.]

B. The Role of Social and Personal Resources

Different people respond to the same stressful event in different ways. Why might this be so? A number of investigators interested in stress and illness propose that the relationship between stress and illness varies with both the personal and social characteristics of the individual. That is, differences in social support systems, skills, attitudes, beliefs, and personality characteristics render some persons relatively protected from stress-induced illness and others relatively susceptible. Social and personal characteristics are thought to influence whether stressful events result in psychological distress (negative emotions), although they may also influence manifestations of distress such as physiologic or behavioral responses. These social and personal characteristics are commonly referred to as stress-buffering resources because they are presumed to protect or buffer people from the pathogenic effects of stress. For example, perceptions of availability of stress-responsive social support provides protection from stress-related symptomatology. People who believe that others will provide aid in times of stress are likely to believe that either they or someone they know will have the resources to meet the demands of the stressor. Personality characteristics or personal resources that have been found to be important in coping with negative events include feelings of control over one's life and self-esteem. People who have feelings of control and high self-esteem are likely to believe that they have the resources to meet the demands that require the strengths they possess. Believing that resources are available may lead a potentially stressful event to be interpreted as a challenge rather than a threat. [*See* CONTROL; SELF-ESTEEM.]

The *Type A behavior pattern,* or Type A personality, is a personal characteristic that has been the focus of much research in the context of coronary heart disease. In contrast to those attributes just described, *not* being Type A appears to protect people from the effects of stress. Type A people are involved in a constant struggle to do more and more things in less and less time, and are sometimes quite hostile or aggressive. People with Type A behavior pattern always seem to be under the pressure of time, and live a life characterized by competitiveness. They are always striving for achievement, are hasty, impatient, and very tense. When under pressure, most people exhibit some behaviors that are similar to this Type A pattern, but Type A individuals exhibit this behavior very often, even during an objectively fun and relaxing situation. Thus, in contrast to having feelings of control or high self-esteem, where stress-buffering results from the *presence* of the personal characteristic, stress-buffering effects associated with the Type A characteristic may be attributable to its *absence*. This is due to the fact that persons with Type A behavior pattern seem more likely to appraise situations as stressful and to cope inappropriately once a stress appraisal is made. Thus, Type B people (people who do not show Type A characteristics) may have a health advantage simply because they are not Type A. Rather, they are able to relax, do not worry about time, are less hostile and less concerned with accomplishments, and are more content with themselves. [*See* TYPE A–TYPE B PERSONALITIES.]

In sum, there are a number of social and personal characteristics or resources that influence how people respond to stressful events. Some resources, such as social support, control, and self-esteem may lessen the effects of stressors. Other resources, such as the Type A behavior pattern may accentuate the effects of stressors.

C. What Is Illness?

When the terms "illness" or "disease" are used in health psychology, they generally refer to a variety of health conditions, including infectious disease (colds, flu, sexually transmitted diseases), autoimmune disease (e.g., lupus, rheumatoid arthritis), cancer, hypertension, coronary heart disease, gastrointestinal disorders (e.g., ulcers, inflammatory bowel disease), asthma, and chronic headaches. Also included in these terms are medical conditions resulting from accidents and other kinds of trauma.

Research in health psychology, however, uses specific indicators of illness and disease. Typically, researchers assess disease symptomatology using one (or both) of two approaches. First, disease symptomatology can be quantified using observable *signs* of illness (e.g., rashes, swelling, blood pressure, pulse). Trained clinicians usually identify and document these observable signs. Second, disease symptomatology can be quantified using *symptoms,* which are not observable but are reported by an individual (e.g., chest pain, headaches, stomachaches). Although these self-reports may reflect underlying disease pathology, they may also reflect influences of stress on thought processes and self-perceptions that are not associated with disease. That is, people may report symptoms or illness episodes without actually experiencing clinical illness, or may not report symptoms or illness episodes when they do have clinical disease. The pathways we discuss below primarily involve those where tissue damage or disease occurs. Symptom reporting that is not based in organic disease is discussed later (see section on Illness Behavior).

D. Summary

Stress arises when a person appraises a situation as threatening or demanding, perceives that it is important to respond, and does not have an appropriate coping response immediately available. A number of social and personal characteristics or resources seem able to either lessen or accentuate the effects of stressors. The specific mechanisms through which stress is linked to physical illness, however, remain to be clarified. At a general level, it is assumed that stress leads to negative psychological states such as anxiety or depression. In turn, stress, as well as these negative psychological states, is thought to influence physical health, either through a direct effect on biological processes that influence susceptibility to disease or through behavioral patterns that increase risk for disease and mortality. These biological and behavioral pathways are discussed below.

II. PATHWAYS LINKING STRESS TO ILLNESS

Figure 1 illustrates a model of the pathways through which stress is able to influence illness. The model suggests that stress can result in negative emotional states (e.g., anxiety, depression). Next, either stress or these negative psychological states lead to physiologic responses and behavioral responses, either of which is capable of resulting in illness. For brevity, the model indicates paths moving in only one causal direction, from stress to illness. It is possible, however, for the direction to be reversed. In some cases, for example, illness might lead to further stress.

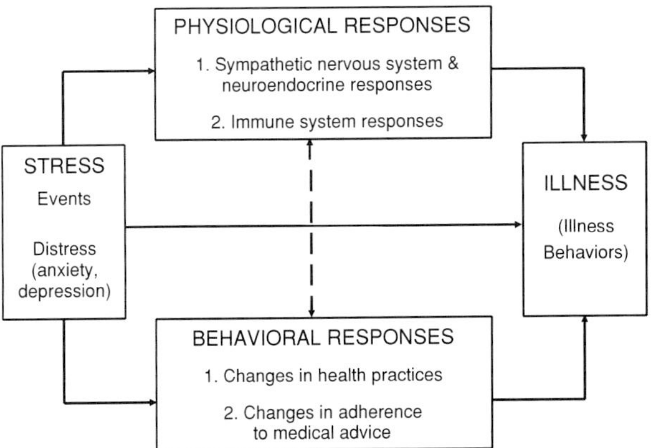

FIGURE 1 Pathways linking stress to illness.

A. Physiological Responses

Two kinds of physiological reactions in response to stress are indicated in Figure 1: sympathetic nervous system and neuroendocrine responses, and immune system responses. In both cases, stress may be related to physiologic responses either directly or through behavioral changes resulting from stress. Here, we focus on the direct physiologic link. The behavioral link is discussed later.

1. Central Nervous System and Neuroendocrine Responses

Stress appraisals affect the nervous system and the endocrine (hormonal) system. The part of the nervous system that controls the internal organs is the autonomic nervous system (ANS). The ANS has two parts: the *sympathetic nervous system,* which mobilizes the body's resources during emotional, stressful, and emergency situations (e.g., increases heart rate); and the *parasympathetic nervous system,* which generally restores the body's energies (e.g., decreases heart rate). Thus, stress appraisals following an environmental event may cause the sympathetic nervous system to signal the heart to beat faster, the energy system to make glucose available, and the blood flow to be shifted toward the muscles that will be needed to fight or flee.

The sympathetic nervous system also affects the endocrine system. It signals the adrenal medulla (a gland on the kidney) to secrete two hormones, epinephrine and norepinephrine. These hormones, more commonly known as adrenaline and noradrenaline, are part of a family of hormones called catecholamines. These hormones enter the blood, travel throughout the body, and increase the general level of arousal. [*See* HORMONES AND BEHAVIOR.]

The second important part of the endocrine system is the hypothalamic–pituitary–adrenocorticol axis. The pituitary, which is controlled by the hypothalamus, is a gland located in the base of the brain near the hypothalamus. The hypothalamus signals the pituitary to secrete adrenocorticotropic hormone

(ACTH). ACTH stimulates the adrenal cortex (a gland on the kidney next to the adrenal medulla) to secrete corticosteroids. The most important of these for humans is cortisol. Cortisol has an anti-inflammatory effect, providing the body with a defense against swelling from injuries that might be sustained during a fight or flight. Because the endocrine system involves the release of hormones into the blood, it is slower to respond, but has longer lasting effects, than the ANS response. [*See* Hypothalamus.]

Thus, the physiological responses in the context of stress are very complex. In short, when someone is threatened or challenged, the sympathetic division of the ANS rouses them from a resting state and stimulates the adrenal medulla to produce epinephrine and norepinephrine. The pituitary releases ACTH, which in turn affects the adrenal cortex. Corticosteroid release prepares the body to resist the potential effects of stress, and even to cope with injury by the release of cortisol. The sympathetic nervous system activation is rapid, as is all neural transmission, whereas the action of the neuroendocrine system is slower. Together, the two systems form the most well-documented physiological responses to stress.

How might sympathetic nervous system arousal or the release of epinephrine, norepinephrine, or corticosteroids lead to illness? One route is through their effect on the immune system, and this is discussed later. Another route is through their effect on the cardiovascular system. For example, an intensely stressful situation may result in extremely high levels of arousal, which can cause the heart to beat erratically or quickly, which may lead, in turn, to cardiac arrest or sudden death in a person with pre-existing heart disease. In addition, chronically high levels of epinephrine, norepinephrine, and corticosteroids appear to increase the growth of plaques (fatty patches) on artery walls. This condition, called atherosclerosis, narrows the inside diameter of the arteries. As the plaques harden, the narrowing and hardening of the arteries increase the blood pressure of the cardiovascular system. Less oxygen is allowed to reach the heart muscle, causing pain (angina) for the individual, and in some cases, muscle death (i.e., heart attack or myocardial infarction). In this context, it is interesting to note that people with the Type A behavior pattern show a heightened vulnerability to developing atherosclerosis and other coronary heart diseases. People with Type A behavior pattern are also more likely to show an increased epinephrine and norepinephrine response when subjected to environmental challenge and have higher blood levels of cortisol in such situations. This is an example of the way a personal characteristic might exacerbate the effects of stress on physiologic processes.

2. Immune System Responses

The immune system protects people from disease-causing microorganisms and other harmful materials (antigens). Cells of the immune system (i.e., white blood cells) circulate throughout the body in the blood and are also located in various organs of the body, including the bone marrow, thymus, lymph nodes, and spleen. There are a number of different kinds of white blood cells, but those most important for this discussion are lymphocytes. Several different types of lymphocytes exist, including natural killer, T, and B cells.

A variety of ways to test the integrity of the immune system exist. For example, some tests simply assess the number of specific cell types or the quantity of specific substances circulating in the blood. One substance often quantified is the amount of antibody in circulation. Antibodies are substances produced by white blood cells (B lymphocytes) when a specific antigen invades the body. Once the antibodies are produced, they attach to the antigen, mark it for destruction by other white blood cells, and prevent it from causing infections.

Another popular test of the immune system is to determine how well specific kinds of white blood cells are functioning. One functional test assesses "lymphocyte proliferative response." In this test white blood cells are incubated for several days with substances that cause them to divide (proliferate). More proliferation is thought to reflect better white blood cell (primarily T and B lymphocyte) functioning. Proliferation is important because when an antigen invades the body, immune cells must divide to increase their numbers before they can successfully eliminate the antigen. Another functional test assesses "natural killer cell cytotoxic activity." In this test white blood cells are incubated for several hours with tumor cells, and the effectiveness of the immune cells (natural killer cells) in killing tumor cells (i.e., their cytotoxicity) is determined. More killing is thought to reflect better natural killer cell functioning. The killing potential of natural killer cells is important because they are one of the fastest responders of the immune system in the fight against viruses and tumor cells.

Many studies have been conducted to determine the relation between stress and the immune system in humans. Studies have investigated the effects of stressors as diverse as medical school examinations, bereavement, divorce, unemployment, and caregiving of a relative with Alzheimer's disease. In general, these studies find that stress is related to changes in both the numbers and quantities of substances in blood, as well as changes in the functioning of the immune cells. Thus, in the context of these kinds of stressors, antibody levels change, as do the number of white blood cells circulating in blood. Moreover, stress is associated with relatively large decreases in both measures of cellular immune function (i.e., lymphocyte proliferative response and natural killer cell cytotoxic activity).

A body of research has also explored connections between negative psychological states (e.g., anxiety and depression) and immune system variables. This research suggests that depressed and anxious mood states are associated with decreased white blood cell function (lymphocyte proliferative response and natural killer cell cytotoxic activity). Negative mood states are also related to changes in the numbers of immune system cells and quantities of substances circulating in blood. Moreover, it appears that the body's ability to produce antibody to an antigen is related to the level of anxiety individuals report—the more anxious someone is, the less antibody they produce after they are injected with the antigen. [*See* Anxiety and Fear; Depression.]

How could stress alter the immune system? Both physiologic and behavioral pathways are plausible. In the case of physiologic mechanisms (behavioral pathways are described below), stress may influence the immune system because some sympathetic nervous system nerves end on the organs of immune system. In fact, a number of direct pathways linking the sympathetic nervous system to the immune system have been identified. This is important because neurotransmitters released from nervous system fibers (like norepinephrine) can influence immune cells directly. Stress may also influence the immune system through neuroendocrine pathways (i.e., release of more far-reaching hormones). A wide range of hormones released under stress have been implicated in influencing the immune system. Examples include epinephrine, norepinephrine, and cortisol, as well as growth hormone, prolactin, and the natural opiates (β-endorphin and enkephalin). At a cellular level, these hormones have been shown to be able to affect immune cells, because there are receptors on white blood cells that allow hormones to attach to and to affect the immune cells. Blood levels of these hormones are also related to immune functioning. For example, acute increases in blood levels of cortisol and epinephrine are related to decreases in the number of lymphocytes in circulation. Immune cell function (lymphocyte proliferative response and natural killer cell cytotoxic activity) also decreases with acute increases in the blood levels of cortisol and epinephrine.

Although both functional and quantitative measures of the immune system are altered by stress, interpreting these changes with respect to health is difficult. The health consequences of changes in the quantitative immune parameters, such as numbers of lymphocytes circulating in blood, have not been determined in otherwise healthy populations. Even though decreased natural killer cell cytotoxic activity has been implicated in certain human diseases (e.g., progression of cancer, chronic viral infection, autoimmune diseases), the direct health consequences of a decrease in natural killer cell cytotoxic activity have not been established. A decreased lymphocyte proliferative response is associated with increased levels of mortality and an increased number of hospitalizations among the elderly. There appears to be no relation, though, between the decreased lymphocyte proliferative responses and mortality or hospitalization due to specific disease entities that are clearly mediated by the immune system. At this point, therefore, it is difficult to outline the implications that stress-induced immune alterations have for health.

B. Behavioral Responses

Two kinds of behavioral responses to stress are indicated in Figure 1: changes in health practices and changes in adherence to medical advice. Changes in behavior in the face of stress can be seen in many upsetting situations. For example, when the spouse of an elderly person dies, lifestyle, habits, and routines are often disrupted. Thus, meals might become haphazard and less healthful, sleep might be more irregular, and more alcohol might be consumed. These changes might be especially problematic if, for example, the surviving person was supposed to be following a strict medical program for his own health condition (e.g., diabetes, heart disease). Thus, stress can influence health by increasing the frequency of unhealthful behaviors, by decreasing the frequency of healthful behaviors, or by disrupting needed and prescribed healthful patterns and regimens. The pathways through which these behavioral responses, in turn, can affect illness include neuroendocrine or immune processes. Behavioral responses can also have more direct effects on health or illness, for example, if someone does not take their medication in the way that was suggested by their physician.

1. Changes in Health Practices

One often hears people saying that they are attempting to lead a healthy lifestyle, "keep fit," or "stay in shape." There are a variety of behaviors that people engage in for the purpose of staying fit. These activities, or health behaviors, include exercising, eating a healthful diet, sleeping regularly, avoiding alcohol, cigarettes, and other illicit drugs, engaging in breast self-examination, wearing seat belts, and having regular dental checkups. Research shows, however, that people who experience high levels of stress tend to perform behaviors that increase their risk of becoming ill or injured. For example, stressed people tend to consume more alcohol, cigarettes, and coffee than people who experience less stress. Thus, it is assumed that persons' psychological responses to stress lead them to engage in unhealthful practices such as cigarette smoking, excessive alcohol consumption, poor diet, and lack of rest and exercise.

Engaging in these unhealthful behaviors as a result of stress, or not engaging in healthful behaviors because of stress, may then result in disease or trauma. For example, there is a well-documented relation between smoking and the development of lung cancer. Cigarette smoking has also been linked to coronary heart disease, strokes, ulcers, infectious diseases, and periodontal disease. Excessive alcohol consumption is also linked to a variety of organic diseases, including those of the liver, cardiovascular system, specific cancers, as well as to bacterial infections. In addition, failing to engage in a regular program of exercise has been linked to coronary heart disease as well as osteoporosis. Exercise also has been reported to increase feelings of self-esteem, as well as alleviate feelings of anxiety and depression—effects that might help to prevent a stress appraisal from occurring in the first place. Changes in health practices due to stress may also influence the duration or severity of disease by directly affecting disease-involved tissue. For example, if an individual with a cold increases the number of cigarettes smoked daily because they are under stress, nasal and lung tissues will become more inflamed and irritated.

In addition, behavioral factors, such as alcohol use and carelessness, probably play a role in the relatively high accident rates of people under stress. Studies have found that children and adults who experience high levels of stress are more likely to suffer accidental injuries at home, in sports activities, on the job, and while driving a car than individuals under less stress. A simple example would be an accident that happened because someone was driving while they were distracted by thinking about a stressful occurrence. Another example involves traumatic injury, that is, stress may lead to alcohol consumption, which may lead to careless or fast driving, which can then lead to injury in an automobile accident.

Finally, in the context of infectious disease, behavioral changes under stress may also influence susceptibility to infection by influencing whether and for how long persons are exposed to infectious agents (e.g., viruses). For example, stressed persons often engage in social coping, that is, they draw on the resources of their social networks. Increased interaction with others results in greater probability of exposure to infectious agents and consequent infection. Other behaviors that may be more likely when an individual is experiencing stress, for example, unsafe sexual practices or poor hygienic practices, could also increase exposure to infectious agents.

2. Changes in Adherence to Medical Advice

Adherence refers to the extent to which a person's behavior (in terms of taking medications, following diets, or executing lifestyle changes) coincides with medical or health advice. Thus, adherence can be viewed in specific terms (e.g., taking medications) as well as in more general terms (e.g., maintaining healthy lifestyle practices). For some individuals, maintaining a healthy lifestyle or practicing a daily regimen is a medical necessity rather than a way of "keeping fit." For example, it is critical that a person who is diagnosed with cancer not smoke, just as it is necessary that a person with insulin-dependent diabetes monitor their blood glucose levels and inject insulin on a regular and prescribed basis. In these and other cases, adherence to a medical regimen is very important, if not life-saving.

The average rate of patient nonadherence to medical advice across a variety of conditions is about 40%. That is, two of every five patients fail to follow the advice of their physicians regarding a desirable medical program. Nonadherence can take many forms, all of which are more likely to occur when an individual is experiencing stress. For example, patients may fail to take their medication as directed, may not show up for a recommended appointment, may skip or stop doing rehabilitation exercises, or may "cheat a little" in following a specific diet or other lifestyle change that was advised. Moreover, each of these forms of nonadherence can itself have many faces. In failing to take medication as directed, for example, persons might omit some doses, use a drug for the wrong reasons, take medication in the wrong amount or at the wrong time, or discontinue the drug before the prescribed course of therapy ends.

Adherence varies considerably, depending on the type of medical advice, and the duration and complexity of the recommended regimen. In addition, long-standing habits are very hard to change. Someone quitting smoking because of cancer or heart or lung disease, for example, might have an especially difficult time not smoking during stressful times. Smoking, after all, was one of the behaviors this individual used to cope with stress. A new or alternative coping mechanism needs to be developed for this person to be successful in adhering to their regimen.

Failure to adhere to medical advice under stress could result in more severe and longer-lasting illness through influences on immune function or through influences on disease-involved tissue. For example, existing problems might be aggravated if an individual engages in restricted behaviors (like smoking cigarettes or drinking alcohol). In addition, failure to perform prescribed behaviors or to adhere to medical programs (e.g., insulin injection schedule) can result in disease progression (e.g., complications due to diabetes).

C. Illness Behaviors

An illness behavior (subsumed in Fig. 1 under Illness) is any activity undertaken by a person who feels ill, to define the state of their health and to discover a suitable remedy. These activities generally include talking or complaining about symptoms and seeking help or advice from relatives, friends, and medical practitioners. Of course, before one can talk about either a symptom or seeking help for it, the symptom needs to be identified and interpreted. There are a number of cultural, social, and individual determinants of illness behaviors. However, stress and other psychological factors are able to independently influence illness behaviors, and this is our focus here.

Unlike the physiologic and behavioral factors described earlier, illness behaviors do not *necessarily* reflect organic conditions such as heart disease, infectious disease, or cancer. That is, people sometimes perceive symptoms with no actual physical basis. These stress-triggered illness behaviors are actually thought to be general in nature, that is, they do not fall within the domain of a single disease. Therefore, to the extent that stress effects on illness behaviors are not disease specific, there is reason to assume that they are caused by psychological processes influencing symptom reporting and care seeking rather than by underlying organic pathology. These processes are discussed below. Physiologic and behavioral mechanisms may also operate in conjunction with stress-induced pathology, however, to influence illness behaviors.

1. Labeling Symptoms

Labeling symptoms really involves two processes. The first thing that has to happen is that symptoms must be noticed. Because psychological stress often triggers physiologic arousal, people under stress may be more attentive to their internal physical states. Just because individuals are more attentive, however, does not mean that they are more accurate about their internal states. On the contrary, research shows that people who are internally focused overestimate changes in their bodily functions (e.g., heart rate). Stress may also facilitate the labeling of sensations as symptoms because people are reminded of previous times when stress was associated with symptoms, or simply because they believe that stress triggers symptoms.

Once symptoms are noticed, the second process that occurs is their interpretation. Here, stress may result in physical sensations being mistakenly attributed to disease symptoms. For example, stress results in sympathetic nervous system arousal which, in turn, results in an increase in heart rate. A person with a history of coronary heart disease, however, may interpret this stress-induced increase in heart rate as a symptom of their disease. Symptoms may also be interpreted as disease because people believe that certain symptom constellations represent certain diseases. For example, many people believe that stress is a major cause of heart attacks. Therefore, under stress, minor chest pains that would be ignored under nonstressful conditions may be defined as possible disease recurrence. Of course, the opposite scenario also occurs. That is, individuals under stress might sometimes ignore pain or other signs of disease in order to focus on the stressful tasks at hand. Finally, reports of symptoms and illness are ways to avoid stressful situations. The prototypic example is the child who reports symptoms to avoid attending school on an especially stressful day (i.e., playing ill).

2. Seeking Health Care

Seeking medical care involves first defining a constellation of symptoms as an illness, discussed above, and then deciding to seek care. Again, such behavior may be driven by underlying organic conditions but can also occur independent of pathology. Stress may influence the seeking of health care in several ways. First, stress may influence the decision to seek medical care when persons label themselves as ill by interfering with the decision to seek care. Stress could also increase care seeking for minor symptoms because people are more likely to notice symptoms under stress, or decrease care seeking for serious ones because the time demands of many stressors make medical care visit inconvenient. Once a person makes the decision to seek health care, stress may also influence the amount of time it takes before they actually do it. Finally, persons under stress may also seek medical care unnecessarily because medical providers are viewed as persons to whom one can confide problems.

D. Summary

In sum, Figure 1 depicts a model of the pathways through which stress is able to influence illness and illness behaviors. We described the way stress and the negative emotional states resulting from stress can lead to changes in the sympathetic nervous system, the neuroendocrine system, and the immune system, as well as the way health practices and adherence to prescribed medical advice are affected. The relation of stress to changes in illness behaviors in the absence of organic pathology were also described. We would like to again point out that it is plausible for the pathways in the model to move in the opposite direction, for example, for illness to lead to further stress.

III. CONCLUSIONS

We have focused on relations between stress and illness, and the pathways by which these relations might exist. In general, it can be concluded that stress arises when a person appraises a situation as threatening or demanding, perceives that it is important to respond, and does not have an appropriate coping response immediately available. Stress may then lead to negative psychological states such as anxiety or depression. These negative psychological states are then thought to influence physical health, either through a direct effect on biological processes that influence susceptibility to disease or through behavioral patterns that increase risk for disease and mortality. Negative psychological states can also influence symptom reporting and seeking medical care without directly influencing organic conditions.

It is important to point out that stress is not the primary etiologic agent in disease, but rather, may be but one of many contributors. Other factors that also influence risk for disease include social and personal resources, immunity (in the case of infectious and neoplastic disease), nutritional status, previous history of illness, presence of other disease, genetic factors, age, race, gender, pregnancy, biological rhythms (e.g., circadian, menstrual phase, annual), and seasons of the year (e.g., temperature, light exposure). Thus, although the association between stress and illness is one that is often studied, it is clear that it represents only one small piece of the puzzle of psychological factors and disease.

Bibliography

Ader, R., Felten, D. L., and Cohen, N. (Eds.) (1991). "Psychoneuroimmunology." Academic Press, Orlando, FL.

Cacioppo, J. T., Andersen, B. L., Turnquist, D. C., and Tassinary, L. G. (1989). Psychophysiological comparison theory: On the experience, description, and assessment of signs and symptoms. *Patient Education and Counseling,* **13,** 257–270.

Cohen, S., and Edwards, J. R. (1989). Personality characteristics as moderators of the relationship between stress and disorder. In "Advances in the Investigation of Psychological Stress" (R. W. J. Neufeld, Ed.). Wiley, New York.

Cohen, S., and Williamson, G. M. (1991). Stress and infectious disease in humans. *Psychol. Bull.,* **109,** 5–24.

Glass, D. C. (1977). "Behavior Patterns, Stress, and Coronary Disease." Erlbaum, Hillsdale, NJ.

Herbert, T. B., and Cohen, S. (1993). Depression and immunity: A meta-analytic review. *Psychol. Bull.* **113,** 472–486.

Herbert, T. B., and Cohen, S. (1993). Stress and immunity in humans: A meta-analytic review. *Psychosom. Med.* **55,** 364–379.

Lazarus, R. S., and Folkman, S. (1984). "Stress, Appraisal, and Coping." Springer, New York.

O'Leary, A. (1990). Stress, emotion, and human immune function. *Psychol. Bull.* **108,** 363–382.

Pennebaker, J. (1983). "The Psychology of Physical Symptoms." Springer-Verlag, New York.

Subjective Culture

Harry C. Triandis
University of Illinois at Urbana-Champaign

Glossary

Associations Connections among the elements of subjective culture, e.g., the categories used by a cultural group.

Attitudes A disposition to respond favorably or unfavorably to an aspect of the environment.

Beliefs Judgments concerning how categories are related to each other.

Categorizations Members of a cultural group make the same response to discriminably different stimuli.

Evaluations Judgments of the worth of a category, e.g., that a category is good or bad, desirable or undesirable, wise or foolish.

Expectations Anticipations of the future state of the social environment.

Ideals Models of excellent states of the social environment.

Meanings What is understood by a symbol.

Norms Beliefs that members of a particular group or culture ought to behave in specific ways.

Roles Beliefs that individuals that hold a position in a social system ought to behave in specific ways.

Self-Definitions Beliefs about attributes attached to the self (all ideas that include words such as me, mine, myself, I).

Stereotypes Beliefs about attributes of a group of individuals, an ethnic group, people who are in specific roles, a country.

Values Conceptions of desirable endstates that transcend specific situations, guide the selection of behavior or events, and are ordered by relative importance. Principles that guide a cultural group's life.

SUBJECTIVE CULTURE is a cultural group's characteristic way of perceiving its social environment. Culture is here defined very broadly to include everything that is human-made. It includes both objective (tools, road, buildings) and subjective (associations, attitudes, beliefs, categorizations, evaluations, expectations, ideals, norms, meanings, roles, self-definitions, stereotypes, and values) elements. Of special importance are meanings and symbols. Culture is to society what memory is to individuals. Elements of culture that proved adaptive, satisfying, or helpful at solving the problems of existence are transmitted through inter-generational socialization, and become widely shared among the members of the culture. [*See* CATEGORIZATION; PREJUDICE AND STEREOTYPES.]

I. MEASUREMENTS

Each of the elements of subjective culture can be measured with paper-and-pencil methods. Other methods are also applicable; convergence across methods is highly desirable to determine the validity of the measurements.

Detailed methods can be found in the bibliography. Among the most widely used instruments for the measurements of the elements of subjective culture are standard attitude items and the behavioral, semantic, and role differentials. Survey methods are quite appropriate in studies of subjective culture.

II. STRUCTURE

The elements of subjective culture tend to be organized around major themes, such as the number of different elements that guide behavior (complex–simple cultures), the relative importance of the individual or the group (individualism vs collectivism) in the judgments of the elements of subjective culture, how do members of a culture utilize and exchange resources, the appropriateness of equality or inequality in social relations (power distance), and the extent to which people are allowed to deviate from the modal position of the members of the culture on cultural elements without being rejected by the majority of the members of the culture (looseness–tightness). These themes are themselves complex, multidimensional constructs.

III. RELATIONSHIP TO BEHAVIOR

The elements of subjective culture are related to behavior. A person's *behavioral intentions* (self-instructions about how to behave that occur just before behavior takes place) are influenced by the norms, roles, self-definitions, and values of that person. Models that predict behavior from attitudes also use the utility of the behavior for that person. Utility reflects expectations and evaluations. The way members of the culture perceive the social situation reflects all the elements of subjective culture.

Bibliography

Fiske, A. L. (1990). "Structures of Social Life: The Four Elementary Forms of Human Relations." The Free Press, New York.

Schwartz, S. (1992). Universals in the content and structure of values: Theoretical advances and empirical tests in 20 countries. In "Advances in Experimental Social Psychology" (M. Zanna, Ed.), Academic Press, San Diego.

Triandis, H. C. (1972). "The Analysis of Subjective Culture." Wiley, New York.

Triandis, H. C. (1980). Values, attitudes, and interpersonal behavior. In "Nebraska Symposium on Motivation" (H. E. Howe and M. M. Page, Eds.). University of Nebraska Press, Lincoln NE.

Triandis, H. C. (1994). "Culture and Social Behavior" McGraw-Hill, Boston.

SUBSTANCE ABUSE

Bernard Segal
University of Alaska Anchorage

Glossary

Addiction A condition brought about by the repeated administration of any drug such that continued use of the drug is necessary to maintain normal physiological function, and discontinuance of the drug results in definite physical and mental symptoms.

Drug Any substance, natural or synthetic, that by its chemical nature alters structure or function in the living organism.

Drug-taking behavior A neutral term that describes drug use, inferring that use of drugs can be explained in the same terms as any other form of behavior.

Physical dependence A physiological state, usually following the development of tolerance, that results in the onset of withdrawal symptoms following cessation of drug-taking behavior.

Psychoactive drug Any chemical substance that alters mood, perception, or consciousness.

Substance abuse Drug use that is excessive, dangerous, or undesirable to the individual or community.

Tolerance A diminished response to the same dose of a drug as a result of prior use of the drug.

SUBSTANCE ABUSE, which can be considered to be synonymous with the phrase *drug abuse,* has been used to describe drug use that is excessive, dangerous, or undesirable to the individual or community. The terms substance abuse or drug abuse have also come to mean the use of any drug to the point where it interferes with one's health or with one's economic or social adjustment. Another definition is that substance abuse represents the recreational use of any illicit *psychoactive* substance—whether or not there is any demonstration of individual harm or adverse social consequences. Regardless of how the terms substance and drug abuse may be defined, they have been used with a great deal of imprecision and confusion, and in a highly subjective manner, to refer to drug use in our society.

I. REDEFINING SUBSTANCE ABUSE

Despite controversy and uncertainty about the meaning of the phrases substance and drug abuse, they have generally acquired the connotation of social disapproval and illegal behavior. Neither of these terminologies, however, offers a precise definition in reference to the actual use of a drug. Thus, what one person or group may define as "drug abuse," may not be perceived similarly by others. For example, some members of our society, depending on their religious, social, or political affiliation, tend to perceive alcohol, tobacco, and caffeine as substances that are abused along with illegal drugs. In contrast, a professional athlete who used anabolic steroids to "bulk up" to achieve a performance edge, for example, may not be seen as having "abused" a drug, while a youth who tried marijuana only once to find out what it was like may be characterized as a "drug abuser."

The use of drugs, however, is too complex a phenomenon to be described primarily as abuse. Drug-related experiences can be better understood when such behavior is devoid of any possible emotional overtones. Based on the premise that the use of drugs is a form of behavior, then the phrase "*drug-taking behavior,*" rather than "substance abuse," or "drug use," implies that such behavior follows the same rules and principles as any other behavior, and as such can be discussed or studied in a more exact and scientific manner. Moreover, the neutral term "drug-taking," helps to explain why, when, and where people use drugs, how they use them, who uses them, and what drugs are being used. Thus, the context of drug-taking becomes an important factor in understanding and evaluating the behavior.

II. DRUGS AND DRUG EFFECTS

A scientific definition of a *drug* is any substance, natural or synthetic, that by its chemical nature alters structure or function in the living organism. This broad definition encompasses many chemical compounds, some of which have the capacity to induce an altered state of consciousness. Those drugs that particularly affect one's level of awareness have been referred to as *psychoactive* substances. A psychoactive drug is thus defined as any substance that alters consciousness, mood, or perception. Many of these psychoactive drugs have found their way from prescription pads to the street, where their use, albeit illicit, has become widespread among large segments of society, particularly youth and young adults.

The types of psychoactive drugs that are available in our society can be grouped into five major categories based on their behavioral effects: (1) sedative–hypnotic compounds; (2) behavioral stimulants; (3) narcotic analgesics (opiates); (4) antipsychotic agents; and (5) psychedelics and hallucinogens. This behavioral classification system is just one of many schemes that have been developed to classify drugs according to how they alter consciousness, mood, or perception. This system is especially useful because it provides a convenient framework within which to describe the many psychoactive drugs that are taken in order to obtain specific psychological effects.

Such effects, however, are not the same for all individuals, nor even necessarily similar for the same person at all times. Drug effects vary widely and are often unpredictable, depending on such factors as mood, expectations of what the drug will do (set), previous experience with the drug, the route of administration, the nature of the drug used and its potency, and the setting in which it is used. What follows is a very brief description of some of the major chemical agents that are used to alter mood, perception, or consciousness. [*See* BEHAVIORAL MEDICINE; BEHAVIORAL PHARMACOLOGY.]

A. Sedative–Hypnotics (Central Nervous System Depressants)

Sedative–hypnotic drugs depress the functioning of the central nervous system (CNS), resulting in a reduction of neural activity and level of awareness. They include barbiturates and nonbarbiturate hypnotics, anti-anxiety agents (minor tranquilizers such as Valium or Librium), and alcohol, which is classified as a sedative–hypnotic because of its behavioral effects, but it is not structurally related to the barbiturates or other such compounds. Some of the better known barbiturates are secobarbital (Seconal) and pentobarbital (Numbutal) and methaqualone (Quaalude).

Physiologically, CNS depressants lower blood pressure and respiration, slow speech, and alter consciousness. Tolerance develops from use over a lengthy time period, and physical dependence may also occur.

At low doses many of these drugs induce a feeling of relaxation and a sense of well-being and drowsiness, which may make the user seem more sociable, jovial, and impulsive. At higher doses they reduce reaction time and impair functioning; there may be a feeling of sedation or mild euphoria. Higher doses evoke behavior that is virtually indistinguishable from alcohol intoxication, including behavioral disinhibition; negative or violent reactions are possible. Very high doses can lead to behavioral depression and sleep, and even higher doses can result in a coma and death.

Intravenous injection of barbiturates may bring on a "warm rush," but not of the same intensity or quality associated with other drugs such as cocaine or amphetamines. The most common street use of barbiturates, aside from seeking the high they provide, is for coming "down" from a high obtained from other drugs, chiefly stimulants.

Alcohol, a sedative–hypnotic drug, is a substance that most people do not think of as a drug, but it is a very powerful mind altering chemical. Alcohol is the most used drug in our society, largely because of its relaxing and euphoric effects. It is also the most misused and abused drug, significantly contributing to health and social problems, such as highway deaths, drowning, suicides, violent injuries, homicides, burns, unwanted pregnancies, and sexually transmitted diseases. As many as 10.5 million people may have some form of a drinking problem, while 7.2 million drink heavily. Alcohol-related problems cost the nation an estimated $85.8 billion in 1988, of which 39% is attributed to reduced productivity, and 33% to mortality losses. The cost in 1990 is estimated to have been $136 billion.

Although there are many more people who drink and do not experience an alcohol-related problem, among the 20% of our population that does drink, 5% will have their lives affected adversely by alcohol. A discussion of the nature of alcohol problems, their etiology, and treatment, however, is beyond the scope of this article.

B. Central Nervous System Stimulants

CNS stimulants represent a major classification of drugs that are used to increase alertness and physical activity. They consist of a variety of chemical agents that vary in mechanisms of action and chemical structure. Four categories of CNS stimulants have been described: (1) behavioral stimulants, which include cocaine and amphetamines; (2) clinical antidepressants; (3) convulsants such as strychnine; and (4) general cellular stimulants, which include caffeine and nicotine.

In low to moderate doses, behavioral stimulants can elevate mood, induce *euphoria,* and increase alertness. At high doses they can produce irritability and anxiety. With repeated use they can induce a psychotic-like reaction that is characterized by aggressiveness and marked paranoid ideation.

1. Amphetamines

There are three chemically similar types of amphetamines: (1) amphetamine (racemic amphetamine sulfate, formerly Benzedrine), (2) dextroaphetamine sulfate (Dexedrine and Obetrol), and (3) methamphetamine hydrochloride (Desoxyn). Use of methamphetamine, in the form of "ice," has exploded in recent years because of illicit manufacturing. Ice, or "crystal meth," is an extremely pure form of methamphetamine (between 98 and 100%) that looks like rock candy.

Amphetamines cause an increase in heart rate and body temperature, and can raise both systolic and diastolic blood pressure, increasing respiration and circulation. Pupils, blood vessels (vasodilation), and the air passages of the lungs (bronchodilation) are dilated. The mouth becomes dry and there can be hyperactivity in speech and movements. Appetite is suppressed.

Shortly after taking a low to moderate oral dose of one of the forms of amphetamines, usually methamphetamine ("speed"), or smoking "crank" or "crystal," the user tends to feel more alert and energetic. A larger dose, particularly when intravenously injected, can induce a "rush," "flash," or "splash," which is a sudden, overwhelming intense pleasurable sensation involving a feeling of euphoria and physical well-being immediately after the drug has been injected, an experience akin to orgasm-like feelings, referred to as a "full body orgasm."

Ice or crystal meth is usually smoked, but it can be injected intravenously. When smoked the effects begin to be experienced fairly quickly, about 7 seconds, resulting in an intense physical and psychological exhilaration, lasting between 4 to 14 hours. A severe overdose can lead to death through respiratory failure.

2. Cocaine

Cocaine is an alkaloid obtained from the coca plant found in the higher elevations of the Andes mountains. It is a short-acting but powerful stimulant similar in many ways to the amphetamines. It can be sniffed or snorted, smoked, or injected. It is used primarily as either a white, crystalline powder or as freebase, which is a purified form that is suitable for smoking. Cocaine freebasing has recently been carried a step further with the conversion of cocaine hydrochloride into an even more concentrated freebase form called "crack." Crack is cocaine mixed with nonvolatile chemicals, such as common baking soda and water, to create a paste, which is usually at least 75% cocaine, that hardens into chips. The resulting intoxication is far more intense than either snorting or smoking other types of freebase cocaine.

Regardless of the form, cocaine's ultimate effect is an intense feeling of euphoria, experienced as a rush, which provides a sense of well-being and exhilaration. This experience, while extremely pleasurable, is rather short-lived, peaking within 15–20 minutes, followed by a feeling of depression. In order to avoid this let down users seek to regain the feeling of euphoria by taking the drug again. This cycle may be repeated until the user collapses from exhaustion.

Crack cocaine use has become widespread in larger cities in the United States, but its use is not restricted to urban areas. It is considered to be injurious to the users and to the social system, sapping productivity, increasing health problems, and creating an underground and criminal distribution system and profiteering. The rise of "crack houses" has also become a concern not only because of the criminal behavior associated with them, but also because of the health problems that have arisen, such as AIDS. Crack houses, roughly analogous to the "heroin dens" noted in the 1970s and early 1980s, are a place where crack users go to smoke or "shoot-up" cocaine, spending hours, sometime days, maintaining a constant high, eating rarely, never sleeping and, primarily among women, trading sex for drugs. These settings place the users at high risk for victimization and for sexually transmitted diseases.

Concern has also risen about maternal use of cocaine and its contribution to pregnancy complications. Pregnant women using cocaine have been found to have higher rates of pre- and postnatal problems and babies with neonatal neurobehavioral disorders. Pregnant women using cocaine have been found to exhibit higher rates of spontaneous abortion, detached placentas, and babies with neonatal disorders. Cocaine has also been related to more frequent premature deliveries, sudden infant death (SID), fetal urogenital anomalies, and low birthweight.

C. Narcotic Analgesics (Opiates or Opioids)

The term *narcotic* has generally been used to refer to opium and opium derivatives that are obtained from the oriental poppy, but it has also come to be used to include other drugs that are semisynthetic or wholly synthetic. Three types of opiates are defined as: (1) natural opiates, which are obtained directly from opium, such as morphine and codeine; (2) semisynthetic opiates, which are chemically prepared derivatives of morphine or codeine, such as Dilaudid (dihydromorphine), heroin, and Metopon (methyldihydromorphine); and (3) synthetic opiates, which are chemically synthesized analgesics whose effects are similar to those of morphine, such as propoxyphene (Darvon), methadone (Dolphin), meperidine (Demerol), and pentazocine (Talwin).

Opiates, especially heroin, are used because they can induce an extremely pleasant euphoric state, and feelings of warmth, well-being, peacefulness, and contentment. A pleasant dreamlike state of consciousness can also be experienced. Not all reactions to opiates are pleasant, but opioids seem to be used primarily in anticipation of the feeling of relaxation and the euphoria they induce.

Heroin is a euphoria-producing opiate derivative that generates a rapid and intense high that is characterized as a rush, followed by a feeling of contentment and detachment from reality. Anxiety and feelings of inferiority disappear. A dreamlike state occurs in which fantasies are experienced as a form of escape from the world and from oneself.

Heroin, and other forms of opiates, can be injected, smoked, or sniffed, but it is "the needle" that is the most popular, particularly when using heroin. The dangers of needle use, because of contamination or unsterile needles, are high, and AIDS has become particularly associated with heroin intravenous (i.v.) users. The number of i.v. users diagnosed with AIDS, according to Sorensen, has risen steadily from 1981 to a high of 43,339 cases in 1991, representing 28.4% of i.v. users. He states that "Heroin accounts for 90% of illicit opiate use in the United States and is most frequently used by injection, which is the major route by which drug users transmit HIV."

D. Hallucinogens (Mind-Altering Drugs)

Hallucinogens refer to the different classes of drugs that induce mind-altering or mind-expanding experiences, which involve visual, auditory, or other hallucinatory experiences, and which create a sensation of feeling separated from reality. These drugs are also known as "psychotomimetics" and "psychedelics." The principal use of such drugs is to induce an altered state of consciousness, the specific nature of which varies with the user's drug experience, the nature of the drug taken and its potency, and the setting in which it is used, among many other factors. The experience can be summarized as "mind expanding," but individual reactions vary greatly. Some of the more frequently used hallucinatory drugs are described as follows:

1. Lysergic Acid Diethlamide-25 (LSD)

LSD is obtained from the ergot fungus found on the rye grain. Its effects include vivid perceptual alterations, including illusions or auditory perceptions, often involving the crossing of different sensory sensations, called synesthesia. LSD is one of the most potent hallucinogens known to man, a very small amount—20 μg (1 μg is one-millionth of a gram) or approximately 1/700,000,000 of the average man's body weight—will produce effects. The usual dose of LSD is about 100 to 200 μg. In powder form LSD is odorless, colorless, and crystalline. It is available on the street as a tablet, a capsule, or, occasionally, as a liquid, which may have a slightly bluish cast. One way of taking LSD is to place a small amount of liquid on a (colorful) blotter or similar material, and chew it.

The effects of LSD vary extensively among its users and are largely related to the purity and dose of the drug, the user's set and the conditions under which the drug is taken (setting). LSD's effects are not predictable and can vary from extremely pleasant to very unpleasant; an individual user can experience either effect at different times or may experience both "good" and "bad" effects within the same trip. One usually begins to feel the effects 30–90 minutes after taking the drug. A good trip may involve such experiences as heightened visual effects—for example, perceiving intensified colors, distorted shapes and sizes, and movement in stationary objects. Auditory distortions and distortions of time and place also occur. Several different emotions may be felt at once, or there may be a rapid swing from one emotion to another. The effects can last from 2 to 12 hours. A bad trip can occur when the user experiences the induced sensations as unpleasant and perceives them as frightening, which contributes to create a feeling of panic. The frightening effects may last a short time or the length of the total trip, and can range from mildly frightening to intensely terrifying.

2. Psilocybin and Psilocin

Psilocybin is a hallucinogenic alkaloid that occurs naturally in a variety of mushrooms found in southern Mexico and Central America. Psilocin is an unstable alkaloid also contained in the mushroom but in smaller quantities than psilocybin. Psilocin is the hallucinogenic compound to which psilocybin is converted in the body, and it is thought to be the active hallucination-producing ingredient.

The nature of the hallucinatory experience induced by these two compounds resembles that of other hallucinogenic compounds, but the most prominent effect induced by psilocybin is one of dramatic sensory changes that heighten sensory input; some individuals may experience feelings of euphoria.

3. Dimethyltryptamine (DMT)

DMT is a fast-acting hallucinogenic compound whose chemical structure is similar to that of psilocin. Its effects are similar to those of LSD and begin almost immediately, but last for less than an hour.

4. Mescaline

Obtained from mescal, the surface top (mescal buttons) of the peyote cactus, mescaline is the active ingredient of the hallucinogenic alkaloid extracted from the plant. The tops of the cactus are cut at ground level and dried into peyote "buttons." They are either eaten or boiled and drunk as a tea. The primary effects of mescaline do not differ significantly from those induced by LSD.

5. DOM (STP)

DOM (STP) is a synthetic hallucinogenic drug chemically related to amphetamine and mescaline, estimated to be at least 100 times more potent than mescaline, but 30 to 50 times less potent than LSD. It produces an intense psychedelic effect that lasts up to 3 days. Soon after its introduction to the drug scene, emergency rooms were flooded with persons who experienced marked adverse reactions—tremors, convulsive movements, and prostration—which could be followed by death. These "toxic reactions" resulted in diminished use of the drug.

The psychological effects of DOM are analogous to those of other hallucinogens and are largely influenced by set and setting. The drug affects mood (feeling happy and sad simultaneously or at different times) and induces intense visual imagery, distortions of perception in time, and feelings of depersonalization—a sense of loss of one's own reality or feelings that one's body is unreal; everything seems dreamlike, and actions of oneself or others are watched with indifferent detachment—among other sensations. The overall effect of DOM appears to be one of interfering with sensory input, thereby altering perceptual sensations.

6. MDA, MMDA, TMA

MDA (methylenedioxyamphetamine), chemically related to mescaline and amphetamine, induces feelings of well-being with a heightened sense of self-reflectiveness. Illusions and hallucinations may occur at high doses.

Chemical manipulation of MDA led to the derivatives of an additional hallucinogen, MMDA (3-methoxy-4,5-methylene dioxyphenyl isopropylamine). MMDA differs from MDA only because it has a methoxyl group in its chemical structure.

TMA (3,4,5-trimethoxyphenyl-β-aminopropane) is a hallucinogenic substance derived from mescaline. It is more potent than mescaline, but not as strong as LSD.

MDA, MMDA, and TMA have similar chemical structures that are closely related to amphetamines and to norepinephrine, a synaptic transmitter found in the nervous system. The hallucinogenic properties of these three drugs produce mescaline- and LSD-like effects. At low doses one tends to experience a feeling of well-being and a heightened sensitivity to one's feelings; few or no hallucinations or perceptual distortions may be present. Higher doses induce more intense hallucinatory experiences that encompass perceptual distortions. The effects last about 7 to 8 hours. Very large doses of these drugs can be toxic, and even fatal, to those who are sensitive to them.

7. Phencyclidine (PCP)

Phencyclidine ("PCP," "Angel Dust") is not a hallucinogenic drug found in nature. It is a product of recent pharmacological research that has been channeled into street use because it was found to have hallucinogenic qualities. Pharmacologically PCP is not a hallucinogen, stimulant, or depressant; it is a drug that was originally intended for use as a clinical anesthetic. But because of its ability to induce hallucinations it came to the attention of the drug culture of the 1950s, who were searching for greater levels of consciousness expanding. It is believed that PCP first hit the streets in San Francisco in 1967, with its popularity subsequently peaking and declining over the years.

Any PCP that is available today has been illicitly made. It can be inhaled, smoked when sprinkled on parsley or marijuana, snorted, swallowed, or injected. At low doses the major reactions may involve feelings of changes in body image, sometimes accompanied by feelings of depersonalization. Perceptual distortions, involving visual or auditory hallucinations and other sensory disturbances, and distortion of time may also be experienced. The reaction may also include a pronounced feeling of apathy or may generate a state of hyperactivity. Severe adverse reactions are known to result when large doses are consumed, involving an intense psychotic-like reaction.

E. Marijuana

Of all the illicit substances, marijuana has achieved the most notoriety, perhaps because it was used extensively by youth in the 1960s and 1970s to symbolize discontent. Accordingly, marijuana has come to be perceived by large segments of the "older" more established segments of American society as symbolic of a counterculture movement that is "destroying the very fabric of American society." Regardless of the controversy associated with marijuana during the past 30 years, its use has persisted and differing claims have been made about its effects.

Marijuana is derived from the dried and chopped-up leaves, flowers, stem, and seeds of the hemp plant, of which there are two varieties—*Cannabis indica,* which represents the East Indian hemp plant, and *Cannabis sativa,* the American hemp plant. There are both male and female plants, and both plants have been found to produce active products, but the female plant yields a higher concentration.

Over 400 closely related chemicals have been isolated from the cannabis plant, which are collectively called cannabinoids, of which THC (δ-9-tetrahydrocannabinol) is believed to be the primary psychoactive or mind-altering compound. Today's marijuana is 10 times more potent than that used in the early 1970s, ranging up to 20%, and as the potency of the plant increases there is a corresponding increase in its psychopharmacological effects.

A typical experience may consist of a sense of well-being, a dreamy state of relaxation and euphoria, alterations in thought formations, a more vivid sense of touch and perceptions, and distorted concepts of time and space. Symptoms fairly commonly (but not always) associated with marijuana use are reddening of the eyes, dryness of the mouth, hunger, a mild rise in heart rate, and reduction of pressure in the ocular fluid of the eyes. A bad trip, experienced mostly by new users, tends to involve symptoms that resemble an anxiety attack, such as feelings of panic, intense anxiety, and restlessness. A unique characteristic of marijuana is that it remains in the body for a long period of time because cannabinoids are eliminated at a very slow rate; traces of the drug can be found in the body up to 50 hours or longer after its use.

F. Volatile Solvents (Inhalants)

Volatile solvents or inhalants are chemicals whose vapors, when inhaled, can produce psychoactive effects. Many of these chemicals are industrial solvents or aerosols, not pharmacological remedies. The pharmacological chemicals included in this category are anesthetics and other compounds that are inhalable. Volatile inhalants are grouped into three categories: organic solvents (hydrocarbons), volatile nitrates, and nitrous oxide.

Since the early 1960s, the practice of solvent sniffing or inhalation of solvents and aerosols for their intoxicating effects has emerged as a widespread phenomenon of major proportions. Some of the products that are used are gasoline, lacquer and lacquer thinner, acetone, benzene, hair sprays, spray starches, chloroform, lighter fluid, carbon tetrachloride, and aerosol products. Many of these aerosols contain not only a conventional solvent, but also one of the freons, a chlorinated, fluorinated methane or ethane derivative, as a propellant.

The most common methods of using these substances are (1) to place the solvent in a plastic bag and inhale the fumes, (2) to soak a rag or handkerchief in the solvent and inhale the fumes; and (3) to sniff or inhale the fumes or vapors directly from the container.

The effect of these chemicals is a rapid general depression of the CNS, characterized by marked inebriation, dizziness, floating sensations, exhilaration, and intense feelings of well-being, which are at times accompanied by reckless abandon. A breakdown in inhibitions and feelings of greatly increased power and aggressiveness can also take place; these sensations are very similar to alcohol intoxication. Vivid visual hallucinations may also be present. These effects last from about 15 minutes to a few hours, depending on the substance and the dose. The use of these solvents or inhalants is predominantly associated with youth (mainly boys ages 6 to 14). Young children are particularly vulnerable to trying such chemicals, which are easily obtainable (e.g., gasoline) and do not generally cost a lot of money, nor do they have to be obtained illicitly.

Chemical solvents can be highly toxic and death or severe physical damage can result from their use. Death occurs from liver, kidney, bone marrow, or other organ failure; asphyxiation; paralysis of breathing mechanisms; or accidents as a result of being inebriated. Continued use of these drugs can lead to kidney, liver, lung, and brain damage.

Two other inhalants, amyl and butyl nitrate (volatile solvents), have achieved special "notoriety." Amyl nitrate is used to treat a heart condition and to relieve asthma attacks. The drug produces a drop in blood pressure, an expansion of the arteries (especially those around the brain), an increase in heart rate, and pressure in the eyeball. The overall effect may be experienced as a feeling of lightheadedness and relaxation of muscles. Amyl nitrate has gained a reputation for prolonging or heightening sensations of sexual climax, with the user breaking the capsule and inhaling the vapors just before orgasm. When amyl nitrate became a prescription drug, *butyl nitrate* replaced it.

Butyl nitrate is used to induce a rush that lasts from 1 to 2 minutes. Like amyl nitrate, it lowers blood pressure and relaxes the smooth muscles of the body. There is some danger involved in using either substance because persons with defective blood vessels may not be able to cope with their sudden constriction.

G. Look-Alike Drugs

The "drug scene" in the United States not only generated an underground or illicit market for drugs diverted from the pharmaceutical industry, but it also resulted in drugs being produced in clandestine laboratories to meet the street demands. Given the profitability involved, it soon became evident that there was a market for drugs that could be made cheaply and serve as substitutes for the "real things." Wesson and Morgan stated that "Look-alikes are dosage forms of a psychoactive drug whose name or appearance would lead a reasonable person to believe that its psychoactive effects were the same as, or similar to, the emulated, controlled psychoactive drug." Many look-alikes are sold as drugs of deception, and do not contain the drugs they are represented to be. Look-alike drugs, according to Wesson and Morgan, "generally contain non-controlled drugs or drugs of a lesser level of control, which have effects that mimic to some extent the effects of the emulated drug."

Another form of look-alikes is counterfeit substances, which, according to Wesson and Morgan, are "dosage forms of a controlled drug which contain the controlled substance they are sold as, have markings which duplicate or closely resemble the original manufacturer's trademark, but are manufactured without permission of the original manufacturer." Look-alikes generally consist of three substances: caffeine, ephedrine (or pseudoephedrine), a CNS stimulant, and phenylpropanolamine (PPA), a bronchodilator and respiratory decongestant. The substitute or look-alike drugs can cause serious side-effects ranging from sleep disturbances to psychotic episodes. With look-alike ingredients readily available from many sources, the illicit manufacture of look-alikes is unlikely to decrease in the near future.

H. "Designer Drugs"

In addition to producing look-alike drugs, underground chemists were also searching for ways to enhance different synthetic compounds to mimic scheduled psychoactive chemicals. By changing molecular structure, a drug's potency, length of action, euphoric effects, and toxicity can be modified. These drugs, introduced in the early 1980s, represent a class of substances called "designer drugs"—whose actions mimic the effects of illegal drugs. Because their chemical structure differed from those of federally scheduled drugs they were initially legal. The Federal Drug Enforcement Administration, however, quickly invoked its emergency authority, in 1985, to place an immediate ban on these drugs by declaring them federally scheduled drugs under the Comprehensive Crime Control Act of 1984. Subsequent Federal legislation in the form of the Controlled Substances Analog Enforcement Act, Anti-Drug Abuse Act of 1986 (public law 99-570), prohibited the (illicit) manufacture of chemically modified drugs (designer drugs) regardless of whether it had been duly scheduled under the DEA's Controlled Substance Act.

One of the first designer drugs was MDMA (similar in structure to MDA), known by the street name of "Ecstasy." The molecular alteration of drugs has also produced new generations of other illicit designer drugs that are more potent and potentially more dangerous than existing chemical substances. The ease with which drugs can be modified is evidenced by the identification of 35 variants or analogs that have been synthesized from PCP; several dozen analogs of methamphetamine have also been produced. Such drugs proved to be exceptionally potent and presented significant health hazards.

The designer drugs that have been described represent only a few that current technology has produced, but there is the potential to synthesize many other drugs that could continue to revolutionize illicit drug production, and which would place the user at considerable risk for severe adverse effects. Techniques are now being acquired to manufacture these extremely potent drugs at a fraction of the cost it takes to produce other illicit drugs.

III. TOLERANCE, PHYSICAL DEPENDENCE, AND ADDICTION

The brief pharmacological review presented above is meant not only to provide a concise introduction to some of the substances being used, but to also emphasize that while they are all psychoactive drugs, except for some volatile solvents, there are differences with respect to their chemical structure, how they are used, and their long- and short-term effects. One of the factors involved in these effects is tolerance.

Tolerance represents the process in which a change occurs in the relationship between the dose of a drug and the effects it produces. Specifically, tolerance is defined as a diminished response to the same dose of a drug as a result of prior use of the drug. Tolerance can be quantified by the increase in dosage required to produce a response equal to the initial response. In essence, tolerance refers to the need for a larger dose of a drug to achieve the original effect obtained through a smaller dose. Most all of the psychoactive drugs being used are capable of inducing tolerance, but the nature of its onset varies with different substances.

It has been noted by Julien that the mechanisms involved with tolerance are becoming clearer, and that two process have been identified.

> One type of tolerance occurs as a result of increased synthesis of drug-metabolizing enzymes that are involved in the metabolism of drugs and other chemicals by the liver. The clinical significance of this *drug-metabolizing* (or *enzyme induction*) *tolerance* is becoming increasingly important. A second type of tolerance, *cellular-adaptive* (or *pharmacodynamic*) *tolerance* involves the adaptation of receptors in the brain to the continuing presence of the drug. (p. 28)

The latter type of tolerance, cellular-adaptive or pharmacodynamic, involves a need for more of the drug to be present in the brain to interact with an increasing number of receptors that developed to accommodate the drug in the body. With respect to the process of enzyme induction, more of the drug would be needed to maintain an effective level within the body.

Another factor involved in drug-taking behavior is physical dependence, a term used to describe a physiological state, usually following the development of tolerance, that results in the onset of withdrawal symptoms. The characteristic of physical dependence is that it is a condition only revealed when a withdrawal or abstinence syndrome is manifested, which becomes evident only after cessation of the drug.

The withdrawal symptom consists of acute physical symptoms, such as nausea, vomiting, or cramps. Heroin, alcohol, opiate derivatives, barbiturates, and some tranquilizers, such as Valium and Librium, are some of the substances that have been associated with physical dependence; cocaine, which was originally not associated with physical dependence, is now believed to produce a strong physical dependence.

Abstinence or withdrawal symptoms, however, do not always occur after cessation of a drug associated with physical dependence. Under conditions in which a person is highly self-motivated to give up drugs, even heroin, abstinence or withdrawal symptoms may be inconspicuous or absent.

Addiction, according to Ausubel, is a term that has been used historically to describe "a condition brought about by the repeated administration of any drug such that continued use of the drug is necessary to maintain normal physiological function, and discontinuance of the drug results in definite physical and mental symptoms." Although it has been recognized that not all drug users experienced the same degree of addiction, and that not all drugs produced addiction, the term continues to be used, and it has become synonymous with physical dependence.

IV. INITIATION INTO AND MOTIVES FOR DRUG-TAKING BEHAVIOR

There is little question that initiation into drug use is a function of a complex interaction involving, among many other factors, age of initial exposure to drugs, availability of drugs, and drug trends. Chronological age and first experience with illicit drugs are highly related, but this relationship differs for different drugs. Research findings have suggested that there appears to be a specific age-related sequence for trying illicit drugs. This sequence primarily begins in early adolescence, with different peak years apparently existing for trying different drugs. Thus, although first use of a drug for some youth may occur as early as age 10, and extend up to age 18 for others, there does not seem to be any single peak year at which any one drug is tried. Rather, there tends to be a range of peak years for initiation into drugs that extends primarily from 13 to 16 years. After age 16 initiation rates tend to plateau for some drugs and then decline slowly, while for other drugs there is a sharp drop in initiation rates after age 16. Within this peak period, inhalants and marijuana tend to be tried first, followed by stimulants and cocaine. Although inhalants are initiated by many youth during their adolescent years, inhalants, as noted earlier, are also tried by younger children, many before their 10th birthday. This phenomenon has raised concern about patterns of inhalant use among younger children and about the consequences of such use.

These four substances, it is interesting to note, all induce highs. Inhalants (e.g., gasoline, spray cans) for example, produce an intoxicated, euphoric-like state, marijuana induces a pleasant, mildly euphoric feeling state, and both stimulants and cocaine induce intense euphoria.

These drug effects correspond to reasons given by adolescents for trying drugs. Research has identified three motives for trying drugs given by adolescents:

1. Tension reduction or coping, which involves seeking the euphoric effects of drugs or alcohol to change consciousness to reduce or cope with stress, tension, or unpleasant or unwanted emotions.
2. Drug effect, which involves using drugs to obtain an altered state of consciousness primarily to experience the drug's effect(s).
3. Peer-related, which involves using drugs chiefly in a social context, largely at the urging of friends, to enhance good times.

Each of the above motives has implications for patterns of drug use. For example, adolescents, and even adults, who use drugs primarily to reduce tension are at risk to progress from experimentation with drugs to more sustained use, and to use a variety of drugs to satisfy their needs. Those who mostly experiment with drugs to experience their effects may limit their behavior to trying different substances a few times, but some may be at risk to seek different and more intense experiences which may potentially lead to drug-related problems. Others who try drugs as a function of peer pressure, or who start their drug use largely for social-recreational purposes, also share a potential for broadening their drug-taking behaviors and place themselves at risk for drug-related problems. The question which arises for adolescents is: to what extent are these behaviors normal manifestations of adolescents, and to what extent do they represent an emulation of the messages about drug use conveyed by the culture-at-large?

While each of these reasons for trying drugs may in and of itself serve as a primary motive to start drug-taking behavior, it is more probable that they interact, with each exerting a stronger influence at different times during an adolescent's development, and also vary in conjunction with the social context in which adolescents find themselves.

V. THE DRUG CRISIS IN THE UNITED STATES

While drug-taking behavior has become a problem of national concern, particularly among youth, a characteristic of such behavior, it should be noted, is that it appears to be more prevalent among specific racial groups. American Indians and Alaskan Native youth, for example, show exceptionally high levels of drug use, especially alcohol, while African American and Latino adults also tend to be overrepresented among drug-using populations, particularly when narcotics and cocaine may be involved. Alaskan Natives and American Indian adults also show extremely high levels of drinking-related problems. Thus, while we perpetuate a "war on drugs" at the national level, which focuses on interdicting drugs, principally cocaine, at their source, and investing resources in destroying the drug distribution system, the problem of drug use does not go away.

Questions have been raised about whether this war is really being won. Billions have been spent, but the problem persists. While some improvement has been noted, such as a decline from 33 to 29% between 1990 and 1991, with respect to the number of high school seniors trying drugs, other indicators are less promising. For example, a recent report from the Drug Abuse Warning Network (DAWN) indicated that the number of hospital emergency room drug-related episodes increased 12% during the first two quarters of 1991. This rise represents an increase in the medical consequences among those involved in drug-taking behavior.

And these consequences are largely a function of a changing drug scene. As Inciardi notes, "There are fads and fashions in drugs and drug use, suggesting that persistent vigilance is needed. Different drugs come and go." This is evident in the distribution of designer drugs, which will continue to simulate the effects of opiates, stimulants, and hallucinogens, and in the new forms of smokeable cocaine and amphetamines. Polydrug use is also becoming more prevalent as users combine drugs to achieve specific effects or to moderate drug effects, such as using heroin to extend the high induced by crack cocaine or to mellow the effects of stimulant use. Searching for new highs also reaches new limits, as illustrated by the recent discovery of a hallucinogenic substance obtained from toads. Bufotenin [2-methylserotonin (5-hydroxydimethyltryptamine)] was isolated from the skin and parotid glands of toads, and used in the treatment of low blood pressure. However, after it was found to induce an LSD-like experience, "toad licking" became a new way to get high. Licking toads, however, can produce intense side-effects. The user experiences walking difficulties and paralysis, and a reddening and swelling of the face may occur. Following the drug's effect the user falls into a pronounced stupor-like sleep lasting many hours, from which it may not be possible to wake.

Is there a solution to the problem? While it may be difficult to develop a solution, part of the process of finding a way to deal with it has to begin by a recognition that our national policies on drug abuse have failed. There is a clear need to reexamine these policies. This need came to the forefront when the mayor of Baltimore, Kurt L. Schmoke, at a meeting of the U.S. Conference of Mayors, in April, 1989, called for a national debate concerning our current drug policy and the potential benefits of decriminalization of illicit drugs. In August of 1989 he brought together 50 expert panelists and guests to discuss the medical, legal, economic, and ethical issues associated with reforming our national drug policy. This action by Mayor Schmoke sparked a dialogue that has not diminished, and has initiated an ongoing discussion on policy alternatives. It remains to see what effect this policy debate will have on drug-taking behavior in our society.

Bibliography

Anglin, M. D., Thompson, J. P., and Fisher, D. G. (1986). Personality and peer correlates of psychoactive mushroom use. *J. Drug Ed.* **16**(3), 245–265.

Ausubel, D. P. (1958). "Drug Addiction." Random House, New York.

Chasnoff, I. J., and Schnoll, S. H. (1987). Consequences of cocaine and other drug use. In "Cocaine. A Clinician's Guide" (A. M. Washton and M. S. Gold, Eds.). Guilford, New York.

Chasnoff, I. J., and Griffith, D. R. (1989). Cocaine: Clinical studies of pregnancy and the newborn. *Ann. N.Y. Acad. Sci.* **562,** 260–266.

Gibbons, B. (1992). Alcohol: The legal drug. *Natl. Geographic* **181**(3), 3–35.

Inciardi, J. A. (1992). "The War on Drugs II." Mayfield, Mountain View, CA.

Institute on Medicine (1990). "A Broadening the Base of Treatment for Alcohol Problems." National Academy Press, Washington, DC.

Julien, R. J. (1992). "A Primer of Drug Action," 6th ed. Freeman, New York.

Mieczkowski, T. (1992). Some observations on the scope of crack use and distribution. In "Drugs, Crime, and Social Policy: Research, Issues, and Concerns" (T. Mieczkowski, Ed). Allyn and Bacon, Boston, MA.

National Council on Alcoholism and Drug Dependence (1990). "NCADD Fact Sheet: Alcoholism and Alcohol Related Problems." NCADD, New York.

National Institute on Drug Abuse (1985). Designer drugs: A new concern for the drug abuse community. *NIDA Notes* 2–3.

National Institute on Drug Abuse, (1991). Data from the Drug Abuse Warning Network (DAWN). *NIDA Statistical Series: Emergency Room Data 1990.* NIDA, Rockville, MD.

Ray, O., and Ksir, C. (1993). "Drugs, Society and Human Behavior." Times Mirror/Mosby, St. Louis, MO.

Segal, B. (1985–1986). Confirmatory analyses of reasons for experiencing psychoactive drugs during adolescence. *Int. J. Addict.* **20**(11,12), 1649–1662.

Segal, B. (1991). Adolescent initiation into drug-taking behavior: Comparisons over a 5-year interval. *Int. J. Addict.* **26**(3), 267–279.

Segal, B., Huba, J., and Singer, J. L. (1980). "Drugs, Daydreaming and Personality." Earlbaum, Hillsdalle, NJ.

Sorensen, J. L. (1991). Introduction: The AIDS–drug connection. In "Preventing AIDS" (J. L. Sorensen, L. A. Wermuth, D. R. Gibson, K-H. Choi, J. R. Guydish, and S. L. Batki, Eds.). Guilford, New York.

Stock, S. (1982). The look-alike explosion. *Grassroots* **11**(82), 17–21.

University of Michigan. (1992). "Results of the 17th National Survey of American High School Seniors." News and Information Services. The University of Michigan, Ann Arbor, MI.

Wesson, D., and Morgan, L. (1984). Drugs of deception. I. Stimulant lookalikes. *Grassroots* **3**(84), 3–4.

Zinberg, N. E. (1984). "Drug, Set and Settings: The Basis for Controlled Intoxicant Use." Yale University Press, New Haven, CT.

SUICIDE

David Lester
Center for the Study of Suicide

Glossary

Altruistic suicide In Durkheim's theory of suicide, altruistic suicide is committed by people with strong interpersonal ties who commit suicide in order to help others, such as a soldier throwing himself on a hand grenade in order to protect his fellow soldiers.

Anomic suicide In Durkheim's theory of suicide, anomic suicide is suicide by someone who has not adopted the prevailing norms and values of the society, as perhaps a person who commits suicide despite belonging to a religion which views suicide as a sin.

Chronic suicide Self-destructive behavior whose impact shortens the life span of the person, such as alcohol or drug abuse.

Egoistic suicide In Durkheim's theory of suicide, egoistic suicide is suicide by someone who does not have strong social ties, such as an elderly widower living alone.

Fatalistic suicide In Durkheim's theory of suicide, fatalistic suicide is suicide by people who are strongly regulated by the social norms and customs and commit society because they are "supposed to," as in suttee in which Indian widows throw themselves on their husband's funeral pyre.

Focal suicide Behavior which intentionally (and sometimes unintentionally) destroys a part of the body, permitting the organism to survive, such as blinding oneself intentionally or losing a limb in a piece of industrial equipment.

Parasuicide A term suggested by European scholars to refer to self-destructive behavior in which the person intends to survive and, in fact, does so. This behavior is more commonly called attempted suicide.

THE TERM *SUICIDE* can be used both narrowly and broadly. In the narrow sense, suicide refers to the actions of people who possess a mature concept of death and who kill themselves intentionally. In order to choose death, a person must understand what death entails. This criterion, therefore, rules out suicide as a possibility in animals, in young children, and in those who are mentally retarded, for such individuals may not have a mature concept of death. Most children, for example, think of death as like a temporary sleep from which it is possible to return. The criterion of having an intent to die rules out some psychiatrically disturbed people whose intent to die is in doubt. For example, a psychiatric patient may hear voices commanding the patient to jump in front of a train. In responding to such hallucinations, the patient may not intend to commit suicide.

However, scholars have begun to use the term suicide in a much looser sense in recent years. This broader use of the term permits the suicidal desire to operate in a covert, unconscious, and partial manner, as described in Sigmund Freud's psychoanalytic theory. In this view, the suicidal impulse may manifest itself in partial ways which do not necessarily lead to immediate death. For example, people with self-destructive lifestyles, such as drug abusers and alcoholics, can be viewed as suicidal (*chronic suicides*), as can those who injure or destroy part of themselves intentionally or accidentally (*focal suicides*). Many people, especially the elderly, refuse to take the medication necessary for their continued physical health, while others may refuse to eat. These indirect life-threatening behaviors can be seen to have suicidal motivation.

Encyclopedia of Human Behavior, Volume 4

While sociologists tend to adopt the narrow definition of suicide, psychologists and psychiatrists tend more often to adopt the broader definition, perhaps because they encounter so much nonfatal self-destructive behavior in the patients whom they treat. Biologists are also using the term suicide more often these days to describe self-destructive behavior in animals.

Many individuals make self-destructive acts but survive. They may take an overdose of a medication which fails to kill them or they may cut their wrists but not bleed to death. Sometimes survival may be planned (as in a person who knowingly takes one-half of the lethal dose of a medication) or unplanned (as in a person who runs a car engine in a closed garage but is quickly discovered by an unexpected caller). This behavior is usually called *attempted suicide*, in contrast to an act where the person dies, which is called *completed suicide*. Some investigators have pointed out that many attempted suicides do not intend to die and, thus, the term attempted suicide is inappropriate. Such individuals may be communicating distress to significant others in their life by their suicide attempt, or perhaps they are ambivalent in their decision to die. (Many suicide attempters, however, do admit to some intent to die even though their suicide attempt is not lethal.) *Parasuicide* has been proposed as an alternative term and is still used, particularly in Europe, but researchers have switched to using the term *deliberate self-injury*, a term which eliminates the presumption of suicidal motivation. Attempted suicide, however, is more serious than *self-mutilation* (a behavior in which people inflict mild harm on their bodies, usually motivated by frustration or boredom).

Recently, feminist scholars have objected to the terms attempted and completed suicide since they suggest that the behavior more commonly found in men (completed suicide) is the only possible goal of the behavior, and that women typically attempt to achieve this goal but fail to do so. They have suggested that the terms be replaced by fatal and nonfatal suicidal behavior.

I. EPIDEMIOLOGY OF SUICIDE

A. Accuracy of Suicide Rates

It has been well documented that coroners and medical examiners often fail to certify suicides correctly. For example, in a study of deaths in one county in Ireland, investigators found an actual suicide rate of 13.1 per 100,000 per year rather than the officially reported rate of 5.8, and this undercounting of suicide has been documented in many other regions of the world also.

Despite this, it has also been noted that the relative ranking of suicide rates of nations is similar to the relative ranking of suicide rates of immigrants from those nations to countries such as the United States and Australia, where their deaths are certified by the same coroners and medical examiners. Thus, though the underreporting of suicide may affect the *absolute* suicide rate of a particular group, it may not change the *relative* suicide rates of different groups by much.

B. Incidence of Suicide

The completed suicide rate in the United States in 1988 (the latest year for which complete statistics are available) was 12.4 per 100,000 inhabitants per year. There were 30,407 suicides out of 2,167,999 deaths. It is estimated that there are 8 to 10 suicide attempts for every completed suicide in the United States which means that about a further 300,000 Americans made suicide attempts in 1988.

Community surveys of the suicidal history of people reveal a wide range in the estimates of prior suicidal behavior. The percentage of residents who report having attempted suicide in their lives is usually in the range of 2 to 10%, and for reports of having thought about committing suicide is in the range of 10 to 50%. This percentage differs from community to community, on the country studied, and on the way in which the question is phrased.

C. Variations in Rates of Completed Suicide

In almost every nation of the world, men have higher suicide rates than women. For example, the United States in 1980 the rates were 18.6 (per 100,000 per year) for men and 5.4 for women, in Japan 22.2 and 13.1, respectively, and in France 28.0 and 11.1, respectively. The relative difference between the suicide rates of men and women is less in Asian nations than elsewhere. In a rare reversal of this gender difference, mainland China has recently reported suicide rates for about 10% of the population and has indicated a higher suicide rate for women.

The variation in suicide rates by age differs from nation to nation. Typically suicide rates increase with age, sometimes peaking in middle-age but sometimes continuing to increase into old-age. In the United States, the suicide rates of men increase steadily with age whereas the suicide rates of women peak in middle-age. However, in less privileged groups in wealthier countries (such as native Americans) and among women in poorer countries (such as Thailand) suicide rates tend to peak in young adults.

The 1970s witnessed a rise in the suicide rates of those ages 15–24 in many nations of the world, including Canada, the United States, and most European nations. The late 1980s, however, have witnessed a rise in the suicide rates of the elderly.

The nations with the highest suicide rates in the world are Hungary (with a 1988 rate of 41.3), Sri Lanka (35.8 in 1985), Denmark (26.0 in 1988), and Austria (24.4 in 1988). The nations with the lowest suicide rates are Islamic countries in the Middle East (for example, Egypt 0.04 in 1987, Syria 0.5 in 1980, and Kuwait 0.8 in 1987).

II. SOCIETAL SUICIDE RATE

The suicide rates of societies remain quite stable over time. The relative suicide rates of nations 50 years ago are similar to the present rates, despite changes in the absolute size of the rates. For example, Hungary, with one of the highest suicide rates now, also had one of the highest suicide rates in the world at the beginning of this century and between the two World Wars, and Hungarian immigrants to the United States have one of the highest suicide rates of all immigrant groups.

The stability of the societal suicide rates means that it is meaningful to inquire whether the characteristics of the society are associated with, and perhaps cause, the suicide rate.

A. Social Causes of Suicide

Emile Durkheim in his book on suicide published in 1897 suggested that two broad social characteristics of a society determined its suicide rate: the degree of social integration (that is, the degree to which people are involved in social relations) and the degree of social regulation (that is, the degree to which people's desires and attitudes are governed by the societal norms). Durkheim felt that suicide would be especially common where social integration was very weak (leading to *egoistic* suicide) and where social regulation was very weak (leading to *anomic* suicide). These suicides are committed by people who are relatively socially isolated and whose values are less often congruent with the prevailing social norms.

To a lesser extent, Durkheim felt that the other extremes of social integration and social regulation might also cause some suicides: too strong a level of social integration leading to *altruistic* suicide (where individuals kill themselves to help others) and too strong a level of social regulation leading to *fatalistic* suicide (where individuals feel so oppressed that suicide is chosen as a means of escape). Later sociologists have, on the whole, disregarded these latter possibilities, claiming that such suicides are rare in modern societies. They have proposed simply that suicide rates are higher where social integration and social regulation are weak.

Possible indices of these social characteristics are indeed associated with suicide rates, over nations of the world, over regions within nations, and over time. For example, suicide rates are typically associated with the divorce rate, the extent of migration with the nation, alcohol consumption, and unemployment (positively) and with church attendance (negatively). Interestingly, where these indices of a lack of social integration and regulation are strong, suicide rates are higher in all groups in the society. For example, in regions where divorce rates are high, suicide rates are higher in the single, married, and divorced, indicating that social integration and regulation are broad characteristics of the *whole* society.

Another variable associated with suicide rates is unemployment, an indicator of hard economic times. Suicide rates tend to be higher in times when unemployment rates are higher and, among individuals, suicide rates are higher in the unemployed.

B. Publicity and Suicide

A great deal of recent research has shown that temporary changes in the society's suicide rate can be brought about by short-term social events. For example, the suicide of a celebrity (such as Marilyn Monroe in 1962) or a character in a fictional television film typically leads to an increase in the suicide rate in the following 7 to 10 days, particularly in those similar to the suicide in age and sex.

This imitation effect in suicide is also present in the existence of suicide venues, places where people go in large numbers to commit suicide, such as the Golden Gate Bridge in San Francisco and the Eiffel

Tower in Paris. The 1980s also saw the documentation of clusters of suicides occurring in communities, for example, among teenagers in small towns, on some native American reservations, and among some groups of Pacific islanders.

III. CAUSES OF INDIVIDUAL SUICIDE

A. Psychiatric Disorder

The most notable personal characteristic associated with suicide is psychiatric disturbance. Persons with an affective disorder (in particular, a major depressive disorder) have a very high suicide rate. Those with schizophrenia and those who are substance abusers also have high suicide rates. It has also been documented that particular personality disorders (that is, chronic maladaptive lifestyles) are associated with a higher risk of suicide and suicide attempts, in particular, borderline personality disorder.

Depression can refer to a mood as well as a particular psychiatric disorder, and the mood of depression is strongly associated with and predictive of suicidality. In those suffering from any psychiatric disorder, the level of depression predicts the degree of suicidality. Aaron Beck has suggested, further, that one component of depression is particularly useful as a predictor of suicidality, namely, hopelessness, a feeling that life will not get better in the future. [*See* DEPRESSION.]

B. Biochemical and Genetic Factors

Biochemical and genetic factors have been shown clearly to have a role in the etiology of psychiatric disorders. For example, studies of twins and adopted children have shown that both affective disorders and schizophrenia have a genetic component. The neurotransmitter serotonin seems to play a role in affective disorder while dopamine seems to play a role in schizophrenia. [*See* SYNAPTIC TRANSMITTERS AND NEUROMODULATORS.]

This association of suicide with psychiatric disorder makes identification of biochemical and genetic factors for suicide difficult. It has proven difficult to show that biochemical or genetic factors play a role in suicide above and beyond increasing the likelihood of psychiatric disorder which itself increases the risk of suicide.

C. Medical Illness

The increasing frequency of long-term debilitating medical illnesses (such as Alzheimer's disease, AIDs, and cancer) has led to the documentation of many suicides committed by people dying of these illnesses or afraid of what their condition will be like as the disease advances. Some people commit suicide motivated by the fear that they might develop these conditions. The fact remains, however, that the vast majority of people suffering from these illnesses do die from the illness rather than suicide.

D. Childhood Experiences

Several childhood experiences have been found to increase the later risk of psychological disturbance and, therefore, suicide. Among these is the loss of parents (through death or divorce) in the first 15 years of life. Although loss of a parent in the first 6 years of life is thought by many developmental psychologists to be especially traumatic, many eventual suicides have lost a parent during the period when they were 6 to 14 years of age and have failed to resolve and complete the mourning process. In some cases, the suicide can be motivated in part by a desire to be reunified with the lost parent after death (as in the case of the American poet Sylvia Plath).

The experience of physical and sexual abuse as a child increases the risk of later self-destructive behavior, and dysfunctional families of all kinds (including those with parents who have psychiatric disturbance or who are substance abusers) also increase the risk of later self-destructive behavior. However, researchers have not yet shown that these experiences lead to suicide *per se* rather than merely increasing the severity of psychological disturbance which in turn increases the risk of suicide.

E. Personality

Several personality traits have been associated with suicidal behavior, including a depressed mood, feelings of hopelessness about the future, low self-esteem, a belief that what happens to you is outside of your control, poor problem-solving skills, and irrational thinking patterns. There is also the suggestion that less lethal suicidal behavior is more common in those who behave impulsively.

F. Interpersonal Relations

Suicidal behavior, especially among adolescents and young adults, is often triggered by interpersonal friction and loss. Although suicide in the elderly is more often the result of long-term psychological distress, elderly men seem less able to cope with the loss of their spouse than elderly women. The significant others of potentially suicidal people sometimes harbor hostile and death wishes (both conscious and unconscious) toward them, and this increases the risk of suicide.

G. Recent Stress

Most of those who experience a psychiatric breakdown have experienced a recent high level of stressful life events. Similarly, those who attempt and complete suicide are generally found to have experienced a particularly high level of recent stress in the past year and to have had this stress level increase markedly in the weeks prior to the suicidal behavior. [*See* STRESS.]

IV. PREVENTING SUICIDE

There have been two major methods of preventing suicide in the past. First, the treatment of those with psychiatric disorders, and in particular depressive disorders, by medication and by psychotherapy can prove useful in reducing the risk of suicide. A program in the Swedish island of Gotland to train physicians in the detection of depression and the prescription of appropriate medication reduced the suicide rate there.

A second method for preveting suicide has been the establishment of suicide prevention centers. In many countries (such as the United States) these centers are set up independently by different kinds of groups, while in others there is a centralized and uniform organization (such as the Samaritans in the United Kingdom). These centers typically establish crisis counseling services, using the telephone as a medium for communication, which are available 24 hours a day and 7 days a week. Clients in distress can call and discuss their problems and search for alternatives to suicide as a solution for their problems. Some centers also have walk-in clinics for face-to-face contact, some have outreach services which can visit people in the community, and others have organized groups for those who have experienced the suicide of a loved one and are finding it hard to cope with the loss.

Recently, it has been noted that elimination of lethal methods for suicide, often inadvertently, can result in a reduction in the suicide rate. Domestic gas companies in many countries (such as the United States, England and Japan) switched from highly toxic coal gas to less toxic natural gas for economic reasons, but the switch has virtually eliminated suicide by domestic gas. Emission controls on cars (which reduce the toxicity of the exhaust) reduce the lethality of cars for suicide. Several investigators have suggested, therefore, extending this tactic to other methods and have advocated, for example, reducing the amount and toxicity of prescribed medications, reducing the availability of guns, and fencing in bridges and subway platforms from which people jump. There is the possibility that some potential suicides will switch to an alternative method for suicide, but the evidence suggests that not all will do so.

V. SURVIVING SUICIDE

Surviving the suicide of a loved one appears to be especially traumatic for people. Not only is there the loss of the person, but there is often a feeling of stigma associated with the death. The survivors feel guilty for not recognizing and responding to the suicide's distress. Often neighbors and friends do not know how to react to the survivors and withdraw, so that the survivors feel rejected and isolated.

In addition, many suicides commit suicide at home where they are discovered by their loved ones, often horribly disfigured (especially if they used a gun for their suicide). This trauma can haunt survivors for the rest of their lives and is similar to the trauma in those who witness murder and war. A posttraumatic stress disorder is not uncommon.

Furthermore, the risk of suicide in the relatives and especially the children of suicides is greater. For example, Ernest Hemingway's father committed suicide, and Ernest and two more of the six children also killed themselves.

VI. IS SUICIDE IMMORAL?

The morality of suicide has been a subject of debate for many thousands of years. There are those who set up a clear principle, such as "Thou shalt not kill," and apply it to every situation. For these, suicide is immoral. There are others who place more importance on other principles, such as freedom of choice for autonomous individuals. For these people, suicide may be moral.

Utilatarian ethicists weigh the harm and the good from alternative actions and suggest minimizing harm and maximizing good. The problems here are that the weights are often subjective and we can argue about for whom should we minimize the harm and maximize the good—the suicide, the survivors, or the society.

Suicide is, however, not illegal in many countries (including the United States), though assisting someone else to commit suicide may, in some jurisdictions, be a crime. Attempting suicide in such a way as to endanger the health and safety of others may be an offense, either in the criminal code or the public health code. However, contrary to popular belief, insurance companies in the United States do pay the full amount for suicides who bought the policy more than 2 years before their death.

VIII. CAN SUICIDE BE RATIONAL?

There has been a great deal of debate over whether suicide can be rational, especially as many of those dying from chronic diseases commit suicide or ask for help to do so. Some argue that suicide can never be rational for the suicide is almost always psychiatrically disturbed or, at least, psychologically distressed. If they could be helped through this period, their desire to live could be rekindled. Others argue that people are capable of weighing the disadvantages and advantages of continued life quite appropriately and of making a rational decision to die.

There are two issues here. First, are the premises of the suicidal person rational and, second, is the reasoning, given their premises, logical. Typically the reasoning of suicidal people (other than those who are grossly psychotic) is quite logical. It is the rationality of the premises that we dispute. However, these are subjective. Pain (physical or psychological) which is bearable for one person may be unbearable for another. The only sensible resolution is to permit each of us to decide what is bearable for ourselves.

Bibliography

Battin, M. P. (1982). "Ethical Issues in Suicide." Prentice-Hall, Englewood Cliffs, NJ.

Fremouw, W. J., de Perczel, M., and Ellis, T. E. (1990). "Suicide Risk: Assessment and Response Guidelines." Pergamon, New York.

Hendin, H. (1992). "Suicide in America." Norton, New York.

Leenaars, A. A., and Wenckstern, S. (Ed.) (1991). "Suicide Prevention in Schools." Hemisphere, New York.

Lester, D. (1989). "Questions and Answers about Suicide." Charles Press, Philadelphia.

Lester, D. (1989). "Suicide from a Sociological Perspective." Charles Thomas, Springfield, IL.

Lukas, C., and Seiden, H. M. (1987). "Silent Grief." Scribners, New York.

Pfeffer, C. R. (1986). "The Suicidal Child." Guilford, New York.

Stillion, J. M., McDowell, E. E. and May, J. H. (1989). "Suicide across the Life Span." Hemisphere, New York.

SURPRISE

Wulf-Uwe Meyer and Michael Niepel
University of Bielefeld, Germany

Glossary

Emotion Hypothetical entity that can be inferred from verbal reports about subjective experience, specific physiological reactions, and behavior (including facial expression).

Orienting response Syndrome of changes in behavioral and physiological components that can be evoked by the introduction, change, or removal of a stimulus.

Schema Part of an individual's knowledge structure representing abstract or generalized knowledge about events, objects, or situations.

Startle Complex response pattern consisting of physiological, behavioral, and subjective components that is elicited by abrupt and intense stimulation.

SURPRISE can be regarded as a hypothetical entity that can be inferred from three classes of observable events: specific physiological changes, behavior patterns, and verbal reports about subjective experience. Surprise is *elicited* by unexpected events, that is, events that deviate from a schema. A schema is part of the organism's knowledge structure. Schemata form a kind of private, normally unreflected theory about the nature of events, objects, or situations. In order to provide an accurate account of our surroundings, schemata have to be monitored continuously with regard to their compatibility with currently available data. When a discrepancy between schema and input occurs, surprise is elicited. The main *function* of surprise is to enable or facilitate processes directed at removing this discrepancy, eventually by revising our action-guiding schemata or theories.

I. THE ELEMENTS OF SURPRISE

Surprise is a short-lived phenomenon elicited by unexpected (schema-discrepant) events. Because surprise can be observed not only in humans but also in infrahumans, and because it is characterized by a specific facial expression, many authors have conceived of surprise as a "primary" or "fundamental" emotion that has been established through evolutionary–biological processes.

In common sense, surprise is equated with the phenomenal experience (subjective feeling) of being surprised. From a scientific perspective, however, this way of conceptualizing surprise raises at least two problems: First, the total set of phenomena that occur when one is surprised comprises more elements than just a specific quality of experience. Second, and more importantly, if "surprise" were defined as a subjective feeling state, it would be directly accessible for observation and analysis only to the person concerned. External observers, including scientists, have no direct access to the experience of surprise of another person. They have access only to the (presumed) observable manifestations of this state. Therefore, when seen from a scientific perspective, which accepts for theory construction only those data that are accessible in the same way to all observers, surprise is a *theoretical entity* or *hypothetical construct* that can only be *inferred* from its manifestations at an observable level. These manifestations of surprise can be observed at three levels: (a) verbal reports about subjective experience, (b) specific physiological reactions, and (c) behavior (see Fig. 1).

Verbal reports, such as "I'm surprised," constitute the most direct index of the subjective experience of being surprised. Whereas the experience of

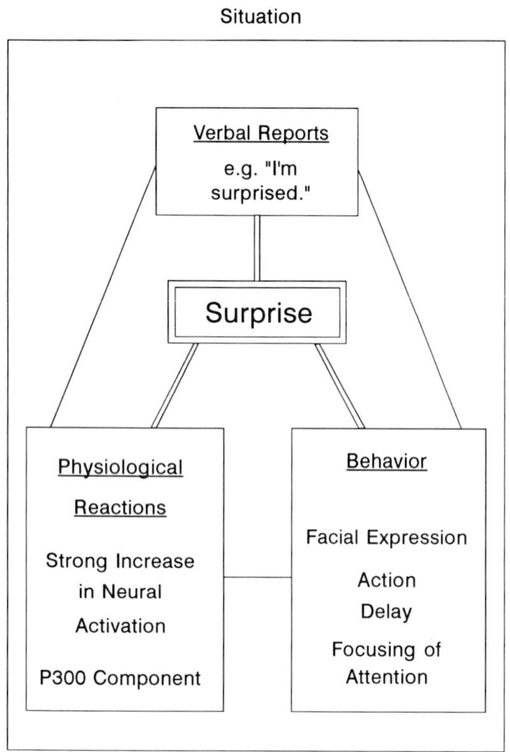

FIGURE 1 The inference of surprise. Simple lines represent observables and relationships between observables. Double lines represent the inferred entity and inferred relations. [Adapted from A. Öhman (1987). The psychophysiology of emotion: An evolutionary–cognitive perspective (p. 83). In "Advances in Psychophysiology" (P. K. Ackles, J. R. Jennings, and M. G. H. Coles, Eds.), Vol. 2. JAI Press, Greenwich, CT.]

most emotions is characterized by a specific hedonic tone, which is either pleasant (e.g., proud, happy) or unpleasant (e.g., fearful, angry), this seems not to be the case for surprise. Although some researchers have found that experiences of surprise in everyday life are frequently characterized by pleasantness, there are clearly also instances of surprise that are hedonically negative (e.g., when an unexpected failure has occurred) or neutral. The fact that the hedonic tone of surprise can be both pleasant and unpleasant (and, in the case of "neutral" surprise, can be completely absent) suggests that the feelings of pleasantness and unpleasantness frequently connected with surprise are not a characteristic of surprise itself, but result from processes other than those that elicit surprise; specifically, an evaluation of the surprise-eliciting event as positive or negative. This evaluation, when it occurs at all, usually takes place very rapidly after the onset of surprise and results in pleasant or unpleasant feelings, which are then attached to, or blend with, surprise—thus giving the experience of surprise a positive or negative quality.

Concerning the *physiological reactions* characteristic for surprise, very little systematic research exists to date. Some authors assume that surprise is characterized by a sudden and strong increase in neural activation. It has also been suggested that the orienting response is a component of surprise (for a more detailed description of this response, see Section IV of this article). Furthermore, recordings of brain waves by means of electrodes attached to the skull (a technique referred to as electroencephalography) have shown that rare or unexpected (i.e., surprising) events evoke a cortical response that differs in waveform from the response evoked by common or expected events. This response is designated the P300 component of the event-related brain potential, and its amplitude correlates with the degree to which a stimulus is unexpected or new. Therefore, it has been proposed that the P300 component might be the electrophysiological manifestation of the surprise process. [*See* BRAIN ELECTRIC ACTIVITY.]

With respect to *behavior,* surprise is characterized, first, by a distinctive facial expression already described by Charles Darwin: The eyebrows are raised, creating wrinkles across the forehead and giving the eyes a large, rounded appearance; and the mouth is opened in an oval shape. Second, surprise is characterized by an interruption or delay of ongoing activities and a spontaneous focusing of attention toward the surprise-eliciting stimulus. This attentional focusing on the surprise-eliciting event typically leads to enhanced memory performance for these events as compared with unsurprising ones.

Perhaps the most systematic research on surprise stems from studies investigating the facial expression of emotions. These studies have revealed two main, robust findings. First, there exists a facial response pattern specific to surprise. Second, the manifestation and recognition of this pattern are not limited to Western cultures, but are universal across different cultures. For example, it has been found that, when confronted with pictures of Americans displaying facial expressions of surprise, American, German, Greek, Chinese, and Turkish observers recognized the expressions about equally well. From the high degree of intercultural universality of facial expression and recognition, it has been inferred that the expression of surprise, as well as that of other emotional states, is governed by genetically encoded programs, and that facial expressions have biologically adaptive value (see Section III of this article). [*See* FACIAL EXPRESSIONS OF EMOTION.]

II. THE CAUSES OF SURPRISE

From the psychological literature dealing with surprise one can compile an extensive list of conditions that are considered to elicit surprise. These conditions have been variously described as unexpected, misexpected, contrary to expectations, unknown, novel (new), unusual, extraordinary, contrary to the natural course of things, rare, improbable, or sudden. This list, which is still not complete, reflects the diversity as well as the overlap in different authors' conceptions of the causes of surprise.

Some of the terms (like "novel," "unusual," or "improbable") do not necessarily allude to an internal state of the person concerned, but describe only (probabilistic) properties of the situation accessible to an external observer. Other terms, like "unexpected," "misexpected," "contrary to expectations," or "unknown," refer to a prior condition or mental state of the surprised individual. These latter attributes, furthermore, may be classified according to the role they ascribe to explicit expectations in the elicitation of surprise. The terms "misexpected" or "contrary to expectations," for example, suggest that, in order to be surprised, people must hold a prior belief about the course of events that is then disconfirmed by a subsequent event. The terms "unexpected" or "unknown," in contrast, suggest that it is sufficient for surprise that the surprising event was *not* the object of a prior belief or expectation.

No matter if the above attributes allude to properties of the situation alone or refer to some internal representation (an expectation or prior knowledge) as a mediating entity between these earlier experiences and the elicitation of surprise by a given event, there has to be some kind of trace or residual originating from previous experience for surprise to occur. However, novelty or rareness can easily be overruled by explicit information. If you have trustworthy information that event E is going to happen next, you will not be surprised, even if, during an extended learning experience, E has never occurred before.

A comprehensive account of the internal representation that serves as a reference against which an event can be classified as discrepant has to consider both cumulative experience over an extended period of time and explicit information as a source. As a concept that leaves open both possibilities, the schema concept promises a description of adequate breadth. If we define a schema as an organized part of an individual's knowledge, we may conceive of surprising events as those that are not consistent with the current state of our schemata, irrespective of the existence of a concrete expectation. Recent schema theories postulate that schemata become activated as a result of our current experiences. An activated schema then serves as a reference against which subsequent experiences are evaluated; events that deviate from the currently activated schemata will elicit surprise.

It should be noted that the activation of a schema need not be accompanied by an explicit (conscious) expectation; schemata can be activated and events can be monitored as to their compatibility with the activated schemata on a nonconscious level.

III. THE FUNCTION OF SURPRISE

Surprise serves to remove the discrepancy between an activated schema and the schema-discrepant event. The removal of the discrepancy may require an extension, correction, or restructuring of the relevant schema, that is, an updating of knowledge. Such an updating enables the individual: (a) to anticipate and, possibly, to control (i.e., to bring about or to prevent) future occurrences of the previously discrepant event; (b) to avoid the event if it turns out to be negative and uncontrollable; or (c) to ignore the event if it proves to be irrelevant for further action. Thus, the ultimate function of surprise is to ensure an effective control of the environment by permitting processes that serve to update our action-guiding schemata. Let us briefly consider how the different components of the surprise reaction contribute to this goal.

The most basic and perhaps the most essential aspect of the updating process consists of two of the *behavioral components* of the surprise reaction, namely the interruption of ongoing activities and the focusing of attention on the eliciting stimulus. Because the individual is most likely engaged in some other activity when confronted with the surprising event, in a first step, the requirements for its further processing have to be met. To permit an undisturbed concentration on the surprising event, other ongoing activities are momentarily interrupted. The available processing resources are redistributed, now favoring processes that serve the analysis of the surprising event and the updating of the currently activated schemata. This reallocation of processing resources is accompanied by the focusing of attention on the unexpected event, which amplifies information relevant for the updating process and simultaneously attenuates potentially interfering information from other sources. It should be noted that, although turning to the surprising event as a prerequisite for updating is in many cases functional, it is not always so, because there are situations in which even the shortest interruption of the person's momentary activities would be inappropriate. This is the case when, for example, the continuation of the ongoing activities is vitally necessary, as may be the case for a fighter pilot or a cat burglar.

As mentioned, the specific *facial expression* of the surprised individual is easily identified by observers, largely irrespective of their cultural background. By signaling the individual's state of surprise to an observer, the facial pattern serves an important communicative purpose, and in some cases may be equivalent to a verbal request for information. Indeed, a deliberately produced, stylized form of the surprise expression, namely raising the eyebrows to form an enquiring look, is frequently used for this purpose in everyday conversation. In this way, the facial expression of surprise may contribute to the updating of knowledge by stimulating support from the social environment.

The *subjective experience* of surprise can be regarded as the manifestation in consciousness of the encountered discrepancy between activated schema and current experience. Current views of consciousness stress the importance of consciousness for planning. Whereas the routine execution of simple activities may be carried out without conscious control, the generation of action plans for exceptional situations requires conscious processing. In addition, the subjective component of surprise can be ascribed a motivational role, for it is most likely the experiential aspect that triggers the extended preoccupation with the surprising event.

A. A Note on Surprise and Learning

As mentioned, surprise serves to remove the discrepancy between an activated schema and an event, eventually by revising our action-guiding schemata or theories, that is, by updating our knowledge. If schema revision or knowledge-updating can be equated with "cognitive development" or "learning," then surprise obviously has an important function for the development of cognitive structures or learning. Indeed, many developmental psychologists have assigned surprise the status of an important motivational factor in childrens' cognitive development. And contemporary learning theorists have stressed that conditioning (learning) is not simply based on the pairing of events (stimuli). Learning is rather seen as a process in which the organism's schemata are brought into line with events that deviate from those schemata. This implies that learning will occur only if events (stimuli) are surprising. [*See* COGNITIVE DEVELOPMENT.]

IV. SURPRISE, STARTLE, AND THE ORIENTING RESPONSE

Closely related to the study of surprise are two further areas of research: startle and the orienting response. From these two research areas stems a large body of empirical literature dealing with human subjects and animals.

A. Startle

In humans, the startle response is characterized by a pattern of muscle movements, varying considerably in completeness, that spreads from the head over the rest of the body. Its most reliable component is the eye blink, but it may also include forward head movements and a specific facial expression (characterized by the widening of the mouth), drawing forward of the shoulders, abduction of the upper arms, bending of the elbows, pronation of the lower arms, flexion of the fingers, forward movement of the trunk, contraction of the abdomen, and bending of the knees. These behavioral responses are accompanied by physiological changes that include an increase in skin conductance, a rise in blood pressure, an increase in pulse rate, and an initial holding of the breath followed by an acceleration of respiration rate.

The startle response is elicited by abrupt and intense stimulation. *Abruptness,* in this context, does not mean unexpectedness, but primarily a sudden onset and fast rise of the eliciting stimulus. For example, an acoustic stimulus with a high peak intensity will elicit startle only given a short rise time (in the range of some 10 msec), but not when it rises gradually. The *intensity* of the stimulus is one of the main determinants of the magnitude of the startle response. Within a wide range of intensities, higher stimulus intensities result in larger responses.

It is not fully clear to what extent the startle response can be reduced by prior knowledge of the eliciting stimulus or by repeated exposures to the stimulus. However, there is some evidence that the startle response may occur even with perfect knowledge of the nature and the time of the critical stimulus, and that it shows marked, but usually not perfect habituation with repeated exposures. In fact, in some human subjects, only minimal habituation to the startling stimulus has been found—even with a large number of repetitions.

The first components of the startle response occur with very short latencies. Its earliest manifestation is an increase of muscle activity at different sites of the head that occurs only 14 to 40 msec after the onset of the stimulation. Hence, startle is apparently a very early response system that requires only little information processing.

It can be concluded that the characteristics of a stimulus that elicits a startle response (high intensity and abrupt onset) need not lead to surprise (if the stimulus has been announced or has been presented repeatedly). On the other hand, a stimulus that elicits surprise (i.e., one that is not anticipated or contrary to expectations) need not elicit a startle response (if it is of low intensity or rises gradually).

B. The Orienting Response

The orienting response (OR) has been described as a syndrome consisting of changes in a variety of components. These include behavioral as well as physiological components, the latter being of primary interest to most researchers in this field. Behaviorally, the OR includes movements of the sense organs toward the source of the eliciting stimulus, as well as an interruption of overt actions, accompanied by an increase in general muscle tonus. Physiological changes occur in at least three domains. (a) Electroencephalographic recordings show alterations in the direction of faster activity with a lower amplitude. (b) Vegetative changes include the decrease of heart rate and respiration rate, an increase in skin conductance, and two opposing vascular changes: vasoconstriction in the limbs and vasodilation in the head. (c) There is evidence for an increase in sensitivity of the sense organs, manifested by the lowering of sensory thresholds.

The conditions that evoke the OR have been classified into three broad categories. The first category, novelty, can be subdivided into (a) novelty of a stimulus or an elementary event, (b) novelty in the sequence of events, and (c) novelty in the patterning of stimuli. The second category, conflict, refers to situations in which an ambiguous stimulus leads to the activation of conflicting response tendencies (e.g., in a perceptual discrimination task). The last category, previous conditioning, includes high-importance stimuli (e.g., one's own name or a warning call like "watch out"), which have acquired their significance as a result of the individual's learning history.

In contrast to the startle response, the OR does not require an increase in the intensity of stimulation. In fact, an event evoking an OR may consist of the *introduction* as well as the *change* or even the *removal* of a stimulus.

The resemblances between the manifestations of surprise and the OR are obvious. There is also a considerable overlap in the typical procedures used to induce either the OR or surprise in humans. Still, surprise stimuli constitute only one class of events that are able to elicit the OR. A stimulus classified into the "novel" category (as defined above) may well lead to surprise, whereas stimuli that satisfy the "conflict" or the "previous conditioning" criterion may not be surprising at all. Nevertheless, it is possible that the OR is an obligatory part of the surprise reaction, in the sense that all events that lead to the subjective state of surprise also trigger an OR. If so, the physiological components of the emotion surprise may well consist of the physiological aspects of the OR.

V. IS SURPRISE AN EMOTION?

Whereas some authors classify surprise as an emotion, and often even as a "fundamental," "primary," or "basic" one, other authors do not regard surprise as an emotion at all. This divergence of opinion is due to the fact that there exists no generally accepted answer to the questions "What is an emotion?" and "What is a basic emotion?"

The criteria for assigning an emotion the status of "basic" vary across different authors. Some authors have approached the issue of basic emotions from an evolutionary perspective. From this viewpoint, the term "basic" is commonly used to denote emotions that are assumed to have importance for basic biological adaptive processes and, therefore, have a strong biological basis. Although these authors do not deny that learning processes (which may be culture-specific) can affect different aspects of basic emotions, such as the control of emotional expressions, it is assumed that there are strong biological constraints on the modifiability of basic emotions by learning processes. Furthermore, one of the most important features of basic emotions, according to these authors, is that the facial expression associated with such an emotion is universal. Because the expression of surprise is characterized by universality, both across infancy and adulthood and across cultures, surprise appears on the list of basic emotions of these authors.

Other authors do not dispute that surprise is an emotion, but deny that it is a basic one. And still other authors do not regard surprise as an emotion at all. According to these latter authors, emotions are "valenced" states, that is, states that are either positive (pleasant) or negative (unpleasant) in hedonic tone. As mentioned, the hedonic tone of emotions may be conceived of as resulting from an appraisal or evaluation of the significance of what is happening for one's own well-being. Because surprise can be affectively neutral (see Section I of this article), these authors exclude it from the list of emotions. Instead, they view it as a *cognitive* state that may play an important role in the elicitation and intensification of emotions or as a *pre-emotion* that prepares the individual for the subsequent evaluative appraisal of events.

Bibliography

Charlesworth, W. R. (1969). The role of surprise in cognitive development. In "Studies in Cognitive Development" (D. Elkind and J. H. Flavell, Eds.), Oxford University Press, New York.

Desai, M. M. (1939). Surprise: A historical and experimental study. *Br. J. Psychol. Monogr. Suppl.* **22.**

Meyer, W.-U., Niepel, M., Rudolph, U., and Schützwohl, A. (1991). An experimental analysis of surprise. *Cognit. and Emot.* **5,** 295–311.

Shand, A. (1914). "The Foundations of Character. Being a Study of the Tendencies of the Emotions and Sentiments." Macmillan, London.

SYNAPTIC TRANSMITTERS AND NEUROMODULATORS

Stephen M. Stahl
University of California at San Diego and Veterans Affairs Medical Center, San Diego

Glossary

Enzyme A specialized protein which converts one molecule (the substrate) into another (the product).

Neuromodulator A naturally occurring chemical messenger which has two functions. First, it can act as a neurotransmitter itself by transmitting a message from one neuron to another. Second, a neuromodulator can influence and modulate the transmission of a message by another neurotransmitter.

Neurotransmitter A naturally occurring chemical messenger which transmits a chemical message from one nerve to another. Release of neurotransmitters is key to converting an electric impulse in one nerve into an electrical impulse in another nerve, with the translation of this message between the nerves being accomplished with a chemical signal.

Receptor A specialized protein which receives chemical input from a neurotransmitter and passes this input along to other molecules.

Synapse The area of connection between two neurons where chemical neurotransmission occurs.

SYNAPTIC NEUROTRANSMITTERS AND NEUROMODULATORS are chemicals made by the brain so that neurons can communicate with one another. Neurotransmission is both chemical and synaptic. That is, the signal between neurons is a chemical. Also, neurotransmission occurs at specialized sites, called synapses, which connect two neurons. This article defines the principles of neurotransmission and discusses how neurotransmission is the target not only of drugs but also of diseases that affect the brain.

I. PRINCIPLES OF CHEMICAL NEUROTRANSMISSION

A. Anatomically Addressed versus Chemically Addressed

Neurons are organized not only so that they can *send* information to other neurons, but also so that they can *receive* information from other neurons. Classically, the central nervous system has been envisioned as a series of "hard-wired" connections between neurons. This idea has been referred to as the "anatomically addressed" nervous system. The anatomically addressed brain can thus be compared to a complex wiring diagram. Electrical impulses are carried along these "wires."

Neurons do send information from one part of the cell to another part of the same cell via electrical impulses. However, these electrical impulses do not jump directly to other neurons. Neurons communicate instead by the first neuron throwing a chemical messenger, or neurotransmitter, at the receptors of a second neuron. This happens only at synapses. A diagram of a synapse is shown in Figure 1. Communication between neurons is therefore chemical, not electrical. That is, an electrical impulse in the first neuron is converted to a chemical signal at the synapse between it and a second neuron. This process is called both chemical neurotransmission and synaptic neurotransmission (see Fig. 1). [*See* BRAIN CHEMICALS.]

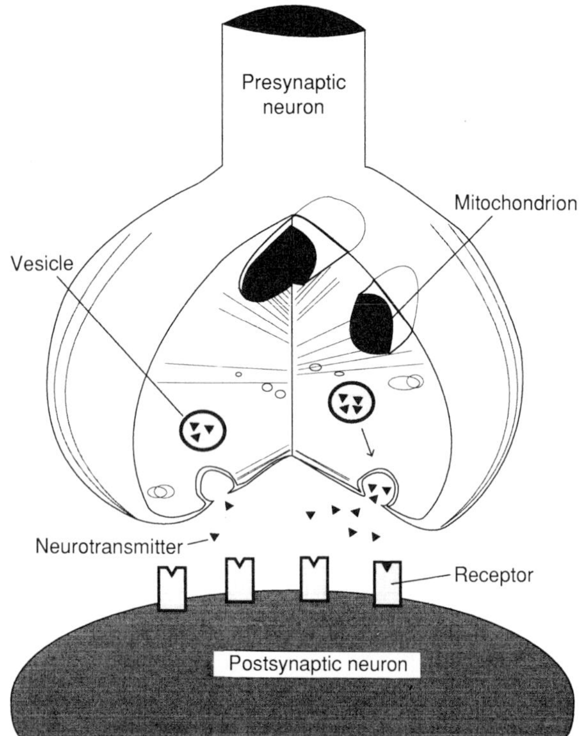

FIGURE 1 The synapse. This is the junction where communication between two neurons takes place. The communication begins with an electrical impulse in the presynaptic neuron. This impulse becomes a chemical message when it causes the release of chemicals called *neurotransmitters* into the synapse. The neurotransmitter crosses the synapse and binds to receptors on the postsynaptic neuron. The neurotransmitters fit the receptors selectively, much as a key fits into a lock. At this point the chemical message is reconverted into an electrical impulse. The process of communication is called *chemical neurotransmission*.

Thus, the principles of chemical neurotransmission demonstrate that the brain is not only a collection of wires, but also a sophisticated "chemical soup." To say it another way, neurotransmission is not only anatomically addressed, but also chemically addressed.

B. Fast versus Slow Signals and Neuromodulators

Some neurotransmitter signals are very brief, lasting only milliseconds. Two of the best examples of fast signals are the neurotransmitters glutamate and GABA (γ-aminobutyric acid). Glutamate is a neurotransmitter which universally stimulates almost any neuron, whereas GABA is a messenger which inhibits almost any neuron. Both of these neurotransmitters act by fast signals.

On the other hand, signals by different neurotransmitters can be longer. Sometimes these longer-acting neurotransmitters are called neuromodulators, since slow signals may last long enough to carry over and modulate a subsequent neurotransmission by a second neurotransmitter. Thus, a long-acting neuromodulating signal can set the tone of a neuron. Setting the tone amounts to a secondary action of the neuromodulator. The primary action is its own direct neurotransmitting signal. The secondary action is a modification of neurotransmission by another chemical message sent before the first signal is gone. Examples of slow-signaling neurotransmitters are *norepinephrine, serotonin,* and various *neuropeptides*. A list of known or suspected neurotransmitters is given in Table I.

C. Excitation–Secretion Coupling, Receptor Occupancy, and Second Messages

An electrical impulse in the first neuron is converted to a chemical signal at the synapse by a process known as excitation-secretion coupling. Once an electrical impulse enters the presynaptic axon terminal in the first neuron, it causes the release of the neurotransmitter stored there (see Fig. 1). Chemical communication is already prepared for action in the first neuron by previous synthesis and storage of neurotransmitter in the first neuron's presynaptic axon terminal. Enzymes and chemical supplies are sent there from the neuronal cell body, being transported down the axon to the terminals. Neurotransmitter is packaged and stored in the presynaptic neuron in vesicles, ready for release by an electrical impulse.

Once neurotransmitter has been released from the presynaptic neuron, it crosses the synapse where it seeks out and hits receptor sites on the second neuron (see Fig. 1). The neurotransmitter acts as a key fitting the receptor lock quite selectively. This opens a process which reconverts the chemical message back into an electrical impulse in the second nerve. It also sets into motion numerous biochemical consequences in the second neuron.

The neurotransmitter is considered the first messenger in chemical neurotransmission, but not the only messenger. Once the neurotransmitter has occupied its receptor on the second neuron, it initiates a cascade of messengers there. The "second messenger" and other subsequent messengers are intracellular chemical signals in the second neuron. These are triggered by the first messenger neuro-

TABLE I
Neurotransmitters in Brain

Amines	*Amino acids*
Serotonin (5HT)	γ-Aminobutyric acid (GABA)
Dopamine (DA)	Glycine
Norepinephrine (NE)	Glutamic acid
Epinephrine (E)	Aspartic acid
Acetylcholine (ACh)	
Pituitary peptides	*Gut hormones*
Corticotropin (ACTH)	Cholecystokinin (CCK)
Grown hormone (GH)	Gastrin
Lipotropin	Motilin
α-Melanocyte stimulating hormone (α-MSH)	Pancreatic polypeptide
Oxytocin	Secretin
Vasopressin	Substance P
	Vasoactive intestinal peptide
Circulating hormones	*Opioid peptides*
Angiotensin	Dynorphin
Calcitonin	β-Endorphin
Glucagon	met-Enkephalin
Insulin	leu-Enkephalin
	Kyotorphin
Hypothalamic releasing hormones	*Miscellaneous peptides*
Corticotropin-releasing factor (CRF)	Bombesin
Leuteinizing-hormone-releasing hormone (LHRH)	Bradykinin
Somatostatin	Carnosine
Thyrotropin-releasing hormone (TRH)	Neuropeptide Y
	Neurotensin
	Proctolin
	Substance K

transmitter occupying the receptor outside of the cell, in the synaptic connection between the first and the second neuron. The best examples of second messengers are cyclic AMP and phosphatidyl inositol. Some receptors are linked to one type of second messenger, and others to different second messengers.

The second messenger intracellular signal tells the second neuron to change its ionic fluxes, to start or stop neuronal electrical impulses, and many, many other events. Most of these events are still mysteries to neuroscientists. Currently, our best information about neurotransmission concerns that part of the process starting from the manufacture and storage of neurotransmitter, through the release of neurotransmitter, interaction with synaptic receptors, and triggering of second messengers intracellularly in the second neuron.

Drugs affect nearly every conceivable component of this process of chemical neurotransmission. Mental and neurological illnesses are thought to affect the various parts of this process as well.

D. Multiple Neurotransmitters

1. Known or Suspected Transmitters

The number of known or suspected neurotransmitters in the brain already numbers several dozen (Table I). Theoretically, there might prove to be several hundred to several thousand unique brain chemicals. About half a dozen "classical" neurotransmitters have been known for several years. These are the *biogenic amines* and *amino acids*. In recent years, an ever increasingly number of neurotransmitters are being discovered as new members. We now know that strings of amino acids known as *peptides* can also have neurotransmitter actions, and many of the newly discovered neurotransmitters are peptides.

Some of the naturally occurring neurotransmitters may be similar to drugs we use. For example, it is well known that the brain makes its own morphine (endorphin). The brain may even make its own antidepressant, its own anti-anxiety agent, and its own hallucinogen.

2. Cotransmitters

Each neuron was originally thought to use one neurotransmitter only, and to use it at all of its synapses. Today, we now know, however, that neurons can have more than one neurotransmitter (Table II). Thus, the concept of cotransmission has arisen. The physiological function of many neurons may thus be to communicate by using more than one neurotransmitter.

E. Plasticity: Aging, Development, and Growth Factors

Thinking of neurons as telephone cables can inaccurately imply that the brain is "hard-wired," and stays that way forever. However, this is not true. Neurons are quite changeable and malleable, char-

TABLE II
Cotransmitter Pairs

Amine/amino acid	Peptide
Dopamine	Enkephalin
Dopamine	Cholecystokinin
Norepinephrine	Somatostatin
Norepinephrine	Enkephalin
Norepinephrine	Neurotensin
Epinephrine	Enkephalin
Serotonin	Substance P
Serotonin	Thyrotropin releasing hormone
Serotonin	Enkephalin
Acetylcholine	Vasoactive intestinal peptide
Acetylcholine	Enkephalin
Acetylcholine	Neurotensin
Acetylcholine	Leuteinizing hormone releasing hormone
Acetylcholine	Somatostatin
γ-Aminobutyric acid (GABA)	Somatostatin
γ-Aminobutyric acid (GABA)	Motilin

acteristics sometimes called "plasticity." It is true that neurons do not replicate after birth, and that new neurons do not grow when other neurons die. However, the parts of the neuron known as *axons* and *dendrites* are constantly changing, establishing new connections, removing old connections, in a manner reminiscent of the branches of a tree. Indeed, the "arborization" of neuronal terminals and the "dentritic tree" are terms implying a constant branching and pruning process throughout the lifetime of that neuron.

It is suspected that neurons elaborate various growth factors which promote or destroy their synaptic connections, allowing for constant revision throughout the lifetime of that neuron.

II. CHEMICAL NEUROTRANSMISSION AS THE TARGET OF DRUG ACTION

A. Receptors and Enzymes as the Targets of Drug Action

Most drugs act in some manner upon chemical neurotransmission. They do this either by acting on receptors or by acting on enzymes.

B. Three Parts of a Receptor

Receptors are proteins which exist in neuronal membranes. Neurotransmitter receptors can be thought of as containing three portions: an extracellular portion which interacts with the neurotransmitter itself, a transmembrane portion which interacts with other elements within the membrane, and an intracellular portion which converts the extracellular message into an intracellular message.

The extracellular portion of a receptor is the part of the receptor which contains its highly selective binding site for its neurotransmitter. This portion of the receptor is the site where a great majority of drugs are targeted, either to mimic the neurotransmitter, which normally binds there, or to block it. The recognition site of the neurotransmitter receptor is quite unique from one receptor to the next, and indeed may be the major distinguishing characteristic of one receptor versus another.

The second portion of a receptor is its transmembrane regions. These portions of the receptor probably serve a structural purpose, holding the receptor in place, or allowing a certain movement of the receptor relative to the membrane itself. In contrast to the external recognition sites, the transmembrane regions of one neurotransmitter receptor can be quite similar to those of another neurotransmitter receptor.

The third part of a neurotransmitter receptor is intracellular. This part of the receptor interacts with intracellular proteins in order to generate second messengers. Numerous drugs interact with second messenger systems to modify the translation of information from neurotransmitter first messengers to various second messengers.

C. Synaptic Teamwork

Although the interaction of neurotransmitter with its unique extracellular binding site on its receptor is a key element of chemical neurotransmission, this is far from a complete description of chemical neurotransmission. The neurotransmitter is only one member of a synaptic neurotransmission team of molecules.

Other participants in synaptic transmission include channels to help ions go through the membrane, the ions themselves, enzymes, transport carriers, active transport pumps, and second messenger systems. Each is not only a key aspect of chemical neurotransmission, but also a possible site of drug action.

The physical and spatial arrangements of these different participants in chemical neurotransmission are organized to enable function as well as structural interactions. Numerous specialized molecules are thus positioned at the synapse in order to coordinate the multiple actions comprising chemical neurotransmission.

1. Ion Channels

Some molecules line the neuronal membrane in order to form a channel for ions to get into or out of the neuron. Channels exist for sodium, potassium, and calcium. Neurotransmitter binding sites sometimes cooperate with ion channels, thus directing the channels to open or close. Neurotransmitter receptors can thereby act as ionic gate-keepers, controlling the membrane's ionic permeability which in turn modifies the excitability of the neuron. Cooperation among the participants in synaptic transmission is a common theme in chemical neurotransmission.

2. Transport Carriers and Active Transport Pumps

Membranes serve to keep the inner environment of the cell constant by acting as a barrier to the intrusion of outside molecules and to the leakage of internal molecules. However, the neuron also has mechanisms to allow certain molecules to get into the cell, and others to exit. This applies not only to ions, but also to certain other molecules. For example, glucose is transported into the cell in order to provide energy for neurotransmission, and released neurotransmitters are recaptured for repackaging and reuse in subsequent neurotransmission.

In order to ferry molecules across an otherwise unpassable membrane, other molecules known as *transport carriers* work to bind that molecule needing to enter or to exit the cell. The transport carrier is thus itself a type of receptor. In order for the transport carrier to concentrate molecules inside the neuron, energy is required.

a. Neurotransmitter Synaptic Reuptake as an Example of Molecular Transport Using an Active Transport Pump

The presynaptic neuron has an active transport pump for its neurotransmitter. This pump begins to work when the neurotransmitter is finished binding to its postsynaptic receptor binding site. After the presynaptic neuron fires and releases its neurotransmitter, the neurotransmitter crosses the synapse, and binds to its receptor on the second neuron. This triggers all the subsequent events in the postsynaptic neuron which translate that chemical message into another electrical impulse in the postsynaptic neuron. The neurotransmitter then diffuses off its receptor, and can be destroyed by enzymes, or transported back into the presynaptic neuron.

When neurotransmitter successfully diffuses back to the presynaptic neuron, a transport carrier is waiting there for it. The active transport carrier binds the neurotransmitter and, with the help of a energy-providing enzyme system, transports the neurotransmitter back into the first neuron for repackaging and reuse. Inhibiting this transport system is the mechanism of action of most antidepressant drugs.

3. Second Messenger Systems

As mentioned above, neurotransmitter receptors can also cooperate with specialized molecules in order to produce second messengers. The first messenger is the neurotransmitter. It hands off to a second messenger which is intracellular. As mentioned above, the two best known examples of second messengers are cyclic AMP and phosphatidyl inositol (PI).

The transition of first messenger to second messenger is accomplished by means of a molecular cascade. That is, the receptor for the first messenger interacts with other receptors and enzymes. The net effect of all of this is to have the first messenger cause the second neuron to do something through the actions of a second messenger. The types of things which a second messenger can cause the second neuron to do are to change firing rate, alter receptors, turn an enzyme on or off, or manufacture a chemical product.

These are specific examples of the generalized theme whereby a neurotransmitter occupying its receptor precipitates a cascade of molecular events, carried out by a team of molecular players who interact with one another cooperatively, handing off the message from one molecule to another. The further one gets from the first messenger, however, the less well understood are the nature and function of the subsequent molecular events.

4. Allosteric Modulation

By now, it should be clear that a neurotransmitter and its receptor function as members on a team of specialized molecules, all working together to carry out the specialized functions necessary for the chemical transfer of information between neurons. Not only can the members of one such team work cooperatively among themselves, but a second team can be so organized so that its numerous members give a hand to the first team in order to alter the output of the first team. This second team is an *allosteric* (literally, "other site") modifier of the first team. The allosteric modulation can be either amplifying or blocking.

An example of this is the way in which drugs called *benzodiazepines* alter the neurotransmitting signal of GABA. Benzodiazepines are anti-anxiety, sleep-enhancing, and anticonvulsant medications. Valium (diazepam) and Xanax (alprazolam) are examples of benzodiazepines. GABA is an inhibitory neurotransmitter which causes its inhibition by increasing the ability of chloride to get into neurons through a membrane channel.

Nearby the receptor for GABA is not only the chloride channel, but also a receptor for benzodiazepines. Benzodiazepine receptors can also affect the conductance of chloride through the channel. However, the benzodiazepines do this not by directly increasing chloride conductance, but by helping GABA to do so. When benzodiazepines bind to their own benzodiazepine receptor, this causes GABA to be more powerful in increasing chloride ions getting through the membrane channel. The benzodiazepines therefore dramatically amplify the effect of GABA. Other drugs such as alcohol and barbiturates may also mediate their psychotropic properties by allosteric modulation of GABA.

The GABA–benzodiazepine interaction is an example of *positive* allosteric moderation. An example of *negative* allosteric modulation has already been discussed above. That example is the case of the antidepressants which act as neurotransmitter reuptake blockers. When reuptake blockers bind to their own selective receptor sites, they do not allow neurotransmitter to bind to their presynaptic transport carrier. Thus, neurotransmitter can no longer be shuttled back into the presynaptic neuron. Another way of saying this is that the neurotransmitter reuptake blockers' receptor allosterically modulates the presynaptic neurotransmitter transporter negatively and thereby blocks neurotransmitter uptake.

It should thus be clear that when they are arranged as next-door neighbors, neurotransmitter receptors can interact with each other allosterically as members of different teams to promote or control some aspect of neurotransmission. This may also underlie the process of neuromodulation, where one neurotransmitter acts long enough to modify a subsequent message from a second neurotransmitter acting at a neighboring but not identical receptor.

This theme is repeated over and over again throughout neuropharmacology, with varying receptors, transmitters, ion channels, and allosteric modifying receptors and their transmitters. The exact architecture of specific sites is being discovered at a fast pace and is only well worked out for a few specific neurotransmitters. Drugs can act at a myriad of sites, to influence this process. So can diseases. There are at a minimum ion channel sites, neurotransmitter sites, and allsoteric sites as targets of drug (and disease) action.

D. Multiple Receptor Subtypes

Neurotransmitters can act on more than one neurotransmitter receptor. This increases the options for brain communication. That is, there is not a single acetylcholine receptor, nor a single serotonin receptor, nor a single norepinephrine receptor. In fact, multiple subtypes have been discovered for virtually every known neurotransmitter receptor. It is as though the neurotransmitter keys in the brain can open many receptor locks. The neurotransmitter itself is like the master key. Drugs generally act at only one of the receptors, like a submaster key for a single lock.

The system of chemical neurotransmission by multiple neurotransmitters each working through multiple receptors enables communication to be simultaneously selective yet amplified. That is, while there is a great variety of neurotransmitters, there is an even greater variety of neurotransmitter receptors. Every individual neurotransmitter is selectively different compared to other neurotransmitters. The multiplicity of receptor subtypes for each neurotransmitter, however, also enables a single neurotransmitter to interact at multiple receptor sites.

E. Agonists and Antagonists

Naturally occurring neurotransmitters stimulate receptors. These are called agonists. Some drugs stimulate receptors just like the natural neurotransmitter, and are therefore agonists. Other drugs actually block the actions of the natural neurotransmitter at its receptor, and are called antagonists. In addition, drugs can also be inverse agonists or partial agonists.

F. Inverse Agonists

Inverse agonists do the opposite of agonists. One example of the actions of inverse agonists can be taken from the opiate system. That is, opiates stimulate opiate receptors as agonists, and thereby relieve pain. An opiate antagonist such as naloxone, on the other hand, *blocks* the actions of the opiate agonist, and stops opiates from relieving pain. By contrast, an inverse agonist neither stimulates the opiate receptor like an agonist nor blocks it like an antagonist. Rather, it binds the receptor in a fashion so as to provoke the opposite effect of the agonist, and thus actually causes pain.

It might seem at first that there is no difference between an inverse agonist and an antagonist. However, there is a very important distinction between them. Whereas an antagonist blocks an agonist, it has no particular action in the absence of the agonist. However, an inverse agonist has the opposite action of an agonist. An example can be drawn from the benzodiazepine family. That is, a benzodiazepine agonist *relieves* anxiety and a benzodiazepine antagonist *blocks* the ability of the agonist to relieve anxiety. However, a benzodiazepine inverse agonist causes anxiety.

G. Partial Agonists

Additional actions of drugs other than agonist or antagonist actions can also occur at neurotransmitter receptors. Such actions can influence neurotransmission in even more ways. This is true for a class of agents known as *partial agonists*. This means that there is a spectrum of degree to which a receptor can be stimulated. At one end of the spectrum, there is the full agonist, which elicits the same degree of physiologic receptor-mediated response as the natural neurotransmitter agonist itself. At the other end of the spectrum is a full antagonist which blocks the effects of agonists, but has no agonist properties itself. (The same would be true for a spectrum of inverse agonists, going from full inverse agonist to antagonist).

What is so interesting about partial agonists is that they can appear as a net agonist, or as a net antagonist, depending upon the amount of naturally occurring full agonist neurotransmitter which is present. When neurotransmitter is absent, a partial agonist will be a net agonist. When neurotransmitter is present, the same partial agonist will, however, be a net antagonist. Thus, a partial agonist will boost deficient neurotransmitter activity yet block excessive neurotransmitter activity.

An agonist and an antagonist in the same molecule is quite a new dimension to therapeutics. This concept has led to proposals that partial agonists could treat not only states which are theoretically deficient in neurotransmitter (such as depression), but also states that are theoretically in excess of neurotransmitter (such as anxiety). What is not yet known is what degree of partiality is optimal.

H. Receptors and Enzymes as Sites of Drug Action

Most of the known drugs act in the brain in one of two manners: by interaction with receptors, or by interaction with enzymes. In the case of receptors, we have already discussed how drugs can be agonists, antagonists, partial agonists, or inverse agonists. In the case of enzymes, a great many of these are involved in various aspects of chemical neurotransmission. Every enzyme is the theoretical target for a drug acting as an enzyme inhibitor. However, in practice, only a minority of currently known drugs are enzyme inhibitors.

There are two major types of enzyme inhibitors: reversible and irreversible. The irreversible types are sometimes called "suicide inhibitors" because they permanently inhibit the enzyme, therefore essentially "killing" it. Enzyme activity in this case is only restored when new enzyme molecules are synthesized. By contrast, the reversible type of inhibitor binds the enzyme in a manner which can be reversed because the inhibitor can come off the enzyme. When the enzyme's substrate is able to compete with the enzyme inhibitor for binding to the enzyme, each can shove the other off the enzyme. The one which "wins" or predominates is the one with the greater affinity for the enzyme and/ or with the greatest concentration.

III. CHEMICAL NEUROTRANSMISSION AS THE TARGET OF DISEASE ACTIONS

A. Receptors and Enzymes as Targets of Disease Action in the Central Nervous System

There is a frustrating lack of knowledge of specific disease mechanisms for neurological and psychiatric disorders. However, a good deal of progress has been made in our thinking about mechanisms whereby such diseases modify synaptic neurotransmission. The resulting abnormality in neurotransmission may in fact be the etiological core of the mental illness itself. This problem may create a cascade of other changes in neurotransmission as well.

B. How Diseases Modify Synaptic Neurotransmission

1. Neuronal Plasticity and Neuro-Psychiatric Disorders

The synapse is a dynamic and constantly changing area of the brain. Synapses are created, maintained, and in some cases removed. Many things influence this process of adding, keeping, and getting rid of synapses. Since the synapse is the where chemical neurotransmission occurs, information transfer in the brain is vitally dependent upon the integrity of the synapse. If synapse formation is interrupted early in development, the brain may not reach its full potential, such as in mental retardation, and as is now speculated to occur in schizophrenia. If synapses are destroyed later in life, the brain may regress from the potential it has realized, such as in various dementias. [*See* BRAIN DEVELOPMENT AND PLASTICITY; DEMENTIA; MENTAL RETARDATION; SCHIZOPHRENIA.]

Drug treatments themselves not only may modify neurotransmission acutely, but could potentially interact with neuronal plasticity. Harnessing the brain's plasticity is an important goal of several areas of new drug development. For example, certain growth factors may provoke the neuron to sprout new axonal or dendritic branches, and to establish new synaptic connections.

Other factors may be involved in the opposite process of the natural pruning of the branches, destroying and turning over old, useless, or unused synapses. If a disease makes the destruction of synapses get out of control, this may cause the permanent degeneration of certain neurons. Some diseases may be caused by a genetically programmed mechanism which gets out of control, and eventually prunes neurons to death. Other diseases could be caused by the ingestion of toxins, or toxic drugs of abuse.

The role of plasticity in the action of drugs or diseases upon neurotransmission in the central nervous system is only beginning to be explored. Drugs are not yet available which can turn on and direct the plasticity process. Theoretically, it should become possible to establish new synapses or to re-establish lost synapses. Such possible modifications of degenerative nerve diseases are being pursued in two different ways. First, the search is on for abnormal genes or abnormal gene products which are mediating the breakdown of neurons. Once identified, it should theoretically be possible to stop the production or block the action of unwanted gene products or to turn on the production or provide a substitute for the desired but absent gene products, depending upon the specific need for the specific disease. Second, transplantation of neurons is being investigated as a manner of substituting new neurons for degenerated neurons. Surgical insertion of highly specialized nerves which produce specialized chemicals and neurotransmitters is under study to see if the transplanted neurons are capable of compensating for and replacing the functions of the degenerated and destroyed neurons which caused disease in the first place. This is already occurring in Parkinson's disease where dopamine-producing neurons have been successfully transplanted into the brains of animals and patients with this condition. Experimental use of cholinergic neurons holds promise for the treatment of experimental models of Alzheimer's disease. [*See* ALZHEIMER'S DISEASE.]

2. Excitotoxicity

One current mechanism causing neuronal cell death is that of excitotoxicity. An excitatory amino acid, like glutamate, can overexcite a cell, causing too much calcium to enter the cell through ion channels, eventually poisoning and killing the neuron. This has been theorized to occur in certain hereditary degenerative disorders such as Huntington's disease. It could also occur in certain disorders which release too much glutamate, such as ischemia and stroke. Still other disorders could be related to excitotoxicity from toxins taken in from the environment. This has been shown for the toxin MPTP, which causes a form of Parkinson's disease, and is speculated to be the case for idiopathic Parkinson's disease itself, as well as perhaps amyotrophic lateral sclerosis (i.e., Lou Gehrig's disease), Alzheimer's disease, or other disorders of neuronal cell death.

Discovery of antagonists to excitotoxicity, such as exemplified by the glutamate antagonists, may portend the possibility of developing new drug therapies for neurodegenerative disorders, and other disease processes related to plasticity and neurodevelopmental dysfunction.

3. No Neurotransmission

Other mechanisms exist by which diseases modify chemical neurotransmission. These can vary from no transmission, such as in the case of a degenerated and absent neuron, to too much neurotransmission from a malfunctioning of the synapse. One of the key consequences of loss of neurons in neurodegenerative disorders such as Parkinson's disease, Huntington's disease, amyotrophic lateral sclerosis (i.e., Lou Gehrig's disease), and Alzheimer's disease, is the fact that no neurotransmission occurs subsequent to neuronal loss. This is a simple mechanism of disease, and it can have profound consequences. It is also the mechanism of other disorders such as stroke, multiple sclerosis, and virtually any disorder in which neurons are irreversibly damaged.

One successful approach to therapeutics in the central nervous system is simply attempting to replace the neurotransmitter in cases of lost neurotransmission. Indeed, this can happen in certain instances such as Parkinson's disease, where the loss of the neurotransmitter dopamine can be replaced.

4. Too Much Neurotransmission

Another possible disease mechanism is too much neurotransmission. An extreme example of this is excitotoxicity. Other examples of excessive neurotransmission are diseases in which neurotransmission stops short of actually destroying the neuron, but cause the neuron to be overactive. This may be the case for epilepsy, psychosis, and panic. In the case of epilepsy, neurons fire when and where they should not, leading to seizures. It is not yet known why this occurs, but is theorized to be related either to deficient inhibitory neurotransmission or to excessive excitatory neurotransmission. [*See* EPILEPSY.]

Psychosis is somewhat analogous to a seizure, in that excessive transmission of dopamine in the mesolimbic areas of brain may lead to symptoms of delusions, hallucinations, and thought disorder in various psychiatric disorders.

Panic disorder may be analogous to a seizure in areas of the brain controlling emotions. This may be the mechanism whereby the symptoms of a panic attack are produced, namely a massive emotional discharge of panic, shortness of breath, chest pain, dizziness, and feelings of impending death or of going crazy. [*See* PANIC DISORDER.]

5. Other Mechanisms of Abnormal Neurotransmission

Several other mechanisms can be conceptualized whereby diseases might disrupt chemical neurotransmission both by primary disease action on neurotransmission and by the secondary consequences of the disease on neurotransmission elsewhere in the brain. These include the imbalance between two neurotransmitters required to regulate a single process. This has been theorized as the mechanism of many of the movement disorders, where balance is off between the two neurotransmitters dopamine and acetylcholine. Another possible aberrancy of neurotransmission is that of the wrong rate of neurotransmission, possibly disrupting functions such as sleep, or biorhythms. The wrong neuronal wiring of the anatomically addressed nervous system could be problematic. This may occur in disorders of brain development in which synapses are laid down incorrectly (perhaps in autism, mental retardation, or even schizophrenia). We have already discussed how degenerative disorders lose neurons and synapses, and the net result of loss of key synapses is an abnormal remaining wiring system of the brain.

Bibliography

Bloom, F. E., and Lazerson, A. (1988). "Brain, Mind and Behavior," 2nd ed. Freeman, New York.

Cooper, J. R., Bloom, F. E., and Roth, R. H. (1991). "The Biochemical Basis of Neuropharmacology," 6th ed. Oxford Unviersity Press, New York.

Gilman, A. G., Rall, T. W., Nies, A. S., and Taylor, P. (1990). "The Pharmacological Basis of Therapeutics," 8th ed. Pergamon, New York.

Groves, P. M., and Rebec, G.V. (1992). "Introduction to Biological Psychology," 4th ed. Brown, Dubuque, IA.

Iversen, L. L. (1986). Chemical signalling in the nervous system. In "Progress in Brain Research" (T. Hokfelt, K. Fuxe, and B. Pernow, Eds.), Vol. 68, pp. 15–21. Elsevier, New York.

Meltzer, H. Y. (Ed.) (1987). "Psychopharmacology: The Third Generation of Progress." Raven Press, New York.

Siegel, G., Agranoff, B., Ablers, R. W., and Molinoff, P. (1989). "Basic Neurochemistry," 4th ed. Raven Press, New York.

Yamamura, H. I., Enna, S. J., and Kuhar, J. M. (1985). "Neurotransmitter Receptor Binding," 2nd ed. Raven Press, New York.

SYNTAX

Howard Lasnik
The University of Connecticut

Glossary

Ambiguity Property of having more than one meaning.

Anaphor Linguistic expression entirely dependent on another linguistic expression in the same sentence for its interpretation: e.g., *himself* in "John injured himself" is dependent upon *John*. Simple pronouns such as *he* are not anaphors, since they can stand alone, as in "He left."

Argument Semantically contentful expression in an argument position.

Argument position Subject position, direct object position, indirect object position, etc., in a sentence.

Embedding Process of inserting one phrase or sentence inside another.

Grammar Theory of a language.

Language Computational system enumerating, for each of an infinite set of expressions, a full array of phonetic, semantic, and structural properties.

Parameter Two (or more) valued choices determining a general property distinguishing one type of language from another.

Phonology Sound pattern of a language; the theory of such sound patterns.

SYNTAX is concerned with the structural properties of languages. The term "syntax" is used ambiguously to refer both to those structural properties and to the branch of the field of linguistics concerned with investigating them. Included in this topic are the regularities governing the facts of word order as well as the grouping of words into larger units relevant to semantic and phonological interpretation. How these regularities are represented in the mind of the speaker, how they arise in the mind of the speaker, and how they are put to use in the production and comprehension of sentences are the psychological aspects of these issues.

I. PHRASE STRUCTURE

A person who knows a language knows a large number of words, including properties relevant to their pronunciation and semantic interpretation. In addition to this "lexicon," he or she has command of a productive system for the appropriate arrangement of words into sentences, the syntax of the language. Given the fact that brand new sentences are routinely used and understood, it could not be true that the syntax of a language consisted merely of a list of sentences which are memorized in the course of language acquisition. Rather, a set of processes, syntactic rules, must be involved in this creative use of language.

The computational system of language including these syntactic rules determines mental representations expressing not only the sequencing of words, but also their grouping into hierarchical structural units intermediate between word and sentence. Even a simple sentence such as (1) is not just a sequence of three autonomous words:

(1) The man left.

The and *man* are closely associated in a way in which *man* and *left* are not. The former pair of words constitutes a unit based on the noun *man*. We can see this in a number of ways. First, that sequence can be substituted for by a "pro-form," in this case a pronoun:

(2) He left.

No comparable substitution is possible for the sequence *man left* in example (1). Further, an adverb modifying the sentence can be inserted between *man* and *left*, as in (3), but not between *the* and *man*, as in (4):

(3) The man obviously left.
(4) * The obviously man left. [* indicates an ungrammatical sentence, a sequence of words that is not a sentence of the language under investigation.]

This same structural grouping is evidenced in the phonology. A longer pause is possible between *man* and *left* than between *the* and *man*, again indicating that the sequence *the man* constitutes a unit while the sequence *man left* does not. There is a division of sentence (1) into two major parts, or "constituents." The first constituent, based on a noun, is called a "noun phrase" (NP). The second constituent, based on a verb, is called a "verb phrase" (VP). A typical English sentence like (1) consists of an NP followed by a VP, roughly corresponding to the traditional division of a sentence into subject and predicate. Example (5), a "phrase structure rule," is a shorthand way of stating this property of English sentences:

(5) S[entence] → NP VP

A simple NP, in turn, consists of a noun (N) preceded by a "determiner" (*the, a,* etc.) or not ("John left"), and a VP consists of just a verb (V), among many other possibilities.

(6) a. NP → (Det) N [Parentheses indicate an
b. VP → V item that may or may not be present.]

These can be thought of as part of the system of knowledge underlying the procedures for the analysis and the production of sentences. Someone who knows English knows these rules, though the knowledge is not generally conscious. The structure that the rules in (5) and (6) determine for sentence (1) can be represented by the "phrase structure tree" in (7).

(7)

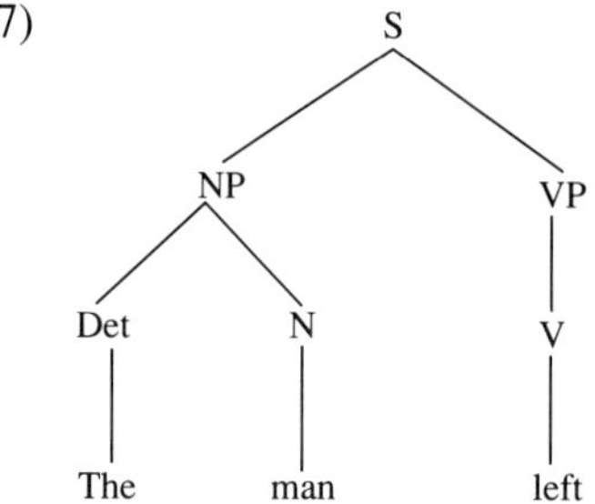

Such a diagram represents the linear and hierarchical properties of the sentence. Two standard relations defined on such structures are "precedence" and "dominance." In (7), NP precedes VP, V, and *left*, but does not precede Det, *the,* N, S, etc. NP dominates Det, N, *the,* and *man,* but does not dominate VP, V, S, etc. Another way of representing precisely the same information is the "labeled bracketing" in (8):

(8) $[_S\ [_{NP}\ [_{Det}$ The] $[_N$ man]] $[_{VP}\ [_V$ left]]].

Phrase structure trees and labeled bracketing representations are both widely used in the syntax literature. A structural representation (in either format) is called a "phrase marker."

In addition to very simple VPs containing only a verb and nothing else, there are also VPs that contain NPs, as in (9):

(9) The man saw the woman.

Rule (10) allows for this additional possibility of a "direct object" for the verb.

(10) VP → V (NP)

As in (6a), the parentheses are to be understood as allowing, but not demanding, that the enclosed material occurs in a structure. Taken together, (5) and (10) correctly assert that just the same kinds of sequences of words that can be subjects of sentences can be objects of sentences, since it is the constituent NP that occurs in either position.

The constituent structure analysis given by phrase structure rules provides part of the basis for the creative use of language. There is no limit on how long a sentence of English (or any other human language) can be. Thus, given a sentence of any length, a speaker can always create a longer novel one. One of the major ways in which ever longer sentences can be constructed is by "embedding" one sentence inside another. We have already seen a VP consisting of just a V, and also one consisting of a V followed by an NP. In addition to these possibilities, the material following the V can be an entire sentence:

(11) The child thinks [$_S$ the man left].

In (11), the direct object of the verb is not an NP but rather is our original sentence, (1). The structure of (11) is represented in (12).

(12)

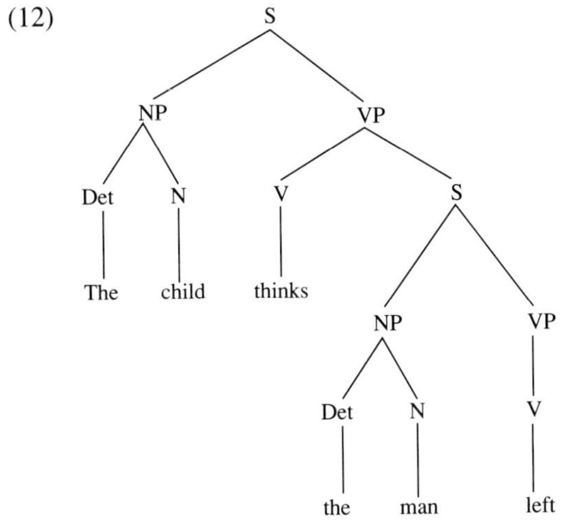

An additional VP rule of the standard sort allows for this possibility:

(13) VP → V S

Now the structure in (12) can be produced by application of rule (5) followed by, among other things, application of rule (13), followed by another application of rule (5). Then, the usual rules for NP and VP can apply. This process can be continued indefinitely, with rule (13) introducing as S which, by rule (5), introduces (in addition to another NP) another VP, and so on. Systems of phrase structure rules with this property are called "recursive." It is important to note that with the addition of the simplest possible rule for generating structure (12), namely rule (13), the system of rules (the "grammer") becomes recursive. Thus, with just the rules we already have, (12) can be further embedded to produce a still more complex sentence such as (14).

(14) The woman knows the child thinks the man left.

The structure of (14) is as in (15).

(15)

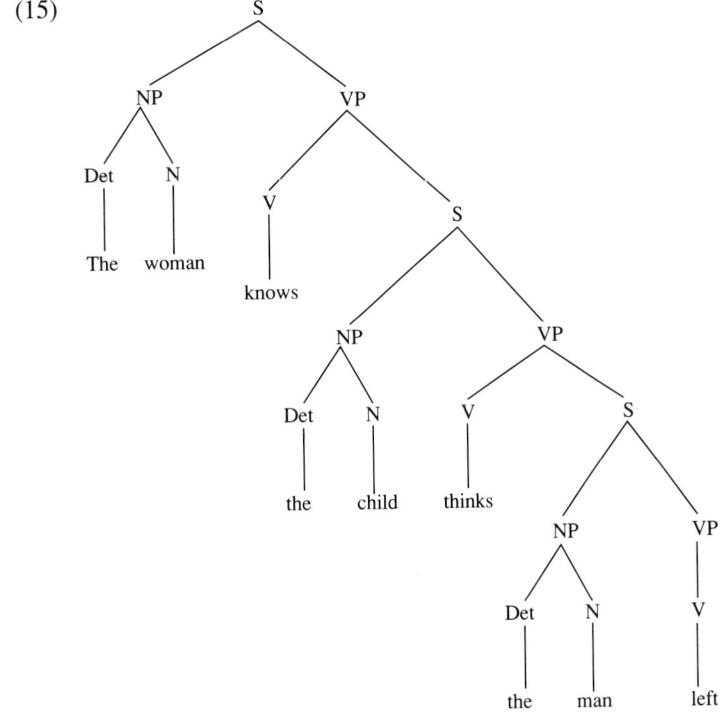

Recursive rules thus provide finite means for generating an unlimited number of sentences. Given the interpretation of syntactic rules as pieces of a speaker's knowledge, this is crucial, in light of the finite character of the human brain.

The VP structures considered so far all contain a V. Similarly, the NP structures contain an N. The hypothesis that this is true more generally—that XP always contains X, for any choice of X (both for all structures of English and cross-linguistically)—is one of a complementary pair of fundamental tenets of what is called "X-bar theory." The name derives from a particular notation used for phrase structure rules, as in (16):

(16) a. $\overline{\overline{X}} \rightarrow \ldots \overline{X} \ldots$
     b. $\overline{X} \rightarrow \ldots X \ldots$

By (16), $\overline{\overline{X}}$ always introduces $\overline{X}$ into a structure, which in turn introduces X. The complementary claim is that whenever X is present in a structure, it must be by virtue of (16). $\overline{\overline{X}}$ must have as its "head" X, and X must "project" the phrasal category $\overline{\overline{X}}$.

There are proposals that not just lexical categories, but also "functional" categories conform to X-bar theory. According to these proposals, S is actually IP, a projection of INFL, a head embodying tense and agreement information. Similarly, Det is not merely a modifier of nouns but is the head of DP, with N-headed NP a constituent of DP. Given the cross-linguistic similarities between pronouns and determiners, and the dissimilarities between pronouns and nouns, pronouns are sometimes analyzed as Ds heading simple DPs.

II. THE LEXICON

As noted earlier, VPs occur in a variety of forms (though all of them contain V). We have observed VPs containing just a V, ones containing a V and an NP, and finally, ones containing a V and an S. Examples (17) to (19), repeated from above, illustrate these three respective types of VP.

(17) The man left.
(18) The man solved the problem.
(19) The child thinks the man left.

Left unexpressed so far, however, is the fact that not just any verb can appear in any of these VP types. For example, the verb in (18) would be ungrammatical in the VP of (17):

(20) * The man solved.

Similarly, the verb in (19) is incompatible with the VP in (18):

(21) * The child thinks the problem.

Lexical properties, that is, properties of particular lexical items (words), thus play a major role in determining syntactic well-formedness. (Categorial grammars express an even stronger view: that all syntactic properties are encoded in lexical category specification; there are no separate syntactic rules as such.) In traditional terms, there are transitive verbs, such as *solve,* which require a direct object. Alongside these are intransitive verbs, such as *sleep,* which do not tolerate a direct object:

(22) * Harry slept the bed.

Further, among the transitive verbs, there are those like *solve* which take an NP, but not an S, for a direct object:

(23) * Mary solved Bill left.

And, as just noted, there are those like *think,* which take an S, but not an NP, as direct object. The large lexical category V is thus divided into smaller lexical "subcategories," each with its own special privileges of occurrence. The properties of the subcategories are expressed in "subcategorization frames" like the following:

(24) a. sleep [__]
     b. solve [__NP]
     c. think [__S]

The categories that appear in the subcategorization frame of a particular verb are called "complements" of that verb. Example (24a) is to be interpreted as the requirement that *sleep* can occur only in a $\overline{V}$ that has no complements for the head V, i.e., one like (25).

(25) $\overline{V}$
     |
     V

A verb with the subcategorization frame in (24b) can only occur in such a $\overline{V}$ as (26).

(26)
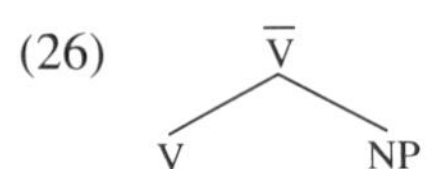

And so on. These syntactic properties of verbs follow, in large measure, from their semantic properties. Thus, in a sentence with *solve*, there is a semantic function for a direct object to fulfill, while there is no such function in the case of *sleep*. These semantic functions that arguments (direct objects, subjects, indirect objects, etc.) fulfill are called "thematic (θ-) roles." It is thus plausible that what is wrong with (20) is that a necessary semantic function has not been fulfilled—a θ-role associated with the verb *solve* has not been assigned. Conversely, the violation in (22) is that there is an argument NP, *the bed*, with no θ-role at all, since *sleep* has no θ-role to assign to an object, just one to assign to a subject. These paired requirements on assigners and recipients of θ-roles are called the θ-criterion: Every θ-role must be assigned, and every argument must receive a θ-role.

Example (27) illustrates several additional subcategories of verbs. The corresponding subcategorization frames are given in (28):

(27) a. Susan put the book on the desk.
b. Oscar convinced Harriet that she was brilliant.
c. Richard envies Marie her intelligence.
d. Stephen looked at the picture.

(28) a. put [__NP PP]
b. convince [__NP S]
c. envy [__NP NP]
d. look [__PP]

As expected, given the $\overline{X}$ schema for phrase structure, other lexical heads besides verbs can also take complements. For example, there often occur pairs of verbs and nouns with similar structure, meaning, and subcategorization, as in the following:

(29) a. John believes that Mary saw Fred.
b. John's belief that Mary saw Fred.

(30) a. Marion lectured about semantics.
b. Marion's lecture about semantics.

The nouns in the (b) examples are known as "derived" or "deverbal" nominals.

In all of the examples in (24) and (28), the head precedes its complement(s). In fact, that is more generally true in English: heads invariably precede their complements in basic "unmarked" word order. This property should thus be factored out of particular lexical entries, since a lexical entry contains only what is idiosyncratic about individual lexical items. However, the property does not hold of all languages. Japanese, for example, is just the reverse of English in this regard: heads invariably *follow* their complements. Simple, general differences of this type between languages are called "parameters." This particular parameter is known as the "head parameter," and it is assumed to be two-valued: a language is head-initial (English) or head-final (Japanese). Learning this structural property of a language involves setting the value of the parameter, based on simple input data.

III. SYNTACTIC TRANSFORMATIONS

The phrase structure rules (arguably reduced to the $\overline{X}$ template plus a specification of a value for the head parameter) along with the lexicon constitute the 'base component' of the syntax. The base component determines the structural representations of an unlimited number of sentences. However, there are sentence types requiring further machinery for an adequate characterization:

(31) a. Which problem did John solve?
b. This problem, John solved (. . . but not that one).

Solve belongs to the subcategory of verbs that can occur only in VPs of the form (26), since they have an object θ-role that they must assign. Yet the examples in (31), which both apparently violate this requirement, are grammatical. The key is that in these examples, although *this problem*, or *which problem*, is at the front of the sentence, it functions just as if it were in the VP. Considerations of this sort lead to the hypothesis in one leading approach to syntax that sentences have not just one structural representation, but (at least) two. For the examples in (31), one representation, the more "superficial" one, determines the pronunciation of the sentence. Another more "abstract" representation determines the thematic relations of the sentence, and is thus responsible for the satisfaction of subcategorization requirements. In this more abstract representation, the so-called "D(eep)-structure" of the sentence, the understood direct object will actually be in direct object position in the VP. In the more superficial representation, the so-called "S(urface)-structure," the direct object NP is displaced leftward from the position that determines its θ-role. The D-structure of (31b) is then (32).

(32) (D-structure of (31b))

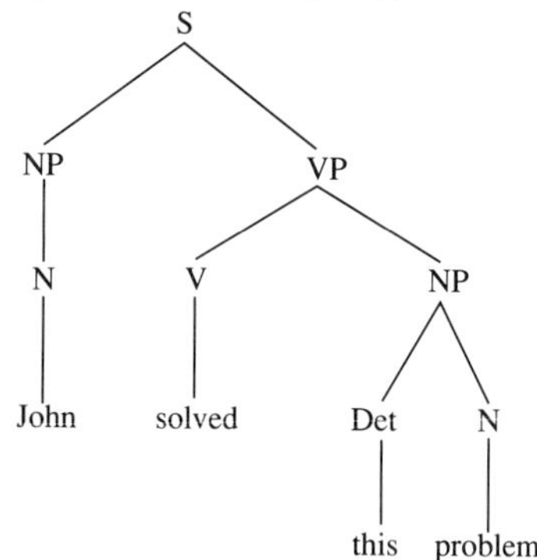

Example (32) accounts for the major θ-relations of (31b), and is consistent with all of the principles and lexical requirements considered so far. It does not, however, account for the structure of the sentence as it is immediately perceived. Rather, the S-structure, in which the direct object has been displaced to the front of the sentence, as in (33), has that function.

(33) (S-structure of (31b))

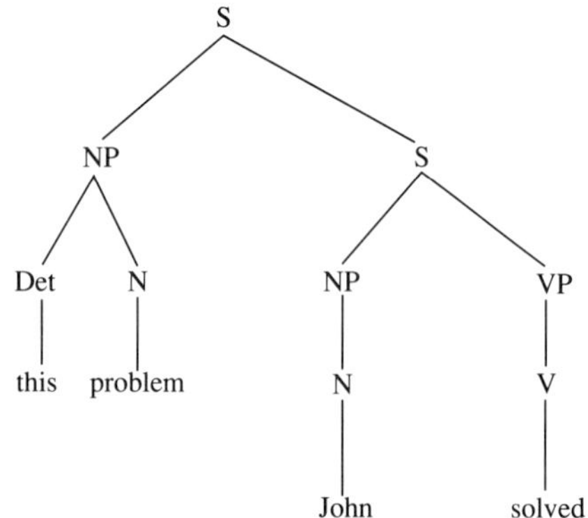

A displacement operation of this sort, relating one phrase marker to another, is known as a syntactic "transformation" (hence, the name "transformational grammar" for this general approach to syntax).

The sequence of successive phrase structure representations of a sentence is known as a "(transformational) derivation."

One alternative syntactic theory, generalized phrase structure grammar, posits a more powerful form of phrase structure rule instead of transformations, and, consequently, only one level of syntactic representation. Another alternative, lexical functional grammar, posits two representations: c(onstituent)-structure and f(unctional)-structure, but with only the former a phrase structure representation. The latter, which is not related to the former by any syntactic derivation, takes as primitives grammatical functions such as SUBJ(ect) and OBJ(ect). In this, it follows in the tradition of relational grammar.

The set of transformations in a given language constitutes the "transformational component" of the grammar. Schematically, the grammar has the following organization (to be slightly revised below).

(34) Lexicon—D-structure—Determination of θ-relations
|
Transformations
|
S-structure
|
Phonological rules
|
Phonetic form (PF)

The transformation which relates (32) to (33) is standardly called "topicalization." (The transformations responsible for (31a) include "WH-movement.") The mode of attachment of the fronted NP to the S in (33) is "adjunction," a transformational process attaching a moved item (in this case, an NP) to a target category (in this case an S) by creating a "higher" instance of the target category from which both the moved item and the original target category hang.

(33) displays left adjunction (i.e., attachment on the left) of NP to S. The structural representation in (33) captures one striking phonological property of sentence (31b): there is a major pause between the fronted NP and the remainder of the sentence, corresponding to the major constituent break created between that NP and the residual S.

IV. TRACE THEORY

A question arises concerning the position from which movement takes place. Example (33) indicates that that position is totally eliminated by the operation of the transformation, but work of the 1970s–1990s suggests that a marker of the previous occupant remains, in the form of a "trace." Example (35) represents this second possibility (which is known as "trace theory," with *t* a silent trace of the moved NP, *this problem:*

(35) (S-structure of (31b) with a trace)

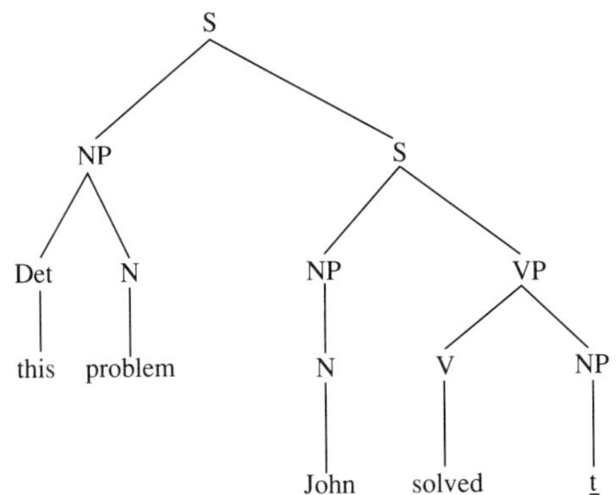

The arguments for traces are based, among other things, on properties of a particular contraction phenomenon in English, and on patterns of subject–verb agreement, whereby the form of a verb depends on properties of the subject of that verb ("He *comes*" but "They *come*"). Three facts are relevant background for the former argument. First the topicalization transformation is not limited to direct objects of simple sentences. The displaced item can come from an embedded sentence, as in (36), where the topicalized NP is the direct object of the lower verb, or (37) where it is the subject of the lower verb.

(36) This problem, [$_S$ Mary thinks [$_S$ John solved *t*]].

(37) This student, [$_S$ Mary thinks [$_S$ *t* solved this problem]].

Second, an embedded sentence need not be "finite," with a verb in the past tense (like *solved*), or the present tense (like *thinks*). An embedded sentence can also be "infinitival," as in (38):

(38) I want [$_S$ this student to solve this problem].

Third, colloquial English has a contraction process by which *want* and *to* become *wanna* when they are immediately adjacent:

(39) a. I want to solve this problem.
b. I wanna solve this problem.

That this process demands adjacency between *want* and *to* is shown by the impossibility of (40), based on (38):

(40) *I wanna this student solve this problem.

The relevant (and surprising) property of *wanna* contraction is that even if *this student* in (38) is displaced by topicalization, contraction is still blocked:

(41) a. This student, I want to solve this problem.
b. *This student, I wanna solve this problem.
(cf. This problem, I wanna solve.)

Though there does not seem to be anything intervening between *want* and *to* in (41a), hence, nothing to prevent contraction, under trace theory, there is, in fact, something intervening—the trace of the moved NP, *this student*. Example (42) represents this hypothesis.

(42)

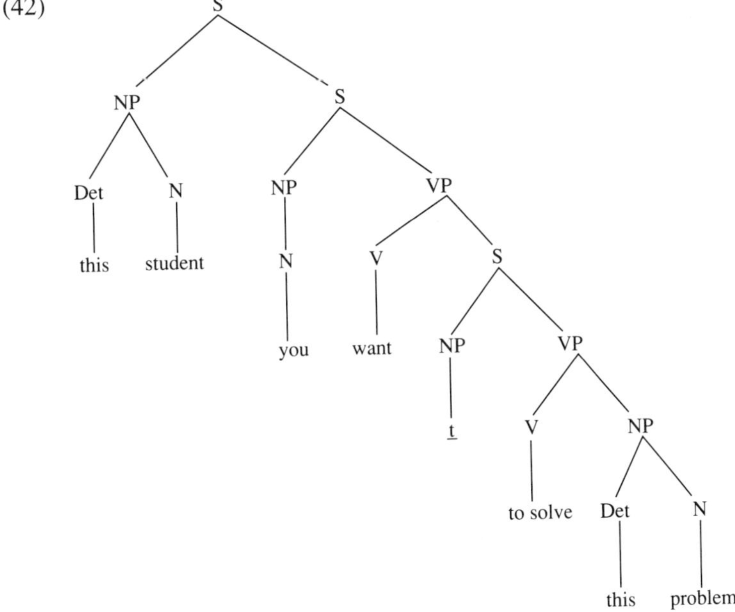

The same array of facts obtains with WH-movement:

(43) Which student do you want *t* to solve this problem?
(44) *Which student do you wanna solve this problem? (cf. which problem do you wanna solve?)

Again, the trace of the moved phrase blocks the adjacency needed for contraction. Even though they are silent, traces are evidently real, as far as the syntax is concerned.

Properties of subject–verb agreement provide a second source of evidence for traces. Generally, such agreement is a strictly local process, relating elements within the same S, for example, *they* with *think,* and *he* with *likes* in (45):

(45) *They think* [$_S$ *he likes* psychology].

Agreement with a more distant NP is impossible:

(46) **They* think [$_S$ he *like* psychology].

However, when topicalization or WH-movement has taken place from the subject position of an embedded sentence, apparent long distance agreement obtains:

(47) *This student,* they think [$_S$ *likes*/*like it].
(48) *Which student* do they think [$_S$ *likes*/*like it].

This dependency between a moved NP and a distant verb can be reduced to standard local agreement on the assumption that movement leaves a trace, and that the trace of a moved NP has the same agreement features (for person and number) as the moved NP. This is illustrated in (49).

(49) *Which student* do they think [$_S$ *t* likes/*like it]
third person *third person*
singular *singular*

V. CONSTRAINTS ON TRANSFORMATIONS

As just seen, the topicalization transformation can move an NP to the front of its own sentence as in (31b), and can also move an NP out of its own sentence to the front of the next "higher" sentence as in (36), (37), and (41a). In fact, an NP can move still farther, as in (50):

(50) This problem, Mary thinks John said Susan solved *t*.

Similarly for WH-movement:

(51) Which problem does Mary think John said Susan solved *t?*

However, there are certain constraints on the operation of these transformations. Consider sentence (52):

(52) I like this magazine and that book.

In this example, the object NP is a "coordinate structure" consisting of two NPs joined by the coordinating conjunction *and.* But while (53) is a good instance of topicalization, (54) is entirely ungrammatical:

(53) This magazine and that book, I like.
(54) *That book, I like this magazine and.

As (54) illustrates, extraction out of a coordinate structure is prohibited. This is schematized in (55).

(55)

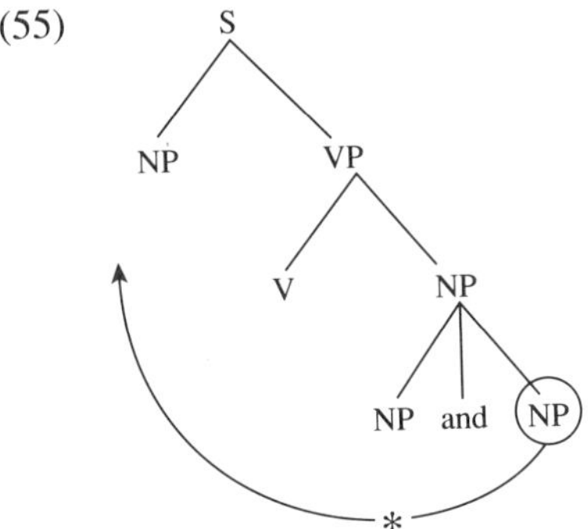

Example (56) is another illustration of the general prohibition, this time with extraction of just a part of one of the coordinate NPs:

(56) a. The true cross, John collects fragments of *t*.
b. *The true cross, John collects [$_{NP}$ [$_{NP}$ bibles] and [$_{NP}$ fragments of *t*]]

Examples (54) and (56) raise in very clear form the general question of acquisition of complex knowledge such as the coordinate structure constraint. It is not plausible that the child learning English is presented with evidence for the constraint (for example, via correction). Thus, it is reasonable to conjecture that the relevant bit of linguistic knowledge is innate. If that conjecture is correct, we should expect the constraint not to be particular to English, since, as a well known, any normal human child can learn any human language. Hence, we should expect the constraint to show up in human languages in general. This expectation is confirmed. Of the hundreds of languages that have been investigated, no clear instances have emerged of languages that permit extraction out of a coordinate structure.

Coordinate structures fall into the class of syntactic "islands" (or, as they are now often called, "barriers"), structural configurations blocking extraction. "Complex NPs," such as the noun complement constructions of the type seen in (29b) above, also constitute islands, as evidenced by the following contrast:

(57) Which problem did you announce [$_\beta$ that John believed [that Mary solved *t*]].
(58) *Which problem did you announce [$_\beta$ John's belief [that Mary solved *t*]].

When β is a sentence containing another sentence, extraction from the more embedded S is possible (57). But when β is an NP containing an S, such extraction is not allowed (58), a typical island effect. There have been a number of attempts to reduce the entire class of island constraints to one general locality condition on movement known as "subjacency." If subjacency and other general constraints on the operation and output of transformations are factored out of particular transformations, the statements of these particular transformations are correspondingly simplified. In fact, one major research direction within transformational grammar is to reduce the transformational component to one maximally simple, general transformation, "Move α" (move anything anywhere), or even "Affect α" (do anything to anything), with all ungrammatical results "filtered out" by constraints. This research program is far from complete, but has had considerable success.

VI. CASE THEORY

WH-movement and topicalization both have the effect of moving a constituent to a "non-A(rgument) position" to the left of the subject of an S. There are other movement operations that move a constituent into the subject position, an "A-position." Consider the following pair of sentences:

(59) It seems Harry knows the answer.
(60) Harry seems to know the answer.

In (59), *Harry* is in subject position of the embedded sentence. On the other hand, in (60), *Harry* is in subject position of the higher sentence, as evidenced by the agreement pattern on the verb: third person singular in (60), but third person plural in (61):

(61) Harry and Bill seem to know the answer.

However, given the close semantic parallelism between (59) and (60), especially with respect to θ-relations, their D-structures are assumed to be similar. In particular, since *Harry* is the understood subject of *know the answer* in both examples, it must be in the subject position of that predicate in the D-structues of both examples. The D-structure of (59) is identical to the S-structure in relevant respects.

(62)

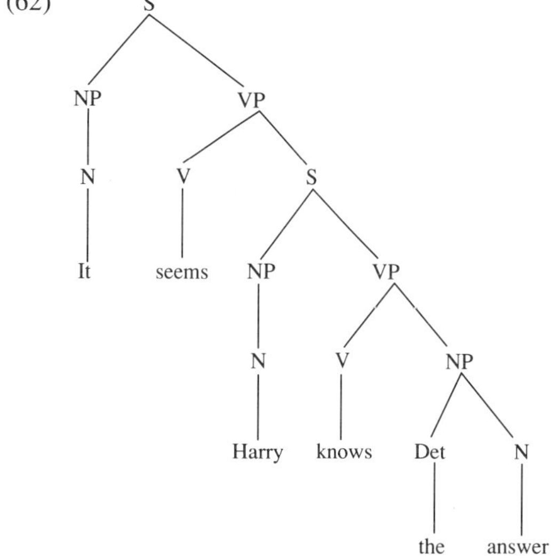

In (62), the subject of the main sentence *it* is not an argument, but rather, an "expletive," a place-holder lacking semantic import (unlike the referential *it* in "It is on the table"). The D-structure of (60) is similar, the only differences being that the main subject position is empty, and the embedded sentence is an infinitive.

(63)

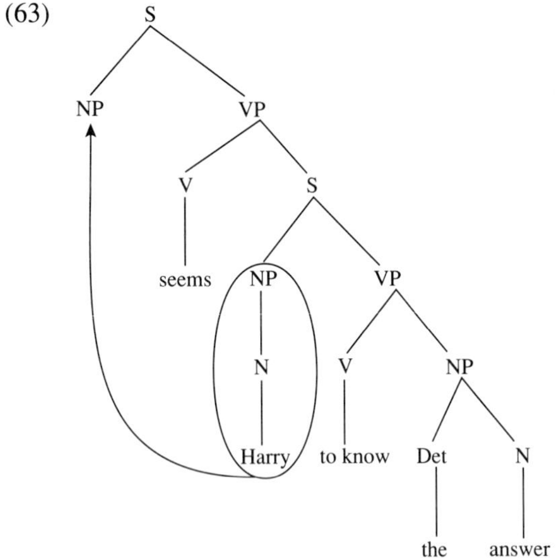

To derive the correct S-structure, the NP *Harry* raises into the empty higher subject position, as indicated by the arrow in (63). The movement is obligatory in this instance. If *Harry* remains in the lower subject position, the result is ungrammatical, whether or not the expletive *it* occurs as the higher subject:

(64) *Seems Harry to know the answer.
(65) *It seems Harry to know the answer.

This obligatoriness of movement of the subject has been analyzed as a requirement of abstract "case," in the following sense. There are characteristic structural positions that "license" particular morphological cases, as in the following table.

(66)

Position	Case	Example
Subjects of finite sentence	Nominative	*He* left
Direct object of transitive verb	Accusative	I saw *him*
"Subject" of NP	Genitive	*John's* belief that Mary solved the problem
Complement of preposition	"Oblique" [in English, indistinguishable from Accusative]	near *him*

In many languages (such as Latin, Russian, German), these case distinctions are overtly manifested in the morphology of nouns, pronouns, articles, etc. In English, only pronouns show an overt distinction between nominative and accusative, but Case theory posits that all NPs have abstract case (henceforth, Case), even when it is not morphologically visible. The requirement that all NPs occur in appropriate Case positions is called the "Case Filter." The Case Filter is a well-formedness condition on the S-structure level of representation. The NP *Harry* in its D-structure position in (63) lacks a legitimate Case, since that position does not license nominative, accusative, genitive, or oblique. Movement of *Harry* to the higher subject position salvages the construction, since that position licenses nominative Case. Such "subject raising" is not possible for structure (62), where the embedded sentence is finite:

(67) *Harry seems [*t* knows the answer].

This, too, has been analyzed in terms of Case: movement of an NP from one Case position to another is prohibited. Metaphorically speaking, movement to a Case position is a "last resort," an option taken only if necessitated by the Case Filter.

Case theory also has been used to explain some of the properties of "passive" sentences, such as (68):

(68) This problem was solved.

The S-structure subject, *this problem,* bears the object θ-role assigned by the verb *solve*. Hence, by hypothesis, it must have originated in object position in D-structure. But as in (63) through (65), movement is obligatory when the verb is in the passive form:

(69) *Was solved this problem.
(70) *It was solved this problem.

Passive verbs lose the ability of the corresponding active verbs to license Case. It has occasionally been suggested that this is because passive verbs are not fully verb-like, in that they share some properties with adjectives (cf. "the solved problem"). The morphological process creating a passive verb from an active one neutralizes its verbal properties.

Adjectives, like passive verbs, lack the ability to license Case on a complement, as seen in the contrast between the VP in (70) and the corresponding adjective phrase (AP) in (71):

(70) I [$_{VP}$ suspect Harry].
(71) *I am [$_{AP}$ suspicious Harry].

For (71), another saving strategy is available: a semantically null preposition is inserted to license Case on *Harry*.

(72) I am suspicious of Harry.

Passive verbs differ from adjectives in this respect. The *of*-insertion strategy is not available for the former:

(73) *It was solved of the problem.

One other special property of passive verbs shows up with verbs that take two NP complements. Passives of these verbs still retain the ability to license one:

(74) a. We gave John a book.
b. John was given a book.

Nouns pattern with adjectives with respect to the phenomena just outlined. First, they do not license Case on their complements:

(75) Susan [$_{VP}$ proved the theorem].
(76) *[$_{NP}$ Susan's proof the theorem]

Second, the strategy of inserting a semantically null preposition is available. Example (76), like (71), is salvaged by *of*-insertion:

(77) Susan's proof of the theorem

Additionally, though, when subject position of the NP is not already occupied, movement into that position is often available for the complement of the head N, a process reminiscent of that seen in passive sentences such as (68) above:

(78) The theorem's proof
(derived from [$_{NP}$ — proof [$_{NP}$ the theorem]]).

Of the four major lexical categories V, N, A, and P, V and P pattern together (as opposed to N and A) with respect to licensing Case on a complement, while N and A pattern together in triggering *of*-insertion. The lexical categories can be analyzed as bundles of values for binary (two-way) "distinctive features" in such a way as to capture these various properties.

(79) V [+v, −n]
N [−v, +n]
A [+v, +n]
P [−v, −n]

The "Case-licensing" lexical categories are those specified $-n$. The triggers for *of*-insertion are those specified $+n$. Since passivized verbs neither license normal Case nor trigger *of*-insertion, the formal representation of their "neutralized" status is as a $+v$ category with no specification at all for n:

(80) Passivized verb [+v]

VII. LOGICAL FORM

There are languages, such as Chinese and Japanese, in which interrogative WH-words are not fronted, as they are in English, but remain *in situ* in their D-structure positions. The Chinese sentence (81) contrasts with its English translation in this way:

(81) [ni renwei [ta weisheme meiyou lai]].
you think he why not come
(82) Why do you think [he didn't come *t*].

Even though *weisheme* remains in its original position in the embedded clause, (81) is interpreted as a direct question, like (82). Thus, the interpretation is just as if *weisheme* had moved. Further, the locality effects on movement discussed earlier also seem operational for WHs *in situ* under certain circumstances. For example, when *weisheme* is inside a complex NP, it cannot be interpreted outside of that island, precisely mirroring the island effect on WH-movement:

(83) *ni xiangxin [$_{NP}$[$_{S}$ Lisi weisheme lai] de shuofa].
you believe Lisi why come claim
(84) *Why do you believe [$_{NP}$ the claim [$_{S}$ that Lisi came *t*]].

[The relevant (and unavailable) construal here concerns the reason for Lisi's coming.] This suggests that (81) and (83), like (82) and (84), respectively, do involve movement, though a kind of movement that has no effects on the phonetic form of the utterances. Given the organization of the grammar in (34), that kind of movement is not possible. But a modification introducing the component of logical form (LF) allows for the possibility of "abstract" movement that does not feed into PF:

(85)
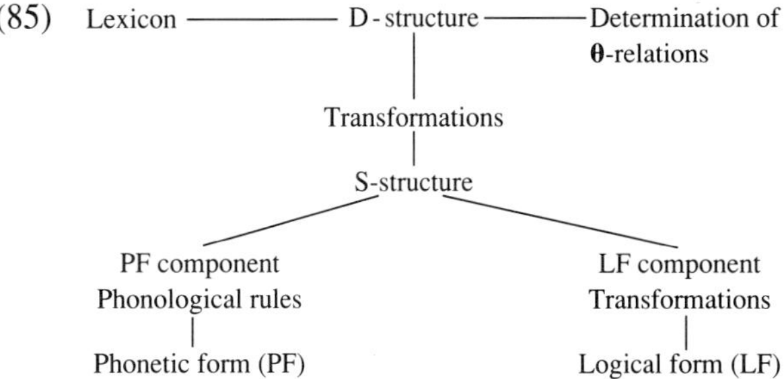

PF and LF specify aspects of sound and meaning, respectively, insofar as they are linguistically determined. [Even θ-relations can be "read off" LF, given that movement processes leave behind traces.]

Transformations do or do not have phonetically overt consequences depending on whether they operate between D-structure and S-structure (as in the English WH-movement examples above) or between S-structure and LF (as in the Chinese examples). As before, language variation of this kind can be stated as a parameter. This parameter distinguishes the languages at the level of S-structure, but at the LF level of representation, in both types of language the interrogative word will be in the position where its semantic scope is determined. The scope of an interrogative "operator" can be an entire utterance, as in the examples considered so far, or it can be just an embedded sentence, as in (86):

(86) John wonders [what Bill bought].

Example (86) is not a question, but it contains within it an "embedded question." The scope of *what* in this instance is the embedded sentence. In a language without overt WH-movement, the same scope effects arise. In (87), *sheme* ("what") is *in situ*, but its scope is the embedded sentence:

(87) Zhangsan xiang-zhidao [Lisi mai-le sheme].
Zhangsan wonder Lisi buy what
Zhangsan wonders [what Lisi bought]
(Zhangsan wonders for which x, x a thing, Lisi bought x)

LF is the level of representation where this semantic parallelism is expressed.

The semantic notion "in the scope of" thus has structural instantiation at the level of LF. This structural instantiation is characterized in terms of the relation "c(onstituent)-command" defined in (88):

(88) A constituent α *c-commands* a constituent β if and only if α does not dominate β, and every ϕ that dominates α also dominates β.

In (89), A c-commands B, C, and D; B c-commands A; C c-commands D; and D c-commands C. No other c-command relations hold.

(89)

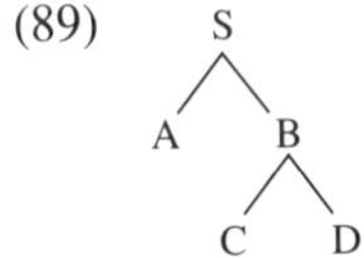

A fronted WH-phrase c-commands the clause that it takes as its scope. Similarly, it has been argued that the scope of a quantifier is determined by an LF operation called quantifier raising (QR), which adjoins a quantificational expression to S, leaving behind a trace. The S-structure of (90) is mapped onto an LF like (91):

(90) John likes everyone.
(91) $[_S$ [everyone] $[_S$ John likes t]]

The interpretation of (91) is then straightforward:

(92) For all x, x a person, John likes x.

"Scope ambiguities," such as that in (93), receive a simple characterization in these terms.

(93) Every student solved one problem.

The relative heights of the raised quantifiers at LF determine the particular quantificational meaning that is assigned to the sentence. Example (94) represents the reading where every student solved some problem or other, and (95) the reading where there is a particular problem that every student solved. [Identical integer subscripts are assigned to a moved item and its trace.]

(94) $[_S$ [every student]$_1$ $[_S$ [one problem]$_2$ $[_S$ t_1 solved t_2]]]
(95) $[_S$ [one problem]$_2$ $[_S$ [every student]$_1$ $[_S$ t_1 solved t_2]]]

VIII. BINDING THEORY

Among the imaginable "anaphoric relations" (relations of referential dependence) among NPs, some are possible, some are necessary, and still others are proscribed, depending on the nature of the NPs involved and the syntactic configurations in which they occur. For example, in (96), *him* can take *John* as its "antecedent," while in (97) it cannot. [The antecedent of an expression E is another expression from which E picks up its reference.]

(96) John said Mary criticized him.
(97) John criticized him.

That is, (97) has no reading corresponding to that of (98), with the pronoun *him* replaced by the "anaphor" *himself.*

(98) John criticized himself.

Apparently, a pronoun cannot have an antecedent that is "too close" to it. In (96), where antecedence is possible, a clause boundary intervenes between pronoun and antecedent. There is no such boundary between pronoun and antecedent in (97). Thus, the presence of a clause boundary between pronoun and antecedent puts them far enough apart to allow a relation of referential dependence.

Distance in this sense does not always suffice to make antecedence possible. In (99), a clause boundary intervenes between *he* and *John,* yet an anaphoric connection is still impossible.

(99) He said Mary criticized John.

Importantly, it is not the linear relation between pronoun and name that inhibits anaphora. This is evident from consideration of (100), in which *he* once again precedes *John,* yet anaphora is possible.

(100) After he entered the room, John sat down.

Similarly, in (101), *his* can take *John* as its antecedent.

(101) His boss criticized John.

The generalization covering (99) to (101) is approximately as in (102):

(102) A pronoun cannot take an element of its c-command domain as its antecedent. [The c-command domain of an item is everything that that item c-commands.]

In (99), the c-command domain of the subject pronoun is the entire sentence. Since the putative antecedent is included in that domain, the anaphoric interpretation is inconsistent with the generalization (102). In (100), on the other hand, the domain of the pronoun is the adverbial clause, which does not include the antecedent *John*. Similarly, in (101), the domain of the pronoun is the subject NP, *his boss,* which does not include *John*.

Supposing that referential dependence is represented in terms of coindexing with identical subscripts, the essence of (102) is as stated in (103) to (105).

(103) *α binds β* if α c-commands β and α, β are coindexed.
(104) If β is not bound, then β is free.
(105) An "r-expression" (fully referential expression—not a pronoun or an anaphor) must be free.

According to (105), often called Condition C of the Binding Theory because it was originally presented as the third of three conditions on anaphora, representation (106) of sentence (99) will correctly be excluded. By contrast, representations (107) and (108), of (100) and (101), respectively, will correctly be allowed.

(106) *He$_i$ said Mary criticized John$_i$.
(107) After he$_i$ entered the room, John$_i$ sat down.
(108) His$_i$ boss criticized John$_i$.

According to (105), (109) is permitted if $i \neq j$.

(109) He$_i$ said Mary criticized John$_j$.

Hence, an interpretation must be provided for the indexing in (109) that explicitly precludes the impossible interpretation. Principle (110) suffices in this case:

(110) If the index of α is distinct from the index of β, then neither α nor β is the antecedent of the other.

Principle (110) also plays a role in the account of (97), along with another binding constraint. The latter must allow (111) and disallow (112).

(111) John$_i$ criticized him$_j$.
(112) *John$_i$ criticized him$_i$.

Condition (105) cannot be generalized to include pronouns as bindees, since that would incorrectly preclude antecedence in (96) by disallowing representation (113).

(113) John$_i$ said Mary criticized him$_i$.

As noted earlier, there is a locality effect involved in this paradigm. A pronoun is able to be within the domain of its antecedent, hence, is allowed to have a binder, but must not be "too close" to it. Condition (114) is a rough statement of the necessary constraint ("Condition B" of the Binding Theory).

(114) A pronoun must be free in a local domain.

The relevant local domain is approximately the minimal clause containing the pronoun. Note that a pronoun can have an antecedent in its clause just as long as that antecedent does not c-command it. In (115), *John's* does not c-command *him* as the former is dominated by an NP, *John's boss,* that does not dominate the latter. Hence, (115) is a permissible representation:

(115) [John's$_i$ boss] criticized him$_i$.

"Anaphors," such as reflexives (*himself, myself,* etc.), and reciprocals (*each other, one another*), require antecedents which bind them. In this, their behavior is quite different from pronouns, which *may* have binding antecedents, but *need* not. Additionally, at least in English and a number of other languages, the antecedent of an anaphor must be local to the anaphor. In particular, we have (116), "Condition A" of the Binding Theory.

(116) An anaphor must be bound in a local domain.

Under the null hypothesis that the "local domain" is the same for Condition A and Condition B, complementarity is predicted between pronouns and anaphors with the same intended referent. This prediction is confirmed to a substantial degree. The ill-formed (112) becomes grammatical, if its bound pronoun is replaced by an anaphor, as in (117).

(117) John_i criticized himself_i.

Conversely, the well-formed (113) becomes bad, if its pronoun is replaced by an anaphor:

(118) *John_i said Mary criticized himself_i.

All that remains for this rough approximation is to specify the interpretation for coindexation. That is, it must be guaranteed that (117) cannot mean that John criticized Harry:

(119) If the index of α is identical to the index of β, then α is the antecedent of β or β is the antecedent of α.

Summarizing, there are three syntactic constraints, repeated as (120a–c), and two principles of interpretation, (110) and (119).

(120) a. An anaphor must be bound in a local domain.
b. A pronoun must be free in a local domain.
c. An r-expression must be free.

The binding conditions, along with the principles of interpretation, determine one aspect of meaning based directly on syntactic structure. The relevant structural representation is, in this case, one of derived structure, rather than D-structure. This can be seen in (121a), derived from (121b), for Condition A, and (122a), derived from (122b), for Condition C:

(121) a. They seem to each other [*t* to be clever].
b. __ seem to each other [they to be clever].

(122) a. [Which of John's teachers] does he admire most *t*?
b. He admires [which of John's teacher's] most.

In (121a), *they* has raised into the subject position of the main sentence. In this position, it can provide an antecedent for the anaphor *each other,* whereas in the pre-raising representation, (121b), the antecedent fails to c-command the anaphor. In (122a), the r-expression *John's* is free, and, as expected, *John's* can serve as the antecedent of *he*. However, in the D-structure (122b), *he* binds *John's,* in apparent violation of Condition C, just as in the ill-formed (123):

(123) *He_1 admires one of John's_1 teachers most.

D-structure is, thus, not the level of representation relevant to the determination of anaphoric relations. Rather, a derived level, S-structure or LF is. The null hypothesis is that LF, the "interface level" with semantics, determines these, along with other, aspects of linguistic meaning, just as the PF interface level determines interpretation in terms of the motor–perceptual system.

Bibliography

Baker, C. L. (1989). "English Syntax." MIT Press, Cambridge, MA.

Baltin, M., and Kroch, A. (1989). "Alternative Conceptions of Phrase Structure." University of Chicago Press, Chicago.

Chomsky, N. (1986). "Knowledge of Language: Its Nature, Origin, and Use." Praeger, New York.

Chomsky, N. (1988). "Language and Problems of Knowledge." MIT Press, Cambridge, MA.

Chomsky, N., and Lasnik, H. (in press). The theory of principles and parameters. In "Syntax: An International Handbook of Contemporary Research." (J. Jacobs *et al.,* Eds). Walter de Gruyter, Berlin.

Cowper, E. A. (1992). "A Concise Introduction to Syntactic Theory." University of Chicago Press, Chicago.

Freidin, R. (1992). "Foundations of Generative Syntax." MIT Press, Cambridge, MA.

Gazdar, G., Klein, E., Pullum, G., and Sag, I. (1985). "Generalized Phrase Structure Grammar." Harvard University Press, Cambridge, MA.

Jacobson, P., and Pullum, G. (Eds.) (1982). "The Nature of Syntactic Representation." Kluwer, Dordrecht.

Lasnik, H., and Uriagereka, J. (1988). "A Course in GB Syntax." MIT Press, Cambridge, MA.

McCawley, J. D. (1988). "The Syntactic Phenomena of English." University of Chicago Press, Chicago.

Sells, P. (1985). "Lectures on Contemporary Syntactic Theories." Center for the Study of Language and Information, Stanford.

Wood, M. M. (1993). "Categorial Grammars." Routledge, New York.

Tactile Perception

Daniel W. Smothergill
Syracuse University

Glossary

Amodal Information specified by more than one perceptual modality or across several modalities.

Haptic Actively touching for the purpose of gathering information.

Introspection Using one's own conscious experience to understand a psychological process.

Local feature A part of an object in contrast to the object as a whole.

Meissner corpuscles Tactile receptors located in papillary tissues.

Optacon A device that converts print into a tactile pattern on the finger.

TACTILE PERCEPTION is a relatively small field of research that is both self-contained and infused thoroughly with the concepts, procedures, and questions characterizing the study of perception at large. It is often turned to by scholars from outside the field itself for answers to questions about the nature and origins of knowledge. It is also of great practical interest to designers of aids and prostheses for persons with visual and hearing disabilities. The basic organization of tactile perception is still a matter of great debate.

I. RELATION TO GENERAL ISSUES IN PERCEPTION

Tactile perception is often appealled to in debates over grand theoretical questions. The great 17th century philosophers, for example, questioned whether a person born blind but suddenly made able to see would recognize by vision the world he had come to know by touch. The British Empiricists believed that the answer was no; they argued that the patently qualitative difference between tactile and visual sensations would require that such a person learn to associate vision with touch before being able to see. Johannes Muller's doctrine of specific nerve energies was a 19th century affirmation of the Empiricist's view. The same school, strongly impressed by the immediacy and apparent certainty of knowledge gained by touch, also advanced the principle that "touch teaches vision" in the development of perception.

A contemporary instance of tactile perception being discussed in a larger theoretical arena recently arose in the psychology of pictures. Phenomenally, pictures seem to possess a strong visual quality. The very expression "picturing in the mind" suggests an experience that is visual-like without something actually being seen. Not surprisingly, most psychological analyses of pictures have taken as their point of departure the visual world of objects and events. Recently, however, several investigators have expressed strong doubts about the visual nature of pictures. These researchers have demonstrated quite convincingly that at least some congenitally blind persons can produce *haptic pictures:* Raised line drawings that when looked at by sighted persons are recognized immediately as depictions of objects and scenes.

Reports of visually recognizable drawings by the blind have appeared sporadically for the past 20 years or more. Recently, the issue has captured center stage as the result of a simple technology for making raised line drawings. Basically consisting of a plastic sheet stretched over a rubber-covered board, a raised line is produced when written on with a ballpoint pen. Drawings by some congenitally blind persons upon first using the device with little instruction are both visually recognizable by the sighted and tactually recognizable by the blind. Other blind persons have been found to require considerable practice with the device and it is by no means clear that all blind people can come to draw simply by being given enough practice. Of course, considerable individual differences exist in the drawing ability of sighted people as well. The important point is that the haptic pictures of the congenitally blind directly challenge the notion that pictures are vision-specific.

They pose a challenge for another popular idea as well. It is commonly believed that touch is a sense of momentary contact; that the kind of information available to touch is sharply constrained in time and space. This suggests as a corollary that the congenitally blind may not so much "perceive" haptic pictures as "understand" what they have touched by integrating a series of momentary percepts. Standing in direct opposition to this position is the testimony of congenitally blind persons themselves who, while claiming to understand quite well the different experiences of perceiving and understanding, say that they do indeed *perceive* haptic pictures. So, haptic pictures are a challenge not only to the idea that pictures are inherently visual but also to the idea that tactile perception is inherently serial and momentary.

These examples make clear that tactile perception has been studied for two kinds of reasons—one narrow and the other broad. Narrowly, tactile perception is a coherent field of research in its own right. More broadly, it is studied as part of inquiry into the general nature of perception and cognition. One group that has been especially interested in tactile perception in the broader sense has been child psychology researchers.

II. DEVELOPMENT

An important component of the explanations psychologists seek is increasingly seen as the process of development. Infancy, the beginning of development, has attracted considerable research in recent years and much that is new has been learned about tactile perception. The origins of this interest trace back to observations made by Jean Piaget of Geneva in the 1920s on the grasping, reaching, and touching of his own infants. These observations led Piaget to propose that hand and eye, beginning as independent sources of information about the world, become increasingly integrated over the course of the first 2 years with reaching and grasping ultimately coming under the control of vision. [*See* PERCEPTUAL DEVELOPMENT.]

Piaget's empirical results have been reasonably well replicated over the years, but new findings have emerged that cast considerable doubt on his developmental theory of touch and vision. Perhaps most importantly, the newer observations reveal the existence of a nascent eye–hand integration much earlier than previously thought. Indeed, film records taken over the *first weeks* of life reveal coordinated patterns of visually initiated reaching and grasping. To be sure, these efforts are rarely successful. Targets are actually contacted infrequently and almost never grasped. Yet the behavior is clearly organized. Reaching is initiated by objects that attract visual fixation; it differs clearly in form from the random flailing about of the limbs. Reaches are also directed toward objects; they are not simply directionless arm movements triggered by visual targets. Some researchers have even reported evidence of *anticipatory hand shaping* preparatory to grasping. It seems fair to say that none of these observations squares easily with the standard Piagetian account.

Surprisingly, early reaching typically declines after the first month or so then seems to disappear for awhile. Several months later, it reappears and 4- to 5-month olds will reach successfully for both stationary and moving targets. Indeed, frame-by-frame analyses of videotapes indicate that babies quickly come to aim their reaches at the point at which the hand will make contact with a moving object rather than at the object's location at the time a reach is initiated. Also, the hand can be observed opening during the reach and beginning to close around the target at the moment of interception. All of this suggests that a highly sophisticated system is in place at a very young age.

The full explanation for the developmental course of events observed over the course of infancy in reaching and grasping is by no means clear, but two broad conceptualizations of development have relevance. First, and contrasting directly with Piaget, touch and vision may be relatively *undifferentiated* in the newborn. Instead of beginning as separate channels that become integrated over the course of development, touch and vision may initially be fused together and only become differentiated with development. This idea is suggested directly by observations of infants' perception of related events in vision and touch and by a general theory which claims that early ontogenesis is characterized by a *unity of the senses*. The modality-specificity of perception so taken for granted by adults, according to this theory, is the developmental product of a process that begins in infancy.

Second, the key to the disappearance and later reappearance of reaching and grasping may lie in the substantial increase in arm mass that occurs over the course of the first few months after birth. As the arm becomes heavier, whatever control that was once possessed over its movement would be expected to decline until the musculature of the arm, shoulder, and related structures become strong enough to permit the regaining of control. This general type of explanation belongs to *dynamical systems theory*, a theory whose successes in accounting for the development of self-produced locomotion has encouraged its extension to the development of reaching.

The similarities between walking and reaching are quite striking. Both are visually guided. The close dependence of walking on vision may be appreciated by the fact that walking is often delayed in blind babies. Also, walking, like reaching, can be observed in rudimentary form for a short period soon after birth—in the stepping reflex—which too disappears. Like the arms, the legs also undergo a relatively large increase in mass coincident with the disappearance of the early form of organization.

Dynamical systems theory encourages the search for those parameters of a system on which a change in magnitude or scale brings about a change in the events within the system: the sequence, for example, of stepping being present (reflex), then absent, then present again in the form of walking. Changes in leg mass and its related musculature are parameters that seem to control this sequence. It seems quite possible that the same parameters might control the development of reaching and grasping.

A related perspective on the development of tactile perception comes from observations obtained on infants under conditions in which an object is placed in the hand when it is out of sight. Prior to 3 months, stereotyped closure movements of the hand, unadapted to the object itself, are typically observed. With further development, attempts to bring the object into view are observed but tactual exploration of the object itself is rare. Not until about 5 months is the object grasped and explored tactually without the accompaniment of visual inspection. A primacy of touch hypothesis would find little encouragement in these findings. Rather, infants seem to use touch to facilitate seeing.

Do infants recognize objects tactually? The most widely used method by which this question has been studied is the *familiarization* procedure. Simply, an object is presented for inspection several times in succession (for either a fixed duration or until the infant loses interest). Immediately thereafter the original object and a new object are presented, either together or successively, and the amount of time the infant spends inspecting each is recorded. If the infant detects no difference between the objects, no basis exists for one receiving more attention than the other. Conversely, more time spent on one than the other would mean that the two were not perceived as the same; that some difference between them was detected.

Studies using such methods indicate that by 12 months infants can discriminate among a large number of shapes by touch (e.g., circles, squares, stars, spheres, etc.). Moreover, by the same age they can discriminate cross-modally. For example, if a square is presented *tactually* and then the infant is presented *visually* with a square and a circle chances are good that by 12 months the infant would look longer at the circle. Such findings, it has been noted, are consistent with the theory of early unity of the senses. Results are more mixed and research less extensive on cross-modal shape perception in infants much younger than 12 months.

An important caution in interpreting familiarization studies: The fact that two shapes can be distinguished between does not mean that either can be perceived veridically. Consider, for example, the finding that 12-month olds have been found to discriminate a circle from a square by touch. That is, 12-month olds will pay more attention to the novel stimulus than the familiar stimulus regardless of whether it is the circle or square that is novel or familiar. Notice that this finding does not in itself indicate the basis for making the discrimination. One possibility is that infants do in fact perceive squares and circles accurately by touch and that they use this ability in discriminating the familiar from novel.

An alternative possibility, however, is that the basis on which the familiar and novel are discriminated is some *local feature*. A machine analogy may be useful here. A machine might categorize objects into two groups on the basis of presence or absence of sharp angles. Such a machine would discriminate circles from squares flawlessly, though it would fail the task of categorizing squares and triangles.

Surprisingly little consideration is given this issue in the by now large literature of familiarization studies of infant perception. It may be speculated that the reason, in part, is related to the very compelling nature of visual shape to adults. Quite simply, it is hard for a sighted adult while looking at an object under normal conditions not to perceive its shape. Given that the vast majority of infant familiarization studies are conducted *visually*, this does little to encourage consideration of local feature hypotheses. *Tactual* familiarization studies, by the same token, may provide something of a corrective here. The common introspection of sighted adults that touch is momentary would tend to make a local features interpretation seem more plausible.

In addition to studies of shape perception, scattered studies can be found on infants' tactual sensitivity to *texture, hardness, volume, temperature*, and *weight*. These studies have often been motivated by questions other than the development of tactile perception per se. Their results consequently hint more about the development of touch than suggest firm conclusions. Nevertheless, as is often the case in tactile perception, intriguing results abound. Consider, for example, the difference between perceiving two ends of one object versus two separate objects. Imagine that while your hands are out of sight a ring is placed in each of them. You are encouraged to move your hands in any way you like so long as your grip is maintained on each ring. If the two rings happen to be connected by a rigid bar, your perceptual experience would likely be that of holding a single object in your two hands since any movement of one of the hands (rings) would be accompanied by a compensating movement of the other. In contrast, movements of one hand (ring) would have no consequences for the other if the two rings were unconnected. Your experience in that case would likely be that two separate objects were being held. A recent familiarization study conducted along these lines found that 4-month olds discriminate the difference between the connected and unconnected conditions. Interestingly, these tactile findings parallel others obtained with vision. Hence, it is possible that an understanding of "objectness" may be present very early in infancy; an understanding that may well be *amodal* in the sense of being independent of any particular perceptual modality.

In research with children, the speed of learning a two-choice discrimination has been compared under tactual, visual, and visual–tactual modes of presentation. In general, faster learning occurs with vision than touch and the combination of the two does not result in improvement over vision alone. This pattern seems to hold across a wide range of ages in childhood. Child psychologists have also studied the ability to feel an unseen object and identify it verbally or select a visual match. Children ages 3 and 4 years typically perform such tasks by moving their hands over the object in a highly unsystematic and irregular manner. Not surprisingly, their ability to identify the object or select a visual match is poor. Somewhat older children explore manually in a more thorough and systematic manner; they also do better at identifying and selecting a visual match. The older the child the more the search is systematic and thorough. Notably older children go back over parts already touched and actively seek out distinguishing features, a pattern that often indicates hypothesis testing.

Information of many kinds is available to touch and some information may be most easily detected by touch. Automobile body inspectors, for example, use touch to judge the smoothness of a surface as do carpenters in working on a piece of wood. Some developmental research has been conducted on sensitivity to the various dimensions of tactile information. Some investigators have asked whether children prefer to discriminate objects on the basis of texture or shape when both are tactually available. In general, school-age children are found to prefer shape over texture even when differences in shape are relatively small compared to differences in texture. Younger children's judgments, in contrast, seem more determined by the degree to which objects differ on a dimension. Kindergartners in one study who discriminated objects on the basis of texture rather than shape showed a greater tendency to discriminate on the basis of shape when texture differences were minor. Hence, haptics—the use of tactile sensitivity—depends not only on the task, and the competing features of the object, but also on biases that may be present at different phases of development.

III. TWO WORLDS OF TOUCH

A distinction is often drawn between "active" and "passive" touch. How touch is *used* in extracting information from the environment is regarded as principally a matter of active touch. Accordingly, most of the topics discussed so far would be classified as instances of active touch. Passive touch, in contrast, refers more to the properties and organization of both the skin and its receptor structures in transmitting sensations to higher levels of the nervous system. The distinction is far from absolute and its significance has tended to blur in recent years, especially in more applied research. Yet it becomes quite plain in surveying the history of research on tactile perception that studies tend to tackle one or the other kind of touch (e.g., most studies of the receptors mediating touch focus on passive touch). Furthermore, it is also clear that the distinction runs deep. It shows up in differences among theorists in what is taken to be the fundamental nature of perception and how "good science" in psychology is best done; hard though it may be to believe that as seemingly innocuous a topic as tactile perception could be at the center of such debate! James J. Gibson, for example, was a leading proponent of the idea that active touch is the proper or natural domain of study. In formulating his "ecological" perception, Gibson held that passive touch is a comparatively minor and even artificial use of touch.

A major topic in the study of passive touch has been the nature of the various sensations arising from deformations of the static skin. It is often pointed out in this context that there have been many challenges over the years to Aristotle's fivefold classification of the senses (taste, vision, smell, hearing, and touch). Critics of this framework typically advocate the partitioning of touch into subcomponents. Pressure, vibration, pain, warmth, and cold have frequently been identified as discrete sensations subsumed under touch. Also, a number of anatomically different cutaneous end organs lying beneath the skin have been identified. These include, in the superficial layers of the skin, Meissner's corpuscles, Merkel disks, and Ruffini cylinders. At a somewhat deeper level are Pacinian corpuscles. A reasonable hypothesis then might be that the various sensations comprising touch are mediated by these end organs; perhaps a one-to-one relation between kinds of sensations and types of end organs. Considerable research has been done on this hypothesis, but relatively little support has been found for it. More encouraging has been research aimed at isolating *functional* receptor systems by means of psychophysical procedures used in conjunction with recordings from cutaneous nerves. Whether discrete sensations in the classical sense are implicated directly in this research is a matter of some dispute, but the technique has yielded important findings. For example, four discrete receptor systems responsive to mechanical stimulation have been found in the palm of the hand. Moreover, each receptor system seems primarily linked to either Meissner's corpuscles, Merkel disks, Ruffini cylinders, or Pacinian corpuscles. There is some suggestion of particular sensations associated with particular systems (e.g., *vibration* seems associated with the system having Pacinian corpuscles as primary neural structures) but linkages of this sort are far from clear. One system, for example, meets all psychophysical criteria as a discrete, functional system, yet seems to produce no specific sensation.

Nerve impulses originating at the receptor level eventually arrive at the somatosensory cortex of the brain. Beginning in the 1930s, researchers have studied how the body is mapped onto the somatosensory cortex. That is, given that the index finger on the left hand is stimulated, what particular location in the somatosensory cortex responds? The map that this research has produced is notable in several respects. First, in partial *isomorphism,* the topology of bodily parts is often preserved at the cortical level. A picture of the various cortical sites that respond when the left index finger is stimulated in various places has roughly the shape of the left index finger. The same is also true for the hand as a whole, the foot, tongue, genitals, etc.

Second, the overall cortical organization of bodily parts is based more on function than proximity. Although, as noted, the cortical representation of the thumb corresponds to the actual thumb the "cortical thumb" is next to the "cortical eye" and an overall cortical picture would *not* look at all like a picture of the body.

Third, the amount of cortical area given over to any bodily part reflects the number of receptors it contains rather than its physical size. The thumb alone gets much more cortical space than all of the back, and the thumb is indeed much more highly innervated than the back.

Research in passive and active touch often proceeds in quite separate directions with little real interaction between the two. The exception is often found in more practical and applied areas; notably, in the design of tactile devices for assisting people with visual or aural disabilities. Collaboration makes good sense here because the design of such devices must take into account both the mechanical aspects of touch and how information is extracted from the world by touch. Moreover, an additional bonus of such work has been to highlight areas in which important knowledge is lacking. Several examples of such devices will serve to illustrate the practical uses to which knowledge about tactile perception has been put.

IV. AIDS AND PROSTHESES

The most familiar example to most people, if only by name, is the braille system of reading by touch. Invented by Louis Braille in the 19th century, braille is a code of raised dots in a field of six locations defined by three rows and two columns. A dot can be present or absent in any one location independent of the others giving rise to 64 distinct patterns. Each letter of the alphabet is assigned one of these patterns with punctuation marks making up some of the rest. Patterns unassigned in either of these ways are used in a more advanced form of braille (Grade II) to signify groups of letters having a high frequency of occurrence in English.

Braille has gained widespread acceptance. It is the "industry standard," so to speak, in an increasingly wide range of communication contexts; in elevators, for example, to designate floor numbers. A variety of devices also now permit the blind both computer access and braille output. These technologies greatly enhance the opportunities for blind people in education, work, and becoming integrated within the larger society.

Two disadvantages of braille should be noted. First, reading braille (touch) is relatively slow compared to reading print (vision). Although individual differences are large (some highly skilled braille readers are as fast as sighted persons reading print aloud), a good braille reader scans at about a third the rate of a normal sighted person reading print. An obvious candidate in accounting for this difference is provided by the notion of perceptual field: how much or little can be taken in at any one time. Intuitively, the field of vision would seem much *wider* than the field of touch. We are able to see many things at once but only a single thing (or part of a thing) can be touched at one time. This difference is sometimes rendered as vision is "parallel" and touch is "serial." Taken to an extreme, it may even suggest that it is a mistake to refer to the "field of touch" as though analogous to the field of vision because touch, by its nature, would be restricted to what the fingers are directly in contact with at any moment.

Although attractive in some respects, this analysis is ultimately unsatisfying because it is clear that perception in any modality is not simply a matter of a series of momentary contacts between individual receptors and small elements of the physical world. Common objects placed in the passive hand are poorly recognized. Objects stabilized on the retina soon fade from view. Compelling as they may be, intuitions about touch based on moment-to-moment contacts between receptors and physical energies should probably be resisted.

An alternative reason for the difference in speed between reading braille and reading print is the nature of the code. In braille, the code is basically binary. Each letter and punctuation mark is specified by some unique combination of the presence or absence of a dot in each of six locations. As such, braille is a logical system, inherently no more suited for perception by hand than by eye. Print is quite different. Although its origins are unclear, print was certainly not the creation of an individual intent on manufacturing a logically clean system. Rather, print characters and the differences among them were shaped over the course of centuries of human usage. This is an important consideration because it implies that the particular features and combinations of features defining print came about at least in part in response to constraints imposed by vision as a perceptual system. In contrast, constraints peculiar to touch played no comparable role in the development of braille as a code (other than the fact that the dots are raised from the background). The suggestion, then, is that one reason print can be read faster than braille is that the compatibility of print with vision may be greater than that of braille with touch.

Conventional reading is sometimes referred to as visible speech, an act braille permits blind persons to engage in by substituting the hand for the eye. Analogously, conventional talking may be regarded as aural speech, an act sign language allows deaf persons to engage in by substituting the hand for the ear. If, as it has been argued here, the nonnatural origins of braille make it a less than optimal code for reading by hand, might there be a parallel in speaking by hand: that is, a nonnatural code that limits functioning in some respect? Recent reports hint of as much.

First, there is a sign code that developed naturally among members of the deaf community in the United States (despite strong disapproval from most authorities on deafness who for years advocated lip reading). It is American Sign Language (ASL), now recognized as a true language possessing all the linguistic complexity of spoken English. The syntax and grammar of ASL are quite different from those of standard English; they are realized more by the *location* of the hand and the dynamics of its movements (befitting a language revealed in spatial gestures) than by sequencing (as in English). [*See* SIGN LANGUAGE.]

Signed English, another sign code, is distinctly different. It did not evolve naturally within the deaf community, but was deliberately created to be isomorphic with spoken English. In contrast to ASL, the syntax, grammar, and lexicon of Signed English map directly onto spoken English. Proponents point out that this makes Signed English easier for the nondeaf to learn: a decided benefit for the deaf in dealing with a world predominantly made up of hearing people.

A significant part of the deaf community is reported to have a strong preference for ASL over Signed English (few, apparently, prefer Signed English to ASL). Complaints about Signed English allude to its "unnaturalness" and lack of "feeling right." Some deaf persons actively resist the use of Signed English: this despite the participation it permits in the majority culture. To be sure, there may be many reasons for the preference for ASL, not the least of which being a sense among the deaf of it being "ours." Yet it would probably be unwise to overlook the significance of the fact that Signed English is essentially a transliteration of a code that developed naturally through use by ear and voice into a eye–hand system.

Besides being read relatively slowly, braille has the additional disadvantage of requiring the manufacture of special books, information panels, computers, etc. This comes at considerable expense as well as limiting widespread availability. Both problems are overcome by devices that provide on-line translation of print into vibrotactile patterns. The Optacon (optical to tactile converter) is an example of such a device. It allows a blind person to read ordinary text by converting an image of the text into a 5 × 20 tactile duplicate on the pad of the index finger. The reader simply moves her index finger along the printed text.

The Optacon eliminates the expense of manufacturing and purchasing materials in braille. It is also portable. A disadvantage is that reading rates are slow; slower even than with static, raised braille on a card. Yet some blind persons are adamant in their support of the Optacon, citing the freedom that comes from being able to read ordinary printed matter.

A step beyond the Optacon is TVSS; the tactile–visual substitution system first introduced in the 1970s. A camera held by either the observer or another person is aimed at various targets producing an image that is translated into a 20 × 20 matrix of tactile vibrators on the back of the observer. Initial reports were quite optimistic. Both blind and sighted observers with some training seemed able to recognize some common objects and performance seemed better when the camera was controlled by the observer—a kind of active touch—rather than stationary—a kind of passive touch. Moreover, there were intriguing reports that some observers came to perceive objects as "out there," in the space surrounding the observer, rather than as impressions on the skin. Indeed, one observer was reported to have moved quickly out of the way when an object was made to appear to loom toward him by rapidly adjusting a zoom lens.

Early enthusiasm for TVSS has waned considerably. Designed as an experimental system, TVSS was not portable. The observer sat in a large chair on the back of which an array of vibrators was mounted. A more serious problem was that the internal details of objects proved difficult to perceive, even by highly trained observers. It seems plausible that the information presented to the tactual system—in this case firings of electronically controlled vibrators in response to a visual signal—was less than ideal. Some investigators have concluded that the limitations of TVSS make a strong case for the need for more basic devices facilitating tactile perception.

Speech is another topic that has attracted the interest of researchers from both the passive and active perspectives on tactile perception. The origins of this interest can be traced to a practical problem; whether the deaf and hard of hearing might be able to perceive speech by the skin. Gault carried out pioneering studies in the 1920s by having speakers talk into a long hollow tube held against the palm of a listener whose hearing had been masked. Results were encouraging. Evidence was obtained that some sentences, words, and even syllables could be discriminated in this way. Phonemes, however, proved very difficult to discriminate because, it is now understood, the temporal resolving power of the skin (which reaches no higher than 600–700 Hz) is insufficient for the high-frequency discriminations phonemes require (more than 3000 Hz).

One approach to this problem has sought to transform the frequency range of the auditory signal to the range of the skin's sensitivity. There have been several attempts to map different speech frequencies (e.g., 500–1000, 1000–3000, 3000–5000, 5000–10,000 Hz) onto different spatial locations of the skin, such as each channel being relayed to a single finger via vibrators.

Observers in such experiments often find the simultaneous activation of several vibrators confusing. Interactions occur among the stimulated locations so that the ability to resolve the signal at any single location is impeded. In general, efforts based on transforming the speech signal have had mixed success, with some combinations of mappings and skin locations found superior to others for reasons that are unclear. Although it seems reasonable to assume that a considerable degree of practice might be needed with any transformation, the role of practice has recieved little systematic study.

Another use of the skin to obtain speech is the Tadoma method—a marked contrast to approaches to the tactile preception of speech in which the auditory signal is broken up into parts and each part relayed to a unique skin location. Introduced to the United States in the 1920s for use by the deaf–blind, the Tadoma method has the perceiver simply place a hand on the speaker's face. This is the method by which Helen Keller came to be able not only to perceive speech but to produce it as well. Some deaf–blind individuals have become quite proficient at perceiving speech in this way, but for others it has been ineffective. Again, the role of practice seems important but has received little research attention. Indeed, systematic research on *any* aspect of the Tadoma method is sparse.

The fact that the Tadoma method is successful at all raises the question of precisely what information the skilled Tadoma perceiver detects. Movements of the lips and jaws in dynamic interaction would seem a likely candidate, but whatever it is the remarkable lesson from the Tadoma method is the fact that speech can be perceived in this way at all. The fact that it can be directly challenges the assumption, common to virtually all evolutionary accounts of language, that speech developed in concert with audition. The clear implication of Tadoma is that normal speech can be perceived bereft of any speficially auditory component. James Gibson often emphasized the concept of *amodal* information in arguing that at least some aspects of perception are based on information that is not tied to any particular sensory modality. Perhaps Tadoma is to be understood in this way, and haptic pictures as well. Both suggest that tactile perception may be more a *way* of acquiring information than a particular *kind* of information.

Bibliography

Bushnell, E. W., and Boudreau, J. P. (1991). The development of haptic perception during infancy. In "The Psychology of Touch" (M. A. Heller and W. Schiff, Eds.). Erlbaum, Hillsdale, NJ.

Kennedy, J. M. (1993). "Drawing & the Blind: Pictures to Touch." Yale University Press, New Haven, CT.

Sacks, O. (1989). "Seeing Voices." University of California Press, Berkley, CA.

Trevarthen, C. (1982). Basic patterns of psychogenetic change in infancy. In "Regressions in Mental Development" (T. G. Bever, Ed.). Erlbaum, Hillsdale, NJ.

Warren, D. H. (1982). The development of haptic perception. In "Tactual Perception: A Sourcebook" (W. Schiff and E. Foulke, Eds.). Cambridge University Press, New York.

TASTE

Ronald Drozdenko
NeuroCommunication Research Laboratories, Inc. and Western Connecticut State University

Curt Weinstein
NeuroCommunication Research Laboratories, Inc.

Glossary

Chemical senses Sensory systems, such as taste and olfaction, which can detect certain chemicals in the environment provided that the chemicals are in a suitable form (e.g., solution).

Neural code of taste A construct based on the premise that the perception of taste is an integration of neural activity originating from different sources in the sensory system.

Palatability A pleasurable response to food, measured behaviorally or with rating scales, which is affected by sensory (including taste), behavioral, and physiological factors.

Taste buds The receptor organs of taste located near the surface of oral structures which contain a collection of chemoreceptor cells.

Taste psychophysics Methods that determine the levels at which taste stimuli can be detected, identified, or discriminated.

TASTE, also referred to as gustation, is a chemical sense which is dependent on receptors located in the oral cavity, especially on the tongue. Four taste qualities, sweet, salty, sour, and bitter, have been identified in humans. Taste is part of a complex physiological and behavioral system which monitors the intake of food.

I. CONCEPTS OF TASTE

There is a distinction between popular notions of "taste" and taste from the perspective of sensory psychology or physiology. Popular and some applied notions of taste also incorporate the senses of olfaction (smell) and somatosensation (touch). In fact, much of what is generally considered as taste is actually the sense of smell. The qualitative aspects of smell are considerable relative to taste qualities and often produce complex perceptions. Volatile molecules in foods reach the nose, mostly through the mouth, and stimulate this other chemical sense. A simple experiment to confirm this theory involves holding your nose closed while eating or, similarly, to monitor your perception of taste when you have blocked nasal passages. Many of the sensations associated with the experience of eating will be missing when the ability to smell is reduced. [*See* SENSE OF SMELL.]

Oral somatosensation also contributes to the experience that is often associated with taste. Nonchemical receptors in the mouth detect texture, consistency, and temperature. Pureed foods do not provide the same experience as the intact version and hot foods do not provide the same experience as cold foods. Studies also have shown that the sense of vision can affect the subjective experience of taste. "Off-colored" foods have been reported as being less desirable, and darker food coloring has been associated with more intense flavor. Additionally, emotional states can affect the subjective experience of taste. Foods taste better when the emotional content of eating is positive.

Therefore, the experience of eating generally associated with the word "taste" is actually a complex interaction of the taste qualities with other senses and the affective state.

II. SIGNIFICANCE OF THE SENSE OF TASTE

There has been considerable speculation on the evolutionary significance of taste. Generally, taste is considered part of a food selection system allowing the organism to sample and accept or reject substances. There is some evidence of innate preferences for certain of the four taste qualities and a rejection of others.

The preference for sweet may have evolved from the need to recognize and to select carbohydrates. Human infants have been reported to suck more when sweet liquids are placed in the mouth as compared to unsweetened water. Facial expressions characterized as reflecting enjoyment and increased autonomic response have been associated with sweet stimuli in newborns. Studies have also found that infants have a higher consumption of water when it is sweetened and tend to prefer the highest concentrations of sugar. Based on these findings there is speculation that the evolution of a "sweet detector" increased the probability of suckling and consequently survival.

Homeostasis of the cell is dependent on sodium balance, consequently, a preference for salt is theorized to have evolved from a need to maintain this balance. Both low levels and high levels of salt are undesirable. However, salt consumption in humans (and some other animals) does not show a clear preference or aversion, but rather a developmental pattern. While newborns show no clear preference for salt and possibly an aversion to it, older infants (4–24 months) have been found to ingest significantly more saline solution than water. Older children (3–6 years) reject saline solutions, as do adults, but prefer salted foods. Therefore, the evolutionary significance of a salt receptor based on innate responsiveness is inconclusive. [*See* HOMEOSTASIS.]

Similarly, early-life responses to sour and bitter tastants also yield inconclusive findings. Amounts ingested of sour and bitter solutions in human infants were found not to significantly differ from the amounts of water ingested. However, there are differences in the facial expressions of infants exposed to sour and bitter solutions. The sour stimuli have been reported to elicit pursed lips, blinking and nose wrinkling, while the bitter stimuli elicited arching of the mouth with the upper lip elevated. Both of these tastants are generally considered to be aversive. Since some poisons are bitter and sourness may indicate the presence of contaminated water, a predisposed aversion toward these stimuli seems consistent with an evolutionary perspective.

Possibly some of the difficulty in interpreting early-life responses to taste and the presence of four taste quality receptors in humans can be attributed to remnant systems which were carried over from other species. For example, some have speculated that salt detection as a primary taste quality in humans has developed from the importance of this receptor in our predecessors, the sea-inhabiting invertebrates.

While there is still controversy regarding the significance of the four taste qualities, there does seem to be a clear preference in early life for sweet substances.

III. BRIEF HISTORY OF THE FIELD

Bartoshuk has documented the history of taste research from ancient to modern times and traces early exploration of taste to the Greeks in the middle of the sixth century B.C. These early investigators thought that tiny pores in the tongue allowed taste stimuli to enter and be detected. Later Greek scholars attributed different tastes to different molecular shapes, and Aristotle developed a list of seven taste qualities. Four of the seven taste qualities proposed by Aristotle correspond with the accepted modern list. Also included in Aristotle's list were astringent, pungent, and harsh.

Galen (A.D. 130–200), considered the father of experimental physiology, attributed taste sensation to two "nerves." The first of these was the lingual (part of the trigeminal nerve) and the second a combination of the glossopharyngeal, vagus, and accessory cranial nerves. Today, sensory physiologists recognize that the chorda tympani (a branch of the facial nerve which enters the tongue with the lingual nerve), glossopharyngeal, and the vagus nerves subserve taste. Despite the errors in defining the specific qualitative, chemical, and physiological aspects of taste, the ancient researchers did provide a framework that is consistent with several modern concepts of taste.

Contributions in the 19th century started to clarify the role of specific cranial nerves in taste and the discovery of taste buds. Different taste buds were thought to have different taste sensitivities, and electrical stimulation of the tongue was found to produce the perception of taste. Psychophysics, the area of psychology that relates physical energy to sensation, also showed much development in the late 19th century and added to the understanding of taste. [*See* PSYCHOPHYSICS.]

Kiesow's classical studies of taste (1894–1898) included papillae sensitivity, adaptation, and interactions among taste qualities. Kiesow found, in agreement with work previously reported by Ohrwall, that the majority of papillae can mediate more than one taste quality. That is, there are no specific receptors for the taste qualities. Kiesow's work on adaptation indicated that, similar to other sensory receptors, taste receptors become less responsive with repeated stimulus exposure.

Kiesow's conclusions on the interactions among the taste qualities was controversial and not entirely supported by more recent research. He argued that taste acted like color vision, when colors are mixed the end perception results in a loss of the original colors. However, when tastants are mixed there is a retention of the original taste quality in most cases. Additionally, he hypothesized that the application of a tastant intensifies the perception of a subsequent tastant. More recent research indicates that this pattern of intensification is not universal.

Henning (1927) is most noted for presenting a tetrahedron with the four basic taste qualities (salt, sweet, bitter, sour) at the corners, two primaries (e.g., sweet–salty, sour–bitter) at the edges, and three primaries (e.g., salt–sweet–sour, bitter–sweet–sour) on the four triangular surfaces. Henning believed that taste was one modality and used the single figure (tetrahedron) as a way to express four qualities within one sense.

Hahn continued the work on primary taste qualities in the 1930s to 1940s by using psychophysical methods of adaptation, that is, the examination of the reduction of taste perception with continual stimulation. Hahn studied a number of factors related to adaptation such as temperature and cross-substance effects. Hahn examined cross-adaptation levels of substances with similar qualities (e.g., acids) and found that not all the substances which stimulate a particular quality cross-adapt. For example, of the salts Hahn tested none showed cross-adaptation.

Psychophysical methods are still widely used in taste studies. For example, researchers such as Booth and Bartoshuk have applied psychophysical techniques to a number of areas in taste research, such as preference and sensory mixture. Additionally, researchers such as Pfaffmann and Beidler have applied electrophysiological techniques to the study of taste. These techniques allow nerve impulses to be tracked during stimulation. Recordings have been taken from taste receptor cells and along points on the neural pathway to the brain. Because there is a lack of a clear relationship between taste stimuli and neural firing patterns of specific receptors, a multiple fiber coding mechanism is speculated. Like other senses, the key to the taste code may be in the firing pattern of numerous cells along the sensory pathway.

IV. ANATOMICAL AND PHYSIOLOGICAL SUBSTRATES IN TASTE RECEPTORS

Taste receptors, called taste buds, have been located in several places in the oral cavity including the tongue, insides of the cheeks, soft palate, throat, and pharynx. The lifespan of the taste receptor cells is relatively short, approximately 10 days, and cells are continually being replaced by new cells. The taste buds are not uniformly distributed over the surfaces of these oral structures and the highest density of taste buds are found on the posterior tongue. Taste buds are generally found in clusters lying within the bumps of the tongue, called papillae, and different types of papillae have been classified on the basis of shape and location. Additionally, certain receptor areas are more sensitive to one taste quality than another. The tip of the tongue best detects sweet substances, the sides sour, the edges salty, and the back of the tongue bitter.

A. Pathways to the Brain

It is generally believed that the facial, glossopharyngeal, and vagus nerve send information from the taste receptors. The facial nerve (chorda tympani branch) innervates the receptors of the anterior two-thirds of the tongue and the glossopharyngeal nerve innervates the posterior section of the tongue. Other areas of the posterior oral cavity are innervated by the vagus nerve.

These taste fibers project to the solitary tract, which ends in the nucleus of the solitary tract in the medulla oblongata. Second-order taste relay neurons project to the pontine taste areas which in turn project to the thalamus, lateral hypothalamic area, and amygdala. From the thalamus, fibers are sent to the sensory cortex where the taste fields are located in the lateral region of the postcentral gyrus.

The taste connections of the thalamus appear to be responsible for the conscious perception of taste. Taste projections to the hypothalamus and amygdala, in contrast, seem to be involved with ingestive reflexes such as swallowing, gagging, and coughing. Possibly the hypothalamic and amygdala connections are also involved with motivational responses to taste stimuli. [*See* HYPOTHALAMUS.]

V. TASTE STIMULI

The potential stimuli for the taste receptors are dissolved or soluble substances. In order for a taste to be perceived, tastable (sapid) substances normally go into solution to some extent when in contact with saliva. Some highly volatile substances may also stimulate taste receptors. Normally the response of certain taste receptors is dependent on chemical factors which include the presence of specific ions, and the particular molecular shape, size, and bonding pattern of a substance. Although there are exceptions, sourness is related to hydrogen ion concentration and saltiness to the presence of sodium chloride or similar molecules.

Chemicals that produce bitter or sweet tastes are more varied. Alkaloids, such as quinine, produce a bitter taste; however, some salts taste bitter as do some chemicals with structures similar to sweet-tasting ones. While sweetness is usually associated with sugars (e.g., sucrose, fructose), a variety of other organic substances also are perceived as being sweet.

VI. RESEARCH METHODS

A. Psychophysics of Taste

Because psychophysics relates quantified levels of physical energy to sensation, stimulus control is an important factor. The accuracy of determining absolute taste thresholds (e.g., the lowest concentration of saline that can be detected), taste-quality recognition thresholds (e.g., the lowest concentration of vanilla extract that can be correctly identified as that substance), and perceived intensity–concentration relationships is dependent on stimulus control. For testing the chemical senses, particular problems arise in controlling the duration and area of stimulation. Tastants applied to the tongue require time to reach and activate receptors; once stimulated it is not easy to remove them rapidly; and because the stimulus is in solution it is difficult to isolate specific areas. In addition, factors such as temperature, chemical state of the mouth, location of stimulation, and receptor adaptation challenge researchers attempting to determine taste thresholds.

Despite these problems, thresholds have been determined for a multitude of tastants including sucrose, sodium chloride, citric acid, nicotine, caffeine, and vanillin. Tastant concentration and perceived intensity are related by a powerful function, but the exponent varies with the tastant tested. That is, for some tastants doubling the concentration doubles or more than doubles the perceived intensity and for others it is necessary to increase the concentration by more than two times in order to double the perceived intensity.

Psychophysical studies of taste have uncovered a number of factors that point to the complexity of taste perception. Researchers have found that the qualitative aspects of tastants change as concentration changes. For example, as the concentration of sodium chloride increases, the perception of the taste changes from sweet to salty. Because taste thresholds are also dependent on temperature, perception of tastant intensity changes as temperature changes, and this temperature–threshold relationship varies with tastant. Additionally, genetic differences exist in taste perception. The perception of bitterness to saccharin and variations in the threshold for vanillin seem to be related to genetic factors.

The psychophysics of various tastants has importance to applied areas such as food technology and contamination detection in addition to adding to the knowledge of sensory function. Threshold compilations, such as the ones published by the American Society for Testing and Materials, containing threshold data on hundreds of tastants, have provided information to scientists in a number of areas.

B. Electrophysiological Measurement and Cross-Species Study of Taste

As in many other areas of sensory research, electrophysiological measures have been used to study taste. Since verbal and some other responses are not obtainable or require complicated conditioning paradigms in non-humans, electrophysiological measures are important in the cross-species study of taste. Additionally, this electrical activity in response to taste stimuli has been studied at several levels of the nervous systems of various animals. For example, sweet tastants elicit little or no electrophysiological activity in most cats, while dogs possess receptors that are activated by sweet stimuli. Further, the sugar preference in rats has been tracked at several levels in the nervous system, in contrast to some birds that have poorly developed electrophysiological responses to sweet tastants. Electrophysiological data have also uncovered a possible gustatory sensitivity to water. Some animals, such as the cat, dog, and squirrel monkey, give electrophysiological responses to water. Other animals, such as the rat, goat, and macaque monkey do not have distinct electrophysiological responses to water. The interpretation of this response is still unclear because of potential intervening factors. For example, adaptation or treatment prior to stimulation with water affects the "water response."

Researchers have used the taste research on various non-human species as a bases for hypothesizing on the role of evolution in the development of existing taste systems. By comparing interspecies taste system differences in light of the environmental demands of the different species, investigators hope to understand why certain sensory capabilities evolved. Since it is still not clear why the four taste qualities have evolved in humans, this interspecies study may prove to be valuable in the understanding of human taste systems.

Additionally, nervous system tracking with nonhumans has provided the basis for understanding the "neural code" for taste. Researchers have been examining the spatial and temporal course of electrophysiological events that occur in the nervous system during stimulation of taste receptors. This research has led to the hypothesis that taste perception is based on the relative activity across a population of neural fibers. Taste perception may be encoded in the pattern of firing of neural fibers in addition to being encoded by the regional differences (e.g., tongue) in sensitivity to particular tastants. Because many taste fibers respond to a number of taste stimuli, coding of taste may occur at a more central level where information on firing rates, patterns, and locations is integrated.

C. Cross-Modality Influences in Taste

As mentioned previously, the popular concept of taste perception includes more than the receptors responding to different chemicals in the oral cavity. In addition to learning associated with a specific sensory quality, taste perception is also influenced by other senses. Olfaction not only influences taste perception but is often mistaken for it. Visual stimuli can also influence the perceived intensity and quality of taste perception. Loss of the tactile capabilities of the oral cavity can dramatically change the overall subjective taste perception. The orotactile and orochemical sensory systems are linked by anatomy, physiology, and learning.

Speculation for the strong influences of other sensory systems and situational factors on taste refers back to the importance of taste as a mechanism for protecting the organism. Information from the other senses allows for a more complete analysis of food prior to ingestion. Based on previous experience with a variety of sensory inputs, an aversion or preference for a food can develop which may increase the probability of survival.

VII. TASTE AND AGING

As mentioned previously, taste changes during early development. Also of concern, are changes in taste capabilities later in life, because these changes relate to applied issues such as nutrition, palatability, and aging. Most sensory systems show some decrements with age and this concept is generally accepted for taste. At the physiological level, the number of taste buds declines throughout life. As many as two-thirds of taste buds may become atrophic in old age. The sensitivity for sweet and salt seems to deteriorate with age, although there is considerable individual variation. Thresholds to electrical stimulation of tongue also show changes with aging in the same direction. It should be noted, however, that some of the data in the area of taste and aging are contradictory, possibly due to the methodological difficulties with taste studies.

While some studies have been conducted on food identification and aging, caution should be used in the interpretation of findings relative to taste capabilities. One study, which compared the ability to identify foods in a group of older and younger persons, found marked differences. The older individuals were less accurate in identifying most foods except for a few foods such as tomato and potato. The two groups were approximately equal in identifying salt. As mentioned previously, the popular notion of taste also includes the sense of smell, and in this study the smell of the food was not controlled. Therefore, some of the deterioration noted with aging may actually be due to loss of olfactory rather than taste capabilities. In fact, in the aforementioned study, when salt and sugar identification capabilities were compared in the younger and older groups, there were no differences found for salt detection and relatively small differences found for the detection of sugar (63% vs 57%). These two tastants directly reflect taste qualities and their measurement is less likely to be confounded by smell relative to the other foods tested such as apple or coffee. While there seems to be deterioration of the sense of taste with aging, more research needs to be conducted in order to determine the specific role of taste decrements in the identification of foods.

VIII. TASTE, LEARNING, AND FOOD PREFERENCE

Genetic predisposition cannot by itself account for the wide variety of taste preferences in humans. Learning, through cultural and individual mechanisms, has an important role in determining preferences and aversions for foods. Taste preference has been studied from a number of perspectives including simple exposure, classical conditioning, reinforcement contingencies, and modeling.

A number of studies, conducted on humans and other species, indicate that familiar tastes are preferred to novel ones. Infants regularly fed sweetened water showed a higher preference for the sweetened water at 6 months of age relative to a group without the exposure. This differential preference was still apparent at 2 years of age; however, it did not generalize to another sweetened substance. Similarly, a study found that bitter and sour solutions were rated as pleasant by Indian laborers who regularly consume bitter and sour fruits. In contrast, other populations without regular exposure to bitter and sour taste generally rate these solutions as unpleasant. Preference for extremely "hot" food (e.g., peppers) is also dependent on cultural factors related to exposure. While there may be a predisposition for familiar tastes based on evolutionary factors related to food safety, particular taste preferences seem to be highly influenced by prior experience.

Familiarity is not, however, the only factor related to taste preference. Association of a flavor with an illness can reduce the preference, or make the flavor aversive. Even a previously highly preferred taste can become aversive if it immediately precedes an illness. On the other hand, if a taste precedes recovery from an illness there is evidence to suggest that the preference for that taste will increase.

Studies on the use of food as a reinforcer denote the complexity of learning on food preference. When fruit juice was consumed as a means to gain access to a play activity, subsequent preference for the fruit juice decreased. On the other hand, when a snack food was used as a reinforcer for "good behavior" the preference for the snack food increased significantly over the baseline.

Modeling and peer influence also influence food preference. For example, the consumption of chili peppers, which is aversive for most individuals on first exposure, becomes pleasurable in many with subsequent ingestion. The consumption of these initially aversive foods is reinforced by social interaction or modeling. The initial negative perceptions may be surpassed by the greater reinforcement of social acceptance. Additionally, some foods and other tastants (tobacco products, liquors) that are hot, bitter, or sour are characterized as "adult" foods and possibly become reinforcers by having that label.

Some theories of motivation have been applied to the hedonics of food. One concept of motivation proposes that an organism strives for an optimal level of stimulation. Within the context of taste preferences, some people are directed toward foods that produce new (and sometimes painful) sensations. The threshold of optimal stimulation may shift with repeated exposure, driving an individual toward hotter or spicier foods. This concept of optimal stimulation level appears to be in conflict with the findings that known foods are more preferred than novel ones. Another type or level of learning may occur which supersedes the reinforcing value of the familiar. Once the potential danger (sickness, disgust, etc.) of novel foods has been removed, the sampling of different tastes may itself become rewarding. The more foods that are sampled, without an aversive consequence, the greater the probability that more new foods will be sampled in the future. With modern food preparation methods which minimize aversive consequences of new food ingestion, there is a trend, as evident in the United States, toward the desire to experience new tastes. [*See* MOTIVATION, EMOTIONAL BASIS.]

The opponent process theory of motivation proposes that a stimulus produces a subsequent response in the opposite direction of the original stimulus. Pain may subsequently yield to an experience of joy (or relief) on a experiential level. In addition, physiological mechanisms, such as the release of endorphins, also may make the subsequent response to an initially aversive stimulus positive.

The literature on the effects of learning on taste preferences shows the complexity of the development of taste preferences. In particular, humans have survived because of the ability to adapt their behavior to a number of environments. While there are genetic and physiological mechanisms which may predispose food preferences in humans, the influences of learning may be even more pronounced. Suppression of food intake, overindulgence, and cravings for particular tastes are probably the manifestations of a complex interaction of a number of types of learning and physiological mechanisms.

IX. APPLICATION AND FUTURE TRENDS

A. Clinical Conditions and Taste

Taste has been studied as a possible factor in the control of eating and obesity. While the literature in this area is quite extensive, the conclusions are equivocal. There is some evidence that obese people are more sensitive to the taste (and also the smell) of food compared to people of normal weight. However, taste sensitivity is not a universal trend with obesity. There is also some evidence from humans categorized as bulimic, that is, exhibiting episodic ravenous overeating, that the taste and texture of food are a consideration in the preparation for the bulimic episode. [*See* APPETITE.]

Animal models have been used to study the control of eating because variables can be more carefully controlled and severe physiological intervention can be employed with animals. In general, the findings indicate that the more palatable the food the greater the intake. Food made less palatable with quinine resulted in lower consumption and weight loss. Physiological correlates of food intake in rats has been related to human obesity. Rats with lesions to the ventromedial hypothalamus have a tendency to overeat (until weight stabilizes at a plateau) in the presence of palatable foods. The preference for highly palatable food is also characteristic of overeating in humans.

While taste seems to be an important cue to eating, and possibly overeating, taste is only one factor in a complex set of factors in the control of eating. There has been little direct application of the research on taste as a means to control eating other than some use of aversive tastes in conditioning paradigms. An interesting theory involving "taste-craving" may have some applied significance. When food is first tasted, a craving or motivation for more tasting is developed if the food is palatable. The greater the duration of time between the first taste and next taste the less the craving. When the taste of food is changed, even if there is satiety, the taste-craving can be reestablished. This concept is subjectively experienced with multi-course meals and is sometimes referred to as the "dessert effect." By controlling the variety of tastes during a meal some control of eating may be achieved. For example, for gaining weight, multiple tastes should be introduced into the meal, but to lose weight, the number of tastes should be limited.

Maintaining good nutrition in advancing age has become an area of concern. Older people often report a lack of appetite which can result in poor nutrition. Since food palatability is a major factor in consumption, researchers are examining ways to enhance the taste of foods for the elderly. The challenge is to determine which tastes are reduced or lost in older populations and isolate (or develop) foods with tastes that are rated as being very palatable with this group. There is also speculation that other sensory systems, especially olfaction and oral somatosensation, may interact with taste in the overall perception of palatability in older populations.

B. Commercial Applications

There has been a continuing trend to apply the scientific methodologies from the psychophysics of taste to food development. These methodologies have been adapted for use in a number of different paradigms (e.g., multiple comparisons) with various populations (e.g., children). Researchers in this area are interested in both the specific taste qualities and also the interaction of sensory systems. The term *flavor* is defined as the sum of the sensations resulting from the stimulation of the sense ends that are grouped together at the entrance of the alimentary and respiratory tracts. A vocabulary of flavors has been developed to describe substances and assist in the evaluation of products.

Developing desired tastes more efficiently and cost effectively is one of the objectives of this applied research. With emerging health concerns, another objective of this research is to develop foods that possess desired tastes while reducing potentially negative consequences. For example, can the taste and texture of fats be reproduced in low fat substitutes? With the application of emerging technologies paired with the incentives of the marketplace, applied taste research is contributing to the overall understanding of the sense of taste.

Bibliography

Bolles, R. C. (Ed.) (1991). "The Hedonics of Taste." Erlbaum, Hillsdale, NJ.

Carterette, E. C., and Friedman, M. P. (Ed.) (1978). "Handbook of Perception," Vol. VIA. Academic Press, New York.

Chapman, R. F., Bernays, E. A., and Stoffolano, J. G. (Eds.) (1987). "Perspectives in Chemoreception and Behavior." Springer-Verlag, New York.

Finger, T. E., and Silver, W. L. (Eds.) (1987). "Neurobiology of Taste and Smell." Wiley, New York.

Meilgaard, M., Civille, G. V., and Carr, G. T. (1990). "Sensory Evaluation Techniques." CRC Press, Boca Raton, FL.

Weiffenbach, J. M. (Ed.) (1977). "Taste and Development." U.S. Department of Health, Education, and Welfare, Bethesda, MD.

Williams, J., and Ostrum, K. M., (Eds.) (1987). "Olfaction and Taste IX." New York Academy of Sciences, New York. [Also see previous volumes of this series.]

Terrorism

Ariel Merari
Tel Aviv University, Israel

Glossary

International terrorism An act of terrorism involving more than one state. The most common form of international terrorism is events in which terrorists belonging to one nation attack the citizens or property of another. Less frequent are incidents in which terrorists attack their own countrymen on the territory of another country.

Propaganda by the deed An anarchist concept referring to acts of terrorism as a tool for attracting attention to the perpetrators' ideas, encouraging imitation of their methods, and arousing potential supporters.

State-sponsored terrorism Terrorism by groups which are logistically or operationally aided by states.

State terror Repressive violence exercised by a state against its own populace.

State terrorism Acts of terrorism by state agents, usually carried out clandestinely.

Urban guerrilla Terrorism. A term which gained popularity especially through the writings of the Latin American revolutionaries Abraham Guillen and Carlos Marighella in the 1960s. It was originally meant to distinguish between classical guerrilla warfare in rural areas and a strategy consisting of armed attacks in the cities. The term was later favored by some writers as a euphemistic substitute to "terrorism."

POLITICAL TERRORISM is the use of violence by subnational groups or clandestine state agents, for obtaining political (including social and religious) goals, when this violence is intended to intimidate or otherwise affect the emotions, attitudes, and behavior of a target audience considerably larger than the actual victims. This definition distinguishes between terrorism and other forms of political violence, such as guerrilla warfare and conventional war, on the one hand, and between political terrorism and violence for personal motives, such as economic gain, on the other hand.

I. DEFINITIONS OF POLITICAL TERRORISM AND THEIR CONCEPTUAL BASES

Numerous definitions of terrorism have been offered by scholars. However, in essence, the constituents of the definition presented above are widely accepted in academic literature and appear in the laws of several countries, although some authors have based their definition on a broader concept of terrorism. In different forms of wording, there are three main elements which are generally recognized as the constituents of terrorism: violence, political ends, and intimidation. Additional elements which appear in academic or official definitions serve, in some cases, to limit the scope of the phenomena covered by the definition, but sometimes simply accentuate one of its three basic elements, such as the mention of the symbolic nature of the targets and the characterization of the violence employed as "extranormal."

A significant difference exists between authors who view terrorism as a mode of struggle, used primarily by insurgents but sometimes also by states against other states, and those who use the term in a much broader sense, to denote any illegal and immoral (usually interpreted as unjustified) form of violent coercion and intimidation for political ends, regardless of the users and the context. According

Encyclopedia of Human Behavior, Volume 4

to this broad concept, terrorism has many forms and contexts (e.g., suppression of the populace by totalitarian regimes, conventional war, limited strikes by one state against another in peace time, and insurgency carried out by a handful of people). It has very diverse aims (e.g., winning a world war, subduing internal resistance, or changing a specific government policy) and completely dissimilar methods (e.g., dropping an atomic bomb on an enemy city or assassinating a political opponent). By this rather general interpretation, terrorism is any kind of unjust or excessive political violence. In the words of Richard Falk, a proponent of this approach, "the opposite of terrorism is . . . permissible violence." It follows, that all nonpermissible violence is terrorism. Because the magnitude of state violence is so much greater than that exercised by insurgent groups, works of advocates of the expansive definition of terrorism devote greater attention to state repression of its own citizens or to the killing of civilians by armies in conventional war than to insurgent terrorism.

Those who view terrorism as a form of struggle apparently constitute the majority of the scholars in the field. Proponents of this approach do not deny the existence of illegal violence by states against their own citizens or of atrocities in the framework of conventional war, and the importance of investigating the moral, political, and psychological questions associated with these issues. However, for the sake of scientific utility they prefer to reserve the term terrorism to a specific type of phenomena, which are mainly associated with a certain mode of struggle of insurgent groups. The obvious need to distinguish between these two interpretations of the term has led several authors (e.g., Frederick Hacker and Paul Wilkinson) to suggest that the word "terror" should be retained for mass state violence, whereas the term "terrorism" should be reserved to denote a strategy of insurgence and clandestine warfare, as it is used in this article.

Most of the literature on terrorism which has been published during the last quarter of the 20th century has dealt with violence exercised by subnational groups and by clandestine state agents against other states. Legal definitions of the term also reflect this interpretation. Actually, anti-terrorism laws have been enacted to cope with insurgent violence, rather than to deal with state violations of human rights or with war crimes. Thus, the commonly used official definition of terrorism by the U.S. Department of State is: "Premeditated, politically motivated violence perpetrated against non-combatant targets by subnational or clandestine agents, usually intended to influence an audience." Similar definitions have been employed by American government agencies for more than two decades.

Some authors have reserved the term terrorism for attacks on noncombatants. The value of this criterion as a distinguishing mark of terrorism is dubious. Although the illegitimacy of attacks on noncombatants is anchored in international accords, particularly the Geneva Conventions, this term is not sufficiently clear, particularly in the context of the terrorist strategy. Not only is it vague whether state functionaries other than soldiers (e.g., decision makers, legislators, police officers, and other civil servants) are included in this category, but the status of off-duty, unarmed soldiers, or military units on internationally authorized peace-keeping missions is questionable. Moreover, by domestic legal standards there is no distinction between attacks on combatants and noncombatants. In all countries the killing of an armed soldier by insurgents is regarded as a murder in its common criminal sense rather than as a legitimate act of war. Thus, the politically motivated killing of an armed American soldier in Washington would be regarded by most people as an act of terrorism, although the victim is a combatant by customary standards. Terrorism differs from other forms of warfare in several important respects, which are summarized in Table I.

II. HISTORY AND CURRENT FEATURES

The term "terrorism" was introduced in a similar sense to its present usage at the time of the French Revolution. The 1793–1794 Jacobin "reign of terror" referred to state oppression of opponents. In the 19th century, however, the term became mainly associated with a form of violent insurgency, as it is usually interpreted today.

Despite the historical recency of the term, terrorism is probably as old as human society. Because it is the most primitive form of organized violent insurgency and internal strife, its age is, undoubtedly, the age of rebellion. Two of the better-known old groups which used terrorism systematically to promote their political interests were the Jewish Sicarii (1st century A.D.) and the Ismaili Shiite Assassins (Hashishin; 11–13th centuries). In modern Western history terrorism gained notoriety with the rise of the anarchist movement in the 19th cen-

TABLE I

Characteristics of Terrorism, Guerrilla, and Conventional War as Modes of Violent Struggle

	Conventional war	Guerrilla	Terrorism
Unit size in battle	Large (armies, corps, divisions)	Medium (platoons, companies, battalions)	Small (usually less than 10 persons)
Weapons	Full range of military hardware (air force, armor, artillery, etc.)	Mostly infantry-type light weapons but sometimes artillery pieces as well	Hand guns, hand grenades, assault rifles, and specialized weapons, e.g., car bombs, remote-control bombs, barometric pressure bombs
Tactics	Usually joint operations involving several military branches	Commando-type tactics	Specialized tactics: kidnapping, assassinations, carbombing, hijacking, barricade-hostage, etc.
Targets	Mostly military units, industrial and transportation infrastructure	Mostly military, police, and administration staff, as well as political opponents	State symbols, political opponents, and the public at large
Intended impact	Physical destruction	Mainly physical attrition of the enemy	Psychological coercion
Control of territory	Yes	Yes	No
Uniform	Wear uniform	Often wear uniform	Do not wear uniform
Recognition of war zones	War limited to recognized geographical zones	War limited to the country in strife	No recognized war zones. Operations carried out world-wide
International legality	Yes, if conducted by rules	Yes, if conducted by rules	No
Domestic legality	Yes	No	No

tury. Anarchist terrorism drew attention not only because of the proliferation of the phenomenon in Europe and in the United States and the prominence of the targets for attacks—often heads of state—but also because this flurry of violence was accompanied by ideological literature, which regarded terrorism as the recommended mode of struggle, giving it an air of a powerful and threatening philosophy, which combined destructive goals with a destructive method. There were also other types of social–ideological movements which used terrorism as their main mode of struggle in the second half of the 19th century and the beginning of the 20th century. These included the Russian Narodnaya Volya (People's Will) and later the Social Revolutionaries which fought against the oppressive Tsarist regime and were influenced by Marxist more than by anarchist ideology. Much of the terrorist violence in the United States was linked to labor struggles between unions and employers, and focused on concrete demands related to labor conditions. A terrorist strategy was also employed by several nationalist movements in Europe, including Irish, Serbs, Macedonians, and Armenians.

In the course of the 20th century terrorism was increasingly used as the principal strategy or as an auxiliary instrument by groups which fought for national liberation as well as by groups which espoused social–ideological issues. It was a common part of anti-colonial campaigns, mainly after World War II, such as in mandatory Palestine, Kenya, Cyprus, Algeria, Angola, and Mozambique.

The late 1960s and the early 1970s were marked by the establishment of many terrorist groups and a corresponding rise in terrorist activity around the world. Since that time, terrorism attracted more attention than ever before. It has become a frequent item on the agenda of international organizations, become a subject of international accords, and generated much publicity. The two main types of goals pursued by the new groups have been social–ideological (various shades of left-wing, right-wing, and religious ideologies) and nationalist (including separatism and irredentism). Some groups, however, often referred to as "single issue groups," have had specific, limited goals, such as "animal liberation," environmental protection, and opposition to abortion.

Most of the terrorist groups in Latin America have been of the social–ideological type. Many espoused radical left-wing ideology (e.g., the Armed Revolutionary Vanguard in Brazil, the FARC and ELN in Colombia, and MIR in Chile). Another frequent brand has been vigilante-type right-wing groups (e.g., the Brazilian Anti-communist Alliance, the Fatherland and Order in Colombia, and the Death Squads in Chile). In Western Europe, left-wing terrorist groups were established in several countries (e.g., the Red Brigades and Prima Linea in Italy, the Red Army Faction and the Revolutionary Cells in Germany, Action Directe in France, the Revolutionary Organization of 17 November in Greece and GRAPO in Spain). Nationalist and separatist groups have been active in Europe (e.g., the Irish Republican Army and the Basque ETA), in the Middle East (e.g., Palestinian and Kurdish groups), in the Indian Sub-continent (e.g., Sikh and Kashmiri groups), in the Far East (e.g., the PULO in Thailand and the Moros in the Philippines), and in Africa, where most of the internal conflicts have primarily stemmed from tribal or ethnic rivalries.

An important cause for the salience of terrorism during the recent quarter of a century was the great increase of international terrorism, especially where it involved attacks by terrorists outside their home countries. Although these kind of terrorist attacks have been much less common than domestic terrorist incidents, they have had a significant effect on international relations and their media coverage has been immeasurably greater. The great majority of this type of international incidents, mainly in western Europe, has been perpetrated by Middle Eastern groups.

The greater impact of modern terrorism is partly attributable to its greater lethality and lesser discrimination. In the course of the 1970s and 1980s the proportion of terrorist attacks that have been intended to kill rather than to damage property has grown, as has the proportion of terrorist attacks which have resulted in multiple casualties. Car bomb attacks on the random public in shopping centers and bombs on board airliners are characteristic of the current variant of this form of struggle.

III. TERRORISM'S STRATEGIC CONCEPTS

Terrorism has often been described as the weapon of the weak. Indeed, there is a manifest disparity between terrorist groups' capabilities and their ambitious goals. Most terrorist groups are very small, numbering tens or hundreds of members. A notorious group such as the German Red Army Faction (widely known as the Baader-Meinhof gang) included no more than 30 active members at any given period throughout its existence. They have been able to assassinate several public officials and businessmen, to kidnap two, and to stage one barricade–hostage incident. Annoying as these actions may be, they constitute a nuisance rather than a threat to the regime. It is not immediately clear how the leaders of this group expected to achieve their far-reaching political goal of overpowering the German government and instituting a marxist regime. This section of the article delineates the main elements and variations of terrorism as a strategy, explaining how terrorists think they may bridge the gap between their meager means and extreme objectives.

A. The Psychological Element

Many scholars have noted that terrorism is a strategy based on psychological impact. This notion has also gained recognition in Western states' official definitions of the term. In a sense, all forms of warfare have a significant psychological ingredient, both in trying to hamper the enemy's morale by sowing fear in its ranks and in strengthening its own forces' self-confidence and will to fight. Nevertheless, conventional wars are first and foremost massive collisions of material forces, and they are usually won by the physical elimination of the enemy's ability to resist, by destroying its fighting forces, economic infrastructure, or both. The psychological basis of the strategy of terrorism is entirely different in nature. Like guerrilla, terrorism is a strategy of protracted struggle. However, guerrilla warfare, notwithstanding its psychological component, is primarily a strategy based on a physical encounter. Although 20th century guerrilla theoreticians have emphasized the propaganda value of guerrilla operations in spreading the word of the revolution, attracting supporters, awakening dormant opponents of the regime, and providing them with a recipe of resistance, the importance of these psychological elements remains secondary. Whereas the physical occupation of territory and the establishment of "liberated zones" is a principal tenet of guerrilla warfare, terrorism only tries to generate a psychological impact on various target audiences.

Although terrorists have been rarely clear enough as to lay down a complete, coherent strategic plan, it is possible to discern several strategic ideas that terrorists have held as the cardinal practical concept of their struggle. These are described below as distinct notions, although they are not necessarily mutually exclusive, and terrorist have often espoused them concurrently.

1. Propaganda by the Deed

The essentials of the psychological basis of a terrorist struggle have changed little since last century, when anarchist writings first formulated the principles of this strategy. The basic idea was phrased as "propaganda by the deed." This maxim meant that the terrorist act was the best herald of the need to overthrow the regime and the torch which would show the way to do it. The revolutionary terrorists hoped that their attacks would thus turn them from a small conspiratorial club into a massive revolutionary movement. In a way, the original concept of propaganda by the deed, as explained and exercised by 19th century revolutionaries, was more refined than its modern usage in the post World War II era. Whereas the earlier users of this idea were careful to choose symbolic targets, such as heads of state and infamous oppressive governors and ministers, in order to draw attention to the justification of their cause, the more recent brand has turned to multi-casualty indiscriminate attacks. In doing so, the terrorists have exchanged the propaganda value of justification for a greater shock value, which guaranteed them massive media coverage. This change seems to reflect the adaptation of the strategy to the age of television. Yet, this basic concept of the nature of the terrorist struggle does not constitute a complete strategy. Like some other conceptions of terrorism, in the idea of propaganda by the deed terrorism is only meant to be the first stage of the struggle. It is a mechanism of hoisting a flag and recruiting, a prelude which would enable the insurgents to develop other modes of struggle. In itself, it is not expected to bring the government down.

2. Intimidation

Another salient psychological element in the strategy of terrorism has been, as the term implies, the intention to spread fear among the enemy's ranks. For a regime and its key functionaries, whose very existence is challenged by the insurgents, the struggle is a matter of life or death and they are generally unlikely to give up because of the terrorists' threat. Nevertheless, terrorists have sometimes succeeded, through a systematic campaign of assassination, maiming, or kidnapping, to intimidate select categories of people, such as judges, jurors, or journalists. An extension of this idea of coercive terrorism applies to the general population. Not only government officials and employees are punished by the terrorists, but all those who cooperate with the authorities and refuse to assist the insurgents. Examples of a large-scale use of this strategy have been the murders of actual or presumed collaborators with the authorities by the Viet Minh and the Viet Cong in Vietnam, the FLN in Algeria, and the Palestinian "Shock Committees" in the Israeli Occupied Territories. An even more extensive use of this type of intimidation is designed to force the population to take a stand. Actually, it is mostly intended to affect the neutrals which, in many cases, constitute the great majority of the public, more than to intimidate the real opponents. Horne notes that in the first $2\frac{1}{2}$ years of the FLN's war against the French in Algeria, the FLN murdered at least 6352 Muslims, as compared with 1035 Europeans. The killings were often carried out in a particularly gruesome manner, in order to maximize the terrorizing effect.

3. Provocation

An important constituent in terrorist strategy is the idea of provocation. Like the theme of propoganda by the deed, this notion appeared in the writings of 19th century revolutionaries. It has, however, gained special prominence in Carlos Marighella's *Minimanual of the Urban Guerrilla,* first published in 1969. Marighella, author of a most influential terrorist guidebook, anticipated that terrorist attacks would provoke the government to resort to harsh measures, which would alienate it from the populace. The idea is, in general, simple and effective not only in the political environment of a Latin American dictatorship but also in many liberal democracies. Terrorist attacks tend to draw repressive responses by any regime, which necessarily affect also parts of the population which are not associated with the insurgents. These measures, in turn, make the government unpopular, thus increasing public support of the terrorists and their cause. When government counterterrorist actions are not only draconic but ineffective as well, anti-government sentiment is bound to be even more prevalent.

A special kind of the provocation doctrine is relevant to a conflict which has an international dimension. When the insurgents represent a radical nationalist faction of a larger political entity, or are supported by a state, they may hope that their acts of terrorism will spark a war between their target country and their state sponsor.

4. Strategy of Chaos

Government ineptitude is the basis for another psychological lever in the strategy of some terrorist groups. The idea can be termed "a stragedy of chaos" and has been typical of right-wing insurgents. It refers to the terrorist attempt to create an atmosphere of chaos so as to demonstrate the government's inability to impose law and order. The insurgents hope that the public will, under such circumstances, demand that the "weak" liberal government be replaced by a strong regime.

In order to create an atmosphere of disorder and insecurity, terrorists have resorted to random bombings of public places. Thus, the Italian neo-fascist Black Order group placed a bomb on a train in August 1974, arbitrarily killing 12 passengers and wounding 48. Another ultra-right Italian group, the Armed Revolutionary Nuclei, was charged with the bombing of the Bologna railway station in August 1980, which caused the death of 84 and the wounding of 200. The same idea presumably motivated German extreme right-wing terrorists, who detonated a bomb in the midst of a joyous crowd celebrating the Oktoberfest beer festival in Munich in September 1980, killing and wounding more than 200. A similar tactic was employed by a Belgian ultra-rightist terrorist group which, in the period of 1982–1985, murdered almost 30 people in random shooting of bystanders during supermarket robberies. There was no apparent reason for the killings other than to create panic in the population. Like the other strategic concepts of terrorism described above, the "strategy of chaos" is not a comprehensive plan for seizing power. It is merely a way to create public mood which, as the insurgents hope, will give them a better chance to continue their struggle in an unspecified way.

5. Strategy of Attrition

Some insurgent groups have viewed terrorism as a strategy of protracted struggle, designed to wear out the adversary. In fact, this is the only conception of terrorism which views this mode of warfare as a complete way of achieving victory, rather than as a supplement or prelude to another strategy. This perception has been typical of modern anti-colonial terrorist groups. The insurgents were fully aware of their inferiority as a fighting force compared to the strength of the government and, unlike the concepts of struggle delineated above, they did not expect that they would ever be strong enough to defeat the government by a physical confrontation. Nevertheless, they assumed that they had a greater stamina than the government and that, if they persisted, the government would eventually yield. Because this strategy assumes that the insurgents can prevail by greater perseverance rather than by building a stronger force, it is patently suitable for conflicts where the issue at stake is not of vital importance for the government. If the government considers the struggle as a matter of life or death, it will not succumb to terrorist harassment, however protracted and unpleasant it may be. What eventually determines the outcome is the relative importance of the struggle for the government and for the insurgents, and the terrorists' nuisance value and durability.

6. Expressive Terrorism

So far terrorism has been treated as a strategy, implying an organized plan to achieve a political end, usually to seize power. Nevertheless, in several cases terrorism has been an emotional response with no clear strategic aim, although the acts of violence have been perpetrated by a group, in a tactically organized manner.

Both South Moluccan attacks in Holland and Armenian terrorism in the 1970s and 1980s are manifest examples of expressive terrorism. The dominant motivation which has driven the young men and women who carried out the acts of violence belonged to the emotional realm rather than to the domain of rational political planning. Terrorism, in these instances, expressed an emotional state, rather than served as a rationally selected instrument in the framework of a strategy of insurgence. Undoubtedly, the emotional element is also part of the driving force behind the activity of other terrorist groups. In most cases, however, the hopelessness of the political case is not as clear as in the Armenian and Moluccan examples, rendering an outside judgment about the weight of the emotional factor impossible.

B. The Co-existence of Terrorism and Other Strategies of Insurgency

In many cases insurgent groups have systematically used a mixture of terrorism and guerrilla. In Peru, the Sendero Luminoso have used a classical guerrilla strategy in the Ayacucho region, where they have occupied towns, carried out attacks on police stations and military convoys, and established control over large areas. At the same time, however, they have conducted a typical terrorist campaign in the cities, which consisted of assassinations, bombings, and kidnapping. A similar mixture has existed in the activities of many other Latin American groups, such as the Colombian ELN, M-19 and FARC, the Salvadoran FMLN, and the Guatemalan EGP. A dual guerrilla–terrorist strategy has also characterized groups in other parts of the Third World. The Viet-Minh and, later, the Viet Cong insurgencies were instances where regular warfare, guerrilla strategy, and terrorism abounded side by side. Similar examples, albeit on a smaller scale, can be found in Asia and Africa.

The co-existence of guerrilla and terrorist strategies is not incidental. Apparently, all insurgent organizations which have adopted guerrilla as their main strategy have also used terrorism regularly. In reality the form of insurgency—terrorism, guerrilla, mass-protest, or any combination of these—is mainly determined by objective conditions rather than by strategic preferences of the insurgents. Usually, the insurgents utilize every possible mode of struggle that can advance their cause. Because terrorism is the lowest form of violent struggle, it is always used in insurgencies. Often, because the insurgents are few, the terrain is not favorable for guerrilla warfare and government forces are efficient, terrorism is the only mode of insurgency available to the insurgents. Thus, there has not been even a single guerrilla organization in Western Europe among the many insurgent organizations which have operated in this region since the 1960s. In other regions, such as Latin America, Africa, and South-East Asia, rebels have been able to conduct guerrilla warfare, although they have continued to use terrorism concurrently. The actual form of contest is forged in a continuous process of friction against hard reality, and terrorism is practically always part of it.

IV. ETIOLOGY

Works on the etiology of terrorism often fail to differentiate between aspects of this phenomenon which are common to all types of violent insurgencies, and aspects that are unique to terrorism. In itself, the resort to violence for bringing about a political change is not specific to terrorism. In this sense, theories which explain rebellion and uprising in general would apply to terrorism as well. These include theories of revolution and uprising (e.g., Samuel Huntington, Chalmers Johnson, Talcott Parsons, Charles Tilly, Ted Robert Gurr) which evolved from sociology and political science. Various theories of criminality and social deviation (e.g., Lombroso, Travis Hirschi, Wilson, and Herrnstein), which emerged from psychology, criminology, and sociology, are germane to terrorism, at least to the extent that they deal with the willingness and inclination to use violence, regardless of the context.

These theories, however, do not explain the resort to terrorism rather than to other modes of struggle. This preference may, hypothetically, be explained by individual psychological traits or by situational factors. To a great extent, these disparate emphases stem from different disciplines. The individual-oriented psychological approach views terrorism as an aberration of the few, whereas the political science, sociological approach and, to some extent, the social–psychological interpretation view terrorism as a product of conditions ("root causes" and opportunities). The two types of explanations are further elaborated below.

A. Individual Psychology Explanations

Psychological explanations of the etiology of terrorism have related to presumed unique characteristics of terrorism: the "extranormality" of the violence; alleged suicidal propensity of the perpetrators, membership in a small group, and the antisocial nature of terrorist groups, which often (albeit not always) act against their society.

Despite some impressions and speculative claims to the contrary (e.g., Cesare Lombroso, Frederick Hacker, Jerrold Post), empirical research has so far failed to find a common psychopathology among terrorists. Indeed, the meager evidence available suggests that members of terrorist groups cannot be characterized as clinically abnormal. Furthermore, no distinctive personality type could be discerned even within a particular terrorist group, let alone across groups. The failure to find common psychological traits is not surprising, in view of the cultural and contextual diversity of terrorist groups. Another cause of variance is the indistinction of the behavioral characteristics of a "terrorist." The term terrorist applies to the ideologue, the finance person, the forgerer, the hitman, and other roles common in terrorist groups. There is no obvious reason to assume that these persons share common personality traits.

A few studies have tried to protray a demographic profile of terrorists. The validity of some of the often-quoted papers of this kind has been questioned on the grounds that they relied on secondary sources (mainly news media reports) and the samples have not been representative of the groups surveyed. Some of the findings (e.g., that most of the terrorists are young and unmarried) add little to layman's knowledge. Some of the data, however, may provide a starting point for further sociological and psychological studies. Such are the differences observed between left-wing and right-wing terrorist groups in gender composition and socio-economic background.

B. Situational Explanations

Factors which have been often proposed as root causes of terrorism include various kinds of grievances and situations which exacerbate feelings of deprivation. The grievances may stem from a perceived condition of unfulfilled nationalist, ethnic, or religious aspirations, economic and social deprivation, or a variety of idiosyncratic causes. Exacerbating conditions are changes which sharpen the grievances and make them appear more salient or more pressing than before. These general factors, however, are suitable for explaining all kinds of violent uprising and to not specifically explain the use of terrorism as a mode of struggle.

The specific use of terrorism by groups or by states is a result of the inability to use alternative forms of struggle or a choice due to special advantages that this particular strategy offers. For reasons explained above, terrorism practically always accompanies other forms of political violence. In some cases, however, notably in Western Europe and North America, objective conditions make terrorism the only form of political violence that can be systematically used by substate groups.

The resort to terrorism where there is a strategic choice, as well as the general rise in terrorism after World War II, can be explained by many features of modern society, which make this form of strife particularly attractive. These include political–strategic circumstances, factors which technically facilitate terrorist operations, and factors which enhance the psychological impact of terrorism.

The changes in the global political–strategic conditions which took place after World War II have made terrorism more attractive for states as a surrogate form of warfare. In this era, wars have become less acceptable as a means of settling disputes. Despite the shortcomings and ineffectiveness of the United Nations as a mechanism of conflict resolution, the influence of the international community on the conduct of individual states is greater than ever before. The introduction and proliferation of mass-destruction weapons have created a situation in which even local conventional wars have global significance, because they may escalate into a nuclear confrontation. Under these circumstances, the international community tends to suppress local wars in the bud. Conflicts between states have persisted, but in many cases they have taken the clandestine or indirect form of terrorism, which has the advantage of unaccountability for the user. By existing international norms, a direct attack by one state on another is a sufficient pretext for war. This is not the case when the adversary state provides support to a seemingly independent group which commits the actual attack, or carries out such attack by its own clandestine agents without claiming responsibility. Another advantage of this method of war by proxy has to do with domestic politics. In many instances, a public which would strongly oppose the idea of starting a war on another nation, would still agree—sometimes even support—the idea of harming an adversary state indirectly, through the sponsorship of insurgent movement's operations. And, of course, compared to a full-fledged conventional war, this form of strife is incomparably cheaper in life and materiel.

Technological changes during this century have provided terrorism with unprecedented capabilities. Modern society is more vulnerable to attacks by small groups. It provides terrorists with many sensitive targets, such as electrical power grids, oil depots, and communication systems. Commercial aviation is not only a highly attractive target for terrorist attacks, but also an important element in international terrorism, as it facilitates terrorists' movement around the world.

The enormous development of the mass media has been a factor of immense importance in enhancing the psychological impact of terrorism. In the age of television and communication satellites terrorist attacks reach, in a vivid form, almost every household. The media qualities of terrorism guarantee extensive and dramatic coverage. Because terrorism, more than any other form of struggle, is intended to create a psycho-political rather than a physical impact, media coverage makes it a more efficient—and more appealing—form of struggle than ever before.

V. THE EFFECTS OF TERRORISM

In the course of the recent quarter of a century, terrorism has become a part of our civilization. It has a conspicuous cultural presence which is expressed not only in media reporting, but also in literature and cinema. However, in view of terrorism's political purpose, the main question in evaluating its outcomes should examine its success in achieving political objectives.

The evaluation of terrorism's success as a strategy depends on how success is defined. Most terrorist groups strive to depose the current government and to seize power. By this criterion of success, taking into account only insurgents which have used terrorism as their main strategy, only some anti-colonial groups, such as the EOKA in Cyprus and the Mau Mau in Kenya, have fully accomplished their goal. The overwhelming majority of the many hundreds of terrorist groups which have existed in the second half of this century have failed miserably to attain their declared objectives. The fact that terrorist success has been limited to the category of anti-colonial struggles is not incidental. The main reason for this phenomenon is that only in this category the issue at stake is far more important for the insurgents than for the government. Where the terrorist organization's struggle is aimed at changing the social–political nature of the regime, such as in the case of right-wing or left-wing insurgents, the incumbent government fights for its life and is ready to take all means necessary to quell the insurgency. There is no room for compromise, as the terrorists' success means the demise of the government. The same is also true for most cases of separatist struggle, where the insurgents' aspirations are perceived by the government as threatening the integrality and intactness of the state. Differences in the degree of success of separatist terrorists stem primarily from the extent to which secession of the disputed part of the country seems, to most citizens of the state, as severing their own flesh and blood. For France, for instance, leaving the protectorates of Tunisia and Morocco or the colonies of Mali and Madagascar was much less painful than relinquishing its rule of Algeria, which was legally part of France and had more than one million French citizens of European origin among its population; giving up Bretagne or Normandy is unthinkable. In this sense, the success of separatist terrorism in obtaining its goals is a yardstick for the degree to which the disputed territory is truly a separate entity.

It is also true, however, that a nationalist cause is generally much more powerful in motivating people than a social issue and, therefore, other things being equal, the intensity of violence which stems from nationalistic sentiments is usually greater than the magnitude of violence generated by social–economical grievances.

Whereas achievement of the insurgents' goals in full is rare, terrorists have more often succeeded in accomplishing partial objectives. Four types of partial terrorist success can be discerned: (1) recruitment of domestic support which enables the terrorists to move on to a higher level of insurrection; (2) achieving international attention to their grievances; (3) acquiring international legitimacy; (4) gaining partial political concessions from their adversary.

The most common outcome of international terrorism is bringing the terrorists' grievances to international consciousness. In itself, this awareness is not enough to effect changes desired by the insurgents and sometimes results in repercussions that are deleterious to the terrorists' cause. Yet, under favorable conditions, it grants the insurgents a ladder by which they can climb further. In Western publics, the initial reaction to a terrorist campaign is, invariably, one of vehement condemnation. This response, however, is often followed by readiness to examine closely the terrorists' case with a tendency to view their grievances favorably. Paradoxically, the public may end up approving of causes while denouncing the method by which they were brought to its attention. The formation of the subsequent benevolent attitude to the terrorists' cause is most likely to occur in publics that suffer from the terrorist attacks, but have nothing to lose from the fulfillment of their demands. In this situation, the initial rage is soon replaced by the wish that the problem will disappear. When a positive political attitude to the terrorists' cause seems to be able to buy peace, governments often adapt their policy so as to gain the terrorists' good will.

Some terrorist groups that have been unable to materialize their whole political objectives, have nevertheless succeeded in driving their adversary to make significant concessions. A typical example is the Basque ETA. Their long violent campaign for secession from Spain has not produced the independence they aspired for, but it has undoubtedly been a major factor in Spain's decision to grant the Basque provinces extensive autonomy.

VI. RESEARCH ON TERRORISM

In the recent two decades the literature on terrorism has grown enormously. Thousands of books and articles have been published on the subject during this period. Alex Schmid and Albert Jongman, who compiled a bibliography on terrorism, estimated in 1988 that 85% of all books on this subject have been written since 1968. This trend—albeit not the volume—of writing on terrorism is also reflected in journals of the academic establishment. In 1970, there were 12 entries under the term "terrorism" in the Permuterm Subject Index of the Social Sciences Citation Index; the number increased to 151 in 1980 and 162 in 1990. The corresponding numbers of entries under the terms "terrorist" and "terrorists" (combined) were 3, 27, and 39. In 1970 neither the Sociological Abstracts nor the Psychological Abstracts had an entry for "terrorism." In 1980 there was one item under "terrorism" in the Sociological Abstracts and none in the Psychological Abstracts. In 1990 there were 30 items under this title in the Sociological Abstracts and 10 in the Psychological Abstracts.

There are several extensive bibliographies on terrorism. Particularly noteworthy are those compiled by Amos Lakos (two volumes), Edward Mickolus (two volumes), and Schmid and Jongman. A few journals dedicated to terrorism and related subjects have been established. Yet, much of the literature on terrorism is nonacademic. Because terrorism is a phenomenon of current political significance and its features make interesting media items, many of the articles and books on this subject were written by journalists, government officials, and politicians.

Terrorism is an interdisciplinary area of study. Academic contributions to research in this field have come from several disciplines, especially political science, psychology, sociology, history, and law. However, the number of scientists who specialize in the study of terrorism as their main academic endeavor is small. Most of the scientific publications in the field have been authored by persons whose main research interests lie elsewhere, in the better cases in fields tangentially relevant to terrorism. Their casual contributions are usually not based on an accumulated body of research in the field. Apparently, no university offers a teaching program on terrorism as a specific discipline or subdiscipline, although courses on terrorism in general or on specific aspects of it are offered at various departments of many universities. A few academic research institutes specialize in terrorism or have continuous projects in this field.

Terrorism is an evolving field of study and terrorism research has not yet crystallized. It has been handicapped by definitional arguments, that have not been devoid of political overtones, which have obfuscated the scope of the field. Although most scholars have focused their studies on the concept of terrorism as a form of struggle used by insurgent groups or a clandestine form of war between states, some have applied it to other violent phenomena as well. The overbroad use of the term by some writers has been one of the main factors which hindered the formation of generally agreed elementary concepts in the field, even at the classificatory level, and the creation of a common language among researchers. Beyond the definitional confusion, the genuine heterogeneity of the phenomena of terrorism makes descriptive, explanatory, and predictive generalizations, which are the ultimate products of scientific research, patently difficult.

Scholarly research on terrorism has also suffered from the derogatory connotation that this term has acquired. The condemnatory approach has permeated academic writing and has interfered with the academic distance which is necessary in scientific research. Moral–judgmental statements can often be found in social science works on terrorism, not only in legal studies or philosophical treatises of the subject.

As an area of study, terrorism is afflicted by a lack of empirical research. Many of the academic works are impressionistic and deductive in nature. Only a small minority of them rely on primary data. This state of affairs is, in part, attributable to the inherent nature of the phenomenon. Terrorist groups are clandestine organizations which are not readily accessible to direct scientific inquiry. It is hardly conceivable that terrorists would make themselves available to answering questionnaires or taking psychological tests, much less so participate in experimental studies which involve a systematic manipulation of independent variables. Sociological and psychological studies based on captured or repented terrorists suffer from inherent artifacts. The subjects are not in their natural habitat, the sample cannot be readily considered as representative of the active terrorist population, and the likelihood of reporting bias is always high. The result is that valid systematic data on terrorism are scanty. Because the physical manifestations of terrorism, the general conditions under which it proliferates and public responses to it are easy to reach, political science research, especially macro studies, is less affected by this difficulty than psychology and sociology.[1]

Bibliography

Gurr, T. R. (1970). "Why Men Rebel." Princeton University Press, Princeton.

Lakos, A. (1986). "International Terrorism: A Bibliography." Westview, Boulder, CO.

Lakos, A. (1991). "Terrorism, 1980–1990: A Bibliography." Westview, Boulder, CO.

Laqueur, W. (1987). "The Age of Terrorism." Little, Brown and Co., Boston.

Merari, A. (1994). Terrorism as a strategy of insurgence. *Terrorism and Political Violence,* in press.

Reich, W. (Ed.) (1990). "Origins of Terrorism: Psychologies, Ideologies, Theologies, States of Mind." Cambridge University Press, Cambridge.

Schmid, A. P., and Jongman, A. J. (1988). "Political Terrorism: A New Guide to Actors, Authors, Concepts, Data Bases, Theories, and Literature." North-Holland, Amsterdam.

Wilkinson, P. (1974). "Political Terrorism." Macmillan, New York.

Wilkinson, P. (1994). "Terrorism and the Liberal State," 3rd ed. Macmillan, New York, in press.

[1] Table I and parts of the text of this article appear in a modified form in the author's article "Terrorism as a Strategy of Insurgence," to be published in *Terrorism and Political Violence,* winter 1994.

TEST BEHAVIOR

David J. Bateson
University of British Columbia

Glossary

Bias The differential effect(s), both positive and negative, on an individual's test scores of systematic sources of variation which are not part of or connected to the construct of interest in a test.

Errors of measurement The random chance differences, both positive and negative, that can occur between an examinee's true score and observed score.

Test Any instrument or method which is used to systematically collect data from an individual or individuals on a particular construct or constructs of interest.

Test wiseness An examinee's ability to use characteristics of the test and/or testing situation, which are independent of the construct(s) of interest in a test, to alter his or her observed score.

True score The score, related to the construct of interest in a test, which would have been obtained by an examinee had there been no bias or errors of measurement present.

TEST BEHAVIORS are the myriad of physical and mental actions and reactions that are displayed or otherwise engaged by individuals when they find themselves in a testing situation—a test being defined an any instrument or process that is designed to systematically collect relevant data regarding the individual or groups being tested.

I. DESIRED AND UNDESIRED EFFECTS OF TEST BEHAVIORS

Tests are designed to measure particular constructs of interest. Since the outcome data, usually in the form of numeric scores, are interpreted in order to make decisions about the individuals or groups, behaviors or cognitive processes that are a part of or are directly related to the particular construct being tested are desired. However, test behaviors that are not related to the construct of interest, but which can have an impact on the scores derived from the tests are cause for concern. Such undesired behaviors or processes can seriously affect the validity of the inferences drawn from test scores; they call into question the interpretation of the score on the test as a valid indicator of the construct intended to be measured. Conditions within the test, the testing environment, and the context of the test can all influence test behavior, and consequently, confound the validity of the test score inferences. Test developers, test administrators, and test users (including those people who make interpretations) should be aware of and understand the sources of such behaviors in order that everything possible is done to reduce the effects of such construct-irrelevant behaviors.

II. MODEL OF TEST BEHAVIOR EFFECTS

Under classical test score theory, the mark or score obtained by any examinee, referred to as the observed score, is made up of three parts: the true score, or the score that would be obtained under perfect and ideal conditions where there are no behaviors or components that are not a desired component of the construct being tested; bias, or the systematic effects of any factor or factors not part of or associated with the construct being tested; and random errors of measurement. For any individual

Encyclopedia of Human Behavior, Volume 4

under a testing situation, the classical test score theoretical model is

$$X_O = X_T \pm \text{bias} \pm E,$$

where X_O is the observed score for the examinee, X_T is the true score for the examinee, bias consists of the systematic effect of factors not associated with the construct being tested, and E is accumulated effect of the random errors of measurement applicable to that examinee.

Theoretically, since the expected value of E is 0, it follows that the expected value of X_O is X_T: for a single test an examinee's observed score is the best available estimate of the true score, and the true score is inferred from the observed score.

In any particular testing or examination situation and for any given individual, construct-irrelevant test behaviors and errors of measurement are governed by a complex interaction of associated factors and causes. If particular and systematic construct-irrelevant behaviors can be anticipated and taken into account, more complex models, developed through generalizability theory, can be constructed and applied to improve the validity of true score inferences. Recent developments in multidimensional or multifaceted polytomous item response theory models also hold promise for detecting and differentiating particular sources of error, thereby improving the validity of observed score inferences.

III. ASSOCIATED TEST BEHAVIOR FACTORS

The factors contingent on test behaviors which contribute to measurement error can be grouped into clusters based on their general similarity.

A. Importance of the Test

The first cluster of factors has to do with the context in which tests are administered. The perceived consequences of degrees of success or failure—often referred to as high stakes or low stakes, generalized test anxiety, and test motivation—all are included in this "importance" cluster. In general, motivation has been found to be a positive factor, and anxiety has been found to be a negative factor. Physical manifestations of the effects of factors in this cluster can range from minor "butterflies," through actual illness, to even suicide, particularly in societies where success on tests is the major determiner of future career and material success. It should be noted that conditions which constitute positive motivational pressure for one individual may very well result in negative anxiety for another individual. Similarly, participation in a high stakes test may be a positive factor for some individuals and a negative factor for others; many individuals thrive on pressure, while others perform much less well under such stress.

Anecdotes told at meetings of international comparative educational researchers describe situations wherein students from one country who were sampled for testing in an international assessment were given uniforms and afforded special status as representatives of their country. They were cheered by their peers and teachers as they entered the room to write the tests. In another country, a selected class was told that they had to write this test and nobody would ever really see their scores, but that they had do it anyway. It is not difficult to conjecture that the scores from the two groups of students would be different, not necessarily because of differences in knowledge, but because of differences in motivation. Given the two situations, conclusions about differences in knowledge based on the scores would most probably not be valid.

B. Construct-Relevant Knowledge

A second set of factors affecting test behaviors has to do with construct-relevant knowledge. These include the degree of cognition or mastery of the material to be tested, and examinee confidence or the examinee's perceived efficacy in the testing situation. In general, the more an examinee knows and the stronger the examinee's confidence in that knowledge, the better the performance. While obtaining differences in results due to differences in knowledge is the goal of tests, the differences can be magnified by examinee confidence and efficacy which result from a high degree of competency and a history of success on tests.

With only two of the groups of test behaviors listed, the complex interaction of these factors can be seen. A given student's level of confidence regarding his or her knowledge of the construct of interest can alter or neutralize what might otherwise be, for that student, negative effects of participating in a high stakes test.

C. Construct-Irrelevant Knowledge

A third cluster, which might be referred to as construct-irrelevant knowledge, has to do with test and/or examinee conditions which are not associated with the particular content or material being tested. These conditions incude the test wiseness or test sophistication of the examinee, the degree to which the test is susceptible to application of various test wiseness skills, and the degree to which the test result can be manipulated by the examinee through bluffing or halo effects which influence the scorer of the test, and cheating. In general, the more developed that the examinee's skill's of test wiseness are, the more susceptible the test is to the application of test wiseness skills, and/or the more favourably the examinee is viewed overall by the scorer, the higher the resultant observed score. Undetected cheating artificially inflates the observed score, and, since the penalty for detected cheating is usually a score of 0, the effect of detected cheating is radical deflation of the observed score.

D. Psychological/Emotional Conditions

A fourth set of factors has to do with the psychological or emotional state of the examinee caused by events not associated with the test. These might include excited anticipation of something such as a holiday, a gift, or a trip; an ongoing severe illness or recent death of a loved one or other important figure such as a pet; abuse by a parent or sibling; or fear of harassment by a "gang." In general, the worse the emotional state of the examinee, the lower the subsequent observed score.

E. Physical Conditions

The final cluster has to do with the physical state of the examinee including conditions such as illness, hunger, fatigue, poor vision, and so on. Physical conditions also include the testing environment. Generally, in order to obtain optimum behaviors and therefore results for a group in a testing situation, the environment should be comfortable and quiet, with provision for adequate lighting, comfortable seating and writing space, normal temperatures and ventilation, and so on. Physical factors are the one set of factors for which the most confident predictions of effects can be made; all other attributes being identical, the examinee who is in better physical condition and is situated in a comfortable and quiet environment will almost invariably perform better than the examinee who is ill, tired, hungry, and/or uncomfortable.

IV. TEST BEHAVIORS AND MEASUREMENT ERROR

Under classical test score theory, it is assumed that the random measurement errors for all tests over all individuals are distributed normally with a mean of zero and a standard deviation of one standard error of measurement. While this model usually leads to relatively narrow error bands and therefore enhanced confidence of decisions based on group performance, unfortunately the behaviors manifested from the interactions of various combinations of the above five clusters of factors cannot be reliably predicted for any given individual in any given situation. Different individuals may behave differently given identical conditions and/or situations. As previously mentioned, if a test is perceived to be a "high stakes" test, that situation will usually provide benefit for one person in that it is a motivational factor which will enhance concentration and therefore performance, but the identical situation may produce strong anxiety in another examinee, which may lead to confusion and depressed performance. Two examinees with identical high degrees of confidence entering a test may react quite differently to encountering an unexpectedly difficult item placed at the beginning of a test; one may have his or her confidence shattered, leading to panic depressed performance on subsequent items, while the other may quickly skip to the next item with his or her confidence virtually intact. While one individual may perform better in an absolutely silent environment, another may only perform optimally with loud music playing.

Another problem that makes successful prediction of measurement errors for individuals difficult is that the correlation of some factors with performance is not linear, but rather curvilinear, and the degree of deviation from linearity may vary across individuals. As an example, the relationship between anxiety and observed score is usually positive up to a "breaking point," after which the correlation becomes negative. The "breaking point" at which the relationship changes from positive to negative may differ substantially among individuals. In a similar vein, examinee confidence has a threshold where the effects go from positive to negative as confidence increases. While an increase in confidence usually is accompanied by increased performance on a test, too much confidence can, at times, lead to inadequate preparation for the test and therefore a decrease in performance.

Even the manifestations due to emotional stress radically differ among individuals. In reaction to the death of a cherished pet, one examinee may be so upset that he or she cannot concentrate on the test and therefore will probably perform below expectations, while the same situation may cause another examinee to use the test as an aid to mentally block out a bad emotional experience. This may lead to greater concentration and attention to detail that, in turn, may lead to a higher observed score than would normally be expected.

The literature on testing includes volumes on the effects of various factors on test scores. Under particular controlled conditions, significant effects on group performance of a wide variety of factors have been isolated, but the specific effects of the complex interactions of all theses factors in the real world of practical testing situations are unpredictable for specific individuals.

V. EFFECTS OF TEST WISENESS

Possibly the single set of factors that can have the greatest effect but can be most easily overcome is the set of construct-irrelevant behaviors, including test wiseness and the susceptibility of given tests to the application of test-wiseness strategies. A seminal article by Millman, Bishop, and Ebel, published in 1965, still provides the best detailed articulation of such strategies. These strategies are listed below in Table I. It should be noted that while there are some generalized strategies which all test constructors and administrators should be aware of for all tests, there are also important strategies that can be employed based on examinee knowledge of a given test constructor. The effect of the application of almost all of these strategies can be considerably lessened if test constructors follow widely documented principles of item and test construction that are available in almost any basic testing and/or evaluation text.

In theory, knowledge of test-wiseness strategies has been held to be independent of construct-relevant knowledge required for any particular test. However, recent examination of student application of test-wiseness principles in testing situations has lead to an empirically tested model of test behavior as shown in Figure 1.

While the model has been validated with typical North American examinees, some research has suggested that it is not applicable to other cultures, particularly Asian and recent Asian emigrants to North America.

As examinees apply test-wiseness strategies, it becomes apparent that while test wiseness in and of itself is independent of construct-relevant knowledge, the ability to apply test-wiseness strategies is often based on partial knowledge of the construct of interest. For example, in order for an examinee to eliminate an option or options known to be incorrect (I.D.1 in Table I), the examinee must have construct-related knowledge that enables him or her to make such decisions of incorrectness. Similarly, the ability to apply strategy I.D.2 from Table I is

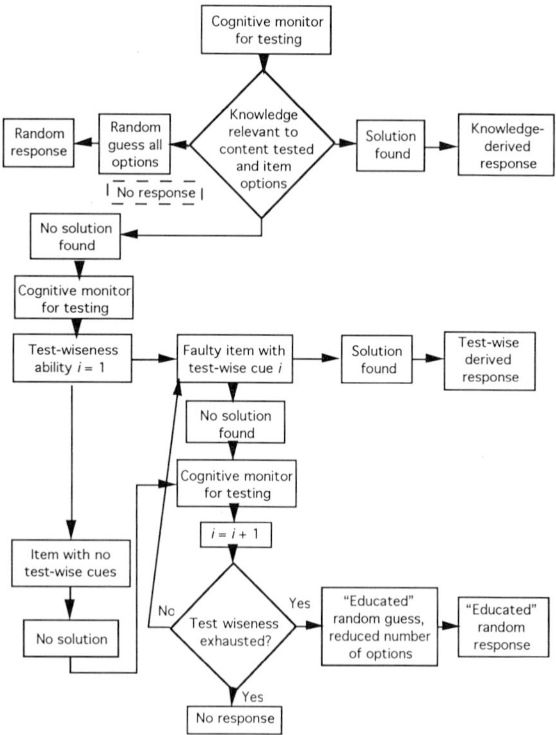

FIGURE 1 Model of test-taking behavior of skilled test takers. [Reproduced with permission from Rogers, W.T., and Bateson, D.J. (1991). Verification of a model of test-taking behavior of high school seniors. *The Journal of Experimental Education* **59** (4); 332. Copyright 1991 by Heldref Publications, Washington, D.C.]

TABLE I

Taxonomy of Test-Wiseness Principles

I. Elements independent of test constructor or test purpose
  A. Time-use strategy
    1. Begin to work as rapidly as possible with reasonable assurance of accuracy.
    2. Set up a schedule for progress through the test.
    3. Omit or guess at items (see I. C and II. B) which resist a quick response.
    4. Mark omitted items, or items which could use further consideration, to assure easy relocation.
    5. Use time remaining after completion of the test to reconsider answers.
  B. Error-avoidance strategy
    1. Pay careful attention to directions, determining clearly the nature of the task and the intended basis for response.
    2. Pay careful attention to the items, determining clearly the nature of the question.
    3. Ask examiner for clarification if necessary, if it is permitted.
    4. Check all answers.
  C. Guessing strategy
    1. Always guess if right answer only are scored.
    2. Always guess if the correction for guessing is less severe than a "correction for guessing" formula that gives an expected score of zero for random guessing.
    3. Always guess even if the usual correction or a more severe penalty for guessing is employed, whenever elimination of options provides sufficient chance of profiting.
  D. Deductive reasoning strategy
    1. Eliminate options which are known to be incorrect and choose from among the remaining options.
    2. Choose neither or both of two options which imply the correctness of each other.
    3. Choose neither or one (but not both) of two statements, one of which, if correct, would imply the incorrectness of the other.
    4. Restrict choice to those options which encompass all of two or more given statements to be correct.
    5. Utilize relevant content information in other test items and options.

II. Elements dependent upon the test constructor or purpose
  A. Intent consideration strategy
    1. Interpret and answer questions in view of previous idiosyncratic emphases of the test constructor or in view of the test purpose.
    2. Answer items as the test constructor intended.
    3. Adopt the level of sophistication that is expected.
    4. Consider the relevance of specific detail.
  B. Cue use strategy
    1. Recognize and make use of consistent idiosyncrasies of the test constructor which distinguish the correct answer from incorrect options.
      a. He makes it longer (shorter) than the incorrect options.
      b. He qualifies it more carefully, or makes it represent a higher degree of generalization.
      c. He includes more false (true) statements.
      d. He places it in a certain physical position among the options (such as in the middle).
      e. He places it in a certain logical position among an ordered set of options (such as in the middle of a sequence).
      f. He includes (does not include) it among similar statements, or makes (does not make) it one of a pair of diametrically opposite statements.
      g. He composes (does not compose) it of familiar or stereotyped phraseology.
      h. He does not make it grammatically inconsistent with the stem.
    2. Consider the relevancy of specific detail when answering a given item.
    3. Recognize and make use of specific determiners.
    4. Recognize and make use of resemblances between the options and an aspect of the stem.
    5. Consider the subject matter and difficulty of neighboring items when interpreting and answering a given item.

Reproduced with permission from Millman, J., Bishop, C. H., and Ebel, R. (1965). An analysis of test-wiseness. *Educational and Psychological Measurement* **25**(3), 711–713. Copyright 1965 by Heldref Publications, Washington, DC.

dependent on the examinee's knowledge that two options, although stated differently, are essentially the same. In most cases, such knowledge is related, at least in part, to the construct of interest. As such, the effects of application of test-wiseness principles may contribute to either true score or to bias depending on the particular situation.

Since the ability to apply test-wiseness strategies is almost always related to the construct of interest, and therefore should not be considered a source of error that could lead to invalid interpretations, ensuring that all examinees have knowledge of test-wiseness strategies would counteract the otherwise negative impact of those testing behaviors.

VI. RECOMMENDED PRACTICES REGARDING TEST BEHAVIORS

More generally, it has been shown that examinees who are aware of the factors that can negatively affect their scores and who develop or are taught methods of counteracting negative effects will perform better than examinees without those skills. Similarly, examinees who develop or are taught techniques and/or skills to utilize performance enhancing conditions will also perform better than those examinees without those developed traits. Practice on similar exams or forms of the test that have been used in the past contribute greatly to both moderation of the negative test behaviors and promotion of positive testing behaviors. All examinee who is well prepared for any test through training or coaching on test wiseness skills, methods of reducing negative emotional and physical stress while retaining motivation, building of self-confidence and testing efficacy, practice on similar old tests, and intensive review and drill of important characteristics and/or components of the construct being tested, will invariably score higher than a person with identical knowledge of the construct being tested, but who has not been so prepared for the test. In fact, Standard 3.11 of the present *Standards for Educational and Psychological Testing* of the American Psychological Association directly addresses the issue of student preparation.

> When test-taking strategies that are unrelated to the constructs or content measured have been found to influence test performance significantly, these strategies should be explained to test takers before the test is administered either in an information booklet or, if the explanations can be made briefly, along with the test directions. The use of such strategies by all test takers should be encouraged if their effect facilitates performance and discouraged if their effect interferes with performance.

When such standards were first proposed, the initial reaction of some test administrators was that such preparation on construct-irrelevant behaviors would constitute cheating. However, based on the spirited discussion that has taken place in the literature over the last several years, the present accepted practice seems to be that any preparation short of teaching the actual items on a test should be considered acceptable, and even desirable practice.

In order to ensure that high validity is a characteristic of decisions regarding groups and, more particularly, regarding individuals, developers of tests should ensure that all testing conforms to the agreed standards of test construction, administration, and interpretation, all test administrators should ensure that examinees receive training in techniques for both counteracting negative factors and utilizing potential positive factors, and all test users should be aware of and take into account the problems with and limitations of the data derived from any test or combinations of tests. In addition, since errors of measurement are assumed to have a mean of 0, decisions about individuals based upon results from a variety of tests over a variety of conditions should have greater validity than a decision based upon one test given at one time under one condition. In practice, for critical decisions made about individuals, undue attention to a single measure should be avoided wherever possible.

Bibliography

American Federation of Teachers, National Council on Measurement in Education, & National Education Association. (1990). "Standards for Teacher Competence in Educational Assessment of Students." Teacher Standards in Student Assessment, National Council on Measurement in Education, Washington, DC.

American Psychological Association. (1985). "Standards for Educational and Psychological Testing," Washington, DC.

Bond, L. (1989). The effects of special preparation on measures on scholastic ability. In "Educational Measurement" (R. L. Linn, Ed.), 3rd ed., pp. 429–444. American Council on Education and the MacMillan, New York.

Joint Committee on Testing Practices. (1988). "Code of Fair Testing Practices in Education." Washington, American Psychological Association and the National Council on Measurement in Education.

Messick, S. (1989). Validity. In "Educational Measurement" (R. L. Linn, Ed.), 3rd ed., pp. 13–104. American Council on Education and the Macmillan, New York.

Millman, J., Bishop, C. H., and Ebel, R. (1965). An analysis of test-wiseness. *Educational and Psychological Measurement* **25**(3), 707–726.

Naylor, F. D. (1985). Test-taking anxiety. In "The International Encyclopedia of Education: Research and Studies" (T. Husen and T. N. Postlethwaite, Eds.), Vol. 9, pp. 5209–5211. Pergamon, New York.

Rogers, W. T., and Bateson, D. J. (1991). Verification of a model of test-taking behavior of high school seniors. *J. Exp. Education* **59**(4), 331–350.

Wolf, L. F., and Smith, J. K. (1993). "The Effects of Motivation and Anxiety on Test Performance." Paper presented at the annual meeting of the American Educational Research Association, Atlanta, GA.

TRAITS

Nathan Brody
Wesleyan University

Glossary

Big Five The name given to the set of five basic traits. The five are extraversion, agreeableness, conscientiousness, neuroticism, and intellect/imagination (or openness to experience).

Correlation Statistical measure of association between a set of paired scores; it varies from + 1.00 to − 1.00. Zero correlation indicates a lack of relation; positive or negative correlations measure the degree of positive or negative relations between the scores.

Extraversion A trait describing the tendency to prefer to be with others, to be talkative, and to be active. One of the Big Five traits of personality.

Factor analysis Statistical procedure used to determine the number of dimensions present in use of correlations among a set of variables.

Idiographic trait Trait dimension describing a single individual.

Nomothetic trait Trait dimension on which all individuals can be rated or described.

TRAITS are terms used to describe differences in the behavior of individuals. Trait terms are assumed to describe consistencies in behavior exhibited by an individual in different situations. For example, if a person is described as impulsive (a trait term), it is assumed that the person will behave impulsively in many different situations. In this article traits are defined and described and their role in providing a comprehensive description of individual differences in personality is considered.

I. DEFINITION

A trait term is a description of the behavioral tendencies of an individual. Persons are assumed to behave in a manner that is consistent with their traits in many different situations. If we assert that a person is friendly, we assume that the person will behave in a friendly manner in many different situations. Trait terms belong to the category of disposition concepts in philosophy. That is, they are characterizations of something that is not invariably present. There are characterizations of things that are invariably manifested. For example, a person's height is a relatively invariant property of a person that characterizes the person constantly. By contrast, a trait remains a latent disposition of a person. Traits are analogous to physical concepts like solubility. Whether a substance is dissolved or not depends upon the conditions surrounding the substance. Solubility is a latent disposition of a substance referring to a capacity that is manifested in certain circumstances and not in others. So, too, traits depend upon the appropriate situations to elicit the behavior that is described by the trait. Individuals are not, in the normal course of events, aggressive when they sleep. Whether a person behaves aggressively depends upon the situations in which the person is found. Aggressive individuals are those who are likely to respond aggressively in a wide range of situations. [*See* AGGRESSION.]

If traits are expressed in some situations and not in others, then descriptions of individuals based on traits are incomplete. When we say that person is friendly we should indicate the full range of situations in which the behavior of being friendly is likely to be exhibited. In the absence of such a specification, trait terms assign a behavioral disposition to a person whose exact meaning and predictive consequences remain vague and partially undefined. Trait terms are unspecified in a second respect. The precise behavior that is expected in the appropriate situations that provides a justification for assigning a trait to a person is usually left undefined. For example, there are many different ways to be friendly and aggressive. We describe individuals by assigning various traits to them. In doing so, we leave unspecified a precise description of an individual's characteristic behavior.

Traits may be construed as continua. Each trait has an opposite. A trait and its opposite form a dimension. Individuals may be described as friendly or, to form the opposite of the trait, as not friendly. Some trait names may be paired with terms that are opposite in meaning that are not the simple negation of the term. For example, individuals may be described as extraverts—a tendency to be sociable and to enjoy the company of others—or, its opposite, as introverts. A trait and its paired opposite define end points on a dimension. The dimension may be scaled and a person may be assigned a number to indicate his or her position on the dimension. If there are a limited number of dimensions that may be used to describe individuals, then all persons may be exhaustively described by their positions on each of several common dimensions. Such a trait description assigning numbers to persons representing their scores on common traits constitutes one way of describing an individual's personality. [*See* EXTRAVERSION–INTROVERSION.]

There are at least three limitations to a trait description of personality. First, individuals may not be adequately described by terms on which all individuals can be rated. Such traits are called nomothetic traits. Some psychologists have suggested that there are idiographic traits that apply only to a single individual. For example, the Marquis de Sade may be described by his unique sexual cruelty. The example indicates the limitations of a descriptive system based on idiographic traits. Cruelty and sexuality are terms that apply to all individuals. Reduced to its absurd conclusion, an idiographic descriptive system for traits requires each individual to be described in terms that apply to that person. And, such a descriptive system would probably require a unique language for each person. There are, however, various trait descriptive systems that fall somewhere between the completely idiographic and the completely nomothetic. For example, it is possible to assert that traits are differentially salient for different individuals. Sexuality and cruelty may be more defining terms for the Marquis de Sade than conscientiousness or extraversion. Second, individuals with the same score on a trait dimension may exhibit trait-relevant behaviors in different situations. One person may be aggressive in encounters with subordinates and not with peers. Another person may be aggressive in encounters with peers but not with subordinates. Third, individuals with the same trait score may express trait relevant behavior in different ways. One person might, for example, be verbally aggressive (or sarcastic). Another person might be described as aggressive because of a tendency to fight and to be physically violent. It is clear that two individuals may be described as having the same position on a common trait dimension, but that description may not do justice to the various ways in which they differ with respect to behavior relevant to that trait.

II. TYPES OF TRAITS

Trait theorists attempted to develop a comprehensive and exhaustive list of nomothetic traits. This task was hindered by an embarrassment of riches—there are approximately 30,000 descriptive terms in the English language that may be used as a basis for a taxonomy of traits. Of course many of these terms are not in common use and many are synonyms or terms that are closely related in meaning. In order to develop a descriptive system containing a limited number of traits, psychologists have relied on a statistical technique called factor analysis. In a typical investigation, individuals are presented with a large and relatively representative set of trait dimensions. Individuals are then asked to describe themselves or others on each of the dimensions in terms of a rating indicating the individual's position on the dimension. The relation between any pair of trait dimensions may be expressed by a correlation. A correlation is a measure of the relation between pairs of scores. Correlations vary from -1.00 to 1.00, with zero values indicating that there is no relation between the scores, such that a score on one dimension may not be used to predict the score on the second dimension. Correlations of -1.00 indicate the presence of a perfect negative relation with high scores on one dimension associated with low scores on the other. For example, a person's trait score on the dimension, neurotic–nonneurotic, is probably correlated with a person's score on the dimension, not adjusted–adjusted. The dimensions are close to being synonymous and individuals who describe themselves as being nonneurotic are likely to describe themselves as being adjusted. Correlations may be used to ascertain the relations among scores on all pairs of trait dimensions. In a typical investigation, individuals may be asked to describe themselves on 100 trait dimensions.

Correlations are obtained among all pairs of dimensions (there are 4950 such pairs for a set of 100). The resulting correlations are then factor analyzed. Factor analysis is a statistical procedure designed to discover the number of dimensions that are present in a set of correlations. The principles used may be elucidated by reference to a hypothetical idealized example. Suppose in a set of all possible correlations among 100 dimensions that all of the correlations for dimensions numbered between 1 and 50 were 1.00. This implies that a single score on any dimension numbered between 1 and 50 may be used to predict a person's score on all other dimensions in this subset. Suppose further that all of the correlations between scores for dimensions numbered between 51 and 100 in the set were also 1.00. And, all of the correlations between a dimension in the first subset (numbered between 1 and 50) and the second subset (numbered between 51 and 100) were zero. It is obvious that the information contained in the set of 100 scores could be summarized by scores on two hypothetical dimensions (or factors) defined by the first and second subset of scores. The set of 100 dimensions would, in this highly artificial and idealized case, be reducible to two dimensions. Factor analysis seeks to discover the number of dimensions that are required to account for all of the correlations among a set of variables.

Factor analysis has been used in many investigations of ratings of personality. Factor analyses have been performed on ratings made by individuals of their own traits as well as on ratings of their acquaintances. These investigations led to the development of a widely (but not universally) shared consensus among trait theorists that the optimal solution has five factors—implying that personality may be described by a person's position on each of five traits. The five traits are: (1) *extraversion* defined as sociable, talkative, assertive, active, and energetic; (2) *agreeableness* defined as sympathetic, kind, and appreciative; (3) *conscientiousness* defined as organized, thorough, and planful; (4) *neuroticism* defined as tense, anxious, and nervous; (5) *intellect* or *openness* to *experience* defined as wide interest, imaginative, and intelligent. Each of these domains includes polar opposites. Individuals may be described as introverted, disagreeable, not conscientious, well-adjusted, and uncultured. Each of these traits subsumes a large number of additional dimensions not included in the brief list of defining terms.

The five traits of personality are sometimes called the "Big Five" and are thought to constitute an optimal trait description of personality. The Big Five descriptive system has some degree of cross-cultural validity. Comparable solutions have emerged from factor analyses of ratings made by individuals in a number of different languages. Thus, the structure is not specific to English.

III. ARE TRAITS LINGUISTIC ARTIFACTS?

In 1968 Walter Mischel wrote an influential book in which he argued that trait descriptions of personality were fundamentally flawed. He indicated that attempts to predict the actual behavior of an individual on the basis of his or her trait ratings were rarely successful. Correlations between trait scores and measures of behavior tended to be quite low, rarely exceeding .3. Consider an example. Assume that individuals who are conscientious tend to be punctual. Imagine an investigation in which information was obtained about the punctuality of a group of individuals—perhaps by noting the time each individual arrived for a class at a college. Correlations between conscientiousness ratings and this measure of punctuality are likely to be low—in all probability below the value of .3 that Mischel assumed was the characteristic upper bound for predictions of behavior from measures of traits. Mischel argued that the low correlations were attributable to the fact that individuals tended to be inconsistent in their behavior in different situations. A person who was described as conscientious might not be punctual and might not behave in a way that was characteristic of conscientiousness in each of the situations in which it is possible to derive a behavioral measure of conscientiousness. Mischel assumed that our tendency to assign trait descriptions to ourselves and others was derived from the way in which we use language rather than from our characteristic behavioral tendencies. He argued that trait descriptions should be abandoned and replaced by descriptions that indicated the characteristic behaviors exhibited by individuals in different situations.

Is Mischel's criticism justified? Are traits nothing more than linguistic artifacts? If trait descriptions are replaced by descriptions that indicate the varying behavioral tendencies of individuals in different situations, there will be a considerable loss of economy of description. Of course, if the economy is attained at the price of distortion of reality it is not very valuable. Let us examine this issue in greater detail. It should be noted that self-reports of trait ratings tend to agree with ratings made by acquaintances. This suggests that we see ourselves for the most part in ways that are congruent with the perceptions of those who know us. Of course, this observation does not really refute Mischel's criticism. Perhaps we and our acquaintances are jointly deluded about the appropriateness of trait descriptions. Agreement between self and acquaintance ratings may best be construed as a necessary rather than a sufficient condition for assuming that trait ratings are valid.

Is Mischel's belief that trait ratings do not predict behavior correct? Consider the hypothetical study relating conscientiousness to a behavioral measure of punctuality. The study is flawed. Punctuality is measured by observations of behavior on one occasion. Such measures may not provide an adequate index of the characteristic behavioral tendencies of individuals. A person may be habitually punctual but on one occasion may have been unavoidably and uncharacteristically delayed. A more appropriate index of punctuality may be attained by observing an individual on several occasions and then averaging the observations to obtain a single measure of punctuality that reflects the characteristic behavioral tendencies of that person. Such a study would probably indicate that individuals tended to be consistent in their behavior. Imagine a study in which 20 observations of the time at which students arrived at a class were obtained. Assume that the set of 20 observations was randomly divided into two sets of 10 observations and an average index of time of arrival at class was obtained for each student for each subset of observations. The average index from the first subset would probably be highly predictive of the average index of the second subset. Mischel would argue that this study would indicate that individuals tend to behave in the same way in the same situation. He would, however, argue that this demonstration is irrelevant to his critique of traits. What is critical is not the demonstration that behavior is temporally consistent in the same situation but rather that trait relevant behaviors in different situations are related. Would a person who is punctual in arriving at class be punctual in arriving at parties? And, would a conscientious person who is punctual also be one who did not act impulsively when faced with a critical decision (another alleged manifestation of conscientiousness): Mischel argued that individuals might be consistent in their behavior in the same situation but inconsistent in their trait relevant behaviors in different situations.

Research on cross-situational consistency in behavior has partially supported and partially refuted Mischel. For example, psychologists have observed the behavior of children in naturalistic settings such as nursery schools and have measured characteristic tendencies to be helpful and supportive of other children. Indices of different behaviors that are assumed to represent such traits as helpfulness or dependency have been found to exhibit considerable cross-situational consistencies. Moreover, when trait ratings were compared to average indices of performance in several different situations, correlations in the .80s have been obtained. This type of research implies that trait ratings tend to be based on observations of the characteristic behavior of individuals in many different situations. Although there may be substantial cross-situational consistency in behavior, behavior in one situation is rarely perfectly predictive of behavior in a different situation. Individuals do have idiosyncratic patterns of trait expression. Individuals who are conscientious tend to be consistently conscientious. But two individuals with the same conscientiousness score might express their conscientiousness in somewhat different ways. One person might be characteristically punctual but not as consistent in acting in a planned nonimpulsive way. A second equally conscientious person might exhibit the opposite pattern of relations between impulsivity and punctuality. Trait descriptions may gloss over many details of the idiosyncrasies that are characteristic of a person's behavior. Whether trait descriptions or more detailed descriptions are correct or optimal depends on the purposes of the description. For certain purposes, a description at the most general level is optimal—for other purposes it may be necessary to describe the idiosyncrasies of a person's manner of expressing his or her traits.

There is evidence in longitudinal research that trait descriptions of persons can have considerable predictive utility. For example, in one study, elementary school children were rated by their peers on aggressive tendencies. Children who were nominated by their peers as aggressive were found to be aggressive and to exhibit a wide variety of anti-social and even criminal behavior as young adults in a 22-year longitudinal study. In another study, trait ratings of neuroticism obtained from peers prior to marriage for a large sample of engaged couples turned out to be the best predictor of the success of the marriage. Individuals whose spouses were rated by acquaintances as high in neuroticism were more likely to divorce or be dissatisfied with their marriage than individuals whose spouses were rated low in neuroticism. In this study, trait ratings were related to marital success measured several decades after the original ratings. There is an emerging body of longitudinal research that indicates that trait ratings, including those obtained in childhood, are related in nontrivial ways to important social indices.

IV. ORIGINS OF TRAITS

Why do individuals have different scores on trait dimensions? Psychologists have used twin studies and adoption studies to answer this question. There are many studies comparing identical (monozygotic or single egg, MZ) twins with fraternal (dyzygotic or two egg twins, DZ) twins in trait indices. The results of these studies tend to be reasonably consistent. MZ twins are more alike than DZ twins on all trait measures. Typically, MZ twins correlate close to .5 on most trait measures and DZ twins correlate .25 or less. What can we infer from these results? The greater similarity of MZ twins implies that there are genetic influences on the trait. This conclusion is based on the following reasoning: MZ twins are genetically identical—they derive from the fertilization of a single egg. DZ twins are genetically similar but not genetically identical. They are roughly 50% genetically similar. Differences among pairs of MZ twins can only be attributable to environmental influences. Differences among DZ twins can be caused by both differences in the environment and differences in their genes. If DZ twins are less similar than MZ twins, we can infer that genes influence traits. [*See* BEHAVIORAL GENETICS.]

Twin studies lead to additional conclusions about genetic and environmental influences on traits. MZ twins reared in the same family do not have a correlation of 1.00 on trait scores. Why? The differences cannot be attributable to the influences of experiences they share as a result of being reared in the same family. Shared experiences can make individuals similar, not dissimilar. It cannot be due to variations in their genes—MZ twins are genetically identical. Differences between MZ twins reared together must be attributable to nonshared environmental differences that cause individuals reared in the same family to differ from one another. We tend to think of environmental influences as those that are associated with the family in which we are reared. But individuals reared in the same family may experience large differences in their environment. Such environmental differences may include differences in prenatal environment. MZ twins are known to experience such differences. For example, the MZ twin whose birthweight is higher than that of his or her co-twin tends to have higher intelligence than his or her co-twin. Also, individuals reared together may be treated differently by their parents or they may believe that they are treated differently. Such differences in actual and perceived environmental differences among individuals reared in the same family may cause them to develop different traits. Individuals reared together may have different experiences attributable to events occurring outside of the context of the family. Two individuals reared together, including MZ twins, may have different friends, fall in love with different individuals, and be influenced in different ways by books, preachers, coaches, and encounters with many different individuals outside of the context of the family.

Same-sex DZ twin pairs reared together may have quite low correlations on measures of personality. They tend to have correlations that are less than half the value of MZ twins, and on some measures they may correlate close to zero. If DZ twins share approximately 50% of their genes and are reared in the same family, why aren't they more alike? There are two different reasons for the relatively low similarity of DZ twins. First, the experiences that are shared by individuals who are reared in the same family do not lead individuals to be similar on trait measures. This conclusion is surprising and counterintuitive but, as we shall see, it is supported by additional evidence. Second, genetic influences can cause individuals who are genetically similar but not genetically identical to differ from one another. In the limiting case, variations in a trait may be determined solely by genetic influences and DZ twins and siblings who share 50% of their genes might have a zero correlation for scores on the trait. In such a case, MZ twins would have a correlation of 1.00 on the trait. If we consider both causes of individual differences among DZ twins (and siblings), we see that for both genetic and environmental reasons, genetically similar individuals reared in the same family may not be similar to each other.

Genetic influences also lead individuals who are genetically similar to be similar in their traits. For example, DZ twins and siblings have correlations of about .25 on neuroticism. These similarities are probably not attributable to environmental influences they share as a result of being reared in the same family. Biologically unrelated siblings reared in the same family (either two adopted children, or the natural and adopted child of the same family) exhibit near zero correlations for measures of traits.

The results of twin and adoption studies are buttressed by a small number of studies of twins reared apart. MZ twins reared apart tend to have similar trait scores. And, in some studies for some measures, they are as similar as MZ twins reared together. In other studies, they are slightly less alike, although they are usually more alike than DZ twins reared together. In a small number of studies of DZ twins reared in different families, it is usually the case that they are as alike as DZ twins reared in the same family.

We are able to reach the following conclusions about the origins of traits. Trait scores are influenced by genes. Some of the genetic influences involved are those that cause genetically similar individuals to be dissimilar in traits. Traits are influenced by environmental influences that are not shared by individuals reared in the same family. In studies of adopted families, individuals reared together who are not biologically related are not similar on measures of personality traits. Most adopted families have had their adoption approved by social agencies. They represent a somewhat restricted range of social privilege. Whether personality traits of individuals reared together in families that are among the least privileged members of our society would be more similar to each other if they are not biologically related is not known. It is possible that extreme conditions of rearing would cause children reared together to have similar scores on personality trait measures. Most of our current studies have not been able to detect large effects of shared family rearing. Such effects may not exist, or they may be too subtle for psychologists to detect.

Perhaps the most interesting and imporant thing that psychologists have learned from studies of environmental and genetic influences on traits is that shared family rearing has so little influence on individuals. There are two different interpretations of this finding: (1) Parents may have relatively little influence on children. Children are influenced by their genes, by the biological environment they experience prenatally, and by experiences that occur outside the context of the home. In this view, children develop their personality traits despite their parents, not because of them. (2) Parents influence children's personality traits, but the influence is different for different children reared in the same family. Genetic differences among children and differences in the way in which parents respond to these differences lead each parent–child pair to develop idiosyncratic sequences of interactions and interdependent influences that have a subtly distinct influence on different children. In this view, each of us is profoundly influenced by the experiences we have had with our parents. These influences, however, are distinct for different children reared in the same family. We do not know which of these two interpretations is correct.

V. TRAIT CHANGE

There is considerable evidence for both continuity and discontinuity in traits over the course of an individual's life. Correlations of .5 have been reported between composite indices of trait ratings obtained in childhood and composite indices of trait related behavior for young adults in longitudinal studies of aggression. These studies, which cover a 22-year period, provide evidence for both continuity and discontinuity in traits. Some individuals who are aggressive as children are not aggressive as adults. Other individuals manifest considerable continuity in aggressive tendencies. Some of the lack of predictability in longitudinal studies is probably attributable to errors of measurement and failures to observe individuals comprehensively in order to obtain the most valid index of aggressive tendencies at different ages. We know that adults exhibit considerable stability of trait scores in longitudinal studies. Correlations close to .7 are common. The correlation is less than 1.00, indicating that individuals do change in their trait scores. There is no doubt that individuals do exhibit genuine changes in their trait related behaviors.

What causes individuals to change their traits? We don't really know. Some psychologists believe that traumas and encounters with unexpected and novel events may cause individuals to alter their personality. This may be correct, but there are at least two reasons to be cautious about evidence that traumatic events (divorce, job loss, etc.) leads to profound alterations in personality. First, some traumatic events may be caused by the individual. Divorce and marital stress may be attributable to neurotic tendencies on the part of individuals. In one study of depressed patients, it was found that individuals who were depressed were two and one-half times more likely to experience personal traumas than individuals who were not depressed. Most of these excess traumas were probably at least partially the result of the actions of depressed individuals and were not solely to be understood as events that occurred for reasons that were independent of the actions of individuals. Second, there is some evidence that traumatic and novel events may actually accentuate preexistent trait differences. For example, early menarche seems to pose problems for adolescent girls. The biological and physical changes that accompany early menarche occur in the absence of social supports and observations of appropriate peer responses to these changes. In one study, girls who had behavior problems prior to the onset of early menarche exhibited exacerbated personal problems and an increase in neuroticism. Girls who experienced menarche early, but who were relatively low in neuroticism prior to the onset of menarche, did not exhibit a large increase in neuroticism. Consequently, early menarche led to an increase in differences in trait scores. Individuals changes in response to novel events by becoming "more like themselves." As individuals encounter novel and stressful events they may change in personality characteristics. These changes in their personality tendencies may actually lead them to change in the direction of pre-existent genetically influenced dispositions. Alternatively, the cumulative effect of a series of novel encounters with the world may cause individuals to slowly change their personality traits and to become different. We do not know which of these two models of personality change is correct. We do know that the influence of genes on intelligence becomes more important as individuals grow older. Genetically identical individuals (MZ twins) tend to remain similar in intelligence over the lifespan. DZ twins slowly drift apart. We do not have enough data on genetic and environmental influences over the lifespan on personality traits to know whether genetic influences become more or less important in determining a person's traits as they grow older.

Can personality traits be altered by planned interventions such as those provided by psychotherapy and other forms of inteventions? We really do not know the answer to this question. Some therapists argue that they do not believe that the goal of therapy is to alter general dispositions or traits. In this view, therapeutic interventions are designed to alter narrower forms of behavior that may be destructive for the individual. Alternatively, some therapists believe that therapy alters basic personality dispositions. There is a large literature that demonstrates that various forms of therapy lead to changes that are larger than those produced by placebo controls. There are, however, two respects in which the literature does not provide evidence for fundamental alterations in personality dispositions. First, most of the changes that occur that are attributable to therapy are small. Although improvements may be clinically meaningful, they do not usually result in changes that lead individuals who are neurotic to behave as if they were no longer neurotic. That is, they may result in changes that leave individuals less neurotic but still more neurotic than the average person. Second, most studies of therapeutic intervention that include attempts to follow individuals after therapy use short follow-ups—rarely exceeding a 6-month period. Longitudinal studies of pesonality traits may extend for a 20- or 30-year period. Viewed against evidence for the enduring significance of personality traits, evidence for relatively small changes that endure for 6 months or a year seems insufficient to leave us with a confident belief that therapy is able to profoundly alter personality traits.

Bibliography

Brody, N. (1988). "Personality: In Search of Individuality." Academic Press, San Diego.

Derlega, V. J., Winstead, B. A., and Jones, W. H. (Eds.) (1991). "Personality." Nelson-Hall, Chicago.

Dunn, J., and Plomin, R. (1990). "Separate Lives." Basic Books, New York.

Pervin, L. (Ed.) (1990). "Handbook of Personality: Theory and Research." Guilford, New York.

Zuckerman, M. (1991). "Psychobiology of Personality." Cambridge, New York.

Type A–Type B Personalities

Jerry Suls and Annette Swain
University of Iowa

Glossary

Coronary heart disease Cardiovascular pathology characterized by an inadequate supply of oxygen to the heart. Major forms include myocardial infarction, or heart attack, and angina, severe chest pain.

Hyperreactivity Excessive cardiovascular, neuroendocrine, or other physiologic responsiveness to environmental stressors.

Potential for hostility Predisposition to react to aggravating circumstances with displays of anger, antagonism, rudeness, resentment, etc.

TYPE A BEHAVIOR PATTERN (TA), or personality, is defined as an action–emotion complex manifesting extreme competitiveness, achievement-striving, hostility, aggressiveness, and a sense of time urgency evidenced by emphatic speech and psychomotor mannerisms. The absence of these features describes the Type B pattern. Early psychosomatic theorists had proposed that hostile, overambitious individuals are at increased risk for coronary heart disease (CHD). In the 1950s, two pioneering cardiologists, Meyer Friedman and Ray Rosenman, formally introduced the constellation of behaviors described above as "Type A" as a risk factor for CHD. Epidemiological studies conducted during the late 1950–1960s, using special measures to assess this complex of competitive, aggressive, and impatient behaviors, indicated that Type A's were at a twofold greater risk of incurring coronary heart disease than their Type B counterparts. These findings were considered important because of the prospect that Type A would improve outcome prediction and identify high-risk individuals for treatment programs beyond that afforded by status on traditional risk factors such as serum cholesterol, hypertension, and smoking. Early findings concerning Type A and CHD encouraged the further development of behavioral medicine and health psychology. TA has been controversial in psychological and medical circles, however, almost from its inception. Some researchers and practitioners have embraced the concept noncritically while others have dismissed it out of hand. The present authors believe the validity and usefulness of TA falls somewhere between these extreme positions.

I. ASSESSMENT OF TYPE A

Friedman and Rosenman initially developed the Type A concept from observations of their own cardiac patients. Six features of the patient's conduct appeared relevant: (1) a strong drive to accomplish multiple poorly defined goals; (2) a propensity to compete; (3) an intense need for recognition and advancement; (4) habitual time-urgent actions; (5) extraordinary acceleration of physical and mental activity; and (6) intense concentration and alertness. Friedman and Rosenman conceived of Type A as a behavioral style resulting from the interaction between a specific set of predispositions and eliciting situations, rather than as a personality trait, to avoid identification with the traditional psychosomatic approach which emphasized case studies and psychoanalytic theorizing about personality and heart disease.

Despite Friedman and Rosenman's emphasis on TA as a behavior pattern, the construct as a whole differs little from those derived from personality theory. The expression of stable attributes similarly requires eliciting circumstances. Conceptualized in trait terms, Type A–B is probably best considered not as a single dimension, but as a composite of facets or subcomponents of several personality dimensions.

Because of Friedman and Rosenman's emphasis on observable activity, in addition to their belief that TA's were either unreflective or consciously defensive, a behavior-based interview was developed to assess the presence of Type A. The "Structured Interview" (SI) consists of approximately 25 questions regarding the individual's typical response to various potentially hostile, competitive, or otherwise stressful circumstances. Type A scoring is based partially upon the content of the interviewee's answers, but more weight is given to both the style of his or her responses (e.g., loud explosive speech) and accompanying behavior (e.g., speech hurrying and anticipation of questions). The interviewer deliberately creates a moderately challenging situation by probing some of the interviewee's answers in a semi-accusatory manner to assess aggressive tendencies and by asking very predictable questions quite slowly to assess impatience. Based on the audiotaped responses, subjects are classified as extreme Type A1, incompletely developed A2, or the converse, Types B3 and B4. The label X is reserved for a small percentage of subjects who exhibit equal amounts of Type A and B behaviors.

Both Friedman and Rosenman's classification system and the use of the term "Type" give the impression that TA is a typology; however, subsequent researchers often treat the construct as a continuous dimension. The validity and relative merits of dimensional versus typological systems is, unfortunately, beyond the scope of this essay. TA is defined by a complex of presumably co-occurring attributes. Confusion is possible, however, because individuals may be grouped within the same category even if they differ in their possession of specific Type A behaviors. For example, some persons may be designated as Type A who are extremely time urgent and explosive in their speech, but only moderate in hostility and achievement-striving, while others might be labeled Type A on the basis of an extreme standing on hostility and achievement-striving. This lack of specificity allows for a diverse population to be categorized as Type A/B and thus may increase the false-positive rate when TA status is used as a predictor of CHD.

Published reports of inter-rater and test–retest reliabilities for the SI are consistent and acceptable, between 79 and 84% agreement for the former and approximately 80% agreement for the latter with an interval of 12–20 months. Although these psychometric properties of the SI are satisfactory, global Type A/B ratings do not reflect or assess all of the central components included in the original conceptual definition (e.g., dissatisfaction with life, worthiness of one's activities). The present version of the SI represents a combination of objective and subjective aspects of measurement. An additional complication is that interviewee's responses, and hence their classification, may be influenced by interviewer characteristics and style.

Construct validity studies of the SI have found that Type A's work longer hours, work more overtime, and travel more on the job. SI-assessed Type A's do not appear to report more psychological strain than their Type B counterparts, either because multiple tasks and time pressure do not bother Type A's or because they are reluctant to acknowledge their distress. Most of these findings are limited, however, by reliance on global self-reports rather than on extensive daily measurements.

An issue related to the reliability, validity, and continued applicability of the SI concerns its vulnerability to change over time. In recent years, interviewers have been trained somewhat differently than those who were employed in the original epidemiological studies of Type A. Although the question content is basically the same, the number of questions has been reduced, and the interview style has been modified. For instance, in comparison to examiners for the first large-scale epidemiologic study of TA and CHD, who were taught to be more gentle and not necessarily hostile, those employed in the later Multiple Risk Factor Intervention Trial (MRFIT) were trained to be more aggressive, rudely interruptive, and confrontational. Friedman also altered the administration procedures for the SI in his Recurrent Coronary Prevention Project (RCPP), under the assumption that the original SI lacked sufficient sensitivity. For the RCPP, videotaping was added to allow visual cues to be incorporated into the assessment process. Although these changes permit the analysis of a greater number of Type A indicators, the revisions make the RCPP interview noncomparable to prior administrations and pose problems for generalizability.

A number of standardized paper and pencil questionnaires have been developed in an attempt to duplicate the evaluation achieved with the SI. The Jenkins Activity Survey (JAS), which is the most popular, uses many of the same questions as the SI, but its validity depends upon the insight and candor of the test taker. This is at odds, however, with Friedman and Rosenman's original belief that Type A's are either too unreflective or too defensive for a self-report questionnaire to adequately assess the presence of TA. Unsurprisingly, the JAS does not correlate with SI assessments of TA at levels significantly above chance even though the JAS attempts to assess similar content. The JAS also has no predictive validity for CHD incidence or mortality after adjusting for traditional risk factors.

The Framingham Type A scale (FTAS) is another popular measure of TA. This 10-item inventory was derived from a pool of 300 questions administered to the participants of the Framingham Heart Study. The FTAS also lacks significant agreement with SI classifications. Its predictive ability is limited solely to the study from which it was derived. Finally, there are no normative data for FTAS, a necessity for the integrity of any psychometric measure.

Given their limited predictive validity, it is somewhat ironic that the construct validity of self-report Type A measures has been studied extensively. This research confirms that persons scoring in the Type A direction prefer higher levels of task difficulty, carry more demanding academic loads, view opponents as more competitive, and attempt to complete tasks as quickly as possible. These results bear on the achievement-striving and job-involvement aspects of TA, but appear uncorrelated with other aspects, such as hostility or nonverbal stylistics, which are assessed by the SI.

Researchers recognized by the late 1970s that only some of the dimensions of TA may represent coronary-prone tendencies. Although attention to particular subcomponents was largely based on serendipitous results, psychosomatic theorists have long advocated a critical role for hostility in the etiology of cardiovascular disease.

In 1977, Matthews and her colleagues examined elements of the SI including anger expressed outward, competitiveness, explosiveness of speech, etc. A more focused component scoring system, emphasizing the anger/hostility aspects of the pattern, was developed by Dembroski soon afterward. Three factors were considered: (1) hostile content—reported frequency of experienced anger and irritation; (2) response intensity—use of emotion-laden, profane, emphatic expressions; and (3) antagonistic interpersonal style—displays of rudeness, condescension, and contempt toward the interviewer. After listening to the taped interview the auditor rates each dimension separately on a 5-point scale. These values are then aggregated (or averaged) to obtain an overall potential for hostility (PH) score. The three sub-component measures have also been used on occasion to predict CHD. Hecker and Chesney at Stanford Research Institute and Barefoot et al. at Duke University Medical Center have recently developed even more elaborate subcomponent scoring systems for the SI which code subject responses question-by-question. The inter-rater reliability of the Dembroski component scoring system falls between .70 and .85, while test–retest reliability has been estimated at .55. Consistency studies for the other systems are still under way, but appear to be in the same range. Evidence for the construct validity of PH is limited, however.

Scores on the Cook-Medley hostility scale (HO), a measure derived from the Minnesota Multiphasic Personality Inventory (MMPI), have also predicted, though less consistently, overall and CHD-related mortality. This standardized inventory appears to measure particular covert facets of hostility, namely cynicism, suspiciousness, distrust, and resentment. The correlation between PH and HO scores is modest (.29–.37). Careful inspection of the Cook–Medley items indicate that most tap subjective aspects of the construct, sometimes referred to as "neurotic" or "experiential hostility." A smaller set of items measures tendencies to express ill will and negativism through verbal or physical aggression, often described as "antagonistic" or "expressive hostility." The latter dimension is more highly correlated with PH, particularly the interpersonal subcomponent. Evidence to be discussed below indicates that the antagonistic style aspect of hostility may be the toxic element involved in the pathogenesis of CHD.

The hostility construct shares the same multidimensionality problems alluded to earlier with respect to global Type A. Separate facets measured with multiple inventories vary in terms of their affective intensity, expression, and direction. Furthermore, the extent to which these negative tendencies are situation-specific is unknown.

II. PERSONALITY CORRELATES OF TYPE A

Conceptualizing TA as a behavior pattern had benefits, but also tended to divorce it from advances in the study of personality and individual differences. The theoretical investigation of TA as a trait was also impeded by past emphasis upon its potential practical uses in identification, treatment, and prevention in medicine. Researchers have only recently begun to examine how TA is related to underlying personality dimensions. [*See* TRAITS.]

One advance has come from researchers employing an interactionist approach, which proposes that particular environmental stimuli may not be necessary to elicit Type A reactions from predisposed individuals. Rather, these people may actually create a personal environment that is physically and psychologically taxing. Their competitive and aggressive demeanor may elicit reactions from others that serve as stimuli for continued Type A behavior. They may also subjectively evaluate situations as being more challenging and stressful. These ideas characterize Type A from a broader, less behaviorist perspective and view Type A as more than simply a response pattern.

Especially relevant is the five-factor model of personality, consisting of the major dimensions of neuroticism, extraversion, agreeableness, openness to experience, and conscientiousness. Within this scheme, TA individuals may be seen as high in conscientiousness and extraversion, and low on agreeableness. These ideas are compatible with results of recent studies examining the dispositional correlates of SI Type A, which indicate modest associations with extraversion, need for power, and achievement, but no relationship with neuroticism. Whether openness to experience is relevant to TA is unclear, though a case might be made that Type A's have a narrow range of feelings and are relatively insensitive to their surroundings (i.e., low in the "feelings" facet of openness). Although Type A measured with the SI is not associated with the general dimension of neuroticism, insecurity, a facet of neuroticism, may characterize Type A's. Otherwise, the extreme need to succeed and heightened tendency to become impatient and openly hostile when threatened or frustrated are without obvious explanation. Since feelings of self-doubt are only one aspect of the basic dimension of neuroticism (which also includes other elements such as tenseness, fearfulness, and impulsivity, that have no obvious connection to TA), SI Type A–B may be uncorrelated with the general dimension of neuroticism. Still another possibility is that Type A's conceal or deny their underlying neurotic concerns. Defensiveness or denial, coupled with insecurity, may be important elements of the behavior pattern. [*See* EXTRAVERSION–INTROVERSION.]

JAS and FTAS Type A are strongly associated with neuroticism and nonpathological, chronic dysphoria, still another indication that the SI taps a different constellation of dispositions. The overlap with neuroticism might lead to the inference that these self-report measures of Type A are predictive of physical disease. Interestingly, contrary to early psychosomatic theorizing, neuroticism is unrelated to morbidity or mortality from physical disease. On the other hand, persons high on this factor report more bodily complaints, apparently because they are somatically overconcerned and frequently label benign physical changes as signs of illness.

Recently, attention has been devoted to the personality correlates of the hostility complex. The overtly aggressive interpersonal style reflected in PH ratings maps well onto the negative pole of the agreeableness continuum (antagonism) and, as noted earlier, is proposed to be the "toxic" component of hostility and global Type A. The items of HO scale that tap experiential hostility demonstrate its similarity to neuroticism. Questions that measure expressive hostility are associated with antagonism.

III. EPIDEMIOLOGICAL FINDINGS FOR TYPE A BEHAVIOR

A. Prospective Studies

The first prospective study of the Type A–CHD relationship and a major impetus for subsequent research was the Western Collaborative Group Study (WCGS). Led by the originators of TA, this investigation followed approximately 3200 middle-aged, white-collar men who were initially free of CHD. After 8.5 years, those men classified as Type A by the SI were twice as likely to develop CHD compared to their Type B counterparts, even after statistical adjustment for the traditional CHD risk factors. Actual CHD mortality, however, was not an outcome measure.

The JAS was also administered to a subset of the WCGS study population. After four years, a comparison of new CHD cases (again, morbidity and not necessarily fatalities—though these were included) with matched controls revealed JAS Type A individuals to be nearly twice as likely to develop CHD. When simultaneous adjustments for other risk factors were performed, however, the JAS ceased to be a significant predictor.

The next major prospective research on the Type A–CHD relationship was the Framingham Heart Study. Unlike the WCGS, this investigation followed a population of both men and women from both white-collar and blue-collar jobs, all diagnosed as CHD-free upon study entry. Type A/B classification, using the Framingham Type A scale, was determined with a median split within sex and age to form the respective groups. Multivariate analyses at 8-year follow-up found Type A to be a significant, independent predictor of total CHD incidence, myocardial infarction (MI), and angina in white-collar men and total CHD and angina in women. However, TA predicted only differential rates of angina after 10 years.

Enthusiasm for the Type A construct reached its peak in 1978 when a distinguished review panel sponsored by the National Heart, Lung, and Blood Institute concluded that Type A was a significant risk factor for the development of CHD, independent of and comparable in magnitude to standard risk factors. The strength and credibility of the Type A–CHD association began to decline in the 1980s, however, following the publication of negative findings.

Outcomes from the Multiple Risk Factor Intervention Trial (MRFIT) provided much of the initial damage to the predictive validity of the Type A construct. Participants of this study were middle-aged males, chosen on the basis of their high-risk status with respect to blood pressure levels, serum cholesterol, and cigarette smoking who were CHD-free at study entry. These individuals were randomly assigned into either a usual care or a special care group, with the latter group exposed to a variety of interventions designed to reduce their high-risk factor status. After being followed an average of 7 years, results indicated that TA classification, assessed either by the SI or by the JAS, did not predict either total mortality or mortality specifically from CHD.

At approximately the same time as the MRFIT investigation was conducted, survivors of acute MI were being followed in the Multicenter Postinfarction Program. The JAS Type A failed to predict mortality at 1- and 3-year follow-up. This analysis was flawed, however, because the sample comprised patients with relatively mild disease. Individuals in the same program who could not be included in the analysis due to loss of their original Type A assessments had more severe cardiac disease and a higher mortality rate.

After publication of these negative results, there was skepticism about the predictive validity of global Type A. This skepticism was increased by the report of the 22-year follow-up of the original WCGS sample by Ragland and Brand, who failed to find a significant association between Type A/B classification and CHD mortality rates while traditional risk factors continued to be significant predictors of CHD. Also, analyses of the subset of 257 WCGS participants diagnosed as suffering from CHD during the 8.5-year follow-up showed that Type B's actually had a significantly higher reinfarction rate. One possible explanation for the discrepancy between the original WCGS findings and later follow-up is that the outcome measure taken at longer intervals was CHD mortality rather than CHD incidence. Hence, Type A may be related to CHD morbidity, but not to CHD fatality. Ragland and Brand also failed to mention the complicating factor that several of the participants who had developed CHD in the 8.5-year follow-up had been simultaneously receiving Type A behavioral counseling in the Recurrent Coronary Prevention Project.

B. Angiography Studies

The development of precise measures of coronary artery stenosis using angiographic imaging provided new means for studying the relationship between the Type A construct and the extent of coronary artery disease. Numerous trials of individuals referred for angiography were conducted, which assessed TA using the JAS. The few investigations employing the SI yielded an overall positive relationship between Type A and the extent of CAD. Those using self-report techniques, however, did not find significant associations.

C. Meta-analytic Studies of Global Type A

By the late 1980s a number of researchers began using quantitative, meta-analytic review methods to aggregate the many studies exploring the Type A–CHD relationship. Results from these reviews indicate a significant, though modest, association between TA, as assessed by the SI, and CHD incidence. Self-report measures, on the other hand, were neither reliable nor valid predictors. These meta-analyses also revealed a trend during recent years toward null findings, possibly due to such factors as insufficient sample size, inadequate disease criteria, the dependence upon questionnaires to determine Type A status, and disease-based spectrum (DBS) bias. This final explanation refers to a type of range restriction problem in studies that employ only high-risk or diseased participants. When the subject sample is limited to such a select group of individuals, the range of disease severity is likewise limited, creating a range attenuation effect and thereby possibly decreasing the magnitude of the relationship between Type A and CHD.

In sum, prospective and cross-sectional investigations have found a significant association between TA and the pathogenesis of CHD, though it is small and is observed only for SI-assessed Type A. This relationship applies to CHD incidence, but not CHD mortality, and is weaker than that of standard risk factors. Finally, the association tends to be restricted to general population studies.

D. Hostility Studies

The hostility complex has emerged as a predictor of CHD, even in those studies such as MRFIT, which failed to show a global Type A–CHD relationship. An assessment of hostility made using standardized measures such as the HO Scale or the SI-based PH suggest that a cynical, mistrusting attitude, evidenced by anger, contempt, and aggression, is a predictor of clinical end points.

The first study that examined the relative importance of the SI subcomponents of Type A compared new CHD cases of WCGS participants with matched controls. Potential for Hostility scores best discriminated cases from controls. This was followed by overt anger, competitiveness, experiencing anger more than once a week, vigorousness of response, irritation at waiting in lines, and explosiveness of speech. Analyses of all available cases from the 8.5-year follow-up of WCGS participants also illustrated that PH (using the Hecker and Chesney coding system) best discriminated cases from controls, independent of traditional risk factors.

Recent research has demonstrated that PH and the HO scale significantly predict angiographically documented CAD severity, even after statistically controlling for age, sex, and traditional risk factors. Prospective studies employing the HO scale have produced inconsistent outcomes. Results from a 20-year follow-up of 1877 males who completed the MMPI in the Western Electric Study demonstrated a significant increase in 10-year CHD incidence in those participants with higher HO scores. A 25-year follow-up of 255 physicians also yielded a four- to five-fold incidence rate among those with an elevated HO scale. However, another study, using a similar methodology, which followed 478 doctors after 25 years failed to replicate these findings. The inconsistent outcomes may be related to the differing circumstances under which the inventory was administered or to the fact that the HO represents a mix of experienced and expressed hostility items.

Accumulated evidence suggests that both global TA and the hostility complex are modestly associated only with CHD morbidity. Although these predispositions predict disease, their predictive utility is modest, and the majority of new CHD cases still cannot be predicted by the best combination of traditional and psychological risk factors. Some researchers have suggested that hostility and Type A are also risk factors for general illness susceptibility, but relevant evidence is scarce.

IV. EXPLANATIONS FOR TYPE A–CHD RISK

The hyperreactivity hypothesis is the most popular explanation for the association between TA (or hostility) and CHD. The theory proposes that persons high in TA or hostility exhibit excessive elevations in cardiovascular and neuroendocrine arousal in response to particular environmental situations, and thereby accelerate the atherosclerotic process and increase the incidence of life-threatening cardiac arrhythmias. This hypothesis assumes that a predisposition to hyperresponsivity creates physiologic changes that eventuate in disease. There is some evidence that sympathetic nervous system (SNS) arousal alters metabolic function in myocardial cells, increases the deposition and incorporation of coronary artery plaques, and may facilitate their rupture. These changes can produce coronary artery thrombosis and myocardial infarction. Catecholamines may also interact with existing atherosclerosis to generate cardiac arrhythmias. The pituitary–adrenocortical system may additionally be implicated in the pathogenesis of CHD. Chronic elevations in cortico-steroids have been linked to elevations in serum lipids, increased atherosclerosis in animals, and higher proportions of dead or injured endothelial cells. Studies using coronary angiography have also found positive correlations between elevated plasma cortisol and early atherosclerosis. Exaggerated physiological responses may also compromise the immune system, thus increasing susceptibility to other illnesses in addition to CHD. Although chronic elevations in these physiologic systems have been alleged as possible mechanisms for CHD development, definitive evidence indicating the degree of risk associated with a given magnitude of reactivity is lacking.

A large number of laboratory-based studies have documented that SI-assessed Type A males manifest larger increases in systolic blood pressure, diastolic blood pressure, and heart rate in response to stressors than do male Type B's. These differences are particularly evident in response to moderately stressful or challenging cognitive tasks. Type B males actually demonstrate higher arousal, however, in situations that are ambiguous or involve role-conflict. Physical stressors have not consistently elicited differences, unless an incentive has been simultaneously provided. There are relatively few studies involving Type A/B females and those available are inconclusive. The failure to produce differential reactivity in Type A/B women may be due to sex-role expectations, inappropriate stimuli, or because of the inapplicability of the global Type A construct to females.

Trait anger and hostility as measured by PH also appear modestly, though less consistently, related to blood pressure responses to anger-eliciting tasks. HO scores are somewhat more consistently related to heightened pressor changes, especially in response to interpersonal stressors. Support for the reactivity model for hostility appears to be dependent upon the assessment measure employed.

The magnitude of physiological responsivity differences between high TA vs low TA (or hostile) persons is modest, raising the question of whether such differences could produce cardiovascular pathology. Whether exaggerated reactivity to laboratory stimuli possesses external validity is still unclear. Research using ambulatory monitors of cardiovascular functioning is, unfortunately, still in its early stages.

The bulk of laboratory research has focused primarily on heart rate and blood pressure changes, indices of SNS arousal. There is some, albeit sparse, evidence to suggest that excessive pituitary–adrenocortical responses may be implicated in the etiology of CHD in Type A's. One problem or ambiguity, however, is that elevated physiological measures may simply be indicative of increased effort to cope with challenges by Type A individuals as opposed to a predisposition or pathogenic mechanism. Human psychophysiological investigations indicate that exaggerated reactivity may be shown using either positively or negatively valenced stimuli (i.e., challenges and threats).

Although most Type A researchers have appropriately assumed that challenging or stressful situations elicit both stereotypical Type A reactions and hyperresponsivity in particular individuals, an equally plausible explanation is that these persons have an underlying diathesis, or physiological responsiveness, which is reflected not only in their reactivity to experimental tasks but also in their Type A personality. A constitutional predisposition for exaggerated responses could be the source of TA itself.

A critical question concerns why TA relates to CHD incidence, but not to CHD mortality. One suggestion is that coronary-prone behavior may be more strongly related to acute precipitating factors (e.g., cardiac arrhythmias, vessel spasm) than to atherosclerosis. Consequently, Type A's may be more likely to experience cardiac events, but are not necessarily destined to die prematurely.

An additional explanation for TA or hostility as risk factors is that coronary-prone persons act in ways, or have health habits, that encourage the disease process. For example, TA's may ignore early cardiac symptoms or create frequent stressful episodes for themselves. Perhaps the difference in arousal between persons high vs low in coronary-proneness is not crucial, but rather the frequency with which such episodes occur. Type A's and hostile persons may also suffer from other inborn physiological weaknesses or liabilities that predispose them to CHD (e.g., greater clotting). Finally, persons presumed to exhibit a high number of coronary-prone behaviors may be vulnerable because they are also high on traditional risk factors. This possibility has been given little consideration because it has been claimed that Type A predicted CHD independent of traditional risk factors. However, epidemiologic studies assess many traditional risk factors in simple ways that may overlook important subtleties in smoking patterns, eating patterns, etc. A recent investigation using improved procedures (e.g., ambulatory blood pressure measurement) showed that Type A's are more likely to be hypertensive, even though TA had been previously assumed to be unrelated to chronically elevated blood pressure.

V. THEORIES OF THE ORIGINS OF TYPE A BEHAVIOR

The search for the origins of TA is dependent upon the researchers' theoretical position on the Type

A–CHD relationship. Cognitive–social learning theory is a popular perspective, but others have argued for a genetic or constitutional basis. Evidence is available for both views.

The psychobiological, or constitutional predisposition, perspective elaborated upon in the previous section is compatible with a genetic basis for the TA construct. Twin studies of the heritability of cardiovascular reactivity have, unfortunately, been methodologically inadequate (e.g., failing to adjust for twin resemblance in baseline blood pressure) and, hence, inconclusive. Research with twins and families has also examined the heritability of Type A and its components. Analysis of the single investigation using SI-assessed twins did not detect a genetic component of global Type A, but did find hostility to be modestly heritable. The inconsistent findings may be due to different evaluation procedures or the possibility of polygenetic influences in TA development.

Social learning theorists emphasize the role of parenting behaviors in the evolution of Type A personality. Parents of Type A's tend to be more critical of their children, but they also provide higher and more ambiguous performance standards in comparison to the parents of Type B children. Such behaviors may foster TA in children to the extent that the children are repeatedly urged to try harder and perform better, yet are not given precise standards with which to gauge their performance. An important point of confusion lies in the direction of effect. Although Type A may be the result of particular environmental elicitors, such as parenting styles, Type A/B children may also evoke differential parenting styles from their caregivers. The latter hypothesis is compatible with the genetic argument. A transactional approach, which assumes that both parenting behaviors and inborn temperament act reciprocally to make significant contributions to the growth of TA, is also compatible with existing evidence.

Cognitions, more specifically personal beliefs, may foster and promote TA. Type A's may equate personal worth with their achievements, believe that there are no universal moral principles, and believe that resources are scarce (thereby justifying hostile, competitive behavior). The Type A personality would then evolve as a coping strategy to deal with these thoughts and fears. Empirical evidence for this view is unavailable. Also, there is no evidence that these kinds of cognitive beliefs are associated with exaggerated physiological responses, poor health habits, or constitutional predisposition. In a parallel literature, hostile persons tend to perceive that they have been treated unjustly and that aggressive behavior may be necessary to maintain their integrity, but there has been no systematic study of how these beliefs relate directly to cardiopathogenic processes.

VI. ISSUES CONCERNING INTERVENTION

Type A has also been the target of intervention measures to improve prevention efforts and prognosis for CHD. Enthusiasm about altering TA pattern has been tempered, however, by ongoing controversy about the nature of Type A, which components of TA are coronary-prone, how accurately TA is measured, and how changes in TA as a result of treatment can be documented.

Clinical research has demonstrated that personality traits are very difficult to change and efforts to do so are generally met with resistance. A number of studies investigating the effectiveness and feasibility of modifying Type A personalities have nevertheless been undertaken. The most impressive of these endeavors is the Recurrent Coronary Prevention Project (RCPP) which randomized 862 post-MI patients into either a control treatment group or Type A counseling group. Controls were counseled to improve their diets, exercise patterns, and medication compliance. In addition to these recommendations, participants in the experimental group were exposed to a variety of cognitive–behavioral techniques (e.g., time management, relaxation) designed to modify daily Type A behaviors. At a 4.5-year follow-up, Type A modification procedures significantly lowered the CHD recurrence rate, although no differences in cardiac mortality rates were found.

With the exception of the RCPP, treatment studies have found little evidence of disease reduction, although a number of investigations have documented significant behavior modifications in Type A participants. Focused approaches using subcomponent models of coronary-prone behavior (e.g., hostility) have also been effective in producing behavior change. None of these studies have demonstrated significant reductions in CHD incidence, recurrence, or mortality rates, however. This may be partially due to the short-term nature of most of the interventions and reliance on healthy samples.

The practicality and feasibility of employing Type A modification procedures to reduce CHD risk needs to be carefully considered. As a CHD-prevention tool for the general population such treatment would be extremely costly in terms of money, labor, and time. Given the small number of actual CHD cases that TA can identify in advance, the benefits would be relatively small. Although TA's may have double the CHD incidence of Type B's, the number of false-positives (i.e., TA's who do not develop CHD) is many times the number of true-positives (i.e., TA's who do develop CHD). (Traditional risk factors also possess this predictive problem, though not as severely.) For high-risk individuals or those who have survived an MI, the potential benefits of intervention may be more substantial.

VII. UNRESOLVED QUESTIONS AND FUTURE DIRECTIONS

The introduction of the Type A construct was a milestone in the study of behavioral factors in disease and in the general development of behavioral medicine. Yet, over 30 years after its formulation, controversy and criticism still surround the relationship between Type A and CHD. Much of this stems from a number of unresolved questions, most of which have already been raised in this article and thus need only brief explication here.

First, the relationship between Type A and the more general theory and measurement of personality needs further examination. The original "behavioral" emphasis had the advantage of avoiding the excesses of psychoanalytic speculation, but also isolated Type A from advances in the study of personality. The Five-Factor Model is relevant to TA, but more research and theorizing are needed. A clearer conception of the attributes underlying Type A may lead to the creation of instruments, or the use of conventional personality measures, which are more objective, convenient, and less costly to both subjects and researchers than the SI.

The relationship between Type A and conventional dimensions of personality also raises concerns about how TA individuals actually behave in their daily life. Researchers of coronary-prone behavior have relied almost exclusively upon global self-reports. Naturalistic observation using state-of-the-art experience sampling and ambulatory monitoring would provide valuable information about whether TA behavior in daily life is similar to responses to the SI, and to Friedman and Rosenman's original conceptions. Such research may also provide opportunities for the design of an accurate, reliable, and more predictive assessment instrument.

Another set of unresolved matters concern the actual size of the relationship between TA and CHD. Meta-analytic surveys indicate that the magnitude of risk associated with the Type A personality is statistically significant, but how clinically meaningful it is remains unclear. Why TA relates to higher morbidity, but not to mortality is an especially puzzling and important question. Perhaps TA is associated only with acute precipitating events, but not atherosclerosis. There may even be protective factors associated with global Type A that allow the individual who experiences a cardiac event to recover.

Similar questions may be raised about the hostility complex. Again, the size of the relationship with CHD is modest at best. Unresolved questions include which components of hostility are general disease factors and which, if any, are CHD-specific. Rosenman and Friedman originally conceptualized Type A as consisting of two components—impatience and hostility—but some research indicates that global Type A and hostility are independent risk factors for CHD.

The developmental origins of TA are also unclear. Type A as a personality construct implies a constitutional, biological temperament as its base, but many researchers subscribe to a social learning model and minimize the role of heredity. More research into genetic factors and mechanisms underlying the temperament of TA is needed.

The mediators linking Type A personality and CHD incidence are currently under investigation. Although chronic sympathetic arousal is a popular explanation for the association, results are inconclusive. Hyperreactivity, by itself, seems unlikely to furnish a complete explanation for the CHD risk conferred by TA or hostility.

Finally, the feasibility, practicality, and necessity of intervention procedures to reduce TA behavior in healthy populations need further attention. If TA modification is promoted, whom should be targeted, what procedures should it include, and how will it be made cost-effective? At this stage, high-risk individuals and persons with existing CHD seem to be the most appropriate candidates for behavioral treatment.

These unresolved and somewhat daunting questions may discourage the prospects of success in understanding how dispositional factors influence disease and the application of this knowledge for medical practice. There are clearly some difficult issues to be faced. Future research should concentrate upon a clearer conceptualization of TA and hostility by drawing upon theoretical advances in the relevant areas of personality and temperament and upon methodological advances in the study of everyday behavior. The recognition that TA is related, albeit modestly, to morbidity, but not to mortality, should also promote research to go beyond a simplistic hyperreactivity explanation for the TA–CHD association. The Type A personality is not a dead issue, as some might suggest; however, some major rejuvenation is in order.

Bibliography

Chesney, M. A. (Ed.) (1988). Area review. Coronary-prone behavior: Continuing evolution of the concept [Special Issue]. *Ann. Behav. Med.* **10**(2).

Houston, B. K., and Snyder, C. R. (Eds.) (1988). "Type A Behavior Pattern." Wiley, New York.

Miller, T. Q., Turner, C. W., Tindale, R. S., Posavac, E. J., and Dugoni, B. L. (1991). Reasons for the trend toward null findings in research on Type A behavior. *Psychol. Bull.* **110,** 469–485.

Smith, T. W. (1992). Hostility and health: Current status of a psychosomatic hypothesis. *Health Psychol.* **11,** 139–150.

Strube, M. (1991). "Type A Behavior." Sage, Newbury Park, CA.

Suls, J., and Sanders, G. (1989). Why do some behavioral styles place people at coronary risk? In "In Search of Coronary-Prone Behavior" (A. W. Siegman and T. M. Dembroski, Eds.), pp. 1–20. Erlbaum, Hillsdale, NJ.

UNCERTAINTY

Michael Smithson
James Cook University, Queensland, Australia

Glossary

Ambiguity A special kind of uncertainty. A concept is *ambiguous* if it has two or more distinct possible meanings.

Fuzzy sets and fuzziness A *fuzzy set* is a set that permits elements to belong to it in degree (rather than having to belong entirely or not at all). *Fuzziness* is a special kind of vagueness that refers to graded degrees of membership in a set.

Ignorance Person A is *ignorant* from person B's viewpoint if A fails to agree with or show awareness of ideas which B defines as actually or potentially valid. Ignorance itself has a passive sense (being ignorant of X) and an active sense (ignoring X).

Irrelevance X is considered *irrelevant* to Y iff X is considered unrelated to Y. Irrelevance therefore leads to X being ignored when considering Y.

Risk Composed of uncertainty (or ignorance) and the prospect of loss.

Uncertainty A special kind of ignorance, namely incompleteness of information. Uncertainty may take nonprobabilistic as well as probabilistic forms.

Vagueness A special kind of uncertainty. A concept is *vague* if its possible meanings extend over a range on a continuum.

UNCERTAINTY may be defined as a particular kind of ignorance, namely incompleteness of information. Traditional approaches to uncertainty were based on probability theory, but more recent approaches have encompassed nonprobabilistic kinds of uncertainty as well. The human sciences have issued two broad streams of theory and research on uncertainty. One of these has antecedents in the psychology of judgment. The other stems from sociology and social anthropology. Both will be discussed in this article.

I. CONCEPTS AND DEFINITIONS

Until the second half of the 20th century, uncertainty was a neglected topic of study. During the past three decades, however, increasing numbers of researchers in several fields have been systematically investigating strategies for thinking about, representing, analyzing, and making decisions under various kinds of uncertainty. There is greater recognition now of the important roles played by uncertainty in scientific research, as well as human affairs, and its profound impact on both modern and postmodern thought. Moreover, a number of scientific fields have experienced a "loss of certainty" during the 20th century and a growing awareness of the importance of scientific ignorance.

Although probabilistic ideas still dominate most writings on uncertainty, mathematicians, engineers, and scientists have recently begun to realize that there is more to uncertainty than probability. As a result, the last few decades have seen an explosion in the study of nonprobabilistic uncertainties such as possibility, fuzziness, and vagueness. Recently several new formalisms have been established for analyzing nonprobabilistic uncertainties, including fuzzy set theory, possibility theory, belief functions, and nonmonotonic logic. Likewise, the human sciences (especially psychology and artificial intelligence) have expanded our knowledge of how people perceive and respond to uncertainty. In the policy domain risk analysis has become a huge growth industry, combining prescriptive and explanatory perspectives and techniques from several fields.

The "modern" approaches to uncertainty, then, are somewhat more tolerant and managerial than their traditional counterparts. Nevertheless, the study of uncertainty is beset with philosophical pitfalls, so we require some conceptual foundations and pathways to avoid such difficulties. Let us begin with probability.

A. Objective and Subjective Probability

The most popular taxonomy of probability theories in recent years is a threefold division of modern approaches into logical (a priori) theory, relative frequency theory, and subjective (Bayesian) theory, with classical theory occupying a fourth, mainly historical category. The first two approaches lay claims to "objective" conceptions of probability.

The a priori theory of probability is exemplified in games of chance, where "fair" gaming devices such as dice, coins, and cards are used for bets on specific outcomes out of a class of possible outcomes. For setups involving the physical propensity of an event to occur out of a finite set of possible events, probability is defined as the ratio of the number of "favorable" cases to the number of all "equipossible" cases. The most obvious problem with this definition is its apparent circularity. Probability is defined in terms of equipossible (read "equiprobable") cases.

The dominant modern paradigm of probability in many fields often is referred to as "frequentist" (relative frequency theory for our purposes), and begins with the premise that under repeated trials, the probability of an event is indicated by the ratio of the number of its occurrences to the number of trials (relative frequency). According to Bernoulli's strong law of large numbers and other similar arguments, with repeated independent trials under stable conditions, relative frequency converges to a limit as the number of trials tends toward infinity.

While the relative frequentist approach does not include such concepts as the probability of a unique event, subjective (Bayesian) theory identifies subjective probabilities with degrees of belief that may be assigned on a rational basis if they obey the laws of probability. Subjectivists claim that their approach ensures that decision makers behave rationally in accordance with their preferences. Repeated applications of Bayes' theorem are used to update prior subjective probability judgments on the basis of new information.

By the 1970s and 1980s, the Bayesian approach became prominent in fields concerned with the mental representation of uncertainty, such as cognitive psychology, artificial intelligence, and knowledge engineering. It is also central to the maximization of expected utility (MEU) framework for rational decision making under uncertainty, which in turn has been widely debated in fields such as economics, management science, risk analysis, military science, and the social sciences.

B. Nonprobabilistic Uncertainty

The claim that there is more to uncertainty than probability is not new. One of the most famous is Max Black's classic distinctions among vagueness, generality (or nonspecificity), and ambiguity. A more modern case in point is the debate in the fuzzy set theoretic literature over the relationship (if any) between probability and fuzziness. Fuzzy set apologists claim that one may have certainty about a fuzzy event (e.g., "right now we have light to moderate drizzle" as an approximate answer to the question "is it raining?") or a graded attribute (e.g., "John is tall" or "this carpet is reddish-brown"). There is no probability there, and no gamble on the "true" state of affairs. Moreover, it seems ungrammatical and/or counterintuitive to describe the vagueness inherent in such events or attributes by subjective probabilities or even degrees of belief.

In recent years there has been a rapid proliferation of alternative frameworks for uncertainty representation. Several extensions of probability theory have been proposed (usually in the form of upper and lower bounds on probabilities) that represent "vague" probabilities; fuzzy set theory and Dempster-Shafer belief theory attempt to formally analyze certain kinds of vagueness and ambiguity; and surprise theory, fuzzy logic, and possibility theory deal with looser kinds of indeterminacies than probability.

Despite sometimes vigorous opposition from Bayesian probabilists, several of these new formalisms have established followings and yielded successful applications in fields ranging from control engineering through the cognitive sciences to the social sciences. It seems unlikely that all of them are passing fads, but it is still too soon to tell which among them will endure as long as probability's 300-year reign. Perhaps the most novel characteristic of recent formal approaches is that they seem to accept varieties of uncertainty and even ignorance that heretofore were either ignored or eliminated.

However, the nonprobabilistic formalisms are not as revolutionary as they might initially seem. They are still largely based on standard logical foundations, and there is a seldom-questioned emphasis on quantifying uncertainty. There is, however, a growing minority of investigators who advocate qualitative approaches to representing and reasoning with uncertainty, belief, and risk.

C. Taxonomies of Ignorance and Uncertainty

Another respect in which the "new" uncertainty frameworks are not entirely revolutionary is their restriction of the topic area to "uncertainty." In this section, we will broaden that to encompass ignorance and also provide a way of addressing ignorance that avoids some well-known pitfalls.

Traditionally, ignorance is treated as either the absence or the distortion of "true" knowledge, and uncertainty as some form of incompleteness in information or knowledge. This position immediately poses difficulties because it requires an objective philosophical basis for knowledge. Also, it seems as though we must fully enumerate the field of "nonknowledge" in order to exhaustively describe ignorance. Clearly, such a task is not only impossible, but also leads to self-referential paradoxes. At first, it might seem that the commonsense distinction between "objective" (real) and "subjective" (perceived) ignorance could suffice, the same duality that is used in probability theory and several other modern formalisms for dealing with uncertainty. But this distinction does not eliminate the problem of defining what "objective" ignorance is.

A famous sociological principle helps us avoid these problems. This is the principle that everything that people consider to be "knowledge" is *socially constructed.* No knowledge is produced without social interaction taking place, and any agreements among people about the nature of knowledge also can only be established through social interaction. Moreover, knowledge itself is represented and communicated via symbolic frameworks (be they natural language, mathematics, or diagrams) which also have a basis in social interaction.

Precisely the same principle may be applied to the study of ignorance. Ignorance is a social creation, like knowledge. Indeed, we cannot fully describe particular instances of ignorance without referring to the viewpoint of some group or individual. Likewise, ignorance is represented within socially constructed symbolic frameworks such as language or mathematics. A working definition of ignorance, then, is this: "A is *ignorant* from B's viewpoint if A fails to agree with or show awareness of ideas which B defines as actually or potentially valid." This definition avoids the absolutism problem by placing the onus on B to specify what she or he means by ignorance. It also permits self-attributed ignorance, since A and B may be the same person. Most importantly, it incorporates anything B thinks A could or should know (but doesn't) and anything which B thinks A must not know (and doesn't).

People's accounts of ignorance include several noteworthy distinctions. One widespread distinction is "ignoring" versus "being ignorant." The act of ignoring is a declaration of *irrelevance,* which is the term that will be used to refer to this kind of ignorance. The state of being ignorant, on the other hand, is in one way or another an erroneous cognitive state, and it may be denoted by the term *error.*

Error may arise from either incomplete or distorted views (or both, of course). *Distortion* usually is referred to in terms of "bias" or *inaccuracy,* on the one hand, and *confusion* on the other. *Incompleteness,* likewise, may be dichotomized in a similar fashion. Incompleteness in kind may be termed *absence,* while incompleteness in degree corresponds to *uncertainty.* Uncertainty, in turn, includes such concepts as *probability, vagueness,* and *ambiguity.* Uncertainty is the subarea to which nearly all existing formalisms for representing nonknowledge are restricted.

Irrelevance, on the other hand, is rather unexplored. The most obvious kind is *untopicality.* For our purposes, it refers to the intuitions people carry with them and negotiate with others about how their cognitive domains fit together. Two other kinds of irrelevance are *undecidability* and *taboo.* Undecidability is attributed to those matters which people are unable to designate true or false either because they consider the problem insoluble or because the question of validity or verifiability is not pertinent. Taboo, on the other hand, is socially enforced irrelevance.

The foregoing elucidation of this taxonomy leads to the following list:

Error (state of ignorance about something)
- Distortion
  - Inaccuracy; confusion
- Incompleteness
  - Absence; uncertainty

Irrelevance (act of ignoring something)
Untopicality; undecidability; taboo

This typology and the social construction thesis underlying it will provide an overarching framework to guide our tour through uncertainty and related topics.

II. UNCERTAINTY PERCEPTION AND JUDGMENT

A. Uncertainty, Rationality, and Judgment

Broadly speaking, psychological theories have provided clear but conflicting messages concerning the functions of ignorance (and especially uncertainty). Perhaps the oldest is contained in the psychoanalytic canons for the well-adjusted individual, and has since been carried into personality and motivation research and indeed most branches of ego psychology. This is a view that favors the person who seeks novel information and experience, tolerates uncertainty in the short run in order to gain knowledge, and who is not defensive about prior beliefs. The healthy person is an ignorance-tolerant "knowledge seeker."

A second tradition emphasizes the debilitating effects of uncertainty, unpredictability, and uncontrollability on affective, cognitive, and physiological functioning. According to this view, people are averse to uncertainty. Most of the impetus and evidence for this viewpoint have come from behavioral research and theories concerning learning and adaptation, and it portrays the individual as a "certainty maximizer."

Attempts to study uncertainty from a human standpoint have a somewhat uneasy relationship with the older intellectual traditions of rationalism. The psychological study of judgment and decision making under uncertainty is a good example of how debates between rational and descriptive perspectives have developed. Until very recently, probability theory has been widely accepted as the sole rational guide for uncertainty representation and analysis. [*See* DECISION MAKING, INDIVIDUALS.]

As a result, the psychological study of human judgment and decision making under uncertainty has been dominated by a statistical normative orientation that entails a strict Bayesian interpretation of perceived uncertainty and a prescription for decision makers to maximize subjective expected utility. Although alternative normative perspectives on uncertainty are available and there are competing schools of probability theory, none of those factors have guided mainstream cognitive and social psychologists in their studies of judgment. Few of them have questioned the normative appropriateness of maximizing subjective expected utility, although many have questioned its feasibility in real world situations.

It is small wonder, then, that most of the research on judgment under uncertainty initially focused on judgmental errors in handling subjective probability. Influential researchers in the area justify the focus on errors by arguing that we may learn about our intellectual limitations from them, they may reveal to use the processes by which we make judgments and arrive at decisions, and they also may reveal which principles of statistics are nonintuitive. A minority have argued that the study of errors is misguided, or at least overemphasized at the expense of understanding judgment processes and heuristics. The literature on this topic is large and so is the list of "errors." One reviewer writing in 1980 listed some 27 distinguishable kinds of deviation from probability by human judges.

B. Judgmental Biases and Errors

At least four major kinds of bias in attention to and weighting of evidence have been unearthed by psychologists in the study of judgment under uncertainty. These include a tendency to ignore or discount negative and disconfirming evidence (the confirmation bias), conservative revisions of probability estimates as evidence is presented sequentially (the conservatism bias), ignoring base-rate information about probabilities in the presence of other supposedly irrelevant evidence (the base-rate fallacy), and ignoring sample size in accounting for statistical variation (the sample size fallacy).

Nor do subjects do much better when it comes to combining probabilities. The "conjunction fallacy" and other variants on the same phenomenon have been reported in series of studies in the late 1950s and again in the early 1980s. Their findings, termed by one researcher as "perhaps the most shocking example" of deviations from logic, point to a consistent violation by both naive and well-trained subjects of the rule that $P(A\&B) \leq \min(P(A),P(B))$.

An intriguing class of "errors" refers to people's perceptions of and responses to randomicity and "chance" or "luck." Unlike the deviations from the standard probability calculus, these are violations against normative criteria for defining and detecting randomicity itself. One of the oldest, gambler's fallacy, is a special case of a general tendency for people to see patterns, predictability, and even causation in random data. Given a long run of heads in coin-tossing, the gambler who believes the coin is fair will also believe that a run of tails is now due because in the long run, the number of heads and tails should balance out. A related finding is that people tend to underestimate the extent to which "patterns" in the form of long runs, clustering, and seemingly regular subsequences occur in randomly generated data. Moreover, several researchers find that people believe they can exert control over random events. The most popular examples come from studies of gambling behavior, and this tendency is often called the "illusion of control."

Lastly, there are a number of studies that concern "framing effects" on people's decisions under uncertainty. One of the most famous hypotheses in this vein is that people are risk-averse regarding possible gains, but risk-seeking when faced with possible losses. For example, the "sure thing principle" predicts that if someone is offered a choice between getting \$100 for sure or entering a lottery with $\frac{1}{2}$ probability of getting \$200 and otherwise nothing, that person will elect the \$100 certainty option (even though their expected payoff in both situations is \$100). The opposite choice would be the more attractive, however, if the prospect were to *lose* \$100 for sure versus undergoing a probability of $\frac{1}{2}$ of losing \$200 and otherwise nothing.

This corpus of research which in effect criticizes human judgmental abilities is not without its own critics. Various studies have been taken to task for mistakenly claiming that the tasks or problems posed to subjects have a normatively unique solution; for not ascertaining that subjects and experimenters share the same understanding of tasks and problems; and for failing to consider alternative "rational" explanations for subjects' judgments. More serious criticisms have addressed the normative criteria themselves. For instance, some critics have questioned the primacy of long-run over short-run decisional rationality in studies using one-shot gambles against a rationalistic template that appeals to long-run expected payoffs.

C. Heuristics and Explanations

What are people paying attention to, and why, when they ignore or discount information that probability theory says they should use in arriving at probability judgments? Having shown that people deviate from probability theory in their probabilistic judgments, during the 1970s and 1980s cognitive psychologists strove to discover the heuristic strategies being used instead.

One of the most widely studied is the "availability" heuristic, which is the tendency to assess likelihood by the ease with which cases can be retrieved, imagined, or associated. People feel that more likely occurrences or cases are easier to recall or imagine than unlikely ones, and so the argument is that they make use of this apparent association to judge the probability of a case.

Another popular heuristic is "representativeness" which concerns the degree to which an event or object: (a) is similar in essential characteristics to its parent population; and (b) reflects the salient features of the process by which it is generated. A number of studies provide evidence that the probability that an event or object is in a given category is judged by the extent to which it seems prototypical or representative of that category. A related heuristic is called "anchoring and adjustment," and refers to a strategy for updating initial probability judgments on the basis of new information. The "anchoring" of the estimate refers to a tendency for people to readjust their estimates to a lesser extent than Bayesian probability would dictate, indicating that the initial estimate exerts a disproportionate influence.

In decision-making, the most famous proposal for explaining people's deviations from MEU rationality is "prospect theory," whose major hypotheses rest on two points. The first is that decision-makers' choices must be understood in terms of relative change rather than simple absolute values, and the second is the "reflection hypothesis," which holds that people are risk-seeking when faced with the prospect of a loss and symmetrically risk-averse when faced with the prospect of a gain.

Not only have these heuristics been widely debated, they have also been criticized on several counts. Chief among them are two arguments, one castigating them for being too vague and difficult to falsify scientifically and the second pointing out that they are not clearly linked to any current theories or models of human information processing.

D. Words versus Numbers

Every area of the human sciences has some kind of a debate between quantitativists and qualitativists, and uncertainty judgment is no exception. Nearly all of that debate has focused on representing uncertainty probabilistically, and it has two main streams. One of them concerns the reliability and validity of measuring people's meanings and assessments of uncertainty by verbal phrases versus numerical estimates. The other focuses on how well numerical subjective probability estimates are "calibrated."

Traditionally researchers in this area have asked subjects to make numerical pointwise estimates of the probability represented by selected phrases (e.g., quite likely, probable, almost impossible, good chance). Although several such studies report reasonable within-subject reliability, most find considerable intersubjective variation, overlap between phrases, and variability with changes in context.

One difficulty with this research is the assumption that the meaning of a phrase like "somewhat likely" could ever correspond to a pointwise probability. Recently some studies have utilized fuzzy set theory to model verbal probability expressions as fuzzy sets in the probability interval [0,1]. Its simplest version involves eliciting from subjects lower and upper bounds for a probability interval that would represent the range of possible probabilities for a given phrase. These studies have accounted for some of the apparent unreliability and intersubjective disagreement cited in previous investigations.

The calibration literature, on the other hand, is solely concerned with whether people's direct probability estimates adhere to the distributional requirements of probability theory. A large number of studies of laypeople and various experts (such as weather forecasters or clinical psychologists) show a general tendency toward overconfidence in their predictive abilities. Furthermore, overconfidence appears to increase with task difficulty and varies inversely with knowledge. A second widespread finding in calibration research is that when people are asked to provide quantile or other distributional estimates involving the spread of probabilities, they tend to construct distributions that are too tight (i.e., they underestimate spread).

Both sets of research results, then, seem to argue that numbers are better than words for expressing subjective uncertainty, but that when people's numerical estimates can be checked against real data or the laws of probability, they are found to be using the numbers incorrectly. Ironically, little research effort has been devoted to describing how people like to express and receive uncertain information. Some evidence suggests that they prefer using words to express uncertainty but would rather receive such information numerically (as long as they can understand the numbers).

E. Judgment Research on Nonprobabilistic Uncertainty

There has been comparatively little investigation into human judgments of nonprobabilistic uncertainty. The 1970s and 1980s saw a brief flurry of interest in empirically testing fuzzy set theory against human performance, and more recently some decision researchers have examined people's aversion to vagueness in probabilities.

Empirical research on fuzzy set theory has been conducted chiefly in the domains of prototypicality and category membership judgments. Unlike research on judgments of probability or logic, these domains have not been dominated by a concern with "erroneous" information processing. In fact, when fuzzy set theory and human judgment disagree, researchers usually conclude that fuzzy set theory is mistaken.

For example, in contrast with their attitude toward human deviations from probability theory, several cognitive psychologists reject fuzzy set theory out of hand for its failure to model what their Bayesian colleagues describe as the "conjunction fallacy." To them, the fact that a guppy receives a higher membership value in the category of "pet fish" than it does in either the category of "pets" or "fish" is no violation of logic at all but merely an unproblematic feature of natural language.

F. Behavioral Research on Uncertainty

In the 1930s and 1940s, some of the leading figures in behavioral psychology argued that animal behavior studies of choice would eventually provide the evidence and insights for generalizable laws of human choice behavior. During the 1980s there has been a resurgence of interest in this claim, or at least a modified version of it, from three related streams of research: (1) neobehaviorist models of choice under uncertainty, (2) studies of animal behavior in stochastically uncertain environments, and (3) recent developments in theories of evolution.

Animal and human behavioral studies of choice under uncertainty have operationalized uncertainty primarily in two ways: reward variability and reward delay. The linkage between reward variability and probabilistic uncertainty is straightforward because it is based on a frequentist account of probability. Accordingly, studies have been conducted on risk aversion and preference for a variety of foraging animals, revealing striking similarities between animal and human preferences. More recently, several experimenters have made a case for linking findings that people are risk-averse under positive outcomes with another body of research showing that people and other animals prefer immediate to delayed positive reinforcement, and correspondingly linking the findings that people are risk-seeking under negative outcomes with the findings that people and animals prefer delayed to immediate aversive stimuli.

III. SOCIAL CONSTRUCTIONS OF UNCERTAINTY

A. Ignorance and Uncertainty as Social Constructs

From a sociological perspective, ignorance is made possible and usable by particular properties of natural language, social interaction processes, social norms, and negotiated agreements, all of which pervade everyday social life. First, natural language is sufficiently flexible and unspecified to permit partial communication or even total misunderstanding. Second, those properties of natural language are used strategically in, for example, polite conversation and self-disclosure to generate acceptable levels of ignorance. Third, there are pervasive social norms which encourage and legitimize less than fully informative communication (e.g., politeness requirements and the maintenance of personal privacy). Finally, there are norms restricting information-seeking and curiosity (e.g., constraints on reality testing and question asking).

A considerable component of being polite, for example, involves the avoidance of messages that might induce discomfort or social conflict (e.g., deference, apologies, white lies), and the promotion of approval and camaraderie. These subgoals may be achieved either by distortion or by vague or ambiguous expressions. Strategies for polite communication are mediated by widely shared norms restricting what should be communicated. An example of a well-known norm is the reluctance of people to transmit bad news to someone who is directly affected by the contents of the message. Moreover, good news tends to be communicated more frequently, more quickly, more fully, and more spontaneously.

A related concern in social psychology has been the study of self-disclosure. Initially, the main research topic in this area was the apparent norm of reciprocity in self-disclosures between people. However, violations of the reciprocity norm soon came to light and research interest shifted to them. A variety of studies indicated that lower-status individuals are expected to self-disclose more intimately than higher-status individuals, with most of the direct evidence for this coming from studies comparing subordinates with superiors, and men with women. More recent findings suggest not only that women are expected to disclose more intimately than men, but that women are also expected to accept more intimate disclosures from others. These findings raise the possibility that women are accorded less of a right to privacy than are men.

Privacy and secrecy both are buttressed by a variety of norms that limit people's information-seeking and reality-testing behavior, or that promote the "social control of curiosity." Children everywhere quickly learn not to ask too many questions and to avoid certain kinds of questions altogether. Overinquisitiveness is widely censured in many societies. Anthropologists such as Mary Douglas argue that the larger patterns of taboos, privacy and secrecy arrangements, and social norms guiding selective attention all are driven by a concern to avoid danger and pollution. Furthermore, societies possessed of either high cohesiveness or complex hierarchical structures will also have the most intricate and vigorously enforced taboos.

Social scientists have attempted to account for selective information-seeking in other ways. One line of argument leads to an "economics of attention" in which various information sources compete with one another to persuade people that attending to them is worth their time and effort. A person is limited in the information to which she or he can simultaneously pay attention. In an information-saturated world, therefore, people cannot afford to indulge in an unselective consumption of information. Ironically, some studies indicate that forbidden or scarce information not only is valued more highly than easily accessible information, but also is more likely to grab people's attention and is more persuasive when obtained.

B. Ignorance and Uncertainty in Organizations

The literature on organizations and management has long included uncertainty as one of its primary agenda items. Unfortunately, this literature frequently has confused various kinds of uncertainty, so that the concept and its measurement have been rather muddled. Nevertheless, a number of useful ideas and findings have emerged during the past 40 years.

The dominant normative message from the classical works on organizational uncertainty was that effective managers either eliminate or absorb uncertainty. During the 1950s and 1960s organizational writers admonished managers to eliminate uncertainty and buffer the technical core of the organization. The most popular proposals for adaptation to uncertainty included buffering, smoothing, forecasting, and rationing. Forecasting and rationing are strategies for outright elimination of uncertainty but buffering and smoothing are attempts to absorb uncertainty. Buffering involves maintaining resources whose supply is uncertain, while smoothing is an attempt to reduce fluctuations.

Most of the early descriptive studies of organizational decision making appeared to support the uncertainty-eliminative view as well. Cyert and March summarized their findings by coining the phrase "uncertainty avoidance." Other writers claimed that bureaucrats and managers may wish to minimize or even cover up the extent of their ignorance to avoid discreditation, loss of control, complicated negotiations, and controversies.

During the 1970s and 1980s the literature took a somewhat more tolerant view of uncertainty. One crucial shift has been due to the realization that not all adaptive strategies are uncertainty-averse. Some high-performing managers strategically select uncertain environments in which they will have a competitive advantage. In a similar vein, some writers suggest that organizations may choose strategies that create uncertainty but also result in a relative information advantage for themselves.

Moreover, uncertainty reduction may not always be adaptive. Some researchers have argued that organizations which eliminate uncertainty, induce conformity, and reduce internal competition may behave maladaptively. Those which attempt to control the sources of uncertainty in the environment also are making a futile attempt to turn the environment into a closed system.

In this connection, some writers criticize uncertainty-avoiding practices for their inhibiting effects on organizational learning. They point out that overcontrol of behavior and standardization of procedures may prevent individual members from responding creatively to novel situations or knowledge. Second, since learning occurs most rapidly when the coupling between the organization and individual is loose, increased regulation can retard the acquisition of knowledge. Recently risk researchers have sounded a similar warning about overregulation in respect of hazardous technologies: without the uncertainties of trial and error there is no learning or innovation.

There is a gadfly literature whose theme is that ignorance and uncertainty are actively sought out and created by people in organizations. Early on, Goffman remarked that every team needs its secrets maintained in order to function effectively. Notably, every organizational role brings with it ignorance-bearing requirements. Formal organizational boundaries are protected through ignorance, and the informal organization thrives on it. Additionally, several theories suggest that when a high rate of change and great insecurity are coupled with increasing regulation of behavior (one of the most frequently observed responses by managers to environmental volatility), organization members will innovate in secret, thereby increasing the extent to which members of the organization are ignorant of one another's activities and goals. The literature on the hidden economy and related activities is relevant here because those activities are based on the creation and maintenance of systematic ignorance.

Critics of conventional control practices point out that ignorance (and in particular, the intentional creation and use of it) is here to stay; it can be turned into a collective benefit rather than a threat. Smart managers should recognize the benefits of unregulated, secret innovation, and set up systems of "soft control" that are receptive to fiddling but also monitor and establish limits for it. Likewise, the widespread use of on-the-job secrecy in the service of getting things done should signal managers that something is wrong with how those jobs are structured.

These writings also have indicated a fundamental type of dilemma in control when ignorance is useful. Attempts to reduce organizational ignorance by seeking information about people and regulating their behavior may provoke them into witholding or giving false information, thereby actually increasing organizational ignorance. On the other hand, as several economists have observed, distorted feedback can mislead organizations and perturb economies. In the case of the hidden economy, a number of national governments are caught between the desire to eradicate the hidden economy and the realization that its unregulated activities contribute substantially to economic performance.

C. Risk, Uncertainty, and Public Culture

In the last decade or so, a literature on the links between risk and culture has begun to emerge, partly motivated by a widespread realization that psychological factors alone do not account for how people perceive and respond to risk. Its origins may be traced to earlier anthropological work on taboo, studies during the 1970s and 1980s of public risk perceptions and attitudes, and an earlier tradition of research on the effects of the media and mass communications on the public. Much of this literature, unfortunately, fails to separate ignorance or uncertainty in risk from the threat of loss. It also fails to integrate ignorance generated by, for example, secrecy and miscommunication into a common framework with ignorance arising in connection with knowledge of risks themselves.

One strand in this literature grew out of the 1982 book by Mary Douglas and Aaron Wildavsky on risk and culture, in which they argued that certain features of social structure and culture influence the ways in which people perceive and respond to risk. They pointed out that although life in modern industrial nations now is generally less risky and more healthy than it has ever been, Western societies have become markedly more risk-averse since World War II. Yet, increased risk aversiveness does not necessarily correspond to increased overall awareness of risks. Instead, some risks have become the selective focus of public concern, and these risks are not the most consequential. Nor are the selected risks always large-scale, involuntary, or irreversibly harmful, even though it is well-established in the psychological literature that those features do make people more averse to risk. One is left, therefore, with an appeal to cultural and social factors to explain this trend.

The type of perspective dominating this literature is exemplified by the "grid-group" approach (also called "cultural theory"), which identifies attitudes toward risk (e.g., fatalism, identification of risk with opportunity, or reliance on experts) with cultural worldviews or "cosmologies." This approach claims that risk is a forensic resource used to defend preferred lifestyles or institutions and place blame on rival groups. It also implies that no common metric for risk can be constructed to link competing worldviews. While this perspective is interesting, it has been criticized for lack of supporting empirical evidence.

Another strand of research has scrutinized the media's role in setting public agendas for risk, and an offshoot has focused on risk communication generally. Considerable evidence suggests that the media are "biased" in their coverage of risks, emphasizing those aspects and topics that increase subscriptions and sales. However, studies are less conclusive about the actual impact that media coverage has on public attitudes and responses. A more sophisticated framework gets away from bias and focuses instead on the ways in which experts and the media frame risk communications, thereby affecting public judgment along the lines suggested by framing effects experiments in the psychological literature.

Moreover, there are recognized dilemmas faced by experts, authorities, and/or the media over whether to fully communicate current knowledge about risks to the public. An important example arises from fears that informing the public about a hazard will panic or enrage them, and yet not informing them will cause them to be incautious or underprepared. This dilemma has been called the "reassurance–arousal paradox."

There is also a growing realization that much of the information on risk provided by authorities is viewed by the public as irrelevant to their concerns. Some writers have suggested that ignoring large-scale hazards which laypeople can do nothing about (e.g., nuclear war) may be more adaptive than social scientists had thought. Others have pointed out that in some cases, public definitions of and concerns about risk have been passed over by attempts to "inform" them, resulting in the public ignoring the information.

D. Strategies for Coping with an Uncertain World

There are competing views on "rational" strategies for dealing with uncertainty. Writing about risk assessment, Wildavsky borrows a useful dichotomy from ecology to distinguish between two ways of coping with an uncertain future: *anticipation* and *resilience*. Anticipation requires that we accurately predict future dangers in order to ward them off before they arise. It is compatible with the traditional orientations toward rational decision making under uncertainty and the "certainty maximizer" thesis, both of which emphasize reducing or banishing uncertainty so as to maximize predictability and control.

Resilience, on the other hand, refers to learning how to "bounce back" by utilizing change to cope with the unknown, and it entails dealing with dangers as they arise. In the managerial and helping professions this is often referred to as "crisis management." Far from relying on uniformity and regulation as does anticipation, resilience becomes most feasible under conditions of variability and spontaneity, or at least freedom of action. Entrepreneurs and creative intellectuals both require such environments in order to be innovative and flexible. Resilience, therefore, is compatible with those newer frameworks that emphasize a tolerant, managerial approach to ignorance or, at least, uncertainty. Resilience also entails the development of a shared language for communicating perceptions of ignorance, uncertainty, and risk among people whose cognitive frameworks may nevertheless differ considerably.

Ironically, resilient systems may be more robust than anticipatory ones if unexpected developments occur. Following a widespread "loss of certainty" in many fields of intellectual and practical endeavor, Western cultures have seen an explosive increase in creative work on uncertainty, which may herald a shift from the traditional preoccupation with anticipation, prediction, and control toward a more resilient and uncertainty-tolerant style of coping with the future.

Bibliography

Arkes, H. R., and Hammond, K. R. (Eds.) (1986). "Judgment and Decision Making: An Interdisciplinary Reader." Cambridge University Press, New York.

Cvetkovich, G. T., and Earle, T. C. (Eds.) (1991). Special issue. Risk and culture. *J. Cross-Cultural Psych.* **22**(1), 11–149.

Dawes, R. M. (1988). "Rational Choice in an Uncertain World." Harcourt Brace Jovanovich, Orlando, FL.

Douglas, M., and Wildavsky, A. (1982). "Risk and Culture." California University Press, Berkeley, CA.

Gardenfors, P., and Sahlins, N.-E. (Eds.) (1988). "Decision, Probability, and Utility: Selected Readings." Cambridge University Press, New York.

Johnson, B. B., and Covello, V. T. (Eds.) (1987). "The Social and Cultural Construction of Risk." D. Reidel, Dordrecht, Holland.

Kasperson, R. E., and Stallen, P. K. M. (1991). "Communicating Risks to the Public." Kluwer, Dordrecht, Holland.

Oakes, M. (1986). "Statistical Inference: A Commentary for the Social and Behavioural Sciences." Wiley, London.

Rachlin, H. (1989). "Judgment, Decision, and Choice." Freeman, New York.

Smithson, M. (1989). "Ignorance and Uncertainty: Emerging Paradigms." Springer Verlag, New York.

VARIABILITY IN BRAIN FUNCTION AND BEHAVIOR

Paul Grobstein
Bryn Mawr College

Glossary

Information An increasingly difficult and important term to define. Central to the concept is that there are aspects of reality which need to be characterized not in terms of matter or energy but rather in terms of the particular organized forms taken by one or the other or both. Similar information, for example, can be embodied as signals in motions of the air (sound waves), ink on a page (printed text), or a series of ones and zeros (on a hard disk in a computer).

Input/output device for information Any physical system whose primary function is to receive, transform, and emit signals (information, as opposed to matter or energy—see Information). Examples include thermostats, radios, computers, neurons, and the brain.

Levels of organization A term emphasizing the reality that virtually all interesting systems (the brain and behavior providing two examples) are made up of identifiable subsystems, which are in turn made up of identifiable subsystems, and so forth. As a general rule, the properties displayed at one level of organization reflect the properties of the subsystems at the next lower level of organization together with the particular way those subsystems are organized in relation to one another. The properties of the subsystems typically constrain but do not determine this organization (which reflects information over and above that inherent in the subsystems). For this reason, interesting systems can productively be explored at all levels of organization, and need to be so that they can be fully understood.

Membrane potential The electric field which exists across the limiting membrane of a neuron (and many other cells). The value of the potential at any given time reflects the current and recent movement of charges across the membrane due to both intrinsic properties of the neuron and signals received from other cells. The value of the potential at any given time in turn determines the signals sent to other cells.

Nervous system The most sophisticated known input/output device for information. The term is a general one which, in animals with backbones (humans and frogs among them), includes the brain, spinal cord, and other related components. Other animals (including leeches) have nervous systems which, while somewhat differently organized, are fundamentally similar in terms of their basic function.

ACCORDING TO THE Harvard Law of Animal Behavior, "under carefully controlled experimental circumstances, an animal will behave as it damned well pleases." An informally propagated and often ironically intended summary of large numbers of observations, the Harvard Law in fact has quite concrete and deep significance for understanding the basic information processing characteristics which underlie the behavior of all organisms, humans very much included. An appreciation of this requires drawing together threads from a variety of lines of inquiry, and is facilitated by a perspective which treats both behavior and the nervous system as nested sets of interacting information-processing boxes each with more or less clearly defined inputs and outputs. Briefly put, the Harvard Law provides the basis for a desirable and productive fusion of scientific and folk perspectives on the determinants of behavior, one which acknowledges that some degree of unpredictability is not only inevitable but desirable.

I. THE PROBLEM OF VARIABILITY AND ITS SIGNIFICANCE

A fundamental question about behavior, whether explored informally as all humans do all the time or formally as done under experimental conditions by scientists, is why a given organism at a given time under given environmental conditions behaves in a particular way. For many investigators, "understanding" behavior is equated with being able to predict for a given subject what behavior will occur at a given time. For others, the ability to study particular components of behavior depends on being able to reliably observe that behavior. In both cases, many investigators are predisposed to treat behavioral unpredictability as not only an inconvenience but also, quite commonly, as a clear indication of the failure of the experimenter to control the circumstances with sufficient precision so that meaningful observations can be made.

This general perspective on variability has contributed importantly to a style of inquiry into behavior whose record of successes is both long and enviable. At the same time, it contributes to a dissociation, to the detriment of both, between the more formal and "scientific" study of behavior, and the common sense informal body of wisdom people are constantly creating in their day to day lives ("folk psychology"). Explanatory frameworks and models of behavior emerging from mindsets predisposed to dismiss variability tend, for obvious reasons, to have a deterministic character to them. These impact less than they might on folk psychology both because they appear somewhat threatening to human dignity, and because they fail to speak to a question central to informal understandings of behavior: they explain why a behavior occurs when it does, but not why it does not *always* occur. Conversely, the very real insights from the common sense body of wisdom about behavior, phrased as they are in terms of both puzzlement about its unpredictability and enjoyment of its playfulness, impact less than they might on more formal inquiries.

Mindsets, of course, influence the accumulation of data sets, and there is a corresponding bias against the reporting of variable data sets in the scientific literature. This of course in turn influences mindsets, reinforcing those that dismiss variability as a meaningful and explorable phenomenon. Against this background, the existence of descriptions of behavioral variability in the biobehavioral literature is quite significant, and such descriptions do indeed exist. In the area of movement control, for example, there is a well-established body of phenomena under the rubric of "motor equivalence": under apparently identical task descriptions and circumstances, the particular movements made by even highly trained subjects vary for largely unknown reasons for occasion to occasion. Well-known ambiguous figures, such as that shown in Figure 1, reveal a comparable largely mysterious variability in perceptual processing: while the particular figure seen can be influenced by prior suggestion, either form of the figure may be seen on successive presentations under apparently identical circumstances. Other examples where substantial variability has been documented include the processes of language acquisition in humans and song acquisition in birds. Both involve "babbling" phases during which largely unpredictable sound sequences are produced. More generally, the careful observational studies of ethologists have led some to suggest that the concept of a "fixed action pattern" should be replaced with that of a "modal action pattern" in recognition of the reality that even relatively stereotyped behavioral acts are not in fact identical when looked at more carefully.

In short, the scientific literature does in fact include fragmented supporting evidence for the Harvard Law of Animal Behavior. Despite this, there remains in many scientists' minds a general skepticism of the Law, and an associated reluctance to take it seriously. This is partly a methodological

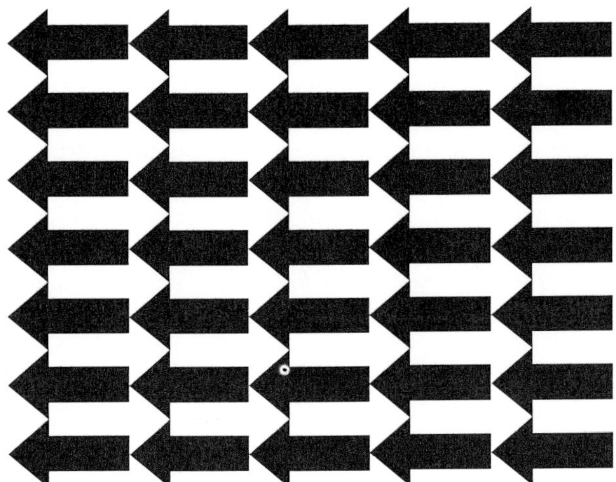

FIGURE 1 An ambiguous figure. The figure, sometimes seen as a series of arrows pointing to the left and other times as a series of arrows pointing to the right, provides a striking example of the importance of an appreciation of intrinsic variability for the understanding of behavior. [Created by the author based on a figure by Roger Shepard in *Mind Sights* (W. H. Freeman and Company, 1990).]

matter (how is one to study a mysterious variability?), and partly a pragmatic bet on the odds (if I work very hard to understand this variability it is just going to turn out to reflect my experimental inadequacies and disappear; besides, some imprecision and "noisiness" is inevitable in any real system). It also, however, reflects a deep-seated discomfort (not restricted to scientists) with the mysterious and uncontrollable, a combination of characteristics which smacks a bit too much of the supernatural. In the following sections are outlined a perspective which removes the taint of the mysterious and supernatural from the Harvard Law (without removing its core or its interest), providing as well both a methodological framework for further inquiry and a rationale for a pragmatic judgment that the phenomena are indeed worth exploration.

II. BEHAVIOR AND THE NERVOUS SYSTEM: INPUT/OUTPUT BOXES WITHIN INPUT/OUTPUT BOXES

Two general presumptions accepted to one degree or another by most neurobiologists underlie this discussion. The first is that behavior and the nervous system are in some sense the same thing: all aspects of behavior correspond in one way or another to phenomena of nervous system structure and function. The second general presumption is that an understanding of nervous system structure and function provides special advantages for better understanding behavior. An implication of the first general principle is that the Harvard Law ought to be understandable in terms of properties of the nervous system, and of the second is that knowing something of how the nervous system works should help to make sense of the Law. In this section is provided a description of some basic organizational features of nervous system structure and function relevant to these considerations.

To a good first approximation, the nervous system can be regarded as an input/output device for information which is made up of interconnected input/output information devices which are in turn themselves made up of interconnected input/output information devices. A convenient stopping point for what might, perhaps correctly, be regarded as an infinite regress is at the level of neurons, the cells which represent similar building blocks for all parts of the nervous system. Each neuron is itself an input/output device, receiving information (typically from other neurons) on receptor surfaces and transmitting information (typically to other neurons) from specialized effector regions. Two aspects of this picture are particularly important to appreciate, both at the level of the neuron and at the levels of each of the successive larger boxes of which they are a part. The first is that one can, with a fairly high degree of rigor, identify and independently monitor inputs and outputs. The second is that the input/output relationship of neurons is in general neither obvious nor stereotyped. It depends on intrinsic properties of the neuron itself, properties which can and do vary from neuron to neuron. That one can identify and independently monitor inputs and outputs, and in many cases control the former, provides the experimental ability to show the dependence of input/output relationships on intrinsic properties and, if one chooses, to characterize aspects of those properties, a point of substantial importance to what follows.

The same two principles hold for the nervous system as a whole, the highest level input/output box under consideration here (there is every reason to believe that a similar analysis can be usefully extended to still higher levels of organization, one in which individual organisms represent interconnected input/output boxes from which emerge, for example, properties of social organization). Like neurons, the nervous system has reasonably well-defined inputs (sensory neurons, the generally quite small percentage of the total neuronal population which consists of neurons whose receptor surfaces are outside the nervous system, rather than in contact with other neurons) and outputs (a second distinct set of neurons (including motoneurons), again generally a quite small percentage, whose effector regions are outside the nervous system, rather than in contact with other neurons). Here too, the input/output relations are neither obvious nor stereotyped (individual organisms behave differently from one another). They depend on intrinsic properties of the nervous system as a whole, a reality which can (as with neurons) be both verified and explored because of the ability to control inputs and monitor outputs.

Between the level of the nervous system as a whole and that of neurons, there are a variety of levels of organization at which the description of interconnected input/output boxes each with significant intrinsic properties continues to hold. The neocortex, for example, has well-defined input and output connections (restricted to other areas of the nervous system), and an internal organization which influences its input/output characteristics. So too does the spinal cord, which is interconnected by input and output pathways to other parts of the nervous system, and has, as well, associated sensory and motor neurons. These in turn are made up of smaller interconnected input/output boxes, each with characterizable and distinct intrinsic properties, such as different cortical regions and spinal cord segments associated respectively with forelimbs and hindlimbs. There is no unique way to describe the interconnected boxes within boxes which represent levels of organization between neurons and the nervous system as a whole, and it remains to be seen whether there is some best way. Regardless, the more general point holds. One can identify (perhaps inevitably with some degree of arbitrariness) at several levels of organization systems of related neurons with well-defined inputs and outputs, each having intrinsic organizations which are significant for determining their input/output characteristics.

III. INTRINSIC VARIABILITY IN INPUT/OUTPUT BOXES AT ALL LEVELS OF ORGANIZATION

The discussion of basic features of nervous system organization in the previous section provides the basis for a useful rephrasing of the Harvard Law of Animal Behavior in terms which make it not only admissable but productive for scientific inquiry. What the Harvard Law in essence asserts is that there is some intrinsic variability in the intrinsic properties of the nervous system as a whole which influences its input/output relationships. To eliminate the taint of the supernatural, this property of the nervous system as a whole should be understandable in terms of the properties of the smaller boxes which make it up. To make the inquiry productive, it should be both explorable in terms of small boxes and meaningful for the understanding of the largest box (behavior). Central to all of this is the ability to specify rigorously what is meant by "intrinsic" variability, and to establish its existence.

The general point is both demonstrable and significant at the level of individual neurons. The output of a neuron is in general due to a time-varying membrane potential which most typically results in a time-varying pattern of action potentials and neurotransmitter release. Given that the inputs to a neuron are known, it is possible in principle (and, in many cases, in practice) to ask whether a time varying output pattern persists in the absence of any inputs (or at least of any time varying signal on the inputs). For many neurons, perhaps most, the answer is yes. Variations in membrane potential can persist in individual neurons totally isolated from any input pathways. Under normal circumstances, the outputs of these neurons reflect not only their inputs but also the membrane potential variations intrinsic to the neuron. To put the matter slightly differently, the Harvard Law of Animal Behavior holds for neurons. No matter how rigorously an experimenter ignorant of intrinsic variability controls the inputs to a neuron, its outputs for a given input can and, in many cases will, vary from trial to trial. While this may at first glance seem mysterious, the underlying cellular and molecular mechanisms are extensively studied and reasonably well understood. Suffice it here to say that within neurobiology it raises no eyebrows whatsoever to assert that the outputs of a given neuron reflect not only its inputs but also variations in signal processing characteristics which occur for reasons largely or entirely intrinsic to the neuron.

The ability to eliminate inputs and monitor outputs makes possible, at the level of the nervous system as a whole, a comparable demonstration and conclusion that one is dealing not with a simple input/output box, one in which a detailed knowledge of inputs suffices to predict outputs, but rather with an input/output box with intrinsic characteristics that vary with time. Figure 2A shows a continuous record of activity from the output nerves of the isolated nervous system of the leech, a preparation in which all input paths have been interrupted. It is clear that variations in output occur in the absence of any variations in input (and, indeed, in the absence of most if not all input of any kind). Preparations of this kind can in principle provide answers to the question that inevitably occurs to most students studying the brain: would a brain in a dish continue to think? The answer, at least in the case of the leech, is clearly yes. While much of the output activity in the isolated leech nervous system has unknown behavioral significance, some periods of this activity are clearly identifiable by their patterns as corresponding to meaningful behavior. The rhythmic activity following the arrow in Figure 2A, for example, is the output pattern corresponding to swimming movements. Though comparably controlled observations have not, for obvious reasons, been done with human brains, there is every neurobiological reason to believe that they too would exhibit variable and behaviorally meaningful output patterns despite isolation from inputs. In addition, "perceptual isolation" studies in humans clearly show that variations in brain states not only persist but may in fact be enhanced (yielding, for example, hallucinations) by reducing variations in input signals. That people frequently seek out quiet spots in which to think is unlikely to be a coincidence.

Figure 2B shows that the intrinsic variability present in the leech nervous system is relevant for under-

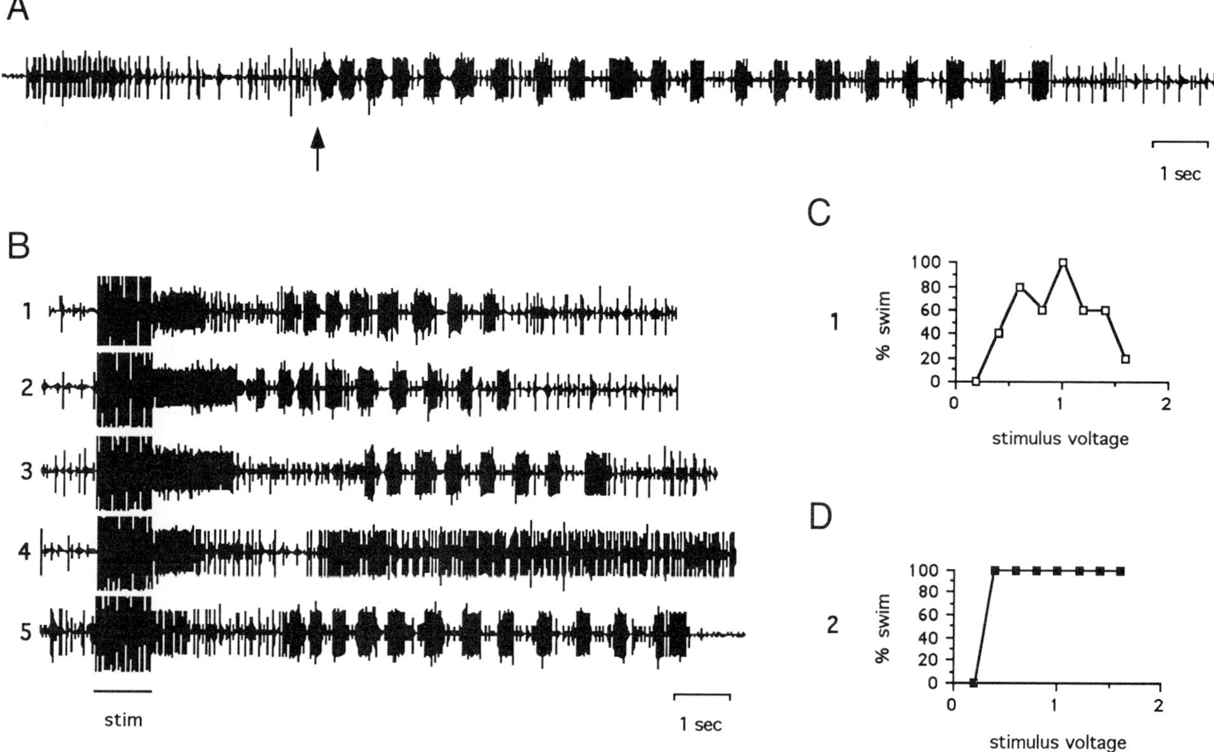

FIGURE 2 Intrinsic variability in the leech nervous system. (A) A record of continuous electrical activity from one peripheral nerve of an isolated leech nervous system. The observed activity varies with time despite the absence of variations in input, and includes periods of activity known to be associated with well-defined output behaviors such as swimming (the bursting activity beginning at the arrow). (B) Variability in response to a fixed stimulus. Shown are five trials on each of which the same electrical sitmulus (line below bottom trace) was applied to a nerve different from the one being recorded from. Notice that the same stimulus sometimes, but not always (B4) causes swimming. Even on trials when swimming does result, there is substantial variability in the pattern and duration of activity prior to the initiation of swimming, as well as in the swimming activity itself (B1,2,3,5). (C). A stimulus–response curve for the isolated leech nervous system. For each of a series of stimulus voltages (abscissa) the figure shows the percentage of trials (ordinate) using that voltage on which a swimming episode resulted. Notice that, over a wide voltage range, the same stimulus sometimes does and sometimes does not trigger a swim. (D) A stimulus–response curve for the isolated leech nervous system in the absence of the most headwards ganglia. Conventions as in C. Notice that there is now a sharp transition between stimulus voltages which reliably do and do not trigger swimming episodes. [Unpublished studies by Peter Brodfuehrer and Paul Grobstein.]

standing the Harvard Law of Animal Behavior. A cutaneous stimulus delivered to an intact leech sometimes, but not always, triggers swimming behavior. Such input/output variability might, in principle, be attributed to slight variations in the cutaneous stimulus itself, or to differences in other sensory inputs at the time the stimulus is delivered. In fact, as shown in Figure 2B, input/output variability persists in the isolated nervous system. Identical electrical stimuli delivered to a peripheral nerve sometimes, but not always, trigger swimming. Notice also that, even when the stimulus does trigger swimming, there is substantial variation from trial to trial in the latency, swim robustness, and motor activity preceding the swimming episode. In short, the Harvard Law of Animal Behavior holds for the nervous system as a whole.

Comparable observations have shown that intrinsic variability may also be a characteristic of the intermediate size boxes of which the nervous system as a whole is made. The significance of this will be discussed further below. Here it is only necessary to stress that neither the intrinsic variability of the nervous system as a whole nor that in any of the various intermediate boxes which make it up requires any appeal to the supernatural. Given intrinsic variability in neurons, there is every reason to expect its existence in the assemblies of neurons which make up both intermediate size boxes and the nervous system as a whole. In short, the failure of an experimenter to be able to predict the behavior of a given organism at a given time under particular environmental circumstances does not necessarily indicate either a failure of the experimenter to adequately control the circumstances or an external deus ex machina. It may simply indicate a phenomenon which can be rigorously documented, the existence of intrinsic variation, and which can, as discussed further below, be taken as a legitimate subject of study in its own right.

IV. THE NATURE OF INTRINSIC VARIABILITY

In the following, it will be useful to focus on the "nature" of variability, the particular form variability takes in a given situation, rather than on its causes. However, one subtlety in the definition of intrinsic variability where issues of nature and cause are unavoidably intertwined needs to be dealt with first. As is evident from the various phenemona of learning and memory, the state of the nervous system at a given time depends not only on its inputs at that time but on the history of its past inputs as well. Such dependence can certainly contribute to difficulties in predicting the response of a given organism to a given input at a given time, but it is in principle at least a correctable problem (by due attention to controlling prior inputs, and/or to invariant correlations between prior and present events) and not the one of primary concern here. "Intrinsic variability" is intended to refer to changes in the state of the nervous system which occur largely or entirely for reasons independent of input signals at both present and prior times.

With this understanding, intrinsic variability can be conceived to take one of three forms: orderly, deterministic but ill-mannered, and probabilistic. Circadian rhythms, and other periodic phenomena known to be present in the nervous, neuroendocrine, and neuromuscular systems, provide clear examples of the first kind of intrinsic variability. Widespread, coordinated changes in the state of the nervous system on a roughly 24-hour cycle can persist for long periods of time in the absence of any driving variations in the input pathways of the nervous system, and there is every reason to think would occur in the absence of any experience at all with daily variations in input. They can occur as well in isolated parts of the nervous system, of various sizes down to the level of individual neurons. Periodic heartbeats are similarly largely independent of driving input at any point in time, and characterize the whole heart, as well as parts down to the level of single cells. Though not directly relevant to the concerns of this article, it is worth noting that, in both cases, the periodic intrinsic variability at the highest level of organization is not explained entirely by that at the lowest but depends as well on the interactions among those elements. Isolated heart cells may beat at frequencies quite different from each other and from that of the heart as a whole, which reflects not only the intrinsic properties of the individual heart cells but the interactions among them as well. Noteworthy too is that both heartbeat and daily activity cycles can indeed be affected by input signals. Orderly intrinsic variability, indeed intrinsic variability in general, is a contributor to behavior, not an explanation of it.

There is a useful, if somewhat fuzzy, border between "orderly" and "deterministic but ill-mannered." Periodic intrinsic variability is well studied at cellular and molecular levels, and raises no spector of the supernatural whatsoever. It also provides an equally safe route into the terrain of the "deterministic but ill-mannered." Any time varying signal, periodic *or* aperiodic, can be approximated as closely as one wants by the sum of a sufficiently large number of periodic signals (sine waves, for example) of different wave-lengths, amplitudes, and phase relations to one another. In particular, by summing the signal from a sufficient number of different elements, one can generate a signal (corresponding, for example, to the internal state of the nervous system) which is equivalent to the output of a random number generator. The resulting behavior would be deterministic, in the sense that it could be predicted if one had a knowledge of the underlying periodic elements. It can nonetheless be very "ill-mannered" in the sense that an outside observer, lacking a knowledge of the mathematics necessary to analyze the observed output, would see the behavior as highly or completely unpredictable. The category of "deterministic but ill-mannered" includes as well the various phemonena increasingly and popularly known as "chaotic." It is now well recognized that the behavior of even relatively simple systems involving small numbers of interacting nonlinear elements (such as neurons) can be highly unpredictable. Such systems are unpredictable but determinate, in the sense that the time evolution of their activity can be calculated algorithmically given known starting conditions. The observed activity pattern itself, however, may, like that of summed periodic elements, exhibit little or no discernable order. An additional noteworthy feature of chaotic systems is a "strong dependence on initial conditions." Very small changes in the starting conditions can lead to very large differences in subsequent behavior. What this means is that chaotic systems, while determinate in principal, may not be so in practice. An observer is inevitably limited to a particular level of precision in the measurement of starting conditions, and the range within which the actual starting condition falls may well be early enough to yield a range of entirely different outcomes.

In popular parlance, events are either predictable or unpredictable, with the former corresponding to "orderly" and the latter to "random" or "probabilistic." The recognition of the category of "deterministic but ill-mannered" is a generally important intellectual development which, however, seriously muddies this neat dichotomy. "Orderly," as already described, grades into "deterministic but ill-mannered," and there is some tendency to equate the second with "unpredictable" in general. In fact, there is an important conceptual distinction between "deterministic but ill-mannered" and random or probabilistic. The latter terms, at least in their strongest sense, refer to systems in which it is presumed that the unpredictability is not a matter of practice but instead one of principal. Quantum mechanics provides the most explicit modern conceptualization of the intuition that such in principal unpredictable systems exist; coin flipping or dice-throwing are vernacular metaphors for the same intution that some phenomena have a truly indeterminate character. It is not at all clear at the moment whether there exists an operational criterion by which an observer can distinguish between variabilities which are "deterministic but ill-mannered" as opposed to probabilistic. Nonetheless, the distinction is conceptually clean, and has at least one quite important general implication, as discussed further below.

Orderly intrinsic variability is a well-documented aspect of nervous system function. So too is less orderly intrinsic variability in neuronal activity, falling into the general area of the second two classes mentioned. There exists an older literature describing "noise" in both single neuron activity and such monitors of global activity as the EEG (such observations were not always done under conditions adequate to rigorously demonstrate that the activity was intrinsic, but such is very much consistent with the trend of the evidence). More recently, evidence of chaotic activity has been obtained in a variety of systems, including invertebrates as well as the olfactory bulb and neocortex of mammals. While there are varying degrees of uncertainty (both practical and conceptual) in these observations, there is no question but that a substantial degree of unpredictability characterizes the physiological activity of many parts of all nervous systems under conditions of substantially controlled input activity.

V. THE ANALYSIS AND SIGNIFICANCE OF INTRINSIC VARIABILITY

Preceding sections have provided neurobiological evidence in support of the notion that the Harvard Law of Animal Behavior may reflect actual variability in nervous system function, rather than supernatural forces or the failure of investigators to adequately control experimental circumstances. What remains for discussion is whether this understanding yields productive new lines of investigation. Two questions are at stake. One is whether there are ways to usefully explore observed variability, and the other is whether variability has any functional significance.

A. Methodology: A Case Study in Frog and Leech

Figure 3A provides a concrete illustration of the Harvard Law of Animal Behavior, drawn from studies of frog prey-orienting behavior. In each of a series of trials, a live prey item was confined in a cup at a fixed angle and distance from a given frog. The frog oriented accurately on all trials, in the sense that a line corresponding to the midsaggital plane of the head passes, when extended outward, through the cup containing the prey item. The actual position and head angle, however, varies substantially from trial to trial, as shown in the figure. Most people's presumption is that such variability relates to a trial to trial variability in the input signals, an obvious possibility being a variation in those related to prey location (which can vary somewhat within the cup) or in the frog's posture at the time the stimulus was presented. The variability is, however, neither decreased by decreasing the size of the cup (Fig. 3B) nor increased by causing the frog to adopt a wider than normal range of initial postures (Fig. 3C).These findings do not preclude some more elaborate explanation of the observed variance in terms of variations in input signals. They do, however, provide the kind of evidence (equally attainable in humans) which would support further consideration of the likely existence of intrinsic variability, and motivate additional experiments (of the kind discussed in previous sections where possible) to try and rigorously establish its existence.

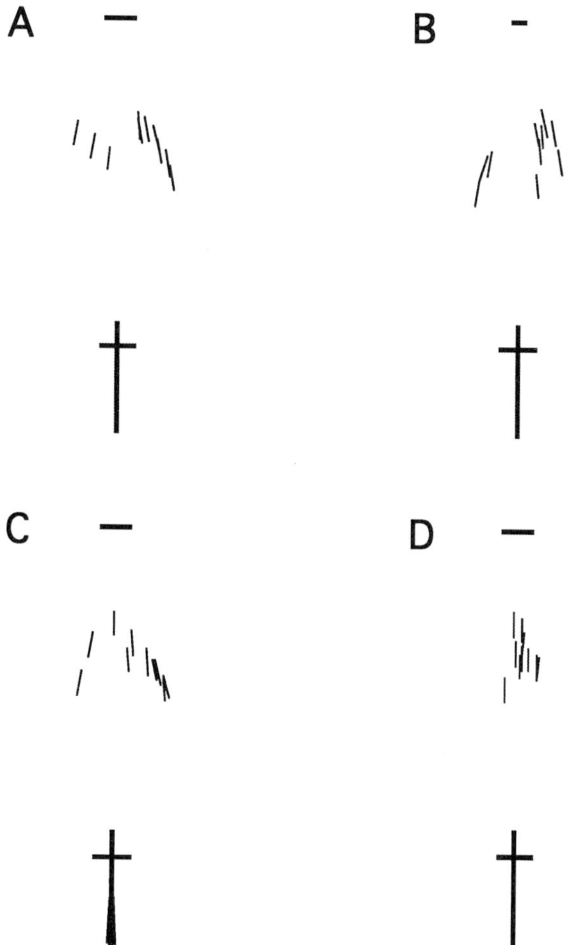

FIGURE 3 Behavioral variability in the frog. (A) Base line behavior. On each of 10 trials, the frog was positioned at the lower cross (long vertical line is body axis; short horizontal line is the line between the frog's eyes) and presented with a live mealworm confined in a cup (short upper horizontal line). Thinner oblique lines show the position and angle of the frog's head after the first movement on each trial. Notice that both position and angle vary substantially. (B) Reduction of stimulus cup size (shorter upper horizontal line). Notice that there is no corresponding reduction in the variability of final head position. (C) Increase in variability of initial posture (broadening of line corresponding to body axis). Notice that there is no corresponding increase in the variability of final head position. (D) A richer visual environment. Notice that, under this condition, the observed variability in final head position significantly decreases. [Unpublished studies by Paul Grobstein, Jeff Oristaglio, and others.]

Even given such a demonstration, many people might discount the significance of the observed variability, on the grounds that the nervous system is a complex physical device and that a certain imprecision in the function of any such device is inevitable. That the observed variation has an organized character (the frog is always pointing at the prey item) rather than being random provides some argument against this interpretation but an even stronger case can be made (here and in other situations). The observed variability is not constant, but instead varies depending on the circumstances. In a more complex visual environment (Fig. 3D), the variability is less. This clearly indicates that the variability evident in Figure 3A is not simply that inherent in the limits of precision of a physical device, but rather an independently variable property of the physical device.

The same is true for the rigorously verified intrinsic variability described in an earlier section for the leech. Figure 2C illustrates the stimulus–response curve for the isolated nervous system, showing that over a substantial range of stimulus voltages, the response in terms of the presence or absence of swimming is unpredictable (response percentages neither zero nor 100%). The behavior is much more predictable when the head ganglion is removed from the nervous system, as shown in Figure 2D. For each stimulus voltage the preparation reliably swims or fails to swim. Here too the intrinsic variability is not an expression of a constant inevitable imprecision but rather a characteristic which can be reduced under certain circumstances.

The findings in the leech further suggest that different regions of the nervous system (different intermediate size boxes) may play different roles in intrinsic variability, with some areas increasing it and other areas decreasing it (removal of the tail ganglion in the leech tends to increase observed variability). Interestingly, the history of neurobiological research, viewed in this light, suggests a similar conclusion. Experimental neuroscientists, interested in stable and predictable preparations in which to explore the details of particular pathways, long ago discovered that removal of the more rostral parts of the nervous system yields more reliable input/output relations in the spinal cord. While it is possible that this increased stability results from elimination of sensory input paths associated with the more rostral parts of the nervous system, it is equally possible that the observed reduction in variability would also be observed in a totally isolated nervous system. This possibility seems worth serious attention, and may relate to the experience of skilled athletes, whose performance at times seems to depend on blocking out not only input signals but their own thinking as well.

The general problem of how the nervous system is organized so as to potentially and somewhat unpredictably associate a given input with any of a number of outputs similar in overall objective but differing substantially in detail is a wide open area for new investigation. Related to this are a series of open questions about the nature of the variability itself (some form of orderly but ill-mannered, or statistical?) and how it is created (molecular noise or something at a higher level of organization?). Clearly, an inquiry proceeding from a presumption of the likely existence of intrinsic variability not only is achievable and opens new lines of scientific investigation, but also can usefully bridge between the latter and folk psychology as well.

B. Significance

The physicist Erwin Schrödinger, in his classic *What is Life?*, remarked 50 years ago on the remarkable stability and predictability of biological systems, noteworthy not only in comparison to the thermal noise of all physical systems but also because the biological systems are, of course, made up of noisy physical elements. From Schrödinger's perspective the problem of biological systems was one of how to combine physical elements so that their inevitable noise was reduced in the combination. The discussion to this point suggests that aspects of nervous system organization may well have evolved with exactly the opposite tendency: to enhance some kinds of noisiness or variability. There is, in fact, some reason to believe this is true of biological systems in general. If intrinsic variability is not actually the residual noise of imperfect machinery, the question to be treated at this point is what functions might it serve?

There is, across the sciences generally, an increasing interest in, and inquiry into the properties of "complex systems." Associated with this is the emergence of new and useful metaphors to try and imagine how properties like those displayed by the brain can emerge from simpler elements. "Complex systems" in general display substantial form and organization in the absence of anything corresponding to either an external planner or an internal blueprint; their properties instead emerge simply from the interactions of large numbers of elements. In this sense, neither the "machine" explanatory metaphor of the 19th century nor the "computer" metaphor of the later part of the 20th century is appropriate.

A more useful metaphor for "complex systems," suggested by some workers in the area, is that of a sandpile, as it might emerge from a continuous flow of sand dropping onto an elevated dish. The sandpile will grow until it reaches a particular size and shape. Despite the absence of any planner for the sandpile, either external or internal, its subsequent size and shape will persist more or less unchanged, as comparable amounts of sand enter and leave the sandpile by falling off the edge of the dish. The sandpile is an "open" and "self-organizing" system. Its form depends on a continuous flow of matter and energy through it, and emerges entirely from the interaction of large numbers of elements. Such systems in general display both homeostatic and adaptive properties. If the pile is disturbed by flattening it, it will, over time, return to its original form. If the dish is made larger, the sandpile will, over time, modify its shape and form to make use of the additional space. Most importantly, in the present context, such open, self-organizing systems are in general "noisy." While the overall size and shape of the sandpile is constant, there are continous and substantially unpredictable small changes in its form: at one point the addition of a few grains of sand results in a comparable number of grains leaving the pile, at another point the same few grains added triggers a major avalanche. Despite the appearance of relatively constant form, the sandpile is in fact constantly in a state of flux, indicated by its noisiness, and it is in fact precisely because of this flux that the sandpile displays both homeostatic and adaptive properties.

The sandpile is an instance of a "determinate but ill-mannered system," one in which substantial unpredictability in practice emerges as a property of the quite determinate interaction of quite determinate elements. It is a particularly simple example of such a system, having only one relatively stable form. More interesting, but not enormously more elaborate, systems can have many relatively stable forms, and shift among them relatively unpredictably (imagine an appropriately sized hole in the center of the dish, so that every once in a while, the pile collapses in the center, changing from a mountain into a volcano). Nonetheless, the sandpile serves to illustrate an important general point: that variability is not only not inconsistent with either homeostasis or adaptability but in fact reflects precisely those phenomena (large numbers of interacting elements in an open system) which give complex systems their adaptive and homeostatic characteristics. Phenomena of both perception and movement control are currently being usefully explored from this perspective. Object recognition, for example, may be best thought of as a variability-added search for a stable configuration of a large number of interacting elements (two such roughly equivalent stable points corresponding to the left and right arrows of Fig. 1). [*See* HOMEOSTASIS.]

There are, however, additional and more direct possible significances of "noisiness" which should also be born in mind. Game theory illustrates one such. The success of an organism at any given task is frequently dependent on the playing out of interactions with other organisms, interactions in which the behavior of each influences the behavior of the other. If the nature of the task is such that greater success of one organism necessarily implies lesser success of the other, then there exists an optimal strategy for the "game," a well-defined set of rules which will assure the maximal achievable score, assuming both participants behave "rationally." In many cases (poker providing one example), it can be proven that this optimal strategy includes deliberate randomization of behavior. Variability in the frog's prey-orienting movements may, for example, make it more difficult for the prey to successfully escape.

Variability can also be used to achieve an objective in the absence of existing information about exactly how to achieve that objective. Here the chemotactic behavior of many protozoans is instructive. In the absence of a chemical gradient of an attractive substance, these organisms move continuously with intermittent and apparently random changes of direction. The frequency of direction changes is, however, a function of the concentration of attractive substances, decreasing with higher concentrations. Because of this, an animal in a concentration gradient will reliably end up at the source, always, of course, by a different path. There is some evidence that frogs, once they acquire information about target location, may have a related capability to use their variability to create novel ways of reaching that target when more straightforward methods are unavailable. Indeed such a "creative" use of available variability may be a quite general property of movement control systems which display "motor equivalence", and perhaps contribute to explaining how it comes to be that years on a playground basketball court can yield performances never before seen.

The discovery, exploration, and creation of novelty has, of course, significance beyond the restricted domain of movement control, and in this wider terrain too variability plays obvious roles. "Noise" is an important element in artificial intelligence systems, where it is used to prevent premature settling on a less good solution to a task so as to ensure the search continues until better ones are found. Most humans have similar experience with needing to "get out of a rut" in their own day to day lives. More generally, substantially unpredictable variability must necessarily underlie all genuinely creative processes, since by definition they represent ways of dealing with phenomena for which the underlying rules are unknown. Dreams provide a familiar archetype of this kind of variability: while the elements in dreams (blue, three horns, snake, woman's head) are frequently familiar, the particular ways they are put together (a blue three-horned woman's head on a snake's body) frequently display a substantially unpredictable variability. The experiences one has with such things represent useful (and used) explorations of the novel, and the unpredictable combinations themselves sometimes emerge as quite significant insights (the "Eureka!" phenomenon).

The preceding is intended to establish that variability is by no means the residium left over when everything else is understood, but may instead in many cases be part of the very essence of what is to be explained, since many aspects of behavior relate more or less directly to problem solving, exploration, and creation. It is not intended to be a complete catalogue of the possible significances of intrinsic variability, and the issue of whether one is dealing with "determinate but ill-mannered" as opposed to probabilistic has deliberately been left vague for the cases discussed. If there is in fact a real distinction between a sufficiently chaotic process and a random number generator, it is probably not a distinction which matters for the situations described (though this is in fact a matter worth exploration). There is, however, one additional phenomenon worth mentioning in a discussion of variability where the distinction is in fact critical.

The existence and nature of "free will" is a major unsettled issue in western philosophy, one for which the Harvard Law of Animal Behavior is relevant. Roughly speaking, the question is whether the output of a given organism is under its own control, as opposed to being fully determined by in-principle-knowable causal factors. In neurobiological terms, one component of the question can usefully be rephrased in terms of whether complete information about the genome of an organism, together with similarly complete information about all input signals which the organism has received during its lifetime, would suffice to make the next output predictable. The discussion of intrinsic variability given to this point implies that the answer to this question is no: even identical twins reared under identical circumstances would behave differently if a sufficiently chaotic intrinsic variability influenced their output, either directly or via the longer lasting effects of intrinsic experiences associated with dreaming or thinking. And they would certainly behave differently if the relevant intrinsic variability was truly probabilistic. This frees one to entertain the possibility that behavior is not fully determined. Finding oneself behaving unpredictably does not, however, fully satisfy the notion of "free will." The remaining question is that of control. Does an individual organism in fact have any control over its output? [*See* FREE WILL.]

A reconsideration of Figure 1 suggests that some organisms, at least, can in fact exert meaningful control over their own output. As earlier described, the figure can, somewhat unpredictably, be seen either as arrows pointing to the left or to the right. Most individuals, staring at the figure for a sufficiently long time, can in fact see it at one time as one and at another time as the other. It is also possible for humans (at least) to withhold output (in response, for example, to the question "what do you see?") until the picture is seen as one or the other of the two images. One is, in short, capable of monitoring the consequences of the intrinsic variability of one's own nervous system, and withholding an output until that variability yields something with which one is satisfied. Individual organisms, including individual humans, are both made up of and are a part of complex causal webs of interacting elements. That they are fully under their own control is clearly not the case. The present discussion, however, suggests that the combination of intrinsic variability and a monitoring/editing function may indeed endow at least those organisms which possess the combination with a quite satisfying degree of "free will."

VI. CONCLUSIONS

The Harvard Law of Animal Behavior clearly warrants more serious attention than it usually receives. A reasonable skepticism about observed behavioral variability, due to the possible existence of unknown but identifiable uncontrolled variables, is both reasonable and demonstrably productive as a research strategy, insofar as it results in the identification of new causal influences. At the same time, the phenomena of intrinsic variability discussed here provide viable alternative explanations of behavioral variability, potential explanations which are at least as likely, rigorously explorable, and significant as an unknown uncontrolled but potentially controllable variable.

Two more general implications of this conclusion are worth making explicit. The first is that the equation between "understanding behavior" and "being able to predict the behavior that a given organism will display at given time," no matter how obvious it might seem or how useful in particular inquiries, is fundamentally flawed as a general prospectus for the behavioral and biobehavioral sciences. Some degree of unpredictability is, as suspected by the common sense view, a fundamental aspect of behavior. This raises some interesting questions about the meaning of "understanding" in the context of the scientific study of behavior, but other disciplines, notably physics, have managed to incorporate "uncertainty'' into their prospectuses, and there is no reason to believe that the scientific study of behavior cannot successfully incorporate a ''biobehavioral uncertainty principle'' as well. Acknowledgment of such a principal would, in any case, contribute to a rapprochment between the common sense and scientific explorations of behavior, reducing the perceived threat to human dignity associated with a presumption that behavior (including that of humans) can in principle be fully predicted, while at the same time making clearer the successes inherent in being able to say why an organism behaves the way it does *when* it does. Intrinsic variability not only removes the spectre of absolute predictability, but may, as discussed, provide a basis for admitting more fully into scientific discourse the concept of free will.

The second, important general implication is that intrinsic variability is not necessarily ''noise,'' in the sense of being an inevitable byproduct of any real system, but instead is, in many cases at least, an essential ingredient of successful behavior. Scientists tend to focus on the ''adaptiveness'' of behavior, on the underlying organization which yields an ''optimal'' behavior in a given context. What game theory established is that, in many contexts at least, ''optimal'' is not a particular behavior, but rather variable behavior. Even more importantly, however, what is forgotten in the emphasis on ''adaptiveness'' and ''optimality'' is that much of behavior is fundamentally exploratory. Even when the task is known, as in the case of frog orienting, the underlying neuronal organization seems to be organized so as to explore various ways of achieving that task. To put the matter differently, ''play'' (and its associated behavioral variability) is not purely entertainment or a luxury to be given up when things get serious. It is itself a highly adaptive mechanism for dealing with the reality that the context for behavior is always largely unknown. Given that the adaptiveness of behavior itself derives from an evolutionary process in which variability and play are absolutely essential (and that no more successful mechanism for creating adapted systems is known), this should not be surprising. Scientists have, however, tended to focus more on the selection process than on the underlying variability without which it cannot act. In any case, recognition of intrinsic variability in the nervous system provides a second basis for rapprochment between the scientific and common sense perspectives on behavior: playfulness is indeed not only to be enjoyed but to be accorded high value for its fundamental role in the success of all organisms, including humans.

Bibliography

Abbs, J. H., and Cole, K. J. (1987). Neural mechanisms of motor equivalence and goal achievement. In ''Higher Brain Function'' (S. P. Wise, Ed.), pp. 15–44. Wiley, New York.

Bak, P., and Chen, K. (1991). Self-organized criticality. *Sci. Am.* January, 46–53.

Barlow, G. W. (1977). Modal action patterns. In ''How Animals Communicate'' (T. A. Sebeok, Ed.), pp. 98–133. Indiana University Press, Bloomington, IN.

Berkinblitt, M. B., Feldman, A. G., and Fukson, O. I. (1986). Adaptability of innate motor patterns and motor control mechanisms. *Behav. Brain Sci.* **9,** 535–638.

Grobstein, P. (1988). From the head to the heart: Some thoughts on similarities between brain function and morphogenesis, and on their significance for research methodology and biological theory. *Experientia* **44,** 960–971.

Grobstein, P. (1992). Directed movement in the frog: Motor choice, spatial representation, free will? In ''Neurobiology of Motor Programme Selection'' (J. Kien, C. R. McCrohan, and W. Winlow, Eds.), pp. 250–279. Pergamon, New York.

Kauffman, S. L. (1993). ''The Origins of Order.'' Oxford University Press, New York.

Linsker, R. (1990). Perceptual neural organization: Some approaches based on network models and information theory. *Annu. Rev. Neurosci.* **13,** 257–281.

Llinás, R. (1990). Intrinsic electrical properties of nerve cells and their role in network oscillation. *Cold Spring Harbor Symp. Quant. Biol.* **55,** 933–938.

Pittendrigh, C. S. (1993). Temporal organization: Reflections of a Darwinian clock watcher. *Annu. Rev. Physiol.* **15,** 17–54.

Poundstone, W. (1993). ''Prisoner's Dilemna.'' Doubleday, Anchor Books, New York.

Ruelle, D. (1991). ''Chance and Chaos.'' Princeton University Press, Princeton, NJ.

Shepard, R. N. (1990). ''Mind Sights.'' Freeman, New York.

Skarda, C. A. and Freeman, W. J. (1987). How brains make chaos in order to make sense of the world. *Behav. Brain Sci.* **10,** 161–195.

Violence, Observational Effects on Behavior

Russell G. Geen
University of Missouri

Glossary

Arousal Activation of physiological processes associated with the autonomic nervous system (e.g., heart rate, skin conductance, respiration) usually accompanied by subjective experience of increased excitation.

Aversive condition Any condition of the person that is experienced as an unpleasant feeling state.

Cross-lagged panel correlation Correlation of data on one variable from one observation period with data on another variable from a later observation period; most likely cause–effect relationships are inferred from relative magnitudes of several such correlations.

Habituation Loss of reactivity with successive presentations of a stimulus.

Social comparison Drawing of conclusions regarding one's abilities, opinions, motives, and/or emotional states from observation of other people in similar conditions.

OBSERVATION OF VIOLENCE, according to a large body of evidence, can elicit or facilitate the expression of aggressive behavior in the viewer. The original theory linking observation of violence to aggressive behavior was built on the concepts of modeling and imitation. Although these explanatory concepts persisted until recent times, they have been superseded by other constructs, such as arousal, cognitive labeling, and cognitive association.

I. HISTORICAL BACKGROUND

Social scientists have long been interested in the question of whether the mass media of communication play a role in the acquisition and maintenance of aggressive behavior. With the rapid spread of informational technology in the 19th century, persons interested in the social bases of mental and behavioral problems began to regard such media as newspapers, popular books, and magazines as potential sources of antisocial influence. The French physician Paul Aubrey (1858–1899) was instrumental in propagating a theory of mental contagion that explained some psychoneurotic behaviors in terms of these influences. A similar viewpoint was held by the sociologist Jean-Gabriel de Tarde (1843–1904), who observed that "epidemics of crime follow the line of the telegraph," thereby indicating a belief that the reporting of acts of violence in the news may disseminate violent images that can elicit aggression. [*See* AGGRESSION.]

In a manner consistent with prevailing social theories, observers such as Tarde attributed this apparent cause–effect relationship between symbolic presentations of violence and subsequent aggressive behavior to processes of suggestion and imitation. It was commonly believed by social and medical theorists in 19th century France, for example, that certain types of persons who inherit "weak" or degenerate dispositions are especially susceptible to nervous trauma induced by vivid images of criminal or antisocial behavior and are also likely to act out the ideas elicited by the imagery without interference from other ideas. Eventually the theory of nervous trauma was abandoned. However, the concepts of imitation, inhibition, and individual differences implied in that theory were assimilated to more modern approaches to the investigation of mass media effects. [*See* Individual Differences in Temperament.]

With the advent of the radio, motion pictures, and television in the 20th century, even more powerful images of violence became widely disseminated in news broadcasting and the entertainment media. During the 1930s, numerous investigations were carried out to explore a possible effect of movies on violent and criminal behavior. These early explorations were addressed to a number of issues that would be studied again in the 1960s and 1970s, such as the possible identification of the viewer with the actors in films, the role of maturation and development in responses to movies, the factors involved in individual preferences for aggressive film content, and the possible role of individual differences as moderators of film-induced effects. Unfortunately, the results of these early investigations yielded few reliable results, mainly because of their relatively unsophisticated methodology.

Interest in the study of media violence increased with the advent of widespread home television in the 1950s. Although some interest in movie research remains, over the years the problem of "media violence" has become defined mainly as one involving the effects of violent television programs on aggressive behavior. There is little question that television is a major purveyor of violent stimuli. Studies by the National Coalition on Television Violence and by social scientists at the Annenberg School of Communication at the University of Pennsylvania show a high level of violence in prime-time programming that has remained fairly constant for many years.

II. THE IMITATION–MODELING HYPOTHESIS

Research efforts on media violence during the late 1950s turned with increasing frequency to the use of experimental designs as investigators sought to discover not only whether such violence had effects on the viewers, but also what the intervening variables in any such effects might be. Initial attempts at theorizing used the familiar concepts of suggestion and imitation, recast in the conceptual language of social learning theory. This approach led to a number of experiments in the early 1960s by Bandura in which it was shown that children responded to an aggressive adult female model by imitatively aggressing against a clown doll. The research showed the operation of two processes in imitative aggression: observational learning of new aggressive behaviors and the emission, presumably due to the model's influence, of aggressive acts already in the subject's behavioral repertoire. The latter is usually attributed to a reduction of social restraints against aggressing.

In several subsequent elaborations of his original modeling experiments, Bandura explored such matters as the effects of quasi-cartoon figures on imitative aggression, the influence of models presented in films rather than live, the effects of observing punished as well as rewarded aggression, and the role of inducements in acting out aggressive behaviors learned through imitation. In general, cartoon-like models elicited less imitative aggression than either live models or realistic ones shown on the screen. Furthermore, whereas punishment inhibited the expression of modeled aggression, it did not hinder the learning of the punished acts. Given strong enough incentives to perform, children imitated a model's punished aggression as much as aggression that had been rewarded. More recent studies of modeling have shown that observed aggression is more likely to be acted out by children when adults present at the time of viewing express approval of the acts or when other children act out the observed behaviors in the viewer's presence.

III. THE MEDIA AS A SOURCE OF INFORMATION

A. Justification of Observed Violence

Despite the adequacy of the concept of observational learning to account for the acquisition of novel or unusual aggressive behaviors, such learning alone does not explain the more general phenomenon of media-induced aggression. Most experiments on the effects of observing violence show that such observation increases the level of many aggressive responses that bear little similarity to the ones observed. Obviously, processes other than observational learning are involved in this sort of aggression. Observing violence in media presentations may influence aggression by providing information about aggressive behavior. It may, for example, inform the observer that aggression is a permissible or even desirable means of solving interpersonal conflicts and, by so doing, help to reduce any inhibition against aggressing that the person may have. Several studies have shown that when violence is presented as morally justified behavior because the victim deserves to be attacked, it elicits aggression, whereas violence that is described as being morally unjustified either has no effect or inhibits the expression of aggression.

B. Social Comparison with the Observed Aggressor

Judgment concerning the motives of the observed aggressor may also influence the ways in which media violence elicits aggression. Of the many motives that may animate aggressive behavior, vengeance is one that most people would probably agree is at least somewhat morally justified. A series of experiments by Geen and his associates has shown that when violence is described as motivated by a desire for revenge, it evokes more aggression from an observer than does the same violence when it is attributed to other motives, provided that the observer has first been insulted, attacked, or otherwise provoked to retaliate. Provoked persons who observe a scene of revenge also describe themselves as less restrained in aggressing than similarly provoked subjects who observe violence due to other causes. On the other hand, when provoked persons observe a media portrayal of an *unsuccessful* attempt at revenge they are later *less* aggressive than those who see successful vengeance.

It is important to note that in these studies, as in others showing the aggression-facilitating effects of observing revenge, only subjects who had first been angered behaved aggressively after observing violence. These findings suggest that one function of observing portrayals of revenge in the media is the facilitation of a social comparison process. The prospects of attacking another person may ordinarily raise inhibitions and aggression anxiety in angry subjects, thereby prohibiting retaliation. If, however, the subject is able to observe in the media an angry character who successfully exacts revenge, his or her own desire to retaliate may seem more appropriate. In the same way observation of an unsuccessful attempt at revenge may remind the person that retaliation can have punishing consequences and may thereby reinforce inhibitions.

It should also be noted that the studies showing that aggression is influenced by the perceived motives of an observed aggressor were all carried out with young adult viewers. The cognitive processes involved in this effect are moderated by the age and developmental level of the viewer. Whereas very young viewers such as kindergarteners tend to comprehend the violence that they see only in terms of its intensity and ultimate consequences and to be relatively unaffected by the aggressor's motives, older children and adults are more likely to judge violence in terms of its motivation than in terms of its intensity or consequences.

The social comparison hypothesis is further supported by studies that have shown that when subjects are instructed to identify with the winner of an act of observed violence, their aggression against a victim is enhanced. These studies suggest that "identification with the aggressor," or covert role-taking, facilitates the expression of media-engendered aggression. Consistent with what has been proposed above, such role-taking may facilitate a social comparison process whereby the person interprets the correctness of her or his motives to aggress on the basis of what is seen on television or in a motion picture.

C. Reality of Observed Violence

When violence in the media is thought to be real it elicits more aggression than when it is regarded as fiction. This finding suggests that the former has greater impact on the person than the latter. Realistic violence may be processed as a more intense informational input than fiction. As a consequence it may be more likely to occupy the observer's attention.

D. Sex Differences

Differences in responses of males and females to observed violence has not been studied systematically in laboratory experiments. There is some evidence that women may not become as aroused as men by televised violence, and that school-age girls may be less likely than boys to aggress as a consequence of viewing such material, but other studies indicate no sex differences. The conflicting state of the evidence on this matter prevents further conclusions.

IV. EFFECTS OF OBSERVED VIOLENCE ON AROUSAL

A. Arousal and Elicitation of Aggression

Observation of violence may facilitate the expression of aggression by causing increased autonomic arousal. Three processes have been suggested as causes for this facilitation. First, autonomic activation produced by watching violence may simply raise the person's overall activity level and intensify all responses. If the person has been provoked or otherwise instigated to aggress at the time the increased activation occurs, aggression will be a likely outcome. This line of reasoning is supported by the fact that most studies reporting a positive relationship between observation of violence and subsequent aggression find that relationship only in persons who have previously been provoked. A second, as and yet untested, possibility is that high levels of arousal may be aversive to the observer and may therefore stimulate aggression in the same way as other aversive or painful stimuli.

A third possibility is that arousal elicited by media portrayals of aggression may be mislabeled as anger in situations involving provocation, thus producing anger-motivated aggression. This mislabeling process has been demonstrated in several studies by Zillmann, who has named it "excitation transfer." Zillmann's theory is especially interesting because it addresses a problem not covered by some of the viewpoints reviewed above: the length of time during which a person is likely to be affected by the observation of violence. Whereas most experiments show an immediate effect that persists for a very short period after observation, the notion of excitation transfer suggests that the effect may be extended over a longer period. Even after the initial arousal has dissipated, the observer may remain potentially aggressive for as long as the self-generated label of anger persists. [*See* ANGER.]

B. Habituation with Repeated Exposure

As is the case with arousal elicited by any stimulus, that elicited by media violence habituates with repeated exposure. Some investigators have therefore suggested that a "desensitization" to observed aggression may follow extended viewing. At the level of psychophysiology, reduced activation as a function of exposure to violent videotapes has been shown in laboratory experiments. There is also evidence that people who watch large amounts of televised violence are generally less reactive to new depictions of violence than are those who watch less. The effects of desensitization on aggressive behavior are not obvious, and data bearing on the subject are scarce. At this time we cannot conclude whether the habituiation to violence that occurs with extended television viewing has any effects on aggressive behavior evoked by that viewing.

V. PORNOGRAPHY AND AGGRESSION

Certain kinds of pornography, in which persons are sexually assaulted, tortured, or placed in bondage, represent a special type of violent stimuli. Although the content of such material is sexual, sex is not treated as an end itself but rather as a means to the real purpose of the drama: aggression against a human victim, who is almost always a woman. Research on this matter is especially important in that it speaks to the question of whether observation of pornography engenders or facilitates aggression against women. [*See* PORNOGRAPHY, EFFECTS ON ATTITUDES AND BEHAVIOR.]

The role of pornography in violence against women has been studied extensively, and there is some evidence from experimental studies that observation of such material is sometimes associated with male violence against women. These controlled studies involve the use of videotapes that have been carefully selected to depict sexual activity carried out in either aggressive or nonaggressive contexts. Research by Donnerstein and his associates has shown that whereas observation of erotic but nonviolent videotapes does not elicit more male aggression against women than nonsexual control tapes, those showing a violent rape scene are associated with significantly more aggression against a female victim. This is true even when the subject has no reason to be angry with his victim. Aggressive-pornographic video material also elicits more aggression against women than against other men. Donnerstein has also shown that when the woman in a rape scene appears to enjoy being assaulted, aggression by men against women is further enhanced. In addition, studies by Malamuth have shown that male belief in the "rape myth"—that women secretly enjoy being sexually abused by men—is fostered by exposure to violent pornography.

Men also show considerable individual differences in their attitude toward women and in the likelihood of aggressing against them. Likelihood of raping (LR) is a motivational variable that moderates some of the situational effects associated with observation of pornography. It is measured by means of a self-report rating scale by which the male respondent indicates how likely he would be to commit rape if he knew that he would not be punished for it. The

LR variable is positively associated with aggression against women. Men who score high on this variable are more likely than low scorers to report that they have used force against women for sexual purposes and that they will probably do so again. Under laboratory conditions, men high in LR are more aggressive toward women than those low in LR, but not against other men. LR also moderates the amount of arousal that men experience when exposed to certain types of pornography. Those high in LR become more excited while listening to an audiotape in which a woman ostensibly becomes sexually aroused while being raped than when she is aroused in consensual intercourse.

To summarize, the effects of pornography on male aggression toward women appear to involve several of the processes noted earlier in this review. Presentations of pornography are likely to elicit aggression to the extent that they (1) provide information about the acceptability of such behavior, (2) reduce inhibitions against aggressing in men who are normally disposed to commit such acts, and (3) arouse male viewers.

VI. NATURALISTIC STUDY OF MEDIA EFFECTS

A. Types of Naturalistic Study

Experimental research such as that reviewed in the preceding sections allows investigators to test causal hypotheses. By controlling sources of extraneous variation in their studies experimental researchers are able to isolate certain other variables (such as arousal, disinhibition, and social comparison processes) and to test whether such variables are antecedents of aggression. For this reason, experimental studies constitute an important part of the literature on the effects of media violence. However, experiments have limitations as well as advantages. They examine behavior over short periods of time only. They involve behaviors that usually bear little relationship to the sort of aggression in which people engage on a daily basis. The samples of television programs that they use represent only a small portion of the wide array of programs seen in the medium. At best, therefore, experiments may involve analogs of aggression rather than cross-sections of it. A more complete analysis of media effects must include results from studies carried out under natural conditions. Three such types of study have been conducted: field experiments, longitudinal correlational investigations, and archival analyses. In many cases, these studies have been designed to test hypotheses derived from laboratory findings and therefore provide a test of the external validity of the latter.

B. Field Experiments

In a field experiment, independent variables are manipulated and controlled, and dependent variables measured, much as in a laboratory experiment. However, the entire procedure takes place in a natural setting. The degree of control is not as high as in the laboratory, but external validity tends to be greater. Findings from such studies are largely inconclusive. Some field experiments have produced data that agree with laboratory findings and others have not. Some impressive effects on aggression of observing violence have been reported in studies carried out in well-controlled settings such as theaters and correctional institutions. Investigations conducted in settings that do not allow a high degree of control over what people watch have tended to show that observing violence has no effect on aggressive behavior.

C. Longitudinal Studies

Longitudinal studies involve the repeated measurement of television viewing and aggressive behavior under real-life conditions over a period of time. A major investigation by Eron and his associates began with a study of third-grade children in a rural county in the state of New York in 1960, in which each child's aggressiveness was assessed through ratings made by the child's peers and parents and by the children themselves. Each child's preference for violent television programs was also measured. Ten years later, the same variables were measured in a large number of children from the original sample. The data from the two periods were analyzed by means of cross-lagged panel correlations. This analysis revealed that preference for television violence among boys in the third grade was positively and significantly correlated with aggressiveness 10 years later, whereas aggressiveness in the third grade was not correlated with preference for televised violence a decade hence. This pattern of correlations supports the hypothesis that, for boys, observation of televised violence in childhood contributes to aggressiveness in young adulthood. Additional analyses showed that the results were not due to differences in the level of aggressiveness among children who did or did not like violent television in the third grade. Across all levels of aggressiveness—high, moderate, and low—in the third grade, an early preference for television violence was correlated significantly with aggressiveness 10 years later. The relationship was not weakened by controlling several possible contaminating variables, such as socioeconomic status of the boys' parents, the boys' intelligence, parental aggressiveness, and the total number of hours of television watched. All of these results pertained only to boys. Among girls, preference for violent television in the third grade was not significantly related to aggressiveness in young adulthood.

In a subsequent report, Eron and his associates noted the results of a second follow-up study of individuals from their original pool 22 years after the first study. Data were gathered from interviews with the subjects, interviews with spouses and children of the subjects, and archival records including criminal justice files. Childhood aggression was a predictor of both aggression and criminal behavior 22 years later. Furthermore, the seriousness of the crimes for which males were convicted by age 30 was significantly related to the amount of television they had watched as 8-year-old boys. The findings of this study therefore support and extend those of the 10-year follow-up cited above.

The results of still another study by the same investigators in the Chicago area support the conclusions of their earlier research. Cross-lagged correlations over a period of 1 year (1977–1978) showed that among boys the correlation between frequency of observing violence on television in 1977 and aggressiveness in 1978 was positive and larger than the correlation between aggression in 1977 and frequency of viewing violence in 1978. Among boys, therefore, the findings were similar to those of the earlier studies. Among girls, however, the results differed from previous ones. All correlations between observation of televised violence and aggressiveness were positive, but their pattern was *opposite* that of the boys. The correlation between aggressiveness in 1977 and viewing of violence in 1978 was greater than the obverse. How may this finding for the girls be explained? Possibly girls learn a sex role that they are encouraged to play as they mature. In part, this role prescribes passive and nonaggressive behavior in response to interpersonal conflicts. A girl who is typically aggressive must therefore find outlets for her emotions that do not include aggressive behavior. One such outlet could be vicarious aggression. During childhood the aggressive girl may turn to violence on television as a means of expressing her feelings.

Another major longitudinal investigation of the effects of televised violence has been reported by Singer and Singer, who studied a sample of nursery school age children for 1 year. At four times during the year, 2-week periods were used as "probes," during which the parents kept diaries of their children's television viewing. Meanwhile, observers recorded instances of aggressive behavior by the children in school. When data were combined across all four probe periods, aggressive behavior was significantly and positively correlated with the total amount of time spent viewing "action–adventure" programs, which had a high level of violence, among both boys and girls.

The pattern of cross-lagged correlations over the four probe periods again supported the hypothesis that viewing violence on television produces subsequent aggression. In general, the magnitude of the correlations between violence viewing in early probes and aggression in later ones was larger than the correlation between aggression in early probes and violence viewing in subsequent ones. However, this usual effect was not found in the analysis of effects from probe 2 to probe 3. Viewing of action–adventure programs in the second probe period was correlated with aggression in the third, but in addition aggression in the second period was correlated with the viewing of action–adventure shows in the third. This finding suggests that a liking for aggressive television programs may be engendered by personal aggressiveness. Overall, the Singers' data may reveal a circular process: observing violence early in the year leads to aggression, which in turn fosters an appetite for more of the same sort of program.

Additional evidence of a connection between viewing televised violence and aggression comes from a series of cross-cultural longitudinal studies carried out by Huesmann and Eron and their associates in the United States, Australia, Finland, Poland, and Israel. The time period of the study was 3 years, and more than a thousand boys and girls were tested. Aggressiveness was studied as a concomitant of several variables, including the violence of preferred programs, overall viewing of violence, identification with televised aggressors, and judgments of realism of televised violence. In general, the results were consistent with the earlier findings from American studies. Early television viewing was associated with aggressiveness among boys in the United States, Finland, Poland, and Israel. Among girls, early television viewing was related to aggression in Israel and the United States. Moreover, early aggression was associated with subsequent increases in viewing violent television among both boys and girls in the United States and Finland, and among girls in Israel.

D. Archival Analysis

Experimental and longitudinal studies are different in many respects but in one way they are similar: at least some of the people involved (e.g., the experimental subjects, the parents who monitor the child's viewing, the teacher who rates the child's aggressiveness) realize that they are participating in an investigation. To some extent, therefore, the measurements are intrusive in that they break into the ongoing flow of behavior and possibly remind the participants of the purpose of the study. Research based on the analysis of public records and other archival data is free of this potential pitfall. Such research involves the search for a spatial or temporal relationship between media violence and aggression, with an inference of cause-and-effect drawn from such evidence. Some observers have suggested, for example, that certain types of aggressive acts appear to occur in clusters following some spectacular and well-publicized event, such as an airplane hijacking or mass murder. The proximity of the aggressive acts to the preceding violent event may suggest the possibility that the latter somehow elicits or facilitates the occurrence of the former.

An attempt to account for normally occurring aggression with a hypothesis derived from experimental research has been made in a series of investigations by Phillips. Dealing entirely with archival data, Phillips has sought to show a causal connection between events related to violence shown on television or reported in other news media and increments in aggression among the public in the immediate aftermath of the reports. Phillips based his studies on a hypothesis of social learning and imitation derived from Bandura's experimental work. For example, Phillips has shown that the incidence of suicides increases immediately after a suicide has been reported in the newspapers, reaching a peak during the month immediately after publication of the story. In addition, the increase in suicides appears to be directly related to the amount of publicity given the original one. Phillips has described this phenomenon as the "Werther effect," after the character in Goethe's novel whose self-inflicted death was said to have elicited many real suicides among readers. [*See* Suicide.]

In related studies, Phillips has shown a correlation between publicized suicides and the incidence of automobile fatalities. Interpretation of this finding rests on the assumption that some motor vehicle accidents may be due to suicidal intentions on the part of the drivers involved. For example, in one study the number of motor vehicle deaths occurring over an 11-day period following each of 23 front-page suicide stories was compared with the average number of such deaths during four control periods in which no suicides were reported. In the case of all but five suicides, the number of automobile fatalities was greater following the story than during the control periods. Overall, the average number of fatalities increased significantly following suicide stories. The peak incidence of traffic deaths occurred, on the average, 3 days after the suicide stories were reported. In still another study, Phillips reported a positive relationship between suicides shown in television fiction and acts assumed to reflect suicidal motives. Thirteen suicides shown in televised soap operas during 1977 constituted the eliciting stimuli. The number of motor vehicle deaths, nonfatal traffic accidents, and suicides all increased, compared to rates during a control period consisting of the latter part of the weeks in which the fictitious suicides were shown.

In a study that pertains more directly to evidence from experimental research, Phillips has reported a positive relationship between televised heavyweight prize fights and the incidence of homicides in the United States over a 10-day period following each fight. It should be noted that some of Phillips' findings involve the operation of variables not yet accounted for theoretically and that the findings and conclusions of the research have been criticized on methodological grounds. Nevertheless, this research program represents an extension of a hypothesis developed in the experimental laboratory to aggressive behavior in the settings of everyday life.

VII. COGNITIVE PROCESSES IN MEDIA-RELATED AGGRESSION

Phillips' invocation of modeling and imitation to account for his findings raises once again the question of the limits of this theoretical formulation. Terms like "observational learning," "imitation," and "modeling" are little more than labels for the emission of aggressive responses in specific settings and hardly explain the wide range of complex effects found in the research. Likewise, the other explanatory variables that have been suggested—those involving disinhibition, arousal, and the acquisition of aggressive attitudes—are not sufficient to explain the general processes that underlie the findings. What is needed is a level of theorizing that goes beyond the invention of labels and links the processes involved in media-elicited aggression to more general psychological constructs. Recently, two such theoretical explanations have been proposed. Each provides a more comprehensive explanation than did earlier viewpoints. Both are derived from the premises of contemporary cognitive psychology.

A. Retrieval of Violent Scripts

Huesmann has proposed that when children observe violence in the mass media they learn complicated scripts for social behavior. The fundamental element in the script is a *vignette* consisting of both a perceptual image and a conceptual representation of a briefly occurring event. A simple vignette, for instance, would be that of one person shooting another with a gun (the perceptual image) out of anger over something the first person has done (a conceptual representation). A script consists of a sequence of vignettes. It defines situations and guides behavior: the person first selects a script to represent the situation and then assumes a role in that script. Once a script has been learned, it can be retrieved at some later time as a guide for behavior.

How does one know which of the many scripts in memory will be retrieved on a given occasion? Granted that some aggressive scripts may be learned through observation of violence, why should one of them, and not some other, be recalled when the person has been provoked? One answer to this question involves encoding specificity: the recall of a script depends in part on the similarity of the recall situation to the situation in which the script was formed and encoded. In addition, certain characteristics of the situation may determine what happens in encoding. Any characteristic of observed violence that makes a scene stand out and attract attention can enhance the degree to which that scene is encoded and stored in memory. For example, acts of violence that are judged to be real may be regarded as more instrumental to the solving of future conflicts than less realistic ones. As we have already noted, when portrayals of violence are said to be of real events, they elicit more aggression than when they are described in less realistic terms. [*See* MEMORY.]

B. Priming of Aggressive Associations

A line of reasoning similar to Huesmann's has been taken by Berkowitz, who argues that aggressive ideas elicited by a violent stimulus can "prime" other semantically related thoughts. This, in turn, increases the probability of the viewer's having other aggressive ideas. Berkowitz bases this "priming" hypothesis on the concept of spreading activation: thoughts send out radiating influences along associative pathways, thereby evoking related cognitions. In this way, ideas about aggression that are not observed in the media may be elicited by the latter. In addition, thoughts are linked, along the same sort of associative lines, not only to other thoughts but also to emotional reactions and behavioral tendencies. The observation of violence can therefore engender a complex of associations consisting of aggressive ideas, anger, and the impetus for aggressive behavior. The hypothesis of cognitive priming may also help explain the finding that the presence of weapons is sometimes associated with aggression. This finding, first reported by Berkowitz and since replicated and extended by others, may indicate that weapons, because of their association with violence, prime aggressive thoughts, emotions, and behavioral dispositions that facilitate the expression of aggressive behavior following provocation.

VIII. TELEVISED VIOLENCE AND FEAR

Viewing violence in the media may have long-range effects on behavior that do not have any obvious connection with the immediate effects described above. In an extensive series of studies, Gerbner and his associates have described one such long-range consequence: extended viewing of television brings a person into contact with a high level of violence, and this violence generates fear, suspicion, distrust, and an attitude toward the world in which violence is assigned an importance disproportionate to its prevalence. Studies conducted in both the United States and Europe have shown that fear may be an immediate consequence of observation of televised violence. [*See* ANXIETY AND FEAR.]

Whether fear engendered by televised violence actually causes aggression is not known. However, it is possible that such fear, and the associated belief that the world is a threatening place, could lead people to feel a need to protect themselves against a clear and present danger. Among the consequences of this feeling could be public demands for punitive justice, authoritarian control, and vigilantism. One finding reported by Gerbner and his associates, for example, is that heavy users of television are more likely than lighter users to believe that too little money is being spent on fighting crime.

Bibliography

Berkowitz, L. (1984). Some effects of thoughts on anti- and prosocial influences of media events: A cognitive neoassociationist analysis. *Psychol. Bull.* **95,** 410–427.

Geen, R. G. (1990). "Human Aggression." Brooks/Cole, Pacific Grove, CA.

Geen, R. G. (1993). Television and aggression: Recent developments in research and theory. In "Media, Family, and Children: Social Scientific, Psychodynamic, and Clinical Perspectives" (D. Zillmann, J. Bryant, and A. C. Huston, Eds.). Erlbaum, Hillsdale, NJ.

Huesmann, L. R. (1986). Psychological processes promoting the relation between exposure to media violence and aggressive behavior by the viewer. *J. Soc. Issues* **42,** 125–139.

Huesmann, L. R., and Eron, L. D. (Eds.) (1986). "Television and the Aggressive Child: A Cross-National Comparison." Erlbaum, Hillsdale, NJ.

Phillips, D. P. (1986). Natural experiments on the effects of mass media violence on fatal aggression: Strengths and weaknesses of a new approach. In "Advances in Experimental Social Psychology" (L. Berkowitz, ed.), Vol. 19. Academic Press, New York.

Wood, W., Wong, F., and Chachere, J. (1991). Effects of media violence on viewers' aggression in unconstrained social interaction. *Psychol. Bull.* **109,** 371–383.

Visual Motion Perception

Stephen Grossberg and Ennio Mingolla
Boston University

Glossary

Contrast A local gradient or discontinuity in luminance.

Grouping The perceptual union of discrete or disconnected elements or features into coherent regions, based on detection of common properties of elements, continuation of partial geometric forms, or correlation of temporal events.

Luminance Amount of light available to the eye from a region of a scene, weighted by a function characterizing human sensitivity to wavelengths of light.

Receptive field The area on the retina within which stimulation can excite a given neuron.

Segmentation The perceptual partition of the visual field into regions, based on detection of edges demarcating the borders between regions or of statistical difference of properties (such as contrast or color) between regions.

VISUAL MOTION PERCEPTION comprises the brain's ability to process the spatiotemporal structure of light stimulating visual receptors to perceive environmental events and to control tracking movements by the eye and other actions. The importance of being able to detect change or temporal variation of light stimulation in evolution is underscored by the inability of many species to respond to spatial patterns in their environment unless either the seeing animal or the object to be seen is moving. Evidence suggests that many lower species can respond only to gross evidence of temporal change (e.g., a rapid, global diminution) in the light of their environment and lack the ability to discriminate the forms of objects in their environment. In humans, however, the motion perception system is so evolved as to permit fine-grained resolution of the forms of objects, even though those objects may at no single instant be revealed by a spatially consistent pattern. For example, when gazing at the reflection of a distant light on rippling water, we perceive the relatively flat horizontal extent of the water as a coherent environmental structure, even though spatially inhomogeneous scintillations of light are our visual inputs through time. Our abilities to quickly and effortlessly organize rapidly changing visual stimulation, to detect which parts of the visual input during some event "belong with" which other parts, and to thereby recognize the structure and motion of objects in our environment are among the most sophisticated feats of intelligent design in biology. [*See* Visual Perception.]

I. FUNCTIONAL IMPORTANCE OF MOTION PERCEPTION

Our ability to perceive moving forms underlies a number of important activities, including the control of our eye movements to detect and track moving objects, the control of our path of locomotion to explore and carry out planned behaviors, and our ability to represent and recognize the layout of envi-

Encyclopedia of Human Behavior, Volume 4

ronmental surfaces in three-dimensional space. In particular, the detection of different velocities in different parts of the visual field is needed for the visual *segmentation* and *grouping* processes by which we separate the spatially and temporally dense stream of optical stimulation into units originating from different environmental structures or events. In our everyday perceptions the unity and persistent identity of objects undergoing motion is so immediate that we may all too readily take for granted the subtle problems posed in discriminating such unity within the scintillating mosaic of visual stimulation. When trying to detect a leopard leaping through a forest canopy, the change in the optic array over time is a jumble of contrast changes whose local components point in a variety of directions, due to the vagaries of the shadows of rustling leaves and of the occlusions and disocclusions of markings on the leopard's surging body. For a leopard to be spotted (by a visual system) in such contexts, several problems must be solved: How can the locally ambiguous local motion signals corresponding to the many parts of the leopard's body be *reorganized* into a coherent object whole with a unitary motion? How can these signals be distinguished and separated from the signals due to other scenic objects and landmarks?

This process of reorganization transforms environmental motion signals into a global motion percept that may replace the directions of motion on the retina with a different perceived direction of motion. In this sense, the perceived motion direction is a visual illusion, albeit a useful type of illusion. It is a type of apparent motion, sometimes call motion capture. This fact illustrates why apparent motion percepts and other motion illusions are so important for understanding how we perceive moving objects.

The example of the leopard illustrates that the payoff for being able to cope with visual motion signals, as opposed to analyzing only static time-slices of visual information, is great. In fact, many ecologically significant events are revealed *only* through motion perception. In addition to the camouflage afforded by shadows or variable light, an animal may display its own protective camouflage that enables it to visually blend in with its surroundings, even to an extent of being nearly indistinguishable from its environment from many static viewpoints. The markings on the animal's body may, however, generate easily detectable optical trajectories if that animal moves across its surroundings. Even if the camouflaged animal remains perfectly still, the difference in depth of its body surfaces from the surfaces of its surroundings may generate differential motion signals, particularly at the edges of its body parts, with respect to a moving animal gazing in its direction. The ability to form a rapid and accurate partition of the visual field into regions based on coherence of motion signals is thus a crucial factor in separating "figure from ground," so that higher mental processes may more easily interpret the meaning of the figural motion signals.

II. LONG-RANGE APPARENT MOTION

In the 1870s, Exner provided the first empirical evidence that the visual perception of motion was a distinct perceptual quality, rather than being merely a series of spatially displaced static percepts over time. He did this by placing two sources of electrical sparks close together in space. When the sparks were flashed with an appropriate temporal interval between them, observers reported a compelling percept of continuous motion of a single flash from one location to another, even though neither flash actually moved. At shorter temporal intervals, flashes look simultaneous and stationary. At longer intervals, they look like successive stationary flashes, with no intervening motion percept. When the spatiotemporal parameters of the display are suboptimal, a "figureless" or "objectless" motion called *phi motion* is perceived. The smooth and continuous motion of a perceptually well-defined form is called *beta motion,* and typically occurs at a larger interstimulus interval, or ISI, between the offset of one flash and the onset of the next flash.

This classical demonstration of apparent motion was followed by a series of remarkable discoveries, particularly by gestalt psychologists, concerning the properties of motion perception. It was noticed that a decrease in ISI causes the speed of the interpolating motion to increase. A motion percept can also smoothly interpolate flashes separated by different distances, speeding up if necessary to cross a longer distance at a fixed ISI. If a more intense flash follows a less intense flash, the perceived motion can travel backwards from the second flash to the first flash. This percept is called *delta motion*. *Gamma motion* is the apparent expansion at the onset of a single flash, or apparent contraction at its offset. A similar expansion then contraction may be perceived when a region is suddenly darkened relative to its background, and then restored to the background luminance.

If a white spot on a gray background is followed by a nearby black spot on a gray background, then motion between the spots can occur while the percept changes from white to black at an intermediate position. Likewise, a red spot followed by a green spot on a white background leads to a continous motion percent combined with a switch from red to green along the motion pathway. These results show that the motion mechanism can combine visual stimuli corresponding to different colors, or even opposite directions-of-contrast. Complex tradeoffs between flash luminance, duration, distance, and ISI in the generation of motion percepts were also discovered. For example, the minimum ISI for perceiving motion increases with increasing spatial separation of the inducing flashes (Fig. 1). This property is sometimes called Korte's Third Law. A similar threshold decrease with distance occurs in the minimum stimulus onset asynchrony, or SOA, which is the difference between the flash onset times. Interestingly, whereas the minimum ISI decreases with flash duration, the minimum SOA increases with flash duration.

These discoveries raised several perplexing issues concerning the nature of the long-range brain interaction that generates a continuous motion percept between two stationary flashes. Why is this long-range interaction not perceived when only a single light is flashed? In particular, why are not outward waves of motion signals induced by a single flash? How does a motion signal get generated from the location of the first flash after the first flash terminates, and only after the second flash turns on? How does the motion signal adapt itself to the variable distances and ISIs of the second flash, by speeding up or slowing down accordingly? What use do these properties play under more normal perceptual conditions?

The figural organization of motion stimuli can also influence motion percepts. The Ternus displays provide a classical example. In Frame 1 of a Ternus display, three white elements are placed in a horizontal row on a black background (or conversely). After an ISI, in Frame 2 all three elements are shifted to the right so that the two rightward elements in Frame 1 are in the same locations as the two leftward elements in Frame 2. Depending on the ISI, the observer perceives either of four percepts. At very short ISIs, all four flashes appear simultaneous. At long ISIs, observers do not perceive motion at all. At

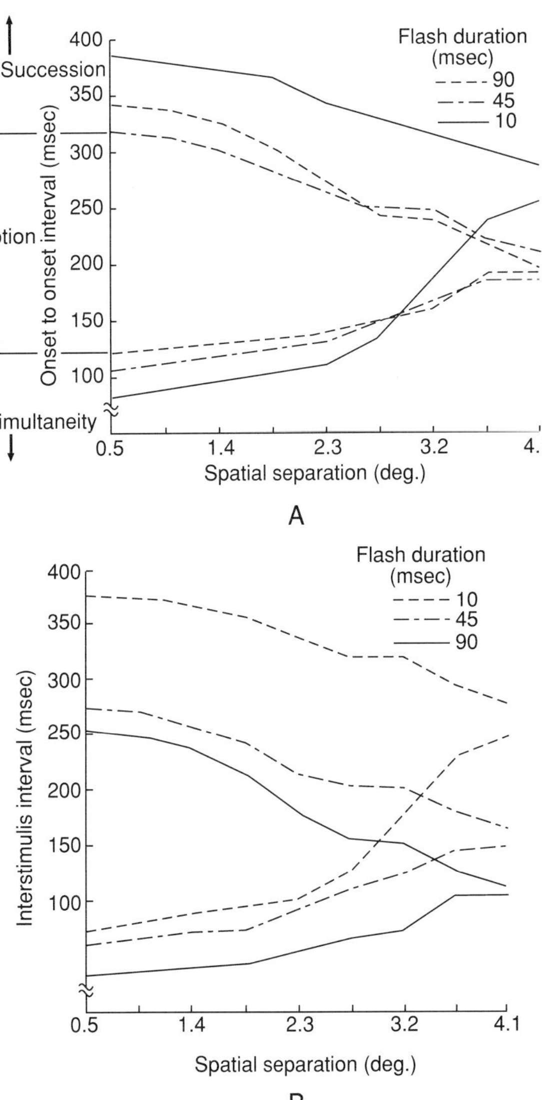

FIGURE 1 Upper and lower thresholds as a function of flash duration for two-flash apparent motion. Adapted from Neuhaus (1930). The lower threshold represents the transition between the percept of simultaneous flashes and continuous movement. The upper threshold represents the transition from perceived movement to perceived succession. (A) Threshold interstimulus intervals (ISIs). (B) Threshold onset to onset intervals (SOAs). [From Kolers (1972). Reprinted with permission from Pergamon Press, Ltd.]

ISIs slightly longer than those yielding simultaneity, the leftmost element in Frame 1 appears to jump to the rightmost element in Frame 2. This percept is called *element motion*. At somewhat longer ISIs, all three flashes seem to move together between Frame 1 and Frame 2. This is called *group motion*.

The percept of group motion might suggest that Ternus percepts are due to a cognitive process that groups the flashes into attended objects, and that motion perception occurs only after object perception. Such an explanation is not, however, made easily consistent with the percept of element motion. It has been argued, for example, that at short ISIs, the visual persistence of the brain's response to the two rightmost flashes of Frame 1 continues until the two leftmost flashes of Frame 2 occur. As a result, nothing changes at these two flash locations when Frame 2 occurs, so they do not seem to move. This type of explanation suggests that at least part of the apparent motion percept is determined at early processing stages. It does not, however, explain how we see element motion. In particular, why does not the element motion percept collide with the two stationary flash percepts? What kind of perceptual space can carry element motion across, or over, the stationary flashes?

Reverse-contrast Ternus motion also suggests that motion properties may be determined at early processing stages. In this paradigm, three white spots on a gray background in Frame 1 are followed by three black spots on a gray background in Frame 2. Here, at the ISIs where element motion previously occurred, group motion now occurs. How does a change of contrast between Frame 1 and Frame 2 obliterate element motion? Does it do so by altering the effects of visual persistence on Frame 2? An answer to these questions is outlined below in terms of neural models of motion perception that clarify the functional significance of many apparent motion percepts.

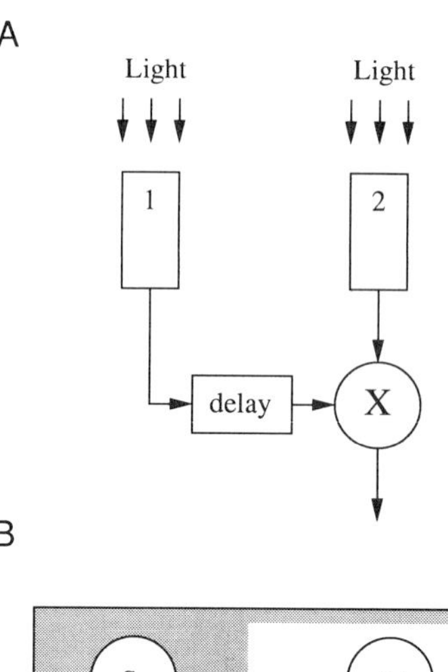

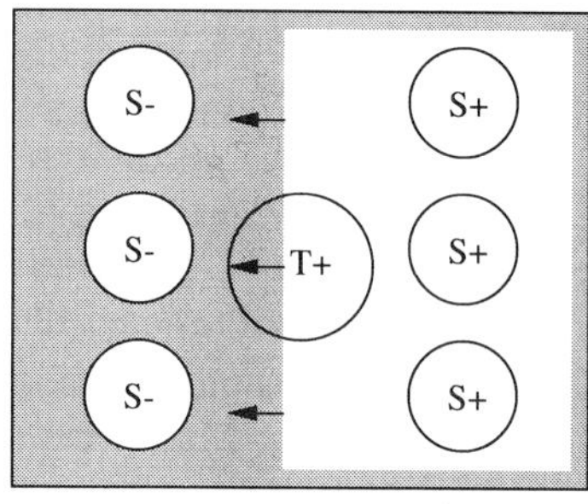

FIGURE 2 (A) The basic principle of the Reichardt motion detector is to compare the temporal stream of luminance values at location two with a delayed—or time shifted—stream of values at location one. A high correlation indicates rightward motion. (B) The Marr-Ullman motion detector determines whether the temporal derivative of luminance at an edge is increasing or decreasing. For example, increasing luminance at an edge that is dark-to-light (reading left to right) is associated with leftward motion.

III. SHORT-RANGE MOTION AND MOTION DETECTORS

Another rich source of early knowledge about motion perception came from neurophysiological studies. In the 1950s and 1960s Reichardt and his colleagues conducted extensive electrophysiological studies of the visual system of the fly, resulting in the development of a mathematical model for a motion detector which remains the foundation of many motion models to this day (Fig. 2A). Barlow and Levick arrived at a similar model in 1965 through their neurophysiological studies of the rabbit retina. The Reichardt model samples the change of luminance over time in two (possibly overlapping) regions and detects correlations in the pattern of change, whereby the temporal profile in one region matches that in the other after some fixed time lag. Such a correlation detector responds preferentially when a pattern of luminances sweeps across its receptive field over time in a prescribed direction.

Variations on the general idea of the correlation detector have proven capable of accounting for a great deal of psychophysical and neurophysiological data on motion perception. Using more elaborate operations than those of correlation detectors, a related class of models, called "motion energy" detectors, approach the problem of motion detection as one of passing the time-varying luminance stream through sequences of filters sensitive to those particular combinations of spatial and temporal variation in luminance that indicate motion. While some disagreement exists among current researchers regarding the details of operation, correlation detectors and motion energy detectors provide essentially equivalent output for a variety of stimuli.

A qualititatively different class of models of local motion detection, popularized by Marr and Ullman, are the "gradient" models (Fig. 2B). Here the fundamental operation is to compute the direction-of-contrast (light-to-dark versus dark-to-light) in the orientation of maximal change of luminance at some region, and to detect whether luminance is increasing or decreasing at a given moment in that same region. For example, if there is more luminance on the left than on the right, and luminance is increasing, then the detected motion direction is computed as rightward.

The correlation, energy, and gradient models focus on "short-range" motion—the type of motion that may be perceived when an image moves a small amount across a scene. The study of short-range motion processes accelerated after Braddick published experiments in 1974 which used random dots to measure the maximum displacement (called D_{max}) that could be seen as moving coherently. His estimate that D_{max} equals approximately 15 arc min was consistent with the short-range receptive field models of Reichardt and Barlow-Levick. This simple but useful viewpoint was complicated by subsequent experiments in which it was shown that D_{max} increases with decreasing element density, with increasing field size, with increasing element size, with retinal eccentricity, and with decreasing spatial frequency. These results are, however, consistent with the idea that a range of receptive field sizes exists and that D_{max} tends to covary with them.

Each class of short-range motion models has its adherents, and all appear to have certain advantages in explaining particular experimental results. No one of these models, however, can explain all the existing data on motion perception, suggesting that additional processes or some hybrid of those models may be needed, as described under Section XI. In particular, these models cannot explain the types of "long-range" motion data, including the long-range apparent motion data that were described above. Further constraints on long-range interactions are described in the next section.

IV. MOTION AMBIGUITY AND THE APERTURE PROBLEM

The transition from locally ambiguous visual signals to globally coherent visual perceptions is a fundamental problem in all aspects of early vision. In the motion domain, one type of local ambiguity is referred to as the *aperture problem,* which can be described both perceptually and in terms of receptive fields of individual neurons. Many perceptual consequences of the aperture problem were described by Wallach. The basic observation is that when a straight contour moves within a circular aperture, the contour is often perceived to move in a direction that is perpendicular to its own orientation, no matter what its true direction of motion might be.

The physiological analogue of this observation concerns the limited "field of view" afforded by an individual neuron's receptive field. As shown in Fig. 3, whenever a straight contour is long enough to completely overlap a cell's receptive field, that cell cannot in principle distinguish among a family of velocities all having the same normal component. If a cell's receptive field is elongated in one orientation, then the cell may be nost sensitive to motion perpendicular to its oriented receptive field, as well as to other directions of motion that have a component in this direction. This property may also be viewed as a distribution of probabilities that a cell detects a motion direction, with the trajectory perpendicular to its major axis being preferred.

In the early 1980s Adelson and Movshon proposed a way to overcome the perceptual ambiguities arising from the aperture problem through computation of an "intersection-of-constraints," whereby the direction of motion for displays containing contours with multiple orientations is determined by a two-stage process. The first stage in the model is performed by a network of directionally sensitive, orientationally tuned cells. A local signal at the first stage is proportional to the normal component of the velocity of stimulus contrast in a direction per-

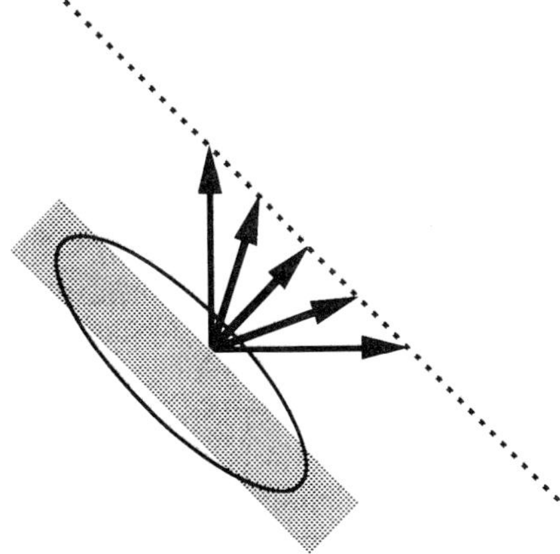

FIGURE 3 The aperture problem: A cell that has a preferred orientation is maximally sensitive to the normal component of velocity for any edge that expands beyond its receptive field.

pendicular to the orientational preference of each cell. Signals are next processed by mechanisms with different orientational preferences but overlapping spatial domains. For example, suppose that a stimulus contains components in two distinct orientations, such as a plaid pattern made of overlapping stripes of different orientations, but similar sizes and contrasts. As the field drifts over a given region, two populations of oriented detectors at the first stage respond. The computed motion follows a trajectory predicted by the intersection of constraints, as shown in Fig. 4. Correspondingly, the reported percept is typically of a single coherent motion in a direction which is not perpendicular to either grating.

Figure 4 also depicts other possible solutions besides intersection-of-constraints to the problem of resolving multiple or ambiguous motion directions within an aperture. The visual system could instead compute a vector average of the two directions that are normal to the orientations of contours. A number of researchers have recently provided psychophysical evidence that vector averaging takes place under many perceptual conditions. That is, where intersection-of-constraints computations are at odds with those of vector averaging, the latter appear to dominate.

Another potentially powerful resolution of the aperture problem would be for the visual system to pay particular heed to the trajectories of particular features in a scene. For example, where contours cross one another or meet at a corner, a perceptually useful feature may exist. The visual system may be able to track that feature and choose those motions of the oriented contours that are consistent with feature motion. While the computation of an intersection-of-constraints has enjoyed popularity in recent years as an explanatory mechanism, a combination of vector averaging and tracking of features may be a better description of human psychophysical data.

This description of how the aperture problem may be resolved is incomplete, no matter what combination of constraints and features may be active during motion perception. The computation of an unambiguous motion percept *only* at locations where salient features or constraint combinations obtain, such as at the intersection points of a plaid pattern, is insufficient to generate a coherent motion percept over an entire moving object. An additional process needs to impart the motion percept to all regions of the object, even those regions that may locally compute only ambiguous aperture motion.

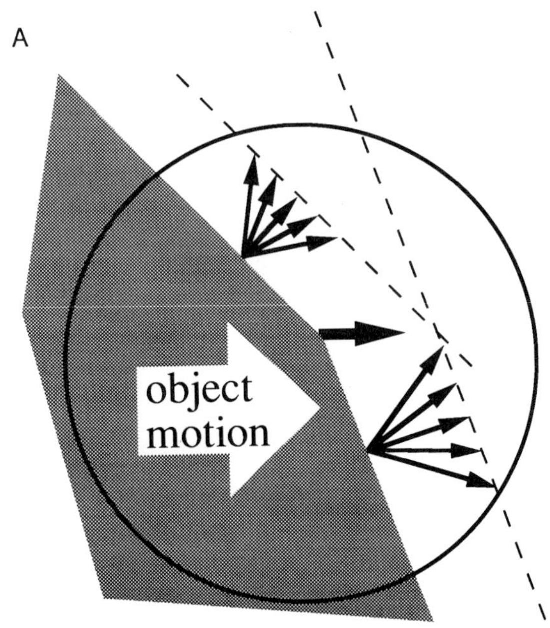

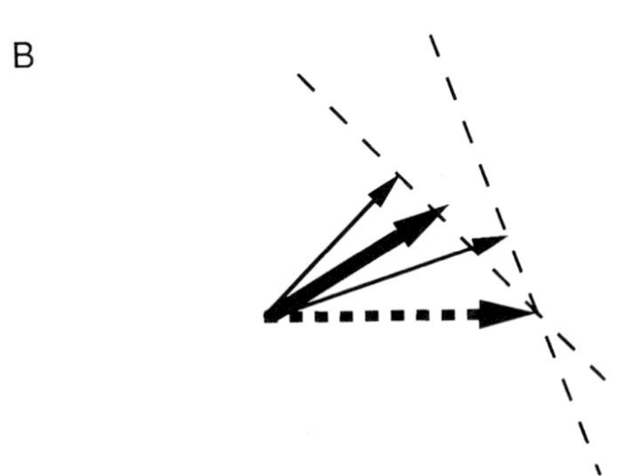

FIGURE 4 (A) An object with a corner moves horizontally behind a circular aperture. The thick arrow indicates the trajectory of the corner, while the thin ones indicate some of the motions consistent with local information at straight edge segments. (B) The two thin arrows indicate the component motions for the diagram in (A); the thick arrow represents the average of the two component vectors, and the dashed arrow represents the velocity space solution, which corresponds with the trajectory of the corner in (A).

V. LONG-RANGE MOTION SEGMENTATION AND CAPTURE

Some of the contextual factors that disambiguate local motion signals are clarified by varying the shapes of the apertures that surround moving lines, dots, or other image elements. These bounding forms also clarify how some features can determine global motion percepts more than others.

Suppose, for example, that the bounding region is a rectangle. Then the perceived direction-of-motion tends to be parallel to the long axis of the rectangle (see Fig. 5A), rather than perpendicular to the diagonal orientations of the moving lines. This percept is called the barberpole illusion. For sufficiently large displays whose length-to-width ratio is not too far from unity, the motion percept may vary across different areas of the display. The perceived motion near the lower left and upper right corners of the rectangle may be diagonal, while horizontal motion is seen through the bulk of the display (Fig. 5B). Unambiguous motion signals are generated in the region where each moving diagonal line meets the horizontal and vertical contours of the rectangle. These signals are diagrammed outside the rectangle for clarity. These unambiguous signals exert an influence on the percept that is disproportionate to their areal extent. In particular, the percept tends to be of diagonal motion if it is on a line whose ends move vertically and horizontally. Horizontal motion is perceived if both line ends move horizontally. The discontinuities at the line ends are "features" that tend to "capture" the motion percept along the entire length of the line, thereby overcoming the aperture ambiguity at all interior points of the line.

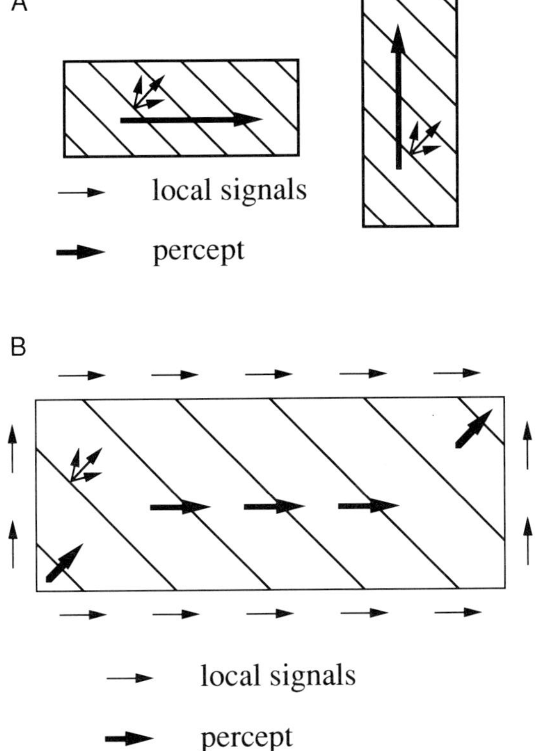

FIGURE 5 (A) In the barberpole illusion a striped pattern is perceived as moving in the direction of elongation of a rectangular frame (or aperture). Local motion signals, indicated by thin arrows at only one location within each rectangle, are generated throughout the interior lengths of each diagonal line. As indicated in Figure 3B, these local motion signals express both ambiguity and preference regarding direction of motion. Despite the large area covered by the ambiguous and diagonal motion preferring local signals, the resulting percept is horizontal or vertical, depending on the configuration of a visible frame (or aperture). (B) For sufficiently large displays, the overall motion percept may vary across different areas of the display. The perceived motion near the lower left and upper right corners of the rectangle may be diagonal, while horizontal motion is seen through the bulk of the display.

The barberpole illusion illustrates several key properties of the global motion segmentation, or motion capture, process. The process interacts *inwardly,* from pairs or greater numbers of inducing elements to the ambiguous elements between. The process can combine different motion directions at the bounding inducers into a composite motion direction between. The process can suppress the locally favored perpendicular direction and supplant it with the inwardly propagated direction. Said in another way, a long-range cooperative process is activated by motion signals at the boundaries of a moving region or object. This cooperative process acts at interior regions of the region by pooling bounding motions into a consensus motion, such as a vector average. The interior motion signals favored by the cooperative process feed back to competitively inhibit other interior motion signals. The boundary motions hereby capture the interior motions, much as the bounding contours of a leaping leopard capture the scintillating motion signals on the leopard's body that could otherwise obscure its fateful leap.

Scintillating patterns of dots have been used to study motion capture in the laboratory. In experiments by Lappin and Bell, and by Williams and Sekuler, for example, random dot cinematograms were displayed in which successive displacements of dots over frames were not uniform across all dots, but rather were sampled from a rectangular distribution of possible directions. On any frame, each dot's displacement was independent of both its own history of displacements and the displacement of other dots in that frame. For appropriate parameter choices, observers reported perceiving a coherent global motion in the direction of the mean of sample local dot motions, as well as perceiving the individual motions of each dot. Hysteresis effects were also reported, whereby the percept of coherent motion persisted while motion distribution parameters were altered from a relatively narrow range, which easily supported the coherent percept, to a wider range, for which coherent motion was not ordinarily seen if presented initially. The persistence of coherent motion signals involves averaging of directional information, long-range cooperative feedback, and short-range competitive sharpening and choice, just as in the barberpole illusion.

Ramachandran and his colleagues have provided additional evidence for cooperation among motion signals to achieve motion capture. In these studies, a two-frame apparent motion display contains an unambiguous rectangular bounding region and an ambiguous interior region of randomly moving dots. For appropriate displacement, flash duration, and interstimulus intervals, the outer rectangular contour provides strong and unambiguous signals for rightward motion. The interior region contains random dots whose distributions are uncorrelated between frames. Local motion signals are thus generated in all directions within the interior. The percept is nonetheless described as being one of rightward motion for both the rectangular contour and the interior dots. Here again, motion signals from an ambiguous interior are captured by signals from an unambiguous boundary. The enhancement of horizontal motion signals in the interior is accompanied by the suppression of random diagonal and vertical motion signals. Long-range cooperation and short-range competition are thus once again at work in generating a coherent global motion percept.

VI. FIRST- AND SECOND-ORDER MOTION STIMULI

Vision researchers have distinguished two classes of motion that are suggested by the example of the leaping leopard. *First-order* stimuli contain are characteristic of the motions of regions of a given lumi-

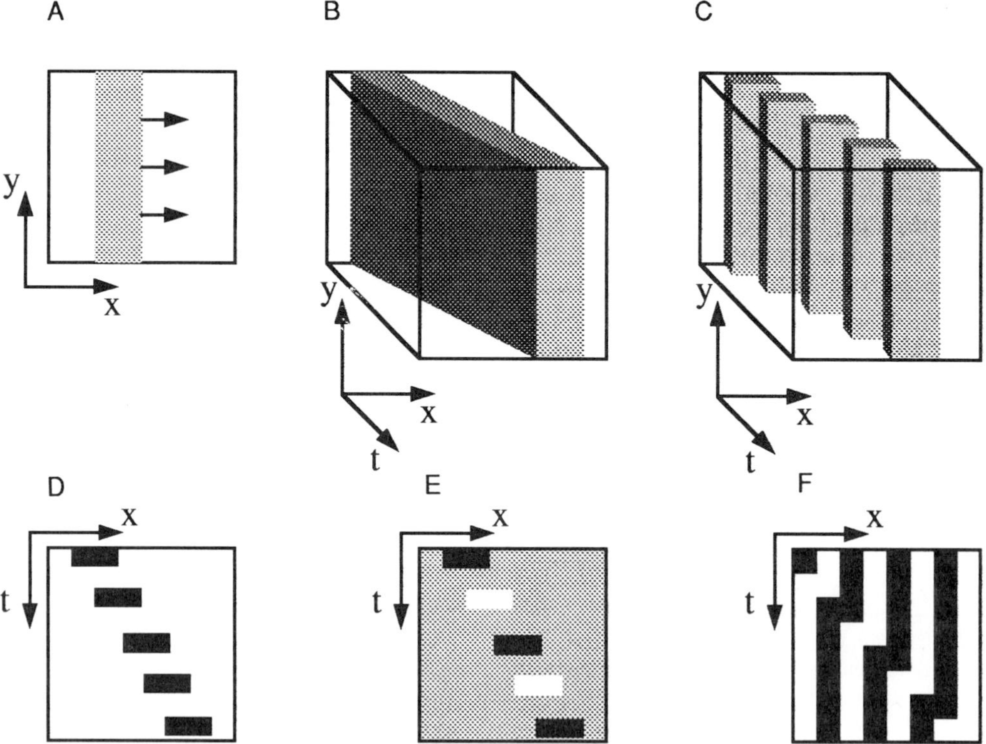

FIGURE 6 (A) A picture of a vertical bar moving to the right. (B) A spatiotemporal picture of the same stimulus. Time forms the third dimension. (C) A spatiotemporal picture of a moving bar sampled in time (i.e., a movie). (D) A cross-section of (C), showing only the x and t dimensions. Because the luminance of the time sampled bar is of the same direction of contrast with the background for every frame, the motion is called first-order. (E) Second-order motion is generated when bars in alternate frames have opposite directions of contrast with the background. (F) Another way of generating second-order motion. Black and white stripes "flip" their luminance in a succession of steps going from left-to-right in time.

nance over backgrounds of another luminance. For *second-order* stimuli, the object in motion has the same mean luminance integrated over time as its background (Fig. 6). Second-order motion is characterized by flickering patterns in which the persistent identity of an object relative to a background is not signaled by any particular static luminance distribution in a given temporal cross-section or frame.

Motion perception in response to second-order stimuli has recently been analyzed using the hypothesis that some first-order neural units are excited by light-to-dark patterns of edge contrast and others by dark-to-light edge contrasts. While each of these units may be inhibited by edges of opposite contrast polarity than the one preferred, higher-order units could be assembled that are sensitive to contrasts of either polarity by adding the *rectified* outputs, consisting of only the positive output signals of the first order units (see Section IX). A similar pooling arrangement could produce cells that are sensitive to temporal *change* in luminance by pooling the rectified outputs of cells sensitive to temporal increase in luminance with the output of cells responsible to temporal decrease in luminance (see Section XI). While rectification is evidently important for the processing of second-order motion, the question of where and when rectification should be applied is subtle and intimately intertwined with issues of size, distance, or temporal delay. An indication of the issues may be quickly gained by considering analogous issues in static form perception.

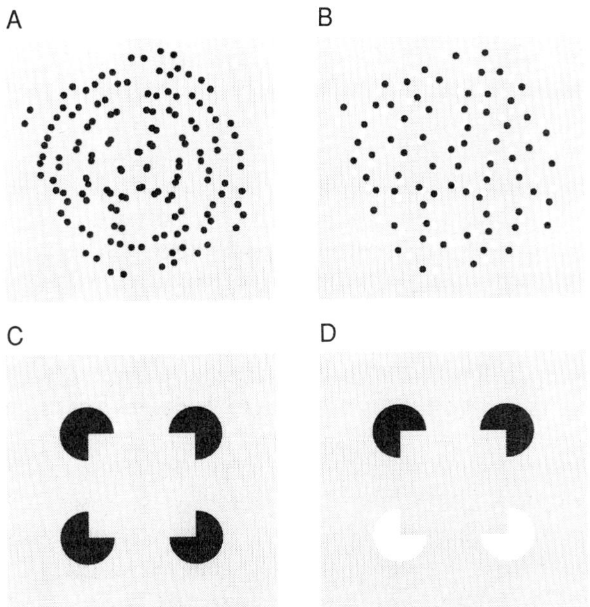

FIGURE 7 The subtleties of the interaction of spatial scale and direction-of-contrast are revealed by the juxtaposition of two classical visual phenomena. Parts (A) and (B) [Adapted with permission from Prazdny, 1984] illustrate how the formation of Glass patterns is destroyed by reversing the contrast of one field of dots, while the reversal of contrast of inducers in the Kanizsa square configuration from (C) to (D) does not significantly weaken illusory contour formation.

Figure 7A displays a Glass pattern, named after its inventor Leon Glass, formed by a random distribution of dots that is replicated and rotated slightly. Strong circular groupings are evident in the pattern. Figure 7B shows an identical distribution of dots, but this time the replicated distribution of dots has an opposite contrast with the background than that of its twin distribution. In this case the circular groupings are no longer perceptually evident. Grouping can, however, be accomplished in some circumstances between elements of opposite contrast polarity, however. Figures 7C and 7D display a Kanizsa square and a reverse-contrast Kanizsa square. Here such groupings can be as vivid between reverse-contrast elements (Fig. 7D) as among like-contrast elements (Fig. 7C) if the elements are sufficiently far apart.

Figures 7A and 7B depend upon a short-range interaction wherein only like contrasts group together. Figures 7C and 7D depend upon a long-range interaction wherein either sign of oriented contrast can group together. Our own modeling work has clarified how individual simple cells with oriented receptive fields can be activated when they are sufficiently stimulated by like-oriented contrasts, as in response to Figure 7A but not to Figure 7B. The responses from these detectors can then be rectified and added to form complex cells which respond to either sign of contrast. These complex cells can, in turn, cooperate across larger distances to form the illusory boundaries that are perceived when we view either Figure 7C or Figure 7D.

A similar type of interaction can be used to clarify how first-order motion stimuli and second-order motion stimuli may be perceived, and how spatially separated stimuli with opposite directions-of-contrast may be grouped into a motion percept, as during reverse-contrast beta motion or Ternus motion. These remarks focus attention upon a fundamental problem for students of motion perception. If indeed the form and motion perception systems share many perceptual properties, then why has Nature evolved separate form and motion systems in the first place?

VII. THE PARVOCELLULAR AND MAGNOCELLULAR CORTICAL STREAMS

This ambiguity is reflected in properties of the parvocellular and magnocellular visual processing streams which have been associated with percepts of form and motion, respectively (Fig. 8). As Schiller and his colleagues have shown, both systems can process coarse form, coarse stereo, slow motion, and flicker at high contrast. Moreover, even the earliest stages of visual cortical processing, such as the simple cells in visual area V1, require stimuli that change through time for their maximal activation and are direction-sensitive. Why could not V1 be used as the gateway to a single cortical stream that processes all aspects of form and motion? What computational properties are achieved by the magnocellular $V1 \rightarrow MT$ cortical stream that are not achieved by the parvocellular $V1 \rightarrow V2 \rightarrow V4$ cortical stream? The beginnings of an answer to this question have been derived from an analysis of a neural model of static form perception by the parvocellular stream. Properties of this model clarify why it cannot solve some of the ecological problems that an animal faces in environments wherein scintillating illumination and camouflaged predators exist.

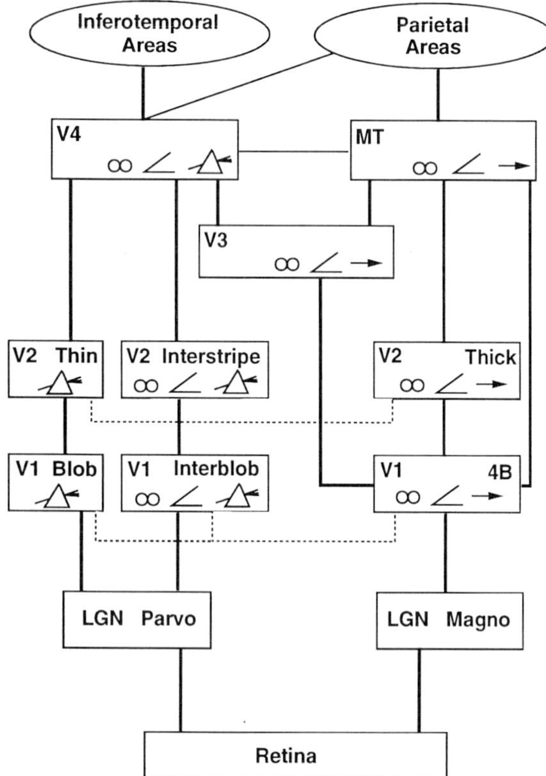

FIGURE 8 Schematic diagram of anatomical connections and neuronal selectivities of early visual areas in the macaque monkey. LGN, lateral geniculate nucleus (parvocellular and magnocellular divisions). Divisions of V1 and V2: blob, cytochrome oxidase blob regions; interblob, cytochrome oxidase-poor regions surrounding the blobs; 4B, lamina 4B; thin, thin (narrow) cytochrome oxidase strips; interstripe, cytochrome oxidase-poor regions between the thin and thick stripes; thick, thick (wide) cytochrome oxidase strips; V3, visual area 3; V4, visual area(s) 4; MT, middle temporal area. Areas V2, V3, V4, MT have connections to other areas not explicitly represented here. Area V3 may also receive projections from V2 interstripes or thin stripes. Heavy lines indicate robust primary connections, and thin lines indicate weaker, more variable connections. Dotted lines represent observed connections that require additional verification. Icons: rainbow, tuned and/or opponent wavelength selectivity (incidence at least 40%); angle symbol, orientation selectivity (incidence at least 20%); spectacles, binocular disparity selectivity and/or strong binocular interactions (V2) (incidence at least 20%); pointing hand, direction of motion selectivity (incidence at least 20%). [Adapted with permission from DeYoe and van Essen (1988).]

VIII. INTRODUCTION TO FACADE THEORY

This new theory of static form perception was introduced in 1983–1988 by us in collaboration with several other colleagues, notably Michael Cohen and Dejan Todorović. A key new insight of the static form theory can be summarized by the paradoxical phrase that "all boundaries are invisible." An illustration of this property is provided by the percept of a reverse-contrast Kanizsa square (Fig. 7D), whose significance for perceptual psychology was first emphasized by us, Cohen and Grossberg, Prazdny, and Shapley and Gordon, around 1983–1985. In this percept, a square boundary emerges between the four pac man inducers. The vertical components of this boundary join together dark–light vertical contrasts with light–dark vertical contrasts. Thus, the boundaries can form between opposite directions-of-contrast. Another way of saying this is that the output of the boundary completion process is insensitive to direction-of-contrast, even though it is sensitive to amount-of-contrast. A process whose output does not distinguish between dark–light and light–dark cannot carry a visible signal. Hence, "all boundaries are invisible."

This boundary completion system has been called the Boundary Contour System, or BCS, in order to emphasize that its boundaries emerge from contrast-sensitive processes. The boundaries formed by the BCS are not created only in response to edges.

Rather, they may be generated in response to combinations of edge, texture, shading, and stereo information at multiple size scales. That is why the term "boundary completion" rather than "edge detection" is used. We have called these form-sensitive boundary structures *boundary webs*.

Since the BCS does not represent visible percepts, another process than boundary completion must also exist that does generate visible percepts. This process has been suggested to discount the illuminant, or compensate for variable illumination conditions, and to fill-in surface properties of brightness, color, and depth using the discounted signals. It has been called the Feature Contour System, or FCS, because it generates the visible percepts that scientists had earlier attributed to "feature detectors," and it does so using a contrast-sensitive process.

What is the relationship between the contrast-sensitive processes of the BCS and the FCS? Remarkably, these processes obey laws that are computationally complementary. Figure 9 summarizes three of the dimensions along which BCS and FCS processes are complementary. The BCS and FCS overcome the limitations of their complementary processes by interacting with one another through both serial and parallel pathways undergoing both feedforward and feedback interactions. One answer to the question of why the visual cortex needs several levels of processing is so that it can hierarchically resolve the uncertainties caused by the complementary processing within each cortical stream. These interactions give rise to a visual representation that is called a FACADE representation because it suggests how properties of Form-And-Color-And-DEpth are combined in a visual percept. The theory that explains how BCS and FCS interactions generate these representations is called FACADE Theory.

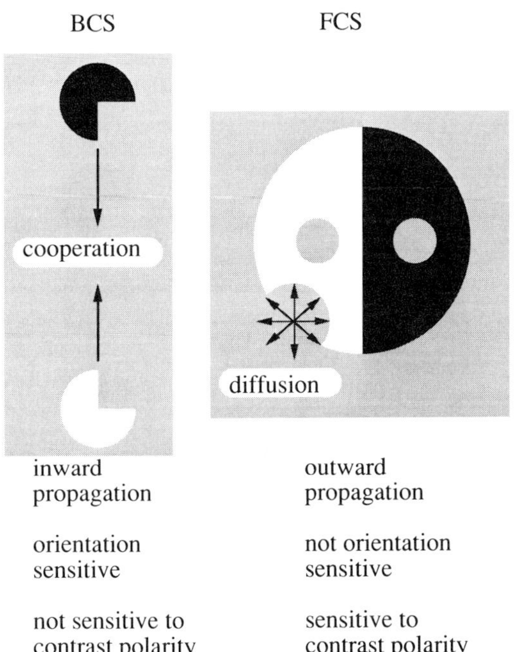

FIGURE 9 Some complementary computational properties of the Boundary Contour System and the Feature Contour System.

FACADE representations are predicted to occur in prestriate area V4 of the visual cortex. More generally, BCS and FCS processes have been used to explain and predict perceptual and neurobiological data about the regions V1, V2, and V4 of visual cortex, notably the cortical stream $V1 \rightarrow V2 \rightarrow V4$ that has been linked to perceptual properties of static form, color, and depth. In keeping with these properties, the BCS is called the *Static BCS* in order to differentiate it from the *Motion BCS* that is used to explain data about motion perception and the magnocellular cortical processing stream.

The need for a Motion BCS came into view through an analysis of why the Static BCS is not adequate for motion processing. This inadequacy of the Static BCS is a consequence of the fact that "all boundaries are invisible." In fact, the process which makes the output signals of the Static BCS insensitive to direction-of-contrast also makes them insensitive to direction-of-motion. A perceptual system whose output is insensitive to direction-of-motion is certainly not well suited to be a motion processor.

This observation led Grossberg to the following theoretical question: What is the minimal change of the Static BCS with which to fashion a Motion BCS whose output signals are insensitive to direction-of-contrast—which is just as important for processing static images as moving images—yet are sensitive to direction-of-motion? The Motion BCS of Grossberg, Mingolla, and Rudd has been used to explain a large data base about motion perception, including all the motion data reviewed above. As a result of this approach, the Static BCS and the Motion BCS can be viewed as variations of a common design for the architecture of visual cortex. This perspective clarifies how the parvocellular and magnocellular processing streams support overlapping but distinguishable combinations of visual properties. The theory suggests, moreover, that the Static BCS and Motion BCS are parallel subsystems of a single total BCS system. This prediction claims that the total BCS system arises during cortical development as an expression of a global symmetry principle, called FM Symmetry (F, form; M, motion). Manifestations of this symmetry principle are familiar to us in our daily perceptual experiences. In particular, why do the geometries of static and motion form perception differ? For example, why is the opposite orientation of a static vertical a static horizontal—a difference of 90°—whereas the opposite direction of motion upward is motion downward—a difference of 180°?

IX. JOINING SENSITIVITY TO DIRECTION-OF-MOTION WITH INSENSITIVITY TO DIRECTION-OF-CONTRAST

We now summarize how the output of the Static BCS becomes insensitive to direction-of-motion due to the interactions that render it insensitive to direction-of-contrast. Simple cells of the visual cortex, which are modeled as the earliest stage of the Static BCS, are sensitive to direction-of-contrast. The Static BCS provides a new computational rationale, as well as a model of the neural circuits governing classical cortical cell types such as simple cells, complex cells, and hypercomplex cells in the interblob and interstripe regions of cortical areas V1 and V2 (Fig. 10). The theory also predicted in 1984 a new cell type, the bipole cell, whose properties were soon after supported by neurophysiological experiments of the von der Heydt laboratory in Zurich. These bipole cells carry out the cooperative grouping function within the Static BCS. This grouping function is homologous to the grouping within the Motion BCS that accomplishes motion capture, as during the barberpole illusion. The Static BCS model consists of several parallel copies, such that each copy is activated by a different range of receptive field sizes. These different receptive field sizes carry out size-and-disparity filtering operations within the Static BCS. These operations are analogous to the filtering operations within the Motion BCS that calibrate the varying sizes of $D_{\max}$ in response to different motion conditions.

Corresponding to these filtering and grouping operations, each Static BCS copy is subdivided into two hierarchically organized systems (Fig. 10): *a Static Oriented Contrast Filter*, or *SOC Filter*, for preprocessing quasi-static images (the eye never ceases to jiggle in its orbit); and a Cooperative-Competitive Feedback Loop, or CC Loop, for generating coherent emergent boundary segmentations of the filtered signals. The SOC Filter contains simple, complex, and hypercomplex cells. The CC Loop contains hypercomplex and bipole cells. Interactions between the Static BCS and FCS model how a FACADE representation may emerge in cortical area V4.

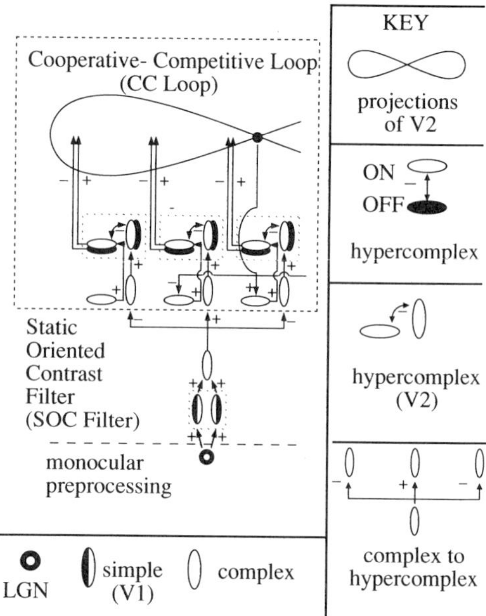

FIGURE 10 The static Boundary Contour System model described by Grossberg and Mingolla. The circuit is divided into a static oriented contrast-sensitive filter (SOC Filter) that preprocesses and locally sharpens and completes oriented image contrasts, followed by a cooperative–competitive feedback network (CC Loop) that globally groups, or segments, preprocessed image contrasts. Multiple copies of this circuit are used, one corresponding to each receptive field size of the SOC Filter. The depicted circuit has been used to analyze data about monocular vision. A binocular generalization has also been developed. In the SOC Filter, simple cell receptive fields are oriented and sensitive to direction-of-contrast. Rectified outputs from pairs of simple cells sensitive to opposite direction-of-contrast input to complex cells, which are sensitive to amount-of-contrast, but not to direction-of-contrast or to direction-of-motion. Complex cells input to two successive stages of hypercomplex cells. At the first competitive stage, a complex cell excites like-oriented hypercomplex cells at its position and inhibits, via an endstopping operation, hypercomplex cells at nearby positions. At the second competitive stage, hypercomplex cells sensitive to different orientations compete with one another. Inhibition is maximal between perpendicular orientations. The CC Loop describes feedback interactions between hypercomplex cells and bipole cells. The latter cells fire only if they receive sufficient activation in both of their oriented receptive fields.

The output of the Static BCS becomes independent of direction-of-contrast due to the way in which its model simple cells combine their outputs to model complex cells. As indicated in Figure 10, each simple cell has an oriented receptive field, represented by an elliptical region. In the illustrated receptive fields, inputs to the white side add up to activate the cell, whereas inputs to the black side add up to inhibit the cell. The cell fires, or emits an output signal, only if the net cell activity exceeds a threshold. Thus, the output signal is rectified. Further increments in cell activity give rise to proportional increments in the output signal. As a result of this rule, the model simple cells are sensitive to direction-of-contrast. In particular, a cell with a white–black vertical receptive field can fire to a white–black (nearly) vertical image contrast, but not to a black–white contrast. This property helps to explain how we perceive Figures 7A and 7B.

Figure 10 illustrates how these simple cells combine their output signals to activate complex cells that are sensitive to the *amount* of image contrast, but not to the *direction* of image contrast. In particular, a pair of vertically oriented simple cells are shown inputting to a single complex cell. The complex cell response is insensitive to direction-of-contrast because it adds output signals from a pair of simple cells which are sensitive to opposite directions-of-contrast.

This construction also renders the model's complex cells insensitive to direction-of-motion. Inspection of Figure 10 shows that a vertically oriented model complex cell could respond, say, to a black–white vertical edge moving to the right or left *and* to a white–black vertical edge moving to the right or left. Thus, the process whereby complex cells become insensitive to direction-of-contrast has rendered them insensitive to direction-of-motion. This combination of properties of cortical complex cells has been reported by several laboratories. Figure 11 summarizes neurophysiological data of Foster *et al.* that illustrate both properties. Our construction of the Motion BCS focuses upon how oriented receptive fields that are sensitive to direction-of-contrast, such as those of simple cells, can be combined to give rise to cells that are not sensitive to direction-of-contrast, such as complex cells, without causing these cells to lose their sensitivity to direction-of-motion.

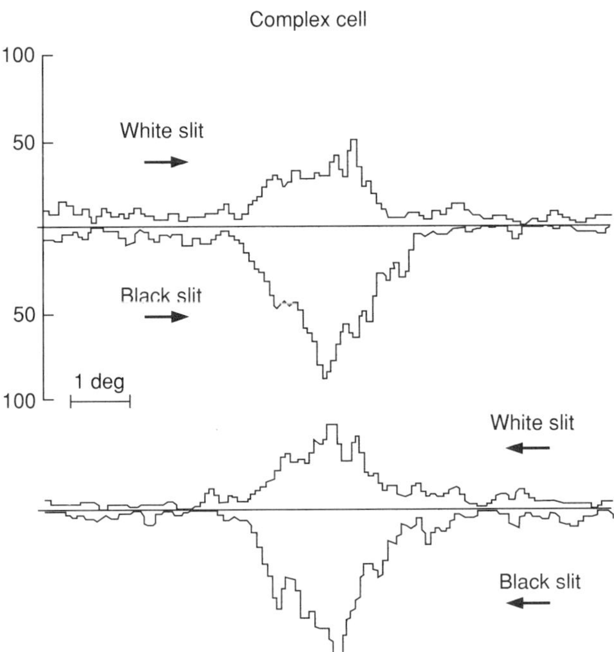

FIGURE 11 Responses of a complex cell to a thin bar drifting first in one direction and then in the opposite direction. The response to the light bar is plotted above the dividing line. The response to the dark bar is plotted below the dividing line. [Reprinted with permission from Foster, Gaska, Nagler, and Pollen (1985).]

X. MANY ORIENTATIONS CAN MOVE IN THE SAME DIRECTION

The cooperative bipole cells of the Motion CC Loop also need to differ from their homologs in the Static CC Loop of Figure 10. Certain images by John Kennedy are helpful in making this distinction. As shown in Figure 12, static bipole cells can respond to orientations which are not locally preferred by generating positive feedback to cooperatively link and complete static boundaries. Each bipole cell can generate an output signal only if *both* of its oriented receptive fields receive large enough inputs from cells with similarly oriented receptive fields. These input cells at the previous processing level consist of formal analogs of hypercomplex cells (Fig. 10). The output signals from the bipole cells feed back to the hypercomplex cells, where they bias the competition among the hypercomplex cells toward grouping the orientations and positions that are most favored by the bipole cells. The properties of these cells help to explain how we perceive Figures 7C and 7D.

The Motion Loop must, however, cope with an additional degree of freedom, since it considers direction as well as orientation. Thus, motion bipole cells are organized in a fashion that differs somewhat from that of their static analogs. As indicated in

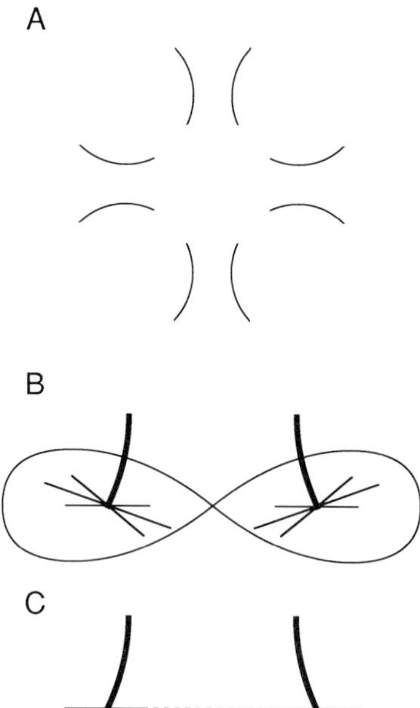

FIGURE 12 (A) This illusory contour display [adapted with permission from Kennedy (1979)], indicates that boundary completion in the static CC Loop can choose orientations that are not locally preferred if global organizational factors are sufficiently powerful. (B) The locally preferred directions at the bottom ends of the two top curves of (A) are perpendicular to the ends of the curves and thus tilted off the horizontal. (C) Cooperation among signals that are horizontal enhances and completes horizontal signals (cooperation) while suppressing nonhorizontal signals (competition) along the illusory contour.

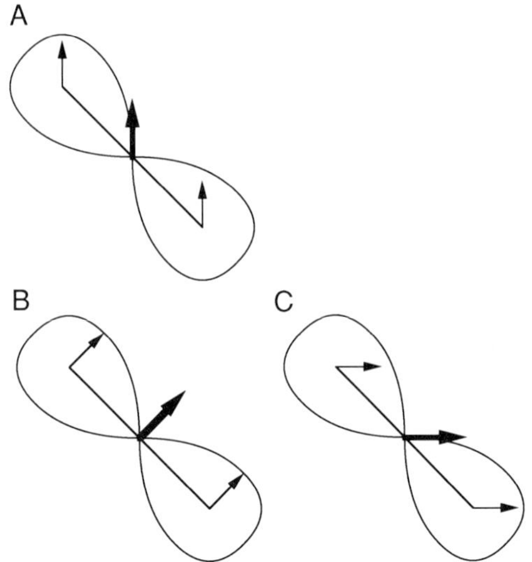

FIGURE 13 As with static bipole cells, motion bipoles are sensitive to bottom-up direction signals from motion hypercomplex cells (indicated by thin arrows), which send excitatory signals to each lobe of the bipole cell. If sufficient excitatory activity is sensed in *both* lobes, the bipole sends feedback signals of like direction (indicated by thick arrows) to the hypercomplex layer. While analogous to their static counterparts, motion bipole cells are fundamentally different, insofar as they must cope with the additional degree of freedom imposed by the simultaneous determination of a globally consistent motion direction over many possible contour orientations. Thus, families of bipole cells are presumed to exist, such that cells whose major axes are the same (diagonal in the present case) can be maximally sensitive to motion signals of different directions, ranging from (A) vertical to (B) diagonal (perpendicular to the major axis) to (C) horizontal for the three bipoles shown here.

Figure 13, motion bipole cells are postulated to exist in families sensitive to motion signals of similar direction but whose sources are arrayed in patterns of different orientations. Expressed differently, while some motion bipole cells are assumed to favor the direction of motion perpendicular to the orientation induced by the elongated axis of their two lobes (Fig. 13B), others have a similar spatial layout but different preferred directions of motion (Figs. 13A and 13C).

As in the Static CC Loop, each bipole cell of the Motion CC Loop can generate an output signal only if *both* of its receptive fields receive large enough inputs from cells that are sensitive to a similar direction-of-motion. These input cells at the previous processing level again consist of formal analogs of hypercomplex cells. The output signals from the bipole cells feed back to the hypercomplex cells, where they bias the competition among the hypercomplex cells toward the directions and positions that are most favored by the bipole cells.

It is intuitively clear that this is just the sort of cooperative feedback, propagated inward between pairs, or larger numbers of flanking inducers, that is needed to explain motion capture phenomena like the barberpole illusion (Fig. 5). Both orientationally sensitive grouping during static form perception and directionally sensitive grouping during motion form perception are thus predicted to utilize bipole cells. The explanatory power of this homology strengthens the case that both the Static BCS and Motion BCS architectures model variations of a common cortical design.

XI. THE SIMPLEST MOC FILTER

The simplest MOC Filter was mathematically defined by Grossberg and Rudd in 1989. Its five processing stages are qualitatively summarized in Figure 14. This MOC Filter was used to carry out 1-D simulations of motion data. We have developed a more complex MOC Filter that can disambiguate

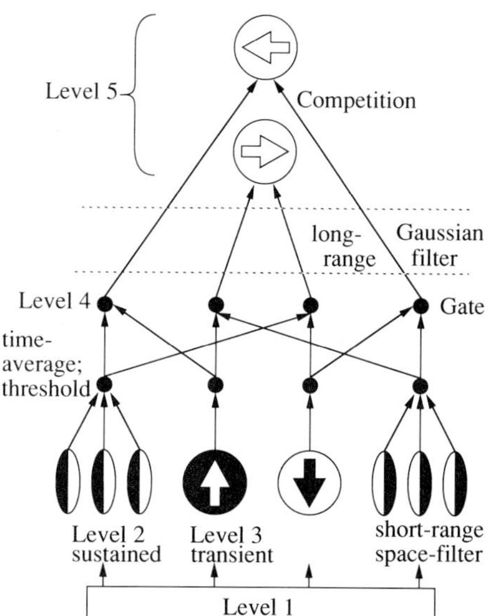

FIGURE 14 The simplest 1-D MOC Filter. The input pattern (Level 1) is spatially and temporally filtered in parallel by both sustained response cells with oriented receptive fields that are sensitive to direction-of-contrast (Level 2) and transient response cells with unoriented receptive fields that are sensitive to the direction-of-contrast change in the cell input (Level 3). Level 4 cells combine sustained and transient cell signals multiplicatively and are thus rendered sensitive to both direction-of-motion and direction-of-contrast. Level 5 cells sum across space and across two types of Level 4 cells to become sensitive to direction-of-motion but insensitive to direction-of-contrast. [Reprinted with permission from Grossberg and Rudd (1992).]

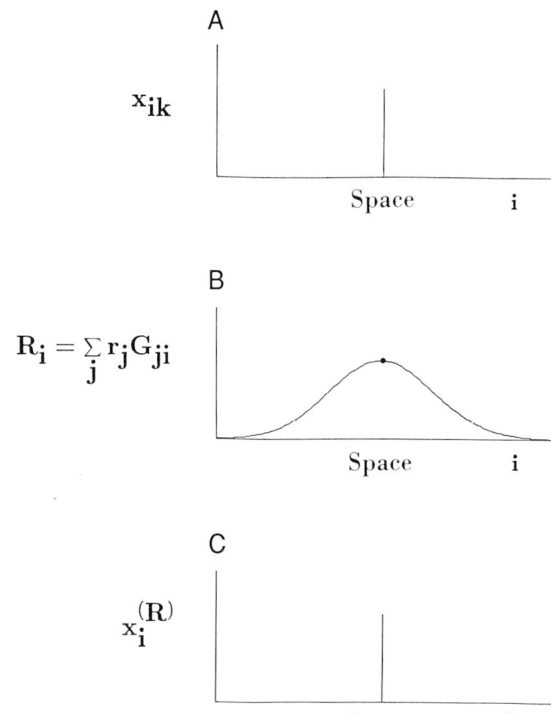

FIGURE 15 Spatial responses at various levels of the MOC Filter to a point input. (A) Sustained activity of a Level 2 cell. (B) Total input pattern to Level 5 after convolution with a Gaussian kernel. (C) Contrast-enhanced output of Level 5 centered at the location of the input maximum. [Reprinted with permission from Grossberg and Rudd (1992).]

orientation and direction in response to 2-D moving figures, and to thereby offer a solution to the aperture problem. In the present brief survey, it suffices to notice that the 1-D MOC Filter possesses both a short-range spatial filter at Level 4, that helps to model D_{max}, and a long-range spatial filter at Level 5, that helps to model long-range apparent motion. Note that opposite directions-of-contrast input to Level 5 to enable long-range motion signals to be derived, say, from combinations of white spots on a gray background and nearby black spots on a gray background, as during reverse-contrast beta motion and Ternus motion.

XII. G-WAVES FOR LONG-RANGE MOTION

How are long-range apparent motion signals generated in such a model? First note that outputs from Level 4 input to the same Level 5 cell only if they correspond to the same direction-of-motion. Figure 15 schematizes how a flash at Level 1 (Fig. 15A) leads to a focal activation at Level 5 (Fig. 15C) after it activates the long-range Gaussian filter that joins Level 4 to Level 5 (Fig. 15B). The broad Gaussian activation of Level 5 is sharpened into a focal activation by lateral inhibition, or competition, among the Level 5 cells.

Figure 16 shows how this input activation looks in time. The input to Level 1 (Fig. 16A) generates a slowly decaying temporal trace (Fig. 16B) that has been called "visual inertia" by Anstis and Ramachandran. When this trace is fed through the Gaussian filter, it generates a spatially distributed input to Level 5 that waxes and wanes through time, without spreading across space (Fig. 16C). The maximum value of this input does not move. Hence, a single flash does not cause a movement across space.

Suppose, however, that two locations both input through the same Gaussian receptive field, and that the activation in response to a flash at the first location is decaying while activation is growing in response to a flash at the second location (Fig. 17).

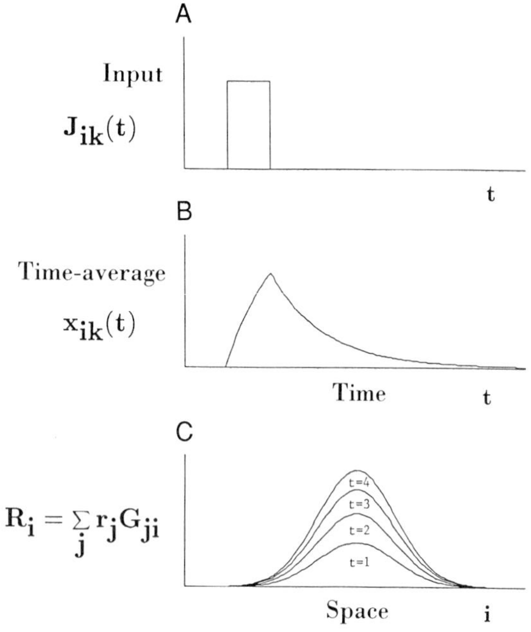

FIGURE 16 Temporal response of the MOC Filter to a point input. (A) The input is presented at a brief duration at location 1. (B) Sustained cell activity at 1 gradually builds after the input onset, then decays after offset. (C) Growth of the input pattern to Level 5 with transient cell activity held constant. The activity pattern retains a Gaussian shape centered at the location of the input, that waxes and wanes through time without spreading across space. [Reprinted with permission from Grossberg and Rudd (1992).]

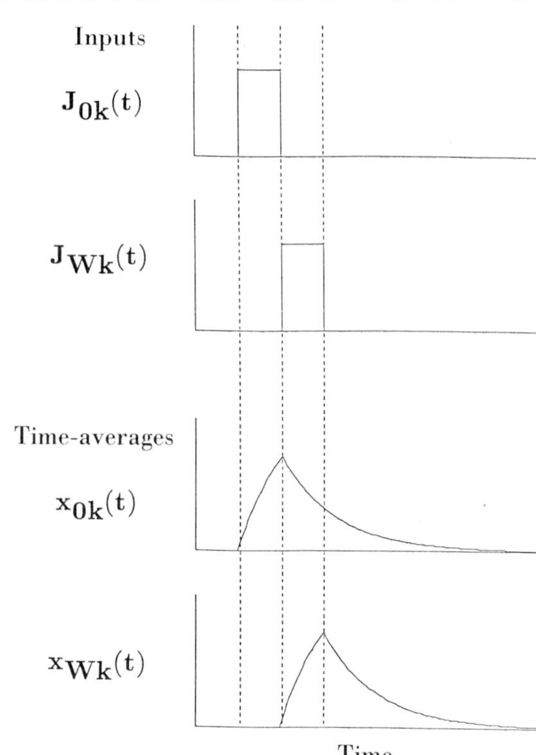

FIGURE 17 Temporal response of the sustained cells at Level 2 to two brief successive point inputs at locations 0 and *W*. For an appropriately timed display, the decaying response at position 0 overlaps in time the rising response at position *W*. [Reprinted with permission from Grossberg and Rudd (1992).]

Under these circumstances, the *total* input to Level 5 from both flashes is the sum of a temporally waning Gaussian plus a temporally waxing Gaussian, as in Figure 18. Under appropriate conditions, this sum represents a wave whose maximum travels continuously in time from the location of the first flash to the location of the second flash.

This Gaussian wave, called a G-wave, was discovered in 1977 by Grossberg. It occurs whenever waxing and waning activation traces interact via a spatial Gaussian kernel under appropriate spatiotemporal conditions. The properties of such a G-wave correspond closely to properties of long-range apparent motion, including the remarkable properties whereby an apparent motion percept can speed up when the ISI is decreased at a fixed interflash distance, or when the ISI is held constant and the interflash distance is increased.

XIII. SPATIAL ATTENTION SHIFTS AND WHAT AND WHERE CORTICAL STREAMS

Grossberg has also suggested that a G-wave may subserve certain spatial shifts in attention. From this perspective, apparent motion percepts take on a new functional meaning. For example, if a targeted predator or prey is rapidly moving across a scene, perhaps darting behind protective cover, than an animal may be able to see the target only intermittently. A G-wave can interpolate these temporally discrete views with a continuous motion signal that adapts its speed to the varying speed of the target. Such a continuous motion signal can be used to predict the location and speed of the target, and to command motor responses accordingly.

The hypothesis that a G-wave may subserve a spatial attention shift is consistent with the fact that the motion perception, or magnocellular, cortical processing stream is part of a larger Where processing stream that includes region MT as well as parietal cortex (Fig. 8). The Where processing stream computes the locations of targets with respect to an observer and helps to direct attention and action toward them. In contrast, the form perception, or parvocellular, cortical processing stream is part of a larger What processing stream that in-

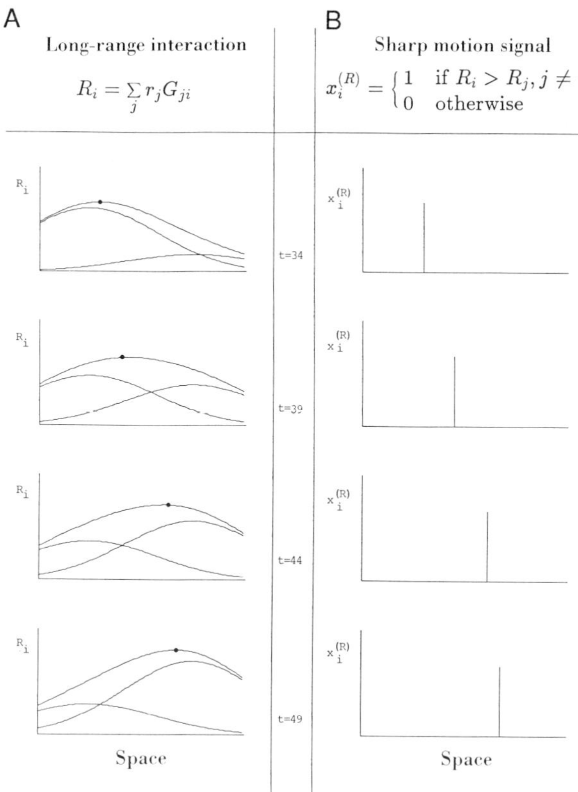

FIGURE 18 Simulated MOC Filter response to a two-flash display. Successive rows correspond to increasing times following the Frame 1 offset. (A) The two lower curves in each row depict the total input to Level 5 due to each of the two flashes. The input due to the left flash decreases while the input due to the right flash increases. The summed input due to both flashes is a traveling wave whose maximum value across space moves continuously between the two flash locations. (B) Position over time of the contrast-enhanced Level 5 response. [Reprinted with permission from Grossberg and Rudd (1992).]

cludes region V4 as well as inferotemporal cortex (Fig. 8). The What processing stream is used to recognize targets based upon prior learning.

From this larger perspective, the parallel but specialized architectures of the Static BCS and the Motion BCS take on new functional meanings in terms of the relationships that exist between perception and action, and seeming perceptual curiosities such as long-range apparent motion begin to look like manifestations of adaptive brain systems whose perceptual properties may be crucial for survival.

Acknowledgments

This research was supported in part by the Air Force Office of Scientific Research (AFOSR 90-0175 and F49620-92-J-0334), ARPA (ONR N00014-92-J-4015), the Northeast Consortium for Engineering Education (NCEE A303-21-93), and the Office of Naval Research (ONR N00014-91-J-4100). The authors thank Cynthia E. Bradford for her valuable assistance in the preparation of the manuscript.

Bibliography

Adelson, E. H., and Movshon, J. A. (1982). Phenomenal coherence of moving visual patterns. *Nature* **300,** 523–525.

Anstis, S. M., and Ramachandran, V. S. (1987). Visual inertia in apparent motion. *Vision Res.* **27,** 755–764.

Barlow, H. B., and Levick, W. R. (1965). The mechanism of directional selective units in rabbit's retina. *J. Physiol.* **178,** 477–504.

Braddick, O. J. (1974). A short range process in apparent motion. *Vision Res.* **14,** 519–527.

Carpenter, G. A., and Grossberg, S. (Eds.) (1992). "Neural Networks for Vision and Image Processing." MIT Press, Cambridge, MA.

Cavanagh, P., and Mather, G. (1990). Motion: The long and the short of it. *Spatial Vision* **4,** 103–129.

DeYoe, E. A., and van Essen, D. C. (1988). Concurrent processing streams in monkey visual cortex. *Trends Neurosci.* **11,** 219–226.

Foster, K. H., Gaska, J. P., Nagler, M., and Pollen, D. A. (1985). Spatial and temporal frequency selectivity of neurons in visual cortical areas V1 and V2 of the macaque monkey. *J. Physiol.* **365,** 331–363.

Goodale, M. A., and Milner, D. (1992). Separate visual pathways for perception and action. *Trends Neurosc.* **15,** 20–25.

Grossberg, S., and Mingolla, E. (1992). Neural dynamics of motion perception: Direction fields, apertures, and resonant grouping. *Percept. Psychophys.* **53**(3), 243–278.

Grossberg, S., Mingolla, E., and Todorović, D. (1989). A neural network architecture for preattentive vision. *IEEE Trans. Biomed. Engineer.* **36,** 65–84.

Grossberg, S., and Rudd, M. E. (1992). Cortical dynamics of visual motion perception: Short-range and long-range apparent motion. *Psychol. Rev.* **99,** 78–121.

Kolers, P. A. (1972). "Aspects of Motion Perception." Pergamon, Elmsford, NY.

Landy, M. S., and Movshon, J. A. (1991). "Computational Models of Visual Processing." MIT Press, Cambridge, MA.

Mingolla, E., Todd, J. T., and Norman, F. (1992). The perception of globally coherent motion. *Vision Res.* **32,** 1015–1031.

Nakayama, K. (1985). Biological image motion processing: A review. *Vision Res.* **25**(5), 625–660.

Neuhaus, W. (1930). Experimentelle untersuchung der scheinbewegung. *Arch. die gesamte Psychol.* **75,** 315–458.

Ramachandran, V. S., and Inada, V. (1985). Spatial phase and frequency in motion capture of random-dot patterns. *Spatial Vision* **1,** 57–67.

Reichardt, W. (1957). Autokorrelationsauswertung als Funktionsprinzip des Zentralnervensystems. *Z. Naturforschung* **12b,** 447–457.

Schiller, P. H., Logothetis, N. K., and Charles, E. R. (1990). Role of the color-opponent and broad-band channels in vision. *Visual Neurosci.* **5,** 321–346.

Sekuler, R., Anstis, S., Braddick, O. J., Brandt, T., Movshon, J. A., and Orban, G. (1990). The perception of motion. In "Visual Perception: The Neurophysiological Foundations" (L. Spillmann and J. S. Werner, Eds.), Academic Press, San Diego, CA.

van Santen, J. P. H., and Sperling, G. (1985). Elaborated Reichardt detectors. *J. Optical Soc. Am.* **2,** 300–321.

Wallach, H. (1976). "On Perception." Quadrangle/The New York Times Book Co., New York.

Watson, A. B., and Ahumada, A. J. (1985). Model of human visual-motion sensing. *J. Optical Soc. Am. (A)* **2,** 322–342.

Yo, C., and Wilson, H. R. (1992). Perceived direction of moving two-dimensional patterns depends on duration, contrast, and eccentricity. *Vision Res.* **32,** 135–147.

VISUAL PERCEPTION

W. Lawrence Gulick
University of Delaware

Glossary

Acuity The capacity of the visual system to detect small differences in stimulation according to brightness, color, saturation, or form.

Diopter A measure of the power of a lens expressed as the reciprocal of focal length in meters.

Illuminance The amount of light falling upon a surface, measured in foot-candles (ft-C).

Luminance The amount of light reflected by a surface, measured in apparent foot-candles (aft-C).

Nanometer A unit of linear measure equal to one-billionth of a meter.

Receptive field An area on the retina which when stimulated by light modifies the behavior of a retinal ganglion cell or a visual cortical cell.

TO PERCEIVE is to select and organize sensations into unified wholes that carry meaning. From among the many energy forms that bombard our senses continuously, the *selection* is determined by internal physiological states, by voluntary attention, and by expectations derived from the environment while the *organization* is guided primarily by past experience.

I. LIGHT AND THE EYE

A. Light

An incandescent source gives off a spectrum of electromagnetic radiation, only 1/70th of which has the capacity to activate the eye. This portion of the radiation constitutes the visible spectrum called light, with wavelengths between 380 and 760 nm (nanometers, billionths of a meter).

When light strikes an object in its path, it may be transmitted, reflected, or absorbed by the object. These three outcomes always are compromised because we know of no objects that are perfect transmitters, reflectors, or absorbers of light.

1. Parameters of Light

There are three physical parameters of light: *wavelength, wave amplitude,* and *wave complexity*. Each physical parameter is related to a different perceptual effect. Wavelength determines hue (color), wave amplitude determines brightness, and wave complexity determines saturation, or the vividness of color. It is important to keep separate the physical parameters from their psychological correlates. Color, brightness, and saturation are qualities added by the visual system. They are not present in the light itself.

Light of a single wavelength is pure, and it often is described as a sinusoidal wave, examples of which are depicted in Figures 1a and 1b. Wavelength (λ) is measured in nanometers from corresponding places in the repeating patterns. The relationship of wavelength to hue is as follows: blue (460 nm), green (530 nm), yellow (590 nm), and red (650 nm). Intermediate hues such as aqua, greenish yellow, or orange would have approximate wavelengths of 500, 560, and 620 nm, respectively.

The second parameter is amplitude. If we increased the amplitude (A) of the wave shown in Figure 1a without changing its wavelength or shape, we would have a light that maintained the same hue and saturation but appeared brighter.

The final parameter of light is its complexity. In Figure 1c is illustrated what happens when two simple waves (a and b) are added together. Note that the algebraic summation produces a wave that is no longer pure. Not only is amplitude more variable, but its wavelength exceeds those of the component waves which gave rise to it. Nevertheless, the com-

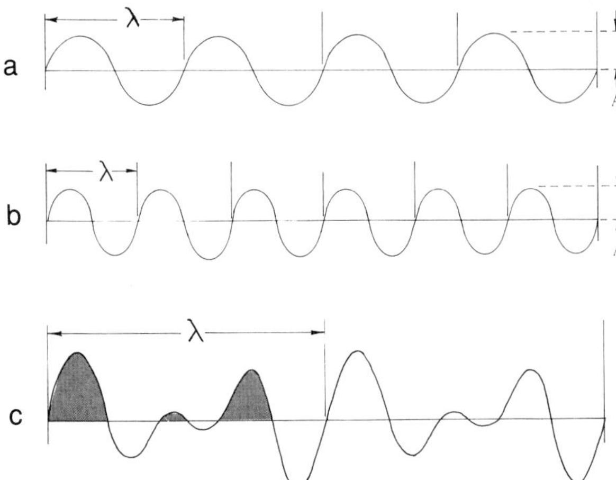

FIGURE 1 Two sinusoidal light waves and their summation. (a) and (b) Pure waves of equal amplitude (A) but different wavelengths (λ). (c) Their summation, a periodic complex wave of different amplitude (shaded areas) and different wavelength (λ).

plex pattern remains periodic and therefore has the capacity to elicit color, but the color sensation is muted and less vivid than that produced by pure waves. Pure waves (monochromatic) are fully saturated, whereas complex waves lose saturation to form tints and shades. A light may contain so many different pure components that it loses its periodicity and, therefore, its capacity to elicit color. Aperiodic waves are achromatic (without color) and appear as black, gray, or white, depending upon amplitude.

2. Measurement of Light

Wavelengths are measured in nanometers. Relatively pure light of known wavelengths can be generated with spectrometers and monochromators. More common is the practice of passing white light through monochromatic filters. Ideally such filters would "pass" a single wavelength and absorb all others. However, virtually all filters are less efficient than this ideal because they also pass light of nearby wavelengths. Hence, the use of the word monochromatic, literally, is a misnomer. Sometimes an interference filter is employed. Unlike the monochromatic filter, which uses the principle of selective absorption, the interference filter uses the principle of wave cancellation, and it transmits light of greater purity.

Complexity measurements involve the synthesis of complex waves by the addition of some number of pure waves or the passing of white light through a series of filters the absorption properties of which are known. In either case the complex wave has known characteristics.

Measurements of amplitude are more complicated. In visual perception one seldom exposes the eye to light emitted directly from a source. Instead, the light we see is reflected from objects. Accordingly, major interest in visual perception centers upon the amount of light that falls upon surfaces (illuminance) and the amount reflected from them (luminance) rather than upon the sources themselves. However, because illuminance and luminance are related to sources, we begin with sources.

The intensity of a source is measured in standard units called *candles*. The intensity of a standard candle is about what you think it to be. The concept of illuminance involves the idea of the interception of light by a surface. There are many units to measure illuminance, but the more common one is the foot-candle. A *foot-candle* is defined as the amount of light falling on a 1-ft^2 surface at a distance of 1 ft from a source with an intensity of 1 candle. Illuminance follows the inverse square law which states that illuminance is inversely proportional to the square of the distance between the surface and the source. The reason for this is that the density of the light flux decreases with distance from the source in much the same way that the streams of water from a shower nozzle become less dense (farther apart) with distance from the nozzle, assuming, like light, that the ever-diverging streams of water continue to travel in straight lines.

In visual perception the concept of luminance is the most important because measurements of it tell us about the level of light reflected from a surface toward the eye. The unit of measure is the apparent foot-candle, defined as the amount of light reflected from a perfectly diffusing 1-ft^2 surface illuminated by 1 ft-candle. Obviously, the luminance of a surface is determined by the capacity of the surface to reflect and absorb light. Greater absorption leads to less reflection and lower luminance. Luminance does *not* follow the inverse square law because light reflected from a surface travels in many directions of scatter so that density does not change with distance. Photometric methods are used to determine luminance by employment of a calibrated instrument (illuminometer).

In summary, a point source of light with an intensity of 1 candle produces an illuminance of 1 ft-candle on a 1-ft^2 surface located at a distance of 1 ft, and the surface produces a luminance of 1 apparent foot-candle if the surface is a perfect diffuse reflector. The difference between incident light (foot-candles) and reflected light (apparent foot-candles) is a measure of the reflectance of the surface.

3. Principles of Refraction

Refraction refers to the bending of light rays as light travels from one medium into another one.

Every medium through which light can be transmitted has an optical density. When media have different optical densities, the rays bend at the boundary, with the degree of bending (index of refraction) directly related to the magnitude of the discrepancy in density.

Consider Figure 2a. Here a light ray (L) traveling in air from left to right encounters a block of optical "B" glass which has a higher optical density (+) than does air. To determine the direction of refraction one constructs a "normal," defined as a perpendicular into the encountered medium from the point of incidence, P_1. The "normal" is illustrated by the dashed line. Whenever light goes from a medium of lower density into one of higher density, the ray is bent toward the "normal," as shown by the solid line. At point P_2 the ray encounters a medium (air) of lower density. Again one constructs a "normal" into the newly encountered medium from the point of incidence, P_2. Whenever light passes from a medium of higher density into one of lower density, the ray is bent away from the "normal," as shown by the solid line. There is one exception to the principles of refraction: regardless of density discrepancies, rays that encounter a different medium perpendicular to its surface do not refract.

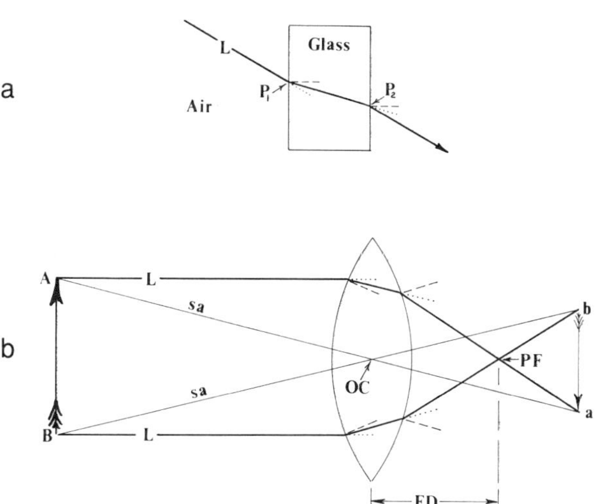

FIGURE 2 Illustrations of refraction. (a) How a light ray L is refracted first in one direction as it enters glass and then in an opposite direction as it re-enters air. Dashed lines represent "normals," lines perpendicular to surfaces at points of incidence (P_1 and P_2). Dotted line is direction of ray without refraction. (b) How parallel light rays are refracted by a convex lens to converge on a point, the principal focus (PF). Dashed lines represent "normals" and dotted lines the direction of the rays without refraction. Focal distance (FD) is distance between optical center of lens (OC) and PF, in meters. Secondary axes are shown as (sa). See text for discussion.

In Figure 2b two parallel rays (L) encounter a lens that has a greater optical density. Application of the principles of refraction requires that the "normals" be constructed into the new medium (lens) as lines perpendicular to the tangents at the points of incidence, shown as dashed lines. As the light rays enter the lens, they bend toward their "normals," as shown by the solid lines; and as they re-enter the surround, they bend away from their "normals," as shown by the solid lines.

A convex lens (Fig. 2b), with appropriately curved surfaces, has the capacity to refract parallel rays upon entrance into rays that converge upon exit to a single point known as the *principal focus* (PF). The focal length of a lens is the linear distance (FD) between the center of the lens (OC) and PF. The power of a lens is measured in diopters, the reciprocal of focal length, where 1 diopter equals a focal length of 1 m. A lens with greater curvature with a focal length of 0.5 m would have a power of 2 diopters, and so on.

The term *principal focus* is somewhat misleading because *focus* evokes notions of image clarity. Were the film in a camera or the retina in the eye located at PF, our photographs and vision would consist only of single points of light devoid of representations of external objects.

Image formation occurs at locations more distant from the lens than PF, as illustrated in Figure 2b. From an external object, such as an arrow, parallel rays from points A and B converge at PF to continue beyond it. The images of A and B occur at the intersection of secondary axes (sa) with their respective light rays at a and b. A secondary axis is a geometrical construct consisting of a straight line from the external point in question through the center of the lens (OC) to its intersection with the light ray emitted from the same external point. Note that the image is inverted, and because the lens is three-dimensional, there occurs as well a right–left reversal.

B. The Eye

The physical structure of the eye allows light from external objects to be focused on the retina where, through photochemical means, light is transduced (converted) to neural impulses conducted via the optic nerve to the visual areas of the brain. Such neural activity leads to visual sensations from which visual perception arises through interpretation of these sensations within the context of expectation and past experience. While visual perception depends upon visual sensations, the two are not synonymous.

1. Gross Structures

The eye is formed of three concentric spheres, two of which are partial spheres. The outer sphere, known as the *sclera,* is a tough, whitish, rigid membrane with a diameter of about 22 mm. Except in its anterior region, where it bulges outward to form the transparent cornea through which light enters the eye, the remainder is translucent.

Whereas the sclera serves primarily a protective function, the middle sphere has entirely different functions. Commonly called the choroid layer, *chorioid* is to be preferred as etymologically closer to the intended meaning, "resembling the chorion." This layer is absent in the anterior region of the eye so that light passing through the cornea can reach the retina. The chorioid has two important functions: first, as a reddish-brown pigmented layer, it absorbs stray light; and second, it is the singular blood supply to the receptors and neural cells that form the retina, the third and innermost of the three concentric spheres.

As shown in Figure 3, there are several additional structures of importance beside the sclera, chorioid, and retina. The first of these is the convex lens suspended within the eye just behind the cornea by a series of suspensory ligaments attached at one end to the lens and at the other end to a ring called the *ciliary body*. The ciliary body lies behind the cornea

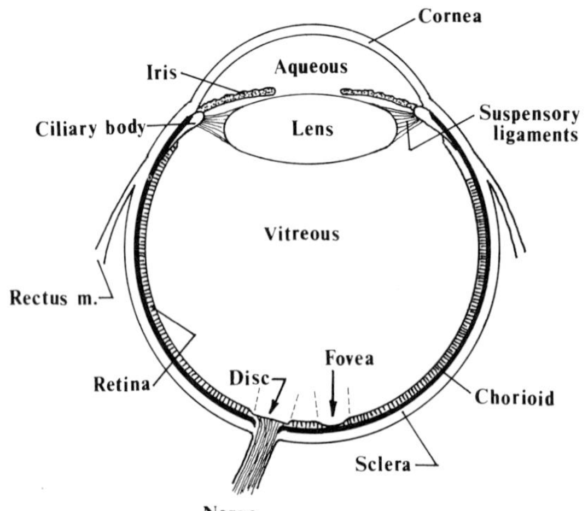

FIGURE 3 Horizontal cross-section of the right human eye showing gross structures. See text for discussion.

and is attached to the sclera at the place where translucency gives way to transparency, near the anterior terminus of the chorioid.

Because the lens has elastic properties, at least until old age, its convexity can be altered by changes in tension exerted by suspensory ligaments. When viewing distant objects, the lens plays virtually no role because the light from such objects is essentially parallel and the cornea alone produces sufficient refraction to focus the image on the retina. The cornea has a refractive power of about 40 diopters. However, when nearby objects are viewed, the light striking the cornea is diverging and the cornea alone cannot focus the image on the retina. Therefore, with close vision, the lens is needed to increase refraction.

With distance vision (objects farther away than 10 ft) the lens is under tension and remains relatively flat. With close vision, the tension is reduced and the lens assumes naturally greater convexity and thus greater refractory power, up to a maximum of about 20 diopters. This is possible because ciliary muscles exert a pull in an anteromedial direction, which moves the body slightly anterior *and* reduces the diameter of the ring, thereby reducing tension. The process of changing the shape of the lens is called *visual accommodation*.

A second structure of importance is the iris, a pigmented tissue housed in the anterior chamber adjacent to the anterior surface of the lens. It operates as a diaphragm with an opening at its center called the *pupil*. The iris contains radial muscle fibers which, when contracted, increase the size of the pupillary opening (dilation) and sphincter (circular) muscle fibers which, when contracted, let in less light (constriction). The iris can effect a 14-fold change in the areal size of the pupil.

The interior of the eye is fluid-filled and has a positive internal pressure to prevent its collapse. The anterior chamber is filled with aqueous humor and the posterior chamber is filled with vitreous humor, yellowish and viscous.

2. The Retina

The retina is an extension of the brain consisting of three layers situated 20 mm from the cornea. The outer layer (I) contains two kinds of receptors called *rods* and *cones,* with their light-sensitive outer segments illogically oriented toward the chorioid. Rods contain rhodopsin and are located primarily in the periphery away from the fovea. They mediate achromatic vision. The cones contain iodopsin and are concentrated at and near the fovea. They mediate color vision. The middle layer (II) contains *bipolar* cells the function of which is to integrate activity of the receptors and communicate that integration to the inner layer (III) which consists of ganglion cells whose axons exit the eye just nasal to the fovea to form the optic nerve. Within and between layers are horizontal and amacrine cells that assist in integration by allowing activity in one region of the retina to influence other regions. The rods, cones, and the bipolar cells are highly specialized cells and give only graded potentials, but the ganglion cells are true neurons and show in their axons all-or-none neural behavior.

The photochemical pigments in the receptors absorb light which, in turn, leads to changes in the polarization of bipolar cells. Hypopolarization is excitatory and leads to the release of neurotransmitters at the synapses between layers II and III. Hyperpolarization is inhibitory. Accordingly, receptor activity can lead to either initiation or inhibition of impulses in ganglion cells.

Rhodopsin (rods) and iodopsin (cones) differ in two major ways. Rhodopsin is absolutely more sensitive to light and so is important at low levels of illumination (scotopic or twilight vision). It also is maximally responsive to the shorter wavelengths. Iodopsin requires more light (photopic or daylight vision) and is maximally responsive to the longer wavelengths.

C. Neural Projection

Neural projection begins within the eye and ends in the visual cortex located in the occipital lobes of the brain (Brodmann's area 17).

1. Retinal Neurology

Rods converge upon bipolar cells which converge upon ganglion cells, sometimes with ratios as high as 200 : 1. Through spatial summation the scotopic (rod) system is able to detect small amounts of light, but convergence robs this system of the ability to make pattern discrimination (acuity). By contrast, there is little convergence in the cone system, since cones have their own bipolars and ganglion cells. Accordingly, the photopic (cone) system serves acuity well even though more light is needed to activate it.

2. Optic Nerve

Axons of the ganglion cells, wherever situated, course through the eye to exit together at the optic disc, a small area devoid of receptors 4 mm nasal to the fovea. To activate the receptors, note that incoming light must filter through thousands of ganglion and bipolar cells to reach the receptors. Upon their exit the ganglion axons comprise the optic nerves and form a cross (optic chiasm) below the frontal lobes as they connect with the lateral geniculate nuclei of the thalamus. Figure 4 illustrates the arrangement. Note that half the cells from each eye stay on the same side of the midline whereas the other half decussate (cross-over) to the other side. Accordingly, the right visual field is represented in the left cortex, and the left field in the right cortex.

3. Central Pathways

The lateral geniculate nuclei preserve the spatial properties of the retina, but additional integration is achieved through the assignment of incoming neurons to layers within each nucleus that represent different specific kinds of visual features detected and coded at the retinal level. From the thalamus

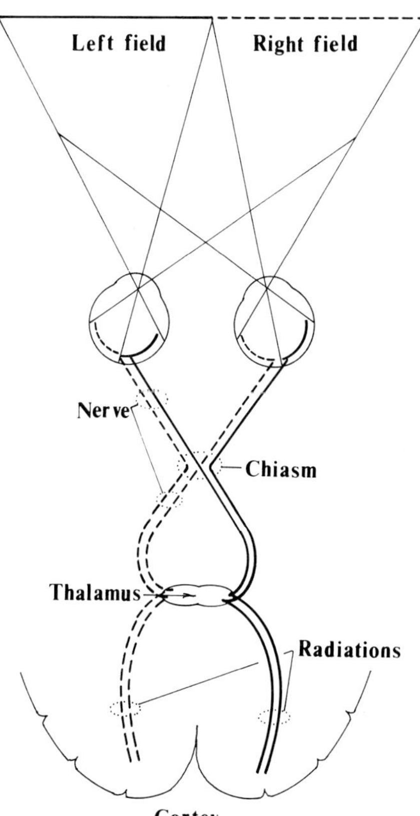

FIGURE 4 Diagram of the neural projections from the eyes via the optic nerves to the thalamus and primary visual cortex. See text for discussion.

higher-order neurons carry information to the primary visual cortex by way of the optic radiations.

A small proportion of optic nerve fibers do not penetrate the thalamus, but rather descend to the superior colliculi of the mid-brain or enter visual motor nuclei from which efferent feedback loops arise to control the motor aspects of vision, particularly the extra-ocular muscles that mobilize the eyes in their sockets and the intra-ocular muscles that control actions of the lens and iris.

The primary visual cortex has elaborate connections with the visual association areas located deeper in the brain (Brodmann's areas 18 and 19).

The eye often is compared to a portrait camera, but consider the changes in the camera necessary to make it similar to the eye: first, place the film in backward so that its light-sensitive surface faces away from the lens, as is the case with rods and cones; second, put a few holes in the bellows to simulate light leakage; third, put yarn and string in the bellows to simulate the neural tissue through which light must pass on its way to the retina; fourth, fill the bellows with lemon jello to simulate vitreous humor and its color aberration; and finally mount the camera on a rapidly vibrating tripod to simulate physiological nystagmus, the small 120/sec oscillations of the eye produced by the rectus muscles. Some camera!

D. Acuity

Acuity refers to the capacity of an observer to detect small stimulus differences, and it differs greatly from one retinal region to another. Generally, images focused on and near the fovea provide the best acuity because in this region one finds the highest density of receptors (cones) and the lowest level of synaptic convergence.

1. Acuity Measurement

There are several concepts in the measurement of acuity, the first of which is *detection,* defined as the least angular subtense of a target that can be seen. The second is *recognition* acuity illustrated by the Snellen eye chart with which, from a distance of 20 ft, one identifies printed letters of decreasing size. An acuity of 20/20 means that an individual sees at 20 ft what the average person sees at 20 ft. As acuity declines, the second numeral increases (e.g., 20/30). Thus, what one sees at 20 ft the average person can see at 30 ft.

A better way to measure spatial acuity is to determine the least angular separation of two contours or edges that continue to appear as separate. Such tests involve the use of Landolt rings (broken circles), gratings, grids, and checkerboard designs. Normal thresholds approximate 1′ of arc and are measures of minimum separable acuity. Another way to measure spatial acuity is with use of a vernier, the detection of a break in a vertical line produced by a lateral displacement of one segment of the line. Normal thresholds approximate 10″ of arc.

A final form of spatial acuity deals with an observer's capacity to resolve differences in the depth (distance) of objects. Stereoscopic acuity is based upon retinal disparity, a topic considered under Depth Perception.

Beside spatial measures of acuity stands temporal acuity, the ability to continue to see a physically interrupted light as a series of flashes. Normally, when the rate of interruption approaches 60/sec, an observer no longer sees a series of flashes. Instead, the target appears continuous (critical flicker fusion, CFF). The highest rate that still leads to flicker is the measure of temporal acuity, and at low luminance levels, CFF can be as low as 5/sec.

2. Spatial Frequency

Imagine a square visual target comprising bright and dark vertical bars of equal width arranged in an alternating pattern, as illustrated in Figure 5, and viewed

FIGURE 5 An illustration of contrast and spatial frequency, the latter defined as the fineness or coarseness of the textures, measured as the number of vertical bars per 1° of visual angle.

in a plane perpendicular to the line of sight. Without changing the size of the square, two manipulations are possible: the contrast between the bright and dark bars can be changed, and the width of the bars can be made wider or more narrow. The number of bars presented obviously increases as bar width decreases. *Spatial frequency* refers to the number of dark or light bars per degree of visual angle.

When the contrast ratio of the bright and dark bars is plotted as a function of spatial frequency, the resultant modulation transfer function shows an interesting interaction. When the vertical bars are wide, resolution of the grating contours occurs even when the contrast is low. However, when the bars are narrow, a much greater contrast is necessary for contour resolution, probably because optical aberrations and diffraction produce on the retina a much lower degree of contrast than that actually present in the target. The relative visibility of targets declines as spatial frequency exceeds six bars per 1° of visual angle.

3. Determiners of Acuity

There are many factors that influence the degree to which the visual system leads to the effective detection of small stimulus differences. Foremost is the clarity of the image on the retina. If the curvature of the cornea is not normal, or if it has been injured or scarred, its refractive powers will be irregularly influenced so that image clarity is wanting. The lens, too, can lead to a similar want. This is known as *astigmatism*. More common is the formation of the image in a plane in front of the retina (myopia) or behind it (hyperopia).

The location of the image on the retina obviously influences acuity because the retina is homogeneous neither in receptor density nor in receptor type. The foveal region is best, which is why we direct our gaze to objects so that the image falls on the fovea.

Acuity improves directly with levels of luminance provided the pupillary size is appropriate and the light is not so great as to be painful. Extended exposures give better acuity than brief ones. Finally, acuity is improved when fixation is maintained and the level of involuntary eye movements (physiological nystagmus) during fixation is minimal. The eye is never stationary.

E. Coding: Feature Detectors

It is important to realize that the visual system does not produce images in the visual cortex as though it contained a television screen. Once an image forms on the retina, the visual system abstracts certain features from the image, features which are coded by neural cells. Accordingly, in the cortex there are no contours, no brightnesses, and no colors. There is only neural activity that represents, or symbolizes, these features attributed to the external environment. What is not coded lies outside consciousness.

1. Receptive Fields

The axons of ganglion cells show spontaneous firings in the absence of light. The behavior of these cells can be modified in two ways: the cell can be shut down (inhibition) or its response rate can be greatly increased (excitation). When the behavior of a particular cell is monitored, we find that there is a small region on the retina in which the presence of light modifies that cell's behavior. This region is known as that cell's receptive field. The fields of ganglion cells are small and circular and come in two different forms, both of which contain a central circle and a larger circular surround (annulus). In the first form, light that falls on the center of the field excites the cell whereas light that falls on the surround inhibits the cell. These are called "on"-centered. In the second form, stimulation of the center inhibits the cell whereas stimulation of the surround excites it. These are called "off"-centered.

Through elaborate and quite wondrous neural organization, the axons from ganglion cells stimulate higher-order cells that converge on cortical cells in the primary visual cortex. When the behavior of cortical cells is monitored, we find that they, too, have receptive fields but they are no longer small circular retinal regions. Instead, cortical cells have larger elongated fields designed to detect lines in a visual scene.

A vertical line imaged on the retina will affect the receptive fields of as many ganglion cells as are stimulated. The result, after synapses at various locations in the projection, is to have the effects of this retinal activity converge on a single cortical cell. It does not respond to spots of light, as do ganglion cells, but only to a series of "spots" from the retinal image of a vertical line. Its receptive field thus is an elongated retinal region with vertical orientation.

The visual cortex contains functional columns of cells oriented perpendicularly to its surface. A single column of cortical cells contains only cells responsive to lines (contours) of a given orientation, with each cell responsive to specific but different retinal regions. Adjacent columns include cells responsive to different line orientations. Other cortical cells have curved receptive fields and seem "tuned" to specific curvatures contained in the visual array.

Further levels of abstraction are coded when, for example, these cortical edge detectors converge on other cortical cells that lie deeper in the visual brain. If four cortical edge detectors, two with horizontal and two with vertical receptive fields, drive a deeper cell, then the deep cell responds only when the retina receives the image of a square of a given size and orientation located at a specific retinal place. The higher one goes in the neural projection, the greater is the integration and the more specific are the characteristics coded by single cortical cells, finally to encompass not just contours, but contrast and color as well.

2. Lateral Inhibition

The presence of horizontal and amacrine cells and the multiple connections made by bipolar cells produce regional interactions at the synapses that involve the ganglion cells. An important aspect of this interaction is called *lateral inhibition,* defined as the capacity of an excited cell through lateral connections to inhibit completely or partially the activity of adjacent cells that otherwise would be excited.

The interaction is understood best by reference to Figure 6. The rectangle depicted (Fig. 6a) is divided equally into dark and light regions with one common contour. The luminance differs for each region but remains constant within regions, as shown in Figure 6b. The amount of inhibition by an active cell upon its neighbors is directly related to the level of its own activity. Accordingly, cell 4 is less inhibited than cells 1–3 because of the weak inhibiting influence by cell 5, whereas cell 5 is more inhibited than cells 6–8 because of the strong inhibiting influence by cell 4. In Figure 6c the activity for each cell is expressed as impulses/sec. Even though each region has constant luminance, lateral inhibition enhances the boundary so that perceptually the region at A seems brighter and at B darker (Fig. 6a) than the remainder of their respective regions. These brightness enhancements, contributed by the eye and not present in the stimulus, are called *Mach bands,* named after the visual scientist who first observed them a century ago.

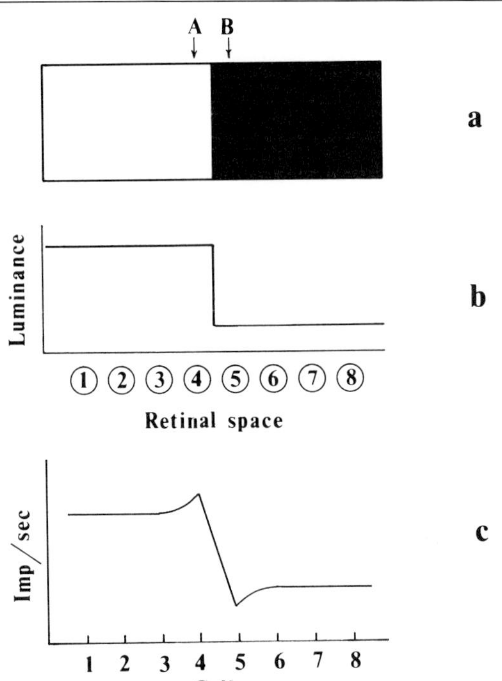

FIGURE 6 Analysis of lateral inhibition. (a) A bipartite field of white and black separated by a single sharp edge. (b) The distribution of light reflected onto the retina where the abscissa is retinal space and the ordinate is luminance. The numbered circles represent a line of ganglion cells stimulated by the target shown in (a). (c) The relative response rates of these ganglion cells in impulses/sec as a function of their retinal location. See text for discussion.

3. Motion

The perception of motion is determined by the retinal blur of a fast-moving target, by voluntary tracking movements of the eyes when target velocity is not too great, or by motion detectors when the eye is stationary.

A motion detector depends upon the receptive field of a ganglion cell wherein the central area is eccentric to its surround. Assume the annulus to be a clock face and the "on"-center circle to be displaced well toward 9 o'clock. The response of this cell remains invariant when an image crosses the receptive field from 12 to 6 or from 6 to 12 o'clock. Therefore, it can not code vertical motion. However, when the image moves horizontally across the field, from left to right, the "on"-center is first encountered followed by the "off" surround. As a result, the cell gives a burst of activity and then shuts down. However, when the image moves from right to left, the inhibitory influence of the "off" surround shuts the cell off; and because inhibitory influences outlast excitatory ones, the cell never fires. Such a cell codes the direction of horizontal movement, and depending only upon the direction of displacement of the "on"-center, other cells can code vertical and oblique motion. [*See* Visual Motion Perception.]

4. Color

Photochemical pigments contained in the outer segments of cones fall into three classes according to their spectral absorption properties. Some cones absorb the longer wavelengths from 580 to 700 nm with a maximum absorption at 650 nm (seen as red, R), others absorb the middle wavelengths from 480 to 600 nm with a maximum at 530 nm (seen as green, G), and still others absorb the shorter wavelengths from 400 to 510 nm with a maximum at 460 nm (seen as blue, B). There are no cones with maximum absorption in the yellow region of the spectrum. Accordingly, yellow must be coded beyond the level of the primary receptors. The receptors operate on a three-color system (*trichromaticity*).

When the spectral properties of the three classes of cone are simulated in the laboratory by passing white light through each of three appropriate filters, the output of each can be focused and superimposed upon a single screen to form an additive product. From laboratory experiments we know that any spectral color (C) can be obtained according to the formula $C = x_R + y_G + z_B$, where the coefficients x, y, and z represent the proportions of the mixture which always must add to 100%. Contrary to intuition, the sensation of yellow arises when x_R and y_G both equal 50% (and z, therefore, equals 0%).

When within the optic nerve the axons of ganglion cells that code color are monitored, we learn that ganglion cells work in opposition within the color pairs of red–green and yellow–blue. Some cells are excited by red (R^+) and inhibited by green (G^-) while others are excited by green (G^+) and inhibited by red (R^-). It is surmised that the receptive fields of such cells have centers that lead to ganglion excitation by one "color" but include surrounds that lead to inhibition when stimulated by the opposing "color." Similar arrangements occur for the yellow–blue pair.

The lateral connections that allow the combined "red"–"green" cone activity to stimulate a ganglion cell for the coding of yellow, while inhibiting its response to "blue," are quite well understood, but beyond the scope of this treatment. However, the important conclusion to bear in mind is this: whereas the retina follows trichromaticity, the optic nerve follows quadrichromaticity. This model of color theory is called *opponent process theory*. Since the last century the three-color theory of Helmholtz and the four-color theory of Hering have been at odds. Current theory brings them together by showing how one stage of coding (retinal) can give rise to a different later stage of coding (postretinal).

Cells in the primary visual cortex that detect color also are organized in columnar patterns in close proximity to the columns of contour and edge detectors, thus providing opportunity for interaction and the combination of features by cells located deeper in the cortex.

II. BASIC PERCEPTUAL PHENOMENA

In this section we consider four basic aspects of visual perception: brightness, form, space, and color. While occasional reference is made to important physiological correlates not heretofore discussed, major emphasis rests upon the global aspects of sensation and perception.

A. Brightness

Brightness has its primary physical correlate in the amount of light reflected from objects (luminance). However, beside luminance there are some intraocular and some extraocular (contextual) factors that also influence perceived brightness.

1. Intraocular Factors

Recall that the outer layer of the retina contains two different types of receptors, and that these receptors contain different photochemical pigments of unequal sensitivity both to light absorption and to light wavelength. Further, these receptors are distributed differently within the retinal mosaic, with the 100 million rods in the periphery and the 6 million cones at and near the fovea. Accordingly, even when luminance is held constant, the effects of light upon the retina vary and depend upon the retinal location of the image and the complexity of the reflected light. For example, if the reflected light is of the shorter wavelengths for which the scotopic (rod) system is especially sensitive, then brightness will be greatest when the image falls upon the retinal periphery where the rods are located. An object that is visible with the scotopic system may become invisible when the image falls on the foveal cones because their thresholds are higher. On the other hand, if the reflected light is of the longer wavelengths, brightness will be determined entirely by the photopic (cone) system since long wavelengths do not activate the rod system. However, if the complexity of the wave is increased by the addition of some shorter waves, then both kinds of receptors are activated and brightness is thereby enhanced.

A third intraocular factor is *retinal adaptation.* The absorption of light by rhodopsin and iodopsin leads to their chemical breakdown, and while this is occurring in some rods and cones, the by-products are being resynthesized into rhodopsin and iodopsin in other receptors. This is why, unlike the camera, the retina operates continuously. At any given moment, the eye is in some state of balance between the breakdown and the buildup of photochemicals, called *level of adaptation,* and whenever there occurs an abrupt change in luminance, the retina seeks a new level of adaptation.

If the change involves a decrease in ambient luminance, as when one goes from sunlight into a darkened movie theater, the retina dark adapts, a process that takes about 30 min for completion. Accordingly, objects that reflect low levels of light are, at first, impossible to detect, only later to be seen with more than marginal brightness. Upon going from the theater back into sunlight, the retina light adapts so that objects that at first produced almost painful glare soon appear normal. Light adaptation reaches completion in about 2 min.

In summary, perceived brightness depends upon luminance, image location, light complexity, level of adaptation, and lateral inhibition, the latter as previously considered in connection with Mach bands.

2. Extraocular Factors

At low levels of luminance the duration of stimulation also influences perceived brightness, a phenomenon not unlike that observed with the use of time exposures in photography. Under some limited conditions, those wherein luminance is near threshold level, duration becomes important. There appears to be a trade-off between duration (D) and luminance (L) such that $D \times L = C$, where C is a constant. A loss of brightness produced by a decrease in luminance can be balanced by an increase in stimulus duration (Bloch's Law).

With targets of small angular subtense, there occurs a similar trade-off between target area (A) and luminance (L) such that $A \times L = C$ (Ricco's Law). For larger targets, the relationship becomes $\sqrt{A} \times L = C$ (Piper's Law).

Another factor that influences brightness is simultaneous brightness contrast. The perceived brightness of a particular object or surface is heavily influenced by the luminance levels of adjacent objects and surfaces simultaneously present in the visual field.

Unlike Mach bands, in which the induced brightness effects occur only near boundaries and contours, simultaneous contrast involves entire surfaces and works in the direction of enhancing brightness differences between adjoining parts of the visual field, with the enhancement related directly to the luminance differences (contrast). Two identical grey surfaces will appear equally bright until one is seen against a dark background while the other is seen against a light background. The former now appears brighter than the squares when seen alone, whereas the latter appears dimmer.

These effects are not one-way. Every part of the visual field influences the brightness of every other part, with the influence greatest with spatial contiguity. The influence declines as the interacting areas become spatially more remote one from another.

Brightness contrast can also occur through time (successive contrast), but this form of influence on brightness is better considered as a variation of the eye's level of adaptation, previously discussed.

Finally, the brightness of objects is influenced by cognitive factors, expectation, and past experience. For example, when an observer views two unidentified targets, each in an adjacent compartment, no difficulty is met when the observer is instructed to make the brightnesses of the targets equal. The observer controls the illumination on each target so as to make them equally bright, as confirmed afterward with an illuminometer. However, as soon as the observer is informed that one compartment contains a piece of anthracite coal while the other contains snow, the coal appears "black" and the snow appears "white," even though their luminances remain equal. In instances such as this, past experience "corrects" sensory impressions to add stability to the perceptual world. If perception begins with sensation, it does not end with it.

B. Form

The visual system evolved to detect changes in stimulation rather than unchanging steady states, for nothing produces less neural activity than the inspection of a visual field of homogeneous luminance (Ganzfeld). Activity is produced by abrupt gradients in luminance that produce edges and contours, by textured and colored surfaces, and by the objects thus formed, the images of which relocate on the retina as points of fixation change during inspection of a scene. The visual nervous system detects these changes and encodes their features almost instantaneously to be combined into recognizable forms that are named and attributed to a knowable external world. Perception is the agent through which constantly changing retinal events are made stable and meaningful, and without which the visual environment would be nothing more than a buzzing confusion of perpetual change. Perceptual stability begins with the recognition of forms, parts of the visual pattern that take on object qualities.

1. Pattern Recognition

The recognition of patterns depends upon the detection of edges and their correspondence with an internal template. The capital letter L may "drive" a cortical cell fed by vertical and horizontal edge detectors, and perhaps by a 90° corner detector. Through complex processing, this pattern can be recognized as an L no matter where on the retina its image falls. Indeed, certain invariances present in this pattern can transcend its orientation so that rotation does not eliminate its recognition since the quality of L-ness remains.

Whether the template occurs naturally or is developed through experience is presently unknown, but the labeling of it clearly shows the role of experience. One unfamiliar with the printed alphabet could recognize this pattern and yet not label it as a capital L. One who knows only the English alphabet might label this pattern rotated 180° as an upside-down L while another, also familiar with the Greek alphabet, might label the same pattern as a backward capital gamma.

Templates obviously are based upon the detection of stimulus features like straight and curved edges, whether they be for lines, letters, or geometrical shapes like quadrilaterals, arcs, or circles. What is remarkable about the resultant forms is that the templates used in their abstraction tend to ignore irrelevant features. A square is a recognizable form regardless of its size, color, brightness, or location. [*See* PATTERN RECOGNITION.]

2. Figure–Ground

While a hierarchical feature-extracting system is responsible for pattern recognition, we do not perceive form directly, as for example "squareness." Instead of perceiving conceptual abstractions like squareness we perceive particular squares, and by so doing such squares become figures that have a "thingness" about them.

Consider the pattern shown in Figure 7a. The central area is not just an area set off by greater luminance than its surround; instead, it becomes a figure because it appears as an entity, it is solid, it is closer, and the edges that separate it from the background belong to it. These are general characteristics of figures.

Shifts in perceptual set can alter figure–ground relationships, as illustrated in Figure 7b. If the light-grey central square remains the figure, then it continues to appear as a solid entity and the edges that define it belong to the square. However, if the dark rectangle becomes the figure, where the background can be seen through a square hole in its center, then the darker area becomes a solid entity, appears

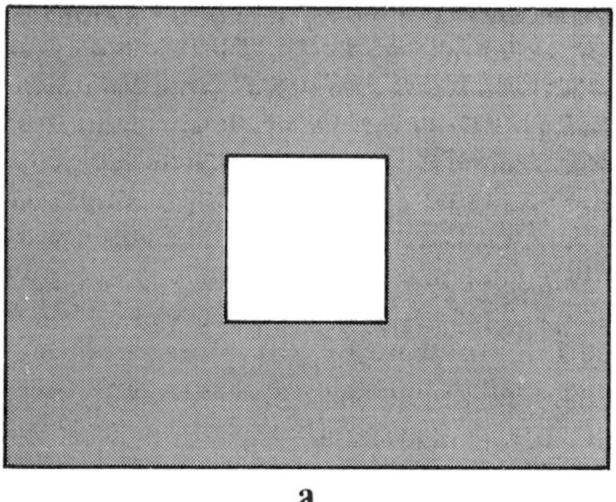

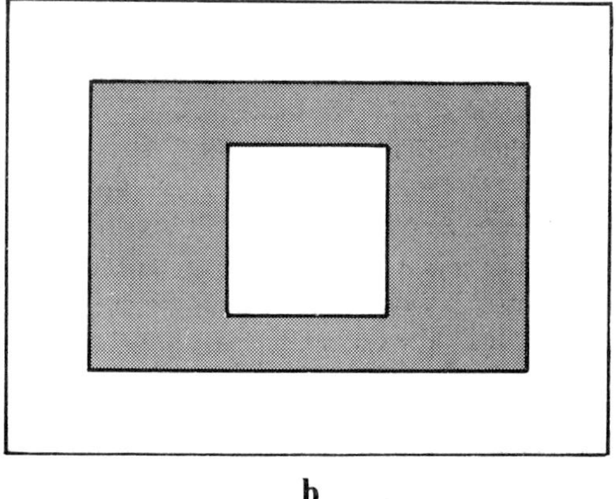

FIGURE 7 Illustrations of figure–ground relationships. (a) A simple square figure upon a dark surrounding. (b) An ambiguous pattern in which the figure changes from the central square to the dark rectangle to the bright surrounding frame. See text for discussion.

closer, and the edges that earlier were seen as belonging to the central square now belong to the new figure. Yet another organization comes about when the figure becomes the bright rectangular frame. Note that the outer edges that earlier defined the dark area as figure now become the inner edges that define the frame as figure.

3. Organizing Principles

The emergence of figures from visual patterns seems to depend upon some innate organizing principles, the more dominant of which represent unconscious efforts to achieve simplicity, balance, symmetry and coherence. Clear demonstrations of these organizing principles during the perception of our usual visual environments are nearly impossible, and so evidence for them comes from simpler patterns like those shown in Figure 8. Note that in part (a) the elements can be organized into either rows or columns. However, when spatial proximity is altered, as in part (b), the columnar organization prevails. In part (c), grouping into rows occurs on the basis of similarity rather than proximity. We also organize enclosed areas into forms and encode them according to the geometrical figures they most nearly approximate, and when the enclosure is not complete, as in part (d), we code them as closed (closure) and so perceive a square and a circle.

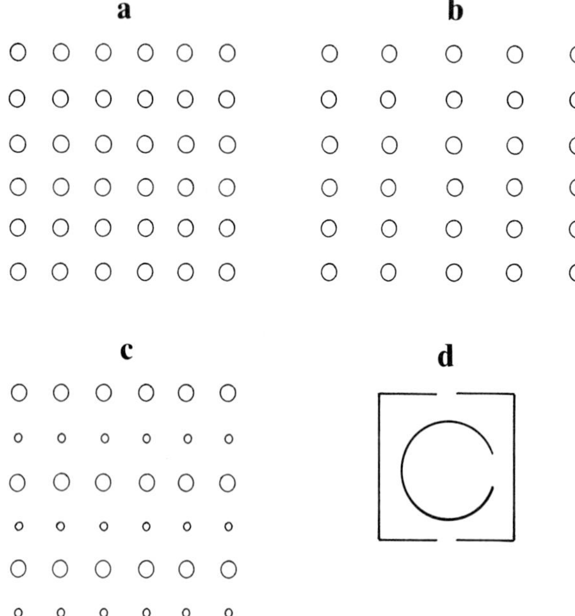

FIGURE 8 Principles of perceptual organization. In (a) all elements are identical and equi-distant and can be organized into rows or columns. (b) Proximity favors columnar organization, while in (c) similarity favors row organization; (d) illustrates closure.

These principles have been taken by psychologists as evidence of Prägnanz, a German word meaning "to convey the essence." Perceiving is a process to convey the essence of the environment as efficiently as possible by representations that are as simple as a given visual array allows. As a pedestrian about to cross a street, we need only identify the approaching target as an automobile at a particular distance traveling at a particular velocity. Efficiency toward our safe passage does not require detail of the style, color, or manufacturer of the automobile. On the other hand, were we watching a parade of antique cars at an auto show, our attention would, no doubt, be directed toward other aspects of the changing visual array. Here we note the influence of context on perception.

C. Depth

Even though the retina is a curved surface, its capacity to code space is two-dimensional. In this section we consider the factors that allow us to perceive the third dimension called *depth*. There are two classes of cues that operate in visual depth perception: primary cues and secondary cues. [*See* DEPTH PERCEPTION.]

1. Primary Cues

There are three primary cues, so-called because they have a physiological basis and are innate (unlearned). Two of them involve the muscle sense known as *kinesthesis,* a sensory system that detects changes in muscle tension.

When we view objects that are 40 ft or more distant from us, the optical axes of the eyes are virtually parallel. However, as objects come closer and closer, for them to remain singular, the attitude of the eyes must change by their rotation in a nasal direction. With the interocular axis (center of one eye to center of other eye) as the base of a triangle, the ocular axes converge to form a triangle, the apex of which is at the object of fixation. This is called *ocular convergence*. The angle of convergence (apical angle) increases as objects grow closer as a consequence of increased nasal rotation produced by the lateral rectus muscles. Kinesthetic signals from the rectus muscles give the central nervous system (CNS) information about the angle of convergence and, therefore, the depth of the fixated object. This cue usually is classified as a binocular cue since both eyes are involved. However, even when sight is limited to one eye, the eyes continue to converge, though with less exactitude, so that convergence continues to have some utility even during monocular vision.

When objects are within 10 ft, clarity of retinal imaging requires lenticular accommodation through involvement of the ciliary muscles. Again, kinesthetic signals from these muscle fibers provide information to the CNS about the shape of the lens and therefore the depth of the focused object. This cue operates during binocular and monocular viewing.

The third primary cue is *binocular disparity* and it operates only with binocular viewing. Disparity refers to small differences in retinal images produced by the fact that we normally see with two eyes which are located in different places in space. If one were to take two photographs of the same scene with the camera moved a few inches before the second photograph was taken, then superpositioning of the respective negatives would show slight disparities. The visual cortex includes cells sensitive to disparities, and these disparity detectors are responsible for stereoscopic depth perception. The normal eye can detect disparities as small as 9″ of arc. Disparity magnitude is directly related to the separation of objects in the third dimension. When disparity exceeds the resolution capacity of the visual system, we see double images in place of a single image in relief.

2. Secondary Cues

Secondary cues are learned and widely employed by artists who wish to give impressions of depth while being limited to a two-dimensional canvas.

The apparent *size* of known objects decreases with their distance from us with the result that size is an excellent cue to depth provided the perceiver has foreknowledge of the object. Closer objects often obscure portions of more distant objects, such as when a tree in the front lawn occludes part of the house behind it (sometimes called *interposition*). Objects of known brightness grow dimmer with distance (brightness gradient). Linear perspective is an important cue as when one stands between railroad tracks and notes that they appear to converge to a vanishing point near the horizon. Further, the gravel between the tracks at one's feet has a coarse texture that appears to grow finer with distance (texture gradient). The clarity of objects also declines with distance because of aerial haze, light diffraction by dust and other impurities in air. Light and shadows also give impressions of depth, as when a flat circle appears bright in one region with the remainder shown as increasingly darker so as to effect the appearance of a sphere. We also make judgments about the distance of objects by their relative motion when we move. Imagine looking out a window while riding on a train. Objects close by appear to move rapidly in a direction opposite to our own. A farm house in a distant field also appears to move in an opposite direction, but much more slowly. This cue is called *motion parallax*.

D. Color

We know that any spectral color can be matched by some combination, through addition of three "primary" sources, each with a dominant wavelength in the red (650 nm), green (530 nm), and blue (460 nm) parts of the spectrum, respectively. The relative contributions of each primary, expressed by their coefficients x, y, and z, allow a particular hue to be defined according to its tri-stimulus specification. When considered in this way, there are about 130 distinguishable hues. However, in this section the treatment centers on direct descriptions of visual color experience rather than upon physiological processes that give rise to them.

1. Nomenclature

In normal experience the large number of detectable hues is collapsed to 10, a number established by the U.S. Bureau of Standards to include the following: red, orange, yellow, green, blue, violet, purple, brown, pink and olive. Intermediate hues are obtained when wavelengths not too divergent are mixed, such as blue and green to form aqua. When the wavelengths are too divergent, the mixture does not appear as a single, stable hue, and instead alternates from the hue of one component to the hue of the other. This phenomenon is called *color rivalry*. When the mixture leads to grey, the components are said to be *complementary*. This occurs when the combination has a spectrum that is so broad (complex) that periodicity is lost.

2. Color Zones

As mentioned, color is mediated by cone receptors; and because they are distributed only in the foveal region, the retinal periphery is not directly sensitive to color. Color zones refer to retinal regions sensitive to color as measured in the laboratory with a perimeter. With the eye fixed upon a point of light straight ahead, a small target imaged on the periphery is moved slowly so that its image moves toward the fovea. If the target has color, its color cannot be identified by the observer until the image enters the color zone. While its presence is detected in the periphery, it appears there as colorless. By using different targets for red, green, yellow, and blue, color maps can be "drawn" on the retina for each color. The boundaries for yellow and blue are almost congruent and form the largest zones. Red and green color zones, also nearly congruent, are smaller but lie within the yellow–blue zone.

There is a remarkable caveat to retinal differences to color. When the test target first is imaged on the fovea so that its color is known, then movement of the image toward the periphery and out of its color zone does *not* lead to a loss of color. Why this happens is unknown, but if it were not so, then inspection of large colored surfaces, like the wall of a room, would appear to carry color only in the immediate area of our gaze while the remainder would appear as colorless.

3. Color Interactions

While wavelength is the major determinant of hue, certain minor interactions occur as a function of wave amplitude. Stimuli of the shorter wavelengths that mediate blue seem not to induce a shift in hue as their amplitudes increase. So, too, is the hue of yellow light (572 nm) immune from hue shifts with wave amplitude. However, stimuli with wavelengths between 520 and 570 nm have their hues shifted slightly toward green as amplitude rises whereas those with wavelengths longer than 575 nm show slight hue shifts toward red. The pattern of these shifts in hue brought about solely by amplitude increases is regular, but they do not show themselves unless amplitude changes are fairly large (2 log steps or more). The interaction of hue with amplitude is known as the Bezold–Brücke effect.

Like the case with brightness, colored surfaces also interact to produce simultaneous contrast effects (simultaneous color contrast). The perceived hue of one surface shows the influence of the presence of other hues in contiguous or nearby regions. Color induction also occurs when a colored region induces "color" into an area that otherwise would appear achromatic. For example, a colorless grey square will appear to have a reddish tint when surrounded by green and a greenish tint when surrounded by red. Similar effects are obtained with yellow and blue. Induced colors are, of course, consistent with the opponent process theory of color vision discussed earlier.

Another form of contrast involves succession rather than simultaneity. When extended gaze is directed first toward a red target and immediately afterward toward an achromatic target (grey), the latter for a time appears greenish. If the first target had been green, then the grey appears reddish; if yellow, then bluish, and if blue, then yellowish. These effects are known as *negative after-images*. Presumably, the first inspection partially depletes the receptors that mediate its color, so that when the retina later receives a broad spectrum of light from the grey surface, the receptors that mediate the opponent (complementary) color are "fresh" and so dominate. In a relatively brief period, the retina reaches equilibrium and the induced color fades, finally to be absent.

4. Color Blindness

Total color blindness is exceedingly rare, and so it is better to describe anomalies in color perception as color weaknesses. Categories of color weaknesses are based, not on the number of hues that an individual perceives, but rather on the number of primaries within the tri-chromatic system that one needs to match the hues an individual sees. Accordingly, the normal eye is called *tri-chromatic* because all three primaries (R, G, and B) are necessary to match all the hues contained in the full spectrum and available to such persons.

The most common form of weakness involves red and green. While these colors are detectable under high luminance levels, they become confused at lower levels. Such persons still require the three primaries, and so remain tri-chromatic, but the proportions of red and green needed to match certain hues deviate from the normal. Such people are called *anomalous trichromats,* and if the weakness centers on red, then they show *protanomaly,* and if on green, then *deuteranomaly*. About 8% of the male population suffers from red–green weakness, a genetically caused disorder carried by women but from which they remain immune.

When only two of the three tri-chromatic primaries are required to match seen hues, the eye is partially color blind and is labeled as *dichromatic*. Usually, it is the red–green system that is absent, for yellow–blue blindness is very rare. Nevertheless, weaknesses may be present in yellow (tritanopia) or in blue (tetartanopia).

When there is total absence of color sensation, the eye is said to be *monochromatic*. This label is consistent with prior principles on the categorization of color blindness and weakness, but the label is unfortunate in that it suggests that such eyes see one color when, in fact, they see none. Any single primary can match everything the visual system detects because the match simply is one of brightness. In the monochromatic eye, the cones are either absent or failing entirely in their function.

III. PERCEPTUAL PROCESSING

As mentioned at the outset, perception involves the selection of certain sensations from among the many that ongoing stimulation could provide. Those aspects of an ever-changing stimulus array to which attention is directed are determined partly by internal physiological states that orient the eyes to seek particular targets relevant to current biological needs. Attention also shows the influence of the perceptual context in which stimulation occurs. The context typically leads one to hold expectations which, given the circumstances, are formed on an assessment of probabilities that particular consequences are imminent, based on past experience.

Expectations lead to the development of what appear to be instantaneous perceptual hypotheses which, in turn, "direct" on-going behavior. The visual system abstracts information through the detection of stimulus features that are relevant to a current hypothesis while ignoring sensations deemed irrelevant. The critical features are matched against past experience, are coded into meaningful wholes, and lead to either the confirmation or the infirmation of the perceptual hypothesis. The following narrative should help understanding.

A. Narrative

Suppose you and a friend are on your way to Boston by car, several hundred miles distant. Because you have just had sandwiches and soda from your cooler, your appetites are satisfied. Unknowingly, you pass a number of roadside billboards announcing restaurants ahead. They are present in your visual world but attention is directed to other matters like conversation and mileage signs to Boston. As evening falls, hunger reappears (physiological state), with the result that you now take note of signs of places to eat that earlier were not processed.

You stop the car in a gravel parking lot beside the restaurant selected. Gravel is recognized by its visual texture and the sound it produces under the car's tires (past experience). As you exit the car, you hear a metallic object hit the gravel, a sound (metal on a hard surface) also recognized from past experience. You conclude that you dropped your ignition key, and this becomes the perceptual hypothesis that directs your gaze downward. In the moonlight you squat to pick up the key only to discover that what glistened was a broken piece of glass (hypothesis infirmed). Note that you attributed relevance and meaning to the glistening glass because you believed that you had dropped your key. Had you not heard something metallic drop, you would have no reason to interpret that stimulus as you did, if indeed you even took note of it. The perceiver attributes meaning to the environment.

You reassess your hypothesis by frisking your pockets, by checking the ignition, and by searching the floor boards—all to no avail. The hypothesis (I dropped my key) now is strengthened. After a long search you discover your key in the cuff of your trouser. The sound earlier heard was its deflection from the car door. You did not immediately hold this hypothesis because its probability of confirmation was low, and perceptual hypotheses usually first follow high probabilities.

Now found, you and your friend walk toward the restaurant as he relates how the sound of the train whistle through the adjacent woods had brought back childhood memories. The sound was there for you, too, but you did not process it because it was irrelevant to your perceptual world during your search.

Dinner concluded, you go to retrieve the car while your friend pays the bill. You enter the car to find that the ignition key will not turn. You might have considered that you were in another person's car, but this idea contradicted your perceptual hypothesis. As you fooled with the key you noticed a hole in the dashboard where your radio had been. Only when you recognized a foreign briefcase on the passenger seat did these lines of evidence infirm your hypothesis. Sheepishly, you discovered your car in an adjacent space. Here we note the role of expectancy. When expectancy is high, perceptual hypotheses require substantial contrary evidence to be infirmed.

B. Perceptual Constancies

Perceptual constancies refer to the tendency of percepts to remain stable (constant) even when stimulation changes. It is as if we cognitively "correct" changes in stimulation in order to preserve a stable and meaningful environment. Thus, a white house appears white whether seen in sunlight or moonlight (brightness constancy), a dinner plate remains circular from any vantage point even thought its retinal image may be, and usually is, elliptical (shape constancy), and a person remains of the same size as he walks away or approaches us even though retinal image size undergoes vast changes in size (size constancy). If perception were no more than a direct reflection of environmental energy, then our world would be entirely without order.

Bibliography

Coren, S., and Ward, L. M. (1989). "Sensation and Perception," 3rd ed. Harcourt Brace Jovanovich, New York.

Gulick, W. L., and Lawson, R. B. (1976). "Human Stereopsis." Oxford University, UK.

Levine, M. W., and Shefner, J. M. (1991). "Sensation and Perception." Brooks Cole, Pacific Grove, CA.

Sekuler, R., and Blake, R. (1990). "Perception," 2nd ed. McGraw–Hill, New York.

VISUAL REPRESENTATION

Michael J. Tarr
Yale University

Glossary

Frame of reference The coordinate system used for encoding the spatial positions of features located within visual input.

Object representation A mental structure that encodes selected properties of a given physical object, most often including shape information.

Perceptual organization Processes by which spatially discrete local features within visual input are grouped to form meaningful structures, such as surfaces and objects.

Structural description An object representation composed of three-dimensional parts and explicit relationships between them in a frame of reference based on the object.

View-based representation An object representation composed of images, each depicting the characteristic appearance of an object from a particular viewpoint in a frame of reference based on the observer.

Visual search The process by which a set of features defining a unique element within a scene is located using both preattentive and serial attention mechanisms.

LIGHT ENTERS our eyes as an undifferentiated array of luminance points. However, because most of the light within the optic array is reflected off of surfaces and objects in the environment, inherent within this array is a tremendous amount of information about the structure of the world around us. Reconstructing this structure, that is, recovering the layout of the scene, is perhaps the most important goal of human visual perception. Accomplishing this involves many complex processes that work toward converting patterns of light and dark into visual representations. Much like the physical world, visual representations are coherent, organized structures that correspond to surfaces, objects, and scenes. It is these mental representations, not the patterns of light that fall upon the retina, that form the basis of our visual percepts and cognition, being used in mechanisms as varied as object recognition, visual reasoning, linguistic descriptions of the environment, and categorization.

I. FEATURE PROCESSING

A. Preattentive Vision

It is generally understood that our visual system does rudimentary feature analysis at the earliest stages of processing. In particular, the existence of cortical cells differentially sensitive to stimulus orientation indicates that a series of orientation-selective filters are used to locate the position and orientation of local edges within visual input. Likewise, a variety of other early visual pathways apparently serve as filters to locally compute properties such as size and color. At this stage, the output of visual processing may be considered a set of *feature maps* that independently code for the value of a given feature at each position within a scene. For instance, given the letter "A" as visual input, a feature map for orientation would encode a distinct local orientation at each spatial position covered by the "A"—creating an array of oblique left, oblique right, horizontal, and possibly indeterminate local features (see Fig. 1). In a similar manner, maps may be formed for color, size, motion, depth, as well as other properties of the scene.

Evidence from visual search tasks indicates that different locations within an individual feature map are processed in parallel. For instance, imagine trying to locate a single vertical bar target among ran-

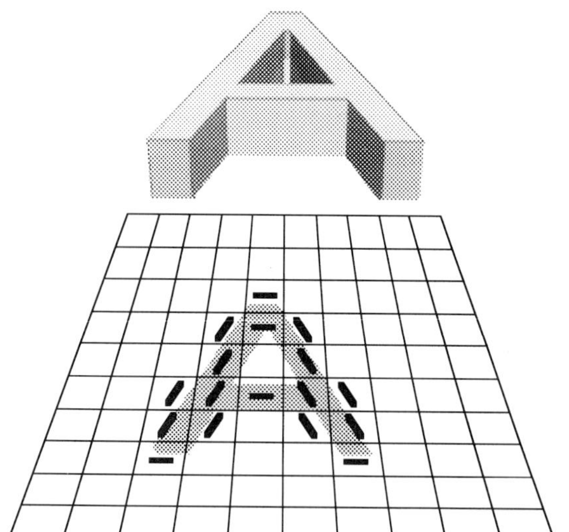

FIGURE 1 A feature map for orientation given the letter "A" as an input. Dark bars in each cell indicate the computed local orientation for that position. The shadow of the "A" is provided for clarity and is not part of a feature map.

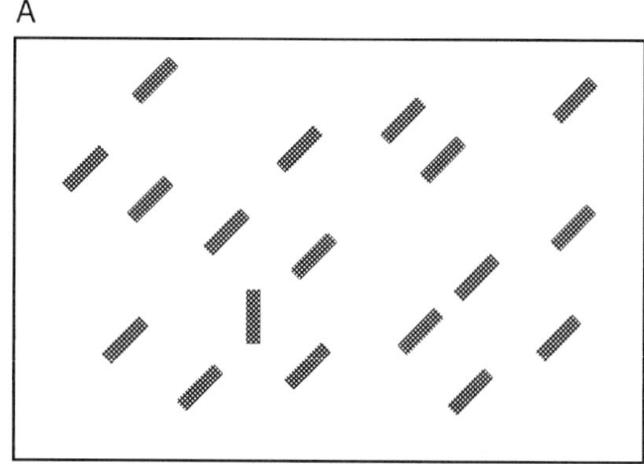

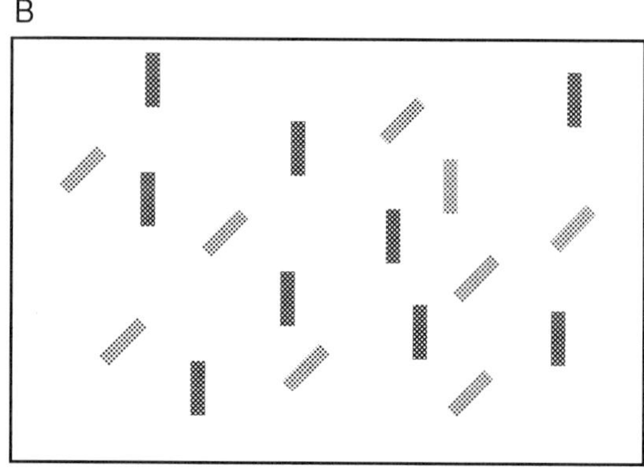

FIGURE 2 Visual search tasks. (A) A preattentive search task: Find the vertical bar among the oblique bars. (B) A conjunction search task: Find the light-gray vertical bar among the light-gray oblique and dark-gray vertical bars.

domly placed distractors composed of oblique bars of the same shape and color (see Fig. 2A); the time to perform this task is independent of the number of distractors present in the display. The target is said to "pop-out." That is, determining the presence of a target based on a feature difference within a single map does not require the application of a serial attention mechanism and, hence, is *preattentive*. Indeed, a similar "pop-out" effect has been found for target/distractor feature differences across color, size, motion direction, simple shape, and many other properties—each suggesting that there exists an independent feature map for a given perceptual dimension.

B. Conjunction Search

1. Feature Integration

In contrast to preattentive processing, a somewhat different situation exists when features must be combined across maps. For instance, imagine trying to locate a light-gray vertical target among randomly placed light-gray oblique and dark-vertical distractors (see Fig. 2B); the time to perform this task is dependent on the number of distractors present in the display, that is, increasing the number of distractors increases the time to locate the target. Therefore, determining the presence of a target based on a *conjunction* of features across two or more maps requires a serial item-by-item search. Furthermore, if a serial attention mechanism is used to locate a conjunction target and is moved randomly from location to location without repetition, then on the average the target should be found after searching through one-half of the items in the display. In contrast, displays with no target present should result in a search in which every distractor item is examined. Empirical evidence bears out this prediction, with no-target displays producing response times approximately twice as long as target-present displays with the same number of distractors. Thus, while individual perceptual dimensions may be processed in parallel, it is only through the application of serial attention to discrete locations that coherent percepts may be formed.

This role for serial search is consistent with earlier models of serial attention that center around the "spotlight" metaphor. The fundamental assumption of such models is that serial attention has the characteristics of a spotlight: it selects items within the spotlight, it is indivisible over spatial location, must be spatially moved from one location to another, and may be expanded or contracted to cover greater or smaller regions. However, while recent evidence suggests that there are many conditions under which this metaphor does not apply, questions about how attention is allocated do not significantly alter its role in the integration of features across maps.

2. Guided Search

While double conjunction searches (e.g., a conjunction between color and orientation) support the concept of serial search that combines information across feature maps, there is also evidence that additional information is used in guiding which items are actually examined. For instance, imagine a triple conjunction search in which the target is a large green vertical bar and the distractors are small red vertical, small green oblique, and large red oblique. In such a search, the target shares exactly one feature with each of the distractors; the time to perform this task is actually less than that found for a double conjunction search using the same number of distractors. Moreover, the time to locate a target increases at a slower rate as the number of distractors is increased when compared to the rate of increase for double conjunctions. A simple serial search model would not predict these results: rather, it would predict that regardless of the number of features shared between the target and the distractors, once features must be combined across maps, a serial search must be used to locate the target. Consequently, the integration of features cannot simply be a matter of searching item by item. Thus, more complex visual searches may be *guided* in some manner so as to reduce the overall number of items searched.

Another type of triple conjunction search yields evidence that helps to illuminate some of the mechanisms underlying complex visual search. For instance, imagine trying to locate a large green vertical target among small green vertical, large green oblique, and large red vertical distractors. In this search, the target shares two features with each of the distractors; the time to perform this task is comparable to that found for a double conjunction searches using the same number of distractors and the rate of increase per additional distractors is comparable as well. These results indicate that the information available to guide serial search mechanisms is dependent on the *relative* number of features present in the target as compared to the distractors. In both a double conjunction search and a triple conjunction search with double-feature distractors, the target differs from each distractor by only a single feature. However, in a triple conjunction search with single-feature distractors, the target differs from each distractor by at least two features. More recent evidence suggests that such examples reflect a more general principle in which visual searches become easier as the target and the distractors become less similar.

How might such information be represented preattentively so as to guide the serial stage in which features are combined? One possibility is that there exists an additional preattentive map that encodes the overall activation of all feature maps—an approximate sum of the features in common between the target and that distractor at each location. For a given location, the larger this sum is relative to other locations and noise inherent within the map, the more likely is the item at that location to be the target. Therefore, when the feature difference between the target and the distractors is great, the information provided by this map will allow the serial search mechanism to ignore some distractors and overcome any noise so as to quickly locate the target; in contrast, when the feature difference is smaller, the information provided by this map will not facilitate excluding many of the distractors or locating the target above the noise, consequently it will be less reliable in guiding the serial mechanism. Thus, preattentive mechanisms guide serial search so that the positions examined are not random; however, this guidance varies in efficiency depending on the featural relationship between the target and the distractors.

C. Combining Features

Beyond visual search tasks, there is the more general question of how disparate features within a given object are combined to form a coherent percept. One final piece of evidence adds further weight to the hypothesis that serial attention is necessary to integrate features. Imagine very briefly viewing a display containing a green "X," a red "S," and a yellow "T" adjacent to each other; observers often report seeing *illusory conjunctions* of features, for instance, a red "X" or a yellow "S." Apparently, without the benefit of time to allocate serial attention, features corresponding to a given spatial location are not *bound* together, that is, they may be combined incorrectly. The binding together of features across preattentive maps is one of the primary functions of serial attention. Moreover, as will be discussed in the following sections, a similar ''binding problem'' occurs at many levels of visual processing.

One highly speculative, but intriguing, neural mechanism for possibly solving the binding problem may involve the temporal responses of the neurons that serve as feature detectors throughout visual processing. While the concept of encoding stimulus properties through the firing pattern of populations of neurons is accepted in audition (i.e., to encode a sound with a frequency higher than the firing rate for individual neurons, a group of neurons may fire in a ''volley'' sequence that collectively indicates the frequency), it is relatively novel in vision. The essential idea is that neurons that encode individual feature properties for a given spatial location may be bound together by synchronizing their firing to a common rate. In this model there is no single neuron that represents the complex structure formed by a conjunction of features; instead, it is a population of neurons and their *temporal pattern* that represent this information. This hypothesis suggests at least one clue to the neural basis of serial attention: rather than simply being located in a particular brain structure, attention may involve mechanisms that enable representations of elements of an object or scene to be combined by the imposition of a common temporal code. As we shall see, this is a problem that must be solved not only for how features processed in parallel at each spatial position are combined, but also for the equally important issue of how features across *different* spatial locations are combined to reconstruct the more complex structures that are the basis of visual perception.

II. PERCEPTUAL ORGANIZATION

Subsequent to the feature analysis performed by early visual processing, the layout of the scene is represented as an array of spatially discrete local features. While such representations implicitly encode the structure of surfaces and objects depicted within the array, it is the goal of perceptual organization to make these and other structures explicit. Two distinct kinds of processes may be available to accomplish this: first *grouping* processes may be used to identify commonalties among local features indicating that they should be combined into more complex structures; second, *segmentation* processes may be used identify differences among local features indicating that they should be separated into discrete structures. Both kinds of processes may be said to be *inferential* in that they operate without the benefit of complete information about the scene (for example, viewing a house partially obscured by trees), instead relying on inferences based on partial data and regularities inherent in the physical world.

Perceptual organization is central to vision, as well as other perceptual modalities, in that it is only by first organizing and marking structure within perceptual input that more complex representations may be created. Indeed, the mechanisms that carry out this task are some of the most sophisticated and impressive to be found in human cognition—a fact that is obscured by the many salient demonstrations of perceptual organization. However, while perceptual organization forms a cornerstone of visual processing, it is perhaps one of the most poorly understood mechanisms of perception. Conversely, perceptual organization is also a mechanism that has generated a wealth of phenomena. Therefore, one common starting point for its study has been to enumerate its specific principles of operation.

A. Principles of Grouping

The most fundamental principles of perceptual organization were established by the gestalt school of psychology in the early part of the century. All of these principles are based on the idea that complexity should be minimized, that is, mechanisms of perceptual organization will ''prefer'' simpler interpretations over complex interpretations. The operation of this principle may be easily illustrated by several demonstrations among the many available phenomena associated with principles of organization. For instance, upon inspecting Figure 3A, most observers will report perceiving three rows of spheres rather than four columns. This illustrates the principle of *proximity,* whereby, all else being equal, elements that are spatially nearer to each other are more likely to be grouped together to form a larger structure. Likewise, upon inspecting Figure 3B, most observers will report perceiving four columns composed of either spheres or cubes rather than four rows of alternating elements. This illustrates the principle of *similarity,* whereby, again all else being equal, elements that are similar in shape, color, or other visual properties are more likely to be grouped together. Finally, upon inspecting Figure 3C, most observers will report perceiving lines that extend from disc to disc forming a triangle. This illustrates the principle of *good continuation,* whereby collinear edges or boundaries are grouped together.

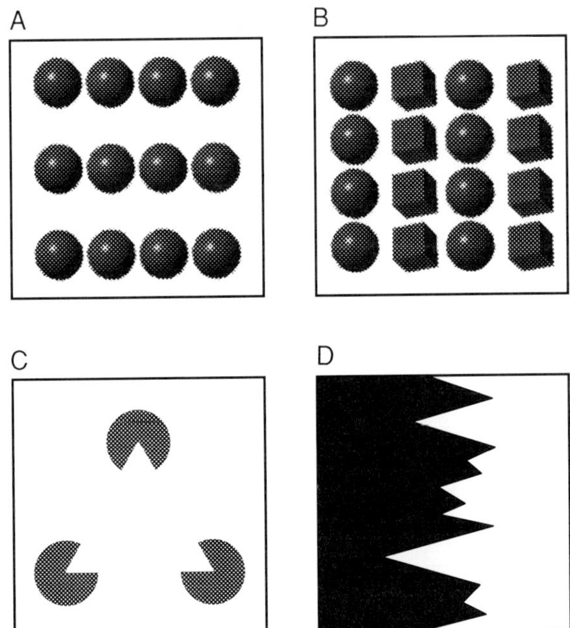

FIGURE 3 Principles of perceptual organization. (A) Proximity: Spheres are grouped into rows based on the proximity between elements. (B) Similarity: Spheres and cubes are grouped into columns based on the similarity between elements. (C) Good continuation: Collinear boundaries of triangular gaps in each disc are grouped to form continuous contours. Panel (C) also illustrates subjective contours; notice that a complete triangle is perceived, even though at some points there is no physical basis for inferring a boundary. (D) Figure–ground segregation: Depending on which side is considered the figure, a range of light or dark mountains may be perceived.

Figure 3C also demonstrates the efficacy of perceptual organization. In this display, not only are collinear boundaries grouped together, but there is an overall perception of an opaque triangle floating above three discs, each partially occluded by one point of the triangle. While edges of the triangle appear quite vivid, there is actually no physical basis for inferring a boundary between each of the discs (prove this by covering the discs). Such illusory edges are referred to as *subjective contours* and may function exactly like physically based edges in many perceptual phenomena, including optical illusions, further perceptual organization, and object perception. Thus, not only does perceptual organization mark structure within visual input, but it can serve to ''fill in the gaps'' in degraded or occluded objects.

B. Segmentation

While grouping processes are used for combining features, segmentation processes are used for segregating features and feature assemblies into discrete structures such as objects and parts. Segmentation often operates in conjunction with grouping, so for instance, two adjacent textures may be segregated into separate regions based on the similarity or proximity of elements within each texture. Another example of segmentation is illustrated in Figure 3D. This figure has two distinct interpretations: either a dark range of mountains with a plateau in the center or a light pair of mountains with several valleys in between (whatever the initial perception, the alternate may be easily perceived by attending to the half that is seen as sky). In each case, one half of the figure is considered to be most salient, called the *figure,* and the remaining half is considered to be background, or simply the *ground.* Notice that when one half is perceived as figure, the other half is always perceived as ground—only one interpretation is available at a time. This process of making one object or set of objects stand out from the rest of the scene, referred to as *figure–ground segregation,* is often considered a prerequisite for recognition mechanisms that match individual objects to stored object representations.

Another form of segmentation that may facilitate recognition is the segregation of objects into discrete parts. As will be discussed in the next section, part-based object representations offer a natural description of complex objects and categories. The decomposition of a given object into parts is consistent across different observers, indicating that a common mechanism is used to arrive at such a description. One possibility is that surfaces and objects are divided into parts by defining part boundaries at the points of greatest curvature within inward facing concavities along a surface or object contour. For instance, imagine a dumbbell shape; the part boundary will be located at the vertical midpoint of the dumbbell. This simple principle has a great deal of explanatory power for how parts are determined. In Figure 3D, it may be used to account for the boundaries between mountains: when the dark half is perceived as the figure, the divisions between the peaks are located in the lightly colored valleys; when the light half is perceived as the figure, the divisions shift and are located at the darkly colored valleys—always corresponding to the points of greatest curvature along inward facing concavities.

C. Nonaccidental Properties

By what general principles does perceptual organization operate? While it is often stated that ''simpler'' interpretations are preferred, it is difficult to arrive at a precise definition of what constitutes simple. One alternative is that preferred configurations of features are those that correspond to properties of meaningful physical structures, e.g., surfaces and objects. Consequently, perceptual organization may operate by exploiting regularities in input that are *nonaccidental* in that they arise due to regularities that are likely to occur in the physical world. A nonaccidental property may defined as a configuration of features for which the probability of occurring due to chance is essentially zero; or conversely, as a configuration for which the number of times it arises due to a coherent structure in the physical world is large compared to the times it arises through chance. Thus, it is to the advantage of the perceiver to consistently infer that particular feature configurations correspond to structure.

The principle of nonaccidentalness may be used to account for the grouping phenomena discussed earlier. For example, the principle of proximity may be explained by the fact that if two features are adjacent in an image, they are likely to be adjacent in the three-dimensional world. Because objects are composed of coherent surfaces and not random points, adjacent features are likely to sit on the same surface, and, consequently, should be grouped together. A similar explanation may be offered for the principle of similarity: because the textures of surfaces tend to be coherent, features that are similar are likely to have arisen from the same surface. Finally, good continuation may explained by the fact that surfaces tend to be smooth over large areas; therefore, collinear edges within an image are far more likely to correspond to a single boundary than to an accidental alignment of disconnected surface features. This explanation also accounts for the perception of subjective contours; in such instances, it is more likely that apparent gaps in objects and the alignment between gap boundaries arise because of occlusion by a single, coherent structure, than because of accidental collinearity between irregularly shaped forms.

Nonaccidentalness has been used to enumerate several additional properties of perceptual organization. In all such cases, a preference for particular feature configuration is based on the likelihood that the two-dimensional configuration reflects the presence of a similar property in the three-dimensional, physical world. Many of these "nonaccidental properties" are closely related to the principles of grouping: for instance, proximity of endpoints reflects a common termination point at a corner; collinearity and curvilinearity reflect features that are elements of a common edge or contour in three dimensions; and parallelism reflects edges that are parallel in three dimensions and therefore likely to denote the boundaries of an object. Finally, the property of symmetry about an axis has been identified as reflecting structures that are symmetrical in three dimensions. As will be discussed in the following section, nonaccidental properties may form the basis for recovering the structure of parts within objects.

III. OBJECT REPRESENTATION

A. Properties of the Representation

Following the perceptual organization of visual input, the layout of the scene is represented as a collection of coherent surfaces and objects. Indeed, there are many situations in which this representation may be sufficient for successful task completion. For example, navigating a hallway may only require detecting the presence of obstacles; likewise, grasping an object may only require noting its size and rough shape. In contrast, many of our interactions with the environment necessitate not only a knowledge of the physical properties of the scene, but the recognition, including both identification and categorization, of objects within the scene. In order to achieve recognition, two fundamental problems must be addressed: first, object representations must be *recovered* from perceptually organized visual input; second, recovered object representations must be *matched* to like-format representations stored in memory. Given this model of object recognition, it is the properties of the representation that will determine the efficiency and robustness of both recovery and matching. Therefore, this section begins with an introduction to four dimensions along which specific formats for object representations may vary from each other. It should be emphasized that these dimensions are independent of one another, so that a format formed by any combination of values along each is theoretically possible. However, as discussed in the latter part of this section, in practice, particular settings tend to co-occur, forming two major families of object representations.

1. Frames of Reference

In order to encode object shape, as well as other spatial properties, object representations employ a coordinate system in which the spatial positions of features are defined. Such a coordinate system is commonly referred to as a *frame of reference*. Generally, two distinct types of reference frames have been proposed for object representations; *object-centered* and *viewer-centered* (a third type of reference frame, environment-centered, is rarely posited for object representations, but has been implicated in spatial representations that are used for navigation). Object-centered and viewer-centered reference frames may be differentiated by whether the coordinate system is based on the object to be represented, or, alternatively, is based on the viewer (encompassing possibly the viewer's retina, head, or body). This distinction is illustrated in Figure 4. In an object-centered frame of reference (top to lower-left panels), the coordinate system moves with a rotation of the object; therefore, the description of the object is not altered by changes in viewpoint. In contrast, in a viewer-centered frame of reference (top to lower-right panels), the coordinate system does not move with a rotation of the object, but instead, remains based on the position of the viewer; therefore, the description of the object is altered by changes in viewpoint.

Given that successful recognition depends on a match between a stored object representation and perceptual input, the reference frame used will have consequences for how recognition mechanisms compensate for discrepancies in orientation. The fundamental property of an object-centered frame is that it is orientation independent: so long as the frame used to represent perceptual input is the same as that used for the corresponding object representation, the descriptions will match regardless of viewpoint. By comparison, the fundamental property of a viewer-centered frame is that it is orientation dependent: because changes in the orientation of either the viewer or the object will alter the description of perceptual input, the perceiver must normalize the orientation of the input to match the viewpoint of the corresponding object representation. This normalization may be accomplished by a mental transformation process in which the orientation of the perceptual input is modified by a transformation analogous to a physical rotation.

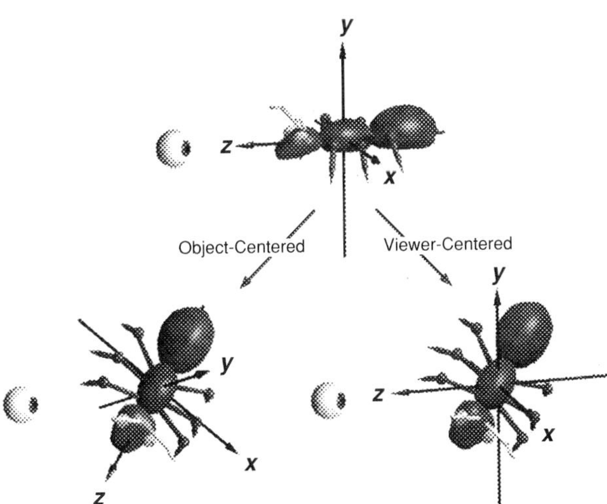

FIGURE 4 Object-centered and viewer-centered frames of reference. In an object-centered frame (top to lower-left), the coordinate system is based on the object, moving with the ant regardless of the position of the viewer. In contrast, in a viewer-centered frame (top to lower-right), the coordinate system is based on the viewer, remaining with the viewer regardless of the position of the ant. [Illustration by Scott Yu.]

2. Dimensionality

A second property of an object representation is the number of *spatial dimensions* encoded, varying from two to three dimensions. While physical objects are three-dimensional, the pattern of light that impinges upon the retina is two-dimensional. Because it is widely held that early visual processes use a variety of cues to recover depth, it is likely that object representations include at least three-dimensional distances between surface points. This relative depth coding has been referred to as "two-and-one-half-dimensional." In contrast, a complete three-dimensional reconstruction of the object would include information about the structure of all surfaces of an object, including those not present in the current viewpoint. One consequence of this is that three-dimensional representations may only be formed by exposure to many different views of an object or by inferences about unobserved structure from a limited number of views.

3. Parts

One of the most salient properties of physical objects is that they are composed of *parts*. Likewise, object representations may employ one of several schemes to encode the part structure of objects. Generally, parts have been defined in two ways: parts may be represented by *volumetric primitives* that are three-dimensional and capture the approximate shape of a given part of an object (see Fig. 5A); alternatively, as discussed in the previous section, parts may be delineated by a principle for locating the boundaries that specify where one part ends and another begins. These mechanisms are not mutually exclusive; the latter may be used to establish the locations of indi-

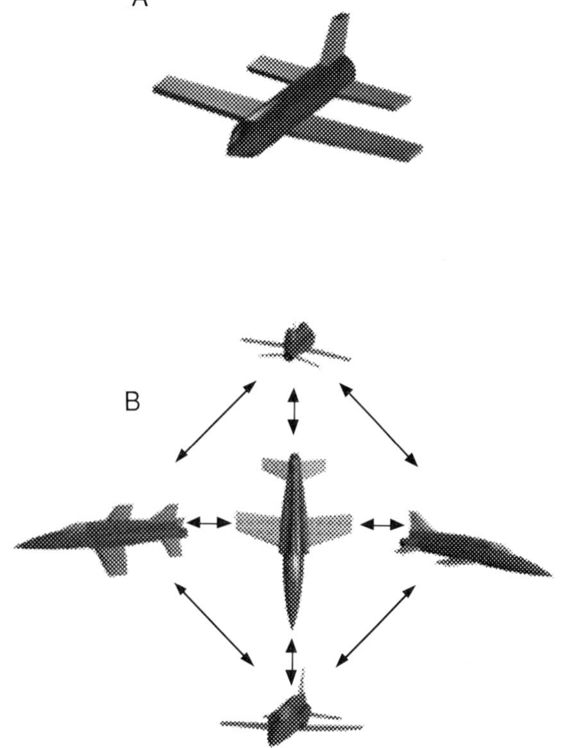

FIGURE 5 Families of object representation. (A) A structural description of an airplane composed of volumetric primitives. (B) A view-based representation of an airplane composed of multiple viewer-centered images. [Illustration by Scott Yu.]

vidual parts within an object, and the former may then be used to capture the shape of each part.

One of the most appealing aspects of using volumetric primitives to represent parts is that they facilitate the *coarse coding* of object shape. To understand why this is desirable, envision a model of object representation in which every variation in the shape of every part is encoded as a distinct entity. In such as scheme, even the most minute change in shape would result in a new part being represented, thereby producing an astronomical number of stored representations. Moreover, it would be difficult, if not impossible, to recognize two variants of the same object class as members of the same category (i.e., a kitchen chair and a desk chair). Even worse, it would be difficult to identify two variants of the *same object*—slight differences in shaping leading to completely separate representations. In contrast to this hypothetical model, a model employing a restricted number of volumetric primitives can represent many parts in an efficient manner. Not only does this reduce the amount of distinct information that must be represented, but it suggests that the same primitive may be used to approximate many variations in part shape. For instance, in Figure 5A, the primitive used to represent the fuselage of the plane may subsume many differently shaped fuselages. Therefore, many variations on this particular plane, as well as many somewhat differently shaped planes, may be categorized as the same type of object.

While volumetric primitives provide an elegant solution to the problem of representing parts, they also present two obstacles: First, primitives must be recovered from visual input with some consistency over changes in both part shape and position; second, it is unclear as to whether a restricted set of volumetric primitives is sufficient to capture all of the meaningful variations in part shape that may be encountered. These limitations may constrain the role of part-based representations in human object recognition.

4. Spatial Relations

Knowledge of parts alone is often inadequate for uniquely recognizing an object; for example, a cup and a bucket may be composed of the same two parts, a curved handle and an open-ended cylinder. In order to differentiate between objects sharing parts, the *spatial relations* between parts must be specified. One method of encoding spatial relations is to represent them implicitly. For instance, by preserving the spatial configuration of visual input within a two- or three-dimensional image array, the spatial positions of each of the parts are preserved. Because the relative positions of the parts are known, spatial relationships between them may be computed, although only by inspecting the image to determine a desired relation. Alternatively, spatial relations may be represented explicitly; that is, there may be a particular value assigned to the relationship between a part and a reference point. Explicit spatial relations may be highly specific, for instance, by using numerical measures of distance and angle, or categorical, for instance by using relations that correspond to spatial terms used in language (i.e., "above," "below," and "on"). As with volumetric primitives, using a restricted set of more general spatial relations offers advantages in terms of coarse coding and reducing the overall information load.

The choice of a reference point in explicit spatial relations suggests an additional property of object representations: whether spatial relations are encoded hierarchically or with regard to a single reference point for the entire object. For instance, [torso]

→ [arm] → [upperarm, lowerarm, hand] → [palm] → [fingers] is an example of a part hierarchy, while positioning all of these parts relative to the center of the torso is an example of a single-point representation. While descriptions using hierarchical spatial relations are likely to be somewhat more complex than single point arrangements, they offer certain advantages. First, at the highest level of the hierarchy the description of an object may be quite simple, including only a small number of diagnostic parts. Second, hierarchical representations capture the fact that objects frequently contain parts of many different sizes. Third, hierarchical representations facilitate the encoding of articulated parts in which spatial relations between two adjacent parts vary over a restricted range. This latter point is crucial for representing many natural objects; for example, the spatial relationship between our upper and lower arms is not fixed, but rather should be represented as a range of acceptable configurations.

B. Families of Object Representation

Combining variations of these four properties produces a wide range of possible formats for object representations. However, current research indicates that properties of object representations apparently cluster into two families: structural descriptions and view-based representations.

Object representations based on *structural descriptions* generally share the following defining properties: they are object-centered, composed of volumetric primitives, encode complete three-dimensional information, and use explicit categorical spatial relations between parts. Additionally, they often contain a hierarchical description in which smaller parts are located relative to adjacent relatively larger parts. Figure 5a illustrates a structural description for an airplane (although the representation can only be displayed two-dimensionally from one orientation and without explicit spatial relations). Two attributes are characteristic of structural descriptions. First, because they encode information in an object-centered frame of reference, visual tasks relying on structural descriptions are unaffected by changes in orientation, size, and position, as well as mirror-reflection of the object. Object identification tasks in which performance is invariant over variations in viewpoint are typically interpreted as evidence for structural descriptions. Second, because structural descriptions use volumetric primitives that produce a coarse coding of object shape, they are suitable for determining the basic categories of objects (e.g., "car" or "person"), but not specific individuals (e.g., "'65 Mustang" or "Bob").

One variant on structural description models uses a highly restricted class of volumetric primitives to represent parts. The complete set of primitives is generated by combining attributes of the cross-section and the axis of three-dimensional volumes that reflect any of several different nonaccidental properties. Each combination forms a unique three-dimensional volume, such as a brick or a cone. For example, a brick would be defined by edges terminating at common points at each of the corners and parallel edges along each of the faces. This approach offers a possible solution to the problem of consistently recovering volumetric primitives from visual input: because the primitives are based on combinations of nonaccidental properties, once a given configuration of properties is identified, the corresponding volumetric primitive may be inferred. Furthermore, this scheme has the advantage of basing part representations on features that are known to exist within visual input; therefore, the structure of these primitives is based on regularities of physical objects, thereby possibly having greater generality for adequately capturing variations in part shape.

One alternative to structural descriptions is the *view-based* family of object representations. View-based representations generally share the following defining properties: they are viewer-centered, use a boundary locating principle to define parts, encode two-dimensional information plus depth, and implicitly encode spatial relations. View-based representations depict the appearance of an object from a single viewpoint (sometimes called a "view"). Figure 5B illustrates several view-based representations for an airplane; each image differs from the others in viewpoint, representing different surfaces, parts, and object shape. Two attributes are characteristic of view-based representations. First, because they encode information in a viewer-centered frame of reference, visual tasks relying on view-based representations are affected by changes in the orientation, as well as possibly size and position, of objects. Identification tasks in which performance is systematically related to viewpoint are typically interpreted as evidence for view-based representations. Second, because view-based representations preserve the original viewpoint and shape of parts within objects, they are suitable for making fine discriminations between objects from within a category (e.g., differentiating between two faces or two models of cars).

One variant of view-based representations uses *multiple-views* to represent the three-dimensional structure of objects. While a view-based representation depicts an object from a single viewpoint, a more comprehensive representation may be formed by linking a set of nonoverlapping, or characteristic, views. For instance, in Figure 5B, five characteristic views of the airplane cover many of the part and surface configurations that are likely to be observed. A multiple-views model also introduces several associated mechanisms. First, in order to achieve a match between a view of an object and the same object observed in a nonmatching orientation, a mental transformation is used to *align* the object with the stored view. Mental rotation is a well-documented visual process that produces systematically longer response times for greater angles of rotation, a pattern consistent with the systematic effects of orientation found in identification tasks. Second, mechanisms are required for determining which viewpoints of an object should be instantiated as views. Research suggests that familiarity with a given viewpoint and the geometry of an object both play a role in this process. Therefore, the greater the number of times an object appears at a given viewpoint and the more that viewpoint does not overlap with stored views, the more likely it is that a view will be stored for that orientation. Indeed, the most familiar and visually salient viewpoint of an object, referred to as *canonical,* is the orientation from which an object is typically imagined and most easily identified.

Converging evidence from studies of object recognition, human memory, and human neuropsychology indicates that both structural descriptions and view-based representations are used in visual cognition. One robust finding has been systematic effects of object orientation on recognition times. The use of view-based representations is supported by naming tasks in which response times increase with distance from a familiar view of an object, rather than just the upright orientation. In contrast, the use of structural descriptions is supported by somewhat different recognition tasks in which responses times are unaffected by object orientation, for instance, categorizing objects. In human memory, conscious, or "explicit," memory for previous exposure to an object is sometimes impaired by changes in orientation, size, or mirror-reflection, indicating that explicit memory may be mediated by representations that are view-based. However, unconscious, or "implicit," memory for previous exposure to an object is sometimes unimpaired by changes in size or mirror-reflection, indicating that implicit memory may be mediated by structural descriptions. Finally, in human neuropsychology, there is a dissociation between the recognition of words and the recognition of visually similar objects, such as faces. This finding has been interpreted as evidence for two types of representations, one in which there is an extensive decomposition of parts into a structural description, and one in which there is little part decomposition, but detailed information about the appearance of the object. Together these results point to two systems for object representation: a structural description system most suited to categorizing objects according to their parts, and a view-based system most suited to recognizing objects from a specific viewpoint.

Bibliography

Biederman, I. (1987). Recognition-by-components: A theory of human image understanding. *Psychol. Rev.* **94,** 115–147.

Cooper, L. A., and Schacter, D. L. (1992). Dissociations between structural and episodic representations of visual objects. *Curr. Directions Psychol. Sci.* **1**(5), 141–146.

Farah, M. J. (1992). Is an object an object an object? Cognitive and neuropsychological investigations of domain-specificity in visual object recognition. *Curr. Directions Psychol. Sci.* **1**(5), 164–169.

Osherson, D. N., Kosslyn, S. M., and Hollerbach, J. M. (Eds.) (1990). "Visual Cognition and Action." MIT Press, Cambridge, MA.

Pinker, S. (Ed.) (1985). "Visual Cognition." MIT Press, Cambridge, MA.

Plaut, D. C., and Farah, M. J. (1990). Visual object representation: Interpreting neurophysiological data within a computational framework. *J. Cog. Neurosci.* **2**(4), 320–343.

Tarr, M. J., and Pinker, S. (1990). When does human object recognition use a viewer-centered reference frame? *Psychol. Sci.* **1**(42), 253–256.

Treisman, A. (1990). Features and objects in visual processing. In "The Perceptual World" (I. Rock, Ed.), pp. 97–110. Freeman, New York.

Wolfe, J. M., Cave, K. R., and Franzel, S. L. (1989). Guided search: An alternative to the feature integration model for visual search. *J. Exp. Psychol. Hum. Percept. Performance* **15,** 419–433.

VOCATIONAL CHOICE

Gary W. Peterson
Florida State University

Glossary

Career decision making A process that not only encompasses vocational choice, but also involves making a commitment and carrying out the actions necessary to implement the choice.

Career development The implementation of a series of integrated career decisions that provide a guiding direction to one's work.

Lifestyle The integration of decisions in the realms of career, personal and family relationships, and leisure that result in a guiding purpose or direction in one's life.

Vocational problem solving A complex set of thought processes involving the acknowledgment of a state of career indecision, an analysis of the causes, the formulation of alternative courses of action to achieve a state of decidedness, and the choosing of one of these alternatives.

VOCATIONAL CHOICE may be defined as a process of selecting an appropriate occupation that effectively matches one's personality characteristics and needs to the requirements of a given occupation. An appropriate choice may be considered as one in which there is a high probability that an individual will be able to successfully perform the work and to derive a sense of personal satisfaction. Thus, the act of choosing a vocation involves two important aspects: (a) the cognitive and affective processes involved in making a career decision at any point in time and (b) an estimation of the likelihood that a choice will result in occupational productivity and feelings of satisfaction and accomplishment. The text that follows examines the act of choosing a vocation from historical, psychological, and social perspectives.

I. OVERVIEW AND HISTORICAL PERSPECTIVES

Early accounts of process of choosing a vocation may be traced to the turn of the century when Frank Parsons wrote in his book *Choosing a Vocation* (1909) that there were three key factors in making a career choice: a clear self-understanding, a knowledge of occupations, and the ability to draw relationships between them. He reasoned that if individuals possessed these attributes, not only would they make more effective vocational choices, but that society in turn would be better served by greater efficiency in matching persons to appropriate kinds of work. Since then, this three-dimensional model may be considered as providing the fundamental framework for the investigation of how individuals make vocational choices.

Several principal lines of inquiry have emanated from this early work of Parsons. One has been directed toward helping individuals acquire self-understanding through the development of measures of interests such as the Kuder Preference Record in 1946 and the Strong Vocational Interest Blank (SVIB) in 1943. The original Kuder required individuals, using a pin-punch, to choose the most liked and least liked activity from a series of triads. The results of this interest inventory provided relative estimates of preference in seven areas of interest, including science, computational, art, music, literature, social, and persuasive. The SVIB, on the other

Encyclopedia of Human Behavior, Volume 4

hand, compared one's likes and dislikes for activities to the likes and dislikes of individuals successfully employed in a variety of occupations. Since the development of these early prototypes, more refined assessments have recently evolved to relate abilities, interests, and values to occupations such as the Kuder Occupational Interest Survey, the Strong Interest Inventory, and the Self-Directed Search. This direction of inquiry has now culminated in the introduction of sophisticated technological advancements in the development of computer-assisted career guidance systems such as SIGI PLUS and DISCOVER.

A second line of investigation sought to help individuals to become more knowledgeable about the world of work. Occupational classification systems, traced back to the U.S. Census Bureau's classification system in 1820, were developed to facilitate the storage and retrieval of information about related occupations. Modern classification systems include *Standard Industrial Classification Manual,* the *Dictionary of Occupational Titles,* and the *Dictionary of Holland Occupational Codes*. Computer-assisted career guidance systems have now incorporated these classification systems in their data bases and are able to link internally the results of the assessment of abilities, interests, and values to occupations.

A third line of inquiry has sought to develop psychological and sociological theories concerning how self-knowledge and occupational knowledge are integrated in the process of making vocational choices. These theoretical approaches may be categorized into five domains. The actuarial approach sought to identify empirical and rational linkages between measures of personality characteristics and attributes of occupations using successful job incumbents as population samples. Decision theorists describe stages of cognitive process in arriving at a vocational choice. Self-theories focus on the role of the self-concept as a referent in making vocational choices and career decisions. The impact of one's social context is described in social psychological approaches. And finally, cognitive information processing has been recently introduced as a comprehensive theoretical system integrating the four preceding approaches. These five theoretical domains will be heretofore presented in terms of their principle assumptions and propositions, most important concepts, and how the respective theories may be applied to help individuals make more satisfying vocational choices.

II. ACTUARIAL APPROACHES TO VOCATIONAL CHOICE

Theories of vocational choice included in this domain emphasize the derivation of empirical and rational estimates of the congruence between measured personality factors and occupational characteristics. The purpose of this approach is to provide precise information about one's self or occupations that will assist individuals in identifying appropriate occupational alternatives for further consideration. The fundamental assumption is that the greater the correspondence between personality characteristics and the requirements of an occupation, the greater the probability for successful performance and satisfaction. Important personality characteristics typically used to make predictions of success include cognitive abilities, scholastic aptitudes, interests, values, and special cognitive or psychomotor abilities. To illustrate this principle of using measures to make the best estimates of matches between persons and occupational environments, three types of actuarial approaches are described, trait-factor, the Holland Hexagonal Theory, and computer-assisted career guidance systems.

A. Trait-Factor Theory

From the standpoint of trait theory, personality may be considered as comprising a set of theoretical constructs, or dimensions, that exist along a continuum from low to high. Important personality dimensions in vocational choice relate to cognitive abilities, interests, values, and cognitive and psychomotor skills. An awareness of the extent to which certain dimensions are possessed allows individuals the opportunity not only to compare the strengths of their personality characteristics relative to others but relative to members of norm groups as well. Such information facilitates the acquisition of self-knowledge, one of the cornerstones in the Parson model. It also provides more precise information with which to estimate the degree of match between individual characteristics and the requirements of an occupation.

A *trait* may be defined as an enduring or persisting personality characteristic that provides a means by which individuals can be distinguished from one another, and is manifested consistently across a wide range of circumstances or situations. A *factor* is considered the operational form for measuring the existence of a trait such as an intercorrelated set of test items comprising a scale on an aptitude test or an interest inventory. Further, while traits were at one time assumed to be enduring neurologically based structures, many psychologists now believe that traits are highly influenced by learning and that they are task- or situation-specific. Nevertheless, while the nature–nurture aspects of traits are still unresolved, the kinds of human traits that play an important role in making vocational choices—such as interests, aptitudes, abilities, and values—do appear to be relatively stable over time. [*See* TRAITS.]

There are several key assumptions or propositions in relating trait and factor theory to vocational choice. One is that each individual possesses a unique and stable pattern of traits that can be measured empirically. Second, for each occupation, there is a unique pattern of traits required of individuals to perform the critical tasks of an occupation successfully. Third, the closer the match between a person's traits and the trait requirements of an occupation, the greater the likelihood of successful job performance and personal satisfaction. Thus, given these assumptions, if measures of traits could be developed with sufficient validity and reliability, individuals could use such information about their abilities, interests, and values to formulate appropriate occupational alternatives and to make more informed vocational choices. Measures such as the Kuder Preference Record, the Strong Vocational Interest Blank, the Differential Aptitude Test, and the Alport-Vernon Study of Values were developed to assist individuals in acquiring accurate appraisals of important job-related traits. In the early stages in the development of the actuarial approach, the drawing of relationships between measured traits and appropriate occupations was left to the individual and the assistance of a knowledgeable professional. The professional helped individuals identify possible career alternatives, located and presented the individual with relevant occupational information, and helped formulate a plan for an occupational search strategy. In some instances, a professional assisted individuals in locating and in obtaining appropriate training or job opportunities.

B. John Holland

The Holland typological theory relates personality characteristics to occupations on the basis of the old adage, "birds of a feather flock together." He extended the work of the trait and factor theorists by drawing empirical (in addition to logical) relationships between personality traits and selected occupations, of which there are over 1100 listed in the Occupations Finder. The principal theoretical presupposition undergirding Holland's work is that when individuals are classified on the basis of measured traits as belonging to a given occupational category, they can be linked to many occupational alternatives within that category. The empirical matching process enables individuals to quickly identify themselves as belonging to an occupational subgroup and to develop an array of corresponding occupational alternatives for consideration.

There are several key assumptions on which the Holland theory is based:

- Most individuals can be placed into one of six personality types: realistic, investigative, artistic, social, enterprising, or conventional (RIASEC). The relationship among these six personality types is portrayed in the form of hexagon (see Fig. 1) in which adjacent occupational groups on the hexagon have more in common in terms of personality characteristics than groups that are opposite one another.
- There are six occupational environments corresponding to the six personality types. According to Holland, people tend to surround themselves with others like themselves and hence create environments that reflect the type they are. Hence, R-type personalities are more congruent with R-type environments than S-type environments.
- An individual's behavior is determined by the interaction of personality and the environment.

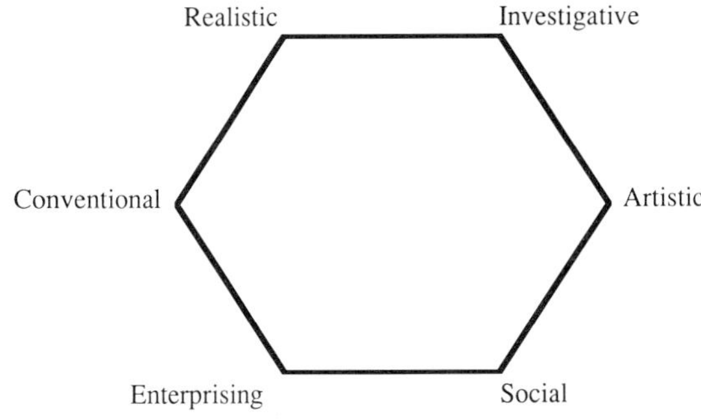

FIGURE 1 Holland hexagonal theory.

Thus, career phenomena such as vocational choice, career development, job satisfaction, and career achievement may be predicted from degree to which there is a match between personality and occupational environments.
- The degree of differentiation affects the strength of the match between person and the occupational environment. Differentiation refers to the strength of the person–environment match and the extent to which one or two interests are clearly different from the others. The more an individual is similar to one environment (S, for example) and less like others (for example R, C, or I), the greater the likelihood of satisfaction in that environment.

The six personality types and environments may be described as follows: *Realistic* personalities prefer things such as money, power, and status and possess mechanical and athletic abilities, whereas the corresponding R-type environment demands the explicit, ordered manipulation of objects, tools, machines, or animals as in automobile mechanic, surveyor, farmer, or electrician. *Investigative* people enjoy scholarly and intellectual activities and have mathematical and scientific interests, while the investigative environment demands systematic observation of physical, biological, or cultural phenomena as in biologist, chemist, medical technologist, or anthropologist. *Artistic* persons prefer ambiguous, free, unsystematic activities that lead to the creation of art forms or products, whereas this environment may be portrayed as unstructured and encouraging individuals to perceive the world in complex, unconventional, and flexible ways as in writer, musician, artist, interior decorator, and stage director. *Social* personalities like to help and understand others and prefer activities that entail informing, training, curing, developing, or enlightening people, while the social environment demands manipulation or the development of others to achieve social goals as in teacher, psychologist, social worker, or the clergy. *Enterprising* individuals prefer activities that entail persuading others to attain organizational or economic goals and possess leadership and speaking abilities, while the corresponding environment demands the manipulation of others to attain certain economic or organizational goals as in salesperson, buyer, manager, sports promoter, and television producer. *Conventional* people prefer activities involving the systematizing and manipulation of data, and the operating of data processing and work processing machines, while the conventional environment requires the manipulation and systematizing of information as in bookkeeper, financial analyst, banker, or tax accountant.

The Holland typological theory has been operationalized through the development of the Self-Directed Search (SDS), a measure that helps individuals determine their three highest personality codes (e.g., SAE or RIE), and the Occupations Finder, a resource that helps individuals locate occupations consistent with their three-point code. The three-point codes of many occupations were derived empirically from having job incumbents take the SDS, while the three-point codes of other occupations were derived from expert consensus and job analysis.

The compelling nature of Holland's theory lies in its parsimony as a theory, the ease of administration and scoring of the SDS, and the high degree of efficiency in locating potential matching occupations listed in the manual. The predictive validity of the three-point code in terms of training performance and job performance and satisfaction varies considerably across the codes and occupations. Thus, in vocational choice, the primary use of the SDS and the Occupations Finder should be to assist individuals in expanding their horizons of possible occupational alternatives to consider for further exploration. Following the identification of plausible occupations, individuals can obtain further occupational or educational information for the planning of an occupational or job search.

C. Computer-Assisted Career Guidance (CACG) Systems

CACG systems may be considered as representing the state-of-the-art in actuarial approaches to vocational choice. Almost all CACG systems provide an on-line interactive instructional medium that allows individuals an opportunity to assess some combination of interests, abilities, and values, to conduct a search for potential occupational alternatives, and to gain access to built-in career libraries of educational and occupational information. Some CACG systems may also include modules on such topics as career decision-making strategies, developing action-plans to implement a choice, the assessment of needs, an orientation to the world of work, information on financial aid, and assistance in coping with constraints that impede vocational choice and career decision-making. Examples of some of the more prominent comprehensive CACG systems are annotated as follows to provide a representation of the technological capabilities and features of these systems:

DISCOVER for College and Adults, developed by the American College Testing Program, is designed to assist individuals in identifying potential occupational alternatives through the assessment of interests, the self-rating of aptitudes, the evaluation of job experiences, and the prioritization of values. The DISCOVER program is partitioned into nine modules, examples of which include "Beginning the Career Journey," "Learning about the World of Work," "Learning about Yourself," and "Planning Next Steps." The program includes information about work tasks, salary range, and employment outlook on 497 occupations. It also contains information about 6,746 2- and 4-year colleges, graduate schools, and training institutions. A junior high school version of DISCOVER is also available.

SIGI PLUS, developed by the Educational Testing Service, helps individuals identify occupational alternatives based on a systematic exploration of values along with expressed interests, abilities, skills, educational objectives, or college major. The program introduces users to a decision-making paradigm, and provides strategies for securing jobs in the area of one's vocational choice. SIGI PLUS comprises nine modules, some of which include: "Self-Assessment," the assessment of values, interests, and abilities; "Search," the generation of a personalized list of potential occupations; "Information," the answers to 27 critical questions about 230 occupations; and "Preparing," descriptions of educational or training requirements for selected occupations. Information is also included on 800 educational and training institutions.

The Guidance Information System (GIS), developed by Riverside Publishing Company, contains information about colleges, professional schools, occupations, military careers, and financial aid. Information is available for over 489 occupations and over 5,200 educational and training institutions. While GIS does not possess an on-line assessment, it does allow for the input of the results of external assessments such as the Self-Directed Search, Career Assessment Inventory, and the Strong Interest Inventory. Six segments of the program include information about occupations, armed services occupations, 2-year colleges, 4-year colleges, graduate schools, and financial aid.

Even though CACG systems possess vast capabilities for the efficient storage and rapid retrieval of information, and contain information about a wide range of occupations and educational institutions, they are not recommended as stand-alone instruments to facilitate making vocational choices. The research literature suggests that even though individuals seeking career assistance express a strong liking for their experience with these systems, clients still prefer to use them as a helpful adjunct to the career counseling process. Further, the psychometric qualities of the embedded interest assessments, as well as the predictive validity of suggested occupations in terms of success in training programs or job satisfaction, have yet to be ascertained by well-controlled studies.

III. DECISION THEORIES

We turn now from theories that emphasize the development of measures and technology to increase the precision and capabilities of the person–occupation matching process to theories that focus on the actual thought processes that individuals might use in making vocational choices and career decisions. There is also a philosophical shift from deterministic views of vocational choice, in which career development is seen as a shaping process leading toward an optimal person–environment fit, to a more self-determined view in which individuals are seen as rationally choosing their optimal environments.

Some of the principal assumptions on which decision theories are based include: (a) the extent of freedom (and hence responsibility) one exercises in career choice depends on the amount of effort invested in thinking through one's vocational choices and career decisions; (b) making vocational choices and career decisions are cognitive processes that take place in a sequence of stages; and (c) the degree to which individuals can become self-determined career decision makers is related to the extent to which they master the cognitive skills, knowledge, and decision rules in the career decision-making process. Several decision-making models are presented that illustrate the application of these assumptions. While these may be considered by some to be relatively minor career theorists, they are nevertheless the principal theorists within this domain of career theory.

A. The Gelatt Model

A good decision is considered as one in which a systematic process is used to arrive at a choice and one in which the decision maker is willing to accept responsibility for his or her choice. The decision process may be described in five sequential stages as follows:

1. Define the purpose or objective of the decision.
2. Gather data from cognitive tests, performances in educational endeavors, and measures of personality characteristics.
3. Formulate a prediction system in which one examines plausible educational and occupational alternatives, anticipates possible outcomes, and estimates the probability of attaining the outcomes.
4. Engage one's value system by examining the desirability of each alternative in light of its relationship to all other important individuals, and social and spiritual dimensions of life.
5. Select a course of action and evaluate the outcomes according to one's individual success criteria.

After completing Stage 5, the decision maker returns to Stage 1 to ascertain whether the initial purpose of the objective of the decision has been met and to assess the extent to which the decision has influenced the attainment of short-term and long-term career goals. According to Gelatt, the overarching aim of career guidance is to teach "reflective thinking" and "positive doubting"—that is, the viewing of any choice as tentative and changeable in light of new information about one's self and the world of work. In his most recent writing, Gelatt refers to this state of tentativeness and ambivalence toward vocational choice as *positive uncertainty*.

B. The Katz Model

Career decision making, according to Katz, is based on the determination of values that undergird one's career goals. Examples of prominent values that bear on vocational choice are achievement, relationships, prestige, income, and leisure. The basic proposition is that a thorough examination of values will assist individuals in identifying occupations that will maximize the expression of these values. A computer-assisted career guidance system, the *System of Interactive Guidance Information* (SIGI), a forerunner of the SIGI PLUS CACG system described above, was based on this premise. Using the capabilities of an interactive computer program, an individual is systematically guided through a valuing paradigm which compels the clarification of the value system. This values clarification process culminates in a list of possible career alternatives.

Basically, the valuing process begins by having individuals estimate the strength of each given value relative to others. They are then given an array of career options generated by the computer and directed to examine each option in terms of its potential strength of return with respect to their value systems. The higher the value return for an occupation, the greater the person–job fit. Finally, the program calls for individuals to estimate the capability of attaining each high value-match option. The career options with both the greatest value-match (i.e., reward) and self-perceived likelihood of attainment (i.e., risk) would constitute the most appropriate career options.

The reason why this decision paradigm is placed here in decision theories rather than in the actuarial theories is that occupational alternatives are generated from a self-determined value structure and one's own knowledge and perceptions of a variety of occupations. In the strict actuarial approach, a manual or a computer provides options given certain score parameters on interest, ability, or values measures. With SIGI, individuals must not only actively derive a value structure, but they must also determine the relationships between their values and their perceptions and knowledge of computer-generated options. In other words, individuals are more active participants in the person–occupation matching process.

C. The Miller-Tiedeman Model

The following is a four-level stage theory advanced by Miller-Tiedeman, which also provides a heuristic for career decision-making:

- *Level 1:* Learning about the problem. Here an individual attempts to differentiate among alternative career goals; collects and lists occupational alternatives; selects viable alternatives; lists advantages and disadvantages of each alternative; and finally considers his or her values to arrive at a first choice.
- *Level 2:* Initiating the solution. The individual now converts thinking into action by orienting his or her behavior in a particular direction.
- *Level 3:* Carrying out the solution. The individual now becomes fully committed to carrying out the choice.

- *Level 4:* Reviewing the solution. The effectiveness of the solution is examined in light of the problem defined in Level 1.

With this decision model, Miller-Tiedeman recognizes that the greatest amount of cognitive energy is invested in the first stage and progressively decreases to Stage 4. At the same time, there is a constant tension between what one feels is right for one's self and what our culture says is right. The awareness and reconciliation of these forces enables one to transfer the decision process to other spheres of life.

One of the important contributions of the above career decision theorists is that they call our attention to the complex thought processes involved in making and implementing a vocational choice. Moreover, these cognitive processes can be described in terms of a systematically ordered sequence of events which can serve as an overarching heuristic to guide the process. Finally, by focusing on the process of career decision making and helping individuals master a decision paradigm, individuals acquire the ability to make subsequent vocational choices more independently. The old adage, "Give a man a fish and he eats for a day, but teach a man to fish and he eats for a lifetime," captures the essence of the ultimate aim of the decision theory approach. While the decision theorists believe it is important to help individuals make an appropriate vocational choice at given point in time, it is more important to provide the learning experiences that will provide the foundation to make appropriate choices anytime a career decision is called for in the future. Thus, the decision at hand is viewed as an opportunity to assist individuals in mastering career decision-making skills.

IV. SELF AS AN INTEGRATING FACTOR

Self theorists allude to a higher-order cognitive process that transcends such activities as the consideration of occupational alternatives or the making of specific career decisions. Phenomena such self-concept and self-efficacy not only provide an integrating force that bears directly on the consideration of occupational alternatives in the making of a career decision at any point in time, but they also span successive career decisions over the lifespan and give a career or one's life continuity. When individuals possess positive self-concepts or a high degree of self-efficacy, career decisions are made as a matter of course in moving through the life span. However, the process of vocational choice and career decision making become excruciatingly difficult in the presence of a negative or fragmented self-concept or when one's self-efficacy is low. Self-concept theory and self-efficacy theory are presented below to illuminate this important dimension of vocational choice.

A. Donald Super

Over his long career, Super has developed one of the most comprehensive theories of vocational choice. However, for purposes of this article, only the components of his theory concerning the role of self-concept is described, which incidentally constitute a major part of his writings. Some of the key propositions of his theory concerning the development of the self-concept include:

- Career development is essentially a process of developing and implementing one's self-concept, or in later writings, self-concept systems. A *self-concept* is the product of the integration of inherited aptitudes, physical makeup, the opportunity to play various roles, and the extent to which these roles are reinforced by peers, parents and superiors. [*See* CAREER DEVELOPMENT.]
- While the self-concept begins to stabilize in late adolescence, it continues to evolve throughout the life span as a result of life's experiences and making choices.
- The degree of satisfaction people attain from work is in proportion to the degree to which they are able to implement their self-concepts.

The implementation of self-concepts may be thought of as a matching process in which individuals relate their perceptions of attributes of themselves to their perceptions of attributes of occupations. This matching process may be *static,* focusing on a single vocational choice; or it can be *developmental,* relating a series of vocational choices to a common integrated theme. The implementation of the self-concept in making career decisions over time enhances the evolution of one's identity; and as one's identity develops and becomes clearer and attains a more stable and complex structure, one's self-concept becomes more positive as well.

One of the implications of self-concept theory for vocational choice is that the degree to which a self-concept varies from positive to negative, or the extent to which it is developed in terms of its structural complexity, directly influences how occupational alternatives are viewed. Negative self-concepts will overly restrict the formation of an array of viable options. Thus, even though an individual may use an interest inventory or a CACG system to generate a list of plausible options, because of a negative self-concept, the individual may likely reject many, if not most, of the alternatives.

An immature or undifferentiated self-concept will often result in the inability to discriminate among interests such that either almost all occupations generated by an interest inventory or a CACG system may seem plausible or, on the other hand, very few seem plausible. Undifferentiated self-concepts may also result in computers producing long, nearly randomly generated lists of occupations without focus. Finally, undifferentiated self-concepts may foster a lack of consistency among vocational choices over time. Thus, when there is no consistent self-referent to guide lower-order decision-making processes, wide-ranging and frequent changes in educational or career aspirations are a common outcome.

Another common occurrence in the vocational choice process is that even if an individual arrives at a first choice of an occupation, a person with a negative self-concept will tend to disconfirm the choice because it is perceived to be unattainable, thus fostering a state of chronic indecision. In the presence of a negative self-concept, group career counseling interventions have been found to be effective, such as a job club, where individuals may express their fears and doubts while obtaining social support in the formation and exploration of career alternatives.

B. Self-Efficacy

Bandura defined *self-efficacy* expectations as people's judgments of their capabilities to organize and execute actions necessary to attain specific kinds of performances. These expectations influence whether a course of action will be initiated, the amount of effort invested in the action, persistence in attaining the desired level of performance, the amount and kinds of cognitive processing, and the affective reactions when confronted with obstacles. Self-efficacy is viewed as a dynamic aspect of the self-system that is primarily domain-specific and interacts with other persons in the immediate environment. The principal proposition of the theory is that accurate and strong self-efficacy expectations are vital to the initiation and maintenance of any goal-directed behaviors. Bandura speculated that self-efficacy beliefs pertaining to a task may be shaped or modified by (a) perception of past performance, (b) modeling the behavior of others, (c) verbal support or persuasion, and (d) emotional or psychological arousal experienced in the conduct of the task.

Hacket and Betz extended self-efficacy theory into the area of career development proposing that self-efficacy influences career decisions, achievements, and occupational adjustment. Self-efficacy beliefs have been found to be related to other career phenomena including the range of perceived options, educational attainment and persistence, career indecision, work performance, and the effects of job loss. Additionally, Hacket and Betz have found that self-efficacy is related to the extent to which females pursue traditionally male-dominated academic subjects and occupations. Nevertheless, while the application of self-efficacy theory into the realm of vocational choice appears to be a promising avenue of investigation, little is known at the present time about how self-efficacy beliefs develop, how they are maintained, or how they can be altered through education or therapeutic intervention. [*See* SELF-EFFICACY.]

V. SOCIAL PSYCHOLOGICAL PERSPECTIVES

From this theoretical viewpoint, vocational choice is seen as a process heavily influenced by the interaction with important individuals in one's social context. Ann Roe is selected as one of the representatives of this domain of career theory because she speaks to the importance of the family environment in shaping predispositions toward certain kinds of careers. Krumboltz, on the other hand, describes how vocational choice is shaped through social learning processes.

A. Ann Roe

Roe hypothesized that early childhood experiences and relationships between offspring and parents significantly influence vocational choice in adulthood. The fundamental premise is that individuals gravitate toward and feel most comfortable in occupational environments that resemble the ones in which they were raised as children. She formulated six types of parent–child relationships and corresponding occupational environments:

1. *Protective*. This is a child-centered environment where parents are indulgent, demonstrably affectionate, and grant the child special privileges. Children will gravitate toward the service occupations, the arts, and entertainment fields.
2. *Demanding*. The demanding environment may be described as one in which parents set forth high expectations for accomplishment, impose strict rules, and require obedience to them. Children growing up in this type of environment may be oriented toward general culture (lawyers, teachers, scholars, librarians) or to the arts and entertainment fields.
3. *Rejecting*. In this environment, the child is not accepted as a child, perhaps not even as an individual, and it may be described as cold, hostile, and derogatory, thus making the child feel inferior and unaccepted. Children from rejecting environments tend to pursue occupations in the sciences.
4. *Neglecting*. Parents provide minimum physical care and less emotional sustenance, giving little attention either positive or negative. Children from neglecting environments develop science or outdoor interests.
5. *Casual*. This environment may be described as conditional, where parents give emotional or physical attention only after higher-priority needs in their own lives have been met. Children treated casually gravitate toward technological occupations such as engineers, aviators, and applied scientists, or to organizational occupations as bankers, accountants, and clerks.
6. *Loving*. The parents are warm, helpful, and affectionate and set limits and guide behavior through rational problem solving. They help the child with activities, but are not intrusive. Children from such an environment tend toward service or business contact occupations, for example promoters or salespersons.

These six types may be envisioned as aligned in a circle in which adjacent environments are most similar. Children who experience loving, protecting, or demanding environments move toward occupations involving people, whereas children from rejecting, neglecting or casual parent–child environments gravitate to occupations involving the manipulation of objects or things.

An assessment of ostensible influences of one's parent–child relationships on occupational considerations may be conducted through the use of a genogram in which the family tree is portrayed in the form of a diagram spanning three generations. Family rules and themes emerge as individuals trace their occupational histories over the generations. Another assessment technique is an occupational card sort in which individuals sort cards, each with an occupation printed on it, into groups of related occupations. Individuals are asked to label each group and to designate the one that is most like father, like mother and like one's self. Inquiries about family relationships may be made following the labeling of the groups. Further, through an exploration of family histories and relationships, individuals acquire additional perspectives that bear on occupational adjustment, such as how they respond to authority figures, the kinds of socio-emotional environments that seem most familiar or comfortable, how work and leisure are balanced, and attitudes toward task completion and accomplishment. By becoming aware of such unarticulated forces in one's life, self-knowledge is enhanced thereby increasing one's capability for critically evaluating plausible occupational alternatives.

B. John Krumboltz

From the standpoint of social learning theory, the social environment provides the context for learned behavior. Since vocational choice can be ultimately thought of as an instance of learned behavior, it can be understood from the behavioral paradigm. According to proponents of social learning theory, such as Albert Bandura, there are three principal types of learning: *Instrumental learning or operant conditioning,* in which the probability of a response is altered by the frequency, recency, and intensity of events contingent upon the response; *associative or classical conditioning,* in which the learning is the result of the pairing of a significant event with a neutral event and the latter acquiring the power to invoke the same response as the initial significant event; and *modeling,* in which a behavior is acquired by observing and copying others and then being reinforced for the mimicked behavior. Krumboltz applied these principles of social learning to the realm of vocational choice. Some of the important factors that influence vocational choice and career decision making include:

- *Genetic endowment and special abilities.* Personality characteristics such as race, gender, and physical abilities or disabilities, as well as particially-determined genetically determined talents such as intellectual, musical, artistic, and kinesthetic may delimit career options open to individuals.
- *Environmental conditions and events.* These are factors that are out of control of the individual, which may either enhance or constrain the array of career options open to individuals for consideration. Examples of such factors include the availability of jobs or educational opportunities, job entry criteria, salaries, labor laws and policies, family expenses and resources, and community resources.
- *Learning experiences.* Every individual possesses a unique repertoire of learned responses through the interaction between one's inherited characteristics and the environment. Instrumental learning, those responses reinforced through contingencies such as grades earned in school; associative learning, responses acquired through paired conditioning, such as attitudes toward and occupation held by someone admired or disliked; and modeling, a form of associative learning, are additional factors that influence the attractiveness of potential career options.
- *Task approach skills.* These learned skills interpret the environment in relation to self-knowledge and world knowledge and make predictions about future events. Such skills include perceptual and cognitive processes (such as symbolic rehearsal), attention and memory, mental sets, and work habits.
- *Self-observational generalizations.* These comprise the learned elements of self-knowledge and are general conclusions about ourselves resulting from self-observations in a variety of situations. These generalizations can be subdivided into three domains; task efficacy, the evaluation of our performances compared to others; interests, the conclusions of whether we like or dislike certain kinds of experiences; and values, generalizations about the desirability of certain behaviors.
- *World-view generalizations.* These generalizations are conclusions, derived from instrumental and associative learning, about the social and physical environment we have experienced. Also included in world view generalizations are the stereotypes and impressions of occupations and the occupational world.

Krumboltz' application of social learning theory to vocational choice calls our attention to the many factors in one's life history and in the environment that influence the consideration of career options and our career decisions over the lifespan. Further, while the theories of Roe and Krumboltz are perhaps more explanatory than predictive, they nevertheless demonstrate how the act of choosing a vocation is influenced by social learning from a myriad of environmental events occurring throughout life. [*See* CLASSICAL CONDITIONING; OPERANT LEARNING.]

VI. COGNITIVE INFORMATION PROCESSING

Recently, Peterson *et al.,* in their book *Career Development and Services: A Cognitive Approach,* introduced from the field of cognitive psychology a new and comprehensive perspective on vocational choice and career development that seeks to integrate earlier theoretical viewpoints described above. The cognitive information paradigm (CIP) was initially formulated in works of Newell and Simon in their book *Human Problem Solving* and from other cognitive scientists in the late 1970s. CIP concerns the thought and memory processes involved in making vocational choices and career decisions as contrasted with the decision theorists who thought mainly in terms of stages in a process. Further, in applying the CIP theory to practice, the emphasis in career counseling and guidance shifts from helping individuals to make an appropriate choice at a given point in time, to the acquisition of knowledge and cognitive skills to solve career problems and to make career decisions over time. Therefore, the aim of this approach is to help people become skillful vocational problem solvers.

A. Assumptions

Some of the key assumptions on which the application of CIP to vocational choice is based include:

- *Making vocational choices is a problem-solving activity*. A *vocational problem* is defined as a gap between a state of indecision and a state of decidedness pertaining to a career goal or direction. *Vocational problem solving* is defined in terms an information transformation process in which a series of thought processes is used to arrive at a course of action to remove the gap. Thus, vocational problem solving involves the transformation of information through the recognition of a gap (problem definition), an analysis of its causes, the formulation of alternative courses of action, and the selection of one of the alternatives that represents the most optimal solution. Career problems are exceedingly complex involving an ambiguous cue function, the optimization of solution alternatives, and the lack of certainty that the anticipated outcomes of the choice will remove the gap.
- *The capabilities of vocational problem solvers depend on the availability of cognitive operations as well as knowledge*. An analogy can be made to the functions of the computer. Data files represent occupational knowledge and self-knowledge stored in long-term memory, while the programs are cognitive algorithms, also stored in long-term memory, which are used to transform the data into new, and more useful and meaningful forms of information. In this way, relationships between self-knowledge and occupational knowledge are formulated through a series of problem-solving and decision-making algorithms.
- *Career development involves continual growth and change in knowledge structures*. Self-knowledge and occupational knowledge consist of sets of organized memory structures called *schemata* (singular schema) that evolve over the lifespan. Since both the occupational world and individuals are ever changing, the need to develop and integrate these domains never ceases.
- *The aim of career counseling and guidance is to facilitate the development of information processing skills*. From a CIP perspective, career counseling involves providing the conditions of learning that enhance the acquisition of self and occupational knowledge and the development of cognitive problem-solving and decision-making skills that are necessary to cope with inevitable occurrence of gaps between indecision and decidedness that arise in the course of a lifetime.

B. Structural Attributes of CIP

In order for individuals to become independent and responsible vocational problem solvers and career decision makers, certain information processing capabilities must undergo continual development throughout the life span. From an adaptation of the works of Robert Sternberg, these capabilities may be envisioned as forming a pyramid of information processing domains with three hierarchically arranged domains. Two knowledge domains, self-knowledge and occupational knowledge, lie at the base of the pyramid with the decision skills domain placed above it and the executive processing domain at the apex.

Information from the respective knowledge domains is combined using the information processing skills of the *decision skills domain*. These skills, referred to as generic information processing skills, are configured in the form of a recursive cycle (i.e., the CASVE cycle). They are used as a heuristic in the career decision-making process as follows:

1. Information is received which signals that a problem exists. One then queries oneself and the environment to formulate the gap (or discontinuity) that is the problem. This receiving and encoding of signals and sending out queries, *communication* (C).
2. The causes of the problem are identified and the relationships among problem components are placed in a conceptual framework, *analysis* (A).
3. Possible courses of action are formulated, *synthesis* (S), through the elaboration of possibilities and the subsequent narrowing to a manageable set of viable alternatives.
4. Each course of action is evaluated and prioritized according to its likelihood of its success in removing the gap and its probable impact on self, significant others, and society, *valuing* (V). Through this process a first choice emerges.
5. A planning strategy, related to educational or training programs, reality testing, or employment, is formulated to implement the choice, *execution* (E).
6. Upon executing the plan, there is a return to the communication phase to evaluate whether the

decision successfully removed the gap. If so, the individual moves on to solve succeeding problems that arise from the implementation of the solution. If not, one recycles through the CASVE cycle with new information about the problem, one's self and occupations acquired from the initial passing through the CASVE cycle.

There is yet a set of higher order of cognitive functions that guide and regulate the lower order functions in the pyramid, the executive processing domain. This domain comprises metacognitions that (a) control the selection and sequencing of cognitive strategies to achieve a goal, and (b) monitor the execution of a given problem-solving strategy to determine if the goal is being reached. A third vital component of this domain consists of the beliefs, assumptions, and awareness of one's self as a vocational problem solver that are necessary to effectively carry out the lower order functions of the pyramid. Dysfunctional beliefs or assumptions pertaining to any facet of the respective domains will inhibit the development of career problem-solving and decision-making skills. Extending the computer analogy, they default lower-order information processing. [*See* METACOGNITION.]

A career counseling environment emphasizing self-directed exploration can be developed along the lines of the paradigm to assist individuals in progressing through the various stages in the career decision process. Self-instructional modules can be made available to assist individuals in progressing through the phases of the CASVE cycle; a comprehensive career library may serve as a resource center for acquiring occupational information; and computer assisted career guidance systems help individuals to clarify interests, abilities and values and to formulate possible career options when individuals reach the synthesis phase of the decision cycle. Career advisors and counselors provide assistance in defining and analyzing the career problem, diagnosing one's capabilities as a vocational problem solver, designing individualized learning plans (ILPs) to master components of the pyramid, and achieving mastery of the paradigm so that each client uses his or her presenting problem as an instance in becoming a more proficient career decision maker.

VII. SPECIAL CONSIDERATIONS

Race, gender, ethnicity, age, family background, socio-economic status, and physical disabilities all may be considered as psychological "background factors" that bear on the vocational choice process. All of these actively influence such career phenomena as stereotyping, academic self-confidence, fear of success or failure, levels of career aspiration, mastery strivings, career commitment, risk-taking attitudes, work motivation, and opportunities for access and advancement in the workplace. Such factors also influence the development of one's personality structure that forms the basis of identity, knowledge structures of the world of work, meanings that are derived from work, the ways life and career problems are framed, the thought processes used to derive career options and evaluate their prospects, and one's view of personal success.

Differences among individuals in background factors such as race, gender, ethnicity, age, disability, and socio-economic status and their effects on vocational choice can perhaps be understood from the standpoint of culture. From a career development perspective, *culture* is defined as a system of beliefs, values, customs, and institutions shared and transmitted by members of a particular society, from which people derive meaning from their work, love, and leisure activities. Thus, each factor may be thought of as contributing to forming a basis for belonging to a certain subculture of society, each sharing its unique values, beliefs, and career orientations. The following assumptions regarding cultural differences may be applied to how these background factors influence vocational choice:

1. *Culture is a determinant of meaning.* Each subgroup possess its own meanings regarding the nature of work itself, the relation of work to family and leisure, and the relative importance of intrinsic and extrinsic motivational factors.

2. *Culture as determinant of communication.* Misunderstandings between members of different cultures occur not because people use different vocabularies or languages to describe the same constructs, but because common words are used with different semantic meanings, and because different cognitive reasoning processes are used to arrive at truth. Thus, the pragmatic aspects of human communication influence not only internal thought processes involved in making individual choices, but also interactions within and between members of different subgroups. As our society moves toward a more pluralistic work force, the pragmatics of human communication will play an

increasingly important role in maintaining productive work groups.

3. *Cultural relativity*. Even though there are differences among cultural subgroups, no subgroup is objectively superior to another. Further, we come to know our own group through the formation of contrasts between one's own and others. Thus, instead of differences serving as a basis for dividing people and forming barriers to access and opportunity, differences should become vehicles to higher understandings of ourselves, our groups, our work, and our society.

Differences among individuals, as determined by membership in subgroups or cultures, introduce important factors in shaping one's identity, and therefore how vocational choices are made and integrated over the lifespan in a consistent, unified direction.

VIII. SUMMARY

Vocational choice, as a field of inquiry in psychology, has received the attention of theorists and researchers for almost a century, and has been driven by a very practical issue; namely, How can individuals select meaningful and satisfying work in which they can become productive members of pluralistic and free society? The theories vary in terms of descriptive, explanatory, predictive, and heuristic emphases. For example, the trait and factor theories emphasize prediction, decision theories are heuristic, self theories and social theories are descriptive and explanatory, while cognitive information processing theory seeks to be comprehensive but is still explanatory and heuristic. All theories are useful and provide essential perspectives for practitioners of the science and craft of career counseling. Some of the emerging issues in the field of vocational choice include the expanding of a theoretical and research base on the influences of gender, culture, ethnicity, and physical disabilities on vocational decision making, job satisfaction, and job performance. Moreover, the role of mental health in career choice, the optimal use of technology, and ascertaining how the knowledge structures, cognitive skills, and attitudes can be developed through education and career guidance are additional important research thrusts leading into the next century. Expectations are that the field will continue to evolve as the ability to make sound vocational choices becomes an increasingly important survival skill in a rapidly changing society—a society wrought by powerful global and national forces moving us toward greater pluralism in the labor force, a peacetime market economy, an expanding population growth, and an ever greater use of technology in the production of goods and services.

Bibliography

Brown, D., and Brooks, L. (1990). "Career Choice and Development: Applying Contemporary Theory to Practice," 2nd ed. Jossey-Bass, San Francisco, CA.

Herr, E., and Cramer, S. (1992). "Career Guidance throughout the Life Span: Systematic Approaches," 4th ed. Little, Brown and Co., Boston, MA.

Isaacson, L., and Brown, D. (1993). "Career Information, Career Counseling, and Career Development," 5th ed. Allyn & Bacon, Boston, MA.

Jones, L. (Ed.) (1992). "The Encyclopedia of Career Change and Work Issues." Oryx, Phoenix, AZ.

McDaniels, C. (1990). "The Changing Workplace: Career Counseling Strategies for the 90's." Jossey-Bass, San Francisco, CA.

Peterson, G. W., Sampson, J. P., Jr., and Reardon, R. C. (1991). "Career Development and Services: A Cognitive Approach." Brooks/Cole, Pacific Grove, CA.

Super, D., and Hall, D. (1978). Career development: Exploration and planning. *Annu. Rev. Psychol.* **29,** 333–372.

Walsh, B., and Osipow, S. (Eds.) (1990). "Career Counseling: Current Topics in Vocational Psychology." Erlbaum, Hillsdale, NJ.

Walsh, B., and Osipow, S. (Eds.) (1988). "Career Decision Making." Erlbaum, Hillsdale, NJ.

Wegmann, R., Johnson, M., and Chapman, R. (1988). "Work in the New Economy." AACD Press, Alexandria, VA.

War

Richard A. Gabriel
U.S. Army War College

Karen S. Metz
Saint Anselm College

Glossary

Cerebral cortex The frontal lobe of the brain within which is located the ability to process and abstract information. These abstractions form the basis of reality for the human animal.

Conoidal bullet A type of bullet made of soft lead with a hollow rear area that expanded under the gas pressure of exploding powder. Upon expansion, the rear area pressed outward against the rifle grooves of the barrel, which provided greater stability for the bullet. It increased the range of the musket by a factor of three.

Cordite An explosive, initially of British manufacture, that was more stable and powerful than black powder. When used in artillery shells, it increased both range and explosive power.

Dispersion The ratio of fighting men or vehicles per given area of ground. With increases in mobility and firepower, smaller numbers of men could control larger areas thereby reducing the number of soldiers required to perform a given mission.

Factory system A system of manufacture that permitted large numbers of workers to work within a single work area. This system replaced the traditional crafts system and laid the groundwork for the Industrial Revolution.

Interchangeability of parts Machining parts to specific tolerances allowed their assembly much more rapidly and with fewer errors. It also allowed the decentralization of the manufacturing process so that no one person was responsible for the entire assembly process. Generally attributed to Eli Whitney, the concept permitted a great expansion in the numbers of weapons that could be manufactured by semi-skilled labor.

Peacening response The instinct/reflex of animals to cease combat once one combatant sends submissive signals. This response is generally absent in human combat or, at least, severely reduced.

Psychology of war The general tendency to see war as a normal social function where once it had been regarded as merely ritual or sport. Unless populations regard war as a normal part of their social existence, war is not possible.

Social primate carnivore A unique development attributable only to man wherein his physiology is derived from primate roots while his social behavior is derived from social carnivores such as pack dogs and wolves.

Strategic range The distances over which armies can project power and conduct military operations over time.

THERE WAS LITTLE in the origins of the human species that suggested it would become the most aggressive and expert predator on the planet. Although originally derived from primate stock, man evolved into a social primate carnivore, a development unique on the planet. As a social carnivore, man is equipped by his evolutionary biology with the means to be a highly efficient predator. At the same time, however, this predatory primate demonstrates a high degree of social cooperation that can place limits upon the degree of savagery he is willing to inflict upon members of his own species. And yet, more than any other predator, man demonstrates a willingness to kill his own kind more frequently and on a larger scale than any other social carnivore. Are the roots of this behavior, which we call warfare, truly sown into his genes?

I. ORIGINS OF WAR

In explaining the tendency toward war among the human species, it is often suggested that the roots of war lie in the aggressive instinct that men share with animals. This view finds its normative expression in the argument that all animals are aggressive and that, as a species of animal, man has aggression deeply embedded in his biological and social nature. Accordingly, the manifestation of aggression and warfare must be accepted as an unchangeable fact. This view ignores considerable evidence to the contrary. [*See* AGGRESSION.]

It is commonly assumed that aggression and killing in man and animals are one and the same thing, and that killing follows routinely from aggression. In the animal world, aggression is central to the successful hunt and kill, but such aggression is normally directed at targets outside the species. Aggression among animals within the species is almost never directed at achieving a kill. When directed at members of the same species, it serves more useful functions such as obtaining mates, territory, and food. Killing members of one's own species as a consequence of aggression is a rare occurrence among animals, and most often seems to occur by accident. It may be correct that man's biological roots propel him toward acts of aggression against members of his own species. It is not true that the point of these aggressive acts is necessarily to kill.

Aggression in the world of social carnivores is not aimed at killing members of the same species nor, in practice, does it result in death very often. For the most part aggression within a species takes the form of symbolic conflict with one animal (or group of animals) driving off the other by making threatening gestures and appearing more aggressive. Thus, aggression among social carnivores aims not at killing but at gaining dominance, that is, winning the contest short of killing one of the combatants. From an evolutionary perspective, the reason for this state of affairs is obvious: large-scale killing of members of the same species by their brethren would be both biologically and evolutionarily dysfunctional. In man, of course, aggression assumes a very different character. Only man, of all the social carnivores, seems addicted to the regular, systematic, and large-scale killing of his own species. Unlike animals, aggression in man seems precisely directed at killing or wounding. The most obvious result of this proclivity is war.

What provoked this bizarre tendency in man? Man's propensity for killing seems less connected to his animal (primate and carnivore) roots than to his unique development as a separate species. And what sets man apart from all other species is his unique brain. The human brain is the most efficient mechanism in existence for converting sensory perceptions into patterns. The ability to further organize these patterns is the basis for conceptualization, which is an absolute prerequisite for the development of basic and, later, creative intelligence. Man stands alone as a creature who can manipulate concepts and engage in abstract thought. How does this unique brain explain the specific form of aggression that is present only in the human species?

Although initially based on empirical sensory impressions, the concepts to which man assigns meaning and value are abstractions, simplified portrayals of the empirical world. As such, man's reality is essentially artificial. Yet, this reality is as real for the human mind as the smell of another animal is real to the animal brain. Unlike animals that fight for specific and limited objects, only the human animal fights for conceptual realities. Thus, the scope of aggression or, at least, the reasons for which aggression might be provoked are much greater in man than in animals. Moreover, since the reasons for which man fights require no direct empirical referents to make them "real" for him, the connection between mounting sufficient aggression to obtain them and the means employed has no objective basis. This proportionality, so basic in the animal world and vital to limiting aggressive damage, is missing in the aggressive behavior of man.

The development of the cerebral cortex introduced into the human brain the ability to ignore or override those instincts and reflexes that limit aggressive behavior in animals. The physiologically triggered "peacening" responses that occur in an aggressive animal when submission is signaled by his opponent are easily overridden by the press of the human intellect determined to achieve the conceptual goal for which aggression is initiated. The ability of the intellect to override the physiological responses that limit aggression found in other carnivores results in aggressive behavior on a scale not found in the animal world. In man, therefore, a once socially valuable behavior, aggression, has evolved to the point where much of that behavior has become an end in itself instead of a means to survival.

If it is true that the roots of war lie in the evolutionary development of the cerebral cortex of the human brain, and that war is a manifestation not of man's animal impulses but of his human uniqueness, it is also true that it is not evolutionary developments alone that urge humankind toward warfare. Equally important are cultural factors, and man is the only species with a culture. While brain biology provides the potency, it is culture that provides the specific actuality of war. Aggression may be innate enough, but the specific forms that aggression takes, the weapons it employs in its pursuit, and the goals for which it is undertaken are more a consequence of cultural learning than of physiology.

II. ARCHAEOLOGY OF WAR

War is a social invention that requires specific conditions to bring about its emergence. Because war has been present from the very beginning of man's recorded history, about 4000 B.C., it has also been mistakenly assumed that it must have been present even before that. If in fact war as a social institution is placed in historical perspective, it becomes obvious that war is among the most recent of man's social inventions. Using the more recent Stone Age cultures of Homo sapiens and Homo neanderthal, which survived approximately 100,000 years ago as a baseline of measurement, archaeology reveals some remarkable data about the development of war. Man required 30,000 years from the baseline to learn how to use fire and another 20,000 years to invent the fire-hardened, wooden-tipped spear. Sixty thousand years after that, the bow and arrow made their appearance. Ninety thousand years after the beginning of the Homo sapiens Stone Age, man learned to herd wild animals, and 4000 years later he learned to domesticate goats, sheep, cattle, and the dog. At about the same time there is evidence for the beginnings of systematic harvesting of wild grains, but it took another 2000 years to learn how to transplant these wild grains to fixed campsites, and another 2000 years to learn how to plant domesticated strains of cereal grain. It was only after these major developments, around 4000 B.C., that warfare made its appearance as a significant human social institution. Man has practiced war for only about 6% of the time since the Homo sapiens Stone Age began.

To trace the development of war requires a working definition of warfare. War involves conflict, but clearly not all conflicts are wars. It is likely that men, either as individuals or in small groups, engaged in conflicts from the very beginning. The evidence concerning life patterns in hunter–gatherer groups suggests that their small size (usually fewer than 50 people), the vast distances over which they roamed, the necessity for constant food gathering, and blood ties all worked against the formation of any sort of warrior class. Rather, the most that could be accomplished in these small conflicts was for hunters to double as warriors when the need for protection arose. The emergence of larger clans or tribes brought into existence a surplus of hunters who often served as warriors. But again, the available evidence suggests that war among clans or tribes as mostly ritualistic, highly structured, a kind of rough sport, in which lethal weapons were often not used, conditions that clearly limited casualties to minimal proportions.

Warfare, as distinct from primitive conflicts, requires larger size combatant groups, a distinct killing technology, a higher degree of societal organization, and role specialization. Thus, warfare can be defined as a level of organized conflict that involves forces of some size rooted in the larger society's organizational and role differentiating structure, applying a killing technology with some degree of organization and expertise. If these conditions are not present, one might find murder, small-scale scuffles, raids, and ambushes, but one does not find warfare. War requires the systematic, organized application of orchestrated violence.

For the first 90,000 years after the Homo sapiens Stone Age began, no evidence exists that man engaged in war on any level, let alone on a level requiring organized group violence. The thousands of discovered cave paintings reveal fewer than 130 paintings that seem to incorporate scenes involving human beings. Of these, none reveal evidence of organized violence of man against man. The first evidence of truly organized violence on some scale occurs sometime around 6500 B.C. at Jebel Sahaba in the Sudan. The skeletal remains of 59 people, including women and children, suggest that these people were killed by repeated arrow wounds and spear thrusts. A Neolithic site in the Transcaucasus reveals the first rock painting of the same period, which shows what seems to be a small armed squad attacking and killing other men with bows and arrows. Another 1500 years passed before there is evidence of a level of organized violence that can be unequivocally identified as warfare. It seems clear that by 6000 B.C. man had learned to use organized groups to kill other men.

The connection between the development of agriculture and warfare has been noted by such scholars as Quincy Wright in his study of 633 primitive cultures. The post-Neolithic period (or Bronze Age) witnessed a great explosion in the spread of large-scale agricultural communities and, with it, the spread of large-scale war. Large agricultural communities made it possible for nomadic tribes to stop their seasonal wandering and occupy a single site. Stability of place naturally increased the human tendency toward territoriality since the fate of the entire group was now tied to occupying a common site. The practical identity with a single site was strongly bolstered by religious beliefs that certain areas were defined as sacred or god-given. Successful agriculture made it possible to sustain populations larger than man had ever seen, and a smaller percentage of the population was required to provide food for all. A surplus population also made possible a greater degree of social differentiation based around function, and the priest and warrior classes came into existence. For the first time in human existence there emerged an entire social class whose sole reason for being was to wage war. Within a relatively short time of a thousand years the warrior class laid claim to rule, and the military society came into being.

For the first time there were social pressures within society to prepare for war and develop weapons in times of peace. When these structures were linked to the operations of man's conceptual brain and its ability to conceive any number of artificial realities for which to engage in war, the last limits on warfare enforced by his physiology and his formerly less-sophisticated social order were removed. Once warfare became an established social institution, it is difficult to find any other social institution that developed as quickly. By 2000 B.C., war had become a dominant social institution in almost all major cultures of the Middle East.

III. EVOLUTION OF WARFARE

The period from 4000 to 2000 B.C. was a seminal period in the development of the institution and instrumentalities of war. This period saw the emergence of the world's first truly urban complexes with large populations, the development of state political and bureaucratic institutions that permitted the mobilization of resources for war, the establishment and stabilization of the world's first military castes, and the rise of the first standing professional armies. As a mechanism of cultural development, the conduct of war became a legitimate social function supported by an extensive institutional infrastructure. In less than 2000 years man went from a condition in which warfare was relatively rare and mostly ritualistic, where combat death and destruction were endured at low rates, to one in which death and destruction were attained on a modern scale. During this period warfare assumed modern proportions in terms of the size of armies involved, the administrative mechanisms needed to support them, and the scope of destruction achievable by military force.

The world's oldest armies appeared in Sumer (modern Iraq) and Egypt. Between 3000 and 2000 B.C., Sumer developed a professional army which fought in phalanx formation and was the first to be equipped with body armor and helmets. Sumerian military technology brought into being the first military application of the wheel, the chariot, and the inventions of the socket axe, the penetrating axe, and the composite bow. The Sumerian states were at war with one another almost constantly over a thousand year period culminating, around 2400 B.C., in the appearance of the world's first military dictatorship under Sargon the Great. The chronicles of the period detail the slaughter of entire armies, the destruction of cities, and the wholesale deportment and enslavement of entire peoples, all indicators of a large increase in the scale and destructiveness of war.

The advances in weapons and warfare introduced by the Sumerians were not evident in Egypt until 1700 B.C., when they were adopted by a generation of warrior kings who established an Egyptian empire by force of arms. Until that time, Egyptian armies were relatively primitive in weaponry and tactics, although they were generally larger than in Sumer. After 1700 B.C., the Egyptian military became larger still and was equipped with new weapons, including a newly designed chariot which introduced mobility and lethality to the battlefield at hereto unforeseen levels. The Egyptian talent for social organization, a talent that had allowed them to build the pyramids almost a thousand years earlier, produced a modern logistics organization that permitted Egyptian armies to operate great distances from the homeland with the result that, for almost 500 years, Egyptian military power was the strongest in the ancient world.

The period from 1500 B.C. to A.D. 100, the Iron Age, was characterized by almost constant war, a time in which states of all sizes came into existence only to be extinguished by the rise of still larger empires which, in their turn, were destroyed by military force. During this period humankind refined the social structures essential to the functioning of genuinely large and complex social orders and, in doing so, brought into existence a new and more destructive form of warfare.

An important stimulus for this military revolution was the discovery and use of iron, first introduced as a technology of war by the Hittites around 1300 B.C. The importance of iron was that it was widely available (unlike tin that was needed to produce bronze weapons) and easy to extract from its carrier ore. The plentiful supply of this new strategic material resulted in a weapons explosion in which even small states could afford large numbers of weapons. An important technological limit on the size of armies was thereby eliminated.

The armies of the Iron Age were larger, more mobile, more logistically sophisticated, more complex, better organized, better trained, and more capably commanded, and, thus, more lethal than anything the world had seen to this time. Iron Age armies were the first to practice conscription on a regular basis which, paradoxically, required a large corps of officers to train conscripts leading to the increased professionalization of armies throughout the period. Conscription was extracted as a normal price of societal membership required by the need to control far-flung empires over large geographical areas. The Iron Age gave birth to the national standing army based on citizen service and, thus, preceding by almost a thousand years the same practice by Napoleon, itself perceived as a revolutionary development at the time.

The size of Iron Age armies was enormous, and not generally surpassed until the 18th century. The Persians, for example, routinely deployed armies 10 times the size of Bronze Age armies. While the armies of Sargon of Akkad (2300 B.C.) numbered perhaps 20,000 men, the army of Ramses II (1300 B.C.) was easily 100,000 men. The Assyrian army of the 8th century B.C. comprised 200,000 men, and the Persian army could deploy 300,000 soldiers. Sustained by larger populations, cheap and plentiful weapons, the need to govern large areas of imperial dimensions, and the evolving ability to exercise command and control over large military establishments, the armies of this period were truly modern in almost all respects.

Iron Age armies were also more complex. The introduction of new equipment and battle formations, the chariot, cavalry, siege engines, artillery, and the need to feed large numbers of soldiers and supply animals, provoked a revolution in logistics. The introduction of the ox-cart, the horse, mule, donkey, and camel as beasts of burden, and the use of ships to support armies moving along friendly coasts, combined to make it possible to sustain large armies in the field over considerable distances for long periods. This increased the strategic range of the armies. Compared to an army of the Bronze Age, an Egyptian army of the Iron Age had twice the strategic range, 1250 miles by 200 miles. The Assyrian army had five times the strategic range of the armies of Sumer, and the armies of Rome had a strategic range of 1500 miles by 3000 miles. On average, the armies of the late Iron Age had a strategic range nine times greater than the range of armies in the Bronze Age.

Supplied with better equipment—boots, uniforms, knapsacks—and better nutrition, the armies of the Iron Age were far more mobile than earlier armies. The introduction of accurate maps and the construction of military roads increased both tactical and strategic mobility. The Romans, for example, constructed 250,000 miles of paved, permanent roadways over which they could move troops. The effect of permanent roads on military mobility was amazing. On dry, unpaved roads a Roman legion (6000 men) could move about 8 miles a day. In wet weather, movement of any kind was almost impossible. On paved roads, however, a legion could move 25 to 30 miles a day. The tactical flexibility of these armies, with the introduction of the chariot, cavalry squadrons, engineers corps, professional military staff, and formal combat training also increased greatly. The military revolution of the Iron Age qualitatively increased the combat capabilities of armies to levels never seen before in history.

For more than 4000 years warfare and weapons technology had grown continually in an upward trend with each succeeding age witnessing larger, more sophisticated, and more complex armies. All this came to an end with the collapse of the Roman imperium in the fourth century A.D. The period from the fourth century to the Renaissance was a period of violent transition in which Europe witnessed the complete barbarization of its civilization followed by 700 years (800–1453) of dynastic struggles, religious wars, and renewed invasions. Under these conditions, the sophistication of war declined to the level of the early Bronze Age. The decentralization of the feudal social order produced decentralization in everything else with the result that there were no centralized arms industries, no permanent standing armies, and no logistical or training establishments. Military doctrine and tactics were almost nonexistent, and war was characterized by a period of "squalid butchery" in which corps of armed knights engaged in battles that were little more than armed scuffles. The rise of the armored knight and mounted individualized combat swept the infantry from the field for almost a thousand years until at Paupen (1339) and Crecy (1346) infantry forces reemerged once again.

This period was marked by a constant tension between the decentralized feudal order and the beginnings of centralized monarchies. Gradually, as monarchs consolidated their power, armies again began to develop military structures, permanent pay, regular garrisons, and military ranks. By the 1600s, for the first time since Rome, Europe once again began to develop stable, permanent armed forces directed by central national authorities and supported by taxation. It was these national authorities, the absolute monarchs of the day, that spurred the organizational, tactical, and technological development of the armies during this period, and set the pattern for the next four centuries. By the time of the Thirty Years War (1618–1648), most of the major elements of the modern army had once again been set into place.

The Thirty Years War began as a clash of feudal armies and ended by setting the stage for the development of modern war. During this period, the full promise of gunpowder technology, introduced 300 years earlier, began to strongly influence warfare. The musket revolutionized the role of infantry. The matchlock gradually gave way to the firelock and, shortly, the wheel lock rifle. A century later this was replaced by the flintlock and, by the early 1800s, the percussion cap made its appearance. With each new development, including rifling, the infantry became more lethal in delivering fire. One result was the ability to thin out infantry formations into lines, an innovation of Gustavus Adolphus, making linear tactics possible. Linear tactics, in turn, made possible larger and more mobile infantry formations. During the Thirty Years War the paper cartridge was introduced, as was the standard-length packing rod, both of which greatly increased the rate of fire of infantry weapons. Gradually, the pikeman was replaced as the bayonet allowed each infantryman to be his own pikeman. The introduction of the first hand grenade also gave the infantry more punch.

The most significant advances in range and lethality came in artillery. During the Thirty Years War artillery production was standardized and the caliber system for shot introduced. Within a century, the wheeled gun carriage and trunion improved mobility and accuracy, and Frederick the Great introduced the idea of mounting guns and crews on horseback and wagons, introducing the first horse artillery. In the 1740s artillery gunners experimented with different types of shells. Over the century, rounds that exploded on impact were supplemented by canister, chain, and grapeshot, and the introduction of timed wicks made possible the first shells that exploded overhead. By the Civil War, advances in breech loading, gas sealing, recoil mechanisms, and new explosives increased the range of artillery to over a thousand yards.

The significance of all these developments was most strongly felt on cavalry. The increased range of the rifle and artillery made the cavalry charge terribly vulnerable. As a consequence, cavalry was no longer able to act as the main striking force of armies, and was relegated to minor roles like reconnaissance, guarding strong points, pinching the flanks, or engaging in the pursuit. Cavalry did not reemerge as a major combatant until the introduction of the tank at Cambrai in 1918.

By the 1800s standing armies in a genuine modern sense had come into being once again, with organization, logistics trains, and hierarchical structures comparable to those found in modern-day armies. It was Napoleon who introduced an element not seen for a thousand years into this equation. Napoleon's revolution was to introduce the mass citizen army based on conscription, and to develop an officer corps selected for its talent rather than its social origins. However, the size of Napoleonic armies was impossible to maintain unless the entire social and economic resources of the state were also mobilized for war. The age of modern war was beginning to dawn.

IV. MILITARY TECHNOLOGY

The American Civil War (1860–1865) was the first truly modern war, for it was the first conflict to take maximum advantage of the new efficiencies of production brought into being by the Industrial Revolution. The Industrial Revolution, particularly the factory system and machine mass production, along with technological innovations in metallurgy, chemistry, and machine tools, provided for an explosion in military technology. New means of economic organization and impressive increases in productivity made it possible to free large numbers of men for military service. The new railroad system allowed the transport of men and supplies needed to support military operations on an unprecedented scale. It was, as well, the first time that the production base and the civilian industrial manpower pool became legitimate and necessary military targets.

The Crimean War (1853–1856) saw the first use of rifled and breech-loading cannon by the British Army. In the Civil War half the Union artillery was composed of rifled and breech-loading guns. Rifled cannon had longer ranges, more penetrating power, greater accuracy, and greater rates of fire than the old smoothbore cannon. Improved black powder also added to the shell's velocity and range. Small arms weapons improved greatly as well. The introduction of the conoidal bullet in the Civil War along with better gas sealing and rifled barrels made the Civil War musket capable of killing at 1000 yards and deadly accurate at 600 yards. Near the end of the war, the repeating seven-shot carbine was introduced. A rifleman could now fire seven rounds in the time it took a musket rifleman to fire a single shot. Infantry firepower increased with the introduction of the Gattling Gun, the first primitive machine gun. This weapon fired 100 rounds a minute, equal to the rate of fire of 40 infantrymen. By 1900, Hiram Maxim invented a truly modern machine gun capable of a sustained rate of fire of 600 rounds per minute.

A number of other technologies of the Industrial Revolution were turned to military use, including Eli Whitney's concept of interchangeability of parts which made mass production possible. With the railroad, mobility of deployment increased dramatically as did the means of sustaining large forces in the field over vast distances by supplying them by rail. Tinned and condensed foods were first used as military rations during this time, and the telegraph greatly increased the level of tactical and operational control of armies by their commanders. The ironclad steam ship signaled the end of the era of wood and sail, and the regular use of the balloon for military purposes presaged the use to which the early airplane would be put in the next century.

The lesson that the European powers learned from the Civil War was that military power now required a sufficient industrial base and supply of manpower that had never before been placed under arms. The result was that European powers created large-standing armies supported by even larger reserve forces that could be quickly mobilized for war. As the Industrial Revolution developed one innovation after another, more and more military applications were found. The armies of the early 20th century had at their disposal a killing and destructive capacity greater than anything the world had ever seen. The fatal flaw was that they did not know it. As the European armies adopted each new weapon, they foolishly retained their traditional unit formations and battle tactics, both of which had already been made terribly obsolete by the range and firepower of new weapons. The result was the horrendous slaughter of World War I.

Among the more important developments in the period between the end of the Civil War and the start of World War I (1914–1918) were the following: the total replacement of smoothbore cannon with rifled breech loaders, artillery time fuses (1877), smokeless powder (1884), cordite explosive (1891), long-recoil hydraulic cylinders to stabilize artillery (1888), fixed ammunition, shrapnel shells, wire wound guns, (1896), and frettage manufacture of artillery barrels, all of which allowed the manufacture of more durable, higher caliber guns. Infantry weapons saw the introduction of the firing pin (1870) and the magazine (Lee-Enfield) and clip-fed (Mauser) bolt-action rifles that increased infantry firepower yet again.

In 1820, the first steam-powered naval combatants were produced and, by 1850, the first screw propeller made the side wheeler obsolete freeing up more deck space for guns. In 1855, the French introduced iron plating for the wooden hull and, in 1860, the British launched the world's first iron-hulled warship, *H.M.S. Warrior*. The armored turret was first used aboard ship in 1868, and by 1900, four guns per turret was the standard for naval combatants. The caliber of naval guns increased from 12 in. (1908) to 15 in. by 1914. In 1913, oil burners replaced coal boilers in ships. All of these advances culminated in the production of the first modern battleship in 1913, *H.M.S. Dreadnought*.

The invention of contact mines and the guided torpedo, however, soon made these large ships obsolete. The first torpedo was introduced in 1866 and, within a decade, the first contrarotating propeller was fitted to a torpedo. By 1895 the invention of the gyroscope improved the torpedo's accuracy to where it could carry a 300-pound warhead 1000 yards at 30 knots. This weapon called into existence a new class of naval combatants, the torpedo boat.

The most revolutionary naval advance of the period was the submarine. By 1900, steel hulls, the internal combustion engine, the accumulator battery, the gyroscope, and gyrocompass combined to make the submarine possible. In 1905 the *USS Holland* introduced water-tight compartments while, the British contributed the conning tower and periscope. The Germans invented double-hulls and twin screws. By 1914, the six major naval powers of the world put 249 submarines to sea.

1911 saw the first use of the airplane in war by the Italians and, in 1912, the Royal Flying Corps in England gave birth to the first official air force. In 1913, speed (127 mph), distance (635 miles), and altitude (20,079 feet) records were set as the airplane began to improve its capability as a new weapon of war. World War I brought the wide range of military technological inventions of the Industrial Revolution to bear on the battlefield, and the world has never been the same since.

The technology of war continued to produce more accurate, longer range, and increasingly lethal weapons until the present day where armies are equipped with the means to literally destroy the entire planet with weapons of war. With the exception of nuclear weapons, the advanced prototype of every modern weapon had been invented by World War I. The important point for understanding the evolution of war, however, is that by World War I, the pattern of societal–technological–military integration, commonplace from the Bronze Age to the collapse of Rome, though interrupted for a millennium and a half by the fragmentation resulting from Rome's collapse, reestablished itself. Once again the world witnessed large standing armies, the integration of the political and economic institutions of the state for military purposes, the propulsion of national interests by state and religious ideologies, and the ability of political institutions to marshall the entire range of social resources for war. The psychology of war, requiring identification with national entities embodying the highest moral obligation of its citizens, was resolidified, and service in war became the citizen's most compelling social obligation. In this sense, war as a social institution remains firmly embedded in man's social structure and psychology and, barring some major change in either, is likely to be so for the foreseeable future.

V. PSYCHIATRIC CASUALTIES

Although a social invention whose persistence is far from inevitable, war has generally been accepted by most men as an inevitable condition of societal existence. Yet, this acceptance and participation, although considered "normal," is not without limits. One of the major limits on the conduct of war is the increasing inability of the human psyche to endure war without succumbing to psychiatric collapse. While warfare has become incredibly intense when measured objectively against its past levels of violence, the propensity of large number of participants to psychiatric collapse under the strain of war is as old as historical records.

There are clear descriptions of soldiers suffering psychiatric symptoms—called at different times in history "madness," "general insanity," "neurasthenia," "nostalgia," "shell-shock," "battle shock," etc.—as early as the Egyptian armies of the Bronze Age. The ancient Greeks were well aware of psychiatric conditions induced by exposure to war, and had specific treatment centers for soldiers. The Romans were the first to incorporate psychiatric wards in their military hospitals, and the warrior chronicles of the Middle Ages—*The Song of Roland* and the *Anglo-Saxon Chronicles*—testify to examples of battle-shocked soldiers.

While the intensity of modern war seems to have increased the numbers of psychiatric casualties suffered by armies, the rates at which these casualties are suffered appear from the limited data to be relatively constant over history. Thus, for example, in every war since 1905, the rate of psychiatric casualties has been approximately 35 per 1000 men exposed to combat. In every war in this century more than twice as many men have been lost to armies through psychiatric collapse than have been killed by hostile fire. This suggests that the human psyche itself sets objective limits upon the levels of stress it can withstand in war.

Psychiatric collapse is a result of prolonged physiological stress. Prolonged physiological stress consumes psycho-chemicals required for rational thought and behavior, inevitably producing psychiatric collapse. Studies conducted in World War II demonstrate that 98% of soldiers exposed to 30 days of combat suffered debilitating psychiatric symptoms. Examination of the remaining 2% showed them to be psychopathic personalities prior to exposure to combat stress. If the data are correct, then, the intensity of modern war—itself 7 to 10 times as intense as World War II—can be expected to result in psychiatric collapse for most of the participants not already killed or wounded within 30 days. Levels of psychiatric collapse in modern war are so high that they threaten to cripple the ability of modern armies to engage in long-term battles. [*See* STRESS.]

VI. MEDICAL CASUALTIES

Lethality in war is always the sum total of a number of factors that go beyond the inherent death-dealing capabilities of military technology. Before a new weapon can reach its killing potential, military commanders must discover new methods of fighting in order to bring the new weapon to bear in a manner that maximizes its killing potential. But once the weapon's killing power is exposed, one's opponent adopts passive and active means for limiting the weapon's most deadly effects. This brings about changes in tactics in an attempt to preserve the killing power of the new technology. Inevitably, the result is a dynamic balance of behavior and technology that results in a state of affairs where the killing power of the new weapon exceeds its replacement, but often not greatly so. It cannot be stressed too strongly in calculating the killing power of weaponry that any failure to adapt either weapons or tactics to new circumstances can be catastrophic. Thus, the failure of the armies of World War I to alter their battle tactics in light of new weapons capabilities resulted in horrendous casualties.

T. N. Dupuy has calculated the effects of modern weapons as their killing power is affected by a number of objective factors such as rates of fire, availability of targets, range, weather, and terrain. When measured against the non-gunpowder weapons of antiquity, excluding nuclear weapons of course, modern weapons have increased in lethality by a factor of 2000. At the same time, however, changes in mechanization, the ability of fewer soldiers to deliver more firepower, and mobility have resulted in battlefield dispersion having increased by a factor of 4000. The result is that wars since 1865 have killed fewer soldiers as a percentage of the deployed combat force than was the case in previous wars. Except for the Napoleonic wars, which used combat formations that packed men into tight battle phalanxes, every war since 1600 has resulted in fewer and fewer casualties as a percentage of the committed forces for both victor and vanquished. Adamson's study of casualty rates from antiquity to Korea reaches the same conclusion. Even in the Gulf War of 1991, which saw a force of almost 400,000 hammered by unlimited conventional airpower for a month and attacked by a large modern mobile armored force with an enormous technological advantage in weaponry, the estimated casualty figure for the Iraqi army was only 7.1%.

Other factors have limited casualty rates in modern war. Among the most important is the progress that has been made against contagious disease and wound infection. A wounded soldier in the Civil War was at seven times greater risk of dying from an infected wound than he was of being killed outright had he fought through all 3 days of the Battle of Gettysburg. Until the Russo-Japanese War of 1904–1905, every army in history suffered many times more casualties to disease than to enemy fire. In every war from 1600 to World War I, the number of casualties lost to disease was, on average, eight times larger than casualties caused by hostile fire. Advances in medicine, particularly the introduction of antiseptic surgery by the German army in 1870, as well as sulfa drugs, antibiotics, and blood transfusions, all worked to save wounded and diseased soldiers from death. In the Crimean War, no fewer than three-quarters of all wounded soldiers succumbed to infection. By Vietnam, the rate had fallen to 2%.

Advances in body armor have also helped reduce casualties. Armies equipped with modern protective helmets and body armor can expect to suffer at least 6% less casualties than those without them. Moreover, once the threat of infection and disease is removed, sheer statistical probability works to limit casualties. Studies of wound rates demonstrate that among wounded soldiers, only one-third require serious medical attention to save the life of the soldier. Even with modern weapons, two-thirds of all combat wounds are not life threatening and, given time, most wounded soldiers could recover without medical treatment.

VII. CONCLUSIONS

For more than 5500 years of man's existence in organized human societies the means and methods by which men fought wars changed little. In the last 400 years marking the introduction of effective gunpowder weapons, wars have changed so drastically as to be quite literally beyond the imagination of soldiers and commanders who have gone before. In this sense, the advent of modern weapons and war can be seen as being among man's most ingenious innovations. And the psyche which rests at the core of man's humanity must still endure the terrifying fear of death and maiming that drove the ancient and modern soldier alike to psychiatric collapse.

War remains a social institution. There is nothing in man's genetic legacy that propels him toward it. Its form and substance have varied widely over history, as has its technology of destruction. Perhaps, like other social inventions of man's brain which have been abandoned as no longer useful to the species' survival, one day war, too, will be abandoned by a species that is already beginning to recognize that it has brought into being the very means to terminate its own existence. Whatever else is true about war, its continued occurrence is not inevitable. Man has both the right and the ability to choose.

Bibliography

Delbruck, H. (1980). "History of the Art of War within a Framework of Political History," 4 Vols. Greenwood Press, Westport, CT.

Dupuy, T. N. (1990). "Attrition: Forecasting Battle Casualties and Equipment Losses in War." Hero Books, Fairfax, VA.

Dupuy, T. N. (1986). "The Encyclopedia of Military History." Harper & Row, New York.

Dupuy, T. N. (1980). "The Evolution of Weapons and Warfare." Bobbs-Merrill, New York.

Gabriel, R. A. (1990). "The Culture of War: Origins and Development." Greenwood Press, Westport, CT.

Gabriel, R. A. (1986). "No More Heroes: Madness and Psychiatry In War." Hill and Wang, New York.

Jones, A. (1987). "The History of War in the Western World." University of Illinois Press, Chicago.

Keegan, J. (1977). "The Face of Battle." Vintage, New York.

Metz, K. S., and Gabriel, R. A. (1992). "A History of Military Medicine," 2 Vols. Greenwood Press, Westport, CT.

Metz, K. S., and Gabriel, R. A. (1991). "From Sumer To Rome: The Military Capabilities of Ancient Armies." Greenwood Press, Westport, CT.

Word Retrieval

Deborah M. Burke
Pomona College

Lori E. James
Claremont Graduate School

Glossary

Activation The process of exciting a representation or node in memory so that the information it stores becomes available.

Aphasia An impairment of language production and/or comprehension often caused by brain damage resulting from a stroke or head injury.

Lexicon A part of memory that stores information about the meaning, syntax, and sound of words.

Phonology The sound pattern of words. The smallest unit of these sounds is the phoneme.

Semantic That which is related to the meaning or concept associated with a word.

WORD RETRIEVAL is the mental process of accessing a word in memory that expresses an intended meaning or names a referent. It is the fundamental process responsible for translating thoughts and ideas into language. Word retrieval begins with a meaning that evokes a corresponding word in memory; for example, naming an object in a picture, say a horse, occurs when the perceptual information in the picture triggers corresponding perceptual information in memory, which in turn activates an associated word, "horse." Retrieval of the word enables its production, either overtly as in speaking or covertly as in thinking about the word.

A word that is required to express a thought usually comes into consciousness automatically with little awareness of what is being done to produce it. Indeed, the speaker is often concentrating on other things, such as planning what they will say next or interpreting the response of the person they are talking to. Word retrieval is an impressive ability especially since most English speakers must select each word from vocabularies of many tens of thousands of words represented in a part of memory called the mental lexicon. The lexicon contains information about the meaning, syntax, and phonology (sound) of each word known by that person. Successful word retrieval depends on selecting the word meaning in the lexicon that corresponds to the intended meaning and activating the phonology of the corresponding word, all of which normally transpires within a fraction of a second.

I. COMPONENTS OF THE LEXICON: WORD MEANING AND PHONOLOGY

The distinction between the meaning of a word and its sound or phonological code is reflected in the way words are represented in the lexicon. That is, meaning and sound are represented separately and may be retrieved independently. One good source of evidence for this is the tip of the tongue (TOT) state in which a person cannot think of a word (i.e., its phonological code) even though they are certain that they know the word. People in the TOT state can usually retrieve many different aspects of the meaning of the TOT word, but are unable to retrieve its sound. Thus, representations of meaning are fully accessible, but the representation of the phonology is temporarily inaccessible.

Further evidence for the distinction between sound and meaning comes from patients suffering from aphasia, often as a consequence of brain damage following a stroke or other trauma. In one type of aphasia, called anomia, the ability to retrieve

Encyclopedia of Human Behavior, Volume 4

words is impaired although the ability to understand words may be normal. For example, an anomic patient may exhibit impaired performance in naming objects in pictures, but perform normally when given the name of an object and asked to point to the corresponding picture. In this case, the patient is unable to retrieve a word on the basis of its meaning, but is able to retrieve the meaning of a word on the basis of its sound. This suggests not only that word meaning and sound may be retrieved independently, but also that the connection between them may be damaged in one direction but not the other. [*See* APHASIA.]

Even when word retrieval is normal and successful, there are several factors that affect how easily it is accomplished. These factors provide insight into the nature of the mental operations that underlie word retrieval.

II. FACTORS INFLUENCING SPEED AND ACCURACY OF WORD RETRIEVAL

How many times we have previously encountered a word has a large effect on the speed and accuracy of retrieving the word. Estimates of the frequency of occurrence of English words have been established by counting how many times a word occurs in samples of printed material or samples of speech. Using such records to estimate the relative frequency of occurrence of a word, it has been shown that low frequency words take longer to retrieve and are more prone to error than high frequency words. For example, pictures of objects with high frequency names (e.g., common words such as "chair") are named more rapidly than pictures of objects with low frequency names (e.g., rare words such as "trellis"). Errors in producing speech during everyday life are more likely for low than high frequency words. For example, mispronunciation of a word is more likely for low than high frequency words as is substitution of a wrong word for an intended word. Finally, low frequency words are more likely than high frequency words to be involved in word retrieval failures as in the tip of the tongue experience. Thus, frequent encounters with a word speed its retrieval and reduce the probability that an error will be introduced during retrieval or that retrieval will fail.

Another factor that influences the ease of word retrieval is how recently the word has been produced. Words that have been produced recently are more easily retrieved than words that have not. Moreover, this effect of prior experience with the word does not require conscious recollection of those experiences. For example, a word is more likely to be produced as the correct answer to a definition (e.g., "An insect that travels in destructive swarms that can have devastating effects on crops") or as an instance of a category (e.g., "an insect") if the word (e.g., "locust") was recently encountered. This occurs even when the person has no conscious recollection that the word was just encountered.

These recency effects have been demonstrated in the laboratory by asking people to perform a task such as pronouncing a list of words followed by a definitions test in which they are to supply a word that fits a definition. Some of the definition answers are words that appeared on the previous list. These words are more likely to be correctly produced than words that did not appear on the previous list, regardless of whether the participants are able to remember that the word was on the pronunciation list. The effect of recent experience on retrieval when there is no conscious memory for the experience is known as implicit memory. [*See* IMPLICIT MEMORY.]

This beneficial effect of recent experience on retrieval can become a liability when a person repeats recently encountered words or ideas of another person while claiming and believing to be the original source of the words or ideas. This phenomenon has been named "unconscious plagiarism" and is the consequence of the increased availability of recently encountered words without conscious recollection of their prior occurrence. It is unknown how often actual cases of plagiarism are an inadvertent consequence of this basic characteristic of language, namely that recency increases word availability.

Word retrieval is also affected by the context in which it occurs: Retrieval of a word is faster when it follows a word that is related in meaning, rather than unrelated. For example, naming a picture of an object is faster when it is preceded by a semantically related picture or word compared to a control condition where it is preceded by an unrelated picture or word. Thus, naming a picture of a table is faster when it is preceded by naming a picture of a chair rather than a picture of a giraffe. This facilitation of retrieval when successive words share aspects of meaning is called the semantic priming effect. [*See* SEMANTIC MEMORY.]

Semantic priming is probably an important factor in explaining the rapid rate at which we produce speech in everyday life. Semantic priming occurs during a conversation when words within a sentence are related to a common theme and the sentences themselves are related to a common topic. Priming would speed word retrieval enabling typical rates of speech production of three or four words per second.

Semantic priming effects also provide important information about the nature of the memory system involved in word retrieval. These effects are evidence for pathways in the lexicon among words that are related in meaning. Retrieval of a word initiates a spread of activation to semantically related words and this increases their accessibility. We consider next a specific model of the memory structure and processes involved in word retrieval. This model provides an explanation of how semantic context, as well as frequency and recency, affects word retrieval. It also provides a framework for the discussion of TOT states and speech errors that follows.

III. AN INTERACTIVE ACTIVATION MODEL OF WORD PRODUCTION

One of the most popular models of speech production postulates that words are represented in a vast memory network of pathways connecting representational units called nodes. Nodes are organized into a *semantic system* which represents word meanings and a *phonological system* which represents word sounds. Figure 1 illustrates a portion of the representation of *frisbee* in the semantic and phonological systems. Lexical nodes do not store either phonological or semantic information, but rather are connected, in the phonological system, to hierarchically organized nodes which represent syllables and phonological compounds and features, and in the semantic system, to nodes which represent aspects of meaning or experience corresponding to the word. For example, the lexical node for *frisbee* is connected to the syllables *fris* and *bee,* and to nodes representing conceptual information about frisbees such as the fact that they are playthings and are thrown. Representational nodes in the phonological and semantic system are connected to all lexical nodes whose words include that component.

Activation of a node causes retrieval of the information it represents and may occur in one system independently of the others. When a node is activated, "priming" spreads along connections within and between systems to related nodes increasing subthreshold levels of excitation which increases the availability of the information at these nodes.

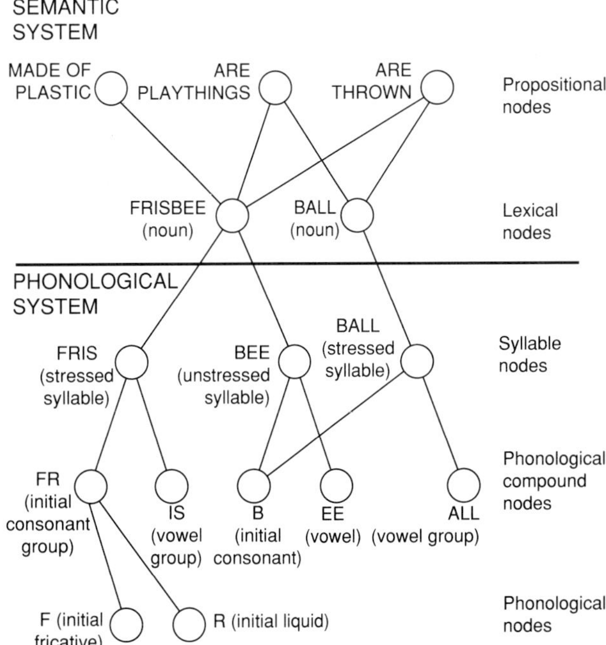

FIGURE 1 An example of representations of the semantic and phonological systems in an interactive activation model. [Adapted from Burke *et al.* (1991). *J. Memory Language,* **30,** 542–579.]

Activation of a node occurs when a threshold level of priming has been achieved and the node is the most primed in its syntactic category.

During normal, error-free word production, the translation of thought into speech begins with activation of a propositional node representing a concept in the semantic system, such as, *They were throwing a frisbee.* Activating this propositional node transmits priming to the lexical node for *frisbee,* so that it becomes the most primed node in its domain and is activated. Priming then spreads from the lexical node to connected phonological nodes. Retrieving the complete phonology for *frisbee* requires activation of nodes at all levels of the phonological system, including phonological feature nodes. Phonological nodes corresponding to the target word are normally activated because top–down priming from lexical nodes suffices to ensure that these phonological nodes are the most primed in their domains.

Semantic priming effects on *frisbee* are caused by production of words that share features of meaning with *frisbee,* such as other playthings; activation of shared semantic nodes causes a spread of priming to the lexical node for *frisbee,* increasing its availability for retrieval. Activation of the *frisbee* lexical node would occur when additional priming was generated by, for example, activation of several connected semantic nodes, so that *frisbee* became the most primed node in its syntactic category.

The strength of connections between nodes determines the rate and amount of priming transmitted between them. Thus, connection strength is an important determinant of what information represented in memory becomes available. Both frequency and recency of occurrence of a word affect retrieval by modifying the connection strength among nodes corresponding to the word. Strength of connections is increased by frequent and recent activation of nodes which enables more efficient transmission of priming. Thus, frequent production of *frisbee* would increase the strength of connections among nodes at all levels. As a consequence, subsequent activation of semantic nodes connected to *frisbee* would transmit greater priming to the lexical node for *frisbee* which in turn would transmit greater priming to the phonological nodes which must be activated for production of "frisbee." This increase in strength of connections caused by activation decays over time. The facilitation of retrieval by recent production is because the connection strength decreases over time since last production.

Errors in word retrieval occur when transmission of priming from the lexical node through the phonological system goes awry. The consequences include activating a wrong phonological node which causes a slip of the tongue, or failing to activate a phonological node which causes a tip of the tongue state. We consider now the nature of these errors in word retrieval.

IV. WHEN WORD RETRIEVAL FAILS: THE TIP OF THE TONGUE EXPERIENCE

One of the most dramatic instances of word retrieval difficulty is the tip of the tongue (TOT) state in which a person is unable to produce a word although absolutely certain that the word is known. The sense of imminent retrieval is like being on "the brink of a sneeze" and is sometimes accompanied by an intense feeling of frustration or irritation.

The basic cause of TOTs in the model described above is a deficit in the transmission of priming across critical connections required for producing the target word. When a TOT occurs, a lexical node in the semantic system becomes activated, giving access to semantic information about the target word, but at least some phonological information remains inaccessible because insufficient priming is transmitted to enable activation of connected phonological nodes. This transmission deficit is related to frequency and recency of use and thus TOTs involve words with a low frequency of occurrence, or words that have not been used recently, such as the name of a cousin who has not been contacted for many months. In Figure 1, a TOT for *frisbee* would occur if its lexical node became activated, but connections to the phonology were weakened from disuse so that there was insufficient transmission of priming to enable some of the connected phonological nodes to become activated.

Despite the inaccessibility of the TOT target, people can typically report partial phonological information which remains available in a most tantalizing fashion. For example, people in the throes of a TOT can typically specify the number of syllables, the stress pattern, and the initial and final sounds or letters of an otherwise irretrievable target. However, reports of final letters of TOT words may be attributable to guessing based on general knowledge of English morphology.

How can we recall parts of a word when we cannot say what the word is? Within the model, only some of the phonological nodes for producing a word may be suffering a transmission deficit due to infrequent or nonrecent use. Some subset of the remaining phonological nodes may in fact become activated, providing a basis for partial recall.

The strong sense of imminent retrieval that is the hallmark of TOT states has been quantified via ratings of the feeling of knowing (FOK). These ratings are correlated with the probability of recalling the TOT target: The higher the rating of feeling of knowing, the higher the likelihood that the word will be recalled. How can we accurately judge that we know a word when we cannot say the word? The distinction between semantic and phonological nodes is essential for explaining this characteristic of TOTs. Activating a lexical node indicates that the word is known and provides one basis for FOK. Activating its connected semantic propositions provides another basis for FOK and enables the rich descriptions of the meaning of the target word given in the TOT state.

Similar factors underlie our ability to reject other, inappropriate words that come to mind instead of the target. In William James' (1890) memorable description, "It is a gap that is intensely active. . . . If wrong names are proposed to us, this singularly definite gap acts immediately so as to negate them."

The "active gap" corresponds to the phonological nodes that cannot be activated, and "wrong names" are rejected because they do not fit the already activated semantic and phonological information. For example, conflicting propositions within the semantic system rather than conflicting phonology will enable rejection of words that are phonologically similar to the TOT word.

Another characteristic of TOT states is that a word related to the target in meaning and/or sound often comes repeatedly and involuntarily to mind. For example, a person experiencing a TOT for *Winnabego* reported that all that came to mind was *rutabaga*. Another person persistently thought of *dacron* while having a TOT for *velcro*. How do these persistent alternate words come initially to mind? For example, how is a persistent alternate such as *charity* retrieved instead of the TOT target *chastity?* The meaning of *chastity* involves propositions such as "is a virtue" and "take a vow of," some of which are shared with *charity* which becomes primed via such shared semantic propositions, e.g., "is a virtue." Some of the phonological nodes for *chastity* receive too little priming to enable activation (causing the TOT), whereas others such as the initial consonant cluster *ch* do receive sufficient priming and in fact become activated. These activated phonological nodes are shared by *charity* and thus are an additional source of priming. Priming from both semantic and phonological representations therefore summate on *charity* increasing the probability that it will be the most primed lexical node enabling retrieval of its phonology (which is not suffering from weakened connections).

Why do persistent alternates come repeatedly and involuntarily to mind? The spread of priming to phonologically similar words is automatic and involuntary, and once an alternate is activated it becomes easier to activate in the future because recent use increases the strength of connections and enables more efficient transmission of priming.

There are a variety of ways in which people attempt to resolve TOTs, that is, to retrieve the TOT target word. Some people use retrieval strategies, for example, thinking of contextual information such as the last time they had seen a target person or place, or going through the alphabet letter by letter as a cue to the TOT word. The effectiveness of such strategies is uncertain. Although people in the TOT state can describe characteristics of the target as they become available, retrieval of this partial information, and the target itself, involves retrieval processes that are themselves not available to awareness or conscious control.

Consistent with this, TOTs are often resolved spontaneously when the target word pops into mind at a time when the person's conscious attention is directed elsewhere and the particular TOT experience is temporarily forgotten. Although people frequently report that they know a TOT word will pop up on its own, the cause of these pop ups remains a mystery. One possible explanation is that the pop up is caused inadvertently when the person hears another word that shares phonology with the target and thus boosts priming of the phonological nodes that suffered the deficit in transmission of priming. For example, if the critical phonological components occur accidentally during internal speech or everyday language comprehension, the full phonology of the TOT word may become available and enable the word to pop into mind.

This inadvertent cuing account is consistent with some descriptions of TOT resolutions. For example, a man suffering a TOT for the name Ojai (a small town in California) was overcome with frustration leading to the utterance, "Oh hell" (pronounced oh'-hell). This utterance immediately triggered recall of the missing target (pronounced oh'-hi). The phonological similarity of "Oh hell" and "Ojai" enabled retrieval of the TOT word.

V. ERRORS IN WORD RETRIEVAL: SLIPS OF THE TONGUE

Another type of error in word retrieval is the slip of the tongue in which we produce an incorrect word or mispronounce an intended word. These errors occur in the speech of most people and while they are relatively infrequent, they are notorious for creating embarrassing messages, as in the following examples:

A former U.S. president said, "I don't want to run the risk of ruining what is a lovely recession" (reception).

A famous general was described as "a battle scared, excuse me I mean bottle scarred general" (battle scarred).

Slips of the tongue are of considerable interest to linguists and psychologists because they allow inferences about the otherwise hidden mechanisms underlying everyday word retrieval and production.

Several collections of slips of the tongue are available from the records of researchers monitoring the speech of friends, acquaintances, and public figures. Analysis of these collections has demonstrated that slips show systematic characteristics and occur in consistent patterns.

The two overarching categories of slips are those which occur at the level of an entire word (word errors), and those which involve only a part or parts of a word (phonological errors). Moreover, slips are called contextual errors when they have been influenced by other elements of the intended utterance and noncontextual errors when they have been influenced by factors outside of the intended speech components, for example, by something that one thinks but does not mean to say as in the case of the general above. Table I presents a categorization of the major types of slips of the tongue, as well as an example of each type.

TABLE I
Major Categories of Slips of the Tongue

Type of slip	Example
Word errors	
Contextual errors	
Substitutions	
Exchanges	Threw the clock through the window → . . . window through the clock
Perseverations	Class is about discussing the text → class is about discussing the class
Anticipations	Sun is in the sky → sky is in the sky
Additions	These flowers are purple → these purple flowers are purple
Shifts	Something to tell you all → something all to tell you
Noncontextual errors	
Substitutions	My boss's wife → my boss's husband
Blends	Recognize/reflect → recoflect
Additions	The only thing I can do → the only one thing I can do
Deletions	I just wanted to ask that → I just wanted to that
Phonological errors	
Contextual errors	
Exchanges	Copy of my paper → poppy of my caper
Perseverations	How the leaflet's written → leaflet's litten
Anticipations	Its a real mystery → meal mystery
Noncontextual errors	
Deletions	Split brain → split bain
Substitutions	Paradigms → paratimes

A. Word-Level Errors

Contextual word errors include substitution of a word in an utterance for an intended word, addition of a word, and shifts of one or more words in an utterance. (See Table I for examples of these errors.) In a substitution involving an exchange, the error is a direct swapping of two words' intended positions in the phrase or sentence (e.g., "threw the window through the clock" instead of "threw the clock through the window"). Perseverations involve the unintentional repetition of a word found early in the utterance at a later point in the utterance. Anticipations are the opposite of perseverations because a word which is planned for a later part of the utterance is said instead of a word intended for the current part of the utterance. Additions of words, on the other hand, involve information which is relevant to the intended utterance but is added in unnecessarily, often duplicating speech (e.g., "these purple flowers are purple" instead of "these flowers are purple"). Shifts of words are those instances when the intended words are all included in the utterance and no extra words are added, but one word moves to a different location in the phrase or sentence than planned.

Although shifts, by definition, are always contextual slips, word errors involving substitutions or additions can be either contextually or noncontextually based. Other noncontextual whole-word slips of the tongue (those which are influenced by thoughts that are not intended to be articulated) are deletions and blends. Deletions are the omission of a word from the planned utterance. Blends are the instances in which two words which are both appropriate in the utterance are combined into one articulated nonword ("grisly" and "ghastly" become "grastly.")

One salient characteristic of word-level slips of the tongue is lexical bias, or the tendency for slips to create words instead of nonwords. This bias has been explained in different ways. One explanation is that there is a mechanism that monitors or "listens to" speech before it is produced and compares it with the intended output. Nonword errors are easier to detect than word errors because of their uniqueness and thus are corrected before they are produced. Alternatively, lexical bias may reflect the structure of the lexicon. Priming accumulates in lexical nodes representing words, but will not affect nonwords since by definition only words have lexical nodes. This increased priming of words will lead to an increased likelihood of a word rather than a nonword being produced in a word retrieval error.

Whole-word substitutions (exchanges, perseverations, and anticipations) demonstrate another general characteristic: syntactic class regularity. This means that in slips of the tongue the intruding word will almost always be the same part of speech or syntactic class as the intended word. For example, nouns will be replaced with nouns, and adjectives with adjectives. This suggests that word retrieval is restricted to the syntactic class of the intended word because activation of lexical nodes occurs within one syntactic domain at a time. [*See* SYNTAX.]

In addition to being semantically and syntactically related to the intended word, substitutions are often phonologically related to the planned word. The model explains this in terms of priming of lexical nodes via shared phonological nodes: When a lexical node is primed, this priming spreads to the connected phonological nodes, which in turn send priming back up to all lexical nodes which contain these phonological components. Thus, words which are phonologically similar to the intended word have increased levels of priming. If any other lexical node accumulates more priming than the lexical node for the planned word, a phonologically related word substitution will occur.

Slips of the tongue resulting in blends of words occur when two lexical nodes in the same syntactic class receive exactly the same amount of priming because the meaning of each is equally appropriate in the given context (e.g., "The competition is a little stougher" [stiffer/tougher]). Thus, both nodes are simultaneously activated. Although semantic and syntactic similarity of the words are the most important determinants of blends, there are also phonological influences. For example, the blend *sotally* involves *solely* and *totally*, which are not only similar in meaning, but also in sound. Again, the influence of priming via both phonological and semantic nodes is demonstrated.

B. Phonological Level Errors

Slips of the tongue at the phonological level are important for models of language production because they indicate the nature of phonological units in the lexicon (see Table I). That is, these errors involve a sublexical component of the word's phonology which is moved or deleted; identification of this component indicates the units of sound that are assembled during word retrieval to create a word.

The most infamous and most studied of these errors (and possibly of all speech errors) is the Spoonerism, or the exchange of sounds within a planned utterance. The Reverend William Spooner, for whom these errors are named, was famous for speech in which he transposed letters or syllables between words. Quite often these transpositions resulted in real words, but the meaning of the sentence was dramatically altered by the error. There is some question as to whether Spooner's errors were truly accidental or carefully planned, but in either case the results are interesting: Speaking to a student, he declared, "I see you have hissed all my mystery lectures. I saw you fight a liar in the back quad. In fact, you have tasted the whole worm."

Phonological perseverations and anticipations are much like their whole-word counterparts, except that only a part of the word is unintentionally duplicated. In these errors, additional sounds are not merely added to the planned speech, but rather they replace the correct phonological components. Noncontextual phonological errors include: elisions, which are the deletion of a phonological component of a word, and substitutions, which are the replacements of phonologically correct parts of a word with inaccurate parts. These phonological level slips of the tongue display consistent characteristics just as do word-level slips. For example, similar to the lexical bias in word errors, there is a bias toward the creation of phonological strings which are acceptable and pronounceable in the language being spoken.

Anticipations at both the word and phonological level are the most common type of speech error and provide evidence for planning before articulation occurs. That is, a word or phonological component of a word cannot be anticipated if it has not been retrieved; the fact that anticipatory errors occur several words in advance of the intended location of a word or sound suggests that planning has occurred by this point. Anticipations may result when priming spreads down from the semantic nodes relevant to the topic and intended meaning to lexical and phonological nodes. This priming of to-be-articulated components prior to their activation produces errors involving anticipations.

C. Freudian Slips

One important and well-known kind of noncontextual word error is what is commonly referred to as the Freudian slip. Freud claimed that slips of the tongue were almost always caused by influences external to the intended utterance, in particular "a single unconscious thought" or "a more general psychic motive." These unconscious processes were believed by Freud to be uniquely responsible for unintended utterances, to the near exclusion of phonological or other influences. Careful analysis of collections of slips, however, has revealed the variety of slips caused by contextual, linguistic influences seen in Table I. Thus, Freudian slips are one example of a more general phenomenon and they too conform to linguistic regularities seen in other types of slips, for example, syntactic class regularity. Nonetheless, they are a colorful reminder of the potent effect of nonconscious thoughts on behavior.

A typical Freudian slip is found in ex-President George Bush's statement "I don't want to run the risk of ruining what is a lovely *recession,*" when he intended to say *"reception."* A Freudian explanation of this mistake would be that Mr. Bush was so concerned with the state of the American economy that this thought was inadvertently articulated during his speech. Thus, this is a case of repressed concern about the economy of the United States coming to light. However, this Freudian interpretation omits some other qualities of the utterance which suggest additional causal factors. The similar phonological components of the two words are something which Freud underestimated as influential in the formation of the error.

The role of both "unconscious thoughts" and phonology can also be seen in a slip reported by Freud: "I call on you to belch to the health of our chief" (drink a toast). The language being spoken was German in which the word for *belch* is *Aufzustossen,* which has obvious phonological similarity to the word for *drink a toast, Anzustossen.* Thus, the error in word retrieval probably reflects both phonological priming and semantic priming from "unconscious thoughts."

Thus, Freudian analyses may be at least partially correct in describing the underlying causes of speech errors, but they do not tell the whole story. They ignore linguistic factors such as the phonological relatedness or syntactic regularity. Current models of language production can account for the existence of competing plans more thoroughly than can Freudian interpretations.

D. Experimental Induction of Slips

Historically, slips of the tongue have been analyzed based on collections of natural errors occurring in everyday life. These collections of errors have provided insight into the nature of word retrieval and speech production, and they have demonstrated the broad range of types of slips, but they also have some drawbacks. There are two main criticisms leveled against collections of naturally occurring speech errors. The first is that the collections may somehow be unintentionally biased by the collector. Misrecorded errors and undetected errors are two sources of such bias. Second, such collections only allow for post hoc interpretations of the causes of the errors. Only educated guesses and inferences can be made about the source of the errors because hypothesized causal relationships have not been tested.

These criticisms have prompted researchers to develop experimental techniques for eliciting speech errors in the laboratory. There are two important components in eliciting speech errors: creating two speech plans which are directly in competition with one another, and providing insufficient time to self-monitor or edit the competing plans.

A successful method has been found for inducing Spoonerisms, which can be defined as errors in which two phonemes within an utterance involuntarily switch places, for example, saying "blue chop sticks" instead of "blue chip stocks." Several word pairs are presented to a person who reads them silently. These word pairs are phonologically related to the desired Spoonerism. Target phrases are cued to be read aloud and these phrases are expected to produce Spoonerisms, based on the composition of the silently read pairs. For example, the person would read silently the first three phrases, and read the final target phrase aloud:

flat freight (silently)
fly free (silently)
flag fraud (silently)
fruit fly (aloud)

The phonology of the first three phrases should cause "fruit fly" to be said aloud as "flute fry," due to the priming of the competing phonology in the preceding phrases.

Slips are also elicited in the laboratory using tongue twisters. For example, subjects read phrases such as "a soldier's major shoulder surgery" or "a bucket of blue bug's blood" several times at a set pace. The structural properties of these phrases make it likely that slips of the tongue will occur.

The problems encountered in identifying the cause of speech errors (e.g., Freudian vs phonological) are reduced when experimental manipulations cause the error. Furthermore, the elicited slips are carefully recorded in the laboratory and thus are less subject to recording errors such as being undetected. The major drawback to reliance on errors induced in the laboratory is a very general criticism of all laboratory research: The influences present in the experiment may not be those which are present in the natural situations in which slips occur. Additionally, the variety of types of slips which occur is severely underrepresented in experimentally induced speech errors. Thus, experimentally induced and naturally occurring slips of the tongue should be considered complementary sources of information about the nature of errors in word retrieval and production.

VI. ADULT AGING AND WORD RETRIEVAL

Verbal ability is thought to be relatively preserved in normal old age despite the decline in some other cognitive abilities, for example, the ability to remember new information. However, older adults' difficulty in retrieving well-known names and vocabulary words is proverbial ("I'll never forget what's-her-name") and figures prominently in their reports of cognitive problems in everyday life. Healthy older adults complain that failures in retrieving well-known words increase dramatically over the years and become an irksome problem. Thus, word retrieval may be an exception to the generalization that verbal ability and existing knowledge are relatively immune to aging. There are at least four sources of evidence that suggest that word retrieval declines in old age.

First, there are age-related decreases in the *accuracy* of naming pictures of objects or actions and age-related increases in the *time* to name pictures. These differences appear to reflect deficits in access to the sounds of words because the age difference decreases when phonological cues are provided.

Second, older adults are slower and less accurate than young adults in producing a target word corresponding to a definition. On fluency tests in which people are asked to produce words that are an instance of a specified category (e.g., "animals," "words that start with P"), older adults usually produce fewer words than young adults in a given amount of time.

Older adults' greater word finding difficulty is also reflected in their spontaneous speech. Relative to young adults, older adults produce more pronouns and more ambiguous references (e.g., "thing," "stuff") than common or proper nouns in describing experiences. The reason for this appears to be that they are less able than younger adults to retrieve the appropriate words. Speech rate is also slower for older than young adults. This is probably partly because of slower word retrieval, but also because of changes in respiration and articulatory musculature that slow articulation.

Finally, older adults experience more TOTs than young adults and take more time to resolve them. However, older adults report fewer persistent alternates and are less able to retrieve partial phonological information about the target. These word retrieval deficits may reflect an aging process that weakens the strength of connections among nodes in memory reducing the rate and amount of priming transmitted across connections. Whatever the explanation may prove to be, a characteristic of normal, healthy aging is greater difficulty in word retrieval, a process that may no longer be taken for granted.

Bibliography

Brown, A. S. (1991). The tip of the tongue experience: A review and evaluation. *Psychol. Bull.* **109,** 204–223.

Burke, D. M., and Laver, G. (1990). Aging and word retrieval: Selective age deficits in language. In "Aging and Cognition: Mental Processes, Self-Awareness and Interventions" (E. A. Lovelace, Ed.), pp. 281–300. North Holland, Amsterdam.

Burke, D. M., MacKay, D. G., Worthley, J. S., and Wade, E. (1991). On the tip of the tongue: What causes word finding failures in young and older adults. *J. Memory Language* **30,** 542–579.

Dell, G. S. (1986). A spreading-activation theory of retrieval in sentence production. *Psychol. Rev.* **93,** 283–321.

Ellis, A. W. (1985). "Progress in the Psychology of Language." Erlbaum, Hillsdale, NJ.

Fromkin, V. A. (1973). "Speech Errors as Linguistic Evidence." Mouton, The Hague.

Levelt, W. J. M. (1989). "Speaking." MIT Press, Cambridge, MA.

MacKay, D. G. (1987). "The Organization of Perception and Action: A Theory for Language and Other Cognitive Skills." Springer-Verlag, New York.

Roediger, H. L., Weldon, M. S., and Challis, B. H. (1989). Explaining dissociations between implicit and explicit measures of retention: A processing account. In "Varieties of Memory and Consciousness: Essays in Honour of Endel Tulving" (H. L. Roediger and F. I. M. Craik, Eds.), pp. 3–41. Erlbaum, Hillsdale, NJ.

WORK EFFICIENCY AND MOTIVATION

Elizabeth Goldsmith
Florida State University

Glossary

Attitudes A state of mind or feeling about objects, people, or events.

Commitment The degree to which an individual identifies with and is involved in a particular activity or organization.

Efficiency Acting in such a way as to use a minimum of time, money, or unnecessary effort, and the ratio of effective output to the input required to achieve it.

Effort The use of energy to do something; exertion.

Goals End results toward which human activity is directed.

Motivation Effort expended to perform work.

Persistence Directed effort over time.

Satisfaction Contentment derived from a relationship or a level of living or working.

Work Physical or mental effort expended to produce or accomplish something.

WORK EFFICIENCY AND MOTIVATION have emerged as concerns of managers and researchers in the 20th century. From its beginning in the United States with the assembly line efficiency studies of Frederick Taylor, this arena of study has grown into a sophisticated science applicable to all organizations. The interest in the topic has emerged because of the recognition that successful organizations need people who are motivated and efficient. How to increase motivation and efficiency in workers are ongoing issues throughout the world. It would be difficult to find a recent research journal or book on industrial psychology, organizational behavior, or management that does not address these issues. [*See* MOTIVATION.]

I. INTRODUCTION

A unified treatment of work efficiency and motivation must begin with the phenomenon of human behavior. Each individual is unique, and placed in similar situations all people do not act alike. However, certain fundamental consistencies that underlie behavior can be identified, measured, and predicted. This predictability allows for the systematic study of human behavior. The aspects of behavior to be discussed in this article are work efficiency and motivation.

II. THE NATURE OF EFFICIENCY

Many practical problems are associated with how efficient workers are. The overall productivity (output) of an organization is linked to the way workers perform. How to encourage efficiency and maintain high-quality performance in workers are problems for everyone from line foremen to company presidents. This problem permeates all organizations, large or small, for profit or nonprofit.

Since the 1940s, the emphasis has shifted from increasing efficiency to increasing effectiveness as a means for boosting productivity. For example, a department store is considered effective when it successfully meets the needs of its shoppers. It is efficient when it can do this and still keep costs low. Thus, a store is most effective when it attains its sales or market share goals in a productive and efficient manner. The emphasis is not purely on making the most number of sales in record time, but on making sure that the sales are well handled, to encourage repeat business, and good "word of mouth." The concept of effectiveness implies a concern for the long haul as well as for short-term gains.

The roots of efficiency studies that eventually led to the more global concept of effectiveness can be traced to the early 1900s when Frederick Taylor proposed scientific management principles designed to maximize production efficiency. The goal of these principles was to eliminate wasted time and motion in repetitious work, especially assembly-line work. By carefully studying the most efficient ways jobs could be performed and implementing changes to increase efficiency, he was able to achieve productivity improvements from 200 to 300%. Naturally, Taylor became the favorite of managers. Because of his contributions, Taylor is often called the father of management or the father of time and motion studies.

Eventually, his methods were criticized because many previously creative, personally satisfying jobs became routinized and boring leading to increased absenteeism, and in some cases disruptive and even destructive behavior by employees. In highly routinized jobs, workers can begin to feel like "cogs in a wheel" rather than as intelligent, skilled human beings. Managers who are aware of this problem try to resolve the creativity/efficiency conflict through a variety of ways. Most typically, jobs are redesigned to make them less routine and more meaningful. For example, encouraging team work stimulates workers' interest in their jobs and increases productivity. Ultimately, organizations need to develop a strategy and a structure that address the needs of its workers as well as its clientele.

By the 1940s and 1950s, concern for the plight of the individual worker became the subject of many management and industrial psychology studies. During these decades, worker motivation became increasingly recognized as a contributor to productivity. Closely allied to the subjects of efficiency and effectiveness is the concept of motivation to be discussed next.

III. THE NATURE OF MOTIVATION

Motivation comes in many forms. The word motivation was originally derived from the Latin word "movere," meaning "to move." In current management theory and practice, motivation refers to movement and also direction, vigor, persistence, creativity, and sustained energy.

To increase worker motivation, employers can choose from several methods. Some of these are enriching job skills through workshops, on-the-job training, workplace seminars, courses, job rotation, and other forms of job/skill enrichment or by providing promotions, bonuses, or raises. Complications arise from the fact that what motivates one worker might not motivate another. The skilled manager tries to match the person with the most appropriate type of motivation. Keeping job skills up-to-date and providing a stimulating workplace are two ways that usually ensure a continual reservoir of highly trained, motivated employees.

The previously mentioned methods to motivate employees are all extrinsic. In other words, they describe ways employers or managers (outside sources) can motivate workers. Another form of motivation is intrinsic. In intrinsic motivation, the effort, comes from within the worker. The concept of intrinsic and extrinsic motivation provides many puzzles for human behaviorists. Origin is one. Some individuals need very little external push to work harder while others seem to need a lot. Are the differences caused by genetics? By childhood experiences? By early work experiences? Another puzzle is how to stimulate intrinsic motivation.

Studies on intrinsic motivation date back to the 1920s, but the concept became more widely known in the 1950s. Intrinsic motivation implies enjoyment in an action, a feeling of being totally immersed by an activity. Far more is known about extrinsic than about intrinsic motivation. It is generally agreed that to increase productivity, organizations need to tap both intrinsic and extrinsic motivation. Since motivation appears to be affected by both personal and situational factors which interact with one another, managers need to address both sets of factors. [*See* MOTIVATION, EMOTIONAL BASIS.]

Many previous studies on motivation have centered on three main concerns: (1) what motivates or energizes human behavior, (2) how this behavior can be stimulated and sustained, and (3) what organizations can do to initiate, direct, and channel motivation. The rest of the article addresses these concerns.

IV. CENTRAL ISSUES IN EFFICIENCY AND MOTIVATION

One specific efficiency issue, efficiency versus effectiveness, has already been discussed. Generally, organizations today stress effectiveness. Also the problems inherent in overemphasizing efficiency and routinization and underemphasizing creativity and individualism in jobs have been mentioned in the Frederick Taylor discussion. A more central issue germane to both efficiency and motivation is how to stimulate and reward people who work hard.

A. Influences

Why is that some workers can be depended on to work hard while others cannot? There are many influences on worker efficiency and motivation. The most basic ones are personality, heredity, environment, and situations. Personality, the qualities, traits, and personal characteristics of a person, appears to be a result of both heredity and environment. The way it is enacted depends on the situation in which people find themselves.

Probably the best known theory of motivation was developed by psychologist Abraham Maslow. He hypothesized that each individual has a series of needs ranging from lower order needs to higher order needs. He called this series a hierarchy of needs. The lower order needs include physiological needs (i.e., thirst, hunger, shelter) and safety (i.e., security, safety from danger). The higher order needs include love (i.e., affection, acceptance), esteem (i.e., respect, admiration, status), and self-actualization (i.e., the development of full potential, fulfillment). According to Maslow, physiological needs have first priority and must be partially met before a person can fulfill higher order needs. All people seek to fulfill their needs, but each individual fulfills them in a different way.

Given this hierarchy, an organization that wants to motivate an employee should try to assess where that person is on the hierarchy and focus on satisfying that level of needs before proceeding to the next level. For example, during a recession or a period of down-sizing, the emphasis should be on safety needs (level two). During high growth times, the emphasis may shift to esteem or self-actualization (levels four and five).

Motivation can be envisioned as a process that originates with unsatisfied needs (see Fig. 1). In Figure 1, unsatisfied needs lead to tension which in turn stimulates drive and search behavior. The process ends when needs are satisfied and tension is reduced.

FIGURE 1 The Motivation Process. [From S. Robbins, "Organizational Behavior: Concepts, Controversies, and Applications," p. 192. Reprinted by permission of Prentice-Hall, Englewood Cliffs, NJ.]

An individual as well as an organization can seek to influence the motivation process. Ideally, individual needs should be compatible and consistent with organizational needs. Unfortunately, it is not unusual for these needs to not match and to prove counterproductive. For example, a worker may be seeking solutions to problems which no longer hold importance for his or her manager. Communication and a shared vision are the keys to creating the right fit between individual effort and organizational output.

By the 1960s a philosophical shift was taking place in the field of organizational behavior. The human factor became an even more important subject of study than it had been previously. Jobs were no longer looked at as strictly technical, but as socio-technical systems. This approach took into consideration the individual's response to their job as well as to the actual mechanics of the job. Technical tasks were viewed within the greater context of the work culture and environment. The narrowly defined concept of scientific management, i.e., efficiency first and foremost, gave way to a much broader definition of management and all its permutations.

For example, in 1960 Douglas McGregor suggested in his book *The Human Side of Enterprise* that the manager's view of the nature of human beings is biased toward two main groupings of behavior assumptions which he labeled Theory X and Theory Y. Theory X assumes that the lower order needs identified by Maslow dominate the individual so that under Theory X, the assumptions held by managers are:

1. Employees inherently dislike work and will avoid it if they can.
2. Since employees dislike work, they must be coerced, controlled, directed, or threatened with punishment to put forth adequate effort toward the achievement of organizational objectives.
3. Employees will try to avoid responsibilities and seek security and direction whenever possible.

The assumptions underlying Theory Y are:

1. Employees view work as being as natural as rest or play.

2. Employees will exercise self-direction and self-control if they are committed to organizational objectives.
3. Employees are committed to objectives that are related to the rewards associated with their achievement.
4. Employees under normal conditions seek responsibility.
5. Most employees will exercise a relatively high degree of imagination, ingenuity, and creativity.
6. Under the conditions of modern life, most employees' intellectual potentialities are only partially utilized.

McGregor thought that Theory Y assumptions were more valid than Theory X. He believed that most people would thrive on opportunities for growth, challenging jobs, good interpersonal relations, and responsibility.

Motivation took on a more complicated formula with the introduction of the motivation–hygiene theory of psychologist Frederick Herzberg. He asserted that intrinsic factors such as achievement, recognition, responsibility, and growth were related to job satisfaction whereas extrinsic factors were more associated with dissatisfaction. A person's attitudes, therefore, have a great deal to do with that person's satisfaction and job success.

Just as with Taylor, the theories of McGregor and Herzberg have their detractors. For example, Herzberg's theory is criticized for emphasizing satisfaction over productivity and McGregor's for being too simplistic. However, all three theorists along with Maslow have had an enormous impact on the way organizations manage workers and design jobs. There are a number of newer theories that fall into the following categories: (1) needs, (2) goal-setting, (3) reinforcement, (4) equity, (5) expectancy, and (6) stress and fatigue. Due to space limitations not all can be sufficiently addressed in this article. What they have in common is that they try to explain and predict motivation, and many build on the works previously cited.

The field of psychology has always had a strong influence on the theories, research, and applications in organizational behavior. As an example, the roots of needs theory can be traced to Maslow's hierarchy of needs and those of reinforcement theory to the work of Harvard psychologist B. F. Skinner. Since Skinner found that rewards are most effective when they immediately follow the desired response, his research influenced when and how managers rewarded positive work behaviors. [*See* OPERANT LEARNING.]

Probably of the six theory categories listed, the one most relevant to the subject of motivation is expectancy theory. According to this theory, a person's motivation is a function of (1) matching effort to performance expectancies, (2) matching performance to outcome expectancies, and (3) the perception of attractiveness of outcomes. Satisfaction is conceived as a result of performance rather than a cause of it.

B. Job Attitudes and Performance

Attitudes are thoughts or feelings (positive or negative) about objects, people, or events. For instance, people like or dislike opera. They also like or dislike certain aspects of their work. People have thousands of attitudes, but for the purposes of this chapter the focus will be on job attitudes, specifically, job satisfaction, involvement, and commitment.

Job satisfaction refers to the general attitude people have about their jobs. There are many measures of work satisfaction. Most attempt to determine whether workers are challenged in their work, feel adequately compensated, rewarded, and comfortable in their work environment including the physical facilities and interpersonal relationships.

Job involvement has to do with how strongly people identify with and really care about the work they do. Commitment refers to how much the person identifies with the overall organization. Research indicates that high job involvement and commitment result in lower absenteeism and job turnover. Job satisfaction, involvement, and commitment are all subject to change, but usually people strive to maintain a consistency or balance in their attitudes and behaviors. This is consistent with McGregor's Theory Y discussed earlier, most people want to do well at their work.

In regard to performance, individuals are motivated if they can see that their performance is appreciated, noted, and rewarded. They need to know what the organization's performance expectations are and what the outcomes of their individual performance will be. Unclear objectives and a lack of consistency or confidence in the organization to define and recognize good performance will decrease worker motivation, and productivity may suffer.

C. Diversity in the Workplace

In the 1990s, a concern emerged about how well past motivational and efficiency theories fit the changing composition of the workforce. The growing number of women, minorities, and older workers in the labor force led organizations to reassess previously held notions about workers and their motivations. Appropriate changes in reward systems have begun to be implemented. As one example of a policy responsive to changes in the work force, the popularity and pervasiveness of flextime (flexible hours of work arrival and departure) can be partially traced to the growing number of working parents who are trying to balance work and family responsibilities.

In addition, the recognition of diversity in the workplace has brought to question the notion that an organization has a uniform culture to which all employees subscribe. Typically in organizations there is a dominant culture and several subcultures. A subculture is a set of values and attitudes held by a minority of the organization's members. Subcultures may fall along the lines of specializations, interests, or in a variety of other ways. Subcultures can weaken and undermine an organization, but more likely they will ascribe to and support the values of the dominant organization culture while seeking to maintain their own identity.

Respecting diversity and working with it rather than against it will be the key to the continued success of organizations. In order to remain competitive, employers are making an effort to recognize, recruit, and manage an older and more culturally and racially diverse work force. While practical applications are moving ahead, research on workplace diversity in relation to motivation and efficiency is in its infancy.

V. MOTIVATIONAL TECHNIQUES

The concept of goal motivation is used to explain how direction, effort, and duration/persistence affect goal-setting. Goals direct action and behavior. It has been established that higher goals produce higher performance. If goals are set too low they are not motivating enough. Conversely, goals set unreasonably high can be frustrating. Thus, finding the right level of goals is a management problem. The words "duration" and "persistence" refer to directed effort over time, a relentless, driving behavior.

Goal commitment implies a determination to continue goal-seeking. Research indicates that self-confidence and previous success at achieving goals positively affect a person's future goal commitment and achievement.

Technique refers to the systematic procedure for accomplishing a task. Motivational techniques, therefore, are procedures that stimulate a person to accomplish a work task. Goal-setting is one technique for motivating workers.

A. Goal-Setting

In 1968, Edwin Locke published a paper that is considered to be the seminal work on goal-setting theory. He wrote that people strive to attain goals in order to satisfy their emotions and desires. Although goal-setting is an important motivational stimulus, the concepts of needs and values are also fundamental concepts of work motivation according to Locke.

More recently, researchers and theorists have concluded that goals direct and focus attention onto certain task requirements, away from conflicting or alternative actions. Thus, goals direct behavior and provide a framework for a strategy of performance. Sometimes intentions and goals are used interchangeably, but they are different in that intentions may be theoretical (a person plans or intends to do something) whereas the word goal implies action. In the terms "goal attainment" and "goal achievement," an end result is assumed.

Before goals can be achieved, they need to be set. Research on goal-setting falls into the following categories: (1) specific versus general, (2) difficult versus easy, (3) owned or shared versus imposed, and (4) timely feedback and progress toward goals. The results of the research indicate that specific, challenging, and owned or shared goals are preferred. The degree of persistence applied to goal pursuance is closely linked to ultimate achievement. And in the end, timely and appropriate feedback is preferable to no feedback. Workers want to know the results of their efforts.

Organizations put a great deal of energy into setting goals and motivating workers to achieve organizational goals. At the same time, workers have personal goals they are trying to achieve. Two examples of worker goals are the opportunity to learn more and move ahead. Organizations try to match worker's needs with organizational needs—enhancing work satisfaction and output for both.

In the 1980s, American business embraced a Japanese business practice called Total Quality Management (TQM). One of the techniques in TQM relevant to goal-setting is the widespread use of quality circles, or QCs. In QCs, a group of employees regularly meets to identify and solve work-related problems.

Their focus is on increasing productivity and meeting department and organizational goals. Improvements are suggested. A group leader reports the proposed improvements to higher management. Steering committees sort through the suggestions and implement the ones they consider viable. With QCs it was thought that everyone benefits from the increased communication between the various levels of the organization and the cooperative spirit generated by teamwork.

By the 1990s, some drawbacks to QCs and TQM were uncovered. This form of management involves many meetings and a lot of paperwork that is time consuming. Some of this time was taken away from the basic organizational functions of serving customers and producing goods. Consequently, TQM and QCs are being reassessed. Research is under way to determine in what situations, settings, and organizations QCs and TQM are most effective.

B. Reward Systems in Organizations

A review of the literature reveals the importance of rewards in the relationship between motivation, satisfaction, and work performance. Lyman Porter and Edward Lawler developers of the Porter–Lawler motivation model recommend that organizations make sure that their reward policies are closely linked to performance. This is suggested because the individual worker's job satisfaction is derived from the difference between the amount of rewards he or she receives and the amount he or she expects to receive. Job satisfaction represents an attitude, positive or negative, rather than a behavior.

Equity is an important part of job satisfaction. Employees want promotion and pay systems that they perceive as just, equitable, and fair. Individuals who perceive reward decisions as unambigious and consistent with their expectations will likely report satisfaction with their job. [*See* EQUITY.]

Closely linked to the concepts of intrinsic and extrinsic motivation discussed earlier are the concepts of intrinsic and extrinsic rewards. The pleasure or value a person derives from the content of work itself makes it intrinsically rewarding. Rewards received from the work environment, the organization, are extrinsic. A company-paid car is an extrinsic reward, whereas the feelings of personal satisfaction from a job well done are intrinsic. Intrinsic rewards may stem from greater job freedom and discretion, more interesting work, opportunities for personal growth, and more participation in decision-making. There are dozens of extrinsic rewards ranging from assigned parking spaces to profit sharing.

To be most effective, rewards should be individualized to meet each person's needs. One employee might value a flexible lunch hour so he can swim every day in the nearby university pool while another employee may put more value on a paneled office with a large desk. Rewards can be used by organizations to recognize an employee's past achievements or to direct him or her toward certain future achievements.

VI. CONCLUDING REMARKS ON EFFICIENCY AND MOTIVATION

Everyone enjoys observing and commenting on human behavior. This article explored how organizations try to direct employee behavior toward higher productivity. The theories discussed in the chapter reveal that there is not one, singular all-purpose way to motivate workers or to make an organization more efficient. Generally it is agreed that satisfied, motivated workers are more productive than dissatisfied, bored workers. Organizations try to identify, recognize, and reward productive workers. Research reveals that rewards should be consistently and fairly distributed. The ultimate organizational behavior goal is a happy/productive/consistent worker—not one alternating between despair and elation. Rewards should not produce ups and downs, but a secure feeling that efforts are noted and rewarded, if not immediately, then soon.

Since its beginnings in assembly-line management, the concept of efficiency has given way to a broader view of productivity encompassing effectiveness and worker satisfaction. The effective organization sets goals and keeps in mind the different levels of job needs of its workers. Organizations in the future will make fuller use of the skills, diversity, and motivational potential of their human resources.

Acknowledgment

The author thanks Dr. Mark Martinko, Professor of Management at Florida State University, for reviewing an early draft of this article.

Bibliography

Herzberg, H., Mausner, B., and Synderman, B. (1954). "The Motivation to Work." Wiley, New York.

Kleinbeck, U., Quast, H., Thierry, H., and Hacker, H. (Eds.) (1990). "Work Motivation." Erlbaum, Hillsdale, NJ.

Locke, E. (1968). Toward a theory of task motivation and incentives. *Organizational Behavior and Human Performance*, **3**, 157–189.

Maslow, A. (1954). "Motivation and Personality." Harper & Row, New York.

McGregor, D. (1960). "The Human Side of Enterprise." McGraw–Hill, New York.

Porter, L., and E. Lawler (1968). "Managerial Attitudes and Performance." Irwin, Homewood, IL.

Robbins, S. (1989). "Organizational Behavior," 4th ed. Prentice-Hall, Englewood Cliffs, NJ.

Skinner, B. F. (1971). "Contingencies of Reinforcement." Appleton-Century-Crofts, East Walk, CT.

Steers, R., and L. Porter (1991). "Motivation and Work Behavior," 5th ed. McGraw–Hill, New York.

Taylor, F. (1911). "Principles of Scientific Management." Harper & Brothers, New York.

Contributors

Numbers in parentheses indicate the volumes and pages on which the authors' contributions begin.

Salmon Akhtar (3:265)
Narcissistic Personality Disorder
Department of Adult Outpatient Psychiatry
Jefferson Medical College
Philadelphia, Pennsylvania 19107

Carolyn M. Aldwin (1:47)
Aging, Personality, and Adaptation
Department of Applied Behavioral Sciences
University of California at Davis
Davis, California 95616

Darlys J. Alford (2:83)
Deductive Reasoning
Department of Psychology
University of Southern Mississippi
Hattiesburg, Mississippi 39406

Scott T. Allison (4:253)
Social Values
Department of Psychology
University of Richmond
Richmond, Virginia 23173

Earl A. Alluisi (3:191)
Military Psychology
Institute for Defense Analyses
Alexandria, Virginia 22311

Madeline N. Altabe (1:407)
Body Image
Department of Psychology
University of South Florida
Tampa, Florida 33620

Bob Altemeyer (1:315)
Authoritarianism
Department of Psychology
University of Manitoba
Winnipeg, Manitoba
Canada R3T 2N2

David G. Amaral (2:509)
Hippocampal Formation
Center for Behavioral Neuroscience
State University of New York at Stony Brook
Stony Brook, New York 11794

Anne Anastasi (1:211)
Aptitude Testing
Department of Psychology
Fordham University
Bronx, New York 10458

W. F. Angermeier (3:351)
Operant Learning
Psychologisches Institut
Universität zu Köln
50923 Köln
Germany

Dick Anthony (1:457)
Brainwashing and Totalitarian Influence
Graduate Theological Union
Berkeley, California 94709

John S. Antrobus (2:165)
Dreaming
Department of Psychology
The City College of the City University of New York
New York, New York 10031

Trevor Archer (1:665)
Conflict Behavior
Department of Psychology
University of Göteborg
S-400 20 Göteborg
Sweden

Martin Arguin (1:71)
Agraphia
Neurolinguistics Group
Montreal Neurological Institute
Montreal, Quebec
Canada H3A 2B4

Robert M. Arkin (4:225)
Social Comparison
Department of Psychology
The Ohio State University
Columbus, Ohio 43210

Roseanne Armitage (4:205)
Sleep: Biological Rhythms and Human Performance
Department of Psychiatry
University of Texas Southwestern Medical Center at Dallas
Dallas, Texas 75235

Mark Attridge (2:689)
Interpersonal Communication
Department of Psychology
University of Minnesota
Minneapolis, Minnesota 55455

James R. Averill (1:131)
Anger
Department of Psychology
University of Massachusetts at Amherst
Amherst, Massachusetts 01003

Efrain C. Azmitia (1:435)
Brain Chemicals
Department of Biology
Center for Neural Science
New York University
New York, New York 10003

Bernard J. Baars (1:687)
Consciousness
The Wright Institute
Berkeley, California 94704

Ronald Baenninger (1:39)
Aggression
Department of Psychology
Temple University
Philadelphia, Pennsylvania 19122

J. Vivien Bainbridge (2:589)
Implicit Memory
Department of Psychology
University of Oklahoma
Norman, Oklahoma 73019

Adriana Balaguer (3:127)
Mate Selection
Department of Psychiatry
Long Island Jewish Hospital
Queens, New York 11042

Janice I. Baldwin (4:159)
Sexual Behavior
Department of Psychology
University of California at Santa Barbara
Santa Barbara, California 93106

John D. Baldwin (4:159)
Sexual Behavior
Department of Psychology
University of California at Santa Barbara
Santa Barbara, California 93106

Albert Bandura (4:71)
Self-Efficacy
Department of Psychology
Stanford University
Stanford, California 94305

Craig R. Barclay (1:337)
Autobiographical Remembering and Self-Knowledge
Graduate School of Education and Human Development
University of Rochester
Rochester, New York 14627

David H. Barlow (1:165)
Anxiety Disorders
Center for Stress and Anxiety Disorders and Department of Psychology
University at Albany
State University of New York
Albany, New York 12203

Melanie K. Barnes (2:701)
Interpersonal Perception and Communication
Department of Psychology
University of Iowa
Iowa City, Iowa 52242

William B. Barr (2:279)
Epilepsy
Departments of Psychiatry and Neurology
Albert Einstein College of Medicine
Long Island Jewish Medical Center
Glen Oaks, New York 11004

David J. Bateson (4:411)
Test Behavior
Department of Mathematics and Science Education
University of British Columbia
Vancouver, British Columbia
Canada V6T 1W5

Roy F. Baumeister (4:83)
Self-Esteem
Department of Psychology
Case Western Reserve University
Cleveland, Ohio 44106

James T. Becker (2:97)
Dementia
Departments of Psychiatry and Neurology
University of Pittsburgh Medical Center
Pittsburgh, Pennsylvania 15260

James K. Beggan (4:253)
Social Values
Department of Psychology
University of Louisville
Louisville, Kentucky 40292

Francis S. Bellezza (1:579)
Chunking
Department of Psychology
Ohio University
Athens, Ohio 45701

Werner Bergmann (3:575)
Prejudice and Stereotypes
Center for Research on Antisemitism
Technical University of Berlin
Berlin D-10587
Germany

Gary R. Birchler (3:103)
Marital Dysfunction
Department of Veterans Affairs Medical Center
and Department of Psychiatry
University of California at San Diego
La Jolla, California 92093

Michael H. Birnbaum (3:641)
Psychophysics
Department of Psychology
California State University at Fullerton
Fullerton, California 92634

Joseph P. Blount (1:473)
Caffeine: Psychosocial Effects
Social Science Division
Widener University
Chester, Pennsylvania 19013

Terry L. Boles (2:297)
Equity
Department of Management and Organizations
University of Iowa
Iowa City, Iowa 52242

Eugene Borgida (4:213)
Social Cognition
Department of Psychology
University of Minnesota
Minneapolis, Minnesota 55455

Robert F. Bornstein (2:105)
Dependent Personality
Department of Psychology
Gettysburg College
Gettysburg, Pennsylvania 17325

M. I. Botez (1:549)
Cerebellum
Neurology Service
University of Montreal
Montreal, Quebec
Canada H2W 1T8

Robert D. Bretz, Jr. (1:223)
Arbitration
Center for Advanced Human Resource Studies
School for Industrial and Labor Relations
Cornell University
Ithaca, New York 14853

Bruce Bridgeman (2:333)
Eye Movements
Department of Psychology
University of California at Santa Cruz
Santa Cruz, California 95064

Chester L. Britt III (2:17)
Criminal Behavior
Department of Sociology
University of Illinois at Urbana-Champaign
Urbana, Illinois 61801

Nathan Brody (4:419)
Traits
Department of Psychology
Wesleyan University
Middleton, Connecticut 06457

Jason W. Brown (1:199)
Apraxia
Department of Neurology
New York University Medical Center
New York, New York 10003

Ronald T. Brown (1:537)
Central Nervous System
Departments of Psychiatry and Pediatrics
Emory University School of Medicine
Atlanta, Georgia 30322

Raymond Bruyer (2:351)
Face Recognition
Department of Psychology
Louvain University
B-1348 Louvain la Neuve
Belgium

Daniel N. Bub (1:71)
Agraphia
Neurolinguistics Group
Montreal Neurological Institute
Montreal, Quebec
Canada H3A 2B4

Christy M. Buchanan (2:543)
Hormones and Behavior
Department of Psychology
Wake Forest University
Winston-Salem, North Carolina 27109

Peter Bull (2:415)
Gestures
Department of Psychology
University of York
Heslington, York YO1 5DD
United Kingdom

Stephen R. Burgess (3:515)
Phonological Processing and Reading
Psychology Department
Florida State University
Tallahassee, Florida 32306

Deborah M. Burke (4:537)
Word Retrieval
Department of Psychology
Pomona College
Claremont, California 91711

John T. Cacioppo (1:261)
Attitude Change
Department of Psychology
and Institute for the Study of Brain, Behavior, Immunity, and Health
The Ohio State University
Columbus, Ohio 43210

Dudley D. Cahn (1:675)
Conflict Communication
Department of Communication
State University of New York College at New Paltz
New Paltz, New York 12561

Vicki Carlson (1:561)
Child Abuse
Department of Psychology
Washington University, St. Louis
St. Louis, Missouri 63130

Peter J. Carnevale (3:271)
Negotiation
Department of Psychology
University of Illinois at Urbana-Champaign
Champaign, IL 61820

Pamela Case (3:499)
Phonetics
Center for Complex Systems and Department of Psychology
Florida Atlantic University
Boca Raton, Florida 33431

Chris Chase (2:177)
Dyslexia
School of Communications and Cognitive Science
Hampshire College
Amherst, Massachusetts 01002

Martin M. Chemers (3:45)
Leadership
Department of Psychology
Claremont McKenna College
Claremont, California 91711

Xinyin Chen (3:431)
Peer Relationships and Influences in Childhood
Department of Psychology
University of Waterloo
Waterloo, Ontario
Canada N21 3GL

Christine Chiarello (4:99)
Semantic Memory
Department of Psychology
Syracuse University
Syracuse, New York 13244

Jan Cioe (1:425)
Brain
Department of Psychology
Okanagan University-College
Kelowna, British Columbia
Canada V1Y 4T4

Jane E. Clark (3:245)
Motor Development
Department of Kinesiology
University of Maryland at College Park
College Park, Maryland 20742

E. Gil Clary (1:93)
Altruism and Helping Behavior
Department of Psychology
College of St. Catherine
St. Paul, Minnesota 55105

Sheldon Cohen (4:325)
Stress and Illness
Department of Psychology
Carnegie Mellon University
Pittsburgh, Pennsylvania 15213

Robert J. Coplan (3:431)
Peer Relationships and Influences in Childhood
Department of Psychology
University of Waterloo
Walterloo, Ontario
Canada N2L 3GL

Stanley Coren (2:123)
Depth Perception
Psychology Department
University of British Columbia
Vancouver, British Columbia
Canada V6T 1Z4

Patrick W. Corrigan (2:645)
Information Processing and Clinical Psychology
Center for Psychiatric Rehabilitation
University of Chicago
Tinley Park, Illinois 60477

Paul T. Costa, Jr. (3:453)
Personality Assessment
Laboratory of Personality and Cognition
Gerontology Research Center
National Institute on Aging
National Institutes of Health
Baltimore, Maryland 21224

W. Miles Cox (1:473)
Caffeine: Psychosocial Effects
Psychology Service
North Chicago Veterans Affairs Medical Center
The Chicago Medical School
North Chicago, Illinois 60064

Phebe Cramer (2:91)
Defense Mechanisms
Department of Psychology
Williams College
Williamstown, Massachusetts 01267

Tony D. Crespi (2:381)
Forensic Psychology
Meriden, Connecticut 06450

Stephen L. Crites, Jr. (1:261)
Attitude Change
Department of Psychology
The Ohio State University
Columbus, Ohio 43210

Denise Dellarosa Cummins (1:125)
Analogical Reasoning
Department of Psychology
University of Arizona
Tucson, Arizona 85721

Rebecca Curtis (4:61)
Self-Defeating Behaviors
Derner Institute of Advanced Psychological Studies
Adelphi University
Garden City, New York 11530

Marvin W. Daehler (1:627)
Cognitive Development
Department of Psychology
University of Massachusetts at Amherst
Amherst, Massachusetts 01003

Nasser Daneshvary (4:35)
Risk-Compensating Behavior
Department of Economics
University of Nevada at Las Vegas
Las Vegas, Nevada 89154

Graham C. L. Davey (2:135)
Disgust
Department of Psychology
The City University
Northampton Square
London EC1V 0HB
England

Lori Dawson (4:183)
Sexual Orientation
Department of Psychology
University at Albany

State University of New York
Albany, New York 12222

Sarah E. Deitsch (1:141)
Antisocial Personality Disorder
Department of Psychology
University of Kentucky
Lexington, Kentucky 40506

Marian Cleeves Diamond (1:443)
Brain Development and Plasticity
Department of Integrative Biology
University of California at Berkeley
Berkeley, California 94720

Keith S. Dobson (3:631, 669)
Psychopathology; Psychotherapy
Department of Psychology
University of Calgary
Calgary, Alberta
Canada T2N 1N4

Jason N. Doctor (4:311)
Stress
Department of Psychology
San Diego State University
San Diego, California 92182
and Department of Psychology
University of California at San Diego
La Jolla, California 92057

Ronald M. Doctor (4:169, 311)
Sexual Disorders; Stress
Department of Psychology
California State University at Northridge
Northridge, California 91330

David S. Douglass (1:271)
Attitude Formation
Department of Psychology
University of California at Santa Cruz
Santa Cruz, California 95064

Ronald Drozdenko (4:391)
Taste
NeuroCommunication Research Laboratories, Inc.
Danbury, Connecticut 06811
and Department of Marketing
Western Connecticut State University
Danbury, Connecticut 06810

Steve Duck (2:683)
Interpersonal Attraction and Personal Relationships
Department of Communication Studies
University of Iowa
Iowa City, Iowa 52242

Terence Duniho (3:13)
Jungian Personality Types
Life Patterns Institute
Providence, Rhode Island 02907

George J. DuPaul (1:253)
Attention-Deficit Hyperactivity Disorder, Assessment
Department of Counseling, School Psychology, and Special Education
Lehigh University
Bethlehem, Pennsylvania 18015

Robert J. Edelmann (2:237)
Embarrassment and Blushing
Department of Psychology
University of Surrey
Guildford, Surrey GU2 5XH
United Kingdom

John A. Edwards (1:291)
Attribution
Department of Psychology
The Ohio State University
Columbus, Ohio 43210

Nancy Eisenberg (2:247)
Empathy
Department of Psychology
Arizona State University
Tempe, Arizona 85287

Robert Eisenberger (3:219)
Motivation, Emotional Basis
Department of Psychology
University of Delaware
Newark, Delaware 19716

Russell Eisenman (1:401)
Birth Order, Effect on Personality and Behavior
Department of Psychology
McNeese State University
Lake Charles, Louisiana 70609

Paul Ekman (2:361)
Facial Expressions of Emotion
Department of Psychiatry
University of California at San Francisco
San Francisco, California 94143

Karen Emmorey (4:193)
Sign Language
Laboratory for Cognitive Neuroscience
The Salk Institute for Biological Studies
San Diego, California 92138

Norman Epstein (3:115)
Marriage
Department of Family Studies
University of Maryland at College Park
College Park, Maryland 20742

F. Eustache (1:525)
Central Auditory Disorders
Université de Caen
and Institut National de la Santé et de la Recherche Médicale
Caen F-14033
France

John Evans (3:115)
Marriage
Department of Family Studies
University of Maryland at College Park
College Park, Maryland 20742

Lynda Evans (3:115)
Marriage
Department of Family Studies
University of Maryland at College Park
College Park, Maryland 20742

H. J. Eysenck (2:321)
Extraversion–Introversion
Department of Psychology
Institute of Psychiatry
University of London
London SE5 8AF
United Kingdom

Beverly I. Fagot (3:411)
Parenting
Department of Psychology
University of Oregon
Eugene, Oregon 97401

William S. Fals-Stewart (3:103)
Marital Dysfunction
Department of Veterans Affairs Medical Center
and Department of Psychiatry
University of California at San Diego
La Jolla, California 92093

Allan Fenigstein (3:401)
Paranoia
Department of Psychology
Kenyon College
Gambier, Ohio 43022

Barbara L. Finlay (3:283)
Neocortex
Department of Psychology
Cornell University
Ithaca, New York 14853

William A. Fisher (3:545)
Pornography, Effects on Attitudes and Behavior
Department of Psychology
University of Western Ontario
London, Ontario
Canada N6A 5C2

Susan T. Fiske (1:719; 2:601, 675)
Control; Impression Formation; Intention
Department of Psychology
University of Massachusetts at Amherst
Amherst, Massachusetts 01003

John H. Fleming (2:689; 4:89)
Interpersonal Communication; Self-Fulfilling Prophecies
Department of Psychology
University of Minnesota
Minneapolis, Minnesota 55455

Michael Z. Fleming (2:143)
Dissociative Disorders
Department of Psychology
Boston University
Boston, Massachusetts 02215

Deborah L. FormyDuval (2:543)
Hormones and Behavior
Department of Psychology
Wake Forest University
Winston-Salem, North Carolina 27109

Nathan A. Fox (2:621)
Individual Differences in Temperament
Institute for Child Study
University of Maryland
College Park, Maryland 20742-1131

Arnold J. Friedhoff (1:505)
Catecholamines and Behavior
Millhauser Laboratories
New York University Medical Center
New York, New York 10016

Howard S. Friedman (3:603)
Psychological Predictors of Heart Disease
Department of Psychology
University of California at Riverside
Riverside, California 92521

Richard A. Gabriel (4:527)
War
Department of National Security and Strategy
U.S. Army War College
Carlisle, Pennsylvania 17013

Lee Galda (3:535)
Play
Department of Language Education
University of Georgia
Athens, Georgia 30602

Eileen Gambrill (1:603)
Clinical Assessment
School of Social Welfare
University of California at Berkeley
Berkeley, California 94720

A. K. Ganzel (4:275)
Socioemotional Development
Department of Psychology
University of Nebraska
Lincoln, Nebraska 68588

Anne E. Garing (4:287)
Spatial Orientation
Department of Psychology
Vanderbilt University
Nashville, Tennessee 37203

Nori Geary (1:187)
Appetite
Department of Psychiatry
Cornell University Medical College
and Edward W. Bourne Behavioral Research Laboratory
New York Hospital–Cornell Medical Center
White Plains, New York 10605

Russell G. Geen (4:459)
Violence, Observational Effects on Behavior
Department of Psychology
University of Missouri
Columbia, Missouri 65211

William L. Gekoski (2:1)
Coping
Department of Psychology
Queen's University
Kingston, Ontario
Canada K7L 3N6

Fred Genesee (1:383)
Bilingualism
Department of Psychology
McGill University
Montreal, Quebec
Canada H3A 1B1

Duilio Giannitrapani (2:225)
EEG, Cognition, and Dementia
Veterans Affairs Medical Center
Perry Point, Maryland 21902

Robert Gifford (2:265)
Environmental Psychology
Department of Psychology
University of Victoria
Victoria, British Columbia
Canada V8W 3P5

Gary Gillund (2:289)
Episodic Memory
Department of Psychology
College of Wooster
Wooster, Ohio 44691

George G. Glenner (1:103)
Alzheimer's Disease
Department of Pathology
University of California at San Diego
La Jolla, California 92093

Elizabeth L. Glisky (1:113)
Amnesia
Department of Psychology
University of Arizona
Tucson, Arizona 85721

Vicki Gluhoski (2:441)
Grief and Bereavement
Department of Psychology
State University of New York at Stony Brook
Stony Brook, New York 11790

Cliff Goddard (4:109)
Semantics
Department of Linguistics
University of New England
Armidale NSW 2351
Australia

George R. Goethals (1:11)
Actor–Observer Differences in Attribution
Department of Psychology
Williams College
Williamstown, Massachusetts 01267

Elizabeth Goldsmith (4:547)
Work Efficiency and Motivation
College of Human Sciences
Florida State University
Tallahasse, Florida 32306

Glyn Goodall (2:567)
Hypothalamus
Institut National de la Santé et de la Recherche Medicale
Bordeaux 33077
France

Stephanie A. Goodwin (2:601)
Impression Formation
Department of Psychology
University of Massachusetts at Amherst
Amherst, Massachusetts 01003

Irving I. Gottesman (4:41)
Schizophrenia
Department of Psychology
University of Virginia
Charlottesville, Virginia 22903

Suzanne Greist-Bousquet (4:297)
Spatial Perception
Department of Psychology

Kean College of New Jersey
Union, New Jersey 07083
Paul Grobstein (4:447)
Variability in Brain Function and Behavior
Department of Biology
Bryn Mawr College
Bryn Mawr, Pennsylvania 19010
Stephen Grossberg (4:469)
Visual Motion Perception
Center for Adaptive Systems
Boston University
Boston, Massachusetts 02215
R. Sergio Guglielmi (3:651)
Psychosomatic Illness
Department of Psychology
Lake Forest College
Lake Forest, Illinois 60045
W. Lawrence Gulick (4:487)
Visual Perception
Department of Psychology
University of Delaware
Newark, Delaware 19716
Judith A. Hall (3:293)
Nonverbal Behavior
Department of Psychology
Northeastern University
Boston, Massachusetts 02115
N. Gregory Hamilton (3:321)
Object Relations Theory
Department of Psychiatry
Oregon Health Sciences University
Portland, Oregon 97201
Robert E. Hanlon (1:199)
Apraxia
Neuropsychology Department
Baylor Institute for Rehabilitation
Dallas, Texas 75246
Ken-ichi Hara (1:233)
Associative Learning
Faculty of Science and Engineering
Ishinomaki Sensyu University
Japan
Allen J. Hart (3:29)
Jury Psychology
Department of Psychology
University of Iowa
Iowa City, Iowa 52242
Timothy S. Hartshorne (2:397)
Friendship
Department of Psychology
Central Michigan University
Mt. Pleasant, Michigan 48859
John H. Harvey (2:701)
Interpersonal Perception and Communication
Department of Psychology
University of Iowa
Iowa City, Iowa 52242
John P. Hatch (1:395)
Biofeedback
Department of Psychiatry
The University of Texas Health Science Center at San Antonio
San Antonio, Texas 78284
Elaine Hatfield (3:93)
Love and Intimacy
Department of Psychology
University of Hawaii at Manoa
Honolulu, Hawaii 96822
Joseph B. Hellige (2:491)
Handedness
Department of Psychology
University of Southern California
Los Angeles, California 90089
Tracy B. Herbert (4:325)
Stress and Illness
Department of Psychology
Carnegie Mellon University
Pittsburgh, Pennsylvania 15213
Leif Hertz (2:429)
Glial Cells
Department of Pharmacology
University of Saskatchewan
Saskatoon, Saskatchewan
Canada S7N 0W0
Steven R. Heyman (4:305)
Sport Psychology
Department of Psychology
University of Wyoming
Laramie, Wyoming 82071
Robert M. Hodapp (3:175)
Mental Retardation
Graduate School of Education
University of California, Los Angeles
Los Angeles, California 90024
Harmon R. Holcomb III (4:263)
Sociobiology
Department of Philosophy
University of Kentucky
Lexington, Kentucky 40506
Grayson N. Holmbeck (1:17)
Adolescence
Department of Psychology
Loyola University Chicago
Chicago, Illinois 60626
Ralph W. Hood, Jr. (3:619)
Psychology and Religion
Department of Psychology
University of Tennessee at Chattanooga
Chattanooga, Tennessee 37401
David A. Houston (3:563)
Preference Judgments
Department of Psychology
Memphis State University
Memphis, Tennessee 38152
Rick E. Ingram (2:113)
Depression
Department of Psychology
San Diego State University
San Diego, California 92120
Vasudeva G. Iyer (1:449)
Brain Electric Activity
Department of Neurology
University of Louisville School of Medicine
Louisville, Kentucky 40292
Carroll E. Izard (3:219)
Motivation, Emotional Basis
Department of Psychology
University of Delaware
Newark, Delaware 19716
Nancy Ewald Jackson (3:407)
Genius, Eminence, and Giftedness
Division of Psychological and Quantitive Foundations
University of Iowa
Iowa City, Iowa 52242
Lori E. James (4:537)
Word Retrieval
Department of Psychology
Claremont Graduate School
Claremont, California 91711
L. B. Jorde (2:611)
Inbreeding
Eccles Institute of Human Genetics
University of Utah School of Medicine
Salt Lake City, Utah 84112
R. Joseph (3:67)
Limbic System
Neurobehavioral Center
San Jose, California 95126
and Department of Speech Pathology and Audiology
Palo Alto Veterans Affairs Medical Center
Palo Alto, California 94304
Steven J. Karau (4:237)
Social Loafing
Department of Psychology
Clemson University
Clemson, South Carolina 29634

Martin M. Katz (1:375)
Behavior Measurement in Psychobiological Research
Department of Psychiatry
Montefiore Medical Center
The University Hospital for the Albert Einstein College of Medicine
Bronx, New York 10467

Richard Katz (3:555)
Post-Traumatic Stress Disorder
Division of Pharmaceuticals
CIBA-GEIGY Corporation
Summit, New Jersey 07901
and Department of Neuroscience
Rutgers University
Summit, New Jersey 07901

Kathryn Kelley (4:183)
Sexual Orientation
Department of Psychology
University at Albany
State University of New York
Albany, New York 12222

I. W. Kelly (3:611)
Psychology and Pseudoscience
Department of Educational Psychology
University of Saskatchewan
Saskatoon, Saskatchewan
Canada S7N 0W0

Dacher Keltner (2:361)
Facial Expressions of Emotion
Department of Psychology
University of Wisconsin at Madison
Madison, Wisconsin 53706

John F. Kihlstrom (1:113)
Amnesia
Department of Psychology
University of Arizona
Tucson, Arizona 85721

Young Yun Kim (2:31)
Cross-Cultural Adaptation
Department of Communication
University of Oklahoma
Norman, Oklahoma 73019

Erika G. King (2:53)
Crowd Psychology
Department of Political Science
Chatham College
Pittsburgh, Pennsylvania 15232

Howard S. Kirshner (1:175)
Aphasia
Department of Neurology
Vanderbilt University School of Medicine
Nashville, Tennessee 37232

Tatsuo Kitajima (1:233)
Associative Learning
Faculty of Engineering
Yamagata University
Yonezawa 992
Japan

Bryan Kolb (1:425)
Brain
Department of Psychology
University of Lethbridge
Lethbridge, Alberta
Canada T1K 3M4

Stephen M. Kosslyn (3:165)
Mental Imagery
Department of Psychology
Harvard University
Cambridge, Massachusetts 02138

Stanley Krippner (3:481)
Persuasion
Saybrook Institute
San Francisco, California 94133

Jerome Kroll (1:415)
Borderline Personality Disorder
Department of Psychiatry
University of Minnesota Medical School
Minneapolis, Minnesota 55455

Jon A. Krosnick (1:279)
Attitude Strength
Departments of Psychology and Political Science
The Ohio State University
Columbus, Ohio 43210

J. Lambert (1:525)
Central Auditory Disorders
Université de Caen
and Institut National de la Santé et de la Recherche Médicale
Caen F-14033
France

Yair Lampl (3:377)
Pain
Department of Neurology
Edith Wolfson Medical Center
Holon 58100
Israel
and Sackler Faculty of Medicine
University of Tel Aviv
Tel Aviv 69 978
Israel

Jonas Langer (3:83)
Logic
Department of Psychology
University of California at Berkeley
Berkeley, California 94720

Kim Langfield-Smith (1:647)
Cognitive Maps
Department of Accounting and Finance
Monash University
Clayton 3168
Australia

Pascale Lapeyre (2:517)
Homeostasis
Laboratoire de Physiologie de la Perception et de l'Action
College de France
CNRS, UPR2
Paris 75231
France

Daniel K. Lapsley (2:579)
Id, Ego, and Superego
Department of Psychology
Brandon University
Brandon, Manitoba
Canada R7A 6A9

Howard Lasnik (4:369)
Syntax
Department of Linguistics
University of Connecticut
Storrs, Connecticut 06268

Dawn Latta (2:655)
Inner Speech, Composing, and the Reading–Writing Connection
College of Education
Grand Canyon University
Phoenix, Arizona 85017

Howard Lavine (4:213)
Social Cognition
Department of Psychology
University of Minnesota
Minneapolis, Minnesota 55455

Julie Leader (2:441)
Grief and Bereavement
Department of Psychology
State University of New York at Stony Brook
Stony Brook, New York 11790

B. Lechevalier (1:525)
Central Auditory Disorders
Université de Caen
and Institut National de la Santé et de la Recherche Médicale
Caen F-14033
France

Mark F. Lenzenweger (4:41)
Schizophrenia
Department of Human Development
Cornell University
Ithaca, New York 14853

Stephen J. Lepore (2:43; 4:247)
Crowding: Effects on Health and Behavior; Social Support
Department of Psychology
Carnegie Mellon University
Pittsburgh, Pennsylvania 15213

Jennifer S. Lerner (1:1)
Accountability and Social Cognition
Department of Psychology
University of California at Berkeley
Berkeley, California 94720

David Lester (2:529; 4:347)
Homicide; Suicide
Center for the Study of Suicide
Blackwood, New Jersey 08012

Michael R. Levenson (1:47)
Aging, Personality, and Adaptation
Department of Applied Behavioral Sciences
University of California at Davis
Davis, California 95616

Stephan Lewandowsky (2:589)
Implicit Memory
Department of Psychology
University of Oklahoma
Norman, Oklahoma 73019

Pierre-Marie Lledo (2:517)
Homeostasis
CNRS
Institute Alfred Fessard
91198 Gif-sur-Yvette Cedex
France

Elizabeth F. Loftus (2:341)
Eyewitness Testimony
Department of Psychology
University of Washington
Seattle, Washington 98195

Oscar L. Lopez (2:97)
Dementia
Departments of Psychiatry and Neurology
University of Pittsburgh Medical Center
Pittsburgh, Pennsylvania 15260

Mary E. Losch (1:639)
Cognitive Dissonance
Institute of Social Science
University of Iowa
Iowa City, Iowa 52246

John A. Lucas (3:389)
Panic Disorder
Psychology Service
Department of Veterans Affairs Medical Center
San Diego, California 92163
and Department of Psychiatry
University of California at San Diego
La Jolla, California 92093

James K. Luiselli (1:359)
Behavioral Medicine
Psychological & Educational Resource Associates
Concord, Massachusetts 01742

William J. Lyddon (2:83)
Deductive Reasoning
Department of Psychology
University of Southern Mississippi
Hattiesburg, Mississippi 39406

Steven Jay Lynn (2:555)
Hypnosis
Department of Psychology
Ohio University
Athens, Ohio 45701

Kevin MacDonald (3:461)
Personality Development
Department of Psychology
California State University at Long Beach
Long Beach, California 90840

Brian MacWhinney (4:141)
Sentence Processing
Department of Psychology
Carnegie Mellon University
Pittsburgh, Pennsylvania 15213

Eugene J. Mahon (3:345)
Oedipus Complex
Columbia Psychoanalytic Center for Training and Research
and Department of Psychiatry
Columbia College of Physicians and Surgeons
New York, New York 10032

Debra J. Manning (4:89)
Self-Fulfilling Prophecies
Department of Psychology
University of Minnesota
Minnepolis, Minnesota 55455

Howard Markman (3:127)
Mate Selection
Department of Psychology
University of Denver
Denver, Colorado 80208

Dominic W. Massaro (3:441)
Perceptual Development
Department of Psychology
University of California at Santa Cruz
Santa Cruz, California 95064

Richard E. Mayer (3:599)
Problem Solving
Department of Psychology
University of California at Santa Barbara
Santa Barbara, California 93106

Charles G. McClintock (2:297)
Equity
Department of Psychology
University of California at Santa Barbara
Santa Barbara, California 93106

Michael McCloskey (1:487)
Calculation
Department of Cognitive Science
Johns Hopkins University
Baltimore, Maryland 21218

Robert R. McCrae (3:453)
Personality Assessment
Personality, Stress, and Coping Section
Gerontology Research Center
National Institute on Aging
National Institutes of Health
Baltimore, Maryland 21224

Katharine McGovern (1:687)
Consciousness
The Wright Institute
Berkeley, California 94704

William A. McKim (1:365)
Behavioral Pharmacology
Department of Psychology
Memorial University of Newfoundland
St. John's, Newfoundland
Canada A1B 3X9

Jo-Anne E. McKinnon (3:431)
Peer Relationships and Influences in Childhood
Department of Psychology
University of Waterloo
Waterloo, Ontario
Canada N2L 3GL

Daniel W. McNeil (1:151)
Anxiety and Fear
Department of Psychology
Oklahoma State University
Stillwater, Oklahoma 74078

Elizabeth A. Meadows (1:165)
Anxiety Disorders
Center for Stress and Anxiety Disorders
University at Albany
State University of New York
Albany, New York 12203

Ariel Merari (4:399)
Terrorism
Department of Psychology

Tel Aviv University
Tel Aviv 69978
Israel

Mary Ann Mercier (3:489)
Phobias
Department of Psychiatry
George Washington University
Washington, D.C. 20052

Karen S. Metz (4:527)
War
Library
Saint Anselm College
Manchester, New Hampshire 03102

Robert G. Meyer (1:141; 3:469)
Antisocial Personality Disorder; Personality Disorders
Department of Psychology
University of Louisville
Louisville, Kentucky 40292

Wulf-Uwe Meyer (4:353)
Surprise
Department of Psychology
University of Bielefeld
D-33501 Bielefeld
Germany

David J. Miklowitz (2:371)
Family Systems
Department of Psychology
University of Colorado at Boulder
Boulder, Colorado 80309

Arthur G. Miller (3:303)
Obedience and Conformity
Department of Psychology
Miami University
Oxford, Ohio 45056

Ennio Mingolla (4:469)
Visual Motion Perception
Department of Psychology
Boston University
Boston, Massachusetts 02215

Margaret L. Moline (3:587)
Premenstrual Syndrome
Department of Psychiatry
The New York Hospital–Cornell Medical Center
White Plains, New York 10605

Beth A. Morling (1:719)
Control
Department of Psychology
University of Massachusetts at Amherst
Amherst, Massachusetts 01003

Mary K. Morris (1:537)
Central Nervous System
Department of Psychology
Georgia State University
Atlanta, Georgia 30303

Donald L. Mosher (2:467)
Guilt
Department of Psychology
University of Connecticut
Storrs, Connecticut 06269

Craig T. Nagoshi (1:345)
Behavioral Genetics
Department of Psychology
Arizona State University
Tempe, Arizona 85287

Bryan Neff (4:169)
Sexual Disorders
Department of Psychology
California State University at Northridge
Northridge, California 91330

Thomas O. Nelson (3:187)
Metacognition
Department of Psychology
University of Washington
Seattle, Washington 98195

J. T. Newton (3:213)
Motivation
Dental Public Health Unit
Guy's Hospital
University of London
London SE1 9RT
England

Michael Niepel (4:353)
Surprise
Department of Psychology
University of Bielefeld
D-33501 Bielefeld
Germany

Elijah Ocherashvili (2:429)
Glial Cells
Institute of Physiology
The Beritashvili Institute
Tbilisi 380060
Republic of Georgia

Kevin N. Ochsner (3:165)
Mental Imagery
Department of Psychology
Harvard University
Cambridge, Massachusetts 02138

Brona O'Dowd (2:429)
Glial Cells
Department of Psychology
La Trobe University
Bundoora, Victoria 3083
Australia

Samuel H. Osipow (1:497)
Career Development
Department of Psychology
The Ohio State University
Columbus, Ohio 43210

Willis F. Overton (4:13)
Reasoning
Department of Psychology
Temple University
Philadelphia, Pennsylvania 19122

Thomas J. Page, Jr. (1:709)
Consumer Psychology
Department of Marketing and Logistics
Michigan State University
East Lansing, Michigan 48826

Adrian Parker (1:665)
Conflict Behavior
Department of Psychology
University of Göteborg
S-400 20 Göteborg
Sweden

Lawrence N. Parker (1:29)
Adrenal Glands
Department of Medicine
University of California at Irvine
Irvine, California 92664

Jim H. Patton (4:121)
Sensation Seeking
Department of Psychology
Baylor University
Waco, Texas 76798

Paul B. Paulus (2:457)
Group Dynamics
Department of Psychology
University of Texas at Arlington
Arlington, Texas 76019

A. D. Pellegrini (3:535)
Play
Institute for Behavioral Research
University of Georgia
Athens, Georgia 30602

Nancy E. Perry (2:213)
Educational Psychology
School of Education
University of Michigan
Ann Arbor, Michigan 48109

Jacqueline B. Persons (1:617)
Cognitive Behavior Therapy
Department of Psychiatry
University of California at San Francisco
San Francisco, California 94143

Christopher Peterson (3:57)
Learned Helplessness
Department of Psychology
University of Michigan
Ann Arbor, Michigan 48109

Gary W. Peterson (4:513)
Vocational Choice
Counseling Psychology and Human Systems

Florida State University
Tallahassee, Florida 32306

Richard E. Petty (1:261)
Attitude Change
Department of Psychology
The Ohio State University
Columbus, Ohio 43210

John R. Pierce (2:187)
Ears and Hearing
Center for Computer Research in Music and Acoustics
Stanford University
Stanford, California 94305

Quentin J. Pittman (2:567)
Hypothalamus
Neuroscience Research Group and Department of Medical Physiology
University of Calgary
Calgary, Alberta
Canada 2TN 4N1

Kirsten M. Poehlmann (4:225)
Social Comparison
Department of Psychology
The Ohio State University
Columbus, Ohio 43210

F. Clark Power (3:203)
Moral Development
Program for Liberal Studies
University of Notre Dame
Notre Dame, Indiana 46556

Anthony R. Pratkanis (1:271)
Attitude Formation
Department of Psychology
University of California at Santa Cruz
Santa Cruz, California 95064

Johnny R. Purvis (2:23)
Crisis Management
Education Service Center
University of Southern Mississippi
Hattiesburg, Mississippi 39406

Dennis Pusch (3:631, 669)
Psychopathology; Psychotherapy
Department of Psychology
University of Calgary
Calgary, Alberta
Canada T2N 1N4

Howard Rachlin (2:389)
Free Will
Department of Psychology
State University of New York at Stony Brook
Stony Brook, New York 11794

K. J. Radford (2:73)
Decision Making, Individuals
Department of Systems Design Engineering
University of Waterloo
Waterloo, Ontario
Canada N2L 3G1

Rudolf E. Radocy (3:257)
Musical Ability
Department of Music Education
University of Kansas
Lawrence, Kansas 66045

Gabriel A. Radvansky (3:137)
Memory
Department of Psychology
University of Notre Dame
Notre Dame, Indiana 46556

Richard L. Rapson (3:93)
Love and Intimacy
Department of History
University of Hawaii at Manoa
Honolulu, Hawaii 96822

Paul Reading (2:477)
Habit
Department of Experimental Psychology
Cambridge University
Cambridge CB2 3EB
United Kingdom

Judith W. Rhue (2:555)
Hypnosis
Department of Family Medicine
Ohio University College of Osteopathic Medicine
Athens, Ohio 45701

Barry J. Ries (1:151)
Anxiety and Fear
Department of Psychology
Oklahoma State University
Stillwater, Oklahoma 74078

John J. Rieser (4:287)
Spatial Orientation
Department of Psychology
Vanderbilt University
Nashville, Tennessee 37203

Shannon Riley (1:291)
Attribution
Department of Psychology
The Ohio State University
Columbus, Ohio 43210

John H. Riskind (3:489)
Phobias
Department of Psychology
George Mason University
Fairfax, Virginia 22030

Thomas Robbins (1:457)
Brainwashing and Totalitarian Influence
Santa Barbara Center for Humanistic Studies
Santa Barbara, California 93190

Karlene H. Roberts (3:367)
Organizational Behavior
Walter A. Haas School of Business
University of California at Berkeley
Berkeley, California 94720

Raymond G. Romanczyk (1:327)
Autism
Institute for Child Development
Department of Psychology
State University of New York at Binghamton
Binghamton, New York 13902

Mary Ann Romski (3:39)
Language Development
Department of Communication and Language Research Center
Georgia State University
Atlanta, Georgia 30303

Eleanor Rosch (1:513)
Categorization
Department of Psychology
University of California at Berkeley
Berkeley, California 94720

Robert Rosenthal (3:293)
Nonverbal Behavior
Department of Psychology
Harvard University
Cambridge, Massachusetts 02138

Kenneth H. Rubin (3:431)
Peer Relationships and Influences in Childhood
Department of Psychology
University of Waterloo
Waterloo, Ontario
Canada N2L 3G1

Laurie A. Rudman (4:213)
Social Cognition
Department of Psychology
University of Minnesota
Minneapolis, Minnesota 55455

Mark A. Runco (2:11)
Creative and Imaginative Thinking
Department of Child Development
California State University at Fullerton
Fullerton, California 92634

D. H. Saklofske (1:245; 2:321; 3:611)
Attention-Deficit Hyperactivity Disorder; Extraversion–Introversion; Psychology and Psuedoscience
Department of Educational Psychology
University of Saskatchewan
Saskatoon, Saskatchewan
Canada S7N 0W0

H. R. Schiffman (4:297)
Spatial Perception
Department of Psychology
Rutgers, the State University
New Brunswick, New Jersey 08903

Louis A. Schmidt (2:621)
Individual Differences in Temperament
Institute for Child Study
University of Maryland
College Park, Maryland 20742

Thomas J. Schoeneman (2:631)
Individualism
Department of Psychology
Lewis and Clark College
Portland, Oregon 97219

Gerald Schoenewolf (2:501)
Hate
The Living Center
New York, New York 10003

Ellin Kofsky Scholnick (3:525)
Planning
Department of Psychology
University of Maryland at College Park
College Park, Maryland 20742

Earl D. Schubert (1:301)
Auditory Discrimination
Department of Music
Stanford University
Stanford, California 94035

V. L. Schwean (1:245)
Attention-Deficit Hyperactivity Disorder
Department for the Education of Exceptional Children
University of Saskatchewan
Saskatoon, Saskatchewan
Canada S7N 0W0

Bernard Segal (4:335)
Substance Abuse
Department of Health Sciences
University of Alaska Anchorage
Anchorage, Alaska 99508

Rose A. Sevcik (3:39)
Language Development
Language Research Center
Georgia State University
Atlanta, Georgia 30303

Ariana Shahinfar (2:621)
Individual Differences in Temperament
Institute for Child Study
University of Maryland
College Park, Maryland 20742

Steven J. Sherman (3:563)
Preference Judgments
Department of Psychology
Indiana University
Bloomington, Indiana 47405

Etay Shilony (2:143)
Dissociative Disorders
Department of Psychiatry
Harvard University
Cambridge, Massachusetts 02138

Raul Silva (1:505)
Catecholamines and Behavior
Millhauser Laboratories
New York University Medical Center
New York, New York 10016

Harinder Singh (2:203)
Economic Behavior
Department of Economics
San Diego State University
San Diego, California 92182

Jan D. Sinnott (4:151)
Sex Roles
Department of Psychology
Towson State University
Baltimore, Maryland 21204

Jonathan C. Smith (4:25)
Relaxation
Department of Psychology
Roosevelt University
Chicago, Illinois 60605

Wendy R. Smith (1:279)
Attitude Strength
Department of Psychology
The Ohio State University
Columbus, Ohio 43210

Michael Smithson (4:437)
Uncertainty
School of Behavioral Sciences
James Cook University
Queensland 4811
Australia

Daniel W. Smothergill (4:383)
Tactile Perception
Department of Psychology
Syracuse University
Syracuse, New York 13244

C. R. Snyder (2:535)
Hope and Optimism
Department of Psychology
University of Kansas
Lawrence, Kansas 66045

Peter J. Snyder[1] (2:279)
Epilepsy
Departments of Psychiatry and Neurology
Albert Einstein College of Medicine
Long Island Jewish Medical Center
Glen Oaks, New York 11004

Robert Sommer (2:197)
Ecological Psychology
Department of Psychology
University of California at Davis
Davis, California 95616

Nicholas P. Spanos (2:555)
Hypnosis
Department of Psychology
Carleton University
Ottawa, Ontario
Canada K15 5B6

Christopher Spencer (2:255)
Environmental Cognition
Department of Psychology
University of Sheffield
Sheffield S10 2TN
United Kingdom

Steven Stack (2:153)
Divorce
Department of Sociology and Criminal Justice
Wayne State University
Detroit, Michigan 48202

Stephen M. Stahl (4:359)
Synaptic Transmitters and Neuromodulators
Department of Psychiatry
University of California at San Diego
La Jolla, California 92093
and Veterans Affairs Medical Center
San Diego, California 92161

Melinda A. Stanley (3:333)
Obsessive–Compulsive Behavior
Department of Psychiatry and Behavioral Sciences
University of Texas–Houston Health Science Center
Houston, Texas 77225

[1] *Present address:* Behavioral Epilepsy Program, Allegheny Neuropsychiatric Institute, Oakdale, Pennsylvania 15071.

Peter N. Stearns (3:1)
Jealousy
College of Humanities and Social Sciences
Carnegie Mellon University
Pittsburgh, Pennsylvania 15213

James A. Stephenson (2:645)
Information Processing and Clinical Psychology
Center for Psychiatric Rehabilitation
University of Chicago
Tinley Park, Illinois 60477

Robert J. Sternberg (2:663)
Intelligence
Department of Psychology
Yale University
New Haven, Connecticut 06520

Laura E. Stevens (2:675)
Intention
Department of Psychology
University of Massachusetts at Amherst
Amherst, Massachusetts 01003

William F. Stone (1:701)
Conservatism/Liberalism
Department of Psychology
University of Maine
Orono, Maine 04469

Jerry Suls (4:427)
Type A–Type B Personalities
Department of Psychology
University of Iowa
Iowa City, Iowa 52242

Annette Swain (4:427)
Type A–Type B Personalities
Department of Psychology
University of Iowa
Iowa City, Iowa 52242

Stephan Swinnen (3:229)
Motor Control
Department of Kinanthropology
Catholic University of Leuven
3001 Herverlee
Belgium

Michael J. Tarr (4:503)
Visual Representation
Department of Psychology
Yale University
New Haven, Connecticut 06520

Henry L. Taylor (3:191)
Military Psychology
Institute of Aviation
University of Illinois
Savoy, Illinois 61874

Philip E. Tetlock (1:1)
Accountability and Social Cognition
Department of Psychology
University of California at Berkeley
Berkeley, California 94720

Mark Thayer (4:35)
Risk-Compensating Behavior
Department of Economics
San Diego State University
San Diego, California 92182

Steven L. Thomas (1:223)
Arbitration
Department of Management
Southwest Missouri State University
Springfield, Missouri 63804

J. Kevin Thompson (1:407)
Body Image
Department of Psychology
University of South Florida
Tampa, Florida 33620

Laura A. Thompson (3:441)
Perceptual Development
Department of Psychology
New Mexico State University
Las Cruces, New Mexico 88003

Robert L. Thompson (1:591)
Classical Conditioning
Department of Psychology
Hunter College
City University of New York
New York, New York 10021

Ross A. Thompson (4:275)
Socioemotional Development
Department of Psychology
University of Nebraska
Lincoln, Nebraska 68588

Geoffrey L. Thorpe (1:57)
Agoraphobia
Department of Psychology
University of Maine
Orono, Maine 04469

Linda Tickle-Degnen (3:293)
Nonverbal Behavior
Department of Occupational Therapy
Boston University
Boston, Massachusetts 02215

Joseph K. Torgesen (3:515)
Phonological Processing and Reading
Psychology Department
Florida State University
Tallahassee, Florida 32306

Daniel Tranel (3:149)
Memory, Neural Substrates
Departments of Neurology and Psychology
University of Iowa
Iowa City, Iowa 52242

Harry C. Triandis (4:333)
Subjective Culture
Department of Psychology
University of Illinois at Urbana-Champaign
Urbana, Illinois 61801

Warren W. Tryon (2:313)
Expectation
Psychology Department
Fordham University
Bronx, New York 10458

Irving F. Tucker (3:13)
Jungian Personality Types
Departments of Psychology and Geography
Shepherd College
Shepherdstown, West Virginia 25442

Betty Tuller (3:499)
Phonetics
Center for Complex Systems and Department of Psychology
Florida Atlantic University
Boca Raton, Florida 33432

Cynthia L. Turk (1:151)
Anxiety and Fear
Department of Psychology
Oklahoma State University
Stillwater, Oklahoma 74078

William R. Uttal (3:421)
Pattern Recognition
Department of Industrial and Management Systems Engineering
Arizona State University
Tempe, Arizona 85287

Steve Van Toller (4:131)
Sense of Smell
Department of Psychology
University of Warwick
Coventry CV4 7AL
United Kingdom

Robin S. Vealey (1:655)
Competition
Department of Psychology
Miami University of Ohio
Oxford, Ohio 45056

Alisha L. Wagner (3:333)
Obsessive–Compulsive Behavior
Department of Psychology
University of Houston
Houston, Texas 77044

John N. Warfield (2:63)
Cybernetics
Institute for Advanced Study in the Integrative Sciences

George Mason University
Fairfax, Virginia 22030

Gifford Weary (1:291)
Attribution
Department of Psychology
The Ohio State University
Columbus, Ohio 43210

Charles A. Weaver III (4:1)
Reading
Department of Psychology
Baylor University
Waco, Texas 76798

Curt Weinstein (4:391)
Taste
NeuroCommunication Research Laboratories, Inc.
Danbury, Connecticut 06811

Scott Wetzler (1:375)
Behavior Measurement in Psychobiological Research
Department of Psychiatry
Montefiore Medical Center
The University Hospital for the Albert Einstein College of Medicine
Bronx, New York 10467

John Whalen (1:487)
Calculation
Department of Cognitive Science
Johns Hopkins University
Baltimore, Maryland 21218

Ian Q. Whishaw (1:425)
Brain
Department of Psychology
University of Lethbridge
Lethbridge, Alberta
Canada T1K 3M4

Michael P. Wilbur (1:81)
AIDS and Sexual Behavior
Department of Educational Psychology
The University of Connecticut
Storrs, Connecticut 06269

Kipling D. Williams (2:341)
Eyewitness Testimony
Department of Psychology
University of Toledo
Toledo, Ohio 43606

Michael Winkler (3:481)
Persuasion
Department of Psychology
University of North Carolina at Asheville
Asheville, North Carolina 28804

Philip H. Winne (2:213)
Educational Psychology
Faculty of Education
Simon Fraser University
Burnaby, British Columbia
Canada V5A 1S6

Daniel Wolverton (1:141)
Antisocial Personality Disorder
Department of Psychology
University of Louisville
Louisville, Kentucky 40292

Camille B. Wortman (2:441)
Grief and Bereavement
Department of Psychology
State University of New York at Stony Brook
Stony Brook, New York 11790

Robert S. Wyer, Jr. (3:137)
Memory
Department of Psychology
University of Illinois at Urbana-Champaign
Champaign, Illinois 61820

David Yaden (2:655)
Inner Speech, Composing, and the Reading–Writing Connection
Division of Curriculum and Teaching
School of Education
University of Southern California
Los Angeles, California 90089

Edward Zamble (2:1)
Coping
Department of Psychology
Queen's University
Kingston, Ontario
Canada K7L 3N6

Index

Volume numbers are boldfaced, separated from the first page reference with a colon. Subsequent references to the same material are separated by commas.

A

B

C

D

E

F

G

H

I

L

M

N

O

Q

R

S

T

U

V

W

X

Y

Z